highland cows

A History of Sailing in Scotland
through the lens of
HUNTER'S QUAY

First Edition, Second Revision
February 2021

EUAN ROSS

With a foreword by
Ian Howlett

"Hunters Quay"
· Hotel and Club-house ·
Royal Clyde
Yacht Club :

Looking outward

Lifelines from Low Latitudes

Other credits: editing, layout, book design, artwork, graphics, and DTP typesetting, are not separately credited as these tasks remained within the compass of the author.

for

Kathryn

&

Samuel

The Clyde

The shadows flew upon the sunny hills;
And down the river, 'gainst the pale blue sky,
A town sat in its smoke. Look backward now!
Distance has stilled three hundred thousand hearts,
Drowned the loud roar of commerce, changed the proud
Metropolis, which turns all things to gold.
Blotting the azure too, we floated on,
Leaving a long and weltering wake behind.
And now the grand and solitary hills
That never knew the toil and stress of man,
Dappled with sun and cloud, rose far away.
And far above the region of the wind
The barred and rippled cirrus slept serene,
With combed and winnowed streaks of faintest cloud
Melting into the blue. A sudden veil
Of rain dimmed all; and when the shade drew off,
Before us, out toward the mighty sun,
The firth was throbbing with glad flakes of light.

Alexander Smith

Contents

An introduction to Hunter's Quay: sporting gentlemen take up yachting – the Clyde's rise from the margins of the yachting world to sit at its very heart – the Royal Marine Hotel as the focus for Scottish yachting – a nod to Anthony Heckstall-Smith's *Sacred Cowes* – the Highland Boundary Faultline and the character of Highlanders.

BOOK ONE – Down the Rabbit Hole

The scope of our yachting history: the 'first' Scottish yachtsman – the Highland Clearances – the aristocracy discover a surpassing adjunct to their sporting paradise – royal antecedents – the House of Stuart – the Victorians – George, Edward and *Britannia* – Britain as a colonial superpower – Pax Britannica – *coda*: The Freedom of the Seas.

The Clyde: sailing through pre-history – dug-out canoes, the trough – the courich – clinker-built boats – the arrival of the Romans – the seafaring Picts – itinerant boatbuilding in the pre-nation state – the Norsemen arrive – Viking longships and Scottish galleys – the stern-hung rudder – birlinns and battle-wagons – the Lords of the Isles – the Battle of Epiphany – the Battle of Largs – the enduring bond with Norway – the Maid of Norway – Edward and the Bodleian Map – Robert the Bruce.

The Royal Scots Navy: the Scots ensign as a symbol of independence – the age of the galley – naval warfare with Norway and England – the naval ambitions of James I, II, III, IV, V, & VI – Sir Andrew Wood – naval dockyards – the advent of naval gunnery – the *Saint Salvator* – the *Great Michael* – the Daunting of the Isles – Flodden – the Act of Union and the demise of the Scots Navy – the rise of the West Coast economy – *coda*: The Galley, Workhorse of Pre-industrial Navies and the trials of John Knox, galley-slave.

Sailing and the British Royal family: the Princess Royal – Queen Victoria beats the bounds – the Age of Exploration and advances in global navigation – witches and weather systems – Charles II, the 'Father of *English* Yachting' – the Duke of York – the Great Fire of London – Admiral de Reuter – yachting diplomacy – the Cork Water Club – Peter the Great and Admiral David Mitchell – William III – 17th century yachting in Russia – Professor Henry Farquharson – the Campbells – *coda*: a House of Stuart Royal Yacht.

Contents

BOOK TWO – The Evolution of the Species

BOOK THREE – Sailing for Sport

Contents

BOOK FIVE – Northern Lights

BOOK SIX – Holy Loch – Holy Grail

on *Sirocco* – a Tigerfish lose in Clyde waters – fun and games aboard HMS *Conqueror* – yachting's torpedo boat heritage – the 'gold ships' *Gometra* and *Sinbad*.

Men are using aluminium, plastics and even glass for their yachts. There are even the theorists who gleefully envisage the yacht of the future as a saucer-shaped affair, without a keel but with a very tall mast, that will be propelled by a rather horrid combination of aerofoils and hydrofoils.
So be it. George Blake envisages the AC75 in 1959.

Author's Notes

The biggest yacht squadron ever seen on the Clyde lay at anchor in the Holy Loch on Monday evening. Some eighty anchor lanterns illuminated the loch, and in the shadow of the hills the flare of the light was curious. The CCYC Regatta of 1890. Image: James Meikle at work in a Rothesay seaside shelter, crafting a race report.

Why a History of Scottish Yachting?

Sailing is arguably the most diverse and multifaceted of all leisure pursuits, thus it is also perhaps the sport most richly endowed with specialist literature. Consequently, countless well-researched histories of yachting have been published since Victorian times. But, unaccountably, not one has focussed on Scotland. While individual Scottish designers have been lauded, even lionised, in lush biographies, the wider story of sailing in Scotland has been marginalised. This rich and colourful vein of incident and anecdote is acknowledged only in passing.

Yachting historians have certainly contemplated the challenge, but at the time of writing, nothing has appeared in print. This reticence is understandable. Any attempt to redress the north-south balance and bring the wider story of Scottish yachting into the mainstream is faced with a century of neglect. In order to render this challenging task manageable, *Highland Cowes* employs a substantially thematic approach. Inevitably topic timeframes overlap and sometimes run in parallel. Hopefully, this welds thirty-seven stand-alone essays into a coherent volume. The intention is to present a diorama of events, viewed 'through the lens' of Hunter's Quay – the heart of sailing in Scotland, during the 'golden age of yachting'.

The Second Revision

This revision reflects minor changes incorporated in the manuscript to provide the British National Yachting Archive with a searchable text that reflects insights gained during the nine months since initial publication. The page count has also marginally increased to accommodate a few nuggets of additional information which I believe are germane to this particular history. To those passionate bookworms who have contacted me with additional details, drawn attention to a specific omission, offered a minor correction, or simply supported the project with their accounts of happy browsing, my sincere thanks.

The Piper Calls the Tune

Highland Cowes carefully skirts the existing body of well-trodden research and material already published on individual designers. Moreover, the author has attempted to respect the oeuvre of others working in the field.

Finally, historical material already published in *The Piper Calls the Tune* has not been duplicated. That earlier book addressed the following:

- A biography of David Boyd describing his childhood, his apprenticeship with the Ardrossan Shipbuilding Co, his employment with Fife's of Fairlie, British Marine, and Alex Robertson & Sons of Sandbank.
- A review of the 'classic yacht revival'.
- A discussion on the role of the draughtsman/yacht designer/naval architect in corporate design offices and where 'the buck stops'.
- A review of the complete Boyd design-portfolio, as of our research to 2017.
- The emergence of organised offshore racing in Britain.
- An analysis of the seminal design competition of 1932 organised by the Royal Corinthian Yacht Club and the Royal Ocean Racing Club.
- A partial account of the Seawanhaka Cup focussed on the three wins by David Boyd-designed yachts – *Circe* in 1938 and 1939 and *Titia* in 1956.
- Detailed accounts of the British American's Cup challenges of 1958 with Sceptre and 1964 with *Sovereign* and *Kurrewa V*.
- A history of Alexander Robertson's boatyard in Sandbank.
- The story of the marine industry's post-war transition from wood to fibreglass construction.
- Notes on the Clyde's premier yacht clubs and well-known Scottish yachtsmen.
- The British School's Yachting Championship (the Clark Cup) 1933-1995 organised by the Mudhook Yacht Club.
- The ethics of 'cloning', 'flopping', and yacht design copyright.
- .....and much more.

A Note on Spelling

In the text, 'Argyle' is used when referring to both the Campbell family and historical references to the county when that spelling was used. The Argyle Papers, in 1834, are close to the cross-over date. 'Argyll' is used for references to events in modern times. The commonly accepted 'Firth' of Clyde is employed throughout, except where quotations use the archaic spelling 'Frith' (derived like fjord from the Old Norse fjörthr). Hunter's Quay is commonly spelt without the apostrophe, but the grammatical correctness of the original has been revived here. Where likely meanings of Gaelic place names are included, these interpretations are as published by Gaelic speakers. Where possible, they have been independently corroborated, however, spelling and usage have changed over the centuries.

A Note on Equivalent Costs

In calculating costs, the 'National Archives Converter', which begins at 1270 AD and estimates by decade, has been used for early equivalents. For the last hundred years or so, the 'CPI Inflation Calculator', which provides year-by-year estimates (based on the Office for National Statistics composite prices), is used. This suggests, for example, that prices in 2019 are 11,830% higher than the year 1880. The average inflation rate for the Pound Sterling during this period was 3.5%. All on-line calculations should be taken with a generous pinch of salt, or a snort of salt water if you are reading this at sea. As for snorts of derision, no claims to any special accuracy are made. The 2019 equivalent costs, quoted in brackets throughout this book, simply contextualise expenditure in a useful and sometimes surprising way.

A Note on Abbreviations

For non-sailing readers: 'tons' descriptions with a hyphen, as in '100-tons' refers to Thames Tonnage, a long-running classification, and indicator of internal volume that usefully indicates size, but has nothing to do with the weight of a vessel. Similarly, the variously designated metre classes, for example the 6-metre, reference a calculated rating and not actual length, as with many other systems. Only restricted and 'box rule' classes, like the Clyde 23/30, refer to actual length on the waterline (expressed throughout as 'LWL') and length overall ('LOA'), not including bowsprits and bumpkins, which in some 19th century racing yachts might add 40% to LOA. The metre-boat classes of the International Rule are abbreviated as follows – 6-metre class as '6mR', 12-metre as '12mR', etc.

A Note on Terminology

In this book, ships are 'she', even if they are named after men or attributes associated with men. This is a delightful convention, worth defending. The author is aware that some Millennials have taken umbrage against the gender tenets of the old patriarchy. But surely, when our neighbours across La Manche are content to endow all manner of inanimate objects with a gender, it is churlish to protest. In the same way, the weight of cultural baggage associated with the terms 'yachts', 'yachtsmen', and 'yachtswomen' is cheerfully accepted. This terminology is free to use, no matter how small your yacht is, or how modest your sailing programme. Assume the mantle, own it, feel like a king and enjoy it.

A Note on Ancillary Detail

Readers who 'switch off' when faced with mathematics can safely skim over the rating formulae, dotted throughout these pages, without affecting the run of the narrative. Similarly, auxiliary information, which is cordoned off from the main text in grey boxes, can be glossed over too.

A Note on References

Highland Cowes is 'key-word, source-referenced'. This facilitates follow-up enquiries through an Internet-search, rather than via reference libraries. The order is article, publication, author, date – or variations of that depending on the material cited. The author-led system is not considered helpful in this type of work as, in some cases, he or she is an unnamed correspondent. And, in respect of the many titled authors cited, the selection of a lead moniker becomes arbitrary. In-text summary references are avoided as these interrupts the flow. References and supplementary notes are listed at the end of each chapter, and like rating formulae, may be happily ignored.

Acknowledgements

The late Theo Rye encouraged the author to question the established narrative. Theo left us in his prime shortly after the publication of *The Piper Calls the Tune*. Together with Martin Black and Jeremy Lines, Theo digitised the entire Lloyds Yacht Register, from its inception in 1878 to its final edition in 1980. This work, carried out on behalf of the Association of Yachting Historians, provided the essential foundation for *Highland Cowes*. In the same context, we would also highlight the valuable work of the Caledonian Maritime Research Trust. Their Clydeships Database is a labour of love, still evolving, but already indispensable.

The author would like to thank:

- Ian Howlett, naval architect – for his generous advice on yacht design-related matters and unstinting collaboration in respect of various technical elements of this book. Ian's contribution to our joint research on the design heritage of the Stephen family, the designs of Thomas Glen-Coats, and the life of Erik Maxwell has been substantial.
- Alison Spice, linguist – for meticulous proofreading and standard English style advice, usually followed but sometimes flouted, and for heroic forbearance.
- Dr. Kate Simpson, née Ross, Lecturer in Digital Studies & Information Media at Glasgow University – for her cheerful assistance and careful research work at the National Library of Scotland in Edinburgh.
- Martin Nichol, stalwart of the Clyde Cruising Club and Scottish Tourist Board Blue Badge Guide – for his support and informed review of the introductory historical chapters. Most of the changes advised to align the text with the orthodox narrative, have been incorporated but by no means all. Any errors which remain are the sole responsibility of the author.
- Bob Donaldson, HLSC Historian, and my long-time collaborator – for his support and inputs concerning the early years of the Holy Loch Sailing Club.
- Jon Reid, Royal Northern & Clyde Yacht Club Historian – for sharing his intimate knowledge of the history of both clubs, and early Clyde yachting generally. Also, for being helpful beyond the call of duty.
- The Stephen Family, descendants of the famous shipbuilding dynasty – for access to the family archive covering the work of Fred J. Stephen and John G. Stephen.
- Brent Maxwell, Erik Maxwell's son – for access to the Maxwell family's newspaper cuttings archive covering the yachting life of Erik Maxwell.
- The late Ian Mitchell – for his research on Dunoon boatbuilders and Clyde yachting recollections. And, more importantly, for a lifetime of friendship and support, from our first national junior championship under his direction to the last cup of coffee in the summer of 2019. We'll nae see his like again.
- The late Andrew Paterson renowned auctioneer and raconteur – for his Holy Loch and Kilmun memories, specifically in relation to Holy Loch mooring rights, Holy Loch in wartime, and the tragic loss of Lt. Col. MacAlpine-Downie

and Major Richard Weston Brooke from the Brixham trawler-yacht *Servabo*. Andrew auctioned off the last artifacts of the legendary Fife yard on Fairlie beach. He also sold us my first boat – a Yachting World Cadet, *Candy*, CK 42.

🐌 David Gray, naval architect of Mylne Yacht Design – for permission to reproduce Mylne drawings and sharing our common interest in Sir Thomas Glen-Coats.

🐌 Molly McLachlan née Lorimer, a member of the HLSC since 1947 – for her lively reminiscences of her father's yard, Morris & Lorimer's, and sailing on the Clyde.

🐌 June Collyer, daughter of the late Peter Collyer, renowned boatbuilder, marine engineer and yachtsman – for access to Peter's extensive personal archive, the generous gift of so many valuable sailing books and the return of my late father's oak roll-top desk, after a sojourn of 56 years in Peter's office.

🐌 Dr. Jeremy Thomson, still a competitive sailor in his eighties – for his endless stories about yachting on the Clyde since WW2, and excellent sundowners.

🐌 Clair McComb, yachting historian, and researcher – for information and advice concerning Mylne, T. C. Glen-Coats, E. G. Martin, Morgan Giles, and *Kelpie*.

🐌 Ian McKenzie, past Commodore of the Royal Gourock Yacht Club – for information on the Clyde 'Straight-eight' revival, the zenith of the 8CR fleet, his memories concerning the last days of the Royal Clyde Yacht Club at Hunter's Quay and teaching me how to sail a Piper keelboat one breezy afternoon in 1968.

🐌 Andy and Cushla Thoms, of the Majestic Line – for access to their extensive early-20th century Yachting Monthly archive and various materials concerning yachting life on the Clyde in the old days.

🐌 Stan Ferguson, of the Ardmaleish Boatyard – for his insights, recollections of his apprenticeship at the Stephen Yard and a lifetime of boatbuilding, and for access to Mylne materials at the former Mylne boatyard.

🐌 Alison Turner, of the Turner Boatbuilding family of Dunoon – for access to her family's boatbuilding archive, and for all the coffee and biscuits.

🐌 Martin Black, G. L. Watson and classic yacht expert – for advice and support, especially, for leading the AYH team who digitised *The Yachtsman* magazine in its entirety from first publication in April 1891 to the final issue in January 1940.

🐌 Ewan Kennedy, of the Scottish Sailing Blog – for his encouragement and advice on early Clyde level-rating and one-design classes.

🐌 David Elliot, instigator, and custodian of the British National Yachting Archive – for his advice and information on specific yachts.

🐌 David Hutchison, Robertson's Historian – for access to his well-researched writings on Hunter's Quay and archive materials about Alexander Robertson's Yard transferred to this volume.

🐌 Bobby Salmond, doyen of the Flying Fifteen Class – for his historical anecdotes and memories of the class.

🐌 Eileen Lea née Waddell, of the Sandbank family of ferrymen and boatbuilders – for advice and access to archive materials.

🐌 Charles Darley, past Commodore of the Royal Northern & Clyde Yacht Club and stalwart of the Gareloch One Designs – for his interest and support.

🐌 Tim Henderson, pillar of the Royal Northern & Clyde Yacht Club – for his observations and recollections transferred to this volume.

🐌 Howard Morrison and Alan Dundas, of the venerable Mudhook Yacht Club – for their support and access to Mudhook publications.

🐌 Gael Pawson – for free and full access to her *Yachts & Yachting* archive.

- May Fife McCallum, yachting historian – for clarifications concerning her book 'Fast and Bonnie' and advice on earlier work transferred to this volume.
- Iain McAllister, yachting historian – for his interest and advice on various aspects of Clyde yachting.
- Joe Graham, descendent of Graham Brothers Boatbuilders, Dunoon – for information on the family firm.
- Dave Fletcher, descendent of Fletcher Brothers Boatbuilders, Dunoon – for information on the family firm.
- Terence Brownrigg, International Judge of 30 years standing, ex-Commodore of the Royal Northern Yacht Club and navigator of Dick Carter's *Rabbit* when she won the 1965 Fastnet Race – for his interest and advice.
- Andrew Cully, of 'Classic Yacht Info' – for his interest and advice.
- David B. Boyd, son of the designer and America's Cup crewman – for his advice on earlier work transferred to this volume.
- Duncan Walker of Greybeard Yachting, formerly of Fairlie Yachts – for access to the Fife design archive at Hamble Yacht Services.
- John Rousmaniere, yachting historian – for his advice on earlier work concerning 12-metre and 6-metre yachts transferred to this volume.
- Jim McIlraith, naval architect, of Survey One – for his interest and advice.
- The late Peter Fairley, formerly Managing Director of Robertson's Yard – for his advice on earlier work transferred to this volume.
- Alan Waugh – for his recollections of the Pleiade Class and the Scottish Council for Physical Recreation Sailing School in the Holy Loch.
- Iain McLeod, former President of the Scottish Schools Sailing Association and the National School Sailing Association – for his interest and advice.
- Andy Postle, of Allspars Ltd – for his insights into the 3rd Rule International 6 Metres yachts for his advice on earlier work transferred to this volume.
- Jim McNair – for his archive on the 'old hands' and full and free access to his excellent photographs of classic yachts on the Clyde taken over the last 25 years.
- Staff of the Dunoon Observer and Argyllshire Standard – for their advice and access to their archives, specifically concerning the *Servabo* tragedy.
- Argyll and Bute Council (Rory Crutchfield and Jackie Davenport) – for facilitating access to the Boyd and Robertson's archives.
- The Royal Institute of Naval Architects (Sally Charity and Lisa Staples) for research into, and information on, Institute membership.

In connection with the additional information contained in this revision, the author would like to thank:
- Colin Litster, of the well-known Litster boatbuilding and sailing family – for access to his nascent archive on the Litster and the Bergius families and insights into the fascinating life of marine professionals in the 'great days of yachting'.
- Tim Street, former Chairman of the Six Metre Class, historian, and a key actor in the renaissance of the 6mRs – for his remarks and observations.
- Glyn Foulkes, sculptor, and yachting enthusiast with a fair few 6mR professional sailors in his family tree – for his *Fane* and *Royal Thames* 6mR memories.
- Jamie Campbell – for information on the fascinating saga of the three Crossbow speed record contenders designed by Rod MacAlpine Downie.
- Nigel Sharp, yachting historian – for his advice on the ratings of the inter-war '24-metre' or '75ft- LWL' cutters racing in British waters.

🐟 Cornelius van Rijckevorsel – owner of the Fife yacht *Ensay*, now *Sibyl of Cumae*, a 36-linear-rater built for J. Stewart Clark in 1902 and still delighting all who sail in her.

🐟 Scott Rohrer, yachting historian – for his David Boyd stories and *Iskareen* memories.

🐟 Graham Ferguson – for detailed information on the Scottish 7CR fleet.

🐟 Chris Freer, yacht designer and professional sailor, for his insights and opinions on grand prix yacht racing, and David Boyd memories.

🐟 Douglas Reincke, Finnish metre-boat enthusiast and instigator of the excellent 6mR Facebook page – for his information concerning the location of the 6mR *Circe*, thought destroyed at the time of writing *The Piper Calls the Tune*, but now provisionally identified as a red hulk rotting contentedly in Estonia.

🐟 Gavin Watson, of the Royal Northern and Royal Gourock yacht clubs, and former Secretary of the CYCA – for his recollections of the post war years, specifically the merger of the Royal and Northern Royal Clyde the in 1978.

🐟 Simon Jackson, sail designer, and much else, for his information on the subsequent life of the 8mR *Coila V* and other topics.

🐟 Guy Tyrwhitt-Drake, 6mR afficionado – for his information on *Josephine*.

🐟 The author would like to thank the following original contributors who have taken the time to offer additional comments and clarifications, now reflected in the current work: Bob Donaldson, Martin Black, Ewan Kennedy and Clair McComb.

The much-admired cover image, taken by Olga Darroch during the British Youth Championships at Largs in April 2018, shows the Laser fleet spread out across the Clyde, with the snow-clad hills of Arran as a dramatic backcloth. This panorama, taken from the Skelmorlie shore, is the view looking down the Clyde Estuary, clean over the low-lying Isle of Bute to the heights of Arran, fully 13 miles distant. Olga's long-lens brings a wealth of our best scenery into frame, with Goatfell and Caisteal Abhail looming menacingly over tomorrow's champions, as they brave the chilly, early-season waters. The ghostly image of a Watson 5-tonner sailing across the back cover depicts *Vril*, photographed off Hunter's Quay in 1876 by John Adamson Jr of Rothesay, possibly the Clyde's finest photographer, who passed away at just 45 years of age in 1896.

The Frontispiece image is a sketch of the Royal Clyde Yacht Club that appeared in the *Daily Graphic* on 26th April 1890, and possibly the work of Henry Charles Seppings Wright. The 'In Memoriam' page portrays *Neptune*, a 10-tonner, designed by William Fife in 1880, photographed by Washington Wilson. The etching on the first page of each section, depicting the mouth of the Holy Loch and Hunter's Quay, is the work of William Lionel Wyllie (1851-1931). The faux 19th century dedication frame is a sampled composite from various sources by the author. The image heading Ian Howlett's Foreword, as is fitting for the designer who made the famous winged keel possible, depicts one of his recent 6mR keels. Below: what is lost need not be forgotten – the author in his thirties when 'young at heart' was not a euphemism. Image Stephen Lim.

For book related matters, the author can be contacted at:
pipercallsthetune@gmail.com

Parable of Immortality

I am standing upon the seashore.
A ship at my side spreads her white sails to the morning breeze
and starts for the blue ocean.
She is an object of beauty and strength,
and I stand and watch until at last she hangs
like a speck of white cloud
just where the sea and sky come down to mingle with each other.
Then someone at my side says,
" *There she goes!* "
Gone where?
Gone from my sight . . . that is all.

Henry Van Dyke 1853-1933

In Memoriam
Ian Mitchell & Andrew Paterson
who contributed their time, knowledge and memories

Prologue: The Martyrdom of Highland Cows

It is lawful for you to eat the flesh of the oxen. For it might chance owing to the hurry of your setting out that ye could not prepare food for your journey, and in the skins of your oxen shall ye prosperously sail to the Holy Land of Promise. God[1]

This divine edict was issued to Saint Fintan Munnu, hard man of Irish hagiography, who gave his name to Kilmun and blessed the Holy Loch. St. Munnu sanctified every harbour he visited, but still, we are grateful. He is here anointed 'Patron Saint of Yachting on the Clyde'. Fintan is primarily a source of inspiration but we might also daub him in as the harbinger of 'creative malapropism' in sailing literature – a pulp-genre inadvertently staked out in these pages. In the Munnu legend, Highland cows, were once marinised in pursuit of a spiritual agenda native to the Celts of the North Channel, albeit in a whimsical context of doubtful veracity.

If we take the almighty spirit of the great monotheistic religions at his word, we find him to be a deity with a working knowledge of Celtic aspiration and a wry sense of humour. The voyage of St. Fintan Munnu and his companions to the Holy Land in the 7th century is one of our earliest sailing stories.[2] This Celtic pilgrimage followed a set of detailed instructions issued by none other than God himself. The sea is acknowledged to be 'a hard life' but for the oxen, press-ganged to assist in the venture, it was the ultimate sacrifice. These cows were not 'going for a sail' in the usual way; they would, in effect, transcend their corporeal existence to become one with the voyage.

In the *Lives of the Saints*, we discover that their cowhides were sewn together to skin a twelve-beam sea-going currach, which is about the size of the St Brendan replica. The flayed flesh of our bovine brothers fuelled the mission – salted-down as beef jerky for the long voyage. It seems that the monks used everything but the 'moo'; or maybe even that too as cow horns make fine fog horns.[3] Monks and deconstructed cows embarked from Slieve League in County Donegal in north-west Ireland. Many years later, Fintan Munnu and his companions returned home after completing the round trip to the Holy Land. Alas, there was no way back for the cows; their hides would be recycled as footwear for the final push to Jerusalem.

The tale recalls *Gulliver's Travels* through allegorical kingdoms and his escape from the land of the Houyhnhnms.[4] Gulliver absconded in a canoe framed with basketwork, like a currach, and covered with the skins of Yahoos, a humanoid species. The Houyhnhnms were an equine race who farmed the Yahoos like domestic animals.[5] Swift's callous hero, always keen to plumb new depths of depravity, also clothed himself in the supple hide of Yahoo adolescents and set a sail made of this same leather. *"I finished a sort of Indian canoe, but much larger, covering it with the skins of Yahoos, well stitched together with hempen threads of my own making."*

Jonathan Swift was an Irish Anglican, but as an educated man he would have been familiar with Catholic mythology and the *Lives of the Saints*. Possibly, he was inspired by the fate of Munnu's highland cows to construct his own metaphor portraying the lives of the Irish under English colonial rule.[6] It is, however, more likely that Swift scandalized society just for the hell of it as he later wrote that his intention was *"to vex the world"* rather than entertain it.

Fintan Munnu was a less complex character with no ambitions to vex or entertain. He would eventually become Saint Fintan, lend his name to Kilmun and consecrate the holy grail of yachting. But, as we have described, the credit is not his alone. So, to redress an ancient injustice, we might make a case here to the Congregation for the Cause of Saints to consider beatification, canonisation, and perhaps collective sainthood for Munnu's selfless 7th century herd.

---

[1] Vita Columbae, Saint Adamnan (624–704).
[2] The Scottish Historical Review, Volume 10th, the Origin of the Holy Loch in Cowall Argyle, Niall D. Campbell, 1913.
[3] Blown correctly, the noise is ear-splitting and remarkably melodic for an instrument without a reed. Our family trumpets few musical accomplishments, but we can make a cow horn bellow.
[4] The Houyhnhnms were horses rather than cows, but it is close enough.
[5] Gulliver's Travels into Several Remote Nations of the World, Jonathan Swift, 1726. In the story, the canoe was a success. After making a landfall, in what was then New Holland, Gulliver eventually secured a passage home on a Portuguese ship.
[6] The Yahoo and the Discourse of Racialism in Gulliver's Travels, Lumen, A. Stewart, 1993.

Childe Harold's Pilgrimage (extract)
And I have loved thee, Ocean! And my joy
Of youthful sports was on thy breast to be
Borne like thy bubbles, onward: from a boy
I wanton'd with thy breakers – they to me
Were a delight: and if the freshening sea
Made them a terror – 'twas a pleasing fear.

Byron, 1818

It may be that yachting history, like love, is better when had by word o' mouth than when printed on a caird and we have sometimes been apt to think that the old stories must have gained by being preserved in kindly memories rather than in the cold, dead pages of newspapers and magazines.

James Meikle, doyen of Clyde yachting journalists

Altair, William Fife III 1931, sailing in the 2008 Fife Regatta on the Clyde   Image: the author

Foreword by Ian Howlett

Accumulating an excess of old books on yachting has been a vice of mine since the early 1970s, when hidden gems were still to be discovered in the little bookshops of Southampton. These writings from the past feel of a different quality to almost all those of today. *Highland Cowes* is a most noteworthy and pleasing exception. This book, like old volumes of the *Yachting Monthly*, is to be savoured in front of a log fire along with a glass of malt. Races under sail, in times of old, were described by men who knew and cared about such things; the results and how events unfolded would be recounted with style and documented with accuracy and spirit. No doubt the readership was inspired by these writings to be part of those delights. Notable also, at least to my eye, is how the 'aesthetics' of the modern sailing craft, whether labelled 'super yacht', 'spirit of tradition' or otherwise, compare so unfavourably with almost all of the beautiful creations of the past, that are pictured in the book.

Highland Cowes is a 'magnum opus' in all senses of the phrase, both in scope and content, describing the history of this extraordinary and beautiful area that was for so long the richest centre of all, for the design, building and racing of yachts. Euan Ross has a special talent for covering much ground in fine detail whilst rooting out the most entertaining stories. It is, of course, the latter that makes history interesting. Euan's approach and the resulting text is in marked contrast to what might be termed the 'dumbed down' museum techniques of today. He combines accuracy, along with the entertainment of many good stories, and like a good malt there is a complexity and depth to be appreciated. The references, at the end of each chapter, will be invaluable to those who would like to discover more, and the illustrations tell a history in their own right.

Interestingly, my own and Euan's backgrounds in dinghies have much in common, though of course there is little similarity between the spacious waters of the Clyde and the narrow constraints of the Upper Thames at Medley, Oxford, where, very early in life, my sailing and racing began. We might, however, recall Linton Hope's 1906 observation in the *Yachting Monthly* that *"river sailing is to ordinary sea sailing as fly fishing is to bottom fishing, or as snipe shooting to shooting tame pheasants"*. Such contrasts are the very essence of racing under sail, and the sport is also blessed in that we are able to enjoy our boats from the age of three to eighty-three, or perhaps even more in these days of greater longevity. The mention here of the Medley stretch alongside Port Meadow and its sailing club merits further observations about such institutions. When I was young, the membership seemingly did include the butcher, the baker, and the candlestick maker. Members from a multitude of backgrounds were brought together in a most beneficial way by shared enthusiasm for 'messing about in boats'.

What is more, the scrubland was cleared away, the boatshed, essential for the drying of cotton sails, constructed and then the clubhouse designed and put up by the membership. Stalwarts included a Commander, a Brigadier and Oxford dons of various disciplines, along with those whose day job involved the assembly of motor cars. The 'dinghy boom' that occurred in the 1950s/60s, nurtured in particular by that outstanding, philosophical, editor of *Yachting World*, E.F. Haylock, brought about many such positive developments in these Isles, but sadly today, many clubs of like kind struggle and have lost the old sense of common spirit. It might be noted too that the costs for the complex apparatus of competitive coarse fishing, such as carbon poles that seem to stretch halfway across the river, are far more than that needed to buy and race dinghies there.

The words of Douglas Phillips-Birt, writing as Argus, in the 1960s *Yachting Monthly*, seem particularly prescient *"The cult of over efficiency in sport or games destroys what it seeks to improve. It produces in a short time the spectator sport or game, which is a different commodity altogether. Sport, like love, must have running through it a thread of the gay and spontaneous if it is to preserve its purity of purpose which is to make the lives of people fuller and their hearts more generous"*. From many years later, the quotation in *Highland Cowes* from Stuart Walker's writings echoes the same theme, and of course, we are now much further along the same 'trajectory'. I share that view; the very term 'professional sport' is an oxymoron. We should take part in sport to enrich our lives.

Perhaps the dreadful pandemic that is now spreading its lethal tentacles around the world will cause us to re-evaluate what is really important and how should we conduct our brief time on earth. As our *Lionheart* America's Cup Challenge unfolded in 1979/1980, I became increasingly aware of how much we had to learn from those who had tackled just the same problems in previous challenges, and how much more we would have been able to achieve if only we had been tuned to the right frequency; but of course, it takes time to learn who to listen to. I should note that the people involved in the small craft business are generally very nice folk. I have long thought of the boatyards and suppliers with whom I have contact, as being part of a large extended family, and many of these became lifetime friends. In early 1983, when the 12mR, *Victory '83*, was in build at Fairey Marine in Hamble, the production manager in charge of the project asked if he might accompany me on my planned 'round trip' to visit some of the key suppliers. He did so, and on our return, he made a point of remarking to me that in a lifetime in the marine industry he had not before come across so many excellent people. So it was when first I visited the Lloyd's Register office in Southampton in 1973; here were men of great experience who were also most amiable and anxious to help.

There is no better teacher than history, and Euan's fine account contains important truths, which need to be taken account of, if in the years to come, the sport of sailing for pleasure is to flourish and we with it.

Ian Howlett, Oxford, March 2020

Ian Howlett (left) and John Prentice sailing the 6mR, *Battlecry VI*   Image: Jason Holtom

Battlecry (Howlett 1983) won the Seawanhaka Cup in 1987, chartered to Erik Maxwell for a shilling!

Britannia and the Scottish Islands Class, *Bernera*, Holy Loch, 1933   Image: RNCYC Collection

Introduction: The Bay of Ferns

Hunter's Quay: perhaps the most picturesque yachting rendezvous on the Clyde, or anywhere upon our coasts. The reach of the Clyde towards Greenock, the estuary running southwards, the Holy Loch and Loch Long, like the meeting of separate waters, bewilders the eye, and fills it with the charms of many pictures. The Field[7]

Hunter's Quay, the one-time Bay of Ferns, was at the very heart of the 'golden age of yachting'. Together with the resorts of Dunoon, Rothesay, Helensburgh, Largs, and Gourock, Hunter's Quay grew to prominence through a powerful combination of new money, increasing leisure-time, and the fruits of the Industrial Revolution. Cut-throat competition among the steam-packets brought the middle-reaches of the Firth of Clyde within daily commuting distance of Glasgow. Paradise was just an hour away.

An increasingly cosmopolitan society was prepared to invest in this sublime coastline. As coastal villages grew into fashionable watering-places, local entrepreneurs, eager to provide the goods and services that upwardly mobile Victorians demanded, made hay. In these circumstances, it was perhaps inevitable that the Clyde should have flourished as a playground for the 'workshop of the British Empire'.

Elsewhere in Britain, with the coming of the railways in the 1830s, the new commercial sector of 'leisure and recreation' lit up rural economies. Yachting outgrew its traditional heartland in the Thames Estuary to enjoy the open waters of the South Coast. The whole circus decamped from the London to the little town of Cowes on the Isle of Wight. Sailing became ensconced there, inheriting the baggage of bloodstock to share the sobriquet 'sport of kings' – a pastime pursued by aristocrats and conferred with the mixed benefits of royal patronage. Evoking these origins, over all this action floated a miasma of spent cordite as the stentorian blast of shotgun cartridges heralded regattas large and small.

The early growth of competitive sailing owed much to the esoteric rituals of contemporary, well-established, sporting communities. The British aristocracy pursued the country life of hunting, shooting, and fishing to an obsessive degree and they brought this same passion to yachting. Among the early members of the Yacht Club, established at Cowes in 1815, were Scottish landowners and Englishmen with extensive estates in the North. Then as now, gentry from the British outlands, maintained households in the South to attend to business in the City of London, to play politics, sustain hereditary licence, and 'network' among men of influence.

When these influential gentlemen congregated in Scotland for the 'Glorious 12th', it was, perhaps, inevitable that their conversation drifted from red grouse to the sport of yachting. Shooting parties, surveying our sparkling waters from the hilltops, scoped-out the Clyde as the next 'field of play'. Subsequently, enthusiasts on both sides of the North Channel got together to establish the Northern Yacht Club in 1824. Sailing, it transpired, was a movable feast. For the next century, well-off yachtsmen would shuttle their racing yachts and support vessels between the Clyde and the Solent, duplicating infrastructure and multiplying operational costs.

When the newly minted tycoons of Caledonia brought their resources to the table, the small fortune necessary to compete on the water became a large one. By the late 1800s, yachting was, arguably, a game played harder, and with more ingenuity, on the Clyde than on the Solent. In the arcane world of yacht racing, the period 1839-1939 might be tagged the 'Caledonian century'. Our best designers and boatbuilders fed upon one another's successes, while their owners indulged in a more genteel battle for bragging rights over a glass of whisky in the smoking rooms of the Royal Northern and Royal Clyde yacht clubs.[8]

In later years, as the Corinthian ethos developed, our native Scots sailed well too. Jimmy Howden Hume (1903-1981) was a good example of the complete sporting gentleman. Jimmy shot countless pheasants on the boggy banks of Loch Lomond and spent long hours salmon fishing on the Spey. He kept a fishing diary meticulously for 30-years. In this little notebook, Jimmy listed details of the more-than 550 fish he had landed with rod and reel. It is, therefore, no surprise that his yachting obsession also exhibited a rare attention to detail. Howden Hume was a talented helmsman with the means to take on the best, but he was just one of a hundred similarly talented, similarly competitive, all-round sportsmen to emerge through the golden era.

However, as we all must acknowledge, things have moved on and times have changed. Caledonia has been cut loose from the leading edge of maritime innovation. The Clyde is again a serene backwater, as it was before the thrashing paddlewheels of countless steamers brought the Highlands and Islands within the compass of Glasgow. While this fall from grace is a matter of enduring anguish, nostalgia too endures. There is much to be said for a quiet life and we still have a rich heritage to look back on and savour. In doing so, we might recover a vital element of our social history. Following the fortunes of racing yachts was once as much a part of daily life on Clydeside as watching football is today. *"The interest in yacht racing increases so steadily that, in spite of the International Exhibition and the joys of the switchback, the shores of the Clyde were lined with admiring crowds."*[9]

The old Royal Marine Hotel, once owned by the Royal Clyde Yacht Club – for a time, perhaps, the largest yacht club in the world, still stands proudly facing the Tail o' the Bank. The Royal Marine enjoys a view that includes the grand villas of long-dead members and encompasses the snow-capped skyline of the Arrochar Alps in the far distance. But, if you are looking for any trace of our yachting heritage at Hunter's Quay today, you are out of luck. In the summer of 2019, there is nothing to see and the very idea of a 'Highland Cowes' seems ridiculous. The anchorage has fallen out of favour, even among owners who still live on the point.

Not many yacht clubs have ever owned full-sized hotels. The present Royal Marine replaced a more modest pile, leased 'off-plan' from James Hunter in 1872, and subsequently bought outright in 1875. This earlier building suffered a disastrous fire in 1888 – recalled as the *"most spectacular terrestrial event in the history of the club"*.[10] The new building was designed by Tom Lennox Watson, a cousin of the legendary yacht designer. But genius dances to the music of chance. Tom's hotel is a flawed masterpiece.[11] *"The general appearance of the house is indescribable without the aid of sketch."*[12] Tom was an antiquarian with a weakness for 'neo-genres' – in this instance, mixing elements of Scottish Baronial with Mock Tudor. Nevertheless, when the Royal Clyde was in residence, with the blue ensign fluttering from *Valkyrie IIs* mast, salvaged from the depths of the Holy Loch and planted in the lawn, by God the old pile looked the part!

Our 'Highland Cowes' was perhaps *the* most significant centre of yacht racing in the 1890s. Through the crucial decades that shaped the modern sport, the Clyde was renowned as a cradle of innovation and a northern counterpoint to offset the perceived uniqueness of Cowes. The analogy of our title with a still-vibrant Solent might offend the ardent nationalist, but old hands will understand the tribute paid here to *Sacred Cowes*, Tony Heckstall-Smith's affectionate portrait of that otherwise unremarkable little Isle of Wight town, glimpsed through a sprinkling of fairy dust.

The full title of Heckstall-Smith's book is *Sacred Cowes or the Cream of Yachting Society*.[13] His deadpan account of the jaw-droppingly decadent social scene in Victorian Cowes pilloried the elite without so much as a snide remark or a déclassé sneer. The dissolute society of great wealth and hereditary privilege did not need any help from satirists to appear ridiculous.

As our formidable old French teacher at Dunoon Grammar School used to inform us daily in Class 1A1, *"it's not only the cream that rises to the top"*. Then, and still today, the residue of the old aristocracy, captains of industry, and career politicians march lockstep in mutual backscratching. Heckstall-Smith recorded all this cliquey nonsense with a light hand and heavy irony. Those familiar with Greydon Carter's editorial tenure at Vanity Fair will understand the skill and ingenuity this requires.

More literally, genuine highland cows are now stationed far and wide throughout the British Isles, to enliven parkland and punctuate vistas beyond the ha-has of stately homes. Here in Hampshire, where we live in happy exile, they are everywhere. However, the first such herd, to be brought 'south' (56°N, 4°W) from the frozen north for purely decorative purposes, was penned in central Scotland at Cambuskenneth in 1888, to serve as life models for a colony of timorous artists.[14]

The Highland Cows, perhaps the most docile of all domestic beasts, were sketched from the safety of a 'shed-on-wheels' like an English shepherd's caravan. In that vein, hopefully, more seriously minded readers will forgive the literal 'Heilan coo' logo that heads each chapter to temper this excruciating pun. What to say? In the perpetual low tide of the 21st century, it's as well not to take life too seriously.[15]

When we were young, Scottish history was handed down as a romantic legend of myth and majesty. Bloody tragedies and fluky windfalls were strung together in a broad sweep of post facto rationale. Our little hearts raced fit to bust. Such innocence is hard to recover today when we no longer see ourselves as the proud scions of mighty warriors. Nevertheless, we will try to separate the threads of achievement from the fabric of happenstance, and if we may, take a certain satisfaction in the former.

When my son was just four years old, he asked: "*What do mighty worriers worry about Dad?*" The answer, of course, is that they worry about being forgotten. Scotland is full of mighty worriers. Alba is a bit like Atlantis; just as that mythical city slipped beneath the sea, our plucky nation has slipped under the radar. It is a wistful analogy that might be inverted. In this uncertain age, when the virtual reality of digital navigation leaves us in God's hands, the hypnotic sweep of radar picks up the real world as a ghostly outline. That, perhaps, may be an apt metaphor for the empty estuary of the River Clyde today.

It is not surprising, therefore, that we Scots tend to live in the past. "*They will defend their unique Scottishness, in terms of events and grandeurs long past and sadly soiled. For the most part they sit, curiously complacent, amid the ruins of their own civilisation, such as it was.*"[16] As a member of the Scottish diaspora, and a 'citizen of nowhere', as ex-prime minister, Theresa May, would have it, I take a very different view.[17] Yes, we have left the stage, but we have not turned out the lights. Across the length and breadth of the Clyde Estuary, the sun still shines, and the wind still blows, even as fine threads of Victorian ectoplasm dance at the masthead.

The spirit of innovation and industry that characterised the Scottish Enlightenment is also still alive today, as are our global networks – interpersonal, institutional, and electronic. 'Civilisation' is expanding at light-speed in real-time. Our finite planet is now the physical core of a virtual reality, growing exponentially to encompass everything that ever was, and much of what will be. In this unsettling, but undeniably 'brave new world', the Scots gain leverage through a remarkable diaspora of perhaps 40-million compatriots, driven still by an eternal flame of raw ambition that owes nothing to nostalgia.[18]

The story of Caledonian yachting is a parable of pride and privilege. 'Pride' might be a Scottish invention, so tightly is it woven into the fabric of our feisty self-image. The Scots as a nation routinely take exception to 'privilege. However, at the same time, we revel in revisionist retellings of our history. The vassal state, feudal servitude, and maudlin tolerance of outrageous hereditary licence have been harnessed to the bandwagon of romantic fiction. Filibustering monarchs, vainglorious princes and rapacious clan chiefs – all have been honoured on the dubious grounds that, 'he may be a bastart, but he's oor bastart'.

Highland Cowes no doubt reflects that conflicted view, with respect to the sometimes-ignoble company of dead and buried Scottish yachtsmen. The relatively few affluent and empowered yachtswomen of the past, on the other hand, get an unqualified free pass. Surely the 'lassies' who broke through the 'glass-scuttle' deserve a break. *"It was a dirty day, and there were skinned knuckles and forceful epithets among our four grown men. Yet the girls (three hefty, oily-covered lassies) sailed a grand race and got their 2nd prize – they had got a 1st the day before. One could not look at these girls handling their plunging boat without thinking of the great object lesson they presented."*[19]

More generally, the story of Scottish yachting reflects the rank inequalities that blighted British society in the 19th century. However, the world of seafaring is a generous microcosm – there is as much to admire as disparage. That said, while generosity mitigated injustice, the scourge of paternalism never engaged with it. The Corinthians of the Victorian era laughed and joked with their crews, then sent them off to the pub with a few shillings in their pockets. The local professionals knew their place. They were character actors performing rope tricks against the sweeping backcloth of the Arrochar Alps and the Arran skyline.

In these circumstances, unless there is clear evidence to the contrary, *Highland Cowes* attempts to redress the balance in a small way: firstly, by 'turning the knife' occasionally when attitudes of entitlement on the part of old-time yachtsmen overwhelm a standing obligation to avoid 'retroactive liberalism'; and secondly, by characterising the honourable company of forelock-tugging maritime professionals as 'the salt of the earth'.[20]

For boat-daft children growing up on the West Coast, our perceived maritime heritage began with the Victorians, even though there were traces of the remote past everywhere, if one cared to look. The County of Argyll, the towns of Dunoon, Campbeltown, Rothesay, and the once-suzerain Clan Campbell all feature a sailing warship on their coats of arms.[21] Indeed, the heraldry of countless local authorities and institutions all around our coasts incorporate cartoons of medieval vessels.

Graphic anomalies aside, the ships which feature regularly in the heraldic crests of the Highlands and Islands are intended to represent the birlinn – a robust Western Isles galley, with fighting castles fore and aft, evolved from the classic Viking longship. There are exceptions; the citizens of Largs, still proud of their eponymous battle, boast a longship on their coat of arms, as does the district of Cove and Kilcreggan, and for less obvious reasons, my old alma mater, Dunoon Grammar School.

Those of us born in the Highlands, we lucky few, were raised believing that a geological event, now more than 400 million years past, somehow elevates us above our Lowland peers in virtue as in geography. In Cowal, we know exactly where the boundary-fault lies, certain that we are on the right side of it. And fortunately, as a radical nation compromised by an uncritical bardolatry before the rough and sentimental charm of Robert Burns' vision of Scotland, our southern neighbours generally humour us.[22]

My heart's in the Highlands, my heart is not here, My heart's in the Highlands, a-chasing the deer; Chasing the wild deer, and following the roe, My heart's in the Highlands, wherever I go. Robert Burns[23]

Scottish geology generally trends north-east/south-west, so the Highlands extend further south than most folk realise, further even than tartan shortbread tins might suggest. The Highland Boundary Fault Line runs right down the middle of the Clyde Estuary. It divides the ancient metamorphic rocks of the Scottish Highlands from the much younger sandstone of Scotland's Central Lowlands. Rothesay has a foot in both camps, built atop the dormant fault-line, marked here by Rothesay Bay and the valley of Loch Fad.[24] Gourock, Helensburgh and Largs are all in the Lowlands and enjoy fine views of the 'promised land', but Hunter's Quay welcomes you to the Highlands.[25]

While our primary interest is 'the racing yacht', *Highland Cowes* also considers 'sailing' more broadly. This approach allows excursions into ancient history, to sample the aeons before the 19th century, when shipbuilding on the Clyde blossomed in a fever of inspired invention. The evolutionary timescale of boatbuilding before the Industrial Revolution was glacial, but there is still technical and social interest, and there are always anecdotes to discover.

Today, the 'identity politics' of resurgent Scottish Nationalism has boosted interest in toe-curling Celtic myths and legends. This fascination with the genesis of our society has also brought the back-story of our maritime history into the light. Obscure tracts, formerly languishing within the dusty confines of our reference libraries, have been 'unpacked' and 'repackaged'. Readers of an enquiring mind can now rediscover the Royal Scots Navy. In comparison to our neighbours, south of the border, who have always revered their naval heritage, we have a lot of catching up to do. Ripping yarns, and otherworldly tales of derring-do on the high seas, surely enrich the narrative of Scottish sailing.

This book is written as a series of thematic essays, organized as an 'interstitial' history, which recognises the futility of parroting good, and in some instances excellent, material that is already in the public domain. While there is a global perspective, *Highland Cowes* seeks to identify gaps in the pantheon and 'slot in' lesser known, but no less worthy, figures. Consequently, the stellar talents of Watson, Fife, Mylne, McGruer and Boyd are recognised primarily through the wider context of excellence they represent.

Hopefully, the book can spark an interest in Scotland's maritime heritage among both sailing folk and the 'lay reader'. Recognising that the latter group far exceeds the former, and is, by definition, less conditioned by preconceptions, there is perhaps an opportunity to 'spread the word'. At the same time, in order to respect the knowledge base of our well-informed readers, the author and his collaborators have attempted to be both technically correct and as accurate as our sources allow.

7 The Field, April 1872.

8 It was not until the 1890s that Scotch could claim to be sophisticated enough to compete with Brandy, which by this time was extremely expensive. While we like the romantic image of the wealthy owners sitting back with a cigar and a glass of malt, it was most likely to be a glass of brandy.

9 The Glasgow Herald covers the 1888 Largs Regatta.

10 Cruise in Company, the History of the Royal Clyde Yacht Club, 1856-1956, George Blake and Christopher Small, 1959.

11 George and Tom shared ownership of *Peggy Woffington* in 1871. This was George's first design and one of his rare failures. Perhaps Tom was an albatross.

12 Royal Clyde New Clubhouse, Glasgow Herald, 30th December 1889.

13 Sacred Cowes, or the Cream of Yachting Society, Anthony Heckstall-Smith, 1955.

14 The Artistic Etruscan School set up several artists' colonies in Britain, inspired by examples

in Brittany. Such colonies flourished at Brig o' Turk, Kirkcudbright, Cockburnspath and Cambuskenneth.

[15] Our cow lives a life of new-found celebrity on Beacon Hill, Hampshire; the lifebelt is from the *Waverley* and the cap was an exhibit in the Scottish Maritime Museum.

[16] The Heart of Scotland, George Blake, 1934.

[17] Theresa May, Speech to the Conservative Party Conference on 5th October 2016.

[18] The Scottish Diaspora and Diaspora Strategy, the Scottish Government, May 2009.

[19] The Clyde 19/24 Footers, William Barclay, Yachting Monthly ca.1912.

[20] 'Creeping Determinism' is a phenomenon identified in 1970's psychology. It is the effect of thinking that something *was* predictable, but only *after* it happens.

[21] From the 1880s to the 1930s, Dunoon substituted an excursion steamer in its coat of arms, reflecting the lifeblood of the community during that period.

[22] In Burns' greatest poem, *Tam o' Shanter*. 'Shanter' is from Seanntor, in the ancient tongue and 'Tam' borrowed from a boat called *Tam*, owned by a tenant of the Burns holding.

[23] My Heart's in the Highlands, Robert Burns, 1789.

[24] As this chapter was being written, a restored *Bluebird*, Donald Campbell's ill-fated water-speed record holder, was seen puttering up and down Loch Fad during the summer of 2018.

[25] Technical Paper No.78, Landscape Assessment of Argyll and the Firth of Clyde, Scottish Natural Heritage, Environmental Resources Management, 1996.

The head of the Holy Loch under winter snow, 1868   Artist: James Docherty (1829-1878)

It must not be imagined that the yachtsman is like the dormouse, sleeping away his time till the summer sun awakens him. The Field, Issue No.1, 1st January 1853

Holy Loch anchorage, off-season, 1920s   Image: old postcard

Hunter's Quay anchorage, 1920s   Image: old postcard

Hunter's Quay jetty, 1930s   Image: old postcard

The Firth of Clyde
for pleasure sailing

The wonderful estuary of the Clyde, with its islands, sea lochs, mountains and bright resorts, is one of Britain's premier holiday areas.

There are regular sailings between the popular holiday places and day cruises to the many beauty spots by the Caledonian Steam Packet Company's fleet of modern pleasure steamers and motor vessels, all with excellent catering.

Fast and frequent train services connect with the steamers at Gourock, Wemyss Bay, Craigendoran, Ardrossan and Fairlie.

Car ferries link Gourock and Dunoon; Wemyss Bay and Rothesay; Ardrossan or Fairlie and Brodick; and Wemyss Bay and Millport —drive on and drive off at all states of the tide.

The Caledonian Steam Packet Company Limited

Clyde Cruising Poster, 1960s   Caledonian Steam Packet Company

A CCYC start from Hunter's Quay Pier   Image: Yuile

Water polo at Hunter's Quay, 1890 (see Chapter 11)   Image: *The Graphic*

BOOK ONE
Down the Rabbit Hole

Chapter 1: Yachts & Yachting, a Chequered History

Ned had tried shooting, hunting, and every other amusement which the brain of man has invented to kill time; and he was now trying yachting, which he seemed to enjoy amazingly, though practically he knew very little about it. William Kingston 1860[26]

Scottish national dress does not lend itself to yachting. Fortunately, clan tartans and all the other kit-and-caboodle we Scots sport so gallusly at weddings and formal dinners are not obligatory. In any case, in these more-informed days, we are bound to concede that our swaggering regalia did not emerge until long after the Forty-five Rebellion. In the old days, plaid patterns were optional, reflecting available local dyes and the innocent sartorial ambitions of colour-blind highland dudes.

Once the ban on highland dress was lifted in 1782, our chequered history began in earnest and grew to incorporate all manner of romantic nonsense. Disconcertingly, much of this mythology was conjured up by the Sobieski Stuarts from Godalming in Surrey.[27] In the same vein, since the advent of the first regatta for classic Fifes on the Clyde in 1998, there has been no shortage of yachting myths and legends shovelled into the mix by the wider community of historians in thrall to Caledonia.

The Scots are prone to recycle history, but hopefully, we don't hanker back beyond the bounds of reason. Nostalgia is leavened with a healthy dose of scepticism, and heresies are couched in speculation. Self-deprecation may be one of our more engaging national traits, but any failure to recognise it as such, wounds deeply. Our friends south of the border need not be concerned, however. The Scots will *"accept harsh criticism from a foreigner; but shy away, as from a betrayal, from criticism of Scotland by Scotsmen in contemporary terms."*[28] So, our pitfalls lie closer to home.

The Clyde's maritime heritage has been stripped back to a handful of clichés concerning clipper ships and paddle steamers. It is a matter of regret that no one was taking notes. We had no Samuel Pepys. So, the origins of recreational yachting in Scotland have been lost in the chaos of our social history. But even if they had not been, the search would still be aimless, as neither the genus 'yacht', nor the activity 'yachting', has ever enjoyed a commonly accepted definition. Moreover, the meaning of these terms has varied widely over time.

Onomastics, or splitting the fine hairs of nomenclature, often takes precedence over the nature of the thing itself. However, in this instance, the word 'yachting' did not become important until it became common currency in the 1850s. A hundred and seventy years later, that currency has been devalued and the once-essential term is being ditched as fast as you can change a letterhead. No matter, *Highland Cowes* will honour the genre. As we travel back in time, the theatre of life becomes ever more absurd and arguably more fun too.

In yachting histories, 'yachts' are characterised in terms of what they are not. The consensus seems to be that such vessels 'did not ply for trade'. This negative definition leads historians, ancient and modern, to conflate the equipment – 'yachts' with the activity – 'yachting'.[29] Together, we will endeavour to unravel these strands, although there is the danger, as always with traditional ropework, that working against the lay can result in a God-awful fankle. Dabbling in the latter, the opposed twist of traditional laid rope both facilitates, and complicates, the task.

Fortunately, the story of the sailing yacht is readily told, and indeed has been told well by fine writers over generations. In Scotland, that story is uncomplicated, at least initially. The private 'yachts' of the 17th and 18th centuries were no more than well-appointed versions of the common wherries which attended commerce, and the navy's fleet-ancillaries which shuttled communiqués on the Clyde. These early yachts met the logistical needs of the wealthy, just as private planes do today.

That much is a given, but as messing about in boats evolved, the quest for suitable vessels left a grey wake as wide as the North Channel. A Brixham trawler is not a yacht, no matter what colour you paint the topsides or how hard you polish the brass, because it was conceived, designed and built as a fishing boat. Post-war lotus-eaters and working boat enthusiasts may not agree, but you don't make a table a chair by sitting on it. The activity of yachting, on the other hand, is simply sailing for pleasure and you are as much a yachtsman, or indeed yachtswoman, at the helm of that rustic Brixham trawler as an elegant 6-metre.

Yacht racing is an even more inclusive concept that does not even require a racing yacht. Of course, it helps, but equally, if you are radio-controlling a one-metre model on a pond or making tea for a boatload of hung-over east-coasters aboard an old gaffer in a Medway drifting-match, you are yacht racing. In fact, we'd even go so far as to include the 'grain races', graphically described by Eric Newby, and perhaps even Pooh-sticks with a following wind. In this spirit, agonising over whether this or that event in the distant past constituted a yacht race misses the point entirely.

Since the dawn of man, when only the fittest survived, our species has been hard-wired to compete. As soon as we got afloat, yacht racing was inevitable; to be swifter, stronger, or just more lethal is as much a part of human evolution as the pursuit of sustenance and shelter.

The quest to build our history from a web of antecedents and the holy grail of priority seems eternal. Early writers followed the yachting spoor back through the ages to the earliest recorded civilisations. This was, and remains, substantially meaningless. However, rummaging through the wealth of historical documents, there is much to savour, even if there is no 'genesis moment'. Boatmen of centuries past surely found joy in an effortless passage before the wind. Sailors have hoisted sail with no other purpose than to avoid a squabble across the scullery table since time immemorial. If that is not sailing for pleasure, then what is?

There is more ambiguity; amateur yachtsmen and yachtswomen have appropriated a proud heritage to which they can lay no legitimate claim. They consider themselves to be 'sailors', but few could make an honest living at sea. In our age of euphemism, this might be called out as 'cultural appropriation'. It is certainly a valid point of view, but it is also one which would make a book such as this impossible to write. So, reluctantly borrowing the counter-thesis; today's community of recreational yachtsmen may be said to share a common heritage with the society of professional sailors, and that Kevlar thread goes right back to the dawn of seafaring.

There is no real need to identify the first Scottish yachtsman, nevertheless, Robert the Bruce has been thus anointed in these pages. Such a designation requires us to marginalise less prominent antecedents, but it plays well for reasons both sentimental and narrative, and it does contain an element of truth. Robert went sailing simply for the hell of it; he was, ergo, a proper yachtsman. And as a proper rogue to boot, the Bruce comfortably inhabited the sailor archetype. As for being one of our own, that is a more difficult call. The man was an unscrupulous French-speaking, Anglo-Norman adventurer from Essex, even if his mother was a Scot. What can one say – sailors are what they are.

The only problem with this designation is that it obliges us to populate our quixotic account of Scottish sailing with anecdotes, from the Bruce's death in 1329 to the Restoration of the Monarchy in 1660, when Charles Stuart returned to curate the next chapter of yachting history in a gingerbread encrusted 'Jaght Schip'. These are 350 long, empty years from any rational perspective. Fortunately, timelines are as compressible as they are elastic. Readers reincarnated from that turbulent period in history may substitute their own tales of mystery and imagination and move on.

40

The origins of sailing for pleasure, rather than business, are entwined with the history of vessels of state or royal yachts. But floating bordellos only become yachts in the modern idiom when they transcend state business. Otherwise, they are simply well-appointed ferryboats. Cleopatra cruised the Nile in sybaritic splendour in the 1st century BC, and the Song Dynasty Emperors of China (960-1279) luxuriated in Haw Ting junks.[30] These famous yachts in early history were all notable for their fine craftsmanship, if not always for their rational design.

The Brobdingnagian pleasure vessels of ancient Mediterranean civilisations have been the subject of enduring speculation. The mind-blowing, or possibly mythic, flagship of Ptolemy Philopator in the 2nd century BC is thought to have been about 400ft LOA. Such a vessel would have been so clumsy as to be useless as a warship. More likely, it tested the laws of Archimedes as a fabulous houseboat with an exceptionally commodious wine cellar.

Caligula's yachts a few centuries later ca.40AD were almost as impressive and enjoy much better provenance. The wrecks recovered from the land-locked Lake Nemi in 1929 attest to vessels 230ft LOA. Structural and propulsion limitations surely confined them to sheltered waters. These huge wooden vessels were venues for Bacchanal excess, with both ships and behaviour transcending subsequent maritime high jinks in Europe until the 1800s. And they presaged the vulgar superyachts that cluster like sweat bees on the rim of Mediterranean honeypots today, cluttered with Arab sheikhs, American billionaires and Russian oligarchs.

Forty years ago, Her Majesty's Crown Agents dispatched the author to Brunei Darussalam as a governance advisor. Late one afternoon in the mid-1980s, a 281ft LOA silver and grey superyacht ghosted into Muara Port. The rumour mill suggested that *Nabila* had been posted as collateral in an arms-deal with Adnan Khashoggi that 'went south'. The Sultan of Brunei may have lost his investment but came into possession of perhaps the most elegant large yacht ever built in the modern era, and the star of the 1983 James Bond film *Never Say Never*.
A bemused Sultan would drive down to the docks occasionally, and according to the increasingly bored crew, sit by himself in the yacht's disco, listen to a few popular dance tracks and play with the light-show console. Then he would drive his Bentley home to the Nurul Iman Palace and doubtless twiddle his thumbs some more. A few years later a notorious vulgarian acquired the boat, painted it white and gold and renamed it *Trump Princess*. He didn't know what to do with the bloody thing either. But then, the wheeler-dealer from Queens ran up more than a billion dollars of debt and the vessel was once again seized by creditors. That's superyachting for you.

Yachting history often dwells on the antics of Charles II, a scion of the Scottish royal house of Stuart. However, in 17th century Holland, when Charles was in exile incognito, as plain 'Mr Jackson', it was the gentlemen of the *Vereenigde Oost-Indische Compagnie* or VOC, kings only of commerce, who chose to show off their wealth on the water.[31] And even then, the shallow waters of nomenclature shoaled with the VOC's use of yachts as fast packets for under-the-counter company business – a common duality that blurs the evolution of the species.

Despite his Scottish origins, Charles is generally credited as the 'Father of English Yachting'. He certainly spent a lot of English money on yachts. But perhaps the emphasis placed on this colourful scoundrel has more to do with deference than priority. Pepys's diaries provide historians with an absorbing ready-made narrative. While respecting a host of caveats, the Pepys narrative effectively downplays all prior threads of evolution. Edgar the Peaceful (r.959-975), for example, is remembered, albeit dimly, as not just the smallest English King ever to clamber up onto the throne, but also as an early pioneer in the hedonistic pursuit of royal yachting. Edgar's *"sommer progresses and yerely cheife passtimes were the sailing round about this whole Isle of Albion"*.[32]

Most historians accept that the sport we know today evolved in Victorian times (r.1837-1901). The lady herself, Alexandrina Victoria, was said to be 'very fond of boating'.[33] In 1848, *"the Queen, accompanied by the royal family visited the Argyle Battery, where a halt was made. Here, Her Majesty stayed about half-an-hour, one portion of which she occupied in surveying the spectacle which stretched beneath her. The procession accompanied her Majesty to the wharf, where she re-embarked for her yacht, the Fairy."* HMY *Fairy*, a fully-rigged steam-auxiliary, acted as escort and tender to accompany the royal party on the first *Victoria & Albert*, designed by William Symonds 1843.

The old *V&A* was a cumbersome vessel in the restricted waters of the West Coast, so *Fairy* – shallow-draft and a quarter of the displacement, was often called into service.[34] Shoal waters are increasingly a problem for the super-rich of today. Yachts dimensioned to secure bragging rights are substantially useless for cruising. They have become too large for most harbours and draw too much to enter the prettiest anchorages. This is how natural selection can lead to extinction, or so one hopes.

The Queen's convoy through coastal waters was borne on a tide of popular enthusiasm. The future Empress demanded a uniquely glamorous travelling circus: *"the day became the occasion. The royal squadron appeared in all its pomp and beauty. A fleet of small vessels, gorgeous in excess of flags and streamers, lay around at a respectful distance. On shore, all was gaiety and enthusiasm."*[35] Victoria's gossipy diaries popularised holidaying in Scotland and sparked an interest in coastwise cruising as venturesome subjects retraced the royal Hebridean wake. The glamour of the Highlands, and the romance of our wild places, were already firmly lodged in the national consciousness through the novels of Sir Walter Scott (1771-1832), and the sentimental paintings of Sir Edwin Landseer, David Wilkie and Horatio McCulloch. If good Queen Vic was game to see all this for herself, well, so were her loyal subjects.

However, sightseeing from the promenade deck is not yachting as the author would seek to present it. In the context of Scottish sailing, the defining moment came when touring parties saw something more than scenery in the Highlands. An effete interest in the 'sublime' gave way to more manly pursuits, with the theatre of the natural world relegated to the status of a sporting arena.[36] Men-of-action can only stare in awe at nature's grandeur for so long before they see a field-of-play upon which to test themselves. "*Everybody who was anybody in 1850 wanted a Highland sporting estate. There were plenty of takers in the Victorian world of burgeoning industrial capitalism – an emergent class of nouveau riche, redolent with competitive snobbery, desperate to emulate a traditional land-owning aristocracy.*"[37]

The roots of our earthly sporting paradise were established much earlier, as the Highland Clearances (ca.1750-1860) took effect. Remote and unaccountable in common law, clan chiefs and landowners were often mired in debt, recklessly courting bankruptcy for generations. The birth of a formal banking sector relieved family, friends, and neighbours from the burden of constant scrounging.[38] But this temporary liquidity came with strings attached. Inevitably, the banks foreclosed on collateral when repayments lapsed. This action incurred the sale of vast tracts of hereditary acreage in the first half of the 19th century, disrupting rural life and leading landless Scots to the water's edge.

The first phase of the Clearances (ca.1760-1815) was a belated fall-out from the Jacobite Rebellion of 1745. The Board of Annexed Forfeited Estates was established in 1752 to manage the land lost by Catholic clans on the wrong side of history. However, the old clan system in its entirety was already in decline.[39] The Dukes of Argyle auctioned the leases of farms and bailes (townships), first in the remote reaches of Kintyre in the 1710s, and more widely through 1737.[40] The net result was an endemic surplus of labour. Displaced peasants were marginalised to scratch a living from tidal kelp or follow the herring.

The second, yet more brutal phase of the Clearances (ca.1815-1850), was triggered by the victory at Waterloo. The downscaling of the economy after 23 years of Napoleonic Wars, reduced employment opportunities for both civilians and military men. The new world order set out by the Congress of Vienna (1815) led to intercontinental migration on a biblical scale. Economically redundant families were shipped overseas en masse to

North America, and later to Australia.[41] In retrospect, it is evident that this phase of the Clearances opened the way for sporting estates, as hill land was first consolidated for sheep-farming before being converted to deer-forests, which were equally profitable and required even less labour.

To don, if just for a moment, the bunnet of Red Clydeside, the saga of the 'sporting estate' remains a festering sore in the hearts of Scots everywhere. These Scottish domains are unique among modern industrial democracies; the closest parallel is the private game reserve in Africa. The number of 'game-reserves' in Scotland grew, from perhaps half-a-dozen in 1811, to 80-odd in 1873, with a significant element of this additional acreage bought courtesy of the iniquitous slave compensation scheme of Earl Grey's Whig Government in 1833.[42]

There were around 150 'deer forests' covering 2.5 million acres at the close of the 19th century. By 1906, 3.5 million acres of Scotland had been surrendered to this vast exclusive network of outdoor amusement parks. Adding gripe to grievance, in the same period, the cultural icons of the Highlands were adulterated and hijacked by the new social élite. This process kicked off with the visit of King George IV (r.1820-1830) to Scotland in 1822. 'Balmorality', a term coined by George Scott-Moncrieff, thinly ridiculed Prince Albert's legacy of kitsch architecture on Deeside, and the southern aristocracy's weakness for tartan and tweed.[43]

As the 19th century progressed, Britain's rich and famous descended from their grouse moors to enjoy the open waters of the West Coast. Initially, days on the water were an adjunct to their 'sporting life' in Scotland but sailing soon took on an almost sorcerous life of its own, driven by competitive extravagance and one-upmanship.

Clyde yachting blossomed as the Industrial Revolution accelerated the growth of Glasgow to deliver an enterprising population of newly minted millionaires; self-made men who would swamp the society of aristocratic pioneers and recreate the sport in their own image. Royalty was welcomed to Mammon's new top table. Victoria's playboy son, Albert (later Edward VII, r.1901-1910), made the whole thing irresistibly fashionable when he sold his flotilla of pied-à-terre superyachts and graduated to the nation's much-loved 221-ton Watson cutter, *Britannia*, in 1893.[44]

Albert Edward, or Bertie, as he was known, was long Britain's most iconic yachtsman.[45] He lent weight to his afterguard, although he was not especially talented as a helmsman. As Prince of Wales, before taking the throne in 1901, he legitimised a cult of boorish anarchy that forms a common bond among yachtsmen even in the age of #MeToo.[46] The British public was tired of gloomy reclusiveness, and they have always been susceptible to the outré charm of the philanderer. George MacDonald Fraser's *Flashman* series of novels might have been written about Bertie.

Most references to the King's well-publicised yachting in *Britannia* omit the crucial context – that his passion for sailing equalled his passion for the ladies. The former was consummated in 1863 when, as Prince of Wales, he accepted the Royal Yacht Squadron's invitation to become Patron, succeeding his father Prince Albert. Bertie was both a titular and experienced yachtsman when *Britannia* slipped into the water at Henderson's Meadowside yard in 1893.[47] And, as would be expected, he had owned some impressive yachts through the intervening decades.

Prince Edward acquired an almost-new 37-ton Wivenhoe cutter in 1866 and renamed her *Dagmar* after his sister-in-law.[48] *Dagmar* was followed by the 40-ton cutter, *Alexandra*, in 1871, the 40-ton cutter, *Princess*, in 1872 and the 38-ton, *Zenobia*, in 1873. In 1876, the prince bought the 198-ton schooner, *Hildegarde*, winning the Queen's Cup at Cowes the following year. He then raced the crack 104-ton cutter, *Formosa*, in which he repeated his Queen's Cup win in 1880 and 1882, the latter while Commodore of the Squadron.

The 216-ton Nicholson schooner, *Aline*, in her time a famous racing yacht, was added to the royal flotilla in 1882 as a mothership to *Formosa*. She was sold to the Pasha to make way for *Britannia*. G. L. Watson's *Britannia* was that rare beast, a comfortable racing yacht with no need for a mothership to host après race cocktails, although, when Edward VII became king, the demands of protocol had the 4,700-ton royal yacht *Victoria and Albert III* fulfil that role. As for *Britannia's* lack of auxiliary motive power, that is where having one's own Royal Navy and a stout hawser comes in handy.

The armed forces contributed more than an occasional tow. Victories at sea with the Battle of Trafalgar in 1805, and on land with the Battle of Waterloo in 1815, put Britain in an unassailable position on the world stage. The 'Pax Britannica' of 100 years, lasting until 1914, promoted free trade and enabled the Industrial Revolution. Yachting around our island shores, and indeed far beyond home waters, was for the first time safe, viable and attractive as a leisure pursuit. Then self-seeding intellectual capital, limitless material resources, the end of the Little Ice Age in 1870 and loads o' money gave us the 'Golden Age of Yachting'.

As sailors, we acknowledge a debt to the swashbucklers of the great British Empire for their boundless ambition. We all take the security of our coastal waters for granted these days, but life has not always been so easy. *"It is a general stipulation too, in most of our treaties, that ships may sail to, and trade with, all kingdoms, countries and estates which shall be in peace, amity, or neutrality, with the princes whose flags they carry, and who are then at peace with the contracting parties, and are not to be molested, provided such ships are not bearers of contraband goods."*[49] The Freedom of the Seas was never inevitable, and it was won at great cost. Sailors of all nationalities 'going foreign' benefit from a century of British sea power. With the exception of some notorious regions, like the waters around Socotra at the entrance to the Arabian Gulf and the Sulu Sea in the Philippines, we sailors can tramp the oceans with our canons run in and our gunports sealed.[50]

In modern usage, the phrase 'Down the Rabbit Hole', referencing *Alice's Adventures in Wonderland* (pub.1865) by Lewis Carroll (1832-1898), is a metaphor for something that transports you into a wonderfully surreal state, or it may simply refer to an engrossing and time-consuming topic.

---

[26] The Cruise of the Frolic, Barnaby Brine, Esq. RN. (William Kingston) 1860.

[27] The Sobieski Stuarts (John Carter Allen and Charles Manning Allen from Godalming in Surrey) wrote the Vestiarium Scoticum, to establish a mythology of tartan traditions in 1842.

[28] The Heart of Scotland, George Blake, 1934.

[29] The Equipment Rules of Sailing (ERS) reference: *"The boat, the sports equipment used in sail racing and the personal equipment."* We can only apologise for using this unromantic term.

[30] The Qing Dynasty marble boat (ca.1755) at the Summer Palace elevated such vessels of state to *objects d'art*. Renovating this transcendentally heavy displacement yacht by Empress Cixi is said to have pilfered a budget earmarked for the renovation of the Imperial Navy.

[31] Our last house in Indonesia had the VOC coat of arms moulded on the classical portico above the front door and picked out in gold. I always got a kick out of that!

[32] A Summary History of Yachting, the Lotus Magazine, May 1914.

[33] National Record of the Visit of Queen Victoria to Scotland, September 1842, James Buist, 1848.

[34] HMY *Fairy* was built in 1844 by Ditchburn and Mare at Leamouth. She was 146ft LOA and 312 tons burden.

[35] The History of Dunbartonshire, Civil, Ecclesiastical, and Territorial, with Genealogical Notices of the Principal Families in the County: the whole based on Authentic Records, Public and Private, Joseph Irving, 1860.

[36] Philosophical Enquiry, Edmund Burke, 1757. This book is credited with stimulating interest in the 'romantic sublime'. Burke saw nature as the ultimate sublime object. The Romantic Sublime influenced generations of artists like Stubbs, Haydon and Constable.

[37] Ill Fares the Land: A Sustainable Land Ethic for the Sporting Estates of the Highlands and Islands, J. Lister-Kaye, 1994.

[38] Scottish banking dates from the formation of Bank of Scotland in Edinburgh in 1695. The overdraft incurring interest was introduced by the Royal Bank early in the 18th century and others followed suit. The Committee of Scottish Bankers (CSCB) website.

[39] Scotland's Empire, 1600-1815, Tom Devine, 2003.

[40] *"The tacksman is a lease-holder, (who) keeps part as a domain, ….and lets part to under-tenants. The tacksman is necessarily a man capable of securing to the laird the whole rent and is commonly a collateral relation. These tacks were long considered as hereditary."* A Journey to the Western Islands of Scotland, Samuel Johnson, 1775.

[41] The population of Argyle in 1819 was about 85,500, in 1931 it was approximately 63,000. The impact of depopulation remained through into the 20th century before recovering to ca.87,000 today – the new growth being mainly in small towns.

[42] Guyana's Scottish-owned sugar plantations were compensated at £100 for each slave compared to £18 for an unskilled field worker. The Baillie family, for example, received £110,000 (£9.2m) for their 3,100 slaves, which they invested across the Highlands to become

one of the largest landowners in the north of Scotland. How Scotland Erased Guyana from its Past, Yvonne Singh, the Guardian newspaper, 16th April 2019.

[43] The Cultural Politics of Hunting: Sporting Estates and Recreational Land Use in the Highlands and Islands of Scotland, Andy Wightman, Peter Higgins, Grant Jarvie and Robbie Nicol, Culture, Sport, Society, Vol.5, No.1 Spring 2002.

[44] The King's Sailing Master, Douglas Dixon, 1948.

[45] The Britannia and her Contemporaries, Brooke Heckstall-Smith and E. DuBoulay, 1929, and The Kings' Britannia, John Irving, 1937.

[46] Bertie's introduction to the pleasures of the flesh by an Irish actress deeply wounded his mother, and by her account, 'killed' his father. It also scuppered Victoria's model family as an icon of the Empire. But the lad was nineteen and no one, apart from his mother, really cared.

[47] *Britannia* and *Valkyrie II* were built side by side and both supervised by the great J. R. Barnett of the W. L. Watson office. The owner's representative in the case of *Britannia* was William G. Jamieson who would become her professional skipper.

[48] Maria Feodorovna, Dagmar of Denmark.

[49] The Ship-Master's Assistant and Owner's Manual, containing complete information relative to the mercantile and maritime laws and customs, 15th edition, David Steel, 1821.

[50] Even so, I have sweated at the approach of a 'pirate' outrigger, seemingly hell-bent on maintaining a converging course on the oily waters of the South China Sea.

Royal yacht, *Aline*, Camper & Nicholson, 1860   Setting up for a spinnaker hoist

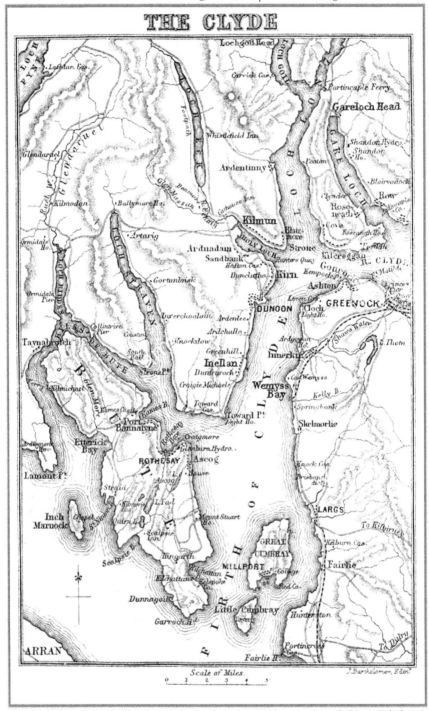

THE CLYDE

The Clyde from Loch Goilhead to Little Cumbrae, late 1800s   A. & C. Black, Edinburgh

Spritsail sand barge and local cows, Holy Loch   Artist: Claude Rowbotham (1864-1949)
From the author's collection. The cows, wandered from Orchard Farm, are entirely fortuitous

The Arrochar Alps, 1810   Artist: Robert Salmon (1775-1845)

Rare bird's eye view of a race off Rothesay, 1890s   Image: Adamson

Chapter 2: Watersheds

In the molten mass there has appeared a vast intricate confusion of different sorts of people, some sailing about upon floating masses of irresponsible property, some buoyed by smaller fragments, some clinging desperately enough to insignificant atoms, a great and varied multitude swimming successfully without aid. H. G. Wells[51]

The Clyde is the largest deep-water estuary in Europe; it is a harbour large enough to swallow an armada in any one of its labyrinth sea-lochs. But only when global trade reached critical volumes, and little boats became big ships, was this generous canvas of any relevance. The Upper Clyde slept through millennia as a quiet backwater; it was a marshy tidal river with endless shifting mudbanks and enigmatic riparian communities.

What would later become the hub of a major European transport system was, for centuries, on its margins. However, if one goes back far enough, long before the river ran where it runs today, archaeologists believe that the Upper Clyde was an important boatbuilding centre.

From prehistory through to the present, as Scottish society evolved and local economies developed, the archipelagic geography of the West Coast dictated the design and construction of suitable vessels and the form of sea-transport networks. With each wave of socio-economic change and each advance in technology, the tide of history has brought demands for all types of specialist craft. However, at the dawn of antiquity, the principal need was for simple open boats to serve as ferries and cargo carriers.

The Log-boat

Most of the early vessels to have survived through the centuries are log-boats.[52] In 1780, workmen digging the foundation for St. Enoch's Church in Glasgow unearthed a log boat, 25ft below the 18th century ground level.[53] To date, 34 ancient boats have been recovered from the Clyde Estuary and along its fossil shorelines.[54] Across Scotland, 154 examples have been discovered, of which just 19% survive.[55] These finds are generally recent in the context of marine archaeology. They are mostly dated around the turn of the first millennium AD, suggesting gaps in the evolutionary sequence. The discovery of the Dover Boat in 1992, one of 20 Bronze Age vessels found in Britain, confirms that significantly larger, more sophisticated vessels had been in use for thousands of years.[56]

The Clyde log-boats therefore merely represent a single strand in the evolution of maritime technology. The largest log-boat found in Scotland was recovered from the banks of Loch Arthur in Dumfries and would originally have been about 45ft LOA. Examples that have been carbon-dated range from prehistory (perhaps 2,000BC) to around 1,500AD. However, historical accounts record their use well into the 18th and 19th centuries. There was evolutionary and regional divergence encompassing inserted frames, false keels, notched-in transoms, built-up topsides, and sometimes even carved and coloured animal 'figureheads' fore and aft.

The 'ammir' or 'trough' was a small dug-out propelled by a standing paddler, like the challenging dugouts that still exist in Papua New Guinea, or indeed as in the hipster affectation of the paddleboard. It is likely that the Scots ferrymen would have wrapped a leg around the paddle as the natives of Papua still do today. However, when confronted with headwinds, it makes more sense to paddle sitting down, just as our early sailors would have set a mat or blanket to enjoy rudimentary sail-assistance downwind. *The desire of early man to get 'something for nothing' led him to use the free-blowing wind to move him and what he wished to carry from place to place on the seas and rivers.*[57]

Field Work – a Cautionary Tale

We might leaven this ancient history with a digression. Many years ago, in the interests of ad hoc maritime research, your author commissioned a dug-out canoe, similar to the Scottish trough pattern, from a boatbuilder deep in the heart of Borneo. Arriving after a tortuous journey at the end of the logging road network, the prospective owner and his advisor clambered up a steep and slippery path to the old man's stilt hut, passing the new boat on the way. It was full of water so as not to dry out and split. Saturated, this miniature vessel weighed-in at about 200lbs. It was also much bigger than we expected.

The master shipwright appeared decrepit and frail, but clearly tough enough to wield an adze with industry and precision. He could also hold his drink. Business began with formal introductions. We sat down cross-legged on the split-bamboo balcony and began the ritual cautiously, with sweet tea. Payment was up to me; whatever 'tuan' thought the boat was worth, and anyway, there was other ground to cover first. That concerned a bottle of Black Label, a down payment on the purchase price, to be consumed in its entirety before addressing the balance.

Meanwhile, across the valley before us, the day wore on, warping the view of rainforest and rice fields with a shimmering heat-haze. Then we tackled the magic demijohn. Had I not just put away a third of a bottle of whisky, the contents of that huge glass jar might have intimidated me. As it was, I was merely mesmerised. There was everything in there: the bottom third of the vessel contained an intriguing sediment of wadded leaf-litter that would have excited the curators of Kew Gardens. And among the twigs and pickled vegetables, there were dead lizards, a small snake and a selection of disconcerting embryos – translucent songbirds and small, huddled rodents. It had all been fermenting for about four years; it was, truly, 'designer arak'.

Even our host approached the stuff with respect; shot-glasses, oily, smoother than expected, slightly meaty; in sum, a cocktail of exotic relish. The effect was immediate and disturbingly hallucinogenic. We had arrived at ten, but when we got up to take our leave, it was four in the afternoon. I think it was the same day, whether it was the same planet, I'm less sure. We blundered home through whorling kaleidoscopic netherworlds, bogged down for a while, then hitched to the back of a passing timber-truck, skating along effortlessly for mile-after-mile in its wake, like an inflatable yacht tender. I was still stoned at work on Monday morning, belched like a seasoned corpse for days, and endured terrifying nightmares for weeks. As for the dugout, the paddle came in useful.

Variations

When considering artefacts buried in mud for hundreds of years, oak log-boats would clearly be the most enduring type-form. Thus, they are no doubt overrepresented in the archaeological legacy. It is likely that a wide range of simple construction technologies using animal skins, bladders, soft-wood and withies were applied to meet the demands of coastal and inter-island transport. The human narrative is, of course, a story of endless innovation and adaptation.

Conjoined log-boats in a catamaran pattern were concurrent with trough dugouts. This type of primitive vessel makes the best use of small timber and remains in use in many parts of the world today. Paired log-boats were recorded on the Solway Firth as recently as 1760. Among various short-crossing ferryboat uses, they linked the all-important drove roads, ferrying livestock where swimming was hazardous. There are no surviving examples of such vessels in Scotland, but that just shows how random our inherited legacy of early craft is.

Northern maritime cultures generally ignored the catamaran, although double-hulled vessels did make an occasional appearance on the Mediterranean. It remains a mystery why outriggers were not developed here, if only for inland waters. South Asian cultures worked out how to incorporate raised platforms on low freeboard outriggers to keep the sailors dry.[58] Our experience with the type in South East Asia suggest aeons of lost opportunity. The belated popularity of small fast multihulls in this country in the 1960s may be attributed to the adoption of divers' wetsuits by dinghy sailors. Scotland's multihull pioneers appear in Chapter 7.

Log boats are routinely made more seaworthy and versatile by building-up the topsides with overlapping planks. It is an easy way to increase carrying capacity and cope with the evolving scarcity of suitable 'donor trees' within dragging distance as coastal logging proceeds apace.[59] Where this set of circumstances exists, the response is universal. More and more of the boat is planked-up as the size of the primary keel log diminishes. Over time, evolution leads boatbuilders to execute the entire shell with overlapping planks built-out from a vestigial backbone.

Trading vessels operating from beaches with heavy bulk cargoes require a flat and robust bottom if they are not to be racked or otherwise damaged when taking the ground. As a response, in another branch of evolution, log floors were engineered with edge-joined planks in a model which developed over 3,000 years and became the ubiquitous cog of the 12th to 15th centuries, before segueing into smooth-skin carvel construction. However, evolution sometimes stutters, so that there are still turn-of-the-century Norfolk Punt sailing dinghies gracing the waters of the Broads with the ancient combination of carvel floor and clinker topsides.[60]

The Currach

Archaeologists have recently turned their attention to the ruins of remarkably sophisticated Mesolithic communities in Orkney and Lewis. This civilisation, which predated Stonehenge, may have spread south bringing its characteristic stone circles with it. No one really knows what Mesolithic boats looked like, but while covering the diggings at the Ness of Brogar, TV presenters tested a currach-like vessel. They crossed the Pentland Firth, albeit within a cocoon of 'health and safety' support boats. Our knowledge of the Mesolithic in Scotland increases year by year, but it seems unlikely that any trace of skin boats from 8,000 to 10,000 BC will ever be discovered.

The Scottish courich was a wicker-framed skin-boat, like an Irish curragh or an English coracle, built to carry two or three people in sheltered waters.[61] Early examples were woven like baskets concentrically from the centre, a method unsuited to larger boats. Courichs endured until the 20th century, later skinned with tarred canvas rather than cowhide. The English and Irish variants were framed with two sets of ribs at right angles, which can be readily scaled-up by multiplying the rib count.

Scottish boats used for inter-island transport would surely have followed that more rational pattern. Seagoing Irish curraghs, like Tim Severin's 36ft

LOA 1976 replica, best represent the type. Celtic monks, engaged in missionary work on the West Coast, likely used lozenge-shaped boats more closely resembling the Irish pattern. They floated like corks but were hardly weatherly. Ninth-century chronicles relate the loss of a fleet of 50 curraghs on passage from Ireland to Scotland which foundered in the Gulf of Corryvreckan separating the islands of Scarba from Jura.[62]

When the Romans arrived in the form of land armies, armed to the teeth in AD79, they had already scouted the coasts of Caledonia in a cursory way, calling at Orkney and doubtless other islands too. It is possible that the Romans' circumnavigation of the British Isles followed in the virtual wake of the Greek explorer, Pytheas of Massalia, who may have voyaged these waters in the 4th century BC. Pytheas probably did not complete the trip, but his account was still the best available set of 'sailing directions' to guide the Romans three centuries later.

Roman scholars believed our island to be triangular. However, in time they learned that beyond the Forth and Clyde lowlands – a line they later demarcated with Antonine's Wall – the lands of Albion spread out east and west. The intriguing table of coordinates set up by the Greco/Roman geographer, Ptolemy (AD 100-170), demonstrates a working knowledge of the coast. Admittedly, an astronomical sighting error rotated the landmass north of the Solway Firth ninety degrees to the east, but that idiosyncrasy had long been recognised and corrected.[63]

The courich type of boat, which requires little technical skill to build, endured for centuries, as highlighted in the chronicles of the saints. Monks favoured the courich for its simplicity and light weight. However, the rudimentary double-ended clinker model that we associate with Celtic sailing was more seaworthy for open-water voyaging, and more durable. Crucially, such craft were less reliant on favourable wind and tide as they could complete passages with the wind on the beam, and even slightly ahead, under both sail and oar.

Julius Caesar wrote about the sea-going currachs of the North Atlantic but was more impressed by the planked boats he came across in the Channel when he was conducting naval operations against the Veneti.[64] The latter *"were made with much flatter bottoms, to help them ride shallows caused by shoals or ebb-tides. Exceptionally high bows and sterns fitted them for use in heavy seas and violent gales, and the hulls were made entirely of oak to enable them to stand any amount of shocks and rough usage. The cross-timbers are secured with iron nails as thick as a man's thumb. Their anchors are secured with iron chains instead of ropes. They used sails made of raw hides or thin leather,"*[65] These robust boats were referred to as 'pieta' by the Romans and renowned for their speed.

The Annals of Tigernach

The Roman army encountered both Celts and Picts as they ranged north, with the latter presenting a more organised resistance on land and sea. The Picts were already a sophisticated people and the dominant terrestrial and maritime power in Caledonia when the Romans arrived. After the Battle of Mons Graupius 83-84 AD, the defeated nobles of the Caledonian Confederacy warmed to Roman technology and civilisation, with some adopting Roman names, customs and manners.

We do not necessarily think of the Picts as a seafaring people in the way that we regard the Celts, but it seems that they were not so different. *The Annals of Tigernach* (AD 729) record that *"a hundred and fifty Pictish ships were wrecked upon Ros-Cuissine"* – said to be Troup Head on the north coast of Aberdeenshire.[66] The annals do not say whether this was a seasonal fishing fleet or a raiding force. It is not clear where they were going and what they intended to do when they got there, but the fact that so many were in close company might support either scenario.

The best-known representation of a Pictish vessel is the carving on St Orland's Stone (AD 700-800). This cartoon-like image depicts four paddlers and a VIP personage in the stern – over-scaled to indicate his importance. Such a depiction says nothing useful about the size or detail of such a vessel, but the general shape shows that the Picts' boats had much in common with Celtic and Viking models.

Early Clinker-built Vessels

Clench-built or nailed clinker vessels appeared during the 4th century BC. These are differentiated from the 'evolved' log boat where the topsides were built up with overlapping planks sewn together with yew withies, like the Dover Boat. Scandinavian shipwrights appear to have led the way for any number of reasons connected with social organisation, geography and natural resources. Clinker construction surely reached Scotland via itinerant craftsmen, word-of-mouth and local innovation long before the Vikings arrived here in force in the 8th century AD.[67]

Although located well to the south in East Anglia, there are 6th and 7th century ship burials featuring well-constructed, nailed clinker-built boats. The lines of the 90ft LOA Sutton Hoo longship equal, or surpass, the Gokstad Ship in sophistication, with waterlines and sections that make the Oseberg Ship appear crude. In the lineage of 'Viking' style ships, it is a very fine example, 200 years before the raid on Lindisfarne that generally marks the start of Viking mischief. Clearly, there was considerable contact and cross-fertilisation among shipwrights even at this early date. Sutton Hoo grave goods originated from as far afield as Constantinople and India.

In the pre-nation state, ships and shipbuilding could not be said to exhibit 'national' characteristics, but an element of regional type-forming was reinforced by the bailiwick of itinerant shipwrights. The archipelagic geography of north-western Europe facilitated sea-borne communication between coastal communities. Efficient land-based road networks that could compete with sea transport did not emerge until the 19th century.

This meant that there was a generous ongoing interchange of ideas to inform the design of sea-going vessels. In this context, it is relevant to note that both Scotland and England only emerged in a recognisable form in the 10th century, when the first elements of our current national identities took root. While there are many different interpretations of early British history, it is generally agreed that Scotland had been substantially united and pacified by Constantine II, who reigned through the period 900-943, while England was ruled by Æthelstan from 927 to 939.[68]

A Furore Normannorum, Libera Nos, Domine![69]

The popular history of Caledonia is bound up in myths and legends and steeped in a formative legacy of the sea and ships.[70] Initially, these ships were in the hands of neighbouring territories to facilitate brutal occupation on the one hand, and tedious evangelising, on the other. Anecdotal accounts of Norse incursions have been preserved within the boastful sagas of rampaging warlords, and the, equally potent, Irish assaults on the soul are celebrated in the chimerical chronicles of proselytizing monks. Inevitably, then, this account is their account, albeit taken on trust and rehashed from a more sympathetic Caledonian perspective.

As the 1st Millennium drew to a close, our islands were vulnerable and disunited. Meanwhile, south of the border in 1066, William, Duke of Normandy's expeditionary force landed at Pevensey Bay. William was surely fortunate to meet an English army already depleted and battle-weary after their hard-won, but ultimately Pyrrhic, victory over the Vikings at the Battle of Stamford Bridge a few weeks earlier. In these circumstances, the Norman Conquest was something of a walkover.

Scotland fared little better. When the Norse raiders first came ashore, they encountered little resistance. The Western Isles with their small and scattered populations were particularly vulnerable. *"The Scots, after being attacked by the Northmen for very many years, were rendered tributory; and the Northmen took possession, without resistance, of the islands that lie all round, and dwelt there."*[71] Across the North Channel, the same thing was happening.

The Norse-Gaels, Hiberno-Norse or simply blended 'Scots' after they settled here, were the dominant society.[72] Godred Crovan (ca.1045-1095), a warlord of Norse/Gaelic blood, who had supported the Norwegian invasion of England, coveted the Western Isles. Godred *"so tamed the Scots that none of them durst build a ship or a boate with above three yron nailes in it."*[73] He became the first secular 'Lord of the Isles' and would establish a powerful, native defensive capability.

In 1156, Somerled (1113-1164), another Norse/Gaelic Lord of the Isles engaged a Norwegian force at the Battle of Epiphany off Islay.[74] The romantic name ascribes from the date of the battle, 12th Night, or 17th January in the old Julian calendar. The first engagement of this legendary sea battle was inconclusive, but two years later, in a more decisive re-run, Somerled was victorious. Epiphany is remembered as a Scottish victory, but it was really just another pointless internecine squabble. The Norsemen in this instance had settled on the Isle of Man for generations and were led by Somerled's brother-in-law, Godred.

However, perhaps the best-known West Coast battle of the Viking period was the Battle of Largs in 1263, during the reign of King Alexander III (r.1249-1286). This debacle put paid to an ill-judged expeditionary campaign mounted by King Haakon IV (r.1217-1263). Haakon had 120 warships at his command and boasted 20,000 battle-hardened men, yet he singularly failed to exploit these assets. The Norsemen met their match in the Largs Channel, where Alexander of Dundonald, High Steward of Scotland, enticed Haakon's warriors to fall on their swords.[75]

Under Dundonald, the Scots relied on a disciplined land army and a small, but well-organised, navy. Dundonald was a cautious man; he kept a weather-eye open and contrived to avoid direct confrontation. The Scot's stand-off emboldened the Norse to the point of carelessness. However, coastal marauding during equinoctial gales is an intrinsically hazardous business. Haakon's mighty fleet dragged anchor, many ships were lost, and the few survivors who struggled ashore were slaughtered.[76]

Three years after the Battle of Largs, the two sides faced-off again, but this time in diplomatic negotiations leading to the Treaty of Perth in 1266. This treaty formally leased the Western Isles and seaboard back to Scotland. However, and perhaps inevitably, the Scots failed to maintain the tribute and the Norwegians were not in a position to enforce payment. Two centuries later, accumulated tribute was expeditiously written off when King James III (1460-1488) married Margaret of Denmark (who was, critically in this context, also Princess of Norway) in 1468.

Meanwhile, through the intervening period, the Scots developed close ties to Norway through strategic marriages between our two royal families. Princess Margaret of Scotland (1261-1283) married the Norwegian King Eric II (r.1280-1299). In 1290, Margaret's daughter, Margaret, Maid of Norway, then just seven years old, fell heir to the Scottish throne. After a rough passage across the North Sea, Margaret became ill and passed away in Orkney, while en route to her coronation. Her tragic death sparked a succession dispute between thirteen contenders for the Scottish crown. This tragedy is said to have inspired the marvellous old poem *Sir Patrick Spens* which has become integral to the myth of the Scottish seafaring man.[77]

> *O whaur will I get a skeely skipper*
> *Tae sail this new ship o mine?'*
> *O up and spak an eldern knight,*
> *Sat at the king's richt knee;*
> *'Sir Patrick Spens is the best sailor*
> *That ever sailt the sea.*

In very different circumstances, we welcomed the Norwegian royal family back to these shores in 1940.[78] The Royal Navy evacuated Haakon VII (r.1905-1957) and his family from Norway during WW2. Haakon organised special operations training at Cairndow for the Free Norwegian forces to support clandestine operations in Norway. The Duke of Argyle entertained Churchill, Mountbatten and Haakon VI for strategy meetings at Inveraray Castle.[79] And, in another Clyde sailing link, the Stephen family's steam yacht, *Medea* was requisitioned and allocated to the Norwegian Navy as an accommodation ship for commando officers during WW2.[80]

The Viking Legacy

With the dispatch of King Haakon IV in 1263, Scotland saw the last of the Vikings as marauders.[81] However, those 'blended' Scots left behind would make a substantial contribution to our maritime heritage. Nearly 30% of Shetlanders have Norse DNA. This declines gradually to 25% in Orkney, 18% in Caithness and 11% in the Western Isles. For comparison, in the Pictish heartlands of Tayside, Perthshire, Fife and Angus, less than 20% of the population show Pictish male lineage.[82]

The Norse-Gaels, Hiberno-Norse, or simply 'Scots' after they settled here, were not to be trifled with.[83] There is a dark side to the Scottish psyche; it rarely surfaces unless you inadvertently nudge a local hard-man and over-brim his pint in a crowded Gallowgate pub. We might attribute this glitch in character to a tell-tale Hiberno-Norse strand of DNA. Trace DNA is substantially meaningless in relation to the inheritance of culture, but it emphasises the extent of assimilation.

The Vikings did not just offer their own blood; centuries of Norse slave-trading also added to the mix. Jim O'Donnell notes: "*As evidence of the far reach of the Dublin slave trade researchers in the past few years have found that a certain portion of the population of Scotland can trace their ancestry to particular Saharan tribes whose ancestors came to Spain with the Moorish conquest and who were then captured in slave raids on Spain, taken to Viking Dublin and sold as slaves to Scottish landowners sometime in the 9th century.*"[84] This abhorrent trade continued until the Norman Conquest of Ireland in 1169. These findings, nevertheless, spice up our ancestry, although it is doubtful whether our passion for indigo banners, or the admonishment 'toe-rag' really stems from Tuareg DNA.

Popular historians like to impart balance to the Viking legacy, arguing that they were benefactors as much as they were butchers.[85] Certainly, the Norse were not unalloyed barbarians; their culture was sophisticated, and self-interest eventually moderated their ruthlessness. They had no special quarrel with the Scots; they had been raiding each other's villages for a thousand years before they ranged overseas. Our coastline was just the next waypoint, as was Iceland, as was Greenland, and as was America.[86]

The modern English language is indelibly imprinted with the Viking's reign of terror, incorporating loan-words such as: 'berserk', 'slaughter' and 'ransack' among countless innocent everyday words like 'give' and 'take'. And of course, in Scotland we have 'braw', the meaning of which is now familiar world-wide through the popularity of Scandi Noir. Scots might also concede that 'haggis' is the Norse word for a small bag and even the pudding itself is probably a culinary relic.

Norwegian paternalism left behind a valuable maritime legacy. Norse practice influenced both seamanship and ship design, while Norse skills in wood and metalworking were held in high esteem by native boatbuilders, keen to learn. What is now known as 'technology transfer' was absorbed through racial blending, cross-cultural sampling and consolidation.[87] Hence the arcane language of sailors is also replete with Norse words like: 'aloft', 'keel', 'knot', 'thwart' and 'windlass'.

Yet, it remains difficult to write the word Viking, or indeed say it, without a virtual exclamation mark. 'Vikings vi et armis!' In an age of brutality, the Vikings notably revelled in gratuitous violence, and the Berserkers, who fought in a trance-like fury of bloodlust, appear not to have worried too much if the blood spilt was their own. "*Let loose the hounds of war, the whirling swords! Send them leaping afar, red in their thirst for war. Odin laughs in his car at the screaming of the swords!*"[88]

Early Double-ended Warships

The classic Viking ship was sophisticated in terms of construction, but it was by no means a unique model. Double-ended, shallow-draft, clinker-built ships with the sheer-line raised fore-and-aft evolved independently around the world and reflect the common challenge of operation from exposed beaches where harbours are few and far between. Moreover, the familiar undulate shape occurs naturally, as a 'least-intervention' form, when edge-fastened planks are bent and twisted. The elegance, light weight and superior sailing performance of such simple, intelligible construction may have been serendipitous, but it certainly reinforced this line of evolution.

The Norse invaders had larger, more powerful, and more elaborately decorated ships than the North-British natives, but they were all of the same genre, built plank-on-plank with the frames added later. A Viking shipyard from the 12th century has recently been discovered on the Rubh an Dunain peninsula in Skye which promises to give some insight into shipbuilding during this key period in maritime evolution.[89]

Over time, our boatbuilders would come to rival the carpenters of Scandinavia with cumulative adaptations to the longship model, albeit that distinguishing Scot from Viking became ever more arbitrary. Scottish longships were classified in ascending size-order as lymphads, galleys and birlinns, type-formed models with a shared lineage. All were easily driven, whether by sail or oar.

Both Scottish and Viking longships are likely to have diverged significantly from the classic model in the 12th century with the introduction of stern-hung rudders. A bas-relief on the Tournai Font in Winchester Cathedral depicts such a rudder ca.1160, concurrent with the legendary Battle of Epiphany (1156-1158) described later in this chapter.[90] Scottish stone carvings through the following centuries consistently depict over-canvassed vessels with sternpost-hung barn-door rudders.

The transition from a steering oar lashed on the quarter to a mechanically integrated stern-post rudder was a key innovation in naval architecture that presaged the eclipse of the open, low freeboard, double-ended hull shapes that required a chain-gang of frightened men with buckets to stay afloat. Over time, the birlinn increased in displacement to acquire better weight carrying capacity and the ability to look after itself in a seaway – essential attributes to both wage war on the high seas and survive the Scottish winter in peacetime with smaller crews.

This same basic model, albeit wider, deeper, fuller in the ends, with less sheer and more stoutly built, was the all-purpose coastal trading vessel of the period. Meanwhile, in an evolutionary convergence, cargo ships, Hanseatic cogs and suchlike were evolving too and could now perform a similar role. Heavy vessels – of whatever parentage, acting as capital ships, are likely to have formed the backbone of defensive raft-up formations, while fleets of lighter, faster galleys were retained to engage the enemy under sail and oar in more tactical one-on-one situations.

The stern-hung rudder would have been a mixed blessing during pitched sea-battles when the boats were crowded with amphibious forces and heavily laden with their associated kit and weaponry. The classic double-ended Viking ship, with a central mast and a squaresail set with minimal standing rigging, has the sailing gear laid out so that it can make way astern almost as efficiently as ahead. This was critical in melées, when congregating and dispersing multi-vessel raft-ups.

When the oppressed people of the Western Isles eventually prioritised shipbuilding, marauding Norsemen would become more vulnerable to interceptions by local warships and forced to engage in ship-to-ship skirmishes. Commanders on both sides quickly realised the value of higher freeboard, fighting forecastles and stern-castles, and later crows' nests to direct operations. Local shipwrights could make these modifications to standard designs, post facto, and with little difficulty.

However, as the threat from Norway receded in the 12th century and England became the prime concern, the lion's share of Scotland's martial resources shifted to land armies. In these circumstances, our nascent navy withered and died, as did the specialisation of warships that had been developed to counter the Viking menace.

More Trouble with the Neighbours

Released from the dread of Viking mischief, Scotland lost its sense of common purpose. Machiavellian politics and relentless internecine enmity with the English marginalised Scottish sea power. Seafaring disappears from our popular history and the chronicle is primarily concerned with pointless gory land battles. Scots look back with unwarranted nostalgia at 250 years of escalating bloodshed with the battles of Stirling Bridge in 1297, Bannockburn in 1314, Flodden in 1513 and Culloden in 1746.

King Edward I of England (1239-1307), the 'Hammer of the Scots', apprehended Scotland as many, even today, purport to understand our brooding nation. He saw a people incubating time-worn ambitions – a common political id rendered impotent by remote decision-making. He saw a cultural landscape seething with suppressed anger like Tam o' Shanter's long-suffering wife: *"Gathering her brows like gathering storm, nursing her wrath to keep it warm."*[91] It seems that Scotland was literally beyond the pale. Edward claimed federal suzerainty over Scotland and our kingdom was a vassal state from 1292 to 1296, first under puppet King John I (r.1292-1396), and then under direct rule from England through the Second Interregnum until 1306.

King Robert I (r.1306-1329), or Robert the Bruce, as beloved in the monologue of primary school history, eventually restored some dignity to the Scots nation when he was crowned in 1306. A king without a country, Robert embarked on a guerrilla war that would last for eight long years.[92] By 1314, he had captured most of the English strongholds in Scotland and was now sending raiding parties into England. Edward II's inevitable response was to invade Scotland with massive force. This was a complex period in our history that defies free rendition, but it appears that Robert now canvassed the Lords of the Isles and his friends in the low countries for naval assistance. Western Isles warships, with the aid of the Flemish Navy, allowed the Scots to blockade the English army's vital supply lines.

Edward's ships were merchantmen manned by civilian crews eager to avoid conflict. So this ad hoc line of defence may have facilitated the famous victory at Bannockburn in 1314.[93] After national liberation, and perhaps as a result of this success, the Bruce was attracted to naval adventures, supporting futile attacks on the Isle of Man and Ireland. More successful, however, was the blockade of Berwick, which fell to the Scots in 1318.[94] But it was not until a decade later, in 1327, that Robert launched Scotland's first purpose-built man o' war at Cardross.

The Ambassadors of the Scottish and the English king co-signed the Treaty of Edinburgh-Northampton in 1328 to end the First War of Scottish Independence after 32 years of intermittent conflict. This treaty must have been a bitter pill to swallow after the loss of so many lives. Scotland was required to surrender Northumberland and compensate England for notional damages to the tune of £20,000 (£10 million). During the run-up to the Scottish Independence Referendum in 2014, we discovered that the perennially marginalised Geordies still harbour ambitions to bolster an autonomous Scottish nation.

Early Shipyards

When population densities were low and economies at subsistence level, building a boat was a major project. New orders were intermittent, so boatbuilding was a peripatetic trade. Shipwrights could not expect a settled or comfortable life. They travelled between seafaring communities, fulfilling their commissions on the local beach. And again today, competitive margins are so fine that the very best craftsmen in advanced composites are locked into a life of vagabondage, moving from one leading-edge racing yacht project to the next, leveraging shortages in their particular areas of expertise in the global marketplace for technical services.

More exalted ships, such as the galleys of King Alexander III's (r.1249-1286) small navy, were built at the ancient royal dockyard at Ayr. Other permanent boatyards eventually grew up at Cardross, near Dumbarton, and at Greenock. The better-known yard at Cardross, where Robert the Bruce built his great warships, was established early in the 14th century hard by Robert's fortress on Dumbarton Rock.[95]

In later life, Robert the Bruce supervised the building of at least one royal galley at Cardross, and surviving accounts suggest that he enjoyed recreational sailing. It is serendipitous that this quintessential Scottish hero heads up our chronology of titular Scottish yachtsman: *"At one time he is in company with his nephew Randolph, making experiments in ship-building, and at another, he is found sailing his vessels on the Clyde, or harbouring them in the Leven."*[96]

Robert is said to have lived out his final years modestly in a simple unfortified manor house with a jetty extending to give access to the river. We might imagine the crusty old warrior enjoying a stiff sundowner on the boardwalk with his old mates, recalling past battles and admiring "*his 'grete schippe, a heartfelt reflection of his western spirit*" lying at her mooring just offshore.[97] As an armchair sailor, who bought a Boyd yacht to moor in front of the house and admire over sundowners, I can empathise.

---

[51] Anticipations, H. G. Wells, 1902.

[52] The Logboat in Scotland, Archaeonautica, vol. 14, 1998, Robert J. C. Mowa.

[53] Pre-historic Annals of Scotland, Dr Daniel Wilson, 1863, cited in Yachting Monthly, 1919.

[54] Glasgow, Elizabeth Williamson, Anne Riches, Malcolm Higgs, 1990.

[55] A Comparative Study of Irish and Scottish Logboats, N. T. N. Gregory, PhD Thesis, University of Edinburgh, 1997.

[56] The Dover Boat was built-up from substantial component parts carved from the solid (resembling multiple dugouts laced together with yew lashings) and would have been about 40ft LOA. It has been dated to ca.1500BC. It is a marvellously complex and sophisticated vessel.

[57] Something for Nothing, Beecher Moore, Colin Mudie, the Dinghy Yearbook, Edited by Richard Creagh-Osborne, 1965.

[58] The Bajau Laut (an ancient culture of sea gipsies) of Sabah, Malaysia, for example, build raised platforms on their boats and protect them with woven dodgers.

[59] This practice of building up the gunwales of log-based hulls is near-universal wherever dugouts are found. For example, South-seas outriggers based on a dugout central hull generally have a sheer strake or gunwale timber added amidships to increase freeboard.

[60] Shooting the Breeze, Euan Ross, Classic Boat, March 2018.

[61] Water Transport Origins and Early Evolution, James Hornell, 1946.

[62] Sanas Chormaic (Cormac's narrative), also known as Cormac's Glossary, Cormac mac Cuilennáin (died 908), King-Bishop of Munster, ca.900 with 19th century translations.

[63] There are other less convincing theories. However, as the 'map' is a series of coordinates, it surely cannot have been that he started at the bottom and ran out of paper.

[64] The Sea-Craft of Prehistory, Paul Johnstone, 1989.

[65] The Conquest of Gaul, Julius Caesar, 58-49 BC, translation by Jane Gardner, 1983.

[66] Matrilineal Succession in the Pictish Monarchy, A. Boyle, Scottish Historical Review, April 1977.

[67] The oldest such boat found in Scandinavia so far is from 320 AD.

[68] Æthelstan invaded Scotland unchallenged in 934. This prompted an ad hoc alliance with Owain, King of Strathclyde and Olaf, the Norse King of Dublin and Constantine's son-in-law, to engage Æthelstan's combined forces at Brunanburh (probably on the Wirral Peninsula although there are five possible sites). The Scots were defeated but the English were unable to capitalise on this success. It was a Pyrrhic victory.

[69] Translation is: "*From the fury of the Norse, O Lord deliver us!*" A History of the Vikings, Gwyn Jones, 2001. The quotation is apocryphal.

[70] The Picts, Benjamin Hudson, 2014.

[71] Annals of Prudentius of Troyes for the year 847.

[72] The Norse-Gaels became the dominant in the Western Isles and peninsular mainland from the Isle of Man in the south to the Shetland Isles in the north.

[73] Sailing ships; the story of their development from the earliest times to the present-day, Edward Keble Chatterton, 1909.

[74] Venturing beyond the bounds of ecclesiastical terminology, an 'epiphany' is a sudden revelation or insight into the nature, essence or meaning of something.

[75] The Vikings had it coming; they fetishized and named their weapons; bloody anthropomorphic affectation ran riot in their pagan culture.

[76] The battle is remembered on the cove-line of Scottish yachts: the motif is believed to be the work of an itinerant craftsman, inspired by the dragonhead on King Haakon's warship at the Battle of Largs. The dragon carvings appeared initially on Fife III's first *Clio* and later spread to other builds. Fife's small boats never had dragons, nor did the original Fife-built *Dragon* or her successor. Dickie's and other yards also carved dragons. Theo Rye.

[77] There are 18 versions of the ballad, but not one is definitive because history does not record a Patrick Spens, although his grave is said to be in Orkney, and the Maid of Norway's ship may have been tossed about, but it did not sink.

[78] The Union between Sweden and Norway was dissolved in 1905. Haakon became Norway's first independent king since 1387.

[79] Villages of Northern Argyll, Mary Withall, 2004.

[80] Steam Yacht Medea, Maritime Museum of San Diego, website.

[81] Haakon died later that year. His successors did not press their claims to the Isles.

[82] Further south, 12% of men in Argyll and South Scotland still carry Irish DNA brought over from the 5th century onwards. But even there, 5% have traces of Viking blood. Vikings still running rampant in Scottish DNA, Glasgow Herald, Lizzy Buchanan, 23rd May 2015.

[83] The Norse-Gaels became the dominant racial group in the Western Isles and peninsular mainland from the Isle of Man in the south to the Shetland Isles in the north.

[84] The Slave Market in Dublin, Jim O'Donnell, April 2013.

[85] For example, BBC documentaries, including Vikings! a Bolt from the Blue, 1980.

[86] The tools for the job were already highly evolved ca.400-300 BC, as evidenced by the Hjortspring Boat and weapons hoard.

[87] Apparently, some 500,000 people alive today are descended from Somerled – a number only bettered by Genghis Khan, who, among historical figures studied to date, has an estimated 16 million living descendants. The MacDonald, MacDougall and MacAllister clans all claim descent from Somerled, between 25 and 45% of them shared the same Y-chromosome, of a kind normally found in Norway. The Scotsman newspaper, 26th April 2005.

[88] Washer of the Ford, Fiona Macleod, apocryphal Celtic, William Sharp, 1896.

[89] Dave Cowley from the Royal Commission on the Ancient and Historical Monuments of Scotland believes that the shipyard could have supported 'an extensive maritime network'.

[90] Tournai fonts were common throughout Northern Europe. Between 50 and 80 were carved by Belgian artisans and exported as finished sculptures. Three or four featured longships with a stern rudder. See also the Port of Poole seal dating from 1325 and the stone-carving of a birlinn in MacDufie's Chapel, Oronsay, from 1772, for example. Barn-door rudders had been in use at least a century before all this during the Han Dynasty in China.

[91] Tam o' Shanter, Robert Burns, 1790.

[92] The warring elite shared a common Norman aristocracy. Bruce was 'de Brus' and his family owned more land in England than Scotland. At one stage, Bruce treasonously swore fealty to Edward. The Fitzallans of Renfrew supported Bruce as did the Campbells of Argyll. The Fitzallans became the Stewards of Scotland and established the Stewart dynasty through marriage to Marjorie, Bruce's daughter.

[93] Bruce's sailors were mercenary Scots, Flemish and French and his fleet included merchantmen and privateers.

[94] It seems that we had a long-standing grudge against the men of Man dating from internecine Norse/Celtic squabbles of the distant past.

[95] This rock, incidentally, is eternally protected by the 'Act of Union' with England.

[96] Robert was of Anglo-Norman and Gaelic stock. The History of Dumbartonshire, Civil, Ecclesiastical, and Territorial, With Genealogical Notices of the Principal Families in the County: the whole based on Authentic Records, Public and Private, Joseph Irving, 1860.

[97] The Kingship of Robert I (1306-29), Michael Penman, 2005.

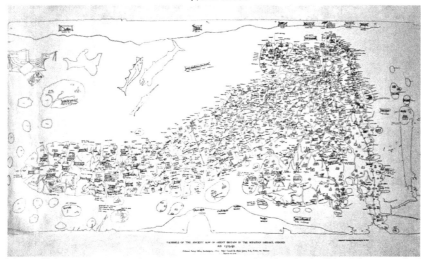

The Bodleian Map. East is 'up'.   Original held at the Bodleian Library, Oxford

The Bodleian Map was drawn post facto during the period 1355-1366 from information gained by a cartographer travelling with Edward's expeditionary forces. It is said to be the first map to depict Britain's coastline with some accuracy. Of course, that accuracy is only in relation to England. Scotland is depicted as the spluttering head of a giant penis. No one appears to have speculated on whether this depiction was accidental, ill-informed or merely provocative. As a map, this image is considerably less accurate than Ptolemy's, drawn a millennium earlier.

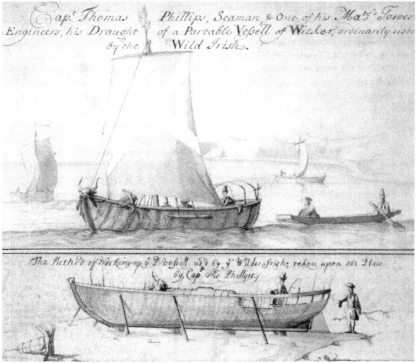

Currach, 17th century interpretation by Captain Thomas Phillips   Note anchor at bottom left

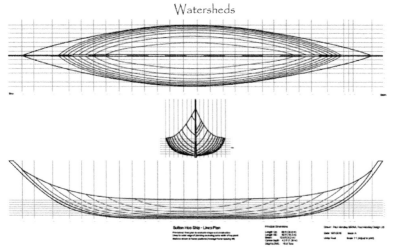

The Sutton Hoo Ship, 7th century, lines plan.   Woodbridge Riverside Trust

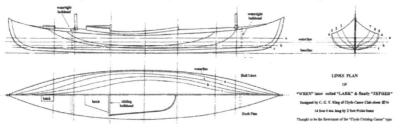

Wren, C. G. Y. King, 1874, prototype Clyde Cruising Canoe   Compare sections with the above.

Dragon Harald Fairhair, the largest Viking ship replica afloat today   Image: Arne Terje Saether

Chapter 3: Monstrous Grete Schippes

He superintended each minute detail, conversed with artisans of every country who flocked in from France, Italy, and the Low Countries; while, under the tuition of Wood and Andrew Barton, the King received lessons in navigation during the trips along the coast and to the Isles. Referring to King James IV.[98]

The ensign of the long-defunct Royal Scots Navy has been informally reintroduced by Clyde yachtsmen in the 21st century. It is flown on a significant percentage of Scottish yachts in what is basically an 'act of civil disobedience'. George McKenzie petitioned the government to have the ensign officially recognised in 2015.[99] However, after some cursory deliberation in the devolved Scottish Parliament, the petitioners received a negative response from Derek Mackay MSP, Minister of Transport and the Isles.[100] Mr MacKay is not a sailor.

Traditionalists initially disparaged the resuscitated Scottish Ensign as a nationalist aberration and just another aspect of the West's regression from the outward-looking cosmopolitan worldview of the late 20th century. Like the St George's Cross in England, the Saltire is associated with populist nationalism and intolerance. However, when inserted into the red ensign, the Saltire becomes satire and a much more subtle comment on a Westminster government that is deeply unpopular north of the border. It becomes, in effect, a 'flag of connivance'.

Whatever the impetus, the flag seldom looks well since almost all examples, fluttering from flagstaffs on the Firth of Clyde, are mean, printed synthetic bunting and horribly undersized. In fact, most British ensigns are much too small. In this, we might look to American practice. If you are going to fly the flag, for God's sake do it with style and conviction! Your ensign should almost kiss the water at rest; it must be sewn not printed, headed with tabling, toggle and cord, and with a field large enough to stir the ghosts of empire. A warrant for a blue or white ensign requires a vessel to be over 7-tons and 30ft LOA; but perhaps that ship has sailed.[101]

However, if your ensign is flown as a tribute to the Royal Scots Navy, it must evoke a time when Scottish diplomacy was 'sleekit' (sly), our foreign policy 'confoutered' (disingenuous) and our glorious military adventures often 'wanchancy' (suicidal). Renaissance Warships were festooned like a Balinese beach café with pennants and streamers in a riot of vainglorious bunting, and sails dyed purple, emblazoned with national regalia. Our ancestors really knew how to dress a ship overall.

Ensigns are important. The ensigns of the English Royal Navy were formerly associated with theatres of operation, but they had also been assigned to divisions within battle fleets, and in various other ways, with the hierarchy of colours not always consistent. At least as far back as 1627, the English fleet was divided into the Red, White and Blue squadrons. In 1665, when the fleet was commanded by the Duke of York as Lord High Admiral, old drawings show the three divisions wearing ensigns of their respective colours.

The colour-coded squadron designations were discontinued in 1864. From that date, the white ensign has been worn by all British warships in commission; the blue ensign by British merchant ships commanded by officers of the Royal Naval Reserve, and the red ensign by all other British registered vessels. Members of the Royal Yacht Squadron have defended their vainglorious right to fly the white ensign of the Royal Navy, while ensuring that the vessels of lesser royal yacht clubs wear defaced blue. Everyone else is required to fly the humble unadorned 'red duster'.[102]

That said, there is no law to stop you flying the rainbow flag, for example, but some familiar bunting is actually illegal.[103] The unadorned Union Flag is reserved for her Majesty's vessels, and if you plan to display the red lion of Scotland, make sure that, if the Queen is not aboard, you hoist the version without the double treasure. That embellishment may still trigger a new life in the Tower of London. And finally, the St. George's Cross is reserved for Dunkerque 'little ships', even if they fly the burgee of a Scottish yacht club.

Today, the Union Flag carries the weighty baggage of empire – the rise to eminence, the assertion of entitlement and the bittersweet tragedy of greatness squandered. Whether this is an arc of catharsis or pathos depends on your politics. Viewed objectively as a graphic design, our national flag is an over-wrought mishmash. But when reduced and set in the canton of the plain red ensign of the British merchant fleet, the overall composition is undeniably magnificent.[104] Certainly, it is a flag we are all proud to fly, and as a bonus, with the troublesome jack thus incorporated, it is impossible to commit the faux pas of flying the damn thing upside-down.

Prior to the union of parliaments, and at least since the 1620s, distinctive English and Scottish red ensigns were flown by our separate navies. There never was a white or blue Scottish ensign, so perhaps that is another point in its favour. These flags included the St. George's Cross and the St Andrews' Cross respectively in the canton. An unadorned Saltire may have been in use as an ensign in Scotland as far back as the mid-1200s.[105] Our discrete national ensigns finally disappeared in 1707, becoming obsolete with the adoption of the mighty Union Jack.[106]

The Royal Scots Navy

All this vexillology justifies a renewed interest in the story of the Royal Scots Navy. Scottish yachtsmen who fly the Scots Ensign should know something of its history and its contribution to the story of sea power. Such naval operations as we embarked upon often involved vessels under charter, manned by mercenaries, and empowered by letters of marque. Even so, the Scots Navy had its moments, through its ups and downs, from its origins back in the Dark Ages.

Fourth century Irish marauders harassed our western seaboard in vulnerable bath-shaped currachs. More weatherly, timber-hulled vessels supported a transformation of intent from coastal raiding to settlement and colonisation. The Irish Scots interbred with the local population and became the dominant bloodline in the region. The blended Celts of Argyle brought with them a social structure that included the autarchic due of 'ship service', i.e. a militia-like people's navy. Arbitrary quotas, bearing little relation to local prosperity or assets, were ruthlessly imposed. The method paralleled the recruitment of land armies raised in times of war by clan chiefs.

The 7th century 'Census of the Men of Alba' recorded that every 20 households in the Kingdom of Dalriada (Earaghaidheal) were obliged to supply two vessels and 28 men, when required.[107] This equates to 170 to 180 'warships' and about 2,500 fighting men.[108] Fishing boats, ferries and coastwise traders could be pressed into service to meet whatever quotas were imposed by the Lords of the Isles, Lord High Stewards, Kings and the like, and served as warships when crewed by angry, frightened men.

In this age before heavy ship-mounted armament, humble little double-enders after the Viking pattern, would have been used primarily to transport troops and provide logistical support, rather than engage enemy vessels on the high seas. The sovereign state could offer little or no naval protection for small coastal vessels preyed upon by marauding Norse, or later by Barbary corsairs and other buccaneers. Then, there was the domestic piracy to contend with – English freebooters and wayward local bullies like the Campbell Clan.

By the late 14th century, naval warfare between Scotland and England had degenerated into the occasional desultory scrap. For both sides, this martial side-show was a mercenary activity, sub-contracted to Dutch and

French merchantmen, independent privateers and locally hired thugs and freebooters. The time was ripe for rekindling, but as a perennially insolvent nation, we could never afford a world-class navy. Nevertheless, the House of Stuart transformed Scotland for a time into a credible, nay formidable, sea power.

When King James I (r.1406-1437) was just 11 years old, he was sent into exile in France. However, British coastal waters were a free-for-all in those days and his ship was boarded by Norfolk pirates who cashed in their prize at the English court. Henry IV pampered his hostage, attended to his education and saw him assimilated into the court when he attained his majority. Consequently, when James eventually returned to Scotland to assume the throne after a hiatus of 18 years, he wisely sought to redefine his image from quisling to staunch defender of the national interest.

In mid-life, King James channelled his boyhood humiliation into a keen interest in maritime affairs. He spent lavishly on shipbuilding and established a naval dockyard at Leith in 1424. However, in many respects, James's new Navy was more akin to a fleet of royal yachts – an armada, built and equipped to transport personages of rank in comfort and safety. The vessels were arranged to trade as well as wage war, not necessarily a bad thing, but in this instance, it appears that the Royal Scots Navy served king rather more than country.

During the reign of James II (r.1437-1460) the navy was obliged to replace their armed merchantmen with purpose-built warships. Not that James could claim much credit; his early reign saw the Royal Scots Navy reach its nadir, with just a single war-surplus Portuguese caravel in commission. Scotland was to all intents and purposes undefended at a time when the art of war at sea was about to undergo a revolution.

With the advent of heavy gunnery, the design of ships changed, as did the order of battle. For four centuries, from 1460 through to the 1860s, large, heavily armed wooden dreadnaughts would defend the interests of maritime nations. Warships would be classified by their firepower and defined by their heaviest armament. Sea battles would no longer be fought with ships grappled together, unless that was necessary to close out an engagement. Capital ships were manoeuvred to stand-off and exchange bombardment. Ships with long-range cannon were favoured.

Perhaps unexpectedly for a small country with limited resources, Scotland muddled its way into the vanguard of this revolution. Even more unlikely is that Scotland's prototype warship was financed by the Holy See. The innovator was a 'canon' who was also an expert in 'canon law'. This homographic tour de force was Bishop Kennedy of St. Andrews (1406-1466). Through Kennedy, the Church enabled the Royal Scots Navy to meet the challenge of the new age of gunnery-based warfare. The result was the 500-ton, *Saint Salvator*, a carrack built with the assistance of Europe's best shipwrights and inevitably tagged 'The Bishop's Barge'.

The *Saint Salvator* was launched in 1458. She was Scotland's first truly 'great ship', incurring a build-cost of some £10,000 (£6.25 million). Clearly, there was money to be made from ecclesiastical council in these bygone days, with kings and bishops in a cosy conspiracy, independent of Rome. The pre-Reformation Catholic Church of Scotland had become an immensely wealthy institution. It is also clear that, for the leadership of the country, the divisions between personal wealth, national assets and God's own estate were blurred to say the least.

The *Salvator* was designed as a warship but served as an old-style armed merchantman, tasked to develop trade between Scotland and the Low Countries. However, in appointments as in armaments, she was no salt-encrusted trampship. The *Salvator* was lavishly outfitted with a suite of luxurious staterooms. While notionally the property of the church, the *Saint Salvator* was often requisitioned by the royal household to serve as a fabulously ostentatious private yacht. Early yachting in this country was often pursued in naval vessels, or non-commissioned ships supported by naval resources. So, for decades at a time, regal duties and autocratic whims took precedence over the defence of the realm.

The *Salvator* was wrecked on the Northumberland coast near the Farne Islands while on passage to Flanders in 1472. The carcass of this innovative sailing vessel was picked clean by Geordie looters; a sad end to a great ship.[109] The people of the north-east of England were notorious wreckers, active across centuries. When Philip II of France sent funds to Mary Queen of Scots a century later in 1565, the treasure ship got into difficulties off the same coast. The Earl of Northumberland seized the bullion, and despite claims by both England and Scotland, kept it.[110]

James II was killed when the barrel of a field-cannon exploded beside him. It was an ironic end for a gung-ho warrior and advocate of gunnery. Subsequently, his partner in crime, Bishop Kennedy, served as regent, caretaking the government until the nine-year old James III (r.1460-1488) attained his majority. James III was an unpopular Anglophile, but his marriage to Margaret of Denmark was welcomed. This union brought Orkney and Shetland, in Scottish possession since the Battle of Largs in 1263, formally into the Scottish realm.[111] James III is known to have had at least two warships at his disposal, the *Flower* and the *King's Carvel*.

Progress made by James III would be continued under James IV. James Grant, an influential 19th century Scottish naval historian, made the following assessment: "*During the reigns of James III and James IV the Scots navy probably reached its highest development. The old alliance with France against England continued, and Scots naval power rose concurrently with the expansion of Scotland's foreign trade and with England's exhaustion through the civil wars of the Roses.*"[112]

James IV (r.1488-1513) came to power in 1488. Through his reign, the king would eventually build a powerful navy boasting 34 ships, including three mighty carracks – the *Great Michael*, the *Margaret* and the *James*. The latter two were about the size of the better-known English vessel, *Mary Rose*, but the *Great Michael*, named after the archangel who led the Army of God against the forces of evil, marked the genesis of the battleship.

James' revitalised navy was tasked to provide leverage in diplomacy, contain foreign piracy in the North Sea and support his crusading ambitions. However, the King's vainglorious character compromised each and every one of these undertakings. The Royal Navy of James IV, nevertheless, became a formidable force, significant even in the global context of sea-power. It was built up from a base tier of coastal defence organised under legislation enacted in 1493 and 1503. Seaside towns were obliged to keep busches (wherries) of at least 20 tons manned by 'idle, able-bodied men'.[113] The King and the nobility saw a good supply of stout seafaring men as essential to expand fisheries, seed a mercantile marine and man the navy.[114]

Noble intent went quickly awry. James's first use of the Royal Scots Navy was against his own people during the Daunting of the Isles (1490-1493), a brutal campaign to suppress dissent and bring the Lords of the Isles to heel.[115] Our king took this opportunity to test his gunnery within suzerain territory in 'an experiment' – possibly, the earliest recorded use of heavy calibre ship-borne weapons to bombard coastal targets.[116]

The legendary might of the Isles had already been weakened a decade since by internecine fighting – in particular, the Battle of Bloody Bay. This engagement was fought off Tobermory ca.1483, between the Lord of the Isles, John MacDonald of Islay, and his son, Angus Òg. Angus prevailed to seize power from his father.[117] However, as half of the McDonalds' fleet was sunk, it was a Pyrrhic victory of the kind we Scots relish. Angus Òg, the last autonomous Lord of the Isles, was murdered in 1490.

Angus Òg reappeared as a comic strip drawn by cartoonist Ewen Bain. It featured from 1960 to 1989 in *The Glasgow Bulletin*, *The Daily Record* and *The Sunday Mail*. Òg of the Isles, and the tabloid Angus both led sketchy lives. Angus's adventures ran riot through the gamut of West of Scotland humour. The storylines accurately reflected, and perhaps to some extent defined, the better half of the Scottish psyche. The other half, of course, remains under the enduring Calvinist influence of killjoy and one-time galley slave, John Knox, and his muse Augustine of Hippo.

King James IV subsequently signed an act of revocation in 1493, formally bringing the Isles within the Scottish kingdom and rescinding

Gaelic self-rule. The troublesome archipelago was annexed to the crown.[118] James established a special naval force on the Clyde to project his authority on West Coast waters via letters of marque to the Argyle clan-Campbell and the Gordons of Aberdeen. Scotia's sovereign territory was now extensive. In fact, the country was as large as it ever would be, as it still included Northumberland at that time.

Freebooting agents of the crown inevitably took advantage of the situation. The Dukes of Argyle swaggered at large on these fickle waters with their private navy of trigger-happy mercenaries. Argyle piracy was a frequent complaint in the Scottish Parliament. Specifically, the Campbells' armed yachts were inclined to stop and search civilian vessels going about their lawful business and rob them with impunity.

James appointed his cousin, the Earl of Arran, as Lord High Admiral, but in practice, he relied more upon the able sailor-statesman, Sir Andrew Wood of Largo, and the rascally Captain Barton. Sir Andrew was something of a buccaneer too. In 1489, with the *Yellow Carvel* and the *Flower*, he captured five English merchant ships off Dunbar and stirred a hornet's nest. In consequence, three warships under Henry VII's *"stout sea captain"*, Stephen Bull, arrived off Edinburgh spoiling for a fight. The ensuing battle was a close-run thing, but the Scots prevailed, and every last English vessel was taken into Leith as a prize. This triumph, before a crowd of enthusiastic shoreline spectators, made Wood something of a national hero.[119]

King James exploited the victory. He released Henry's seamen and sent them south with a message that *"the Scots could fight by sea as well as land"*. Unusually in the Scots' eternal saga of English nose-tweaking, we got off with it. Over the longer term, however, national security was not enhanced. Even so, five years elapsed before a new warship building programme began. The records of the National Treasury show that a galley and two smaller boats were built at Dumbarton in 1494, using timber from Loch Lomond-side and ironwork forged at Leith.[120]

Through the ensuing decade, warship construction moved from the West to the East Coast. James revived the old naval dockyards on the Firth of Forth. He built a new slipway and harbour at Newhaven in 1504, and a new yard at the Pools of Airth in 1506. Substantial fortifications were built on Inchgarvie. This little island stands sentinel to the upper Firth (and supports one leg of the iconic 1889 rail bridge). With all this investment, James was clearly hedging his bets as the Scots had recently signed the airily-named Treaty of Perpetual Peace (1502) with England.[121]

The first great warship launched under the new programme was the *Margaret*, a carrack of 500-tons. She was the largest Scottish vessel afloat, but not for long. In 1505, even before she was ready for sea-trials, King James IV was thinking of yet larger ships. Then as now, commissioning a warship was a long and involved process. *Margaret* would be Scotland's flagship for just four years. Her operation and maintenance became unsustainable in the wake of James's next project, and she was lent to Louis XII of France in 1513 on a two year charter, doubtless in lieu of debts.

James' next project, the *Great Michael*, was laid down in 1507; she would test the technologies of the age.[122] Construction of the great ship demanded the collaboration of skilled craftsmen and the import of materials from far and wide. *Pitscottie's Chronicle* described the ship as a carrack, 240ft LOA and 36ft beam, planked in oak. Specialist craftsmen were recruited from France, Holland, Spain and Portugal.[123] The *Great Michael*, said to be the largest ship in the world at that time, was launched in 1511.

Sourcing materials for the 'monstrous grete schippe' deforested large tracts of Fife. Additional timber was imported from Norway and the Baltic states.[124] The final cost of £30,000 (£20 million) was roughly a year's income to the Scottish Treasury; albeit that the expenditure was spread over five years. More onerous yet was the recurrent operation and maintenance of this one ship, which exceeded 10% of the entire state budget. It is no wonder that the *Great Michael* was said to have 'cumbered all Scotland'.

As for armament, while some canons were cast in Edinburgh Castle, the *Great Michael's* heavy guns came mostly from Flanders, along with hundreds of 'gun-stanes'. Sailcloth and cordage stock were also sourced from Flanders, while standing rigging was spun in the lofts of Dieppe and Rouen. Pitch and tar, like so much of the timber, was bought from Denmark and other countries round the 'Estland Seys'.[125] The *Michael* would have displaced around 1,000 tons, and reportedly carried 24 cannons and 36 pieces of smaller artillery. "*She bore many cannons, six on every side, with three great bassils, two behind on her deck, and one before, with three hundred shot of small artillery – that is to say mijand, and battered falcon, and quarter falcon, slings, pestilent serpents, and double dogs, with baytor and culvering, cors bows and hand bows.*"

If the 20-inch calibre Mons Meg was indeed one of "*three great bassils*" described by Lindsay of Pitscottie, the *Great Michael* would have boasted the largest-calibre gun ever deployed in the history of the world's navies, even to the present day.[126] 'Mons Meg' was cast in 1449 by master iron-founder Jehan Cambier and given to James II in 1457 by the Duke of Burgundy "*desiring to interfere in English affairs*". Weighing 15,366lbs, this weapon cannot have facilitated rapid deployment. Nonetheless, while in service as an artillery piece, 'Meg' was allegedly hauled to England in 1497 to bombard Bishop Foxe's Norham Castle in a typical cross-border action of the time.

The *Great Michael* was manned by 300 seamen and 120 gunners, while up to 1,000 marines might barrack aboard. Sir Andrew Wood of Largo was quartermaster and Robert Barton the skipper.[127] James visited the ship frequently during her construction and often took his lunch there. He loved to show the ship off to friends and acolytes. One such 'exhibition' had her well-tested: "*When this ship passed to the sea and was lying in the road, the King caused shot ane canon at her, to essay if she was wight, but the canon deered her not.*"[128] The proud monarch even had the *Great Michael's* deck-plan planted out to scale in hawthorn trees at Tullibardine Castle.

James intended to employ the *Great Michael* as his flagship in a crusade to free the Holy Land from the Ottoman Turks. The King saw himself as the saviour of Christianity against the dark forces of Islam. However, he failed to mount a crusade, or indeed engage his new ship in any bold and glorious adventure. And so, the most powerful navy ever to defend these shores blossomed briefly before withering away like a mirage.

The new Scots Navy saw limited action in Scandinavia and the Baltic, and coastal patrols successfully deterred privateers in home waters, but the force was never deployed effectively. On one typically errant mission, James Hamilton, Earl of Arran, was tasked to intercept Henry's invasion of France. Hamilton took the Scottish fleet north-about through the Pentland Firth and looted Carrickfergus en route to Brest, arriving too late to influence events. Then, on passage home to the Firth of Forth, the flagship, *Great Michael*, ran aground at Honfleur to remain stranded for a month.

The Scots' new warships precipitated an expensive arms race with the English. Henry VIII commissioned the 700-ton, *Mary Rose*, and the *Great Harry* (*Henri Grace a Dieu*), which at 190ft LOA, approached the size of the *Great Michael*. However, in relation to wielding effective naval power, as opposed to the pursuit of maritime prestige, these vessels were highly inefficient. Their construction squandered the lion's share of the defence budgets of both countries in a largely symbolic projection of sea-power.

The *Great Michael*, like others of her ilk through history, represented a concentration of investment that could not be risked in most theatres of conflict. The great battleships of the 20th century, like the *Hood* and the *Tirpitz*, were similarly vulnerable, as are today's aircraft carriers. They become key targets in themselves and require a small navy to defend them.

Captain James Wood found the *Great Michael* unwieldly and painfully slow to manoeuvre. Drawing more than any other ship in Scottish waters, she ran aground frequently. Three French pilots were recruited – their skill presumably transcending local knowledge. That said, the vessel appears to have been adequately seaworthy for her intended purpose, being in commission long enough under the flags of both the Scots and French navies to encounter and survive bad weather. As she was too big for most harbours, she must have possessed some fairly impressive ground tackle.

The *Great Michael* and the *Great Harry* were very similar in design detail and rigged to sail off the wind. The combined windage of topsides, forecastle, sterncastle and the cats-cradle of rigging would make any attempt to come beyond a beam-reach futile. While smaller warships could make ground to windward, the vulnerability of capital ships of this era meant that weather gauge was decisive in sea battles.

In Nelson's time (1758-1805), weather gauge was still important, but by then even the capital ships enjoyed some windward ability in favourable conditions. That said, even into the clipper ship era, when the square rig was thoroughly optimised, these 'ocean greyhounds' might spend a week gaining, then losing, ground before breaking out of British coastal waters.

We know little about how such behemoths handled, but it is clear that managing the great ships of the Tudor and Jacobean periods could not have been easy. Modern replicas of carracks, as used in the Age of Discovery, are not comparable. They are much smaller and generally enjoy the design oversight of qualified naval architects to ensure certification, and with this comes a fair chance of staying right-side-up. Even then, *"the small body of literature describing practical seamanship in sailing vessels is largely anecdotal. In many cases, the information only applies to specific vessels; in some cases, it is simply wrong."*[129]

Modest success at sea emboldened Scotland to violate the Treaty of Perpetual Peace with a poorly planned invasion of England in 1513. The adventure was invoked by France under the terms of the Auld Alliance.[130] As might have been predicted, such a gratuitous escapade did not end well. James, rashly leading from the front as usual, lost his life on Flodden field. Although this was perhaps *the* archetypal land battle in British history, 26 naval vessels were deployed to support the Scots, including 16 capital ships.

This debacle threw Scotland's institutions of state into turmoil and brought the financial houses of the City of Edinburgh close to bankruptcy. The Royal Scots Navy was emasculated as our nation's finest warships were sold to the French in 1514. The *Great Michael* was brokered by the Duke of Albany to Louis XII for just 40,000 livres (18,000 pounds Scots). The pride of Scotland was renamed *La Grande Nef d'Ecosse* and became the de trop flagship of the Vice Admiral of Brittany, even though she was too big for the harbour at Dieppe. In 1521, *La Grande Nef* led the siege of Fuerteventura, and there is some evidence to suggest that she may still have been in commission as late as 1545, participating in the French raid on Plymouth 34 years after her launch.

James V (r.1513-1542) did not share his father's interest in the navy, but he did revitalise it, mainly by virtue of a strategic marriage to Mary of

Bourbon. The union yielded the French-built warships, *Salamander* and the *Great Unicorn*, as wedding presents, gifted by King Francis.[131] In 1538, James departed Leith for Kirkwall, then Lewis, on official duties aboard the newly refitted *Salamander*. He was accompanied by the *Mary Willoughby*, the *Great Unicorn*, the *Little Unicorn*, the *Lion* and 12 other ships.

The cruise was to fly the flag and hold a series of justice ayres, or local courts – a cornerstone of government in that period. Young James appears to have been a nervous sailor as he signed his 'last will and testament' before his essential but *"uncertane aventuris"*. Writing his will turned out to be time well-spent; James V was barely 30 years old when he died. During his reign, the navy was occupied with domestic duties acting as armed transports on expeditions to the Isles and France. However, these day-to-day operations were compromised when the *Salamander*, together with the Scots-built *Little Unicorn*, were captured by the English.

James VI (r.1567-1625), *"the wisest fool in Christendom"*, made his mark on the high seas in the bureaucratic realm, asserting the sanctity of Scottish territorial waters.[132] Following the Union of the Crowns in 1603, he decreed that all warships under the joint-command of a British Royal Navy should fly the Union Flag as a jack. English warships were sent north on manoeuvres under the still-extant Lord High Admiral of Scotland. In 1616, Scottish captains, David Murray and John Brown, joined the fisheries task force and the consolidated navies finally ended English piracy in Scottish waters.

King James had John Seldon draft the *Mare Clausum* (Closed Seas) decree in 1619 to enable a levy on foreign fishermen. The territorial waters of the British Empire, as claimed by the English, Scots and Irish, were generously drawn to include the North Atlantic all the way to the Americas.[133] James (and later Charles I) stoutly defended these claims.[134] The potential significance of Selden's work was widely recognized when the book, *Mare Clausum,* appeared in 1635.[135] But the argument was already lost; a growing spirit of freedom throughout the world favoured the principle of *Mare Liberum* (freedom of the seas).[136] Following the Vatican's imperious gift of hemispheric trade monopolies to the Spanish and Portuguese in the 1494 Treaty of Tordesillas, Britain too saw wisdom in the *Mare Liberum* too.

King James VI advanced the fortunes of his Scottish acolytes, but he was a not a people's monarch, and he was certainly no sailor. Following the union, he decamped to London, returning to Scotland only once in 1617. Opening Parliament on that occasion in Scotland, he declared his countrymen a *"barbarous people"*, and *"hoped that they would be as ready to adopt the good customs of their Southern neighbours as they had been eager to become their pupils in the arts of smoking tobacco and of wearing gay clothes"*.[137] It seems that James was a demanding individual, disinclined to make the best of things.

With the King in residence, Captain David Murray was kept busy running errands. Murray and the royal yacht *Charles* were dispatched to London *"at the first occasioun of wynd and wedder"* to collect a boatload of unnecessary regalia and regal trappings for the king's use in Edinburgh. Meanwhile, the nobility scrambled to reassemble the royal kit and caboodle they had pilfered over the years of the king's absence. James's visit turned Alba upside-down, and we were glad to see the back of him.

With the Union of the Crowns, Scotland was now inexorably drawn into England's foreign adventures. Our trading vessels were vulnerable on the high seas, but it was not until 1626, after Charles I (r.1625-1649) took office, that a squadron of three guard ships (*Lion, Unicorn* and *Thistle*) was commissioned. The following year, this small Scottish flotilla was sent to support the English in the Bay of Biscay but arrived too late to contribute.[138] The unsuccessful siege of La Rochelle signalled the start of the Anglo-French War of 1627-28.

The Scots Navy, as represented by ships with 'letters of reprisal', or subsequently 'marque', returned to patrol the West Indies intermittently and took part in the capture of Quebec from the French in 1629. During the Interregnum (1649-1660), after going over to the Royalist camp, the Covenanters established patrol squadrons for the Atlantic and North Sea coasts, known collectively as the Scotch Guard. However, they were no match for Oliver Cromwell's republican forces; the ships were seized, and their crews pressganged into the Commonwealth Navy.

Following the Restoration of the Monarchy under Charles II (r.1649-1651, 1660-1685) a small, but unwelcome, task force of the English Royal Navy patrolled Scottish waters. HMS *Kingfisher*, a small ship-of-the-line, remained on-station, able to call in reinforcements when required. Even such little ships could cause trouble along the endless seaboard of the Scottish highlands and islands, as when *Kingfisher* bombarded Carrick Castle on Loch Goil during the last days of Archibald, 9th Earl of Argyle's 'rebellion' in 1685, see Chapter 4.

The English Royal Navy boasted 323 warships in 1697. By contrast, Scotland was essentially defenceless with just a handful of merchantman and privateers on-call for naval duties. The need to protect commerce in home waters was eventually recognised towards the end of the 'Nine Years War' (1688-97). The Scots bought three purpose-built warships from English shipbuilders in 1696: *The Royal William*, a 32-gun fifth rate, and two 24-gun frigates, the *Royal Mary* and the *Dumbarton Castle*.

After the eventful years of the Dissolution, the Commonwealth and the Restoration, one last King James was 'inflicted' upon the long-suffering

British people. James VII (r.1685-1688) was Charles II's younger brother. In his youth as Duke of York, James VII was kept out of mischief aboard his various yachts, venturing the odd braggartly wager with Charles when the mood took him. The two brothers, partners in crime, liked nothing better that messing about in boats and obliging the royal court to bundle-up for endless days on the water too.

As a child, James VII was a precocious mariner. When he was just three years old, he was appointed Lord High Admiral. This was one of the Great Offices of State, albeit rendered absurd in this context. Later, while in exile during the Interregnum, King Philip IV (r.1621-1640) invited James to serve as an admiral in the Spanish Navy. However, this opportunity was declined as the Restoration of the Monarchy allowed him to return home and take charge of the Royal Navy in his native land. While still Duke of York, James commanded the Royal Navy during the 2nd (1665–1667) and 3rd (1672–1674) Anglo-Dutch Wars. Both conflicts were futile, but they enabled James to muscle in on the trade networks of Dutch slavers in Africa. In addition to revenue from the slave trade, James financed his household with profits from the post office and wine tariffs.[139]

For a minor figure in the pantheon of sailor kings, thanks primarily to his brother's largesse, James VII's titles could match the self-aggrandizing knavery of any yachting monarch: Lord High Admiral, Governor of Portsmouth; Lord Warden of the Cinque Ports; Governor of the Royal Adventurers into Africa; and Governor of the Hudson's Bay Company. James was, nevertheless, a real seafarer with the requisite sea-miles under his bunnet. James VII rather than his brother (Charles II) has been described as the true father of yachting.[140] In 1675, during his tenure as Lord High Admiral, vessels of state were first recognised as yachts in official papers. James oversaw significant advances in naval architecture, and the seminal book of charts by Grenville Collins, while dedicated to Charles II, was an initiative approved by James at a cost of £1,914 (£230,000) in 1670.

James ascended to the throne as James VII in 1685 after Charles II suffered a fatal stroke. However, as an ardent Roman Catholic convert in an obdurate Protestant country, his reign was chaotic. He may have worked harder at the business of government than Charles, but his 'Declaration of Indulgence' was too much for Britain to accept. This proclamation, which ostensibly promoted religious freedom, was more concerned with James's ambitions to consolidate an eternal Catholic dynasty in Britain.

A group of senior establishment figures, who came to be known as the 'Immortal Seven', sent a letter to James's daughter, Mary, inviting her to assume the British throne. She agreed, but only if the invitation extended to a partnership with her husband, William of Orange. This was no less than a formal invitation to invade Britain. The 'Immortals' rashly assumed that the English people would rise up to support William and Mary. And indeed, the gamble paid off. The navies of Britain and Holland did not engage, allowing William's vulnerable troop transports and their small armed escort safe passage. So, the 'Glorious Revolution' of 1688 was a bloodless affair in more ways than one.

King James VII had *"ingratiated himself with the sailors of the fleet, behaving with great affability, and taking notice of every particular officer"*. But it was to no avail. Indecision *"paralysed James's vigour of mind"* and in any case, as it transpired, half of his line-of-battle ships were commanded by defectors to the cause of William and Mary. James fled in a blind panic, allegedly casting his Great Seal into the Thames en route, thus de facto abdicating the British throne and leaving it unchallenged for the coronation of William III and Mary II (r.1689-1702).

The Demise of the Royal Scots Navy

The Darien disaster finally drew a line under Scotland's independent naval ambitions. The English had passed protectionist Navigation Acts in 1660 and 1663 which prevented Scottish trade within England's bailiwick. Trade, then as now, was the lifeblood of the Scottish economy. In response, the Company of Scotland was established in 1698 to found a colony at Darien in Spanish-controlled America. The scheme was poorly thought out in almost every respect. When it collapsed with great loss of life and 20% of Scotland's liquid capital, the financial crash that followed ushered in five years of phoney war with the English.[141]

The poorly planned Darien colony was always going to be unproductive and vulnerable, but English action to foil the initiative raised hackles in Scotland. In 1705, the Scottish ship, *Annandale*, was seized on the Thames on behalf of the East India Company on the dubious grounds of breaching the company's charter. When the English ship, *Worcester*, sought shelter in the Firth of Forth, the Scots retaliated with summary brutality. The captain and two of his officers, men guilty only of prudence and good seamanship, were condemned as pirates and hanged from a scaffold erected on Leith sands.[142]

The Act of Union, long on the table, then became inevitable if another pointless war was to be avoided. The long-mooted union became, in effect, an ultimatum. The English parliament passed two bills in 1705 which gave Scotland little choice. The first offered a full union, with a single parliament and common access to the English free trade area, but it obliged the Scots to recognise the Hanoverian succession. Failing agreement, the second bill on the statute book would choke off Scottish exports to England and imperil English property acquired by Scots during the reign of James VI.

This 'carrot and stick' legislation was unpopular on both sides of the border so perhaps it was more even-handed than it appears. On 1st May 1707, the two antagonistic nations merged into a single state.[143] While Scotland may have morphed from a sovereign state to a gelded nation, centuries of ruinous war ended, and with secure borders, the raison d'etre for the Royal Scots Navy expired too. The Scots' enthusiasm for a scrap had also invoked squabbles with the Habsburg Empire, Spain, France, the Dutch Republic, Norway and Denmark. All this was subsumed within a new framework of British foreign policy.

As a small state prone to martial overreach, an effective navy would have been invaluable to Scotland. However, the institution was unreliable and such sea-power as we enjoyed was seldom wielded effectively. Control of the Royal Scottish Navy and its privateer ancillaries lay in the hands of hereditary office-bearers who appear to have known little of the sea and ships. These music hall admirals were not just incompetent, but corrupt, sometimes treasonous, and routinely missing in action. Consequently, no clear naval strategy was ever established.[144]

The passing of the Royal Scots Navy did not, of course, curb our nation's disposition to serve aboard warships. Perhaps a third of the Royal Navy's commissioned officers at Trafalgar were from Scotland. Admiral Adam Duncan (1731-1804) was a fine example. He was born in Dundee of an aristocratic family and joined the navy as a fifteen-year-old. While in command of the North Sea Fleet, Duncan reputedly put down a mutiny by holding one of the ringleaders over the side with one arm, while haranguing the rest of crew with the other. Then, with just two loyal ships, he maintained the nation's defences until the remainder of the fleet submitted to naval discipline.

However, Duncan is best known for leading the British fleet to victory over the Dutch at the battle of Camperdown in October 1797. This was a significant action in naval history. The Dutch Vice-Admiral, Jan de Winter, fought with typical Kampen stubbornness to make this one of the Royal Navy's hardest-won victories. Casualties were high, but the final result was a rout; the British captured seven of de Winter's 11 ships-of-the-line, including his flagship.[145]

The Rise of the West Coast Economy

The Act of Union shifted the focus of economic growth from the Forth to the Clyde and transformed the Scottish economy with Glasgow becoming the 'second city of the empire'. The Scottish merchant class had been enthusiastic advocates of the Union. The English Navigation Acts of 1651 were ostensibly designed to thwart Dutch engagement with the

American colonies, but the East India Company, among others, had been happy to see their neighbours enmeshed in the same trade-war.

Glasgow was at the heart of populist protest in the run-up to the union. But now its status as an ecclesiastical burgh enabled a transformation. As the 18th century dawned, the city's ancient traditions concerning religion and education were side-lined in the relentless pursuit of Mammon. Seeking a toehold in transatlantic commerce, the Glasgow merchants somehow secured the lion's share. So, for them the Union was game changing. The newly empowered merchant class established themselves like pantomime royalty, swaggering abroad in the silks and scarlet cloaks of the Italian Renaissance, holding court in the new coffee houses, and plotting the course of commerce.[146]

This success was interrupted by the American Revolution (1765-1783) which wrecked the tobacco trade. Glasgow merchants suffered heavy losses of £1 million (£150 million) when the Virginia tobacco planters repudiated their debts, en masse. Fortunately for the city, this was just a speedbump and two hundred years of economic growth lay in prospect. The Glasgow merchant class would prosper to mimic the trappings of the aristocracy. Through the 19th century they would embrace a sporting society, yacht racing and 'Highland Cowes'.

CODA: The Galley, Workhorse of Pre-industrial Navies

Mary, Queen of Scots embarked for France in 1548, escorted by a small fleet of French galleys. Marjorie Boden evokes the scene at Dumbarton: *"The sympathetic eye can visualize the appearance of the splendid fortress, flying the beautiful banner of the Stewarts, as it rose along the waters of the Clyde where the French ships, with chained galley-slaves, furled sails, and martial pomp lay at anchor."*[147]

The departing monarch was just six years old and fleeing for her life. *"I inform you that she prospers and is as well as ever you saw her. She has been less ill on the sea than any one of her company, so that she made fun of those that were. We landed in this place, Saint-Pol-de-Leon, on the 15th of this month of August, having been eighteen days on board ship, amidst heavy storms."*[148] Mary's mother, Mary of Guise, sailed from Scotland two years later. By some accounts, her reception at Rouen was florid to excess; even the galley-slaves and sailors of her ship had been attired in white damask. A giant wood and canvas whale floated on the river while Brazilian 'savages' set fire to a tar-ship. Meanwhile, Mary's men behaved badly, 'fighting and brawling'.

Galley-slaves were still common in 16th century France and the practice lingered on until the 18th century throughout Mediterranean Europe. John Knox (1513-1572), the dour lodestone of Scotland's moral compass, was a galley-slave for nineteen long months, sustained only by his faith. *"The more*

I suffer, the more I love the truth that makes me suffer." So wrote French protestant, Pierre Serres, aboard the ironically named *Fortune* a century and a half later in 1700.[149] It is therefore understandable that Knox would hate the Queen, the French and the Catholic Church with a passion. The French routinely consigned convicts and prisoners of war, usually Protestants, to this gruesome fate; few survived the sentence.

A French galley of the period was around 150ft LOA, powered by 150 galley-slaves or 'forsairs', six to an oar. Calculations of horsepower and displacement suggest that better progress would be made under sail in any sort of a breeze; nevertheless, rowing was the norm. 'Motor-sailing' would only have been possible in the lightest of airs or on a dead run, as rowing when heeled was not feasible. With their low freeboard, these ships could only sail to Scotland during the summer months.

"A galley is a long flat one-deck vessel; and tho' it hath two masts, yet they generally make use of oars, because they are built so as not to be able to endure a rough sea, and therefore their sails for the most part are useless, unless in cruising, when they are out of sight of land; for then, for fear of being surprised by ill weather they make the best of their way. There are five slaves to every oar, one of them a Turk, who being generally stronger than Christians, are set at the upper end to work it with more strength: There are in all 300 slaves, and 150 men, officers, soldiers, seamen, or servants."[150]

To our credit, whatever else the British got up to – and our mischief knew no bounds, neither Scotland nor England routinely employed galley-slaves, although Knights Hospitaller of both countries condoned the practice in the Mediterranean. Henry Mainwaring (1586-1653), a lawyer and naval officer turned politician, was an exception. Henry was once a pirate himself; nevertheless, he advocated pressing captured buccaneers to the oar as a deterrent to deal with piracy. Most European countries reviled France's religious persecution. Anne of England finally took a stand in 1713, securing the release of many condemned men, but by no means all.

---

[98] The Stuart Dynasty: its Rise, Course, and Early Exile, Percy M. Thornton, 1891.

[99] This petition was based on the fact that the Merchant Shipping Act of 1995 permits Her Majesty the Queen in Council or a Secretary of State to approve *"any colours consisting of the Red Ensign defaced or modified"*. Supporters cited the States of Jersey, who were permitted to use a voluntary or informal red ensign, adorned with a Plantagenet crown in 2010.

[100] Petition PE1569 – The re-introduction of the Scottish Ensign. *"Calls on the Parliament to urge the Scottish Government to seek a warrant from the UK Government in terms of Part 1, Section 2(3)(a) of the Merchant Shipping Act 1995, for the re-introduction of the Scottish Red Ensign as an 'informal or voluntary' ensign for Scottish vessels."* A negative response was received, dated 22nd December 2015, but this matter has not been laid to rest, by any means.

[101] In 1985 it was as noted. Size limitations have been reduced over the years for specific ensigns.

[102] *"A UK flagged vessel must wear her ensign as required by the Merchant Shipping Act, which includes*

when entering or leaving a foreign port and on demand. It is recommended that the ensign is worn at all times in daylight, especially when near to or in sight of land or another vessel. A UK registered vessel should wear the national maritime flag, the Red Ensign, unless entitled to wear a special Ensign. Wearing anything other than an authorised Ensign is a violation of British and International Law". RYA. The blue ensigns of yacht clubs are 'defaced' with a badge or emblem. The Squadron's white ensign is not defaced.

[103] The RYA's advice is: "*Wearing anything other than an authorised Ensign is a violation of British and International Law*".

[104] Charles II confirmed the Red Ensign as the appropriate flag to be worn by English merchant ships via a royal proclamation in 1674.

[105] The earliest Scottish records concerning these matters were carried off with the Stone of Destiny and lost at sea when the ship returning these documents foundered.

[106] Despite the enthusiasm of James VI/I for the Union Flag, the Scottish Red Ensign is shown on the flag charts of William Downham 1685-6, Allard 1695 & 1705 and Lens ca.1700. So, it seems likely that it survived until 1707.

[107] The Senchus fer n Alban is Britain's earliest native census dating from the 7th century, long before the Domesday Book. It concerns the population of Dalriada, the Kingdom of the Gaels on the West Coast of Scotland. The Senchus contains the oldest reference to a naval battle in the British Isles – an engagement between rival Dalriadan groups in 719AD.

[108] The Safeguard of the Sea, N. A. M. Rodger, 1997.

[109] The Border History of England and Scotland, New Edition, George Ridpath, 1810.

[110] In the Steps of Mary, Queen of Scots, Marjorie Bowen, 2013.

[111] The young King was just 17 when his marriage was arranged. Robert Boyd (a regent) sailed to Denmark to make the preparations. However, while Boyd was engaged in this diplomacy of great national import, he was arraigned for high treason. Such was court life in the 13th century.

[112] The Old Scots Navy from 1689 to 1710, edited by James Grant, 1844.

[113] The 'busche' was probably a wherry, as in the following: "*About the year 1750, this fishery was prosecuted on these coasts by a good many small vessels, named wherries from Ireland; each wherry being about 20 tons burden, manned by 8 or 8 men.*" Transactions of the Highland & Agricultural Society of Scotland, Vol.1, 1799.

[114] The reference to 'idle' able-bodied men is not a reflection on the Caledonian character, it merely confirms that jobs were few and times were hard on the West Coast.

[115] Warships of the World to 1900, Lincoln P. Paine, 2000.

[116] James III had been an unpopular king. James IV was a genocidal despot to the West Coast islanders but enjoyed the common touch with mainlanders and was able to raise large armies at short notice. His court was said to be 'flamboyant, creative and cosmopolitan, patronising poets, writers and artists' and it seems that he was also interested in law and medicine.

[117] The Angus Òg comic strip by cartoonist Ewen Bain appeared from 1960 to 1989 in the Glasgow Bulletin, the Daily Record and the Sunday Mail.

[118] James III annexed Orkney, Shetland and the Western Isles in 1472, but the Isles still enjoyed reasonable autonomy.

[119] Tales of a Grandfather, Sir Walter Scott, 1828. Written as an abridged history of Scotland for young people, Scott's account on this occasion is factually based.

[120] The Old Scots Navy from 1689 to 1710, ed. James Grant, 1844.

[121] James IV married Margaret Tudor, Henry VIII's sister and so there may initially at least have been a genuine desire for a long-term reconciliation of the north south differences.

[122] "*The 'Micheall' was ane verrie monstruous grete schippe for this schippe tuik so meikle timber that schoe wasted all the woodis in Fyfe.*" The Chronicles of Scotland, Vol.1, Robert Lindsay, 1814.

[123] Warships of the World to 1900, Lincoln P. Paine, 2000.

[124] The Shipbuilders' Complete Guide: Comprehending the Theory and Practice of Naval Architecture, with its Modern Improvements, Charles Frederick Partington, 1826.

[125] The Ship, W Clark Russell, 2012.

[126] The largest Great War gun, as used on a few English battlecruisers, was 18-inches. During WW2, the Japanese mounted some 18.1" guns, but they fired a lighter shell.

[127] The Old Scots Navy from 1689 to 1710, edited by James Grant, 1844.

[128] The Historie and Chronicles of Scotland, Robert Lindsay of Pitscottie, 1728. According to the Biographical Dictionary of Eminent Scotsmen "*his credulity, in particular, seems to have been boundless, and is remarkable even for the credulous age in which he lived*".

[129] CFD Analysis of the Survivability of a Square-Rigged Sailing Vessel, W. C. Lasher and L. S. Flaherty. Engineering Applications of Computational Fluid Mechanics Vol. 3, No. 1, 2009.

[130] The Auld Alliance had been renewed 14 years previously in 1499.

[131] The best Scots Whisky is matured in old Bourbon casks, but alas, not as an intrinsic result of this association; the casks come from the USA where this rough spirit was concocted by émigré Scots, a diaspora evidently without prior distillery experience.

[132] This epithet is attributed to well-known deprecator of all things Scottish, Sir Anthony Weldon.

[133] The Law of Nations developed along the lines of the Mare Liberum proposed by Hugo Grotius. It was recognized that the high seas should be open and free. Exclusive sovereign claims over vast areas of the sea were abandoned. But there was general recognition that a littoral state had the right to claim sovereignty over the waters near its coast. Mare Clausum et Mare Liberum, the journal Arctic, Vol.37, No.4, Bo Johnson Theutenberg, 1984.

[134] While collecting taxes from foreign fishermen, a Scottish pinnace commanded by Captain John Brown was seized and taken to the Dutch Republic. James considered the detention unlawful and a personal affront. The Dutchmen were summoned to receive a severe berating from King James personally. James VI reinforced the authority of all his officers, be they commissioned by the Royal Navy or the Scottish Lord High Admiral. 'The Terror of the Seas? Scottish Maritime Warfare 1513-1713', Steve Murdoch, 2010.

[135] Mare Clausum: The Right and Dominion of the Sea, John Selden, 1663. The draft was completed in 1618, but James was concerned that some parts of it might upset the King of Denmark. James was aye short of money and trying to secure a loan from Denmark at that time.

[136] These days, however, the 'freedom of the seas' is still being tested by China in the South China Sea and by Russia in the Bering Sea, for example.

[137] The Scottish Progress of James VI, F. M. Powicke, George A. Sinclair, the Scottish Historical Review, Volume 10th 1913.

[138] In another telling, the three Scots ships were employed as troop transports.

[139] When the British took New Amsterdam, the city was renamed New York in James' honour, and Albany on the Hudson is named after his Scottish dukedom.

[140] When the Sailor Kings were Crowned, Noel Methley, The Yachtsman, 22nd June 1911.

[141] The Scots invested £400,000 (half the money in circulation in Scotland). English investors initially put in £300,000 and the Germans £200. However, the English trading community lobbied Parliament and most English subscribers withdrew. Moreover, when the enterprise got underway, English 'diplomacy' meant that the Scots were denied sustenance and succour in the New World by the governors of Jamaica, New York, Barbados.

[142] Glasgow and the Clyde, W. Dodgson Bowman, 1928.

[143] Scotland was 'allowed' to retain its legal and education systems and our religion retained its hard-won independence from both Rome and the Crown.

[144] Blood on the Wave, Scottish Sea Battles, John Sadler, 2010.

[145] Admiral Duncan Facebook post, Philip K. Allan, 28th January 2019.

[146] Glasgow's Tobacco Lords: An Examination of Wealth Creators in the Eighteenth Century, Carolyn Marie Peters, PhD Thesis, 1990.

[147] In the Steps of Mary, Queen of Scots, Marjorie Bowen, 1952 (ref. background research).

[148] Apocryphal, quoted in, The girlhood of Mary Queen of Scots from her landing in France in August 1548 to her departure from France in August 1561, Jane T. Stoddart, 1908.

[149] A sentiment expressed by Pierre Serres, a Frenchman put to the oars, that Knox would have endorsed. It was not until 1713 that Queen Anne of England successfully pressed for the release of Protestant galley slaves.

[150] An Account of the Torments which the French Protestants endured aboard the Galleys, Jean François Bion, 1712.

The *Great Michael*, 1511

Birlinn Stone carving, tomb of Alasdair Crotach
MacLeod, 8th Chief of Clan MacLeod, 1528

Birlinn Stone carving, on display at the
Abbey Museum on the island of Iona

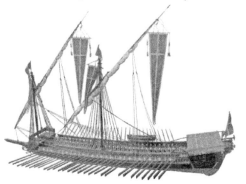

16th Century Mediterranean Galley, Maltese flagged

Image: Myriam Tyhes

Chapter 4: Royal Yachts in Absurdia[151]

Yacht: a vessel usually employed to convey princes, ambassadors, and other great personages, from one kingdom to another." Abraham Rees 1819.[152] *Yacht: a vessel used for private cruising, racing, or other non-commercial purposes.* Dictionary.com[153]

Just one 'royal yacht' has survived the demystification of the British monarchy. The Princess Royal, President of the Royal Yachting Association, owns *Ballochbuie*, a royal blue Rustler 44. The current 2012 vessel replaced another Rustler product, an R36 named *Blue Doublet*, which she bought new from the builders twenty years earlier in 1992. Through the past three decades, Princess Anne and her husband have kept their boats at the Ardfern Marina in Loch Craignish. Anne has remained loyal to this part of the West Coast, a secluded bolthole that invites hyperbole, even among our guests who are neither habituated to the climate nor the midges.

These days, even royalists are embarrassed by a royal family 'gone rogue' and seemingly bent on draining Elizabeth II's reservoir of goodwill, but the Princess Royal has earned herself a free pass in Scotland. When we were young, there was great excitement each summer as the Windsors arrived at Crinan for their West Coast cruise on board the 1936 C&N yawl, *Bloodhound*, a venerable classic even in the 1950s. The family sold the boat in 1969 and today she has found a new role as an exhibit and occasional training ship, curated [sic] by the executive of HMY *Britannia* at Leith.

It is sobering to observe that there is not a boatyard in the Clyde today that can meet the needs of discerning clients and compete with Rustler's products in the niche market for small luxury yachts. Even the David Boyd-designed Piper, which has provided some of the best class-racing on our estuary this past half-century, is now built by Rustler at Falmouth. The Rustler 24, as the Piper is now tagged, is marketed in a day-sailing configuration with a deluxe fit-out as befits her new role as a 'second yacht'. Wealthy owners of much larger craft can relish the tactile pleasures of sailing a thoroughbred without hired hands and enjoy time on the water shorn of desensitising intermediary hydraulics.

Our royal yachts were all sailing vessels until 1842 when Queen Victoria lost patience with the uncertainties of a passage under canvas in the *George*. It seems that it was simply too much for the Empress to drift becalmed on oily seas as sooty steamers went whizzing by. *HMY Royal George* was a small frigate without auxiliary power.[154] That summer, Victoria abandoned the yacht in the Firth of Forth and chartered the SS *Trident*, a 1,000-ton commercial steamer, to complete her cruise. On hearing news of the royal tantrum, Robert Peel, the pitifully eager-to-please Prime Minister, immediately promised a replacement vessel. The first of three steam-yachts to carry the name *HMY Victoria & Albert* was launched the following year.

Victoria carried on the tradition of 'beating the bounds' of her kingdom each year in the comfort of her new steamship.[155] This first *V&A* later became the much-loved *HMY Osborne*, which ferried the royal family to and from the Isle of Wight in later years. Victoria was keen to sail in a manner befitting an empress with a global dominion. Once she had discovered the sybaritic joys of superyachting, the old girl constantly petitioned Parliament for upgrades: *V&A II* followed in 1855 and *V&A III* was launched in 1899, the latter remaining in commission until the outbreak of WW2 in 1939. The replacement, HMY *Britannia*, was launched in 1954. This austere 412ft LOA turbine vessel was built by John Brown in 1953 and decommissioned with much handwringing in 1997.[156] *Britannia* is now quiescent, her decks trodden by day-trippers at Leith. It is heart-rending to see an ocean-going ship reduced to the status of a static exhibit.

Tub-thumping politicians still see a glimmer of hope for a new royal yacht to market their nostalgic rebranding of our diminished nation as 'Global Britain'. However, this idea is dead in the water: mere royalty cannot compete with the mind-boggling super-yachts of today's super-rich. At the time of writing, a nameless billionaire was building a vessel, which at 728ft LOA, diminishes any regal aspirations. Such a vessel dwarfs even the Queen's requisite Royal Navy Type 45 destroyer escort by 228ft, or the length of a small football pitch. And with that thought, chronicles of royal yachting steeped in a cocktail of megalomania and madness, look more rational.

Through our history, the times have not always been propitious for yachting, royal or otherwise. The 100 Years War (1337-1453) between England and France was a pointless conflict between rival dynasties that sapped the resources of both nations to benefit only third-party states. The Scots sided with the French under the banner of the Auld Alliance (1295-present?).[157] As we share a small island with the English, this was awkward to say the least. Then the Black Death (1347-1355) crossed the North Sea. Before 1349, when this foul plague reached our shores to strike for the first of seven times, Scotland had been a relatively prosperous country. However, this pan-European scourge hit our small nation hard. A substantial proportion of the common people were relegated to a subsistence existence, with fatalities disproportionately impacting on the very poorest. Scotia did not begin to recover until the 16th century.[158]

There are few stories from the 14th, 15th and 16th centuries that bear on the history of Caledonian sailing. However, towards the end of the period, in the early 1500s, James IV and his nemesis Henry VIII of England brought in shipwrights from Genoa and Venice to rebuild their navies, as described in Chapter 3. With design and construction now coloured by Mediterranean practice, our capital ships appeared vulnerable on hostile northern seas, like England's *Mary Rose*, which "*turned, the water entered, and sodainly she sanke.*"

We might note, however, that this was also the glorious 'Age of Exploration', when small sailing ships voyaged to the far corners of a still unknown world. However, the bold mariners of Europe sailed precariously in slow and cranky vessels with heavy, clumsy gear. Successful global voyaging depended on trans-generational experience and God's will – the same god, we might remember, who sanctioned the Spanish Inquisition. So, even though this was an age of unmatched seamanship, a liberal slice of secular luck was obligatory too.

From the navigator's perspective, the essential tools of the trade (the astrolabe, telescope, barometer and charts) were not refined to useful levels of accuracy until the early years of the 1600s, sometime after the most significant trans-oceanic voyages had been achieved. Sir Isaac Newton (1642-1747) considered the climate of invention to have attained a peak during this era: "*It is certainly apparent that the inhabitants of this world are of a short date, seeing that all arts, as letters, ships, printing, the needle, &c., were discovered within the memory of history.*"[159] In his defence, Isaac claimed no expertise in social anthropology, archaeology or history. Newton's confident, if misguided, point of view reflects a society before specialisation, where polymaths of genius could grasp all the intellectual advances of the age.

For those intent on yachting during the Age of Discovery, the Little Ice Age (ca.1275-1875) delivered some truly dreadful summers. In these years, the attractions of employment with imperial trading companies in the tropics must have been considerable. Both the British East India Company (1600-1874) and the Dutch East India Company (1602-1799) introduced yachting to the languid waters of the tropics as a suitable diversion for their senior officers in the late 18th century.

The Governor of Bombay, Sir John Gayer, owned an armed yacht called the *Benjamin* in 1698. A feature on 100 years of Indian yachting in *Yachting* by Scot Kenneth McIver commemorated the first regatta in 1830, won by the cutter *Rob Roy*.[160] The Scottish expatriates were clearly well represented, with Robert McGregor a popular, long-serving commodore of the Bombay Sailing Association.

The end of the Little Ice Age (1275-1875) is seldom cited as a factor in the growth of yachting, but if not instrumental, the onset of more benign sailing conditions through the summer months was surely serendipitous. While pre-1875 temperatures only averaged a degree less than 'normal', we are currently less than a degree above that virtual benchmark now and already experiencing dramatic change. The Dickensian scenes of winter with deep snow and families skating on frozen rivers, that still adorn Christmas cards today, depict the usual winters of the Little Ice Age. In that era, the salt water of coastal harbours and sheltered straits froze over too. There were three particularly cold spells around 1650, 1770 and 1850. Summers were shorter and less attractive for yachting. In these circumstances, boatbuilding out of doors on exposed beaches must have been challenging to say the least.

On home waters, interest was stirring too. There are well-documented references to English royal yachts in the Tudor Period (1485-1603), although the modality of their use is unclear. Henry V was said to have sold his yachts to clear debts, but they were brokered into commerce as demand for yachts was non-existent. Henry VIII, always something of a poseur, was reputed to have sailed aboard a yacht with sails of gold-tinted cloth in 1520. While the spectacle of gilded ships adrift on the River Thames at sunset must have been magnificent, most yachting histories wisely give this period a wide berth.

We are on firmer ground following the accession of James VI of Scotland to the English throne in 1603. Celebrated shipwright Phineas Pett built a much-admired pleasure boat for Prince Henry of Wales (1594-1612), eldest son of the monarch, in 1604.[161] The *Distain* was a miniature ship-rigged yacht, measuring 28ft LOA x 12ft beam, mimicking the English flagship, *Ark Royal*. Beneath the styling, she was a well-designed sailing boat, seaworthy enough for open water.

This fabulous toy was presented to the young Prince at St. James's *"who entertained it with great joy, being purposely made to disport himself withal".*[162] Through his childhood, Henry revelled in watersports and swam regularly in the dangerously polluted waters of the Thames. As a result, the heir to the throne died of typhoid at just 18 years of age. His brother, the Duke of York, was next in the line of succession and would become Charles I (1600-1649) on the death of his father, James VI, in 1625.

While such a needless death is poignant in itself, when James VI lost his first-born son, perhaps an element of Old Testament retribution adhered to the tragedy. Back in 1590, James's mother, Anne of Denmark, endured a rough passage across the North Sea to Scotland from Oslo aboard the *Charles*.[163] Seasickness was inevitable, but while the royal party was merely inconvenienced, the Danish admiral accompanying the fleet insisted that only witchcraft could explain such a storm. This casual assertion led to the scapegoating and execution of Agnes Sampson, the 'Wise Wife of Keith'.[164]

Agnes was brought before the notorious North Berwick Witches Court and accused of invoking malicious mischief upon the royal yacht. She was a convenient suspect, as were all midwifes and 'barefoot doctors' when such courts were convened. Agnes was brutally tortured before conceding that she raised the tempest.[165] The Scots were particularly enthusiastic witch hunters during the reign of James VI.[166] King James is well-remembered as patron of the definitive English Bible, but *Daemonologie*, the work of his own hand, published some years before, was sadly the work of the devil.[167]

This unhappy voyage also saw two Danish womenfolk put to death for the same crime, sending devils to shiver the timbers of the ship. Surely, if bad weather is attributable to witchcraft, we must have an impressive coven of witches in Scotland. Writers cashed-in on all this naïve nonsense. Shakespeare referenced the voyage, when one of his witches claimed to have set sail in a sieve; and then Edward Lear brought satire to the drama.[168]

The Jumblies
They went to sea in a Sieve, they did,
In a Sieve they went to sea:
In spite of all their friends could say,
On a winter's morn, on a stormy day,
In a Sieve they went to sea!
And when the Sieve turned round and round,
And everyone cried, 'You'll all be drowned!'
They called aloud, 'Our Sieve ain't big,
But we don't care a button! we don't care a fig!
In a Sieve we'll go to sea!'
Far and few, far and few,
Are the lands where the Jumblies live;
Their heads are green, and their hands are blue,
And they went to sea in a Sieve.

Peter and Phineas Pett built the *Charles*, an 810-ton, 44-gun warship for the English Navy of King Charles I in 1633. In the account of the maiden voyage, we find King Charles enjoying the sail and later returning home up-river in the royal barge.[169] Baby Charles, Duke of Rothesay, later to become King Charles II and the first 'sailor king', would have been three years old and not yet able to join such excursions. However, in his later youth Charles appears to have been indulged in the same manner as his late uncle, Prince Henry of Wales.[170]

Thus, perhaps, were the seeds a lifelong enthusiasm for yachting sown in the constitution of the House of Stuart's proto yachtsmen. But before Charles II, could take the stage, there would be a significant hiatus in royal yachting. The English Civil Wars of 1642-1648 and Britain's dalliance with the republican model of government marginalised such trivial pursuits for the best part of two decades.[171] There were no 'presidential yachts'. Prince Charles, later to become Charles II, led a charmed life that bridged these tumultuous years. His father, Charles I, was beheaded in January 1649. For Oliver Cromwell, it was *"an unfortunate necessity"*, as the old king had refused to relinquish the royal prerogative.[172]

Charles's quest to regain the throne began in June 1650 when he landed at the mouth of the River Spey to receive the title of King of Great Britain, France and Ireland, conferred four months previously by the Scottish Parliament. This rash assertion prompted a full-scale English invasion. The Scots were routed at the Battle of Dunbar in the autumn of that year. Undeterred, the Duke of Argyle, formally crowned Charles at Scone in January 1461, when Cromwell's victorious army was still camped on Scottish soil. As the English troops rested and regrouped, Charles seized the opportunity to march an army of Covenanters south to invade England.

Cromwell was on their heels in an instant and once again fatally outmanoeuvred the Scots. The ensuing Battle of Worcester ended in a brutal street-fight. Charles watched from the tower of the city's cathedral. After the rout, he fled the field of conflict to scramble aloft into the generous canopy of a local oak tree. The agile royal rogue shared his perch with Colonel William Careless – surely ill-advised company? Charles absconded with a bounty of £1,000 (£103,500) upon his head. He embarked for Normandy in the *Surprise*, a little vessel owned and skippered by Captain Tettersell, a native of Brighton. The 8,000-odd mercenary Scots roped into the fighting were not so lucky. They were deported to New England, Bermuda and East Indies to work as indentured labourers. But for their descendants, we might say, who is laughing now?

The promotion of sailing, as a fashionable pastime in 17th century Britain, owes much to the patronage of Charles II, the first 'sailor king'. While it is perhaps disingenuous for Scotland to lay claim to the 'Merry Monarch' in the context of Caledonian yachting, since he was a scion of our very own Royal House of Stuart, we must accept the chaff with the wheat.

Charles already knew something about small boat sailing from the early years of his exile in the Channel Islands, where he had found little else to do.[173] He lodged in Elizabeth Castle, accessible by causeway at low tide, but otherwise an island. It is a good place to learn to sail as you can go over the side and walk home if anything goes wrong. The Jersey interlude inspired a life-long interest in boats.

Charles subsequently found refuge in Holland until he was recalled as the figurehead for the Restoration of the Monarchy. Dutch mercantile society had been yachting on the Zuider Zee for a century, at arm's length from the moral strictures of a rather strait-laced Presbyterian culture. As a competent sailor and bon vivant, Charles would have fitted in nicely. The Dutch thought him an amiable fellow with a 'genius for amusing himself', not perhaps the sort of genius that is universally admired, but certainly a valid entrée into the world of yachting.

Once the ink had dried on the Restoration, in 1660 this once-and-future king was ferried to a rendezvous with a waiting British warship on a Dutch yacht. Charles took a fancy to this fine little vessel. Initially, the newly installed monarch had two yachts at his disposal – the *Mary*, bought from the Dutch East India Company and presented to the newly reinstalled monarch by the City of Amsterdam, and the *Bezan*, also relinquished by the same company.

Naturally, the King was keen to see if the shipwrights of Deptford and Woolwich could match the speed and utility of these little Dutch vessels. Whether Charles understood the limitations of Dutch design, or was simply exercising his national chauvinism, we do not know. Certainly, the English shipwrights did not take the continental model as a point of departure. Rather than copy, and reluctant to innovate, they reverted to the old practice of miniaturising well-known warships, a grovelling ruse generally well-received by royal clients with aspirations to sea-power.

The first new yacht was based on the hull design of a sixth-rate man-of-war, recalling Pett's earlier effort for Henry of Wales in 1604. The new English-built yachts were deeper-bodied than the Dutch vessels and did not require leeboards. As for rig, the stump-topmast was retained, but a standing gaff was used in place of the Dutch-style sprit we now associate with Thames barges. A typical royal yacht of this period was 130-tons, 70ft LOA, 56ft along the keel, with 20ft of beam and 8ft depth of hold. Buffed-up armament was part of the show, and such a vessel could mount eight little 3-pounders to deliver an appropriate level of ceremonial cacophony.

King Charles and his younger brother James, Duke of York, sponsored a squadron of royal yachts which cruised in company as 'party boats' on the Thames. Charles is said to have commissioned 14 English yachts and there may have been 25 in all, including those used by family and courtiers. Diarist Samuel Pepys lauded the occasional point-to-point wager between bouts of gluttony, heavy drinking and high-jinks.[174] The sport has been associated with the patrician buffoonery of hell-raising rogues ever since.

Charles was an unabashed rogue, and unsurprisingly, the spectre of divine retribution dogged his career. A sepulchral gloom fell over London in 1665, with a quarter of the population dying from the last great outbreak of bubonic plague. Then a mishap in Farriner's Fish Yard bakehouse ignited the Great Fire in 1666, rendering 80,000 long-suffering subjects homeless. Charles and his brother James took an interest for once, albeit a self-interest, to score a rare PR coup. However, we may reasonably doubt the motives of the more servile accounts of these two lads, stripped to the waist, wielding fire beaters and quenching the flames with their noble sweat.[175]

Meanwhile, Charles had fallen out with his old friends in Holland. In 1667, Admiral Michiel de Reyter crossed the Channel with a well-armed raiding party. The English fleet was laid up for want of funds in the Medway, secured behind a heavy chain barrage. The king had pilfered the defence budget and frittered away the assets of the Exchequer. De Reyter broke through the barrage and ran riot. He sank 23 English warships and spirited away the English flagship, the *Royal Charles*. The pride of the Royal Navy was displayed as a trophy in the heart of Rotterdam. The counter decoration of the *Charles* remains an exhibit in the Rijksmuseum today.

Yachting Diplomacy

Bridging the yawning gap from the Stuarts to the Victorians has always been a challenge for yachting historians. And yet, yachting survived the 18th century, and arguably emerged stronger without the high-profile patronage of unpredictable British monarchs. A common description is that "*yachting appears to have sunk into a stupor after the death of Charles II and did not revive again until nearly a hundred years later*".[176] Most histories restart the narrative with the Cumberland Sailing Society in 1775 – generally recognised as the first 'proper' sailing club in Britain.

The Cork Water Club may have appeared half-a-century earlier in 1720, but it bore little resemblance to the clubs we know today. In that same year, even as the Irish gentry frolicked in the sunshine, the British Government in London passed the Dependency of Ireland on Great Britain Act, declaring the right of Britain to legislate for Ireland and emasculating the Irish House of Lords. Not, perhaps, a year for the Irish to remember then? In any case, if we view the slate objectively, the earliest yacht club in the world is the Russian Flotilla of the Neva in 1718. The Neva was resuscitated in 1892, revived again in 1958, and is still active.

In the 1720s, the Cork Water Club exerted negligible influence on an apathetic society. Apparently, sporting gentlemen in the rest of the British Isles had no real desire to re-enact archaic sea battles in tedious pantomime format conceived by the Dutch, as in the painting depicting "*the Amsterdam Yachts enacting a battle on the occasion of the visit of Peter the Great, in 1697*".[177] Not everyone revels in the minutiae of nautical etiquette, or is willing to subject themselves to the childish whims of putative admirals, nevertheless, in the early years of yachting it was the only game in town.

The following year during the reign of William III, Peter the Great, Czar of Russia (r.1682-1725), and an enthusiastic amateur yachtsman, visited Britain. 'King Billy' had no interest in yachting but arranged for his guest to spend time at the Royal Dockyard at Deptford, with excursions to the Greenwich Observatory, the Arsenal, the Mint and the Royal Society. Peter is credited with an enquiring mind, but he made no attempt to meet Isaac Newton, Christopher Wren, or Edmund Halley. The Czar's visit to Deptford is well-documented, incorporating key details on the evolution of efficient fore-and-aft rigged yachts in an indigenous British idiom.

No efforts were spared to facilitate this early eastern bloc 'espionage'. The host's underlying motives were, as ever with UK plc, commercial. The Crown sought to re-establish the Muscovy Company's recently lapsed trading monopoly. Consequently, Peter was given unrestricted access to the Royal Navy's inner workings, installations, and facilities during a period of significant advance in the field of naval technology.[178]

Peter's sojourn in Deptford cues another self-made Scot into the story. Admiral David Mitchell (ca.1650-1710) rose from humble beginnings to become one of our finest seamen. On the outbreak of the Third Anglo-Dutch War in 1672, young David was abducted by the English Royal Navy. In his memoirs, John Macky recalls: "*David Mitchell was born in a little fisher town in Scotland, and was pressed into the English Service, when but a boy: he hath past through all the degrees of a sailor, and without any recommendation, but his own merits, hath raised himself to the honourable post he now enjoys and had risen faster had he been an Englishman.*"[179]

Mitchell travelled the world and rose rapidly through the ranks, gaining his first command in 1684. However, his career faltered in 1686 when the fleet was rationalised, and like many others on the Navy list at that time, he lost his ship. Ashore, on half-pay, he joined a coterie of discharged, and generally disgruntled, naval officers who subsequently travelled to Holland to throw their lot in with William and Mary. The defection was timely and prescient; the 'Glorious Revolution' was both successful and bloodless.

Catholicism was unpopular in England in the late 17th century. Thus the 35,000-strong Dutch force landed unopposed at Brixham and secured a quick and efficient 'regime change'. This unequivocal invasion is forgotten by a nation that cites 1066 as the last time a foreign army took possession of English soil. James VII was allowed into exile to live in France with his cousin Louis XIV. He was the last king of Britain to have much interest in sailing until Edward VII in 1901.

David Mitchell prospered in King Billy's navy, with a fair collection of ensigns to his name. He was promoted to Rear Admiral of the Blue in 1693, and knighted in 1694. He served as Rear Admiral of the Red in the Mediterranean and later Vice Admiral of the Blue. He was a Commissioner of the Admiralty and a Member of the Lord High Admiral's Council. This ambitious Scot revelled in his honours and appointments, which included 'Gentleman Usher of the Black Rod'.[180] "*He is a very just, worthy man, of good solid sense, but extremely afflicted with the spleen, which makes him troublesome to others, as well as himself; he was the author of that commendable order, in the Navy, of preferring the officers according to their seniority, which takes off the powerful solicitations of great men for commands for their creatures, greatly to the prejudice of the service."*[181]

David Mitchell was Captain of the flagship, HMS *Yorke*, which brought Peter to England. Both men were fluent in Dutch, so at the Czar's request Mitchell was assigned as his official escort and translator. For a strait-laced protestant, spending time with this uninhibited character was surely a mighty sacrifice for king and country. But then, while babysitting his wayward charge, David was able to go yachting regularly on the Thames.

Peter's 'Great Embassy' was based in Deptford, home of the diarist, John Evelyn. Peter never met Evelyn; he sub-leased the house from Captain (later Admiral) John Benbow. Benbow was himself a less than satisfactory tenant, however, the Russian delegation was far worse. Like a boisterous rock band on tour, or indeed some late-20th century yacht crews that we all might recall over the years, Peter and his entourage ran riot. Evelyn's housekeeper wrote to complain of *"a house full of people right nasty. The Czar lies next your library and is very seldom at home a whole night"*. Peter's crew used valuable oil paintings for target practice. The 'great ambassadors' destroyed Evelyn's well-tended garden, ploughed the bowling green, flattened the flowerbeds and somehow devastated a 400 feet long holly hedge.[182]

Evelyn called in His Majesty's Surveyor, Sir Christopher Wren, *"to view how miserably the Czar of Muscovy had left my house"*. Wren's account of *"goods that is lost, broake, and damage done to them includes 3 wheelbarrows broke and lost, eight fether beds, eight bolsters, twelve pair of blanketts very much dirtyed and spoyled"*. The damage estimates totalled £350 (£25,000). Peter was a large man at 6ft 7", and by all accounts, dangerous to know. The young Czar endorsed 'recreational vandalism' as the new 'sport of kings' and left chaos and the weighty judgement of history in his wake.

The Czar's interest in ships and shipbuilding was genuine enough, however. Indeed, his naval ambitions became something of an obsession. Earlier in his fact-finding tour, Peter had worked alongside the carpenters at the Dutch East India Company's yards to learn the business. A young shipwright employed at Deptford said later *"the Czar of Muscovy worked with his own hands as hard as any man in the yard"*. Alas, his dark side was transcendent. Peter offered up one of his own men so that he might witness a demonstration of keelhauling, still on English Navy statutes at that time. It must have taken courage, but David Mitchell stood his ground and refused to countenance such wonton savagery 'on his watch'.

King William gave Peter the sixth-rate, *Royal Transport*, as a gift. This was a luxurious armed yacht, formerly deployed as a VIP taxi, shuttling members of the royal family and British envoys back-and-forth across the Channel. She was one of England's most modern small sailing ships, reportedly built to an 'experimental' hull-shape and rigged as a schooner. The *Royal Transport*'s talented amateur designer was a young, hard-drinking

English nobleman, Peregrine Osborne, Marquis of Carmarthen, also known more commonly as the Earl of Danby.

Danby was a man with flexible morals and too many names. But he was by all accounts an excellent sailor and an original designer, even if he was perhaps better-known for suicidally hard-drinking, bribery and embezzlement. No matter, in the world of yachting, these ancillary characteristics can be attributes. More positively, Danby's pioneering work on schooners cements his place in the history of yachting.

Czar Peter often went sailing in the company of the like-minded Marquis. Danby was "*a bold, volatile, and somewhat eccentric young man, fond of the sea, (who) lived much among sailors and was the proprietor of a small vessel of marvellous speed*".[183] This particular vessel does not feature among the Royal Navy's fleet, but she was already renowned for her sailing qualities in 1690 and was a good model for his subsequent series of handy, fore-and-aft rigged vessels. Danby's design talents might just have produced the first yachts that were actually responsive enough to make sailing them more than an ego-trip. It is possible that a turn at the helm came with the prospect of genuine tactile pleasure.

Peter had caught the sailing bug as a teenager, messing about in a 'botik' on the restricted waters of the Yauza River in Moscow. Peter's *St. Nicholas* was either built in England or built by Danes in Russia to an English design; there are alternative histories. More certainly, the yacht originally belonged to Peter's grandfather and dated from as early as the 1580s to as late the 1640s. Peter came across the *St. Nicholas* in 1688 and had it restored. Reputedly, and unlike most Russian vessels of the time, *St. Nicholas* could make ground upwind. Her fine handling surely inclined Czar Peter to admire the work of the Deptford yards.

The *St. Nicholas* was clearly a well-built vessel as she is still exhibited today at the Naval Museum in St Petersburg. In form, she resembles the shallow-draft Dutch-inspired yachts of Charles II's era, with a single mast stepped well forward, fore-and-aft rigged and cheekily armed with four miniature cannons. She is 23ft LOA x 6'7" beam. The oldest surviving yacht in Britain is the 26ft 6" LOA, *Peggy*, dating from 1789 and now at Castleton on the Isle of Man.[184] If *St. Nicholas* is in any part authentic, she would predate *Peggy* by a century.[185] More likely, the Russian boat merely represents the type, which is interesting in itself.

The Czar was having fun, but it was apparent that he had his eye on a greater purpose – the projection of sea-power. Peter had established a naval dockyard in Archangel in 1683, and on his return to Russia, would prioritise the construction of a grand navy. In the early years of this ambitious project, many Scots travelled to the Baltic to build, maintain and man Peter's ships. With the assistance of the Earl of Danby, the Czar recruited about 60 British experts, including: Major Leonard van der Stamm, a master shipwright at Deptford; Captain John Perry, a hydraulic engineer; and Professor Henry Farquharson, a Scottish mathematician, who was assigned the daunting task of transforming intellectual life in Russia. David Mitchell, perhaps wisely, passed on this opportunity.

Henry Farquharson (ca.1675-1739), an Aberdeen Professor, was a key agent of Peter's ambition, enjoying a level of resources, influence and patronage he could never have achieved at home. He established a School of Mathematics and Navigation in Moscow and a naval academy in Saint Petersburg. Farquharson might be said to have curated the 18th century intellectual life of Russia, such was his reach and authority.

During his tenure in Russia, Henry Farquharson inspired a generation of explorers, land surveyors, cartographers and astronomers and opened lines of communication with the European scientific elite in these disciplines. He personally corresponded with the 'great minds' of his age such as Leibniz. And he translated the seminal scientific papers of the time into Russian, giving local intellectuals access to works like *Euclid's Elements* for the first time.

Peter created a great and powerful fleet. By the close of his reign, there were 28,000 men employed in the dockyard and as serving sailors on 49 capital ships and 800 smaller vessels. However, these proud Russian vessels never saw action. Peter's glorious fleet would simply rot contentedly at moorings for years, before suffering the indignity of being handed over to the Ottoman Empire following the 'Treaty of Adrianople' in 1713. Ultimately, this was sea-power without a purpose, consigned to the marginalia of history.

Meanwhile in Scotland – Campbells vs the Crown

Yachting on the Clyde before the 19th century was enlivened by life-or-death competition. In the early 1600s, Archibald Campbell, 8th Earl and Marquis of Argyle (1607-1661) and Chief of the Clan Campbell was effectively the head of government in Scotland. Argyle commanded a stout little armada – three armed yachts and sundry smaller vessels which later came under the control of his son Archibald, the 9th Earl (1628-1685). When these toy warships sailed in company, martial intent was very real; they were not aping naval manoeuvres.

The Campbell yachts: the *Anna*, the *David* and the *Sophia*, sported 36, 12 and 6-guns respectively. They were withdrawn from domestic service in a last-ditch attempt to rally the clan in 1685. Archie marshalled his forces on the Isle of Bute; however, discipline was breaking down. They looted the island and sacked Rothesay Castle. Argyle's recruits had both outstayed their welcome and established the Scottish yachting archetype.

News of an English force on the horizon prompted a move to Eilan Dearg where they fortified the old castle.[186] The Scots assumed that the notorious Kyles of Bute narrows would be impassable to the much larger English warships. Alas no, while Argyle was absent fighting skirmishes elsewhere, Captain Hamilton warped the *Kingfisher* through the East Kyle. In a coordinated assault, he sent the *Falcon* the long-way-round via the West Kyle and had the *Mermaid* and *Charlotte* stand by in Rothesay Bay.

The unexpected arrival of the *Kingfisher* inspired Argyle's men to desert the Eilan Dearg garrison rather than defend it. The mutineers mined their arsenal, but cautiously left themselves plenty of time to escape. Arriving on the island, Hamilton's commandos were able to extinguish the slowly fizzling gunpowder trail before it reached the magazine. Booty seized by the English included 300 Dutch rifles with latch-fixed bayonets, the first seen in Britain, and unforgivably, Argyle's bragged standard. *"For God and religion, against poperie, tyrannie, arbitrary government, and erastianism"*.[187]

The secluded waters of Loch Striven would again see pioneering weaponry again, 260 years later. During WW2, the Royal Navy tested perhaps 200 of Barnes Wallis's 'Highball' and 'Upkeep' bouncing bombs. These were smaller versions of the famous Dambusters' bomb and were designed specifically for naval action. Two decommissioned battleships, *Admiral Courbet* and HMS *Malaya,* were anchored in the loch as targets. The Highball was initially intended to attack the *Tirpitz*, but that ship was dispatched in a conventional bombing raid. The proposed target was then changed to Japanese ships in the Pacific theatre, but WW2 ended before Highball could be used.[188] The loch was also used for midget submarine (X-craft) testing and planning for another *Tirpitz* operation. The Kyles Hydro Hotel in Port Bannatyne was requisitioned as HMS *Varbel* and 'Ardtaraig House', at the head of Loch Striven, was a satellite naval base for the 12th Submarine Flotilla as HMS *Varbel II*.

The extensive interests of the Campbell family, up and down the West Coast and on the East Coast too, justified the trouble and expense of maintaining a well-equipped fleet of private yachts. In peacetime use, the term 'yacht', as used in the 17th century, may have encompassed later definitions associated with sailing tours and yachting for sport. So, were the Campbells yachtsmen? Their boats were certainly well-finished and emblematic of status, but whether any member of the family sailed for the hell of it, like the Bruce in his twilight years, we are less sure[189]

The Argyles' place in the annals of Scottish sailing was affirmed when Archibald, the 8th Earl and 1st Marquis (1607-1661), persuaded Charles Stuart (1630-1685) to sign the Covenant in 1650 and crowned him King of Scotland at Scone the following year. However, as events transpired, the Campbells' dalliance with Charles II, the 'father of English yachting', 'father of tennis' and father of fourteen acknowledged illegitimate offspring, and countless other poor wee bastards, did not end well.[190]

Archie suffered the ultimate fate of those who play both sides. Archibald Campbell, 8th Earl and 1st Marquis, was beheaded on the block at the Maiden in Edinburgh, and his son Archie, the 9th Earl and 2nd Marquis (1629-1685), suffered the same grisly fate. Their heads were spiked on the "*the prick of the highest stone*" on the northern gable of the Old Tolbooth in Edinburgh High Street. The corporeal remains of father and son were later reconstituted and now rest beneath the tar-black dome of the Campbell family's forbidding crypt on the north shore of the Holy Loch.

The 10th Earl (1658-1703) acquired the more familiar title of the 'Duke of Argyle' in 1701.[191] Archie Campbell, 10th Earl and 1st Duke, broke with family tradition, to depart for the next world with his head still firmly attached. But this Archie's exit was hardly quiescent either. The Duke was well-known for his debauched lifestyle, which he pursued with vigour when residing at his estate on Tyneside. Even so, his death from knife wounds after a fight in a Newcastle brothel shocked polite society. Then the family discovered that Archie had left Chirton Manor to Mrs Alison, his paramour. Inevitably, the bequest was contested by the Campbells and the bitter struggle fuelled years of litigation and salacious gossip.

There was more misfortune. In the 'Argyle Papers', the Duchess, writing in connection with the settlement of the 10th Earl's affairs in 1704, laments the sinking of one of the family's yachts off Northumberland while on-passage to Edinburgh laden with household effects from Chirton.[192] In this era, the Campbells still maintained yachts on both coasts of Scotland. As for Chirton, the family did eventually recover the estate via an outrageously biased Ecclesiastical Court hearing, where poor Mrs Alison was excommunicated and impoverished for good measure.

As a clan, the Campbells never commanded public sympathy and Daniel Campbell of Skipnish in Kintyre parlayed apathy into open hostility. The Westminster government imposed the Malt Tax in 1725 – effectively a levy on beer-drinkers. The tax applied throughout Britain, but the Scots took it as a personal affront. In Glasgow, the people ran amok to be mown down by musket fire.[193] The target of their anger was tobacco baron Campbell who, as Glasgow MP, had voted for the tax.

Campbell's house, 'Shawfield Mansion', was ransacked. As might be expected when a pillar of the establishment suffers loss, a compensation bill was passed in the Commons. The City of Glasgow was required to pay out £9,000 (£1.5 million). After the renovation of Shawfield, there was enough 'small change' left for Campbell to buy the island of Islay. Although not in the Argyle's direct bloodline, Dan Campbell was loyal to the Argyles and represented Inveraray in the pre-1707 Scottish Parliament. During the 1745 Rebellion, Bonny Prince Charlie made Shawfield his headquarters for ten days while he held the city fathers to ransom.[194]

CODA: A House of Stuart Royal Yacht

The Science Museum in London holds a model of a 17th century yacht (70ft LOA; beam 20ft 4") dating from the reign of Charles II. This scale model is thought to be one of the 14 royal yachts built in England, either the *Katherine* or the *Portsmouth*, both built by Phineas Pett at Woolwich in 1674, so it could be either. A third option is that it may represent a design proposal as it does not display the royal coat of arms worked into the stern of full-sized royal vessels. The model is well-preserved and nearly all elements are original, so it provides an insight into the detail of early British yachts. Also, see drawing at the end of this chapter.

The English model of this period superficially resembled the *Mary* and the *Bezan*, as gifted by the Dutch, but was fundamentally different in hull-form as it sprung from a diverse tradition of ship design. The Dutch yachts of this period were beamy, carrying this beam to the stern; they had heavy quarters, flared bows and more freeboard aft than forward. In section, they were basically semi-circular with maximum beam at deck level, like the lethal and late-lamented Division II sailboards.[195]

So, while the British and Dutch models had much in common above the waterline, beneath the waterline our yachts were considerably more sophisticated; they were deep-bodied, with enough lateral area for good performance upwind without leeboards. The Stewart yachts resembled a sixth-rate man-o'-war with the typical long rudder-post and maximum draft at the stern. The aspect ratio of the rudder is twice that of the shallow-draft, *Mary*. Note that the keel-line is not parallel to the waterline. While built-up from a long straight keel, sailing trim was quite different. The vessel rotated onto designed waterlines with the less buoyant stern sections settling into the water to level the sheerline and raise the bow.

The most significant attribute to recognise is that, beneath all the baroque clutter of gilded gingerbread and pomp-encrusted upper-works, sits a nicely proportioned, well-formed hull. On the deck-line, the shape is very bluff and typical of the 'cod's head and mackerel-tail'. However, on the waterline the entry is surprisingly fine, and the run, as usual on English vessels, is very clean and easy. Shorn of all decoration, she would be a handy, good-looking vessel and lively enough to maintain the interest of a recreational yachtsman.

As to the rig, that also is fundamentally correct. The model carries a single pole-mast to set an efficient sloop rig. The recently evolved standing gaff is potentially unwieldy, but in this instance is controlled by a pair of powerful vangs or braces. The loose-footed mainsail is the main driver, but there is also a generous staysail and a jib on a bowsprit. The free section of the pole-mast above the gaff carries a square topsail sheeted to a yard. Gaff topsails were not then common. There was no reason why such a vessel should not have been able to turn to windward with reasonable efficiency in skilled hands.

[151] Søren Kierkegaard (1813-1855) influenced the development of 20th-century philosophy, in particular, existentialism and postmodernism. His Absurdist Philosophy is an affirmation of the inherent meaninglessness of life. More recently, 'Absurdia' became a crazy dreamland of wardrobe monsters, dragons, where nothing is quite what it seems. Trees are birds, umbrellas are trees, and the sky is thick with snoring fish. See: The Emperor of Absurdia, Chris Riddell, 2007.

[152] The Cyclopædia or Universal Dictionary of Arts, Sciences, & Literature, ed. Rev. A. Rees, 1819.

[153] Dictionary.com 2019.

[154] HMY *Royal George* resembled a small frigate and would have been classed as a sloop. On her retirement, the yacht was used to accommodate members of the Royal Service until 1901.

[155] While we use the term figuratively, the literal meaning is not so far adrift; 'beating the bounds' is an ancient custom from before the Norman Conquest. The community would walk the boundaries of a parish, led by the parish priest.

[156] The new Labour government in 1997 announced that *Britannia* would be decommissioned, and no replacement would be built. Her last official duty was associated with the handover of Hong Kong to China in July 1997. The Queen wept at the decommissioning ceremony.

[157] The original formal alliance that granted dual citizenship in both countries was eventually revoked by the French government in 1903, but some aspects were never annulled, and De Gaulle refreshed the Auld Alliance in 1942. They are all dead now, but Scots born before 1907 arguably enjoyed dual nationality from the residual legal standpoint.

[158] Scotland, a History from Earliest Times, Alistair Moffat, 2015.

[159] Men of Invention and Industry, 1884.

[160] A Hundred Years of Yachting in India, Kenneth McIver, The Yachtsman, 22nd March 1930.

[161] The Autobiography of Phineas Pett, Edited by W. G. Perrin, 1828.

[162] However, this same comment is attributed to Prince Charles on receiving a model yacht in 1637, as noted in Men of Invention and Industry, 1884.

[163] Prince Charles, later King Charles I, was born ten years later in 1600, but we doubt whether his father's enthusiasm for boats extended to christening his son after the royal yacht Charles.

[164] Witchcraft on the High Seas: King James and the North Berwick Witch Trials, C. Emerick.

[165] James married Anne of Denmark in 1589. He sailed to Denmark to collect the lady. On the return voyage, they were battered by storms, thought to be the result of witchcraft.

[166] Between 1479 and 1727, more than 2,500 'witches' were executed (just 15% were men). Thousands more were tried and tortured. Scottish persecution was notably savage.

[167] James VI of Scotland and I of England was obsessed with witches. He published *Daemonologie* in 1597. This philosophical dissertation on necromancy and ancient black magic included sections on demonology, werewolves and vampires to educate the populace on the perils of sorcery.

[168] The Jumblies (first verse), Edward Lear, 1812-1888.

[169] The Autobiography of Phineas Pett, Edited by W. G. Perrin, 1828.

[170] Pett may have built a similar model to Henry's *Disdain* of 1604 for Charles in 1637, but the references concerning the circumstances of the gift are conflicting.

[171] The Commonwealth of England, Ireland and Scotland was only in existence from 1659 to 1660. However, the monarchy was deposed for eleven years from 1649-1660.

[172] In 1653, in an ironic twist, Cromwell assumed that reviled prerogative himself with all the hereditary privileges of a transmissible dictatorship. Charles II would later bestow sainthood on his Scottish father, an honour unique in the annals of the Church of England, and one seemingly conceived solely to torture the ghost of Cromwell. This footnote comes into the 'not relevant, but fun', category.

[173] The King's Sailing Master, Douglas Dixon, 1948.

[174] Previous British monarchs had vessels of state, sometimes five or six of them. Henry V was obliged to sell off his royal yachts to pay debts and fund his wars with France. Charles II had no fewer than 25 royal yachts during his reign, some small, others large and opulent. When Victoria succeeded to the throne there were still 5 royal yachts in service.

[175] Glasgow had already fought the plague in 1645 and seen the city laid ruin by its own fires in 1652 and again in 1677. These fires are not as well-known as Pudding Lane (or Monument Street as new research suggests), but equally devastating to the little university town.

[176] British Yachts and Yachtsmen, a complete history of British yachting from the middle of the sixteenth century to the present day, The Yachtsman, 1907.

[177] The History of Yachting, 1600-1815, Arthur Hamilton Clark, 1903.

[178] The Great Stone Dock at Depford was designed by Edward Dummer and first used by the Royal William. This was not the first such dock by any means; the dry dock in Portsmouth of 1595, which currently accommodates the Victory, was already 100 years old.

[179] Memoirs of the Secret Services of John Macky, 1833.

[180] Biographica Navalis, John Charnock, 1795.

[181] Memoirs of the Secret Services of John Macky, Esq, during the Reigns of King William, Queen Anne, and King George I, John Macky, 1833.

[182] History of the county of Kent, Alfred John Dunkin, 1855.

[183] The History of England from the Accession of James II, Thomas Macaulay, 1855.

[184] There is a restoration programme underway with more experts on hand than might seem strictly necessary. However, it is proposed to replace rusting iron fastenings (clenched not riveted) with treenails. If this is the case, it is wrong in any circumstances.

[185] The St. Nicholas was reputedly discovered by Peter the Great at the Royal Izmaylovo Estate in 1688. It was then restored by Karshten Brandt. This old botik was constructed in England, or to English design by Danes in Russia, and is said to date from the 1640s. An alternative, more nebulous, theory suggests that the boat was a gift from Queen Elizabeth to Ivan the Terrible in the 1580s. From the museum video, it is more than likely that it is a replica.

[186] Referenced as Eilan Gheirrig in the old writings, however, Gheirrig or Greig does not appear on the charts. There is a Creyke – a submerged rock just to the west of the Kyles of Bute. The well-known, if almost invisible, ruins are on the tiny island of Eilan Dearg (Gaelic for Red Island).

[187] For those of enquiring mind, 'erastianism' is the control of the church by the state.

[188] Three of the bombs have been recovered recently. In relation to design, these bombs were spherical rather than the barrel shape of the Dam Busters' bomb, some were smooth skinned and some featured golf ball dimples. The footage of bouncing bombs in the Dam Busters film was recorded in Loch Striven.

[189] A New and General Biographical Dictionary, Alexander Chalmers, 1795.

[190] On checking usage, we find 'Poor wee bastards' officially ascribed as Scottish slang.

[191] On 21st June 1701, the 9th Earl's son was created Duke of Argyle, Marquises of Kintyre and Lorne, Earl of Campbell and Cowal, Viscount of Lochow and Glenyla, Lord Inveraray, Mull, Morvern, and Tiree for his services to William of Orange.

[192] The Argyle Papers, National Archives of Scotland, Edited by J. Maiment, 1834.

[193] The tax was sixpence a barrel, reduced to threepence a barrel after a public outcry. It was levied to pay debts accrued through containing rebellion at home and fighting foreign wars. Glasgow and the Clyde, W. Dodgson Bowman, 1928.

[194] Charles Edward Stewart extorted cash and complete sets of uniforms for his army of 5,000 Highlanders. At least they died well-clad with new breeks and brogues and fine blue bonnets.
[195] The Corinthian Yachtsman, or hints on Yachting, Tyrrel E. Biddle, 1881.

Fortuna (replica)   Image: Boatyard Varyag   *Fortuna*, said to be Peter's original boat ca.1698-92

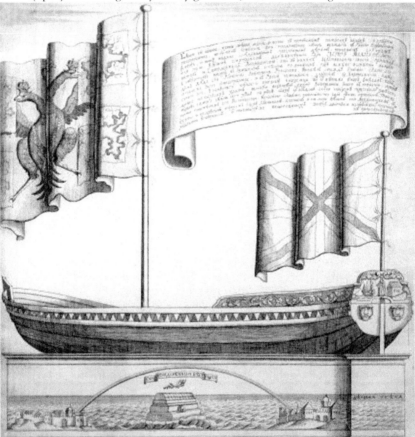

Engraving of Peter's *St Nicholas*, ca.1580-1640   Военная энциклопедия (Сытин, 1911-1915)
The *St. Nicholas* was built for Peter's grandfather in England or built by Danes in Russia to an English design. The depiction of a vessel flying an early flag of the United Kingdom as an ensign suggests that the British connection is after 1603 and the Union of the Crowns.

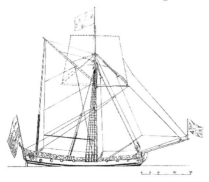

House of Stewart Royal Yacht, 1690   *The Royal Transport*, Sixth-rate ship, 1695

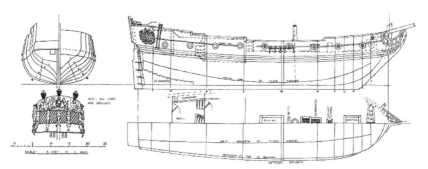

A House of Stewart Royal Yacht, 1690   Image: G. K. Chatterton

The *Kathryn*, a Samuel Pepys yacht of 1661 for Charles II   Drawing: Leslie A. Wilcox

BOOK TWO

Evolution of the Species

Chapter 5: Shipwrightery

The naval novelist Frederick Marryat, casting aspersions on the honour and background of the graduates of the School of Naval Architecture, declared that out of the whole only two are respectable, while some of them cannot legally make claim to any father! William Symonds[196]

The emergence of naval architecture, as an honourable profession for a gentleman, is generally correlated with the European Renaissance. Inquiring minds began to break free from the strictures of metaphysical oppression to rediscover the natural philosophy of the Greeks and the real world.[197] However, shipbuilding has always been a deeply conservative industry, and experience accumulated over generations did not disappear overnight. A mastery of traditional craft skills was still essential if you intended to build a boat in the pre-industrial age. So, initially, the theoretical papers published by intellectuals outside the industry exercised limited influence.

Nonetheless, the best of 'hands-on' shipwrights of the era, often with self-taught mathematical skills, certainly understood the benefits of more systematic approaches. And when compiling 'existing best practice' they took the opportunity to advance their own ideas and pet theories. In ship design, most advances have been grounded in experience, just as most have been trumped by it eventually. There is nothing new under the sun, or more graphically, rusting and forgotten beneath leaden skies.

Revisiting well-known challenges will often cast even tried-and-tested solutions in a new light. Shipwrights, and later specialist ship designers, have nearly always addressed new commissions by finessing existing work. Ship design is substantially evolutionary and incremental, and every boat owes some sort of debt to precedent. However, while modifications may appear to be vanishingly small, this does not diminish their significance.[198]

In that respect, naval architects are no different from wheelwrights – wheels can be bigger or smaller, wider or narrower, and the material may change, but they are always round with a bearing in the centre. Indeed, the Fifes of Fairlie started out in that circumlocutory profession. Just as attention to detail characterises the wheelwrights' craft, the Fifes broke the bounds of traditional demarcation to apply the magic of the perfect circle to increasingly sophisticated boatbuilding processes.

Variation and divergence, which may appear radical at the time, routinely fall into the broad stream of progress. As an example of this, the latest fashion in inshore racing yachts is to wash away the foredeck after the style of the wave-piercing amas of offshore multihulls. Of course, monohulls racing round-the-cans do not benefit from the safety margins conferred by surface-piercing dynamics in Southern Ocean nose-dives. In these boats, the foredeck is simply made uninhabitable.

There are some useful structural gains and weight-management benefits, and hull windage is marginally reduced when sailing to windward, however, the ruse ignores the gargoyled wall of crewmen on the weather rail. Airflow is accelerated onto these poor sods, as indeed is solid water. No matter, the big-ticket asset is the 'appearance' of technological advance, which trumps a host of operational disadvantages. The latest yachts are not revolutionary, but the new brutalism is certainly intimidating on the racecourse.[199]

Throughout its history, naval architecture has been closely tied to naval shipbuilding programmes. Anything other than incremental change incurs significant risk capital, which before the Industrial Revolution, might only be wheedled from national exchequers, or occasionally, from wealthy men of an enquiring mind. Through the 17th to the 19th century, the pursuit of speed and sea-kindliness, in respect of both racing yachts and private steamships, often underpinned advances in naval technology.

There have been many significant game-changing initiatives influencing the course of ship design. The Venetians and Spaniards are regarded as the pioneers in the abstraction of 'ship design' from the practice of 'ship construction'.[200] In the early 15th century, the 'sesto e partixon' system of proportion, was influential as the first conscious step away from artisanal shipbuilding, leading to the working-up of hull lines on paper.[201]

The first paper plans of a British ship were drawn by Mathew Baker, the man who prepared the English fleet to face the Spanish Armada. Despite his palpable expertise, Baker was far from popular, so his unfinished manuscript, *Fragments of Ancient English Shipwrightry* (1586), which heralded the integration of graphic and numerical methods in ship design, languished unread.[202] However, the following year, Spanish shipbuilder, Diego Garcia de Palacio, published *Instrucción Náutica para Navegar*, advocating the same thing.[203] This manual was commercially printed and widely circulated. It would influence generations of European shipwrights, but the English remained unconvinced.

During the 16th and 17th centuries, the industrious Pett family flourished in the dog-eat-dog world of Admiralty shipbuilding contracts. Peter Pett (ca.1525-1589), the father of the dynasty, was a master shipwright at Deptford. But it was his second son, Phineas (1570-1647), who would be celebrated as the first great shipbuilder in these islands. Phineas attended the University of Cambridge for three years until, after the death of his father, his allowance ceased when his mother remarried. Phineas was then obliged to earn a living shipbuilding, before embarking on an interlude of seafaring adventure.

When he returned to shipyard work, Phineas immersed himself in the business. He spent his evenings in study, working on his drawing skills and improving his grasp of mathematics. And in his free time, he shaped models of ships. Phineas Pett successfully institutionalised the scientific methods pioneered decades before by Mathew Baker. Pett's commitment in attempting to master both the theory, and the practice, of shipbuilding served as an example to inspire generations of shipbuilders.

Phineas Pett's son, Peter Pett (1592–1652), followed in the footsteps of his father, producing some exceptionally fine sailing vessels,.[204] His first frigate, HMS *Constant Warwick*, was said to be "*an incomparable sailer, remarkable for her sharpness and the fineness of her lines; and many were built like her.*" Peter "*introduced convex lines on the immersed part of the hull*". His contemporaries described him as the best ship architect of his time. Unfortunately, he is remembered principally for the scandal and gratuitous controversies that dogged his career.

Naval architecture as a profession has its origins in warship design – hence 'naval architecture' rather than 'ship architecture'. Among 17th century maritime nations, the defence of the realm was paramount and elevated naval architecture above less vital arts. In these circumstances, ship design was a subject upon which everyone held an opinion. Those with influence at the highest levels of government played for high stakes, seeking prestige through the success of their favoured experts.

As naval architecture transitioned from 'craft' to 'science', and gained credibility as an honourable profession, shipwrights of the royal dockyards became upwardly mobile and able to consort with the gentry without undue deference. As is typical with the nouveau riche, they revelled in the trappings – formal portraiture and coats of arms. However, these ambitious shipbuilders missed out on the ultimate prize of knighthood.

When Sir Walter Raleigh defrauded Pett in the construction of the *Destiny* in 1617, James VI sought to make good the debt. Phineas Pett records that the king "*bestowed upon me, for the supply of my present relief, the making of a knight-baronet*". All parties understood that the title was a readily convertible asset. Phineas sold the baronetcy to a recusant, Francis Ratcliffe, for the sum of £700 (£80,000). However, he was swindled in the transaction, saw nothing of the money, lost his title and ended up £30 out-of-pocket.

Sir Anthony Deane (1638-1720), who wrote the *Doctrine of Naval Architecture* in 1670, was among the first of his profession to be knighted properly.[205] The *Doctrine* has been described as *"marking the point when naval architecture became a modern science"*.[206] Deane's knighthood was bestowed in 1675, and he assumed the role of Master Shipwright at Portsmouth the following year. Deane served his apprenticeship at Woolwich under Christopher Pett, becoming a competent mathematician. Dean shrewdly dedicated his 1670 manuscript on naval architecture to Samuel Pepys, then Secretary of the Navy Board.

Pepys lauded the famous shipwright as *"the first that hath come to any certainty beforehand of foretelling the draught of water of a ship before she be launched"*.[207] Deane was indeed able to calculate displacement and the load waterline accurately. This was particularly crucial when determining the freeboard to gunports and it also enabled him to make useful predictions of performance under sail. Deane certainly constructed notably fast vessels, whether diminutive royal yachts or majestic ships-of-the-line, and he also pioneered the use of forged iron fastenings and structural components.

Meanwhile, in the traditional craft industries, stubborn resistance to change endured. This tendency was closely linked to the protection of proprietary assets. William Bushnell wrote about the impediment of self-interest in the handing down of arcane knowledge in 1664. Bushnell highlighted a situation where, although a shipwright's apprenticeship was meant to be equal parts theory and practice, the usual result was that apprentices learned *"nothing more than to hew, or dub, to fey a piece of timber when it is moulded to the place it is assigned"*.[208]

In the 17th century, England, France, Spain and The Netherlands all sought dominance on the high seas. King Louis XIV held ambitions to increase France's maritime commerce and naval power. In 1666, Louis' Finance Minister and Minister of the Navy, Jean Baptiste Colbert, founded the Académie des Sciences to specialise in maritime matters. Colbert's school promoted design research using model ship basins and simple testing equipment, precursory to the more controlled environment of test-tanks.

In a further significant initiative, Colbert brought together prominent French shipbuilders to share expertise and disseminate existing best practice in 1680. It was, in effect, an attempt to advance ship design by committee, establishing classifications and standard warships designs – a practice that became common among all navies. Standardisation resulted in general improvement before stultifying innovation, as was perhaps inevitable. Whether contemplating warships or racing yachts, naval architects remain sceptical of one-designs to this day.

French works on naval architecture were highly influential in the 17th and 18th centuries. Paul Hoste's *Théorie de la Construction des Vaisseaux* of

1697 highlighted essential principles of statics and mechanics. Ironically, this influential French school was inspired by an Englishman, albeit *the* Englishman. When Isaac Newton published his *Principia Mathematica* in 1687, it is likely that he had never given a moment's thought to ship design. And when French naval architect, Pierre Bouguer (1698-1758), first read the thesis three decades later, he had never built a ship either, but he had given a great deal of thought to the behaviour of floating bodies in motion. Now, he pondered over the application of Newton's 'solids of least resistance' to ship design.

In the 18th century, Newton's work influenced the approach of just about everyone involved in the emerging fields of three-dimensional geometric modelling and fluid mechanics.[209] Newton's scholium is central to Bouguer's *Traité du Navire* of 1746.[210] Bouguer developed a new language of practical hydrodynamics that would guide shipwrights through the century. The 'solids of least resistance' theory encouraged designers to minimise resistance caused by the 'shock' of the water against the bows, ignoring the drag caused by wave-making and skin friction. Newton's theory influenced ship design until the 19th century, before succumbing to mounting theoretical and experimental evidence from the test-tank.

Although based on a historic misconception, the *Traité du Navire* represents a milestone in the development of naval architecture. It was the first credible attempt to grapple with the mysteries of hydrodynamics in a systematic way. Duhamel du Monceau (1700-1782) of the same school reinforced France's pre-eminence in ship design with *Elémens de l'Architecture Navale*, published in 1752. Like Hoste and Bouger before him, Monceau's works were translated into English and were widely read.

Mungo Murray

Mungo Murray (ca.1705-1770) was Scotland's first naval architect of note. The Victorian historian, Nathan Dews, considered Murray's magnum opus to be *"the only English Treatise on ship-building that can lay any claim to a scientific character"*.[211] Dews further declared that Mungo was a man *"whose conduct was irreproachable"*. He may be forgotten today, but back in 1939 a *Yachting Monthly* article on John G. Stephen's designs, referring to balance and handling, quoted a Mungo aphorism: *"There is one thing not to be forgot, that a ship that goes well will certainly steer well."*[212]

In 1846, in the introduction to a section on shipbuilding, the marine editor of *Encyclopaedia Britannica*, surely a fellow Scot, wrote unequivocally: *"Mungo Murray was most undoubtedly a man of thought and ability, and his acquirements were very far superior to his station. Had he been advanced in the service, it is more than probable that his country would have had ample reason to be grateful to him for the benefits which he would then have had the power, as he certainly had the ability, to render her."*

However, in the body of the above work, the acid-tongued Augustine Creuze has this to say: *"Britain has not to this day one original truly scientific treatise on the subject in her language; and, passing by some few papers and tracts of modern times, she can only cite the writings of uneducated and unlearned men, as Mungo Murray, Hutchinson, and Stalkart, against those of such names as the Bernoullis, Euler, Chapman, Don Juan, Bouguer, Clairbois, Romme, and a host of others."*[213] No comment is necessary about a snob who revelled in such bile.

Mungo Murray was born in rural Perthshire, but a precocious interest in shipbuilding led him south to seek an apprenticeship. As a young Scot, he displayed all the characteristics of the classic working-class autodidact. Inspired by the practice of shipwrightery, and blessed with an aptitude for mathematics, Mungo rose quickly through the ranks to come up against the glass ceiling early in his career. He arrived at Deptford in 1738, as well-qualified as any of his generation to practice naval architecture but bereft of influence. Mungo's optimism and palpable naiveté are still apparent across three centuries. Inevitably, he had trouble gaining a suitable position in the royal shipyards, but in time he would become part of 'the establishment'.

Initially, there were additional barriers beyond social class and contacts; Mungo's early years at Deptford coincided with the outbreak of the 'War of Jenkin's Ear' in 1739, which prioritised the supply and repair of ships built to standard, proven models.[214] The naval dockyard's war-footing effectively stultified design development for a decade. In any event, shipbuilding in this era was a deeply conservative trade where entrenched past-masters held their cards close to their chests. Youthful ambition was seen as a threat.

Although denied a senior appointment, Mungo supplemented his shipwright's wage by advertising his services as a tutor of mathematics and navigation. In the evenings, he immersed himself in the theory and practice of ship design and published a *Treatise on Shipbuilding and Navigation* in 1754. In the book's introduction, he acknowledged the relatively lowly position he occupied in Deptford society, citing *"the great obligation I am under to the principal officers and gentlemen in his majesty's service, not only in the yard where I have the happiness to be employed, but in several others"*. This book also annexed abridged versions of selected French works on naval architecture by De Monceau, and Bouguer. Clearly, Mungo's self-taught French was fluent. It says much about the man that, largely at his own expense, he translated and promoted works, which he judged worthy of a wider readership, among fellow British shipwrights who did not possess his linguistic skills.

Mungo's book was widely read and well-received, and he would have been optimistic about his employment prospects for a time. However, despite an expanding network of friends, contacts and admirers, he seemed destined to remain on the shop floor. Nevertheless, Mungo has been cited in relation to using his connections to further the career of one John Rose, who eventually formed a shipbuilding partnership with Mungo's nephew, James Stuart, in Charleston USA.[215] This partnership tapped the resources of the Scottish diaspora to purchase slaves, then trained these new 'employees' through an apprenticeship in boatbuilding. Stuart later committed suicide and Rose swindled his heirs. This disreputable conduct was considered an affront by Stuart's nephew, Charles Irvine, who felt that Rose had let down Mungo, a man he held in high regard.

Eventually, Mungo secured a permanent appointment aboard the HMS *Magnanime*, with Lord Howe, who recognised his expertise in the theory and practice of navigation. The post as midshipman would seem to have undervalued his abilities, but of course, Mungo was not a 'gentleman'. He was employed as a teacher of mathematics and navigation and he received a warrant as Schoolmaster in 1760.[216] In that same year, he invented the Armillary Trigonometer, an instrument designed to facilitate spherical trigonometry calculations at sea.

Mungo Murray was marginalised by naval architects of his generation and has been almost forgotten today. He may have possessed one of the best minds in the business, but his influence was compromised by his social status as a salaried artisan. Consequently, during his lifetime, well-connected contemporaries freely accessed his ideas without attribution. His worth was only recognised by later generations of ship designers.

By contrast, Mungo's contemporary, Frederik Chapman (1721-1808) was the right man in the right place. Chapman has been dubbed the "*first naval architect*" by his biographer, or perhaps hagiographer, Dan Harris.[217] To be fair to Harris, others have made this claim. However, bearing in mind the pioneers name-checked in the previous paragraphs, the case for priority is not especially convincing. Nonetheless, Chapman's contribution to the nascent discipline was indeed significant, and his fashionable career raised the profile of the whole profession.

Fred Chapman was born to Thomas Chapman, a British naval officer from Yorkshire, and Susanna Colson, the daughter of a successful London shipwright. So, naval architecture was certainly in his blood, and that of course, was all English. Thomas Chapman was a well-connected ex-pat in the service of the Royal Swedish Navy. As a young man, Fred kick-started his career with a small shipbuilding enterprise that yielded enough profit to set him on his travels. He already had the access and introductions via his maternal grandfather, and now he had the resources to study shipbuilding in Britain, France and The Netherlands.

Over the following seven years, with a sojourn in his own small yard, Fred studied shipbuilding and mathematics. He was in England shortly after Mungo published his seminal work. Fred Chapman would certainly have read Mungo's *Treatise on Shipbuilding and Navigation* and the two would surely have met and discussed their passion. Mungo also had blood-relations in Sweden but was not tempted by the opportunities there.

However, while Mungo Murray remained enmeshed in the labyrinth bureaucracy of Deptford Dockyard, the ambitious Chapman secured a job as Assistant Shipwright in the Royal Swedish Navy through the good offices of his brother, who had risen to become a councillor of the Swedish realm. Chapman published *Architectura Navalis Mercatoria* in 1768. This book comprised drawings of ships that he found interesting and merely demonstrated his surveying skills and fine draftsmanship. His *Tractat om Skepps-Byggeriet* or *Treatise on Shipbuilding*, published in 1775, was a much more important work, influencing the course of the ship design process throughout Europe.[218]

Chapman wrote of the need for a grasp of science and mathematics in 1775. To paraphrase: *"it may be said to suffice if (the naval architect) knows enough to calculate: draft vis-a-vis load carrying requirements; stability within the range mandated by function; handling characteristics in respect of rolling, pitching and 'quickness' of motion; sailing performance off the wind and close-hauled with predictions of leeway; whether weather-helm is anticipated and the balance of the ship in relation to her ability to come about easily"*.[219]

Chapman's advocacy of mathematics was perhaps more of interest than practical use in the early days of naval architecture, and in many respects remained so until the advent of desk-top computing two centuries later. It was said that the calculation of the centre of gravity in the two-decker, HMS *Bulwark*, took two men working full-time one whole year to complete. However, Chapman eventually devised a system which involved moving weights (usually the ship's guns, being a known and very considerable weight, and moreover, already mounted on wheels) a specified distance across the deck. After measuring the change in heel angles, Chapman was able to calculate the centre of gravity in about an hour. For this alone, Chapman deserves his place in the pantheon.[220]

As the 18th century came to a close, British ships remained a formidable presence on the world's oceans, but few of our naval architects could compete with Chapman in Sweden, or indeed the French pastmasters, who still built the fastest and most weatherly ships. We had some of the best craftsmen in Europe and our shipyards turned out stout men o' war, but the design of these warships was now perceived to be outmoded rather than well-proven. The fleet was technologically obsolete, something that would soon become apparent when the Napoleonic Wars (1803-1815) broke out.

French mathematician Charles Bossut (1730-1814) is given substantial credit for the superior sailing qualities of French navy vessels at the start of the 19th century. The Frenchman's seminal work on hydrodynamics and the stability of ships was published towards the end of his life. Bossut is credited with advancing fluid dynamics and hydrostatics as applied sciences. He established his reputation as a hydrodynamicist with his *Traité élémentaire d'hydrodynamique* 1771, appearing again reworked in a 1787 publication. Bossut would later influence David Napier, as described in the next chapter.

In the 1790s, British naval officers were fully cognisant of scientific advances in France. The navy was a notably well-read and numerate profession in those days, active in promoting independent research on ship design. While senior naval officers continued to consult with time-served shipwrights in the naval dockyards, they were open to the advice of independent experts. Among these authorities, Colonel Mark Beaufoy (1764-1827), was that rare combination of scientist and sportsman.

Beaufoy is credited with significant advances in naval architecture. He studied hull-form resistance and the physics of sailing vessels in the 1790s through controlled experiments. His work would later exert a significant influence on the work of Isambard Kingdom Brunel.[221] Colonel Beaufoy also played a leading role in the formation of the Society for the Improvement of Naval Architecture in 1796. This became an influential think-tank, networking the community of civilians and naval personnel involved in ship design and construction.

Samuel Bentham (1757-1831) and Robert Seppings (1767-1840) of the Royal Dockyard at Deptford supported progress in detailed design and engineering of large wooden structures.[222] Bentham, a mechanical engineer turned naval architect, was also instrumental in founding dockyard schools for the Royal Navy's shipwrights.[223] He devised machinery to mechanise the production of pulley blocks – a game-changer in naval dockyards, and among myriad other inventions designed amphibious craft and articulated barges while working in Russia.

Britain's first college of Naval Architecture was established at Portsmouth in 1811, half a century later than the École d'Application du Génie Maritime in Toulon in 1741. The French school subsequently moved to Paris, closed then opened again in 1765. The British school also enjoyed mixed fortunes before closing its doors in the 1830s. It appears that naval officers considered the supervision and instruction of shipwrights to be within their existing domain and skillsets. Forty years on, the Admiralty set up the Royal Naval College in the old Royal Hospital for Seaman at Greenwich. Existing courses, taught at Kensington and Portsmouth, were transferred to Greenwich in 1873.

At this point in the story, British yachtsmen take matters in hand, or at least attempt to. The Yacht Club, precursor to the Royal Yacht Club and Royal Yacht Squadron, was established in 1815. From that date, the First Lord of the Admiralty had an official yacht registered with the club. So, 1815 also marks the start of a period where yacht design heavily influenced naval architecture – in effect, the tail wagged the dog. Trials invariably showed that privately-owned yachts of comparable size had the legs on the navy, with superior speed and better handling characteristics.

This might be expected as yachts were lighter and displaced less. But even so, yacht design informed the lines of the Admiralty's smaller vessels like frigates. Influential members of the Yacht Club were able to lobby their friends in the Admiralty to promote specific designers and design concepts. One such champion was William Symonds (1782-1856), an RYC member who would eventually design around 200 warships.

Symonds was a serving naval officer who joined the Yacht Club in 1817 with his boat *Cornwallis*. He initially pursued naval architecture as a hobby, experimenting on his frigate HMS *Pique*. He designed his first yacht in 1821, financed by his sister's legacy. This schooner, *Nancy Dawson*, was beamy in comparison to her contemporaries, with a fine entry and 'wedge-shape' sections – the latter referring to deadrise, not the entry on the load-waterline.[224] In fact, all Symonds' vessels would exhibit a bold rise-of-floor.

George Vernon, a wealthy yachtsman, admired Symonds' work and built a sister-ship. He then petitioned the Admiralty to build the *Columbine*, a Symonds 18-gun corvette. Vernon demonstrated considerable faith in his protégé's ability by standing surety with a bond of £20,000 (£2 million).[225] In 1826, Vernon introduced Symonds to William Cavendish-Scott-Bentinck (1768-1854), 4th Duke of Portland, who owned a boatyard in Troon, see Chapter 20. Sir Henry, as the 4th Duke was known, was another influential yachtsman and amateur designer. The collaboration led to the Troon shipyard becoming a centre of excellence and innovation.

In 1827, Sir Henry built a hull-sister to the Symonds-designed warship, *Columbine*. This was the ketch, *Clown*. A few years later, he commissioned Symonds to design the famously beautiful *Pantaloon* (1831). Both yachts were constructed by Robert Thomson at Sir Henry's yard in Troon. The later yacht was so quick that she was bought by the Admiralty. Both boats competed in the Admiralty's sailing trials of 1827 and 1831, which cast Symonds' entries in a favourable light.

A century later, James Meikle would recount the role of Sir Henry, the Royal Northern and the Ayrshire yard in the service of naval architecture and the defence of the realm.[226] At the time, the *Sporting Magazine* noted that *"the Pantaloon is a fine brig of 350 tons with 4ft 6" more beam than the common 10-gun brig. The increased beam of this yacht gives her great power under canvas, and from her having to carry less cumbrous weight, her projector is enabled to give her a much finer bottom. This would give her the weathier qualities and must necessarily add to her speed.*[227] Also helping *Pantaloon* along was a mizzen the size of a schooner's mainsail.

Symonds had friends in high places, and his honorary position as a lieutenant on the King's yacht secured his establishment credentials. Remarkably for an 'amateur' in the field, he was appointed Surveyor to the Navy in 1832. Symonds' yachts were designed after the pattern of small warships, but with greater beam than the norm for British fighting ships. Beneath the waterline, these vessels resemble the work of Fred Chapman.[228] The *Pantaloon* reportedly made 11½kts on the long heavy weather beat to windward from Falmouth to Land's End. Surely the tide was favourable? Through the 1830s Symonds' designs were relatively restrained but became more 'experimental' in the 1840s.

These beamy yacht-like warship designs generated increasing resistance among more conservative critics. In his 1824 pamphlet on *Naval Architecture*, published by his friend George Vernon, Symonds advocated the 'cod's head and mackerel tail' form and curiously criticised existing warship designs as *"reversing the fish-form"* which they did not.[229] Symonds' designs were all characterised by high deadrise (confusingly referred to as a 'fine bottom' or a 'fine entry'), which seems to have been what the reactionary lobby disliked. As an aside, we might note that Atlantic cod, when viewed in section, are also generously endowed with deadrise.[230]

Symonds was obsessive in his attention to sail shape, rigging details and trim. Modern yachtsmen are acutely aware that these critical elements can override and obscure significant differences in hull-form. Symonds and his supporters made this a doctrine, advocating ship design based on practical experience. *"In making this claim, he and his allies even questioned the value of other types of experience required for holding that office, including the hands-on experience in ship design and construction that shipwrights possessed."*[231] Symonds himself boasted that he had *"hit upon a secret of naval architecture"*.

William Symonds designed some of the fastest men-o'-war ever to grace the age of sail, even if their merits were lost in a long-running partisan debate; his doctrine of rationalism pleased no one. By disparaging both the conservative instincts of shipwrights, and the academic approach of avocational naval architects, he alienated both camps. Consequently, his impact on warship design was not long-lasting, and in retrospect, his 'broad church' was an outlier in our chronology. Symonds was eventually outwitted by the modernisers' lobby and forced from office in 1847.

Fincham's *History of Naval Architecture* provides a window through which to view the 'state of the art' in 1851.[232] John Fincham (1785-1859) was a towering figure in 19th century warship design and responsible for the introduction of the screw propeller into the Royal Navy. He was a Master Shipwright at the Portsmouth Dockyard and Superintendent of the School of Naval Architecture at Portsmouth.

Reading Fincham, it is clear that while Britain was a great maritime power in the 19th century, naval architecture was a discipline in crisis. The Royal Navy was acutely conscious that we had fallen behind our neighbours across the Channel. Britain had been obliged to periodically review and re-conceptualise its warship designs, for example during the Napoleonic Wars (1803-1815). Going back further, captured French frigates had been acknowledged as superior as early as 1712.

Fincham wrote: *"In several of the European states, the science of ship-building has long been an object of national interest. It has occupied a higher position as a subject of literature than in England. Spain, France, Russia, and Sweden have successively made naval architecture a national object, and each of those countries has produced one work or more of distinguished merit on ship-building."* Fincham then cites Don George Juan, Pierre Bouguer, Daniel Bernoulli, Vial du Clairbois, Euler, Romme, and Chapman.[233]

John Fincham is notable for the time he invested in a comparative study of fast sailing ships.[234] In the 1820s, he took the lines off five Squadron yachts and analysed them. *"Many of our builders are distinguished for producing beautiful models and fast-sailing cutters without any scientific skill in their constructors, but the excellence of these vessels is only established by the inferiority of others, and it is necessary to obtain certain data from the application of mathematical science to the result of practical experience to enable us to determine the principle on which the vessels are constructed."*[235] Fincham was writing in 1827, but when he repeated the exercise in 1855 with seven later-model yachts, transcending the schooner *America's* visit in 1851, he found that nothing much had changed. *"Those flat sails are good for nothing, at least with a craft that has a decent pair of bows of her own and something of a tournure behind her."*[236]

Yacht owners of that period, unwilling to recognise in shipwrights the intellect they associated with men of good breeding, showed little interest in Fincham's work initially. And of course, competing builders were hostile to any systematic deconstruction of their trade secrets. In 1852, *Hunt's Universal Yacht List*, a register established in 1846, published the following: "*The publishers regret that builders are not more anxious to publish to the world the deeds of their yachts; the pages of the List are open to them and we hope they will avail themselves of the offer. Our desire is to create a feeling of friendly rivalry, and to prove that Old England yet stands A.1. in yacht building*".[237]

In the words of French polymath, Monsieur Bouguer: "*It always happens that they think differently from each other; and yet each alleges, with equal confidence in his favour, his own practice, or a tedious list of ships which he has already constructed.*"[238] Once again, there is still more than an element of truth in this today, and it is indicative of how little things have changed when we look for a learning curve vis-a-vis critical matters like accumulated top-hamper on cruising yachts and fin-keel attachment. "*We learn from history that we learn nothing from history.*"[239]

Philip R. Marett, a young English yachtsman, suggests that nothing had changed in the years following *America's* visit. In his book, *Yachts and Yacht Building* (1856), Marett stressed the importance of owners understanding the principles of yacht design if they were to supervise their builders and take advantage of new developments. "*At present there seems to be no prospect that a class of scientific yacht constructors will arise. Owners should learn to construct their own vessels; or, at all events, to understand the drawings and calculations and thus be able to control construction.*"[240]

Marett advocated a complete change in the way yachts were produced, detaching design from build. "*In yacht building, the separation* (of designing and building) *is even more necessary than in other constructive arts, for the designer should be not only a scientific constructor, but also an experienced yacht sailor otherwise he can form no correct estimate of the probable effect of the combinations of his design.*"

He was right, but he was ahead of his time. A few remarkable families bucked the trend. The Fife dynasty operated an efficient 'design and build' operation for 126 years from the yawl, *Lamlash*, in 1812 to the cutter, *Madrigal*, in 1938, then there were the Herreshoffs in the States, the Nicholson family on the Solent and many others. All that was still to come in the early years of the 18th century when most builders of sailing yachts learned their trade constructing coasters and fishing boats. The old school was replete with confident gung-ho artisans, but at the same time conservative to a fault. Crack cutters were built on windswept beaches, where equinoctial gales rocked the cradle of innovation.[241] Even through the 20th century, wooden boats by famous designers, built by reputable boatyards, were often re-ballasted and waterlines re-scribed before they were handed over.

As for the alchemy of traditional craft skills – fast forward through the years to the 1970s, when the best small boat designers – Dick Carter, Ron Holland and Doug Peterson all designed fast yachts 'by the seat of their pants' and only brought in specialist engineering expertise when 'big-budget' clients insisted on due diligence and proper risk management.[242] However, today, intuition, insight and a 'good eye' are unlikely to lead to success on the race-course. While precedent is still reassuring, it is merely a point of departure to support the latter-day alchemy of simulation.

Meanwhile in Scotland

As elsewhere in Europe, the enlightenment in Scotland (1685-1815) created an intellectual climate of enquiry and advance. Shipbuilding played an unacknowledged part in this. In the late 1700s, the seeds of a great shipbuilding dynasty were being sown in the northeast of Scotland. The Stephen story illustrates how most shipbuilders entered the business north of the border, and indeed for all our emphasis on the growth of naval architecture as a distinct profession, south of the border too.

Alexander Stephen built ships on the Moray Firth. Alexander's brother William Stephen (1720-1799) was a farmer who survived the battle of Culloden in 1746. His son, William (1759-1838), joined Alexander to serve 10 years in his Burghead yard before returning home to Aberdeen in 1787. Notwithstanding his decade of practical experience, William immediately embarked on a paid apprenticeship with James Cochar, a local shipbuilder. The tuition fee of precisely £3 seems modest today, and it was, even then.[243]

October 10th, 1787

Sir,

I do hereby oblige myself to pay you the fee of Three Pounds sterling money for teaching me the art of ship drafting as you practice it yourself, the one half when entered to said drafting, and the other when I can lay down a draft by myself.

I also bind myself to teach no other person the same under the fine of Ten Pounds sterling money. I acknowledge to have received your letter agreeing to these terms and to renew them on stamp paper when required.

Sir, I am yours,

William Stephen

Three pounds in 1787 is just £460 today and that £10 penalty is £1,560. So, to become a ship designer at the end of the 18th century was not expensive, but it still required a level of skill and abstract intelligence that the average shipwright did not always possess. Ship drafting, as it was known, was even then acknowledged as a separate profession. For William Stephen, this new qualification transformed his prospects in the industry. He returned to Burghead with the means and ability to transform his uncle's business.

The Stephen family became one of the most significant shipbuilding dynasties anywhere in the world. As the decades passed, each generation became more knowledgeable and technically proficient. The Stephens showcased hereditary career development in a way that became a model for institutional succession on the Clyde. The boys combined university degrees with practical experience, both with competitors and the home firm, before taking on lead design responsibilities in the drawing office or attending to logistical planning and business development.

David Elder (1795-1866) is credited as one of the founding fathers of marine engineering on the Clyde. He was a working-class autodidact who excelled at mathematics.[244] Elder was Works Manager with David Napier at Camlachie. In 1824, Elder's expert team built the engine for the *Clarence*, the fastest boat on the river. She was 99ft. LOA, 16ft. beam, with a 45hp engine. At the Royal Northern Regatta in August 1827, under the command of Captain Turner, she won the trophy for the steamship race. The *Helensburgh*, also built by Napier, was second.

Perhaps unusually for such a famous family, the Napiers were generous in acknowledging David Elder's indispensable contribution to the fame and prestige of the Napier marque.[245] The *Clarence* and the *Helensburgh* established the reputations of both men in the field of marine engineering. The great steamship race also inspired Assheton Smith, who crops up in the next chapter, to flaunt the regulations of the Royal Yacht Club in Cowes and order one of these fine vessels himself.

James Napier, son of Robert Napier, and no mean engineer himself, in a paper to the Institution of Engineers and Shipbuilders in 1866 said "*The history of so remarkable a man* (David Elder) *must be interesting to many on account of his connection with works which have made Glasgow and the Clyde famous, and given to his employer a fame which is known over the engineering world.*"

David Elder's widow, Grace, sponsored the first chair in Naval Architecture at Glasgow University in 1883.[246] That same year, William Froude, who had worked for Brunel, built a test-tank in Torquay and the famous Denny Test Tank at Dumbarton followed in 1884.

CODA: Biomimicry in the 18th Century

"*Most fish offer us the same external form; sharp at either end and swelling in the middle; by which they are enabled to traverse the fluid which they inhabit with greater celerity and ease. That peculiar shape which nature hath granted most fishes, we endeavour to imitate in such vessels as are designed to sail with the greatest swiftness.*

However, the progress of a machine moved forward in the water by human contrivance, is nothing to the rapidity of an animal designed by nature to reside there.

Any of the large fish (sic, they would be dolphins) *overtake a ship in full sail with great ease, play round it without effort, and outstrip it with pleasure.*

The chief instruments in a fish's motion, are the fins, which, in some fish, are much more numerous than in others. A fish completely fitted for sailing, is furnished with, at the least, two pair: also, three single fins, two above and one below. Thus equipped, it migrates with the utmost rapidity, and takes voyages of 1,000 leagues in a season."[247]

John Knox (1790-1720), an advocate of fisheries reform, unwittingly opens a window into a future where sailing craft cross oceans borne aloft on foils.

[196] Shaping the Royal Navy, Don Leggett, 2016, referencing: School of Naval Architecture, Metropolitan Magazine, 8th November 1833.

[197] The European Renaissance blossomed through the 14th to 17th centuries. The age of enlightenment (17th & 18th century) and the Scottish enlightenment (18th and early 19th century) interrogated the status quo and encouraged innovation.

[198] The Piper Calls the Tune (Dolly and other Clones) Euan Ross and Bob Donaldson, 2017.

[199] These comments concern canoe bodies and do not address the rampant iterations of 'Swiss Army knife'-type foils exercising dynamic lift.

[200] Cog and Galley blog, Naval Architecture, Mich Williamson.

[200] Of Ships and Stars: Maritime Heritage and the Founding of the National Maritime Museum, Greenwich, Kevin Littlewood and Beverly Butler, 1998.

[201] Kaufmannsbücher und Handelspraktiken vom Spätmittelalter bis zum 20 Jahrhundert, Markus A Denzel, Jean Claude Hocquet and Harald Witthöft, 2002.

[202] English Shipwrightery, Mathew Baker (First Master of the Company of Shipwrights), 1586

[203] Instrucción Nautica Para Navegar, García de Palacio Diego,1587.

[204] Phineas was 'knighted' in 1680 in that he was given the title of knight-baronet by the King in 1616 – he sold the title for £700 but was defrauded. This would have made him the first naval architect to be so honoured. The Pett 'autobiography' appears to confuse Peter with his son Sir Peter Pett (1630-1699), the fourth Peter Pett. I leave this to the many Pett scholars.

[205] Other naval architects to receive a knighthood include: Sir Anthony Deane (1638-1720); Sir Thomas Slade (1703-1771); Sir Samuel Bentham (1757-1831); Sir Robert Seppings (1767-1840); Sir William Symonds (1782-1856); Sir Edward Harland (1831-1895); Sir Alfred Yarrow (1842-1932); Sir John Thornycroft 1843-1928; Sir James Flannery (1851-1943); Sir Thomas Thurston (1869-1950); Sir Westcott Stile Abell (1877-1961); Sir James Matthews (1887-1981); Sir John Brown (1901-2000); Sir Alexander Belch (1920-1967); Sir Clifford Skeggs (1931-present); Sir John Parker (1942-present).

[206] The Flowering of a Tradition: Technical Writing in England, 1641-1700, Elizabeth Tebeaux, 2016.

[207] He divided the hull body into equidistant sections, calculated the area of each and obtained a figure for displacement by a rough process of quadrature. However, there is no record of such calculation for a ship of the period, so this exercise was rare at best.

[208] The Island Nation: A History of Britain and the Sea, Brian Lavery, 2005.

[209] Philosophiae Naturalis Principia Mathematica, Isaac Newton, 1687 (Eng. trans. 1728).

[210] Traité du Navire, de sa Construction, et de ses Mouvemens, Pierre Bouguer, 1746.

[211] A treatise on shipbuilding and navigation. In three parts, wherein the theory, practice, and application of all the necessary instruments are perspicuously handled, Mungo Murray 1754.

[212] The Racing World, speed and balance, HB, Yachting Monthly, May 1939.

[213] Treatise on the Practice of Naval Architecture: being the article Shipbuilding in the Encyclopaedia Britannica, Seventh Edition, Augustine F. B. Creuze, 1846.

[214] The War of Jenkins' Ear (1739-1748) was a conflict between Britain and Spain. The name was coined by Thomas Carlyle and refers to Captain Robert Jenkins' ear, severed by Spanish

Coast Guards and apocryphally waved before Parliament to justify action against the Spanish.

215 'A Global Clan: Scottish Migrant Networks & Identity since the 18th century', ed. Angela McCarthy, 2006.

216 During his service in the *Magnanime*, which included the battle of Quiberon Bay, Murray published a pamphlet on the Rudiments of Navigation, 1760. In 1764, he wrote a short note on an eclipse of the sun, which was printed in the Philosophical Transactions. He issued a new and enlarged edition of his Treatise on Shipbuilding in 1765. He also published various volumes of elevations, sections, and plans of different vessels.

217 F. H. Chapman: The First Naval Architect and his Work, Daniel Harris,1989.

218 A Treatise on Shipbuilding, with explanations and demonstrations, Frederick Henry De Chapman, Knight of the Royal Order of the Sword, Chief Shipbuilder of the Swedish Navy, and Member of the Royal Academy of Sciences at Stockholm, 1768.

219 Chapman, the First Naval Architect, Captain Henry P. Boyd, R.N. (Retired), published in Thoughts on Yachts and Yachting, Ed. Uffa Fox, 1938.

220 Ibid

221 Nautical and Hydraulic Experiments with numerous Scientific Miscellanies, Mark Beaufoy, published posthumously in 1834.

222 Of Ships and Stars: Maritime Heritage and the Founding of the National Maritime Museum, Greenwich, Kevin Littlewood and Beverly Butler, 1998.

223 Bentham was an Advisor to the Imperial Russian Navy. During this sojourn, he came across the use of watertight bulkheads in the Chinese ships he encountered in Siberia. Subsequently, Bentham oversaw the construction of prototypes for the Navy.

224 Facts versus Fiction; or, Sir W. S's principles of naval architecture vindicated by a compilation of official and other documents; with introductory remarks. By one who has served, William Symonds, 1848.

225 The Nautical Magazine: A Magazine for those Interested in Ships and the Sea, 1832.

226 Leaves from the Logbook of an Old Clyde Journalist, XXXV, James Meikle, The Yachtsman 15th August 1925.

227 Hampshire Telegraph, July 1808.

228 Symonds acknowledged no others in his design philosophy, but he has been considered a disciple of Fredrick Chapman, whose technical works he was known to possess.

229 This pamphlet was distributed to influential friends and Edinburgh intellectuals. 'A few observations upon architecture or construction for the purpose of proving that the present system of admeasuring British vessels and the duty of tonnage are injurious to the British navy and in every way hurtful to the encouragement of shipbuilding for the purposes of navigation and commerce', William Symonds, 1824.

230 Symonds' designs look well-proportioned to modern eyes, and despite contemporary reservations, seem to have adapted fairly well to auxiliary steam-power when this was introduced, and his finished hulls were handed over to the Steam Department. The 'stink-pot' engineers had to work out the details of engine installation in a dedicated sailing boat. History of Technology, Volume 21, Graham Hollister-Short, 2016.

231 Shaping the Royal Navy: Engineering, Authority and the Ship in the Long Nineteenth Century, Don Leggett, 2016.

232 A History of Naval Architecture – to which is prefixed an introductory dissertation on the application of mathematical science to the art of naval architecture, John Fincham, 1851.

233 Work carried out for the renowned French Académie de Sciences in 1735. We might single out Pierre Bouger (1698-1758), a Cape Horner with seven years served at sea in pursuit of science, including the measurement of a degree of the Meridian on the Equator.

234 Directions for Laying-off Ships on the Mould-Loft Floor with some Instructions for Drawing Ships in Perspective, etc, Originally Designed for the use of the late School of Naval Architecture, and the Shipwrights in the Mould-Loft, John Fincham, 1840.

235 Report on the utility of the yachts of the Royal Yacht Club by John Fincham, Superintendent of the School of Naval Architecture at Portsmouth, 1827.

236 A Tale of a Tub, Hunt's Yachting Magazine, April 1854. 'Toumure' is French for bustle and is used here to denote a steep stern wave of the sort that breaks at hull-speed.

237 W. P. Stevens, incidental comments on a paper on tank-testing. Some Experimental Studies of the Sailing Yacht, Kenneth S. Davidson, 1936.

238 Traite du Navire, Pierre Bouguer, 1746.

239 George Bernard Shaw (1856-1950).

240 Yachts and Yacht Building, Philip R. Marett, 1856.

241 In many parts of the developing world this is still the case, for example, dhows in Arabia, phinisi in Sulawesi and outriggers in the Pacific Islands.

242 Dick Carter Yacht Designer in the Golden Age of Offshore Racing, Dick Carter, 2018, and All the Oceans, a memoir, Ron Holland, designing by the seat of my pants, 2018.

243 Stephen of Linthouse, a Record of Two Hundred Years of Shipbuilding – 1750-1950, published by Alex Stephen & Sons Ltd and written by John L. Carvel, 1951.

244 David Elder began his career on the shopfloor as a millwright under his father and progressed rapidly to become the chief millwright and architect for the Clark family. Elder would design and supervise the construction of some of the largest factories in Scotland: the Clark family's Mile-end Thread Works, Broomward Mill for James Dunlop, William Gillespie's Woodside Mills, and Chemical Works for Charles Tennant and the Hurlet Alum Company. The board members of all these firms became clients of Fife and Watson, stalwarts of the Northern and famous patrons of yachting.

245 Elder found his greatest success working at Robert Napier's yard, where he designed and built some of the finest machinery ever to come to life on the Clyde.

246 Acumfaegovan ('I come from Govan' – a rather special district in Glasgow, for English readers) website.

247 A View of the British Empire, More Especially Scotland, with some Proposals for the Improvement of that Country, the Extension of its Fisheries, and the Relief of the People, John Knox, 1785. Disambiguation: Disambiguation: this is not John Knox, our moral compass (1514-1572).

Pantaloon, William Symonds, 1831   Artist: J. Rogers Snr

Pantaloon was built by Robert Thomson in Troon. Few paintings accurately convey the art of working a square-rigged vessel to windward, in this case a barque. Rogers painting shows perfect sail-set, if a little idealised, and the contribution of a mizzen sized like the mainsail of a schooner.

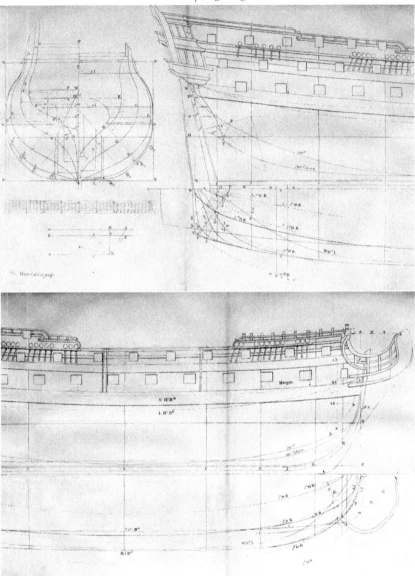

Warship, Mungo Murray   A treatise on shipbuilding and navigation

ADVERTISEMENT.

THE feveral Branches of Mathematicks treated of in this Book are expeditioufly taught by the AUTHOR, at his Houfe in *Deptford*; where may be had all Sorts of Sliding Rules and Scales: As alfo Sectors for delineating Ships, Diagonal Scales, &c. on Brafs, Wood, or Pafte-board. Attendance from fix to eight every Evening, except *Wednefdays* and *Saturdays*.

Mungo advertises private tuition services. The income was important but he enjoyed teaching too.

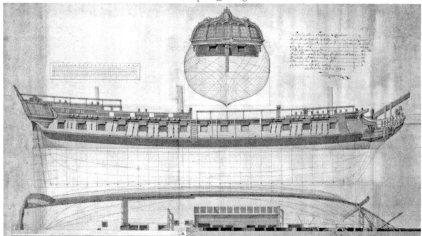

Frigate, *Venus*, Fred Chapman, 1783   Image: *A Treatise on Ship-building*

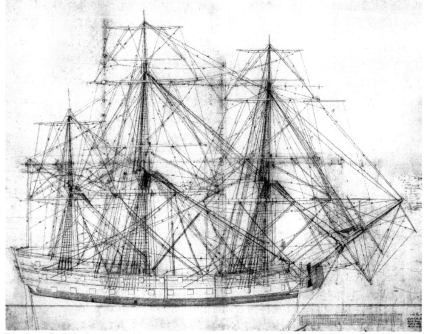

Rigging of a British 60-gun ship ca.1770, designer unknown   Image: Chapman biography

There is more to sailing ship design than the hull shape, but much as the Admiralty vacillated over design, they seem to have been remarkably complacent about rigs. This, despite the ongoing development of fore and aft rigs by the Earl of Danby and others. This rigging plan, which was picked up by Chapman in 1745 during his 'study tour' through Europe, illustrates the extraordinary complexity of the simplest square rig. Standing and running rigging were organised on the same pattern and remained virtually unchanged for 300 years. The importance of ropemaking as an industry was reinforced by the short operational life of 18th century rope. Outward voyage, end for end the ropes; homeward voyage, replace and repeat.

Chapter 6: McBoffins

If there is any flair or artistry involved, it is only to bridge the gulf where ignorance prevails. 'Argus' of the *Yachting Monthly* on naval architecture[248]

The classic elliptical shape of all primordial seagoing craft mimics a floating leaf. There must have been innumerable 'genesis moments' as early man observed random flotsam in happenstantial 'test-tanks'. Northern Europe's deciduous trees like ash, beech, elm, cherry and rowan shed their leaves in autumn. When elliptical leaves dry, they curl into boat-shapes. Surely there can be few children who have not set these little vessels afloat upon a stream or puddle.

Insight is multifaceted, yet it is difficult to conceive of a development pathway that did *not* progress from fallen leaves, seedpods, and the like to include models, whittled into pleasing shapes by the earliest boatbuilders. Inspiration from the natural world, and materials availability, naturally led to double-ended, clinker-built boats. The lanceolate ellipse remains the most logical response to the challenge of working sawn planks into a useful buoyant volume. As a path of least resistance, this shape evolved independently throughout the world and contact between seafarers refined it.

Like much of sailing history, it is impossible to date, or identify, the first attempts to refine a hull-shape by testing models or by assessing the performance of comparable full-sized boats to determine hull-forms of least resistance. However, just as shapes evolved to address perceived deficiencies in capacity, stability, dryness, leeway, and indeed, any number of attributes, so too the yardstick of 'speed achieved for power applied' would have been tested a million times in a million different ways. Within the parameters of intended use and operational requirements, no one ever knowingly built a slow boat.

The story of tank-testing, in the common meaning of the term, began after vessels of most types had already evolved into highly efficient archetypes. Steamships, being initially trapped in sailing ship hulls, were the principal exception. Crackpot theories, prejudice, self-interest and even fashion, impacted on the state-of-the-art, but over time change was cumulative and the net result positive. Purpose-built test-tanks came into use alongside comparative testing using full-sized ships, as still today alongside virtual modelling via computational flow dynamics (CFD). Such models run in digital environments that far exceed the combined calculating capacity of every mathematician in the world. Supercomputers can carry out 200 quadrillion calculations per second if that means anything.

Naval architects do not yet have access to such computing power, and few require it, but the days of physical models and load-gauges on tank-test carriages may be numbered. Virtual models analysed via CFD software may already have condemned tank-testing to the status of a mere blip in the history of naval architecture. However, not everyone thinks this way. Ian Howlett, the top metre-boat designer in practice today, remarks: "*If tank-testing is considered unreliable, then CFD work on metre-boats takes prediction to new levels of randomness. Properly designed and conducted tank-tests are still by far the most reliable method available for* (conventional) *yacht development.*"[249] So, let's keep an open mind.

We begin the story with Frederick Chapman, the first-generation Swede of expatriate English parents, who featured in the last chapter.[250] When Chapman was sixty years old, and had already made his name as a naval architect, he was appointed to run the naval dockyard at Karlskrona. There, he developed advanced prefabrication and series production methods. In just three years, he delivered 10 ships-of-the-line and 10 frigates. More significantly, his ship designs were guided by extensive use of computational methods which were sophisticated for the time.

As a key element of this approach, in 1794 Chapman built a test-tank at Karlskrona to trial and compare hull shapes. His models were small – just 28" long, 8" beam and of various shapes. The tank was 74ft long and each run was accurately timed.[251] The test-models were pulled through the water using a rope and pulley structure. A similar system, but using much smaller weights, held the models in line to eliminate yawing. These Swedish experiments presaged the methodology adopted 23 years later by Scottish tank-test pioneer David Napier in Glasgow.

Chapman was said to have gained 'realistic' comparative values which informed his later design work, and indeed, influenced a generation of naval architects. It does not diminish Chapman's efforts to note that, while good 'real world' results were achieved, almost everything about his testing conformed to the paradigm we now refer to as 'GIGO', or garbage in – garbage out. Today, with more than two centuries of hard-won experience, we are still sorting through the garbage.

Writing in 1891 in his formidable tome *Yacht Architecture*, Dixon Kemp explained why this early work reinforced the old dogma of the 'cod's head and mackerel tail'.[252] Before William Froude came up with his useful rule of thumb ($\sqrt{LWL}$ x 1.4) based on work by Rankine and Scott Russell, scale speed was somewhat arbitrary.[253] For a model towed at twice her scale speed, the principal drag is not from the bow wave but the quarter-wave. Thus, attenuating the tail reduces resistance more than fining the entry. For the tank-test pioneers, who considered resistance to be a function of Bouguer's erroneous 'bow shock', their inverted research environment skewed the whole process until factors concerning scale and the relative density of the medium were better understood.

With his model testing, as with much else, David Napier (1790-1869), first son of the famous shipbuilding dynasty, was both ahead of his time and in debt to precedent. He was a well-read man and a keen student of design, so he would have been aware of Chapman's work. Napier's crucial insight was to tow his models much more slowly. This allowed him to observe waveforms and relate them to his full-scale observations, clinging to the guardrails of his North Channel steamers in foul weather.

David Napier is curiously considered as a lesser figure in the pantheon of great shipbuilders than his cousin, Robert. Robert Napier (1791-1876) was a few months younger than David, "*born with a hammer in his hand*" and a natural businessman. He took over Camlachie three years after David vacated the yard and would go on to construct many more ships (260+). Robert began as an engine builder and did not launch a ship until 1843 when the paddle steamer, *Vanguard,* went down the ways at his new yard in Govan. In this period, when an engine might outlast a hull by a factor of three, vessels were often attributed to the engine-builder, rather than the naval architect or shipbuilder. Robert's son, James Robert Napier (1821-1879), would take over the family yard in 1842.

In 1858, we find David Napier, in his late sixties and drifting into eccentricity, writing to *The Glasgow Herald* about a proposal for shipping sewerage by tanker from Glasgow to the lower Clyde as an interim solution to environmental problems.[254] It was a wide-ranging letter; Napier first digresses to criticise asinine assertions in a paper recently published by an eminent engineer, before describing his early experimental work: "*I have at present before me a number of your papers, in which there is an article headed 'Institution of Engineers of Scotland'. I have often had grave doubts of the utility of some of these self-constituted self-elected associations.*"[255]

Napier particularly took issue with the following: "*It may be regarded as certain that experiments on the resistance of models are almost worthless for the purpose of determining the propelling power required by ships of figures similar to those of the models.*" Napier dryly observed that there had been no shortage of full-sized practical experiments: "*One would have thought that there are sufficient number of real ships launched every day, on which the owners, who are most deeply interested in these matters, are doing everything in their power to surpass their neighbours."* He then went on to describe his own pioneering experiments in 1817-1818 and the successful outcomes he obtained.

The target of this particular rant was a Mr Rankine, a man of whom Napier claimed ignorance. He was being facetious of course; Rankine was a giant among 19th century engineers. However, in respect of assessing the value of design research using test-tank models, rather than experimenting with alterations to full-scale ships, Napier had the practical experience and the insight, and Rankine's scepticism could not have been more misplaced.

Professor William John Macquorn Rankine (1820-1872) was a world-famous engineer, a pioneer in the field of ship science, and instrumental in establishing the credibility of naval architecture as a legitimate engineering science. In 1857, the year before the events recounted here, Rankine had been elected as the first president of the Institution of Engineers & Shipbuilders, Scotland, an academic forum disparaged by Napier. Adding fire to the feud, Rankine's good friend and life-long collaborator was James Robert Napier, David Napier's nephew.

David Napier is usually characterised as a hands-on engineer rather than a theoretician. He was indeed an essentially practical man, but he was also a visionary and a fine example of the Scottish autodidact. *"In my younger days, the French being far ahead of us in scientific works, and being desirous of obtaining all the knowledge I could on the division of fluids, I sent to Paris for the works of Bossut and other celebrated writers, and not then being satisfied with the knowledge I acquired from these books, I commenced a set of experiments for myself."*[256] Napier resolved to measure the resistance of hull-shapes using towed models on the still water of the millpond which bordered his works at Camlachie.

The Camlachie Burn, which would charge Napier's millpond test-tank, is a tributary of the Molandiner Burn, that joins the larger stream before it debouches into the Clyde. The Glasgow burns were utilised to power waterwheels during early industrialisation before the steam engine. Camlachie was an old weaving village that developed into an important industrial suburb during the late 19th century. Foundries and engine shops were set up there to take advantage of local coal supplies. David Napier transferred his business to Camlachie in 1814. With room for expansion, Napier soon had the measure of Duncan McArthur, then regarded as the best marine engine builder in the West of Scotland.

David Napier was certainly a talented mechanical engineer, but our main interest here concerns his contribution to ship design, wherein progress towards seaworthy, low-resistance hull lines was clearly a painstaking, iterative process: *"I cannot, at this distance of time, recollect the various improvements, or more correctly the alterations, I made on steamers. I recollect that they were generally built with a full round bow, which, with a clear run, was considered at that time the best shape for speed; but on perusing the works of Bossut on the resistance of fluids, I began to have serious doubts of the full bow being the proper shape"*[257] Naval architecture was clearly a world for the taking in 1817.

The Camlachie pond *"afforded great facilities."* Napier's test-rig featured a precision weight-drive, like the gravity mechanism on a grandfather clock. This was suspended from a tripod to drive a towing reel with a known and consistent force. *"A framework close to the water of considerable elevation, at the top of which was a roller or drum for winding up a weight, the other end of the line being attached to the experimental block. I carefully noted the time the weight took to descend, dragging the block at the same time through the water."*

Wooden block-models were towed to compare relative drag via a simple time over distance calculation. Despite best efforts, model speed would have varied over the course of the run, but as it was total drag that was being measured in seconds, this was less important than it might seem. Comparison of cumulative measurements did not require precision tools, and in any case, accurate mechanical dynamometers, to measure resistance in real-time, still lay in the future. Napier's biographer, David Bell, noted that, while these early 'tank-tests' lacked the precision of subsequent mechanisms to measure resistance, they served Napier's purpose adequately.

Napier describes the process: *"I then launched the block on the mill dam and noted accurately the time the weight took to descend, drawing the block after it through the water, and every alteration I made on the shape of the block I took care to keep the weight always the same and I continued altering until the difference of time the weight took to descend was imperceptible."* As Napier whittled away at his model, he settled on a shape far removed from the old cod's head and mackerel tail.

The location might have fostered divine insight: Saint Kentigern, Glasgow's patron saint, dwelt by the Molandiner Burn in a simple shack furnished with a stone bed, stone pillow and a stone bedside chair. He would bathe in the icy waters each morning before (reputedly) drying himself on a 'stone towel' and setting forth on his day's work proselytizing.[258] Sadly, in view of the irrevocably lost environmental benefits, these burns were culverted and built over during Glasgow's urbanisation in the 1870s.

The traditional full entry, common among sailing ships, and indeed as used on early steamboats too, had evolved to maintain fore-and-aft trim when subjected to the long lever arm of lofty topsails. Driven before fair wind and a following sea, a buoyant entry was deemed essential.[259] And of course, fish were that shape, although you had to reference two separate species to make the connection – hence the 'cod's head and mackerel tail' sobriquet for this enduring hull-form.[260]

Napier understood that a steamship requires a different distribution of volume, determined by different parameters. He spent hours observing the behaviour of hull-forms at sea in his attempts to understand this. He perceived that a powered vessel could be much finer forward to reduce wave-making. With the power source applied below the waterline, there was no tendency to bury the nose. And hull-forms could be fuller aft to reduce squatting, as paddle wheels, and to a greater extent, screw propellers, reduced effective buoyancy aft of midships by introducing aerated water into the flow. He discovered that in terms of generating a quarter-wave, a broad, fairly shallow, straight run aft could be as clean as the traditional fined-down, tucked-up run of a sailing vessel.

Napier's model which ran with least resistance was given to William Denny at Dumbarton, where the yard's shipwrights took off the lines for what would become the *Rob Roy*, a paddle-steamer 81ft x 15ft 8" with a depth of 9ft. "*I gave the model to the shipbuilder to take off his lines for building the Rob Roy. When it was launched nautical people said I had put the wrong end foremost; however, when it was tried it was found that they were wrong, and the old boats were put into dock to have their bows sharpened, which was found invariably to increase their speed.*"[261] Denny's built the first commercial test-tank 66-years later in 1884.

Walter Scott's romantic novel *Rob Roy*, published in the same year as Napier's experiments took place, promoted the Trossachs and the Scottish Highlands. "*It seems clear that David Napier had a vision of how to use steam-boats to develop tourism and other enterprises. Extensive experiments were conducted to determine the best hull-lines and positions for the paddle wheels. The result was the Rob Roy, a most notable vessel.*"[262]
David Napier was indeed a tireless promoter of steamships as a tool to develop Scottish tourism, in which he had business interests, and he was also something of a showman, ref 1817: "*Mr David Napier, engineer, made such alterations on the vent of his steamboat, the Marion, as enabled him at high water to sail her through the different bridges. …..at almost every turn of the river loud acclamations encouraged the undertaking. The public are certainly much indebted to Mr Napier for the zeal and spirit evinced by him in this memorable experiment.*"

Rob Roy's fine lines heralded a brave new approach to steamship design. The benefits were legion and included improvements in speed, range, economy of operation, ease of motion and seaworthiness. Charles McIntosh, the inventor of the seminal waterproof and a good friend of Napier was on board for the maiden voyage across the Irish Sea – the first such crossing by a steamboat.

David Napier's contribution to naval architecture was a product of that rare ability to run simulations in his head and visualise the performance of a ship at sea. He saw the obvious – that a powered vessel, stripped of top-hamper and the press of sail could handle bad weather more comfortably than a sailing ship. Even today, if you are trying to make ground to windward under storm-canvas in a full gale, it is a whole lot easier with a diesel auxiliary quietly working its magic in the bilges – to keep the yacht's head up and maintain drive in the wind-shadow of the oncoming seas.

The all-weather steamship was a major break with orthodoxy and one reliant on the three essential factors that Napier championed: slim, low-drag hull-forms; powerful motive machinery, and absolute reliability. This latter attribute, in particular, was a major challenge for Napier because his mantra of constant improvement meant that he never made two engines the same. Napier's boats sliced through gales upwind and down with the ease of a WW2 Russian destroyer.

The anonymous author of the *Scottish Gazetteer* noted that: "*At first it was supposed that steam-vessels were only capable of navigating the smooth waters of lakes or rivers, and for two or three years the trade of carrying passengers was confined to the Clyde. The matter was put to the test, however, by Mr David Napier who was the first to employ his vessel, the Rob Roy carrying goods and passengers on the open sea; the trial was so successful that its result may be found, not only in every creek and arm of the sea on our coasts, but in the waters of the Mediterranean and the Indian and Atlantic oceans.*"[263]

After a period of initial hesitation, Napier's contemporaries boarded the bandwagon. The new generation of steamships that followed would be fine forward, with easy waterlines. *Rob Roy* was admired and widely copied, but few appreciated that the real prize underlying her success was empirical tank-testing. The value of Napier's experimental work was not, and indeed never has been, fully recognised by his peers. For decades afterwards, as Napier himself observed, our shipbuilders persisted with the infinitely more expensive process of design development at a scale of 1:1.

Multiple contemporary accounts attest to this extravagant trial and error approach. References concerning the design development of steamboats of that time note the craze for 'cut and paste', described as follows: *rebuilt sharper and deeper; a new sharp bow, lengthened five feet, sailing improved; bottom twice altered; bottom rebuilt and sharpened, sailing improved; lengthened six feet forward and eight feet abaft, with a fine entrance and run, went much easier through the water, etc.*[264]

It took another fifty years to bring about a fair perception of what a steamship's form should be in relation to her designed operational speed, but eventually the value of models was recognised. Methodical testing protocols arrived with the construction of the first commercial facility at Denny's yard in 1884. This produced remarkable hull-lines that are still strikingly elegant today. The Atlantic greyhounds and the formidable dreadnoughts signalled new levels of performance and seakeeping.

David Napier continued to plough his own furrow. He was a man of enormous energy and commitment with an endlessly enquiring mind. As is typical with such characters, he struggled to deliver products on time to agreed specifications. His obsession with refinement, even during the course of a fixed-price contract with a firm delivery date, was almost ruinous. Sometimes this impacted on costs, but he was content to assume the associated financial risk.

In effect, Napier put his money where his mouth was, and in the course of time, his friend and patron Royal Yacht Club stalwart, Assheton Smith, put his money there too. Napier recalled that *"Mr Smith first turned his attention to shipbuilding in 1829. He had been for many years a member of the Royal Yacht Club and had built no fewer than five sailing yachts."* Smith found a kindred spirit in Napier and the maverick Scot found a sponsor at the heart of the British establishment. So, they launched into a fulsome co-operation.[265]

In 1858, after Assheton Smith passed away, David's cousin, Robert Napier, sparked a pointless post-mortem dispute, championing the ideas of Smith in opposition to the work of Scott Russell. This squabble was conducted at arm's length through Smith's grieving widow, Maria. Robert had enjoyed Smith's patronage, but other than that, his motives are unknown. Robert asserted that while theoreticians had dabbled in hollow entries, Smith's *Fire King* was the first practical application.[266] *Fire King* was built in 1838 by Thomson's in Troon and engined by Robert.[267]

Robert curiously ignored his cousin's earlier, more carefully grounded, pioneering work on fine entries. If a slight was intended, it missed the mark. David Napier too deferred to the late Assheton Smith. In a letter to Maria, he wrote: *"From all that I know of these hollow lines, I am decidedly of the opinion that the theory of them may belong to this or that person; but that the practical introduction and adaption of hollow water lines to steamers entirely belong to your late husband, and cannot, I think, be honestly gainsaid by anyone."*[268] This was a sentimental indulgence. David did not meet Smith until 1829, almost two decades after his own success with the seagoing steamer, *Rob Roy,* in 1818.

While he would not have acknowledged the lead, John Scott Russell's experiments of 1834 effectively followed in David Napier's footsteps. Russell built and tested more than 100 hull shapes, from 3ft models to 200ft full-sized ships. His test-protocol was similar to Napier's two decades before, with both models and canal boats towed in flat water by systems of pulleys and suspended weights.[269] From the diagrams, half-a-dozen horses were required to tow a full-size test vessel back to its release point, while hoisting the drive weight to a height of approximately 60ft.[270]

Again, more efficient hull-forms simply went faster. However, the underlying basis for this progress remained a matter of speculation and hyperbole. The precise relationship between resistance and speed was difficult to quantify until Russell replaced the old system of suspended weights with the 'spring dynamometer'. This instrument, invented in 1798 by French gunsmith, Edmé Régnier L'Aîné (1751-1825), was sufficiently accurate to equate hull resistance with the horsepower required to propel it.

During trials within the 'boxed' waterways of canals, at the end of each run Russell was struck by the curious solitary wave that continues independently after a vessel is halted. The discovery was intriguing but predated any practical use. Such waves are now dubbed 'solitons' and have become important in the fields of optics and communications. Russell explained the propagation of the 'constant velocity wave-packet' in his 'wave-line' theory. This theory was quite wrong, but that did not negate its enduring influence on naval architecture. Wave-line Theory informed the design of more efficient hull-forms and underpinned the development of tank-testing protocols. As a practical result, coal-hungry steamers could now achieve trans-oceanic range.[271]

Russell built several experimental vessels based on his 'wave principle'. The first was *The Wave*, a 75ft iron vessel launched in 1835. The records of the first trials noted that, at a hull-speed of 17 mph, "*there was no spray, no foam, no surge, no head of water at the prow, but the water is parted smoothly and evenly asunder*". The following year, Russell built a larger steamer to this same design, being 120 feet long by 12 feet wide, and of 30-horsepower. This second boat performed equally well and was notable for its frameless construction with transverse bulkheads and longitudinal stringers.[272]

Unfortunately, Russell's ideas about the compressibility of water meant that he was unable to conceptualise flowlines beneath a vessel. As Dixon Kemp noted, the theory could not address the real-life performance of the deep, heavy-displacement yachts of his time, and by some interpretations, precluded the possibility of fish, cod and mackerel both![273] Nevertheless, the man was celebrated and showered with honours.[274]

Meanwhile on the Clyde, also in the 1830s, the Duke of Portland, credited elsewhere in these pages as an influential progenitor of one-design yacht racing, was also testing the relative resistance of towed models on flat water.[275] Always an innovative operation, the Troon shipyard carried out their testing in a specially constructed tank with the towing carriage mounted on an overhead railway. Robert Curle, later to become a partner in Barclay Curle & Co Ltd of Stobbcross, another famous yard, served his apprenticeship at Troon, where his duties included model-making and conducting the Duke's tank-testing.

Apparently, test runs were carried out using various liquid mediums. In addition to water, the Duke's team experimented with more viscous materials like tar.[276] Quite why they did this is unclear, although they may have thought that the super-viscous medium, coupled with super-slow-motion carriage speed, might facilitate observation and approximate to the real world. It was a mad idea; one of the scale effects incurred in model testing is that the water becomes a denser medium, which is why larger models are generally preferred and small ones require artificially induced turbulence. Even changes in ambient water temperature can introduce variations in viscosity of up to 10%. Issues like this are grist to the mill of VPP modelling.[277] So, while these gooey experiments may be intriguing historically, they were well out of the mainstream.

In the 1840s, Scotts of Greenock set the standard with their fast clipper-ship designs for the East India Trade. These famously quick sailboats were finessed via a basic form of tank-testing overseen by Charles Cuningham Scott. Clippers built on Clydeside and in America at that time normally had a length to beam ratio of five or six, as compared to four for the more conventional East India Company's ships. At Scotts, *"an ingenious method of making model experiments in the graving dock at the works was evolved in the 'forties, whereby the firm were able to arrive at the most satisfactory form of hull to give the minimum of resistance, and at 4the same time a large capacity for cargo per registered ton."*[278]

Robert and Colin Scott carried out model testing on Loch Thom, a secluded beauty-spot high above Greenock, invariably blessed with a good stiff breeze.[279] The firm *"prepared fully-rigged models, about 5ft long, for experimental trials as to the ship's form and rudder on Loch Thom, an exposed place where the conditions of wind were analogous to those at sea. In these years, when the Minerva, A-bar, and other noted clippers were built, the care used in design and construction was almost as great as that now devoted in the case of racing yachts.*[280] Scotts prioritised 'handiness', as how a vessel answered to the helm was critical to both speed and safety in the days of the square-riggers.

Thomas Seath (1820-1902), an outlier in this story, used a much simpler method on the Johnstone Canal. He attached an evaluation model to each end of a 'jack-stick' (a light beam-balance), which 'weighed' the relative resistance of each when towed from a line fastened at its centre. This simple apparatus was reeled in with a fishing rod and line. The method takes 'rule of thumb' to new heights, as there are issues with consistency over a series of runs, but as long as a 'control' hull-form was set aside after each phase of whittling to ensure consistent progress, it works well enough to confirm or question hunches.[281]

Seath went to sea at the age of fourteen. He was a self-taught builder and designer, and a very successful one too. In 1854, he began building ships at Meadowside in Glasgow and two years later he moved his yard to Rutherglen. The Clyde Weir was completed the year Seath died in 1902 and put an end to shipbuilding in the upper reaches. Thomas Seath's yard built 272 ships, of which more than 40 were yachts.[282]

Of the establishment figures, one man who seems to have really understood what he was doing, was Professor Rankine, cited earlier in connection with Napier. Rather annoyingly, Rankine was neither designer nor builder, but an academic.[283] He theorised that the passage of water around a ship's hull followed neither the horizontal nor vertical plane, but rather took the shortest distance, as seems obvious now.

One wonders why these early theorists did not simply attach a field of tell-tales over the bottom of a small boat and observe the immersed bottom in motion to see how they streamed. The *Dialogue on the Art of Swimming* had been published in Germany in 1538 and 18th century Polynesian pearl divers already had goggles with glass lenses.[284] Surely a quick dip, or in winter, a simple box-and-mirror periscope, was not beyond the luminaries of the Industrial Revolution.

After this late start, Rankine's insight changed everything. Robert Montague in his influential publication, *Naval Architecture* of 1852, stressed the importance of designing ships by what he termed 'dividing lines', rather than the then-current practice of drawing waterlines only.[285] Dividing lines, ribband lines or diagonals are the first thing anyone looks at when studying plans of conventional racing yachts. If the diagonals are fair, we can be sure that no matter how weird the boat looks in plan or profile she will perform well both upright and at moderate angles of heel.

In the matter of fine entries, smaller sailing yachts powered by fore-and-aft rigs followed in the turbulent wake of the steamers. Thomas Assheton Smith's 163-ton cutter, *Menai*, of 1826 was reputedly the first sailing yacht with hollow lines following major surgery in 1828. However, as the plans for *Menai's* new bow were lost, so too was Smith's priority. In any case, the yacht did not perform much better after the surgery.[286]

The 45ft cutter, *Tiara*, built by Simons of Renfrew in 1850, also had a long fine, cut-away entry and sailed extremely well. *Bell's Life* declared that, had she been available for the Squadron's race around the Isle of Wight in 1851, she would have beaten the visiting schooner, *America*, but then so might several other yachts if the stars had not aligned so favourably for the visiting Yankees.[287] Nevertheless, the home fleet's reaction to *America's* fluky line honours was an unseemly rush to rebuild with entries lengthened and fined down: "*the old round bow was utterly condemned, and everyone went more or less crazy on the long hollow bow*".[288]

It is salutary to reflect that existing 'wave-line' yachts, with fine and even hollow entries, had raced successfully in home-waters for years, but these boats had singularly failed to impress the establishment. As for the rebuilds, some of these worked and some did not. "*As is often the case, the pendulum swung too far the other way; bows were built on old boats, and the moderately hollow bow was caricatured in some instances to a ridiculous extent."*[289]

America's good fortune was curiously a national humiliation. Certainly, she was a good boat with good sails, but her influence was transient, and even then, more style than substance. *America* was designed and built by George Steers for the Stephens brothers. Steers developed her rakish lines from the *Mary Taylor* which he had rebuilt in accordance with Scott Russell's wave-line theory the previous year. According to W. P. Stephens, the leading light of mid-19th century American yachting journalism, Steers was inspired by the encouraging performance of the *Mosquito* in Britain.[290]

Mosquito, designed by Tom Waterman and built by John Mare at Blackwall on the Thames, could certainly have matched *America* around the Isle of Wight. G. L. Watson recalled that *"the yacht Mosquito astonished the yachting world in 1848"*. And, even before she was remodelled to follow the new fashion, the evergreen *Arrow* was also more than capable. *Arrow*, built by Joseph Weld in 1823, remained competitive for six decades, even while developments in yacht architecture, rigs and sailing techniques continued apace. Her bow was fined down in 1837, and she was rebuilt again for the 1852 season with an even finer entry.

The key innovation was to slim down the entry, not to hollow it. For most purposes, adding volume behind the midship-section was a blind alley too. There was never anything wrong with the traditional clean run of sailing vessels. For steamers, the calculation of required buoyancy aft was more complex to take account of, inter alia, i) the propensity of some hull-forms to squat under power; ii) the need to ensure a clean water-flow to the propellers; iii) the required operational speed, and iv) the horsepower necessary to achieve that. Scott Russell's prototype was fast because she was super-slim, like a rowing skiff, not because she had a needle-sharp entry or plump quarters transitioning to a wine-glass transom.

The extraordinary passion of the debate on hollow entries, particularly Russell's obsession with the curve of versed sines, seems pointless today. The real lesson concerned the futility of the trial-and-error experiments, which involved chopping and changing full-sized ships. While this approach can sometimes produce a good result, it is uneconomic, and as promising alterations cannot be 'bracketed', it virtually precludes optimisation.

Napier understood that steamers and yachts required different lines and distribution of buoyancy; it is not clear in their writings whether Assheton Smith and Scott Russell did. Slim, low-prismatic entries (less volume/buoyancy in the bow) work well with powerboats that operate at displacement speed, whereas a relatively higher prismatic coefficient (more volume/buoyancy in the ends) is necessary for high average speeds under sail, and for good performance to windward when heeled.[291]

Low prismatic shapes have particular problems in displacement sailing yachts as the bow wave and quarter-waves are closer together, limiting top speed, and when heeled, the new distribution of immersed volume may lift the ends and shorten the effective waterline. The prismatic coefficient is defined as *"the ratio of the immersed volume to the volume of a prism with its length equal to the waterline length and cross-sectional area equal to the maximum cross-sectional area"* and can be quantified as follows:

Prismatic Coefficient $(Cp) = \dfrac{(A \times L)}{V}$

Where:

    V is the immersed volume of the hull in cubic feet

    A is the maximum cross-sectional area in square feet.

    L is the waterline length in feet.

In 1884, the Denny shipyard built the first commercial test-tank. The facility was designed by William Froude, a contemporary of Scott Russell, but a scientist working on a sounder theoretical basis. The Denny test-tank was a 100-metre commercial version of an 85-metre prototype built privately by Froude at the Torquay Experimental Station in 1871. Froude's first tank was funded by a British Admiralty contract to investigate the performance of full-sized ships at sea.[292]

Froude's 19th century manual computations struggled to replicate the complexities of real-world cause-and-effect. While Russell's deeply flawed wave line theory was more influential at the time, Froude's approach, together with his signature 'numbers', have endured. The Froude Number remains a useful rule of thumb to estimate the likely maximum speed of real-world displacement yachts, the scale speed for tank testing, and in evolutionary robotics, the running speed of dinosaurs.

Froude was a key figure in the development of both experimental tank testing in a controlled environment and the mathematical models that have evolved to make sense of the results. Today, his work is still manifest in the modelling techniques of computational fluid dynamics (CFD). Here, we might also acknowledge the work of Lewis Fry Richardson in the birth of modern CFD. Richardson was a long-term Kilmun resident and not much interested in sailing, as far as we know, but his remarkable insights into turbulent flow inform naval architecture to this day.

Richardson's seminal work on weather forecasting presaged finite element analysis and the now ubiquitous CFD calculations where physical space is divided into cells. The inherent complexity of this approach and the need to address the wall of 'big data' precluded practical application until developments in electronic computing finally caught up to deliver useful outputs in real-time. Richardson's laborious long-hand calculations were initially thought erroneous, however, when a 'smoothing' algorithm is introduced they are found to be impressively accurate. Richardson's book, *Weather Prediction by Numerical Process*, and his published worksheets are the well-buried foundation stones of modern CFD.[293]

> *Big whirls have little whirls*
> *that feed on their velocity,*
> *and little whirls have lesser whirls*
> *and so on to viscosity.*[294]

Richardson was a remarkable character to whom we also owe fractals and the Richardson Effect, which proved mathematically, to the joy of sailors everywhere, that the length of a coastline is infinite. However, a deeply held pacifism limited his influence through WW2 and marginalised his research. When Richardson discovered that his meteorological work could be applied to the deployment of chemical weapons, he abandoned this field and destroyed his unpublished findings. Following the loss of the *Titanic*, Richardson registered patents for iceberg detection using acoustic echolocation in both air and water, anticipating the 'invention' of sonar by Langevin and Boyle six years later.[295] And among other, often astonishing, achievements, he reduced our inherent propensity for conflict and war to a mathematical model.

Clyde shipbuilder, John Inglis (1842-1919), lobbied unsuccessfully for a research test-tank to be built at Glasgow University and was an enthusiastic advocate of the process as a design aid. Inglis was married to James Denny's daughter, Agnes, so he was familiar with the Dumbarton facility and enjoyed unparalleled access.[296] G. L. Watson was much influenced by Inglis and respected Froude's work, so we might assume that he had coveted a tank-test budget since his apprenticeship. That opportunity arose in the late 1890s, with a 2,082-ton steam-yacht commission for American publisher and playboy, Gordon Bennett Jr. Watson tested a range of design options in the Denny test-tank before finalising the lines. The result was *Lysistrata*, built at Denny's yard, and by all accounts something of a masterpiece.

Watson normally favoured D. & W. Henderson, who built *Britannia* and the *Valkyries II & III*, for Big Class sailing yacht commissions. There were good reasons for this. In the words of yachting correspondent James Meikle: "*So proud over her building were the men, that the putting of her together was a real labour of love. Really it was not difficult to imagine that the framework was woven together, so beautifully were the many parts joined in to and on to each other.*"

Certainly, quality-control at Henderson's was almost unnecessary as pride in fine craftsmanship was institutionalised in that yard.

However, when he was awarded the commission for *Shamrock II*, the opportunity to return to the Dumbarton test-tank sealed the construction contract for Denny. Prior to the *Shamrock II* challenge, while the benefits of tank-testing were already well-established, the world's best yacht designers had yet to capitalise on its possibilities. Watson changed all that, taking full advantage of the Denny facility and in the process establishing the generic protocols for tank-testing racing yachts.

Tony Browning, who was fascinated by ship models and tank-testing, revisited Watson's test methodology in 1951. Browning made it his life's work to secure the maritime history of the Clyde. He was born on the Isle of Wight but is eternally associated with Glasgow and Clyde shipbuilding as he graduated in naval architecture from Glasgow Tech and gained his post-qualification work experience at Fairfield's and Denny's. He was appointed Curator of Technology at Kelvingrove Museum in 1955, from which he spun off the Museum of Transport. Tony Browning's legacy is the fine collection that first expanded into the Kelvin Hall, before migrating once again to the custom-built facility of Glasgow's Riverside Museum.[297]

Watson appears to have been the first naval architect to both carry out comparative tank-testing using models of existing racing yachts, and to develop a new design using an accurately calibrated commercial testing facility. As this was also the first serious work on sail-driven vessels, he had to design the tools to obtain consistent angles of heel and introduce yaw to simulate leeway.[298] Off and on, he spent more than a year at the test-tank – tinkering even as *Shamrock II* was under construction.[299]

Watson recognised that recent America's Cup matches (1893 through 1895 to 1897) had seen elapsed race times for the full Cup Course reduced from between 4 to 7 minutes seriatim. To be competitive in 1901, he was, therefore, seeking a gross performance gain of 15 minutes, including a margin to accommodate wind strength variations and distance sailed. This target translated into a required net average speed of 7.9 knots over the 30-miles Cup Course. Thus, *Shamrock II* would have to achieve an average speed through the water of 10kts over the combined windward, leeward, reaching cycle, and a maximum hull-speed, in ideal conditions, well in excess of that.[300]

During the period September to November 1900, and again through the early months of 1901, Watson tested models of *Britannia*, *Valkyrie III* and *Shamrock I* to establish a known datum for comparison. William Fife gave Watson the design of his *Shamrock I*, which had lost to *Defender* in 1899, and appears to have been generally supportive, if not enthused.

The second phase involved modifying the best of these base models to explore specific design features that might speed them up or slow them down. Watson tested line-of-motion resistance and side forces at typical angles of yaw and heel experienced when racing.[301]

To arrive at the final hull-form, eleven separate designs were tested. Watson was generously funded to iterate variations of the most promising base models; something our 1958 *Sceptre* challenge, for example, could not do. He was thus able to bracket, refine and optimise his final lines. As both existing and new designs were subject to this optimisation process, close to 100 discrete variations were eventually tested.

This painstaking process was facilitated by the paraffin wax model system used at Dumbarton. The models were milled by a precision cutting machine, then finessed by hand and ballasted to their marks with lead shot to maintain identical weights and moment of gyration. A century later, when Ian Howlett, an advocate of tank-testing, made a pilgrimage to the Denny Tank, he was *"struck by the darkness of the wax bound up with the dust of ages"*. Then he wondered, almost devotionally, *"whether some of the same wax used for 'Shamrock II' might just still be embodied in the surviving models – the ultimate in recycling – no waste to dispose of or models to store"*.

Watson's tank-test models were built at 1/10th scale (a 120ft LOA yacht is a 12ft model). The wax milling machine could not cut to the full keel depth required, so the lower elements of the models were carved in wood. This drawback was turned to advantage as the wooden fins were stiffer when running at high yaw and heel angles, and moreover, could be readily interchanged. Testing addressed a range of ship speeds from 3 to 15kts.

Model speed is calculated in relation to the Freud number, which determines hull speed in displacement-mode. Effectively, when a single wave formation peaks at the extreme ends of the effective waterline. So, for *Shamrock II*, sailing on an effective LWL of 105 ft at a conservative hull-speed, that would be $\sqrt{105} \times 1.34 = 13.73$kts, which would be 4.34kts for the 1/10th scale model.

The first trial was of the *Valkyrie III* model, designed by Watson in 1895 and known to be a good boat. She was tested at five angles of yaw, varying from 0° to 5° and at 90° to the line-of-motion, and at angles of heel from 0° to 20°.[302] These early tests suggested that 2° of yaw and 10° of heel were mathematically fundamental to other yaw and heel angles. Resistance curves were drawn for *Valkyrie III* in this condition and for 0° of yaw and 0° of heel – hull upright, line-of-motion along the centreline. Variations of these angles could, therefore, be determined by proxy calculations.

The test procedure was as follows: models were run to measure resistance over a range of 9 to 12kts ship speed, with 2° of yaw to port and at 10° of heel to starboard. If a model showed initial promise the speed range was increased, and the model was also run upright with 0° yaw. If a model performed especially well, further tests explored broader operational conditions. Side forces were also measured to determine the centre of lateral resistance.[303]

A series of preliminary optimisation tests were based on *Valkyrie III*. The first test compared keel-fin entry and waterlines. Unsurprisingly, a fair rounded edge was best, and the bulbed-keel also performed well. The waterlines of the canoe body were then alternately fined down within the constraints of a fair and feasible hull shape. Both interventions suggested possible marginal gains from finer ends, as long as the lateral centre of buoyancy remained approximately amidships.

The benefits of overhangs were then assessed. It transpired that *Valkyrie III's* overhang aft was longer than necessary, but not by much and her bow was about right. Over 10kts of ship speed, the benefits of these long overhangs were pronounced. Tests on keel fin placement suggested that moving the fin aft, always within practical limits, reduced overall resistance and was indeed a feature of the final model.

Following the *Valkyrie III* tests, the lines of *Shamrock I* (Fife 1899) were put through the mill and are believed to have been marginally slower all round than the *Valkyrie III* model (Browning says the reverse). Of interest is that the optimum fin keel shape for this model was found to be very close to *Shamrock I's* original keel – a fin symmetrical in planform and located slightly abaft midships, with the keel-foot parallel to the load waterline and gently bulbed. Subsequently, models representing other promising variations were tested. These explored 'beam and depth ratios' and a 'fin depth series' – all assessed on a constant midship section.

These tests demonstrated the performance gains that could be achieved by fining down the garboards – reducing total resistance and leeway. This was not news, but it was useful to quantify the benefits. The 1897 class rules for 19/24 included a tax on garboard hollow, paid for in sail area. Many years later, in 1906, the new International Rule would severely tax garboard hollow, measured as skin girth minus chain girth.

G. L. Watson synthesised the wealth of original data generated by the tests into a new lines-plan. While the lines were initially based on *Valkyrie III*, as informed by the test results, they now diverged considerably. The result was a more radical scow type of hull-form. The final design for the full-size build was developed from this model, with the leading edge of the keel cut back to provide a leading edge which was nearer the vertical. The numbers suggested that, while the *Valkyrie III* base model was already a good light airs design, when the breeze came up the new boat, *Shamrock II*, would be considerably quicker.

After applying a scale factor correction to reflect relative viscosity, Watson concluded that for a race run at a mean windspeed of 10 to 12kts he had reduced resistance by 10 to 12%, equivalent to his original target of 10 to 15 minutes shaved from an average race time. However, as events transpired, when *Shamrock II* came up against *Columbia* (the same boat that had easily defeated *Shamrock I* and of similar performance to *Valkyrie III*) in 1899, the margins gained, expressed as a percentage, were in low single digits.

Predicted Performance improvement *Shamrock II* over *Valkyrie III*

Boat-speed (ship speed) knots	8	9	10	11	12
Reduction in resistance %	0	2	6	11	11

So, Watson's new design was indeed a lot better than Fife's last effort, but still only on a par with Herreshoff's *Defender* from 1899; and that yacht was drafted without the benefits of tank-testing. We might also consider that the average windspeed on the America's Cup Course off New York is below 10mph (8.7kts) for 25% of the time in September, the month in which the match took place, and the last Cup competition had been dominated by light airs for two out of three races. So, perhaps performance in light airs should have received more attention?

"*When the underwater form of Shamrock II was laid bare in the Erie dry-dock, two facts were at once made evident: first, that G. L. Watson has designed an entirely original boat; second, that the much-talked-of towing experiments in the Denny testing tank were evidently responsible for the most striking departures in her lines from what might be called the orthodox form of a ninety-foot racing cutter.*"[304] Arguably, *Shamrock II* came undone through a series of basic errors in her campaign. Her tune-up time was limited, she suffered from the lack of a trial-horse in the USA, then, she came against émigré Scot, Charlie Barr, in his pomp.

W. P. Steven was certain where the blame lay: "*As to the failure of that yacht, she was in form quite up to the very high standard of all of Watson's work. Though she was handled by the ablest Corinthian and one of the best of British professionals, it was quite generally recognized in this country that her failure to defeat the two-year-old Columbia with two-year-old sails was due in no way to the quality of her design.*"[305] This painful defeat, however, might now be seen as a mere blip in history.

Watson's tank test methodologies, by contrast, represented a sea change. From this date forward, no serious yacht designer would willingly forgo the opportunity to use these tools when tank-access was available. Watson's careful benchmarking laid bare the suspicion that William Fife's *Shamrock I* for the 1899 America's Cup was slower than Watson's own *Valkyrie III*, designed four years previously for the 1895 competition. Nevertheless, Lipton was advised to return to the Fairlie drawing office for *Shamrock III*. It seems a pity that Watson could not build on his existing progress. However, his health was failing, and he was unable to commit to the all-consuming effort of another America's Cup.

Watson was still keen to support the challenge. He handed over his most promising models from the *Shamrock II* test sessions and offered further support via an informal peer-review process. Unfortunately, Fife did not capitalise on this generous offer. Perhaps the great William Fife III, consummate artist, but a relative novice in these technologies, apprehended the whiff of condescension? Certainly, Fife did not fully take advantage of Watson's progress, so industriously developed in the Denny tank, nor indeed did he employ the tank effectively himself.

Fife and Watson were personal friends who held each other in high regard professionally. Yet pride is a curious thing; Fife lobbied Lipton's people to use the obsolete *Shamrock I* as a trial horse rather than the more recent and considerably more-sophisticated Watson boat. In effect, he knowingly buried his head in the sand. So, the manifest shortcomings of *Shamrock III* were not exposed until she reached America. This debacle reflected on the sterling reputation of the Scottish yacht design community as a whole. Tommy Lipton's advisors counselled change. Lipton's next, and easily his most dangerous, challenger – the radical *Shamrock IV* would be designed by the new master, Charles E. Nicholson.

While Watson was testing yachts in the late 1890s, another talented designer was similarly engrossed in tank-testing. Fred J. Stephen, who features in Chapter 27, routinely tested new ship design ideas in his tank at Linthouse. Shipbuilding was extremely competitive in this era and shipowners were able to caveat orders with performance and efficiency specifications that required an incremental advance on the state of the art. A new vessel underperforming on the measured mile invoked ruinous penalties or might simply be rejected. In 1902, the Stephen-built *Wyandra* achieved her contract speed with a wafer-thin margin of 0.002kts. After this close call, Stephen commissioned a larger purpose-built tank.

The original test-tank at Linthouse was built as a condenser-tank. It was just 45ft long and formed part of the roof of the Powerhouse. On Sundays, with the machinery shut down to eliminate vibration, ship models were towed, and their performance evaluated. A striking element of the original apparatus was a pendulum, adjusted to record half-second beats on a rotating drum. Fred Stephen's results were said to match those used in the much larger and more sophisticated Denny Tank.[306]

This testing was carried out about 15 years before the National Physical Laboratory at Teddington built their ship test tank in 1911. After that more advanced facility became available, Fred lobbied his clients to incorporate a budget for testing at Teddington, particularly when guarantees concerning operational speeds formed part of the contract. In-house tank-testing endowed Alex Stephen & Sons with a competitive edge in commercial shipbuilding.

In light of Stephen's ready access to a tank and command of the testing process, we are bound to consider whether his racing yacht designs benefitted. However, while Fred's designs were indeed preternaturally quick out of the box, it is unlikely that this was a result of work in the tank. The Stephen's tank-test was limited to measuring upright resistance. Moreover, the scale of Fred's free-sailing models, which were built to the 6-metre model rule, were really too small for reliable results. On the other hand, we do know that Fred, his son, John, and Tommy Glen-Coats, all employed free-sailing models in both comparative tests and open competition.

Following the tank-testing carried out under the direction of G. L. Watson, the technique failed to gain traction on either side of the Atlantic for 40 years. There was occasional America's Cup work, most notably for the Burgess-Stephens J-class, *Ranger*, before Olin Stephens went back to the tank to work-up the lines of the 6-metre, *Goose*, over the winter of 1937-8.

As an essentially self-taught designer, Olin built up his toolbox over the years, reinventing what he failed to discover, like the lateral dynamometer, a device that G. L. Watson had used nearly half a century before. There were setbacks, however; David Boyd's *Circe*, the product of a fine eye and years of experience in the Fife design office, trounced *Goose* in the Seawanhaka Cup in three straight races – two in heavy airs and one in light weather. Writing in his autobiography 60 years later, Stephens still could not believe it. "*I wish I could clarify the question of Goose losing to the Scottish Six*".[307]

The traditionally conceived *Circe* was a beautiful anachronism. The work on *Goose* laid the foundations for post-war metre-boats and informed their offshore variants. There was the seminal 12-metre, *Vim*, and an entire generation of successful Stephen's designs at 6, 8 and 12-metre ratings – including *Iskareen*, *Llanoria*, *Iroquois*, *Columbia*, and *Constellation*. Also, in 1937, innovative English designer, Laurent Giles, was working in the same Davidson Tank. Giles's work on the 12-metre, *Flica*, for Hugh Goodison produced an enduringly quick boat and another fine advertisement for the Fairlie boatbuilder's skills.[308] Goodison would later underwrite the 1958 *Sceptre* challenge for the America's Cup.

Through the inter-war years, Scottish designers like Alfred Mylne, James McGruer and David Boyd coveted the budgets necessary to tank-test racing yachts. Boyd, for example, was forced to follow in the path of Fife, trusting to luck that each iteration might result in a small performance improvement – as had so often transpired through the history of yacht design. Boyd recalled: *"William Fife had a 'golden rule': Never alter the waterline length of a new Six design by more than 2 inches between seasons, nor that of an Eight by more than 3 inches."*

David Boyd's view was that, without recourse to a test-tank, any other evolution of an already successful design with no apparent vices, was simply guesswork. Ian Howlett summarised the situation after WW2: *"The dominant designer of the immediate pre-war era in the USA was the incomparable Olin Stephens, whilst in Britain David Boyd held sway. The plateau of development for full-keel designs had been scaled by the late thirties, so it was inevitable that the first post-war designs from these masters showed little change of character."*[309]

However, when David Boyd did get access to a tank, he made the most of the opportunity. *"It is an open secret that the tank tests of designer David Boyd's models at Stevens Institute in Hoboken were, in the words of Olin Stephens, 'better than anything tested to that time', so it seems certain the challenger will go to the line with a hull that is not outclassed."*[310] Chapter 30 touches on some lesser-known stories concerning the tank-testing of Boyd's 12-metres that were received after *The Piper Calls the Tune* was published.

Finally, we might close this chapter with a full-scale test of the type common before custom-built test-tanks – but with an unusual twist. In 1939, some bright spark in the United States had the idea to paint stripes at right angles to the centreline on a 6mR and tow the boat with the paint still wet.[311] If nothing else, the perfect parallel paint runs of this messy exercise demonstrated that the pre-war 6-metre is one of the slipperiest shapes, next to an Orca, that is ever likely to grace our waters.

CODA: William Fife II, William Fife III and *Shamrock I*

Why *Shamrock* Lost: Letter to the Editor of *The Yachtsman* magazine in January 1900 from William Fife II, concerning *Shamrock I* designed by his son William Fife III. Fife Snr was then 79 years old, but with a mind as lively as it ever was.[312] He passed away two years later.

11th January 1900, Fairlie

Dear Sir,

It is not often in a long life that I have taken to the pen in defence of remarks made in the various yachting papers criticising yachts and their performance, but when I see paragraphs in The Yachtsman, I cannot resist stating that none of the reasons given why Shamrock was beaten for the America's Cup are correct. The true cause why the Shamrock sailed so poorly in the last two races was that she was screwed up. In all my 60 years of experience, I have never known a yacht sail her best with tight rigging and tight sheeting. And from all that I learn from some aboard the said yacht, she was pinned up to an extraordinary degree.

I believe that the Columbia is as good a yacht for her inches as has ever been built, but I believe Shamrock is as good as Columbia under equal management, and I am not often wrong in my opinion. I built the Cuckoo more than 20 years ago. I thought her the best thing I had turned out. She was unfortunate in falling into hands that could not take the best of her and made no name until she was nine years old. I still had the belief that the lines were alright, so much so that I built Neva, Cynthia, Bloodhound and Neptune, 50-ton yawls, all on nearly the same lines. They were all successful in their different classes; and when Captain o' Neil got in charge of Cuckoo, in her ninth year, she was at the top of the tree, and I have not the least doubt that the Shamrock will be there before long, without altering her lines or sailplan.[313]

William Fife Snr

There is little doubt that Fife Snr was correct in his assessment of the two hull-shapes – as we have seen, Watson found *Shamrock* to be a very good boat when he tank-tested the model; and the fact is that she was not sailed particularly well. As to the matter of rigging, Fife's letter prompted a lengthy response from H. Wheatley Ridsdale, an eminent engineer who had worked on the Parsons Steam Turbine.

Ridsdale hypothesised that slack rigging can be beneficial in some conditions – light, fluky or puffy winds where micro-changes in strength and direction occur constantly. Micro-changes can, to a certain extent, be absorbed by deflections in the sailplan – rather than heeling and recovery, stored and returned to even out the drive provided by the rig. There may be an element of truth to this, in terms of keeping a boat 'in the groove', but it is an idea rejected today as every element of the rigging is engineered to minimise stretch, and deflection is confined to the spars and upper roach.

While these conditions are common on the Clyde where the hillsides come down to the sea, the scenario was not relevant in the 1899 America's Cup match on the New York Yacht Club course. Ridsdale then went on to explain the engineering reasons why the change-over to steel masts required tighter rigging and made stiff hull structure essential. First, he suggests that aluminium alloy spars would be better and in this he was right. He was right again when he explained why a thin-wall, substantially incompressible spar must be correctly stayed to remain 'in column' and to prevent sidewall buckling.[314]

On the Clyde, Herbert Thom was the great advocate of slack rigging and such was his influence, he was not alone. Thom also advocated a fair degree of movement in the hull structure, favouring an element of torsional flex and specifying a maximum-sized cockpit (where he had that option) to let the boat 'give'. With the rig 'breathing' and the hull 'giving', a good helmsman today would tear his hair out. While some one-design classes today, notably the Sonata where the jib is cut for this set-up, are sailed successfully without running backstays and without much forestay tension, where a straight forestay is possible it is usually desirable. As for the benefits of hull flex, this is an old wives' tale laid to rest more than a century ago; there are none.

248 Reflections on Yachts, Designers and Designing, Douglas Phillips Birt, 1968.
249 Ian continued: *"For example, my 1/5 scale 6-metre tests in the period 1984-1988 provided excellent data. But I was present for every run and designed the experiments which were conducted by highly capable friends and colleagues. My choice of 1/5 scale was the largest that could sensibly be tested into the Southampton tank, and resulted in a model weight four times that of the Davidson lab 6-metre tests, i.e. the measured forces would scale similarly."* Correspondence with Ian Howlett, January 2018.
250 F. H. Chapman, the First Naval Architect and his Work, Daniel Harris,1989.
251 Chapman, the First Naval Architect, Captain Henry P. Boyd, R.N. (Retired), published in Thoughts on Yachts and Yachting, Ed. Uffa Fox, 1938.
252 Yacht Architecture, Dixon Kemp, 1891.
253 The square root of the waterline length multiplied by one point 'something', usually between 1.2 and 1.5 in traditional longkeel sailing yachts.
254 Napier was prescient here again. The Glasgow Corporation 'sludge fleet' operated from 1904 to 1998. I remember the *Shieldhall* best, but the *Gardyloo* surely had the best name!
255 A Letter to the Editor from Mr David Napier, Glasgow Herald, 10th November 1858.
256 Charles Bossut (1730-1814) was a French mathematician and expert on hydrostatics, hydrodynamics and the stability of ships.
257 David Napier – Engineer (1790-1869) Autobiographical Sketch with Notes, 1912.
258 Folklore of Scottish Lochs and Springs, James Murray Mackinlay, 1893.
259 This was certainly true from the years of European exploration through the great years of the East Indiamen. However, clipper-ships in a speed-competitive market demonstrated the viability of lines which eventually became quite fine forward too, but then again, they plumbed the Southern Ocean like submarines.
260 There are 'lifting sails', which can bodily elevate small craft like windsurfers – where the whole rig is canted to windward, and well-trimmed spinnakers might be lifting slightly more at the bottom than they pull down at the top (drive remains substantially parallel to the water). However, on square-riggers, even if topsails are lifting, the 'centre of effort' is so far above the sectional 'centre of resistance' that these sails are still depressing the bow.
261 David Napier – Engineer (1790-1869) Autobiographical Sketch with Notes, David Napier and David Bell, 1912.
262 Early Clyde Steamboats III, Dalmadan Blog, 14th May 2015.
263 The Topographical, Statistical, and Historical Gazetteer of Scotland, Volume First, 1843.
264 Observations of David Bell, who annotated and enlarged Napier's autobiography, 1912.
265 Other joint experiment with hull design which includes 'cathedral' hull developments (see the pre-WW1 Hickman Sea Sled and the Ray Hunt-designed Boston Whalers from 1956) and a number of steam-yachts with hollow waterlines in the period 1830-1851. Reminiscences of the late Thomas Assheton Smith, Esq, Sir John Eardley Eardley-Wilmot, 1859.
266 Reputedly, while at Eton, Assheton Smith *"discovered the principle of hollow lines for yachts"* by throwing stones into the water. Judge that as you will. Smith was instrumental in legitimising steam yachts for the British establishment; as these vessels were initially associated with vulgar new money and people 'in trade'. One of Russell's early commissions was for Smith.
267 *Fire King*, 1838, built for Smith by Thomson, engined by Robert Napier who later acquired her.
268 Letter to Assheton Smith's widow, 4th April 1859.
269 Clippers, Yachts, and the false promise of the wave-line, L. Ferreiro & A. Pollara, 2017.

270 Full-scale tests were carried out on the Union Canal at Hermiston, near the Riccarton campus of Heriot-Watt University, Edinburgh. Subsequent model testing would be carried out in a 30ft tank in Scott Russell's back garden.

271 Re-inventing the Ship: Science, Technology and the Maritime World, 1800-1918, Don Leggett and Richard Dunn, 2012.

272 The egg-box construction was patented by David Napier.

273 Yacht Architecture, Dixon Kemp, 1891.

274 Scott Russell was awarded the 1838 Keith Prize by the Royal Society in Edinburgh for a paper on wave-line theory. He held this as his badge of priority on hollow waterlines.

275 G. L. Watson, the Art and Science of Yacht Design, Martin Black, 2011.

276 Ibid

277 Tank Testing and Data Analysis Techniques for the Assessment of Sailboat Hydrodynamic Characteristics, Claudio Fassardi, conference paper, December 2002.

278 Scotts' Shipbuilding & Engineering Co Ltd. Two Centuries of Shipbuilding by the Scotts at Greenock, Offices of Engineering, London, 1906.

279 Circumnavigating the loch on my bicycle, always a joy, it strikes me as an arena better suited to kid's sail-training programmes and RC yachting than angling.

280 Two Centuries of Shipbuilding by the Scotts at Greenock, 1906.

281 The Clyde Passenger Steamers: From the Comet of 1812 to the King Edward of 1901 James Williamson, 1904.

282 There is a suggestion that Thomas Seath built the G. L. Watson cutter, Leila, of 1879, a 5-tonner. However, Leila was wood and every other Seath ship was steel, so this seems unlikely.

283 Rankine served his time as a surveyor after dropping out of his first degree-course.

284 Der Schwimmer oder ein Zwiegespräch über die Schwimmkunst, Nikolaus Wynmann, 1538.

285 Naval Architecture, a Treatise on Shipbuilding and the Rig of Clippers, with suggestions on a new method of laying down vessels, Lord Robert Montague, 1852.

286 The 163-ton Menai, of 1826, had a conventional entry (as insisted by Ransome of Hastings, the original builders). She had her bow extended in 1828 by Rubie of Southampton, with hollow waterlines to Smith's original design concept bringing her displacement to 180 tons. The Napier steamer, Menai, built by Wood and Richie in 1830, had an entry 'based on Assheton Smith's sailing cutter of the same name' – the Menai.

287 Bell's Life, August 1850.

288 The Badminton Library of Sports and Pastimes: Yachting, Volume 1, The Evolution of the Modern Racing Yacht, G. L. Watson, 1894.

289 Bell's Life, August 1850.

290 American Yachting, W. P. Stephens, 1904.

291 Modern wedge-form semi-displacement and foil-assisted yachts play a different game, as do the latest generation of square-planform scows, now performing well offshore too.

292 Denny's designs were tested in the tank to confirm performance targets and avoid the contractual performance penalties clauses that made steamer contracts a game of 'Russian Roulette' in that era. The Denny facility is now managed by the Scottish Maritime Museum.

293 Prediction by Numerical Process, L. F. Richardson, 1922. Written while serving with the Friends' Ambulance Unit on the front line. The manuscript was lost during the Battle of Champagne in April 1917, then found months later, under a pile of coal.

294 Ibid

295 Lewis Fry Richardson: scientist, visionary and pacifist, Lettera Matematica, Angelo Vulpiani, September 2014.

296 The Auld Mug, the Scots and the America's Cup, Len Paterson, 2012.

297 Browning's magus opus was a History of Clyde Shipyards, A. S. E. Browning, 1991.

298 G. L. Watson, the Art and Science of Yacht Design, Martin Black, 2011.

299 Letter from G. L. Watson to William Fife, 13th February 1902, sourced by Martin Black.

300 Some Factors in the Tank Testing of Shamrock II, A. S. E. Browning, June 1951.

301 As these elements of resistance are unique to sailing craft, specialist gear had to be

developed within the project. Time constraints meant that this had to be very simple.
[302] Consistent heel angles, which were difficult to maintain, were resolved through trial and error using a sliding weight on a calibrated arm.
[303] This was certainly an advance on the old tradition of balancing a cardboard cut-out of the underwater profile on a knife, which requires some latitude in mast position.
[304] The Lawson History of the America's Cup, Thomas W. Lawson, 1902.
[305] W. P. Stevens, incidental comments cited in a paper on Tank-testing & some Experimental Studies of the Sailing Yacht, Kenneth S. Davidson, 1936.
[306] Said to be "*crude but remarkably accurate*". Stephen of Linthouse, a Record of Two Hundred Years of Shipbuilding – 1750-1950, John L. Carvel, 1951.
[307] All this and Sailing Too, Olin Stephens, 2001.
[308] 'Jack' Giles tested five models. Olin Stephens remembers that Giles did a fair bit of 'fishing' on the protocols, procedures and costs of model testing in tanks. *Flica II* incorporated so many innovations she took an age to reach her potential. Many years later, after conversion for cruising, she served as an able trial horse in the 1964 *Sovereign* campaign.
[309] David Boyd conceded that most of his design development was in the spacing of the sections. "*What could you do without being able to test in a testing tank?*" Lines for the Layman, Ian Howlett, The Yachtsman, Issue No.3, Nov/Dec.
[310] Of two better boats, which is more better? C. Mitchell, Boating, June 1964.
[311] Yachting, April 1939, composite image credited to John A. Davis.
[312] Why Shamrock Lost, William Fife Snr. The Yachtsman 11th January 1900.
[313] Ibid
[314] Setting-up Rigging & Steel Spars, H. Wheatley Ridsdale, The Yachtsman 25th January 1900.

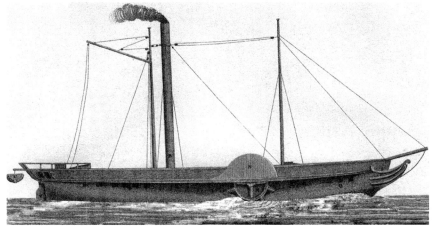

Believed to be *Rob Roy* (1 of 4 possible candidates) designed by David Napier built by Denny, 1817

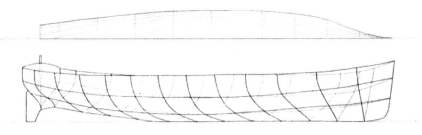

The Wave, 1835   Design: John Scott Russell

Models by William Froude. *Swan* (top) and *Raven* (bottom) on display in the Science Museum. These 12-foot scale models were used in towing trials to establish resistance and scaling laws. *Raven's* fine entry followed John Scott Russell's wave-line theory. *Swan's* rounded entry presented lower resistance. Ship hydrodynamics in the 19th century was heavily influenced by John Scott Russell's wave-line theory. From the 1840s to the 1880s, the design of many famous clipper ships and yachts followed this theory before it was eclipsed by William Froude's laws of ship resistance. The Science Museum, London.

Shamrock II, G. L. Watson 1903, in dry dock   Image: James Burton
The radical shape that emerged from Watson's methodical tank testing programme is apparent. The extreme overhangs extend the sailing waterline to optimise hull-speed in moderate wind strengths. Note: i) the snubbed termination of the bow overhang; ii) the engineering required to maintain forestay tension – the loads on the extended cantilever at the extreme end of the bowsprit were challenging to say the least; and iii) the keel design, with a close to vertical leading edge for windward performance and an aft location for least drag and good handling downwind.

Early Denny test carriage (steam powered)   Wax model cutting machine

Denny Test Tank, Dumbarton, 1884, images: the author   *Shamrock II*, G. L. Watson 1903

The waterway of the Denny Test Tank is 300ft long, 22ft wide and 8ft in depth. The tank was modernised between the world wars.

A gangway running the full length of the tank and supports rails for the model testing carriage carried the recording apparatus, an operator and any observers. The carriage railway is subtly curved to match the curvature of the Earth. Temperature and salinity levels in the tank were constantly monitored.

The wax model cutting machine was invented by the tank's designer, William Froude.

Worldwide, when new test tank facilities are comissioned, they are christened before first use with a bottle of water from the 'Mother Tank' at Dumbarton.

Chapter 7: Bottomless Double-bottomed Machines[315]

South of the Equator in the steady Trade Winds and warm water, catamarans have existed and flourished for hundreds of years and have been noted for their high speeds and ability. Uffa Fox[316]

The pirogues of Oceania were described as 'flying objects' by Antonio Pigafetta during Magellan's first circumnavigation in 1521. Pigafetta was Magellan's supernumerary and chronicler of the expedition. And, as one of just 18 souls to return from the original company of 240, he was something of a survivor too. Initially, Pigafetta's reports of 'flying objects' belonged to the mythical realm of giant octopuses and sea monsters.

However, as it transpired, this tall tale was true. Cephalopods may not be able to drag seagoing vessels down to the depths of the ocean, but they represent an entirely different evolutionary path to vertebrates, opening our eyes to what might be encountered in other worlds. Similarly, the flying objects of the Pacific represented an entirely different way to go sailing in machines that appeared radically configured to European eyes.

Scotland's on-off love affair with catamarans began in 1786, with Patrick Miller's innovation and investment, and ended in 1980 with the last designs of Rod McAlpine Downie. Generally, however, sailors north of the border have been indifferent to the fickle charms of multihulls. The Scots are not alone in this, but we do seem to have made our minds up, and the community of peripatetic cruising cats generally avoid Scottish waters too.

There are good reasons for this. Sailing conditions on the West Coast are characterised by long periods of calm when multihulls simply stick to the water. Then, when it does blow, the Scottish fjords are notorious for unexpected changes in wind strength and direction, backing gusts and brutal squalls. In such conditions, traditional self-righting keelboat designs promote a good night's sleep. Finally, our sailing waters and roadsteads are deep and our shores are rocky, so there is no intrinsic virtue in shallow draft.

Even dinghy sailors do not show much interest these days. Half-a-century ago we had good class-racing in Shearwater cats at Largs and most clubs had a few cats in the dinghy park. Today, you will have to look much harder. There are still catamarans at Largs, but no two are the same. The only regular class racing we can discover is provided by the Dart fleet at the Royal Tay. To witness a healthy pride of cats in Scotland, it is necessary to track down the small band of diehard travellers at one of their open meetings. This disinterest belies the fact that the Scots played a small, but significant, role in catamaran development.[317]

Early European catamarans were seen as oddities and confusingly known as double-bottomed boats, or sluice-boats, the latter term referencing the tunnel between the two hulls.[318] The earliest recorded examples were designed by Sir William Petty (1623-1687). "*Anno Domini 1663 he made his double-bottom'd vessell (launched about newyeere's tide), of which he gave a modell to the Royall Societie made with his owne hands and kept it in the repository at Gresham College.*"[319] Appended to the text above, which appears in Aubrey's *Brief Lives*, there is an intriguing reference to a contemporary, or possibly earlier, vessel: "*there is yet a double bottomd vessell in the Isle of Wight, made by one Mr .... which, they say, sailes well: quaere Captain Lee.*"

William Petty's *Simon & Jude* was launched on the 28th October 1662. She was assembled from two cylindrical floats 20ft long and 2ft in diameter connected by a platform 9ft wide. She was rigged with a spritsail sloop rig.[320] The *Simon & Jude* was apparently fast and was even faster when she was lengthened to 30ft.[321] This prototype was a 'proper' catamaran with separate, independent hulls as found in the Asia Pacific region, and as we understand the type today.[322]

Petty's early success encouraged him to build a much larger double-bottomed machine in 1663. The *Invention II* was clinker-built with 'boat-shaped' hulls. This was the celebrated vessel that beat the regular Irish packet boat, which ran between Holyhead and Dublin, in a wager each way. On the basis of this achievement, Petty built the *Experiment* in 1664. Tragically, the boat went down with all hands in a severe storm in the Bay of Biscay. However, the fact that she was even sailing there in the depths of winter in the Little Ice Age is impressive.

However, going down fighting is still going down. The calamity set back the multi-hull cause by two decades. Petty tried his hand again in 1684 with a fourth design, *St Michael the Archangel*. In Christian mythology, the Archangel was indestructible and slew dragons, but in the real-world *St Michael* succumbed to the pitfalls of technological overreach. The big catamaran proved unmanageable and was such a complete failure that the debacle overshadowed his earlier success. Nevertheless, the seeds of an idea lingered, and many others would take up the challenge. In later life, Petty moved on to experiment with paddlewheels, to give ships "*fresh way at sea in a calm*", as he termed it.

Through the following period, tunnel-hull configurations, as used today in modern pickle-fork powerboats, held sway. This style is effectively a conventional vessel split down the centreline with the two halves set some way apart. The flat inner elevations form a parallel-sided tunnel.[323] This is fine for a prop-riding powerboat but is less convincing in a sailing vessel.

> The proas of the Pacific islands evolved over centuries with asymmetric hulls which present their flat buttocks outboard. The asymmetric foil of the depressed lee hull is an unsophisticated attempt to reduce leeway. The twin-wire Hobie 16, for many years the most popular multihull in the world, has this ancient configuration. However, in practice, Hobie sailors sail the boats quite differently, raking the rig quite dramatically to bring the centre of effort back and load-up the rudders.[324]

Admiral Sir Edward Spragge, a contemporary of William Petty, was also intrigued by the prospect of sluice-boats and manual paddle-power. Following more than a decade of experimental work with small-scale models, Spragge commissioned a full-scale prototype which was launched at Chatham in 1683. However, the engineering necessary to achieve the required power-to-weight ratio did not exist in the 17th century. Ten strong men might sustain one horsepower, but not for long.

Undaunted by Spragge's experience, Patrick Miller (1731–1815), a wealthy Scottish banker and amateur naval architect, invested in the same basic idea a century later in 1886, with the 60ft LOA triple-hulled *Edinburgh*.[325] Miller's paper to the Royal Society also references 60ft and 35ft catamarans, but it is doubtful whether these 'experiments' were built. More certainly, the next in the series, *Experiment of Leith*, was launched in June 1787. This ambitious vessel was 105ft LOA and 25ft beam. John Laurie's shipyard in Leith invoiced Miller £3,000 (£500,000) for the work. The vessel resembled William Petty's *Experiment* of 1662, after which it was named in tribute.

> Patrick Miller's 'double boat' was patented in 1787. The documentation described two ordinary skiffs joined by a common deck. The paddlewheel was sited between the hulls at the stern. Miller's patent was ostensibly for manually driven paddle wheels, but crucially, his vision included the possibility of steam power. So, Miller effectively patented the steamship in 1787. However, as far as we have been able to determine, he spent £30,000 (£4m) but derived no subsequent benefit from his idea.

The *Experiment of Leith* was fully rigged as a five-masted sailing ship. Like previous sluice-boats she resembled a conventional vessel sliced down the centre line with the two halves spaced apart by a hull's breadth. All else being equal, designs like this add wetted surface and waveform interference drag, without returning much through increased sail-carrying power. None of this bothered Miller who had mounted no less than five in-line paddlewheels in the tunnel between the hulls, wound by geared capstans, with each wheel in the sequence rotating a little faster.

On trials, with this labour-intensive arrangement whirling at full-gas, *Experiment* touched an impressive 4.3 knots. While this scenario seems unlikely, Miller was a major shareholder in the Carron Company, one of the largest iron works in the world at that time. This association gave him access to Carron's expertise in designing and casting specialist machine parts and to the company's engineers, who were entrusted with the design of the complex gearing system.[326] Nevertheless, it was hard work aboard the *Experiment*. The long-suffering 'chain gang' complained bitterly of exhaustion, no matter how generous the rum ration.[327]

Miller was undeterred by these operational constraints. In 1790 he tendered a proposal for a shoal-draft vessel to King Gustavus III of Sweden, then embroiled in the 11th Russo-Swedish War. This was for a double-hulled, 144-gun ship-of-the-line – 246ft LOA, 63ft beam, and 17 feet draft. The two hulls would be set 16 feet apart to accommodate a cascade of manually powered paddlewheels. Miller sent his prototype, *Experiment of Leith*, over to Sweden as proof of concept. King Gustavus despatched an aide to welcome the curious vessel to Stockholm and arranged for trials to be conducted by Fred Chapman.

> On a personal level, the King was not ungrateful; he gave Miller a golden snuff box and a painting of the ship. The snuffbox contained seeds which Miller planted to become the ubiquitous 'neeps', otherwise known as swedes or turnips. Neeps are served with haggis and 'tatties' as a Scottish staple. When this whole mess is steeped in whisky, it is enjoyed by unselfconscious Caledonian Societies celebrating Burn's Nights throughout the known world. This root vegetable would be the only enduring legacy of the *Experiment of Leith*, but we cannot in all fairness complain. Neeps added a generous tang of 'basse cuisine' to the myths of Balmorality.

Frederick Chapman, who crops up in prior chapters, jealously guarded his position as the Swedish Navy's principal shipwright and was sceptical of innovation by others. His personal agenda was clear from the first; he disparaged the big cat as a 'sea-spook'.[328] Chapman was a well-travelled man of English parents, who had worked for a time at Deptford. He would thus have been familiar with the history of the early English catamarans but had no personal experience of the type. Nevertheless, his appraisal, while brutal, was sound.

Chapman considered that, in operational trim, Miller's proposal would exceed its designed displacement – the Achilles heel of all early European multihulls, and still far too many today for that matter. Chapman was also concerned about manoeuvrability and structural integrity, although as regards the latter, extended sea trials in the *Experiment of Leith* had exposed no significant weaknesses. He predicted that speeds under both sail and capstan would be disappointing.[329] Fred Chapman summed up the Miller proposal as follows: *"Despite all this, two-hull vessels are completely sound when the theory can be properly applied; that is in vessels of very light weight, and of small size, with crews of one or two men."*

Chapman was both oh-so-right, and rather unfairly, oh-so-wrong. Weight is certainly the enemy of catamarans but as regards size, his considered opinion, prescient for two centuries right up to the launch of Eric Tabarly's floating junkyard, *Pen Duick IV*, in 1968, has now been dashed. New materials have overcome the engineering challenges posed by joining two or three hulls together. If he were alive today, Chapman would, like the rest of us, simply marvel at the extraordinary performance of the foil-assisted Ultime trimarans, the size of a five-a-side football pitch, that traverse the world's oceans, on occasion touching 45kts with a lone Frenchman coolly catnapping below on a beanbag, podcasting to a global following.

When the Russo-Swedish War ended with the Treaty of Värälä in August 1790, the prospect of a commission disappeared. Miller's bold creation languished at anchor off Skeppsholmen Island, unattended and unloved. Four years later in 1794, in what seems to be the most reliable among conflicting accounts of her fate, she was scuttled to form the foundations for a bridge.[330] As for positive outcomes, the *Experiment* safely completed a good many sea-miles during eight-years of operational trials, and no one drowned; a record later multihull designers would come to envy.

Patrick Miller's 'tunnel-hull, central paddle-wheel' concept may have been impracticable in a pre-industrial world, but it was just about perfect for steam power. After the Stockholm debacle, Miller was fortunate to team up with pioneering engine-builder William Symington. In 1788, they built a second *Experiment*, a little 25-foot catamaran of iron construction, powered by a miniature steam engine. The paddlewheels were again located between the hulls, sited fore and aft of the horizontal engine.

The *Experiment* was an immediate success, making 4½kts on Dalswinton Loch. Much encouraged, Miller commissioned a larger boat, again named *Experiment* in 1789. William Symington returned to superintend the engine design and construction of the vessel. On trial on the Forth and Clyde Canal, near the Carron engine works, the *Experiment II* achieved a consistent speed of 6kts. Miller enjoyed the success; it had been a long time coming. However, he had sunk a fortune into his multihull experiments and his largesse was not limitless. He would now pass the baton to others.[331]

Thomas Dundas, an investor in the Forth and Clyde Canal, saw the potential of Miller's research work. He employed Symington to build a 60-foot version of *Experiment II*. This was the first *Charlotte Dundas*, which matched the prototype's 6kts on the canal. Dundas then transferred the same steam engine to a conventional single-hull 56-footer. This second *Charlotte Dundas* became the first commercially viable steamboat in 1803.[332]

Meanwhile, across the Atlantic, Miller's and Symington's ideas enjoyed one last copy-cat iteration. Robert Fulton's *North River Steamboat* of 1807, built by Charles Browne in New York and engined by Boulton and Watt in England, is celebrated in the USA as the first commercial steamboat.[333] Fulton was a wealthy impresario and undoubtedly a magpie. He visited and inspected the *Charlotte Dundas* in 1801.[334] Fulton patented a tunnel-hull paddle-steamer and built the East River ferryboats *Jersey*, *York* and *Nassau* (1812-1814), and a floating battery or blockship, the *Steam Battery*, for the US Navy to this basic pattern. Thereafter, the catamaran fell out of favour on both sides of the Atlantic for the best part of a century.

Unfortunately for the development of the catamaran, succeeding generations of steam-ship designers were unconvinced by the virtues of a tunnel-hull. They returned to the proven hull-forms of contemporary sailing ships, with a tucked-up run to keep the sternwheel in a well-charged waterflow. Then, when the steamship entered the mainstream, shipyards would favour an entirely different model, with over-large paddle boxes sited amidships, astride ever slimmer hulls.

George Mills' *Twin* was the last big tunnel-hulled central paddle-wheel steamer to be launched in Scotland. Built by Tod & MacGregor in 1857 and licensed to carry 500 passengers, the *Twin* was distinctive, with three funnels athwartships. She was also popular as the first 'saloon' steamer on the Clyde, where the day-trippers could enjoy the pleasures of al fresco travel, up on deck writhed in the choking downdraft.

Among other innovations, the *Twin* sported a bow thruster between the hulls.[335] In 1863, she was converted to side-wheel paddles, lengthened and given more powerful engines, bringing her registered tonnage up to 460-tons. She was a fascinating vessel; her hulls, eventually 110ft long, were just 9ft wide. This length-to-beam ratio presaged the modern seagoing catamaran ferry as revived by Norwegian and Australian boatyards in the 1970s. Today, such vessels are simply more efficient than hydrofoils or hovercraft with regard to operational and environmental costs, and significantly more comfortable too.

The *Twin's* owners cashed in on the American Civil War, selling the boat to the Confederates for service as a blockade runner. She sailed for Nassau in 1863. After a brief career evading the Yankee's Atlantic blockade without actually penetrating it, the *Twin* – then sailing as the *Alliance*, was captured at Savannah in 1864. After service as a troop ship, she was auctioned as a prize in New York. The last tunnel-hulled Clyde paddler then appears in New Zealand for the 'gold rush', making one successful round trip to Britain, before ending her days as a wreck on Hokitika Bar in 1865.[336]

As a postscript, we might note that Hawthorn, Leslie & Co of Newcastle-on-Tyne had one last crack at the double-hull paddle steamer in 1876. The *Express*, later renamed the *Calais-Douvres*, was a much larger vessel, 2,000-tons and 300ft LOA, built for the Dover to Calais route. She was fast and popular, but her high coal consumption made her uneconomic to run. This fine ship is included because Newcastle was part of Scotland from 1139 to 1157, and the eminent historian Howard Chapelle thought it still was in the 1960s.

Western Replicas of Polynesian Designs

François-Edmond Pâris (1806-1893) published the first well-informed treatise on South Seas multihulls in 1839. François' interests ranged from engineering through painting, draftsmanship, hydrography and ethnology. He joined Dumont d'Urville's 1926-29 circumnavigation as Hydrographer but was also tasked to *"record all the canoes of the various peoples we would visit"*. The expedition trawled the coasts of East Africa, India, China and South America, allowing Pâris to accurately survey over 250 types of vessel.[337] This ethnographic diversion did no harm to his career. Pâris attained the rank of Vice-Admiral and served as President of the Academy of Sciences.

Uffa Fox had a story about a proa replica, perhaps informed by the work of Edmond Pâris, which allegedly attained 20-knots in Portsmouth Harbour in the 1750s.[338] Better documented, however, is an experiment at the Royal Mersey Yacht Club in 1860, with a Marianas Islands-type proa, built by a local boatbuilder. This replica, with a flat outer-face on the main hull, worked well and was also extremely fast, although the unique end-for-end style of tacking a proa perplexed the assembled throng of gawping Scousers. *"It was for a short time a great attraction, as one of the most remarkable novelties ever seen on that river."*[339]

Through the great age of exploration, the remarkable speed of native craft did not go unnoticed. Small Polynesian outrigger canoes and similar craft were brought home as souvenirs from South Seas voyages and later sailed with varying degrees of success by unskilled and inappropriately clad Western tyros. However, in Scotland, our seafaring diaspora seem to have shown little interest in replicating this simple technology until the Parkers, a wealthy family with trading interests in the East, bought land in Fairlie and built a summer villa in 1818.

In 1831, George Parker, a young man familiar with outrigger canoes through his East Indies contacts, began to look into the design of proas and ordered a replica from John Wood of Port Glasgow, the shipwright who had built the original *Comet*. George's proa, the *Flying Fish*, was 22ft LOA, 15ft at the crossbeams with an 11-foot-long float or 'ama'. William Fyfe drew the sailplan and the mast was made at Steele's in Greenock. Young George inveigled Fyfe to join him on the maiden voyage. First the yard of the flimsy lateen rig broke and then they capsized.[340] These initial trials ended with a punt lashed to the ama, which rather defeats the point of a proa. Design issues are understandable, but it is not clear why things literally fell apart with such an experienced boatbuilding team on the case.[341]

Undeterred by the wreck of *Flying Fish*, and intrigued by their brief exposure to the idiom, George Parker and Fyfe teamed up to build the *Ruby Queen*, a much larger lateen-rigged proa built at Fairlie to George's own design.[342] George seems to have carried out some research on end-for-end tacking techniques over the winter of 1831/32. The *Ruby Queen* performed well in her first season, but there was scope for development. After the craftsmen at Fairlie rebuilt and lightened the boat, performance improved. The *Ruby Queen* could now keep pace with the Largs steamer. The *Caledonian Mercury* described the dramatic end of this bold experiment.

"Loss of the Flying Fish. This vessel, well known to the visitors at Largs was, on the 23rd of last month, unfortunately wrecked on the northern headland of the Little Cumbrae. The proa was beating out against a strong breeze, accompanied with a rolling swell which caused her to lurch heavily, and which at length broke her outrigger, when she immediately capsized to windward. Her crew clung to her side and were directed to cut the shrouds and halyards to relieve her; but she was fast drifting towards the rocks. She was observed by the vessel Georgina, of the RNYC which was run alongside. Her commander succeeded in rescuing Mr Parker and his companions from their perilous situation. The proa was soon afterwards dashed upon the rocks and may be considered a total wreck."[343]

Contemporary newspaper accounts referred to the ill-fated proa as the *Flying Fish*, but from the date and description she was the *Ruby Queen*. In any event, she was simply known as the 'flying proa'. This was a substantial vessel at 41ft 6" LOA, although the breadth of main hull was just 4ft 6".[344] The name suggests that she 'flew' a short ama to windward, with the crew lined out on the crossbeam, like Rod MacAlpine-Downie's record-breaking *Crossbow* in the early 1970s. Conversely, a proa, like the Dick Newick-designed, *Cheers*, which performed so well in the 1964 Transatlantic race, employs a full-length, buoyant ama to leeward.

The *Caledonian Mercury's* yachting correspondent considered the saga of the flying proa to be significant in the story of yachting. He noted that *"she was an experiment on a large and somewhat expensive scale for ascertaining whether a vessel of her construction would, in our climate, excel vessels of the usual form, as much as the proas of the Ladrone and South Sea islanders are said to have excelled the European ships which have visited those distant coasts"*.

The correspondent conceded that the proa was *"not much admired by the practical seaman, nor considered very picturesque in form by our dilettanti"*. The 'proletariato' disagreed. Sailing at the Largs Regatta earlier that year, the flying proa made quite an impact. Day trippers, thronging the esplanade, were impressed by this colourful craft parading before them in a welter of spray, flaunting her exceptional performance and easily outpacing all the other yachts on the free legs of the course. However, not privy to protocols of the Royal Largs, shoreline spectators were aghast when Robert Morris's staid three-masted schooner, finishing long after, lifted the Town Cup.

George Parker, speaking to a correspondent of *Hunt's Magazine* in 1851, confirmed that his proas were modelled on the Ladrone Island Prahu and carried the outrigger on the weather side. He said that they achieved close to 20mph sailing in smooth water along a weather shore in an easterly gale. George conceded that the outrigger frequently failed, and he cheerfully acknowledged that duckings were an everyday occurrence. *"On a wind she was useless, off a wind but middling, but with the wind abeam nothing could touch her; at last, she broke her out-rigger once too often and left her bones on a desert island as a warning to all too venturous voyagers."*[345] *Hunt's* depiction of the Wee Cumbrae as a 'desert island' epitomises the lost art of joyous hyperbole.

After the wreck of the *Ruby Queen/Flying Fish*, George Parker had one last crack at the proa model, with a new boat referenced in *The Glasgow Courier* as a 'proa junior', spawned by the *Flying Fish*. George sailed this smaller successor for a season or so until, under pressure from his elderly parents and his new wife, he finally wrung-out his neck-towel in 1836 and threw it in. Subsequently, he would cruise the Western Isles in the fishing-yacht, *Phantom*, built by John Fyfe to William Fyfe's design.

George had not lost his interest in novelty, however. In 1840, he launched a 16-ton, three-masted schooner, *Doria*, that was in a category of its own. She was 60ft LOA, with just 9ft of beam, described as *"round-stemmed and without counter, upright stern-post but raking stem, her lines were graceful, and she had the look of a fast craft."*[346] Fyfe built the boat, then he and Parker chopped and changed her every year in a quest for perfection that seems to have become an end in itself. *"The owner stated that this extraordinary vessel had been originally laid down as a large rowing barge."* We do not know why George would build something resembling a Mediterranean galley in Scotland in the mid-19th century. In any event, he had second thoughts and *Doria* morphed into a three-masted schooner.

The Lowestoft lateeners, much-loved by engravers of the 1850s, set huge lateen foresails for racing, so *Doria* was not unique in combining lateen and gaff-rigged masts on the same platform. However, George fused the felucca of the Nile with the schooner.[347] *"Doria appeared at Cowes towards the end of the season of 1851. Instead of a foremast she had a pair of light sheers, between which she set a large lateen sail with the usual long bent yard aloft and another along the sole of the sail, which was made fast about the centre to the deck on which it moved as on a pivot. The main-mast was rigged like a fore-and-aft schooner, with main-sail and gaff-topsail."*

George had set sail from the Clyde, with his wife, children and two seamen aboard. *Hunt's Magazine* records that *Doria* made an extremely fast passage south through the Irish Sea. George reported that they had no problems with the lateen foresail, except that, when reefed, with the luff-spar slung low between the shear-legs, it lacked lateral support. After George and the family left Cowes, they visited the Thames before continuing their circumnavigation of England via the East Coast. *Doria* and the Parkers arrived home safely, most likely via the Forth and Clyde Canal. That route had opened in 1790 and could accommodate a vessel of *Doria's* dimensions by 1831. Alternatively, the Caledonian Canal, which opened in 1822, was also available.

Yachtsmen tend to associate the first viable Western multihulls with Nat Herreshoff (1848-1938). Herreshoff's *Amaryllis* and her successors certainly made an impact on the sailing world through the late 1870s. Subsequently, Ralph Munroe, a good friend of Herreshoff, built a successful proa in 1898. This was based on drawings by Piercy Brett made during Admiral Lord Anson's circumnavigation in 1742. Anson marvelled that the pirogues were *"able to close the wind better than any other known vessel"*.

In 1892, perhaps inspired by Herreshoff's catamarans, William Fife II made a model of *"a double boat and conducted sailing experiments with it near his own yard. The model is 30-inches long and rigged with a shoulder-of-mutton mainsail and large jib, and under some conditions of the wind and water Mr Fife got interesting sport out of it, and I believe it is his intention to experiment still further"*.[348] The *Yachtsman* observed that *"the double boat is not altogether a novelty at Fairlie"* and referenced Parker's proas which still *"haunt Fairlie yet"*. The magazine recalled that *"on a night when the water was smooth and the wind of the desired kind, she easily beat the river steamer, Hero."* As far as we are aware, Fife's model tests came to nought.

The commentators of the period made much of flexibility as an essential pre-requisite for success. Herreshoff built in a complex 'suspension system' with ball-and-socket joints. In fact, flexibility was only useful in relation to holding the elements together before modern materials were available to enable rigid construction. Independent movement is energy-sapping, plays havoc with rig tension, creates undesirable trim issues and generally makes for a slow boat. Cats perform much better when wracking is minimised.[349]

However, not all revolutions end gloriously. In 1876 with *Amaryllis* and then again in 1898, with the Seawanhaka Cup-winning *Dominion* – an innovative, catamaran-like, tunnel-hull scow, designed by George Duggan, the impact of cats on the sport of yachting was spectacular, but transitory. Sailing instructions and rating rules in America and Europe were swiftly amended to exclude such aberrant types from open competition. Yacht club committees have a long history of impulsively rejecting any innovation that might endow an unfair advantage.

Resistance to change in this context was not an irrational fear of the unknown. It was a rational desire to maintain the current value of the established yacht racing fleet. Such concerns dogged every perceived discontinuity in the continuum of design development. That said, yachtsmen, while an inherently conservative community, have always been prepared to write down their investment when a workable consensus emerges. This willingness to embrace progress has been despite the disproportionate cost of our 'equipment' vis-à-vis nearly every other sport.

Herreshoff's *Amaryllis* challenged the essence of 19th century yachting, moving sportsmen from a secure cockpit-well, where they enjoyed a fair prospect of returning home in the evening dry-shod, to perching on a tea-tray, inured to a long, wet afternoon in damp, itchy breeks. Which is not to say that catamarans disappeared entirely. *Heavenly Twins*, a cat which measured-in as a 5-rater under the Length & Sail-area Rule, appeared on the Solent to 'scare the horses' in 1895.

Nat Herreshoff had boasted in 1893 that he could *"lick creation"* under the L & SA Rule with a double-hulled boat, and of course, he could have done exactly that. However, after experience with several boats of this *"out-of-the-way description"*, Colonel Conway Gordon had constructed *Heavenly Twins* from steel. The boat was certainly bullet-proof, but her weight was crippling. Ironically, the bold Colonel came to grief in a monohull; he was run down in fog while sailing his 25-tonner and died shortly after rescue.[350]

George Parker's experiments, in collaboration with the first William Fyfe, must have been distant memories in the 1890s. Parker's proas were fast, wet, and downright dangerous but they represented a stunning 'proof of concept'. However, in 1894, any lessons learned had clearly been forgotten. In the spring of that year, the Allan brothers, Henry and Robert, challenged the Bergius boys (see Chapter 34) to a match in 17ft catamarans. The Allen family, enabled by the success of their eponymous shipping line to devote an inordinate amount of time to yachting, owned the rambling Hafton estate on the south shore of the Holy Loch.

The Allan cat was inspired by Ladrones proas and the fast outriggers of the Indonesian Archipelago. The hulls carved from two huge cedars felled in the estate forest. Surely few families, then or now, can source such yacht building materials from their back garden. The logs were squared off to form identical blanks, which were then bored vertically and horizontally at close intervals. This ensured that the hollowed-out hulls would have a constant skin thickness. Shaping was carried out by adze, and finally the augur holes were plugged with claret corks – of which there were no shortage on the Allen Estate.

In sharp contrast, the Bergius cat, *Gemini*, was based on the familiar lath and canvas touring canoe, of the type later popularised by Klepper. Narrow, octagonal-sectioned hulls were decked over and linked with a rudimentary bridgedeck. *Gemini* carried a lugsail rig with bamboo spars, as at that time in small boats. A blow-by-blow account of the challenge has not survived, but we do know that the lighter boat was clearly faster. Unfortunately, it was also more fragile; so, after a series of pitchpoles and capsizes, *Gemini* was scrapped mid-season. William Bergius never built another catamaran, but he had established a lifelong preference for light, easily driven designs, as we describe in *The Piper Calls the Tune*.

And so, established conventions won out and multihulls lost decades of evolution before their reincarnation as series-produced recreational craft in the 1960s. As Uffa Fox observed: *"the catamaran has had to wait until sailing has become the full-blooded sport it now is, with enough enthusiasts willing to endure the cold flying spray of these waters, before it flourished"*.[351] Fortunately, time lost has been recovered in the context of performance gains over the last 50 years, which owe more to the palette of new materials than incremental design improvements. So, while the banishment of multihulls for the best part of a century undoubtedly limited market penetration, the current state-of-the-art shows no signs of arrested development.

The multihull scene, and indeed the whole culture of small-boat sailing in beach-launched boats, enjoyed a renaissance in the early post-war years. Returning ex-servicemen were game for anything. New materials developed during WW2 made all this possible, particularly the advent of waterproof marine plywood and thermo-setting adhesives. And then, when series-production in fibreglass finally arrived, the industry capitalised on the knowledge gained from the countless 'flying string-bags' built on dining room tables by DIY chemists.

Rod McAlpine Downie

Scotsman Rod MacAlpine-Downie (1934-1986) was the high priest of the era, taking the multihull world by storm with a series of elegant high-performance designs encompassing beach cats, ocean racers and spidery record breakers. Rod was born and brought up in Argyll, son of the Laird of Appin. He attended Eton school, where he studied biology and gained one of the 14 King's Scholarships in his year, although the family were not exactly short of money. Rod returned home after university without clear ambitions. He considered a career as a concert violinist before becoming a less-than-enthusiastic gentleman farmer in Appin.

Rod's father, Archibald McAlpine Downie, a retired Lieutenant Colonel, was a specialist in hypervelocity artillery shells during WW2. Archie was something of an athlete in his youth, running the mile for Scotland. Rod, by comparison was not. He never looked comfortable on a trapeze, even when sailing at the top of his game. After the war, Archie become an enthusiastic offshore sailor Sadly, he and his companion Richard Weston-Brooke drowned in the Holy Loch in 1958, as described in Chapter 33, concerning the *Servabo* tragedy.

The MacAlpine-Downie family occupied Appin House, an imposing 17th century pile overlooking Loch Linnhe.[352] When his father died, Rod became the new laird, a designation that counted for little when the bill for death duties came in. After a few years it all became untenable. Rod's stepmother returned to Ireland, and Rod moved south to join boatbuilder Reg White in Brightlingsea, where he would enjoy success in his new egalitarian career as a yacht designer. However, the inimitable Jack Knights noted that charts of the London Stock Exchange remained a feature of the MacAlpine-Downie drawing office.

Rod had no formal training as a yacht designer. As the story goes, a Shearwater cat caught his eye, most likely on the seafront at Largs, where there was a good fleet at that time. The Prout Shearwater was the best of the first-generation cats and widely adopted for class-racing in the UK. It was a good looking cold-moulded boat, if rather heavy and narrow in planform. Early examples were fitted out dinghy-style with a solid deck platform in varnished ply. Today, as a development class, they have been transformed with lightweight carbon construction, mesh trampoline, twin trapezes, and a feathering fat-head mainsail.

Back in 1961, Rod thought that he could improve on the design. The obvious point of entry was to increase the width and power of the boat and to develop more modelled hull sections. Rod's seminal Thai-cat prototype was followed by three rapid design iterations, with the boat becoming progressively lighter and more powerful and eventually sporting the now-ubiquitous beam-spar and trampoline platform.[353]

In the early days of racing catamarans, the boats were divided into three IYRU open development classes: the popular singlehanded A Class (18ft LOA), the mid-sized B class (20ft LOA), the legendary C class (25ft LOA), and the vanishingly rare D class (32ft LOA). Today, only the A and C types still race as development classes, both now locked into constantly evolving foiling configurations. The other size bands have lapsed with the original divisional designations almost forgotten. The former B class market is now firmly the preserve of manufacturers' one-designs

Rod's Thai Mk.III won half the races in the 1961 UK 'one of a kind' regatta, and the Mk.IV followed this up with a clean sweep of the 1962 European one of a kind. One-of-a-kind regattas were popular in the 1960s when small-boat classes were competing in a marketplace crowded with prototypes and optimistic start-ups. The Thai Mk.IV went into series production with Reg White's Sail Craft in the UK, and Dick Gibbs in the USA. The boat was nicely detailed and streets ahead of the competition as an affordable high-performance one-design.[354]

In 1960, a small group of Yankee boffins in baggy shorts from Long Island Sound hatched an idea that would ignite an arms race on both sides of the Atlantic. They invited their friends in Britain to compete in a match-racing series in C Class cats. John Fisk of the fledgling IYRU Multihull Committee, accepted the challenge on behalf of the UK. There may have been considerably less experimental activity in this country, but the sophistication of MacAlpine-Downie's early work belied the cliché of the small pond. The first International Catamaran Challenge was the beginning of something quite wonderful. Bullshitting on the beach led to an enduring match-racing series that transcended the initial vision to redefine the boundaries of high performance under sail.

With John Fisk at the helm, Rod's *Hellcat II* won the first series in 1961.[355] The Brits were invited back for a rematch, but Fisk, describing the event as a 'Little America's Cup', told the Yanks to come over here and get it. British cats defended seven consecutive series to hold onto the trophy until the Danes broke the winning streak in 1969. Rod crewed in the 1961 and 1963 Cups. Initially, having the designer's technical know-how on board was invaluable, but as the competition heated up, Rod stepped down to make way for more athletic sailors.[356]

The original *Hellcat I* won in 1962; *Hellcat IIIS* in 1963; *Emma Hamilton* in 1964 and 1965; and *Lady Helmsman* in 1965, 1966, 1967 and 1968. *Lady Helmsman*, Rod's most famous cup-winning boat was, paradoxically, a Reg White variation, where the spray rail was converted to a knuckle, with a consequent increase in hull volume above the crease. MacAlpine-Downie had jumped ship in 1966, to design *Wills Venturer II* and *Wills Venturer III* for Excel boats, so Reg took matters into his own hands and modified the *Hellcat III* mould. Rod's Excel cats had the vertical stem we are familiar with today but were not as quick as the more refined Hellcats.[357]

In the annals of Scottish yacht design, the 'Hellcat' C Class variations were an important contribution to 1960s naval architecture. However,

Lady Helmsman's success merits shared honours. As the hull design was getting long in the tooth, the winning edge of this beautifully integrated 1966 design package was provided by the innovative wing-mast and soft-sail combination, designed by Austin Farrar in association with Seahorse Sails. The wing section was thick and deep with an arced trailing edge that blended into the soft sail. The whole package was more elegant and simply much better thought-out than anything that had gone before.

Another factor touted extravagantly at the time was the Graphspeed hull coating supplied by International Paints.[358] 'Helmsman' was one of their brand-names and the International Catamaran Challenge, a high-profile competition at the leading edge of the sport, was a match made in Heaven. Moreover, the prosaic brand-name offered good cover to circumvent IYRU rules on commercialisation.

Readers once tempted by the product's extravagant promises will have their own memories of Graphspeed. Our school sailing team won an enormous pot of the stuff at the GP14 National Junior Championships in 1965. It was tenacious, like the UV security paint they use to protect the copper and lead on church roofs. Graphspeed seemed to reduce the friction coefficient of underwater surfaces in relation to everything but water and brought 'miners chic' to sailing. Boats slipped off trailers, and mounting a capsized hull was akin to clambering aboard a greased Orca.

MacAlpine-Downie's *Crossbow* prototypes for Sir Tim Colman held the World Sailing Speed Record for many years, winning Weymouth Speed Week from 1975 to 1984, and topping out at 36 knots, although higher speeds were claimed at the bar.[359] Colman's wealth derived from the mustard 'left on the side of the plate', but he also benefitted from the main dish, roping in turkey tycoon, Bernard Mathews, to support his early record attempts. Clearly, on this occasion, the sponsorship defied allegory.

Crossbow I and *II* both appeared advanced for the time, sporting radical and extreme geometry. However, they were essentially conventional. The first *Crossbow* (1972) was a catamaran with tandem wishbone una rigs stepped in the centre of both hulls, stayed laterally with rigid, cross-braced links. Her hulls were 60ft long, skewed to an LOA of 72ft. The staggered mast separation enabled the twin rigs to operate in relatively clean air.

Crossbow II (1980) was a unidirectional proa, 56ft LOA, 22-inch hull width, boasting a 30ft outrigger carrying a vestigial 'control pod' ama. Like her predecessor, the boat's hulls were cold-moulded-ply. She carried a fully battened sloop rig on a slim 60ft aluminium 'noodle' mast with a birdcage of rigging. There was limited rig tension and her sail-set spoke of limited sail control.[360] The crew ran up and down the outrigger to balance the boat. When up to speed, they perched on the little ama, full-face into the breeze.

Then came *Crossbow III* (1986), a 65ft LOA surface-skimming foiler with an unstayed wingsail, daringly mounted just 7ft from the transom of the weather hull.[361] Ostensibly a catamaran, Rod described her as a *"canard configuration, flying proa, sailed on the lee hull with the crew to weather"*. A supercavitating foil (effectively a planing foil) was mounted on the weather ama to ameliorate splashdown drag. Only the lee daggerboard (aft) and the lee rudder (forward) were operational. Tacking was possible but it required reconfiguration: both appendages and rig had to be swapped over, and the lee foxholes had to be sealed with watertight covers.

Performance Sailcraft built the boat to the following specs: hulls, carbon epoxy over a low-density core; crossbeams, carbon fibre epoxy with Kevlar fairings; and, wing and tail plane, Kevlar carbon skinned with aircraft-grade Dacron. It is unfortunate that this ambitious project never saw salt water as it collapsed with the death of the designer. However, the whole wonderful contrivance still exists, lodged in the rafters at the late Tim Whelpton's Eastwood boatyard in Upton, Norfolk.[362]

Rod's other high-profile designs towards the end of his working life included the 70ft *British Oxygen* and the 65ft *British Airways I* – the former comfortably in the vanguard of offshore multihull development, the latter a bit of a 'truck'. More prosaically, the 30ft Iroquois and 32ft Comanche cruising cats, designed for Sailcraft, exhibited a rare blend of performance and style that has yet to be matched by the wall-sided offerings of the principal builders today.

In his later years Rod seems to have been content turning out dozens of docile, not to say dull, production dayboats for the American market. However, a few years before he passed away, Rod became involved in an eccentric project for the 1984 Observer Single-Handed Race (OSTAR) from Plymouth to Newport, Rhode Island. The client was Rob Denny, a young New Zealander with a plan to enter a 40ft windmill-powered trimaran in the race. It was not a new idea – back in 1811, Robert Dawson had used a vertical axis impulse rotor to propel a ship from Bristol to London, and in 1870, Croatian adventurer, Nikola Primorachad, crossed the Atlantic, sailing from Liverpool to New York and back assisted by windmill power on the 20ft LOA, *City of Ragusa*.[363]

Windmill enthusiasts in yachting history include Lord Brabazon, who fitted a turbine to a Bembridge Redwing keelboat in 1934; uniquely rule legal in this class.[364] Brabazon experimented with a Flettner rotating cylinder mast.[365] His final trial employed an autogyro or windmill. The rotor powered Redwing performed impressively, until the device took off and chewed up several neighbouring yachts, innocently laying at their moorings nearby, before self-destructing.[366] More recent designs have benefitted from half-a-century of wind-power in electricity generation.[367] This has radically altered the equation. "*The technology of the time, in both materials and availability, severely limited the application of this approach to sailing.*

169

Today, with the availability of 'off the shelf' components for wind turbine electricity generators, the general approach is almost childishly simple to implement."[368]

Denny's tri was to have had a three-bladed turbine on a horizontal axis, 28ft in diameter, driving a 40-inch marine prop.[369] A kite was planned for extra propulsion down-wind. However, as often when kites are flown in yachting, sponsorship did not materialise, and the initiative lapsed. Two years later in 1986, Denny teamed up with Neil Bose of Glasgow University to install a 3-bladed turbine on his MacAlpine-Downie Iroquois catamaran.

The turbine-tri highlighted the potential of wind-power and McAlpine Downie's elegant design solution generated considerable press coverage at the time. Today, turbine power remains potentially viable, but experiments to date fall woefully short of designer's expectations. Equally interesting was the Royal Western's acceptance of the entry. *"It is wind-driven, and we will accept it,"* Mr Lloyd Foster, club secretary said. *"Because it can sail directly into the wind, the club is reserving the right to treat it as a powered vessel so far as the 'rules of the road' are concerned. The craft would then have to stay well away from all the conventional yachts."*[370]

The following list contains all the McAlpine Downie's designs we have been able to identify, although there are surely others. For the most part, his cats and more popular monohulls carry through a recognisable aesthetic, characterised by soft 'U'-shaped sections to minimise wetted area and fine entry with a nicely proportioned stem-line. The bow profile resembles a classic spoon, but functions in a quite different way to ramp-up buoyancy forward and maintain longitudinal stability when bearing away.

Rod MacAlpine-Downie – Design List 1958-1980

No	Date	Design	LOA	Notes
1.	1958	Thai Mk I	17.00ft / 5.18m	Catamaran, B class
2.	1959	Thai Mk II	17.00ft / 5.18m	Catamaran, B class
3.	1960	Thai Mk III	17.00ft / 5.18m	Catamaran, B class
4.	1961	Thai Mk IV	17.00ft / 5.18m	Catamaran, B class
5.	1961	*Hellcat*	25.00ft / 7.62m	C-class cat
6.	1961	Hellcat II	25.00ft / 7.62m	C-class cat
7.	1963	Hellcat III	25.00ft / 7.62m	C-class cat
8.	1962	Shark Catamaran	20.00ft / 6.10m	C-class cat
9.	1963	Dingo 15	15.00ft / 4.57m	Singlehanded cat
10.	1964	Barracuda 13	13.00ft / 3.96m	Lateen/ una-rigged scow
11.	1964	Man-o-War 15	15.00ft / 4.57m	Una-rigged beach scow
12.	1964	Phoenix 18	18.00ft / 5.49m	Catamaran
13.	1964	Yachting World Cat	15.50ft / 4.72m	Catamaran
14.	1966	*Lady Helmsman*	25.00ft / 7.62m	C-class cat, Reg White mod.
15.	1966	*Wills Venture II*	25.00ft / 7.62m	C-class cat
16.	1966	*Wills Venture III*	25.00ft / 7.62m	C-class cat
17.	1967	Upstart 16	16.50ft / 5.03m	2/3-man dinghy
18.	1968	Buccaneer 18	18.00ft / 5.49m	2-man dinghy – heavy for type
19.	1968	Iroquois 30 Mk.I	30.00ft / 9.14m	Cruising catamaran
20.	1969	Iroquois 30 Mk.II	30.00ft / 9.14m	Cruising catamaran
21.	1969	Sidewinder 16	15.50ft / 4.72m	Sloop/una-rigged hybrid dinghy
22.	1970	Apache 41	40.83ft / 12.44m	Cruising catamaran

23.	1970	Apache 45	45.00ft / 13.72m	Cruising catamaran
24.	1970	Copperhead 14	13.75ft / 4.19m	Standing lug singlehander
25.	1972	Bandit 15	15.25ft / 4.65m	2-man dinghy
26.	1972	Bandit 17	17.00ft / 5.18m	Miniature sloop-rigged trailer/sailer
27.	1972	Mutineer 15	15.00ft / 4.57m	2-man dinghy – heavy for type
28.	1972	Navaho 46	46.00ft / 14.02m	Cruising catamaran like Apache
29.	1973	Cherokee 35	35.00ft / 10.67m	Cruising catamaran
30.	1975	*Crossbow*	60.00ft / 18.29m	Speed-week Proa
31.	1973	Musketeer 17	16.50ft / 5.03m	Catamaran, big rig, genoa
32.	1974	Pirateer 13	13.00ft / 3.96m	2-man dinghy, heavy for type
33.	1974	Whip 17	17.00ft / 5.18m	2-man trapeze dinghy, heavy
34.	1974	*British Oxygen*	65.00ft / 19.81m	Offshore cat, Sailcraft, later *Kriter*
35.	1976	Dagger 14	14.50ft / 4.42m	Big, heavy singlehander
36.	1977	Aztec 23	23.00ft / 7.01m	Big, heavy 2-man cat
37.	1978	Comanche 32	32.18ft / 9.81m	Cruising catamaran
38.	1979	*Crossbow II*	60.00ft / 18.29m	Skewed cat, side-by-side masts
39.	1982	Starwind 18	18.00ft / 5.49m	2-man dinghy – heavy for type
40.	1984	Rob Denny (Client)	40.00ft / 12.19m	Windmill trimaran, not built.
41.	1984	Starwind 15	15.00ft / 4.57m	2-man dinghy – heavy for type
42.	1985	Gloucester 18	18.00ft / 5.49m	Ballasted cruising dinghy
43.	1985	*British Airways*	60.00ft / 18.29m	Offshore catamaran, Sailcraft
44.	1986	*Crossbow III*	65.00ft / 19.80m	Canard, flying proa
45.	1987	Gloucester 15	15.00ft / 4.57m	Heavy cruising dinghy
46.	1989	Ultimate Concepts 32	32.00ft / 9.75m	Cruising catamaran like Iroquois

Dick Gibbs (in partnership with RMD from 1964) claims 80 designs and 15,000 units. Number of separate designs is unlikely, but total numbers built corresponds with individual class data.

CODA: South Seas Outriggers

Living in the tropics for thirty years, spending many happy hours treading the hot sand and pondering the infinite variety of multihulls that have evolved to fill every niche in the maritime ecology, one remains eternally mystified as to why replicas consistently underperformed when in Europe.[371] The best East Indies outriggers embody a host of innovative design features which are only now becoming common in the West.

The Balinese outrigger is a particularly sophisticated variant that has remained unchanged since the first colonial-era encounter. The main hull has elliptical sections and a rockered profile to balance low-wetted-area with good-weight-carrying. The sailing platform is almost as wide as it is long, with 9" diameter bamboo floats extending fore and aft beyond the main hull, providing both floatation and dynamic stability. The weather float rides clear of the water to reduce resistance, while a 10-degree toe-in allows the lee float to develop lateral resistance for windward work. The rudder is scimitar shaped with a stall-tolerant, blunt nosed section to overcome innate directional stability.

The stubby mast requires no standing rigging. An extravagant luff-spar provides a long leading-edge for upwind performance, while the equally long boom controls both the foot and the lower leech. On the wind, as the breeze rises, the single large sail automatically reduces in aspect ratio, flattens and releases excess power from the short, open leach. Though the fabric sets in an even curve from one spar to the other, when the rig is raked aft, the breeze strikes at an oblique angle, and 'reads', not a catenary curve, but a perfect aerofoil.

Off the wind, as the rig rotates it cranks forward automatically, to raise the sail-plan aloft. In this configuration, the foot becomes the leech and the airflow exhausts behind the spar, through a slot formed by the loose cat's-cradle lacing. The siting of the rotational axes minimises sheet loads. Even with 200ft^2 of sail-area, the mainsheet is just a single length of string attached to the boom by a cascade of bridles to 'fix' the spar's profile.

The characteristic 'prawn-head' of the Bali boats is the mythical Gajah Mina (elephant-head fish), an elegant alternative take on the figurehead. This goggle-eyed sea monster transports Varuna, the Hindu God of the oceans, and protects him when he inspects the deep. Whimsy aside, the outriggers are far from primitive curiosities.[372]

CODA: Black Leading

Lady Helmsman's Graphspeed was not the first black-lead composition to be applied to a yacht. The historical antecedent, black-leading, was no more durable but it was the best available in the mid-1800s, before hard enamels and dry sailing big boats became de rigueur for serious competition. Blackleading was popular on racing yachts in the 19th century. *"It was formerly a common practice to blacklead the bottom of boats, especially for match sailing, and the custom is still much followed. There were several methods of getting the lead on, and the following is as good as any: First scrape the bottom clean of old paint, tar, etc, and stop open seams, nail holes, shakes, etc. Then put on a thin coat of coal tar, reduced by turpentine or naphtha until quite liquid. When dry and hard put on another coat, and if the boat is a large one this second coat should be put on by instalments. When nearly dry, but yet sticky, put on the blacklead, which must be mixed with water (and well-stirred), and make a solution about as thick as paint.*

To get the mixture on, a dabber must be used; a sponge tied up in a soft piece of cotton cloth is the best thing for the purpose. Care must be taken not to attempt to put on the blacklead in the sun, or the tar will come through. On the other hand, if the tar is hard the blacklead will not 'take hold'. When the whole is thoroughly dry and hard, polish up with the ordinary brushes used by housemaids for grates.

Mayflower, Puritan and Galatea had blacklead mixed with copal varnish put on their hulls. The same was sand-papered and brushed smooth with hard shoe brushes, taking care to have a good smooth body of paint underneath. Galatea was also coated with blacklead on gold size (not as extravagant as it sounds, gold size is the adhesive used when applying gold leaf), *the blacklead being put on dry and brushed afterwards. This is the best method. Blacklead acts on steel. After being in the water three- or four-month's rust will show in beads. A blackleaded bottom will last clean for match sailing about five weeks.*"[373]

Hull finish is a fascinating subject in itself as the shift to wrought iron, steel and alloy constructions meant that it was no longer possible to tack copper sheets over the bottom. Fouling, an issue solved in the 1750s, was back with a vengeance until durable paints, incorporating copper and toxins, were formulated.

---

[315] Sir William Petty's description of his catamaran *Experiment II*, the *"fantastical bottomless double-bottomed machine"*, was launched in October 1662.

[316] The Bell Cat, Uffa Fox, published in Catamaran Developments No.18, the Magazine of the Amateur Yacht Research Society, April 1958.

[317] 'Catamaran' is a French word derived from the language of the Tamil ethnic group. 'Kattu' means 'link' and 'maran' means 'wood'.

[318] Though the double canoes of the Pacific Islands were probably known to some in Europe in 1662, these early English designs were an independent line of development.

[319] Aubrey's Life of Sir William Petty (1632–1687) from Brief Lives, chiefly of Contemporaries, set down by John Aubrey, between the Years 1669 & 1696, Andrew Clark, 1898.

[320] That is how the model in the Royal Museum at Greenwich is rigged, however, according to other accounts she carried a single gaff sail.

[321] Fulton's Steam Battery: Blockship and Catamaran, Howard I. Chapelle, 1964.

[322] A full-size replica was built by Hal Sisk in 1991, Multihull Pioneers, Theo Rye, published posthumously in Classic Boat, March 2017.

[323] The cutter-rigged catamaran *MacKenzie*, built in Belfast in 1868, still had the asymmetry backwards, with shell volumes reduced inside the tunnel.

[324] During a 30-year sojourn in Asia, the author owned a series of Hobie 16 cats, used mainly to burn-off the local outriggers and for surf-sailing rather than round-the-cans racing. They are poorly engineered from primitive material, but are nonetheless, great boats.

[325] Patrick Miller built the short-lived triple-hulled boat, *Edinburgh*, in October 1786, publishing the drawings in January the following year. The boat carried a generous sailplan with staggered paddlewheels between the hulls for auxiliary manual power. She has been described by David Bell as *"the eight* (vessel) *he had experimented with"* but she was just one of eight in total.

[326] The Carron Works fired up their first furnace in 1760. The company is forever associated with the development of the carronade (a short-barrel cannon); and, more specifically in the maritime context, with the manufacture of excellent anchors up to 70 cwt (7,840 lbs).

[327] In 1789, Mr Sandeman, a wealthy citizen of Glasgow, commissioning a catamaran christened *Sandeman*. A Brief History of Multihulls, Catavore, Voiles News, March 2005.

[328] Det skotska fartyget Experiment of Leith och Sverige, Marcus Hjulhammar, 2014.

[329] Ironically, this was an issue Chapman had to address when his own designs missed operational targets – magnificent war-galleys which struggled to touch 1½kts under oar.

[330] Another story, related by Howard Chapelle, the oracle for this type of maritime history, suggests that the vessel was badly strained in a storm and was finally abandoned at St. Petersburg.

[331] Miller had also been disappointed by Symington's steam engines. Robert Cullen wrote to Boulton & Watt on Miller's behalf. James Watt was disinclined to help and considered Symington's engines as *"attempts to evade our exclusive privilege"* despite their separate patent.

[332] Dundas also later lost enthusiasm, primarily because the action of the paddles raised concerns about bank erosion in the canal.

[333] As a 'first' in respect of practical use as opposed to experimentation, the claim is muted as the American vessel followed two years after the *Charlotte Dundas*, a hard-working tugboat. In any case, Fulton may have been born in Ayrshire….though we have no wish to claim him.

Symington had successfully trialled steamboats in 1788 and there is no doubt that Fulton knew about this as he kept abreast of progress. Later, working for the Duke of Bridgewater between 1796 and 1799, Fulton assisted Benjamin Powell with a prototype engined by Bateman and Sherratt of Salford. Symington and the Steamboat, B. E. G. Clark, 2010.

[334] This date has been revised to 1804 by Fulton's biographer The Steamboat Era: A History of Fulton's Folly on American Rivers, 1807–1860, S. L. Kotar & J. E. Gessler, 2009.

[335] William Clark of Greenock, a painter of maritime subjects and occasional inventor, supposedly proposed the bow thruster in 1859, so there is an unresolved mismatch here. Registered with the Office of the Commissioner of Patents, 23rd May 1859.

[336] Clydeships search, Scottish-built Ships, the History of Shipbuilding in Scotland, website.

[337] Essai sur la construction navale des peuples extra-européens, François-Edmond Pâris, 1841.

[338] The Bell Cat, Uffa Fox, April 1958.

[339] Paris underpins the English-language works of Folkard and Warington Smyth on the subject. Sailing Boats from around the World, Henry Colman Folkard, 1906 and Mast and Sail in Europe and Asia, Herbert Warington Smyth, 1906. William Ackland built another successful proa replica in 1938.

[340] We follow the precedent set by Fife biographer May McCallum and use the 'Fyfe' spelling for William I and 'Fife' for Williams II and III.

[341] Fast and Bonnie, May Fife McCallum, 1998.

[342] May also refers to this vessel as the *Flying Fish* when she cites an article in the Glasgow Courier which refers to the *Flying Fish* spawning a 'proa junior'.

[343] Shipping Intelligence, Caledonian Mercury, 10th July 1834 and Loss of the Flying Fish, Belfast Newsletter, 15th July 1834.

[344] May suggests a boat 60ft LOA, but the *Mercury's* precise dimensions are more likely.

[345] Hunt's Yachting Magazine, Volume the 3rd 1854.

[346] Ibid

[347] The Nile felucca is a wide, stable platform with a length to beam ratio of 2.5 to support the towering lateen rig. A felucca is three times as wide proportionally as George's *Doria*, which by contrast, was just 8ft beam on a LOA of 60ft – a length to beam ratio of 7.5.

[348] Clyde, The Yachtsman, 25th February 1892.

[349] The foil-borne America's Cup catamarans introduced deliberate wracking as a way of altering the angle of attack of the weather rudder foil to increase sail carrying power. This was an aberration caused by rule restrictions. The old boats have been reborn as F50 cats and can now adjust rudder-mounted foils without resorting to this undesirable ruse.

[350] Notes & Notions, The Yachtsman, 4th July 1895.

[351] The Bell Cat, Uffa Fox, April 1958.

[352] Demolished and rebuilt in 1970 after the MacAlpine-Downie family moved to Ireland.

[353] The Thai Cat is a Western Siamese, backcrossed with indigenous Whichianmat.

[354] Rod would go on to collaborate with Dick Gibbs in the production of some 80-odd designs. Reputedly, the combined production of this diverse design portfolio, by builders in the United States Britain, Germany, Italy and Japan, totalled 150,000 units.

[355] Catamaran Sailing to Win, Chris Wilson and Max Press, 1973.

[356] Richard Creagh-Osborne thought Rod to be a better designer than sailor. The Dinghy Yearbook 1964, the Dinghy Yearbook 1965 – both edited by Creagh-Osborne.

[357] Multihull Design and Catamarans, 1966, the Amateur Yacht Research Society, Issue 59, articles by Jack Knights and others.

[358] After a few graphite-bespattered years, during which we all looked like newly off-shift coal miners, Graphspeed disappeared without trace leaving behind a nightmare to overcoat. An equally short-lived white version followed; that one suckered me too.

[359] *Crossbow* maxed out at 30.1kts in 1975. *Crossbow II* extended the World Sailing Speed Record to 36 knots in 1980. She held the record for six years.

[360] Crossbow 40 Years On, Stephen Pullinger, 21st October 2012.

[361] Proposed World Sailing Speed Record Attempt, Rod MacAlpine-Downie, ca.1984.

[362] Jamie Campbell writes: *"Timothy Colman wasn't a bad helm and once came within a broken genoa halyard of winning the Edinburgh Cup. He part owned his Dragons (all called Salar) with his cousin, who had won a gold medal in 1936 in 6mRs. Since he married the Queen's cousin, Tim was desperate to stay out of trouble."*

[363] There is some doubt about whether the windmill on the mizzen mast of the *City of Ragusa* was used during the crossing. Croatian Life Stories, Croatian World Network.

[364] Moore-Brazabon was an aviation pioneer. In 1934 he fitted a gyro-rig to a Bembridge Redwing. The boat is currently in the Classic Boat Museum on the Isle of Wight.

[365] Flettner rotors have been trialled on cargo ships to harness windpower as a fuel-saving measure.

[366] The Royal Yacht Squadron, 1815-1895, Ian Dear, 1985.

[367] As noted above in relation to the Flettner system with the current emphasis on reducing operational costs and harnessing alternative power sources for commercial craft, this type of system of great interest today. Designs have been developed from the original power generation turbines pioneered by Denmark in the 1970s.

[368] Malcolm Tennant, Multihull Design Limited, website.

[369] Malcolm Tennant's *Revelation II*, a catamaran launched in 2001, is a similar concept but the rotor diameter is 50% greater.

[370] Whirring across the Atlantic, Financial Times, 5th March 1983.

[371] Before the advent of modern materials and construction techniques, it may be argued that bamboo spars and rattan lashings were the essential magic that enabled fast South Seas multihulls. But these materials were imported into Britain at that time and light bamboo yards were used in small conventional sailing craft.

[372] The vessel described is a Jukong of the Eastern Islands of the Indonesian archipelago. Text summaries from a piece in Seahorse Magazine, Euan Ross, November 2005.

[373] Manual of Yacht and Boat Sailing and Architecture Dixon Kemp, 9th edition, 1900.

Experiment of Leith, Patrick Miller, 1790   Sourced by Marcus Hjulhammar

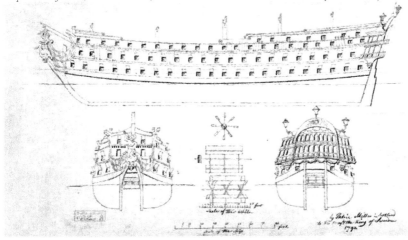

Miller's '*Sea Spook*' proposal for a 144-gun ship-of-the-line catamaran pitched to King Gustavus, 1790

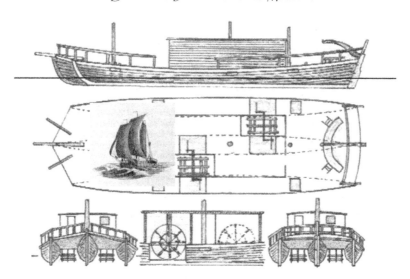

Edinburgh, Patrick Miller, 1786, which may have been used for subsequent steam-powered experiments

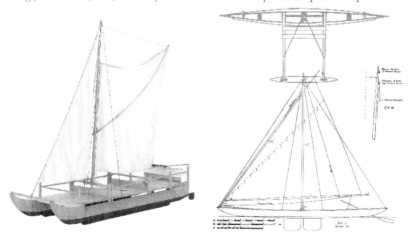

Model of *Simon and Jude*, William Petty, 1663   *Proa 1*, Ralph M. Munroe, 1898

City of Ragusa, 1870   Turbine-powered Tri, McAlpine Downie, 1984

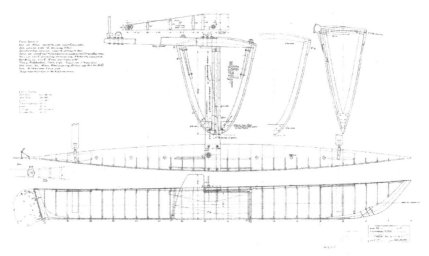

Amaryllis, 33ft catamaran,1876   Nathaniel Herreshoff

Gemini, 17ft lath and canvas catamaran, 1894   William Manera Bergius
There is no known image of her opponent, the Allen family's unsuccessful dugout catamaran.

Lady Helmsman, MacAlpine-Downie/Austin Farrar/Reg White. International Catamaran Trophy, 1966

Slingshot, Clark Thomas, 1978, built by Gougeon. An unsuccessful American 'interpretation' of the concept with a canting rig and a planing hull. Image Epoxyworks.com

Crossbow I, 1972   Rod McAlpine Downie, built by Reg White

Crossbow II, 1980   Rod MacAlpine-Downie, built by Tim Whelpton

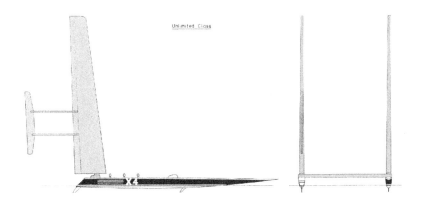

Crossbow III, 1986   Rod MacAlpine-Downie, built by Performance Sailcraft

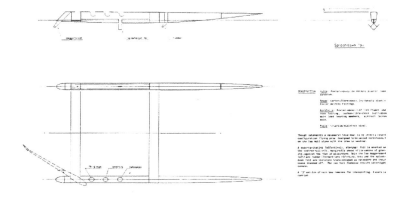

Crossbow III, Speed Record Contender 1986   Rod MacAlpine-Downie, built by Performance Sailcraft

British Oxygen, Offshore cat, 1985.   Hellcat on steroids for Robin Knox-Johnston and Gerry Boxall
Inset: *Heavenly Twins*, 5-rater, Col Conway Gordon, 1895   Image: The Yachtsman

Bali outrigger, as built today and since first European contact   Drawn by Aldo Cherini

Chapter 8: Caledonian Cockiness

The Marjory, of 70 tons, built in 1814, with one engine of 14 horsepower, was the first steam vessel on the Thames. She was taken south along the east coast of Scotland; and, when she reached the Thames, passed close to the English fleet, there at anchor, and her appearance created great commotion amongst the officers and men, as none of them had ever seen a steamer before, and by some wag taken for a fire-ship. Andrew Scott[374]

Through two centuries, the Clyde was synonymous with shipbuilding. As may be expected, the odyssey of yachts and yachting on the river is inextricably linked with our commercial shipbuilding heritage. Without this nidus of innovation, cutting-edge technology and hard-won expertise, Caledonia's sailing legacy would be as a pale shadow. But, more than anything, the extraordinary league of shipbuilders and engineers imparted a certain cockiness – swelling hearts, broadening minds and instilling a 'can-do' mentality that acknowledged few peers and recognised few limits.

The legendary shipbuilders of Clydeside endure today only in sepia-tinted time-exposures. Bewhiskered grinches glare cholericly at the lens, impatient to get back to work. But these momentarily petrified Victorians were ballsy risk-takers with lively minds, often leavened with unexpected dry humour. They were the acknowledged masters of their craft. In economic and social terms, the scale of their collective achievement marginalised the cottage industry of yachting. Nevertheless, skills and personnel overlapped, and the two camps entertained considerable mutual respect.

From the Industrial Revolution (ca.1760-1840), through to the early 20th century, Britain harvested her geopolitical dominance in the form of one-sided trade deals. The industrialists of the British Empire enjoyed access to limitless natural resources and could call on a global pool of skilled and still-malleable labour. Our engineers and chemists routinely broke new ground with innovations that were fast-tracked and unregulated. Financiers and entrepreneurs, often qualified engineers and ideas men themselves, invested in new technologies with an enthusiasm bordering on recklessness. The result was an industrial base that became the envy of the world for a hundred-and-fifty years. The Clyde was at the heart of this machine, breasting great social and political change, indiscriminately monetising both war and peace.[375] Through a tumultuous century of wars and social upheaval, Scotland's marine industry consistently punched above its weight.

Clyde shipbuilding would collapse under the overhead-costs of its own weighty reputation in the 1960s. We lost our claim to the premium on excellence that international clients had been happy to pay. The shipyards fell silent through corporate neglect, with middling managers blind to the slow slide into mediocrity. Financial prudence, and breaking with its very genesis, absence of vision, combined to erase the raison d'être of the industry. Ironically, a yachtsman wielded the axe. Ted Heath's free-market Tory government sounded the industry's death knell, and the 'Iron Lady' herself drove in the nails to seal the coffin.

Meanwhile, around the world, less-doctrinaire national governments, recognising that sea-freight was the lifeblood of globalisation, maintained a weather-eye on the emerging new world-order, and quietly invested in this key strategic sector. Government subsidies of any form may be inconsistent with our economic model, but we have seen other key sectors closer to the heart of Westminster 'bailed out' repeatedly. It is therefore not difficult to understand why most Scots considered the mishandling of shipbuilding as a calculated ideological confrontation with the romantic working-class rabble of 'Red Clydeside'.

The story begins with William Patterson, a Scottish financier, who raised £1.2 million (£144 million) to re-equip and remobilise the English Navy in 1694. None of this money found its way to our shipyards as the Clyde had yet to acquire expertise in warship construction, but it was the spark that lit the industry. The Bank of England was formed to manage the loan and would become a model for such institutions. Then came our ill-fated colonial adventure at Darien, a debacle which exposed the underlying fragility of Scotland's economy. Patterson and other major investors were now motivated to campaign for a union with England. Even today, many Scots liken the Union of 1707 to a 'hostile takeover', but it removed long-standing barriers to trade and kick-started the Scottish economy.

In the early years of the 18th century, the Clyde was a cul-de-sac, remote from established trade links between Britain and mainland Europe. It was not an obvious location for a revolution in shipbuilding. Our only regionally competitive yards were on the opposite side of the country – on the Forth, Tay and Dee estuaries. In the 1700s, Glasgow merchants had their vessels built in Cumbrian yards or bought them second-hand from shipbrokers in Europe. Access to the Americas changed the game entirely.

In the wake of the Union, our business houses quickly capitalised on trade opportunities across the Atlantic, but that also meant that it was now simply good business to buy their ships there too. American yards dominated the shipbuilding industry in that era. In 1769, they built 389 vessels totalling 20,000-tons, far exceeding the total British output. The Americas enjoyed a limitless supply of fine timber, while the London government imposed crippling import duties to favour English oak, which tripled in price as a result. This was obviously unsustainable; oak is a slow-growing species taking 150 years to become a useful boatbuilding material.

John Scott opened his books for business at Greenock in 1711.[376] While the Scott family would eventually graduate to ocean-going vessels, John initially specialised in fishing boats, coastal trading craft and 'herring buses' – small sailing ships used to take the catch to market. In 1728, the fishing fleet comprised upwards of 900 locally built boats. Scotts was the name that would endure to symbolise the industry, but the yard was just one of many on the Clyde competing for orders in the early 18th century.

The first ship to be specifically built for the Atlantic trade after the Union was a 60-tonner, built at Crawfordsdyke in 1718, but almost half-a-century would elapse before Clyde-built products became competitive.[377] Early Clyde-built ships enjoyed a small cost advantage over the products of London and Bristol, but even 60 years after the Union, there was still a strong prejudice against Scottish shipping. However, attitudes were changing. The *Greenock*, a fast square-rigger of the type that would make the Clyde famous, was launched at Peter Love's yard in 1764. Then, James & William Scott built the first ship for a 'foreign' client (a consortium of merchants in Hull) in 1765, using timber from the Ducal woods at Hamilton.

A century later, secure in a well-respected dynasty, John Scott's descendants could afford to take time out to design and build our first 'proper' yachts, which the family raced with considerable success. Most of our shipyards, while renowned for their great liners, freighters, steamers and warships also built yachts in their early years, albeit in small numbers. At first, the only differences between working boats and private yachts were the names of the clients and the standard of finish. However, as the shipbuilding industry upscaled, yard managers were content to cede their relatively unprofitable yacht work to the smaller, low-overhead boatyards, now springing up around the coast. The two branches of the business would briefly come together again when steam yachts became fashionable in the 1870s.

It should be emphasised that Clyde shipbuilding owes nothing to any long-standing ship-building tradition.[378] The labour-force that worked on the ways and in the sub-assembly shops, brought no specific skills. But they learned on the job and quickly built a formidable reputation. If the industry can trace any native stimulus – that derived from the expertise of a talented generation of engineers working in the mines of Lanarkshire and Ayrshire. And it benefitted immeasurably from the transferrable skills honed in that industry – specifically, the techniques and machinery developed to tunnel and extract coal from galleries and dewater the workings.

The Clyde's new shipbuilding industry was receptive to progress from the start, developing rapidly without the stultifying baggage of tradition. Growth accelerated when corporate entities and public institutions saw the benefits of coordinated investment. Glasgow entrepreneurs opened a new economic front with a 500-ton capacity dry dock at Port Glasgow in 1762. The magistrates of the city then commissioned civic works contracts to dredge access up-river. And the Forth & Clyde Canal was started in 1768, although it would take 22 years to complete. These major public works encouraged shipyards to establish premises on the upper reaches of the river. Eventually, they would line the banks and dominate the landscape.

By the 1770s, Glasgow controlled the world tobacco trade, adding to a slate of major existing investments that included cotton, sugar and its by-product rum, a spirit beloved of sailors now through five centuries.[379] These industries have one thing in common. Shipbuilding cannot be dissociated from the dreadful corollary of these boom years; the trade-triangle that delivered raw materials to Glasgow began with a voyage to Africa, where trade-goods were exchanged for slaves. Scotland's share of this trade was small, but it was not insignificant, especially when proxy trading through Bristol, Liverpool and London is included.[380]

The nation, at home and abroad, was up to its neck in a moral morass, even while our courts determined that slavery simply did not exist.[381] The profits of this traffic in human misery purchased 'respectability' via grand houses, splendid churches, neo-classical civic buildings, fine art, university bequests, and quite a few yachts. The merchant princes of the city assumed the trappings of a dissolute aristocracy and their descendants became the recreational sailors who populate the later chapters of our story. While none of this was remarkable for the age, it is no less abhorrent.[382]

Up until the American War of Independence (1775-1783), Glasgow merchants, as we have noted, enjoyed artificially low shipping costs. With America otherwise occupied, the order-books of Scottish shipbuilders began to fill, sparking a flurry of new investment. Three yards were set up at Saltcoats in the period 1775-1790. The earliest of these was run by William Ritchie, who moved on in 1791 to establish an important new centre of Scottish shipbuilding expertise in Belfast. The Ayrshire yards would contribute to advances in ship and engine design during the heyday of the industry, even if they represented a small percentage of tonnage launched.

When the American war eventually ended, 'Clyde-built' commanded a premium that would endure for 200 years. Across the Atlantic, history was repeated with the Civil War of 1861-1865. This ugly conflict kept Clyde shipbuilders on perpetual overtime. Famously quick local steamers were sold at ransom prices to act as blockade runners, and of course, these ships had to be replaced. In the early 1860s, close to 27,000 jobs were associated with this work. The Clydeside economy essentially cashed-in on a shameful conflict and thus prolonged the war, perhaps by as much as two years.

Clyde yards were soon busy openly flouting the law by fulfilling direct orders from Confederate agencies. Scots were also involved in financing these vessels. Perhaps a hundred Clyde-built ships crossed the Atlantic, of which 42 were new-builds. On the yard books, the client might have been the 'Emperor of China' or whatever notional entity was then in vogue with the Bridge of Allen spy-ring. This surely adds insult to injury when we consider Britain's state-sanctioned drug-running. Any objective review of the First Opium War (1839-1842), and the Second Opium War (1856-1860) also invokes regrettable shipping associations.[383]

Growing up on the Clyde, we were completely taken in by the romance and daring of blockade running. Schoolboys thought it was wonderful that our elegant paddle-steamers, which still plied the river in the 1950s, were seaworthy enough to cross the Atlantic and fast enough to run the Yankee blockade, shuttling back and forth between Bermuda and the Southern States.[384] We had no idea that all this nose-thumbing by the Southerners was to defend the indefensible.[385]

In the late 18th century, the Clyde yards embarked on the vital transition from wooden sailing ships to steel-hulled steamships. Shipbuilding and yacht-building would diverge for a time until the craze for extravagant steam yachts through the period 1870-1939 brought them together again. These new developments on Clydeside mirrored the changeover from waterpower to steam in local mills and factories. The yards first employed steam engines in the sawmills. Then, as lighter, more powerful and reliable powerplants became available, the steam-powered ship was inevitable.

Like most aspects of the Industrial Revolution, the genesis of these innovations is disputed. Thomas Savery's steam pump, patented in 1698, was probably the first useable steam engine, but it languished as a curiosity.[386] James Watt, son of a Clyde shipwright, developed the condenser and an efficient transfer of steam power into a circular motion. In so doing, he achieved the first viable commercial engines in 1766. Integral with these inventions, was the Watt system for parallel linkage still used today in high-performance cars to achieve linear suspension travel. The first practical application of steam technology to ships was the work of Patrick Miller and his engineer, William Symington, in the 1780s. Miller's important contributions to steam-ship design and the development of the catamaran are discussed in Chapter 7.

The 56ft *Charlotte Dundas II* was launched on the River Caron in 1801, with Symington's patented horizontal steam engine. She served as a tugboat on the Forth and Clyde Canal, operating efficiently without much fanfare. A decade later, the *Comet*, a 4hp 25-ton sea-going paddle-steamer with engines by John Robertson and boilers by David Napier, would steal the headlines. *Comet* was built in 1812 by John and Charles Wood for Helensburgh hotelier, Henry Bell, who used the boat initially to ferry his guests down-river from Glasgow.[387] As the story goes, when the *Comet* was 'getting exhausted' at the end of a run, the passengers would pitch in, manually turning the flywheel.

The *Comet* legend celebrates her system of propulsion, but the builders were also men of ingenuity and interest: *"Charles Wood was a remarkable man, but perhaps too far in advance of the age in which he lived. Among his other designs, he constructed the great ship-rafts Columbus and Baron of Renfrew as a new expedient for bringing timber to this country* (from North America). *There can be no doubt that these brothers have conferred honour upon their profession and added to the lustre of their native land."*[388] The Wood brothers built many of the early wooden steamships before iron construction became viable.

That same year, 1812, the 'Lang Dyke' hydraulic management project enabled the River Clyde to self-scour. Soon larger vessels were able to access the heart of Glasgow. A decade of innovation and development fostered a confluence of key technologies, so that, by 1824 steam-powered dredgers guaranteed the sustainability of the new deep-water channel. The nascent shipbuilding industry on the upper Clyde could now confidently take commissions for much larger seagoing vessels.

Iron ships were every bit as revolutionary as steamships. Englishman John Wilkinson built the *Trial*, a timber-framed barge with an iron shell, in Shropshire in 1786.[389] However, the first practical all-iron ship might have been Thomas Wilson's *Vulcan,* a Forth and Clyde Canal passenger barge, 61ft LOA, 11ft beam and 4ft 6" depth, built in 1819. The new canal was proving to be an excellent test-tank. *Vulcan* was built of puddled-iron; there were, as yet no rolling-mills to supply plate.

David Napier's *Rob Roy*, as described in Chapter 6, was built by William Denny in 1818, but her 32nhp (5bhp) engine was a product of Napier's own engine works.[390] The idea of a 5hp engine efficiently driving an 80ft LOA vessel offshore is astonishing, but Napier's first venture into naval architecture combined speed and reliability with remarkable sea-kindliness in heavy weather. In 1821, *Rob Roy* was re-engined with a more powerful unit and sent south to shuttle from Dover to Calais, providing a passenger service with a still-respectable operational speed of about 8kts.

The best-known of the early steamship builders was James Lang of Dumbarton. After an unhappy experience with engines supplied by Duncan MacArthur, he turned to David Napier who was now making quite a name for himself. Napier and his wider family were crucial in advancing naval architecture and incidentally, yacht architecture too. The Lang/Napier partnership enjoyed great success in the period before the long-established Scotts of Greenock hit their stride in the 1830s.

Aglaia, 63ft LOA and 30-tons, was the first iron steamer on the Clyde in 1827. She was the first complete vessel built by David Napier at his Lancefield works for service in the sheltered waters of Loch Eck. The ferry link was part of his multi-modal 'road to the isles' through Kilmun. He would have been aware of Admiral Charles Napier (no relation) who conceived and financed the first seagoing iron steamer, the *Aaron Manby*. This landmark vessel was prefabricated at the Manby family's Horseley Ironworks in Staffordshire before final assembly on the Thames. The *Aaron Manby* successfully crossed the English Channel under Charles Napier's command in 1822.

As Loch Eck is land-locked and remote from the workshops of Glasgow, the design of *Aglaia* featured a modular iron bottom with wooden topsides, so that it could be transported in sections and assembled on-site. It was a particularly clever solution in this operational context. The stout iron bottom was dragged up the River Echaig from Kilmun by heavy horses, presumably while the tide was high and the river in flood. The topsides, engine and boiler travelled by road.

Renamed *James Gallaher*, *Aglaia* enjoyed a second life as a ferryboat on the more testing waters of the Clyde estuary. It may be assumed that she left Loch Eck as she entered it, the reverse operation being considerably easier. Tragically, however, this pioneering vessel was the scene of a fatal accident in 1838.[391] Four people lost their lives when the boiler exploded due to a sequence of operation and maintenance errors.[392]

Iron construction required considerable development before it was proven as safe for use in tidal and open waters, where wave patterns induce the complex cycles of sagging and hogging. John Neilson's 1840 iron steamer, *Fairy Queen*, was a valuable proof of concept, shuttling passengers on the Glasgow-Largs-Millport route. Also, in 1840, Tod & McGregor built the *Iron Duke*, a three-masted sailing ship for use offshore. However, as she sank the following year, it is arguable how 'ocean-going' she really was.

Preceding both these vessels was the 30-ton cutter, *Cyclops*, of 1836, which was built with an iron hull up to the waterline and wooden topsides, like the *Aglaia*. Her owner, James MacNair, claimed that she was the first iron-hulled open-sea sailing vessel. Thomas Assheton-Smith's *Water Cure*, an all-iron 25-ton cutter, was constructed by Robert Napier in 1843. He subsequently built the *Spray* in 1852 and many vessels more followed. Iron racing yachts appeared in 1844, when the 25-tonners, *Belvidere*, *Bluebell* and *Ariel*, turned out at Cowes, so we might assume that English yacht builders and designers were in the van of this revolution. The best of the Clyde's iron-pots like *Vanduara* 1880 and *Wendur* 1883, both G. L. Watson/D & H Henderson collaborations for John Clark, followed later with the subsequent introduction of steel.

The changing of the guard in commercial shipping came in the 1850s when iron and steam finally eclipsed wood and sail. In that year, Britain built 84% of all steamships worldwide. The Lloyds Register of 1850-51 shows that Clyde shipbuilders were responsible for 76% of iron steamers built in this country and 90% of their engines. This dominance lasted for twenty years before a more balanced geographical distribution emerged. But Clyde yards retained a competitive advantage in steam power, iron construction and screw propulsion for many years.[393]

The last really big wooden ship launched on the Clyde was the *Canadian*, built by Scotts in 1857. She was a three-masted sailing vessel 167ft LOA. However, it was not until the 1880s, when mild-steel plate of consistent quality became available, that the new material entirely supplanted wood.

With wooden ships, longitudinal stiffness became a critical issue at around 300ft LOA. This upper limit was confirmed notably by the catastrophic failure of B. B. Crowninshield's *Thomas W. Lawson*. The American naval architect knew success in small racing yachts but appears to have lost the plot in 1902 with this 475ft LOA, seven-masted leviathan. Sailing light, the sail-plan was only twice the area of the topsides. She foundered off the Scilly Isles with great loss of life. Ironically, the wreck of this eco-giant caused the first major oil-spill in maritime history as her final cargo comprised 58,000 barrels of paraffin oil.

Iron ships promised a very substantial 25% reduction in operational costs. However, the Admiralty's preferences and Luddite specifications for mail contracts delayed the change-over. There was a real fear that cannon-fire, which could be absorbed by oversized timber construction, would turn iron boats into shrapnel.[394] This did not happen. Even so, the Navy did not get to grips with the new technology until well into the second half of the 19th century.

Tod and McGregor, both protégés of Robert Napier, were first to tool-up for iron shipbuilding, but it was Robert himself who invested most heavily in the new market. Napier, together with Samuel Cunard, had the business acumen to bet the farm on big fast ships for the transatlantic passenger trade. This collaboration culminated in the *Scotia* (1863), the most powerful ocean-going paddle-steamer ever built.

David Napier and his cousin Robert were giants among the big men of the Clyde, innovating and influencing generations of engineers and shipbuilders. Through the 1820s and 30s, the Napier dynasty confidently strode the fine line between reliability and continuing development to make the Clyde world-famous in the annals of steam navigation. Napier engines retained their value, and some did sterling service over decades to outlast three, or even four, wooden hulls.

For shipping companies, it was all about profitability; at issue was the cost per ton of building and operating sailing ships vis-à-vis steamships. The changeover to iron allowed bigger ships and hence a more favourable ratio of cargo capacity to fixed machinery and bunkering. In the 1820s, a steamship cost about £25 (£2,400) per ton and a sailing ship £15 (£1,550) because the powered vessel had to be more substantially constructed.[395]

However, by 1852, the position had reversed. Wooden ships cost £14 a ton, and iron £12 per ton.[396] That said, a steam engine still meant considerably more initial outlay than the most complex sailing rig. Early engines were not particularly fuel-efficient, with onboard bunker space incurring high economic costs. On the other side of the equation, operational crew numbers on steamships could be reduced, although while reliability issues remained, auxiliary sail and a caucus of experienced crewmen standing by still represented essential insurance.

Moving with the times was an expensive business. Shipping lines might issue new shares in stock to cover the up-front investments or prevail on the engine-builder to contribute risk capital. However, as the century wore on, more efficient and reliable motors allowed skippers to stow away their auxiliary sail and pay off the 'Cape Horners'. Manpower savings finally tipped the balance in favour of steam for most commercial applications.[397]

The Clyde yards brought the paddle-steamer to such a high point of development that the industry in Scotland may have been a little late in commercialising the screw propeller. Nevertheless, in 1845, the same year as Brunel's *Great Britain*, Robert Napier launched the *Fire Queen*, the first iron screw-steamer on the river, and in 1850, Tod & McGregor's *City of Glasgow* proved the technology to be safe and reliable on the regular service between Glasgow and New York.

Robert Wilson (1803–1882) had successfully demonstrated a practical screw-propeller to the Highland Society in 1828.[398] Wilson petitioned the Navy for years with little success. His prototype ran at 9kts, but the Lords of the Admiralty saw only witchcraft. They could not understand how the narrow jet behind a small, submerged screw-propeller could compete with the great volume of water accelerated by paddlewheels.

Wilson seems to have deferred to James Steadman of Irvine, who first proposed the idea in 1816. But not lodging a patent in his own name was a costly act for Wilson.[399] This self-effacing gentleman was eventually rewarded by the Admiralty with an award of £500 (£60,000) for the design of an evolutionary spin-off; the coaxial counter-rotating propellers used on early torpedoes, later patented for aircraft by F. W. Lanchester in 1907.

Wilson's contemporary, George Rennie (1791-1866), was the son of John Rennie (1761-1821), designer of bridges, docks and the Caledonian Canal, and brother of Sir John Rennie, who rebuilt Chatham Dockyards in 1862. George was born in England while his parents were resident there, but he remained very much the Scot. George built the engines for the SS *Archimedes* (1839), and the HMS *Dwarf* (1840), the latter being the first propeller-driven vessel in the Royal Navy. As might be inferred, *Archimedes* employed an Archimedes screw, while the *Dwarf* used an early conventional propeller.

David Napier's cousin, Robert, leased the Lancefield Foundry in 1821, eventually purchasing the site in 1841. During these decades, Robert's company not only produced outstanding work, but his yard also spun-off a superior class of apprentices. Napier alumni would carry the baton of excellence through the 19th century. Robert Napier and his right-hand man, David Elder, enabled the talents of, inter alia, Peter Denny, William Denny III, James & George Thomson, John Elder, Charles Randolph and William Pearce. These men would, in turn, institutionalise technical excellence first in steamship and then in yachts too.

Without this impetus, it is doubtful that the yachts of the 'golden age' would have been imbued with such a sublime blend of science and art. Napier tyros lacked neither confidence nor ego. In particular, there was G. L. Watson who worked under the supervision of the highly esteemed marine engineer, A. C. Kirk, and naval architect, John Inglis. Alfred Mylne (1872-1951), another outstanding Scottish yacht designer, was apprenticed to Henry Napier's firm of Napier, Shanks & Bell.[400] Mylne then moved to G. L. Watson's before setting up on his own account in 1896.

J. & G. Thomson and Randolph, Elder & Co were perhaps the two most significant marine engineering firms run by former Napier employees. Elder built the first compound steam engine for the *Brandon* in 1854, an engine significant for its low fuel consumption. In the old days, strong headwinds or bad weather meant that steamships sometimes arrived at their destination stripped down to the essential structure after sacrificing furniture, fittings and non-essential combustibles to the furnaces. The compound engine was around 25% more efficient and therefore ideal for transoceanic travel and service to the increasingly important South American ports where bunker coal was not readily available.

In the mid-1850s, James Howden and Co further refined the design of marine engines by preheating combustion-air with exhaust gasses and using forced-draft systems in the combustion chambers of turbines. The company later pioneered blowers in marinised diesel engines. Those technologies were soon widely adopted by rival firms. New ideas were seldom allowed to languish as proprietary assets in those days. In subsequent generations, the Howden family would become a famous name in yachting circles, as engineers, boatbuilders and clients.

Meanwhile sailing shipbuilders were also driven to innovate in order to remain competitive. Alexander Stephen & Sons was a family business from the east coast which moved to Kelvinhaugh in 1850. The Stephen's yard led the way in composite construction with the *John Lidgette*, *Arima* and *Arriero*, all launched in 1863. William Thomson (later Lord Kelvin), physicist and a keen yachtsman, collaborated in the firm's technical advances. Specific research addressed the engineering challenges of mixed materials, the applied science of new marine adhesives, the formulation of new protective coatings and the insulation of dissimilar materials from galvanic action.

Composite expertise would spin-off into the world of yacht racing. This light, strong construction became de rigueur for fast racing boats, especially those Big Class yachts with long overhangs and low freeboard. Composite technologies diversified to encompass the all-metal America's Cup defenders. Herreshoff's *Defender* employed a mix of steel, aluminium, and manganese bronze with the characteristics of a giant battery, fizzing round the course in 1895. As for *Reliance* in 1903, Cornelius Vanderbilt said: "*Call the boat a freak, anything you like, but we cannot handicap ourselves, even if our boat is only fit for the junk heap the day after the race.*" Lord Kelvin, then enjoying retirement in Largs, must have shaken his head with disbelief.

The East India Company lost their trading monopoly in 1814. Free trade was the spur to develop bigger, faster clipper ships for the Far East. By 1852, there were 200 clippers shuttling around Cape Horn. The famous tea clipper, *Cutty Sark*, was Scott & Linton's swansong, launched in 1869 when the breed was already obsolete.[401] The oldest clipper-ship in existence today is the *City of Adelaide*, better known as the *Carrick*, built in Sunderland in 1864. This vessel has had a long and adventurous life. She was moored in Glasgow for many years as the dank and pokey headquarters of the Royal Naval Voluntary Reserve. The Clyde Cruising Club came aboard as tenants in 1973. RYA Scotland meetings were held there too.[402]

Carrick capsized and sank in 1989, drowning the archives of the CCC. After an exceptionally low tide, her gunwale caught on a wharf timber as she rose on the flood. She was sold to the Scottish Maritime Museum for

£1.00 in 1990, but it wasn't a bargain. After decades of neglect on the River Irvine, the hulk was transported by barge to South Australia, to be restored by the great-grandchildren of the 1864-87 immigrants.[403] By way of compensation, the *Glenlee*, a fine Clyde-built 3-masted steel barque from 1896, was rescued from a Spanish shipbreaker.[404] She was brought home and restored in 2011 and now lies alongside Glasgow's Riverside Museum.[405]

High-performance yacht-like clipper ships would transform the public perception of seafaring.[406] But it remained difficult to insure these boats, or to maintain their value as assets. Alexander Stephen lobbied Lloyds in London intensively and finally won approval for an A1 classification for composite construction to last 15-years. As Alexander himself said, *"this is a national matter and will be a benefit to the country and also the shipowner"*. The Stephens' iron clippers, like the beautiful, 1,466-ton *Maulesden*, built in Dundee in 1875, set records only eclipsed by modern ocean-going multihulls.

Despite this success with Lloyds, a group of Clyde shipbuilders set up an alternative institution in 1890 – the British Corporation Registry. The intention was to foster innovation through a more scientific survey system. The notoriously conservative gentlemen at Lloyds took years to assess new technology. Steel ships were considered higher risk than wood for the first decade of the overlap. The Allen Line ships were the first to be classified B.S.*, the highest grade under the new system. With this endorsement, others followed in Britain, Belgium, Australia and New Zealand. The B.S.* registry was sold to Lloyds in 1949 and folded into the Lloyds Register.

Alexander Stephen wrote in his diary in 1851, *"settled to commence iron shipbuilding"*, but he did not abandon composite construction.[407] His shipyard launched the composite screw-steamer, *Sea King*, in 1863. She was described as an 'extreme tea clipper'. The following year, she was sold to the Confederates and renamed *Shenandoah*.[408] The late-era clipper ships were nearly all built with mild steel frames and internal structures planked over with a timber skin.

Once established in their new yard at Linthouse in 1869, the focus of the Stephen Yard changed to take advantage of Clydeside expertise in steam and steel, building both freight and passenger vessels. Through 222 years of operation, working from multiple locations, the Stephen family pioneered many practices we take for granted today. Perhaps the most important of these followed in the wake of what remains the worst launching tragedy to befall a shipyard on the Clyde. The *Daphne*, a cargo cum-passenger ship of 450-tons, was launched on the 3rd July 1883.

At the launch, there was an unusually large number of men down below, working to complete her fit-out before the Glasgow Fair holiday.[409] A few minutes after entering the water, and without warning, the vessel rolled over and sank, taking 124 men with her. Remarkably, the Special Commission of Enquiry did not hold the builders liable. Shipyards in those days did not routinely carry out stability calculations. All the 'good and the great' in shipbuilding and academia contributed to the recommendations. The Commission's report subsequently formed a cornerstone of naval architecture and informed the design of large steam yachts which sailed 'light'.[410] The *Daphne* was relaunched as *Rose* and operated successfully for 35 years until she struck a mine in the Aegean in 1918.

When Alexander Stephen (the 3rd of that name) died in 1899, there were more ships afloat designed by him than by any of his competitors, and he had hand-carved the half-models of all of them. Among a long list of pioneering and innovative vessels, the Stephen's yards on the Tay and on the Clyde built specialist vessels for high latitudes. Most were whalers, but the list also includes legendary polar exploration vessels.

> There were many famous polar exploration ships associated with the Stephen family. Captain Scott's *Discovery* (1872) was the fourth of that name to capture the public imagination. (The first 'Discovery' to capture the public imagination was Hudson's *Discovery* of 1607 of the Hudson and Baffin expeditions. The second was *Discovery* (1774), a converted Whitby-built collier which sailed under Cook, the third was Vancouver's *Discovery* of 1789, built at Rotherhithe.) Scott's *Discovery* was built at the Stephen yard in Dundee after it was acquired by the Dundee Shipbuilding Co. Scott also commanded the *Terra Nova* (whaler 1884). Shackleton's *Aurora* (sealer 1976) and *Nimrod* (sealer/whaler 1866), Admiral Byrd's *Bear* (sealer 1874), which went to the assistance of Amundsen and others had seen decades of Arctic service before being repurposed for polar exploration. The *Alert* (1875) and the fifth well-known *Discovery* (1875) were both Stephen steamers used in Disraeli's North-West Passage Expedition of 1875. Joseph Conrad's first command was *Otago*, an iron barque of 349-tons, built at the Stephen's Kelvinhaugh yard in 1869. The Stephen family's contribution to racing yacht design is described in Chapters 27 and 28.

The departure of *Terra Nova* on the 1st June 1910, proudly flying the Royal Yacht Squadron burgee and white ensign, remains an iconic image of the age. Closer to home, Ernest Shackleton's *Endurance* flew the defaced blue ensign of the Royal Clyde Yacht Club when his Imperial Trans-Antarctic Expedition sailed south in 1914. "*She drew away from the wharf to the sound of a pibroch discoursed by a Highland piper in compliment to the Scottish contribution in money and men.*"[411] Scottish Jute magnate and mathematician James Caird was one of the expedition's patrons.[412]

However, prestigious yacht club bunting was not necessarily emblematic of establishment support. Expedition ships invariably embarked on unsupported multi-year voyages with the Plimsoll Line antifouled over. If classed as a 'yacht', they were exempt from troublesome Board of Trade regulations, so avoided inspection to establish whether they were a *"well-found merchant ship within the meaning of the Act"*.

In the mid-1800s, all the great minds in shipping were focussed on developing steam power, but sail had not gone away. While iron steamers carried passengers and the mail, low-value non-perishable cargo was still carried by sailing ships, built of wood. Most of these vessels were lumbering, low-cost carriers able to offer rock-bottom rates for non-perishable cargo that might arrive a few days, or even a month, late.

But not all; some of the most famous clipper ships were as fast as racing yachts, even by today's standards. They may have been old fashioned, but they were relatively cheap to operate for bulk cargo and competitive under certain circumstances. Moreover, clipper-ships were unconstrained by bunkering requirements so there were no restrictions on range. However, through the 1850s, and reprising the story of the 1750s and 60s, the clipper-ship trade was dominated by the Americans.

The lower Clyde yards, like Scotts of Greenock, were prepared to take on the Yanks and persevere with this useful and profitable niche industry. There was great rivalry and public interest in the fastest passages along the major trade routes. Scotts *Lord of the Isles* (1856) eclipsed the best of the Yankees. Robert Steel & Co Ltd of Greenock was another successful yard in this sector, with *Serica* and *Taeping* (1863) notable among their output. The *Leander*, built by J. G. Lawrie in 1867, was rather special with her fully modelled underbody, as opposed to the parallel midsections usually mandated by economic considerations.[413]

Through the 1800s, until the turn of the century, many vessels were built on the Clyde for European and American clients. An intrinsic element of these deals was what we now call 'technology-transfer'. Young hopefuls from France, Germany, Italy, the USA and far-flung outposts of global shipping, were sponsored through these contracts to serve apprenticeships in the yards. After classroom courses became available later in the century, they also studied naval architecture at the local universities.[414]

Inevitably, and partly as a result, more shipyards opened abroad, and friendly collaboration became stiff competition, which of course, is exactly how such programmes are supposed to work.[415] This liberal policy also meant that we shared elements of our comparative advantage with our friends across the Atlantic. William Gardiner (1859-1934) spent years here, studying British methods and befriending the leading naval architects and yacht designers. When he returned to New York in 1888, Gardiner soon established himself as a master in the 'Scottish scientific tradition' with some notable racing yachts in his portfolio, the legendary *Atlantic* (1903) among them. Sherman Hoyt (1878-1961) was another proud Glasgow Tech alumnus. He too was a fine 'technical' designer, achieving great success in the 6-metre class.

The age of steamships ushered in a new age of fierce competition on the transatlantic passenger trade. For the great shipping lines, business was brisk, partially fuelled by unrestricted Scottish emigration to America. However, the financial crisis of 1873 led to devastating layoffs in the USA, and then the Immigration Act of 1882 closed the front door. It was not until 1892, when Ellis Island opened, that the trans-Atlantic passenger trade began to recover. The Statue of Liberty, completed in 1886, was there to welcome a new wave of skilled immigrants, among them my paternal grandmother and her family.

In 1873, the London & Glasgow Engineering & Iron Shipbuilding Co Ltd of Govan launched the iron screw-steamer, *State of Pennsylvania*, for the State Steamship Co. Reflecting the limited range and uncertain reliability of the period this three-masted steamship carried an auxiliary brigantine rig. Later, the vessel would be bought by A & J Allan, a family synonymous with Hunter's Quay, the Hafton Estate and Clyde yachting. The *Pennsylvania* would serve with the Turkish Navy until she was sunk by the Russians. But first, she took our family to America in 1889.

Great Grandpa George Cullen had been head-hunted as an inspector of coalmines; a new post linked to the transcontinental expansion of the railways in the United States. The Cullen family crossed the Atlantic on the SS *Pennsylvania* in the company of a generation of Scottish engineers and technicians who would develop the industrial infrastructure of the New World. The 1889 manifest shows Mr George Cullen, Mrs George Cullen, their daughters, Elizabeth and Nellie.

However, less than two months after the family arrived, Great Grandma Cullen died tragically of an undiagnosed fever. A couple of years later, George's sister Agnes, by all accounts a formidable spinster, visited from Scotland and more-or-less abducted the girls. But that was not the end of it. A long-running turn-of-the-century tug-of-love over two starched and 'pinafored' little girls. Great Grandpa Cullen never did get them back.

On the Clyde, progress continued. Alexander Carnegie Kirk, an engineer formerly at 'Paraffin' Young's works and then with John Elder & Co, took over Robert Napier's yard. He developed the first effective triple-expansion engine installation in 1874. Kirk had the technology finessed for commercial use by 1881, and in 1885 it was successfully applied to the steam-yachts, *Mohican* (Watson, Henderson), and *Nerissa* (Stephen), leading to dramatic performance improvements. Of course, progress did not end there.

With the conventional steam engine, as used in a locomotive, for example, power is generated in a reciprocating motion, which has then to be converted into a circular motion to provide useful motive power. The efficiency losses in this conversion sit uneasily with engineers. The steam turbine, attributed to Hero of Alexandria in the 1st century AD, and introduced in its modern form by Charles Parsons in 1884, was the answer and became synonymous with Clyde shipbuilding.

While this type of motor was not invented in Scotland, it was brought to such high development on the Clyde that when the changeover to more-economical diesel engines was made, our yards were very late to adopt an arguably inferior technology. Parsons' little *Turbina* astounded the naval review at Spithead in 1897, weaving between warships at an impressive 36kts. Charles Parsons was the son of a minor Irish aristocrat (6th son of the Earl of Rosse) but he made his name and his fortune in Tyneside. After excelling at mathematics at Cambridge, he entered a premium apprenticeship with Sir William Armstrong on the Tyne.

Parsons set up his own business in 1889. He was always happy to collaborate with like-minded Clyde yards in commercialising his ideas and reaping the benefits of his patents. In 1901, the Denny shipyard installed the first civilian application of Parsons' technology in the *King Edward*, an excursion steamer, which remarkably for a prototype, remained in service for another half-century. William Denny was confident, but careful. He constructed the vessel to accept both reciprocating engines and paddlewheels, but the fall-back option was never necessary.

In 1904, John Brown laid down the keel for the *Lusitania*, an Atlantic liner which brought turbine technology to new levels of efficiency and won the coveted 'Blue Riband'. However, interference vibration between the two outer and two inner turbine drivetrains persisted until Parsons could refine a system of reduction gearing. The conversion of the *Vespasian*, from direct drive to single reduction gearing in 1909, reduced impeller speed from 1,700 rpm to 74 rpm to match desired revs for propeller efficiency.

Clyde yards, working in collaboration with Parsons were quick to apply the technology. The *Normannia* and *Louvima*, cross-channel ferries built by Fairfield's, were the first new-builds to be propelled by Parsons single-reduction geared turbines in 1912.[416] Denny built the wickedly fast cross-channel ferry, *Paris*, in the following year. The final piece in the turbine puzzle came with Denny's steamer, *King George V*, which employed high-pressure steam turbines operating at 37bar. Parsons made the engines and Yarrows of Tyneside constructed the special high-pressure boilers.

The Clyde's competitive advantage in the emerging technologies of steamships in the 1910s did not go unchallenged. In the 1920s and 1930s, other shipyards around Britain began to catch on, and for a time offered stiff competition. Meanwhile, the long association between shipbuilding and yacht-building faltered as the two industries, now far from their common root, embarked on entirely separate paths.

CODA: No Free Lunches

Before we leave commercial shipbuilding, we might note that the Scot's barefaced aiding and abetting of the Southern Rebels in the American War of Independence did not go unnoticed. The Yankees demanded $2 billion in reparations, or the Dominion of Canada, but eventually they acceded to international arbitration. The 1872 'Treaty of Washington' acknowledged a lack of 'due diligence' on the part of Britain in connection with the Scottish-built raiders supplied to the Confederates. The UK exchequer was eventually stung for $15.5 million (about £240 million today). Even so, the rise in insurance by 800% put many USA ships into British registry. American shipbuilding never recovered and even today limps along, reliant on protectionist legislation.

---

[374] Reminiscences of the Glasgow Custom-house, Trade of Clyde Steamers, Andrew Scott, Glasgow Archaeological Society, Volume 1, 1859. The *Marjory* was an early Clyde steamer built by Archibald McLachlan of Dumbarton with a James Cook engine. She was towed through the Forth and Clyde Canal with her paddles, boxes and sponsons removed.

[375] The Clyde, a Portrait of a River, 1997.

[376] Two Centuries of Shipbuilding by the Scotts of Greenock, corporate author, 1920.

[377] The Clyde, a Portrait of a River, 1997. We have been unable to identify vessel or builder.

[378] The Development of the West of Scotland 1750-1960, Anthony Slaven, 1975.

[379] Rum punches were popular in Glasgow. The 'Glasgow Sherbet' of water, sugar, lemons and limes from the West Indies became the famous 'Glasgow Punch' by adding rum from Jamaica.

[380] Scottish vessels shipped 4,500 slaves out a total of 3.5 million. However, *"estimating the number of ships participating in the 'Triangular Trade' from Glasgow is complicated by these ships often heading to Rotterdam first on their outward trip. Whilst Liverpool's docks recorded 1,011 slave voyages, Glasgow records show 27. Even this seemingly small number of trips accounts for about 3000 slaves. Between 1710-69 British ships transported around 1.5 million slaves from Africa. Many more of these ships may have departed from Glasgow as the Port Books from before 1742 have not survived."* 'Glasgow and the Slave Trade, a Secret History?', 4th February 2014, 'Glasgow Punter' blog.

[381] *"No such thing as slavery."* In 1778, after a series of court cases – Joseph Knight versus John Wedderburn – it was ruled that slavery could not exist in Scotland. The Court of Session upheld the Sheriff's judgement that *"the state of slavery is not recognised by the laws of this kingdom and is inconsistent with the principles thereof"*. Scotland and the Slave Trade, National Trust 2011.

[382] Did Slavery make Scotia great? Tom M. Divine, University of Edinburgh, 2011.

[383] In England, opium was blended with babies' cough syrup, and Victoria's court was replete with 'Pot-head Pixies' but opium was never legal in Scotland.

[384] The paddle-steamers: *Jeannie Deans*, the *Talisman*, the *Waverley* and the *Caledonia*, the *Marchioness of Graham* and the turbine-steamers: the *Duchess of Montrose*, the *Duchess of Hamilton*,

the *Queen Mary* and the *Marchioness of Lorne.*

[385] Today, the protectionist nonsense of the 1920 Jones Act insulates the USA's shipbuilders from international competition. The 2013 America's Cup teams competing in San Francisco had to gain a waiver for their race craft and support boats via a special Act of Congress.

[386] As regards priority, it appears that Blasco de Garay of Barcelona did not actually use steam power to propel the 200-ton *Trinidad* in 1543. Englishman, Johnathan Hulls, patented such a system in 1736, although his practical experiments on the Avon have not been substantiated.

[387] A 1962 replica of the *Comet*, built by Denny apprentices, is on display in Port Glasgow.

[388] The Clyde Passenger Steamers: from the Comet of 1812 to the King Edward of 1901 James Williamson, 1904.

[389] Composite builds, with steel frames and timber planking, were common from the early days of Clyde shipbuilding, but few reversed the principle.

[390] There are about 6 nominal horsepower (nhp) to today's brake horsepower (bhp).

[391] Another Steam-Boiler Explosion, Melancholy Loss of Lives, Liverpool Mercury, 22nd June 1838.

[392] 'Valeman' (Graham Lappin) has made a convincing case that the *Strachur*, a small iron ferry, formerly operating on Loch Fyne and sold in 1837, could have been the *Aglaia*.

[393] The Development of the West of Scotland 1750-1960, Anthony Slaven, 2013.

[394] There were concerns about corrosion in saltwater and the tendency of iron to crack and fracture. At that time running repairs were, of course, more difficult than with wood. The magnetism of iron hulls interfered with the compass. And for commercial vessels, Lloyds initially levied a substantial 'added risk' surcharge on iron ships.

[395] Operational problems of the transfer to steam: Dundee, Perth & London Shipping Company, 1820-1845, Gordon Jackson, in Scotland and the Sea, Ed T. C. Smout, 1992.

[396] These figures are not directly comparable, nevertheless, the pattern is clear.

[397] The Impact of Technological Change: Early Steamship in Britain, Armstrong & Williams, 2017.

[398] The Screw Propeller, who invented it? Robert Wilson, 1860.

[399] Stevens, of the well-known Stevens' Institute at Harvard in the USA, experimented with helix screws in 1802, but these are more akin to screw pumps than marine propellers and represented a blind design alley.

[400] Henry Melville Napier (1854-1940) was Robert Napier's son. He studied marine engineering under Professor William John MacQuorn Rankine.

[401] *Cutty Sark* was started by Linton's but completed by Denny's following expensive delays.

[402] Around the world, many yacht clubs have repurposed old sailing ships or lightships as clubhouses; most are impractical and ultimately unsustainable. That said, the atmosphere in these old boats is magic. The SY *Carrick* was a fascinating 'venue' before she sank and there have been some fine evenings at the Royal Northumberland in the HY *Tyne III*.

[403] Unfortunately, this project appears to be going nowhere at the time of writing. The *City of Adelaide* was still on a barge at the time of writing. Little work has been done on the hulk since she arrived in Australia and there seems to be no agreement on her future.

[404] The *Glenlee* was built by Anderson Rodger & Co in Port Glasgow in 1896.

[405] Another old-timer, the 4-masted ship-rigged *Falls of Clyde*, from 1878, was scheduled to come home from Hawaii. The *Falls of Clyde* was built for general cargo by Russell & Co in Glasgow in 1878. Latterly she became the only surviving sail-powered oil-tanker in the world. As the ship is 140 years old, and one of the last built of wrought iron, a rebuild will be an expensive undertaking and a technical challenge. The latest news is that the project has fallen through due to lack of funding and there is a danger that the ship may be broken up.

[406] *Thermopylae* and the *Cutty Sark* were of composite construction.

[407] Stephen of Linthouse, a Record of Two Hundred Years of Shipbuilding – 1750-1950, published by Alex Stephen & Sons Ltd and written by John L. Carvel, 1951.

[408] Under that infamous name, *Shenandoah* sunk 37 Northern vessels before re-crossing the Atlantic and surrendering to the British.

[409] *Dauphine* was launched with her engines aboard but not the boilers. She was light but should have been adequately stable. The *Dauphine* foundered as she was designed with large cattle

doors, yet to be fitted. Public subscription for the families raised £30,000 (£3.6 million).

410 *"To complete the representation of stability, as it should be known for merchant ships, it is now recognised that curves showing the stability at every possible draught of water and for different positions of centre of gravity should be constructed."* Modern Shipbuilding and the Men Engaged in it: a Review of Recent Progress in Steamship Design, David H. Pollock, 1884.

411 The Life of Sir Ernest Shackleton, Hugh Robert Mill, 2013.

412 After *Endurance* was crushed by the ice, Shackleton's audacious voyage from Elephant Island to South Georgia in the lifeboat, *James Caird,* enabled the entire crew to be rescued.

413 But by 1891, when Russell & Co launched the *Maria Rickmers,* a five-masted auxiliary barque of 3,800-tons, the writing was on the wall for sail. She was lost at sea shortly after delivery.

414 A Shipbuilding History. 1750-1932 (Alexander Stephen and Sons) Grace's Guide, website.

415 For example, American yacht-designer Sherman Hoyt, who was privately funded at Glasgow, returned to the Clyde to win back the Seawanhaka Cup.

416 Fairfield's yachting spin-off came in the form of Robert Lorimer of the Sandbank yacht builders Morris & Lorimer. Robert was a former manager at Fairfield's and retained a loyalty to the firm, naming his house Fairfield Lodge.

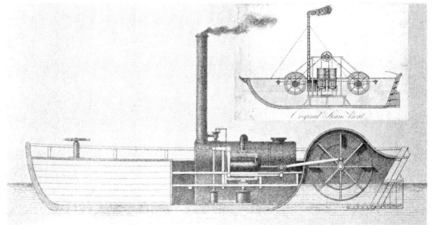

Charlotte Dundas II, William Symington, 1802   Inset: Symington's 'Original Steamboat', 1787

Comet replica, 1962 (original 1812), builder: J. & C. Wood, engines: J. Robertson, boilers: D. Napier

199

Fire Queen, Robert Napier, 1845   Image: Clydeships

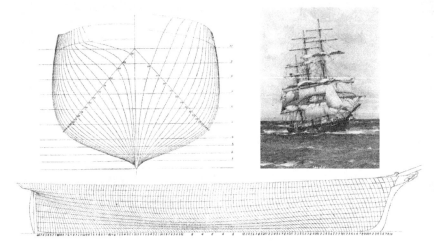

Leander, J. G. Lawrie 1867, extreme tea clipper   Basil Lubbock, The China Clippers, 1919

Meg Merrilies, Barclay Curle & Co Ltd, 1883, leaving the Clyde for Rio de Janeiro in 1902. Note temporary wooden foredeck for Atlantic crossing. Built for Captain Robert Campbell of Kilmun and at one time on the Glasgow – Kilmun run, she was the last iron-hulled Clyde paddle-steamer.

State of Pennsylvania, 1873, London & Glasgow Iron Shipbuilding Co Ltd   The Cullen Family

Fox in the Arctic, a perilous position near Buchan Island   Etching: Captain W. W. May

Fox in the Arctic, a dramatic escape from the pack   Etching: Captain W. W. May

BOOK THREE
Sailing for Sport

Chapter 9: The Rising Tide

There are a few misty memories and time-worn traditions to the effect that yachting of a kind was indulged in on the Clyde in the closing years of the eighteenth century; but there are no authentic records antecedent to the nineteenth century. A History of Scotts of Greenock[417]

Sailing for sport was initially an unplanned spinoff from the more legitimate quest for speed under sail. The century of 'the Georges' (1727-1830) saw Parliament levy heavy import duties upon all manner of attractive and desirable goods. Smuggling evolved to become increasingly profitable, and as often happens when crime is perceived to be 'victimless', glamorous too. As every schoolboy knows, smuggling creates an incentive to design fast and handy vessels, with success stacking up an orderbook of repeat commissions that most naval architects today can only dream of.

"*It is a general stipulation too, in most of our treaties, that ships may sail to, and trade with, all kingdoms, countries and estates which shall be in peace, amity, or neutrality, with the princes whose flags they carry, and who are then at peace with the contracting parties, and are not to be molested, provided such ships are not bearers of contraband goods.*"[418] When it was necessary to describe these boats to inquisitive revenue officers, we find their ascribed status to be 'yachts'.

Clyde boatbuilders rose to the challenge and the success of a local 'yacht' in this hazardous form of pursuit racing could lift the spirits of a community for weeks. Lugger design was an 'open source' milieu when the tide went out, so sequential plagiarism led to rapid refinement before reaching a design plateau which ensured close 'racing'. Shipwrights were open-minded and everyone was keen to learn from everyone else.

These days, smugglers' vessels are still impounded and auctioned off. My pretty little Jeanneau Fun sportsboat, *Gunboat Diplomacy*, was arrested while rum-running in the azure waters of the South China Sea; in subsequent hands I stress. I would say under subsequent 'ownership', but I never did receive the money. The confiscation of the yacht delighted me, until I realised that the vessel's registration documents were probably still in my name. One can only hope that, if there is a statute of limitations in Brunei Darussalam, it has now run its course.

Sometimes, revenue cutters and smugglers' vessels were constructed side by side in the same yard with the clients of both tiptoeing around each other. Otherwise, the builders of revenue cutters were obliged to copy, then seek to surpass, the fleetfooted smugglers if they were to do their job. Yacht design also benefitted. When a famously quick French vessel was finally captured after decades of evasion, she was bought by the Duke of Portland who dissected the battered prize and built one of our earliest racing yachts along the same hull-lines in his yard at Troon, see Chapter 20.

Honourable Men of the North

The Northern Yacht Club was formed by a group of *"gentlemen in the North of Ireland and the West of Scotland who were addicted to the sport of yachting"* If these stout fellows were already deeply 'addicted' in 1824, we must assume that they had been mucking about in boats for quite some time. Indeed, they are described as 'old sportsmen', however, as the sobriquet often referenced equestrian pursuits in that era, we do not know if these gentlemen were indeed sailors. However, while records of organised racing might be lost, there are accounts of cruising, although the term was not necessarily common currency at that time. Like the word 'yacht', 'cruizing' is borrowed from the Dutch and comes to yachting through its use in describing naval patrols in foreign waters.

In Scotland, as in the rest of Europe, recreational sailing was more often constrained by the exigencies of a society on a perpetual war-footing, than the available technical and financial means – a modest requirement, long met. Centuries of war denied our sportsmen the opportunity to disport gallusly upon our splendid waters. However, there was certainly yachting of a sort in the middle reaches of the Clyde Estuary at the close of the 18th century. James Smith made a pioneering cruise through Irish waters in the first decade of the 19th century, in the company of a group of like-minded friends, when he was still a young man. They would later come together to form the kernel of Scotland's first yacht club.

James Smith, the 2nd of Jordanhill (1782-1867), is one of the best-known of the Clyde's early cruising yachtsmen, and certainly the most influential. He is regarded as the 'father of yachting on the Clyde'. Smith was a longstanding member of the Yacht Club in Cowes, sometime commodore of the Royal Northern, and the first commodore of the Royal Clyde. His charm travels across history – a likeable, modest and cultured man; and this he may well have been. However, James was only able to devote his life to science and theology through a family fortune built on the back of slave labour.

James's father and his uncles travelled to Virginia in the 1760s and prospered in the tobacco business. But then, cognisant of the rise of nationalism in America, they returned to Scotland before the Civil War and shifted their focus to exploit new opportunities in the West Indies. They made a great deal of money and all three brothers were able to set themselves up in style by the end of the 18th century, with grand country houses and all the trappings of the *nouveau riche*. After the abolition of plantation slavery in 1834, the family laundered their wealth through investment in heavy industry on Clydeside.[419]

"The glorious histories of Glasgow have portrayed James Smith of Jordanhill, as having limited involvement with the West India firm. This was replicated more recently as he was described merely as a 'sleeping partner' in Leitch & Smith. However, it is now apparent that James was also a leading influence in the successor family firm, and maintained an elite lifestyle based on a West India fortune."[420] The legacies of too many early Scottish yachtsmen, intellectuals, academics, politicians, and even the dilettantes of leading trading families, are poisoned in this way.

James Smith was certainly not a dilettante. He undertook geological and conchological field work on the West Coast of Scotland, and frequently returned to dredge the arctic seas in support of his precocious theories of glaciation in the British Isles.[421] However, his earliest published paper concerned his discovery of a vitrified fort on Eilean Buidhe, one of the three Burnt Islands in the Kyles of Bute.[422] Eilean Dearg to the north also features a vitrified fort in addition to the burnt fortress laid waste by the English Royal Navy when in pursuit of early Scottish 'yachtsman', Archie Campbell, as described in Chapter 4.

James's constant companion afloat was Dr. John Scouler (1804-1871) of the Andersonian (the first technical college, founded in 1796 of which James Smith was later President).[423] John was the perfect crewman, a medical doctor with extensive expertise in natural history and metrology. Scouler launched his career with the Hudson's Bay Company as Surgeon and Naturalist on a mission to the Columbia River in 1824 aboard the *William & Ann*, making calls at Madeira, Rio de Janeiro and the Galapagos Islands.

James Smith lived in Rosneath Castle, built on the foundations of the former home of the Duke of Argyle, burned down a decade before. His first cruise in a yacht of his own was in 1806, and he continued cruising for sixty summers until the season before his death in 1866.[424] *"Most men yacht either from love of the sea, or of sailing, or of the beauties of nature. Mr Smith made his yacht his study and workshop. His freshness of mind and sympathy with youth made him delightful company for the young while to his older and scientific friends those 'voyages of discovery' were equally delightful."*[425]

Smith bought the Baths Hotel at Helensburgh from well-known steamship entrepreneur, Henry Bell, in 1827 and maintained it as a rest house for his extended family. Henry's wife, Margaret, stayed on as Manageress of the 'hotel' after Henry died. James Smith's last yacht was the *Wave*, a 25-ton Steele cutter built for John Cross Buchanan in 1834 and acquired by him in 1851. James Smith had coveted the *Wave* since 1838, when Matthew Preston sailed the yacht to win the 25-ton class at Gourock, beating Smith's *Amethyst*. G. L. Watson notes that Robert Steele's *Wave* was the first yacht on the Clyde with a 'metal keel', or external ballast, pre-dating John Inglis' influential *Hilda* of 1871 by 27 years.[426]

As a keen yachtsman and a man of science, Smith was an acknowledged authority on yacht design and the rules governing yacht racing. He was a good friend and patron of William Fyfe, introducing him to the latest technical advances and discussing the merits of whatever vessel Fyfe had on the stocks at Fairlie. He was certainly a clever man and a gentleman with the common touch. However, he remains a deeply compromised figure and one whom, on balance, we cannot admire, particularly, as not everyone in his position ignored the source of their wealth.

James Smith's nephew, James Brown, was one of the close company of yachtsmen who built villas in Fairlie in an area known as 'Clyde Clapham'. James, together with his brother Robert, his cousin William Euing, Hugh Tennent and his brother-in-law, Charles Parker, were all 'keen yachters' and disciples of Smith. They are recognised here because they did not share their mentor's complacency with regard to slavery. In these years, abolitionists were not universally popular, hence the 'Little Clapham Sect' disparagement. The original Clapham Sect in London was, of course, a society of wealthy evangelical Christians committed to the abolition of slavery and reform of the penal code.[427]

James Brown was hopeless with money; all his business ventures, launched on a sea of inherited wealth, collapsed. James, it seems, was something of an amateur designer, critical of the 'cod-head and mackerel tail' lines and advocating the finer entries recently introduced in steamships by David Napier. But Hugh Tennent (1780-1864), an elder sailor of Smith's generation, is perhaps the best remembered of the group. This pioneering cruising yachtsman left an enduring legacy and remains a household name among sailors today. Hugh took over the famous brewery in 1827, on the death of his uncle, John Tennent.

Notwithstanding the demands associated with slaking the thirst of a hard-drinking nation, Hugh developed into a genuine deep-water sailor. He began his sailing career with a little 8-tonner, the *Helen*, and worked up to the *Saint Ursula*, a square-topsail schooner of 200-tons. This fine vessel was designed and built by Thomas Inman's Lymington boatyard in 1853. In the autumn of his life, after relinquishing control of the historic Wellmark brewery, Hugh and the *Saint Ursula* crossed the Atlantic and voyaged extensively in the Baltic and Mediterranean seas.

These voyages were often in support of James Smith's studies in retracing and analysing biblical voyages.[428] *"The Saint Ursula left Malta for Alexandria, on Thursday, January 10, 1856, and being favoured with fair winds and fine weather, by Sunday afternoon she sighted the west end of the island of Candia, whose snowy mountains stretched for many miles along the horizon."*[429] Hugh Tennent was preparing for a cruise in 1864 when he died, aged 84, on board his beloved yacht in Bantry Bay.

William Stirling (1780-1847) retired early and moved to Helensburgh to focus on yachting in his 50-ton Fife schooner. The *Fiery Cross* was well-known and so was Jamieson, her skipper, who was reputedly something of a character. Stirling himself, however, has been characterised as the most perfect gentleman in Scotland.[430] Today, we associate the 'Fiery Cross' with the scourge of white supremacy, particularly in the United States. But, in Stirling's time, the 'Crann Tara', was remembered as an ancient rallying call for the clans. The last significant use of the cross in Scotland was during the Jacobite rising in 1745. Thereafter, it imparted melodrama to the novels and poetry of Sir Walter Scott, then lay quiescent for 30 years until the Klan, abusing their substantially Scottish heritage, adopted it.

John Houldsworth (1807-1859) was another early yachtsman who made his money in cotton (spinning in this instance) and invested in industry – the Coltness Iron Works in Newmains. John was a cultivated, well-travelled man and an excellent pianist. He combined the pleasures of aesthete and yachtsman, cruising on the West Coast with his many artistic friends. It was an eccentric floating salon des beaux-arts.

Houldsworth passed away on his return from a cruise to Norway. He was Vice-Commodore of the Northern Yacht Club at the time of his death.[431] The famous engineer, Robert Stephenson, made the same voyage at the same time, and he too passed away unexpectedly in 1859. In the press, the loss of these two gentlemen was attributed to the *"exceedingly boisterous"* conditions encountered in northern waters.

Early Clyde Yachting

While royal yachts and vessels of state bedazzled, early yachts were not always masterworks of the shipwright's craft; anything, but as a matter of fact. This would have been especially evident in Scotland, where the new sport was driven by individualists and eccentric enthusiasts, rather than dedicated followers of fashion. The industrial aristocracy of Glasgow was in no way morally superior to their southern counterparts, but we are led to believe that these brusque gentlemen could be genuinely gregarious. Their sense of humour gelled with the hired hands and they were able to share the joys of an impenetrable dialect.

It is also apparent that the earliest Scottish yachtsmen actually enjoyed roughing it. They made do with rough-and-ready vessels, the product of local fishing boat builders who were then still set in their ways.[432] The yachts of the nascent Caledonian fleet were little different from the trading wherries of the day. These stout, multi-purpose sailing boats were the pick-up trucks, white vans and black cabs of their world. The yacht version was better-equipped, better-appointed and generally 'scrubbed up'.

The Highland wherry was an archaic model: *"Previous to the year 1812, according to the Chronicles of St. Mungo, the vehicles of communication to the new port of Greenock were a species of wherry-built nutshells designated flyboats."*[433] Wherries, going about their lawful business and readily identifiable by their distinctive ochre sails, were the only boats abroad most days on the Firth of Clyde when few but the wherrymen dared approach the rocky, and then-uncharted, shores. Wherries were popular fishing boats too, being more versatile than sloops when nets had to be hauled over the gunwales.[434]

However, luggers were faster and thousands of these more specialised skiffs were deployed to follow the herring. But, with all the heavy labour involved in tacking the dipping-lug variant (the tack was tacked to the stemhead), they were well-nigh impossible for short-handed sailing and so less than ideal as yachts. When day-racing 'lugger-yachts' were introduced on the Clyde in the mid-1800s they evolved rapidly to become handy wee craft with little trace of their ancestry. They were rigged with high-peaked (gunter-type) standing-lugs, resembling early Bermudian rigs in profile.

It is difficult today to appreciate just how many sailing vessels were involved in the herring fisheries and to imagine the spectacle they presented. However, comparable fleets of 'working sail' still exist in other parts of the world. While stationed in Lombok I used to take my daily run along the ridgelines at dusk. As darkness fell, the entire Lombok Strait, all the way to Bali, would light up like a magic carpet as the crew of each little outrigger pumped up their Tilly lamp for the hours of darkness ahead. It was always an uplifting display of the human spirit.

And on the Sunda Strait, where we maintained a weekend cottage at Sambolo Beach for many years, it was always a joy to take the Hobie 16 out before breakfast to welcome the fleet returning from a long night spent among the djinns (demons), fishing the weird and disconcerting waters of the Krakatau lagoon (a result of the Krakatoa eruption in 1883). The fishermen would be tired and cramped from their overnight vigil, but they were always game to match up multihulls (a century apart in evolution), in an impromptu race home to the morning fish markets of Labuan.

The arrival of yachting as a popular recreation on the Clyde bridged the technological transition from the antediluvian wherries, with their heavy and ponderous una-rigs, to proper fore-and aft-rigged cutters, ketches and yawls. The first sloop-rigged smacks seem to have arrived in Campbeltown from Ireland in the mid-1800s. This marked a new beginning. Subsequently, handy coastal vessels following this model, with the ability to work to windward efficiently, became common in Scottish waters as both working boats and yachts. Scotts of Greenock, Simons of Renfrew, the Steeles of Greenock and Linton of Dumbarton were the pioneers.

The Duke of Argyle's *Jockey* is one of the earliest documented Scottish yachts in 1703.[435] The 10th Earl was an all-round sportsman and a regular at Newmarket, but his philandering lifestyle, as recounted earlier in this chapter, was the death of him. The Argyle Papers contain a housekeeping entry concerning wages due to James Gordon, the master of the vessel, and itemise the contents of a provisions hamper which suggests passage-making in style. The *Jockey's* inventory included the usual domestic paraphernalia like saucepans, baking tins and a large pewter chamber pot. Like nearly all yachts of the period, the *Jockey* was an all-purpose vessel, in daily use to serve the far-flung interests of the Argyle estate. Her use as a cruising yacht would have been in conjunction with periodically showing the family flag of a feudal overlord.

The first notable Clyde yacht to be owned and maintained simply as a 'big boy's toy' might have been the *Auld Sod* or the *Old Soo* – no one is sure which variant is correct.[436] The *Sod's* long-suffering owner evidently had a sense of humour that would still go down well at the bar of the Islay Frigate Hotel today. We know next to nothing about this boat except that she sailed in the second half of the 18th century and likely before 1775.

This celebrated wherry was hard-mouthed and a challenge to handle. She sailed down-by-the-head and was likened to a stuck-pig by the local longshore-men, so she may have been 'auld soo' as in old sow. However, the use of soo in this context was more or less unknown before 1700 and remained uncommon. Moreover, a 'soo-boat' was a contemporary square-sterned dinghy employed as a tender and towed behind a larger boat, so it is unlikely that the term would have been used for the yacht itself.

Francis Humberston McKenzie, (Lord Seaforth, Chief of the Clan McKenzie) was the MP for Ross-shire, an amateur botanist and a soldier – he raised the Seaforth Highlanders. The National Archives reference his yacht as *Mary of Seaforth*. This might have been *Mary*, a sloop of 34-tons built in Port Glasgow in 1787, which changed hands in 1806.[437] Seaforth returned to Scotland from service as Governor of Barbados in 1806 and would have been 'in funds' and looking to trade up.[438] The McKenzie family had interests on the island of Lewis and used their yacht as a ferry.

Other 18th century Clyde-built yachts include: *The Lady Montgomerie*, a 30-ton cutter built for Lord Montgomerie of Skelmorlie Castle; the wherry-rigged *Aurora* of 9-tons, built for a Mr Cunninghame of Craigens;

and another wherry-rigged boat, the *Heroine*, belonging to Mr Hutcheson of Fairlie. *Lady Montgomerie* and *Aurora* were likely constructed by Scotts in the decade preceding 1775. These early yachts were based on commercial vessels and were reportedly 'short and of barrel-like design'. G. L. Watson described the boats as *"round-headed things, of about three beams in length, in most cases innocent of metal ballast, and kept on their feet by gravel or by iron ore"*.[439] The *Heroine*, as an example of the type, was planked-up with green oak and would have been no lightweight. The *Lady Montgomerie* went 'into trade', for which she would have been eminently suitable, while *Aurora* ended her days as a hulk on Fairlie Beach.

Heroine was one of the earliest yachts launched at Fairlie, but she was surely not the last. William Fyfe's first yacht, of which there are records, was the *Comet*, a 7-ton cutter, built in 1807 for the aforementioned James Smith. The pre-1807 *Heroine* is also listed as a William Fyfe-built boat. McCallum quotes Smith as a client with reference to even earlier Fyfe boats, which were doubtless small boats built on the beach at Fairlie before the shipwrights had a roof over their heads.[440] These vessels are referred to as 'little cutters and schooners' in contemporary accounts. All in all, James Smith seems to have been something of a *patron* to the young Fyfe, and a key client to establish the reputation of the business.

Early Scottish yachts like *The Jockey*, *Old Sod* and *Mary of Seaforth* are all from the late 1700s to early 1800s. These examples were yachts in terms of their function – sailing for pleasure, but not yet yachts in respect of style or quality. Only royal yachts and yachts owned by the great trading houses of the East Indies, aspired to elegance in those days. The Scottish proto-yachts could not hide their working-boat DNA, and as regards craftsmanship, that too was still some way in the future. An early Fyfe was described as being built *"without much attention to elegance or tightness"*[441]

We know of at least two exceptions to this rough and ready model. In 1803, John Stuart, 4th Earl and 1st Marquis of Bute, commissioned a Mr Ferguson to build him a yacht. The vessel was christened *Guildford*, and mainly used to ferry the Marquis and his entourage from Bute to Largs. The *Yachtsman* mused that *"if a yacht be a vessel which is kept for her owner's private use, convenience, sport or pleasure, or for all four, then this boat, by name, built in 1803 might be called a yacht without torturing either language or logic unduly"*.[442]

Guildford was a three-masted lugger, but she might also be termed a galley, as she was double-banked for twelve oars. Her 'curious sails' were made of a *"strong woolleny sort of cloth"*, woven in one of the local mills. She was retired to the boatshed in the policies of Mount Stuart on Bute in the mid-1800s. In 1911, the 4th Marquis had *Guildford* relaunched and towed round to John Fyfe's at Ardmaleish to be refitted for sentimental reasons. It was reported that this beautifully constructed 110-year-old galley made very little water, despite having been out of the water and drying out under cover for decades.

Another 'proper yacht' of the same vintage was the *Roebuck*, a 40-ton, carvel-built cutter, launched by Scotts in 1803 for Colonel Campbell of Inveraray. The cutter was pronounced *"one of the completest of the kind ever built in Scotland up to that time"*.[443] She was finely crafted and well-appointed. Above all, she was intended to be a model that other sporting gentlemen might emulate, but she was not a racing yacht. Both builder and owner were keen to popularise the new pastime of yachting. *Roebuck* was christened with much pomp by the colonel's wife, Lady Charlotte Campbell. The vessel slid into her element to the music of a military band. Charlotte was the youngest daughter of the 5th Duke of Argyle and later became a successful author and celebrated beauty.[444]

Scotts launched just two other ships that year: *Aurora*, a cargo wherry for Neil McKeller of Glasgow, which later sank when she sat on her anchor in Cardwell Bay, and *Princess of Wales*, a cargo sloop for the Scott family's shipping line. As an aside, looking at the fate of the early wooden sailing ships built on the Clyde, we find them ending their days in all kinds of wretched peril. A surprising number were pursued by pirates in the Caribbean, looted and burnt to the waterline. Indeed, a sailor's life was lived close to the edge in those days.

John Scott (1752-1837) built some of the best-known early clippers and the company his grandfather founded went on to build something like 1,250 ships through its long history (1711-1993). John understood the parameters influencing sailing ship performance, and it was clearly with some pleasure that he applied the resources of his yard to building racing yachts. John Scott was a long-time member of the Royal Northern Yacht Club. Charles Cunningham Scott, John's son, was also a founder member, but prioritised the business. Over the longer term, the family were known principally as steam-yacht enthusiasts, but John and Charles played a key role in the early growth of yacht racing on the Clyde.

John built the *Hope* and the *Hawk* (cutters, 19-tons) for family use and the *Clarence* (another cutter, 36ft, 15-tons) in 1830 for Robert Sinclair of Largs, his son-in-law. The *Hope* seems to have been set up more for cruising and the family mainly used her principally for that use. The *Hawk* was John's full-on racing yacht. Most of the Scott-built yachts enjoyed occasional success when competing in the Northern's regattas, but it was the *Clarence* that presaged the potential of Clyde regattas to function as a shopwindow for fast yachts.[445] The *Hope* and the *Hawk* were hull-sisters, and *Clarence* was similar, but a little smaller.

While John Scott and *Hawk* won more than their share of races, Robert Sinclair and the *Clarence* had the edge. The *Clarence* was the first in a long line of dominant Scott yachts, winning more than 30 challenge trophies and recording a clean sweep in her best season. Through 1833-34, John Scott and *Hawk* won the Anglesey Cup at Dublin, the Oban Cup and Helensburgh Cup, while Robert Sinclair, with the *Clarence*, won the Ladies' Cup at Oban, the Kintyre Cup at Campbeltown, the Dublin, Adelaide, and Booth cups at Dublin, the Stewart Cup at Greenock, the Largs Cup and the Dunoon Cup. This enthusiasm for competition triggered an avalanche of silverware, which would continue to accumulate over the next 150 years.

John Scott's grandson, also John Scott, owned several cutters, beginning with *Zingara*. This particular John was elected Commodore of the Royal Clyde in 1894 and occupied the post until shortly before his death in 1904. Commodore Scott was an early 'classic yachts enthusiast'. He pursued an unsuccessful quest to recover and restore the *Hawk*, his grandfather's old boat. After her racing days were over, the *Hawk* was repurposed as a fishing boat, but as she remained a very successful one, John's efforts to purchase her were in vain. When affluent individual yachtsmen have small fleets of racing and cruising yachts and are able to consider the restoration of old boats, these gentlemen are no longer 'roughing it'.[446]

Details of early Scottish yachts are extremely limited. The few that survived until the first edition of Lloyds Register of Yachts are the most accurately recorded.[447] Lloyds set up the Register in 1834, but it was not published and issued to subscribers until 1878. By that date, the wherry-style yachts and converted trading smacks had been superseded by more sophisticated craft incorporating strands of DNA from smugglers, revenue cutters, naval yachts and the pleasure vessels of British royalty.

Robert Thomson, a shipwright at Troon, built the little brigantine, *Pantaloon*, 90ft LOA, as an 'experimental' yacht for the Duke of Portland in 1831. Her speed and handiness suitably impressed the Admiralty and they bought her to deploy on anti-slavery patrols. During this period, the Royal Yacht Squadron, of which Portland was an influential member, collaborated with the Royal Navy to improve the sailing performance of warships as described in Chapter 5.

Sailing on the Clyde might imply sheltered waters, but the reality was very different in the days before marinas. Anchorages are often exposed and sailing conditions can be difficult. It was a challenging environment that slanted the game more towards sport than recreation. 'Handiness' was therefore a priority in cruising yachts. And indeed, the credo of being 'fit for purpose' would distinguish Clyde-built products through the 19th century. The association with a booming commercial shipbuilding sector, as described in Chapter 29, did no harm either. English yachtsmen came north in the summer, liked what they saw and put down deposits. Scottish yards built for English markets and optimised their designs for English waters.

The 'Free Church Navy'

A more unusual entry into the world of early Scottish yachting is represented by the *Breadalbane* of 1844, a John Barnhill schooner, built at his Bay of Quick yard in Greenock for the Free Church of Scotland. The *Breadalbane* replaced the *Betsey*, the first yacht of the so-called 'Free Church Navy' and said to be a modest vessel.[448] This unlikely saga begins when the Reverend John Swanson was summarily evicted from his parish on the Isle of Eigg during the 'Disruption'.[449] Swanson was inspired to lobby the Free Church for a yacht. His plan was to use the boat as a peripatetic manse from which to service his residual flock.

Hugh Miller described the *Betsey*'s accommodations as "*about twice the size of a common bed, and just lofty enough under the beams to permit a man of 5ft 11" to stand erect in his nightcap*". When he viewed her lying off Eigg, Miller thought the little cutter "*wonderfully diminutive, but evidently a little thing of high spirit, taut-masted, with a smart rake aft, and a spruce outrigger* (bumpkin) *astern, and flaunting her triangular flag of blue in the sun*". The bold blue pennant fluttering in the Hebridean sunshine was the house flag of the defiant Free Church Navy.

Miller clearly enjoyed a memorable cruise on the little boat. "*We entered the Bay of Tobermory about mid-night and cast anchor amid a group of little vessels. The water this evening was full of phosphoric matter, and it gleamed and sparkled around the little boat like a northern aurora around a dark cloudlet.*"[450] However, after four years of hard service and zero maintenance, the *Betsey* had deteriorated considerably. She was eventually sold in 1847 for just £40 (£4,100). "*The seams of the Betsey's deck had opened so sadly during the past winter, as to be no longer water-tight, and the little cabin resounded drearily in the darkness, like some dripping cave, to the ceaseless patter of the leakage.*"

Meanwhile the Barnhill schooner, *Breadalbane*, had been commissioned as a more substantial replacement to 'spread the word' up and down the West Coast. Free Church ministers could now proselytise among those outer islands where they could not establish a viable toehold on land.[451] The name, *Breadalbane*, acknowledged the Marquis of the same name, a generous Free Church benefactor, and a valuable ally at a time when most Scottish landowners enjoyed the good life. In fact, many were downright hostile to the sanctimonious agenda of the 'We Frees'.

The *Breadalbane* was said to combine speed with generous internal volume and the necessary steadiness under way to cosset ecclesiastical gentlemen unused to the rigours of life afloat. As 'stiff as a church' perhaps? The new schooner was solidly constructed of British oak, 49ft LOA, with a beam of 13ft 6" and 6ft headroom – unusually generous for the time. Her fixed accommodations comprised a two-berth after-cabin, and two single-berth state rooms. The salon seating could be converted to sleep another six when the boat was in party mode. Once the *Breadalbane* was in commission, the Free Church could dispatch a legion of reluctant clergy around the whole of the West Coast of Scotland, with an annual ordeal to St Kilda thrown in for good measure.

The Free Church Mission evokes the salty yarns of Conrad and the timeless romance of atoll-hopping across the South Seas. When the familiar silhouette of 'God's own schooner' slipped into the bay in the grey light of early morning, it was a major event for the whole island. As we imagine the scene: the sun-bleached vessel brings-up and her anchor is let go with fifteen fathoms of rusty chain rumbling after it. A skiff is slung over the side to take the minister ashore His bare feet are soft and startlingly white. Treading carefully, shoes and prayer-book in hand, he pads up the sandy beach like the avenging wraith of the apocalypse. His self-appointed mission – to spread the word and murder the soul. That is our legacy of cultural insensitivity as we preached our way through the Pacific islands.

Scottish missions to the Highlands and Hebrides were seen as a 'foreign' adventure, and as the programme is understood, it acted as a 'dry run' for future work in Africa and Asia.[452] The only thing 'dry' about this run, however, was the good ship *Breadalbane* herself; more's the pity for the professional crew. The Calvinistic islanders, of course, embraced dry Sundays and loved the 'blessed yat'. At least the womenfolk were not forced to abandon their lavalava and wear a Mother Hubbard – they were already bundled up like bobbins!

David Livingstone, the famous missionary, was funded by the London Missionary Society, but the Free Church would take over and maintain many of his outposts after the great man passed into history. Livingstone received additional financial support from James (Paraffin) Young, the world's first oil man, who appears later in this book when his Steele schooner, *Nyanza*, so nearly eliminated the Fife bloodline of nascent genius, and established my family's proud claim to lead the 5th column of Clyde yachting.[453]

Polar Exploration Yachts

Two Scottish yachts took part in the search for Sir John Franklin. Franklin's party disappeared in the Canadian Arctic while attempting to forge a route through the North West Passage in 1845. The search was an interminable Victorian drama that spurred a decade of risky endeavour on both sides of the Atlantic. Lady Franklin kept the quest alive long after there was any hope of rescue.[454] The mystery is still being solved by stages and the search remains active to this day. HMS *Terror* was found by the Canadian government in 2014 during an exploration and research programme widely seen as a thinly disguised assertion of sovereignty over these remote Arctic waters. The wreck of HMS *Erebus* was located two years later to finally resolve a search of 75 years.

The *Felix* was built in 1850 by Sloan & Gemmel and fitted out as an expedition yacht for Sir John Ross.[455] She was heavily built for the ice with galvanised iron sheathing, but was still on the small side for a polar expedition yacht at just 71ft LOA. She sailed from Ayr in May 1850 and returned safely home in September the following year. This in itself was an achievement, but her voyage shed no light on the fate of the Franklin Expedition. She was sold by auction at Ayr for £755 (£105,000) to Banff owners for use in the arctic seal fisheries.

The *Fox* was a more famous yacht engaged in the same mission. She is better known because of the best-selling book, first published in 1860, and still in print today.[456] The *Fox* was an auxiliary schooner, 122ft LOA, built for Sir Richard Sutton 2nd Baronet (the 5th Baronet of the same name owned the 1885 America's Cup challenger, *Genesta*) and launched from the yard of Alexander Hall & Co, Aberdeen, in 1855.[457] The *Fox* sailed that year for Norway and the Baltic, but Sutton passed away shortly thereafter, and the vessel was laid up and offered for sale by the builders, still unfinished.

The *Fox* was acquired by Lady Jane Franklin in 1857. The interior was completed, and the hull was strengthened to deal with the stresses of overwinter in the icepack. As Lady Jane was now close to penury, the McClintock Arctic Expedition was funded largely by a generous public, susceptible to the entreaties of the resolute widow. Later that year the *Fox* sailed from Aberdeen for the North West Passage. McClintock is credited with substantially solving the Franklin enigma. He interviewed the local Inuit population who confirmed the loss of both the *Erebus* and the *Terror* and described the final purgatory of the expedition members.

The Fox Expedition lived dangerously, but the vessel performed well during her sojourn in high latitudes, returning the crew safely to Portsmouth in 1859. Those expedition members who had not already earned an Arctic Medal received one, and the naval personnel on board were credited with time served. Afterwards, the stout little ship made sealing and whaling voyages under Danish stewardship. She was subsequently fitted out in 1860 to survey landing sections of a Transatlantic Cable to the USA routed via Greenland and Labrador.

Robert Steele & Co

Robert Steele & Co of Greenock were the premier Clyde builders of large yachts in the 1860s. Among these were the 271-ton schooner, *Selene*, built in 1865. The old boat had already paid her debt to society when she was acquired by the Clyde Industrial Training-Ship Society in 1899 under the Industrial Schools Act. The society sought to "*improve the character and efficiency of merchant seamen*", but success was mixed.

The boys had torched *Cumberland*, an earlier vessel, to the waterline in 1889, risking the lives of 390 suspects. Those responsible were birched but escaped prison time. The case was adjudged 'not proven', an idiosyncrasy of the Scottish legal system. However, when the *Empress* was set alight again in 1892 there were no second chances. Fortunately, the blaze was doused with little real damage done, but this time the boys were in real trouble.

The Society's landing stage on the Gareloch became a magnet for local girls, one of the few perks of sail-training; otherwise, discipline was strict. The boys were well-fed and well turned-out, and many went on to become useful mariners. *Selene* survived 22 years of high jinks unscathed and was finally broken up in 1925 after 60 years of service.[458]

Another Steele vessel, the 87-ton cutter, *Condor*, launched in 1866, lasted barely a year with her first owner before she was sold to John Orr-Ewing of the well-known Dunoon family for £3,500 (£389,000). Orr Ewing was on the management board of Young's Paraffin Oil Company, which seeded British Petroleum. Later, in 1880, she would be one of the first yachts acquired by the voracious Clark family. Steele's built the 218-ton composite schooner, *Nyanza*, for the Earl of Wilton, Commodore of the Royal Yacht Club in 1867. *Nyanza* was later sold to James 'Paraffin' Young, of whom more later.

The 163-ton Steele yawl, *Oimara*, of 1867 was owned for a time by John Wylie of the well-known retail concern Wylie & Lochhead, later House of Fraser. Originally cabinet makers and funeral directors, the firm reaped the grizzly benefits of the 1832 cholera epidemic to expand and diversify. Their department store became the go-to supplier for avant garde furniture and all the trappings of Art Nouveau style. In the 1870s, the firm became a key contractor to Clyde shipyards, constructing and fitting high-class ship and yacht interiors.

Other Steele yachts of the period included: the 180-ton schooner, *Ferida*, built for Henry Moore, 3rd Marquis of Drogheda, in 1868. Henry was a dilettante and a figure of fun who may actually have been mad. And there was the 90-ton cutter, *Garrion*, built in 1871 for Thomas Houldsworth, steel industry magnate and scion of another significant Clyde yachting family.

The Fifes vs *Nyanza*

The Fifes built so many yachts over the years that the story of this one remarkable family often overwhelms the wider narrative. Glancing through the boatbuilders listed in Lloyds during the great days of yachting, this family business was, for a time, the most prolific yard in Britain. Fife's of Fairlie occupied a wholly unsuitable site and throughout its long life was remarkably undercapitalised. Yet this quick and dirty 'design and build' operation matched, and occasionally surpassed, the best in the world. Among classic yacht enthusiasts, Fife yachts are uncritically acclaimed and the allure of Fairlie is immune to fashion. There must indeed have been some magic in the water.

William Fyfe handed over the 'unprofitable' yacht-building side of the business to William Fife II (1821-1902) in 1839, the old man continuing with fishing smacks and the like in the meantime. Fyfe's pragmatism might have been better exercised 25 years earlier. He was the man who built the *Industry*, just the seventh Clyde steamship and by far the most enduring of the forerunners. The Beith syndicate, who financed the ship, had pressured William Fyfe, and his brother John, to capitalise on their success. However, the *Industry* was the first and last commercial steamer built at Fairlie, although they did build motor launches.[459]

Through the autumn of his patriarchy, 'Auld Wull' may have been marginalised, but there is an anecdote that suggests a still-active mind. This is a tallish tale, but it is a good story.[460] It concerns Lord Kelvin.

Sir William Thomson, later Lord Kelvin, was born in Belfast but moved to Glasgow as a child. Kelvin can be credited with fashioning physics into a unitary discipline. As a scientist and an engineer, his research into fluid dynamics included work on the behaviour of wetted surfaces in motion that would inform naval architecture, as touched upon in Chapter 6.

Like many wealthy Scots, in 1872 Lord Kelvin joined the Royal Yacht Squadron with the 126-ton Wanhill schooner, *Lalla Rookh*, built in Poole in 1854. This impressive vessel was entirely trumped by his good friend James Lindsay, the 26th Earl of Crawford, also a Fellow of the Royal Society, who joined the Squadron two years later. At the turn of the century, Lindsay owned both the 546-ton auxiliary schooner, *Consuelo* (J. H. Richie, Gourlay Bros, Dundee, 1887) and the 1490-ton, *Valhalla*, one of the largest fully-rigged yachts ever built (W. C. Storey, Ramage & Ferguson, Leith, 1892). Kelvin was a wealthy man, but as the following shows, he retained the 'common touch'.

One afternoon, while out for a stroll, Kelvin met old-man Fyfe on the beach at Fairlie. The two men fell into conversation about what might constitute the perfect yacht. Kelvin took a stick and sketched out his design ideas on the sand. He drew a profile, deckplan, waterlines and sections, all the while explaining to his friend how this should surely result in a breakthrough. In response, the old boatbuilder gathered a pocket-full of pebbles and began to amend the lines. We might imagine there was a running commentary, this time to explain the difference of opinion.

We can find no corroborating details, but as the story goes, both designs were built and match-raced against each other. The suggestion is that these were not models, but little yachts. Fyfe's *Bluebell* was the runaway winner. In the 1860s, before John Inglis came along, it seems that artisans could still hold their own against scientists.

Through the early 1860s, the Fife yard, now managed by William Fife II, dominated the local market for substantial cruisers. There were the schooners: *Wild Flower* of 48-tons in 1860, *Irene* and *Rowena*, sisterships of 62-tons and *Aeolus*, a 63-ton cutter in 1861. This latter vessel was later owned by John Houldsworth of the Coltness Iron Works and subsequently bought back by Fife. Then there was: *Aux*, a 90-ton cutter and *Clutha* a 91-ton yawl in 1862; *Surf*, a 54-ton yawl in 1861; the schooner *Fiery Cross* in 1863; *Xema* and *Leila*, 35-ton cutters in 1864; and *Fiona* in 1865, an 80-ton cutter also picked up later second-hand, like *Clutha*, by Ben Nicholson.

Fife yachts often found their way south, as racing on the Clyde showcased new developments. Buying a yacht in commission, fully fitted-out and 'sorted', as Ben Nicholson of that great Gosport boatbuilding family often did, is simply good business. The number of yacht owners who will turn down a reasonable offer is vanishingly small, and, after the warm glow of divestment subsides, who can resist ordering a new one?

The Culzean Shipbuilding & Engineering Co Ltd was established in 1870 by the 3rd Marquis of Ailsa (1847-1938). The yard moved from Culzean to Girvan in 1883, and then to Troon in 1886. There had been a yard at Troon since 1810, when the 4th Duke of Portland set up operations there. In 1873, the yard built the *Clown*, a 16-ton yawl.[461] During the build, the Marquis appointed William Fife II as Yard Manager, and by some accounts made him a partner too.[462] The 1879 Lloyd's Register had 'Fyfe' as *Clown's* builder.[463] The story is that William signed the builder's certificate, as any master shipwright would, but in so doing incurred the displeasure of the Marquis. Subsequent registers show the builder as the '3rd Marquis of Ailsa' in all his amateur pomp. Fife allowed this slight, so the association must have been financially worthwhile.

William Fife was still on-hand in 1877 when the Troon yard launched the *Beagle*, a 10-tonner, built to one of William's designs for the Marquis' own use. The Fife team took the new yacht over to Rothesay Bay to test her pace at the Royal Clyde's Opening Regatta. It was a maiden voyage from Hell; the *Beagle* was rammed and sunk off Tighnabruaich by the 218-ton Robert Steele & Co schooner, *Nyanza*, then owned by proto-oil-tycoon James 'Paraffin' Young and under the command of Captain Wilson, "*the most careful yacht-master on the Clyde*".[464]

Nyanza, at 110ft between perpendiculars, was four times the size of the next-largest yacht competing. Nyanza is the Bantu word for a large lake and reflects Young's interest in the missionary work and derring-do expeditions of David Livingstone, Richard Burton and Stanley in Africa. The following year, the name 'Victoria Nyanza' became eternally linked with the massacre of every last man of the ill-fated Smith and O'Neil Church Missionary Society Expedition. This retaliation was attributed to the fall-out from Stanley's careless brutality in the region.

With a 218-ton vessel whacking a 10-ton minnow, there was no contest. The little *Beagle*, proud possessor of one winning flag from one race sailed, went straight to the bottom as the only Fife yacht ever to retire unbeaten.[465] In defence of my distant cousin, many times removed, the Royal Clyde had moved the finishing line from the end of Tighnabruaich Pier to a mark-boat off Blackfarlane Bay, apparently to suit the smaller boats. This action by the Race Committee was disparaged in the press as it necessitated an awkward last-minute change of direction for the big boats, which had to sail by the lee to cross the line.

On finishing, *Nyanza* was therefore obliged to luff sharply to avoid a crash-gybe. Unfortunately, the Fifes were in the way and weren't getting out of it. The press observed that the 10-tonner was "*hove-to in an awkward place*". I think we have all been there – hove-to by the line, beer in hand to salute friends and rivals. Unfortunately, on this occasion, the *Beagle* left no place for the big schooner to go. *Nyanza* cut the cutter "*into halves*". William Fife II, his son young William (later to become the legendary Fife III), his brother Allan, and crewman Allan Buchanan scrambled aboard *Nyanza* much relieved, and not a little surprised, to be safe and sound. There was no loss of life, and in our family-tree James Young remains well-hidden in the foliage, absolving his descendants of inherited guilt.[466]

The afternoon's excitement did not end there. Later, fetched-up to her anchor off the Royal an Lochan Hotel, the wayward *Nyanza* sheered across and collided with *Florence*, another innocent 10-ton cutter, tearing her mainsail and breaking her gaff. Practical jokers all, one bright spark went over the side with a lifebelt on and raised the alarm in a theatrical fashion. The near-knuckle humour was not appreciated; Captain Wilson was respected and well-liked. Did I mention that the rain was now torrential, and it was getting dark? Whatever the rights and wrongs, Wilson "*escaped without censure*".

James Meikle, writing in *The Glasgow Herald*, had this to say: "*Certainly, risk to a greater or lesser extent is never wholly absent from yacht racing, yet it is pleasant, reassuring as well, to reflect that while accidents happen in the pursuit of it, deaths or even serious maimings in consequence are gratifyingly few. Our designers and builders, in relation to the smallness of their number, have been in as many adventurers as any class of men intimately connected with the sport, as when the new 10-tonner Beagle was run down in the Kyles of Bute by James Young's large and powerful schooner Nyanza.*[467]

Later that same year, William Fife Jr, his cousin William, and William Boyd set sail in a lugsail dinghy to deliver a punt to Largs.[468] After depositing the punt, on the way back to Fairlie they capsized off Keppenburn. In those days before built-in floatation, personal buoyancy and self-bailers, dinghy sailors had no means of self-recovery, particularly if the water was choppy, so a capsize could be fatal. Fortunately, this incident was seen from the shore and a boat launched to rescue a very wet, cold and dispirited crew.[469]

But all in all, and despite my family's attempts to nip the emerging dynasty in the bud, 1877 was not such a bad year for William Fife II. The Fairlie yard ended the season as the most successful yacht-builder in Britain, with more wins than Hatcher and Ratsey. William's twelve best vessels started 202 races and won 84 of them with thirty 2nd places to boot. The top-scoring *Neva* won £1,350 (£156,000) and the other eleven outstanding Fife yachts were *Bloodhound, Cuckoo, Fairlie, Surf, Torch, Camellia, Cythera, Fiona, Spindrift, Clio* and *Thyra*.[470] However, even such sterling racing success would not have entirely erased the memory of that close run thing in the Kyles of Bute.

The Emergence of a Dedicated Industry

Yacht building became a viable core business in the 1850s. Notable yachts included the 47ft cutter, *Coralie*, built in 1850 by William Fyfe for Andrew Ewing Byrne; *Content*, a 36ft sloop built by Scott & Sons in 1852 for James Ewing, MP for Glasgow, later lost on passage between Montego Bay and Falmouth; the 79ft schooner, *Chance*, built in 1853 to a William Simons design and believed to be the first iron yacht built on the Clyde, and certainly one of the earliest yachts to sail to Australia; the 64ft schooner, *Aurora* of 1854, another William Simons 'iron pot'; and the *Tammie Norie* of 1855, a cutter of 24-tons built at Ayr for the first Marquis of Ailsa.

Yacht-builders active in the 1860's and 1870's included: William Simons & Co Ltd with *Anita*, a 51-ton iron schooner, built in 1861 for prominent Greenock merchant James Ballantine; Wingate & Co with another iron schooner of 116-tons in 1862; and Brown & Simpson with *Mayflower*, a 46ft LBP Dundee-built iron cutter for Colonel David Laird of Strathmartine.

Ambitious builders, the length and breadth of the Clyde, lined up to tender for lucrative private yacht contracts. Some of the more significant through the years 1870 to 1879 are listed in the following box

These included: J. G. Lawrie with *Viking*, a 61-ton schooner in 1870; John Reid & Co with *Leander*, a 19-ton composite cutter in 1871; Charles Connell & Company with *Zampa*, a 19-ton composite cutter in 1871; Hugh Boag with *Gondola*, a 10-ton cutter in 1874 and *Diana*, a 40-ton cutter for James Coats in 1876; A. & J. Inglis, with the 20-ton composite cutters, *Moira* and *Irene*, in the same year; Charles Connell with the *Athene*, an 11-ton composite cutter in 1877; John McAdam with *Quiraing*, a 10-ton cutter Watson design in 1878; Paul Jones & Son with *Foam*, a 15-ton yawl and *Secora*, a 6-ton cutter in 1879; James Adam with *Lina*, a 6-ton cutter in 1879; and John Reid with the 20-ton composite cutter, *Sayonara*, in the same year.

Then in 1880, D & W Henderson entered the field with *Vanduara*, a 98-ton steel cutter for John Clark. David Henderson (1816-1893), senior partner of the firm, came from Pitenweem in Fife and devoted 25 years to excellence in shipbuilding. Meanwhile, the Fifes were still testing the operational limits of a boatyard remote from navigable water with *Melita*, a 161-ton schooner in 1876, and *Condor*, a 159-ton yawl in 1878. Clearly, yacht-building on the Clyde was in good health with good prospects. And through the turn of the century, business only got better.

Henderson's would build 28 superb sailing yachts in the period to 1900. These would be some of the most elegant yachts ever launched on the Clyde, or anywhere else for that matter. Among the best-known were: *Wendur*, 143-tons; *Genesta*, 84-tons; *Thistle*, 170-tons; *Varuna*, 67-tons; *Queen Mab*, 79-tons; *Britannia*, 221-tons; the *Valkyries II&III*, 203 and 191-tons; *Meteor*, 238-tons; *Bona*, 123-tons; *Rainbow*, 331-tons; *Gleniffer*, 496-tons; and *Sybarita*, 214-tons.

CODA: The Last Cruise of the Nyanza

The composite Steele schooner *Nyanza* was a very able cruising vessel. A decade after the Fife debacle recounted above, on the 1st July 1887, the new owner, James Cumming Dewar, and his wife departed for a cruise south, down the Atlantic, and into the Pacific via the Magellan Straits.[471] The vessel grounded in the straits and lost her false keel, main anchor and ground tackle; her copper sheathing was also badly chaffed. The party called in at Lima for drydock repairs.[472] *Nyanza* was one of the first private yachts to attempt that difficult passage, which would be repeated nearly two decades later, singlehanded, by Joshua Slocum in 1896.

In the interconnected world of late-19th century men-of-influence, Slocum met Henry Morton Stanley in 1897, while stopping-over in Durban, South Africa. The great circumnavigator mentions that Stanley was once a nautical man himself, on the *Nyanza*.[473] It is likely that Stanley, who famously met Livingston in 1871, linked up in subsequent years with the philanthropic community of the Free Church of Scotland, who sponsored Livingston's missionary work in Africa, among them James Young, who owned *Nyanza* before James Dewar.

The Scottish schooner visited an impressive number of Pacific island groups, Easter Island, The Marquesas, Tahiti, Samoa, Fiji, New Caledonia,

New Hebrides, and the Sandwich Islands (Hawaiian Islands) then sailed on to Japan.[474] *Nyanza* was wrecked in October 1890, at Ponapi (Micronesia) with all hands surviving.[475] The 18 members of the owner's party and crew then hitched a ride to Manilla in the Caroline Islands (Philippines).[476] In the subsequent enquiry, which took place in Hong Kong, the sailing master, John Carrington, and the first mate, Robert George, were found to have made errors in positioning, but retained their tickets with the admonishment that *"it would be well to avoid like errors in the future"*.[477] The expression 'got away with murder' comes to mind.

Nyanza's cruise, while it ended disastrously, was remarkable for the era. In the three years of her world cruise, she sailed 42,784 nautical miles and averaged 104 miles a day – island-hopping in the Pacific in the 19th century, in a big schooner without an auxiliary engine, this was good going.[478]

CODA: The New Paradigm of Discretionary Spending

Industrialisation enabled discretionary spending, then an entirely new phenomenon. An emergent class of self-made men could engage in outdoor sports. Boy's toys had yet to be targeted as a market sector, but yachts, an aspirational purchase like horses and guns, were one of the few big-ticket items the middle-class professional, or successful businessman, could buy before the advent of motor cars, electronics and white goods. Consumerism dragged yachting from its 'forelock-touching' cottage industry roots. The new clients, from mogul to shopkeeper, saw designers and builders as their intellectual peers, rather than deferential artisans.

Yachts could now be elevated to the status of fine art without upsetting the old status quo. Vessels of the period were incredibly sophisticated artefacts, designed by numerate professionals and crafted by ever-more-capable shipwrights. Floating works of art were an accidental spin-off from the most significant period of technological advance in history, but this digression into truth and beauty, as expressed in performance and aesthetics, became emblematic of what Glasgow could do.

---

[417] Scotts' Shipbuilding & Engineering Co Ltd. Two Centuries of Shipbuilding by the Scotts at Greenock, Offices of Engineering, London, 1906.

[418] The Ship-Master's Assistant and Owner's Manual, containing complete information relative to the mercantile and maritime laws and customs, 15th edition, David Steel, 1821.

[419] The merchant house of Leitch & Smith (later James and Archibald Leitch & Co) operated in Jamaica and Grenada from 1779 to 1867. Initial capital was earned in tobacco trading and then investment in cotton was parlayed into banking, insurance and financial services.

[420] A Glasgow-West India Merchant House and the Imperial Dividend, 1779–1867, Stephen Mullen, Journal of Scottish Historical Studies, 2013.

[421] Cape James, Cape Mary and Jordanhill Island were named after Smith and his family.

422 Smith discovered the remains of a circular vitrified fort about 65ft in diameter when nosing around the islands in his rowing dinghy. The mechanism by which forts were vitrified has long been a subject of speculation and experiment. A temperature of over 1,000°C is required and elements of mystery remain. There are about 100 of these structures worldwide, with 70 or more in Scotland.

423 The Anderson's Institute, founded in 1796, was the first technical college in the world to provide instruction in practical science subjects. It was also the first to run evening classes in science and the first to admit women on the same terms as men.

424 The voyage and shipwreck of St. Paul, with dissertations on the life and writings of St. Luke, and the ships and navigation of the ancients, James Smith, 1880.

425 Memoirs and portraits of one hundred Glasgow men who have died during the last thirty years and in their lives did much to make the city what it now is, James MacLehose, 1886.

426 The Badminton Library of Sports and Pastimes: Yachting, Volume 1, The Evolution of the Modern Racing Yacht, G. L. Watson, 1894.

427 100 Glasgow Men, James MacLehose,1886.

428 The voyage and shipwreck of St. Paul, with dissertations on the life and writings of St. Luke, and the ships and navigation of the ancients, James Smith, 1880.

429 Ibid

430 100 Glasgow Men, James MacLehose,1886.

431 Ibid

432 British Yachts and Yachtsmen, a complete history of British yachting from the middle of the sixteenth century to the present day published by The Yachtsman, 1907.

433 Days at the Coast, Hugh MacDonald, 1860.

434 A View of the British Empire, with some proposals for the Improvement of that Country, the Extension of Its Fisheries, and the Relief of the People, John Knox, 1785.

435 The Argyle Papers, 1734, National Archives of Scotland.

436 British Yachts and Yachtsmen, The Yachtsman, 1907.

437 The website http://www.clydeships.co.uk/ run by Caledonian Maritime Research Trust.

438 As Governor of Barbados, he was a 'reformer' though not an 'abolitionist' of slavery.

439 The Evolution of the Modern Racing Yacht, G. L. Watson, 1894.

440 Fast and Bonnie, May Fife McCallum, 1998. May notes that Smith cruised the Western Isles in 1806 in his yacht, Comet, which was built in 1807. However, as Comet was built in 1807, she cannot have been James' first boat.

441 Ibid

442 Notes and Notions, A 110 Years Old Boat: The beginning of Yachting on the Clyde, The Yachtsman, 16th October 1913

443 Scotts' Shipbuilding & Engineering Co Ltd. Two Centuries of Shipbuilding by the Scotts at Greenock, Offices of Engineering, London, 1906.

444 Interestingly, several of Scotts ships were christened by men, including Lord Carnegie who launched his own yacht, Kittiwake, in 1893. What a cad!

445 Robert's success on the racecourse ended when he was struck by a flaying backstay. The heavy wooden-cheeked block struck him on the jaw. Three operations, apparently without anaesthetics, failed to put things right.

446 The Clarence, in her new role as a pilot boat, was run down off Garroch Head.

447 Lloyd's Register of British and Foreign Shipping: Yacht Register Established 1834. From 1st May 1878, to 30th April 1879. See also Hunts Universal Yacht List.

448 Hugh Miller, a stonemason, geologist and Free Church propagandist, recorded his experiences in The Cruise of the Betsey: or, a summer ramble among the fossiliferous deposits of the Hebrides, 1862. An unusual blend of theology and geology originally written for the Free Church paper, the Witness ca.1845.

449 The 'Disruption' of 1843 split the established Church of Scotland. About 450 evangelical ministers, who disagreed about the relationship of the Church with the State, broke away to form the famously austere Free Church of Scotland.

450 The Cruise of the Betsey: or, A summer ramble among the fossiliferous deposits of the Hebrides, Hugh Miller, 1862.

451 The Naval Policy of the Free Church of Scotland, A. Richie, Podcast, 22nd August 2014.

452 Religion and Society in Scotland Since 1707, Callum G. Brown, 1997.

453 Robert Napier, perhaps the best-known of the Clyde shipbuilding pioneers, was also a close friend of Livingstone. The two men had a keen interest in tropical plants. In Scotland, even now, there is seldom much separation between the Church and men-of-influence.

454 Something like 40 expeditions searched for Franklin over a decade, including those led by Sir John Ross, his nephew James Clark Ross, Horatio Austin, Henry Kellett, John Richardson, Edward Inglefield and Edward Belcher. The search effectively mapped out the whole west arctic region of North Canada. When the story was eventually pieced together it emerged that the expedition had become icebound off King William Island. Franklin died in June 1847, and his crew all died in an attempt to escape south overland.

455 Lady Franklin's daughter named the *Felix* after Sir Felix Booth, who had financed Sir John Franklin's exploration of the North West Passage of 1829-1833. The *Felix* was stove in by an iceberg and the crew took to the boats. Twenty of 26 survived until rescue by a German Sealer.

456 The Voyage of the Fox in the Arctic Seas: A Narrative of the Discovery of the fate of Sir John Franklin and His Companions, Sixth Edition, Sir F. Leopold McClintock, 1895.

457 Sir Richard Sutton 4th Baronet was the father of Sir Richard Sutton, 5th Baronet, who would challenge for the America's Cup in *Genesta* in 1885.

458 Clyde Industrial Training-Ship Empress, Valeman, Dalmadan blog.

459 The Clyde Passenger Steamers: From the Comet of 1812 to the King Edward of 1901, James Williamson, 1904.

460 The normally reliable George Blake specifically sets this story in the period after William Thomson's knighthood; however, according to the *London Gazette*, Thomson was conferred this honour in 1866, a year after William Fyfe passed away. If the events described took place, they would have been in the early 1860s.

461 Not to be confused with the Duke of Portland's better-known 156-ton Symonds-designed ketch of the same name, constructed nearby in Troon, but much earlier in 1827.

462 Initially known as the 'Culzean Steam Launch and Yacht Works'. From 1886, the company was known as Ailsa Shipbuilding & Engineering Co, acknowledging the Marquis as senior partner in the company. John G. Stephen served his apprenticeship here.

463 The Fyfes had become Fifes already by that date, but it is the same man.

464 Yachting, Glasgow Herald, 4th June 1877.

465 Royal Clyde Yacht Club Regatta, Evening Telegraph, 4th June 1877.

466 The author's family's genealogy, as it extends back into the dim and distant past, doubtless incorporates the chronic distortions of all oral history.

467 Leaves from the Logbook of an Old Clyde Journalist, LXXXIX, James Meikle, The Yachtsman 1927.

468 William was an uncle of David Boyd, who would later become a fine yacht designer.

469 Fast and Bonnie, May Fife McCallum, 1998.

470 Yachting, Bell's Life in London and Sporting Chronicle, Saturday, 16th March 1878.

471 The Voyage of the Nyanza, RNYC; being the record of a 3 years' cruise in a Schooner Yacht in the Atlantic and Pacific, and her subsequent Shipwreck, James Cumming Dewar, 1892.

472 News, Shields Daily Gazette, 14th June 1888.

473 There was also a steamer named *Nyanza* on the lake of the same name, but the schooner is more likely in this context. Sailing Alone Around the World, Captain Joshua Slocum, 1900.

474 The Cruise of the Schooner Yacht Nyanza, Southampton Herald, 2nd March 1889.

475 The Voyage of the Nyanza, RNYC, James Cumming Dewar, 1892.

476 Disasters to Shipping, Sunderland Daily Echo and Shipping Gazette, 16th October 1890.

477 Southampton News, Southampton Herald, 7th February 1891.

478 The Encyclopaedia of Sport and Games, Volume 4, Charles Howard Suffolk and the Earl of Berkshire, 1911.

Chance, William Simons, Jordanvale Yard, Glasgow, 1853   Image: Clydeships
Believed to be the first steel yacht built on the Clyde. She ended her days in Australia, decades later.

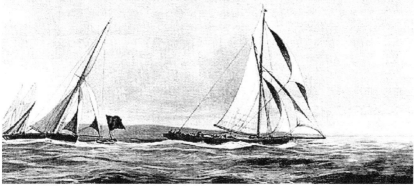

Aurora, William Simons, Jordanvale Yard, Glasgow, 1854   Image: Clydeships

Tern, ca.1870, builder unknown   The famous *Clarence*, John Scott, 1830

Gleam, William Fyfe, 1834   Model: RNCYC Collection

The two models illustrate the subtle shift in underbody from blunt to easy entry over 31 years. Even under the identical paint jobs, there is a strong family resemblance. Note, the change is less than initially apparent as *Fiona* was 80-tons, *Gleam* was 30-tons – considerably smaller with a higher beam to length ratio. 4.4 vs 4.8

Fiona, William Fife II, 1865   Model: RNCYC Collection

Heavy weather in *Chloris,* a big yawl, typical of the 1870s   Barlow Moore, Beppe Croce Collection

Westhill Schooner, *Shark*, in the Kyles of Bute, 1893   Painting: Beppe Croce Collection, Genoa

Wreck of *Nyanza*, 1892   Artist: Algernon Yockney, Fleet Paymaster R. N.

Chapter 10: The Silent Sea in Bureaucracy

A steam yacht of great size and singular grace was anchored far out from the pier, and there was a blank space of water between it and the mark-boat flying a bright red flag. The captains of the river steamers gave these marks a wide berth as they came into Hunter's Quay pier, for this was a Holy Place, the abode of a sacred cow – the starting line. George Blake[479]

Early accounts of yacht cruises describe well-heeled owners and their guests being ferried from place to place, generally looking for something to kill. The Clyde may have been a little late to the party in discovering that type of sailing, but Scottish clubs were in the vanguard of the next phase in the evolution of recreational yachting. The Clyde Estuary became synonymous with the development of 'sailing for sport', from the mid-19th century through to the late-1930s.

As a club activity, yacht racing represented a considerable progression from the fleet manoeuvres and naval etiquette of the Cork Water Club, emulated briefly on the Clyde in the early days of the Northern Yacht Club, before a more relaxed form of cruising in company emerged. This was a participation sport of sorts that placed a value on the palpable pleasures of working a sailing vessel, or simply 'sailing' as we understand it today, but then as now, cruising was more pastime than sport.

Serious yacht racing developed in two stages – initially professionals ran the show and the owners looked on with interest, risking only their bank balance. This is sport like horse-racing is 'sport' – or isn't. But the second phase demanded considerably more of yachtsmen: intellectual engagement, physical exertion and a modicum of grit when conditions became cold, wet and miserable. This was the real thing and a million miles away from Charles II's 'sleep-overs' on the Thames. Well, almost; they still had, and indeed still have, one thing in common – a boozy anarchic sub-culture.

By the 1880s, the perception of yachting as 'cruising in comfort' had been completely supplanted in the public mind by the mock-heroics of Big Class yacht racing. Sailing for sport lit the touchpaper under yacht design. Comfortable and commodious cruising vessels would continue to improve, but the lion's share of design development would go to a new genus of specialised racing yachts that branched off in the 1850s.

Forerunners

Organised yacht racing on the Clyde dates from the establishment of the Northern Yacht Club in 1824, but the first yacht club in the British Isles, the Cork Harbour Water Club, was founded more than a century earlier in 1720.[480] The Starcross Yacht Club, on the west bank of the Exe Estuary in Devon, is also from the 18th century. The venerable Starcross was formed to organise a one-off regatta in 1772 and never looked back. Today, this self-effacing institution caters for dinghy sailors and shoal-draft keelboats. Other sailing clubs predating the Northern include the London-based Cumberland Fleet (est.1775), the Liverpool-based Dee Yacht Club (est.1815), which remarkably has never had a clubhouse, and the Royal Yacht Squadron at Cowes (also est.1815).

Casting the net wider, the oldest yacht club in the world would surely have to be the imperial Russian revellers, a.k.a. the Flotilla of the Neva, founded by the decree of Czar Peter the Great on the 12th April 1718, some two years before the Cork Water Club.[481] Czar Peter's Neva Fleet was a delightful extravagance, almost certainly planned 'under the influence', and just as surely, unconstrained by good council or financial prudence.[482]

The Czar's dockyard started building pleasure craft in 1716, so there were already a good number of boats on the Neva before the flotilla was established. Czar Peter made yachting fashionable, so his recreational flotilla grew to cater for a legion of camp-followers and sundry parasites. By some accounts, the Neva had access to 140-odd yachts *"to entertain people in perpetual tenure"*.[483] The Flotilla of the Neva folded when Peter died. The club has experienced wars and revolutions over the years, but the thread has been maintained and it has never disappeared for long, with the most recent incarnation dating from 1958.

There are some in Ireland who dispute the primacy of the Czar's Neva Club. They do not regard it as a 'proper' yacht club since it was established by decree. However, all yacht clubs are the product of individual initiative (a conversation over a glass of port), followed by the identification of like-minds (an advertisement in a gentleman's magazine) and mobilisation of resources (a meeting where start-up funds are solicited).

There are those who argue that a yacht club is a 'voluntary association of members'. However, such a definition is so arbitrary and open as to be useless. And, for what it's worth, we can readily tuck the Neva into that bunk. The aristocracy of Czar Peter's Russia were not obliged to go yachting, even if it was socially advantageous to do so. And our own royal yacht clubs were also transmogrified into their exalted form at the pleasure of the sovereign.[484] Obsequiousness is integral to that institutional model.

And finally, any member of any club is, by definition, in an association with the other members.

More pertinently, the Flotilla of the Neva was an unconscious forerunner of the 'pay to play' business model. These entities, usually based in a warm-water location with good air connections, reflect an inexorable shift to corporate ownership of leisure-sports facilities and equipment. This may be the future of our sport, or at least a branch of it. The Czar's fleet is echoed today in New York, for example, where the yacht club owns a substantial flotilla of state-of-the-art competition yachts. As we broach the third decade of the 21st century, our traditional yacht clubs, based on individual boat ownership, are in the throes of a slow-motion car crash.

Skimming lightly over the second-tier primogenitors, we might note here that the oldest yacht club in the United States is the Detroit Boat Club of 1829, and the better-known institution of the New York Yacht Club was not established until 1844. As for the other great yachting nations: the Royal Swedish Yacht Club in Stockholm was established in 1830; the Societe des Regates du Havre in 1838; the Segelclub Rhe in Hamburg in 1855; the Associação Naval de Lisboa in 1856; the Yacht Club Italiano in Genoa in 1879; the Royal Norwegian Yacht Club in 1883; the Société des Régates in Monaco in 1888; and the Real Sporting Club, at the port of Bilbao in Spain, in 1898.

Britain's colonies (Canada, Australia, Bermuda, New Zealand, Hong Kong, Malaya, and the rest) all boasted yacht clubs through the mid-1800s to cater for the recreational and social needs of our pampered expatriates, and many petitioned successfully for a royal warrant. Regarding the 25 oldest clubs, just a handful are outside the British Empire and Ireland; so yachting, like football, owes much of its, heritage and arcane rubric to the crack sportsmen of these islands, noblemen, gentlemen and protestants to a man. The genesis of the sport is undeniably Anglo-centric.

Organised yacht racing began with clubs. World, national, regional and sectoral associations came later. While these overarching bodies facilitated yacht racing and have influenced yacht design through rating formulae and common racing rules, they have barely touched on the soul of the sport. Perhaps this is fortunate. Today, the bureaucracy has never been more remote from the aspirations and priorities of grass-roots sailors. World Sailing today is a vast and rambling organisation that lives on overdraft from one Olympics to another.

The Yacht Racing Association

The Yacht Racing Association (YRA) was formed in 1875. The YRA became the Royal Yachting Association (RYA) in 1952 by the command of Queen Elizabeth II (r.1952-present). The YRA was the third attempt to establish a central governing body after the abortive 'Confederation of Commodores' in 1852 and the still-born 'National Yacht Racing Club' a decade later in 1862. Initially many of the leading clubs ignored the association and saw no reason to fall in line with such an undemocratic body. However, notwithstanding enduring controversy on matters of substance, the YRA rules allowed yacht owners on the British regatta circuit to enjoy a consistent system of time-allowances to rate competing yachts and calculate results, and also established a common set of rules to govern the conduct of yacht races.

Scottish yachtsmen, as an integral part of the British 'establishment' who made up the Royal Yacht Squadron, were involved in this new bureaucracy from the first. Later, in 1890, the independent-minded representatives of the Clyde's premier clubs were primarily responsible for introducing an element of democracy in the constitution of the YRA's Council and the conduct of the association's business. These forthright and sometimes 'difficult' northerners kept the YRA on their toes, and to some extent, kept them honest.

While the Scots yachtsmen have always been well represented within the organisation, many on the Clyde considered the YRA to be out of touch with the issues of the day; a view held from day one. The well-known Clyde 20-ton One Design, *Noyra*, owned by Mathew Greenlees, was an acronym for 'no yacht racing association' and was emblematic of a common sentiment. Nevertheless, it is debatable whether the association ignored the concerns of the Scots or acted against their interests. The core issue was simply the matter of centralised decision-making in London. Many Clyde yachtsmen considered that the success of Scottish designers, boatbuilders and sailors through the turn of the century, and the size and influence of Caledonia's royal yacht clubs, belied the perceived vassal status of Scottish yachting.

In 1900, Captain John Orr-Ewing, armed with letters from George Watson and William Fife, petitioned the YRA Council to consider the introduction of rules and regulations to control the scantlings of yachts.[485] To some extent, Scotland's leading designers were more concerned with protecting their business interests than ensuring the longevity of racing craft. Together with Arthur E. Payne, of Summers & Payne in Southampton, who would also submit a letter of support, the Scottish lobby feared that 'lightly-constructed' German imports might show up our more robustly built home-grown products on the racecourse.

Countering initial expectations, the initiative bore fruit with a new set of rules that were well-received in Europe and would influence the scantlings in the International Rule when it was introduced in 1907. Agreement on the First International Rule preceded the essential institutional infrastructure to manage such an ambitious initiative. The International Yacht Racing Union (IYRU, now World Sailing) was finally constituted in October 1907. It was the thin end of a wedge that would eventually split the sport apart, marginalising the core constituency of grass-roots Corinthians from a burgeoning corporate structure of jet-setting committees and messianic chief executives hell-bent on selling the soul of an innocent sport to antithetical corporate interests.

The business plan of our own Royal Yachting Association is less compromised by Mammon and personal ambition. Nevertheless, today, 170 people work for the RYA. At the regional level, the RYA established regional councils, including RYA Scotland in 1971. Whether any substantive purpose is served by this intermediary layer of bureaucracy is a moot point. It has facilitated access to regional government grants, but the question remains: should the public purse (or indeed state lottery funds) ever be used to support a capital intensive, minority sport such as yachting? In terms of community health and wellbeing, the returns from investment in public playing fields and sports centres are considerably higher and more easily justified. And as for NHS trusts spending half a million on a yacht, as reported recently, when basic health care is in crisis; words fail us. But we digress.

The Boat Racing Association

The Sailing Boat Association (SBA) was founded in 1888 to manage racing on the Thames for 1-raters and ½-raters using the YRA rules modified for inland use. The SBA was first of a number of regional bodies organised to promote and regulate small boat racing.[486] The Yachts' Sailing Boat Association (YSBA) was a similar group established in 1890.[487]

Of particular interest is that in 1891, when the YBRA met in Cowes for their annual meeting, they considered the question of lifejackets, citing the Clyde yacht clubs' experience. In the heyday of the plank-on-edge 3-tonners in the 1880s, when *Cora, Daisy, Coila,* and the like provided splendid sport, there was a rigid lifejacket rule in force. Crew members on the Scottish 3-tonners were required to wear lifebelts when racing. At that time 'life-belts' with 10lbs of buoyancy cost about 1/6 (£10). The danger in these boats was not a capsize, but rather *"those who are unversed in acrobatic arts or tight-rope walking"* going over the side.

The YSBA noted that casualties on small racing cutters were frequent and that risk might be reduced by mandating common-sense regulations, such as those tested on the Clyde.[488] However, this YSBA initiative went nowhere as there was no 'decision-making quorum' on that occasion. Apart from the 3-tonners, the Royal Northern seems to have led the way in mandating lifejackets for the open boat classes, but these appear to have been carried rather than worn.

During this period of growth in small boat racing at the turn of the century, the Yacht Racing Association (YRA) was missing in action. The YRA was only interested in larger craft, so early in 1912, following promotion of the idea by *The Yachtsman* magazine, interested individuals and associations like the BSA, the YBSA and others, combined forces to form the Boat Racing Association (BRA). The BRA standardised the rules of measurement for the then fast-developing sport of small-yacht racing, mirroring the work of the YRA for an unrepresented constituency.

It is understood that from as early as 1888, some members of the YRA favoured the expansion of the organization to include owners of small-craft – or *"centre-boarders and other non-yachts"*.[489] However, it was not until 1919, following an impassioned plea by Lieutenant Marks of the Royal Prince Albert Yacht Club, arguing on behalf of Australian yachtsmen, that the YRA was finally shamed into accepting 'tiddlers'. If 67,000 Australians could die for the British flag, surely the YRA could embrace the type of boats sailed down-under?

During the quarter-century of its existence, the BRA generally 'punched above its weight'. It presided over small-craft racing in the UK during an exciting period in naval architecture when fast, light-displacement fin-keelers were de rigueur. The BRA Rule of 1912 is said to have influenced the drafters of the rule adopted for the Fastnet Race by the Ocean Racing Club (ORC) in the late 1920s.

The Clyde Yacht Clubs' Conference

An initiative to establish a 'united yacht club' in Glasgow in 1894 ultimately came to nothing, but what eventually emerged was better in every way. The Clyde Yacht Clubs' Conference of 1898 was formed to coordinate the activities of the Royal Northern, Royal Western, Royal Largs, Clyde Corinthian, Mudhook and West of Scotland Yacht Clubs. There were already more than enough yacht clubs on the Clyde and what they all required was a coherent and coordinated regatta programme.

The original Clyde Conference of boat owners appears to have been less consensual. They immediately began to regulate the Clyde fleet with paternalistic measures that were not always popular.[490] It seems that the arrival of the James Allan's Herreshoff *Wenonah*, while built to the Y.R.A rule, had put Clyde yachtsmen to flight. The *Glasgow Evening Nexus* reported *"Wenonah's success has been a salutary lesson to the conservative class of yachtsmen who object to innovations, since she has shown in all kinds of weather to be the fastest and most seaworthy boat of her class."*

Today, reflagged as the Clyde Yacht Clubs' Association, it remains an efficient umbrella for all the Clyde clubs. The CYCA manages the C-series sail-numbers and their notoriously arbitrary performance handicaps.[491] The CYCA used to manage the Dragon class in Britain and it still owns the Dragon Gold Cup. This oversight dates from the time that the YRA would not have anything to do with the national classes of other countries.

The Glasgow Yacht Clubs' Room was another 1933 initiative. It was conceived to imbue the CYCA with the aura and assets of a gentleman's club. The new 'social headquarters' were opened for a trial period at the Ca' d'Ore Restaurant Buildings in Union Street. The Club Room was open from 9 am to 10 pm as a port of refuge for West of Scotland yachtsmen in Glasgow. Members of Conference-affiliated clubs were entitled to use the room on payment of a small extra subscription.

The CYCC Cadet Scheme

Following a reorganisation in 1933, the Clyde Yacht Club's Conference established cadet centres at both Hunter's Quay and the Gareloch.[492] Cadet members; boys and girls under 21 years of age, were enrolled at a much-reduced subscription.[493] Full members were also eligible for the programme. Candidates were required to swim 100 yards, a deterrent that happily lapsed in the cadet schemes of the Clyde clubs after WW2. A Cadet Captain and Secretary were appointed at each centre to manage the scheme under the supervision of the Clyde Conference.

The scheme initially used the Gareloch class at the Royal Northern, and the lucky Royal Clyde cadets sailed 6-metres and Scottish Islands class yachts. The boats were lent together with their professional skippers. As a follow-up, owners of racing and cruising boats were encouraged to 'sign-on' cadets for the season where they could take the place of paid hands. Reciprocally, the cadets would commit to the owner's programme. In its early years, the programme culminated in end-of-season team racing between the cadets of the two centres, and ultimately led to the better-known British Schools Championship for the Clark Cup, recalled in *The Piper Calls the Tune*, and the Young Cup for universities.

CODA: Shoreline Starts

Shoreline starts, always an anathema to my generation for anything other than beercan races, were first introduced to the Clyde surprisingly late, in 1913. Prior to that date, a starting vessel would always be stationed off the clubhouse. It is a practice which inevitably compromises the clean windward start, although as a finish it is more acceptable. The Royal Yacht Squadron, among others, had been starting from their clubhouse for years. Were this recourse only resorted to in weather that kept the commodore vessel ashore, as described in the report from 1913 cited below, we might have been less antagonistic.

"With a suddenness that was so dramatic as it was undesirable, the wind piped up between Friday night and Saturday morning from the sighing zephyr to the snarling summer hurricane, with the result that while the opening matches of the Holy Loch S.C. on Friday evening were rendered much tamer than they would have been under happier weather auspices, those of the Royal Gourock the next afternoon had to be abandoned altogether. The wind went up from west-south-west to a high west, and at starting time it was blowing so hard and rolling such a big sea up the Firth that everyone was relieved when it became known that it had been agreed to abandon the regatta.

It was not without regret, it is scarcely necessary to add, that such a course, proper and necessary though it was, had to be observed, as the entry-some six-and-twenty boats for five races was the best which had been obtained so far this season, and it had been intended to try an innovation so far as the practice among the more important clubs of the Clyde is concerned in the way of the timing of the boats. Several of the Clyde stations, Gourock and Largs among them, are blessed with such deep water into the very shore edge that it would be such an easy thing to time the boats from the shore instead of from the flagship of the acting officer, that one wonders why it has never been attempted.

Of course, the answer is that it is more sailor-like to do everything from the sea, and a ship, and most of our yachting customs were originally copied from those of the sailors par excellence of the early days of yachting, those of the Royal Navy. On this occasion, however, the Gourock Club people had determined to try the shore plan by means of two posts or flag-staffs close to their own cosy little clubhouse. Mr A. Harvie Anderson, vice-commodore of the club, was officer for the day, and his powerful motor auxiliary ketch Vanora was flagship."[494]

[479] Cruise in Company, George Blake and Christopher Small, 1959.

[480] The London-based Cumberland Fleet (est. 1775), the Liverpool-based Royal Dee (est. 1815) – which, remarkably, has never had a clubhouse, and the Royal Yacht Squadron at Cowes (also est. 1815) predate the Royal Northern.

[481] The first rating rule, to enable yachts of different designs and performance potential to compete, was introduced in 1730. Mr Ackers' tonnage rule evolved from the then current system of builders' measurement.

[482] The Neva's ensign is identical to the national flag of Finland, which must cause some confusion in the Baltic.

[483] Yacht Clubs, Committee of Culture, St Petersburg, Peter the Great Institute.

[484] And not always by petition. The Scottish club, the Royal Western, received the honour in thanks for lending Queen Victoria a rowing boat.

[485] Captain John Orr-Ewing, while of Scottish extraction and a member of the Royal Northern, was based on the South Coast. He was a captain in the 4th Dragoons.

[486] The Sailing Boat Association was formed in 1888 to *"promote the interests of small boat sailing and to obtain a uniform system of measurement and time allowances"*. It comprised recognized sailing clubs on the Thames between Oxford and Teddington and invited *"such other clubs not sailing on tidal waters which might be willing to conform to the rules"*. The association survived until 1948.

[487] The Yachts' Boat Sailing Association catered for *"genuine yachts gigs, cutters and dinghies"*

[488] Notes & Notions, The Yachtsman, 30th July 1891.

[489] Minute by Minute, Gordon Fairley, 1983.

[490] *"The 17ft. class was taken first, and after the owners had given information, and the matter had been thoroughly discussed, it was decided to reduce the sail-area to 470ft², the mainsail, as before, to contain 0.75 of the total sail spread. It was agreed to limit the overall length of the 23ft class to 30ft, and sail area to be restricted to 750ft². Fins, bulb-keels, and centreplates are prohibited in both classes. The rule is to hold good for five years."* Clyde. The Yachtsman, 17th November 1892.

[491] CYCA since 1968. Anyone who has been caught on the wrong side of the CYCA 'performance based' handicapping system which gives identical boats different ratings and smaller boats higher ratings than bigger boats which are acknowledged to be faster, may be forgiven if they bear a lifelong grudge.

[492] Scottish News, The Yachtsman, 25th February 1933, 27th May 1933.

[493] Elsewhere defined as age-group 14 to 23 and introduced in 1935.

[494] Racing on the Clyde, The Yachtsman, 12th June 1913.

THE CLYDE YACHT CLUBS' ASSOCIATION
COURSE CHART 1971

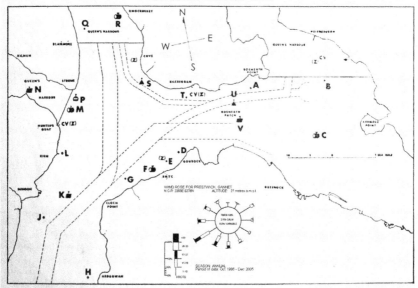

CYCA courses in 1971   Maxwell Family Archive

Note that the lochs are marked out as Queen's Harbours but were not excluded from the racing area. In the Holy Loch, Mark N was the port channel mark in the 'neck' of the loch formed by Lazaretto Point and Grahams Point. The older courses, reproduced on the following page, did not venture into the lochs, although race descriptions suggest that mark-boats were commonly positioned in these locations. Note also from the wind-rose that, with prevailing wind from the WSW, a square beat during a race was a matter of happenstance. The prevailing westerly is redirected to WNW down the Holy Loch and for some distance from its mouth. Note: varying orientations of true north.

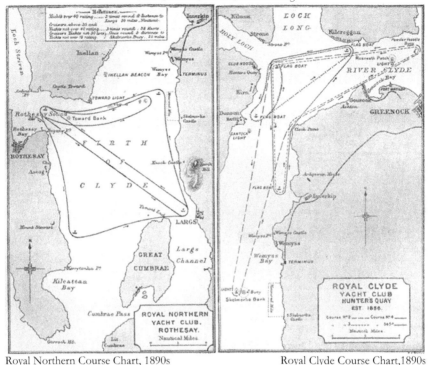

Royal Northern Course Chart, 1890s

Royal Clyde Course Chart, 1890s

Royal Clyde Course Chart, 1896   Charts: RNCYC Archives

The course set here is remarkably short. However, there is a good beat from Kilcreggan back to Hunter's Quay. This may have been specific light airs course, or one designed for the smaller classes.

Chapter 11: Membership had its Privileges

Yachting has always reached its highest point of development in the racing for the cups of the reigning sovereigns, and the same adds a feather to the bonnet of Scotland, for when her comparative poverty and her positive littleness as a nation are taken into account, the success which has attended her in every way in this form of the pastime is nothing short of wonderful. The Yachtsman, 1911[495]

Yacht racing without clubs is much like playing golf, similarly bereft. Clubs are an intrinsic part of the game, and for yacht racing an essential part. That much at least was true, until the 'puppet' clubs of the late 20th century America's Cup years dispensed with the heritage and traditions of the golden age, to usher in a brave new world of rapaciousness and opaque corporate values. The Corinthian ideal has been battered to death under a raft of confidentiality agreements, a fate shared by transparency in yachting administrations. During their tenure of the RTWR, the Volvo management team, less duplicitous perhaps, simply dispensed with the chimaera of an 'organising club' entirely in 2001.[496]

At the close of the 19th century, there were eight Clyde yacht clubs registered with the Yacht Racing Association. The largest of these was the Royal Clyde with over a thousand members and 370 yachts. The collective tonnage of 26,000-tons averages out at 70-tons per vessel. Yacht clubs had sprung up in all the popular watering-places – the Clyde Model Yacht Club (later the Royal Clyde) at Hunter's Quay in 1856, the Western Yacht Club at Millport in 1875, the Corinthian Yacht Club at Dunoon in 1876, the Holy Loch Club in 1888 and the Gourock Club in 1894.

Some of these clubs subsequently gained a royal warrant, but the hierarchy resolved into the major players – the Royal Northern and the Royal Clyde, with all the rest as either second-tier, or spin-offs. This 'second division' followed the lead of the senior clubs, consciously or not. *"At one time, when royal yacht clubs were few and what were called 'recognised yacht clubs' were many, certain coteries in Royal clubs sneered at merely 'recognised' clubs, excluded them from certain races, and excluded them from coveted prizes. And once more the same class, who can only by courtesy be spoken of as 'sportsmen', are intent upon excluding yachts under a certain tonnage from the privileges which the jurisdiction of the Yacht Racing Association entail.*[497]

Membership of the Royal Clyde and Royal Northern yacht clubs varied over the years with the Northern remaining consistent at about 500 and peaking at 571 in 1881, before declining at the turn of the century. The Royal Clyde membership grew steadily over this period to 902 in 1891 and it remained at over 1,000 from 1895 through 1904 and beyond.[498] The Royal Clyde's Corinthian ethos and relative accessibility made it a candidate for the title of the largest yacht club in the world at the time. James Meikle, the doyen of Clyde yachting correspondents, declared that: *"by 1899 the Royal Clyde Yacht Club could claim to be the largest yacht club in the world in terms of tonnage"*.

Estimates of Royal Clyde and Royal Northern Membership 1880-1900

	RCYC			Average	RNYC Members[499]	
Year	Members	Boats	Tonnage	Tonnage	*M. Black*	*J. Reid*
1880	619	187	10,584	57	539	300+
1890	813	213	11,492	54	475	300-400
1900	1,100	389	27,979	72	503	300-400

The principle of rotating race starts among the main yachting venues, that characterised the heyday of the Clyde Yacht Clubs Association, has a long history. The Northern's four-day Annual Regatta in 1835, began in Helensburgh, moving to Greenock, then Dunoon, before ending up at Largs. In the same vein, the Clyde Model Yacht Club's inaugural meeting in 1856 established that *"the annual regatta be held in rotation at the various watering-places along the coast"*.[500]

At the start of the 1877 season, three Clyde clubs (the Royal Clyde, the Royal Northern, and the influential subset of the Mudhook Yacht Club) initiated planning for a coordinated racing programme and a combined regatta to be called 'Clyde Week', later to be extended to the International Clyde Fortnight, drolly dubbed the 'Wee Fortnight', on a two-year cycle. This initiative attracted first-class racing yachts from all over the country to compete in Scotland. Coordinated planning was facilitated by the fact that most 'opinion leaders' on the Clyde held multiple club memberships. We might also note that this widespread networking resulted in considerable double counting in estimated levels of participation, yacht numbers and yacht tonnage.[501]

The Royal Northern Yacht Club

Scotland's first yacht club was the Northern Yacht Club (Royal since 1830), founded in 1824. The Northern has survived through the good times and the bad, through splits and combinations, and the odd takeover to arrive in this century at something of a crossroads. It remains our premier club, but socio-economic trends point towards ever-decreasing leisure time among potential users of such a facility, trends unforeseen even in the 1990s. Serious restructuring is on the cards and its greatest challenges are imminent. These matters reflect global trends in our allocation and use of leisure time, touched on in the conclusion of this book. In the main narrative, the Northern is depicted in its glory days, when yachtsmen had more money than sense, and the prosperity of half-a-dozen seaside towns relied on that oft-used idiom.

Through its early years, the Northern Yacht Club, somewhat ambitiously, encompassed yachting in both Scotland and Northern Ireland. *"It is pleasing to see the honourable men of the north blending the name of Scotland and Ireland under bright friendship."*[502] In these early days this might have made sense. The collaboration reflected a time when adjacent coastal communities often enjoyed better communications than within contiguous landmasses. Even in the days before steamships, travel by sea in a well-appointed vessel was always to be preferred over travel on horseback or rattling along in a coach-and-four.

The age of the steamship would reconfigure the geography of the Clyde and profoundly alter relative accessibility, however, the railway was a prerequisite. The Kilmarnock and Troon Railway, financed by Royal Northern stalwart and long-serving office bearer, the Duke of Portland, provided Scotland's first all-weather land-link in 1812. Progress was rapid and, by the 1840s, a usable rail system served the whole of Central Scotland, with links to London and the South completed towards the end of that decade. On the Clyde, the new railway routes connected seamlessly to the schedules of high-speed turbine steamers. This integrated network expanded rapidly, coinciding with the growth of yachting as a fashionable pastime – hence the location of the Royal Northern at Rothesay, and the Royal Clyde at Hunter's Quay, neither of which were exactly accessible by road. By 1900, there were 300 steamers operating on the Clyde.[503]

The Northern Yacht Club originated in Belfast in 1824. Rather than form their own club in these early days of the new sport, the yachtsmen of the Clyde threw their lot in with the Irish to form a common society the following year. The records of the Scottish division from 1825 to 1846 were lost in the 1930s, but the minute-book of the Irish division survived to attest to the origins of the club in Belfast. A meeting of sporting gentlemen interested in the establishment of a northern yacht club, was held on Guy Fawkes night of 1824. At that meeting, it was resolved *"that the establishment of a yacht club is a highly desirable object"*.

A committee was accordingly appointed to that end, with Mr Robert Thomson acting as secretary, and John Allan of Glasgow representing the interests of the Clyde. The first General Meeting of the new club was held in Belfast on the 8th May 1925, with 22 in attendance. The Marquis of

Donegall, consented to become President, and Thomas Pottinger accepted the position of Admiral for the 1825 season. However, his tenure was short as James Hamilton of Holmhead took over at a second general meeting of the club in Greenock on the 3rd August the same year.

The club's maiden regatta was scheduled to take place on the Clyde on the first Monday in June 1825, when the Irish members declared that "*they were ready to meet the Scotch members in any part of the Clyde*". But, as events transpired, this first gathering of the combined fleets was held in July on Belfast Lough. As for competition, the first prizes offered were for rowing matches, rather than yacht races. The yachts sailed as a fleet and performed "*manoeuvres under the directions of the Admiral*".

The first Northern Yacht Club fleet, mustering on Belfast Lough comprised: *Dasher*, R. & G. Thomson; *Arab*, Thomas Pottinger; *Elizabeth*, James Carrick; *Anna*, Robert Sinclair; and *Ruby*, William Cunningham. All the owners were commoners and designated 'Esq'.[504] For this very first event, spectators were catered for on an accompanying steamer. The club steamer would become an enduring feature of Northern and Clyde regattas over the decades. Today, the spectator ferries that follow the 18ft Skiff races on Sydney Harbour continue the tradition.

The following month, the Northern held a sailing match off Greenock for yachts described as 'wherries'. No winners were declared but the Greenock Advertiser informed its readership that "*the boats started at eleven o'clock and returned in the following order*": The *Brothers*, George Mains, Inverkip; *Argyll*, James McFarlane, Gourock; *Janet*, Alex Campbell, Gourock; *Battlefield*, A McClay, Greenock, and *Maine*, D. Colquhoun, Helensburgh.[505] The paper also described the racing flags by which each vessel was identified.

But the Greenock Regatta was merely "*under the patronage and direction*" of the Northern, and the boats were owned and sailed by local enthusiasts of less elevated station. While there is an element of largesse here, it is also apparent that the competitors were racing, by grace and favour, at the pleasure of the gentlemen. Northern members were still more comfortable with the 'cruise in company' format followed the previous month on Belfast Lough. So, this apparently pioneering regatta was in the pre-yacht club English tradition of fisherman's, or bargees' races for local working boats.[506]

Initially, at least, the gentlemen of the club appear to have been influenced by the old Cork Water Club, dressing-up in faux-naval uniforms of blue coat with turn-over collar, crimson silk lining, braided vest, blue or white pantaloons according to season and silk stockings and indulging in arcane rituals. There was a 10/- (£54) fine for dress transgressions. The club burgee first appears in the signal book of 1828 and there is a painting from the early days of the club, which shows the fleet off Garroch Head flying red burgees with the letters N.Y.C. picked out in white.

While the Northern was established in 1824, the archives of the club include a signal book from 1817. This is the earliest such document in existence and covers a complex vocabulary of 3,000 signals. The number of unique signals would more than double to 6,500 by 1831, as contained in the Royal Yacht Squadron's later copy. This was an arcane aquatic language which would endure until 1896 when pleasure craft adopted the commercial code. The RYS copy includes signals for 14 different types of wine, should you run low and be obliged to issue an 'all-points bulletin' for immediate assistance.

The new Admiral, James Hamilton, owned *Lamlash*, a 51-ton cutter built by Fife in 1812. This fine vessel was the first official flagship of the Northern. Hamilton took her to the Mediterranean in 1819 and indeed had specified gunports with such a cruise in mind. Later, under new ownership, the *Lamlash* voyaged to Tasmania and on to Hawaii.[507] The Admiral led his Scottish flock across the North Channel for their annual regatta in 1826, again held off Belfast with sailing and rowing races. The rowing it seems was a 'members and friends' event, rather than the more usual indulgence of local artisans and seamen. The regatta concluded with manoeuvres under the direction of the Admiral – more Irish madness.

Perhaps this embarrassing echo of the Cork Water Club encouraged the Scottish members to seek a 'trial separation'. This was agreed on the 16th May 1827. The inevitable 'decree nisi' would follow in 1838. The Irish division now flew a red burgee with a harp, and the Scottish division was henceforth distinguished by a white lion. The lion rampart survives within the third quarter of the current burgee, but it is now yellow, and with disconcerting self-effacement, faces backward towards the hoist.[508]

In 1830, there was a perfect balance of members organising separate programmes on both sides of the North Channel: "*The Northern Yacht Club is a highly interesting society. The documents for 1830, with which the commodore, J. E. Matthews, has favoured us, comprise 92 in the Scottish and 90 in the Irish division, with 52 honorary members, in addition to 93 members of the Cork yacht clubs who are also entered in the honorary list. It had, in 1830, 60 yachts not equal in proportion to the tonnage of club, as smaller vessels are permitted.*[509] The Cork yacht club members, who were included on the list but paid no subscription, were an early formalisation of the reciprocal privileges that members of many recognised yacht club around the world enjoy today.

The writer (William Maxwell) noted the high society cross-over with the established social whirl at Cowes, where wealthy Scots and Irish, with interests in the south, had been among the first to take up this new sport of yachting. *Gentlemen found in the Northern club include the Marquis of Donegal, Earl Belfast, the Duke of Portland and the Rev. Denis George and Captain Kean. The commodore of the Irish division is John E. Matthews, who hoists his flag on the Water Witch, a three-masted schooner of 73-tons; and the Duke of Portland, in his Clown, a ketch of 156-tons, still, we believe, presides over the Scottish division.*"[510]

After separation, independence from the colonial baggage of the Irish aristocracy allowed the emergence of an indigenous yacht club tradition on the Clyde. "*Certainly, we are neither Corsairs or Buccaneers, but we have all their mirth and freedom without the smallest oppression of conscience.*"[511] Perhaps not. The fourth day of the Northern's 1835 regatta was devoted to a passage from Dunoon to Largs, during which manoeuvres were carried out under the orders of the Commodore. The buccaneers meekly went through "*several very beautiful evolutions*". And for this we cannot blame the Irish, or for that matter the Dutch before them who dreamt all this nonsense up.

We like to think the culture that evolved became a little more open-hearted, and indeed open-minded, than parallel developments across the North Channel. By 1843, the Royal Saint George Club in Dún Laoghaire claimed to have "*some 400 Irish noblemen and gentlemen, all of them protestants, of course*". We may reasonably doubt the noble Anglo-Irish had much in common with the bluff self-made Scots yachtsmen, unfortunate to have made their fortunes 'in trade'!

Not all of the Scots' new ideas would endure. In 1827, steamers were included in the Northern's regatta programmes on the Clyde. The first vessel to win the steam-boat cup was David Napier's *Clarence*. Captain John Turner's *Helensburgh* was second. In July 1835, while the *Clarence* was preparing for another race, a fatal boiler explosion occurred on board one of her rivals, the *Earl Grey*, moored alongside at Greenock quay. That explosion killed six persons and twenty were injured. From the date of that incident, there is no record of steamers taking part in the Clyde regattas.[512]

The Northern gained a royal warrant on the 10th May 1830, securing the coveted prefix along with the right to fly the blue ensign of Her Majesty's Fleet.[513] Thus, it became the Royal Northern Yacht Club. *Hunt's* had this to say: "*This club is, we fear, not sufficiently noticed in England, but whoever pays a visit to the Clyde, will there find a fleet of first-rate yachts sailing under a blue burgee, (having the device of a crown and anchor,) as fit as any at Cowes to make a passage with rapidity, and with comfort to all on board, to any part of the known world*".

It was not uncommon for clubs to gain royal warrants just a few years after their inception; such warrants could be issued or denied on a whim. The Royal West of Scotland Amateur Boat Club can perhaps boast the best wheeze. That club was granted its charter in 1885 after furnishing "*the handsomest gig procurable in the West of Scotland*" for the pleasure of Queen Victoria during her summer tour of the Highlands. The gig was "*rowed through the still waters of Loch Maree by six stalwart Highlanders*".[514]

The Northern's membership was about 150 in the 1830s, with fifty or so yachts on the club list. Among the most impressive were the Duke of Portland's ketch, the *Clown*, 156 tons; the Duke of Buccleuch's cutter, *Flower of Yarrow*, 145 tons; John Scott's cutter, *Lufra*, 81 tons; Robert Meikles's schooner, *Crusader*, 126 tons; and Lewis Upton's cutter, *Briton*, 91 tons.[515] The first steam yachts joined the fleet in 1855 and grew into a private navy. All the well-known racing yacht owners maintained steam-yachts. The 4th Duke of Portland 1768-1854), Commodore of the RNYC from 1834-53, was a prime mover. Sir Henry, as he was known, was also an early sponsor of one-design racing through his private club at Troon.

The following account of a Royal Northern Regatta off Helensburgh, published in the *Caledonian Mercury* in 1836, describes a long-vanished world of style and privilege: "*On Monday the weather was calm and fine, and the placid waters of the Clyde were studded with craft of every description and size, from the gallant bark, with her graceful lines and swelling sails, to the tiny cock-boat* (yacht tender), *presenting a scene of animation and beauty at once exhilarating and refreshing.*" The splendid rituals may be long-gone, but the Clyde in high summer is still a 'painted ocean' that taxes patience and rewards bold strategies.

This account is also one of the first which emphasises the spectacle of yachting as a spectator sport. Entertainment for the masses may have been a collateral benefit, but it distinguished the first century of Clyde yachting, as discussed in Chapter 17. "*The pebbly shore, along which were stationed groups of delighted spectators, presented a splendid and picturesque panorama, was doubly enhanced by the romantic scenery landward, whilst the Clyde – the majestic Clyde – cradled in slumber, she lay like a queen. The pleasure-boats and steamers plying round and through the fleet, crowded with fashionable company, and gaily decorated with flags and streamers, their snow-white sails glittering in the sun had a very pleasing effect.*"

Fifty years later in the 1870s, the Royal Clyde was chartering its own steamer, usually the *Duchess of Hamilton*, cautiously threading her passage through the fleet. Her taciturn Highland skipper was famously courteous, being acutely conscious of his vessel's wind-shadow and wake, and her effect on the racing yachts. Meanwhile, ashore, "*the coastwise hotels and clubhouses bright with hospitality; the seaside castles and villas crammed with guests and their numerous body-servants; bands playing, coloured burgees streaming in the wind, and the bars of pierhead pubs loud with the boastings of canvassing the niceties of the day's racing.*"[516] It all sounds tremendous fun!

Returning to Helensburgh in 1836: "*At half-past twelve the fleet assembled, and a little after that period the Vice Commodore, John Cross Buchanan was received on board the Orion* (the RNYC club-boat at that time)*; where he hoisted his pennant, under a salute of nineteen guns, the band the while playing 'God save the King'. Previous to twelve o'clock there was not a breath of wind stirring – in fact, it was a dead calm; but shortly after that time a light breeze sprung up from the east, to the no small delight of the yachters.*"[517] Afterwards we understand that the 'yachters' and their friends usually retired to Bath's Inn, where 'Smith of Jordanhill' (a name always geographically qualified) 'in the chair', and Provost Bain, as the croupier, would preside over the gathering.[518] Garrulous toast succeeded garrulous toast and hilarity prevailed until the wee small hours.

The Irish branch of the Northern was dissolved two years later in May 1838, and the balance of funds – £14 17/2 (£165) transferred to the Scottish Branch.[519] This might be the first and last time we got one over on our uber-competitive Irish neighbours. No matter, as recreational yachting grew there was more than enough demand for separate infrastructure on both sides of the North Channel. The Celtic bond is still strong; Clyde sailors happily endure the featureless and unpleasant slog across the North Channel for the warm welcome on arrival at Bangor, cognisant they will face an equally featureless and unpleasant slog back home.

The race to Ireland commands such fortitude among the 'rail fodder' only because a fine welcome is guaranteed at the Royal Ulster Yacht Club, which closet-Glaswegian, Tommy Lipton, used as a vehicle for his America's Cup Challenges. The Royal Ulster was established in 1866 and the Royal North of Ireland Yacht Club was founded in 1899, when two Belfast sailing clubs from the early 1890s amalgamated. Sadly, standards have slipped in the Emerald Isle. The latest sailing instructions for the North Channel Race include the advice that "*the dress code has been relaxed to allow smart denim.*" Cowboy breeks on a yacht? 'Say it aint' so Joe.'

Bells Life described the Royal Northern's 1850 regatta thus: "*The Firth of Clyde presented an uncommonly gay appearance, from the large number of handsome vessels cruising about in all directions, and the many spectators assembled on shore.*"[520] The 1852 regatta, held off Largs, would have presented a similar spectacle. On that occasion, of interest is that a 'first prize' of 50 guineas (£7,270) was on offer for the Big Class, a 'second prize' of 20 guineas (£2,910) for the next size down and a 'third prize', also of 20 guineas, for the winner of the small boat class. Generous indeed, although as the big boats did not finish their course before the fixed finishing time of 8.00pm, the club realised a useful saving. In 1852, the RNYC joining free was £5 (£690), with an annual subscription of £3 (£420).[521]

Generous prize money was not enough to impress J. D. Bell, writing incognito in *Hunt's* in 1865. "*The Royal Northern has done honourable service in vindicating the taste, the wealth and the hardihood of our titled and untitled aristocracy; but the influence of this club was hardly felt beyond the class who liked to own a floating palace and who loved to command a crew. To take an occasional turn at the helm, corroborate his captain's notions about the weather and the trim of the craft, smoke cigars and drink champagne constituted a sufficiently onerous round of duties for a cruise, and those best acquainted with the habits of the 'northern' yachtsmen will be able to recognise the portrait.*" This gratuitous slight cannot have been welcomed, but it was easily ignored.

But then *Hunt's* pitched in again the following year with a more germane criticism: "*The club-yacht belonging to the Royal Northern may be an enjoyable sort of thing to the few who can secure its use, and afford the cost of it, but is by no means a substitute for a club-house, where members could associate, and reciprocate information, and where the business of the club might be transacted.*"[522] *Hunt's* advice was ignored. The Northern was content squatting in Largs. After all, it had originally alternated meetings between Belfast Lough and Oban. It would be another twelve years before the Northern acquired a clubhouse in Rothesay.

Meanwhile, the institution thrived, as demonstrated in this infamous debacle. When the RNYC mark boat at Little Cumbrae drifted onto the beach, only the *Meteor's* pilot, Archie Wright, had the wit to circumnavigate the little island. Unlike Eric Morecambe, not only did the *Meteor* round all the marks, but she also rounded them all in the prescribed order. So delighted were the owner's party that they drank all the champagne in the White Hart Hotel. And it has to be said that, as the regular Glasgow rendezvous of the Northern, the White Hart was lavishly stocked.[523]

The Northern secured rented accommodation on the idyllic Isle of Bute in 1878, shadowing the Royal Clyde's move down-river to Hunter's Quay the year before. During their early years on Bute, the Northern enjoyed the ebullient contributions of Alexander Bannatyne Stewart, a flag officer of the club.[524] The club's first regattas in Rothesay Bay culminated in a magnificent fireworks display set off from the deck of Stewart's steam yacht. His statue still presides over the Rothesay seafront.

Early Clyde yachtsmen were certifiable pyromaniacs. On another occasion, the Clyde fleet was mustered in Loch Ryan, ostensibly on regatta business. Archie Campbell, of the 1850 Inman schooner, *Claymore*, rowed over to Mr Arbuthnot's *Mavis* to offer his condolences after an explosion of gunpowder and fireworks had wrecked her cabins. During Archie's short absence, an identical blast blew the doors off his own boat!

Reminiscing with James Meikle, William Fife recalled the high jinks he witnessed as a boy at Largs: "*the ramrod was omitted to be removed from the*

Commodore's starting cannon. The gun being discharged, the stick went flying amongst a group of men who were busily hoisting a cask of whisky on board, and then through the good new mainsail of a smart cutter called Echo. Happily, no one was injured, although the men in their fright let the precious keg fall into the sea".[525]

The Northern occupied a suite of clubrooms on Craigmore Road with a sea view over Rothesay Bay on a year-to-year tenancy. Catering was provided by the Glenburn Hotel next door. It was a flexible arrangement that left the club free from onerous commitments – so much so that, at the AGM on 30th December 1893, the club reported a healthy balance of £6,897 (£890,000), invested in securities.

However, this happy state of affairs paled beside the Royal Clyde. Clyde members both owned a magnificent clubhouse at Hunter's Quay, and boasted almost as much money in the bank, with reserves of £6,353 (£819,000). Consequently, many of the Northern's more progressive members thought that their accumulated capital surplus should be invested in a permanent home. But the cautious old guard held sway and the Northern would remain footloose and fancy-free for decades. The institution eventually moved to the Gareloch in 1937, two years after the new pier brought steamer services to Rhu.

"The change is to permit quicker road travel to and from the coast by cutting out the steamer crossing involved in the journey to Rothesay. It does not, however, affect the venue of the club's full-day fixtures, which will be still held over the old courses between Bute and Ayrshire. Evening races to take the place of the fixtures of the Gareloch Yacht Club, which voluntarily disbanded when the larger club invaded their territory."[526]

The new Royal Northern clubhouse was the seaside villa, 'Ardenvohr', which offered splendid premises and generous grounds, with the lawns sweeping down to excellent anchorages on both sides of Rhu spit. Ardenvohr was named after the Knight of Ardenvohr, who was pestered to death by Sir Dugald Dalgetty – in the fertile mind of Sir Walter Scott.

The Northern has happily remained immune to the mythical 'Legend of Montrose'. While the institution was surely eclipsed by the Royal Clyde in the years before the Great War, it endured to absorb the dwindling membership of its rival in 1978.

The Royal Eastern Yacht Club

In 1845, Scotland had two royal yacht clubs – the Royal Northern, a conventional club dating from 1824, and the Royal Eastern, a facet of ego which had more in common with Peter the Great's Flotilla of the Neva. The Eastern was ostensibly established by a meeting in Edinburgh in December 1835.[527] However, the Duke of Buccleuch was then developing Granton Harbour, and being a sporting gentleman of means and some considerable influence, thought that he should have a resident yacht club to kick off the venture in style.[528] The Yacht Club Costa Smeralda was similarly established at Porto Cervo, Sardinia in 1967 by the Aga Khan. Unlikely as it may seem today, Granton became equally glamorous for a time.

The Duke's club was constituted on 30th March 1836 as the Eastern Regatta Club. Just a few weeks later, Buccleuch prevailed on his friend King William IV to become Patron, and the little club became the Royal Eastern Yacht Club. Like instant coffee – just add water and there you have it, even if it bears no relationship to the real thing. The *Eastern Regatta Register* declared that the club would promote *"aquatic amusement"* among the *"seafaring population of the Firth of Forth"* through an Easter Regatta.[529]

Edinburgh in March is not for the faint-hearted. One early spring in 1971 the Aberdeen University Sailing Team visited Granton. The Arctic weather recalled Shackleton's epic voyage from Elephant Island to South Georgia in the converted lifeboat, *James Caird*, back in 1916. Not being stranded in the Antarctic, we bought beers; we played cards; we bought more beers and eventually we went home with dry feet. Nineteenth century yachtsmen were surely made of sterner stuff.

The Eastern's maiden regatta 'proper' on the Firth of Forth was a three-day event at Leith in July 1836. The Forth and Clyde Canal Company supported the event by inviting Clyde yachts, going to or from the regatta, to pass through the canal toll-free. As reported at the time: *"Altogether, what with the racing, and the public breakfast, and the dinner, and the ball, 'all went merry as a marriage bell'."* *Gleam*, a cutter of 30-tons sailed by J. C. Buchanan, won the main event. There were sailing races and rowing matches for the local fishermen and boatmen. Such side shows were a common adjunct to regattas all around our coasts for many years.

The Royal Eastern soon lapsed into a gentleman's social club with clubrooms on Princes Street. The sailing programme was limited to an annual regatta. The REYC history records that the club *"fell on hard times in the late 19th century and sold its assets on Princes Street and became a club in name only until the last three members and its remaining assets were absorbed by the Royal Forth Yacht Club in 1969".*[530] There is something terribly poignant about the reference to the 'last three members', conjuring up an image of these impossibly ancient old codgers waffling contentedly into oblivion through a cloud of cigar smoke. Surely the Forth Corinthian club should have made a move on these gentlemen? The reward for three double brandies would have been the right to fly the coveted blue ensign of royal patronage.

So, the current Royal Forth Yacht Club, dating from 1886, only incorporated the old Eastern Club in 1969, but in the interval, it had seen institutional change. Granton Yacht Club was established in 1868 and became the Forth Yacht Club in 1872. With the support of the ubiquitous Duke of Buccleuch, Queen Victoria gave it her blessing in 1883 and it became the Royal Forth Yacht Club. Granton was a busy little harbour during the last decades of the 19th century. It was a period of strong growth, balancing niche interests with incompatible objectives and social aspirations but also, unfortunately, a time of pointless institutional change and dilution of efforts.

The Almond Yacht Club was established at Granton in 1897. This lesser-known society is not to be confused with the charming Cramond Boat Club, which races dinghies on the river Almond. The Almond Yacht Club sailed alongside the Royal Forth for many years and has been characterised as a stronghold of 'active sailors', in withering comparison to the RFYC. However, many inter-club matches were held between the Royal Forth and the Almond, so there must have been genuine sailors within the ranks of both. The two clubs amalgamated in 1957.

Granton Harbour is currently owned by the Forth Ports Authority. There has been infilling over the years, but now with unrealised development plans going back to 1998, the harbour has been rebranded 'Edinburgh Marina', and forms part of an ambitious 346-acre 'Edinburgh Waterfront' site that stretches for two miles along the coast. With 7,500 new homes in prospect, it is obvious where the city's priorities lie.[531] However, sailors might be reassured that Camper & Nicholsons Marinas will design, commission, manage and operate the new harbour.

The Forth Corinthian Yacht Club is entirely separate. It was formed at the Granton Hotel in 1880, and today shares the harbour with the Royal Forth. There was a hiatus of 73-years when the Corinthians removed to Reform Club-type premises in Central Edinburgh in 1895. They returned to the 'scene of the crime' seven decades later, to occupy the former Harbour Master's house and office at Granton in 1968. This is now a more affordable, 'family friendly' club, according to its current management.[532]

Notwithstanding all this worthy activity, the Firth of Forth has never been a major yachting locus, although over the years there have been competitive inshore fleets supported by the wealth of financiers, lawyers, accountants, doctors and other suited and booted professional men bound by their employment to the capital city. The Forth *"has serious disadvantages as a yachting centre, being favoured neither by nature nor circumstances as is the Firth of Clyde, which absorbs all yachting interests"*.[533]

Nevertheless, sailing on the Forth today is supported by a number of which are well-run, if not immune to the decline of club culture affecting all UK yacht clubs. Sadly, the Soling, Dragon, and IOD fleets that marked the Forth out as a hotbed of one-design racing are now gone. Serious racing has given way to all-comers events and knockabout classes. East coasters compete in H-boats, Hunter 707s and handicap fleets.

The Royal Clyde Yacht Club

The Clyde Model Yacht Club was initially formed to give the owners of smaller yachts a voice and a home. The Royal Northern would not accept yachts of less than 8-tons, so the enthusiastic owners of the little boats formed this new club in 1856. Indeed, *Cruise in Company* – the history of the RCYC, noted a *"critical if not positively hostile attitude"* to the Royal Northern. The authors continued, there were *"subtle expressions of a social conflict"*. When we consider that the founding membership included among its ranks, shopkeepers and tradesmen as well as professional people and wealthy merchants, this is understandable.

> The founder-members included: James Sutherland, *Plumber*; James Rankine, *Builder*; John Ure, *Flour Merchant*; James Easton, *Designer*; Thomas Falconer, *Warehouseman*; William McCue, *Fish Merchant*; Alexander Woodside, *Accountant*; Robert McIntosh, *Leather Merchant*; James Grant, *Builder*; James and Andrew Spencer, *Ironmongers*; James Munn, *Agent*; Robert Thomson, *Writer*; Archibald Kennedy, *Wholesale Stationer and Printer*; Captain Small, of Andrew Small & Co, *Ship Chandlers*; John and Richard Ferguson, *Ironmongers and Weighing Machine Dealers*. The influential and popular pioneer of small yacht cruising, James Smith of Jordanhill, was to be Commodore.[534]

Modest beginnings notwithstanding, a good number of these 'humble' tradesmen went on to become successful in business and their families 'weel kent'; this socio-economic trajectory cannot have been unrelated to their membership of the club. The West of Scotland business community was, and to some extent remains, under the influence of the Freemasons, the Palmerston Whigs, and the Church of Scotland. Rule XX of the new club declared *"that no political or theological subject may be discussed at any meeting."* This must have been a breath of fresh air, as the Victorians were already burdened with a surfeit of jingoism: *"The yacht clubs, by keeping alive this feeling, feed the patriotism, and uphold, with just ambition, our hopes, our honours, and our fame."*[535]

Through the good offices of the Duke of Argyle, the Clyde Club obtained an Admiralty warrant in 1857, allowing members to fly the blue ensign with their burgee, the latter being also blue, with a crest featuring a red lion on a yellow shield. However, members had to wait another 15 years before they achieved the 'Royal' prefix and were allowed the privilege of placing a crown over the lion's head in the burgee crest.[536] The pursuit of this honour reflected a rising awareness of 'status' and the value of social entrée among the membership. In 1858, the case for the 'common man' took a further knock when three handsome steam yachts turned up at Rothesay to act as motherships for their owners' racing boats. On the positive side, the Royal Northern was now forced to take notice of the upstart club and confer with its members as equals.

The Clyde Model Yacht Club's over-eager quest to gain the essential cachet of a 'royal' prefix might have been based on the atypical experience of the Royal Eastern. In fact, the committee had followed advice from contacts in the Royal Mersey Yacht Club. It must have been a convivial and well-lubricated evening with the Scousers to precipitate the direct course of action that would cause so much embarrassment. At a meeting on 1st April 1863, it was announced that following a petition from the club, Lord Palmerston had granted the club permission to use the coveted 'royal' prefix. This was not within his gift, however, and moreover, it was not true.

The Admiralty had addressed correspondence concerning their warrant application to the 'Royal Clyde Yacht Club'. Alas, this was an administrative mistake, and the man they knew affectionately as 'Pam' had, in any case, ignored the club's pleas entirely. So, the first iteration of the Royal Clyde Yacht Club existed for just a week. Chastened, the members quietly dropped the 'royal' and operated as the Clyde Yacht Club for the next nine years. Queen Victoria would eventually bestow the 'royal' prefix in 1872, but only after private influence was brought to bear in the normal way.[537] These were not altogether honourable times, and this toadying, in lieu of well-reasoned argument, must have distressed more principled members.

The Clyde Yacht Club's racing programme comprised mainly regatta courses where members could be back in the clubhouse by late afternoon. There were few overnight races of the type we now call offshore, or more accurately, passage races. With a few notable exceptions, this has remained a characteristic of the Clyde clubs, although the Royal Northern has always been more open to the type of open-sea work common in the south of England, and Ireland. The first Clyde Yacht Club race in the North Channel did not take place until 1871.

Before the institution became established in Cowal, the Commodore vessel started the races at any one of the common race venues and members' yachts, and hotels ashore, hosted the après sail. Through the off-season, the Royal Clyde met in the Globe Hotel in Glasgow for many years and latterly, Clarks Hotel in Gourock. The Queen's Hotel in Rothesay and the George Hotel were also patronised at one time or another.

In May 1872, the Royal Clyde established a permanent home at Hunter's Quay when they leased premises in James Hunter's new hotel, designed by Pilkington & Bell of Edinburgh. The location was already a popular venue for race starts, and recent infrastructure investments made it ideal. The original stone pier built by Robert Hunter in 1828 had been rebuilt by James Hunter in 1858 and extended in 1870. The piled timber extension could cater for the larger steamers, then coming into service, at all states of the tide.[538]

The Royal Clyde's annexe had been leased 'off the plan' and was thus specifically tailored to the requirements of sporting gentlemen. The club's two-storey wing included an office and a coffee lounge, along with rooms for reading, billiards, smoking and committee meetings. The hotel proper included a ladies coffee room, various parlours, 12 bedrooms, and all the usual facilities found in a first-class waterfront establishment.

Hunter had little interest in the hotel business; the enterprise had been typical of the man's propensity to show-off. Consequently, in 1875, James offered the Royal Clyde the whole operation – grounds, hotel, club-house and ancillary buildings for £2,400 (£275,000), or something less than build-cost. From the 1876 season, members could enjoy a club with facilities unequalled in this country. Sailing families and their friends could lodge in deluxe quarters on affordable terms, particularly after 1881 when 22 additional guest rooms were added in a major extension to the hotel. With such fine facilities, it was a very attractive 'members club'. In 1877, the club boasted 643 members and an impressive fleet of 195 vessels.

Search for early images of Hunter's Quay on the Internet, and the first picture to pop up is a striking engraving, depicting a game of water-polo, drawn for *The Graphic* magazine. In the summer of 1880, it appears that the Royal Clyde hosted a marine fete at Hunter's Quay, boasting weird and wonderful competitions. These included: swimming for yachtsmen – fully-clothed, with a flag in one hand; and the pièce de résistance – water polo on horseback. The 'horses' were ballasted barrels with equine heads and tails. The players both propelled their steeds and whacked the ball with double-ended canoe paddles.[539]

The progress of the Industrial Revolution had been consolidated by a period of invention and continuing innovation in communications. The Royal Clyde was quick to take advantage of these new technologies. *"Telegraphic communication was opened up between Hunter's Quay, Glasgow, and the outer world in 1887. The club provided an office and guaranteed the sum required by the Post Office authorities, and by so doing conferred a benefit not only on themselves but on the whole surrounding neighbourhood."*[540] The small telegraph and post office of the hotel is located on the roadside opposite the ferry terminal and was a newsagent's until recently.

On the 12th July 1888 (unsettlingly the anniversary of the Battle of the Boyne) the clubhouse burnt down. Almost nothing was saved; just some furniture and one or two half-models. The insurance assessment of damage came to £5,000 (£650,000), which suggests that subsequent investment notwithstanding, the club got a good deal from Hunter, especially considering the residual value of the large waterfront site. Craigend Villa, a five-bedroom house within walking distance of the old clubhouse, was promptly rented as a makeshift club for a year, while the club's committeemen explored their options.[541]

The Royal Clyde's catering inventory included a well-stocked cellar. As the story goes, volunteer firefighters and salvage-workers spirited this away as the big clean-up progressed. When researching the club history sixty years later, Blake and Small quizzed the surviving residents who remembered the conflagration. One grizzled old boy, paused for a moment, put down his dram and gazed into the middle-distance. With a far-away look in his eyes, a nod and a wink, he recalled the best of the good old days.[542] It's a story that might raise a smile, but it is unconscionable that the club's records and a treasure trove of priceless early yachting memorabilia were considered less of a priority than the demon drink.

About 60 Royal Clyde members attended the opening of their new home two years later in 1889. The contractor, Mathew Henderson of Glasgow, had met an extremely tight schedule. Optimism, however, had transcended common sense. The wildly extravagant clubhouse incurred a build-cost of £20,000 (£2.6 million), financed by just 32 trustees among the club's 643 members, or 5%. *The Glasgow Herald's* correspondent was impressed: "*As a yacht clubhouse it is unrivalled in the kingdom. The architect, T. L. Watson, has adopted the style of domestic English building, in which projecting eves and interlacing woodwork play so important a feature, and which gives the rustic architecture of England that adaptation to its surrounding which completes a picture.*"[543]

The *Herald* went on to describe the sporting character and spectating assets of the new clubhouse in some detail: "*Red slates have been used to obtain colour as architectural effect, and the result is very satisfactory and a most agreeable relief on the formality of line and elevation which has done much to disfigure the Clyde. A wide central doorway is aided by an outside corridor in excellent taste. Along the face of the first flat runs a balcony, from which the yacht racing will be advantageously seen; and further point of vantage is the top of a tower.*"

The speeches, apparently, were a welcome departure from "*the tedious oratory of the club's earlier meetings*". Mr William Bergius proposed 'long life and prosperity' to the old institution in its marvellous new clubhouse. Mr Colin Scott, speaking on behalf of the 'kindred clubs', was glad to find that the accommodation for the Mudhook Yacht Club, in particular, had been 'so well attended to'. Mr Bell, replying for 'the gentlemen of the press' contrived to take some credit for the facility. He suggested that, had the fourth estate not lobbied so persistently and effectively, the clubhouse might never have been built.

Bell doubtless raised a few laughs when he observed that the RCYC's palatial new residence would remain incomplete until the America's Cup could be featured among its adornments. Bell reported that he had just heard of a serious offer of £10,000 (£1.3 million) towards equipping another Scottish challenger for the cup. Perhaps wisely, and unlike the Royal Perth Yacht Club, the RCYC had not prepared a secure exhibition niche with a correctly threaded through-bolt in anticipation.

Coinciding with the completion of the clubhouse and representing another reason to be cheerful among the membership, the Greenock to Gourock railway line was opened on the 1st June 1889. The new rail link had been a long time in coming as the tunnelling work along the east bank of the river had been extensive. Hunter's Quay could now be accessed via a fast rail connection to the pier at Gourock. This knocked more than an hour off the three-hour journey and increased the viability of the Royal Marine Hotel as a business venture.

The Good Life at Hunter's Quay

The Royal Marine Hotel was something special. In the good old days, there were 'royal' hotels in almost every town and resort, but this building was, in every sense, regal.[544] It was an extraordinary asset for the membership, but it was also a responsibility. Experienced management staff were required to balance club and hotel functions. The House Committee was forced to terminate the services of the club-master, poached from the Royal Forth, for unspecified 'unsatisfactory' service. After the expense of that payoff, everyone was recruited on contracts with just a month's notice.

The former headwaiter took over; he seems to have risen to the challenge and done a better job. This was a large and complex establishment to manage, with a full complement of butlers, boots, chambermaids, kitchen-maids, footmen, tweenies, head-gardeners, under-gardeners, stable-boys and who-knows-what-else. Life had clearly moved on from the club's professed mission to cater for modest yachts and ordinary people.

As for these extravagant premises, we might refer to *The Glasgow Herald*' correspondent's first impressions. The internal accommodations of the Royal Marine were certainly impressive: "*An extensive corridor gives access to the dining-hall, parlours, bar, and club business rooms on the ground floor. A spacious staircase leads up to the reading-room, smoking-room and drawing-room. Overhead, the space is devoted to bedrooms of which there are forty, bathrooms and dressing-rooms. The billiard-room is unique in its design and lighting. With an oak roof and low-arched windows it has the look of a chapel in which the service would be inspired by a ritualistic tone.*"

The *Herald's* man demonstrated an impressive knowledge of the club's heritage and members' yachts. He waxed lyrical in his account of the décor and new artworks presented by wealthy members: "*The internal decorations are all in harmony with the carved wood-work and artistic elegance that pervade the general design. The reading room is being filled up with models of yachts, among which are the models of Mr E. Paton's ill-fated Oona, and the noble-looking old schooner Salene.*"

It appears that it was an opportunity for rich men to indulge in a little self-promotion to secure their own legend: "*Photographables and pictures are being presented by friends, including a series of portraits of the more famous members. John Clark commodore of the club, Mr James Bell V.C and Mr John Neilson R.C. have made presentations of stained-glass windows* (made by Messrs J. & W. Guthrie, of Sauchiehall Sheet, Glasgow). *Mr York, the club secretary, has presented a bronze panel for the reading-room fire-place, and other adornments are being forwarded.*"[545]

During the Opening Regatta in 1888, another journalist was particularly impressed by the crowded anchorage, commenting "*it looked from the shore as though you could cross dry-shod from the slip at Cammesreinach to Strone Point*".[546] The jetty would have been clustered with dinghies and launches, carriages shuttling in and out of the clubhouse driveway, and a pipe band playing on the lawn. Perhaps it was all too much for some. Before the paint was dry on the new clubhouse, a group of members, owning summer villas locally, established the Holy Loch Sailing Club. In so doing, they salvaged an element of the simple life, racing 'round the cans' on weekdays and nurturing the next generation.

Meanwhile, the Royal Clyde aspired to ever more ambitious heights of grandeur. The club's ball was a highlight of Glasgow's social calendar during the closed season. Something like 800 members and their guests could be accommodated in the St Andrew's Halls at Charing Cross. In 1897, the dancing in the main hall was complemented by the temptations of dining, drinking and smoking which occupied the entire first floor. The St Andrew's Halls were resplendent, decorated with a nautical theme and all the club trophies on display.

The RCYC must be one of a vanishingly small number sailing clubs to have a polka written in its honour. Wilhelm Iff and his orchestra recorded the *Royal Clyde Yacht Club Polka* in Glasgow in the early 1900s.[547] By contrast, the Royal Yacht Squadron boasted less boisterous waltzes composed by T. H. Barnett. Herr Iff was a Glasgow-based German bandmaster who performed waltzes, polkas, ragtime and 'all the most up to date music' for bright young things who lived only to dance the night away. Wilhelm was a naturalised citizen in this country and immensely popular, but inevitably his tenure did not survive the Great War.

The Hunter's Quay anchorage was ruled by customs and routine. After a day's sail, once the decks were washed down and ropes in a harbour stow, galley fires were lit. In the early evening, the professional crews would have their 'tea' (evening meal), while cooks and stewards prepared dinner for those owners and friends dining aboard. The yachts' boats would be on call to look after the ladies and gentlemen who might arrive at the jetty, after tottering down from the Royal Marine, two, or even three, sheets to the wind.

Following dinner, the serious business of after-dinner drinks was an excuse to make the rounds. George Blake describes the scene: "*The yacht-owner starts off, and either rows himself and friends in his dinghy, or is rowed in correct form, to some friend's yacht where he may remain, or after a short visit, proceed, taking with him his host and as many of his friends as he can pack away in the gig's stern-sheets, to some other yacht, and so on, ad infinitum.*" Those who were able to shake off their hangovers might rise on Sunday in time to attend to a stout breakfast before attending 'church parade' onboard Lord Glasgow's yacht. George Boyle (1826-1890), the 5th Earl, was a founder member of the club.

The *Vigilant* vs the *Britannia*

On the 9th July 1884, breakfast was worth getting up for. Sleep, in any case, was impossible as the skirl of half-a-dozen pipers signalled the new day. All the big yachts would have at least one crewman who could play the pipes and that man was more than happy to ship his pipes aboard for a few shillings bonus. The anchorage would have had a festive air with yachts dressed overall. Ashore, as the day's events got underway, the brass band from the sail-training ship, *Empress*, assembled on the lawn of the Royal Clyde and struck up a patriotic air. And on the water, the 1st Volunteer Battalion of the Highland Light Infantry played stirring Scottish airs aboard the club steamer.[548]

The 1893 America's Cup winner, *Vigilant*, had come to town for a series of matches against the Prince of Wales' *Britannia*. Although *Britannia* raced as a 151-rater in Britain, as a near sistership to *Valkyrie II*, the defeated 1893 British Cup Challenger, she complied with the same simple 1882 Seawanhaka Corinthian Yacht Club measurement rule as *Vigilant*. This rule was used for the America's Cup races from 1893 to 1903. Bertie's yacht was fitted out as a cruiser-racer below, and at that stage, so was *Vigilant* for her Atlantic crossing and European season. Thus, expert opinion anticipated that the two yachts would be closely matched.

1882 Seawanhaka Rule

$$\text{Rating} = \frac{\text{Load Waterline Length} + \sqrt{\text{Sail Area}}}{2}$$

Thomas Fleming Day famously said of this rule that "a tax on sail is a tax on skill"

The two SCYC 80-footers arrived at the starting line off the RCYC in dramatic fashion, towed above hull-speed from their moorings in the Holy Loch. It has been estimated that 100,000 people lined the seafront from Hunter's Quay to Dunoon, and between Gourock and the Cloch, while a small armada of spectator boats followed the racing. The races for the Queen's Cup were close and exciting with *Britannia* taking the honours. The cup was a jug with an image in bold relief of a yacht race between *Britannia*, *Valkyrie*, and *Satanita* on one side and a view of the Royal Clyde and the Holy Loch, with yachts at anchor in the forewater.

The yachting correspondent of the *Dunoon Herald & Cowal Advertiser* could not contain his enthusiasm: *"The success of the Britannia throughout the Fortnight has been quite marvellous – having beaten the Yankee flier six times in succession – and should make up for the defeat suffered by this country in American waters last year.…1894 will be memorable in the annals of the sport, as it witnessed the struggle which terminated in the decisive victory of a British yacht over the best boat that America could produce and man"*.[549]

Unsurprisingly, the Yankees saw things differently. They protested that *Britannia* won, only because Captain Nat had taken advice from the local pilot they shipped aboard. This apparently partisan Scot contrived to detour around what was a highly localised, but well-known afternoon breeze that usually originated off a 'point of land' (Toward Point?). Captain Nat wrote in his race notes, *"after this I did no more racing yachts for others."*[550]

On the 16th May 1895, *Yachting* magazine had this to say: *"The Clyde is but a poor racing-ground on which to test the merits of yachts. We may instance the six consecutive defeats of Vigilant by Britannia last season to show that Clyde races are not all fair as regards wind."* After a fluky early season on the Solent, on June 27th of that same year, the editor of the magazine seemed to have had second thoughts: *"On the Clyde we may hope for better sport, it is par excellence the home of real sport in yacht racing."* It is hard to argue with either point of view!

Ladies, Children, Cocktails and other Queer Fish

The Royal Clyde was a palace of plumped-up cushions, antimacassars and extravagant table-settings. Despite these sybaritic surroundings, and excepting the waitresses, Royal Clyde was an all-male domain in the evenings. A notice appeared in 1894 advising the manager to *"keep the bedroom accommodation during regatta time as much as possible for yachting men"*, and *"no children and as few ladies as possible should be received as visitors during that time"*. The half-hearted restriction on ladies was in addition to limiting their admission to the club premises after 4 o'clock p.m. on regatta days.

In the years before the Great War, few yachtsmen took lady sailors seriously. *"The fact that the Countess Fitzwilliam chose to steer her jolly little 6-metre*

'Peterkin' in her races last week has led to the revival of the very old question: Should ladies be allowed to steer racing yachts? The answer is, obviously, why not? Provided they are the bona fide owners and have sufficient knowledge to enable them to keep clear of the other boats in the race – a quality, by the way, that a good many male owners do not always display. Every year ladies are increasing in their knowledge of yachting and are learning to steer their yachts with more confidence than they ever previously possessed."[551]

The more prevalent view was expressed by well-known English professional skipper, Tom Carter. Tom reckoned that *"you can have the best boat in the world and lose race after race through not understanding her. A yacht wants as much handling as a woman"*.[552] As to the first part of that assertion, it is certainly true, but regarding Tom's chosen analogy, we doubt that the old seadog would have had much success in 'handling' the bold Countess Fitzwilliam.

C. L'Estrange Ewen, who translated the specifications of the Pleiade Class when the plans first arrived from Denmark, features in the Royal Clyde's story in 1920, when he proposed that ladies should have free use of the club until 6 o'clock p.m.[553] He was responding to George Paisley's purdah-like proposals to circumscribe a women's place in this male bastion of boorish brouhaha and cigar smoke. After all, women had just got the vote in 1918 – albeit restricted to those *"over the age of 30 who were householders, the wives of householders, occupiers of property with an annual rent of £5, and graduates of British universities"*. God know what they were going to ask for next.

Andrew Mitchel went one further and suggested identical fees and privileges. Neither Ewen nor Mitchel received a seconder and Paisley's resolution was carried. At least ladies could have access, and in exchange for leaving the boys alone in the sanctuary of their smokeroom, they more or less got in for nothing.

Fast-forward to 1968 when we were guests at the Royal London in Cowes, as recipients of Owen Aisher's youth sailing award. One afternoon, our party paid a visit to the Royal Yacht Squadron's clubhouse, and quite by accident it appears, the girls of our squad were the first women to breach that bastion of all-male privilege, as we clambered upstairs en-masse to the forbidden first floor. The Squadron eventually allowed women full equality in August 2013, and yes, the date is correct!

"No matter how expert a boat-sailer you may be, never take women and children out in a boat with only yourself to handle her. Otherwise, leave the women and children ashore and postpone the excursion heedless of the tears and entreaties of your best girl. I know many girls who can beat me easily in yachting and all that appertains thereto; but fair ones of that sort are not so plentiful as they might be."[554]

It seems positively incongruous today, when bars are integral to the social life and bottom-line economics of yacht clubs, that the idea of a bar was as controversial as women members. But the two were linked. Bars then were 'cocktail bars', and cocktails fuelled the jitterbuggery of flappers and bar-flies. Real men simply snapped their fingers for a drink; the staff knew exactly what you wanted from the time of day and the club's conventions. The ladies 'ball-room' eventually became a cocktail bar after WW2, but not without a fight.

The war years empowered women, whether delivering Spitfires, building bombs, salvaging broken bodies or running the country. Now, they faced greater barriers when they asked for a place to drink. The matter was raised formally in 1948. The House Committee seems to have been concerned about the ladies' restrained drinking habits. One motion considered whether "*a large number of lady members would seriously curtail the profit-earning capacity of the hotel*", and if so, perhaps female membership should be capped at twenty-five? Quite what this says about the drinking habits of the men and their tight-fisted attitude to buying a girl a drink, is unclear, but one suspects that in the brief post-war era of 'motherhood and apple-pie', housekeeping allocations did not include much of an allowance for 'spending money'.

As for children, 1933 saw the introduction of 'cadets', a new class of membership with minimal fees. My good friend Jeremy recalls that when he became a cadet member of the Royal Clyde ca.1948, he was thrilled to be summoned into the presence of the club's grandees. Jeremy imagined that perhaps someone had noticed his precocious talent on the water. Perhaps they had, but the young lad's services were simply required to circulate among the overflowing ashtrays and overstuffed armchairs and offer the senior members the snuff box and spittoon. Both, of course, artefacts of solid silver. Where are they now?

Decline and Fall

The life aquatic at Hunter's Quay changed through the thirties and forties in other ways. As the 'queer fish' moved in, the club's éminences grises passed on, one by one, to reunite in the smoking lounge of the 'Valhalla Yacht Club' – influential figures like Duncan Finlayson, Robert Allan, Sir Thomas Dunlop, Maurice Clark, William Bergius and Sir Arthur Young were never replaced. The prestige of events in any sport turns on the pedigree of those in attendance. And as yachting events in the days of Royal patronage were particularly susceptible to stardust, decline was inevitable and self-perpetuating.

Eventually, the Clyde clubs were unable to attract English owners north to compete in International Clyde Fortnight. Then, following WW2, yachtsmen returning home after six long years of conflict were confronted with a new and very different world, where both 'privilege' and 'entitlement' were much diminished. The peace-dividend was an egalitarian society, not prosperity. Attempts to recover the good life came up against a new reality, where businessmen and professional people lost their domestic help. Helpless middle-class families were left to fend for themselves and some of us still feel the pain.

The loss of paid-hands redefined yachting. Just a few businessmen who had profited from the war could maintain big boats and carry on yachting in the old style. But even for that rump of affluent sailing men, the pressures of the working week meant that few could take time out through the sailing season to shuttle back-and-forth to Hunter's Quay. All along the Cowal coastline, summer villas were sold, or simply deteriorated and collapsed in a miasma of wet-rot and decay.

Gavin Watson: "*I once spoke to Alan Birkmyre whose family owned the Gourock Ropeworks at Port Glasgow. His family donated their house and its grounds in Kilmacolm, which became the Birkmyre Park, and is now home to St. Columba's School. Alan reported that after WW I his family had to return £300,000 to HMG as a result of profits made during that war.*"

Of all the Clyde clubs, the Royal Clyde felt the impact most. Uniquely, the club still owned and operated a substantial luxury hotel. Post-war, occupancy rates had fallen and showed no signs of recovering. In 1949, subscriptions were doubled in an attempt to keep the club solvent, but the cash-flow crisis would not go away. Working families still enjoyed the Glasgow Fair holiday and a trip 'doon-the-water', but they were 'not the right sort' of people. They stayed in the grand houses once owned by members, now converted into private hotels.

Money was tight; food was still rationed, and petrol shortages restricted members' use of their cars and motorboats. The Royal Clyde sometimes struggled to fuel-up the club launch. Serious losses stacked up in the hotel accounts and threatened to bankrupt the club; the Marine was not a limited liability company. In 1952, it was losing £2,000 (£55,000) a year. The Royal Clyde had no option but to lease out the hotel side of their operations in 1952 and retreat into the east wing.[555] A worrying financial situation was exacerbated in 1954 when the manager of the hotel stole £807 (£22,000) to settle his gambling debts.[556]

It was a perfect storm of inexorable trends and unforeseen difficulties. Regular steamer services to Hunter's Quay Pier had been withdrawn at the instigation of the Ministry of Fuel and Power in 1951. The pier was scheduled for closure in 1952, but it was reprieved and used by the *Maid of Ashton* serving the Holy Loch to Gourock run until 1964. The loss of the ferry service was not a decisive development in itself, but it was certainly an important contributory factor. Much later, in 1973, Western Ferries established a car-ferry service from Hunter's Quay to McInroy's Point on the Renfrew shore, but by then the Royal Clyde had long gone

Even in retrospect, the 1951 transport rationalisation makes no sense. As events transpired, the ferry services to Dunoon, and even Strone, Blairmore, Kilmun, Kirn and Innellan were uninterrupted, but the die was cast, and Hunter's Quay missed out. Kilmun and the north shore villages were served by the *Maid of Ashton* from 1953-1971, and the little *Countess of Breadalbane* through the period 1972-1978, before the subsidies ran out and the Holy Loch route was abandoned by Caledonian McBrayne.[557]

In 1955, the Royal Clyde leased the Royal Marine Hotel, as a going concern, to William Paisley for a period of seven years until February 1962. The rent was £480 (£12,500) per annum, plus 5% of valuation.[558] The club was to retain exclusive use of the west-wing, where the clubrooms were located, together with the liquor license for that part of the premises. The bunkhouse and cadet hall in the annexe were reserved for the private use of the RCYC, with the hotel operator servicing the rooms on an agreed scale of fees. There were also conditions concerning access to the coveted smoking room and some other choice areas of the main hotel.

The pier, the pier house and the flagpole on the front lawn were not included in the agreement. The *Valkyrie II* mast flagpole commanded a special nostalgia. While boys were not allowed in the 'henhouse' section of bunkhouse, they honoured a perpetual challenge to hoist female lingerie to the yardarm of the mast overnight. Morning glory was only achieved once, as the clubhouse staff were wise to such youthful high jinks.

The lessee had an option to buy at a fixed price of £15,000 (£390,300); this option, which looks like a steal today, to be exercised within three years. The Royal Marine was finally sold during the winter of 1959-60. The buyer was John McLaurin, who owned the prestigious Manor Park Hotel on the opposite shore between Largs and Skelmorlie. So, the old owners were now tenants. These days we call this 'lease-and-lease-back', and it is considered smart business for asset-strippers; back then it was a humiliating and desperate measure. The dwindling band of members 'squatted' uncomfortably in a corner of their old home, holding back time. Once again, they considered their options.

The first serious proposal to amalgamate the Clyde's principal clubs can be traced back to January 1960.[559] The Royal Clyde and the Royal Northern had jointly prepared a detailed feasibility study. After much discussion, the plan to combine assets and form a stronger, more sustainable entity was endorsed unanimously by the committees of both clubs.[560] Their recommendations were circulated to the RCYC and RNYC membership later that year. For most members, this proposal would have brought additional privileges of access and choice. Two parallel racing programmes were envisaged, and it was intended to retain access to the bunkhouse at Hunter's Quay after the expiry of the lease.

Footfall projections suggested that club facilities would see increased use, so that fees could stay the same. However, as 25% of the membership subscribed to both clubs, the base income would have declined, although bar and catering receipts may have increased. Prior to the merger, RCYC contemplated a levy on its members to clear their debts. The circular also noted that the proposal did not preclude the incorporation of the Royal Gourock in the new 'super-club'. Half a century later, intelligent networking of facilities might still be the best hope for the survival of the traditional yacht club, see Chapter 39.

Through the summer of 1961, the Royal Clyde burgee still flew from *Valkyrie's* old mast on the front lawn of the Royal Marine, and the blue ensign still fluttered proudly from the yardarm.[561] Nevertheless, the club appears to have been uneasy patronising the Royal Marine as a client, although this was the original business model of all the major Clyde clubs. Meanwhile, the merger with the RNYC was on hold as the Royal Clyde clung to the receding prospect of a separate existence.

If assessed objectively in the frame of a rational 'corporate rescue and restructuring', the RCYC timeline now becomes increasingly obtuse and erratic. In October 1961, the Commodore circulated the members with a fait accompli. The merger idea had been summarily dropped. Declaring that the club no longer wished to maintain a presence in Hunter's Quay, the committee presented an entirely different proposal. Gallingly, this new plan failed to address any of the perceived issues dogging their old home and added a whole set of new disadvantages.

Following the sale of the Royal Marine, after settling debts, there was £8,000 (£208,200) in the account.[562] It was now proposed to use this modest windfall to move the club to a 2.5-acre site that the committee had identified on Portkill Road in Kilcreggan. And, in an unexpected twist, the RCYC minutes suggest that the proposed new clubhouse would be oriented towards dinghy racing – a constituency that barely overlapped with the existing membership. We might note that Helensburgh Sailing Club had been established a decade before, in 1951, and was already on a trajectory to become the major dinghy club above the Tail o' the Bank.

The Rosneath Peninsula was, and remains, significantly less well-served with essential infrastructure than Hunter's Quay – there is no urban centre as such, and there is no car ferry. Members living in Glasgow, or Paisley, would have to drive past the splendid Royal Northern at Rhu (an hour by road from Glasgow, but also served by rail), then continue for another half an hour to arrive at a little clubhouse lacking even a semblance of the RCYC's former cachet. Without using ferries, it takes two hours to drive from Kelvinside to Hunter's Quay.

Outlining the 'advantages' of the move, the question of moorings arose. The Kilcreggan anchorage, to the east of the pier, is safe enough but hardly comfortable. Nevertheless, the RCYC newsletter suggested, more in hope than expectation, that: "*There is no reason to believe that it will not live down its poor reputation in the same way the anchorage off Royal Gourock has done.*" The analogy dams with faint praise. The west end of the Ashton anchorage remains unchallenged as the worst on the Clyde and is widely acknowledged as a triumph of stout ground-tackle over common sense.

Whatever else, the Royal Clyde was now committed to seeking new premises nearer Glasgow. However, before finally quitting Cowal, the club temporarily moved their operations to 'Creggandarroch', a small but comfortable hotel in Blairmore. The sojourn at Blairmore was not a particularly happy one. One young member recalls, "*I remember coming down to the kitchen one morning for an early breakfast to find the owner with her head in the oven and the gas on*". The annual regatta remained at Hunter's Quay, with the races started from Ron Teacher's big Mylne yawl, *Mariella*. Ron was still Commodore and *Mariella* still evoked the days of style and glamour.

Meanwhile, the Scottish Council for Physical Recreation had returned to 'desecrate' the once-hallowed lawns of the Royal Marine with tartan blankets, Spam sandwiches and bottles of warm beer. The 'Physical Wrecks' had set up their sailing school at Hunter's Quay in 1953 in collaboration with the Royal Clyde, but a few years later, after Alistair Galbraith took over the school from Jock Kerr Hunter, they moved to the Ardnadam Hotel. The 'Wrecks' were evicted from there when the American Navy arrived on the 3rd March 1961, see Chapter 37. With money no object and following the example of the Royal Navy in WW2, the Yanks rented the pier for shoreside operations and the old Hotel became the shabby portal of a sleazy enlisted men's club, which grew like Topsy in tin huts behind. "*Ding Dong Dollar*", as the song goes.

The remaining active members of the Royal Clyde endured this nonsense for a single season before the move to Rhu in the autumn of 1962. The committee had secured premises at Rhu Pier and purchased a 50% share of the equity from the pier operator. As might have been expected, the parties to the agreement had quite different agendas; the club sold their stake in the pier, along with the club launch, two years later. The following year, however, saw progress of a sort. Planning permission was granted for a modest, prefabricated 'Doran-style' clubhouse landward of the pier and a slipway alongside it.[563]

Even though the RCYC could still boast about 800 members, the club operated from changing rooms in caravans at the pierhead, which had to be 'taken ashore' each autumn. In 1967, we find the committee, of what was once one the world's premier yacht clubs, fussing over the cost of a coat of paint on their worthless caravans. After seven years squatting in these old trailers, the RCYC finally moved into the new club bungalow behind Rhu Pier in 1969. Having divested themselves of their equity in the pier, a ground rent of £300 p.a. was now payable.

Two years previously, in 1967, even with the new prefab clubhouse in prospect, the RCYC briefly considered a move back to Hunter's Quay when the pier came on the market.[564] Holy Loch Sailing Club also weighed up this opportunity at a special general meeting. HLSC was considering a move from their site beside Robertson's Yard at the head of the Holy Loch – ongoing silting meant that access to deep water was becoming increasingly inconvenient from mid to low-tide. In the event, neither club made an offer; the pier would be purchased by Western Ferries to become the Cowal terminal for a roll-on-roll-off service to McInroy's Point on the east shore of the Firth. Over the following decades, this quick and efficient new short crossing would, ironically, transform the accessibility of Hunter's Quay, Dunoon and the whole of Cowal.

In November 1976, the RCYC wrote to members advising them that final planning permission had been granted for the new Rhu Marina, which would be sited close to the RNYC clubhouse.[565] As both clubs would soon be mingling at a common location, it made sense to reconsider the long-mooted merger with the Northern. The Royal Clyde was not to know that it would be years before Rhu Marina became a safe harbour, as the floating breakwater system failed repeatedly. While the marina is now secure, with conventional 'hard' breakwaters, swinging moorings still remain a popular option at Rhu and in the Gareloch.

In their May 1977 newsletter, the RCYC committee reported on the following options: a) merger or 'co-existence' with the Royal Northern or Helensburgh Sailing Club; b) a 'club arrangement' with a hotel at Rhu; c) building a new establishment at one of four locations, viz Blairvadach on the Gareloch – where the outdoor education centre is now established, Craigendoran Pier – between Helensburgh and Cardross, Clynder and Fairlie; d) do without a physical base, and e) dissolution.[566] The three favoured options were to associate with the RNYC, build new at Craigendoran Pier, or become a 'paper club' like the Mudhook and the Royal Western.

On the 10th January 1978, at separate 'special general meetings', the members of both RCYC and RNYC finally resolved to unite; and so, from 1st February 1978, a new entity emerged under the clunky banner of 'The

Royal Northern and Clyde Yacht Club'. Queen Elizabeth consented to preside over the union as Patron, with HRH Prince Philip as Admiral.[567] It was the last chapter in a long-drawn-out saga that had taxed everyone's patience and seen the RCYC membership halve, from about 800 at the start of the story to 400 at its conclusion. It has never been satisfactorily explained how a club of that size, history and enduring potential could not command the will and resources to endure as a viable entity. The once-mighty Royal Clyde Yacht Club folded into the Royal Northern in a one-sided merger that had much in common with the Union of Parliaments back in 1707.

During the Royal Clyde's nomadic period, priceless archives of the 'golden age' of yachting were stored in a member's garage where they deteriorated, before finally going up in flames in an electrical fire. All that remains in respect of this crucial period are the fading minute books and financial records held by the RNCYC Archivist. These sparse records throw surprisingly little light on the club's final days in Hunter's Quay, or the fallout when an office-bearer absconded with the club's remaining funds, sometime after the move to Rhu.

And so, the demise of yachting at Hunter's Quay has disappeared into the mists of hazily remembered, and no doubt wildly inaccurate, anecdotes. The story of the merger in 1978 is, fortunately, well-documented. And crucially, the story of the great days of the Royal Clyde, from inception in 1856 to its centenary in 1956, has also been preserved in the inimitable prose of George Blake, as set down the pages of *Cruise in Company*.[568]

CODA: Club-boats

From its early years, the Royal Northern had club yachts available for charter by members for periods not exceeding a fortnight. They were all well-known boats, first, the venerable Robert Steele cutter, *Orion*, originally built for James Smith in 1822 and acquired for club use in 1833, followed by *Mosquito*, the Tom Waterman iron cutter of 1848, and then the 1861 Fife, *Aeolus*. While our major clubs were happy to buy English products, perhaps the best-loved of all the RNYC club-boats was *Ailsa*, a cutter of 67 tons, purpose-built for the job by Fife of Fairlie in 1885.

Taking a cue from the Royal Northern, the Royal Clyde invested £1,000 (£125,000) in their first club-boat in 1881. *Alcyone* was a 35-ton cutter, built by Dan Hatcher in Southampton in 1871 and a successful competitor in the 40-ton class. The yacht was manned by a captain and four paid hands. Of note is that the standard inventory included 7 bottles of whisky, 13 bottles of brandy, 4 bottles of gin, 3 port, 24 claret and 9 magnums of champagne. As each individual hire was limited to two weeks and the charter party would have comprised one, or at most two families, they were unlikely to run out. *Alcyone* was a profitable venture for the club, netting £300 (£36,000) annually after operational costs.

During the winter of 1886-87, the Royal Clyde Yacht Club acquired three 19ft luggers, built by McAllister to a standard G. L. Watson design for day-sailing and match-racing, see Chapter 20 concerning the 19ft OD. They were apparently successful in *"initiating many a tyro into the secrets and mysteries of yacht racing"*. Building on this success, in 1890 the RCYC commissioned a larger 23ft LWL class, designed by Watson and built by McAlister. Two of these little 4-tonners were launched in 1890 and a third followed in 1891. *Mayflower, Thistle* and *Shamrock* were kept on moorings off the clubhouse and proved popular with members

In the post-WW2 years, one-design club-boats were common among all the Clyde clubs, large and small, but the days of lushly stocked cocktail cabinets were over. In 1948, the Royal Clyde bought four Loch-Long keelboats. *Thistle, Rose, Shamrock* and *Daffodil*. It seems that there was an understandable reluctance to use *Leek* as the Welsh icon. A decision was made to replace two of the club boats ca.1961. *Thistle* and *Rose* were sold, and two new boats were ordered from Bert Shaw. At the time, Bert Shaw, like James Litster years before in Kirn, (See Chapter 34) was listed in the Telephone Directory as 'Joiner and Undertaker'.[569]

CODA: Cruel and Arbitrary Exclusion

Early yacht clubs were strictly for Corinthian sportsmen and there are many stories of cruel and arbitrary exclusion. Owners of shipyards, shipping lines and fishing fleets could fall foul of these restrictions, even when they underwrote very large operations and were far removed from the life of a professional sailor. For some, as when the Squadron black-balled Scottish grocer, Sir Tommy Lipton, even being associated with the taint of blue-collar 'trade' was too much. As the King's buddy, Tommy got in eventually, but many others were not so lucky, if 'lucky' is the right word.

Perhaps the best amateur-status story concerns Henley Rowing Club. Rowing clubs, you will note, seldom get the royal seal-of-approval, although the Royal Chester Rowing Club, established in 1838, and our own Royal West of Scotland Amateur Boat Club, established in 1866, are notable exceptions. Jack Kelly was a building contractor and a keen oarsman. Jack was the USA Champion in his discipline, but being 'in trade', he could not compete in the most prestigious international tournament of the calendar. Some years later, Jack's daughter became a famous Hollywood actress. And then, of course, the same Grace Kelly became Princess Grace of Monaco.

"At the lowest computation, the number of vessels at present employed for pleasure in this kingdom cannot be less than from three to four hundred, ranging in bulk from

10 to 350-tons. These craft are variously distributed along our shore, carrying their opulence into every port and harbour in the sister islands. But there is another advantage arising from yacht clubs, which as yet has been slightly touched upon; I mean, that national principle which to a maritime people is above all choice. We must never allow the proud feeling of naval supremacy to wither or decay."[570]

CODA: A Regatta at Kilmun 1850[571]

"The Annual Regatta took place on Friday, under the auspices of the Royal Northern Yacht Club. From the preparations that had been made for a day's good sport, expectations were formed that the competition would be more than usually keen, and in this respect, they were not disappointed, the muster of yachts and boats being exceedingly numerous. The Commodore, George Middleton, Esq, hoisted his flag on board the fine yacht Orion, belonging to the Northern Club, which was gaily decked with a profusion of colours and moored opposite Kilmun.

Unfortunately, the prospects that a fine morning had given of a brilliant day were dispelled about 12 o'clock by a thick drizzle which fell with little intermission till nearly five o'clock in the afternoon. In spite of this drawback, however, the appearance which the unusually quiet waters of the loch presented was transformed into a scene of great panoramic beauty and interest. The course marked out for the sailing boats was from a buoy moored at the head of the loch, round another similarly moored in mid-channel, which, being sailed twice round, gave a course of nearly eight miles.

Shortly after eleven o'clock, a gun from the Commodore gave the signal for the first race to start, which was a sailing match, for 'Gentlemen's Pleasure Boats, not exceeding 8-tons register', for a piece of plate, value ten-guineas (£1,400). For this race, six boats started: the Gipsey, Mr Aitken, Gareloch; the Artful Dodger, Mr Carlisle, Greenock; the Francis, Mr Rattray, Rothesay; the Garland, Mr Walker, Kilmun; and the Naiad, Mr Ronald of Fairley. For the first hour or two, there was little wind, and their progress was very tedious, but a fine breeze gradually sprung up, which gave a grand opportunity for a display of seamanship. The first boat which came in was the Gipsy, closely followed by the Francis and Artful Dodger in the order named.

The second race was a sailing match, for 'Gentlemen's Pleasure Boats, not exceeding 20ft', for a piece of plate, value six-guineas (£830). The course was the same as at the previous race, and the interest excited equally great. The prize was won very beautifully by the Euphrosyne, Fyfe, Greenock, which took the lead-shortly after starting, and kept it; the Dream, Mitchell, Rothesay, came in second, and throughout the Jeanette was third, the others following."[572]

CODA: A Regatta at Kilmun 1870

Regattas were organised locally at short notice by James Hunter. In 1870, the man himself *"acted as Commodore"* to oversee a range of events that included all the usual sailing and rowing races classed by profession, gender and age-group, together with swimming races, and a duck hunt for boats up to 18ft with four amateur crew and 'no helmsman'. This competition required that the duck be caught within 10-minutes, but not until 5-minutes had elapsed from the start. On this occasion, after a fine contest, "*the duck won*".[573]

A lugsail race, for boats not exceeding 18ft with one sail only to be used, promised a first prize of £2 (£270), and a second prize of £1 (£135). Seven boats were entered for this race, which was won easily by *Vesper*, Mitchell of Kirn, with *Midge*, Rankin of 'Langbank', second. A four-oared jolly-boat rowing match, to be pulled by 'gentlemen amateurs', in boats not exceeding 26ft LOA, and not under 4ft beam, was contested for a piece of plate, value 8 guineas, as the prize. First was *Meteor*, Kerr of Dunoon; second *Petrel*, Macdonald also of Dunoon.

Other rowing races were 'open' and not confined to gentlemen amateurs. These concerned 16½-ft skiffs, with crews of four, two and one, prize money £1 (£135), and a race for 8ft punts, which offered 10/- (£67) in prize money. A special four-oared match for boats not exceeding 22ft, owned and pulled by residents of the Holy Loch, saw the *Snake* of Kilmun beat the *Maggie*, of the same village. And, may I say, we still row well today.

CODA: Royal Marine Architect, Tom Watson

Thomas Lennox Watson FRIBA (1850-1920) was a prominent Glasgow architect and interior designer. He is credited with 68 designs of which 6 were yacht interiors, where entrée was provided his cousin, yacht designer G. L. Watson. The yachts were, *Mohican*, *Britannia*, *Foros*, *Irene*, *Margarita II*, *Margarita III*, and *Meteor*. However, his RCYC commission was via an open design competition, rather than via his yachting contacts. Tom's usual style was neo-classical and Romanesque, but the Royal Marine's quirky design, heavily influenced the Arts and Crafts Movement, was quite different.

[495] The Power of Clyde Yachting, The Yachtsman, 6th July 1911.

[496] The Race is now under new management and new arrangements will doubtless follow. Volvo was complicit in the reestablishment of the long-moribund 120-year-old Royal Galway Yacht Club (est. 1892). The 'new' club violated the etiquette of a royal warrant.

[497] Yacht Racing Legislation, Glasgow Herald, 14th September 1891.

[498] G. L. Watson, the Art and Science of Yacht Design, Martin Black, 2011. Black quotes James Meikle and the RNCYC Archive.

[499] John Reid points out that membership numbers were not sequential. For example, in the 1881 Yearbook they start at number 32 and there are many gaps, so although the last member number shown is 571, there were less than that. Martin Black's estimates are also shown.

[500] Cruise in Company, George Blake and Christopher Small, 1959.

[501] Ongoing Research by Jon Reid, RNCYC Historian.

[502] The Field Book: or, Sports and Pastimes of the United Kingdom, W. H. Maxwell, 1833.

503 The Piper Calls the Tune, Euan Ross and Bob Donaldson, 2017.

504 First Meeting of the Northern Yacht Club, the Belfast Chronicle, 7th July 1825.

505 Northern Yacht Club, Greenock Advertiser, 15th August 1825.

506 We cite this tradition as 'English', because occurrences of the word 'regatta', or variations thereof, are vanishingly rare in Scottish newspapers articles published before 1825.

507 G. L. Watson, the Art of Science and Design, Martin Black, 2011.

508 The records of the Scottish division of the Northern Yacht Club, later the Royal Northern Yacht Club, after the dissolution in 1838 and prior to 1846, have been lost.

509 The Field Book, William Hamilton Maxwell, 1833.

510 Ibid

511 The Royal Northern Yacht Club Regatta on the Clyde, 1935, The Sporting Magazine, Vol. XI, No. LXL May 1835, musings of the magazine's Editor.

512 The Clyde Passenger Steamers: From the Comet of 1812 to the King Edward of 1901, James Williamson, 1904.

513 The Squadron secured exclusive rights to the white ensign in 1858.

514 Royal West of Scotland Amateur Boat Club, Diamond Jubilee, John Donald, 1926.

515 Scotts' Shipbuilding & Engineering Co Ltd. Two Centuries of Shipbuilding by the Scotts at Greenock, Offices of Engineering, London, 1906.

516 The Firth of Clyde, George Blake, 1952.

517 Royal Northern Yacht Club, Clyde Regattas, Caledonian Mercury, 1st August 1836.

518 Smith was a talented amateur geologist among other things, with discoveries concerning glacial moraines as between the Holy Loch and Loch Eck.

519 The Badminton Library of Sports and Pastimes: Yachting, Volume 2, Chapter 2 Scottish Clubs, R. T. Pritchett, 1894.

520 Bell's Life, August 1850.

521 For comparison, the Royal Yacht Squadron at Cowes was then three times as expensive. Source: Hunt's Universal Yacht List, 5th annual edition for 1852.

522 Yachting on the Northern Waters of Scotland, Hunt's Yachting Magazine, January 1866.

523 Leaves from the Logbook of an Old Clyde Journalist, V, James Meikle, The Yachtsman 3rd January 1925.

524 Alexander owned Ascog Hall and was a connoisseur of contemporary paintings, early jewellery and illuminated manuscripts. His son, Ninian, was a serial client of G. L. Watson.

525 Auld Lang Syne of Clyde Yachting, The Yachtsman, James Meikle, Christmas Issue, 1895.

526 Various articles in Yachting, 1937.

527 Badminton: Yachting, Volume 2, Chapter 2 Scottish Clubs, R. T. Pritchett, 1894.

528 The Buccleuch Dukedom was twice ennobled when the amorous bloodline of proto yachtsman and serial philanderer Charles II entered the family. The 10th Duke is the largest private (as opposed to corporate) landowner in Scotland.

529 The Nautical Magazine, 1845. The Nautical was published from 1832 to 2012.

530 Royal Forth Yacht Club, History, Bill Titterington, current website.

531 Plans for Edinburgh Marina progress with a £10m loan to snap up more land, the Scotsman, 19th July 2018.

532 Forth Corinthian Yacht Club, current website.

533 Scottish Clubs, R. T. Pritchett and Rev. G. L. Blake, 1894.

534 Smith's son, Archibald, was an influential mathematician, who earned a Royal Society gold medal. His work on ships' magnetism and compass deviation informs the Compass Manual of the British Admiralty, used also by the USA, France, Germany, Russia, and Portugal.

535 The Field Book, William Hamilton Maxwell, 1833.

536 The first issue of The Field (1st January 1853) deigned only to mention the activities and office bearers of the 17 'Royal' yacht clubs in the British Isles in their round-up of the state of play in British yachting. Clearly, it was a 'must have' prefix.

537 There are a few clubs which do not have a 'Royal' in their title but still have an Admiralty warrant to fly a blue ensign; these include the Thames Motor Yacht Club, the Severn Motor

Yacht Club and the Sussex Yacht Club. The Army Sailing Association also flies a blue ensign.

[538] The first James Hunter of Hafton (1780-1834) was a wealthy Greenock businessman. He bought the Hafton Estate ca.1815 and built Hafton House in 1816.

[539] Hunter's Quay's Contribution to Clyde Yachting, David Hutchison, 9th December 2015.

[540] Scottish Clubs, R. T. Pritchett and Rev. G. L. Blake, 1894.

[541] This elegant villa was recently advertised for just £295,000 – where else but Cowal could you find such a house with a matchless sea-view for that modest sum of money?

[542] Cruise in Company, George Blake and Christopher Small, 1959.

[543] Royal Clyde New Clubhouse, Glasgow Herald, 30th December 1889.

[544] In theory, permission is required to use 'Royal', 'King', 'Queen', 'Prince' or 'Princess', 'Duke' or 'Duchess', and 'His or Her Majesty' in most contexts.

[545] Ibid

[546] Cruise in Company, George Blake and Christopher Small, 1959.

[547] This recording is held by the US Library of Congress. Music lovers can relax.

[548] Hunter's Quay's Contribution to Clyde Yachting, David Hutchison, 9th December 2015.

[549] Article in the Dunoon Herald and Cowal Advertiser, 13th July 1894.

[550] Herreshoff Sailboats, Gregory O. Jones, 2004.

[551] Yachting Notes, White Ensign, Sunday Times, 12th July 1914.

[552] Yachting Notes, White Ensign, Sunday Times, 5th July 1914.

[553] Cruise in Company, George Blake and Christopher Small, 1959.

[554] Boat sailing in Fair Weather and Foul, Captain Ahmed. J. Kenealy, 1854.

[555] The committee decided to lease the building ca.1952, but details have been lost.

[556] Hunter's Quay's Contribution to Clyde Yachting, David Hutchison, 9th December 2015.

[557] The *Maid of Cumbrae* and the *Maid of Skelmorlie* were converted to operate as car ferries and still ply scheduled routes in Italy. The *Main of Ashton* is now a Thames excursion vessel. The *Maids'* operational speed was just 14kts as opposed to 18+kts for earlier ferries.

[558] Lease Agreement between Sir Thomas Dunlop and others, and William Paisley and others, 2nd November 1955, RNCYC Archive.

[559] RCYC Newsletter to Members, second draft, private and confidential, 29th January 1960.

[560] RCYC Newsletter to Members, 19th October 1960, RNCYC Archive.

[561] *Valkyrie II* was sunk by the *Satanita* at the mouth of the loch in 1894 with loss of life. The mast served as the Royal Clyde flagpole before the Royal Marine Hotel at Hunter's Quay for many years. When rot was discovered in the spar it was replaced. The remains have been cut lengthways to serve as benches at Lazaretto Point.

[562] RCYC Newsletter to Members, 20th October 1961, RNCYC Archive.

[563] RCYC Minute Book, RNCYC Archive.

[564] Ibid

[565] RCYC Newsletter to Members, 23rd November 1976, RNCYC Archive.

[566] RCYC Newsletter to Members, 12th May 1977, RNCYC Archive.

[567] RCYC Newsletter to Members, 13th January 1978, RNCYC Archive.

[568] Cruise in Company, George Blake and Christopher Small, 1959.

[569] After leaving Blairmore in 1962 the R.C.Y.C. Club Boat Section, effectively the rump of the club, spent a year as guests of Royal Gourock before moving with their boats to Rhu.

[570] The Field Book, William Hamilton Maxwell, 1833.

[571] Neither of these two regatta descriptions involved the Holy Loch Sailing Club.

[572] Holy Loch Regatta, Glasgow Herald, 29th July 1850.

[573] Holy Loch Regatta, Glasgow Herald 15th August 1870.

Royal Marine Hotel main entrance with the Royal Clyde Yacht Club members' automobiles

The Billiards Room   The Annexe   Images: Ormonde Carter collection

The view from Hunter's Quay looking north to the Arochar Alps and Strone Point with Ben Narmain lording it over Dunselma. Also on 'the point' are villas of former yachtsmen, with Strone House far right and Strone Kirk centre.   Image: John Stirling, Castle House Museum

1	J.A.D.MACKEAN	13	WILLIAM FIFE	25	A.J.M.BENNETT
2	JOHN FULTON	14	GEORGE BLAIR	26	JOHN INGLIS, LL.D.
3	HUGH MUIR	15	D.F.D.NEILL	27	W.C.MACNAUGHTAN
4	CAPTⁿ JAMES WILLIAMSON	16	J.J.FRAME	28	A.HARRIS
5	H.S.PAUL	17	J.G.THORBURN	29	JOHN MATHESON
6	W.M.MACKEAN	18	JOHN S.DUNN	30	JOHN McLINTOCK
7	THOMAS DUNLOP	19	Wᴹ BEARDMORE (VICE COM)	31	ALEXANDER HENDERSON
8	WILLIAM ADAM	20	ALEXANDER WALKER	32	THOMAS W.LANG
9	ROBERT WYLIE (REAR COM)	21	GAVIN H.RANKIN	33	J.B.HILLIARD
10	C.F.CRICHTON	22	JAMES S.CRAIG	34	JOHN G.KINCAID
11	JOHN COCHRAN	23	JAMES REID	35	FRANK J.CRUIKSHANK
12	WILLIAM YORK (SECRETARY)	24	THOMAS PRENTICE	36	JOHN HAMILTON
				37	ALEXANDER LANG

Outside the Clubhouse, 1906   Image: Cruise in Company

The group includes several early members of the club. Note the almost ubiquitous bowler hats. Prior to the Great War, it was not customary to wear yachting caps ashore, only Thomas Prentice is wearing one here. Unlike the Boer War, which made no discernible impact on dress, yachtsmen became habituated to uniform during WW1 and appear to have become more comfortable wearing elements of such after their military service.

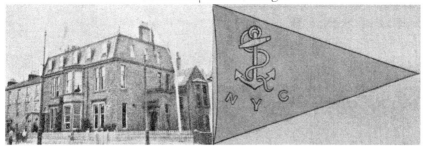

Northern Yacht Club, Rothesay   Northern Burgee, 1829

The old Royal Marine after extension in 1877, and before the fire in 1888   Image: old postcard

Stylised rendition of an RNYC Regatta early 1800s   Image: *The Graphic*

273

RNYC Regatta early 1830s   Artist: William Clark, RNCYC Archives

GRAND SAILING MATCH.

A S it is intended by the NORTHERN YACHT CLUB that a SAILING MATCH is to take place with their Pleasure Vessels, on TUESDAY next, the Steamer BANGOR CASTLE will, on that day, take Passengers from Belfast and Cultra, and accompany the Pleasure Boats, so that a view of this singular and grand spectacle may he had by those who wish to avail themselves of this comfortable conveyance.

JOHN CRAMSIE.

The BANGOR CASTLE will leave Donegall Quay at EIGHT o'Clock to-morrow Morning, to be in time at Cultra and Carrickfergus from either of which places the Pleasure Vessels are to start.

Fare for the Whole Round, only...... 4s. 2d.
Belfast, July 4, 1825.

Advertisement 1825   RNCYC Archive   The Northern Seal, 1890s

Royal Northern Steam yachts racing (organised racing was halted in 1835)   Image: Peggy Brawn

The new Royal Marine after completion 1889 — Image: old postcard

Royal Marine Hotel dining room — Image: Ormonde Carter collection

Vigilant and *Britannia*, 1894   Image: sourced by Martin Black

The band play on the RCYC lawn   Image: McLean Museum Collection, Inverclyde Archives

Chapter 12: Fellow Travellers

The facilities given by the railway and steamboat companies for readily getting from the city to the coast induce most young men who are in the least degree nautically inclined to keep a boat of some sort; and during the summer months, in the bright northern evenings, from every coast village may be seen a fleet of little vessels flitting along the shore in the smooth water, and lying over to the land wind, which in good weather rises as the sun sets. George Blake[574]

As the sport grew, smaller clubs were established to serve the local catchments of seaside towns. Others emerged to cater exclusively for niche yachting activities which warranted a society of fellow travellers. And of course, not everyone relished the trek to Hunter's Quay or Rothesay and others simply disparaged high society. They just wanted to go sailing. Consequently, owners of holiday villas and the better-off local businessmen and professionals got together to organise mid-week racing, or simply to form a community of like minds. A few of these clubs gained 'royal' status, although it was seldom coveted.

The Mudhook Yacht Club

The Mudhook Yacht Club is a society that is not merely unique, it is inimitable. It was established in 1873 with a one guinea subscription, reduced to one pound when decimalisation struck in 1970.[575] The club was founded by Colin Scott, ostensibly to promote amateur seamanship. Candidates were subjected to searching examination on 'the ways of a sailor'. The initiation of a Mudhooker saw him confronted with a *"coil of rope, a small marlinspike, a chart and dividers, a forecastle bucket and other implements; and, before the hand of fellowship was extended to him, he was exercised, with more or less of solemnity, as to their uses"*. This is a society that once had the confidence to ditch yachting caps and sport conspiratorial fedoras afloat.

It is perhaps the most exclusive yacht club in the world, as membership is limited to 'forty and one forbye'. So, to become a new member, not only do you have to pass muster, but you also have to murder an old one.[576] Amicicide apart, the Mudhook has made its mark on Clyde yachting. As an institution, it has been disproportionately influential, assembling the 'great and good' from the other Clyde fellowships in a 'dining club' which often set the direction of the sport in Scotland. The Mudhook Regatta required all helmsmen to be Corinthians, even in Big Class yachts. This dogma was heavily criticised after *Satanita* sank *Valkyrie II* at the mouth of the Holy Loch in 1894, and it remains an open question as there is evidence of a reverse correlation between ability and wealth.

For generations of Clyde yachtsmen, the 'Mudhook' is synonymous with the 'Clark Challenge Cup for Small Yacht Sailing by School Crews', first hosted at Clynder on the Gareloch in 6-metres back in 1933. This regatta was a perceptive and well-timed initiative. The Mudhook became a cherished institution, wherein sailing families packed their youngsters off to the Gare Loch to do battle on the water each August.[577]

There was also a corresponding Universities Championship, but that competition never quite fired the popular imagination in the same way. The Mudhook's Clark Cup was enacted as a parable of youth and skill vs experience and cunning. Mr Clark was a "*sweet-natured and much-loved man*"; would that his inheritors had been the same. *The Piper Calls the Tune* dedicates a bitter-sweet chapter to this fondly remembered, if occasionally acrimonious, microcosm of Clyde yachting.

The Royal Western Yacht Club

The Western was established at Millport in 1875, following a meeting of interested parties at the Waverley Hotel in Glasgow on 23rd August that year.[578] The aim was to "*encourage small boat and dinghy sailing in the Firth of Clyde and especially in the lower reaches*", developing aspects of the sport relatively neglected by the two big clubs. Following the example of the Mudhook, a one guinea subscription was levied, and like the senior club, that was decimalised to £1 in 1971. The £1 fee is maintained to this day, although if you want to fly the club burgee and blue ensign there is an additional £20 to pay for the warrant.

The Western was a surprisingly exclusive little club in its early years, fielding the 'black-ball' in a score-settling way like the past-masters of the Mudhook. But, unlike the Mudhook, the original 24 founder members soon allowed another 100 or so yachtsmen to join the party. The boys had clearly worked out their differences and would unite to harbour more than a modicum of ill-will against the Secretary, who absconded with the club's meagre funds in 1888, leaving a deficit of £50 (£6,450).

While established for 'small yachts and dinghies', the Western is principally known for its offshore and passage races. The first of these was a famously challenging match in 1885. Only two of the seven entries braved the course from Millport around Ailsa Craig and back. James Coats' Steele cutter, *Marjorie* (G. L. Watson 1883), of 72-tons TM beat the D. & W Henderson-built yawl, *Wendur* (also G. L. Watson 1883), of 143-

tons TM. Neither was a small boat, but they were indeed sailing in the lower reaches.[579] In its early years, like the other Clyde clubs, the Western Club's starts moved around, with regattas at Rothesay, Largs, Skelmorlie and Kilchattan Bay, as well as Millport, and later, Helensburgh.

Also, in 1885, the Western gained the 'royal' prefix and a new burgee, quartered red and white, with a red Saint Andrew's Cross on a yellow shield. The history of the Western records that the club had amalgamated with the Clyde Canoe & Lugsail Club (est.1873, Rosneath) the year before in 1884, so in this telling, the humble canoeists also gained the coveted blue ensign. But then, in the eighteen-nineties the club re-divided with the Clyde Canoe Club, decamping to the banks of Loch Lomond and condemned to fly the red duster in 1893.

However, the history of the Canoe Club (now Loch Lomond Sailing Club) records that, between 1894 and 1897, the association simply folded for a time.[580] *"Running expenses had increased and although income stood at £58 (£7,500) for the year 1893, the club treasurer estimated that the club would be £5 in debt at the year-end. For this apparently paltry sum (£650* in today's money) *it was decided to disband the club. All the assets were sold – boats, club canoes, the Rosneath clubhouse, everything."*

This account states that the boats were bought by the Royal West of Scotland Amateur Boat Club, across the water in Greenock. The Boat Club was said to have offered full membership to paid-up members of the Clyde Club. However, *The Yachtsman* reported that the headquarters of the Clyde Canoe Club had moved to Helensburgh, which is more consistent with the Royal Western's account which refers to the club's assets in Helensburgh.[581]

The only plausible explanation for the differences between the two accounts is that the historians of the canoe club have mixed up the 'Royal Western' with the 'Royal West', which coincidentally, bought three 19-footers to the same G. L. Watson design in 1891. *"Gourock had a launch, or rather a triple launch, to itself on May-day, when Messrs Paul Jones & Sons put three large pleasure boats into the sea from their yard, which they have built to the order of the West of Scotland Yacht Club. Nineteen feet long overall, the boats have both good breadth and depth. They are decked all round, with a large well. They are rigged with lug-sail and jib, and the sails are to be tanned."*[582]

The 1884 merger brought the Canoe Club's three Helensburgh-based luggers – *Red*, *White*, and *Blue* into RWYC ownership. These early 19ft G. L. Watson one-designs are discussed in Chapter 20. It seems that the wee boats caused more than a little discord amongst the Western members as, unlike the RCYC experience, running costs exceeded rental income. The experience with the luggers was germane to the Western's key role in the conception and success of the Clyde's iconic and uber-competitive classes – the 17/19s, and the subsequent and larger 19/24s. These two design-development classes are discussed in Chapter 23.

The Royal Western, unencumbered by a clubhouse, moved its regatta starts to Hunter's Quay in 1904. There, it inevitably found itself in the shadow of the Royal Clyde. Nevertheless, the Western would establish an enduring niche in the story of Clyde sailing, and with the first race to Tighnabruaich in 1910, become one of its cherished institutions. For the best part of a century, the Tighnabruaich Race was among the most popular fixtures in the Clyde programme. The pursuit-race format was an enduring novelty, and the course leads competing yachts through the most beautiful waters of the Clyde. Sadly, this wonderful event has now fallen out of favour.

Maurice Clark, one of the Clyde's best and most active sailors, used his position as Vice-Commodore of the Western to revive the Clyde Yacht Club's Conference (first established in 1898) in 1931. As the CYCA, this institution coordinated the post-WW2 yacht racing on the Clyde. The author's generation fondly remembers the season-long series of Saturday regattas organised by each of our clubs in turn. Clyde Fortnight, later reduced to a Week, was the highlight of the sailing season, buttressed by a well-considered calendar of classic inshore passage races and the occasional offshore jaunts.

The Clyde Corinthian Yacht Club

The Clyde Corinthian was the next institution established to recover the essence of amateur competition originally sought by the old 'model' yachtsmen of the RCYC. A coalition of Dunoon-based yachtsmen, who enjoyed each other's company in a more relaxed context, resolved in 1896 to set up an informal yacht club. Their mission was "*to encourage amateur sailing and cut out the professional*". The Western had considered, then rejected, 'Corinthian' as a name the previous year, so that was still up for grabs, albeit that the original Royal Corinthian Yacht Club of Erith had been founded in 1872. There are Corinthian yacht clubs, many now Royal, in Cowes, London, Plymouth, Burnham, Bristol and Teign, to name just a few in Britain alone.

The Clyde Corinthian gave us the Tarbert Race, and that alone justifies the institution. Whatever the weather forecast promises, the tortuous passage usually ensures that competitors are tested in a variety of wind strengths and on every conceivable point of sailing. For example, in one light weather race ca.1980, we found ourselves chasing down the fixed finishing time. It was perhaps the only occasion when the entire fleet wished us well, as by finishing we would extend their time-limit.

The Mudhook, the Western and the Corinthian all exist happily without clubhouses, and piggy-back on the likes of the Royal Northern and the commercial marinas. As the annual fee for membership of the Corinthian, for example, is still just a tenner, there has to be a spark of magic in that back-to-basics formula.

The Royal Highland Yacht Club

The Royal Highland Yacht Club was founded in Oban in 1881, at a time when large yachts from the Clyde took in the Oban Regatta during their summer cruise. Sepia-tinted images from the 1890s show impressive collections of steam yachts mustered in the bay, following the established West Coast cruise itinerary. For West Highland Week, they would be joined by up to 100 racing yachts, most having sailed north from the Clyde.

Like many of the old-school clubs, the RHYC formerly enjoyed substantial premises; their home in Oban is now the Lancaster Hotel. Occupancy was lost through requisition during two world wars and deracination was ratified in the reduced circumstances of post-war Britain. So, as the years passed, yachting in the grand style lapsed and sailing in the bay became a low-key local affair.

Oban was just too far north to attract the prestigious racing classes. In 1947, the RHYC joined forces with Oban Sailing Club and the Western Isles Yacht Club, to re-establish West Highland Week as a popular, low-key booze-cruise series of passage races and inshore events. *"Of course, in those days it would only have been the owners attending the ball – the hired hands would have been expected to entertain themselves at the local public house! The pub tradition still continues – now for owners and crew alike – with the added entertainment of a wide-ranging social programme to accompany the 'craic' and camaraderie that is so much part of West Highland Week."*[583]

The Royal Largs Yacht Club

The Largs Yacht Club was also founded in 1881 or 1882, surprisingly late considering its location as a popular regatta venue and the town's prominent place in the history of the sport. The Royal Largs took over the old Royal Northern courses. These were said to provide *"a test on every point of sailing, besides being as free from flukes as any course on the Clyde can be"*. The Royal Largs, as it soon became, also owned 'the King's Course'.

Founder members such as James Clark, Thomas Dunlop, Fred Stephen and Will Fife were prominent in other clubs. It was a feature of club membership on the Clyde that if you could afford it, you joined them all.

The Royal Largs disappeared in 1975, having been moribund for some years. Rather marvellously, from rise to ruin, the Royal Largs had no rules or constitution. But then, ironically, the club's fortunes waned because of its blinkered 'conditions of entry'.

Local apprentices were obliged to form the Largs Sailing Club because the Royal Largs required an applicant to be 21 years old and a master in his trade. In a morality tale of poetic justice, the senior club was wiped out like skittles as their black balls rebounded. Meanwhile, the humble sailing club, supported for many years by thread-baron John Clark, has endured. Today, RYA Scotland is based at Largs and LSC is the premier dinghy regatta location in North Britain. However, and perhaps rather unsportingly, their burgee continues to feature a rapacious Viking longship, rather than a homely Scottish birlinn.

The Royal Tay Yacht Club

The Royal Tay Yacht Club at Broughty Ferry was founded in 1885. "*At a meeting of gentlemen, favourable to the formation of a Sailing Club, held in Lamb's Hotel Dundee on Friday 27th March 1885, it was unanimously resolved by those present to form themselves into a sailing club to be known as the Tay Corinthian Yacht Club.*"[584] Despite this pedigree, and its undoubted success in retaining a fine Victorian clubhouse and an enthusiastic membership, the club has remained on the margins of the story of sailing in Scotland. Paradoxically, the *Dundee Courier* has furnished a wealth of yachting journalism focussed on events on the Clyde, and commercial shipbuilding on the Tay Estuary was often pioneering and innovative.

The Firth of Tay was, and remains, remote from any other centre of yachting. It can be a grim stretch of water. One morning back in the 1960s, the Holy Loch boys arrived there for team racing. The weather was apocalyptic with a charcoal-black sky, rain squalls sweeping the estuary and navigation buoys surfing crazily on the outgoing tide. The Royal Tay might be the only yacht club in Scotland that can offer homesick Englishmen Solent-type tidal flows.

But the visit was memorable for the race briefing in the 'chart-room' overlooking the estuary. As the RTYC race officer pointed out the windward mark, a mesmerising bolt of lightning split the gloom to electrify the buoy in question. After the ear-splitting crack of thunder that followed, our OOD conceded that such divine guidance might not always be available throughout the afternoon. Neither HLSC nor the home team had any desire to go racing. However, as we successfully disqualified three RTYC boats during the pre-start of the first heat and two in the second, it turned out to be a good day's work.

The Royal Gourock Yacht Club

The Royal Gourock Yacht Club was established in 1894 as Gourock Sailing Club and became 'Royal' in 1908. Largs may have owned the King's Course, but the Royal Gourock owned the King's Cup – a trophy donated by George V in 1920 for competition between 'artisans and working men'. And to be fair to the club, while they have not eschewed prosperity and privilege, they have always tried to cater for "*poor men who have to work for a living*".[585]

The club in Gourock fulfilled a long-expressed need. In 1866 when the Royal Northern was peripatetic, *Hunt's* favoured Ashton: "*Gourock being the place of general rendezvous for yachts, and almost the only place where strangers can safely, or conveniently anchor in the Clyde, seems to be a proper locality for a club-house; and, it is hoped, by many that, ere long, it may be selected for that purpose.*"[586]

The RGYC has enjoyed its present location since 1902, when yachting enthusiast James Coats of the yarn-spinning family, rallied to fund the construction of the Gourock clubhouse. Ashton is a horrible anchorage, particularly at the south end, but the clubhouse occupies a superb position with a 180-degree view of one of the best yacht-racing areas anywhere in the world. The fine prospect is rendered sublime by the backcloth of Cowal and the Holy Loch, with Ben More and the Arrochar Alps in the distance.

The Holy Loch Sailing Club

The Holy Loch Sailing Club sometimes erroneously tagged the 'Holy Loch Yacht Club', was formed in 1888 as an offshoot from the Royal Clyde. However, there are references which suggest a much earlier date, which we have not been able to validate. "*Sir Thomas Dunlop has had many years' experience of yachting in various craft and is as keen as ever over sailing. As far back as 1875 he won the Holy Loch Sailing Club Cup with a small lugsail boat named Dora.*" Sir Thomas was Commodore of the Royal Clyde (1934-1938), the Royal Gourock and an HLSC stalwart.

However, the formation of the current club is not in doubt: "*A meeting of gentlemen was held at Strone three weeks ago to consider the propriety of forming a sailing-boat club. It was stated by several of those present that much greater interest was now being taken in the sailing of small craft than in the matches with large yachts, and as there were over twenty suitable sailing boats owned in the district that a club should be formed, so that matches could be arranged for during the season and a regatta given towards the end of the season.*

A club was formed under the designation of Holy Loch Sailing Club, and that Mar John Hunter Jr, Finartmore, Strone was appointed Hon Secretary. At a subsequent meeting, Mr George Handyside Dick owner of the (40-ton Hatcher yawl) *Dione was appointed Commodore. The first matches of the new club took place on Saturday afternoon. The entries were very numerous, but the wind was light, and the matches were not well-contested."*

In earlier years, the Royal Northern held an annual Holy Loch Regatta for 'gentlemen's pleasure boats' at the lower end of the size scale, and thereafter it seems to have been arranged locally with a secretary and 'acting commodore', without any specific club sponsor. In the 19th century, there were such regattas all around the Clyde coast.

The Hoch Loch Club was based in Kilmun but made use of the RCYC facilities. The new club represented the interests of those sailing families who owned seaside villas on the shores of the Holy Loch and decamped to Cowal for the entire summer season. The HLSC organised weeknight races for all but the larger classes of boat, and other special events slotted between the principal weekend regattas.[587] *"This club exists principally for the purpose of giving a number of evening races during the season, the courses being laid inside the Holy Loch. Once a year they hold a regatta on the outside courses for the 35-ton class and downwards."*[588]

The HLSC races specifically catered for families, with informal 'beercan' racing, and separate starts for the lugsail dinghies sailed by the children of the extended family networks in Cowal. *"Although this body of yachting men and women prefers to call itself a sailing club, it is as good a yachting organisation as any of those with a local habitation about the Clyde, and it was gratifying to learn from the statement of the Secretary at the annual meeting that it had now 166 members, and that generally, it was in excellent condition."*[589]

In some respects, it was a prototype for the tea-and-biscuits sailing clubs of the post-WW2 years, albeit that most of the members could afford Champagne and caviar. Wednesday and Friday evening races were contested in the latest 6-metres. Boats like Fred Stephen's *Coila III*, Tommy Glen-Coats' *Cynthia*, and the McAndrew's *Gonda*, graced the Holy Loch. The club's helmswomen were prominent. *The Yachtsman* noted that *"Miss E. M. Allan is proving quite invincible with the 6-metre Apache."*[590] Similarly, the Morgan Giles Six, *Gonda*, with Charles McAndrew crewing for his daughter, often embarrassed the big guns, especially in the notorious sunset 'drifters' that left precious little time for après sail in the Coylet Inn in my day.

In the early years, the HLSC did not maintain a separate clubhouse. Club business was conducted at 137, Ingram Street, Glasgow. We note in the minutes that a resolution was approved to the effect that *"in view of the European Crisis and the improbability of racing taking place on the Clyde this season"* no subscriptions would be levied for the year 1915. This waiver was later extended 'until resolution of the conflict'. When club life restarted after the

Armistice, evening races only were proposed. This cycle of events was repeated through the course and aftermath of the 1939-45 war.

The 1919 HLSC meeting notes contain a mildly rancorous reference to a Royal Northern initiative (in their capacity as the senior club) soliciting contributions for a retirement gift to Mr Pirrie, the Clyde yacht club's Official Handicapper. This oft-maligned official cannot have been popular in the Holy Loch as just one guinea was donated (the same amount as second prize in one of the club's lugsail dinghy class regattas).

The club minutes are mainly concerned with prize money allocations and long-running deliberations on protests, somehow mixed in the general business. Evening races appear to have been competitive and well-attended. In 1931, the HLSC schedule was amended in coordination with the Gareloch Yacht Club, so clearly there were members of both clubs participating in both programmes. At that time, points series were run for Scottish Islands and Gareloch class yachts in the Holy Loch.

For the 1925 season, it was noted that the mark boats were "*completely done*" and the club resolved to purchase four new ones. With all the sailing clubs on the Clyde employing the same system, orders for replacement mark-boats and the annual maintenance of an oft-neglected asset must have provided a useful income for local boatbuilders. Only in the changed economic environment post-WW2 was the ongoing cost of maintaining and stationing mark boats questioned from the floor.

In 1939, thirty-odd regattas (not including cruising races, schools' races, or the Clyde Fortnight) were listed in the Clyde fixture list. Of these, the little Holy Loch Sailing Club would host five at Hunter's Quay, outside the loch in front of the RCYC. What started as a niche society with modest ambitions had clearly taken on a life of its own. The racing programme catered for old-style 5-raters, 6-metres, 19/24s, and everything up to 35-tonners, mirroring the Royal Clyde.

The Holy Loch was a notable pioneer in organising evening racing on the Clyde. "*Remembering the success which has attended the evening matches of the Royal Western Yacht Club and the Holy Loch Sailing Club, in recent years, it is not at all astonishing to find that evening sailing is likely to be one of the most prominent features of the coming Clyde year. When the weather is at all on its good behaviour there is a wondrous charm about racing in our northern gloamings.*"[591]

Although a small club, the membership was influential and active in the affairs of the Clyde Yacht Clubs Conference, using the HLSC as a lobby channel, rather than one of the senior clubs. The same well-connected summer residents donated fine trophies and underwrote generous prize money. First prize in the principal regatta for the big boats in 1919 was

£8.00 (£410). Today, with the demise of prizemoney, the club's well-buffed legacy of vulgar Victorian silverware reflects this past grandeur.

The HLSC catered for generations of well-known sailing families and inter-war owners including John G. Stephen, T. C. Glen-Coats, Charles McAndrew, Thomas Dunlop, Jimmy Howden Hume, J. Herbert Thom, Ron Teacher, Col. Campbell, Major A. S. L. Young, William Bergius; and industry people such as Robert Lorimer, Alex Robertson, and David Boyd. Nevertheless, the club was inclusive. James Fergusson Jr, Ferryman, was elected to membership at the same meeting as Charles McAndrew MP. Ladies and junior members under 18-years enjoyed full privileges.

Even in 1946, the club still held races for 8mRs at the annual regatta, although now the first prize was just £1 in that class. In 1946, even the Mudhook Yacht Club was feeling the pinch and soliciting assistance to host the Schools Races. The HLSC donated two guineas. At that time, the club subscription was £1 5/-. In 1948, the club's starting canons were discovered in the RCYC changing rooms. However, the ammunition-box, recall-numbers and signal-flags were still missing, and the Secretary wrote to the RCYC to have these returned. The Royal Clyde considered our mark boats theirs too – a downside of consanguinity, but then they did have the clubhouse.

As West of Scotland society rebalanced in the post-war years, the pace of life changed. Fewer 'mainland' families were inclined to maintain weekend villas on the Highland side of the Clyde. At the same time, yachting had morphed from an all-consuming lifestyle to become a mere recreation. This benefitted Clyde yacht clubs within easy reach of the greater Glasgow area, where most members lived and worked. In these changed circumstances, the original HLSC lost its raison d'être.

By 1952, at the club's Spring General Meeting in the Teacher's Whisky boardroom, the order of business referenced stalwart members, like Col. Wordie, Commodore since 1931, passing away and office bearers, like Adam Bergius, intent on resigning as they no longer lived by the loch. J. Herbert Thom declined to take over as Commodore and a reluctant Adam Bergius ended up in that position.

By the following year, restructuring was inevitable. The Cowal Sailing Club, located across the loch in Sandbank, presented the obvious possibility of a merger. The CSC was a 'blue-collar' society, formed in 1947. However, the membership of local boatbuilders and tradesmen was upwardly mobile and keen to embrace change. A full union was arranged after the usual ballots to create the 'Cowal Holy Loch Sailing Club' in 1953. The redundant 'Cowal' in the title was dropped ten years later.[592] When the two clubs merged, there were still 65, long-standing, HLSC members to carry the old institution's traditions forward, including the firearms license for a fine set of starting cannons made by the Winchester Repeating Arms Co.

HLSC is perhaps the only club to have run races concurrently for 12ft National dinghies and 12-metre yachts. This occurred in July 1963, when the newly launched *Sovereign* raced against *Sceptre* on the Clyde in her initial working-up trials. One wonders why these races were held under the auspices of the HLSC rather than one of the Clyde's more senior clubs. Two years later, the HLSC transferred allegiance to the larger National 14ft Merlin Rocket class, precluding further doubles; as, if there ever were any 14-metres built, they were few and far between.

Perhaps the most remarkable aspect of the HLSC is how well the 'toffs' and the 'hoi polloi' have got along over the years. We have members who are entitled to fly the white ensign of the Squadron, and the blue ensigns of the Royal Gourock and the Royal Northern, but who are, nonetheless, happy to substitute the red duster for club events. The levels of factional infighting, political intrigue and sheer bloody-mindedness are much the same as any other club, but with a backbone of enthusiastic Piper sailors and low overheads, it is today a relatively sustainable institution.

Our senior member is Molly McLachlan, née Lorimer, who has been a full member of the Holy Loch Sailing Club since she was elected on the 14th February 1947. Seventy-three years of membership is remarkable for any institution and it is certainly a record in Scotland. Molly is a living link to the yacht building industry on the Holy Loch, when Morris & Lorimer, established in 1885, was the preferred yard for big boats.

Molly was a good sailor in her youth and today speaks about yachting with authority and a lifetime of experience. She is excellent company, and although now in her nineties, her vital spark burns so brightly that she lights up any room she enters. Bob Donaldson writes: "*during a recent morning coffee, we were entertained by Molly with a flood of stories about M&L: how she bought her first boat, a steam yacht, on behalf of her father, when she was only a teenager: how she bought Vadura, on behalf of Jimmy Howden Hulme for the same reason*". Perhaps during their next coffee Bob might ask her exactly how that scam worked!

The Clyde Cruising Club

The Clyde Cruising Club (CCC) emerged from the 'Gluepot' in 1909. The 'Gluepot', or the Argyll Arms, was a notorious drinking den in Rothesay in the days before sobriety was regarded as a virtue. This wee establishment closed recently, out of step with a world of wine-bars and gastro-pubs. There may be members today who are unaware of the Gluepot, but its closure left the CCC as yet another peripatetic institution.

The Cruising Club's dinghy section does, however, have a small pavilion by the tiny Bardowie Loch, where cadet members have bounced off the banks for 80 years. Belying the stereotype of the tight Scotsman, the CCC has invested heavily in this cosy little pond.

The CCC is renowned for its unsurpassed library of 'Sailing Directions', which cover every nook and gunkhole up and down the West Coast. Even experienced cruising yachtsmen clutch a salt-stained copy, white-knuckled, when entering the 'best', or rather most terrifying, anchorages on our shores. A deal of lead shrapnel and paint chips must have been shed to identify all these sub-surface snags in the days before echo-sounders. The CCC also runs offshore racing, or rather 'coastal passage racing', as it is generally played out on the West Coast. But then again, they do disappear in the direction of St Kilda from time to time, so what do we know?

The Cruising Club was once famed for its social life: "*Mr Glen-Coats, as Commodore, presided over a most successful smoking concert a few nights ago in Glasgow. Nothing could better show the great popularity of this, the most recently organised club of the Clyde, than the simple statement that the company numbered over 250.*" *The club was arranging to hold a ladies' night in the future.*"[593] The CCC's well-rounded race programme of the Scottish Series, the Tobermory Race, the Tarbert Race, the two-handed Ailsa Craig Race and the rest, comprise the core of competitive sailing for the cruiser-racer type of yachts that are now the mainstay of yachting on the Clyde.

CODA: An American in Paradise

In his memoirs, Sherman Hoyt describes the young boys of the Holy Loch Sailing Club and their shenanigans during the 1925 Season. After the conclusion of the Seawanhaka Cup match that year, Clinton Crane and his family left Hunter's Quay with the trophy. Hoyt, however, was in no great hurry to go home and hung around the Royal Clyde to socialise with his many friends, and continue his masterclass in the 6-metres, maintaining a perfect record with the Crane-designed, *Lanai*.

Hoyt was bent on having a good time. The American campaign had chartered the 65ft LOA auxiliary sloop, *Iolanthe*, from Captain John Coleville to act as a mothership to the two American 6mRs. She was a good-sized vessel that came with a crew of four. *Iolanthe* had been built by the Ailsa yard in 1922 and was powered by twin Bergius petrol-paraffin motors. Hoyt extended the charter on his own account and made a number of short cruises between the regular RCYC race days. He then embarked on "*a happy summer with many amusing incidents.*"

"*Finding myself short of crew, after Crane and young Dan Cox had left, I adopted a lot of nice Scotch boys called the Holy Loch Sailing Club, rather a cross between a* troop of sea scouts and one of our junior yacht clubs. I would take two or three as crew on 'Lanai' when racing and between races would load up Iolanthe with as many boys as she had bunks for. We made various cruises to Fairlie, Largs, Rothesay, up through the Kyles of Bute to Tighnabruaich, Tarbert and other ports."[594] In these years the senior clubs like the Royal Clyde did not admit cadet members, so the HLSC was home to these 'lost boys'. Hoyt enjoyed the company of our youngsters, even if he did have trouble understanding the accents.

Two years before, in 1923, after sailing the British American Cup races on the Solent, Hoyt had detoured to the Clyde with the 6mR, *Lea*. In this visit, he befriended Sir Thomas Dunlop's grandsons. Dunlop at that time owned *Harbinger*, a 94-ton Stowe yawl, which he described as "*a fine floaty boat.*" Hoyt remembers that the lads "*were normally on hand, eager to row us ashore when we had picked up our moorings. As they were very small boys, the oars in their grandfather's large gig were quite a job to handle, but Clydeside youngsters take to the water about as soon as they can walk, and they managed somehow.*" Hoyt took both boys racing on *Lea*, with dispensation from the committee to carry the extra hand – or to substitute two half-sized crewmen.

Hoyt was not above joshing his young friends for a bit of fun. He asked Tommy, the elder brother, if he would like to race on the Yankee Six the following day. Tommy replied that he "*would luv it fine.*" The boy proved to be an excellent crew, if a little on the small side. But on returning to Hunter's Quay that afternoon Jimmy, the younger brother, was waiting. Hoyt had previously promised to take him along the next day. However, Tommy had proved his worth and earned his place. "*All richt*", said Jimmy accepting his lot with a tear in his eye. Hoyt continues: "*Still poking fun, I asked him if he knew the rule then in force that if one or more of the crew were ladies, an extra hand might be carried; so, I suggested if he had, or could borrow, a kilt that would do.*"

Jimmy's response to this crass insult to both his nationality and his manhood was immediate. Just three feet tall and purple with rage, he gave back as good as he got "*I ken the rules, I'll hae ye understand I've got a kilt of my ain. I'm a proper man (and kin pruv it). I'm nae a lady!*" Of course, he was on the boat next day, but I doubt he ever forgave Hoyt. Six-up, *Lea* won again with Jimmy on the weather rail, risking the famous binoculars, and providing a running commentary on the fortunes of his dad's diminutive Fife 19/24, then in her 24th season: "*Aye, there's Tresta. Look at the damn fou noo; I'll nair let faither go racing wi'out me again!*" Hoyt mused: "*Do you wonder that I loved my Scotch boys as well as many of their elders?*"

Forty years later, but still before the advent of common sense, a new generation of Holy Loch boys would menace the estuary with another 65ft auxiliary yacht. This was a mighty steel ketch, boasting a toy chest to die for, and a roulette table set into the saloon table of the after cabin. *Vaer-Wel* was a battlewagon to encourage bad behaviour. Innocents abroad, we swept the beach-side shelters of the Clyde coast with our wheelhouse searchlight, dazzling courting couples to gratify our youthful sense of fun. I might take this opportunity to offer an unreserved apology on behalf of the entire crew of the *Vaer-Wel*.

Sherman Hoyt (1878-1961) of Long Island Sound was a legend in yachting circles worldwide. He won consistently, both offshore and in America's Cup competition. He was an undiscriminating raconteur, hobnobbing with presidents, kings and princes; he toasted Sir Thomas Lipton, the Dowager Empress of China, and Adolph Hitler. Hoyt was involved in the birth of the 6-metre class in the USA and designed five of these boats: US 12 *Lea*, US 24 *Paumonok*, US 35 *Atrocia*, US 40 *Saleema*, and US 52 *Aprodite*.

[574] The Firth of Clyde, George Blake, 1952.

[575] The Mudhook Yacht Club, 1964 – 1999, A Brief Historical Sketch, M. C. Henry, June 2000. The 'one forbye' arises because a member reappeared after being posted missing, presumed dead.

[576] The Piper Calls the Tune, 2017 where primary sources can be accessed.

[577] The Armstrong and Douglas families, for example, made the 'pilgrimage' for three generations.

[578] History of the Royal Western Yacht Club, Royal Western website.

[579] Between 1966 and 1972, the Western ran the Barra Head Race in alternate years, one of the few 'offshore' races offshore races, in the history of Clyde yachting.

[580] The Story of the Clyde Canoe Club at Rosneath, Baloch & Cashel, 1873-2013.

[581] The Yachtsman, June 1893.

[582] Yachting, 15th October 1891.

[583] Royal Highland Yacht Club, West Highland Week website.

[584] Royal Tay Yacht Club, Club History, RTYC website.

[585] Cruise in Company, George Blake and Christopher Small, 1959.

[586] Yachting on the Northern Waters of Scotland, *Hunt's Yachting Magazine*, January 1866. The quote continues, sagely: *"The probability of a railway being brought there; and, important improvements being contemplated, as regards the harbour, offer an additional inducement to make that selection at once, rather than incur the risk of having to pay an advanced price for a site after its enhancement, by the improvements which are anticipated."*

[587] Minute Book of the Holy Loch Sailing Club – 1914-1954.

[588] Yacht Club News, The Yachtsman, 31st July 1926.

[589] Club Reports, The Yachtsman, 10th April 1913.

[590] Ibid

[591] Clyde, The Yachtsman, 29th November 1894.

[592] Holy Loch Sailing Club, Bob Donaldson, Sandbank, Life and Times of the Village, Ed Anne Galliard, 2009.

[593] Clyde, The Yachtsman, 2nd February 1911.

[594] Sherman Hoyt's Memoirs, C. Sherman Hoyt, 1950.

The Lorimer family's 6mR, *Suzette*, on the Holy Loch   Image: Molly McLachlan née Lorimer

6mR, *Suzette* (ex-*Lucille*, Fife 1928) on the Holy Loch   Image: Molly McLachlan née Lorimer

Rothesay Bay, the RNYC anchorage ca.1890   Image: old postcard

Hunter's Quay anchorage ca.1910   Image: old postcard

Holy Loch today, HLSC at lower centre   Image: incognita

The Holy Loch Yacht Club is giving a spurt to racing in the loch, and the revival will be appreciated by the few who remember the racing of small craft there long ago, when Mr Robertson's little cutter the Clipper, the Banshee, and other Bermuda-rigged boats used to be at it all summer through. The Glasgow Herald, 10th April 1890. The newspaper faithfully recorded the development of the sport through the turn of the century.

Chapter 13: Tip-top Sportin' Chentlemen

If you're a Coats you lose a lot o' time makin' up your mind what boat you'll sail tomorrow; the whole o' the Clyde below the Tail o' the Bank is chock-a-block wi' steamboat-yats and cutters the Coats's canna hail a boat ashore from to get a sail, for they canna mind their names. Still-and-on, there's nothing wrong wi' them – tip-top sportin' chentlemen! Neil Munro satirises the Coats.[595]

Victorian tycoons did not tread lightly on this planet. Perhaps some were lacking something in moral stature, but unquestionably, they all had bigger balls than today's shadowy robber barons. Eccentric men of immense wealth, these magnates could be competent captains of both industry and extremely large yachts, or indeed fleets of the same. The story of Scottish sailing rests on a foundation of patronage and relentless ambition. But then, this is not so different from anywhere else in the world, as yacht ownership is the last refuge of the scoundrel, the recluse and the individual.

In 1982 our family were on holiday in Alaska. A dark-blue T-shirt caught my eye among the Ulu knives and native bead-crafts. It was so 'on-message' I bought two. My daughter, Kathryn, still wears one. The shirt boasted that the 49th State was the *"land of the individual and other endangered species"*. It is undeniable that our designers and boatbuilders made the Clyde a centre of excellence. However, without that celebrated generation of owners, individualists who craved cutthroat competition in all walks of life, who loved the outdoors, and who had money to burn, nothing would have stirred.

But nothing lasts forever; as the global economy moved from burst to boom through the 1990s and into the new millennium, yawning income inequalities, of the scale necessary to support a renaissance in 'first-class' yachting, have re-emerged. But the *"tip-top sportin' chentlemen"*, cited by Para Handy were indeed an endangered species on the road to extinction.[596] They have disappeared from the face of the Earth and the furtive inheritors of the robber baron business now dwell in tax havens, or rather, claim to.

Yachting on the Clyde grew in parallel with Glasgow, and in parallel with Glasgow it has declined. Should we lionise the rich patrons of the past? Certainly not, but we surely can't ignore them. They are an essential part of the story, and if we can cope with the Stuart monarchs, we can cope with anything. *"Here's tae us, wha's like us, damn few, and they're a' deid"*.[597]

The yachtsmen we describe here were Corinthians, but they pursued their passion professionally, with acumen and due diligence. Of course, there were also dabblers who made a virtue of wilful ignorance: *"The 23mR Shamrock led the class up to within 50 yards of the finishing line. Here she fell into a soft patch and was completely becalmed. For two hours she lay there lifeless, watching all the others sail by and cross the line, a thing that dumfounded and angered Sir Thomas Lipton, though he had been, as you might say, brought up on the Clyde; but then Sir Thomas never could be got to understand these things."*[598]

Looking north at the turn of the century, the vigorous yachting scene on the Clyde shadowed the undisputed status of Cowes. Reinforcing our then-dominant marine industry, 41 of the 165 'most influential British yachtsmen of 1907' were Scottish sailors, or active members of Scottish clubs.[599] And, perhaps surprisingly, nine were members of my own little club – the Holy Loch Sailing Club. An early draft of this book told their stories in a 'who's who' of turn-of-the-century Scottish yachting. Perhaps inevitably, that task collapsed under its own weight, so this chapter focusses on a few key individuals and two significant families, the Coats and the Clarks. These gentlemen were not just wealthy, nearly all were keen sailors and serial clients of the Clyde's best designers and boatyards. Moreover, they bred like rabbits and had their fingers in every pie.

James Coats (1774-1857) started yarn-spinning in a small way at his modest premises in Ferguslie, Paisley, in 1826. His sons, James and Peter, were more ambitious. They founded J. & P. Coats, with their brother, Thomas, joining the firm two years later. Andrew, a fourth brother, moved to the United States in 1839 and established the Coats' export business. Steam powered spinning, and the invention of the domestic sewing machine in the 1840s, created a ripe environment for expansion. The Coats business grew rapidly until the American Civil War (1861-65) constricted the supply pipeline. While blockade runners did indeed smuggle cotton out of the Southern States, the supply was limited and unreliable.

It is impossible to overstate the value of the cotton trade to British GDP in the mid-19th century. Fully 54% of British exports in 1851 was earned from cotton fabric, and in 1860, 80% of our raw cotton was imported from the Rebel Southern States.[600] After the North won the Civil War, the USA instituted steep tariffs against British firms who had collaborated with the Rebels. These sanctions inspired J. & P. Coats to become a multinational, protecting their market share by manufacturing in the USA.[601] Other deft corporate footwork allowed the firm to circumvent the penalties assigned to their illegal supply chain. Thus, tacit support for slavery effectively propelled the Coats to the heights of the great panjandra.

James Coats, Peter's oldest son, travelled to New York and helped Andrew to set up the first Coats mills at Pawtucket, Rhode Island in 1864. The success of the first satellite operation led to new factories in Russia, Germany, Austria, Hungary and Spain. In this context, it is important to remember that the USA only overtook the UK in population numbers during the 1850-1860 inter-census period. Home-grown US conglomerates were in their infancy and the Old Country still had much to offer new markets through high-level industrial skills and business expertise. As one of the 'jewels in the crown' of our Empire, the Coats operation was an exemplar of a proud state.[602]

James and Patrick Clark established their first mill in 1755, predating the Coats family by half-a-century. Despite Napoleon Bonaparte's trade blockade (1806-1814), the Clarks' business empire grew rapidly. The family developed new methods of spinning and then industrialised the process in 1812, before going on to dominate the world trade.[603] Clark & Co built manufacturing facilities in the USA in 1864, four years before Coats.

Clark and Co. were an innovative enterprise and represented J. & P. Coats' main competition before the Coats' greater financial clout allowed a relatively amicable take-over. In 1896, J. & P. Coats absorbed Clark & Co Ltd. From then on, the corporate behemoth was unstoppable. The giant combine of J. & P. Coats Ltd grew to become one of the first multinationals and the largest operation of its type in the world. The Coats Group has endured to become one of the oldest companies in Scotland. Today, it still dominates its sector, with no quarter asked or given.[604]

The two yard-spinning families accumulated fabulous wealth, and after belatedly severing their connections with slavery, they were also notably philanthropic. J. & P. Coats Ltd invested in forward-thinking worker welfare programmes, education, health, literacy, museums, parks and gardens, science and religion. The Coats even distributed Christmas gifts to all the lighthouse keepers in Scotland.

A few years after the merger, the Clark family stepped back from the business to enjoy the fruits of what was then a record buy-out. In fact, both Coats and Clark families, having made their millions, began to enjoy more leisure time after 1900. Our tip-top sporting gentlemen were free to party. Perhaps their forebearers' connections with slavery and gunrunning should have left a stain on their collective conscience, but the newly-minted dilettantes stealthily 'sport-washed' the blood from their hands. Former Tory minister, Alan Clark, liked to quote his father's autobiography. "*My parents belonged to a section of society known as 'the idle rich', and although, in that golden age, many people were richer, there can have been few who were idler.*"[605] Alan's grandfather, Kenneth McKenzie Clark, was owner of several large yachts and a man who played billiards every night of his life.

The 1887 *Thistle* challenge for the America's Cup was led by James Bell, then Vice-Commodore of the Royal Clyde. However, the syndicate's real strength lay in their 'money men', included George Coats (James Coats Jr's brother) and John Clark (father of Ken Clark, the famous Riviera gambler who 'broke the bank at Monte Carlo'). Despite the fact that the syndicate might have embarrassed Croesus, G. L. Watson designed the boat for nothing, and the membership of the Royal Clyde pitched in too.

The story of the D. & W. Henderson-built, *Thistle*, and the tip-top gentlemen who funded the 7th Challenge, has been covered in countless histories of the 'Auld Mug'. 'Pierie' McNicol, from Strachur, was among the crew. The nickname endured from McNicol's former employment taking the lines on Strachur Pier. And, when *Thistle* was sold to become the Kaiser's first *Meteor*, several local men stayed with the boat to ease the passage of the imperial German navy into the manifold mysteries of first-class yachting.

The Coats and Clarks owned an awful lot of yachts. The contribution to the local marine industry was extraordinary when we remember that each, from the smallest lugger to the largest steam-yacht, was a hand-crafted object built entirely from raw materials. The yards sawed their own timber, forged their own metalwork and cast or fabricated their fastenings and fittings. These boats were not popped out of a mould on a production-line.

If there is any pattern to be discerned, the Coats built bigger boats on average and more of them. Most were designed and supervised by G. L. Watson. The Clarks tended to patronise the Fifes, first Auld Wull and then William Fife Jr. The patriarchs, James Clark (1813-1889), with his schooner, *Amandine* (Fife 1870), and Thomas Coats (1809-1883), with the steam-yacht, *Hebe* (1869), both enjoyed their leisure-time on the Clyde, but these gentlemen first had fortunes to make. Subsequent generations would have more time and more opportunity to spend, spend, spend.

The two families were nothing if not competitive. In 1901, James Coats Jr. set up a lop-sided wager between the yawl, *Sybarita*, owned by his friend Whitaker Wright, and Kenneth Clark's cutter, *Kariad*. This race was sailed in a north-west gale and "*mountainous seas*" and became part of the legend of yacht racing on the Firth of Clyde. Unlike the close reaching drag-races the region is notorious for, this course serendipitously balanced windward and leeward legs over 76 miles around Ailsa Craig. It was therefore all the more impressive that the winner would charge across the finishing line in an elapsed time of just 6 hours 13 minutes, at an average speed of 12kts, leaving the spectator fleet rollicking in her quarter-wave.

The two Watson yachts were deadly rivals, but neither had established a clear superiority. James thought *Sybarita* to be the faster and backed her unilaterally for 500 guineas (£64,000). *Sybarita* was indeed faster as her rating suggested, but she only 'saved her time' in the final stages. *Kariad* was winning 'on time' until Captain Bevis, *Sybarita's* skipper, ordered a man out along the boom to cut the reef-points. Breaking the reef out while sailing full-and-bye is not easy on a maxi-yacht, but in this case it was worth it. *Sybarita*, took off and "*fled before the gale like a frightened stag*".[606]

James stood to win nothing but had *Sybarita* lost to *Kariad* he would still have been obliged to pay the stake; these were bookmakers odds. Coats and his party followed the race aboard *Gleniffer* (Watson 1899). At 158ft LOA and 500-tons Thames Measurement, this magnificent G. L. Watson schooner could average 16kts on passage and was one of the few vessels able to keep up with the hard-driving cutters. James Coats watched the racing from the companionway. There is an old saying that 'only owners and alseholes block the companionway'; and the consensus is that it's hard to tell the difference. James suffered terribly from rheumatism so perhaps we can give him a pass on this one.

The Coats Family go Yachting

At one time, the Coats family, taken as a whole, had twelve yachts in commission – more than 3,000-tons of boys-toys. They employed around 120 professional seamen and the annual cost of maintaining this small navy on occasion exceeded £20,000 (£2.5 million). Many of these seamen spent the greater part of their working lives in the service of the family.[607] For the time, the Coats' paternalism was generous and enlightened, but for working men these were hardly the 'good old days'. Most laboured for subsistence wages and had no job security. And whether you were mast-man on a first-class cutter, or a miner at the coalface, the Victorian workplace was a very dangerous place indeed.

James Coats Jr. was what my mother used to call a 'confirmed bachelor', a tag surviving from an age when gay men could be nothing else if they wanted to stay out of prison.[608] At the time, competitive mothers with marriageable daughters tagged him as a misogynist. As a yachtsman, James was no more of a misogynist than the usual company in the smoking room of the Royal Clyde. But as a man of wealth and means he was decidedly unusual. His philanthropy exceeded the sum of his peers.[609]

James built 'Dunselma Castle', the fairy-tale baronial tower-house that sits sentinel atop the beak of Strone. 'Dunselma' was designed by Rennison & Scott in 1884. Subsequently, the Bergius family, who revolutionised auxiliary power in sailing yachts, and also feature prominently in the story of Scottish yachting, acquired this rambling nautical monument and maintained it until 1941, after which it became an uncommonly exotic youth hostel.[610] James visited his extravagant eyrie perhaps twenty times in his life, sometimes with years passing between visits. Even so the house was always fully staffed and kept ready for use.

There is a story, likely apocryphal, of James Coats turning up unannounced at 'Dunselma' and being detained at the gate by the gardener. James protested that he just wanted to look around and that in any case he was in fact the owner of the property. The gardener was not impressed. *"You wouldn't believe how many folks come here with stories like that"* he retorted. No offence was taken, and the two men enjoyed a pleasant chat, both extolling the virtues of this fine Scottish baronial house and its magnificent outlook, which extends to Tenerife if not for the curvature of the earth. James thanked his gardener and headed off home, reassured that if nothing else, the security at 'Dunselma' was excellent and the staff were on their toes.[611]

As James aged and debilitating arthritis limited his sport, his great schooner, *Gleniffer*, was fitted out in the James Watt Dock each spring, and moored beside her consort, the steam-yacht, *Triton*, off Ashton. The two vessels were kept in-commission all summer before being laid-up and the cycle repeated. James could not bear the thought of laying-off the two crews, totalling perhaps 60 to 70 men. One doubts if they enjoyed the 'idle life', polishing brass waiting for the old man to show up; but hope springs eternal and bills had to be paid.

When at last it became obvious that this could not go on forever, James still sent round gifts at Christmas to let his old crew know they had not been forgotten. It must have been a sad parting of the ways. If you are destined to 'know your place' in life, it is as well to have a beneficent boss. When *Gleniffer* (Watson 1899) raced the slimmer, racier *Rainbow* (Watson 1898) and the 80-linear-rater, *Bona* (Watson 1897), in 1899, Coats and his crew came a bad last. It was a sporting mismatch; nevertheless, the old man distributed prize money as if the boys on *Gleniffer* had won.

"Mr C. Orr-Ewing's schooner Rainbow arrived in the Clyde from the south yesterday, her mainboom broken in the heavy weather at the beginning of the week while the racing fleet were on their way from the South of England to Queenstown. After the accident, Rainbow came right away to the Clyde. She is now moored near Coats's new schooner Gleniffer, so that there is every opportunity of making a comparison of the two huge vessels, both of them exceedingly handsome. They bear a close resemblance in most points, which is natural, the Rainbow with, if anything, more of the racing look about her."[612]

The big boats were not the only ones mothballed. Coats retained ownership of three Watson-designed yachts until his death: the cutters *Marjorie* (1883), a particular favourite, *Brunette* (1893), and the little 3-tonner, *Sprite* (1881). These treasured yachts would appear in his 'last will and testament'. Before his health deteriorated, James delighted in sailing small craft. When doctor's orders confined him to *Gleniffer*, he acquiesced reluctantly, desperately unhappy to surrender the splashy joys of what he called the 'bantam class'. Among his other good works, James funded research into cancer and TB and equipped the Scotia Antarctic Expedition to the tune of £15,000 (£1.8 million). Sadly, he became an invalid while still in his 60s and was only 72 when he died.[613]

Madge in America

Like many well-read yachtsmen of an enquiring mind, James Coats Jr. admired American catboats, intrigued as to quite how they are able to overcome fatal asymmetries and apparently defy the laws of physics. When money is no object, solutions are often to hand. James ordered a 'Cape Cat' from Thomas D. Stoddart of Newport. The little yacht was christened *George and Annie,* possibly after James's favourite niece and her husband.

The boat's dimensions were: 26ft LOA and LWL, 11ft beam, a frankly terrifying 34ft boom, and a 19ft gaff. She was shipped from New York in April 1880, accompanied by a skilled catboat skipper from Newport, Josiah Albro Jr. She was soon sailing on the Clyde in the capable hands of Josiah, showing off at Hunter's Quay before the Royal Clyde Yacht Club's fleet as they mustered for the day's regatta.[614] It appears that the experiment was not a success.

Lining up against the like-sized 22ft Class of Clyde lugsail boats, *George and Annie* was not impressive. The fat little catboat was comprehensively outgunned. The Clyde luggers of that era were famously quick, boasting stiff, light-weight clinker-built construction, and a plumb stem and transom. Beam was about 7ft, and draft 3ft 2". The luggers were spectacularly over-rigged for 'no-holds-barred' racing, with a large standing lug and a big foresail. They deployed shifting ballast with bags of lead-shot slung onto a special shelf built into the turn of the bilge, see Chapter 18.

Whatever James's intentions, if he wanted to test an American model against our flying death-traps, he should have brought over a Yankee sandbagger. Although the catboat was consigned to a life of pottering, James was still interested in the long-running trans-Atlantic debate about which continent's model was best. This was by no means an East vs West divide. There were many admirers of the beamy American centre-boarders in Britain and a corresponding group of 'cutter-cranks' in the States. James resolved to send his recently outclassed 10-tonner, *Madge*, across to do battle in the United States

G. L. Watson designed *Madge* in 1879. She became one of the most famous yachts in the history of yachting, but ironically not until *after* her days as a top-class racing yacht had ended. The 10-tonner class was a hot-bed of competition in the 1870s and 1880s on the Clyde, with new yachts being launched every year to challenge the established 'cracks'.

W. P. Stephens, who took a keen interest in our design trends, tabulated the changes from 1875 to 1884, highlighting the increasingly radical proportions of the British cutter. Had Stephens waited another year he could have cited the 6-tonner, *Oona*, to complete the picture of a reckless descent into oblivion. During this era, beam was progressively reduced, and waterlines lengthened, although as yet nothing like the dangerous extreme represented by *Oona* in 1885, being 45ft 3" LOA (3ft 4" longer than the longest of these 10-tonners) and 5ft 6" beam.

Leading 10-tonners on the Clyde (1875-1884)

Yacht	Year	Designer	LWL	Beam
Lily	1875	Richardson	36'1"	8'1"
Florence	1876	Reid	38'7"	7'10"
Verve I	1877	Watson	37'0"	7'7"
Volga	1878	Fife	37'0"	8'0"
Quiraing	1878	Watson	38'8"	7'9"
Preciosa	1878	Luke	35'3"	8'4" (outlier)
Maharanee	1879	Waterman	40'8"	7'6"
Madge	1879	Watson	38'8"	7'9"
Verve II	1881	Watson	40'6"	7'7"
Neptune	1880	Fife	39'6"	7'7"
Ulidia	1883	Fife	41'11"	7'2"
Ulerin	1884	Watson	41'6"	7'3"

Madge was beautifully built by J. McAdam of Govan and wanting for nothing. In the capable hands of her professional skipper, Robert Duncan, she was successful on the Clyde from the day of her launching.[615] In the published accounts of this campaign, we find that winning was not just satisfying, but lucrative. In her first year, from 24 starts, *Madge* took 22 wins and 2 minor places; winning a total of £395 (£46,600).[616]

In 1880, she started 35 times, winning 20 firsts and 2 minor places to realise £300 (£35,500). *Florence*, a well-sailed Reid design, limited *Madge's* winnings that year, winning £219 (£27,000) of the available pot. In 1881, her third season, *Madge* came up against the Fife-designed, *Neptune*, and took only £47 (£5,600), while *Neptune* made off with £260 (£31,000). Whether these conversions are accurate or not, anything in that range is confounding, especially in light of the modest outlay required to campaign a 10-tonner.

The 10-tonners were the most competitive class in the country, on the Clyde, and to a lesser extent on the South Coast. So, as a racing yacht just three years old, *Madge* was now reaching the end of her competitive life and ripe for retirement. Superannuated racing yachts of the period were usually converted to cruisers with their overhanging booms cropped and a vestigial mizzen added to gain the yawl's rating bonus. However, in this instance, James Coats saw an opportunity to send the boat across the Atlantic to challenge the American model. In 1881, the *Standard* wrote: "*In the North the Tens had plenty of sport, the Neptune latterly finding her equal in the new Verve and both leading the Madge so completely that she fled to America in despair.*"[617] *Madge* was shipped on the Anchor Line's SS *Divonia* and arrived in New York on August 16th 1881. She was dropped over the side, rigged-up and moored by the Yacht Club off Staten Island.

The locals were unimpressed, at least initially. C. P. Kunhardt, Yachting Editor of *Forest and Stream*, the American's 'Dixon Kemp', commented, "*in point of beam she has been unreasonably squeezed by the English Rule.*" As to being 'squeezed', that could not be denied, but to the surprise of many on both sides of the Pond, this outdated little Clyde cutter turned out to be 'unreasonably' quick. Coats appears to have had no clear plan of campaign; this was left in the hands of W. Lindsay Blatch, a Scot living in New York and a member of the New York Yacht Club.

Coats may have been acting on a whim, but G. L. Watson was not. In a gently provocative letter published in the *New York Nautical Gazette*, he declared, "*I shall be surprised if anything above her inches bothers her in rough water*". Watson did not need to caveat his prediction with a preference for 'rough water'; *Madge* made a great impression and left a lasting impact. Despite scratch crews and chaotic mark-roundings, no one was left in any doubt that the little Scottish cutter was the 'class-act' of the season.[618]

The Yankee sloops might have been more usable dual-purpose yachts and better-looking too, but they were just not as quick. As the story goes, 'the cat was out the bag'. Lessons were quickly learned, and by the time of the 5th Challenge for the America's Cup, Uncle Sam – or more specifically Herreshoff and Burgess were back up to speed. Burgess, in particular, was lightly taunted by Herreshoff as being a 'cutter-crank' and unduly influenced by his friendship with G. L. Watson.[619] Whatever influence there was, it was surely benign. In the 1885 match, Edward Burgess's *Puritan* would best the elegant Beavor-Webb cutter, *Genesta*, built by D. & W. Henderson.

G. L. Watson, among others, considered that *Genesta* was merely a fast cruiser and not in the first rank of British cutters. This was still, however, a contest that could have gone either way, but in what would become a recurring irritation, the Americans just sailed their boat much better.[620] Nevertheless, after the mistakes of the Cup matches, *Genesta* won three prestigious trophies in American waters – a special cup for schooners and 'single-stickers' presented by Commodore Gordon Bennett, the Brenton Reef Trophy and the Cape May Challenge Cup, before sailing back across the Atlantic on her own bottom. As for *Madge*, the 'Pride of Govan' never came home; almost three decades after her launch in Scotland, she was broken-up on the beach at Rochdale, New York, in 1894.

James Coats Jr (1841-1912) was the perfect client. His first racing yacht was the 40-tonner, *Diana* (1876 Boag), quickly followed by the schooner, *Siren* (Cunliff & Dunlop 1877). James' early patronage of Boag reminds us that Fife's yard (est. ca.1803) was not the only one in the village. Hugh Boag, of an old Fairlie family who had worked for Fife II, set up on his own account on the beach north of the Fife yard ca.1870. The 'Clydeships' database lists 14 Boag vessels – starting with miniature cutters, then gradually moving up the size range to a steam-yacht of 63ft LOA.[621] Business was good, apparently, as by 1877 Hugh could afford to buy back *Maggie*, one of his 20-tonners, to go sailing himself.

Hugh Boag is said to have designed and built a number of yachts for the Coats and Clarks in the early days before G. L. Watson and William Fife hoovered up the lion's share of commissions.[622] However, of the yachts listed, only *Diana* was delivered to James Coats Jr. in 1876, and *Minette* to William L. Coats in 1877. Boag's other work included fishing smacks, small pleasure steamers and alterations to Fife and McAlister boats. Clearly, he was a talented designer and builder. Boag's relatively small, but enduring and clearly much-loved, portfolio would reward further study. The fact that Hugh was brought in to alter yachts drawn by other designers and optimise them supports this scenario.

James Coats Jr's long association with G. L. Watson began with the celebrated *Madge*. This was followed by the cutters, *Sprite* (1881) and *Marjorie* (1883) and her steam-yacht mothership, *Express* (1884). The Fife cutter, *Cruiser* (1886), interrupts the Watson series before James commissioned the little match-racing sister-ships, *Gypsy* and *Brunette* (1893). James also owned the steam-yacht, *Iris* (Watson 1892), the fishing-yacht, *Scouder* (Fife 1894) and *Gleniffer* (Watson 1899).

The 131-linear-rater, *Gleniffer* (300-ton TM), was the largest two-masted schooner in the world at the time and she cruised in company with her luxurious 'steam-tug', *Triton* (Watson 1902). Who, after all would willingly suffer the noise and vibration of a stinkpot in the bilges when the breeze drops?[623] G. L. Watson designed a range of powerful steam-launches specifically as yacht tenders for the fashionable Clyde yachting man. *"This screw is to be 70ft long and is to have very considerable cabin accommodation. She will steam fast and will have power to tow a 100-ton cutter at five or six miles an hour."*[624] Perhaps fortunately, the tag 'screw' for propeller-driven steamers did not catch on.

James Coats Jr. was also the registered owner of the 495-tons auxiliary barque, *Scotia* (Jørgensen & Knudsen 1872), in which William Spiers Bruce's '*Scotia* Expedition' voyaged to the Antarctic in 1902. Andrew Coats had established a firm friendship with William Bruce in 1898 when they sailed to the Arctic together in Andrew's steam-yacht, *Blencathra* 424-tons (H. M. Dockyard 1867). The success of Bruce's scientific programme aboard the *Blencathra* led to the Coats' sponsorship of the *Scotia* Expedition.

James and Andrew eventually funded almost all of Bruce's Expedition; as a result, a wedge of Antarctica between 20°W and 36°W was given the name 'Coats Land'.[625] Similarly, James Caird, who made his fortune in jute, sponsored the unsuccessful, yet still inspiring, Imperial Trans-Antarctic Expedition of 1914. Shackleton's Weddell Sea party saw perhaps the lowest mortality of any polar expedition, despite losing their ship in the ice.[626]

Andrew Coats owned the steam-yachts, *Fujiyama*, 170-tons (J. Reid & Co 1895) and *Hecate*, 447-tons (G. L. Watson 1903). His sailing yachts included the cutter, *Ptarmagan* (Fife 1892), the 10-rater, *Woodcock* (Fife 1890), the luggers, *Scowther* (Fife 1894) and *Pansy* (Hatcher 1883), the 23/30, *Fuji* (Fife 1898) and the Clyde 30ft Restricted Class, *Great Auk* (Fife 1905). Larger racing yachts included the 53-linear-rater, *Morning Star* (Fife 1897), the 52-linear-rater, *Camellia* (Summers & Payne 1902) and the 12-metres, *Cintra* (Fife 1908) and *Heatherbell* (Glen-Coats 1907).

Among numerous yachtsmen in the Coats family, James Coats Jr's cousin, George, later Lord Glentanar (1849-1919), owned the 56-ton steam-yacht, *Finuella* (A. & J. Inglis 1883) and the luggers, *Lucifer* (Watson 1895) and *Lottie* (Watson 1898), the 30-linear-raters, *Badger* (Watson 1894) and *Maudie* (Fife 1898). George Coats, the next 'Glentanar', owned the 15-metre, *The Lady Anne* (Fife 1912) and the 6-metre, *Gairney* (Fife 1921).[627]

William Allan Coats (1853-1926) owned the steam-yachts, *Queen o' the May*, 270-tons (Watson 1895) and *Queen of Scots*, 632-tons (Watson 1903), the cutter, *May* (Watson 1881), the cruising yacht *Will-o'-the-Wisp* (Watson 1887), the steam-launches, *Druid* (Ramage & Ferguson 1886) and *Minette* (Boag 1877), and the little lugger, *Hebe* (Watson 1886). Alan's uncle, William, owned the steam-launch, *Express* (Watson 1884), the cutters, *Solan* (Watson 1880) and *Minette* (Boag 1877), and a 'pleasure boat', (Watson 1882).

Peter M. Coats owned the 40-ton steam-yacht, *Jackal* (Cunliffe & Dunlop 1878), the 249-tons steam-yacht, *Zara I* (Watson 1891) and *Zara II* 516-tons (Watson 1895) and the luggers, *Thaber* (Fife 1893) and *Helena* (Fife 1894).[628]

Sir Thomas Glen-Coats 1st Baronet (1846-1922) owned the 310-ton steam-yacht, *Hebe* (J. & G. Thomson 1869), subsequently acquired by Margaret Coats. Sir Thomas's son, Thomas Glen-Coats (1878-1954), later to become the 2nd Baronet, is the subject of Chapter 26. Tommy owned the Clyde 30ft Class, *Thetis*, (Mylne 1904), then the racing yachts, *Pallas*, *Heatherbell*, *Hera*, *Cynthia*, *Clio*, *Ariadne*, *Arethusa*, *Aurora*, *Selene*, *Echo*, *Iris*, *Helen*, *Sapho* and *Pandora*, as described in Chapter 26, and all bar the first designed by himself.[629] Tommy's brother, A. H. Glen-Coats, owned *Elise* (Mylne 1904), a Clyde 30ft Restricted Class, and *Thetis* (Mylne 1904).[630]

The Clark Family go Yachting

The big spender in the Clark family was Sir Kenneth M. Clark, who among other things, owned the entire Ardnamurchan peninsula. Kenneth jointly owned yachts with his brother Norman Clark, principally the *Katoomba* series of steam-yachts: the 169-ton, *Katoomba I* (Scotts 1884); the 437-ton, *Katoomba II* (Ramage & Ferguson 1890); the 270-ton, *Katoomba III* (Ramage & Ferguson 1894); and the Clyde 23/30s, *Lala* (Fife 1893) and *Thella* (Fife 1896). Ken enjoyed the name *Katoomba*, first in partnership with his brother then on his own. There were six *Katoombas* in all. They were not numbered (although that is done here). There can be no reason for this other than a perverse delight in spreading confusion.

Ken's individually owned steam-yachts included the 737-ton, *Katoomba VI* (G. L. Watson 1903), which replaced the 469-ton, *Katoomba V* (Watson 1898) and the little 22-ton steam-yacht, *Katoomba IV* (Adam 1896). For cruising under sail, he had the 186-ton auxiliary schooner, *Stratherric* (J. G. Fay & Co 1898). In the realm of Big Class racing yachts, Ken owned the 65-linear-rater, *Khama* (Fife 1900), which was almost immediately replaced by the 94-linear-rater cutter, *Kariad* (Watson 1901).[631] At the other end of the scale, Ken Clark owned the 17/19s, *Nellie* (Fife 1887) and *Nellietoo* (Fife 1888), the luggers, *Lisette* (Fife 1891) and *Spider* (Fife 1895), the 10-rater, *Encore* (Fife 1890), the Clyde 23/30, *Thela* (Fife 1893) and the centre-boarder, '*Design 499*' (Fife 1903). There was also a little launch named *Puffer* (Adam 1896) and an MFV-type yacht, *The Ketch* (Fife 1906) for use in Suffolk. Norman Clark, left to his own devices, owned the lugger, *Design 238* (Fife 1890), the Clyde 23/30, *Ulva* (Fife 1900), the 2½-rater, *Lizette* (Fife 1891) and the 1½-rater, *Fly* (Fife 1895).

John Clark was a keen racing sailor, particularly in the 1880s. "*The cutter-racing on the Clyde last year was the most marvellous yachting performance ever seen in our waters. It was Erycina, Vanduara, Samoena – sometimes one, sometimes the other; there was no certainty which might win so long as the breeze was not too strong, and the Clyde about its usual.* When it blew, *Vanduara*, an 1880 Watson 90-ton cutter, romped home. Her performance induced John Clark to order a bigger, better and faster yacht from Watson.[632] The result was the famous yawl *Wendur*, built by Messrs Henderson, who had built *Vanduara*. This magnificent vessel was 143-tons, 53-tons larger than Clark's previous cutter and constructed of steel with a lead keel. *The Glasgow Herald* noted that with *"all the latest appliances in ballast, rig, canvas, and outfit the new vessel will be the finest, and probably the fastest racing yacht ever seen on the Clyde"*.

John and William Clark jointly-owned the magnificent 704-ton steam-yacht *Mohican* (Watson 1885), mothership to *Thistle* in 1887. They later commissioned the design of a successor, the 827-ton *Mohican II* (Watson 1895), but she was not built. John Clark had previously owned the steam-yacht, *Bessie* (Watson 1881), 42-tons. He also owned the cutters, *Vanduara* (Watson 1880) and *Ina* (Watson 1881), and the big yawls, *Condor* (Fife 1878), *Wendur* (Watson 1883), and *Atalanta* (D. & W. Henderson 1883) 123-tons.

John Clark became the Commodore of the Royal Clyde Yacht Club in 1889 and held office in that position until his death. The *Mohican* (and the other large steam-yachts of our two yarn-spinning families) served as committee vessels for the RCYC regattas and were quite superb in that role. John's summer residence was 'Curling Hall' in Largs, where he was active in the local community, practically bankrolling the egalitarian new Largs Sailing Club from its inception.[633]

John Clark and his crew made the front pages when the *Mohican*, with Captain Timpson in command, sailed from Largs for New York in 1887 to attend the America's Cup races between the Scottish challenger, *Thistle*, and the defender, *Volunteer*. Captain F. C. Timpson of Southampton worked for the Clarks for many years, first with John and finally finishing his career with William. He was as popular as he was skilful and eventually people of Clydeside came to look upon him as one of their own.

Half-way across the Atlantic, during a difficult passage, the party came across the Canadian yacht, *Lillian*, in a sinking condition after weathering a hurricane. Donald Beaton led a volunteer crew of powerful oarsman. They launched *Mohican's* gig and lifeboat and effected a successful rescue under difficult conditions. The sea was still high in the aftermath of the storm, so it took four hours of strenuous effort to transfer the *Lillian's* complement of twenty officers and seamen, together with the captain's wife, and finally, a *"noble dog of Canadian breed"*. Yachting journalist James Meikle, who was cadging a ride across the pond on the *Mohican*, wrote about the great pride John Clark took in the heroic efforts of his crew and Clark's emotional embrace with the captain of the *Lillian*. The crew of the *Mohican* renamed the lucky dog 'Cyclone' and apparently, by the time they all reached New York, Cyclone was answering to the new name. The *Mohican* was sold to the German Navy during the 1890s.

Stewart Clark was well-known on the Clyde for his 1886 G. L. Watson steam-yacht, *Vanduara* (not to be confused with John Clark's 1880 Watson cutter), at 200ft LOA, she was merely a medium-sized vessel of the type, but she was an especially beautiful one. The D. & W. Henderson-built, *Vanduara*, regularly over-wintered in the Holy Loch. Stewart's son, J. Stewart Clark, owned an extreme, fin-and-bulb keel ½-rater, *Nita* (1893), which hung in slings on *Vanduara's* quarter.[634]

The Watson-designed, *Nita*, was beautifully built by Peter McLean of the finest cedar, the hull planed down to $3/8$th-inch. Her manganese bronze bulbed fin was cast and finished by D. & W. Henderson. *Nita* was rigged with a bamboo-yard lugsail and jib. MacLean was a favourite of Watson's for this type of build. His yard was taken over by James Silver, who made his name with a line of classic motor-cruisers to designs by John Bain.

Stewart Clark owned the steam-yachts, *Morna*, 86-tons (Watson 1884) and the *Vanduara*, 450-ton (Watson 1886). But his son, J. Stewart Clark, was the serial client of brokers and boatyards.

J. Stewart Clark owned the 247-ton steam-yacht, *Rona* (Henderson 1874), the schooner, *Ulva* (Scott 1879), the cutter, *Rona* (Watson 1886), the luggers, *Shuna* (A. Burgoine 1890) and *Jura* (Fife 1896), the Clyde 23/30, *Shuna* (Watson 1893), the ½-rater, *Nita* (Watson 1893), the 1-rater, *Tiree* (Watson 1896), the Clyde 23/30, *Rona* (Fife 1897) and the 36-linear-rater *Ensay*, Fife, 1902.

J. George Clark owned the 100-ton, *Cassandra* (Fife 1886) and the cutter, *Nellie* (Fife 1888). Robert Clark, who had a thing about the letter 'V', owned the cutter, *Vril* (Watson 1876), and the little luggers, *Vashti* (Fife 1891) and *Vis* (Watson 1895) and the sloop, *Valmai* (Mylne 1900).[635]

Fred Clark owned the lugger, *Lizzie* (McLaren 1879). F. N. Clark's *Ailsa* (Fife 1896) appears in the Fife build list but does not feature in Lloyds.

William Clark owned the 5-tonner, *Ivanhoe* (Adam 1876), the 20-rater, *Windward* (Fife 1887/9, the auxiliary cutter, *Bessie* (Watson 1881), the yawl, *Condor* (Fife 1878), the schooner, *Wendur* (Inglis 1882, ex-*Lady Cassandra*) and the yawl, *Wendur* (Watson 1883), acquired from John.

William Clark of Paisley, another family member, owned the 591-ton steam-yacht, *Tuscarora* (Watson 1897).

James Clark owned the cutter, *Snowflake* (Fife 1869) and one of the early *Katoombas*. Other yachts passing through Clark hands include the yawl, *Cee-Mee* (Fife 1892), little lugger, *Winone* (Adam 1883) and the auxiliary schooner, *Lady Cassandra* (Inglis 1882).[636]

From more recent times, the last household name in the dynasty, Kenneth McKenzie Clark (1903-1983) owned the ketch, *Kentra* (Fife 1923), well-known in classic yacht circles and still sailing today.

It seems appropriate to close this section with the words of Neil Munro, as expressed by the garrulous crew of the fairy tale Clyde puffer, *Vital Spark*: *There's an aawful money in them yats!'* said the mate, who was at the wheel. *'I never could see the sense o't,'* remarked the Captain. *'There's the Hera tacking; man, she's smert! Smert! Wan o' them Coats's boats; I wish she would win; I ken a chap that plays the pipes on her.'*

595 Para Handy, Neil Munro, Birlinn reprint, 2015.

596 Para Handy, Puffer (steam coaster) skipper, a delightful figment of Neil Munro (1863-1930). Munro was a local lad, born in Inveraray. He became an influential journalist, novelist and commentator. He wrote beautifully and insightfully, but somehow, he is disparaged in literary circles today.

597 Scottish toast of 19th century origin.

598 Harbours of the Clyde, John Scott Hughes, 1954.

599 British Yachts and Yachtsmen, a complete history of British yachting from the middle of the sixteenth century to the present day, The Yachtsman, 1907.

600 Phantoms of Anglo-Confederate Commerce: An Investigation of American Civil War Blockade Running, Gordon P. Watts, PhD Thesis, St. Andrews University, 1997.

601 Rising tariffs prompted J. & P. Coats to build production facilities in the United States (in 1869) and Russia (in 1889 and 1890), its two largest markets. But competition with Clark & Co and the Nevsky Company contributed to these initiatives. J. & P. Coats foreign direct investments covered 15 countries and 53 investments projects. Dong-Woon Kim, Business and Economic History, Volume Twenty-six, no. 2, Winter 1997.

602 William Thackeray and Napoleon III (not to be confused with his predecessor Bonaparte) were shown around the Paisley mills.

603 Napoleon Bonaparte issued the Berlin Decree in 1806 which prevented imports of silk thread into Britain.

604 Coats and Clark, the binding thread of Paisley's history, Valerie Reilly, RLHF Journal Vol.15, 2009.

605 Rear Window: Why Alan Clark is rich: Three generations prosper on the fruits of the spool, the Independent, Ian Jack 5th June, 1994.

606 The Encyclopaedia of Sport and Games, Volume 4, Charles Howard Suffolk and the Earl of Berkshire, 1911.

607 Harbours of the Clyde, John Scott Hughes, 1954.

608 Homosexuality between consenting adults was only decriminalised in Britain in 1967.

609 Rich Man's Philanthropic Hobbies, Otautau Standard and Wallace County Chronicle, 28th May 1912.

610 'Dunselma' is 'Grade A'-listed and incorporates many nautical themes and elements in the stonework, stained glass and interior details.

611 As 'Dunselma' had a jetty and boathouse at the bottom of the hill, and James would likely have arrived by boat, this story is doubtful.

612 Yachting, Glasgow Herald, 24th June 1899.

613 Death of a Great Scottish Yachtsman, The Yachtsman magazine, 26th March 1912.

614 Traditions and Memories of American Yachting, William P. Stephens, Motor-Boating, February 1945.

615 James McAdam built a handful of Watson-designed boats in his yard at Govan in the period 1879-83. In 1987 we find him in Ambleside on Lake Windermere building a Watson-designed 4-tonner *Wanda* for Charles McIver. McIver, of Scottish parents, was based in Liverpool and began his sailing in the English Lakes before embarking on the long commute to Hunter's Quay and becoming an honorary Scot.

616 In G. L. Watson, the Art and Science of Yacht Design, Martin Black, 2011, Martin Black cites results which differ in detail from those listed here from British Yachts and Yachtsmen, published by The Yachtsman magazine, 1907.

617 The Past Season, the Standard, 24th September 1881.

618 G. L. Watson, the Art and Science of Yacht Design, Martin Black, 2011.

619 Martin Black quotes Herreshoff's letter to the Eastern Yacht Club Ditty Box, "*all loaded up with the English cutter craze*".

620 In contemporary photographs, the 'compromise' sloop *Puritan* does not look the match of the elegant and efficient-looking cutter, *Genesta*. *Puritan's* rig is not as well-detailed, and her

sails did not set as well. Nevertheless, Burgess' 'compromise' would come to dominate.

[621] The Clydeships database seems fairly complete with the exception of *Minette* 1877.

[622] In Fast and Bonnie, her book of the Fife family, May McCallum depicts Hugh Boag as specialising in fishing skiffs and pleasure boats for the tourist trade. Such vessels would not have been listed in Lloyds. May also suggests that Hugh built 'numerous yachts for the Coats and Clark families', but a search of the Register gives little evidence for this.

[623] No machinery is listed in Lloyds, but clearly, she must have had an auxiliary. *Gleniffer* was later modified to be a three-masted schooner.

[624] Clyde Yacht-building, Glasgow Herald, 3rd February 1883.

[625] Coats' Land is a 150-mile-long stretch of the coast of Antarctica discovered by the 1902-1904 Scottish National Antarctic Expedition.

[626] While Shackleton's Weddell Sea party arrived home to acclaim, the less 'glorious' story of Aeneas Mackintosh's unlucky Ross Sea party has been marginalised by history.

[627] Two George Coats lived contemporaneously, Sir Peters son (1849-1918) and Thomas's son – later Lord Glentanar (1849-1919).

[628] George Coats from Ayr, not of the same family, owned the lugger, *Pike*, (Watson 1893), the 1-rater, *Lucifer* (Watson 1895) and the 15-metre, *Alachie,* (Fife 1908).

[629] J. & P. Coats, Grace's Guide to British Industrial History, website, current.

[630] Caveat to the family yacht lists. A given name is not a unique identifier in this context; boats were passed down within families and sometimes shared, and build dates do not chronicle ownership, as not all were new builds.

[631] *Kariad* was built by D. & W. Henderson as *Distant Shore* for A. D. Rose, bought by Clark before launch.

[632] Clyde Yacht-building, Glasgow Herald, 3rd February 1883.

[633] Largs sailor Escaped Hurricane, Largs and Millport Weekly News, 23rd April 2009.

[634] Ian McAllister Classic Yachting, occasional blog, current.

[635] George Clark of Troon, no direct relation, owned the steam launch, *Borboleta* (T. Or Jr. 1893).

[636] John George Clark of Wemyss Bay owned the cutters, *Olivette* (Watson 1881) and *Corrette* (Watson 1883).

Mohican, 704-tons, Watson 1885, for John & William Clark   Image: W. J. Finlayson

Which reminds me of the serious reply of an old Scotsman to a comment of mine, when he was showing me round a large yacht on the Firth of Clyde. "D'ye no ken? Immorality (he pronounced it 'eemorality') is the verra backbone of yachtin."

Edward C. Allcard, writing in *Single Handed Passage*, 1950

Sybarita, G. L. Watson, 1900 for James Coats   *The Lady Anne,* William Fife, 1912, for George Coats

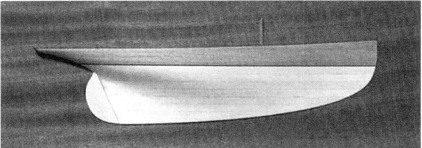

Madge, G. L. Watson, 1879, built by James McAdam for James Coats   Image: Wylieisland model

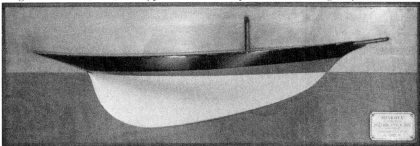

Minerva, Fife, 1888   Model: RNCYC collection

The success of James Coats' *Madge* in America sparked new confidence in the 'cutter craze' and the enthusiastic band of 'cutter cranks'. The Fife cutter, *Clara* (1884), drove the point home. Subsequently, Herreshoff and Burgess produced 'hybrid' designs. The 40ft LWL 23-ton Fife cutter, *Minerva,* was built at Fairlie for Admiral Charles H. Tweed of New York in 1888. Built to the American rule, she was a 'hybrid', wide for a cutter and all the better for that. We see a decade of development from *Madge.* Charles Barr took care of the delivery trip across the Atlantic and also raced the boat. "*In the hands of Captain Charles Barr, winning with a sad monotony, until a cry, almost pathetic went up from the press and from yachtsman, for 'anything to stop Minerva'.*" W. P. Steven.

309

Gleniffer, G. L. Watson, 1899, built by D. & W Henderson for James Coats

Hebe, designed and built by D. & W Henderson, 1869, for Margaret Coats   Image: W. J. Finlayson

Vanduara, G. L. Watson, 1886, built by D. & W. Henderson for Stewart Clark
The rater on davits is *Nita* owned by Clark's son J. Stewart Clark. She was an extreme fin-and-bulb
half-rater designed by G. L. Watson and built by Peter MacLean in 1893. Source: Ian McAllister

Wendur, G. L. Watson, 1883, D. & W. Henderson for John Clark   Artist: Henry Shields
From the Preface of 'Famous Clyde Yachts, 1880-87': *"The years traversed by Famous Clyde Yachts
have been witness to a most gratifying increase of yachting on the Clyde – an increase which would seem to
indicate a wider distribution of wealth and a laudable desire to spend a portion of it on a worthwhile pastime.
These years have been further rendered noteworthy by the gallant attempts of the Genesta, Galatea, and Thistle
to win the America Cup, and by the great and ever-increasing popularity of the steam yacht."*

The Stephens go yachting in style, late 1930s   Headsail change on a big Mylne ketch

12mR, *Jenetta*, Mylne, 1939, to lee of the yawl *Mariella*, Mylne, 1938   Image: Ian Gilchrist

Chapter 14: Tilting at Windmills

I do not deny that what happened to us is a thing worth laughing at. But it is not worth telling, for not everyone is sufficiently intelligent to be able to see things from the right point of view. Cervantes[637]

With so much fast steamer traffic on the Clyde, it was inevitable that accidents might happen and that yachts would occasionally be run down. Three stories with very different outcomes are recounted here.

One moonless night in September 1871, the SS *Eagle*, an iron paddle-steamer of 210-tons, travelling at speed, ran down the yacht, *Miranda*, 25-tons. The *Eagle*, under the command of Captain William Buchanan, was about one-third of the way across the Firth on her route from Gourock to Kirn. The newspapers placed the blame on the *Miranda*, which "*it is alleged, had only one man on deck at the time of the occurrence, and he steered athwart the steamer's bows, whereby the yacht was cut in two.*"[638]

Before going down, the *Miranda* heeled over sharply, and her mast became entangled in the halyards of the *Eagle*. Curious passengers, who had rushed on deck to see the spectacle, were caught up in the stricken yacht's rigging and swept into the water: "*The excitement that ensued was great and was increased when the engineer, Mr Laving, was ordered by some person to 'back-up' the steamer. This increased the distance between the vessel and the victims in the water, thus rendering their rescue more difficult.*" The steamer, *Undine*, proceeding up-river, was a witness to the pandemonium; immediately she stood by to assist and lowered a boat.

Mr Neill, owner of the *Miranda*, and his two sons were down below relaxing in the saloon at the time of the collision. Suddenly, their situation was desperate as they struggled to escape through the companionway. In the chaos, Neill's elder boy drowned. Of those dragged overboard from the *Eagle*, miraculously, no one drowned, and the only injuries were broken fingers. The casualties were attended to by Dr Gemmel at the Argyle Hotel. The Dunoon correspondent reported that Mr Neill's surviving son suffered a bad break with his arm fractured above the elbow.

The second story concerns a collision in August 1899. In this case, as far as may be determined from the newspaper accounts, no blame was attached to either party. Nevertheless, the Belfast mail-boat, SS *Dromedary*, clearly failed to keep a good lookout and navigate with caution. The mail-boat ran down the racing yacht, *Vendetta*, in heavy fog off the Cumbrae Isles, striking her hard and cutting deep into the starboard quarter. Boats were lowered from the steamer, but with zero visibility it was a hopeless task; nothing could be seen, and it was feared the *Vendetta* had gone down.

Onboard the *Vendetta*, help would have been welcome. However, while her foghorn could still be heard, the *Dromedary* had vanished in the mist. The stricken yacht made lot of water but "*her crew manfully stuck to the pumps and kept the vessel afloat off Cumbrae until the morning*".[639] *Vendetta* was a crack Summers & Payne cutter, 65ft LOA and built in 1893. She was under sail at the time of the collision, making for Hunter's Quay. The owner, Mr W. W. McLellan, was aboard with a party of five guests, including three ladies.

Damage to the yacht was serious, but fortunately, the stove-in section did not extend below the waterline. When dawn broke, the owner's party were rowed ashore to recover at a hotel in Millport while they awaited the arrival of a tug and a boatyard team from Greenock to secure the *Vendetta*.

The *Telegraph* newspaper reported that: "*Those on board at the moment of the collision were thrown into a state of alarm, but when it was seen that the craft would keep afloat the sense of danger passed away and was materially mitigated by the steadiness of the crew and the owner.*" All were extremely lucky to escape injury. SS *Dromedary* was a substantial vessel – an iron screw steamer of 922-tons launched in 1891. She would eventually be wrecked herself – off the coast of Newfoundland in 1914.

The last story concerns the Caledonian Steam Packet Company and two notable Clydeside characters. Once again, it is a ferryboat captain vs a yachtsman, although with a different twist. The paddle-steamer, *Ivanhoe*, was said to have set the standard with regard to smartness, sobriety, and good behaviour onboard. The '*Ivanhoe* Assault Case' changed all that. Captain James Williamson, just 34-years old, but already a legend in his own short lifetime, was accused of assaulting a passenger.[640]

Thomas Reid, the gentleman concerned was a bluff 62-year-old retired engineer from Paisley, who kept a boat on the Holy Loch and maintained a holiday house on 'the shore'. He was also a yachtsman and owned *Zephyr*, a 7-ton Fife cutter built in 1859. He was not a 'big-hitter' in any sense, but he was a member of the Royal Clyde, and apparently, well-connected in the Clyde yachting community. Unfortunately, he was also unconventional and somewhat highly-strung.[641]

Reid and his family, together with their dog Jerry, boarded the *Ivanhoe* at Dunoon Pier one Saturday morning in September 1884. The *Ivanhoe* was a dry ship and was presented as 'a cut above' the usual Clyde steamer. It was to be expected, then, that officers and crew carried out their duties with a certain swagger. Dogs were prohibited below-decks. But being a Skye terrier, Jerry was unaware of this and slipped down to explore the forbidden saloon. When Reid attempted to recapture his puppy, he was taken to task by Jane Fimister, a famously bossy stewardess.

A fine day out with the family suddenly went pear-shaped. Somehow, Jane found Reid's, no doubt abrupt, behaviour hostile. So, she had a word with James Robertson, the second cook. Then she spoke to Angus McDougall, the mate. Jane's story was that she had felt threatened by a passenger *"in a highly excited state, swinging and throwing his arms about and swearing"*. Thomas may have resented Jane Fimister's 'telling off' but whether he responded with *"None of your damned tongue"* is arguable. And as to an accusation that he had touched the lady's breast, that would have been entirely out of character. Indeed, Reid's account was very different: *"She said: 'Mind what you are doing. Don't strike me.' And I looked at her in perfect amazement. Strike you, I would be ashamed to strike any woman. I am not sensible of touching you."*

Then the gallant McDougall collared Reid and bundled him forward into steerage. Reid, of course, protested vehemently. In his account, he was *"seized by some of the hands and hustled along the dark passage between engine and paddle box"*. Despite Reid's pleas for assistance, the other passengers were unwilling to become involved, even as the lapels were torn from the Paisley man's jacket. The saloon steward, Jane's husband, followed the fracas and joined the fray. Reid's son, Alexander, then turned up and challenged the steward, while Reid slipped back up on deck to complain to Captain James Williamson.

After supervising the *Ivanhoe's* call at Wemyss Bay, Williamson went below and held an impromptu 'court of enquiry'. Obliged in this instance to support his crew, the young captain told Reid that since he had struck the stewardess, he didn't have a leg to stand on. He then banished Reid from the bridge saying, *"You deserved what you got"* and threatened to have the mate *"kick him like a dog"*. These days, any interaction we might hazard with the staff of service industries is in close proximity to a sign making it clear that you are in a 'zero tolerance' environment, and even the slightest physical contact will be prosecuted as assault. And as for satire at the airport, be warned that the doubtful pleasures of an indefinite holiday at Guantanamo Bay lie in wait.

When Williamson passed through the saloon a little later, the argument resumed, with Reid protesting his innocence. Approaching Rothesay, we find our man, still agitated, holding court before a group of friends, including John Polson, Robert Wilson and George Barclay – all of whom subsequently testified on Reid's behalf. The group, Royal Clyde Yacht Club members to a man, were talking about yachting. However, one witness, who was not part of this circle, described Reid as *"moving himself up and down in a grotesque fashion"* and thought that perhaps he was *"drunk or crazy"*. Another witness, a scion of the Denny shipbuilding family, remarked that Reid was *"the first drunk man he had ever seen on Ivanhoe"* – a temperance steamer. It seems that Reid, a lifelong teetotaller, was still 'hopping mad'.

While berthed at Rothesay, Thomas Reid spoke to the Purser who naturally referred him back to Williamson. In any case, the result was that Reid was *"pitched ashore"*. In his account, Reid was, *"by the defender's orders and personal assistance, carried across the hurricane deck on which he was standing and thrown onto the pier at Rothesay"*. It is not clear how much force was used and whether Captain James Williamson had personally wrestled with the unhappy passenger or not. Reid raised a laugh in court when he described the experience thus: *"I was picked off my feet – a man at every leg and one at the arms…. The mate had my hands twisted behind my back."* The newspaper accounts of the court proceedings are punctuated by 'laughter' in brackets, so there was certainly a fair bit of theatre on both sides, and more than a hint of hyperbole in the testimonies for the defence.

Reid went straight to the police station to have Williamson charged with assault. However, like many local worthies that weekend, the Rothesay Procurator Fiscal was on holiday so there was no immediate result. After an interval of nearly two months, the Fiscal informed the complainant that this was a civil matter and not for the criminal courts. Meanwhile, Reid was inclined to seek redress through a petition for damages and his lawyer added a demand for an apology. As there was no response from Williamson, the matter ended up in the Sheriff Court.

Reid sought £250 (£30,000) in damages, but Sheriff Smith found against him and cleared Williamson of any wrongdoing.[642] After a fruitless appeal before Sheriff Moncrieff, Reid was out of pocket, having been obliged to pay expenses of £100 (£12,000). In his judgement, the sheriff expressed some irritation in having to adjudicate between two *"men high in the estimation of their fellow citizens"* when this should have been a jury trial. He was certain that, if Reid had struck Mrs Fimister, it was accidental. Moreover, he considered that Reid's *"rough and rude language"* did not constitute an assault but could well have been frightening.

Thomas Reid surely did not know when to quit and his performance in the witness box did him no good at all. He was *"hasty, excitable* (and) *impulsive*" in sharp contrast to the urbane Captain Williamson, who spoke "*without the least appearance of excitement or exaggeration*". The court concluded that Reid had been put ashore because he was "*noisy and turbulent*", not because he had actually hurt Jane Fimister in any way. The notion that Reid had 'interfered with' the lady was rightly dismissed as nonsense. However, in Captain Williamson's view, "*his removal was necessary for the peace and good order of the ship*" and the Sheriff had no issue with that. Common sense prevailed over both imaginary injuries and injured pride. Reid was an honourable man and would never have struck a woman, but he was also a right royal pain in the ass.

What happened afterwards, however, makes one wonder about the respective characters of the two men. Among Clyde yachtsmen, there was considerable sympathy for Thomas Reid. Later that summer, "*a large and influential company of gentlemen*" met in the Globe Hotel, a grand establishment favoured by the rich and famous in Paisley, to laud Reid for his "*manly character*". Archibald Coats, of the famous yarn-spinning dynasty, presented Reid with a cheque for £285 (£35,000) and threw in some rather nice jewellery for his wife.[643] Coats launched into a "*highly-embellished address*" waxing lyrical about Reid's "*genuine uprightness and honesty of character*" and his "*fearless contempt for anything which savoured of shams or meanness*".

In 1884, estimating build-costs at £25 a ton, that cheque for £285 could have bought Thomas Reid a 10-ton cruising yacht. However, when Reid did eventually go shopping for a new boat, he bought the little cutter, *Ayrshire Lass*, built at Fairlie in 1887 and just 24ft LOA. Reid spent the rest of the money replanking *Zephyr's* topsides and renewing the decks to make her more saleable. Ewen Kennedy came across *Ayrshire Lass* lying ashore at Rosneath in the late 1990s. Paul Goss saw her in 2004 and committed to a full restoration.[644] Michael Kennedy did the work at his Dunmore East yard in south-west Ireland. *Ayrshire Lass* sailed with distinction at the 2008 Fife Regatta.

Reid was awkward, eccentric and probably a bit deaf. He had no apparent capacity to modulate his voice. Williamson had previously observed his nemesis in Dunoon's Argyll Street "*walking about with his hat off, talking loudly*". In the same way as these days, we look upon people wearing hoodies as potential delinquents, in the old days going bareheaded branded a chap as 'not quite the full shilling'. Thomas Reid's obituary in the Scotsman remembered him as "*a man of striking physique and very original and quaint in his observations*".

And what of Captain Williamson? He said that he had "*never been brought up in this line before, though he had been hauled over the coals for racing and that sort of thing*", but he was familiar with the courtroom. During the early years of his first command, when in charge of his father's paddle-steamer, *Sultana*, Williamson appeared before the Greenock Police Court twice in 6 months.[645] The first time was for navigating without due caution as he passed the harbour. The *Sultana's* wake damaged a ship moored there and "*endangered life*". On the second occasion, he was accused of ignoring the orders of the harbourmaster, steering the *Sultana* recklessly between the *Vivid* and the *Marquis of Bute*, to steal the prime berth at the Custom House Quay.

A fair amount of this recklessness is on record in the news reports and letters to the editor of the local newspapers.[646] Williamson kept out of trouble for most of the next decade, but in June 1885 "*smoke in dense quantities*" drew attention to the *Ivanhoe* when she was berthed at Rothesay. Captain Williamson was ordered to appear before the Sheriff Court, but he sent the First Mate in his place. This arrogance was not appreciated by the sheriff.

Williamson was as successful in business as in his career. He was still a young man when he sold the family's shipping interests to the Caledonian Railway Company in 1889. As part of the deal, he was appointed Marine Superintendent of the new shipping division. But he remained a law unto himself. *Galatea* had been operating in 1891 without proper certificates on display. The sheriff held Williamson to account, although Duncan Bell, the Master, was also in trouble. Captain Bell was a man after Williamson's heart. He was in court again a few years later, when the paddle steamer *Galatea* gazumped *Minerva* at Kirn Pier.

Victorian steamer captains were a law unto themselves, but in truth, it was more good judgement than good luck that kept the public safe. Consequently, Williamson considered all these court appearances to be an insult to his profession. At an enquiry into pier signalling in 1895, he said that "*instead of captains being hauled to a police court and placed side by side with 'drunks' and other riff-raff*" they should be handled by "*experienced nautical men*" or "*a committee familiar with the working of this special traffic*". But it was clear a few months later that this was not a self-policing community when a Board of Trade officer counted 1,619 passengers on the Caledonian Steam Packet's *Marchioness of Bute*. Her Safety Certificate allowed just 1,119 pax.

Captain James Williamson, without doubt, a law unto himself, was unquestionably a skilled seaman, as when one day in 1887, he rescued Mr McCallum, who had removed his hat and jumped from the paddle-box intent on committing suicide.[647] And as for 'pier racing', this opinion from 'Fiat Justitia' (let justice be done) writing anonymously to the Editor of *The Glasgow Herald*, seems to sum up the public's indifference to the odd scrape: "*The captain admitted that he saw the* (berthing priority) *signal, but it was too late* (to do anything about it).... *Happily, we still have captains wise enough not to direct the whole of their attention to one object, no matter how important that object may be.*[648]

In his capacity as Superintendent of the Caledonian Steam Packet Company, and a member of the Royal Clyde Yacht Club, Williamson committed to the provision of an adequate ferry service to support the RCYC at Hunter's Quay. Captain Williamson remained immensely popular with both yachtsmen and the travelling public and finished his career with a best-selling book on Clyde steamers published in 1904.[649]

CODA: Respect for the Fourth Estate

One day the Clyde yachting hacks found themselves in Lamlash without a ride to the race finish at the Kyles of Bute. James Meikle recalled: "*All the captains of the river steamers in those dear old days were interested in yachting and sympathetic to much pertaining to it, including the wants of the journalists. Duncan Bell was the name of the Ivanhoe's commander. Our Duncan was such a real good sort: Weel, you newspaper boys are no blate, but as we canna dae verra weel wantin' you, we'll hae to try an help*". Captain Bell rang the telegraph for another couple of knots and the boys made their connection.[650]

---

[637] Don Quixote, Miguel de Cervantes Saavedra, 1605.

[638] A Yacht Sunk in the Firth of Clyde, Loss of Life, Grantham Journal, 9th September 1871.

[639] The Clyde Collision, Evening Telegraph, 2nd August 1899.

[640] Action Against a River Steamboat Captain, Glasgow Herald, 29th February 1884.

[641] This account also benefits from the research and text of: When intemperance got the better of Ivanhoe (Iain MacLeod, Clyde River Steamer Club, current website).

[642] A settlement of £100 (£12,300) was later agreed. The Expenses in the Ivanhoe Case, Edinburgh Evening News, 25th June 1884.

[643] The National Statistics composite price index inflated this figure to a current value of £35,000.

[644] Goss has been the skipper of *Adix* for more than a quarter of a century. The 213ft three-masted schooner was designed by South African Arthur Holgate and is no classic, nevertheless, she is impressive.

[645] Williamson had many adventures with the *Sultana*. He beached her in a sinking condition after a grounding incident on Crab Island off Gourock in 1879. On another occasion in 1888, he collided with the Sligo steamer, *Ivy*, in thick fog. *Sultana's* watertight bulkheads came in handy. He truly led a charmed life.

[646] Steamers Racing for Clyde Piers, Glasgow Herald, 4th September 1883. Shipmasters Prosecuted for Racing, Edinburgh Evening News, 13th August 1885. The Collision Between *Sultana* and *Adela*, Glasgow Herald, 13th August 1885.

[647] Attempted Suicide from a Clyde Steamer, Edinburgh Evening News, 25th November 1887

[648] Letters to the Editor, Glasgow Herald, 23rd August 1887.

[649] The Clyde Passenger Steamers: From the Comet of 1812 to the King Edward of 1901 James Williamson, 1904.

[650] By Way of a Thank-Offering, from an old contributor, (James Meikle), 6th December 1924

Ivanhoe, the 'teetotal steamer' D & W Henderson 1880. No booze but not 'NO SMOKING' obviously

Cigarette cards advertising *Ivanhoe* cruises   Images: sourced by Dalmadan

Ivanhoe – party boat in picnic mode   Image: Clyde River Steamer Club

Duchess of Hamilton, William Denny & Bros, Dumbarton, 1890   Image Clydeships

Steamers racing past Innellan. The main smoke plume that fills the sky from another steamer off-shot to the left. Note the sailing yacht-like lines of the gentleman's steam launch in the foreground and masts tall enough to allow a passage under sail if the steam powerplant fails.

321

Chapter 15: The Salt of the Earth

It is better if the owner knows most, even if he knows very little. If you don't believe us go into a pub where the paid-hands and amateur pros gather for their pints and listen to what they say about their owners. G. Hackford-Jones [651]

There were many first-rate racing skippers on the Clyde, although few are household names like their English contemporaries from Itchen Ferry, Gosport, Cowes and the Colne: men like Robert McKirdy, Tom McInnes, William Jamieson, Hugh Morris, Robert Duncan, Archie and William Hogarth and Dougald McGlashen. Most of the English greats were seamen born and bred, but many Scots came to the profession by a different route: Robert McKirdy and Matthew Houston were handloom weavers, Billy Blair was a tailor, W. W. Mackie and Archibald Wright were joiners, William King was a stonemason, John Houston owned a grocer's shop and Charlie Barr was an apprentice in the same business.

In the golden era of the sport on the Clyde, professionals were not 'sailmakers' taking time out to disrupt their, curiously compliant, clients at play. They were simply the only people with the experience and expertise to hustle a Big Class yacht around the racecourse with a modicum of safety. On the few occasions when an amateur crew entered the arena, the result was painful. Tom Sopwith fired the crew of *Endeavour* following a pay dispute, thus conceding the 1934 America's Cup to the slower *Rainbow*.[652] It is a fascinating morality tale that began when Sopwith bought *Shamrock V* from Thomas Lipton and inherited his crew.

Sir Thomas Octave Murdoch Sopwith (1888-1989) would learn the hard way that penny-pinching was an even more expensive game than J-class yachting. His scratch crew eventually included 13 Corinthians, all to become well-known names in the world of yachting. One young man, Olympian Beecher Moore, would later present the Endeavour Trophy for a 'Champion of Champions' event in dinghies.[653] There were three amateurs in the afterguard (counting Mr and Mrs Sopwith) alongside Charles E. Nicholson, Frank Murdoch the rig designer; twelve 'blackleg' professionals, including two captains; a navigator and two mates. Two cooks and a steward were also pressed into service on deck. Only four ordinary seamen crossed the metaphorical picket-line. Ironically, the amateurs competed on full wages, guaranteed by their various employers. Scottish owners were perhaps more sensitive to 'how the wind blew'.

In Victorian times we had the likes of 'Hellish Dick' Grierson, once the finest small-boat sailor on the Clyde and described by George Blake as "*a Conradian figure whose reward was the occasional bottle of whisky*". They are long gone now, but in their dotage, these past generations of crusty seadogs were every bit as enthusiastic in their reminiscences as the gentlemen who were ostensibly the beneficiaries of the sport. Indeed, for the old hands, Big Class yachting was their whole life, not a diversion to be fitted into a busy social calendar, so it is likely that their nostalgia was genuine.

Captain Ahmed. J. Kenealy, that grand man of 19th century Yachting journalism, writing in 1854, could square the circle as only a contented man can: "*Personally, I can enjoy a good square meal of sardines and hardtack, wash it down with a cup of coffee and wind up with a pipe of plug tobacco, and conclude that I have feasted like a prince.*"[654] That said, for most old hands they were reminiscing over seasonal work which only came their way if they had the right connections. Was it ever thus? Crewmen were recruited through family networks associated with the various boatyards or drawn from the Highland fishing fleets of Loch Fyne, Port Bannatyne, Tighnabruaich and the Isles as far north as the Glendale district of Skye, with a smattering of lowlanders from Gourock and Saltcoats in Ayrshire.

Only a select band at the top of the game could settle down and live at a racing yacht's home port. The lucky few managed the fit-out and lay-up and kept a watching brief via a retainer over the winter. As for the rest, most went fishing. Successful crews cannily invested their winnings, improving their homes and fishing boats. And a few might sign on for the more secure return of a deep-sea winter voyage.

With the small boats, when an owner formed a bond with his paid hand, the friendship was often enduring. Unfortunately, however, familiarity could be manifest in complacency over working conditions and a steady fall in real income over the decades. And of course, if they fell out, that was that. On bigger boats, often raced with the owner remote from the action, ensconced on his steam-yacht or on the yacht club veranda, it was the skipper you had to keep happy. If you crossed him, you were out, although if the same skipper jumped ship for a better billet, you might follow him. The Board of Trade was kept at arms-length and there were no trade-unions to argue the toss.

The season was just five months, but it was intensive. Big Class yachts were put into commission in early May and remained active until the first week of September. The affluent South Coast yacht owner, if committing to a full season, sailed in about 40 individual races. The circuit kicked off in the Thames Estuary and then took in the regattas at Harwich and Dover, before the long passage around Land's End to the Welsh coast and Kingstown in Éire.

July brought the circus to the Firth of Clyde where they raced for a fortnight – the only regatta of such extended duration. Thereafter, the English fleet and a few Scots attended the regatta at Belfast Lough before proceeding back down the St. George's Channel, and around the Longships to Falmouth. Then it was up the English Channel to the Solent for Cowes Week. At the close of the Solent season, the racing yachts visited Bournemouth, Weymouth Bay, Plymouth Sound, Torbay and Dartmouth.

While the Clyde's best yachtsmen enjoyed Cowes Week, only the highest-profile Scottish campaigns followed such an itinerary, as it involved long delivery trips, often in poor weather. Deliveries were not always under sail. During the 1910 season, for example, the Scottish 12mR fleet were all whisked down South in a small armada at the close of the Largs Regatta. The wealthy owners of *Hera*, *Cyra*, *Javotte* and *Nargie*, clubbed together and chartered a steamer to tow them all to Cowes. *Alachie* and *Cintra* followed on behind their owners' own steam yachts.

A Solent-based yacht could clock-up 1,500 miles of sea passages, while a Clyde vessel would be faced with nearer 3,000 miles and another two weeks at sea. The average yacht-race of the period for Big Class yachts was about 40 miles, taking five hours in a decent breeze. The crew rose before 6.00 a.m. to prepare for the day's racing and were seldom finished before 6 p.m. Then, there were longboat duties, and inevitably, repair work to be carried out in the evenings. In the smaller boats, and for duties like hoisting the mainsail in big boats, the stewards and cooks were also roped into sailing the boat.

James Litster and William Bergius went back a long way. The Bergius family were highly unusual among the company of well-off Scottish yachtsmen, in that they rolled up their sleeves and worked alongside James and his men in Litsters boatyard at Kirn. The Bergius family were good owners of happy ships. They maintained a genuine friendship characterised by mutual respect with the Litster family over more than a century. Alec Litster would later serve as skipper on Walter Bergius's 1927 Fife-built ketch, *Dodo IV*, and *Dodo V*, a 77ft Thornycroft motor launch acquired from Tom Thornycroft in 1957. *Dodo V*, formerly *King Duck*, was subsequently sold to the Marquis of Bute in 1964.[655] In their own understated way, the Litsters are as much a part of yachting on the Clyde as the celebrated Bergius clan. The seafaring Litster family facilitated the birth of the Bergius's small yacht auxiliary, skippered their yachts and went on to become successful professionals in the rarefied world of superyachts. In the process, they became as thoroughly middle-class as their cardinal clients, albeit without the fairy-dust of the Teacher's Whisky empire to lighten the load.

James McNair was a professional sailor from Strachur. James' unequal correspondence with his owners provides an insight into the duties of a typical skipper in the 1920s. They were expected to manage the yacht in its entirety, dealing with all logistics and operational expenditure while keeping the owner informed of every penny spent. We find James dealing with engine failures in the North Channel and making arrangements for the owner's party to watch the iconic Schneider Trophy races in the Solent. That competition was won by the Supermarine S.6 which would form the basis for the legendary Spitfire fighter of WW2.[656]

In 1927, James was offered an improved position as skipper of Major Stuart Black's *Cerf*, a 45-ton motor-yacht, designed by Francis G. Pratt and built by Cox & King in 1913. This proposed appointment was conditional on James's contractual release. Happily, his old owner, Mr James Campbell, congratulated him on his good fortune and signed off as follows: "*With regard to the amount which you have drawn this winter as a retainer, which up to this point I reckon at £10, I am frankly not prepared quite to lose sight of this, but instead of asking you to refund it as our arrangement entitles me to, I have much pleasure in asking you to accept it as a present from me in view of your excellent services and in memory of happy sails which we had together.*"[657]

It is not clear how the move to *Cerf* was a promotion. McNair's previous command, Campbell's 53-ton auxiliary ketch, *Javelin*, built by Summers & Paine in 1897, had been a larger yacht. Moreover, while James' old salary is not known, his winter retainer was certainly more generous. As Master of *Cerf*, James would receive £4 (£250) per week, with £1 (£62) per week as a winter retainer. He would get 'the usual outfit' and might inform Major Black what else he would require in the course of his duties.

Donald McPherson, the cook/deckhand on *Javelin* received £3.10/- (£218), so a good lunch was nearly as important to Major Black as the safe navigation of his ship. The third crew member was a McVicar, so with that name, it seems they all came from Cowal. Unfortunately for these stout lads, the *Cerf* was laid up for sale with Camper & Nicholson's two years later. Hence the crew had been paid off and were now looking for work. As regards the 'value of money' at that time, we may note that their train tickets from Southampton to Glasgow cost a steep £2.13/6- (£42). As for getting from Glasgow to Strachur, a fair trek even today, it seems that the boys were on their own.

Few sailors had formal qualifications, especially those who signed-up to race on yachts as boys, but the skippers would usually have some sort of deep-sea experience and could handle a sextant – if only as a badge of office. These men were yet another example of the Scottish working-class autodidact. Skippers liked to demonstrate superior competence in a specific skill, whether it be navigation, rigging or whatever, but never sailmaking – unlike today, that was a full-time job for specialists. At the turn of the century, a deckhand would be paid about £1 (£122) to £1.15 (£140) a week, and a top-notch captain, perhaps £10 (£1,219) to £12 (£1,463) a week. In addition, crew uniforms were provided, but well-worn or not, they remained the property of the owner.[658]

Setting-up and maintaining the rig on a fabulously over-canvassed cutter or schooner of that era demanded expertise and experience. With inconsistent wooden spars, plough-steel shrouds and hemp rigging this particular skill was more art than science, so confidence and good luck were also paramount. The honorific title 'rigger', in this context, also encompassed the downstream skills of optimising the set and trim of complex overlapping sail combinations, a conjuring trick that requires computer analyses of instrument logs today.[659]

Through the history of yachting, the sustainability of rigs has waxed and waned. When masthead rigs and aluminium spars replaced variable wooden masts and 'hit-or-miss' birdcage rigging in the 1960s and 1970s, the rigger's job was simple. However, through the 1980s and 1990s, multi-panel fractional rigs evolved beyond the safe working limits of their materials to test the bottle of competitive crews. Today, all bets are off; integrated all-carbon rigs are so sensitive to set up, and the consequences of failure so dire, we would all rather not leave that job to a 'be-jandled' pro in board-shorts with a master's degree in composites engineering.

A final word on the crossover between the skipper's and rigger's arts concerns an arcane skill, once essential but no longer quite so vital. When we look at the giant rigs of the Big Class yachts today, we marvel at how skippers kept the boat under the mast. If you are ever at the helm of a 23-metre with a wooden mast, and you hear a worrisome crack or the twang of stranded plough-steel, bear off – immediately! Then the only crewmen in danger are the unfortunate lads in the lee scuppers, the nest of rascals on the foredeck, and of course, the mastman perched on the jumper strut. The brains-trust in the afterguard, your valued gentleman guests, and their precious mistresses, will all be just fine.

Len Patterson tells a fine yarn.[660] He notes that on a Cup yacht of the early 1900s, it took about 40 men to haul the mainsail aloft. A gaff-headed main weighed more than 2-tons, and apart from purchase losses, raising that weight was not helped by the friction of the gaff-jaws and mast-hoops. One method of hoisting was to send half-a-dozen men aloft to the spreaders, where they would all cluster on the fall of the halyard, like a string of French onions – the so-called 'British method'. The combined weight of a jack-yard topsail and its spars was about 1¼-tons to be set, and more onerously, sent-down in a blow. Setting an 80ft spinnaker-pole, weighing 2,000lbs, doesn't bear thinking about; at least twenty hands were necessary to haul in the mainsheet; and the whole crew, plus the gentlemen guests, to 'board-out' the mainsail on the wind.

> The 'British method' is not to be recommended. In 1984, while standing-in for a friend as Sailing Master on a 112ft square topsail ketch, a singular weakness of the technique came to light. The author was up the mainmast, by the spreaders, sweating the throat halyard when it broke. As I plummeted toward the deck with the frayed tail still in my hands, an all-too-short life flashed before me. Fortunately, the 'show' did not reach the final reel; a deck-cargo of rattan peacock chairs broke my fall. I bounced once and went back up the mast to rethread the halyard before my rational alter ego was able to contemplate alternative endings. If you favour traditional materials that is fine, but I would suggest you draw the line at traditional cordage.

In British waters, the nationality of the hands was seldom an issue, although the entirely Scottish crew of *Thistle* in the Royal Clyde Yacht Club's challenge for the America's Cup in 1887 did attract comment – both good and bad. However, rather xenophobically, *The Glasgow Herald* crowed that the crews selected to sail under several well-known Clyde captains for the 1893 British season would be entirely Scottish. It seems that there was no need that year for the usual smatter of experienced men from the South of England. The *Herald* optimistically prophesied that, *"there promises to be a complete change in favour of Scotch sailors as well as Scotch building"*.[661] But national chauvinism aside, surely casting the net wide, served only to raise standards and reinforce our common interests.

That year, John Clark's new steel yawl, *Wendur*, would sail under the command of Captain Mackie. Captain Duncan was in charge of James Coats' new 72-ton cutter, *Marjorie*, while the 40-ton, *May*, after some substantial winter alterations, was in the capable hands of Captain John Barr (1839-1909). These three 'crack' Clyde yachts, and many others, would normally sail with professional crews drawn from Brightlingsea, Wivenhoe, Southampton and the Solent towns, and indeed from all around our coasts. Then as today, declared allegiance among the ranks of top-class professionals was often hard to pin down.

It may be noted that Highland crews were not universally popular, and to be blunt, they were often too fond of the bottle. If our Highlanders were kept occupied, they were among the best; but unfortunately, the long hours of boredom on a cruising yacht drove many to drink. The Steele schooner, *Nyanza*, features in Chapter 9. The owner wrote: *"It may be gathered from various incidents during the latter part of our voyage, several of my ship's crew had worked themselves up into a very unsatisfactory condition of insubordination and want of amenity to discipline. From the experience I had gone through, I became quite disgusted with the class of men who had been serving under me, and nothing would ever induce me to attempt a voyage again with a Highland crew."*[662]

In Dewar's account, the boys were fine at sea but went AWOL in port with tedious monotony, painted the town red and then crept back aboard with a stash of liquor sufficient to disrupt the first few days of each new passage. However, the cruise did take *Nyanza* through the famously tempting honey-traps of the Pacific. And when the schooner was wrecked on the beach in Micronesia, the dipso-Teuchters were entirely free of blame. They were already working their passage home aboard tramp steamers.

In any case, *Nyanza* had probably seen worse. She was built for a member of the Royal Yacht Squadron, where the club's *Black Book* listed offences that were typical of the era and may still be common today. Offences range from drunkenness, insubordination, and desertion to 'bringing a common whore on board and sleeping with her in the owner's cabin'. *Nyanza* went to Cowes in 1867, well before seamen were obliged to obtain the newly introduced 'certificates of conduct', de rigueur from 1874.

Mutiny for Bounty? – the Ailsa Mutiny

The famous 'Ailsa Mutiny' at Cowes during the 1895 season saw a professional crew engage in a criminal conspiracy just to make their yacht more competitive. Much was expected of A. Barclay Walker's new cutter, *Ailsa*, designed by William Fife to match *Britannia*. However, she was hopelessly outclassed. Consequently, when news of the mutiny first leaked out, the press reported that the non-payment of 'losing money' had sparked the unrest. That was half right; the grievance concerned losing but it was not about the money. The gentlemen of the fo'c'sle were mortified, but they were sure they knew how to get *Ailsa* up to speed. Sure enough, in fact, to put their jobs, and perhaps their liberty, on the line.[663]

That June, as *Ailsa* prepared to leave the Cowes anchorage on a delivery trip north, the ringleader of the mutineers, an old hand in the Fletcher Christian mould, told the mate that thirteen of the crew had resolved not to race the boat again unless six tons of lead was taken off the keel. When this ultimatum was delivered to Captain Jay he was outraged and threatened to prosecute the lot. The *Yachtsman* magazine was similarly unsympathetic: "*We are only sorry that Jay did not do his duty in this case. Surely it is intolerable that a set of ignorant men, smart sailors though they be, should be allowed to dictate to not only their Master, but even to the designer and owner of their yacht*". The YRA's 'certificate of conduct' system for paid hands had lapsed through lack of interest. Now *Yachting* proposed a 'register of racing hands' to ensure that crewmen knew their place and would remain bound by it.

Ailsa departed Cowes for Liverpool behind schedule, under tow as far as Land's End while a hastily recruited crew learned the ropes.[664] After such a rancorous and very public defection, one might imagine that the break would be permanent. But no, over the next month the crew quietly returned to their posts one-by-one. Back on the Clyde, when questioned about the crew defections on *Ailsa*, Captain Jay confirmed that "*they were not all back, but that they soon would be*". So, what crucial information had been omitted from the press reports? What was going on?

Ailsa had carried all before her during the early season regattas in the Mediterranean, but back in Britain when the breeze got up, she had proved to be no match for *Britannia*. The yachting press considered *Ailsa* tender and 'over-sparred' and noted that she sailed rail down, tumbling half the ocean around the course with her. Fife's initial response was to add six tons to Ailsa's keel in an attempt to stiffen the boat. But the new lead had been counterproductive. *Ailsa*'s low freeboard, once a source of good-natured banter, was now downright dangerous. Even the normally sanguine yachting press noted that "*Ailsa has suffered grievously from accidents.*"

Barclay Walker's campaign was in disarray. *Valkyrie* was due to join *Britannia* and *Ailsa* for a series of much-anticipated three-way duels, so Walker and Fife invoked desperate measures. On the second day of Clyde Week, *Ailsa* was withdrawn from racing and towed up-river to her builders, A. & J. Inglis, to be reconfigured. She had the six tons of lead recently added to her keel removed and her spars lightened, with the mast chopped by 5ft and the boom by 3ft. To maintain her light-airs edge, the topmast was lengthened. Lapthorn & Ratsey was obliged to rebuild the entire sail wardrobe. After the changes, *Ailsa* was not just improved, she was transformed. What do deckhands know?

Uffa Fox used to say that weight was only useful in a steam road-roller. The following anecdote suggests that there is more than a hint of truth in this old adage. The Fife 6-ton cutter, *Primula* (1886), was built for an Irishman and later sold to an owner in the South of England. *Primula* became the subject of an anecdote that amused the yachting world. She was an absolute dog during her first season on the Solent. But then, while laid up over the winter, 6cwt of internal ballast was arduously spirited away by the hard-working cat burglars of Cowes. The stingy owner was disinclined to replace the lead and relaunched her without it. The result was entirely unexpected; *Primula* became a real flyer and maintained a perfect record through the summer.

Made in Scotland from Girders[665]

Captain John Barr was reckoned by many on the Clyde to be the best sailor in the talented Barr family. John's career-path was perhaps unusual. He achieved success in early middle-age through a route which is common enough now but was rare for the time. As a young man, John assisted his father, Charles Barr, with wintertime trawling in fore-and-aft rigged smacks, and some yachting in the summer months. However, at the midpoint in his career as a professional sailor, he became *"wonderfully clever in the handling of a sailing boat; one of the best steersmen on the Clyde; and with ideas of his own to designing, building and rigging, being a skilful workman and designer"*.

John's elevation from useful hand to maestro came about when he bought the 1874 Inglis 10-tonner, *Blanche*, 'as was', on the seabed off Hunter's Quay in 1877. He raised the hulk and towed it over to Gourock for reconstruction. Racing at Largs, John and *Blanche* had the better of the Watson 10-tonner, *Verve*, and the equally quick *Carina*, designed by Corie of Fairlie. As a result, the following year he was given a paid position as skipper of the new Watson 10-tonner, *Quiraing*. From this point on John Barr's reputation grew until he became acknowledged as the best racing skipper on the Clyde.

"Whatever are yea daein', Mr Watson?" Barr asked. *"Sailing the boat as she was designed to sail"*, said Watson, perplexed. *"Ah, weel, you tak' my word for 't, that's just the way she'll no' sail. See—!"* Barr took the helm from the incorrigible tiller-waggler, and with the delicate touch of his ilk – steerin' sma' as the old hands called it on the Clyde, he soon coaxed her back up to speed.[666] On another occasion, a correspondent on a competing yacht, that had benefitted from a lucky windshift to start the last leg ahead of Barr, observed the maestro's demeanour: *"I think I see his face yet as he passed us, brown as a gipsy's, calm as a judge's, good-natured as that of a man who has just heard that he is heir to a legacy"*.

John was at the helm of *Thistle*, Scotland's America's Cup challenger, in 1887. The partnership lasted until the boat was bought by the Kaiser for 90,000 marks (£587,000) to become the first *Meteor*. John Barr emigrated to the States in 1889. He had one more crack at the 'auld mug' when he skippered amateur yacht designer John Paine's *Jubilee* in the defender's trials of 1893. But *Jubilee* was no match for Herreshoff's *Vigilant*, which went on to successfully defend the Cup. As a popular captain with the rich and famous, John was never out of work until he retired, aged 69. Sadly, his well-earned retirement lasted just two years before he passed away.

The *Times* obituary summarised his character as follows: "*He was accompanied to the United States by a numerous family, and later by his half-brother Charles, to whose remarkable ability in sailing against the three Shamrocks it is mainly due that the Cup remains with the Americans. Captain John Barr was a typical Scot, reserved, self-contained, strong in moments of crisis. On neither side of the Atlantic did he seek to form a numerous company of friends, but it can be said with truth that those who knew him most intimately never faltered in their loyalty and attachment.*"[667]

However, it was John's half-brother, Charlie, who would become Scotland's most famous professional sailor. That remains the case even today when he lies buried in Southampton, dead now for more than a century. Wee Charlie Barr (1864-1911), just 5ft 3" tall, but a man of towering stature, served his time, Tommy Lipton-style, as a grocer's clerk. Charlie learned his trade crewing for his elder half-brother, John. They sailed John's *Daisy*, then *Gipsy King* and the resurrected 10-tonner, *Blanche*. In their own words, it was "*winning always winning*".

This perception of yachting as 'money for old rope', may have set Charlie on a career-path to become a professional hand, but first, he had to become a proper seaman. He quit the grocer's shop to sign-up as a boy apprentice 'in the coasting trade', like the fabled Para Handy. Certainly, after a couple of tough winters, young Barr leapt at the first opportunity to enjoy the more civilised life aboard private yachts. In 1884, he signed up as an ordinary crewman on the new Watson 10-tonner, *Ulerin*, together with his cousin John, Malcolm McPhail, and Andy McDowd.

Once aboard a high-profile racing yacht, the 18-year-old proved his worth and quickly rose through the ranks. In his first season he "*made his reputation on the Clyde.*" In the prose of romantic fiction: "*The agile, muscular young man with black hair, piercing dark eyes and a determined, well-cut mouth and chin, was in demand in fast racing great craft.*"[668] The following year, 1885, he joined John to deliver the 21-ton Fife cutter, *Clara*, across the Atlantic to her new owner, Charles Sweet of Long Island Sound.

They stayed on to race the boat through 1886, enjoying considerable success and delighting Sweet. At the tail-end of the racing programme, young Charlie further impressed the local cognoscenti when he was given an opportunity to steer the Boston boat, *Thana*. Charlie returned to Gourock satisfied with his American debut. On the strength of this 'audition', the following spring he was invited back to Boston to skipper the Watson 5-tonner, *Shona*.

While in the USA, by one account, he took time out to crew for John on *Thistle* in her unsuccessful 1887 challenge, but this seems unlikely.[669] There is also a story that Charlie and John settled for a time in Marblehead, Massachusetts. Barry Pickthall reckons that the Barrs *"built a Scottish-styled fishing vessel, which they worked outside the yacht-racing season and amazed their American counterparts with the size of their catches"*.[670] This sounds like hyperbole; perhaps we should just assume the boys did a bit of fishing over the winter.

Charlie Barr's next job took him back to Britain to collect the new Fife cutter, *Minerva*, for Admiral Charles H. Tweed in 1888. *Minerva*, as is well-known, swept the board in the States. Charlie was also able to take time-out to achieve success with *Queenie* and *Gloriana*, before taking charge of *Wasp* in 1890.[671]

By now well-established as a crack skipper in the United States, Barr was given command of Phelps Carroll's big Herreshoff cutter, *Navahoe*, in 1893, just prior to her departure for a summer of racing in Britain. However, the voyage began inauspiciously. On the first day out of Newport bound for Southampton, *Navahoe* was in collision with a pilot-boat and came off second-best. There was a thick fog at the time and no blame was apportioned. The yacht's bow was badly stove in, she lost her topmast, her bowsprit sprung, and the mainmast was so checked it had to be replaced. The cutter was towed back to the shipyard where a section of the starboard bow was cut out, the area reframed, and the plating replaced. The repairs took just ten days.

Navahoe departed a couple of weeks later to complete the voyage without incident. She did not have a good summer in Europe, coming off second-best again in a hard-fought and much-publicised series of matches against the Kings' *Britannia*, see Chapter 11. Herreshoff disingenuously characterised *Navahoe* as a 'cruiser', but then so was *Britannia* with all the creature comforts down-below that might be expected in a royal yacht with an interior by Tom Watson: *"The main saloon of the vessel is placed amidships and runs the full width of the ship. The Prince's own apartments, handsome and commodious rooms too, are immediately aft of the main saloon to starboard. A large ladies' cabin occupies the after end of the cutter, while a cosy smoking room on the port side is another of the details of the boat's fit-out, which may be noticed in passing. Immediately forward of the main saloon are the galley, pantries, and the quarters of the officers and men."*[672]

Charlie Barr was a crack racing skipper; he was one of the first of his profession to 'weaponise' the racing rules. Charlie turned barging at the windward end of the line into an art-form. The Scot refined his famous starting technique during his tenure aboard the schooner, *Colonia*. With such large, fragile and expensive vessels, right-of-way was often determined by a reckless game of chicken. Charlie Barr got away with it, but he would surely have been hauled up in front of an unsympathetic protest committee after virtually every race under the racing rules as interpreted today.

Although the matter may be settled south of the border and across the Atlantic, there is a continuing debate among the Clyde cognoscenti as to which of the Barrs was 'first among equals'. John, it seems, was a natural leader of the Shackleton type, who inspired his crew to subsume their individuality to his iron will; effectively, they inhabited a common personality. In yachts like *Neptune*, *Ulerin*, *Clara*, and even *Niagara*, the race was over before a gun was fired as he was able to project an aura of invincibility. He really was that good – think Dennis Connor in his pomp.

Charles, on the other hand, became a past-master in the art of optimising the skills and resources he had at his disposal. In really big, complex boats, trust, co-operation and rational delegation can ultimately achieve higher levels of performance than the uncompromising 'team' approach employed so successfully by John with his tight, well-practised crews – think Paul Cayard. If this is an accurate characterisation, John might have had the edge in 20-raters (12mR-sized boats), but in SCYC 90-footers (super-maxi-sized yachts), Charlie was the past-master.[673]

Barr skippered the unsuccessful American defence candidate, *Vigilant*, in 1895 before taking the helm of the successful *Columbia* in 1899 and 1901, then *Reliance* in 1903. Columbia's owners, among them J. P. Morgan, awarded Barr a bonus of $3,965.75 (£98,000) for the campaign.[674] If it were credibly authenticated, Charlie Barr's lifetime pension, said to be £400 (£51,000) per annum in today's money, would have been easily the richest prize in sport.[675]

Charlie took charge of Morton F. Plant's big Herreshoff schooner *Ingomar* for her successful campaign in Europe in the summer of 1904, picking up 17 trophies. Then there was the Trans-Atlantic Race for the Kaiser's Gold Cup in 1905. Sailing the schooner, *Atlantic*, Charlie's crew set a record of 12 days, 4hrs 1min and 19s that stood for 98 years until the Briand-designed *Maria Cha IV* bettered the mark in 2003.[676]

When *Atlantic's* owner, Winston Marshall, put his trophy up for auction in 1917 to support the American war effort, it realised $150,000 ($3.25 million). But melted down, the baroque carbuncle turned out to be nothing more than gold-plated pewter and confirmed the perceived opinion of the Kaiser as a worthless bounder.

Charlie Barr became a 'naturalised' American ca.1899 after the first successful defence but returned home at the close of each sailing season to spend six months of the year in Southampton with his wife and son. It seems that Barr found yacht racing in the United States engaging, and it was certainly lucrative, but at heart, he remained British. *"Barr's remarkable skill, intelligence and racing pedigree with Colonia were principally responsible for him being chosen as the first non-American skipper to lead a US America's Cup defence campaign."*[677] There has been some debate about this, but it is entirely irrelevant whether he took American citizenship before his first cup win or after – he was not a patriot, he was a professional.

A century-and-a-half of America's Cup shenanigans make the matter moot. Foreign mercenaries were common at that time in the America's Cup, after it became competitive and before nationality was raised as a core value. *Defender* was headline news in 1895 because she boasted an all-American line-up. In any case, few if any, native Americans have crewed aboard a first-class yacht.[678] Challengers over the years have learned not to make assumptions about the relationship between nationality and national prestige and what is or isn't in the Deed of Gift.[679]

The Scandinavians who served aboard American Cup defenders through the 1883-1937 period were nicknamed 'Norwegian Steam'. They did not represent any nation, they were just the best power-plant that money could buy – and indeed revelled in the coolest nickname of any racing team before or since.[680] Somehow, designating our ill-disciplined chorus lines of West Coast rail-fodder as the 'Clyde Puffers' doesn't quite merit the same cachet.[681] First-class professional yachting was, and remains, a very different ballgame.

Professionals in Print

Through the great days of yachting, sailing books were invariably written from the perspective of the owner or to address that aspiring demographic niche. When professional seamen appear, they rank below designers and builders and only a little above the anonymous legion of sailmakers. Wading through the turgid exceptionalism of Victorian adventurers, we find that few genuine seamen have put pen to paper. And among those, the majority are petit bourgeoise slumming it by choice, spinning yarns filtered through a middle-class education. There are, of course, notable exceptions, a category led by the preternaturally accomplished Joshua Slocum (1844-1909). *Tom Diaper's Log* (1950) or *Tack Now Skipper* (1979) written by Owen Parker. Neither is a literary masterpiece, but they furnish vital insights into the nexus of classic yachting – the rapport between owner and skipper.[682]

When exploring such narratives, the danger is that we are bound to read both along and between the lines. In the context of 21st century society, acquiescence appears as oppression and loyalty becomes entwined with servility. A conscious reset is required. Only then can we develop an understanding of the history of our sport, if we are to do so with any degree of honesty. Of course, these exceptions provide little more than a fleeting glimpse of a lost world. The vast majority of professional skippers and hired hands were disconnected from aspirations of literary endeavour by the intractable barriers of class. even in Scotland where the tradition of intellectualism among the 'working class' was as strong then as it is today.

Professionals vs Amateurs

In the 21st century, as in the 19th, professional sailors still do the jobs we amateurs cannot do, or at best execute less-effectively at some hazard to life-and-limb. Their services are vital in respect of the growing fleet of large yachts, particularly those traditional rebuilds with manual heavy gear. Happily, in relation to terms and conditions of service, the wider narrative has evolved. Our best sailors are no longer burdened with the casual slights of social apartheid. Quite the reverse; the great-grandchildren of 'Hellish Dick' and his mates are now rock stars. Owners seek the kudos of their company as much as their skill.

That was then and this is now, but the passage of a century and a half encompassed the heyday of the amateur. From 1946 to 1986, post-war austerity and its aftermath limited the size of yachts, their complexity and their incipient danger. Back then, a 12-metre was considered a big boat and an offshore maxi justified the name. But even so, keen amateurs could be trusted with this kit. In the 1970s and 80s, even well-known maxi crews were playing hooky from their day jobs.

When asked if maxi racing was not a rich man's sport, Jim Kilroy, of the all-conquering *Kialoa* series, had this to say: *"No, there's one rich man aboard and 25 poor men, and they enjoy it more than the rich man does!"* Well, it's a 'yes and no' interrogative; Jim probably enjoyed the game at least as much as his crew of professionals and semi-pros when they were on the water winning races. But surely his dedicated amateurs, absolved of writing cheques, had the best of the afterglow when they were all back ashore celebrating their many successes in the pub.

Professionalism returned gradually, top-down from the apex events. Dick Enersen, who crewed on *Constellation* in the match against *Sovereign* for the 1964 America's Cup, has written: *"Today, grinders are being paid like first-year lawyers. But, back then, money never changed hands. On reflection, if they had asked us, we would have paid to be included. Not only were we living like princes, but we were sailing the best boats ever – with, and against, the best sailors on the planet. Those experiences, those associations, and those friendships made that summer and have shaped and enriched my life in ways I could never have imagined."*[683]

Where does the keen amateur fit in today? For most, to be honest, pretty far down the pecking order. But all is not lost. Elite competition is out of reach but not out of sight. There is a growing community of enthusiasts who 'live' the sport through the host of sailing media now dedicated to showcasing the rarefied world of professional yacht racing. However, since all this is 'free to air' on the Internet, it surely undermines the precept that sustainable professionalism must be underpinned by sustainable models of 'service provision'.

Every professional sportsperson provides a service that someone somewhere is paying for. This axiom obviously encompasses working seamen, and the 'horse whisperers' who dangle on the backstay too. But it can now be expanded to take in marketing and PR assignments, on and off the boat. We might also, sceptically, include the holy grail of 'stadium sailing' – conceived as some sort of soggy bullring, where the ever-present prospect of impending disaster is intermittently commercialised.

There are long-standing issues with all these business models, but they are not wholly beyond the pale. The sustainability of 'professional small boat course racing' is much less certain. Sometimes it seems that every good sailor wants to be paid for their participation in both competitive events and training programmes, whether or not they add value to an identifiable income stream in the course of an average day. Arguably, virtually none do, especially those on the RYA payroll. Squad sailing is often disparaged as it generates a 'culture of entitlement'; but a more generous analysis is that motivated young people are able to exploit a niche opened by national chauvinism.

The debasement of the sporting ideal has its roots in the athletic programmes of the former USSR and the equally cynical sports scholarships of American universities. It is manifest in Britain today in the allocation of national lottery profits to sailors who are considered to have 'good medal prospects', whatever that means. And so, the poorest in society who buoy-up their dreams dabbling in sweepstakes, or simply give in to an unfortunate gambling addiction, sponsor middle-class Olympic aspirants. Of course, it is not just sport, it is also 'the arts' – music, opera, art galleries and the whole gamut of elitist culture we yachtsmen disproportionately enjoy.

It is impossible to defend any sort of remuneration in the Olympic classes on cost-benefit grounds, unless the currency is jingoism, and we endorse the xenophobic nonsense about sporting patriotism pedalled by our national authority. Success on the water is not a measure of our Britannic worth or the mettle of our small nation. And it is not a substitute for gunboat diplomacy. Olympic athletes in yachting disciplines do not entertain, provide no useful service, and all the flag-waving notwithstanding, seek only personal glory. Why on earth should anyone get paid for that?

Since yacht racing is primarily a participation game, and struggles as a spectator sport even among enthusiasts, the paradigm-shift to a virtual venue on the Web is a vital lifeline for professionals if they are to earn a living. However, the America's Cup foilers have reduced a surpassingly complex sport to the lowest common denominator – crash and burn. In this brave new world, the coverage of elite competition paradoxically becomes fragmentary when we cut away from virtual reality to live action.

Until recently, it was reasonably asserted that if sailing was engrossing it was only in the same way as golf, or snooker, or maybe even chess is. But the 2017/18 Volvo Ocean Race changed all that; it was a watershed. The advent of camera-drones, skilfully flown by embedded reporters, brings live footage from the wilds of the Great Southern Ocean. This represents a sea change, maybe even a revolution. We can witness the sublime skillset of professional sailors in a way that has never been seen before. Balls-to-the-wall racing among the icebergs is mesmerising; no argument.[684]

This immersive action is enthralling, even without the usual requisite – a lifelong obsession with the minutiae of the back-story. No one saw this coming. However, there is always a downside; now we really know just how good they are, professionals have become even more remote from the world of the weekend yachtsman. Specifically, the maestros who race and break records short-handed in the current slate of blue-ribbon events might be acclaimed unreservedly. They deliver real returns in product exposure, and that rare thing in 21st century sport – favourable product associations for sponsors. These guys now represent the apex of our sport; a summit which might be in hawk to Mammon but is blessedly aloof from the whimsical billionaires who have reclaimed the America's Cup.

However, these guys are an exceptional elite. The bulk of pro-sailor vacancies are on the big yachts that crowd the favoured harbours of the 'beautiful people'. Such assignments incur ethical dilemmas by the boatload. Superyachts require a legion of poorly paid professional sailors, cooks and bottle-washers. Countless starry-eyed young people have been drawn into this superficially attractive lifestyle, postponing career, marriage, family and homeownership for a day in the sun.

Perhaps it is fun for a while; but attending to the every-whim of people who always get what they want inevitably involves huge compromises in terms of self-respect, and ultimately, life-prospects. Only the boat captains transcend this shit; well, that is until the 'hired guns' and 'rock stars' come aboard in the regatta season. Then the regular crew are condemned to ferry the boat to and from the racecourse, man the handles and tweak the running backstays. The sybaritic slavery of superyachts is clearly not for everyone.

CODA: James Hamilton

Certainly, it is not always like that and 'not-always-like-that' has a long history too. James Hamilton was the Commodore of the Royal Northern. This was in 1827, after the bothersome Irish contingent was hived off to obscurity. James was a proper gentleman and that rare beast; an owner who not only looked after his crew but actually liked them. When it came on to rain, Hamilton could be relied upon to 'pop his heid' through the companionway and present the helmsman with a big black golf umbrella.

Hamilton was also famous for his punch, so potent that it was only brewed after a successful cruise and when the ship was secure at anchor in her home roadstead. Jimmy Tait was steward and valet to the Commodore. On one memorable occasion, Jimmy contrived to snaffle a wee bit too much of Hamilton's lethal brew. When the Commodore summoned his well-oiled servant to undress him at bedtime, oor Jimmy was quite incapable. Ruefully contemplating the potency of his own punch, the old-school aristocrat addressed the slumbering valet: "*Weel, Jimmy, I daur say it would scarcely be becoming o' me to do anything in the way o' flytin the noo; but really after this we maun try no baith to get fou at the same time.*"

CODA: Good skippers

In 1899, Captain A. J. Kenealy wrote: "*Whether amateur or professional, the skipper must be a man of dash and daring tempered with a modest soupcon of discretion, active, vigilant, with his weather eye wide open at all times and seasons. He must have the knack of handling men so as to get every foot-pound of energy out of them that is in them. He should be a strict, but not necessarily a stern, disciplinarian; and he should have sufficient diplomatic instinct in his make-up to know when to wink at a slight lapse on the part of a generally capable and faithful bluejacket. A good skipper must therefore be a good judge of human nature, alive to the idiosyncrasies and frailties of sailors, who have in good sooth as many whims and vagaries as silly schoolgirls in the transition stage of development. In fact, he should be quite a past mastering the cunning art of 'jollying along'.*"[685] That job description still stands today as a template for the perfect skipper.

CODA: Sink or Swim?

Through the turn of the century, Edward VII was donating King's Cups right, left and centre, and of course, the Royal Clyde received one. The 1914 Kings Cup at Hunter's Quay was sailed in 15-metres and was notable for illuminating incident which occurred just as the winning yacht crossed the line in a fresh north-easterly. When Sir Charles McIver's *Cestrian* gybed at the finish, two crewmen were caught by the staysail sheet. One was struck on the head by a flailing block and knocked overboard.

An unnamed guest jumped in and kept the unconscious man afloat while the cutter's dinghy was launched. In those days, gentlemen could swim, while most professional seamen were simply fatalists.[686] The two crewmen were rushed ashore in the club launch. After receiving medical aid, they both recovered and would go on to serve in the Great War.

CODA: 'Upstairs-downstairs' on a Clyde 10-tonner

"The Verve's professional crew was Tom McCubbin (a good Dunoon man) and George Tyre (from Largs) and with Mr Wylie, who was a first-class steersman himself, they made a powerful combination in a boat like the Verve. Both of the men were devoted to their young master, and he had a warm regard and respect for them. Tyre was a man of such versatility in a boat that he was as capable in the role of cook and steward, as he was in that of masthead man, and bowspritend man. Soon after coming-to at Blackfarland, Mr Wylie and I were sitting in the cutter's little saloon reviewing the events of the day, while on the other side of a slight bulkhead Tyre was making a meal for us of the kind known in Scotland as a 'toosie tea', and in England as a knife-and-fork-tea, and to judge by the sounds coming through enjoying himself the while.

After some reference to the Mail's aggressive Radicalism, preventing it becoming popular with the great body of yachtsmen, Mr Wylie added with an indulgent smile, 'But its politics will be no different to you, for according to George, you're all Radicals about Largs. On my rejoining, 'Well, the great majority of us', he continued, as he lowered his voice to a whisper, 'Don't you speak a word, no matter how extravagant you may think my remarks are, and I'll let you see me stirring up George beautifully. Sometimes, he roars so loud when I twist his Radical tail, you would think he was going to eat me'. Then he started to show up in no measured terms the sins and shortcomings of the Liberal Party, and to administer a few shrewd but caustic digs at the high priests of it, as he sailed gaily on.

For a short time, there was a significant silence in the galley, then an even more eloquent knocking of things about, but as neither had any effect on checking the stream of intentionally acrid criticism. His weaver-yachtsman servant, all afire with righteous indignation, and completely indifferent as to consequences, burst into the saloon, thundering, 'here, Mr Wylie, you've gaun faur enoch, an' it's too bad – Meikle's as good a Radical as I am, but he disna' care to make a shirra-mair (Jacobite term for an indecisive skirmish) *in your boat the first time he's abaird o' her. If it's a political raw you're wearyin' for, I'm your man'. Wylie's face was a study, as he looked with something approaching admiration at his servant who was man enough to face bravely up to him on behalf of 'the cause' which was dear to him, albeit he attempted the line of correction by saying, 'Now, George, now you forget yourself'.*

He got no further, however, for he noticed that Tyre was beginning to awaken to the real nature of the situation, and so he finished the sentence with as jolly a laugh as ever I heard. 'Done again!' Tyre jerked out, then continued, 'an I woner if I'll never learn to mak oot when you're on the jokin' tack afore I lose my temper. An' noo, Sir, let me beg your pardon'. 'Oh, it's all right, George', Wylie rejoined with a pleasant smile, 'but really it is getting easier to twist your political tail than it once was."[687]

---

[651] Come Sailing, Gilbert Hackford-Jones, 1948.

[652] The pay dispute concerned the professional crew, sailmakers, shipwrights and craftsmen and their claims were justified. Nevertheless, Sopwith contacted 'Tiny' Mitchell, Commodore of the Royal Corinthian (Burnham) to round up a crew of RCYC members.

[653] Corinthians (ironically on full pay) were James Bacon, Alton Bacon, Chris Boardman, Nigel Warrington-Smythe, William De Quincey, Denny Drew, Ernest Moltzer, Miles Belleville, Colin Ratsey, Roy Mitchell, Reginald Droop, Beecher Moore, Jack Martin & Wally Richards.

[654] Boat Sailing in Fair Weather and Foul, Captain Ahmed. J. Kenealy, 1854.

[655] Before selling *King Duck* to Walter Bergius in 1957, Tom Thornycroft used her extensively as a mothership for regattas and carried two International 14s on deck. She served during the 1948 Torquay Olympics and the 1952 Olympics in Helsinki. Bergius had *Dodo VI* built by Berthon's in 1961. *Dodo V* was sold to Alan Fairbrother before being bought by the Marquess of Bute in 1964 and resuming her original name of *King Duck*.

[656] The 1929 Schneider Trophy races were limited to three seaplanes per nation, but that year only the British and Italians fielded teams. H.R.D Waghorn won with the Supermarine S.6 powered by a Rolls-Royce R 1900 to achieve a speed of 528.879kph over a 350km loop off Southsea.

[657] Jim McNair's archives, a letter from Campbell to James McNair, 22nd February 1927.

[658] The skipper's remuneration is higher than one might expect. The Auld Mug: The Scots and The America's Cup, Len Paterson, 2012.

[659] For example, the crews in recent global circumnavigations have used staysails, jibs, yankees and code-zeros, three headsail tight reaching, which taxes even the best sailors.

[660] The Auld Mug, the Scots and the Americas Cup, Len Paterson, 2012.

[661] Clyde Yacht-building, Glasgow Herald, 3rd February 1883.

[662] The Voyage of the Nyanza, RNYC; being the record of a 3 years' cruise in a Schooner Yacht in the Atlantic and Pacific, and her subsequent Shipwreck, James C. Dewar, 1892.

[663] Notes and Notions, The Yachtsman, July 4th 1895.

[664] Yachting, the Mutiny onboard the Ailsa, Dundee Evening Telegraph, 19th June 1895.

[665] The old slogan for Barr's Iron Brew, the quintessential Scottish soft drink containing 0.002% of ammonium ferric citrate. (Apologies to my English friends.)

[666] Leaves from the Logbook of an old Clyde journalist, James Meikle, reproduced in The Yachtsman 21st September 1924.

[667] Captain John Barr – Obituary, The Times, 12th January 1909.

[668] The Outing: an illustrated monthly magazine of recreation, March – April 1889.

[669] "*Another account had it that Charles was a member of the crew of the Thistle in the America Cup races. Such was not the case, however.*" Charles Barr Obituary, The Yachtsman, 2nd February 1911.

[670] Charlie Barr, the Story of a Skipper Supreme, Barry Pickthall, Classic Boat, 2013.

[671] Ibid

[672] Clyde, Yachting magazine, 27th April 1893.

[673] A Great Yachtsman, the late Captain Charles Barr, The Yachtsman, 2nd February 1910.

[674] Some of today's Cup skippers would just laugh at that sort of money. However, more generally, wages are intermittent and fluctuate. Annual salary equivalents are derisory and would not arouse the envy of a new graduate in local government.

[675] A Great Yachtsman Dead, the Western Gazette, 27th January 1911. With regard to the pension, if the amount was in US$ it would be the equivalent of £9,800 today.

[676] Between 1980 and 1990, the absolute record was bettered seven times by very large multihulls before the remarkable *Maria Cha IV* crossed the Atlantic in a time just a few hours

outside the then-current multi-hull record. Since then, *Comanche* has brought the mono-hull record down further to 5 days 14hrs 21min and 25s.

[677] Charlie Barr, Barry Pickthall, Classic Boat, July 2013.

[678] We would be happy to stand corrected here, but while yachts are given native American names and Americans with native DNA will certainly be out sailing somewhere, we have found little to suggest any significant level of participation.

[679] Nationality rules, and then only in terms of residence, were introduced on 15th July 1980, after Andy Rose, an American, sailed for Alan Bond in the 1977 Challenge. A 'trustee interpretative resolution' on 9th March 1982, defined nationality as holding a passport, having domicile, or by having a principal place of residence in the country concerned.

[680] Throughout the 1870s and 1880s, Scandinavians, especially Norwegians, were hired as captains, mates and crew on American yachts, playing a vital role in America's Cup competitions between 1893 and 1937. See Jattlaget, Yacht Sailors from Tysnes. More than 250 sailors came from this austere and thinly populated archipelago alone.

[681] In the 2007 America's Cup, the Spanish yacht *Desafío Español* carried the 'Scottish Power' logo on her mainsail. Scottish Power is part of the Iberdrola group. It was fun while it lasted.

[682] 'Tom Daiper's Log' Tom Daiper, 1950, 'Tack Now Skipper', Owen Parker, 1979.

[683] Memories of a Corinthian Summer, Dick Enersen, December 2014.

[684] We used to top out at about 20kts in the Southern Ocean in IOR maxis. These days, incredibly skilled professional sailors are going twice as fast in much smaller planing monohulls. Now, with foils, the expression 'a wing and a prayer' was never more apt.

[685] Yachting Wrinkles, Duty and Discipline Afloat, Captain A. J. Kenealy, 1899. Kinealy (1856-19xx), became a naturalised American in 1886.

[686] Yachting on the Clyde, The Times, 13th July 1914.

[687] Leaves from the Logbook of an Old Clyde Journalist, LXX, James Meikle, Yachting, 19th June 1926. Sailing on a Watson 10-tonner.

The infamous 'British method' for hoisting sail.　　　　　Charlie Barr (1864-1911)

Charlie Barr working aboard the plank-on-edge, *Shona*, in Lawley's Yard, Massachusetts 1888

Crew and family from steam yacht *Olivia*, A. & J. Inglis 1883   Image: Castle House Museum Dunoon
We assume the fact that the children have clay pipes too is simply a bit of fun. Although many children did smoke in the 19th century, the fact that everyone has a pipe suggests homespun satire.

Chapter 16: The Rag Trade

One of the most striking features of Shamrock is her superb suit of sails. Her capital showing was due in a great measure to the quality of her canvas. The hull of Columbia is superior to that of Shamrock, but the sails of the Yankee yacht are far inferior to those made by Lap thorn & Ratsey. The Outing Magazine[688]

During the 1950s, 60s and 70s, the British coveted the sails built by Ted Hood using cloth woven by his father on a 'junkyard challenge' loom. These sails appeared to give the Americans a critical advantage. *"In 1958, horse track reporters wrote reams of unchivalrous comments about Sceptre's underbody. They neglected to note that the lady was wearing some of the worst fitting suits of sails ever seen in international competition."*[689] These stories obscure the fact that Britain led the world in sail-making. Everyone remembers that when the schooner, *America*, visited our waters in 1851, she boasted a set of well-cut cotton sails that outclassed the baggy flax canvas of the English Channel fleet. Then we fast-forward to find *Sceptre* humbled again in 1958. Invariably, the hyperbole of disappointment means that we gloss over the best part of a century when our sailmaking was second to none.

Writing in 1924, Thomas Ratsey chronicled the sequence of key innovations: cotton sailcloth was not widely taken up in Britain until ca.1870, becoming ubiquitous on racing yachts by 1887. Lacing the mainsail to the boom, a detail considered irrelevant today, did not become popular until 1890-92, and horizontally-cut sails only superseded vertical-cut ca.1900.[690] Ratsey went on to note that *"Herreshoff took to making his own sails following his visit to these waters in the Vigilant in the year 1894, and no one could blame him. The American sails of those times were very discreditable, mostly due to the inferiority of the sailcloth which was woven so irregularly."* Tom Ratsey attributed the decline in quality of American sailcloth to the demise of the American clipper ships in the 1860s.

Matthew Orr and the Scotch-cut

Matthew Orr, a native of Greenock, was an important pioneer in sailmaking, working both before and during the clipper ship era. This master sailmaker has been all but lost in the labyrinth of maritime history. Orr perfected an innovative, perhaps revolutionary, panel layout for headsails during the years 1825 to 1830.[691] He termed this new cut the 'angulated method' of sailmaking. These sails were the first to recognise load paths and orientate traditional cloth, which stretched least along the length of each panel, most efficiently. The flax canvas common in that era was invariably 'double warp' (twice as many fibres along the length of the fabric bolt). In order to achieve this orientation, Orr's foresails crucially featured diagonal seaming, splitting the clew angle with a mitre following the line of the sheet-load. This cut effectively eliminated bias stretch, still the bogey of all conventionally woven sailcloth, even today. Moreover, a sail constructed in this way is almost indestructible.

Orr's sails were quickly recognised as standing better than the traditional vertical-cut where all the panels lay parallel to the leech. However, in spite of the fact Greenock-made sails cut to this pattern were clearly superior, it was upwards of twenty years before Orr's mitre-cut achieved general acceptance in the British Isles. But that, we may note with some satisfaction, was just in time for the bonanza of the clipper ship era. Today, Mathew Orr's angulated method, now known as 'Scotch-cut', is still evident in the pages of *Classic Boat Magazine* when bespoke sailmakers replicate traditional cuts authentically.

'Honest John' McFarlane

In the heyday of the clipper ships, there were seven sailmakers and seven rope-spinners in Greenock alone. One of the earliest lofts was established in Glasgow in 1840 by 'Honest John' McFarlane. The McFarlanes were perhaps the best-known of our early sailmaking dynasties. Archibald Flemington McFarlane, son of the founder, bridged the era. He died in 1937, aged 92. Honest John's loft made sails for clipper ships and early Clyde racing yachts. From the mid-19th century, sailmakers on the Clyde and the sailcloth weavers of Greenock and Arbroath set the standard, exporting their products around the world.

Archie McFarlane retired in 1907, leaving the business, by then exclusively devoted to working canvas, to his sons.[692] Trawling through the early editions of Lloyds Register, it is significant to note that sailmakers are credited in the listings. Lloyds recognised that sails were a significant element of both the cost and the performance potential of a yacht, and thus sailmakers should be recorded along with designers and builders.[693] The Register shows that, from the 1870s, the bulk of the Scottish yacht sails trade devolved first to A. & W. Menzies of Gourock, then to the peerless Lapthorn loft.

What we can take from the Register is that most of the racing yachts built on the Clyde during the golden age – whether from Watson, Fife or Mylne, were dressed in the finest Ratsey, Lapthorn, or Lapthorn & Ratsey rags, with a small but significant contribution from Douglas Menzies. Just as the creations of our talented yacht designers are integral to the story of English yachting, so our neighbour's sail designers became a common denominator in the parallel stories of Scottish, English, and American sailing.

Thomas Ratsey and the Mitre-cut

Mathew Orr's mitred cut played to the strengths of traditional warp-oriented fabrics where sail shape more a by-product of cloth stretch, rather than luff rounding or seam shaping. This was ideal for 'working canvas' on square riggers and traditional craft, but not for lightly constructed racing sails where a whole new slate of design criteria comes into play. It would transpire that cross-cut sails – requiring new types of canvas, meticulous design and flawless workmanship met these criteria. Nathanial Herreshoff is generally credited with the invention. His cross-cut sails appeared on a couple of small boats in 1894.[694] However, while not wishing to spoil a good story, or diminish the legend of Captain Nat, Thomas W. Ratsey had been on the case for some time and patented cross-cut sails two years earlier.[695] Letters of patent were granted in 1892 in England and in 1894 in the United States.

Ratsey rotated the cloths 90-degrees so that they lay at right angles to both the foot and the leech, employing a mitre in both foresails and mainsails. To assist in sail shaping and reduce the friction resistance of vertical seaming, Tom's cut required weft-orientated fabrics with stretch minimised across the weft. The new panel layout also facilitated the use of sail battens to promote a flat-run roach. Vertical-cut sails were usually built with concave leeches to minimise curl. This area lost from a hollow leech had long rankled among sailmakers and early racing sailors.

Tom's mitre-cut mainsails appeared from time to time during the cotton sailcloth era, but the extra work required and more complex sail cutting limited its use. Most sailmakers, and indeed Tom himself, focussed on the simpler cross-cut variant adopted by Herreshoff.

Fast forward to the 1970s, during the early years of the International Offshore Rule, and mitre-cut mainsails became popular again.[696] Over the next 20 years, with continued progress in sail fabrics, ever more complex tri-radial-cuts were favoured before Swiss sailmakers Luc Dubois and J.P. Baudet harnessed the potential of emerging technologies to make the Holy Grail of genuine load-path sails possible. North began production in 1990, and after a protracted struggle, the new sails became commercially viable seventeen years later in 2007.[697] All of these wizards owe a debt to the founders of modern sail engineering, Mathew Orr and Tom Ratsey.

Ratsey, later Ratsey & Lapthorn (nb Lapthorn & Ratsey in Scotland)

The Ratsey family established their loft at Cowes in 1790 and the Lapthorns followed suit in Gosport in 1825. The two rival Solent lofts amalgamated in 1889. Lapthorn's Greenock loft, established seven years earlier in 1882, became the Scottish branch of Lapthorn & Ratsey and part of the largest sailmaking group in the world, which grew to serve the American market with a New York loft in 1902.[698]

Ratsey & Lapthorn could reputedly make up a mainsail for a yacht the size of *Britannia* (1893) overnight, although it is hard to imagine that a hand-stitched sail could be cut and assembled in that time.[699] Technology and orders were shared among the various branches of the organisation so that state-of-the-art sails were available from the Gourock loft. The company was an early multinational, spanning the yachting world like North does today. At the turn of the century, a clear majority of British racing yachts, north and south of the border, set the firm's racing canvas.

Thomas W. Ratsey (1851-1935), who headed-up the British operation during these years, was noted for his diffidence and charm, but 'dedication to the craft' seems to have been his defining attribute. Tom was a key man in four of our six America's Cup challenges. He and his team fettled the Clyde-built series of *Thistle, Valkyrie II, Valkyrie III* and *Shamrock I, Shamrock II* and *Shamrock III*, as well as the Nicholson-designed and built *Shamrock IV*. Tom Ratsey also managed the challengers' sail inventories in the States in this era, a tour of duty spanning 23 years.

Across the Atlantic, despite arguably infringing Tom Ratsey's 1892 US patent, Nat Herreshoff's cross-cut racing sails were highly successful in their home waters. It is unclear whether the additional sophistication of Ratsey's mitre-cut negated his patent in the American market; if so, it would indeed have been ironic. In any event, the Herreshoff loft was still riding the wave in 1902.[700] In that year, Tom Ratsey established Ratsey & Lapthorn's New York loft to bring British sailmaking expertise to the USA and challenge Herreshoff's monopoly. "*Visiting America so many times, as I did in connection with the America Cup, opened my eyes, and I saw there was an opening there for Ratsey & Lapthorn, and so, in 1902, out I went.*"[701]

Ratsey lofts on both sides of the Atlantic would eclipse Herreshoff's cross-cut sail designs. Tom Ratsey continued: "*I knew before I left that I should be welcomed, particularly by such men as the late Commodore Pierpoint Morgan and the late Commodore Adams and Commodore Ledyard, and many other prominent yachtsmen.*"[702] Ernest Ratsey, who ran the New York loft, liked to boast that his great-great-grandfather had made the sails for Nelson's *Victory*. Off-putting, perhaps, but such things play differently over there.

Country of Origin

After the Great War, rigs developed using British aircraft technologies also drew admiration from the American camp, particularly during the *Endeavour* challenges of the 1930s. The Yanks bought our sailcloth and coveted our instruments and electronics too. U.S. defenders, right up until *Ranger*, used British sailcloth. However, we forfeited this lead in sailmaking technology, and much else, during the hiatus of WW2.

Post-war, holding all the cards for once and desperate to hold on to the America's Cup after the scare with *Gretel* in 1962, the New York Yacht Club decreed that sailcloth and sails had to be manufactured in the challenger's 'country of origin'. The irony of this move was missed entirely in the press. In 1903, there was widespread disquiet concerning the use of Ratsey sails on the Vanderbilt syndicate's *Reliance*, chosen to race against *Shamrock III* in that year's contest. The *Pall Mall Gazette* opined: *"This is a most unsportsmanlike proceeding. If the defender wins by means of British canvas it would not be an American victory at all"*.[703] Other papers took up the story: *"The only consolation would be that the superiority of British workmanship received so fine a testimonial."*[704]

Through the 1930 America's Cup summer, Ratsey & Lapthorn built sails for both the defender, *Enterprise*, and the challenger, *Shamrock IV*. George Ratsey's New York loft also supplied the American trialists *Whirlwind*, *Weetamoe* and *Vanity*. Even after WW2, the 12mR, *Columbia*, successful defender of the 1958 America's Cup, sailing for the New York Yacht Club, used sails cut by the American offshoot of the old British firm. The New York loft closed in 1982.[705]

Lapthorn, later Lapthorn & Ratsey (nb Ratsey & Lapthorn)

In setting out the context, we have been obliged to run ahead of the Scottish story. Back in 1867 we find *Hunt's Yachting Magazine* complaining that Clyde yachts really required the services of the English loft on-site in Scotland. *"Indeed, English made sails don't seem to fit Clyde boats with sufficient accuracy, and the fact is that our yachtsmen when they want an extra good job to stand well, prefer a sail from Menzies of Greenock to one of Lapthorne's best make."*[706]

It would be another 15 years before an English loft took the hint. Lapthorn of Gosport set up their Scottish branch in 1882, seven years before their merger with Ratsey in 1889. Lapthorn initially rented space from Scotts and set up their Clyde branch in a vacant loft at the back of the Greenock shipyard. It was a timely business venture; in the boom years of the mid-1880s, local lofts could not cope with an ever-increasing demand for sailmaking services. Both Fife and G. L. Watson were keen to have well-cut sails of Lapthorn quality on their latest creations.[707]

Demand was particularly acute during Clyde Fortnight when an upsurge of repair work and demand for short-notice replacements taxed both local sailmakers and kept the railways busy shuttling sail-bags up and down the length of the country.[708] Additionally, some of the finest yachts in the world, many with sails by Lapthorn, now spent significant periods of time on the Clyde. Spar failures, and the enduring phenomenon of short-life racing sails, meant that specialist on-site support was necessary to keep the fleet in racing trim.

Lapthorn's acquired their own accommodation across the road from Scotts in Forsyth Street in 1886, later moving to Cove Road in Gourock, where the loft prospered under the direction of James Lapthorn, and subsequently, his son, Stanley. *Thistle*, the Royal Clyde's America's Cup challenger of 1887, was dressed by Lapthorn. Most sails were built in Scotland, but the most expensive grand-prix rags arrived on the overnight train from Portsmouth. The capacity to balance the skills and resources in various lofts became a significant commercial advantage when Lapthorn merged with Ratsey in 1889.

Then as now, racing yacht owners might favour a specific sail-cutter, in a particular loft, as still occurs today with global brands like North. So, most of the Scottish America's Cup yacht sails would have been cut down south, although service, alterations and recutting work was handled in Scotland. It was no wonder that *"the prices charged by the firm are high, but their work is maintained at a very high degree of efficiency, and their cut attains perfection."*[709] In 1892, the firm exercised the same kind of dominance as North Sails does today: *"At the sail-making establishment there of Messrs Lapthorn & Ratsey, affairs are very brisk with new canvas for old boats, as well as many of the new ones."*[710]

James Lapthorn was a perfectionist, and his after-sales service followed a pattern that is still common among all the great sailmakers. If an owner, or a skipper, was unhappy with a sail, James would go afloat and observe how the sail was being set up and how the boat was being managed. More often than not, he could tweak a sail to perfection, but in the days of cotton sails, if they had not been 'broken-in' correctly, recutting would inevitably be required. Then, he would ask the skipper to moor the vessel just off the loft with the sails stretched out on the spars. James and his foreman George Knaggs would assess the options and agree on the recut.

George Knaggs was a second-generation sailmaker by trade, learning his craft on the tea clippers. When George came ashore in 1880, he remained with the trade he knew, securing a position with Lapthorn. George soon graduated to building racing sails for Clyde yachts. As Loft Foreman, he was able to assist the firm's clients in setting up their new sails, and of course, he gained additional fees from this advice. George would end his days as a successful technician, able to provide well for his family, owning a spacious upper flat in Gourock with fine views over the Cardwell Bay anchorage and beyond.[711]

By all accounts, the Lapthorn family enjoyed their time in Scotland and became stalwarts of the local community. James was a gentleman of impeccable moral rectitude as the following story relates. Father and sons were cruising in what George Blake describes as *"one of James's rather nondescript yachts"*. The youngest son returned from an early-morning row, having pillaged the pots of a local fisherman to set up a lobster breakfast. James was more than a little dismayed by this dishonest behaviour.

Young Lapthorn argued that they would probably come across the owner of the pots later and they could settle the account then. However, this casual approach to a poor man's livelihood was deemed unacceptable. Taking 7/- from his pocket, James instructed the now-remorseful boy to *"go back, lift the pot, place this money inside, and moor it again"*. Seven shillings (worth about £12 today) was generous for even the finest lobster back then, so one assumes the lad learned his lesson. Later Stanley Lapthorn would buy the old Robertson's built, Watson-designed 23/30, *Xyris (Lottie)*, and convert her for cruising, maintaining the family tradition of non-competitive sailing.

Lapthorn, independently, and later with Ratsey, maintained a Clyde loft for exactly 50 years, with the Lapthorn family finally packing up and consolidating their business back in Gosport in 1932. George Blake, among others, noted that this period coincided with the golden age of yachting on the Clyde.[712] But of course, it was not a coincidence. The Lapthorns left at the height of the Great Depression when the modest Scottish orderbook could be serviced from the main loft on the Solent.

Mackenzie of Sandbank

When we think of Scottish sailmaking, Scots of my generation recall Mackenzie's and Black's, but we generally do not boast about it, although these firms built many serviceable and long-lasting cruising sails. However, while all the fastest racing yachts seem to have been customers of Ratsey & Lapthorn, the native Scottish lofts also had their moments on the racecourse locally, and indeed, on the world stage too, even if the later success passed us by when Bruce Banks set the standard in Britain.

In the post-war years, Tom Black, a keen 6mR sailor, ran Mackenzie's loft at Greenock, while the sail loft in Sandbank was run by his son John. 'Mackenzie of Sandbank' was located at the back of Robertson's Yard, occupying the entire top floor of the Old Distillery building. The loft was a magic place, aromatic with the wonderful smells of tarred hemp and cotton sailcloth.[713] Sadly, Mackenzie of Sandbank did not survive the transition to synthetics, amalgamating with Black's Greenock loft in 1969.

The Mackenzie sail loft was first established in Greenock in the 1880s and moved to Sandbank in 1894 to serve the two increasingly successful yacht-building yards in the village.[714] *"Our crack native sailmaker and clever Corinthian steersman, Mr John Mackenzie, has flitted his sailmaking establishment from Greenock to Sandbank. The change has been attended with success, and never before did the firm do as much work during the winter season as since pitching its tent in Sandbank last October. Mr Mackenzie is getting a 1-rater of the usual bulb-fin type built by Messrs McAlister, Dumbarton."*[715]

John Mackenzie was a talented amateur yacht designer; the 1-rater, *Florence*, was still winning prizes fourteen years later in 1910. John was the official measurer for the Royal Clyde during the Scottish stand-off with the YRA in the 1890s. Prior to this he had insisted on following the spirit, rather than the letter of the rule, where measurement of blatant rule-cheaters was concerned. John was a stickler for correct procedure and thus *"not universally popular, whether as contractor or helmsman"*. John ran the sailmaking business until 1937 when his son Kenneth took over.

Kenneth took time out from the business to serve in the Royal Indian Navy during WW2, and after the conflict, relinquished the loft to his cousin, John Black, who returned from Canada to carry on the family business. However, just a few years later John sold the firm to Stuart Black of the rival loft, Blacks of Greenock. The two families shared a surname and a profession but were not related. Stuart sent his son John across the Clyde to run the operation together with James Leslie (future partner), Duncan Lauder and Alan Mackenzie (sail designer and cutter).

One of the last suits of cotton sails made by Mackenzie was for the Arthur Robb-designed Lion-class, *Siandra*, that won the Sydney Hobart overall and the magnificent Tattersall Trophy in 1958 and 1960.[716] The 35-footer had new, 'made in Australia' Terylene sails for the 1960 triumph, but the Scottish rags appear to have performed well in the ghosting conditions that brought *Siandra* through to an unexpected win by almost an hour-and-a-half, in 1958.[717]

This small, but significant, footnote in Scottish yachting history has been largely forgotten. Firstly, because the Australian press in the 1950s didn't acknowledge sailmakers, and secondly, because when you look for the winners of the Sydney Hobart, it is difficult to get past the bookie's favourites – the big yachts which boast of 'line-honours'; overall winners on handicap are relegated to marginalia.

John Black, writing in 2008, described how Nylon had been in use for some time for spinnakers but the introduction of Terylene in 1958 encountered some resistance and was specified in just 10% of new orders (see coda to this chapter). Nevertheless, initial results on the racecourse were so impressive that, by 1960, the transformation was complete. Unfortunately, Mackenzie's Terylene sails were not as good as their cotton ones had been, but they were well-made and hand-finished and served the West Coast cruising set well for decades. Our National 12ft dinghy, *Hijack*, temporarily back in the hands of her original owner Peter Collyer after my father's death, would continue to lead the Terylene-equipped fleet home with her old cotton Mackenzie mainsail through the 1962 and 1963 seasons.

Stuart Black passed away in 1960 and this left John in charge of both lofts. During the 1960s, the Royal Clyde moved from Hunter's Quay to Rhu and this impacted on the essential personal contacts that led to new sail orders. Subsequently, the two Mackenzie lofts were consolidated in Greenock in 1969. John Black was the fourth generation of sailmakers. His son in law, Andrew Smith, carried the tradition with him when he joined the board of Elvstrom Sails in Aabenraa, Denmark in 1992. More recently, Andrew was the Technical Director for design and production.

Other Lofts

Blacks of Greenock was a separate sailmaking business that made sails for commercial craft in the days of sail. The firm existed as a sailmaker from 1863 through to 1904 when the rise of steamships began to impact on all sailmakers' profits. Blacks responded by using their skills to run-up marquees, tents and camping accessories. The new business made a significant contribution to the war effort through two world wars. Blacks went on to build a substantial industry in outdoor and adventure-wear in the 1960s. Today, the firm has been swallowed by the ubiquitous JD Sports.[718]

While most shipyards had affiliated, or associated, sail-lofts in the days of sail, there were few other sailmakers on the Clyde specifically catering for yacht sails. Leitch of Tarbert, established in 1893, was one. The current 'Leitch of Tarbert' was re-established by Willie Leitch in 2010. While there is no direct line of succession, it is still nice to see a member of the Leitch family making sails at Tarbert. Willie Leitch's grandfather was a sailmaker on the clipper ship, *Cutty Sark*, and, like more than a few of his peers, rounded Cape Horn many times before settling down ashore and starting a sailmaking business.

While there are still local sailmakers in Scotland: Saturn in Largs Marina, Caldwell in Rosneath, Owen in Oban, Leitch in Tarbert and Jessail in Ardrossan, most of these small firms run-up sails cut from well-proven, commercially available computer files.[719] If you sail a Piper, or a Gareloch, or any other similar low-volume craft, you will receive a unique product cut by local craftsmen. However, if you are racing a big boat, sailmaking is now global, and quality is benchmarked by North. Smaller lofts aspire to equal North's technology, and when any one of these upstart firms do nudge ahead with a specific innovation, that situation does not last long.

Ironically, North Sails, the acme of American tech, is now British owned so we have come a full circle and are back in 1902. Peter Dubens' Oakley Capital Private Equity, a 'mid-market' private equity investor with over €1.5bn under its management, acquired a majority stake in the North Technology Group in 2014. Lowell North, who founded the business in 1957, sold out in 1984. He passed away in June 2019.

CODA: Terylene Sails Debut on the Clyde

Englishman, Rex Winfield, developed Terylene fibre and patented the process in 1941. From this, ICI developed a viable yarn for a corporate client, Calico Printers, in 1946. Subsequently, in the autumn of 1951, Gowan & Co, the West Mersea sailmakers, were given access to a small batch of pre-production cloth and invited to build the first Terylene yacht sail.

Gowan's ran up a 7/8ths fractional genoa for the 8-metre Cruiser-Racer, *Sonda* (8CR K1), designed and built by James McGruer the previous year. See Chapter 24. *Sonda* trialled the sail in the spring of 1952, initially on the Clyde, and subsequently at Cowes. Commercial production of Terylene sailcloth followed in 1954. DuPont licenced the patent from Calico Printers and immediately began the manufacture of Terylene under the tradename 'Dacron' in the USA. After Ted Hood's Dacron sails won the Star World Championship in 1954, the new material took the sailing world by storm.

---

[688] The Outing: an illustrated monthly magazine of recreation, March – April 1889.

[689] Boating News, Wm. Taylor McKeown, Times Record N Y, September 1958.

[690] Mr Thomas Ratsey on Sailmaking II, The Field, 3rd April 1924.

[691] Yacht Sails, their Care & Handling, Ernest A. Ratsey and W. H. de Fontaine, 1948.

[692] Clyde Notes, The Yachtsman Sail and Power, December 1937. A few years later McFarlane teamed up with Messrs John McAlister & Sons under the new name of John McFarlane & McAlister, Ltd. John's son carried on the Glasgow-based business through the 1930s, but by then the company was no longer making racing yacht sails.

[693] Of course, sails are replaced regularly, and a change of sailmaker was not often reflected in subsequent entries, but nevertheless, the intention was sound.

[694] Captain Nat Herreshoff, the Wizard of Bristol, L. Francis Herreshoff, 1953. The first of the loft's cross cuts appeared on 21ft fin keeler and the second on Nat's own *Alerion II* – both in 1894.

[695] Yacht Sails, their Care & Handling, Ernest A. Ratsey and W. H. de Fontaine, 1948.

[696] The IOR was established in 1969 and ran until it was 'frozen' in 1993. IOR racing still continues sporadically in Italy and Russia.

[697] Only about 15% of North's early 3DL sails were usable. The development of the current generation of moulded sails was begun in Switzerland by the *Alinghi* 2007 America's Cup team who built sails using PBO fibre. North Sails bought the research which eventually led to 3Di.

[698] English Yachting, Walter Marks, Sydney Morning Herald, 9th January 1909.

[699] Yachting, Hull Daily Mail, 26th July 1899.

[700] Captain Nat Herreshoff, the Wizard of Bristol, L. Francis Herreshoff, 1953.

[701] Mr Thomas Ratsey on Sail Making II, Solent, The Field, 3rd April 1924.

[702] Ibid

[703] Indianapolis Journal, 26th May 1903, citing the Pall Mall Gazette of 19th May 1903.

[704] Sir Thomas Lipton Honoured, the New York Times, 27th May 1903.

[705] Captain Franklin Ratsey came in for some unpleasant chauvinistic abuse for the part his firm played in *Columbia's* victory, but not everyone realised that *Sceptre* was a client too.

[706] Victories of Clyde Yachts, Hunt's Yachting Magazine, Volume 16, 1867.

[707] The Sails of Rhona and Daisie, G. L. Watson, Field, 3rd July 1886.

[708] A hundred years later, yachting life on the Clyde had regressed so that we all became familiar with the goods reception at Glasgow Central Station despatching yacht sails to Southampton for alterations and recuts in the 1970s. But alas, 24hr turnarounds were a thing of the past even then.

[709] Manual of Yacht and Boat Sailing and Architecture 11th Edition, Dixon Kemp, 1913.

[710] Clyde, The Yachtsman, 4th February 1892.

[711] My Father's Family, Artisans in Industrial Scotland, Jenny Blain, 2008.

[712] Cruise in Company, George Blake and Christopher Small, 1959. After the firm returned south, part of the Gourock site was subsequently occupied by James Adams, the boatbuilder.

[713] The author's mother bought what were probably the last hand-finished cotton sails made by John Black for our Cadet (CK 42) in 1962. John had made us a red cotton jib in the late 1950s and at the same time, he ran up a new red mainsail too as he wasn't particularly busy.

[714] Mackenzie's Sail Loft, John Black, Sandbank, Life and Times of the Village by the Holy Loch, Ed Anne Galliard, 2009. John had the 'flitting' date as 1903.

[715] Clyde, The Yachtsman, 14th March 1895.

[716] *Siandra* is an Arthur Robb-designed 35ft Lion Class, built for Graham Newland by Ron Swanson in his spare time in the back-yard of his engineering works in 1956. She was *the* outstanding Australian yacht of the 1950's and 60's. She was 2nd in her division in the Sydney to Hobart of 1956. She went on to win the 1958 race outright and also the Middle Harbour Yacht Club's Racing Shield, their offshore series and the Montague Island race. *Siandra* won the Sydney to Hobart Race again in 1960, giving her a rare double. Source: Boatgen.com.au.

[717] Race to *Siandra*, Seacraft, January 1959.

[718] There was also the Greenock Sail and Tent Co advertising in Lloyds in 1952. This business was incorporated in 1937, and according to the GPO records was active in 1973 and 1981. The name was changed to GST Industries in the mid-1990s and the company now appears to have no connection with sailmaking.

[719] The Nicolson Hughes company was dissolved in February 2019.

Vertical cut lug, *Osprey*, P.R. McLean, 1891   *Siandra*, Arthur Robb, 1956, Sydney Hobart Race

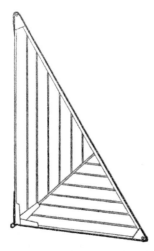

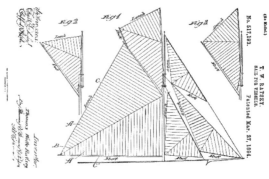

Image at left: Mathew Orr's Scotch-cut, designed ca.1825
Image above: Tom Ratsey's patent as approved in 1892

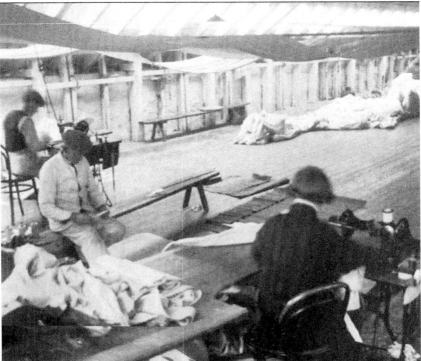

The Mackenzie Loft in Sandbank   Images: Sally-Anne Arnott Collection

BOOK FOUR
Clyde Racing Yachts

Chapter 17: Sport of Kings – Théâtre sans Frontières

Before the Great War, yacht racing had been a popular spectator sport and dense crowds had stood at Hunter's Quay and other viewing points on the Clyde and formed partisan loyalties to boats owned by Scotland's industrial plutocracy. Few other sports could be watched in a Scottish summer; the yachts sailed past resorts crammed with working-class families. Ian Jack[720]

For more than half-a-century, from the 1870s through to the 1930s, yacht racing competition enlivened our society. The yachting calendar was once as much a part of everyday life as the flat racing season at the likes of Newmarket, Epsom and Ascot. Yacht racing occupied an important niche in popular culture in an era when both the scope of sports reporting and the media available to present it to the public were limited.

Both of these leisure pursuits were undeniably extravagant and amply justified the tag 'sport of kings'. And both, with counter-intuitive synchronicity, delivered a fine show to the downtrodden proletariat of an unequal society. But yachting uniquely recast our privileged elite as heroic. 'Sport-washing' is a time-honoured route to makeover any public image.

Yacht racing became an extension of paternalism – the 'grace and favour' entertainment of pre-industrial times with fetes, fairs, race-meets and working-boat regattas. When kings and princes raced on the Firth of Clyde, they shared the water with rowing skiffs and lugsail dinghies raced by local artisans and tradesmen. Even the most prestigious sporting competitions were conducted entirely in the public domain. Sailing presented high society in a flattering soft focus, a flourish on the fabric of our social history, a théâtre sans frontières.

It was a formula that would be overwhelmed by its own success as Clyde coast steamer traffic grew exponentially. "*When the courses of the Clyde were laid off, long ago, the great desideratum was so to place the flag boats that the piers and most prominent parts of the beaches of the chief resorts would become good grandstands, so to speak, for the viewing of the racing. The immense amount of steamer traffic has now rendered the turning of flag boats near piers a most awkward matter.*"[721] With steamers stacked up like aircraft over Heathrow, yachts becalmed off the pierhead became a gratuitous hazard to navigation. And it was no doubt an alarming experience for the crews too.

In 1927, Dodgson Bowman observed that *"in the South of England yachting was, until the late 1870s, the sport of the privileged few and a monopoly of the rich. But on Clydeside, yachting has always been a pastime open to rich and poor alike. Anyone, boy or man, could command the use of a sailing boat as long as he had a few shillings in his pocket."*[722] This may be overstating the case, but yacht racing as a spectator sport in Scotland predates football, tennis and golf.

> We all enjoy a God-given right to view the seascape. That right is intrinsic to the freedom of the seas that our ancestors fought and died for. It is unconscionable that this freedom is threatened today. Recent America's Cup competitions and spin-off 'travelling circus' events, have attempted to monetize round-the-cans racing on the open sea. Exclusive use of common land on coastal promontories has been wheedled from local councils for elite play and pitiful profit. This is the so-called 'stadium sailing' that has upset the locals from Portsmouth, UK to Portland, USA. Stadium sailing is a contradiction in terms. The organisers of such spectacles ignore the more obvious contemporary model of professional road cycling. Cycling is a spectator-friendly competition that takes place on public highways, where the endless 'stand' of the roadside verge is free-to-access. A sequestered 'stadium' for yacht racing is not only of doubtful legality; in attempting to squeeze a quart into a pint pot the grandeur of the sport is trivialised, particularly when the boats are so fast as to render tactical nuances imperceptible, or even irrelevant. We can only hope that 'the free market', always a great leveller, kills this trend.

From Victorian times, right up until the outbreak of WW2, annual regattas hosted by local yacht clubs attracted yachtsmen to compete for 'town cups' presented by supportive local councils. Yachting, particularly Big Class yachting, attracted large numbers of spectators to seaside resorts. As far back as 1865, concerning the Royal Northern's annual regatta held on a Wednesday, *The Field* boasted *"the attendance of spectators and yachts was large"*, 'spectators' significantly being mentioned first.[723]

The 'Big Class', which thrived across the turn-of-the-century and the elegant J Class yachts of the 1930s, were titanic, fast and spectacular. They tested the limits of contemporary technology to impress the holiday crowds massed around our bays and estuaries. The key element of scale made 30-mile trophy races fast and easy to follow. Yacht races on the Clyde estuary might command the attention of a dozen yachting correspondents and a legion of specialist yachting photographers, see Appendix 2. Their analyses and illustrations sold the morning papers.

On public holidays, the races were promoted as the headlining attraction in an afternoon of entertainment that would feature brass bands, street theatre and market stalls. The day was organised to boost local businesses. Listings of the 'runners and riders' were published in lavish programmes, complete with costly colour illustrations of the identifying racing flags and details of the 'field of play'.

Local lads sold these programmes to the crowds on the esplanade, attracting custom with the familiar incomprehensible attenuated cry, now the sole preserve of market traders. Whether you could afford a programme or not, good eyesight and considerable knowledge were required to identify yachts in the old days. It was not until 1910 that the YRA council altered Racing Rule No.17 to mandate sail numbers affixed to both sides of the mainsail at the peak, starboard uppermost. This sensible regulation was not well-received: *"The idea seemed to be regarded as so absolutely foreign to the spirit and the practice of the pastime that it did not provoke a single word of comment, argument or protest – it was simply received with a chilling silence."*[724]

Regattas were a grand day out with preliminaries to entertain the local onlookers before the main event, as in August 1836: *"On Thursday, the regatta amusements were resumed at Dunoon. About noon the wind came up, and to delight both the spectators and the yachters, the sun shone with unusual brilliancy. The sport duly commenced with a number of rowing matches by boats, gigs and skiffs, which excited no small degree of interest among all classes of spectators".*[725] In 1838, Mr William Campbell of Dunoon secured his vantage point on the Castle Hill at the crack of dawn. William had a couple of twelve-pounders mounted on the summit, *"from which the craft and crews, as they kept sailing hither and thither, were ever and anon cheerfully saluted"*.

In these halcyon days, the seafront crowds warranted respect. Today, the marine industry collectively disparages enthusiasts as 'fans', and sees them as gullible commercial targets. But in the heyday of yachting, the toffs-at-play had no interest in commercialising their private wagers and sporting shenanigans. Such base endeavour would indeed have been beyond the pale – the preserve of cads and bounders. But the bourgeoisie today have no such scruples. In this new millennium, ex-professionals turned impresarios, wheedle and deal desperately to sell yacht racing as a viable forum for product marketing.

In the 21st century, racing yachts without names appear as sandwich boards, cling-filmed wrapped with elaborate graphics. Once-proud sailing events are smothered in tacky corporate livery. The entire circus is subsumed to the artless whim of mammon, flogging a sponsor's shoddy product, tacked together by child labour in East Asia, or a financial service dreamt-up by coke-snorting wide-boys and delivered through a labyrinth of tax-friendly havens. The notion that the proletariat might be interested in the outcome of a sailing match is not even considered.

Nineteenth century yacht racing was an essentially frivolous sporting diversion, bankrolled by a motley crew of self-aggrandising landowners, robber barons and materialistic plutocrats. Nonetheless, the objects of their investment were artefacts of great beauty, esteemed by the British people in the same way as thoroughbred bloodstock: *Flying Fox, Man o' War, Seabiscuit* and *Arkle* versus *Britannia, Ailsa, Shamrock* and *Lulworth*. And again, like horse-racing, yacht-racing supported rural communities with investment in local manufacture and service industries, including the employment of expert facilitators and skilled hands.

Today, professional sports teams are owned variously by the world's richest men, pariah states and dodgy commercial institutions. Yet, ordinary people are generally uncritical. Whatever the hidden agenda, sport is entertainment, but yachting spun off a crucial dividend which makes its history so fascinating to study today. Rich men sponsored scientific progress and technical innovation across a wide range of design, engineering and artisanal industries that connected with the pride and passions of the populace. The following dialogue is a glimpse of this innocent pleasure.

At Hunter's Quay – July 1920

"*Do you know Jeanie, that boat over yonder is the Terpsichore, and she has not tried her sails until today, and she is the scratch boat too.*" The speaker, an elderly man with white hair, handed his field glasses to her companion, also a lady well advanced in years.

"*Dear me,*" said the other, "*surely that is very bad management, Laura.*" (refers to her programme). "*And she is a brand-new yacht too, Sir Peter was saying. What a tremendous mast she has.*"

"*A Solent-built vessel*", replied the other. "*Ro-bert always said that the Solent was a puir place for boats after the Clyde. There, Jeannie, here comes the 'Britannia'; I just love that boat – she's like a dear old friend come back. But it makes me sad to think of the terrible changes and all the puir boys killed since 1914. Puir Alec in Gallipoli, and Charlie in France – how they would have loved all this.*"

"*Yes, my dear,*" said her friend, hastily changing the conversation. "*Do you remember, Laura, when the Satanita sank the Valkyrie this time 26 years ago?*"

"*I do indeed, and we were out in the Plover. I remember it well, because I happened to drop my purse overboard that very day. How vexed I was too. There they go. That's Nyria leading, and that's the Britannia next. You can tell her because the crew were not dressed like pastry-cooks, all in white.*"

I'll tell you Laura, if your boat beats the Nyria and the Zinita, I'll give you a shilling. I never gamble, my dear, but we'll just do that – a shilling."

"*Well, Jeanie, you're just throwing our money away; the Britannia is going to win.*"

"*Today, Laura, in this wind?*"

"*Of course, my dear; why I remember the Britannia beating the Vigilant many years ago on a day like this. I've won your shilling already Jeannie.*"

"Well," said the postman, stopping his rounds to view the racing, "*I* would like to see a bit more wind. I'm afraid with this drizzle the wind will fall away by the afternoon. An awfu' pity as there's a fine lot of boats out to-day, with the King's yat."

"Ay!" said the butcher, "it's grand to see the big boats again." (To his assistant) "Hay Jamie, away upstairs and ask the wife for my field-glasses."

"Is yon the Sham-rock, Sir-r?" said a small boy in knickerbockers

"The Sham-rock, laddie? The Sham-rock!" replied the butcher with a sniff of contempt, "are you a Clydeside boy?"

"No, Sir-r, I'm frae Edinburee." "Well you'll have to ask your Granny to teach you the difference between the Brynhild and the Sham-rock."

"Mon, but that's guid," said the postman enthusiastically. "The Britannia is leading the Moonbeam"

"Ay!", said a policeman, who had joined in the conversation "and the Moonbeam is trying to get on the weather of the old boat. Britannia is about again."

"So is Moonbeam", said the butcher, handing his field-glasses to the policeman.

"Ay! Carter will stand in under the Cloch with the other tucked under his lee."

"Hey! But it's no' the Moonbeam, it's the Nyria – number-r four."

"I don't see the Terpsichore," remarked the postman presently.

"No," said the elderly gentleman in a bathchair. "The Terpsichore is away doon to Fairlie to get her mast put to rights: a steel spar: that's what they call a Marconi mast."

"Take the glasses sir" said the butcher, "it's a bonny sight."[726]

An Alternative Take Aboard the *Vital Spark*, 1920s

And in this conversation, the crew of the *Vital Spark*, Neil Munro's fantasy Clyde puffer, watch the yacht racing.[727] Munro was not a racing sailor, but he was a well-informed observer and his insights into the character of Clydesiders remain unparalleled. We join the crew as the engineer mops his forehead fretfully with a fistful of oily waste and shrugs his shoulders. "*If you chaps like to palaver awa' your time,*' said he, '*it's all the same to me, but I was wantin' to see the end o' the racin*."

"*Whatna racin'?*" asked the captain.

"*Yat-racin*", said the engineer, with irony. "*Ye'll maybe hae heard o't. If ye havena, ye should read the papers. There's a club they ca' the Royal Clyde – at Hunter's Quay, and a couple o' boats they ca' the Shamrock and the White Heather are sallin' among a wheen o' ithers for a cup. I wouldna care if I saw the feenish; you chaps needna bother; just pull Cloon the skips o' your keps on your e'en when ye pass them, and ye'll no' see onything.*"

"*I don't see much in aal their yat-racin*", said Para Handy.

"*If I was you, then, I would try the Eye Infirmary*", retorted the engineer, "*or wan o' them double-breisted spy-glesses. Yonder the boats; we're in lots o' time*", and he dived again among his engines, and they heard the hurried clatter of his shovel.

"*Anything wi' Macphail for sport!*" remarked the captain sadly. "*You would *think at his time o' life and the morn Sunday, that his meditaations would be different. Give her a point to starboard, Dougie, and we'll see them better. Yonder's the Ma'oona; if the duvvle wass wise he would put aboot at wance or he'll hit that patch o' calm."*

"I sometimes wish, mysel', I had taken to the yats," said Dougie; *"it's a suit or two o' clothes in the year and a pleasant occupaation. Most o' the time in canvas sluppers."*
"You're better the way you are," said Para Handy; *"there's nothing bates the mercantile manne for makin' sailors. Brutain's hardy sons! We could do withoot yats, but where would we be withoot oor coalboats? Look at them chaps sprauchlin' on the deck; if they saw themsel's they would see they want another fut on that main-sheet. I wass a season or two in the yats mysel' – the good old Marjory. No' a bad job at aal, but aawful hurried. Holy smoke! the way they kept you jumpin' here and there the time she would be racin'! I would chust as soon be in a lawyer's office. If you stopped to draw your breath a minute you got yon across the ear from a swingin' boom. It's a special breed o' sailor-men you need for racin'-yats, and the worst you'll get iss off the Islands."*

"It's a cleaner job at any rate than carryin' coals," remarked the mate, with an envious eye on the spotless decks of a heeling twenty-tonner.
"Clean enough, I'll alloo, and that's the worst of it," said Para Handy. *"You might ass weel be a chamber-maid – up in the mornin' scourin' brass and scrubbin' floors, and goin' ashore wi' a fancy can for sixpenceworth o' milk and a dozen o' syphon soda. Not much navigation there, my lad! If I wass that fellow I would gybe her there and set my spinnaker to starboard; what do you think yoursel', Macphail?"*

"I thocht you werena interested," said the engineer, who had now reduced his speed.
"I'm not much interested, but I'm duvellish keen," said Para Handy. *"Keep her goin' chust like that, Macphail; we'll soon be up wi' the Shamrock and the Heather, they're yonder off Loch Long."*

"That's whit she's aye daein'," retorted the engineer; *"stoppin's her strong p'int; gie me a good substantial compound engine; nane o' your hurdy-gurdies! I wish the wind would fresh a bit, for there's the Shamrock and her mainsail shakin."* He dived below, and in a little while the *Vital Spark* had her speed reduced to a crawl that kept her just abreast of the drifting racers.

"Whit's the use o' hangin' on here?" said the engineer, with a wink at Dougie; *"it's time we were up the river; I'll better get her under weigh again."*

The captain turned on him with a flashing eye. *"You'll do nothing o' the kind, Macphail,'* said he, 'we'll stand by here and watch the feenish, if it's any time before the Gleska Fair."*

The Greatest Show on Earth

Perhaps surprisingly, nineteenth century yachtsmen, and particularly the owners of Big Class racing yachts, expected to receive serious prizemoney. The masters of crack cutters were charged to win, not just for winning's sake, but to help fund their owner's racing programmes. This bare-faced avarice extended all the way up the social scale to the royal yacht *Britannia*. One might have thought that the richest men in the country would have distributed their winnings among the crew, as the winning teams and lead riders in professional cycling teams do today, but no.

James Meikle recalled a blether with James Taylor as to whether the men received anything extra for winning in his *Clarence* days: "*No, we got nae extra money when we won. I hae seen the maister, if he was extra weel pleased owre the way we had sailed a particular race, gie us a gless or twa o' whiskey; that's onything extra ever I saw in thae days.*"[728] *Clarence* was an 1830 cutter of 15-tons, builder unknown. Sixty years later, when the crew did get 'prize money', it reflected a paltry fixed-scale, common among first-class yachts.

Yacht Racing on the Clyde: Winnings 1897 Season

Yacht	Owner	Designer	Winnings
Over 52 ft-linear-rating			
Isolode	P. Donaldson	Fife	£808 (£104,200)
Carina	P. M. Inglis	Watson	£200 (£25,800)
Hester	J. Nairn	Fife	£150 (£19,300)
Over 42ft to 52ft-linear-rating			
Morning Star	A Coats	Fife	£316 (£40,100)
Senga	F. A. Dubs	Fife	£140 (£18,000)
Zinita	K. H. Connal	Fife	£85 (£11,000)
Over 30ft to 42ft-linear-rating			
Westra	J. C. Connell	Sibbick	£92 (£11,900)
Laura	A. C. Connell	Sibbick	£84 (£10,800)
Qinta	T. H. Bennett	Fife	£36 (£4,600)
Over 23ft to 30ft-linear-rating			
Kisyma	B. Donaldson	Fife	£91 (£11,700)
Vida	W. A. Wylie	Fife	£48 (£6,200)
Thaber	P. M. Coats	Fife	£35 (£4,500)
Yachts not exceeding 4-tons old rating			
Badger	G. Coats	Watson	£45 (£5,800)
Cora	D. Holms-Kerr	Watson	£35 (£4,500)
Madgel	Messrs Tullis	Watson	£35 (£4,500)

The owners considered that they were staging a public spectacle, albeit unsolicited, at great personal expense. In these circumstances, it was only right and proper that winnings should contribute to the hefty yard bills of a top yacht. Before we settle this ungenerous mantle on the tight Scots, it is important to note that our southern neighbours did exactly the same thing.

The yacht racing circus visited the South Coast's seaside towns only when the city fathers had been able to raise enough prize money from their hard-pressed business communities to attract the rapacious company of mercenary navigators to their shore. And reciprocally, that is why courses in the 'great days of yachting' generally paralleled the coast with well-placed turning marks and a start and finish off the town pier. When a spectacle is on order, you can whistle for a square beat to windward.

The viewing public knew that the gentry were performing for prizemoney as well as prestige, but this did not alienate them; quite the contrary. The Clydeside spectators were happy to be entertained and often had a stake in the outcome too. The crowd included local punters and skilled artisans enjoying a day out from the clamour and industrial pollution of their weekday lives, working-class cognoscenti bearing treasured 'spyglasses' – telescopes or binoculars, glinting with the dull shine of machine oil and polished leather.

"Many in England find it difficult to understand the passionate interest the Clydesider takes in yachting, but people take an infinitely greater interest in sports in which they have taken an active part themselves."[729] Most of the 'common people' who flocked to watch their chosen champions compete had some experience in boats and they all had an affinity with the sea. These men were often well-informed and well-read. Many shared an engineering heritage; some had built ships and many more had worked in the marine supply-chain.

Threadbare gentlemen ranged along the seafront, occupying the best vantage points and crowding the public benches. Mingling among them, in the manner of the aspirational middle-class at Premier League football-matches today, were chaps with dreams to buy a small yacht, though yet without the means, content for the time-being to enjoy their pleasures vicariously.[730]

In 1922, under the agenda item 'other business', the IYRU prescribed the position and colour of winning flags to inform regatta spectators about the day's events. They specified the owner's racing flag be flown beneath: the burgee for a win; a blue pennant with a '2' for second; and a red pennant with a '3' for third. There is something heart-warming about the sport's highest authority being concerned about matters like this. But, oh, to have Georgian eyesight!

Aficionados of this era embraced their sport with a passion. And it was not just dreamers and old codgers, schoolboys took a keen interest as well. We associate cigarette cards with football, cricket and motor racing, but the America's Cup and the Seawanhaka Cup also commanded their own sporting series, and Clydeside youngsters collected these avidly. The G. L. Watson-designed Royal Yacht *Britannia* was the outstanding crowd-pleaser across decades, and her matches against the *Vigilant* in 1894 were the high point of yachting as spectator sport on the Clyde.

The demise of first-class yachting as a focus of public interest was signalled in 1911. Writing in *The Glasgow Herald*, their correspondent said that it would be *"idle to blink the facts"* that the sport no longer *"designed fervent enthusiasm in yachtsmen not personally engaged or concerned in the racing"*. That year, even the 12-metres were absent, but they would come back the following year and life would go on as before until the hiatus of the Great War.

The cutter, *Britannia*, of 220-tons TM, which was so popular with the public required a crew of 33 men to sail her. The 23mRs, less spectacular perhaps but still imposing, sailed with a crew of 22. This is what killed the Big Class eventually. The build cost of *Shamrock* or *White Heather* in 1907/8 was around £10,000 (£1.2 million), manageable for any wealthy man in Britain at that time. However, sailing with 22 professional hands, the annual upkeep was about 50% of build cost, or £5,000 (£600,000). This restricted such racing to the super-rich.[731]

Post-WW1

Following the Great War, and notwithstanding a global recession, Big Class racing gradually re-emerged. Inherited wealth was substantially intact, industry had made a great deal of money in the war, and professional seamen still needed the work. In these times of hardship, it was deemed 'bad form' to build new vessels, however, recommissioning old yachts and providing employment was admirable.

The first Clyde Week after the Armistice took place in 1919 with a testing race programme in blustery 'jib-headed topsail' weather. Concern that the Big Class might not show up was allayed by the arrival of the maxi yawls from Belfast. All the same, it was a low-key event, and as oft before and many times since, Clyde yachtsmen wondered if anything would ever be the same again. Fred Stephen won both the 6mR class in *Coila II* and the Pleiade class in *Maia* – two events scheduled to allow this.

Everyone was clearly making an effort to recover the old spirit of the Clyde Fortnight when the Big Class raced for the Kings Cup.[732] The Royal Clyde and the Royal Northern joined forces off Hunter's Quay and members dined together in the Royal Marine. The 1920 regatta was another week of strong winds and stoicism. But that year, *Britannia* made the trip north, and while she did not win any prizes, her presence added not just prestige but a sense of optimism to the event.

As late as 1939, under the shadow of the impending conflict, the Royal Northern Yacht Club's Seawanhaka defence attracted thousands of knowledgeable shore-side spectators to witness the first couple of races in an interminable series beset by frustrating drifting matches. These were conditions to truly separate the men from the boys. As for the girls, in 1883, *The Glasgow Herald* informed us that "*ladies with engagements cannot abide flat calms and the profane language which accompanies such weather.*"[733]

Unfortunately, the weather remained uncooperative through the week and the crowd had to go back to work long before a result was declared. This notorious series required 11 starts to achieve a result, with 6 races abandoned before Herbert Thom's *Circe* beat Rolf Svinndal's *Norag III*, three wins to two. It was a successful defence, but it signalled the death knell of what is now called 'stadium sailing' on the Clyde, cementing our estuary's reputation as a light-and-shifty sailing venue and Thom's reputation as a wizard in these conditions.

Post-WW2, First-class Yachting Regression and Rebirth

As post-war Britain laboured to implement long-overdue corrections in the structure of society through the ensuing decade, yachting inevitably lost some of its sparkle. *"The great trophy* (the Seawanhaka Cup) *was stored away in the Royal Northern Yacht Club and its members went to war. Five years later, I escorted a convoy up the Firth of Clyde one moonlight winter night and thought of the great Six-meter racing there of which I had heard so much. I wish I had raced aboard a Six-meter in that beautiful body of water."*[734]

In the years of austerity that followed WW2 there was no question that yachting changed irrevocably. Big yachts may have been back on the water, but the impact of taxation on income and inherited wealth was now undeniable. Wealthy yachtsmen grumbled openly in the yachting press and most yachting writers and journalists, seemingly unaware of their own meagre stipends, agreed with them. This obsequious and self-serving point of view was nonsense; a check on excess was unequivocally a good thing.

A few big boats survived WW2, and in those years before they all slipped off to the Mediterranean or the Caribbean, on the Clyde we could enjoy the sight of Jimmy Howden-Hume's 109-ton Mylne, *Vadura* (1926), Ossie Graham's 80-ton Fife *Griselda*, (1906), Ron Teacher's 74-ton Mylne, *Mariella* (1938), A. M. McGeorge's 62-ton Mylne, *Roska* (1930) and the Mylne, *Mingary* (1929), in the Sandbank anchorage. Then there were smaller vessels like Sibbick's *Saunterer* (1900), Boyd's *Zigeuner* (1935) and Fife's 15-metre, *Kismet III* (1909), joined by the post-war *Lone Fox* (1957), designed by Robert Clark, and James McGruer's 13.5mR, *Stornoway*.[735]

In the post-war years, following Boyd's 1961 'modernisation', *Roska* was perhaps the most beautiful big yacht on the Clyde, slimmer and more elegant that Mylne's *Mariella* and more shapely than Fife's *Griselda*. *Roska* was the last of the breed to be refitted by old hands; she now sails in Spain as *Arosa*. *Mariella*, one of the few classic yachts afloat today to have been maintained regardless of expense throughout her life, is a regular at classic yacht regattas, while poor *Griselda* was wrecked in the Caribbean. Of all these big two-masters, only *Griselda* was a racing yacht. She was still 'scratch boat' on the CYCA handicapping system in the 1960s.

Few today would deny that the ordinary men and women who won the war deserved a country 'fit for heroes'. The social reforms introduced by the incoming Atlee Government included universal healthcare, old-age pensions, a welfare safety-net, free education, public housing programmes, and workers' rights. Indeed, it was a scandal that it took a world war to trigger these basic elements of a caring culture. Britain became, for a short time, a fairly equal society. These days, alas, are long gone. Trace elements of egalitarianism and social care still endure, but yawning inequalities now define our generation.

Eminent maritime authorities who presided over the drawn-out death of first-class yachting would be surprised, but not uncomfortable, with its renaissance over the past twenty years. As we enter the third decade of the 21st century, the top tier of the industry puffs at the same old pipe, chasing the same old dragon. But today, the playground is different. Serial clients no longer entertain an enthusiastic proletariat lined along Britain's piers and promenades. When our new crop of super-rich goes yacht racing in the grand style, they occupy a world apart.

CODA: Ordinary People

When the sailing scene kicked off again in 1946, everything was in short supply. The Clyde shoreline was rimed with emulsified bunker-oil and the surface of the estuary shone with the slick of more volatile hydrocarbons. As children in the early 1950s, we trailed gummy blobs of tar into the house after beachcombing excursions. It found its way everywhere and was as tenacious as chewing gum. Even the post-war minute book of the Royal Clyde bears witness to this forgotten legacy.

The exigencies of war continued into peacetime, with industry now focussed on exports and harvesting foreign exchange. We could not afford a clean river; it was not a priority, and in any case, we had no idea how to achieve it. Consequently, the struggling industries of the Upper Clyde tipped every kind of toxic effluent into the river until relatively recently. Salmon returned to the Clyde just 20 years ago. Two full centuries had passed since crystal waters lapped these shores.

These were not ideal circumstances to ignite a post-war sailing boom based on small, home-built plywood dinghies, launched from the beach and frequently ending up upside-down in polluted waters. So, for all we lament the passing of 'the good old days', decades of methodical rehabilitation work mean that we can now muck about in small boats with confidence and even glimpse the seabed. And on bigger boats, a badly taken wave no longer qualifies the ballast on the weather rail for two weeks off with a sick note for gastro-enteritis.

[720] Ian Jack, writing in the Guardian of 5th July 2013, on the occasion of the Fife Regatta.
[721] Clyde, The Yachtsman, 11th June 1908. The Corinthian Club was reviewing courses.
[722] Yachting and Yachtsmen, W. Dodgson Bowman, 1927.
[723] The Field, 22nd July 1865.
[724] Notes & Notions, The Yachtsman, 2nd March 1911, and subsequent correspondence.
[725] The Royal Northern Regatta, Caledonian Mercury, 8th August 1836.

[726] An imaginary dialogue, George Blake.

[727] 'Para Handy', Neil Munro, Birlinn reprint, 2015.

[728] Clyde, The Yachtsman, 7th April 1892.

[729] Para Handy, Neil Munro, Birlinn reprint, 2015.

[730] Cruise in Company, George Blake and Christopher Small, 1959.

[731] A New Racing Class, Frank B. Cooke, Baily's Magazine of Sports & Pastimes, 1911.

[732] Yachting Notes, White Ensign, the Sunday Times, 26th April 1914.

[733] Clyde Yacht-building, Glasgow Herald, 3rd February 1883.

[734] A History of the Seawanhaka Corinthian Yacht Club, the Great Six Meter Era, undated.

[735] *Griselda* was launched as *Rose*, then became *Thelma IV*, then *Vida IV* before becoming *Griselda*. *Kismet III* was launched as *Tuiga*, then became *Dorina*, then *Betty IV*, and is now *Tuiga* again.

Big Class start off Hunters Quay inc. *Britannia, Ailsa* & *Westward*   Artist: Charles Dixon

Hunter's Quay, ca.1880   Image: old postcard

Kariad, G. L. Watson 1901, off Hunter's Quay, 1906   Artist: J. Young Hunter

The Tail o' the Bank during WW2   Image: Imperial War Museum

Kate leading *Bird o' Freedom* off the Holy Loch   Artist: Gregory Robinson (1879-1967)

Chapter 18: Swinging the Lead[736]

Blair Tuke, who also provides some of the pedal power aboard the Kiwi boat, said there has been an element of 'sandbagging' in Team NZ's build-up, as they try to keep some innovations and sailing techniques under wraps. New Zealand Herald[737]

The well-known open-boat classes of the Clyde estuary developed from traditional fishing skiffs. This type of vessel was found everywhere around our coasts and provided an initial model for affordable leisure sailing nationwide. Over the years, inevitably, racing 'improved the breed', or more accurately, made the boats much faster and a tad more dangerous too. In the 1870s they were still recognisable as simple skiffs, usually ballasted with stone blocks or sandbags.

However, when the famous yacht designers of the day recognised the potential for 'brand exposure', they began to take an interest. The small classes became an arena for low-cost experimentation and rapid incremental development. Big dinghies, built by rule-of-thumb, morphed into remarkable little yachts. While their sophistication was masked by traditional clinker construction, these little boats reflected contemporary progress in design technology, but the development path they represented was ultimately a route to oblivion.

We use the American term 'sandbaggers', but Clyde yachtsmen were made of sterner stuff, performing their ballistic ballet with sacks of lead shot. Alternatively, ingots of lead or iron were lugged from side to side and slotted in behind shallow fore-and-aft stringer-shelves. Mishandled, such ballast could have pierced the hull and sunk the ship, although as far as we can tell that never happened. Shifting ballast was in use throughout the size-range during the second half of the 19th century, not just in the small centre-board classes. A 10-ton racing cutter of the period might ship a ton of shifting ballast, and larger yachts considerably more.

In the days of the 'sandbaggers' the crews worked damned hard, as Folkard explained: "*A peep into the interior of the vessel, however, revealed the whole secret; for there, unseen by all above deck, were four or more men trimming heavy bags of shot — real shot, such as sportsmen use to wing the feathered tribe — and those they shifted from the leeward side to the weather side — or rather from lee-bilge to weather-bilge, according to the tack on which the vessel was sailing — to 'hold her up', or to 'keep her stiff', as they termed it.*[738] The dedicated 'pit crew' spent the windward legs crouched atop the 'stack', after shifting the load across with each cry of 'Ready About, Lee-oh'. When short-tacking aboard a racing yacht, the chain-gang down below worked harder than any crewman above deck.

These sporting vessels, with towering rigs out of proportion to their tonnage, were considered both unsportsmanlike and dangerous, even by their owners. It is amusing to note that they were deemed undeserving of feminine names and disparaged as sailing machines. How times change: today owners of fin-keel yachts seem to be quite happy racing against canting-keel, water-ballast and foil-assisted yachts, which despite rating penalties, enable some crews to get around the course with considerably less physical effort than others. What other sport allows this nonsense?

We may well ask, but it is important to recognise that the issue of shifting ballast waxes eternal. The controversy first raised its ugly head back in the 1820s, two hundred years ago, at the birth of organised yacht racing. The over-canvassed cutters of that era appear cartoonish to the modern eye, apparently defying the limited strength-to-weight ratios of 19th century materials. We can only admire those designers, boatbuilders, spar-makers, sailmakers, riggers and ropemakers who traded in miracles.

Their extravagance and optimism predated low-slung external ballast and deep, efficient fin-keels. Consequently, drastic measures were necessary to keep a racing yacht 'on her feet'. For the prestigious 'cup-races', bulkheads, cabin-soles and internal furniture were dismantled and sent ashore. In their place, temporary stacking platforms were constructed to support ever great quantities of shifting ballast, wedged up to weather, from the stringer at the turn-of-the bilge to the beam-shelf.

This oft-repeated cycle of interior conversion and restitution was expensive and dangerous. It was also counterproductive. Everyone was playing the same game, so no competitive advantage was gained; there was merely a race to the bottom. Even so, very few yachtsmen favoured regulation, arguing instead against the very idea of inshore regatta-sailing. They reasoned that the challenge of racing offshore would impose its own constraints and thus seaworthiness would become self-regulating. This naïve optimism has maintained currency over two centuries, even as our best designers continue to furnish our best sailors with incredibly fast and unreliable vessels. Rigs collapse, keels fall off and canoe-bodies at the leading edge of materials technology self-destruct. We are incorrigible.

Regulation, Honour & Enforcement

Yachting administrators first grasped the nettle in 1828. That season saw the Royal Yacht Club introduce regulations, which had they been more influential, would have changed the game entirely. The RYC 5th Regulation declared that: *"No trimming with ballast or shifting of ballast be allowed, and all vessels to keep their platforms down and bulkheads standing to prevent the unnecessary expense that has heretofore taken place."*[739] Other significant changes banned 'booming out' sails downwind and special downwind sails; multiple entries by the same owner, and handling ballast within the 24-hours of the start.[740] But the Yacht Club seems to have been a lone voice for reason.

In 1854, we find the Royal Thames Yacht Club with an interesting take on shifting ballast. It seems that there was some doubt among members about how these 'new' regulations might be enforced. *"There seems to be but one opinion regarding the necessity of its abolition, but there is evidently a strongly-entertained opinion that the restriction will be subject to constant violation; not by members who it is felt would be governed by too strong a sense of honour to descend to any such violation, but by those who may form a portion of their crew."*[741]

Nevertheless, the *Sunday Times* reported that participating yachts at an early season regatta the following year were inspected at their stations. The mid-1850s was a time of lively debate on what was, and was not, a proper yacht. *The Times* opined: *"The term 'pleasure yacht' was appropriately enough used in the early days, (but) it would be a stretch of fair reasoning to presume that it would ever comprehend within its category some of the skimming dishes of the present day. Pleasure and sport were once to be enjoyed in the same craft, but the former became subservient to the latter, and interior accommodation was entirely lost sight of."*

Writing in *Badminton's* G. L. Watson commented: *"During this season (1862) the principal clubs made a bold stand against the prevalent custom of using shifting ballast, chiefly in the form of bags of shot. It may seem incredible that the prohibition of shifting ballast should have met with strong opposition, yet such was the case. There were advocates in those early days of the useless racing machine, even as in later years there have been staunch defenders of rules producing vessels of a bad and ephemeral type."*[742] Eventually reason prevailed, but while an initial consensus was reached over the winter of 1862/63, change was not immediate.

The Clyde clubs' efforts to abolish shifting ballast were half-hearted and lagged a decade or more behind our friends at Cowes. Even then, the practice continued. The Irish were equally stubborn, although the Royal Cork Yacht Club adopted sensible regulations to outlaw sandbaggers, or more accurately, 'lead-shot-baggers' in 1863.[743] Quite why the Celtic faction of Scots and Irish wanted to hang onto this risky, and wholly unseamanlike, practice into the 1880s remains a bit of a mystery.

The 1868 season saw the Royal Clyde Yacht Club establish an annual match for Corinthian helmsmen. This event paved the way for change on the Clyde. The rules for the match restricted professional crew to just two paid hands for yachts of 15-tons and over, and one paid hand on smaller yachts. The amateur seamen of the club were now game to wrestle with the heavy gear of a big cutter, but it seems that wrestling with shot-bags was another matter. Such coarse manual work was not for gentlemen. So, the 'stack' was abolished for Corinthian races and this ban would later be extended to all competitions organised by Clyde yacht clubs.[744]

As Hunter's Quay, local yachtsmen championed the, then fairly radical, notion that amateur skippers should steer their own racing yachts, invidious comparisons were drawn with the Royal Northern, which was slow to encourage owner-drivers. *"The influence of this club was hardly felt beyond the class who liked to own a floating palace and who loved to command a crew, to take an occasional turn at the helm, corroborate his captain's notions about the weather and the trim of the craft, smoke cigars and drink champagne. This constituted a sufficiently onerous round of duties for a cruise, and those best acquainted with the habits of the Northern yachtsmen will be able to recognise the portrait."*[745] Happily, while such impulses still exist in the wider world of superyachting, things have changed at the Northern, and their current maestro, Olympian Luke Patience, actually steers his own boats!

Agreement was readily reached among club administrators, however, arguments rumbled on through the 1870s and 1880s: *"There is not much doubt that the time has arrived, as we have many times before remarked, when the YRA should re-consider this rule. The death-traps of the American coasts and lakes, the capsizeable sandbaggers could be kept out of competition by some prohibitive clause, but it seems rather hard that because one type is condemned all should die."*[746]

W.J. Miller, in his tribute to the Clyde, published in 1888, noted: *"The racing boats are divided into three classes, the lengths being 17, 19, and 21 feet; the breadths varying from about 5ft to 7ft, and the depths from 3ft to 4ft. The lugsail is principally used. It is of great size, spreading in a 19-feet boat to between 20 and 30 square yards* (180 to 270ft²). *An old rule for an ordinary lug was 1 square yard per foot; but these bigger boats are specially ballasted or have metal keels; some also carry shot in bags, which can be shifted to windward, on the principle of sitting up to windward in the ordinary open lugsail boat."*[747]

G. L. Watson summed up technical progress in the *Badminton's Yachting* edition of 1894: While 'lead mines' remained an issue, in matters of equipment, it seems that steady progress had been made since the 1850s. Wire rope had replaced hemp for standing rigging, sailmaking was becoming more scientific in the hands of Lapthorn and Charles Ratsey; flax canvas was no longer favoured and the prejudice surrounding cotton had been overcome. By 1893, well-cut cotton sails were prevalent throughout the fleet, from Big Class yachts down to the smallest day racers. Watson then went on the discuss the state of the art with regard to hull-form in a fascinating chapter with enduring historical relevance.

Watson looked to ongoing design trends to solve the problem of shifting ballast: *"A considerable factor in modifying form was the gradual abolition of shifting ballast; this, though not yet actually illegal, was being more and more looked upon with disfavour, and as the use of outside lead increased, it was found that depth was a more than sufficient substitute for weather ballast, especially as beam was being squeezed down by the tonnage rule, and a long lever in this direction rendered impossible*.[748] Certainly, with knife-on-edge yachts, shifting ballast made no sense. When such vessels were sailed at the angles of heel necessary to extend the lever arm of their lead keels to balance rig forces, the weather rail was directly over the centre of buoyancy. Notwithstanding the accuracy of Watson's analysis, in this case the antidote (ever deeper and narrower yachts with ever slacker bilges), inflicted more damage on the sport than the venom.

Sandbaggers were still a topic of current interest in 1900, Kemp cited a number of examples from around the world.[749] *"The Mystery (1882) has usually 4½ cwt of shot in square, flat, stout, well-painted canvas bags, a board top, and rope handle. The canvas nailed to the edges of the board, as shown. She has no outside ballast; the inside ballast being increased as required for match sailing."*[750] Kemp thought the Clyde open boats *"most seaworthy little craft"* as long as they were not driven recklessly; noting that they ventured out in almost any weather, snugly reefed-down. Sinkings were rare, and as far as we know, there were no fatal accidents. All the Clyde clubs enforced a rule, that *"every boat shall carry life-saving apparatus sufficient to float every person on board"*.[751]

Henry Folkard, writing early in the early 20th century, confirmed that the 'lead-shot-baggers' had been legislated out of existence: *"Many years ago, a highly discreditable practice prevailed in match-sailing with the smaller class of racing yachts – that of ballast trimming – but which has now long since very properly been discountenanced by all British yacht clubs."*[752] And in the final 1913 edition of *Yacht and Boat Sailing*, Kemp summarised the new status quo: *"Ballast, shifting: to put ballast (usually duck shot in bags) in the weather side of a vessel during sailing. This practice for many years has been strictly forbidden in yacht racing, and if a man were known to practise it, he would be at once debarred from racing under YRA rules. Shifting ballast is of course forbidden on account of its extreme danger."*[753]

Live Ballast

In 1887, the crack Largs 19ft lugger, *Neva*, hung water butts over the side when racing – more efficient than lead and safer.[754] References to 'live ballast' also begin to appear from this period. Fast forward to 1939, and we find Adam Bergius of the well-known Clyde sailing family shipping 'Thurber' aboard *Jura*, their Scottish Islands class yacht. 'Thurber' was a very large white bull terrier who was trained to perch on the weather rail. Renowned dinghy sailor, Paul Elvstrom, combined both the water butt and the slightly demeaning concept of 'live ballast' when he instituted the practice of wearing wet sweaters outside of waterproofs. I well-remember the heft of three wet Arran sweaters when hiking upwind in Merlin

Rockets through the 1960s. Too late for my own bad back and blown knees, the IYRU banned the use of weight jackets in 1994.

In January 1892, the YRA were deep in discussion on the subject of Rule 3, and the excessive use of 'live ballast' on small yachts of 10-rating and under. It was proposed that a yacht be measured with the maximum number of crewmen the owner might nominate, clustered amidships for the purpose. Of course, this was a rule to drive a coach and horses through, so there was no agreement.

> When we see 25ft ¼-tonners (originally sailed by three or four) carrying five or six persons totalling 420kg (925lbs), how little progress have we made? Idiotic lines of evolution are often difficult to reverse: the over-manned, over-canvassed turn-of-the-century skiffs of Australia and New Zealand, the 'fitted dinghies' of Bermuda, the 'sandbaggers' of New England, and the racing dhows of the Persian Gulf all represent a triumph of dumb enthusiasm over intellect. These vessels are limited to sail in semi-displacement mode and consequently just dig a huge hole in the water. Real progress in yacht design prioritises efficiency, not excess, or making 'less' do more. More speed comes from less hull-weight, less ballast, less wetted-area, less wave-making resistance, less sail-area and a whole lot less muscle-bound baggage.

Regarding Centreboards as Shifting Ballast

Solent-centric yachting histories invariably stress what the authors perceived as a great transatlantic divide in relation to preferences for keelboats and centre-boarders. However, on the Clyde, the centre-board luggers were the most active and popular racing classes, as this contribution by *The Glasgow Herald's* yachting correspondent illustrates: *"The next grave subject for the Yacht Racing Association to legislate upon is the question of metal centre-boards and what amount of weight ought to be permitted. It is quite evident legislation is wanted in the meantime in the interests of the owners of keelboats, who are not to be swept off the course without sufficient time to realise the value of their yachts."*[755]

Regarding the big picture, the *Herald* argued that progress must be allowed to run its course, citing the Clyde passenger steamers, which in that era, were engaged in cutthroat competition. Succeeding generations of machinery and hull design were faster and more efficient. Obsolete vessels were simply run off their routes and discarded without sentimentality. No one ever suggested governing down the engines of new steamers to maintain the value of the existing fleet. *"It may be argued that yacht racing is a sport and not a business, and that the cases are not parallel. But they are so. No one will sink money in building racing yachts unless for the object of winning races, and races are only won by speed. The sport would be nothing without racing, and no sort of legislation can stultify this issue."*[756]

Vested interests may delay progress, but they cannot arrest it. There have been notable exceptions over the years, but a new state-of-the-art racing yacht might be competitive for just two years, usually not more than five. Beyond that, the value of the investment cannot be guaranteed. We all accept this. As *the Yachtsman* declared in 1892: "*it can be argued, on the one hand, that putting any restriction on design is an interference with the liberty of the naval architect, and therefore a measure at which the soul of every true-born Briton should revolt*".[757] There is a broad consensus in the marine industry that the pursuit of racing success through constant development can only improve the breed and benefit everyone in the long-term.

The protest made against metal centreboards, that they are an evasion of the rule against shifting ballast, may to a certain extent be true; but the rule against shifting ballast was made to prevent a dangerous arrangement of it. The Clyde centre-boarders are as safe as the Clyde keelboats, the reason for the rule against shifting ballast does not hold good in their case at all. All that the YRA can do is to let the owners of keelboats down easy."[758] Being 'let down easy' is still the best we can hope for unless we sail classic yachts or archaic one-designs.

History is inclined to repeat itself. As we stumble into the third decade of the 21st century, we are burdened with a very considerable 'lost' investment tied up in existing fleets. In the good old days, obsolete designs could be recycled through a wood-burning stove, but things are very different today. These days we are not so confident about the wisdom of evolution and 'survival of the fittest' in the marketplace, and not just because we cannot afford to write-off our old boats and have no idea how to dispose of them responsibly.

These are important issues, but let's face it, the vast majority of yachtsmen are neither savvy investors, nor short of hypocrisy where environmental issues are concerned. No, the truth is that we rather like our antediluvian fleet, replete as it is with yachts that are slow – giving time to think, comfortable – seeking neither to injure nor terrify, subtle – in that they are constrained by the laws of physics to ensure close and competitive racing, and shapely – engendering pride in ownership.

In that respect, nothing has changed much since the 1850s, when it was commonly argued that yacht racing should give "*an impetus to yacht building and yacht sailing and to encourage the spirit of honourable evolution in the science of both, by uniting accommodation with speed*". The *Phantom*, *Truant*, and *Kitten* were contrasted unfavourably with Weld's *Alarm*, Young's *Amazon* and Goodson's *Avalon*, fast craft, which combined "*all the sea-going comforts and qualifications which are so essential desideratum*".[759] On Mr Curling's *Shark*, the owner and crew cooked and dined on board while racing to Lowestoft.

And in another throwback, the rules under which most big boats race today permit, nay encourage, the use of large numbers of human bodies as shifting ballast, crucified like old socks and clothes-pegged over a single 4mm 1x19 wire washing-line. The only positive thing to be said about this is that, unlike lead-shot, people, or most of them, float. There is something deeply dehumanising about being shipped aboard just for your weight – which is what happens after all the cerebral, technical and athletic roles have been handed out on a racing yacht.

After a spell in the 1990s, when water-ballast, pumped from side-to-side was the way to go, swing-keels are now de rigueur on the better-funded campaigns – even when racing on handicap against conventional yachts. The performance vs effort gap continues to open up with the addition of any number of foil-lift systems that reduce displacement. All this is immensely dispiriting for the crew sleeping on the rail of a conventional fixed-keeler. At least the somnambulant brigade are slightly more secure than their 'mechanically enhanced' competition in a marine environment littered with the detritus of our throw-away civilisation, stray containers and more than a few dozy sun-fish.

How do we defend a vulnerable and gratuitous hazard? Swinging a keel reduces its lateral resistance, so additional daggerboards are required to stop the boat sliding sideways. More holes in the boat, more things to go wrong. And, of course, by definition, every type of movable appendage compromises structural integrity, with the potential for control mechanisms to fail, or indeed for the fin to drop off completely, although to be fair, the latter problem is not exactly unknown in simple fixed-keel yachts either.

> Some races, although fortunately very few, like the fully crewed round the world race and short-handed racing in IMOCA and Class 40 yachts, also allow 'stacking' of spare sails on the weather rail, rather than, for example, along the cabin sole (where, admittedly, they get trampled into useless 'garbage bags'). This is another example of the ill-conceived rules that have systematically blighted our sport since its inception. Apart from the mindless hard labour involved in moving weighty and unwieldy objects, crew members sit on the stack, clear above the lifelines. And as you would expect, sometimes a big wave comes along, the crew dive for cover, and a small fortune in sails simply disappears over the side.

Bending the Rules to Breaking Point

Shifting ballast has long been associated with cheating. Polite society didn't think much of sandbaggers in Britain, Europe and across the Atlantic; however, more subtle forms of shifting ballast were hard to stamp out. In this context, the visit of the American yacht, *Niagara*, to our shores in 1896 is worthy of note.[760] Howard Gould's *Niagara* had additional 'wing' water-tanks in the bilges. These were interconnected, and as there is only one reason why such a system might be installed in a racing yacht, the YRA measurer, who had caught wind of the matter, escalated it. *Yachting* magazine called the idea "*a compliment to the owner's ingenious mind*"; but cautioned Gould by citing Punch's advice to those about to marry.[761]

Scrutineers arrived unannounced, as was normal and indeed still is. *Niagara's* professional captain cooperated fully, but on hearing about the inspection, Gould was apoplectic. He complained bitterly and copied his letter, expressing singularly unpersuasive outrage, to the press. In Gould's defence, though we go there reluctantly, there was a widespread and not altogether unjustified perception that this sort of thing was standard, albeit sharp, practice on some suspiciously stiff British racing yachts too.

Gould stooped as low as any man in the history of yacht racing – and that is a very low bar indeed. Racing against Dunraven's *Audrey*, he lost badly, but won after protesting that *Audrey* was 'entered improperly'. Dunraven's skipper had signed himself 'Capt. Bevis' rather than Charles Bevis as the rule, framed for gentlemen, required a Christian name. The famous case of *Navaho's* protest against the RYS to take the Brenton Reef Cup from *Britannia* in 1893 (after the finishing line was repositioned without prejudice) was another example of the Yankee win-at-any-cost mentality. Still, we welcomed the Americans to our shores.

The *Niagara* case recalls Dunraven's complaints to the New York Yacht Club concerning the re-ballasting of *Defender* in the 1895 America's Cup. At the time, public opinion supported the Americans and Dunraven was thought to have behaved in a rather caddish manner. However, there is no doubt that *Defender* was re-ballasted; even if, as claimed, the net result was as before, she should still have been remeasured. More seriously, a Herreshoff letter of 1895 confirms that that *Defender* could fill the hollow fin-keel with water to alter displacement by as much as 19,500lbs (> 8-tons).[762] This letter is inconclusive, but it does lend some support to the 1898 accusation that *Defender* could take on 23,870lbs or 12 tons of water ballast in tanks hidden beneath the sole.[763]

Ever since rating systems changed from an almost arbitrary measurement between perpendiculars to waterline-length, yachts have been measured with dry bilges and are expected to race in the same trim. Herreshoff was more up-front about *Reliance*. She had a hollow rudder with an integral rubber bladder. Ostensibly, this brazen device was to ease steering. However, the rudder of an SCYC 90ft LWL yacht is about 450ft^2 and a foot thick at the leading edge, so between the rudder being flooded or pumped dry, displacement was altered slightly and trim significantly; a change critical to the effective LWL in yachts with very long overhangs.[764] But then after the 'Dunraven affair', and with the compliant Tommy Lipton challenging, who would question the trim of an American defender?

Through the final decades of the 19ᵗʰ century, the collective work of Clyde-based designers and builders relied increasingly on quantitative methods to produce ever more sophisticated yachts constructed with a rare precision. Martin Black's excellent biography of G. L. Watson is subtitled the *Art and Science of Yacht Design*, whereas the 'art and science of sandbaggers' could only be uttered tongue-in-cheek. As the 19ᵗʰ century progressed, we like to think that Clydeside yachtsmen valued more cerebral innovation and sought to set trends rather than follow them.

A century later, during the 1987 One Ton Cup, the yacht, *I-Punkt*, exhibited blazing speed. Thomas Friese and Olympic hero Hubert Raudaschl had installed a Y-valve and a two-way bilge-pump tapping into their engine's water intake.[765] Five hundred pounds of water translated into thousands of pound/foot righting moment. Legendary Olympian, Rodney Pattison, who raced against *I-Punkt* on *Jamarella*, has recently revealed the whole sordid story in a new book.[766] We note here that, although he was born in Machrihanish, while his parents were stationed there with the Royal Air Force, and could thus have played football for Scotland, Mr Pattison is unambiguously English.

After a long and hardly impartial investigation, Friese eventually admitted to cheating and his entire crew were banned, including whistle-blower Andrew Cape, whose big mistake was leaking the story to the press, rather than lodging a formal protest with the Race Committee. Years later when a very successful New Zealand yacht was sold to a new owner in Ireland, mysteriously redundant glassed-in piping was discovered during a refit.[767] As the editor of *The Yachtsman* asserted in 1892: "*it may be taken for granted that owners do not, and will not, break the rules, or do anything unfair*"!

CODA: No Greater Love Hath Any Man

Mr McGrouther died at his own home in Largs on the 17ᵗʰ April 1891. The old seaman had reached the goodly age of 72, before congestion of the lungs took him, after a short illness. *Yachting* magazine described him as "*careful and industrious in the years of his prime*." The magazine noted that, as a sailor in demand and seldom out of work, he had retired comfortably. "*Mr McGrouther was able in his declining days to live at ease, and for many years he did no yachting save a little piloting.*"[768]

McGrouther was an honourable man of the old school. Perhaps he was the inspiration of the cliché 'loyal to a fault'. His passing was celebrated in a famous story in which McGrouther was the hero, prepared to make peace with his god in order to protect the integrity of his gentlemen. Old McGrouther had one weakness, he was a slave to the power of shifting ballast. If the masters were strongly opposed to it, well, all in all, perhaps it was better that way.

One afternoon, beating up the Cowal shore, McGrouther's afternoon was not going well; his master's vessel was staggering under the weight of her jackyard topsail, the skipper had lost the groove and the opposition was slowly edging away, sailing higher and faster. Clearly, the ballast was not 'trimmed' to advantage. The whole crew knew exactly what had to be done. Unfortunately, the owner was a gentleman of irreproachable conduct, and perhaps even worse, sharp-eyed.

McGrouther was immediately spotted as he set out to investigate the problem. Did I say he had a 'reputation'? The owner asked him why he was going below when all hands were required on deck. *"Am aff tae chynge ma breeks, sur"* replied our hero. *"What's wrong with those you have on?"* asked the owner. *"Burst, sur"* says McGrouther. In Scotland, a man's trousers are not to be doubted, so what more could be said?

McGrouther disappeared below and for some reason it took a while to find his damn breeks. As the man himself told the story, *"both the breeks an' a pickle o' ballast were shifted, an' the race won without the maister kennin' aboot ainy o' the shiftings"*. Our hero's enduring love affair with the 'Goddess of Righting-moment' is as old as the sport itself and it has smitten more good men than we will ever know.

---

[736] For a sailor engaged in sounding with a lead-line, retrieving the lead was hard work, so he would just swing it until he was being watched and only then release it.

[737] The other use of the term 'sandbagger'. America's Cup: Team New Zealand walking a fine line in build-up, NZ Herald, 19th May 2017.

[738] Sailing Boats from around the World, Henry Colman Folkard, 1906.

[739] The Royal Yacht Squadron, Montague Guest & William B. Boulton, 1902.

[740] The History of Yachting 1600-1815, Arthur H. Clark, New York Yacht Club, 1903.

[741] Yachts and Yachting Restrictions, The Sunday Times, 31st December 1854.

[742] The Badminton Library of Sports and Pastimes: Yachting, Volume 1, The Evolution of the Modern Racing Yacht, G. L. Watson, 1894.

[743] Royal Cork Yacht Club, Cork Examiner, 11th June 1863.

[744] Scottish Clubs, R. T. Pritchett & Rev. G. L. Blake. Badminton's Yachting, Volume 2, 1894.

[745] Hunts Magazine, anonymously written by J. D. Bell in 1865.

[746] Yachting Notes (from The Field), Southampton Herald 28th December 1887.

[747] The Clyde from its source to the sea, W.J. Millar, 1888.

[748] The Evolution of the Modern Racing Yacht, G. L. Watson, 1894.

[749] These boats were all from the 1880s.

[750] Manual of Yacht and Boat Sailing and Architecture Dixon Kemp, 9th edition, 1900. Contribution by G. L. Watson.

[751] Ibid

[752] The Sailing Boat, a Treatise on Sailing Boats and Small Yachts, Henry Coleman Folkard, 1901.

[753] Manual of Yacht and Boat Sailing, 11th edition, 1913. Contribution by G. L. Watson.

[754] Manual of Yacht and Boat Sailing, 6th edition, 1888. Contribution by G. L. Watson.

[755] Yacht Racing Legislation, Glasgow Herald, 14th September 1891.

[756] Ibid

[757] From the Man at the Wheel, The Yachtsman, 11th February 1892.

[758] Yacht Racing Legislation, Glasgow Herald, 14th September 1891.

[759] 'Desideratum': something that is needed or wanted.

[760] Minute by Minute, the Story of the RYA (1875-1982), Gordon Fairley, 1983.

[761] Punch: *"Advice to persons about to marry ----- Don't!"*

762 Deer Isle's Undefeated America's Cup Crews: Humble Heroes from a Downeast Island, Mark J. Gabrielson, 2013.

763 Which is Right, Captain J. G. Johnson (pseudonym) a pamphlet of 1898.

764 Ships and Shipbuilders: Pioneers of Design and Construction, Fred M. Walke, 2010. Herreshoff Sailboat, Gregory O. Jones, 2004. A Brush with Sail, Jim Boland, July 2012. The hollow rudder contained a rubber bladder that could be filled with air by a foot pump. Letter from Herreshoff to C. Oliver Islin, 21st December 1895.

765 The Racing Yachtsman, Yachting, January 1988.

766 Superdocious! Racing Insights and Revelations from Legendary Olympic Sailor Rodney Pattisson, Rodney Pattisson and Barry Pickthall, 2019.

767 When sold on after first-class racing careers, a number of yachts have been found with tell-tale traces of illegal plumbing.

768 Clyde News, Yachting, 30th May 1891.

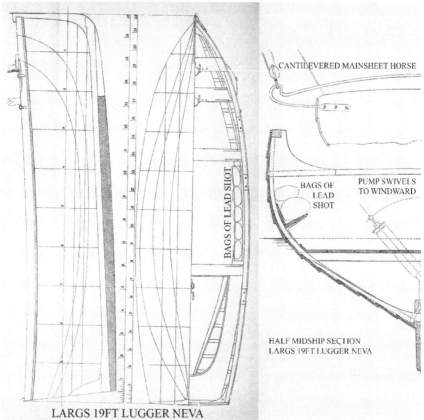

LARGS 19FT LUGGER NEVA

Clyde Lugger ballasted with Lead shot ca.1875   G. L. Watson, in 'Dixon Kemp'

The bags of lead shot are stacked at the point of maximum beam which reduces at deck level with the modest tumblehome on this design. The 'tacking' pump arrangement shows that the boats were also dependent on human ballast and that they shipped a lot of water to windward in a blow. It remains an enduring mystery to the author why a century had to pass before topside flare was introduced to give human ballast leverage in National 12 and 14ft Merlin Rocket dinghies in the 1960s, although Ian Proctor conceptualised the 7ft-wide Merlin in 1955.

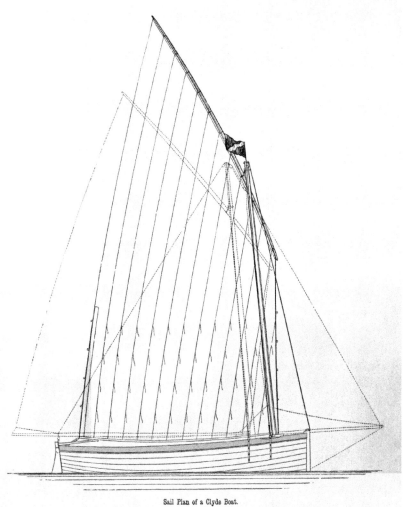

Sail Plan of a Clyde Boat.

19ft Clyde Lugsail boat, ca.1880   Drawing by G. L. Watson Ltd

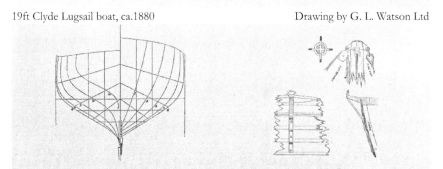

19ft Clyde Lugsail boat sections   Detail – note shroud outriggers or channels

Chapter 19: The Whirligig of Time Allowances[769]

I don't smoke marijuana anymore. I don't drink. Marijuana is a handicap. So is alcohol. Alcohol is a terrible handicap. But in spite of being a handicap, it shouldn't be criminal.
Gary Johnson[770]

Andy Capp is not a Scot, but he could be a role model for many of our finest.[771] Andy is a working-class hero from the harbour town of Hartlepool in north-east England. He loves pigeon-racing, fishing, darts, snooker, football and betting on the horses. Andy is a tireless scrounger at the bar, and although quite the Lothario with the barmaids, he is an enduring trial for his long-suffering wife Flo. Andy's character is blind-sided by both his oversize bunnet and his prejudices. He personifies the folly of self-imposed handicaps. To all intents and purposes, Andy Capp is useless, except as a metaphor for yacht racing with time allowances.

Through the early years of yachting the desire to assert individuality exceeded by far any desire to compete on level terms. Level rating was the preserve of tiddlers and men of modest means. Wealthy iconoclasts saw their yachts as an aspect of self-expression, in effect a manifestation of their ability to do as they damn well pleased. Such men were not amenable to regulation, except in the most general terms. They would agree on a course and the starting time, but other than that there were few limits.

Prior to the publication of Froude's findings in 1879, the relationship between waterline length and boat-speed was an open question, hotly debated and confused by the ability of sprightly small boats to sail circles around ponderous large ones. *"Nothing is more remarkable in the history of yachting than the cheerfulness with which the owners of small boats took the odds of tonnage and sail area without the slightest hesitation or without a single thought of time allowance. The established fact that, other things being equal, the larger boat wins was long undiscovered, we may assume."*[772]

Line 'Honours'

Racing with time allowances, or handicap racing, is simply a fun day out.[773] It is substantially worthless as a demonstration of your ability, or as an indicator of progress when matching your skills against the best. For this very reason, it is eternally popular. Handicap racing is infinitely less stressful than racing level, as it introduces the music of chance to serenade even the worst day on the water with a glimmer of hope – that conditions may change to favour your unique performance profile. Moreover, if you are in the fortunate position of having money to burn, you can strike a match to chase what is ironically known as 'line-honours'.

If you are hell-bent on finishing first in a handicap race, you are not playing the game. There is no 'honour' in reaching the bar first if you have got there aboard the quickest boat; neither are we impressed if you have cheerfully taken rating penalties which preclude any chance of an overall win, or heaven forbid, hired the best crew that money can buy to compete in an all-comers yacht race. Unfortunately, this type of empty braggadocio has thrived under Rolex's lavish sponsorship of the Sydney Hobart, where the real race for overall victory and the Tattersall Cup is a now a side-show.

Where the 'good old days' differed from today is that spectators and camp followers were once more knowledgeable and understood the race, with time allowances integral to their perception of the event. They were not impressed when the biggest, fastest, or most expensive boat crossed the line first. Before Big Class yacht racing was homologated into the J-class of the Universal Rule, the boats may have looked similar, but the larger yachts were always racing on handicap. Similarly, the old level-rating 5 and 10-tonners enjoyed a second life in the small boat divisions. So, we can take some satisfaction in recognising that the unholy quest for 'line honours' in mixed fleets does not form a significant part of Scotland's yacht racing heritage. However, handicap racing, unsatisfactory as it may be, certainly does.

Cannon Fodder – a Necessary Corollary

From the dawn of the sport, owners of uncompetitive boats have been bullied to compete in regattas as cannon fodder for the crack racing yachts of the day. There is no fun in losing, so over two centuries yachting administrators have endlessly tinkered with rating rules, ostensibly to reward sailing skills, rather than disposable income. This admirable task is compromised by the fact that there is a strong correlation between fast crews and fast boats.

Even if the perfect rule were not an impossible quest, clarity in this regard would still be counterproductive. The truth is that all but the very best crews savour an element of randomness in race results – even one-design sailors. Occasionally, a middle-of-the-fleet crew will score a good result and bask in self-delusion for a month. The importance of this for the long-term health of the sport should never be underestimated. Yacht racing is sustained by its diversity, its ambiguity, and the faint possibility of a good result when the stars align. Failing that, a lucky windshift, which reshuffles the fleet for half an hour, is all a stoic backmarker needs to make a day on the water worthwhile.

There are essentially two types of rating: a) performance-based – like the Clyde's arbitrary time allowances, the American PHRF system and the Portsmouth Yardstick; and b) via measurement of the competing yacht and her equipment – like all the systems touched on in this chapter. The first is based on an analysis of 'observed performance' to assign a subjective rating. The second is based on measurement and calculations, often complex, which seek to model 'potential performance' objectively. Both types of rating can be levied on time elapsed or distance sailed.

With a performance-based system, after a few seasons of adjustment, the results are close, and every dog can have his day. Winning may be meaningless but it encourages less able crews to compete, and it is ideal for 'beer-can' racing when folks just want to gabble in good company. Such systems are inevitably influenced by the ability of the crew, so good sailors can expect their expertise to be reflected in their rating. Serious competitors prefer to have their yacht rated objectively, disregarding their arsenal of go-fast equipment and the skill of the crew. In this context, the only way to weight the dice is to invest in optimisation, a procedure which requires endless fiddling, measurement, remeasurement and more remeasurement, creative distraction, and in our experience, the odd bottle of whisky.

All rating systems face a Sisyphean task in their quest for a level playing field. Had this been their only failure, the course of yachting would have run more smoothly. Unfortunately, the impact of rating rules on every aspect of the sport has been profound; the arcane formulae that emerged through the clouds of cigar smoke in ill-lit rooms have sent designers down murky conceptual back alleys and signalled U-turns to coincide with maximum collateral damage to resale values. Sporting owners have been enticed to fund whimsical experiments in yacht design, vulnerable to the winds of change.

Old Thames Tonnage

Thames Tonnage was originally intended to assess the hold size or cargo capacity of a commercial ship to calculate port dues.[774] Builders' Old Measurement was the first revision, with half-beam substituted for 'depth of hold' – that being an essential element in determining capacity. This proxy reflected the average proportions of contemporary vessels and was used because an accurate measurement was often difficult, or impossible, to establish, requiring an empty ship and good physical access. These early tonnage calculations were determined as follows:

Thames Tonnage Rule – used extensively to calculate port dues, pre-1719

$$T = \frac{L \times B \times D}{96}$$

L = *Length*
B = *Beam*
D = *Depth of Hold*

Builders' Old Measurement was used commercially ca.1719 to 1854

$$T = \frac{(L - [B \times 3/5]) \times B \times B/2}{94}$$

L = *Length*
B = *Beam*

In 1829, the Royal Yacht Squadron institutionalised the Builders' Old Measurement with Ackers' scale of time allowances. With beam penalised and draft effectively unmeasured, the archetypical deep, narrow British cutter was born. Large racing yachts never have been, and never will be, a sound investment, but they were perhaps not as ruinous during this era of relative innocence as subsequently. A yacht built to last fifty years might remain competitive for ten or twelve. Then there was a second life in the second division, with a third life as a comfortable cruiser – which might be extended almost indefinitely if the boat was pretty and well-built.

Despite the absence of a sound rating rule, or perhaps due to that situation, the 1830s witnessed a generation of famously long-lived racing yachts, particularly those built in England, like the *Pearl*, *Arrow*, *Alarm*, *Egeria* and the first *Lulworth*. These boats were lengthened, reskinned, reframed and occasionally given a whole new centreline structure, courtesy of cheap skilled labour spun-off by the Industrial Revolution. There was nothing really comparable in Scotland. John Scott's *Hawk* and *Clarence* were the most successful cutters racing on the Clyde and on the Irish Sea, but they passed 'into trade'.

Thames Measurement

Persistent rule-cheating led to change in 1854 with a joint initiative by the Royal London and the Royal Mersey yacht clubs. However, it seems that vested interests prevailed; too many influential yachtsmen owned rule-cheating yachts. The following year the Royal Thames addressed the question. Their new Thames Measurement, as reformulated in 1855, was another bad rule, which quite perversely, penalised wholesome designs even more harshly. There was a glimmer of hope in 1857 when the Royal Yacht Squadron attempted to substitute 'extreme draft' for half-beam in the formula.[775] This proposal would have encouraged more wholesome boats, but unfortunately, it was not widely adopted. No matter, owners were not deterred and so the elegant, but wet and cramped, cutters flourished.

The Yacht Racing Association was formed in 1875 with the express purpose of rationalising and homologating the many different versions of the tonnage rules under which British clubs raced their yachts.[776] Competing rating systems, then as now, are counter-productive in terms of growing the sport. It is axiomatic that yachts should be rated fairly with a universally agreed number that remains fixed no matter where they race. In 1876, after a couple of unsuccessful attempts to establish a consensus, the YRA opted for the lowest common denominator – a virtually useless rating system based on old Thames Tonnage.

Yacht designers of the day, perhaps unable to believe their luck, were free to drive a coach and four through the open gates of the new national rule. Scottish designers, like Fife and Watson, were in the van and alive to every ambiguity. One such ruse was cranking the stern-post vertical and separating it from the rudder stock, see illustration at the chapter break. When this was penalised, G. L. Watson simply moved his rudder stock forward of the waterline. Closing this loophole led to the first attempts to measure actual waterline-length. The 1876 Rule was calculated as follows:

The Thames Measurement Rule, as adopted by the YRA in 1876

$$\text{Rating in tons} = \frac{(L - B) \times B \times B/2}{94}$$

L = *length, in feet, from the stempost to sternpost*
B = *maximum beam, in feet*

This formula is sometimes expressed as $\dfrac{(L - B) \times B^2}{188}$

The Clyde clubs introduced the new system for the 1877 season, and initially at least it was welcomed as it rated the existing fleet without prejudice. Thames Measurement was an 'easy to measure' system, but one with known and fatal weaknesses. As it was based on carrying capacity, minimising internal volume reduced the rating, even while slimming the boat down also made it faster. Thus, began a long tradition of designers circumventing measurement rules in unsporting ways that still detract from yacht racing today. Rule cheating is not like trespass; it is never accidental. So, it remains a mystery quite why the administrators of the sport have never framed, or implemented, a robust 'spirit of the rule' rider.

On the Clyde, RCYC measuring officers did their best when dealing with the old Thames Rule. They were admonished to follow the club rule that *"the length must be taken from outside of the stem to the outside of the sternpost at half the depth of each from the load waterline"*. But even then, they curiously lacked the authority to require the sternpost to be straight. Consequently, as the 1880s progressed, both the rule, and respect for it, were diminished. *"Gentlemen owning wholesome craft were unwilling to compete against such as were purely laid down for racing."*[777]. The seeds of discontent had been sewn up north. The Clyde's designers and boat builders had become too successful in pushing the edges of the envelope. While owners of well-found schooners and yawls on the South Coast gave up racing altogether, their counterparts in the North, often party to the mischief, were loath to 'rock the boat'.

Consequently, as the 19th century drew to a close, The Clyde thrived to become, arguably, the epicentre of the sport in Britain. More generally, English yachting commentators of the period were pessimistic about the future of yacht racing, as steam yachts became fashionable just as race results became essentially meaningless. *"Those who go to sea under canvas are beginning to be regarded as fanatics – who to desire to temper their amusement with penance."*[778]

In the 1882 season, Clyde-built yachts did particularly well on the national stage. The 40-ton Fife cutter, *Annasona*, led the field with cash and medals worth around £1,700 (£203,000). Her near-perfect record fuelled a major controversy about admitting these 'little' yachts into first-class events.[779] Smart designers now looked for rating sweet-spots in the size continuum. A lead-keel 40-tonner could keep up with the old 90-tonners in all but heavy-weather, so they inevitably swept the board in handicap events. However, the 40-tonners were not a good investment. In 1881 *Britannia*, a crack 1873 Hatcher 40-tonner, sold for just £1,000 (£121,000), a derisory amount for a well-found, plumb-stem yacht about 75ft LOA, just a quarter of her value a few seasons earlier.[780]

The Thames Measurement Rule was modified by the YRA in 1881, after much deliberation, but this was still a rule biased to embrace existing 'knife-on-edge' yachts without undue penalties. *Shona*, designed in 1884 by G. L. Watson, was 42ft LOA, 5ft 9" beam, 6ft 3" draft, and carried 1,640 square feet of sail. So clearly, as a type-forming rule for new-builds, it did nothing to temper design decisions. And after a few years, neither did it adequately safeguard the value of the existing fleet, as ever more extreme types made seaworthy, dual-purpose yachts substantially worthless for competition.

The revised YRA Tonnage Rule of 1881

$$\text{Tonnage} = \frac{(L+B)^2 \times B}{1730} \quad L \text{ and } B \text{ expressed in feet}$$

Under this rule *"beam was undervalued, and length was taken at any price, with the result that the adoption of extreme proportions was hastened rather than averted"*.[781] So said G. L. Watson, but he was being slightly disingenuous. Beam is not 'undervalued' in this calculation; incredibly, it is penalised even more than it had been previously had been. One wonders how much port was drunk at the YRA committee meetings if the members thought that this formula would encourage the wholesome vessels that they professed to desire.

However, a major advance of the era was that the mixed racing fleets of the past were channelled more effectively into rating bands. This improved competition and incidentally informed design development decisions. The main classes were designated as 3-tons, 5-tons, 10-tons, 20-tons and 40-tons upwards. "*The year 1882 was notable chiefly for the introduction of a new class in the regatta programmes, viz. that for 3-tonners. Four of these little vessels did battle in all kinds of weather and proved most successfully how much power and what fine sea-going qualities can be obtained by length and depth with almost a minimum of beam.*"[782]

George Blake, an otherwise discerning commentator on the state of the art, was moved to congratulate the marine industry for doing its best to dispense with "*the troublesome dimension of beam*" altogether. How do we address the delusions of rational men? Thomas Huxley's words resonate: "*The scientific spirit is of more value than its products, and irrationally held truths may be more harmful than reasoned errors.*"[783]

The pages of Dixon Kemp's classic *Yacht and Boat Sailing* illustrate a 3-tonner that was too slim to fit port and starboard settee berths abreast. The artfully named *Spankadillo*, designed by Captain H. Bailey in 1882, was innocently presented as a well-thought-out example of the new type. Contemporary authorities seem to have been impressed that such a vessel was indeed feasible. But it was a low bar, and that was just the first season before everything went horribly wrong.

Noted examples of this type on the Clyde were: *May* (Watson 1881), *Annasona* and *Sleuthhound* (Fife 1881), *Wendur* and *Marjorie* (Watson 1883). But that said, it was a relatively small boat that defined the era: William Paton, who had previously designed the successful 3-tonners, *Currytush* and *Cora*, now blazed a trail into the bizarre realm of the 'six-beam' cutters. The 6-tonner, *Oona* (1886), was perhaps the ultimate lead mine. *Oona* was twice the size of an extreme plank-on-edge 3-tonner, but with the same beam.[784]

Dixon Kemp, writing in *The Field*, naively described *Oona* as a marvel. That much was true; she was certainly astonishing, but not in a good way. The contemporary 3-tonners were 'five-beam' cutters, just 5ft and 5ft 6" wide. Note that the length to breadth ratio is calculated on LWL and B-max, not LOA and waterline beam. Revisionist yachting historians have sought to characterise these designs as an intelligent response to the rule as "*all the major designers of the era were doing it*". But surely there is nothing clever about carting countless tons of deadweight around the racecourse when a light and lively boat with good form-stability can lengthen the lever arm to carry the same sail with a fraction of that ballast.

With the tonnage rule, the British design environment of the late 19th century existed in an alternate reality, disassociated from seaworthiness or efficiency. Meanwhile, across the Atlantic, things were moving in a different direction. There are reams of well-documented discussion on the relative merits of the narrow deep-keeled British cutters and the wider American centreboard sloops. While the American boats could also be dangerous when the concept was taken to extremes, as with the sinking at anchor in a squall of the American schooner, *Mohawk*, in 1876, the wider boats were generally more wholesome. After the success of the James Coats' 1879 10-ton G. L. Watson cutter, *Madge*, in the USA in 1881, the two models would converge to mutual advantage between 1887 and 1893 with Scottish designers active in the synthesis.[785]

The Length & Sail-area Rule

The year 1887 saw another change in yacht measurement with the introduction of the Length & Sail-area Rule, introduced by Dixon Kemp. The new rule was based on a system which had been in use in America since 1882, with length measured along the load waterline. Beam was now untaxed, so no one was interested in knife-on-edge yachts. What was once defended was now ridiculed mercilessly. Despite their much-vaunted windward ability, not one was built after 1887.

The Length & Sail-area Rule of 1887[786]

$$R = \frac{LWL \times SA}{6000}$$

LWL *expressed in feet and* SA *in square feet*

Clyde designers and yachtsmen embraced the wider and lighter model with enthusiasm. The new boats sailed more upright, they were drier in a seaway, cheaper to build and offered useful accommodation down below – boats like *Yarana* (Watson 1888), *Deerhound* (Watson 1889) and *Dragon* (Fife 1889), then *Britannia* (Watson 1893) and later *Ailsa* (Fife 1895), *Isolde* (Fife 1895), and *Caress* (Watson 1895). That said, in the early days of the rule, and presaging a more competitive design milieu, the majority of the new crop was from the drawing boards of English designers, like Nicholson and Sibbick. But it did not take long for the Scots to catch up.

For many, this was *the* golden era for large yachts and Big Class yachting, but then something remarkable happened. Smaller racing yachts had long been popular on the Clyde and now the Length & Sail-area Rule sparked a surge of interest on the South Coast. Yachts of 20-rating down to 2-rating were built in large numbers, and because the boats were cheap, designers now experimented with flat shallow sections, scow bows, plate and bulb keels and lightweight constriction. These boats were far from the '*Britannia* ideal' the rule-makers sought. So, while they were excellent sports-boats, the mere thought that such concepts might be replicated in big boats inspired incipient panic. The YRA feared a glut of lightlybuilt 'throw-away' racers.

The prospect of large yachts with shallow bilges and no headroom was a paper tiger. In the USA, inland Europe and the Antipodes, where shallow hull-forms have long prospered, extended deckhouses were engineered to maintain adequate structural integrity. The aesthetic quality of these railway carriage-style carbuncles was mixed to say the least, but nonetheless, they were accepted as a fair trade-off to allow light displacement and shallow-draft. And deckhouses dispelled the gloom of Victoriana, giving light and airy salons a view to the outside world.

> *Oh, here is the useful, 'speedy' craft*
> *Of the Y. R. Association:*
> *Thin hull, bulb-keel, enormous draught,*
> *And no accommodation.*[787]

Matters concerning what was, and what was not, a proper yacht exercised opinion in the 1890s, with proposals to relegate the management of the smaller boats (under 5-tons) to a sub-committee of the YRA. However, on the Clyde, the 2½-raters were extremely popular with yachtsmen and small-class racing enjoyed a legion of enthusiastic followers. Moreover, the leading lights of the 2½-raters included prominent yachtsmen who also owned larger vessels. Clyde sailors believed the 2½-raters to be "*quite as important as any other*" and indeed integral to the continued good health of the sport in developing seamanship.[788]

While the big boats may have commanded the headlines, *The Glasgow Herald's* yachting correspondent stressed the importance of the smaller classes: "*The Clyde above all other racing waters is interested in the progress of the sport, and no one requires to be told that the reputation of the Clyde at the present time has very little to do with 100-tonners. The success of its most sporting and most successful season has lain with its 10 and 2½-raters, sailed by amateurs with a precision and style which cannot be outrivalled anywhere.*"[789]

The *Herald* thought that perhaps "*the origin of the agitation to limit the functions of the YRA has been stirred through the jealousy created by prominence given to the smaller classes, and by rapid spread of public interest in the sport due to their presence.* Surely, to any thinking person, the upsurge in newspaper articles and public enthusiasm for exciting yacht racing, in whatever size of yacht, should have been a cause for satisfaction, not regret. The *Herald* continued: "*The increase of the smaller classes is the healthiest guarantee that the sport is at strength spreading with giant strides, for nothing is more certain the fact that for one owner who can build and uphold a 40-rater, there are twenty that can build and uphold a 10-rater, and perhaps that number doubled who can build a 2½-rater.*"[790]

Clyde yachtsmen were rebellious in 1891: "*The most prominent difficulty to be brought under the notice of the YRA is where the line is to be drawn between yachts the association should recognise and yachts the association ought not to condescend to legislate for. The Squadron has drawn the line at 5-tonners, and of course, a strong feeling of a certain class of followers is in favour of accepting the dictum of the RYS."* A 5-rater in 1891 would typically be 32ft LWL and 45ft LOA – not a small boat. With such congenital instability at the heart of the system, it is easy to see why Clyde yachtsmen engaged in open revolt.

The columns of *Hunt's*, in particular, oozed with Caledonian vitriol: *"it so happens that although the Royal Squadron is filled with noblemen, the club is not recognised outside the walls of its clubhouse as a sporting club. The yachts of the squadron have mainly been outclassed, and so have the opinions of their owners; and any line the squadron may draw is not regarded by Clyde yachtsmen as of any importance whatever."*[791] The Clyde clubs reluctantly accepted the formal oversight of the YRA in 1895, twenty years after the perceived southern mafia first sought to exercise it.

Small-class racing thrived on controversy. Meanwhile, as the 1890s progressed, Big Class racing in British waters also went from strength to strength. It has been said that the slow pace of development during this period, when rule-cheating was kept in check, was good for the sport. But it did not last. There were generous rating benefits for yachts with two masts, initially conceived to encourage cruising schooners and yawls to support round-the-cans racing. This would have repercussions later.

The Linear-rating Rules

After allowing the sailing community the best part of a decade to enjoy high-performance sailing, the Yacht Racing Association introduced a new system of measurement, developed by R. E. Froude, which taxed 'skin girth' and thus penalised draught, beam, tight garboards and light displacement.[792] The plan, it seems, was to legislate skimming-dishes out of existence. The 1st Linear Rating Rule ran from 1st January 1896 until the close of 1900.

YRA 1st Linear-rating system of 1896

$$R = \frac{\text{Length} + \text{Beam} + \tfrac{3}{4}\,\text{Skin-girth} + \tfrac{1}{2}\,\sqrt{\text{Sail-area}}}{2}$$

Length, beam and girth expressed in feet and sail area in square feet

Incipient panic had prompted this course reversal. Perhaps the fast, light flyers of the Length & Sail Area Rule were a century ahead of their time and the materials required to build them. In the 1890s, there was indeed a gap between the bounds of engineering solutions and the boundless ambitions of naval architects. But that gap was narrowing, even as the YRA sought regression to more traditional forms. The emerging discipline of structural engineering in yacht design was an unsung collateral casualty, only recovering when synthetic composites emerged, and fin-keels resurfaced after WW2.

In the interim, very few racing yachts tested the limits of late Victorian materials technology, but the likes of C. E. Nicholson's rather wonderful

Shamrock IV sacrificed the Universal Rule on the altar of high performance, and showed what might have been done, even with conventional low-tech materials, if yacht design had been allowed to develop untrammelled. Today, 'wonder' materials with physical properties that boggle the mind, define new avenues of innovation to push sailing performance past the limits of inconvenient physical laws.

The era of the 1st Linear-rating Rule on the Clyde, saw healthy turnouts in each size class. Perhaps the best example of the new rule was the Kaiser's *Meteor II*, launched in 1896. *Meteor* was virtually unbeatable and hounded *Britannia* off the racecourse. Looking at the two yachts side by side, while built to different rules, they are similar in concept.

1896 Linear-rating Rule: *Britannia* (1893) and *Meteor II* (1896) compared

	TM	LWL	Beam	Draft	Sail Area	Rating
Britannia	221-tons	87.87ft	23.3ft	15ft	10,359ft^2	96.8
Meteor II	238-tons	88.95ft	24.3ft	18ft	11,248ft^2	101.9

However, with *Meteor II*, Watson took *Britannia's* key strengths and emphasised them with more sail-area, a much deeper, more-defined keel fin and longer overhangs. While generally, the dimensions of the two yachts are reflected in their comparative ratings, the race-winning difference is in the tighter garboards and deeper fin keel, giving *Meteor* the power to carry the additional sail. The Kaiser's success, beating *Britannia*, was hugely unpopular, not just with Bertie but also among a people still happy to be regarded as 'subjects'. However, the YRA's knee-jerk response, fiddling with ratings, compromised the whole system.

In 1897, a cumulative penalty of 10%, or 0.12 seconds a mile for each foot of rating, was imposed on yachts rating above 90ft. It appeared as if the YRA had rerun each encounter between the two boats to determine what rating change would have swung the balance of victories in favour of the King's yacht. In any event, *Britannia* was withdrawn from first-class racing that year. The Big Class struggled in this era, uncompetitive against the smaller yachts that now gained access to make up the numbers.

For the larger yachts, the obvious response was to take advantage of the rating concession available to yawls. Cutters truncated their mainbooms and mounted a vestigial mizzen mast as far aft as 19th century engineering, and an apparently otherwise distracted God, would allow. Yachts so altered were slightly slower on a square run, marginally less close-winded in very light airs, and faster reaching in any conditions. But with the rating bonus, they could follow their old sparring partners round the course with more time in hand than they would ever need. *Sybarita*, *Meteor II* and the American yacht *Navahoe* took this to extremes.[793]

As for the little boats: "*There was a general feeling that it required less scientific knowledge or architectural skill to design a successful skimming dish as opposed to a more conventional displacement hull which had more body.*"[794] The 'general feeling' was perhaps a feeling of grievance rather than anything else. While it is certainly true that almost anyone can design a skimming dish, Sibbick, regarded in this context as "*an untrained designer and builder*", could match and sometimes surpass similar radical designs by Herreshoff, Watson, Fife and Nicholson. When stultifying incremental change is lauded as progress, overreaching ambition can only be refreshing.[795]

The 1st Linear Rating Rule penalised fin-keelers, but the conceptual advantages were such that they still outperformed their rating. Victorian yachtsmen were hooked, but these radical, and as yet unrefined, fin-keelers were scaring the pants off yachting administrators. R. E. Froude's second attempt was a real mishmash issued at short notice in another attempt to halt these developments. The 2nd Linear-rating system ran from 1st January 1901 and ended at the close of the 1906 season. The formula was:

YRA 2nd Linear-rating system, 1901

$$R = \frac{\text{Length} + \text{Beam} + \tfrac{3}{4}\ \text{Skin-girth} + 4d + \tfrac{1}{2}\ \sqrt{\text{Sail-area}}}{2.1}$$

$d = $ *skin-girth – chain-girth at* $^6/_{10}$ *back along* LWL

Length, beam and girth expressed in feet and sail-area in square feet

The YRA fixed this rule for a period of seven years. The new measurement 'd' represented the difference between the skin-girth and chain-girth. By taxing tight garboards through a multiplier of four, the rule bludgeoned designers into drawing fuller-bodied sections with generous bilges. The result would be ultimately heavier, slower vessels, and the demise of surfing downwind. The crude way in which the girth penalty was imposed led to triangular keel-profiles, with maximum draft behind the measurement station.

Despite these obvious flaws, the rule produced some superb vessels such as G. L. Watson's cutter, *Bona*, an 80ft liner-rater of 1897. Initially, however, the new builds were scattered through the rating bands. *Bona* was condemned to sail pointless mismatches against the much larger *Ailsa*, which had been re-rigged as a rule-cheating yawl. The 65ft linear-raters, *Isolde* from Fife and *Astrild* by Watson, and the 52ft linear-raters, *Forsa*, by Alfred Mylne and *Viera* from Fife, after an inauspicious debut, eventually provided good close racing for participants and spectators.[796]

Type-forming

All rating rules are unsatisfactory, and these early rules were no exception. Each change was a reaction to trends deemed undesirable, but each intervention fostered a 'typeform', rather than embraced innovation at a measured rate, commensurate with the life of a first-class racing yacht. From 1855 to 1887, all the rules effectively penalised beam and encouraged deep narrow-gutted cutters. Then, from 1887 to 1895 the prevailing rules motivated designers to test the opposite extreme, before an attempt was made to reverse course back to the mythical *Britannia* ideal.

Perhaps fortuitously, the rule makers were blindsighted when the Length & Sail Area Rule produced some wonderful boats. Manifestly unsustainable, yet manifestly fun, this rule produced the first planing keelboats and added spice to the adrenaline-pumping action in big boats. It was a time of fin-keels and spade rudders and the beginning of the quest for decent oilskins that would eventually see us wearing ski goggles.

Judicious length to breadth and displacement ratios, coupled with adequate scantlings, are essential for seakeeping. Equally important is the provision of usable internal accommodation to maintain viability for a post-racing afterlife and hence resale value. There is no magic involved in minimising beam to reduce wave-making resistance in a displacement hull-form, and of course, reducing weight has long been an effective route to all kinds of performance gains. Sail-carrying ability can be compensated through increased draft, while increased beam also does the trick, which is not to say that both will ever settle in an optimum balance.

From its inception, the story of yacht racing has been dogged by the dichotomy represented by, on the one hand, keen sailors who want to sail fast, light, responsive boats and can tolerate their short competitive life and innate capacity to self-destruct; and, on the other, conservative owners who will gladly compromise a little on performance to ensure durability, low maintenance and good resale value.

Naval architects are affronted by any interference with their creative process, but why owners, who outnumber their designers a hundred to one and pay the bills, do not insist on basic safeguards within the rating rules to preserve their investment, such as a minimum LWL to beam ratio, is another mystery. By contrast, the spectre of depreciation has ensured that 'freaks' have never been replicated as one-designs.[797] Competitiveness need not always trump common sense. The rules of the late and unlamented America's Cup IACC Class, drafted in the 1990s by a remarkably short-sighted confabulation of 25 world-class designers, omitted this key restraint.

In the 2nd International Rule, beam was discarded from the formula, replaced four years later by a minimum of one foot per metre rating in 1937, giving a bizarre mix of metric and imperial measurement systems. This forestalled evolution towards increasingly narrow-gutted mid-ship sections; a fate that befell the International America's Cup Class (1987-92).

The various rating classifications around the turn of the century are undoubtedly confusing, for example, yachts of about 40ft LOA are described variously as 2½-raters and 30-raters. The table below is an attempt to broadly compare classifications under four well-known rating rules: old Thames Tonnage (1855-1875), new Thames Measurement (1876-1886), Length & Sail-area (1887-1895), 1st Linear Rating (1896-1900), 2nd Linear Rating (1900-1906) and the International Rule (1907-present.[798] Such a table cannot ever be fully resolved in terms of its internal logic. However, it is still a useful guide as a basic aide-mémoire:

Cross-referencing Rating Rules[799]

Length Measured or LWL	1855-1875 Old Thames Tonnage	1876-1886 Thames Measurement	1887-1895 Length & Sail Area Rule	1896-1900 1st Linear Rating Rule	1901-1906 2nd Linear Rating Rule	1907-present International Rule
≈15ft	≈2-tons	≈1-ton	½-rater	18-rater	-	-
18-22ft	≈3-tons	≈1½-tons	1-rater	20-rater	16-feet	5mR
20-27ft	≈5-tons	≈2½-tons	2½-rater	24-rater	20-feet	6mR
28-35ft	6-9-tons	4-5-tons	5-rater	30-rater	26-feet	8mR
32-40ft	9-12-tons	5-6-tons	10-rater	36-rater	34-feet	10mR
37-48ft	15-25-tons	7-12-tons	15-rater	42-rater	40-feet	12mR
46-65ft	25-40-tons	12-20-tons	20-rater	52-rater	50-feet	15mR
60-73ft	80-100-tons	40-50-tons	60-rater	65-rater	62-feet	19mR
75-115ft	120-165-tons	60-85-tons	75-rater	75-rater	75-feet	23mR

LBP or length between perpendiculars (the outside of stem to the inside of sternpost – usually used in connection with early straight stemmed yachts).

Linear Rating Rule: Yachts were arranged in classes as before. Yawls, ketches, schooners, and luggers received certain advantages as against the 'base-line' configuration of a cutter in the matter of time allowance per knot of the course. Schooners were reckoned at just 85% of their actual measurement and yawls at 92%. The latter was an obvious point of entry to bend the rule.

CODA: The Bermudian Rig

The jackyard topsail was emblematic of the great days of yachting. The majestic cutters, schooners, and latterly yawls, that drew the crowds were all gaff-rigged with extravagant topsails. However, it might be noted that jib-headed rigs were already successful on the Clyde. Notable examples included Fife III's 17/19, *Lapwing*, in 1888, then his little yellow and black-striped 2½-rater, *Mimine*, in 1894. In the smaller classes, Bermudian or 'shouder-o'-muttn' rigs, as they were called locally, were powerful enough to win in any sort of breeze. Nevertheless, Lloyds for 1896 listed just nine Bermudian rigged yachts, five by Fife, and four by Linton Hope, so most owners still favoured gaff, gunter or lugsail rigs.

In the context of first-class racing yachts, Charles E. Nicholson was the 'father of the modern Bermudian rig' with the 15mR, *Istria*, in 1912. The 15-metre is considered a large yacht today, but back then was still classed as a small boat. It was not until 1921, when Elizabeth Workman's 167-ton C&N cutter, *Nyria*, designed back in 1906, substantially larger than a 23mR, appeared at Cowes with a Charles E. Nicholson Bermudian rig that the wider world took notice.

The following season, two 6-metres – the Linton-designed *Scotia IV* and Morgan Giles's *Vanda*, appeared Bermudian rigged. The little boats enjoyed a reduction of weight aloft by 30% to 40%, but still maintained the inefficient low-aspect sail-plan of their gunter predecessors. Observing all this, in 1922, the International Yacht Racing Union resolved to impose punitive limits on the sail-plans of new yachts above 14-Metres to 1.75 x LWL + 5ft. As the 15mR, *Lady Anne*, for example, is about 48.3ft LWL this would give a crippling sail-plan limit of 89.5ft, 8ft less than the length of the yacht (minus bowsprit) which is 98ft overall.[800] Clearly, a gaff rig with a jackyard topsail would have been a more attractive prospect.

The engineering of early Bermudian rigs was bedevilled by inconsistent spar timber and relatively stretchy wire rigging. There have been fine masts built of wood, steel, and in particular, aluminium, but it was not until the advent of carbon fibre spars in the mid-1990s that designers could combine lightness, lateral stiffness, programmable fore and aft bend with user-friendly set-ups and reliability. The 'good old days' produced beautiful boats galore, but their picturesque rigs induced more ulcers than Aspirin.[801] The only bright spots in an otherwise unmitigated horror show were the wonderful 'mandrel rolled' hollow spars of the McGruer sparmeisters.

Ewing McGruer Jr's made hollow wooden spars which have never been equalled. He cut his spar 'planks' (veneers $^1/_8$th" to $^3/_8$th"), with a radial grain 45⁰ to both surfaces. *"This board is flexible, stable but not rigid; it deforms readily when required"*, he wrote. *"It never splits. It is elastic in the direction of the width and shrinkage shakes are absent."* Veneers of neutral grain were cut to match the required circumference of the spar, then rolled into a tube with the edges scarfed and glued together. Additional layers, formed by the same method, were added as required to make up the specified wall thickness. A special tool like a rigger's server was used to wind webbing round the tube to compress each laminate until the glue set. The best wood for the job was Pacific Coast Spruce. Circular, oval, and pear-shaped sections were moulded using a shaped mandrel.

These hollow spars became popular with big-budget racing yachts; *Britannia*, for example, had a boom built by this method. In terms of strength-to-weight ratio, they were unmatched and about 40% more flexible than grown sticks. For these reasons, they were approved by the BoT for use in critical situations like lifeboats and liferafts. They were also used for billiard cues, stretcher poles and organ pipes. Climbers on the 1924 and 1933 Mount Everest expeditions trusted their lives to ice axes with McGruer's high-tech handles.

During the Great War, Ewing was persuaded to establish a factory in London to support the aircraft industry. His McGruer Hollow Spar

Company Ltd of Lambeth supplied the wing-struts for all fighter planes produced after 1916 and eventually, bombers had struts and fuselage longerons (load-bearing longitudinal fuselage members) built in the Lambeth factory too.[802]

CODA: The Essence of the Sport

In October 1922, the IYRU legislated against electrical power-assisted steering on *Terpsichore*, and thus reaffirmed the essentially 'manual' nature of the sport.[803] In the 21st century this later principal is again under threat. Canting keels on big boats are actuated by hydraulics and powered by diesel or electric motors. Super-maxis chasing line 'honours' also use powered winches for sail trim and to shift water ballast. *Wild Oats*, *Black Jack*, *Perpetual Loyal*, *Ragamuffin 100* and many of the other large boats have to keep their engines running all the time.[804]

---

[769] With apologies to William Shakespeare and lovers of Twelfth Night.

[770] Surely the odd heavy session at the pub is all the handicap a yachtsman worth his salt needs.

[771] Andy Capp was created by Reg Smythe and published in the Daily Mirror and Sunday Mirror from 1957 to the present-day.

[772] The Royal Yacht Squadron; memorials of its members, with an enquiry into the history of yachting and its development in the Solent; and a complete list of members with their yachts from the foundation of the club to the present time from the official records, Montague Guest and William B. Boulton, 1902.

[773] *"Handicap: to impose special disadvantages or impediments upon, in order to offset advantages and make a better contest; to place at a disadvantage."* Source: Microsoft Bookshelves Basic Dictionary.

[774] The first tax on the hire of ships was levied by King Edward I in 1303 based on tons burthen. Later, Edward III levied a tax of 3/- tun of imported wine. A wine tun of 252 gallons occupied 100 cubic feet and weighed 2,240lbs and is the origin of the Imperial long ton.

[775] *"Another change in the method of measuring yachts made by the Squadron in 1857, which had a very important effect upon design. At the May meeting in that year, it was decided that 'extreme draught of water' should be substituted for 'half the breadth' in taking the measurement for determining their tonnage."*

[776] Minute by Minute, the Story of the RYA 1875-1982, Gordon Fairley, 1983.

[777] Yachts and Yachting Restrictions, the Sunday Times, 31st December 1854.

[778] Ibid

[779] The Yacht Racing of 1882, The Glasgow Herald, 16th September 1882.

[780] Yachting Gossip, the Isle of Wight Observer, 28th May 1882.

[781] Quotation continues: *"till in 1886 a radical change in the rule was demanded, and in the autumn of that year a Committee of the Yacht Racing Association, after taking most exhaustive evidence from the various experts, decided on the adoption of a rule proposed by Mr Dixon Kemp, based solely on length (which was measured on the load-waterline) and on sail-area".* The Badminton Library of Sports and Pastimes: Yachting, Volume 1, the Evolution of the Modern Racing Yacht, G. L. Watson, 1894.

[782] Ibid

[783] The Collected Essays of Thomas Henry Huxley.

[784] *Oona*, at 34 ÷ 5.4 = 6.3, was extreme but by no means unique. *Currytush* was 28.5 ÷ 4.7 = 6.1. Among 'first-class' racing yachts, the Hatcher 40-tonner, *Tara* (1883), for example, displaced 75 tons, of which 38 tons was lead. *Tara* was 66ft LWL and 11.5ft beam and set the sail-spread of an old 60-tonner. Her beam to length ratio was 5.74.

[785] American Yachting, W. P. Stephens, 1904.

[786] This rule was adopted by the Clyde yacht clubs, and all classes of yachts, bar the 3½ tonners, were so rated. Their six-strong fleet was based at the Royal Clyde.

[787] Douglas Graham, 1895.

[788] Ibid

[789] Yacht Racing Legislation, The Glasgow Herald, 14th September 1891.

[790] Ibid

[791] Ibid

[792] The tape follows the hull section and is not pulled taught as with 'chain-girth'.

[793] Looking at images of these boats today, it is hard to imagine how their mizzen masts stayed up. And as for wringing stresses on a delicate attenuated counter, there must have been half a ton of girders slotted in behind the sternpost.

[794] G. L. Watson, the Art and Science of Yacht Design, Martin Black, 2011.

[795] Charles Sibbick built more than 300 boats before his tragic death in 1912.

[796] Yachting, Glasgow Herald, 28th June 1898.

[797] The exception to the rule is represented here by the RC44, with its monsoon-drain like midship-section designed to resemble the 100-odd, narrow-gutted, now-useless, IACC yachts.

[798] The Encyclopaedia of Sport & Games, Vol.4, Charles Suffolk and the Earl of Berkshire, 1911.

[799] Data from the build lists of Watson, Mylne and Fife. Note that there are inaccuracies in the Fife and Mylne lists which can misassign values due to the nature of early record-keeping. Cross-referencing via Lloyds is not always helpful either.

[800] Yacht Racing Association, The Times, 16th February 1922. While the *Lady Anne* is used as an example, she was converted in 1913, before the short-lived regulations.

[801] Classic yacht owners desperate to ditch their alloy masts and re-rig with authentic wooden spars are advised to weigh the beauty of varnished spruce against peace of mind.

[802] McGruer and Co, a Century of Boatbuilding on the Clyde, Kathy Mansfield, Classic Boat, September/October 1996.

[803] Yacht Racing Association, The Times, 12th October 1922.

[804] Powered winches are ideal for short-handed superyacht owners or even mid-sized family cruisers if you don't rely on them. However, in a racing yacht they are not necessary; on board *Comanche*, with the highest sheet-loads of any full-on maxi-racing yacht, all the power is generated by the crew labouring mightily on coffee grinder winches. Less divisive perhaps is the use of electric Autohelms in the increasingly popular two-person fleets of much smaller vessels, but a crew of three is surely more seamanlike, especially in overnight coastal races. Sydney to Hobart: Comanche may end era of powered boats, D. D. McNicoll, The Australian, 17th May 2019.

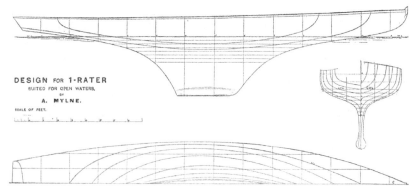

DESIGN FOR 1-RATER
SUITED FOR OPEN WATERS,
BY
A. MYLNE.
SCALE OF FEET.

Mylne, modelled fin-and-bulb 1-rater, 1893   Mylne Yacht Design

The spade rudder is not shown, but it would have 'of the era' - that is, a very low-aspect-ratio foil with a shallow paddle shaped blade, probably constructed in plain steel plate, without profiling.

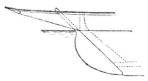

Vanderdeckan's sense of humour   The scurrilous dog-leg sternpost

Nita, 2½-rater, G. L. Watson, 1893   Image: Adamson

Rosetta, 10-rater, Charles E. Nicholson, 1894   Image: Adamson

Rosetta was built by Camper & Nicholson, Gosport, for Robert Allan. Here she is being retrimmed on Robertson's slip at Sandbank, after a rough delivery trip found her down by the head. Lead was removed from the front of the fin and added to the back on the advice of the designer.

Irex, Alex Richardson, J. & G. Fay, 1878, YRA 98-tonner (88-ton TM)   Image: W. J. Finlayson

Reference the images of *Fiona* in the following page: *Fiona's* underbody shows the dramatic shift in fashion from the old 'cod's head and mackerel tail' type, as seen on Fife III's 1834 cutter, *Gleam,* see Chapter 19. Note how half-models of the same yacht vary. In the second model, the so-called 'builder's full-model', the long entry and abbreviated run are considerably more pronounced than in the RNCYC half-model. Also note how different the forefoot cutaway is. The third model also depicts *Fiona* with a fuller run. It is not known whether the builder's model, or the post-facto owner's (?) model best represents her form, as design continued to evolve full-size in frame. Whichever is correct, the boat was fast.

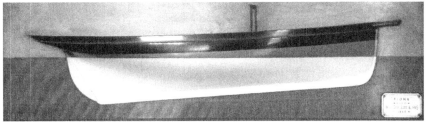

Fiona, William Fife II, 1865   Model in the RCNYC Collection

Fiona, William Fife II, 1865   Model auctioned at Bonhams

Fiona, William Fife II, 1865 (rudder added by author)   John McFie's model in Fast and Bonnie

Fiona, William Fife II, 1865, 80-ton cutter   Image: RNCYC collection

Bloodhound, 40-tonner, Fife II, 1874   Image: RNCYC collection

Zinita, 20-rater, Fife III, 1893   Image: RNCYC collection

Navahoe, Nathanial Herreshoff, 1893, ex-America's Cup   Image: American Library of Congress
Consider the engineering required to mount and stay a mizzen on the counter. Note the trailing dolphin striker strut is sited directly under mast and the two are linked through. The bumpkin is bowsed hard down and the trailing bobstay and dolphin striker are enveloped in the sternwave. The whole counter would have wracked and tilted several degrees in the puffs. The mizzen is about the same size as you would find on a gaff-rigged 8-metre.

Rose (Thelma IV, Vida IV, Griselda), Fife III, 1896   Image: Ian Gilchrist

Chapter 20: Honest Competition

Yachtsmen found the shortness of the life of a class racer the source of expense and irritation; a man wanted a new boat every year to keep pace with the rapid evolution of the rule. This led to the introduction of what is known as the one-design class system of yacht racing. From the year 1894 and onwards many yachtsmen took to one-design racing. Major Brooke Heckstall-Smith [805]

The story of yacht racing on the Clyde includes large and extravagant vessels, owned and sailed by an idiosyncratic bunch of bull-headed industrialists unaccustomed to failure and keen to make their mark on the blank canvas of a new sport. This was where innovation flourished, and boundaries were pushed. Good clients, particularly good repeat clients, enabled the Scottish designers and builders to deliver world-class yachts and marine equipment.

However, since the earliest days of Scottish yacht-racing, there has always been a place in the starting sequence for small yachts, where the nature of the game is very different. Dixon Kemp noted: *"Open-boat sailing has long been very popular on the Clyde; and this is hardly to be wondered at, as the firth offers special opportunities for such a pastime – snug anchorages, fairly smooth water, little or no run of tide. Many of these boats are racing craft, and as each principal watering-place has its club, there is no lack of sport on the Saturday afternoons."* [806]

If you love honest competition and your sport is sailing, the only format that means a damn has everyone starting with an equal chance on a fair course. Then we know what is happening; the first boat across the line wins the race. Time-allowances are an anathema to any racing skipper who has the confidence to compete on level terms. Whether boats are variously equalised to race level, as with the level-rating and restricted classes, or whether they are simply all the same, as featured here and in the following two chapters, is a matter of choice, not principal.

What do we mean by one-design and when can we say a one-design class has been constituted? The position taken here is that 'a one-design class shares the same hull lines and rig measurements. As to, inter alia, choice of builder, deck layout, fit-outs and equipment – these may vary within the umbrella of a one-design class, as for example with the Flying Dutchman. Where some, or all, of these elements are standardised, such a class can be regarded as a 'strict one-design', like the Enterprise dinghy, or where the entire boat is copyrighted by one builder, this is a 'manufacturer's one-design', like the little Laser. Of these options, only the latter offers the possibility of identical boats.[807] Where builders vie for your custom, you can be sure that they will all exploit measurement tolerances to seek a competitive advantage.

Most one-design classes celebrate their anniversaries from the launch date of the prototype, or its first exhibition at a boat show. The Piper class, for instance, started the clock with the prototype in 1966. Strictly speaking, this is wrong. A prototype is just a prototype, even if it is later accepted into the class. And if you have two prototypes, they are merely sister ships. Consequently, it is necessary to have three or more boats on the water in compliance with a common rule before you have a one-design, as the term is universally understood. And, since one-designs are contextualised by racing, 'day one' is when they sail together in an organised competition.[808]

The question of 'priority' in the timeline of invention is always fraught with caveats and vulnerable to challenge. As to the question of the first one-design, the Water Wags of Dublin Bay usually lay claim to this honour, with the double-ended 1886 Design. The 'current' Water Wag design is a much larger boat dating from 1900. However, it is arguable that the Irish have lost out yet again, this time to the Scots, and not just by a year or so, but by more than half a century.[809] The YRA minutes suggest that "*the new sport* (of one-design racing) *was developed in 1896 and in that year a number of 8-ton yachts were built on the Solent and called the Solent One Design Class*".[810] This was, of course, before the Internet.

Cavendish-Scott-Bentinck One Design

William Henry Cavendish-Scott-Bentinck (1768-1854), Marquis of Titchfield and the 4th Duke of Portland, was married to Henrietta, a coal heiress from Kilmarnock, descended from Robert the Bruce, perhaps disingenuously, nominated as 'Scotland's first yachtsman' in these pages.

Sir Henry was a remarkable character in the 'improver' mould, turning his hand to farming, estate management, industrial development, social reform and maritime affairs.[811] He bought the Fullarton Estate to facilitate coal exports from the seams he had acquired through marriage to Henrietta. Sir Henry then tabled a bill in parliament to make Troon harbour a commercial port. This bill is notable in the annals of government legislation as the fastest ever to pass through the labyrinth of the British Parliament; the honourable members were celebrating the Battle of Trafalgar and disinclined to bicker over Henry's plans. Sir Henry presented another Act to authorize a railway from Kilmarnock to Troon (the first in Scotland), then another to authorise the export of coal from the harbour. Troon's coal exports made it one of busiest small ports on the West Coast.[812]

As an experienced yachtsman, Sir Henry saw the possibilities of Troon for boatbuilding. He established a sawmill and boatyard in 1810. Initially, he built his own boats, but as they performed well, his yard took on other work and grew to become a notable builder of fine ships. Sir Henry was a generous patron of naval architecture and a capable designer in his own right. Working in association with his friend, Sir William Symonds (1782-1856), he devoted generous quantities of time and money to the advancement of sailing ship design, see Chapter 5.

It was said that "*No one did more than he, possibly no one did as much, to make boat-sailing popular on the Clyde.*" Certainly, Sir Henry's enthusiasm and hospitality were legendary. Every summer, while holding office as Commodore of the Royal Northern Yacht Club (1834-1853), he and his extravagant entourage would debunk from his ancestral home in Welbeck, Nottinghamshire, to his summer estate at Troon.[813] In the 1830s, he built a fleet of identical 5-tonners, designed in-house, for the use of his Scottish guests.[814] When Sir Henry was 'at home' there might be 40 visiting yachts in the little harbour.

James Meikle wrote: "*The Troon yard was established by himself primarily for the building of brigs and schooners to carry coals dug from his own pits to Ireland. As yachting increased in popularity, he enjoyed laying down in it a yacht occasionally for himself. In this way were built a beautiful brig called the Pantaloon, the ketch Clown, the cutter Mother Goose, and a number of rather smart 5-tonners for private racing.*"[815]

Sir Henry's 40-ton cutter, *Mother Goose*, was the mothership for the little squadron.[816] The 5-tonners were said to be quite good-looking for their day, nicely sheered, fairly sharp-bowed with an easy entry and fast. The yachts carried running topmasts, and in light weather 'quite goodly-sized square-headed topsails'. They were ballasted internally with 'iron bars'. No drawings have survived, but the best 5-tonners of the period were over-canvassed little 30-footers, with minimal accommodation.

As the Duke was a keen student of yacht design, his boats were state-of-the-art. Like the pioneering 'Fleet of the Neva' made available for the gratification of the aristocracy in Russia a century before, this little fleet was maintained regardless of cost. There is no doubt that the Duke could afford it, he was one of the wealthiest men in Britain. And, as the son of the Prime Minister, one of the most influential.

Sir Henry was enlightened and socially progressive by the standards of the time.[817] On occasion, he joined his sailors, boatbuilders and apprentices aboard the 5-tonners. Indeed, he shared the rustic pack-lunches of bread, cheese and ale which were always a popular feature of his 'day-racing package'. When not taking an active part on board, Sir Henry would scout for talent among his seamen, identifying who was ripe for promotion to his famous flyers and speedy Admiralty prototypes. He "*believed the modern gospel of efficiency, and nothing troubled him more than bungling in a boat.*"[818]

The 'Neva' line of semantic argument, see Chapter 11, would say that this was not a proper one-design, as the yachts were the toys of a wealthy man and his fleet of clones did not enjoy the administrative trappings of an organised class. However, administrative trappings and 'club culture' are perhaps uniquely valued by the English; other parts of the yachting world may see things differently. No matter how Sir Henry's modest fleet of sailboats was managed, the boats were built specifically to foster competitive sport, a 'fitness for purpose' that is the very essence of one-design racing.

Sir Henry was ever seeking improvements in performance and redesigning his yachts. The 5-tonner programme surely fertilised his many innovations, while repair and maintenance work on the yachts would have kept the men busy in slack periods too. As the story goes, Sir Henry imported a 'fin-keeler' from London to benchmark the performance of the 5-tonners. This boat was so broad and shallow it was called the *Skate*. The *Skate* ended up as a garden ornament at Fullarton House in Troon.

In his twilight years, Sir Henry retired to the family seat in Nottinghamshire, where he continued his experiments in yacht design with even smaller boats and test models on the lake at Welbeck Abbey. On 9th October 1823, the following advertisement appeared: "*To Shipbuilders and others: To Let, for such term of years as may be agreed upon: that large and commodious and well-established shipbuilding yard at Troon Harbour, belonging to His Grace the Duke of Portland.*" This long-forgotten yard was one of the most important early centres of design development on the Clyde.[819]

With the passage of years, and only the bare bones of a story handed down, it is easy to reinterpret history in a modern social context. Even so, there is surely something rather wonderful about Sir Henry having his workforce out on the water, fired-up, racing 'round the cans', no quarter asked – no quarter given, just for the hell of it.[820] It seems to have been a rare gesture of inclusiveness, half-a-century before the Yacht Racing Association, formed in London in 1875, reserved the sport for gentlemen. And it was a million miles away from the stifling social conventions that existed elsewhere through the 19th century.

Watson 19ft One Design Class

The 19ft Watson One Design is another class that jumps the gun on the Water Wags, albeit by a more debatable margin in this instance.[821] The Clyde Canoe and Lugsail Club approached G. L. Watson to draft a small one-design in 1886. Watson was unenthusiastic, but after his valued client,

James Coats, put in a word, the G. L. Watson office readily complied. R. McAlister and Sons of Dumbarton, at that time a noted canoe-yawl builder, constructed the first three, named *Red*, *White* and *Blue*.

Three more were built the following year and one more boat joined the fleet in 1888.[822] Finally, yet another three were built in 1891, this time for the West of Scotland Boat Club.[823] So with ten boats in total, this was a significant design. However, it is unlikely that they sailed regularly as a combined fleet, if at all. These one-design boats are usually described as belonging to the 19ft RCYC Class. They were not 17/19s and were too big to measure within the 1894 17/19 Rule.

Watson 23ft Royal Clyde Yacht Club One Design Class

The Royal Clyde 23ft One Designs were cutter-rigged, square-sterned 4-tonners of 23ft LWL, designed by G. L. Watson and built by McAlister. *Thistle* and *Mayflower* (later renamed *Rose*) were ordered as club-boats for the RCYC in 1890. *Volunteer*, a 23-footer to similar lines, was launched in the same year for Robert Wylie. This boat was built lighter and to a higher standard with diagonal planking and fitted with a centreboard. A third boat, *Shamrock*, was built to the original specification for the RCYC in 1894. The club-boats were kept on moorings, close inshore, off the clubhouse at Hunter's Quay and proved popular with members.

Watson 'One Design' 1-Raters

After his Irish commission, G. L. Watson again muddied the waters of the one-design ethos in 1895 with a batch-build for his Clyde clients. In May of that year, an initial consignment of 'Clyde 1-raters' arrived in Greenock from Cowes, via a Clyde Shipping Company steamer, and from there, they were towed round to Gourock Bay. The first three new boats enjoying priority shipping on an Allen-owned shipping line were: *Lynette*, Mr Henry Allan; *Nita*, R. G. Allan; and *Vanda*, Mr R. S. Allan. Another five arrived shortly afterwards for more well-known names in Clyde yachting: *Era*, Mr George Moir; *Tiree*, Mr J. Stewart Clark; *Lucifer*, Mr George Coats (Ayr); *Corbie*, Mr Geo. Smith, junior; and *Vis*, Mr R. Clark.

These eight one-design Watson boats were built by Sibbick of Cowes. Sibbick's yard was particularly efficient in the art of building 'down to cost' and he comfortably underbid the established Scottish boatbuilders.[824] The Sibbick boats attracted considerable interest. They were lightly built of cedar, long-ended, with a narrow canoe-body and a fin and bulb keel. They were long for the rating and of particularly light displacement.

The Glasgow Herald noted that "*the class is new to the Clyde, but as all the owners are leading yachtsmen, the fleet is rightly expected to obtain a prominent place in regatta programmes.*" However, the eight one-designs would not have things all their own way on the water as additional boats had been built by other designers and builders. There was Mr P. M. Ingles' *Evoe* from Fife, and John Mackenzie, the Sandbank sailmaker, had commissioned his own design from McAlister's.

The one-design experiment encouraged yachting correspondents to extol all the usual virtues of concept, trusting that the new class would "*bring out the merits of the men rather than of the boats, so that the forthcoming season should witness a series of hard contests between amateurs, every one of whom has already earned a reputation for seamanship and skill*". However, it was conceded that "*should the boats not after the Watson design take part in many of the fixtures, the importance and point of the struggle would probably be shifted back to a question of relative speed from the various designs.*"

As events transpired, Messrs Inglis and Mackenzie did not have an opportunity to match up with the Watson boats, which only engaged in informal racing at Hunter's Quay and Skelmorlie, where the members of the 'Allan's Club', essentially a private clique, had summer residences. A couple of years later, in 1897, we find the odd surviving 'Clyde 1-Rater' competing in a class described as 'yachts not exceeding 4 old-rating', together with the old 30-linear-raters.

Clyde 20-ton One Design Class

After this initiative, there was a hiatus in one-design interest until Mylne became involved in an owner-driven project at the turn-of-the-century. The handsome Clyde 20-ton One Design Class was established in 1899 when a group of enthusiasts met at the Royal Clyde to discuss common ambitions for a new medium-sized class of cruiser-racer. The prospective owners sought the usual trinity of speed, robustness and comfortable cruising accommodation. This was the period when the Scots had begun to rebel against the types of boat 'fostered upon them' by the rating rules of the Yacht Racing Association (YRA) in London.

Alfred Mylne attended the meeting in an advisory capacity. He was the 'designer of the moment' with a sequence of successful designs in the smaller restricted classes. His design proposal was for an elegant one-design 20-Tonner. The assembled yachtsmen were clearly impressed, as Mylne left the meeting with commissions for an initial five boats to be built at his family's yard, the Bute Slip Dock.

The dimensions of the new class were: LOA 50ft; LWL 35ft; beam 11ft; draft 8ft; 10-tons of ballast, all external lead on the keel. These would be fine, roomy, cruising boats, with 6-feet headroom in the saloon amidships. They were rigged as pole-masted cutters carrying 1,700ft^2 of sail with 900ft² in the mainsail, 575ft² in the fore-triangle, and setting a 225ft² topsail. When the first batch debuted in the 1899 season, they were much admired, and in their first competitive outings, they were also seen to possess an excellent turn of speed.

The class was effectively a Clyde one-design, but they also raced and cruised extensively in the Irish Sea and around the Western Isles. This was just the right size of yacht for races to Belfast Lough and Dublin Bay, where they also performed well round-the-cans in local regattas. The new class enjoyed welcome prominence during the 1900 Clyde Fortnight, as that year the Big Class racing yachts had failed to show up. The lively 20-tonners attracted a generous ream of column inches in the newspapers and entertained the informed public with some of the keenest matches of the season.

Over the course of that season's points competition, Charles McIver's *Avalon*, built by MacAlister & Sons at Dumbarton took the honours, Mathew Greenlee's provocatively named *Noyra,* built by P. Jones & Son of Gourock was second and *Vagrant* third. *Noyra* contrived to hijack most of the prizes on offer, and the crew of A. F. Maclaren's Jones-built, *Snarleyow*, had their hands on the silverware too.[825] B. W. Morris's *Rosemary*, another new boat from MacAlister & Sons, appeared to have been uncompetitive, but there would certainly not have been anything wrong with the boat.

Innellan Corinthian Y. C. One Design or 17/15s

The Innellan Corinthian Yacht Club is an impressive-sounding association. However, the village does not have a sheltered harbour and the offshore anchorage is unpopular. From the records, it is not clear how much, if any, racing ever took place directly off Innellan. Certainly, some of the district's most enthusiastic yachtsmen had homes there, but they generally raced with the Royal Clyde at Hunter's Quay and in the Holy Loch.

The Innellan Club was conceived in the winter of 1895 with modest ambitions to establish a reasonably priced one-design for local racing. *"It is intended that these boats will form the foundation of a new sailing club, with headquarters at Innellan, the promoters of which are in hopes that the class will, in addition, receive countenance from the other clubs by occasionally having a line given them on their racing programmes."*[826] As events transpired, the club would turn out to be more in the nature of a class association than a proper yacht club.

Nonetheless, the meeting was successful in bringing like-minded enthusiasts to the table, but as often happens when sailors get together, the end result was not in line with the desired outcome. An unresolved difference of opinion meant that some boats were built to plans by Messrs J. & H. M. Paterson, by Paul Jones of Greenock, and a similar number were built to a slightly different design by John Ninian of Largs. The latter survived a fire in John Ninian's steaming shop during construction.

Folkard records that the boats constructed by the two builders were different in design, but notes from the office of the late Peter Collyer show the two boatyards building to the same design, with whatever differences emerged simply a matter of the execution.[827] In any case, two similar but not identical one-design classes, together fielding 19 boats, appeared simultaneously to sail under the burgee of the Innellan club.[828] Apparently, keen racing ensued, despite a small, but surely perplexing, difference in performance between the two types.

Mr Herbert Brown's *Lola* had the best of the averages in 1896, with 19 firsts, 6 seconds, and 1 third from 34 starts. *Lola* was one of the Largs-built boats, which proved to be a little quicker than their Greenock equivalents. Intriguingly, while three more owners built to this faster design in 1897, the final boat, built in 1898, was to the Greenock model. Ninian built nine 'fast' boats while Jones built 14 'slow' ones, giving a combined total of 23. See list in Appendix 3.

"The new Innellan Club is going to be strong in members as well as boats, and I understand that their first year-book is to be a very neat production, embellished with the racing flags of the members depicted in colour."[829] In fact, the combined fleet was large enough after the first season to disperse into the two centres where members lived. The Largs section (Division No.1) comprised 12 boats and the Gourock section (Division No. 2) boasted 14. As these numbers do not tally with the local boatbuilders, the two fleets were surely mixed, see Appendix 3.

All the boats from both builders were clinker-built to a good standard with larch and yellow pine planking on elm frames, copper-fastened throughout. The critical dimensions were as follows: LOA 17ft; LWL 15ft; beam 5ft 3"; draft 2ft. 6"; 104 cwt lead-ballasted keel; sail area 150/200ft². They were securely decked-over with a full foredeck, aft-deck and 10½" side-decks, leaving a small oval cockpit within high comings, typical of the era. The new boats all displayed unique sail numbers on the mainsail, one of the first Clyde classes to adopt this sensible requirement.

The specifications for the class required that they be cheap, fast, and safe. However, after their first season, the owners agreed that the class could be altered to perform better in the typical light to moderate airs of the Clyde in mid-summer. They were fat little boats that required more sail-area and more grip on the water. Consequently, the entire class was fitted with deeper keels and bowsprits, and the sail area was increased from 150 to 200ft². The revised drawings show the mast to be well-raked, but very far forward, so unless the original design was una-rigged, it would not have been possible to set a jib without a bowsprit.[830]

"I remember being taken out in our little yacht Nada. This was a sloop, one of the early one-designs, the Innellan class. She was about 19ft-long [sic] brown-varnished, gaff-rigged with mainsail and jib. Nada was named after the heroine of Rider Haggard's novel Nada the Lily. The trip, I remember my father taking me more than once, was a quick run down the loch before a north-westerly breeze to bring us to Strone Buoy by about 5 o'clock in the afternoon, so that we might see the 'Isle of Skye' pass across the mouth of the loch on her way back from her daily callings to Lochgilphead. Then we would put about for the beat back up the loch against the wind, an enterprise that would sometimes take a long time to complete if the wind died away too soon." Summer of 1920 at 'Anchorage Villa', Kilmun.[831]

Holy Loch One Design Classes

The Holy Loch One Design tag has been ascribed to four different classes. Folkard describes the formation of the best-documented iteration. This class was first mooted at the 1898 Spring General Meeting of the Holy Loch Sailing Club, held as it usually was, in Glasgow.[832] Members agreed to adopt a one-design class of small centre-boarders, based on lines by Alfred Mylne. The dimensions were: LOA 16ft 6"; LWL 16ft; Beam 6ft. 6"; (6ft at L.W.L); freeboard 1ft 6"; steel centreboard and internal lead ballast 2 cwt; sail-area, 160ft²; foresail, 40ft². The class-rules required all the boats to be built over the same set of frames. The crew was limited to three hands for each boat. The new class was mainly used for evening racing on the loch.

Perusing the Mylne Design List, the only boat of approximately the same size, and designed in the same period, was: *"1898, Olive, Design No.14, centreboard, 16ft 6" LOA"*. We assume *Olive* to have been the second of four Holy Loch ODs, built by McGruer's. These attractive little daysailers were among the first boats which appear on the McGruer's build-list. The full fleet comprised: *Tatiana, Olive, Winsome* and *Gollywog*. The first three were launched in 1898 and a further example followed in 1900.

These were some of the earliest boats built by the McGruer brothers at Rutherglen. In 1903, Ewing McGruer moved to Alex Robertson's yard in Sandbank and then on to Smith's at Tighnabruaich the following year. He would establish his own yard on the west shore of the Gareloch at Clynder in 1914. In time, the little village became synonymous with the McGruer brand and exceptional craftsmanship in wood.

The Mylne Holy Loch ODs appear to have raced through the 1898, 1899 and 1900 seasons with the 'paper trail' disappearing after that date. The drawings show an extremely fat and friendly little vessel, not unlike an American catboat.[833] The absence of a thwart and substitution of a small perch at the front end of the centreboard case is of interest. There is no information on construction, but most dayboats were clinker-built in that period. This was cheap, and crucially for a boat of this size, light and stiff.

However, the Mylne design-list also contains the following entry which describes a very different boat to that which appears in Folkard's: *1903, Sunbeam, Design No.76; Holy Loch Redwing One Design, Sloop; No. of Yachts built – 4; Date 1903; LOA 24.75ft; LWL 16.00ft; beam 5.15ft; draft 3.15ft.* This later design was built by Alexander Robertson's boatyard at Sandbank. The yard's build-list for 1903 contains the following entries covering builds Nos.29, 30, 31 & 32. *Holy Loch Redwing: 4 built; LOA 24ft 7½"; LWL 16ft; Beam: 5ft 1½"; Depth: 3ft to top of coving board to underside of wood keel; Keel, lead, 15 cwt.*[834]

This newer design was for a miniature keelboat, with proportions not unlike the Piper which followed 63 years later – same LOA, same LWL, but a foot narrower. These little yachts had an elegant spoon bow and a counter stern. As to construction, the bottom planking was of pitch pine and the topsides were executed in cedar for the first three boats, and yellow pine for the final build. Depending on batch, these two materials could have had similar specific gravity. Sails: lugsail and jib. The delivered cost, on the water and ready to sail was £89 (£11,000) each. The four boats were: *Sunbeam*, G. P. Collins (the only boat listed in Lloyd's), *Coraline*, *Diana*, and finally, *Redwing II*. These exquisite little yachts rank among Mylne's most beautifully proportioned designs from any era. It is, therefore, a tragedy that they have been entirely forgotten.

One final Holy Loch 'redwing' class, which should not be confused with the older boats, was formed by the three red-sailed clinker dinghies, designed and built by G. & A. Waddell for Leonard Hinge. These were a gift to the HLSC club boats in the 1960s and were also tagged Holy Loch One Designs. They were based on a dinghy owned by Sheila Hinge, who as a young woman, had been one of the best Dragon One Design sailors on the Clyde. See Holy Loch OD lists in Appendix 3.

CODA: 1890s Match-racing Pairs

In 1893, G. L. Watson would design the 23-ft LWL *Gipsy* and *Brunette* for James Coats, as an identical match-racing pair. There must have been earlier examples of this approach, which could have been a precursor of the one-design idea. A 'one design' sailing yacht or dinghy, as defined in these pages, requires at least three boats in commission and on the racecourse at the same time.

Gipsy and *Brunette* were 23ft LWL and 36ft LOA, 7/8th planked and beautifully finished. With their slightly comic clipper bows, they were dated even when launched, nevertheless, they seem to have been successful. They were built side-by-side in James Adam's yard in Gourock. Contemporary images show them to have been dumpy little boats of the sort that roll out of the water when heeled, rather than settling in and extending their waterline.

The two yachts tagged along in tow behind Coats' steam yacht, *Iris*. *"One of the sort of 'side shows' of the Clyde season was the private match sailing of Mr James Coats's two handsome little tan-sailed cutters, Gipsy and Brunette. As like as two peas, and well matched, Mr Coats got a lot of sport by regularly pitting the two against each other."* Watson and Coats, among others, both tried their hand at match racing. As for crews, the pair *"manned, too, by men out of his* (Coats) *steamer, Iris, they were sailed with great keenness."*

Other owners saw the attraction of private racing in matched pairs. Mr Bullough's yacht, *Rhouma*, was accessorised in 1895 with two Fife-built lugsail centreboarders of *"the newer and higher-class examples of this now popular type, suggestive of superior power and speed.* They were clinker-built of the best mahogany, with metalwork of polished brass, over-canvassed and equipped with *"bowsprits of considerable length"*.[835]

Coats ultimately sold *Gipsy* to the son of his skipper, Captain Duncan, for a shilling (£5).[836] Duncan, long in the service of Coats as Master of *Marjorie*, *Gleniffer* and others, had looked after the match-racing pair. French yacht-builder, Hubert Stagnol, who previously reincarnated William Fife's archaic *Seabird* and *Fyne* in modern materials, is building a new boat to this 130-year-old G. L. Watson design.[837] See list in Appendix 3.

Coda: Fife and the Early Irish One Designs

Scottish designers, and particularly William Fife, were popular with Bangor yachtsmen. The Bangor Corinthian Yacht Club had a passion for one-design racing, which of course Fife did not. Nevertheless, through the 1890s he designed several such classes. However, they were mostly built on the other side of the North Channel as the Fife yard was busy with larger, more challenging and more profitable yachts. The *"striking element of fair play and real sporting feeling in the Bangor Corinthian"* was notable. *"He seeks not to plant himself upon his friend's weather bow by obtaining what he may believe to be a superior design, and this praiseworthy desire to keep up the class has its reward in promoting the very best racing in the British Isles"*.[838]

The Irish Corinthians first committed to one-design racing with a 25-foot one-design class. However, it appears that these boats had been expensive to build, and ongoing maintenance costs were burdensome.[839] Consequently, the club replaced the 25-footers in 1889 with a batch of Fife 2½-raters. These raters were now on the market in 1891.[840] The *Yachtsman* reported that the club had adopted an even smaller one-design class, once again designed by William Fife.

The new 18-footer design was described as *"by no means a thing of beauty, everything being sacrificed for speed"*, but the magazine later referred to the finished boats as *"fine, seaworthy little things, with plenty of displacement for their size"*. This was a flattering take on a quartet of fat little barrels that would have been out of their depth in open competition. The first four were built by Robertson of Sandbank. *Helen*, *Mosquito*, *Ulah* and *Miss Mollie*, were delivered by steamer to Belfast. They were later joined by *Antelope* and *Miss Peggy*.

In 1897, the Bangor Corinthians reorganised their one-design racing to support three classes. William Fife seems to have had a hand in all of them. The No.1 class (25ft LWL, 37ft LOA) was *"an able little sea-boat, quite capable of carrying her owner to Strangford"*. They had unusually flared topsides – not normally an asset for boats sailed on their ear in heavy weather. The eight yachts, all named after birds, were built by Hilditch at Carrickfergus. One of the class, *Tern*, was restored in 2015.[841]

Fife also designed the No.2 class (15ft LWL and 24ft 6" LOA). These were built by Hutcheson of Belfast in 1897. As for the 'small' No.3 class, Fife ceded the details to Linton Hope. They ended up larger than Fife's No.3s, although they were indeed cheaper. The 'Jewels of Cultra' (17ft LWL and 24ft LOA) were built by Roberts in Belfast.[842]

Other Scottish commissions of this type included two separate Dublin Bay one-designs, designed by Fife in 1898 and 1892 for different clients. G. L. Watson designed a very odd-looking 1-Rater one-design in 1893 for Queenstown, and Alfred Mylne had a rare opportunity during this period to show his skill with a Dublin Bay OD (21 ft LWL and 32ft LOA) in 1904.

[805] The Complete Yachtsman, Brooke Heckstall-Smith and Captain E. Du Boulay, 1912.

[806] Yacht and Boat Sailing, 9th Edition, Dixon Kemp (Revised and partly re-written by Brooke Heckstall Smith), 1900. Contribution by G. L. Watson.

[807] The Class Association of the Laser dinghy cited here appears to have rather let the side down by allowing additional stiffening in boats built by one of the licensed builders in Australia. *"In late April, LaserPerformance released documentation and correspondence between ILCA management and builder Performance Sailcraft Australia, which outlines construction issues whereby PSA allegedly produced non-compliant boats from 2006 to 2015."* Laser Class Builder Battle Escalates, Dave Powlison, Sailing World, 30th April 2019.

[808] The Piper prototype, *Sandpiper*, is not identical and has never sailed in class. The anniversary of the class as a one-design should date from 1967 when 7 boats raced on the Clyde.

[809] Sixty-eight double-ended Water Wags were built between 1887 and 1900. One survived, but it is not part of the current fleet embalmed in the Maritime Museum of Ireland. Since 1900, there have been 114 of the larger, transom-sterned Water Wags built-in Ireland with more than 50% surviving. Water Wags were also built and raced in other locations in the UK and in our former colonies. The 1900 class is the oldest active one-design dinghy.

[810] Minute by Minute, the Story of the Royal Yachting Association 1875-1982, G. Fairley, 1983.

[811] *"While unable to influence the course of agrarian change in the adverse demand circumstances before 1760, the improvers arguably had a profound impact on the response of the supply side between 1760 and 1820."* T. C. Smout, 2012.

[812] Marr College, Ayrshire, website uploads.

[813] Welbeck passed into the hands of the Bentinck family in the 18th century.

[814] Yachting and Yachtsmen, W. Dodgson Bowman, 1927. The references are to a *"little fleet"*, so we may reasonably think in terms of at least 4 or 5 boats.

[815] Leaves from the Logbook of an Old Clyde Journalist, XXXV, James Meikle, The Yachtsman, 15th August 1925.

[816] Other versions have the *Mother Goose* as 70 or 80-tons.

[817] The Death of the Duke of Portland, Nottinghamshire Guardian, 30th March 1854.

[818] Yachting and Yachtsmen, W. Dodgson Bowman, 1927.

[819] The Troon shipyard became the Ailsa Shipbuilding & Engineering Co in 1886. The 3rd Marquess of Ailsa (1847-1938) had established the Culzean Steam Launch and Yacht Works in 1870. From there it moved to Girvan in 1883 and subsequently to Sir Henry's old yard in Troon in 1886.[819] The Marquess of Ailsa was another well-known yachtsman. Like Sir Henry, he was an amateur designer. The Troon yard finally closed in 2000.

[820] William's gregarious character is in striking contrast to his son, the 5th Duke, an eccentric recluse and the inspiration for Mr Badger in Kenneth Grahame's Wind in the Willows.

[821] Ewen Kennedy has this to say: *"I am aware that the Dublin Water Wags are also contenders for the title of first-ever one-designs, being first proposed by Thomas B Middleton in September 1886. The first boat, Eva, based on Mr Middleton's model, was built for him by McAlisters."* Ewen has generously offered the Irish a dead heat. However, as we need three boats on the water to make a one-design class and just a single Water Wag caught the last days of summer in 1886, so the class dates from 1887. In any case, the matter is moot if we recognise the Duke of Portland's 1830s one-designs.

[822] The Clyde 17/19-foot Class, Scottish Boating Blog, Ewen Kennedy, December 2010.

[823] Est. 1866. Now the Royal West of Scotland Amateur Boat Club.

[824] Yachting Notes, The Glasgow Herald, 13th May 1895.

[825] This yacht is listed as *Snarleyow* in the 1901 Lloyds Yacht Register. Clydeships use the name *Snarley Yow* and suggest that the Lloyds spelling is in error.

[826] Clyde, The Yachtsman, 17th October 1895.

[827] List of yachts and build details contained in notes from the office of the late Peter Collyer – marine engineer, boatbuilder and doyen of post-war small-boat sailing in Scotland.

[828] Sailing Boats from Around the World, the one-design and restricted classes, Henry Colman Folkard, 1906.

[829] Clyde, The Yachtsman, 2nd April 1896.

[830] The drawings in Folkard were originally provided by Messrs Paterson.

[831] For ten years, this family from Lenzie rented 'Anchorage Villa' in Kilmun. The house has been in the author's family since 1948.

[832] Sailing Boats from Around the World, Henry Colman Folkard, 1906.

[833] The beam is quoted at 5.15ft, but on measuring the drawing it's more like 6.8ft, which is close to the Mylne proposal.

[834] The Mylne dimensions are fractional, rendered approximately in decimals, while the Robertson's are in fractions – the Robertson's are presumed correct.

[835] Clyde, The Yachtsman, 5th December 1895.

[836] The Irish restoration, *Peggy Brawn*, is a slightly scaled-up sequel to this design, and we can safely assume that the restoration programme incurred costs of rather more than a shilling.

[837] G.L. Watson website, current projects.

[838] Bangor Corinthian Sailing Club, The Yachtsman, October 1891.

[839] *Bedouin, Halcyone, Fedora, Nita,* and *Primula* were built by the Hutcheson, Hilditch and McKeon boatyards. The Bangor Corinthians maintained their one-design emphasis. They *"prudently disposed of these craft in such a way that now not one remains upon the station"*.

[840] The boats were: *Cora, Shibbeal, Magic, Phryne* and *Brenda*. Fife also designed a 2½ rater OD class for the Clyde. The Yachtsman, 9th May 1891.

[841] Baby Fife Sails Again, Nigel Sharp, Classic Boat, website, undated.

[842] *Amethyst, Beryl, Coral, Iolite, Onyx, Opal, Ruby* and *Sapphire*.

One design 18-footer, Fife 1891, built by Alex Robertson, Sandbank, for Bangor Corinthians

Clyde One Design 1-rater, Watson, 1895   *Brunette*, Watson, 1893

Innellan ODs, J. & H. M. Paterson, 1895   Image: W. Harold Fraser

417

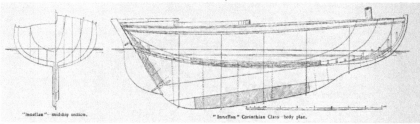

Innellan One Design, J. & H. M. Paterson, 1895   Images Folkard

Enid, 19ft Watson, Helensburgh, ca.1887   One Design 1-rater, G. L. Watson, 1895

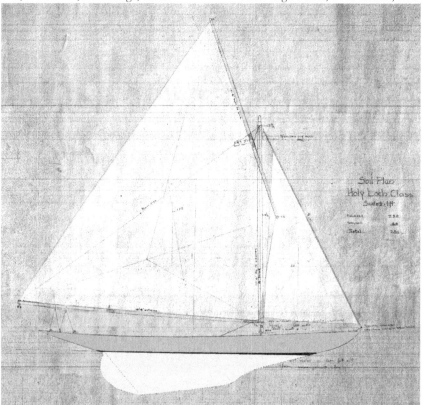

Holy Loch Redwing One Design, Alfred Mylne, 1903   Mylne Yacht Design

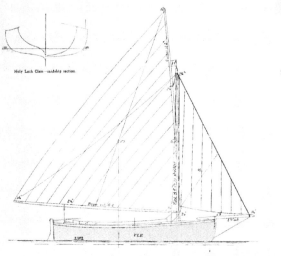

Holy Loch One Design, 16' 6" dinghy, Alfred Mylne, 1898   Image: Folkard

Tigris, Clyde 20-tonner One Design, Alfred Mylne, 1899   Image: RNCYC collection

Tigris is still sailing on the Mediterranean. On the recommendation of Mylne, and in order to reduce the number of expensive professional crewmen required, the Clyde 20-tonners adopted a more modern Bermudian rig with a club-footed jib in 1930

Gipsy and Brunette, G. L. Watson, 1893, match racing pair, and SY *Iris*, 1892   Image: W. J. Finlayson

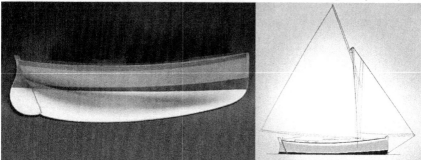

19-ft One Design, G. L. Watson, 1886, for Clyde Canoe & Lugsail Club, West of Scotland Boat Club

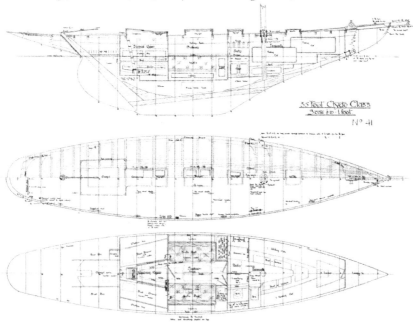

Clyde 20-ton Class (35ft LWL), Alfred Mylne, 1899   Mylne Yacht Design

Chapter 21: Local Heroes

Winning or losing is satisfying when you beat or lose to equally advantaged competitors, dissatisfying when the outcome is predetermined by differences in equipment, training time, technical support, funding etc. When the outcome is more important than the game, the game is no longer a game. Stuart Walker [843]

The second group of one-design classes, once popular on the Clyde and in some cases still active, are the more recognisably modern, Bermudian-rigged yachts, which appeared after the Great War. In the wider context of local classes sailed in the UK, the inter-war day-sailers are of the same generation as Solent Sunbeams, and the Victory on the South Coast of England, and the post-WW2 Piper would be equivalent to the Daring. These boats were intended for 'beercan racing' with family crews, although the Piper's big genoa and even bigger spinnaker challenged that assumption.

Scottish Islands One Design Class

The Scottish Islands Class was introduced at the 1928 meeting of the Clyde Yacht Clubs Conference. The seemingly gratuitous 'Scottish' prefix distinguished it from the Islands Class of Belfast Lough built by the McGruer yard. By this date, the surviving boats in the 19/24 fleet were becoming tired and their designs, some dating back to 1897, were undeniably old-fashioned. In the late 1920s, a decade of metre-boat development had established the superiority of a very different model. Before the classic yacht revival, owners did not spend lavishly on restorations or rebuilds.

While the members of the CYCC selection committee did not request specific new design proposals, they cast their net wide, at least among the 'Alfreds'. They considered the following existing designs: Alfred Westmacott's Sea View Mermaid and Solent Sunbeam – both built by Woodnutts at Bembridge, Alfred Mylne's Belfast Lough River Class, and an as-yet-unbuilt 1927 design languishing on Mylne's drawing board. At this time, Mylne had the successful Kingston 21-footers and the Belfast Star Class in his favour. Westmacott, an alumnus of Glasgow University, had the popular X One Design to illustrate his credentials. The thoughtful consideration of South Coast designs suggests a refreshing lack of national chauvinism, even if the final balance swung in favour of Mylne.

The new boat would be a strict one-design. Mylne conceived a fully decked two or three-berth fractionally rigged auxiliary Bermudian sloop of carvel construction. Alfred followed the brief to keep costs as low as possible. Perhaps this led to the erroneous belief that the yachts had iron keels. That, however, would not have been an acceptable economy for Mylne.[844] Possibly the unique sailing style of the legendary Herbert Thom, gung-ho at high angles of heel, consolidated the misapprehension.

Mylne did not skimp on sail-area either. The working jib was modest, but a powerful mainsail more than made up for that. However, when the breeze got up the mast tended to invert, the sail shape went to hell and the long boom became a liability. Downwind, with no kicking strap, and with the spinnaker set inside the forestay, or left in the bag in the early days, the rig was as unbalanced as a catboat; situations where Thom came into his own.

Ironically, Mylne criticised Johan Anker's Dragon for having too little sail when it arrived in Scottish waters a few years later, with only a high-cut working jib to fill the fore-triangle.[845] However, the two classes were never really in competition. The Dragon might be a foot longer than the Scottish Islands class, but it looks smaller. The Dragon is a much slimmer, more easily driven boat with a higher prismatic coefficient and a more efficient rig, particularly after modernisation in 1945.[846]

"The design selected is that of Messrs Alfred Mylne & Co, Glasgow and the racers will be of the following dimensions: overall, 28ft 6in, waterline 20ft; beam 7ft; draft 4ft 6in; sail area 420²ft (Bermuda rig). Messrs Ratsey & Lapthorn will supply the sails. The boats are to be designed for auxiliary power, with side propellers and should any owner not desire to install an actual motor, he must still fit the propeller and shaft and carry an equivalent weight in the position corresponding to that of the motor." The Watermota 3hp was specified as standard with a 'one-design' propeller and shaft mandatory.

"The names of the prospective owners are Messrs Thos Dunlop, Jr & George Jackson, Dr J. McNaughton Christie, W. M. Dunn, and George Nisbit. It was originally stipulated that there should be a minimum number of six boats, and although it has been agreed to form the class with five, there is still a hope that other owners may come forward."[847] The spring of 1929 saw the first five boats, built by McGruer's, on the water. The subsequent six builds would be entrusted to the Mylne family's yard, the Bute Slip Dock. Alfred Mylne had taken over the day-to-day management of the Ardmaliesh yard in 1924, following the death of his brother Charles. The yard had never been very profitable, and one imagines that, with Alfred shuttling between Bute and his Glasgow office, efficiency did not improve. Alfred Mylne's design work did not enjoy the same premium as celebrity designers like G. L. Watson, neither

did his boatyard benefit from the efficiencies of William Fife III's quick-and-dirty, design-and-build production line.

The Clyde Clubs Conference formulated a tight set of class rules at the outset, with one set of building moulds approved initially. It appears that cost-controls left McGruer's with little profit from the first batch of boats, so Alfred's own yard was obliged to step in and take over production. This might seem like an instance of 'the biter bit', but Mylne was just collateral damage. Well-off syndicates with the leverage of batch orders, more often than not, chisel honest craftsmen to the bone. A second set of moulds was authorised, and fortunately, the same class-appointed measurer was able to oversee production in both yards.

Each year, the owners got together to decide on which sailmakers to bully for that season's orders and which anti-fouling composition to endorse. No haul-outs or surreptitious scrubbing sessions were allowed during the racing season. Some of these rules were adopted many years later in the 1960s, when the Piper One Design class association established their own interpretation of fair play. Like the Scottish Islands, the Piper's scrubbing limitations are honoured in the breach.

Ewan Kennedy records that Herbert Thom initially declined to join the Islanders because he disliked the mandatory auxiliary engine, with the only opt-out possible involving an equivalent weight in the same place and a dummy propeller. After he swallowed his pride, Herbert trounced the homespun Scottish Islands fleet for six straight seasons, initially with *Gigha* and then *Westra*. When Thom eventually started to look for more serious competition, he quixotically rejected the obvious challenge of the Dragons, because they were "*of foreign design*". Herbert would instead subscribe to a new Robertson's built 6-metre.[848] This was the famous *Circe* which established David Boyd as a designer in his own right after the long years honing his craft in the Fife design office. Thom would return to the class post-WW2 with *Canna*. See list in Appendix 3.

Where are they now? No.1, *Westra*, was destroyed by fire during WW2. No.2, *Cara*, was repatriated from Wales in 1990 and restored by John Hill. She was then sold to Kevin O'Farrell in Eire in 2000. She is in excellent condition. No.3, *Bernera*, has been restored and is in good condition. Tom Webster keeps her on a mooring in upper Loch Fyne. No.4, *Stroma*, has been beautifully restored by Ewan Kennedy after he rescued her from the Scottish Maritime Museum. She is now lying at Cairnbaan and is for sale. No.5, *Sanda*, was converted into a cruiser. She was discovered in very poor condition in Hull by the Clyde Keel Boats Association. She is lying next to *Stroma* at Cairnbaan awaiting restoration. No.6, *Jura*, was rescued from the Lowestoft Academy of Traditional Boat Building by the Clyde Keelboats Association and is also at Cairnbaan in poor condition awaiting restoration.

No.7, *Fidra,* is owned by Ricky Standley and has also been converted into a cruiser. She is in poor condition and lies in a shed in Fairlie, awaiting restoration. No.8, *Iona,* was scuppered in the Clyde after lying at Hunterston for many years. No.9, *Gigha,* is owned by Scott Raeburn. She is lying outside in the yard at Port Bannatyne. She last sailed in 2015 and is in fair condition. No.10, *Canna,* is owned by Alastair Thom (Grandson of Herbert Thom). She was professionally restored by Adam Way in 2015/2016 and lies off the Loch Melfort Hotel in summer. No.11, *Isla,* is owned by Peter Wylie. She is in very good condition and lies at a mooring off the Royal Gourock Yacht Club. No.12, *Shona,* is a new boat, built by Richard Pierce in Cedar strip and epoxy in 2000. She is owned by Martin Webster and is based in upper Loch Fyne during the summer months. [849]

Gareloch One Design Class

The Gareloch class was proposed at a meeting of the Gareloch Yacht Club in October 1923. Locally based designer and boatbuilder Ewing McGruer Jr. was asked to come up with a good value-for-money daysailer. The following April, the first boat, *Athene,* was much in demand as prospective owners queued up to test this elegant new keelboat at Clynder. McGruer's production line was fast and efficient. The owners drew lots for their boats prior to painting. There were ten boats on the water for the club's opening regatta in June 1924: *Galatea, Athene, Dione, Ceres, Halcyone, Thalia, Iris, Hermes, Thia* and *Zoe.*[850]

The Garelochs were also built down to a price. This is not always equitable, nor indeed is it a recipe for longevity. Nevertheless, on a unit-cost budget of just £160 (£10,000) McGruer's work could not be faulted. The Garelochs are lightly built, but this has encouraged care and maintenance, and may counter-intuitively have ensured their survival. The author has not sailed a Gareloch for more than half a century, but in 1966 they were just lovely, and as is the way with classic boats these days, they are probably even better now.

Once the Gareloch contract was completed, the yard promptly set to work to build five more boats to the same design for the Royal Forth Yacht Club. In the remarkable time of just six weeks, *Spray* (now *Luna*), *Cockelroy* (now *Zephyrus*), *Fintra* (now *Catriona*), *Jean* (now *Circe*) and *Rosemary II* (now *Teal*) were ready for delivery by rail to the Forth where they would sail together as the Royal Forth One Design. A sixteenth boat, *Juno,* was built four years later and joined the fleet in 1928. Two Scottish fleets created an excellent inter-club dynamic for a time, with team-racing between the west and east coasts for the Barge Cup of 1934.

The class thrived for just a decade or so before the Dragon took Scottish sailors by storm. The glamorous Scandinavian laid waste to the local classes until increasing sophistication elevated the class out of existence in the 1970s. The Aldeburgh Yacht Club took advantage of this opportunity; their members were able to purchase several Gareloch O.D.s from the Royal Forth in 1937, along with others from Rhu. The McGruer design was an ideal replacement for the East Anglican's ageing Sibbick-designed Whitewings. This expatriate fleet of Garelochs and Royal Forth O.D.s – *Luna, Catriona, Thalia, Athene, Iris, Juno* and *Circe*, raced as a class on the River Alde both before and after WW2.

At the end of the 1955 season, however, the Scots had second thoughts and wanted their boats back. John Henderson, whose family had a long association with the class, organised the repatriation, sourcing yachts in Aldeburgh, the Forth and the 'star-buy' – the Gareloch attached to H.M.S. Conway in North Wales. When *Iris* returned from Aldeburgh in 1957, the combined class was complete to race together on the Gareloch for the first time, under the burgee of the Royal Northern Yacht Club.

The Garelochs have maintained this resurgence in recent decades. The complete fleet last raced together in 1984, but there are around 10 boats afloat most seasons. The Gareloch owners have organised reciprocal matches with the owners' associations of traditional one-designs in Ireland and Wales: the Dublin Bay Howth 17, the Fairy Class from Belfast, and the Fife OD of the Menai Straits. The Gareloch Class Championships are held in late July each year for the 50th Anniversary Cup, presented by the RNCYC in 1974.

Relatively Modern Classics

In the 1960s, local one-design keelboat fleets all around our coasts were struggling for survival against the rapid growth in light-weight centreboard classes. Club trots were cluttered with unloved and obsolete wooden keel-boats – hogged and strained, stained by rusting iron fastenings and marked by the nostalgic whiff of decaying garboards. Jack Holt and Ian Proctor, the established high priests of origami in waterproof plywood, had won over the middle-class with a family of cheap and cheerful racing dinghies. A new generation of small-boat builders now sought to expand design horizons and exploit this market. Roving trailer-sailors could take their boats to regional-level open meetings and national championships and make new friends and enjoy new waters.

During this period, the daysailer market on the Clyde was pretty much moribund. The 24ft Garelochs from 1924 were considered a quaint anachronism. The 28ft Scottish Islands class of 1929 had also waned. Even the Dragons were in decline, although that was more the result of an arms race than participation fatigue. However, the 21ft Loch Longs from 1937 still retained sufficient numbers to enjoy good racing. Signals were mixed, but most authorities doubted the wisdom of reviving the obsolete heavy-displacement model in new materials.

The 1960s can be seen in retrospect as a brief period during which time-served classic-yacht design expertise overlapped with early series production polyester construction. Three elegant dayboat classes were conceived in this period: the 5.5 Metre-derived Daring OD, designed in 1961 by Kiwi, Arthur Robb, Olin Stephen's Shields OD of 1963 in the USA, and David Boyd's series-produced Piper OD in 1967. These three transitional designs are all regarded as the epitome of elegance today.

Piper One Design Class[851]

William Fife III was not at all keen on one-designs and his disciple, David Boyd, did not disagree. It was therefore appropriate that when Boyd received the Piper commission from the new owners of Robertson's yard, he referenced the Fife O.D, one of Fife's few examples of the type; in this case produced as a favour for Peter Dickie, another of the master's protégés. Transposing the two boats, the sheerlines and freeboards are identical. The deckline is one and the same until the last two stations, where the Boyd development comes out a little wider.

The Piper shares the same dimensions, but it is not a copy. At this stage in his career, Boyd's style had diverged significantly from Fife's. Moreover, the primitive polyester construction technologies available in 1965 meant that the new Robertson's boat would have to be considerably heavier than the Fife OD. The Piper lines are therefore significantly fuller fore and aft. The keel is a little shorter and deeper and there is a 1960s square-toed rudder. Boyd's signature aesthetic is reflected in slightly flatter curves on the overhang profiles, and the retroussé counter popularised by the elegant 12mR sisterships *Sovereign* and *Kurrewa V*.

Beneath the styling, the essence of the Piper clearly springs from that very special period in sailing yacht design, now all of 90 years past. Intriguingly, the little boat bears more than a passing resemblance to G. L. Watson's *Britannia*, the beau idéal of classic yacht design. Adjusting the length-to-beam ratio, to reflect the difference in scale and make a meaningful comparison, there is a startling similarity in the two classic models demonstrating an unadulterated bloodline.

David Boyd was a notorious perfectionist, so inevitably the design phase of the programme overran. In November 1965, with the Earls Court Boat Show looming, Robertson's made a virtue of necessity and planked-up just one side of the hull. Thus, the prototype, *Sandpiper*, which presaged a GRP production boat, incongruously showcased the anatomy of time-honoured timber construction. No matter – in a letter to Boyd, John Nicholson, son and biographer of the great Charles E. Nicholson and no mean designer himself, enthused: *"Now I see, in this day and age of many odd conceptions, a GEM. I refer of course to your Piper OD. What a sweet thing she is. When I see your great artistry, it cheers me up no end."*

Sandpiper was launched at Sandbank on a typically cold bright spring day in 1966, a masterpiece perhaps, but eternally a niche product. The new boat was a step-up in performance and handling from long-established local one-designs of similar size, but from day one, it was clear that the future, in this market segment, would belong to light-displacement fin-keel yachts, with more nimble handling and much lower sheet loads. Nevertheless, the Piper was so pretty, it found a niche.

The process of reconfiguring *Sandpiper* for series production in fibreglass was carried out over the winter of 1966/7. Cost-effective modular building techniques were outside the Scottish yard's experience. Consequently, the production Piper is basically a wooden yacht built in fibreglass. It is a simple monolith of glass mat and polyester resin. The mouldings do not take advantage of the special 'plastic' properties of composites – there are few integral stiffeners or self-supporting compound shapes and no internal sub-mouldings in a Piper.

Yet somehow all this caution and conservatism resulted in a highly desirable 'classic look' that has played out to the Piper's advantage over fifty years. There have been other serendipitous outcomes. Because fibreglass was a material little understood by Lloyds at that time, there was no skimping on the basic scantlings. The variation in certified weights of the Piper fleet bracket the minimum weight of a Dragon – a yacht five feet longer and designed for traditional carvel construction way back in 1929. Pipers are almost indestructible.

Fibreglass as a boatbuilding material arrived late on the Clyde, although there is a story that G. L. Watson's son turned up at Hunter's Quay in the 1890s in a papier mâché prototype. The first glass fibre patents were lodged in the USA in the mid-1930s, but the imperatives of WW2 delayed commercial production of GRP yachts until the post-war years. In the 1956 Earls Court Boat Show, 17% of the exhibits were built of fibreglass; 21 years later, in 1979, that figure was 70%.

The Piper's 1966 debut breasted this sea-change. The first hulls were moulded by Marine Plastics in Grimsby and fitted-out in Sandbank in an old rubble-walled distillery, which pre-dated Alexander Robertson's land-lease of 1879. Later hulls were moulded by Halmatic and then Mechans of Clydebank before the final batch was produced in-house. The former distillery might have been a romantic cradle for the swansong of Caledonian craftsmanship, but it was hardly ideal in terms of climate control through the Scottish winter. Nevertheless, 57 units were launched through the decade to 1977, a lifecycle trajectory typical of small production yachts.

In the eighties, with no more new Pipers available, the second-hand market slowly picked up. One-by-one, the scattered fleet began to return from remote roadsteads to the diocese of the Clyde Yacht Clubs Association. And when Robertson's offered favourable trade-in terms on their glamorous new Etchells line, yet more passé Pipers were repatriated. Perhaps all this was inevitable; there is a history of Clyde one-designs, such as the Garelochs and the Pleiades, dispersing and then being brought back to home waters.

In 1998, Piper production recommenced at the Cornish Crabbers' yard in Wadebridge. Only half-a-dozen were built. Nevertheless, in 2006 Adrian Jones of Rustler Yachts saw, not a failure, but an unrealised opportunity. He believed that the timeless chic of the Boyd design could still compete alongside the longer, slimmer, lighter displacement 'spirit of tradition' yachts that command the lion's share of the new classics market.

The original Pipers sail on. The Piper's 50th Anniversary Regatta was held on the Clyde in June 2016. There were 26 starters, a record for the class. Today, there are active Piper fleets in the Holy Loch, at Gourock, and in the Gareloch. More than 50 of the original yachts remain in commission. And with continuing healthy sales, there are now similar numbers of R24 clones built by Rustler Yachts on the water.

So, *"A hundred pipers, an' a' an' a'!"* sail in Scotland, England, France, The Netherlands, Sweden, New Zealand, South Africa, Greece, Bermuda, Antigua, The USA, and doubtless other waters too. Almost all the boats are in regular use and Boyd's bijou masterpiece is once again enjoying a popular renaissance among those sailors who enjoy tactical displacement yacht racing. See image on Page 799. The story of the Piper Class is recounted in detail in the concluding chapters of *The Piper calls the Tune.*

---

843 From an article on professionalism by Stuart Walker. Sourced from a clipped photocopy.
844 100 Years of Alfred Mylne, Ian Nicolson, Classic Boat, Dec. 1996, Jan & Feb 1997.
845 Temerity notwithstanding, Mylne's cruising boats, like *Mingary* and *Mariella*, were arguably short of horsepower too.

846 The Dragon 'came alive' with a genoa and spinnaker to morph from a docile family cruiser into a full-blooded racing yacht. The foretriangle was raised, the spreaders were lowered, and the upper forestay was replaced by jumper struts. Mast-height and mainsail remained the same.

847 New Clyde Class, The Times, 24th December 1928.

848 Thom also owned the Scottish Islands Class, *Canna*, which he bought after he sold *Circe*.

849 Sourced from the Clyde Classic Keelboats Association website.

850 Notes are based on the Gareloch website, a brief history written by Iain McAllister.

851 Summarised from The Piper Calls the Tune, Euan Ross and Bob Donaldson, 2017.

Sanda, Scottish Islands Class, Alfred Mylne, 1929   Image: Scottishboating

Halcyone, Gareloch OD, James McGruer, 1923   Image: Tim Henderson

Chapter 22: Much-loved Imports

The squadron of boats in the Holy Loch was so large, and the gathering of Corinthians of such a representative nature, that good as a tonic was the spirit which atmosphered Hunter's Quay just prior to the firing of the first prepare gun. James Meikle reminisces.[852]

In terms of numbers, the most popular one-designs on the Clyde were not products of Watson, Fife, Mylne, Boyd or McGruer, but imports from other renowned yachting cultures – modified national classes, like the Pleiades and Loch Longs, and international classes designed in Scandinavia, like the Dragons, Solings and IODs. Only the US-designed Etchells bucked the trend. Whether our susceptibility to Nordic design reflects an open mind or a shared maritime heritage, who can say. Certainly, through the period in question, we were not short of world-class designers in home waters.

Much as the Scots punched above their weight in the great days of yachting, we have always been open to good ideas from beyond our shores, particularly in the international classes and from the drawing boards of latter-day Vikings, with whom we share a sizable chunk of DNA. The fact that none of these fine craft originates from south of the border is, I believe, merely an accident of history, rather than national chauvinism.

The Clyde Mermaids aka Seamew Mermaids

In the autumn of 1894, the Clyde Corinthian Yacht Club introduced the 'Clyde Mermaids', based on Linton Hope's 'Seamew Mermaids', as the club's new one-design.[853] The class also took root in India where they were known as the 'Bombay Tomtits'. The Seamew Mermaids were unballasted centreboarders, with a straight stem, curved forefoot with a slightly raking transom; 18ft LOA, 16ft LWL, beam 7ft, draught board-up 10", draught board-down 6ft, sail area (actual) 275ft^2, displacement, 1,818lbs and a YRA rating calculated at 0.7 ($^3/_4$-rater).

The Mermaids promised to 'stand a lot of hard driving'. Nevertheless, they were decked fore and aft to enclose watertight bulkheads providing enough buoyancy to support the boat and a crew of three. At least seven were built by McAlister of Dumbarton. During the first season, the 'Clyde' prefix lapsed, and they were referred to simply as 'Seamew Mermaids'. In 1895, the newly formed Clyde Sailing Club at Helensburgh got off to a flying start with the purchase five 18ft Linton Hope Seamew centreboard daysailers as club boats.[854] The new class seem to have been an irreverent company. *Yachting* noted that they had "*brought down upon their heads a journalistic castigation for their frivolous, if not too ready, wit*". A now-defunct Glasgow journal considered that the names: *Ally Sloper, Pick-Me-Up* and *The Pink 'Un*, as typical examples, "*had neither classical association to recommend them nor yet homely dignity*".[855]

The Gaels aka Seabird One Design Class

The 'Seabird' class originated on Merseyside in 1898 and debuted at the Royal Gourock Yacht Club around the turn of the century. They were stout little half-rater centreboard dinghies, 20ft 6" LOA and 16ft 6" LWL, with a standing lug. As the class history has it, the design was drawn by Club Commodore, W. Scott-Hayward, and amateur designer, Herbert Baggs, on the back of a cigarette packet under a streetlamp in Southport after the pubs had shut. The design is workmanlike rather than elegant, so it is quite possible that this defaced fag-packet was given directly to Latham of Crossens, the original boatbuilder.

The Seabirds were known as 'Gaels' on the Clyde. Other fleets sailed as 'Seashells' and 'Cariads'. Whatever they were called, by all accounts they are poorly balanced and cranky little boats. To achieve reasonable balance, the mast must be raked forward and the 560lbs of internal ballast placed towards the front. Surely the good people of the Royal Gourock could have done better? Things have not improved much today; the class association still bans bottle-screws, kicking-straps, tiller-extensions, fairlead tracks, toe straps and centreboard slot gaskets. Remarkably, 65 are still sailing. However, as far as we are aware, none of the Clyde boats has survived.

Pleiade One Design Class

The Hunter's Quay-based Pleiades were built to a Danish design, with some modification to ballasting and freeboards to suit local conditions. In Denmark, they are known as '15m^2 Jolly Boats'. The Pleiades first hit the water in 1914, dispersed through the inter-war years and then re-mustered on the Holy Loch after WW2. The class remained active until the mid-1960s but were already in steep decline when the Pipers arrived to sound their death knell. Unlike most of the other classes described here, very little has been written about the Pleiades in recent decades, so these much-loved little yachts have been given their own chapter, see Chapter 25.

Loch Long One Design Class

On a visit to Norway in the 1930s, Ian Campbell happened upon the little 18ft clinker-built, Stjärnbåt, a Folkboat-type yacht simplified with a fin-keel. The Stjärnbåt was designed by Janne Jacobsson sometime before the Great War. Ian enlisted local boatbuilder, James Croll, to adapt the design for carvel construction and draw out the transom stern into a more elegant counter.

Five examples of the new class took to the water for the first time in May 1937, and to mark the most significant event of that year, were named the Loch Long One Design Coronation Class.[856] However, Robert Colquhoun of Dunoon, the builder, had also built seven very similar 'Coronation One Designs' for the Royal Lymington Yacht Club. And so, to avoid confusion, the 'coronation' tribute was soon dispensed with.

The Loch Longs have had their ups and downs. In the early 1950s, the class was at loggerheads with itself. The moulds and the 'original' lines were lost in a fire in 1940, although Janne Jacobsson's Stjärnbåt lines should still have been available. Bert Shaw of Robertson's and James Rodgers, a small boatbuilder from Glasgow, independently took lines off *Roma*, LL No.11 and 'cleaned them up'. Subsequently, there was a spat of seismic proportions. Rodgers seems to have been concerned that his boats would be uncompetitive. He argued that Robertson's boats, with their spruce hulls and 732lb keels vs 640lbs, *"violated the specification in every conceivable form"*. One can see his point.

It was clearly unfortunate that a rival builder was highlighting non-compliant aspects on the new Robertson's boats. Rather than Bert Shaw having made mistakes, it seems that David Boyd had 'cleaned up' the lines so thoroughly that the class diehards considered it to be a completely new design. Moves were made to throw the whole of the Robertson's sub-division out-of-class. It took two years of acrimonious discussions before *"the rules were altered to accommodate them"*.[857]

The twenty-seven Robertson's boats do look a bit different. To the casual observer, they appear a little 'plumper' than the original boats. Perhaps Boyd could not resist the temptation to fair-up the lines and he certainly found a loophole that allowed him to increase the ballast-ratio. Fortunately, perhaps, these controversial interpretations of the class rules were not notably more successful than the products of any other builder, and the class began to grow again. By 1966, there were 125 boats on the water. Among traditional daysailers in Britain, they were second in numbers only to Alfred Westmacott's evergreen XOD from 1909.[858]

During the 1960s, Boag's of Largs were still able to deliver new wooden Loch Longs at affordable prices. Seventeen boats were launched in the 1966-69 period, almost all credited to old Mr Boag, who built a remarkable 65 in total. Healthy turnouts in the clubs around and below the Tail o' the

Bank during these years, and close competition at Loch Long Week, favoured this established class. After Boag retired in 1970, the supply of new Loch Longs dried up. Small numbers have been built since 1991 but they are no longer 'affordable'. Nevertheless, through the eighties, the second-hand market stayed buoyant and good local racing continued at Cove, Gourock and Largs.

Any number of magazine articles quote the following: "*On the River Clyde they are known as the 'wee Dragons' because of their similarity to the International Dragon.*" Writing for *The Field* in 1951, Ian Gilchrist referenced this description and added wryly "*only in print*".[859] The performance of the Loch Long is in no way comparable with the Dragon, but then the same may be said about the revered XOD on the Solent. In a well-managed one-design, ultimate performance is irrelevant. The Loch Longs offer good close racing and have given immense pleasure to generations of sailors, both on the Clyde and on the Alde in Suffolk.

The Aldeburgh folks have regularly raided the Clyde Estuary. They abducted and fostered the Garelochs for twenty years between 1937 to 1957. These days, it is the turn of the Loch Longs. There are now more than fifty examples of the class on the River Alde, which is more than we can muster anywhere on the Clyde today. The Aldeburgh Yacht Club revere the boats as genuine classic yachts, and consequently, they all look absolutely splendid. Moreover, new boats are once again being built in Suffolk workshops. Such projects require an eye-watering budget for such a small boat. Craftsmanship in wood is not cheap in the 21st century.

International One Design Class

The International One Design, or IOD, was the result of an initiative by America's Cup legend Cornelius Shields.[860] In the spring of 1936, Shields came across an elegant new Bjarne Aas 6-metre called *Saga* at the Royal Bermuda Yacht Club. The boat so-impressed him that he promptly commissioned a new one-design from Aas. Shields was acting on behalf of the members of the Sound Interclub Class who had agreed to replace their ageing fleet.

In what seems a remarkable act of faith, Shields and five friends underwrote the construction of 25 yachts which measured: LOA 33ft; LWL 21ft 5" and 6ft 9" beam. For comparison, the 6mR, *Saga*, was: LOA 37ft 6"; LWL 25ft 4" and 6ft 2" beam. The new boat presumptuously christened the 'International One Design', was smaller and beamier than a 6mR, and to modern eyes better proportioned. As was normal practice at the time, Aas rigged the IOD with a modest working jib and a generous mainsail to compensate. In the 1930s, favourable exchange rates made

Norway an extremely attractive build location. Even with shipping factored in, the boats represented exceptional value.

While the IODs were brought into the USA legally, Yankee sailors of that generation revelled in less conventional delivery methods. These cheerful smugglers imported European-built boats through Canada to avoid import duties. This ruse was sometimes conducted on an industrial scale. The New York Yacht Club once ordered a batch of six Burgess-designed 12-metres from Abeking & Rasmussen in Germany. They were built in just five months and shipped to Halifax, Nova Scotia, where they were rigged-up and sailed offshore down the coast to the United States. Ferrying convoys of low freeboard metre-boats offshore was obviously fraught with risk, but by all accounts, the experience was memorable

Legend has it that during the Nazi occupation of Norway (1940-45), Bjarne Aas buried the IOD construction jigs to safeguard the future of the class. Production recommenced at Fredrikstad after the War. Equalised fibreglass construction was introduced in the 1960s to allow the old boats to compete on level terms. Wooden boats are still being built, however. As metre-type boats go, the IOD is just about perfect in its proportions and the small coachroof in no way detracts from their appearance.

Uffa Fox described the boat's *"lines as clean as a smelt's and each and every line perfect for its purpose"*. The IOD does everything the 6mR, Dragon, Shields, Daring and Piper can do only better, especially if you a have a recent fibreglass model. To date, around 285 have been built, of which about 252 have survived. Fleets are active in the USA (East and West Coast), Bermuda, Norway, Sweden and St. Mawes in Cornwall.

The first IOD did not arrive in Scotland until 1968.[861] *Kyla* (formerly *Windflower*) was joined by *Mitzi* in 1969 and *Arrow* in 1970. By 1973, the Royal Forth at Granton had 13 boats. This was an active fleet, hosting the World Championship on the Forth in 1975, 1979, 1984, and 1998. There was some cross-over with the Dragons. While the IOD is a bigger boat, it is cheaper to campaign. Dragons respond to checkbook optimisation.

The Forth fleet travelled cross-country to compete in the 1973 edition of International Clyde Fortnight at Rothesay. The class caught the eye of discerning Clyde-based sailors, triggering a nationwide search for boats. *Mirenda* was found in Chichester, *Wildgoose* was found in Bangor, and then *Starlight* and *Pirate II*, from the Forth, joined the embryo fleet. With this interest, the class visited the Clyde for their World Championships in 1990, hosted by the Royal Northern. *Jeannie M*, the first of two Scottish fibreglass IODs, was built at Silvers Marine in time for the regatta.

By 1995, the Forth fleet was in terminal decline and the remaining boats were transported to Rhu. However, just a few years later, when the IODs scheduled another visit to the Clyde for their 1998 World's, the local fleet was struggling for numbers. Local enthusiasts, Gilmour and Gilli Manuel, revitalised the class with a much-needed restoration programme to bring *Stallion, Tadpole (Sheen)* and *Kyla* back to racing condition.

Sadly, this brief revival was the Scottish IOD fleet's last gasp. What makes the loss of this beautiful fleet almost unbearable is the fact that to maintain their commitments with regard to reciprocal team racing fixtures such as the venerable Seawanhaka Cup, the RNCYC replaced their gorgeous IODs with Sonar keelboats. The Sonar was designed in 1979 by Bruce Kirby. While the boat is no beauty, I understand it does the job. No criticism of RNCYC is intended here – we all live in a world dominated by the brutal realities of the bottom-line. See class list in Appendix 3.

International Dragon Class

Like many traditional one-designs, the Dragon was initiated by a group of like-minded enthusiasts at the Royal Gothenburg Yacht Club. In 1929, the club invited submissions for a cheap dual-purpose boat with a manageable sail-plan of about 215ft² or 20m². The winning proposal was submitted by Norwegian designer, Johan Anker. He proposed a long, slim yacht in the Scandinavian style, with a tall inboard rig and low freeboard. The dimensions were: LOA 29ft 2"; LWL 18ft 7"; beam 6ft 5"; draught 3ft 11" with a displacement of 3,740lbs. The boat conformed to the Skerry Cruiser Rule and early examples carried the '20' designation on the mainsail.

In 1933, Clyde yachtsman A. H. Ball came across the Dragon while on a sailing holiday in Scandinavia.[862] He liked the look of the boat and secured a copy of the plans which were subsequently circulated around the yacht clubs. During October 1935, the Royal Clyde sponsored a meeting in the Bath Hotel, Glasgow to consider the creation of a new class. George Paisley set out the case for the Dragon. George informed the assembled company that he and James Howden Hume had bought a boat in the Baltic and that it would soon be available at McGruer's Yard for inspection.[863]

The arguments that followed are still remembered on the Clyde. It appears that some crusty old-timers thought that "*foreign-designed and foreign-built boats*" were not wanted here. Herbert Thom, a fine sailor but not always the most rational of technicians, was among them. But the best quotation to survive from that meeting was this: "*the Dragon class was originally started with the idea of encouraging yachting for poor men who have to work*".[864] A new Dragon today will set the 'working man' back £60,000 plus, but there are great-looking boats on the market for less than ten grand.

Fortunately for Clyde yachting, the meeting concluded with an open mind and the embittered old guard reconciled to more Scandinavian designs. The International Rule and the Pleiades originated in these foreign waters, and to add insult to injury, the Loch Longs would soon be on their way too. Howden-Hume's *Anita*, the first Dragon to come to Britain, arrived in the following spring of 1936. That same year, McGruer's built 9, and altogether 14 boats came to the starting line during Clyde Fortnight in that first successful season. As McGruer's were able to deliver the first boats for £280 (£20,000), at a quality comparable with the Danish imports, the fleet was off to a flying start.

Sometime in the 1930s, Alfred Mylne was having dinner with John Nicholson. John's father, Charles E. Nicholson, was arguably the finest of the talented crop of yacht designers active in Britain through the first half of the 20th century. In his book *Great Years in Yachting*, John is generous to the Scots and includes many anecdotes that touch on Scottish yachting.[865] One such delightful tale concerns Mylne and the Nicholson's dinner party.

The subject of conversation was the Dragon. *"Alfred surprised me by squeezing my leg rather hard under the table exclaiming, John, my boy, the Dragons are knocking at the doer."* Mylne saw what was happening. Just as the grey squirrel supplanted our red squirrel, this import would occupy the same niche as a host of local one-designs and prove to be a more enduring species in the Darwinian ecology of maritime evolution.

James McGruer may have liked the boats, but Mylne disparaged the Dragons for their design as much as for their negative impact on Britain's home-grown one-design fleets. He thought they were under canvassed, which in the early years with just a working jib, they certainly were. But his main criticisms concerned the extravagantly long-ended hull-shape and how this behaved in the Clyde chop. Elegant yes, but at the cost of an unfavourable moment of gyration. In some sea conditions, the Dragon's flat scow-entry pounds and the stern 'smacks' too. Consequently, to remain tight in traditional carvel construction it has to be overbuilt. Thus, it is a design that comes into its own as a fibreglass monocoque. Mylne had a point; but even so, the ayes have it and the Dragons have flourished.

In 1938, with 25 Dragons racing regularly on the Clyde, the class spread to other yachting centres in Britain, principally the Forth, the Solent, Burnham-on-Crouch and Bangor in Northern Ireland. When WW2 interrupted leisure pursuits in 1939, there were 120 Dragons registered in the UK with the Clyde Yacht Clubs Conference, an administrative responsibility transferred to the Yacht Racing Association in 1946, after the class achieved 'international status'.[866]

McGruer's were the most productive and successful of the Clyde Dragon builders. During Ewing McGruer's sojourn in London making hollow spars, he became friendly with Johan Anker. Ewing immediately saw the potential of his old friend's design for racing on the Clyde. Subsequently, from 1936 to 1951, the Clynder boatyard would build 46 beautiful Dragons.[867]

The Dragon is quite unlike other classes, defined or influenced by the International metre-boat or Universal Rule classes, which were evolving at the time. The Aas design is now so familiar that we have forgotten how different it is from anything else in international waters. The Dragon, originally known as the '20m² Dragon', is the only example of the wildly extravagant Skärgårdskryssare type to achieve worldwide acceptance.[868] This was the boat that appeared on the Clyde in the 1930s. It looked great but was clearly underpowered and the long overhangs and bluff scow entry made it challenging to sail well in waves.[869]

Still, in this configuration, and with the rudimentary accommodation beneath the extended coachroofs of the era, the Dragons were good family boats, and a decent helmsman did not require an expert crew. The class showcased our best women sailors. Among the best Dragon sailors on the Clyde, bar none, were the talented Simpsons. Mrs Simpson sailed *Emagee* to win the Daly Trophy for three years in succession. And her daughters, Sheila Hinge with the old *Argee II* and Molly McKay with *Lora*, clearly inherited their mother's skill at the tiller. With their husbands crewing, they took the class by storm in the early post-war years.[870] Other leading Clyde Dragon sailors included Miss Sheila Leitch and Miss A. M. Steven.

In 1950, *Yachting World* reported on the early season success, and exemplary sportsmanship, of these ladies: *"In that day's outing the Dragons had rather a surprising finish, following a drift for some time after the start. Mrs Shiela Hinge's Argee II, which had started ten minutes late, was first in by ten seconds, having caught the breeze before any of the others. As it happened, she withdrew later because she had been under tow from the other side of the Firth when the five-minute gun went. Mrs Hinge, and her sister, Mrs Mackay, and mother, Mrs Simpson, have all entered for the Dragon Gold Cup races in Denmark in July."* To balance out the report, we may note that male skippers were also competing. *"Ronald Hesketh is also entered from the Clyde with his Elska."*[871]

The Clyde's love affair with the Dragon peaked in the immediate post-war years, marked by a generous, and possibly unique, gesture. Johan Anker waived the royalties for British-built examples in perpetuity, as a small thank-you for all the assistance rendered by our seaman to Norway during WW2.[872] The programme for the Royal Northern's regatta at Hunter's Quay in 1947 *"for yachts other than the finalists in the International Dragon Gold Cup"* lists 43 Dragons, far and away the largest class competing. The sailing instructions noted that yachts would be split into two flights.

While short-hoist genoas and small spinnakers had been introduced before the war, the sailplan remained unsatisfactory. After WW2, the masts were re-rigged and moved forward, the hounds were raised, and a genoa and spinnaker were added. This brought the upwind sail-area to 297ft^2, and a kite of 254 ft^2 lit up performance downwind. Like the early metre-boats, this extra sail-area transformed the boat. The long hoist overlapping genoa not only gives more power, it provides a useful range of gears to work through a left-over chop. Measurement tolerances were tightened up in 1962 and fibreglass construction was permitted in 1973. Today, a hull measurement tolerance of 0.05% at each of seven template stations gives a maximum tolerance of 16mm, measured away from the hull at midships, and just 8mm in the forward sections.

Pre-war, the Dragons were vulnerable to optimisation within generous tolerances. This was necessary as millimetre accuracy is simply impossible with traditional wooden construction. Very few wooden Dragons have been built since 1972, partly for cost reasons and also because increasingly tight tolerances have made construction expensive. Indeed, when *Lady Jayne*, the first wooden Dragon to be built for some time, was completed in 2006, the cognoscenti considered it remarkable that the boat actually measured.

Over the 1936/37 winter, David Boyd spent many hours refining the lines of the Robertson's-built Dragons to exploit the generous tolerances in the original class rules, slimming the midsection and filling out the ends. Current builders still push the envelope in this direction. He also sought to reduce hull weight and lower the centre of gravity. Robertson's built five Boyd-optimised Dragons, with *Pinta* going to Hugh Somerville's father. Hugh, chronicler of the *Sceptre* project and a good friend of Boyd, later bought *Primula*, another Boyd Dragon.

In 1937, the Clyde Yacht Clubs Conference presented the Dragon Gold Cup, still coveted today as one of the most important international trophies in inshore racing. The cup is solid gold and was made by Messrs R. & W. Sorley of Glasgow. Two winged dragons serve as handles and the decorative and chaste-work was appropriately copied from the carving found on a Viking long-ship from ca.900 A.D. The competition has been held on the Clyde eight times and once at Granton on the Forth.

Among British winners of the event when sailed in home waters were W. H. Barnett, who took the trophy in 1947, then Sir Gordon Smith in 1961, and D. Young in 1973. The Royal Forth had a very competitive Dragon fleet with James Leask, Marshal Napier, Kenneth Gumley, Hamish Mackenzie, David Young and Gilmour Manual winning, not just in Scotland, but internationally. On the Clyde, we had Jeremy Thomson and

Jimmy Gibb's *Tarka II* always pushing hard for the top places. Today, the Dragon is sailed in 26 countries, with over 1,500 registered worldwide and many more serving as elegant daysailers. Counterintuitively, the class has thrived since losing its Olympic status, but not alas on the Clyde.

In *The Piper Calls the Tune*, the late Peter Fairley recalled the decline of the Scottish Dragons and his response to it: *"We identified a need for a new one-design class on the Clyde as the traditional daysailer classes, like the Garelochs, were becoming old and tired. The Dragons were still a well-populated and competitive fleet, but these boats were now extremely expensive to campaign."* Peter had recently chartered the Dragon, *Vodka*, from Tom Cottrell and had been struck by the need for deep pockets and an endless supply of the latest rags from the best sailmakers. These days, the ante continues to climb and the ambitious owner with an eye on the main chance has to secure a couple of extremely skilled professionals to snuggle in between the Corinthians as middleman.

The Dragon became an Olympic class in 1948. Highly competitive Dragon fleets remained a highlight of every Olympics until 1972 when the 3-man keelboat slot was allocated to the Soling. While some Olympic classes lapse into obscurity after losing this honour, the Dragons have thrived. Active class associations can maintain the relevance of an obsolete design for decades. The Dragon, like the Star and Finn, have been allowed to develop incrementally over the years. Even today, if you want to identify the best sailors in the world, these are the three classes to watch.

The Flying Fifteen

Uffa Fox (1898-1972) was a fine dinghy designer in his early years but his yacht designs are less assured.[873] However, the 20ft LOA, 15ft LWL Flying Fifteen keelboat from 1947 is a significant exception. Timeless good-looks, and planing-dinghy performance without the risk of a capsize, ensured that it became an enduring classic. In the days before decent foul weather clothing was available, few ageing dinghy sailors relished a ducking. So, for 20 years before wetsuits, then dry-suits, came on the market, the F15 had the greybeard market-segment to itself.

The design of a popular production keelboat was a rare triumph for Uffa, and he capitalised on its unexpected success with a series of scaled-up, scaled-down, and ultimately irrelevant, clones. He promoted the class tirelessly, taking Fifteens to regattas around the country and writing about his exploits in his best-selling books. Then, he chanced upon the marketing ploy of 'celebrity endorsement', lobbying the people of Cowes to buy a Fifteen for the Duke of Edinburgh and his family. This was the first *Coweslip* – miniature royal yacht and kindred Cowes pun.

There were, in fact, three *Coweslips*, which all sailed under the same name and sail-number. The famous 192 number was originally issued to *Bluebottle*, the Duke of Edinburgh's Dragon. However, when it was issued there were only about 50 FFs on the water, so no doubt Uffa also thought that it would suggest impressive early growth in the class. As the years passed, the Duke found his original gift horse a bit of a donkey and had a new boat built by Woodnutts at Cowes. That Fifteen was unsatisfactory too for a number of reasons and a third (also by Woodnutts) was launched in May 1962, which is the *Coweslip* now on display with *Britannia* at Leith.[874]

Uffa once said "*most designs are the result of a great deal of thought and many hours of work on the drawing board, where every detail is designed and developed. Not so the Flying Fifteen*".[875] While the great man hatched the legend of a Eureka moment in the bath to explain the eccentricities of his design, he was being disingenuous, to say the least; the Fifteen was the result of a life-long fascination with raters and considerable thought. In fact, the boat had a much longer gestation period than most designs.[876]

Before WW2, Sir John Field Beale, then chairman of the YRA dinghy committee, had talked to Uffa about reviving the Linear Rater-type (1896-1906) of planing keelboat which raised pulses through the turn-of-the-century. The two men shared a particular interest in the inspired work of Charles Sibbick, the leading light of British Rater design. Consequently, after the war, the YRA organised a design competition to select a new one-design keelboat for the 1948 yachting Olympics in Torquay. The requirement was for "*a fast and lively boat – easy to handle and cheap to build*". Uffa designed *Pensive Temptress* for the trials.

It was 'typically Uffa' that the boat he submitted was based on his pre-war conversation with Beale, rather than the parameters set by the YRA. While Uffa's design was allowed to compete and proved to be the fastest of the four boats on trial, she remained ineligible for selection. Tom Thornycroft's *Toucan Too*, a less extreme planing keelboat, got the nod.[877] Back home in Cowes, Uffa tinkered endlessly with the boat, and she became known locally as '*Expensive Temptress*' before evolving into the original Flying Twenty, the forerunner of the Flying Series of which the only really successful model was the Flying Fifteen in 1947.[878]

The class was introduced to the Clyde in 1948 when Uffa persuaded his friend David Boyd to build Fifteens at Robertson's yard (4 were produced 1948-9). The Fifteens did not become popular on the Clyde until more recent decades; there were just seven or eight starters in Clyde Fortnight during the 1950s, including the odd visitor. Local luminaries like James Howden Hume, George McGruer, Ossie Graham, A. A. Roberts, Charles Lamb, Arnold Roberts, Douglas Arthur, Jeremy Thomson and Terence Brownrigg all enjoyed the class in the early days, so standards were high.

George Blake wrote in 1952: *"Under the influence of Mr Uffa Fox from the South of England the classes tend to grow smaller and smaller until even an original member of the Clyde Model Yacht Club would have been scared to venture in them...Flying Fifteens...and all manner of strange, dangerous-looking craft."*[879] That said, many excellent sailors either disagree, relish the challenge of sailing sideways, or just enjoy competing against like-minded converts who have swallowed the 'Kool Aid'. My late father aspired to be among them; he had just completed the shell of a cold-moulded Fifteen, using offcut mahogany veneers sourced gratis from a local plywood factory, when he was struck down by a heart attack in 1962.

Uffa visited the Clyde in 1953, and again in 1958, with the first *Coweslip*. With the hull slung on the roof of his beaten-up Humber Super Snipe and the 400lb keel wedged in the boot, man and machine were off up the road, in these pre-motorway days, at a claimed 80mph. But of course, Fifteens were not really 'car-top' boats. Uffa had the idea that travellers might borrow a keel for open meetings. However, apart from obvious logistical issues, the inefficiencies of the keel's ploughshare shape mean that a perfect section and finish are not just desirable, but essential. So, any old keel will not do.

Today, they are trailed with the keel affixed. As all the competitive boats are dry-sailed, that 400lb keel is now simply a dead weight when an efficient vertical lift keel-assembly could give the same righting moment with a 100lb bulb, and transform performance, particularly if allied to a modern rudder. However, discussing the boat with Adam Ovington the response was that the boat was very much 'of a piece' and modernising any one component would leave half-a-dozen other elements begging for attention.[880] Essentially, the Flying Fifteen is a quirky classic with no pretensions to be a modern performance boat, and all the better for that.

That said, the boat has been sensitively modernised over the years. At one stage, Uffa sought to reverse decades of progressive evolution which had made the boat easier and more comfortable to sail. However, he gave his blessing to those cumulative changes (cockpit, sail-plan and other details) before he passed away. This compact sparked a flurry of development with competing builders exploiting the originally very generous measurement tolerances (±1") incorporated into the class rules to allow amateur building.

Reflecting post-war materials shortages, any construction material is permitted. Fifteens have been built of wood, GRP, aluminium, Tufnol, and even Formica. Today, hulls are built of carbon fibre, which is expensive, but ensures a long competitive life, in conjunction with the imposition of much tighter tolerances in 1984 (±¼"). Thus, the current Mk10 design, which dates from 2002, seems to have reached a plateau in performance, fostering very close racing at the head of the fleet. As for the club sailors, who still cherish their old boats, the Fifteens now sail in three divisions: Classic, Silver and Open. This accommodates performance difference across the three main design generations and ensures fierce competition at all levels.

Three hardy Fifteens joined in West Highland Week ca.1969. It was a one-off event as the Royal Highland Yacht Club could not really 'look after' them in these remote waters. As sailing back to the Clyde was a bridge too far, the boats were towed home behind a trawler. The 'Nantucket sleighride', surfing at 12kts on the fishing boat's quarter-wave, appears to have imprinted a memory more exciting, nay nerve-wracking, on the Fifteen crews than anything the class has offered before or since. The national championships have been held on the Clyde many times since 1950 and have always been well-attended.[881] The 1976 event at Rhu saw an entry of 119 boats.

BB11 Class

The BB11 is a 20ft 3" LOA fin-keel boat, designed in 1956 and built in Norway by Bjorge Bringsvaerd. Half-a-dozen of these little yachts were imported in the mid-1960s and sailed keenly during the same decade as the inelegant cruising Folkboats raced as a class. The Clyde fleet comprised *Lestris*, *Cinders*, *Bbet*, *La Forza* and *Anitra*. *Anitra* was moored in front of our house, so my friends and I had the use of her when we were boys. In those circumstances, it seems ungrateful to concede that they are mediocre performers, being both under-canvassed and in want of a heavier ballast keel. The BB11 class is still popular in Scandinavia, where they offer competitive, if undemanding, class racing.

1960s GRP fin-keelers – Etchells and Solings

The Dragon is a traditional heavy-displacement, full-keeled vessel, but the next generation of imports, the Etchells and the Solings are medium-displacement, fin-keeled yachts. Both were designed in 1965 to take advantage of ongoing advances in composites construction technology. They were lightly constructed and involved less material than translating classic keelboats into fibreglass. Consequently, the new boats travelled through the water much faster than traditional daysailers. No one really expected the Etchells and the Soling to plane, but plane they did, making a mockery of the IYRU stipulation that the contenders for the Olympic slot soon to be vacated by the Dragon should "*not be a planing-type*".[882]

The IYRU held selection trials for a new three-man keelboat at Kiel in 1966 and Travemunde in 1967. At the Kiel trial, the Etchells was favoured by a committee of respected racing sailors.[883] Apparently, however, this recommendation did not reflect the IYRU agenda, so they scheduled the second trial at Travemunde. The second observation committee sold their souls to the Devil.[884] While the Etchells was once again outstanding, the Soling was selected.[885]

An argument was made that the Soling offered the same type of yachting but in a smaller cheaper package. That much is true, but the IYRU had specified an envelope of dimensions and the Soling did not conform to these specifications. Bizarrely, while the Etchells was ignored entirely, the mediocre, Van der Stadt-designed, *Thrial* was given a special commendation. The committee's recommendations lacked transparency and had, obviously, been swayed by lobbying. In the USA, where the Etchells originated, the sailing community was apoplectic.

The Soling campaign was supported by the Norwegian Royal Family, who were highly influential in that era.[886] It may be significant that the class rules were cobbled-together one Friday night at the Norwegian Embassy by Beecher Moore, Jan Linge and Finn Ferner. Later, King Harald presented Soling designer, Jan Linge, with the Beppe Croce Award for his 'lifelong contribution to the sport of sailing'. Linge had already received the ISAF Gold Medal with the same citation.[887]

Olympic 'equipment' trials to evaluate new designs are almost always unsatisfactory: either picking the wrong boat – like the Swallow, Soling, Yngling and Tempest; or a reasonable boat hindered by crucial design flaws; or inadequate specifications like the 49er, Laser and Nacra 17; or simply a good boat which fails to convince, like the Contender. The marketplace is no respecter of arbitrary selection.

In June 1967, Tim Henderson was yarning with Kenneth Miller at the bar in the Royal Northern. Kenneth had just ordered a Piper. Tim replied, *"why have you done that, you should get a Soling?"* Ken's reply was, *"what's a Soling?"* They adjourned to the big clubroom, where there were piles of magazines, and Tim showed Ken an article in *Yachting World* about the Soling and her performance at the IYRU three-man keelboat trials.

Tim rashly challenged Ken, *"if you get a Soling, I'll get one too"*. Two weeks later, Ken reappeared. *"Tim you'd better get your cheque book out."* He had been to Norway, sailed a Soling and ordered one; *Solorana* was due to arrive in two weeks. Tim followed suit and took delivery of a second Soling, *Soliris*, at a total cost of £1,250 (£22,500), including sails and shipping costs.[888] This modest investment got sailors on the water for £250 less than a Piper. You also got a faster boat, albeit one made with 1,000lbs less material.

Tim and Martin Miller, Kenneth's son, raced *Solorana* at Clyde Week, held in Rothesay Bay in 1967. One day it was 'howlin' and all racing was cancelled, a rare occurrence during mid-summer. These were, however, the very conditions that the new Soling enthusiasts had been waiting for. Tim took Ken's boat out for a blast, reaching backwards and forwards in front of the Glenburn Hotel in a welter of spray. Happily, after the regatta, Ken got his boat back in one piece. Meanwhile, the Earth-bound Dragon and Piper crews propped up the bar, reassuring each other that this high-performance sailing business would never catch on.

The Soling experience was not all positive, however. New owners discovered that they had to recruit young athletic crews, happy to hike hard, and with the expertise to manage ever-more 'tweakable' rigs. Heavy and light keelboat demographics slowly drifted apart. This divergence became a gulf when Paul Elvstrom turned up at the Soling World's in 1971 with a crew practised in the new technique of 'drop hiking' using ankle hobbles. The great Hans Foch, among others, argued that this mindless bondage was killing the class, as indeed it did.

Through the late 1960s, the Soling battled it out with the Piper in the Clyde day-sailer market. After the Solings reached a fleet of 15 boats on the estuary, the Piper was advertised as having 15 boats on the water too. Today, it seems odd that two boats so completely different in every respect, except price and internal volume, were ever in competition.

The Soling is now considered slow and dated by sports-boat enthusiasts. However, the Etchells, by contrast, has achieved classic status and thrives, even on the Clyde, where a cost-limited fleet still entertains some of our better sailors at Royal Gourock. Perhaps the shenanigans that led to the Etchells being passed over for Olympic service have now played out in its favour. Certainly, the sensible sitting-out regime encourages ageing legends back into the class: "*When hiking in the sitting position, no part of the crew's body between the middle of the thigh and the feet shall be outboard of the sheerline*".

In 1975 Robertson's launched a Piper buy-back scheme to promote the sale of Etchells. Piper owners could part-exchange their boats with a favourable premium and trade-up. This scheme was successful in that, of the 49 Etchells sold, more than half-a-dozen involved a Piper trade-in. While not part of the masterplan, the initiative had the serendipitous effect of bringing the same number of Pipers home to the Holy Loch and thus reinvigorating class racing on the Clyde.

CODA: Classes Missing the Cut

The most popular one-design classes in recent memory were two cruiser-racers from the board of David Thomas, the Sonata, 22ft 7" LOA (400+ built) and the Sigma 33, 33ft LOA (364 built). The Sonata was designed in 1976 and the Sigma 33 came out in 1978. The latter was originally named the Skua 33, but after the Scottish Skua Class Association objected the name was changed. The original Skua was designed for the Royal Forth Yacht Club by Jack Robertson and debuted in 1964. This boat had a 180lb drop-keel and was described as a "*keel assisted sailboat broadly similar to a Flying Fifteen*", but smaller at 17ft LOA, and of hard-chine construction. Fifty-six of these good-looking boats were built, but sadly the class is now moribund.[889]

---

[852] Leaves from the Logbook of an Old Clyde Journalist, James Meikle, The Yachtsman.

[853] The Bombay Tomtit was also built to the Seamew design.

[854] The Yachtsman, January 1895.

[855] Notes and Notions, The Yachtsman, 28th March 1895.

[856] The Piper Calls the Tune, Euan Ross and Bob Donaldson, 2017.

[857] Robertson's built 27 Loch Longs between 1949 and 1966. Loch Longs, the First 50 Years, John McMurtrie, 1987.

[858] There are about 190 XODs still sailing in today and perhaps 130 Loch Longs.

[859] Class Notes, Loch Long OD, Vanessa Bird, Classic Boat, December 2010.

[860] Cornelius Shields on Sailing, Cornelius Shields, 1965.

[861] International One Design Class Association website.

[862] In other versions of this story, it was the Howden Humes on holiday.

[863] Cruise in Company, George Blake and Christopher Small, 1959.

[864] Ibid

[865] Great Years in Yachting, John Nicholson, 1970.

[866] The Yacht Racing Association (YRA) became the Royal Yachting Association (RYA) in 1952.

[867] However, as impressionable young schoolboys in the 1960s, we could not see past the superlative craftsmanship of the all-varnished Dragons built by Borresen in Denmark.

[868] 'Skärgårdskryssare' is usually translated as skerry cruiser, but while you can indeed cruise in one, they are cramped and wet for this purpose and it's more like camping on an actual skerry. The 1907 Swedish Square Metre rule eventually covered a multitude of classes, although only a few were really popular: 22m², 30m², 45m², 55m² 38m²: in 1912: 15m², 75m², 95m², 120m²; in 1913: 150m²; in 1915: 38m² and 45m² classes were combined in a 40m² class. Ironically, throughout the history of these boats, the rules have required accommodation.

[869] The 30m² and 40m² classes were used for the 1920 Belgium Olympics, but as the entry was just three, the Swedes collected two golds and a silver! This situation recalled the two-boat 12-metre class competition sailed on the Clyde for the 1908 Olympics.

[870] Sheila Hinge, née Simpson, later became a stalwart of the Holy Loch Sailing Club when her husband Leonard was Commodore.

[871] On the Clyde and Forth, Yachting World, June 1950.

[872] Anker asked his son to ensure that no British builder or owner paid a royalty on the Dragon design after his death. The 'bequest' was transferred in 1940 when W. M. Mackinlay, Secretary of the CYCC met Erik Anker at the Royal Gothenburg Yacht Club in 1946.

[873] Uffa was gifted his RINA as he was then designing a yacht for the President of the Institute.

[874] Prince Philip's New Yacht, James Ware, The Field, 3rd May 1962.

[875] Sailing Boats, Uffa Fox, 1959.

[876] National Small Boat Collection, Pensive Temptress, tech notes, Lauren Hogan, 27th April 1916.

[877] Renamed the Swallow, Thornycroft's design served for just one Olympiad and never attained widespread popularity. There is a keen fleet at Itchenor.

[878] It is doubtful how much evolving went on, looking at layout and painful cockpit combings.

[879] The Firth of Clyde, George Blake, 1952.

[880] Ovington Boats Ltd. is currently the top builder in the class in Britain.

[881] The class has enjoyed 17 such occasions on the Clyde, plus a visit to the Forth.

882 Both classes were used in the 1972 Olympics. The Star and its (temporary) replacement the Tempest also overlapped in this year.

883 The Kiel Observation Committee comprised: Frank Murdoch, Beppe Croce, Bob Bavier, Costas Stavridis, Hans Lubinus and Gordon Smith.

884 The Travemunde Observation Committee comprised: Jonathan Janson, Beppe Croce, Ding Schoonmaker, Eddie Stutterheim and Herr Hamstorf.

885 The Ugly IYRU, Editorial, Boating, April 1968.

886 The Crown Prince of Norway sailed a Soling in the Olympics when the class was represented for the first time.

887 The selection of the Yngling, another Linge design, was similarly controversial. After losing Olympic status, both Soling and Yngling have sunk without trace.

888 Despite being built in England, a Soling purchased from the Tyler Boat Company in 1966 was a little more expensive at £1,500, complete with sails and all equipment.

889 Design details from respective class associations.

Flying Fifteens on the Holy Loch, 2007   Image: the author

Titania off Hunter's Quay   Image: Gilchrist   BB 11, Bjorge Bringsvaerd, 1956

In the hands of Uffa Fox, the designer, *Titania* won the second National Championships in this boat in 1950. She was sold to J. Heddle and based on the Clyde in 1953.

Seamew One Design, Linton Hope, 1894   Gael One Design, 1898

Royal Yacht, *Bluebottle*, and the Dragon fleet on the Clyde   Image: press photo

Dragons off Hunter's Quay   Artist: Montague Dawson (1890-1973)

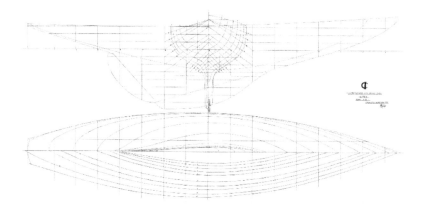

International One Design, Bjarne Aas, 1937   Lines, Bjarne Aas IOD Class Association

Sirocco, Loch Long OD Class, Janne Jacobson / James Croll, 1937   Image: LL Class Association

Sirocco caught here on port tack at the port end of the line, must be a perennially unlucky boat. She was the Loch Long torpedoed in Loch Long in 1957, as recounted in Chapter 36.

International Soling   Image: Class Association International Etchells   Image: Class Association

Chapter 23: Level Pegging

Youngsters with thousands a year are periling their lives in the smaller class of racing boats to have it out with other youngsters who have not hundreds a year, but who are respected all the same, and over whose clever sailing there is quite as much, perhaps a little more, excitement as over the victories of their wealthy rivals. The Glasgow Herald[890]

Rating systems and time-allowances were once seen as essential to racing yacht development. In past times, but perhaps not so much today, sailing enthusiasts were men of independent thinking, committed to advancing the state of the art. They were not an easy bunch to control. Early yacht races were more a question of who had brought the best mousetrap to the party than a contest of sailing ability. In any case, most yachts of any size were managed by risk-averse professionals who were much-of-a-muchness, like flat-racing jockeys. Some well-known owners did not even race aboard.

But when the sport 'settled down' in the second half of the 19th century, amateur yachtsmen were keen to hone and demonstrate their skills in direct competition with their peers. The media spotlight was still on the big boats, but the cognoscenti knew that most design innovation took place in smaller, level-rating classes where blind alleys could be binned without bankruptcy and risk to life and limb was manageable.

Development classes which race without time allowances are perhaps the purest form of the sport of yacht racing, eclipsing handicap racing and even one-designs. We can group 'level-rating', 'restricted' and 'box-rule' classes as a genre that best tests a sailor's all-round ability. Such boats require an understanding of hull-form and design detail in addition to sailing ability and fitness. As the essence of yacht racing is its unique combination of cerebral and physical endeavour, in roughly equal parts, this seems only right and proper.

Level-rating classes are also a hell of a lot more interesting than one-design, where if you have seen one, you have seen them all. In the 1960s and 1970s, most of the young Holy Loch sailors raced Merlin Rockets, an 'open' national restricted class, so perhaps there may be some bias here. But our many subsequent years racing in one-designs and handicap events have not changed that opinion. We do not require cyclists to compete on frames of the same dimensions, skiers to use the same-sized skis or tennis players to use the same racket. Manufacturers of one-designs are even worse. Concerns about product liability mean that they are conservative and thus seldom 'state of the art' in design or construction. Moreover, a single supplier with attendant monopoly pricing can severely impact on the poor consumer's right to 'value for money'.[891]

The Merlins are a good example of the restricted class ethos. With length limited to 14ft LOA and beam to 7ft 2", plus a rise-of-floor limitation, a sail area/mast height trade-off formula and very little else, they demonstrate how a well-considered development rule can keep a class relevant and cool; in this case contributing to seven decades of significant progress in yacht design following WW2.

The Merlins have evolved into the most efficient hull-form, layout and rig for a two-person, non-trapeze dinghy that anyone has been able to come up with, even after the passing of three decades since the sweet-spots were identified. Understandably, the basic form has been extensively copied in one-design production boats. That said, no two Merlins are exactly the same. Assuming you buy, build or carefully choose your boat, it will be tailored to suit your physique, weight-distribution between the crew, your sailing style, your competitive priorities and your aesthetic preferences.

With sailors' strength optimised, and their weaknesses mitigated, almost by magic, individual performance envelopes converge. Counterintuitively, racing can be closer in these restricted classes than in one-design classes under 30ft, where a 'one-design crew' is also required. The equalising attributes of level-rating diminish as vessels become larger and crew weight diminishes as a percentage of displacement. But regardless, when any class of yacht anywhere in the size range from Moth to Maxi embraces different answers to the same question, this immeasurably enriches competition for both participants and spectators.

The Royal Clyde Yacht Club transformed yacht racing on the Clyde in the 1869 season with the introduction of level-rating with the 40-ton, 20-ton, and 10-ton classes. A year later, the club introduced the 5-ton class. The importance of this initiative cannot be overstated. From that date forward, the best, keenest, or simply the most trend-conscious, owners would commission new-builds at regular intervals to compete head-to-head in agreed measurement or rating bands. From this date, racing boats and cruising boats drifted apart in design and specifications as designers now had an unambiguous sense of purpose.

The 1890s saw the introduction of open-cockpit day-sailers. In 1888 Messrs R. Wylie and J. B. Hilliard, two well-known Clyde yachtsmen, canvassed the leading yacht clubs in the north to agree a classification system for smaller, more affordable racing yachts. This collaborative process led to the adoption of the 10-rater, 6-rater and 3-rater 'rating' classes and three 'length' classes, set at 19ft LWL, 17ft LWL and 15ft LWL. The second group were just big dinghies, so existing restrictions on the use of centreboards were lifted. Small yacht racing grew rapidly in popularity to become the mainstay of Clyde yachting, providing excellent sport through the golden years.

Clyde yachtsmen ploughed their own furrow with determination and a growing conviction that they could manage their own affairs without interference from the south. As the turn of the century approached, the Clyde clubs enjoyed a critical mass that made autonomous action entirely feasible. Henry Coleman noted that: *"The type of boat produced by recent YRA measurement rules, has resulted in the practical neglect of the YRA classes, and the development of a type of craft better suited to the physical features of the Clyde."*[892]

Coleman continued: *"The principal characteristics of these boats are considerable proportion of beam and draft to length, and high freeboard, with consequent great sail-carrying power. As overhangs are generally restricted, the boats present a somewhat over-sparred appearance."* While YRA classes would eventually make inroads, the Clyde did not toe the line until 1907 when the International Rule, conceived in the kindred fjords of Scandinavia, appeared.

Recreational sailors, who owned holiday villas on the shores of the Clyde estuary, turned out to race the small level-rating classes twice a week or more during the summer. This was where young talent flourished. As the years passed, while the keenest racing men remained faithful to the small boat fleets, others began to climb the age-old old-age ladder. Aspirational yachtsman traded up to a bigger boat every few years.

And, where there was serious family money in the mix, keen sailors could follow the old adage 'a foot of waterline for every year of age' to compete in big-league yachting on the national stage. Wealthy sailing families accumulated entire fleets: steam yachts, large cruising boats and professionally-managed top-class racing programmes, with motherships and tenders – all in addition to their still-cherished round-the-cans level-raters, see Chapter 13 on our 'tip-top sporting gentlemen'.

Skipping over a few of the rich and famous, Prof. John Teacher of the celebrated whisky family, was a small boat enthusiast, as were others in his family. He wrote a booklet titled: *The Records of the Clyde 19/24ft Class* in 1926. In the next century, Ron Teacher, chairman of the family business, was a keen and successful Dragon sailor. The Clark family, of the global thread spinning business were also involved in the 19/24's. The Bergius family, of marine engines and Teacher's Whisky fame, sailed all manner of small boats including 17/19s, and the wonderfully titled 'Baron MacAndrew of the Firth of Clyde' was a tireless advocate of small boat sailing. Many more such worthies appear in the pages of this book.

Through the mid-1800s, small undecked boats raced on the Clyde in arbitrarily assigned 17ft and 19ft classes. There were also 21ft boats and a few 15-footers, but they were not significant in the early development of class-racing. Prior to 1878, the only measurement was overall length. This was as simple a 'box rule' as could be drafted. Consequently, with sail-area unrestricted, designers sought the most powerful hull-shape possible. The boats were deep, with full ends, straight stems and wide vertical transoms.

The early 19ft Clyde lugsail racing boats displaced little more than half-a-ton and carried about 6-cwt of internal (shifting) ballast. However, as the years passed, the boats became deeper and displacement increased rapidly, edging towards 4-tons with 2-tons of ballast. They all had generous freeboard but were originally left entirely open. The perverse logic for this stipulation remained with the International 14ft dinghy until 1995:

"What was at issue was the degree of penalty for a capsize, how long before the boat was clear of water and racing again. In the past, the class had put a premium on seamanship."[893] In this 'alternate universe', good sailing was about keeping your boat dry, not driving it through the water faster than your competitors. The Largs and Western yacht clubs broke ranks with the Royal Clyde and the Northern to allow decking, making the boats more usable all-round.

Dixon Kemp noted that 'back to basics' weekend cruising was now popular in these short-ended 'racing machines': *"One or two clubs even now permit the boat to be covered from the mast forward, the space below forming what is called 'the den', where provisions, etc, may be kept dry, and where the luxurious owner and friends sleep when away on a cruise, covering the other four feet of their bodies with a tarpaulin."*[894] Oh the 'luxury' of half-in half-out cruising through a wet weekend in July.

The first Clyde 17/19s were a restricted class, established around 1888 and based on prior boats of similar dimensions, described as 'Clyde 17s' by Watson (1886) and Fife (1887).[895] The heyday of level-rating on the Clyde was played out in the three classes designated by LWL and LOA descended from this common root: the 17/19s, the 19/24s and the 23/30s. The addition of a maximum waterline-length allowed designers to build prettier boats with a decent bow overhang. However, the limitations on overall length meant that transom sterns still prevailed.

Ewan Kennedy, of the Scottish Boating blog, curates what might be termed 'open studies' on Scotland's yachting heritage. One of these threads concerns the old level-rating classes. Ewan notes that the classes thrived as a grassroots response to local sailors' needs and the specific conditions on the Clyde: "*There was a lot of hostility to the YRA, which many saw as seeking to impose ideas worked out in the South of England on the Clyde. However, the desire to innovate remained and a small development class would allow designers to experiment without any disasters being too expensive.*"[896]

Clyde 17-Foot Waterline Class (17/19s)

The Clyde 17-footers, as a class-racing boat, first appeared in the records of the Royal Western Yacht Club in 1888, and there is evidence that they had been around for some time by that date. Ewan notes that, in the years prior to that, G. L. Watson drew a small boat described as a '17ft Clyde Class' for P. R. McLean, the boatbuilder. This was *Mollie*, design No.108 of 1886. She would spark an enduring interest in this type of simple, affordable day-racer.

The following year, 1887, William Fife III designed *Nellie* for K. M. Clark of Wemyss Bay. More 17ft Fife designs followed in 1888: *Caprice* for R. M. Donaldson, *Nellie Too* for Mr Clark and *Dorothy* for John Tennant. Watson designed *Nell*, a '19ft Lug', for N. B. Stewart Junior in 1888 and the Bermudian-rigged, *Lapwing*, for E. S. Parker of Fairlie in the same year. Watson followed with *Harlequin*, built by MacLean for Dr Robinson in 1890.[897] Fife's *Katydid* of 1892 for P. P. Nicholl, the Watson design, *Cutty Sark*, built by MacLean of Roseneath for E. C. Richardson and an unnamed yacht for A. Logan also appear to fall into this category.[898]

However, this group of similar small yachts only became a formal class when the boats came under the wing of the 23/30 Committee in 1894 (see 23/30 Class notes below). The following dimensions were retrospectively agreed: 19ft LOA; 17ft LWL; 470ft^2 SA, 75% max in the main. No centreboards, fin, or bulb-keels. The 17/19s became popular in the early 1890s, with *Harlequin*, *Celia* and *Rosalind* heading the class.

Competition hotted up in 1894 when new boats by G. L. Watson, and William Fife III appeared. The Fife boat, *Hatasoo*, owned by James Bain, represented a new approach to the rule. She was wider and more lightly built than anything the class had seen before, and with a remarkable 64% ballast ratio, proved so quick in all but heavy airs that she effectively 'broke' the class. For the next three years, scheduled racing continued, but the pace of design development had led to processional racing.

Fife built two further new boats, but neither was able to challenge *Hatasoo*, launched in 1894, but still dominant through the 1896 season. James Bain and *Hatasoo* amassed a record 100 prizes when class-racing for 17/19s was wound up in 1897. The fact that Fife's new boats could not match his first attempt, suggests that *Hatasoo's* helmsman may have had something to do with the boat's success. However, the denizens of Clyde yachting were convinced that the rules governing the 17/19s had produced an undesirable type of boat, so the class was effectively euthanised. See list in Appendix 3.

A representative selection of 17/19s have endured to the present day, although exactly how many is unclear. *Hatasoo* has been well-maintained over the years and is still active, attracting much attention at the 2008 Fife Regatta.[899] *Fricka*, a William Fife III boat built for Robert Mann in 1895, and a hull-sister to *Hatasoo*, is an incongruous exhibit at the National Maritime Museum in Cornwall.

Yvette is listed as Mylne's only contribution to the class. She was supposedly built by McGruer's in 1897, but the design date is incongruous. *Yvette* was reportedly in storage at McGruer's in 1995. The yard was redeveloped in 2000 and her present whereabouts is listed as 'unknown'. *Banshee*, a G. L. Watson design (No.149) of 1888, is laid-up in a yard on the South Coast after an extensive restoration. However, she is thought to be an original clinker-built 17ft design, not a 17/19.

Other boats that may have survived include Fife's design No.304 of 1894 and No.369 of 1896 (no name or details in the Fife list), a second *Snarleyow* (later named *Vera* and owned by William Manaus Bergius) and Watson's design No.257 of 1892, *Pukerirera*, a Holy Loch-based boat, built by J. Adams in 1893. Finally, at the time of writing, *Golden Plover* is up for sale, a boat which appears to be a 17/19, despite substantial discrepancies in the description and specification.[900] She was referenced in *Leaves from Rowan's Log* by Dr Carslaw, but nothing in those pages sheds any light on her provenance.[901] *Golden Plover* resembles Watson's Royal Clyde OD, built by MacAlister in 1890/91, but that boat is much larger at 23ft LWL

Clyde 19-Foot Waterline Class (19/24s)

Of all the Clyde classes, the 19/24s are perhaps the best-loved, at least by the baby-boomer generation, as half-a-dozen were still racing together in the mid-1950s and a few were actively raced into the 1960s. Following the decision to wind-up the 17/19 class, The Clyde Yacht Clubs Conference held a meeting at the close of the 1896 season to establish a successor. A sub-committee was established with Watson and William Fife II as their main technical advisors. Fife's *Hatasoo* was considered to have taken the 17/19 class in an undesirable direction. Consequently, the conference set out to frame a new rule that would encourage a larger, more 'wholesome', type of racing boat. Inevitably, the new rule was more complex and more prescriptive.

The Royal Western had been largely responsible for the success of the 17/19s, and their representatives ensured that the proposed class would maintain the essential essence of amateur sailing in small, lively yachts. The Western's mission was to provide a more affordable alternative for sailors of modest means. By some perceptions, the 'moneyed style' of yachting promoted by the Royal Northern now prevailed at the Royal Clyde too.

But this was arguable; small boat sailing remained eternally popular in all the Clyde clubs, even among the grandees.

The initial proposal for the new class had come some years earlier from A. W. Steven, a pillar of the Royal Clyde. He suggested a more seaworthy boat than the 17/19, but one which retained scope for individual whimsy. A prototype was built to the basic concept in 1893. This was *Jeanette*, by McLean of Rosneath for J. C. Couper of Rhu. However, when G. L. Watson and William Fife II submitted the draft measurement rules to the Clyde Yacht Clubs Conference, for what would become the 19/24, they defined a larger boat. The prototype was effectively an '18/21' and would be obliged to sail-out her racing life as a 1½-rater.[902]

The leading dimensions of the 19/24 class were as follows: 24ft LOA; 19ft LWL; 500ft² SA, 80% max in the main (foretriangle to be measured from the gooseneck to stem, overlap free); 6ft 6" minimum waterline beam 60% of LWL from bow, to be measured without crew, but with ordinary spars, sails, and gear, including anchor and chain. The sternpost was to be straight, with no part of the hull or bumpkin projecting abaft that plane.

Light displacement was unreasonably taxed by penalising a tight turn of bilge and a slim efficient keel section; then as now seen as desirable characteristics in yacht design. The sagitta was to be measured at LWL section, 60% aft of the entry and if this was in excess of 12-inches, a sail area penalty was incurred. So, for example, if the garboard hollow was 16-inches, the boat sacrificed 58ft² of sail.[903] The penalty reduction in sail-area was calculated according to the following formula:

Clyde 19/24 Class Rule

$S = (\sqrt{MS} - E^2)^2$

Where:

S = *Actual sail area to be carried by the boat*
MS = *Maximum sail area allowed for the class*
E = *Excess sagitta in inches over the untaxed sagitta allowed*

The rule went on to specifically ban bulbed-keels, finkeels and centreboards. The first two restrictions, like the sagitta clause, would increase construction cost and reduce performance. This was unfortunate, but designers would, as usual, push the new rule to its limits. Looking at *Shireen*, for example, Mylne employed a 'bull nose' and an immersed transom to produce a much bigger boat, with a higher prismatic coefficient, than the dimensions would suggest.

The rig was simple – a gaff mainsail and a jib. The 17/19s had sliding gunter rigs that were effectively Bermudian, so the rules of the 19/24 class required that the angle of the gaff could not rise above 65° from the horizontal and had to be more than half the length of the boom – another retrogressive step. Notwithstanding the generally Luddite approach to the class rules, spinnakers would be allowed. Crew numbers were limited to five, although that was a tight squeeze. The sagitta measurement used in the 19/24s, effectively outlawed light displacement. A similar type of penalty but calculated from the difference between skin girth and chain girth, was later adopted for the International Rule of 1906.

The Clyde yacht clubs agreed that the new class should follow the period of rule-stability guaranteed for the larger 23/30s, viz, five years from the close of the 1897 season, but to include any boats built earlier. Several owners took advantage of this grandfather clause to participate in organised racing during 1897. The best of this small bunch was William Fife III's *Verenia*, followed closely by *Trebor*, designed and built by Peter McLean of Roseneath. The next year, the first season proper, a larger fleet was dominated by *Vashti*, designed by Alfred Mylne, with 29 prizes from 40 starts, beating a still-competitive *Verenia*.

In 1899, Fife's *Tringa* and the Mylne boat, *Jean*, joined the fleet. *Tringa*, owned and sailed by W. C. & J. H. Teacher, had the best of the season. The McGruer-built *Zitella* and McAlister's *Ceres*, both boats from the Mylne drawing board, took second and third. The 19/24s gave good racing but numbers grew more slowly than anticipated. Nevertheless, the class rules were seen to have evolved a more seaworthy type of boat than the old 17-footers, albeit not much quicker. There was some regret that counters were not allowed, an amendment which would certainly have improved the yachts' appearance. No matter, the 1900 season saw five new boats added to the fleet. *Valmai*, another Mylne boat sailed by Robert Clark, was the best of the season with *Memsahib II* runner-up.

The *Memsahibs* were commissioned by John Keil Tullis, a successful industrialist, and a long-term Mylne client. The original *Memsahib* had been Alfred Mylne's first racing yacht commission in 1897, after leaving the G. L. Watson office to establish his own practice in Hope Street, Glasgow. *Memsahib II* was another Mylne design. She was built by Gruer and Ewing McGruer at their original yard in Rutherglen in 1900. This was before the McGruers moved their yard to the Gareloch in 1910 and before Ewing took time out from the family business to hone his trade in the Sandbank yard of Alex Robertson.[904]

Mylne contributed substantially to the evolution of the class with fourteen commissions, although Fife maintained a significant presence with four fast boats. Peter McLean and Englishman, Linton Hope, contributed three each, and these too had their moments. Overall, the boats were as well-matched as any development class.[905] See list in Appendix 3.

In the years before the Great War, the 19/24 class was in decline, but the remaining owners were still enthusiastic. William Barclay wrote a charming piece for the *Yachting Monthly* in 1912 describing a race in *Valmai*.[906] "*Puffs came off the land and rain squalls belched out of the Holy Loch*". It was such a horrible day that only three starters came to the line, but the racing was close and the crew of four sat the boat out from the open cockpit and kept their heads down. Appraising the minimal inventory carried aboard, Barclay noted a "*rusted marlinspike and a less-rusted corkscrew*". It was a fine day out. *Valmai* ended her days in Bombay.

As far as we are aware, the only original 19/24s still sailing is *Shireen*, which retains the coachroof from her inter-war cruising conversion. However, she will soon be joined by several more: *Memsahib II* is currently undergoing a refit to return her to her original racing trim. *Ulidia* is in a yard on the Isle of Man awaiting minor repairs after falling over and cracking a few planks. *Robina* is currently being restored. Finally, *Lyvinda* is in a barn at Blairmore. The owner believes her to be a Mylne, but we need her original name to confirm that.[907] *Lyvinda* was tired but complete when she went into storage and represents a feasible restoration project.

Windhover II, ex *Sapphire*, ex *Doreen*, is now owned by the Clyde Maritime Trust, which acquired her in 2006. She is presently lying at Yorkhill Quay in Glasgow. It is intended that she will be based in Largs and sailed by the Glasgow Sea Scouts. There is also a boat called *Tringa*, but she is a 2010 replica which carries the name of the 1899 Fife boat.[908] So there is the prospect of six 19/24s afloat before long to recover the essence of traditional small boat sailing as practiced on the Clyde.

Clyde 23-Foot Waterline Class (23/30s)

The Clyde 23/30 class followed on from the two cutter-rigged, square-sterned boats of 23ft LWL, designed by G. L. Watson for the RCYC. Robert Wylie built *Volunteer* to the same design. At the close of the 1891 season, Wylie sold the boat and commissioned *Verve III*, from G. L. Watson for the 1892 season. *Verve III*, arguably a 'prototype' 23/30, differed significantly in concept, being a much bigger boat, lightly constructed and with powerful overhangs. She was clearly an advance in design over her short-ended predecessors and would spark a decade of development to bring these small yachts to a high level of refinement.

There were other new boats in 1892. This 'second generation' shared *Verve's* generous bow overhang (a feature that would later be limited by the 23/30 Rule), but they were bigger boats all-round, having grown from 4-tonners to 5-tonners. By now the other Clyde clubs were taking an interest in these sporting little yachts. In the autumn of that year, the Clyde Yacht Clubs Conference drew up a set of rules for a new 23/30 Class. The dimensions would be: 30ft LOA; 23ft LWL; 750ft² SA, with a maximum of 80% in the mainsail. Centreboards, fin, or bulb-keels were not allowed.

Six boats to the new rule followed in 1893: *Vida*, *Pike* and *Shuna* by G. L. Watson; *Thaber*, *Lala* and *Norka*, from William Fife III. The Wylie's *Vida* was the best of the bunch with Peter Coats' *Thaber* generally second. The same two boats headed the fleet the following year. Just as *Vida* was waning, *Vida II*, after her late launch in 1895, continued the Wylie family's domination. After a lull in interest for three years, there was a feeling that beating *Vida II* was no longer a hopeless task. In 1898 eight new boats were built to bring the strength of the class up to fifteen.

Nevertheless, *Vida II* still headed the rankings for that season, but *Espada* and *Mavis*, both from Fife, took second and third. In 1899, Patterson's, Mylne-designed *Lola* joined in the fun, but *Vida II* stubbornly retained the top spot. Interest then seems to have waned, even though two new boats joined the class; as in the two previous years, the average number of starters was just eight. *Vida II* withdrew early in the 1900 season and without the Wylie family on the starting line the class seems to have lost some of its drive. The 1898 Fife, *Mavis*, had the best of the averages, followed by *Psyche II*, of the same vintage from Mylne. See detailed list in Appendix 3.

Henry Coleman, writing in 1906, noted that *"the original boats of the class, such as Vida I and Pike, were roomy enough for conversion into cruisers, and are still to the fore in that capacity, while racing more or less regularly in the handicap classes. The development of the type has, however, proceeded in the direction of decreased displacement, with consequent shallowing of the underwater body and lower freeboard, thereby reducing the head-room to such an extent that the modern boats are useless for cruising purposes."*[909]

Clyde 30ft Restricted Class

The popular Clyde 30ft Restricted Class was conceived in 1904. The rating parameters were based on the YRA 30-rater, and indeed all the class measured in as such and could use that rating when participating in handicap racing. However, perhaps reflecting the Clyde's long-standing scepticism of YRA classes, and their perceived unsuitability for northern waters, the organisers of the Clyde class regarded the 1896 YRA rule as just a starting point from which to specify a more wholesome vessel.

The class's technical committee framed supplementary restrictions to reduce expense and produce a seaworthy boat with a useful second life as a cruiser. These objectives were met and the Clyde 30ft Class provided some of the best local competition before the arrival of the International Rule. The 30-rater rule produced a waterline of about 26ft on 40ft LOA with 8ft+ beam. The additional Clyde rules were as follows: draught measured at 0.6 LWL to be 5ft 3"; min beam on LWL at 0.6 LWL from the entry to be 7ft 9"; min freeboard to top of deck at side to be 2ft.[910]

Other restrictions emphasized the desire for a level playingfield. Expensive double-skin construction was not allowed. Hollow topsail yards, spinnaker booms, and jackyards were permitted, but hollow or bamboo masts or other spars were banned. Conventional sternpost-hung rudders were specified, precluding separate fin-and-skeg, or balanced rudders. An ordinary working anchor and chain had to be on board for measurement and while racing.

The anchor rule may be honoured in the breach. At the 1970 Merlin Championships at Pwllheli, Olympian, Rodney Pattison, turned up with a bobbin of twine better suited to wrapping parcels and a little Danforth, like an executive paperweight, executed in polished stainless-steel. As events transpired, difficult conditions and a record fleet stretched rescue services and many crews had to resort to anchoring. This is where the spirit, as opposed to the letter of the law, is important.

Within the layout of cockpits, the 30-footer rules required two fixed platforms, or seats, at least 7ft 6" long, and all such seats and floor-boards had to remain in position when racing. The cutter rig was mandated, comprising mainsail, topsail, and two headsails. The area of mainsail was not to exceed 62% of total sail area. Finally, the class rules emphasized that the linear-rating could not exceed 30-feet as the boats would race level with no time allowances.

The yachts gave excellent racing. In the first year of the class seven were built: two, *Lilian* and *Mikado*, were designed and built by Fife; and five, *Armyne*, *Thetis*, *Psyche*, *Corrie*, and *Vladimir* were designed by Mylne. R. G. Allan's *Armyne* topped the class in her maiden season, closely followed by Sir William Corry's *Mikado*. All, except *Vladimir*, were out again in 1905, together with two new boats designed by Fife – Andrew Coats' *Great Auk*, and T. K. Laidlaw's *Tarpon*. These new boats started the season well, but *Thetis* was the season's top boat with 25 prizes in 34 starts, including 14 firsts. *Armyne* was second and *Lilian* third. The 1906 season saw the departure of *Armyne*, *Mikado* and *Tarpon*. Two new boats arrived: R. G. Allan's *Medora*, by Mylne, and Thomas Glen-Coats' first design, *Pallas*, which replaced his Mylne boat, *Thetis*, see Chapter 26

There was never a points prize for the class. However, Glen-Coats made out a table, adopting Thalassa's system of giving 400 points for a first prize, 200 for a second, and 100 for a third, and dividing by the number of starts.[911] Under this system, Thomas's brother Andrew Glen-Coats came out on top in the Mylne-designed *Thetis*.

Glen-Coats writes: *"Turning to windward in a strong breeze and a jump of a sea, Thetis was probably a little better than any of the others and her excellence in these conditions probably won her a number of races towards the end of the season. As a good all-round boat Thetis was always a difficult one to shake off, and judging by the other yachts of the class, she seemed to be sailing quite as well as in 1905. For the second season in succession, she has finished champion."*[912] Thomas Glen-Coats' self-penned *Pallas* ran *Thetis* a close second. Tommy and Andrew were two of the best helmsmen on the Clyde. Clearly there was some sibling rivalry as Tommy failed to mention his brother's role in the continued success of *Thetis*. Andrew was equally successful when he transferred his skills to *Pallas*, which was kept in the family when Tommy built the 12-metre, *Hera*.

The class thrived until its chief proponents bought into the 6-metre class as the International Rule gathered momentum in the period 1907-09. The Clyde 30ft Restricted Class Rules produced fine, seaworthy vessels which remained popular as a 'second' division and also performed well in handicap racing. After lapsing into inactivity, the 30-footers revived, albeit briefly, in 1938. Five owners committed to race through the season and it was hoped that more would be brought back into racing trim to join the fleet. Unfortunately, WW2 intervened, and the initiative lapsed.

Alfred Mylne, like many designers, was too busy to run his own boat until he acquired *Medea* (ex-*Vladimir*) from his late brother's estate in 1927. Charles had bought the 30-linear-rater (41ft LOA) on Alfred's advice a couple of years before. Mylne had designed *Vladimir* to the Clyde 30ft Restricted Class rule in 1904 and her longevity suggests that she had been well-built by Alexander Robertson in Sandbank. Mylne was at a stage in his life when he could kick back and enjoy life during the summer when business was slack. The old yacht was ideal for this.

Medea raced in the Under 15-tons, or Under 20-tons, handicap division in the 1930s, albeit that she was down on her marks with an excess of cruising gear and truly dreadful sails. Nevertheless, by grit and guile, Alfred usually placed in the top three, although competition was limited in numbers and quality. In 1930, he won 10 times from 15 starts, with four seconds and a third. When Charles Mylne bought the boat, she had already been converted to Bermudian rig, as had most of the other ex-Clyde 30ft Class boats that competed in the small handicap fleet. There must have been a sentimental attachment. Mylne kept *Medea* until his death in 1951; the yacht was then 43 years old. See list in Appendix 3.

The Still-born Clyde 22ft Restricted Class

A Clyde 22ft rating restricted class was proposed for 1913. At this time there was much talk of the need for new classes. However, no boats materialised. The boats were not to exceed 22ft rating, as measured under IYRU Rules, but Lloyds classification was not required. H. C. Smith of Burnham of Crouch produced a design which appeared in the pages of *Yachting*.[913] This shows a heavy boat, beamy with slack bilges but not unattractive. The designer thought she could carry another 100ft^2 of sail, but the rating would go up over half-a-foot. The gaff sloop sail-plan featured a very low boom. She was, basically, a cruiser laid out as a racing boat.

The Short-lived New National Classes of 1919

After the dust had settled on the Great War, there was a mood to make another fresh start on the perennial quest for wholesome boats that would hold their value. J. F. Jellico proposed a resolution to "*meet the demands of younger yachtsmen who want a cheaper form of boat than that produced under the International Rule*".[914] The Yacht Racing Association appointed a learned committee to draft rules for a whole new slate of national classes to cover the small to medium size-range.[915]

The proposed National Classes of 1919 were:

- *30ft Cabin Class*. Max. length on waterline 30ft; actual or calculated displacement 9-tons; max draft aft 6ft 3", at girth station 5ft 9"; min at girth station 5ft 6"; min freeboard at bow 3ft; at girth station 2ft 5" and at stern 2ft 4"; sail area 1,200^{2}ft, max measuring 80% of the fore-triangle only; beam max 10ft, min 9ft.

- *25ft Cabin Class*. Max. length on waterline 25ft; displacement about 6-tons; draught 5ft 6"; freeboard 2ft 10" at bow, 2ft 3" at girth station and 2ft 2" at stern; sail area 850^{2}ft, measuring 80% of fore triangle-only; beam max 9ft, min 8ft.

- *20ft Heavy Displacement Class*. Max length on waterline 20ft; displacement 3-tons; draught 4ft 8"; freeboard 2ft 6" min at bow, 1ft 10" at girth station and 1ft 8" at stern; sail area 540^{2}ft measuring 80% of fore-triangle only; beam 7ft 3" max 6ft 5" min.

- *20ft Light Displacement Class*. Max length on waterline 20ft; displacement 2.33 tons; draught 4ft; freeboard 2ft 5" min at bow, 1ft 8" at girth station, and 1ft at stern; sail area 435^{2}ft measuring 80% of fore triangle only; beam 7ft max and 6ft 5" min.

Fred J. Stephen, council member of the YRA, more than adequately represented Clyde interests.[916] Technical advice was provided by Messrs C. E. Nicholson, William Fife, and Alfred Mylne, so on this occasion at least, there was no question of a stitch-up by the 'southern mafia'. However, very few of the proposed classes were realised in any form. There was a Fife 18-footer for A. S. L. Young, a similar boat from Nicholson's design for the Solent, and a single 23-footer, also by Nicholson, for Thomas Marlowe, Editor of the *Daily Mail*.[917]

A slate that had looked good on paper sank almost without trace. The only enduring dividend was the 12ft and 14ft National dinghy classes, which in turn, morphed into a whole new world of small boat sailing in light-weight dinghies. This is perhaps the principal legacy of the YRA and their collaboration with the BRA. Today the RYA, as successor to both organisations, is all about small boat sailing. It has no significant role in the design of yachts and limited involvement in the larger classes.

There is some interest in reviewing what this august panel of experts considered desirable in 1919. Restricted development classes were generally preferred to one-designs. Scantlings rules and basic cabin fit-out requirements, including a minimum headroom prescription, were deemed necessary in the 30ft and 20ft cabin classes. So far so good, but the committee also sought to typeform an awkward triangular keel with maximum draft aft.

The 19/24 style of profile would become irrevocably dated over the next decade, and of course, they were extremely awkward to slip. A tax on overhangs was agreed, but it was not clear how this would have been applied through the proposed trade-off mechanism. Foresails were still conceived in terms of working jibs set within a limited fore-triangle. In 1919 there were still benefits in assigning most of the allowable area to the mainsail, but all that was about to change as increasing use of the genoa jib in the 1920s favoured taller fore-triangles and longer J measurements.[918] More effective spinnakers resulted from these changes too. So, august as they were, the committee could not see into the future.

The already established 18ft LWL class of the Boat Racing Association was also endorsed for adoption: *"The designer to be given a fixed length on the waterline, a minimum displacement, and a certain minimum and maximum beam, between which he must work, and the same with draught of water. He is then free to solve the problem of getting the fastest boat possible, subject to these restrictions."*

This curious wording suggests that the committee had not considered whether the existing boats met all essential criteria for a YRA national class, whether they should be grandfathered, or whether they were unsuitable. They left the matter to the BRA and a sub-committee. Better, surely, that they had not attempted to specify the class at all.

In addition to fostering 'cheap boats for younger yachtsmen', additional proposals were drawn up in 1919 for larger racing yachts; in this instance to address the presumed requirements of established gentlemen. Two classes, 16 metres (52.5ft) LWL, and 13 metres (42.7ft) LWL, were envisaged. The early thoughts of the committee were that these new classes might be organised as restricted or one-designs, perhaps with a fixed sail area and a choice of rig.[919]

Of the four keelboat classes, it appears that just two 30ft Cabin Class yachts were built in Scotland, both in 1919. Perhaps anxious to promote the class, William Fife III submitted the plans of his new *Clio* (the favoured name for Fife yachts, although they were not numbered) for publication. The second boat was *Ierne*, built the following year for Mr A. F. Sharman Crawford across the Irish Sea in Cork.

As regards *Clio*, *Yachting Monthly* noted: *"For a small fast cruiser, it would be difficult to get a better boat or one more easily handled and more economical to run. The plans show how comfortable she should be to live on. As the sail-plan of these boats last year is being considered, or reconsidered, by the YRA, it cannot yet be shown. It will be Bermuda, however, with one headsail on a boom. No shifting of sheets being required for windward work, the boat, works out at 4-tons TM, may be easily handled by two persons, while three amateurs could race her efficiently."*[920]

Design for a 16-metre (52 ft LWL) National Class Boat

The idea of a 16-metre 52ft LWL National Class boat, as with the smaller classes, went nowhere, but it is interesting that such a large yacht was still seen as a viable national class. It was envisaged as a more commodious successor to both the old 52-linear-rater and the International Rule's 15-metre. In the event, this proposed class was simply unnecessary, and moreover, a recession was on the way.

It is likely that most British design offices devoted time to explore the possibilities of the new classes. Thomas Glen-Coats drew the short straw in the Mylne office. The design was published in *Yachting Monthly* in the summer of 1920. *"I am sending you the plans of the 52 ft 6" LWL fast cruiser as promised. The LWL corresponds to that suggested by the YRA last year for the larger of the two proposed national classes, which classes have, I understand, fallen through, the idea having been abandoned in favour of the new IYRU classes. We were told at the time that these would be classes (with restrictions) for boats of 13 and 16 metres LWL, with as nearly as possible the accommodation of the old 15 and 19-metre boats respectively.*[921]

Tommy then described how he had drawn a set of lines the previous summer to see how the required accommodation would fit into a boat of 16 metres LWL of moderate displacement and conventional hull-form. His objectives in this exercise were: *"i) as good accommodation as possible for the given LWL while keeping the displacement, and thereby the sail area, moderate; and ii) a handy and weatherly type with a good turn of speed."* The final dimensions were as follows: LOA 82.75ft, LWL 52.5ft, beam 17.25ft, with a draft of 10ft.[922] The results were more than satisfactory, and the lines appear at the end of this chapter. In fact, she looks a more wholesome and useful vessel in every respect than either a 15-metre, or a 19-metre of the period.

Design for a BRA 35ft LWL Class

The BRA 35ft LWL class (10.7 metres) appears to derive from the initial proposal for a 13-metre class (42.7ft LWL). *"This month we are able, through the courtesy of Mr T. C. Glen-Coats, to publish the lines, sail-plan and arrangement plan of a 35-ft. load waterline fast cruiser.*[923] The design was for an extremely pretty boat in the old fast-cruiser style, before internal volume trumped all other attributes. *Yachting Monthly* noted that, although not originally intended to fit the BRA Rule, the design conformed to the draught and freeboard restrictions and lay within 1% of the additional draught restriction adopted for the little BRA 18-footers.

The dimensions of Glen-Coats' design were: LOA 55.25ft, LWL 35ft, beam 11.33ft, draught 7.75ft, displacement was relatively light at 13.3-tons, with a tight turn of bilge, sail area 1,900ft^2, BRA rating 40ft. There was 6ft of headroom in the saloon under a low, elegant cabin top. There were two unusually wide settee berths (6.5ft x 3ft) and three folding pipe cots in the very generous forecastle. The drawings follow this section.

Design for a BRA 18ft LWL class

While the BRA 18ft Class became popular for a time and the rule was adopted by model yacht fleets, there were no takers in the larger sizes which became no more than a minor curiosity in the history of yachting. The light displacement BRA Rule yachts were more like raters than the products of the 1906 International Rule. They were good boats. The BRA, which had been a notable champion of dinghy racing and the small keelboat racing classes, folded into the YRA in 1921.

In 1917, Thomas Glen-Coats described a system of designing in the pages of *Yachting Monthly*.[924] This idea appears to have grown in the fertile mind of Tommy's good friend, the late Mr David Dunlop, who passed away in 1914. Dunlop had built a model of a 12-metre yacht, at a scale one inch to the foot, using the mechanism. Tommy felt guilty that he never could find the time to indulge David with a discussion on his friend's favourite topic. So, to make amends, as it were, he trialled the system in the design of a BRA 18ft LWL class yacht.

This was the system, in as much as Tommy could recall: *"The exact shape of the vessel (apart from the keel) can be got from certain lines (three or four in number), the form and adjustment of which are arranged according to the judgment of the designer and as experience dictates."* A common process used throughout the design produces the curve to form the sections. Beam and depth of body (excluding the keel) are decided beforehand and the process starts at the mid-section. *"In the example I have fixed the extreme beam at 6ft, depth of body below LWL. At 1ft, and vertical point where section tumbles home, I have fixed at 1ft 10½ inches above profile line at mid-section. Now I divide the half breadth (three feet) into, say, five divisions of the following proportions, reading from left to right as per my drawing: 1/ 25th, 3/25th, 5/25th, 7/25th and 9/25th.*

Next, the height of the section can be taken from the lowest point of the profile (exclusive of the keel) to the tumble home point (previously fixed in relation to the LWL). *And this we divide also into twenty-fifths in the same proportion as in the horizontal divisions.* (There are the same number of divisions vertically as horizontally). *These are divided as follows: 1/25th, 3/25th, 5/25th, 7/25th and 9/25th, the smallest division being at the lowest point (see drawing). Next, I join the lines as shown, and thus get the form of the section."* Tommy notes that all sections formed in this way will have a common character, but possible variations might give an infinite variety of forms.

Tumblehome on sections was controlled via a 'disappearing line', an entirely unnecessary feature on a BRA 18-footer which complicated the system to an extraordinary degree. *"It seemed to me then that it would be possible to make the disappearing line of a certain form vertico-longitudinally, and to let it govern the design rather than the line of greatest breadths."*

Thomas settled on a disappearing line which was a curve of sines, so that the vertical longitudinal line of greatest breadths also became a curve of sines, as did the profile of the hull proper. *"As to its form, it is simply continued in a perfectly fair line. This controls the line of profile of the forward overhang. It is a correct curve of sines, though with regard to the centre-line it is rather fuller forward than aft, so arranged as to give the desired width of section forward, aft and amidships."*

Tommy summarised that the design exercise is substantially complete when: i) the profile line; ii) the 'disappearing line' (which governs the form of vertical-longitudinal line of greatest breadths); and iii) the half-breadth tumble-home line are all resolved. The rest of the process follows automatically, and theoretically, fairing is not necessary. The system generates sections up to the tumblehome line, or the sheerline if there is no tumblehome. The keel is designed separately and is not part of the system.

While this extensive, and rather esoteric, discussion was substantially a tribute to his old friend (Tommy only used this system once and for this exercise), Glen-Coats did see specific potential in the method, particularly if applied to canoe bodies without a full-keel, such as motor vessels and steamers. The 18ft BRA design follows this section, and hopefully, the above will have explained the unusual accompanying curves.

In profile and sail-plan, the Glen-Coats boat bears a strong resemblance to a G. L. Watson & Co Ltd one-design, built by William Fife at Fairlie. Four 'Salcombe Saints' to the BRA 18-ft Class rule were delivered to Salcombe Yacht Club in 1919. Below the waterline, however, the boats are very different. Tommy's boat draws 4ft 3" and has a short, efficient fin-keel in the modern idiom, while the Watson equivalent is deeper-bodied but still draws just 2ft 2". It has a long shallow fullkeel that harks back to the old days. Only one of the Saints has survived. *Saint Patrick* was rescued from a garden in Dumfries and Galloway in 2009 and beautifully rebuilt by Fairlie Restorations.

The 18-ft Rule spawned a wide variety of interpretations. A couple of contemporary Charles E. Nicholson variations are included to illustrate the scope of this interesting rule. One is a long-ended fin keel interpretation, with a low aspect Bermudian rig. The other is a dinghy type yacht with a fin and bulb keel, bowsprit and long overhanging boom.

[890] Clyde Yacht Racing, The Glasgow Herald,16th July 1888.

[891] Manufacturers' one-designs can be vulnerable to EU anti-trust issues if used in Olympic and related competition.

[892] The Sailing Boat, a Treatise on Sailing Boats and Small Yachts, their Varieties of Type, Sails, Rig, etc, Henry Coleman Folkard, 1901.

[893] The History of the International 14ft Dinghy, J. Vaughan, 2004.

[894] Manual of Yacht and Boat Sailing and Architecture Dixon Kemp, 9th edition, 1900. Contribution by G. L. Watson.

[895] The Clyde Canoe and Lugsail Club corresponds to the Clyde Canoe Club in the description of these boats by Martin Black. The Canoe Club was established in 1873 on the Gareloch at Rosneath and moved to Loch Lomond in 1898. It became the Loch Lomond Sailing Club much later in 1999. Neither the old name, nor the club's diversion into small keelboats in 1886 is mentioned in their official history (The Story of the Clyde Canoe Club, 1873-2013); and the same is true of the story concerning the club's merger with the Royal Western and its subsequently reasserted independence on moving to Loch Lomond.

[896] The Clyde 17/19-foot Class, Scottish Boating Blog, Ewen Kennedy, 7th December 2010.

[897] Ibid

[898] The name *Katydid* stands out. The popular 'What Katy Did' books were written back in the 1870s. Katy is a tomboy, forever getting into scrapes but with a desire to be beautiful and popular. When she becomes an invalid, after an accident, her illness and long recovery brings about a reformed, and sadly, rather pious character.

[899] At the 2008 Fife Regatta, *Hatasoo* was 114 and still in sailing condition. A journalist asked Ronnie McGrouther when they planned to restore her. "*She had a new transom fifty years ago*" came the reply "*what more do you think she needs?*" Theo Rye.

[900] *Golden Plover* is advertised as being designed by Watson and built by McAlister in 1899 – 1903. However, none of Watson's 17/19s were built by McAlister, and Watson's last 17/19 was *Pirouette*, built by Maclean in 1894. She has been diagonally sheathed over carvel planking.

[901] Leaves from Rowan's Log, Dr Carslaw, 1944. Carslaw has *Golden Plover* down as being owned at that time by "*JA and BK*".

[902] Cruise in Company, George Blake and Christopher Small, 1959.

[903] The 'sagitta' is the garboard hollow, or distance of separation between the 'chain girth' (a line stretched tight from gunwale to keel-foot) and the 'skin girth' (a line following the surface of the skin on the same line).

[904] Ewing moved on to the Smith's Rhubaan Boatyard in Tighnabruiach, before establishing Robertson's famous rival-yard at Clynder on the Gareloch in 1910. The rest of the McGruer legend is history, as they say. McGruer Legacy, Kathy Mansfield, Classic Boat, May 2012.

[905] George Watson was not involved in the 19/24s after his work on drafting the rule.

[906] The Clyde 19/24 Footers, William Barclay, Yachting Monthly ca.1912.

[907] *Lyvinda* was surveyed in 1973 and ascribed as McGruer 1905. However, as McGruer did not build 19/24s after 1901, this is incorrect.

908 Helmut and Gisela Scharbaum built a replica of this yacht in 2010. Clyde 19/24 Class website, Ewan Kennedy.
909 Sailing Boats from Around the World, Henry Colman Folkard, 1906.
910 The Clyde 30ft (restricted) Class, T. C. Glen-Coats, the Yachting & Boating Monthly, Volume II, No.9, January 1907.
911 *Thalassa* was the name of a cutter, designed in 1887 by Mr A. E. Payne for Colonel Bucknill, and also the enthusiastic colonel's pseudonym.
912 The Clyde 30ft (restricted) Class, T. C. Glen-Coats, January 1907.
913 Notes and Notions, Yachting 13th January 1913.
914 Minute by Minute, the Story of the RYA 1875-1982, Gordon Fairley, 1983.
915 Yachting, New National Classes, The Times, 27th May 1919.
916 The committee members were the Rev. H. H. Rogers (Royal Norfolk and Suffolk Yacht Club), Mr J. R. Payne (Royal Temple Yacht Club), Mr A. G. McMeekin (vice-president, BRA), Mr Gautier de St Croix (Royal Corinthian Yacht, Club), Mr F. J. Stephen (Royal Clyde Yacht Club), Mr F. A. Richards (Royal Southern Yacht Club), Mr Charles Livingston (Royal Mersey Yacht Club), and Mr R. E. Workman (Royal North of Ireland Yacht Club).
917 These National Classes, The Yachtsman, 10th June 1933.
918 The 'J' measurement is the horizontal distance from the front side of the mast to the intersection of the forestay and the deck.
919 It is interesting to see the YRA's main criteria were then defined in SI units, an influence of the International Rule perhaps, nearly half a century before British government policy set metrication in motion in 1965.
920 The 30ft National Class, Yachting Monthly, bound copies for the year 1919.
921 52.5ft Fast Cruiser, the Yachting & Boating Monthly. Volume XXIX, Nos. CLXIX to CXXXII, May to October 1920.
922 The detailed restrictions were never decided on (at least they were never made public), only the respective LWL limits were announced.
923 35ft Fast Cruiser, the Yachting & Boating Monthly. Volume XXII, Nos. CXXCII to CLXXIV, November 1916 to April 1917.
924 A System of Designing explained by Thomas C. Glen-Coats and illustrated in the design of an 18ft BRA Racing boat, the Yachting Monthly and Marine Motor, Volume XXIII, Nos. CXXXIII to CXXXVIII, May to October 1917.

Susette II, 19/24, Alfred Mylne, 1902   Image: sourced by Scottishboating

Vida, Clyde 23/30, G. L. Watson, 1893, off Hunter's Quay   Image: Adamson & Sons

Shuna, Clyde 23/30, G. L. Watson, 1893   Image: Adamson & Sons
Note the double-diagonal decks which would have imparted stiffness to compensate for the large open cockpit (and maintain a dry deckhead below). Compare this deck layout with *Vida*, above.

Lapwing, 17-footer, Clyde, 1888. Image: Adamson   Harlequin, 17/19, G. L. Watson, 1890

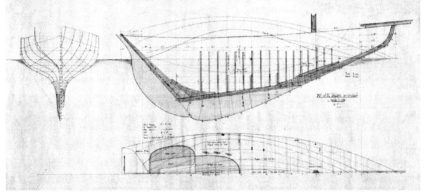

Memsahib II, 19/24, Mylne, 1900, backbone construction detail   Mylne Yacht Design

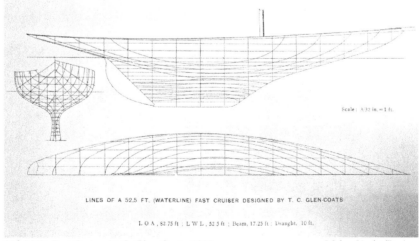

LINES OF A 52.5 FT. (WATERLINE) FAST CRUISER DESIGNED BY T. C. GLEN-COATS

L.O.A., 82.75 ft ; L.W.L., 52.5 ft ; Beam, 17.25 ft ; Draught, 10 ft.

35ft LWL Fast Cruiser T. C. Glen-Coats, 1917   Mylne Yacht Design
Note the vertical section of the keel, swollen/slightly bulbed at the keel-foot to lower CoG
and the slight hollow in the run of the horizontal keel section – an unusual feature.

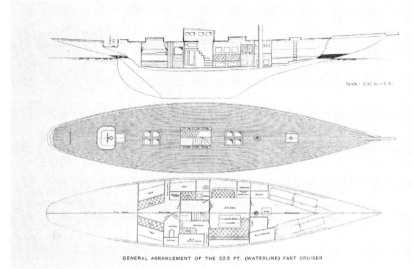

GENERAL ARRANGEMENT OF THE 52.5 FT. (WATERLINE) FAST CRUISER

Thomas Glen-Coats, 52.5ft LWL Fast Cruiser, 1919   Mylne Yacht Design

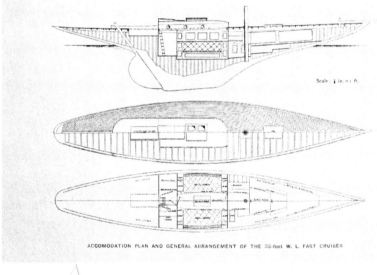

ACCOMODATION PLAN AND GENERAL ARRANGEMENT OF THE 35-foot W. L. FAST CRUISER

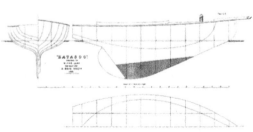

Hatasoo, 17/19, 1894   William Fife III

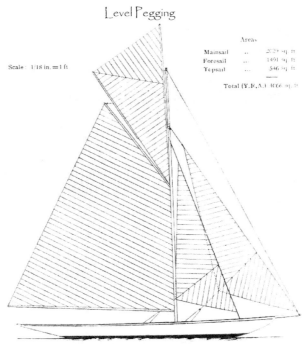

SAIL PLAN OF THE 52.5 FT. WATERLINE FAST CRUISER

52.5 ft LWL Fast Cruiser, 1929   Mylne Yacht Design

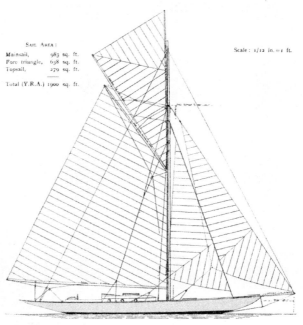

SAIL AND RIGGING PLAN OF THE 35-foot W. L. FAST CRUISER

35ft LWL Fast Cruiser T. C. Glen-Coats, 1917   Mylne Yacht Design

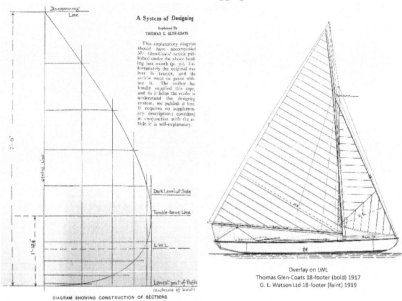

A System of Designing

Explained By
THOMAS C. GLEN-COATS

This explanatory diagram should have accompanied Mr. Glen-Coats' article published under the above heading last month (p. 30). Unfortunately the original was lost in transit, and the article went to press without it. The author has kindly supplied this copy, and as it helps the reader to understand the designing system, we publish it here. It requires no supplementary description; considered in conjunction with the article it is self-explanatory.

DIAGRAM SHOWING CONSTRUCTION OF SECTIONS
Section 5. The others are constructed in the same manner.

Overlay on LWL
Thomas Glen-Coats 18-footer (bold) 1917
G. L. Watson Ltd 18-footer (faint) 1919

Curve of Section · Sailplan

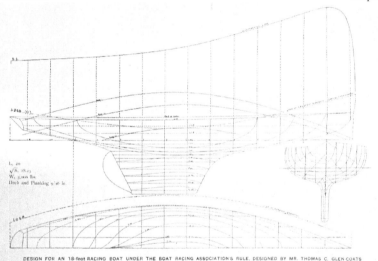

DESIGN FOR AN 18-foot RACING BOAT UNDER THE BOAT RACING ASSOCIATION'S RULE, DESIGNED BY MR. THOMAS C. GLEN-COATS

18ft-LWL BRA Racing Boat, T. C. Glen-Coats, 1917 · Mylne Yacht Design

G. L. Watson & Co designed four identical BRA 18ft Class yachts in 1919 which were built by Fifes of Fairlie. The boats were all named after saints. *St. Patrick* has been restored by Fairlie Restorations for a G.L. Watson & Co client. The topsides profile and sailplan are identical to the Glen-Coats design exercise two years earlier, but the long shallow keel contrasts markedly with the efficient fin on the Glen-Coats boat.

472

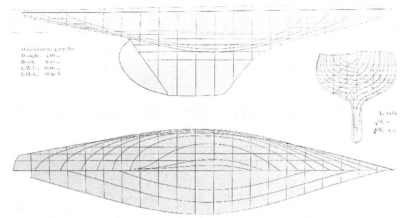

DESIGN FOR AN 18 FT. RACING BOAT (KEEL TYPE) UNDER THE BOAT RACING ASSOCIATION'S RULE. BY C. E. NICHOLSON.

Fin & Bulb BRA 18ft LWL design ca.1915   Charles E. Nicholson

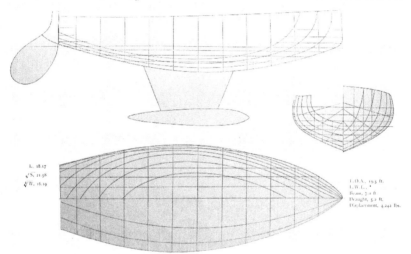

DESIGN FOR AN 18 FT. RACING BOAT (BULB-FIN TYPE) UNDER THE BOAT RACING ASSOCIATION'S RULE. BY C. E. NICHOLSON.

* Being clench-built, this boat gets 1.33 deduction from L.O.A. for L.

Fin & Bulb BRA 18ft LWL design, ca.1915   Charles E. Nicholson

Oban   Artist: William Lionel Wyllie (1851-1931)

473

Chapter 24: Scottish Internationals

Tis true these lean new fashioned half-starved yachts manage to slide along with a flat sail and be hanged to them. But I would not give an old marlin'spike to sail as they do. Why you can't see them go, no foam under their bows, no bright spray tossed on either side, and worst of all no wake behind them. Tale of a Tub, 1854[925]

The International Rule was good for the marine industry on the Clyde. While only the smaller classes regularly mustered healthy fleets on the local starting lines, our designers and builders enjoyed a bonanza of lucrative orders. Metre-boat orders were shared among the 'name' designers for most size classes, but where the lucrative contracts for bigger boats were concerned, the lines of William Fife III and the craftsmen of his Fairlie shipwrights were especially esteemed.

Fife designed and built three 23-metres: *White Heather II* in 1907 and *Shamrock* in 1908, then *Cambria* two decades later in 1927. There were two 19-metres: *Corona* and *Mariquita,* both built in 1911; and eight 15-metres: *Mariska* and *Alachie* in 1908, then *Vanity, Hispania* and *Tuiga* in 1909, *Sophie Elizabeth* in 1910, followed by *The Lady Anne* in 1912, and *Maudry* in 1913. Alfred Mylne designed four 15-metres: *Ma'oona* in 1907, *Ostera* in 1909 and both *Paula II* and *Jeano* in 1910.

The 23-metres, 19-metres and 15-metres raced occasionally during the Clyde Fortnight, but these were special occasions. As for classes turning out regularly, each era saw the mix alter, beginning with the world's first 12-metre fleet, which enjoyed close racing before the Great War. The 8-metre fleet had its moments, but the 6-metre fleet was the hot-house of design and development. Post-WW2, the 8-metre cruiser-racers (8CRs) often provided the best racing, although the 'straight-eight' revival in the 1960s and 70s was also notable. The 6-metres enjoyed a long run through to the 1950s, racing after a time in two fleets – the new and newish boats with certificates, and the unmeasured 'ex-sixes' raced by family crews in the company of a few non-metre boats of similar speed.[926]

In addition to the principal level-rating bands, there were intermediate sized metre-boats that failed to attract enough owners for class racing. Concerning the 12mR and smaller classes, Chapters 26 and 27 on 'gentlemen designers', Tommy Glen-Coats and Fred J. Stephen, describe their outstanding contributions to metre-boat design and campaigning.

The Livingston brothers, who financed the build of the David Boyd 12mR America's Cup triallist, *Kurrewa* V, in 1964, had some experience with an earlier generation of Scottish Twelves. The brothers took line honours in the Sydney to Hobart Race three times in *Kurrewa IV* (1956/57/60). This fine vessel was launched as *Morna* at Morrison & Sinclair's yard in Sydney in 1912. She was designed by William Fife as an 'offshore' interpretation of the 1st International Rule for Sir Alex McCormack. She won the Sydney to Hobart three times as *Morna* (1946/47/48) before the Livingston's triple.

Fife referenced the International Rule again for the famous 15-metre cruiser-racer, *Halloween*, which so nearly revolutionised racing offshore in 1926, setting a course record and placing 3rd on corrected time in the second Fastnet Race. Unfortunately, offshore racing missed the cue and promptly regressed, with ponderous heavy displacement vessels like *Tally Ho*, *Niña* and *Jolie Brise* winning the trophy, before the Stephens brothers crossed the Atlantic with *Dorade*. *Dorade* was another genuine racing yacht; she reprised the lessons of *Halloween* in 1931, but this time more convincingly.

The International Rule, while conceived more than a century ago, still provides an excellent rating formula for close racing in the 12mR, 8mR, 6mR and 5.5mR classes.[927] The process of deliberation and agreement on the new rule also led to the formation of a new institution to regularise and manage international yacht racing i.e. the International Yacht Racing Union (IYRU), now World Sailing.

Estimate of Numbers of Yachts built to the International Rule 1907-2019

Class	Nos Built	Remaining	Notes
23mR	7	3	Only three were built for 23mR level rating
19mR	6	1	classicyachtinfo.com/yclass/19-metre, lists 1
15mR	20	4	-
12mR	≈170	≈90	12mrclass.com. 35 hold valid certificates.
10mR	≈90	≈22+	classicyachtinfo.com/yclass/10-metre
9mR	≈50	≈10	classicyachtinfo.com/yclass/9-metre, lists 3
8mR	≈500	≈177	8mr.org
7mR	≈200	≈30	classicyachtinfo.com/yclass/7-metre lists 2
6mR	1,234	≈450	Tim Street has arrived at this number after much research
5.5mR	≈729	≈557	5.5inventory.org
5mR	≈350	≈150	classicyachtinfo.com/yclass/5-metre lists 1
4mR	≈172	≈136	The Nicholson formula deviates from the International Rule
3mR	≈1	≈0	Stephen family project
Total	3,528	1,630	Published estimates vary wildly

The Illusion-type 1mR is not considered here.

Following the 1st Rule, the 2nd Rule (1919-1933) and the 3rd Rule (1933-present) fostered refinement, while maintaining the essential character of the type. That said, the boats did become longer, narrower, deeper and heavier, built down to the minimum beam. For this reason, many find the wider 2nd Rule boats of the mid to late 1920s to be more shapely. The 3rd

Rule is still the basis of the various metre class rules but is separately modified by individual class associations.

American delegates attended the 1906 and 1907 conferences on the new rule, but only as observers. They had just developed their own Universal Rule in 1903. Although very few boats had been built to this rule in 1906, they were determined to go it alone. The Universal Rule rating bands were classified alphabetically, and, unlike the level-rating International Rule, defined broad bands within which time correction factors would be applied. That said, level-rating competition emerged at the top of some bands, as in the iconic J-class. The divisions were: J-class = 65-76ft, K-class = 55-65ft, L-class = 46-55ft, M-class = 38-46ft, N-class = 31-38ft, P-class = 25-31ft, Q-class = 20-25ft, R-class = 17-20ft, and S-class = 0-17ft.[928]

In 1928, the Yankees reluctantly accepted the European rule for International competition in the 'smaller classes' up to 12-Metres, while Europe agreed to use the North American Universal Rule for larger boats – J-class and up. For the USA, there were few other options if they wanted to enjoy international competition occasionally. In the event, there was no quid pro quo; the agreement coincided with the demise of Big Class racing, so there was negligible impact on European yachting. Only the short-lived J-class in Britain was spun-off from the use of the J 'rating cap' in the America's Cups of 1930 to 1937.

In Britain, in the years before the Great War, the 12mRs were the smallest class considered able to participate in the coastal trek around our seaside resorts in the regatta season. While it was possible to do this in 8mRs, it was not always a whole lot of fun. As for the 6mRs, they were usually transported on flat-bed railway cars and delivered by lorry. *"The smallest racing yacht at the present time which can be used as a residential home is a Twelve Metre, about 21 or 23-tons displacement and 35-tons Thames tonnage.*

The largest class at the present time is the 24-Metre Class. A 24-metre is about 120-tons displacement and 175-tons Thames tonnage. The 12-metre is 41 to 43ft on the waterline, and the 24-metre about 76 to 80ft. The rules of the YRA provide that all large racing yachts must be classed at A1 Lloyds and properly fitted internally with cabins. The larger racing yachts are most comfortably fitted and have every luxury."[929] There was no '24mR Class', as such, only 'Class A, above 23-metres'.[930]

The Twenty-three Metre Class (23mR)

Three yachts were built initially to the 23-metre rule, with a further three racing cutters of similar size built in the 1920s. As class racing seldom materialised, the second batch were rated to optimise performance in open competition.[931] *White Heather II* (Fife, 1907), *Brynhild* (Nicholson 1907) and *Shamrock* (Fife 1908) were designed to the 1st Rule before the Great War, then *Astra* (Nicholson 1928), *Cambria* (Fife 1928), and *Candida* (Nicholson 1929) were drawn to the 2nd Rule in the late 1920s. *Astra, Cambria* and *Candida* have survived. As to the size of these boats, *White Heather II* was 90-tons displacement, 180-tons TM and 82ft on the waterline, with 8,890ft^2 of sail area. For comparison, in 1908 the *Britannia* displaced 115-tons, registering 221-tons TM, with a waterline length of 88ft and 10,359ft^2 of sail.

All three of the 1920s boats were measured under the 2nd International Rule, but only *Astra* briefly rated 23mR. *Cambria* was initially 23.2, as was *Astra* by August 1928 (at that time both *Shamrock* and *White Heather* rated 23.9). In June 1929, *Candida* was 24.0, *Astra* 23.8, *Cambria* 23.7, *Shamrock* 24.7 and *White Heather* 24.5. In the yachting press the 1920s these boats were sometimes referred to as 'the 75-footers' (LWL) and sometimes as 'the 24-Metres'. We might also note that, in addition to the cutters, the splendid Fife schooner *Susanne* rated 23.2mR in her first season (1911).

Shamrock match-raced with the older 82ft-liner-rater, *Nyria* (a slightly shorter, wider boat), on the Clyde in 1908. *White Heather* and *Brynhild* had gone south reducing the anticipated spectacle. The race accounts for the Clyde regattas suggest that when the 23mRs sailed in class in 1909 and 1910, *Shamrock* dominated, with *Nyria* and *Brynhild* perpetual bridesmaids. For the 1910 season there had been a flurry of 'optimisation' with garboards padded to reduce girth difference and allow more sail. In the days before micro-balloon, the rationale for this type of padding was flawed at best, and in this case, self-defeating, as all three underwent the 'Botox' treatment to eliminate any comparative advantage.

23-metre class – active in UK waters in 1910. season's points & ranking[932]

Yacht	Designer	Owner	Races	Firsts*
Shamrock	William Fife III (1908)	Sir Thomas Lipton	28	18
White Heather II	William Fife III (1907)	M. B. Kennedy	27	10
Brynhild	Charles E. Nicholson (1907)	Sir James Pender	2	-

* Note 'firsts', not 'points' in this instance. Note *Nyria* was not active in 1910.

Brynhild sank in May 1910 while racing off Felixstowe. She was dismasted and the mast stump pierced the hull. The crew were fortunately rescued by a torpedo boat on naval operations nearby. However, before the boat could be salvaged, she suffered the unwelcome attentions of the Eastern Railway Co's Harwich steamer. After she was raised, *Brynhild* was found to be beyond repair, leaving the two surviving 23mRs to twenty years of match racing.

In the 1920s, the 23mRs raced in the 'over 70-tons TM' handicap class on the Clyde. Three new boats joined the action towards the end of the decade, but they never mustered as a viable class in Scotland. However, when the 1903 Universal Rule was introduced for the America's Cup in 1930, three of the 23mRs – *White Heather II, Astra* and *Candida* were modified to race in the J-class. The 151-linear-rater, *Britannia*, predating them all from 1893, was also converted to race with the Js in 1931.

Much later, in 2003, *Cambria* was rated as a J, following the resurrection of the J-class and the formation of the J-Class Association in 2000. Since that date, six replicas, or more accurately, new-builds of Js to 1930s hull lines, have joined the resurrected J-class fleet. All these boats now sit much deeper in the water, having been adapted to race with all the weighty kit and caboodle demanded by billionaire sybarites.

Terpsichore, or *Lulworth*, as she is better-known (William Herbert White 1920), also raced with the 23mRs in the Big Class. She has recently been restored with a period-correct rig. The other dissimilar stalwart of the old 'Yachts 21-metres and Over' class was the 1910 Herreshoff schooner, *Westward*, rating 29mR under the 1st International Rule, but the same as *Lulworth* at 25.7 in the Big Class, despite the great variance in configuration. Both of these spectacular big boats visited the Clyde regularly and were popular with local spectators.

The Nineteen Metre Class (19mR)

The six members of the 19-metre fleet were all launched within a three-year window, but they never came under starters orders together. Moreover, the German boats did not visit the Clyde. The fleet comprised: *Corona* (Fife 1911), *Norada* (Nicholson 1911), *Octavia* (Mylne 1911), *Ellinor* (Gerhard Barg[933] 1913), *Cecilie* (Max Oertz 1913), and the sole surviving 19mR, *Mariquita* (Fife 1911, rebuilt by Fairlie Restorations 2001-2004).

The 19mR was introduced with considerable optimism that it might be an affordable, dual-purpose vessel, albeit for the wealthy. *"A new class of 19-metre yachts is in the process of formation and gives every promise of proving a strong and successful one. The existing rule was carefully framed with a view to the encouragement of habitability, and in this it hitherto proved entirely successful. With a long life of general utility assured, there is every inducement to yachtsmen to build to this new 19-metre class, which is likely in the future to be the most popular of the large yacht classes."*[934]

Alas, this was not to be, the class did not have sufficient 'presence', in terms of scale, nor was it sufficiently numerous to present a spectacle for the public. The 19-metres failed to make an impact on the Clyde. Like the 23mRs, they generally found themselves match-racing, or racing on handicap, as in 1908 when *Mariska* prevailed over the Mylne 52ft-linear-rater, *Britomart*, with a clean sheet, despite apparently close racing.

The Fifteen Metre Class (15mR)

Clyde designers were responsible for a dozen 15-metre yachts, but this was another class that seldom saw action on the Firth. The best turn-out was in 1912, when nine 15mRs competed for the season's points around the coast of Britain. That year, somewhat denting local pride, the great

English designer, Charles E. Nicholson, stamped his authority on the 15mRs with *Istria*, against an otherwise all Scottish lineup. That said, the Mylne, *Ostara*, excelled in a blow and Fife's *Lady Anne* was the best boat in light airs, if only just. She won the closest race of the week, overlapped with *Istria* – the latter's bowsprit menacing the owner's party, perched nervously on *Lady Anne's* counter to keep out of the way of the racing crew.

The 15mR fleet endured a famously rough passage north to the Clyde. None more so than the new Nicholson boat which arrived at Hunter's Quay with weeping seams and the paint flaking off. *Istria* was innovative and quick, but she was the Cinderella of the fleet. She was a fast-track design and build contract, afloat and measured less than four months after the order was received. *Yachting Monthly* described her as "*a sad spectacle, so far as her hull went, especially to those accustomed to see the perfect finish of the Clyde boats.*"

Istria was the first substantial yacht in Britain to step a Marconi rig. This was an enormous success. Although occasionally bending like a fishing rod when the topsail was mishandled, the aerodynamic advantage was decisive, and the rig proved to be an important steppingstone on the path to engineering high aspect-ratio Bermudian rigs for the Big Class.[935] The 23mR, 19mR and 15mR fleets, most of which were new boats, now had to consider this new escalation in the design arms-race.

The Fife, *Maudrey*, and the Nicholson, *Pamela*, joined the British fleet the following year in 1913. It is evident from even a cursory glance at the ownership of yachts in this class that only the most wealthy in society could afford to campaign them, despite their being the third ranked level-rating fleet sailing under the International Rule in terms of scale.

15-metre class – active in UK waters in 1912. Season's points and ranking

Yacht	Designer	Owner	Races	Points
Istria	Charles E. Nicholson (1912)	Mr C. C. Allom	36	33
Sophie Elizabeth	William Fife III (1910)	Sophie E. Herr Biermann	35	27
The Lady Anne	William Fife III (1912)	Mr George Coats	29	19
Hispania	William Fife III (1909)	The King of Spain	25	18
Ostara	Alfred Mylne (1909)	Messrs Last	33	17
Paula II	Alfred Mylne (1910)	Herr L. Sanders*	27	16
Vanity	William Fife III (1909)	Messrs Payne and Benn	33	14
Mariska	William Fife III (1908)	Messrs Stamp and Cook	23	3
Tuiga	William Fife III (1909)	The Duke of Medinaceli	17	3

* Herr Sanders commissioned the Nicholson *Paula III* the next year but fared no better.

When looking at the 1912 results we can see that ongoing design development had turned the class inside-out since 1910 when *Ostara*, *Vanity* and *Mariska* led the points, followed by the Mylne, *Tritonia*, and *Ma'Oona*, with *Paula II* failing to complete any of the races she started.

Just twenty 15-metres were built in total worldwide, the first being the 1907 Fife, *Shimna*, built by Robertson's in Sandbank and the last being

Johan Anker's *Neptune* in 1917. Four pampered examples still exist: the sister-ships *Tuiga* (res.1990-1993) and *Hispania* (res.2004-2005) were rebuilt by Fairlie Restorations, as was the *Lady Anne* (res.1998-1999). *Mariska* (Fife 1908) has benefitted from an equally fine restoration by Chantiers Réunis Méditerranée. There are further notes on the class in Chapter 26 concerning Thomas Glen-Coats.

The Twelve Metre Class (12mR)

At the mid-sized level, William Fife III, with twelve 12mRs, shared the Scotland commissions equally with the Mylne design office, Alfred drew ten, with another two from the pen of his protégé Tommy Glen-Coats. The Glen-Coats Twelves are discussed in Chapter 26. The only Scottish Twelves to be built subsequently were associated with Britain's first post-war America's Cup challenges. David Boyd of Robertson's in Sandbank was responsible for all three of these designs. *Sceptre*, *Sovereign* and *Kurrewa V* are discussed in detail in *The Piper Calls the Tune*; also see Chapter 30.

The 12-metres blossomed briefly on the Clyde in the early days of the International Rule with Thomas Glen-Coats' *Heatherbell* (1907), for Charles McIver, and his own *Hera* (1908), the 1908 Mylne's *Mouchette* and *Nargie*. Then there was *Kelpie*, a converted Solent OD (42ft-linear-rater) from 1903, designed by Alfred Mylne, which George Coats replaced in 1908 with the Fife Twelve, *Alachie*. "*There is a thoroughbred look about this class which the one-design Clyde 20-tonners never possessed. They have in addition a turn of speed to which those one-design craft were strangers. It is possible that the one drawback to the attaining of wide popularity by the 12-metre boats will be their cost. It is an open secret that one at least of them cost £2,000 (£239,000).*

It will not be invidious to add that the presence of Mr T .C. Glen-Coats with a boat of his own designing, and that boat one of which even a Herreshoff, or a Fife, a Nicholson or a Mylne might be justly proud, has done much to recommend the class, not only to yachtsmen, but to the general public as well. Hera must be nearly, if not altogether, the best racing yacht designed in modern days by a non-professional draughtsman. The people of the Clyde are justly proud of him."[936]

In these early years, there were few 12mRs outside Scottish waters, hence the paucity of the entry in the 1908 Olympics, as recalled in Chapter 26. In that year, only Max Oertz' *Davo II* and Barg's *Skeaf II* in Germany and Charles E. Nicholson's *Rafaga*, built for an Argentinean client, added to the tally represented by the Clyde fleet. Then, in the period leading up to the Great War, a further 29 would be built. The Twelves endured as a premier racing class for 80 years, and around 170 would be built in total.

The top-end of the 1910 Clyde fleet was very-closely matched, with Fife's *Cintra* and Mylne's *Javotte* sharing the honours. *Alachie* had had her keel recast and was the best-performing of the older boats. *Hera*, now two years old and in new ownership, was still competitive, taking 5 firsts and 5 seconds. The new boats were clearly quicker, although the performance of *Cyra*, the latest from Mylne, suggests that crew work remained the decisive factor. *Cintra*, the season's champion, albeit by a small margin, lost her mast towards the end of August. Dismasting was a common enough occurrence in the days of wooden spars, but it was a tragedy on this occasion as the accident cost the lives of two *Cintra* crewmen.

12-metre class – active in UK waters in 1910. Season's points and ranking

Yacht	Designer	Owner	Races	Points
Cintra	William Fife III (1909)	Andrew Coats	42	29
Javotte	Alfred Mylne (1909)	Charles McIver	40	28
Alachie	William Fife III (1908)	George Coats	37	27
Hera	T. C. Glen-Coats (1908)	J. H. Gubbins	35	13
Nargie	Alfred Mylne (1908)	Jack Little	28	10
Cyra	Alfred Mylne (1909)	A. F. Sharman-Crawford	24	1

Subsequently, the Clyde 12mRs had their moments but relied heavily on visiting yachts to swell the fleet during the Fortnight. Thereafter, they struggled for traction. Wealthy yachtsmen who could afford to own this type of boat, preferred to race in the more competitive 8mR and 6mR classes. After WW2, when the Clyde 12mRs and a number of the 8mRs, had been converted into fast cruisers, they all sailed together in the fast handicap class.

In the years before WW2, Twelves were seen as 'small boats'. *"In some of the smaller racing yachts, I am sorry to say, the spirit of the YRA rules with regard to cabins is not fairly carried out. When a man goes down to a shipyard and sees a small racing yacht such as a 12-metre for sale, and finds her cabins well equipped with beds which are comfortable to sleep upon, chests of drawers which will open and shut and have good capacity, and the cabins well lined, divided by substantial bulkheads, and lit by good skylights, he is attracted by her."*

John Irving continues: *"On the contrary, if her internal fittings barely comply with the YRA rules, and she looks below decks like a third-class railway carriage, he is repelled."*[937] Irving's point is not lost. In the mid-1980s, we chartered the Dubois IOR 1-tonner, *Bimblegumbie*, for the China Sea Race. Below decks, following Keith Jacob's 'weight reduction programme', evidently carried out with a chainsaw, the ambience was that of a vandalised public toilet.

The last 'genuine' new 12mRs were launched for the 1987 America's Cup in Fremantle. Since then, there have been rebuilds and replicas – the most recent being the sensational rebirth of the 'Tartan Twelve', *Jenetta*, in May 2019. Mylne's masterwork was re-created from little more than a whiff of wet rot and the lead of her original ballast keel.[938]

Today, 12mRs are raced in five age and development-based divisions where entries permit. These divisions reflect key turning points in design through the 112-year history of the International Rule and are designated as follows in the list below. The first three divisions are further qualified to fairly allocate innovative yachts among their peers.[939] Similar systems are used in the 8-metre and the 6-metre classes, which also survive in numbers today.

- Division A (Grand Prix): yachts with wing keels and/or constructed 1983-1987.
- Division B (Modern): yachts without wing keels, but with rudders separated from the keel. This corresponds to the period of 1967 to 1983.
- Division C (Traditional): yachts built from 1950 to 1967 with keel-hung rudders.
- Division D (Vintage): yachts built before 1950.
- Division E (Antique): yachts built under the First International Rule.

The early Scottish Twelves, *Hera*, *Mouchette* and *Alachie* would all end up in South America. *Alachie* was shipped across the Atlantic to bolster the emerging 12mR fleet in Argentina. *Mouchette* now lies derelict behind the Tigre Maritime Museum in Buenos Aires. *Hera* arrived in Argentina after a long and interesting life, then disappeared without trace off the coast of Argentina in 1950, a fate shared by underfunded programmes campaigning Scottish classics through the 1950s and 60s.

The Eight Metre Class or 'Straight-eights' (8mR)

In 1937, the 8mR was the class of choice for competitive racing on the Clyde. Of all the level-rating classes under the International Rule, William Fife had most success with the Eights, particularly in the Seawanhaka Cup. Tommy Glen-Coats, John G. Stephen and Alfred Mylne all designed fine examples of the class too. For reasons unknown, James McGruer, master of the 8CR, and on occasion the 6mR class, appears never to have received an 8mR commission, see Chapters 26 and 27.

However, the 8-metre class was a slow starter in British waters. In their first season of 1907, only four boats appeared: *Sorais IV*, *Ythene*, *Julnar* and *Geraldine*.[940] They raced solely on the Solent, where the Fife-designed, *Sorais IV*, won every race and almost broke the class in her first season.[941] The 8mRs returned for the 1908 Olympics at Ryde, where *Cobweb*, a new Fife boat, won.

The following year, a revitalised class mustered for the Solent and Clyde regattas and became immediately popular as a style of boat which offered relatively comfortable passage-making between venues, and even basic live-aboard accommodation for the owner's party, as demonstrated by Thomas Glen-Coats. Fife had another good year in 1910. His boats filled the top three positions for the season, winning 29 out of 52 races. After the Great War, the class was active in the Olympics, the Coupe de France and the Seawanhaka Cup.

The Eights may have been more successful in Britain through the inter-war years if we had embraced the 1927 rule change to make the 8mR a 'cabin class'.[942] Every other member country of the IYRU was in favour, on the very reasonable grounds that a small deckhouse would make the cramped accommodation down below more habitable and thus strengthen the regatta circuit. Boats ordered before the 1927 Conference were 'grandfathered' and allowed to retain flush decks.

In Scotland, the Eights remained eternally popular through changing fashions until the 1970s. Olin Stephens' 8mR, *Iskareen*, came over to sail in British waters in 1939, and together with the 12mR, *Vim*, made a considerable impact on the local metre-boat fleets as WW2 clouded the horizon. As for the post-WW2-war period, one summary mistakenly suggests that: "*sadly, the class did not return to the Solent after 1945, but the Clyde class continued much as before until it began to decline towards the beginning of the fifties.*"[943] For reasons unknown, the second of two important revivals in the fortunes of the class on the Clyde has been forgotten.

8-metre class – active in UK waters in 1910. Season's points and ranking

Yacht	Designer	Owner	Races	Points
Endrick	William Fife III (1909)	Sir A. E. Orr-Ewing	50	38
Spero	William Fife III (1909)	Rev C. Progers	47	35
The Truant	William Fife III (1910)	Sir Ralph Gore	40	24
Folly*	C. E. Nicholson (1909)	Senor C. F. Blanco	22	17
Anemone III	C. M Chevreux (1910)	M. Ph. Fe Vilmorin	20	6
The Nun	Alfred Mylne (1909)	A. D. Grigg	36	5
Bryony**	R. E. Froude (1909)	R. E. Froude	15	1
Antwerpia***	Linton Hope (1911)	Syndicate Antwerpia	7	1
Dilkushi	G. A. Heal (1910)	Capt. F. Guest	13	-
Kathleen	Col Faulkner Brown (1909)	Col Faulkner Brown	6	-

Folly was shipped to South America mid first season. A rotation of guest helmsmen showed her potential. **Robert was the great William Froude's son ***Antwerpia* was built at Bowness on Windermere, as was an 8-metre for Bombay to designs by Mylne. The yachting press were nonplussed, as with the lake being freshwater, trial floatation could not confirm rating marks.

Post-1945, the Clyde class was indeed revitalised for a decade before the remaining yachts scattered to be replaced by the Cruiser Eights (8CR) class. But then, ten years later, and much to everyone's surprise, there was a vigorous revival of 'Straight-eights' on the Clyde. The Clyde fleet soon grew to 10 or more boats, racing as a class until the early 1970s. Astutely rechristened the 'Straight-eights' in the press and among an enthusiastic cognoscenti, the revival attracted great interest. For a few short years, there was lay discourse on yacht racing, a phenomenon rare since the 1930s.

In his entertaining autobiography, Gordon Findlay recounts these times. Gordon's family rented a house near the RCYC at Hunter's Quay in the 'good old days', and his book captures the spirit of the 'Rentokil Fleet'.[944] Gordon invested £2,900 (£52,000) to bring *Wye*, a 1935 Nicholson, over from Cork to join the embryo classic fleet in 1967. *If*, a Bjarne Ass boat from 1930, and *Severn II*, a 1934 Mylne, also migrated across the Irish Sea in the 1960s. The Cork trio joined Peter Fairley's *Christina of Cascais* (1936 Tore Holm), *Silja* (1930 Anker), *Turid II* (1939 Bjarne Ass), *June II* (1929 Anker) and *Carron II* (1934 Fife). This gave a fleet of eight, all of similar potential performance, if not resources.

Later, *Aina*, owned by Kenneth Baird, joined the fleet, but we have yet to establish which 8mR she was. *Margaret* (1922 Anker), *Vagrant II* (1927 Fife), *Sirus* (1925 Morgan Giles) and *The Truant* (1910 Fife) did not race in class. *The Truant* has recently been rebuilt, using a commendably large proportion of original timber, by Adam Way of the boatyard at Crinan. She looks splendid, fitted out in full Edwardian detail with her original gaff-rig and varnished wooden spars.

Some of the Clyde Straight-eight fleet were stripped out below and some enjoyed rather more in the way of creature comforts, but they were all so old and tired this made little difference. Nevertheless, there was a desire to modernise the fleet in the 1960s. Both *If* and *June* had their counters cropped in the manner of *Sceptre* by 2ft 3" and 2ft respectively. Not to be dogmatic, *Sceptre* was perhaps more handsome and 'of her era' with her stern cropped, but the pre-war Eights were simply brutalised, rather than 'modernised'. A number of Olin Stephens' Sixes, like *Goose*, suffered the same fate.[945] Thankfully, in these more enlightened times, with the advent of properly regulated competition in the metre-boat classes the best examples of the period have been reinstated to their original hull design drawings and chainsaw restorations have lost their attraction.[946]

In the 1960s, there were also attempts at 'equalisation' to improve the quality of the competition. Non-engined boats were required to sport dummy 12-inch props and carry an equivalent chunk of lead (or more likely concrete, as the no-engine brigade often didn't have any money). For those who *had* a motor, it was not always an asset. *June*, one of the rougher boats, had an old Leyland bus engine with no gears and no clutch, it was 'on' or 'off'. This made the passage through the Crinan Canal interesting to say the least, even if an RNLI orange paint job signalled her intentions.

Most of the Straight-eight fleet lost their masts in the first season in a single hit to the marine insurance industry – the devil-may-care boat-handling that precipitated these happy dismastings was surely not without risk. *Wye* was re-rigged more ethically when *June* was wrecked on the Ashton shore. The rest of the fleet bid for parts and fittings. By October 1968, six of the Scottish fleet had new metal masts. Ian Proctor surely did good business with the class. Attempts were made to restrict sail wardrobes at the class AGM in 1970. From the following year, they agreed to limit such expenditure to 5 sails in 5 years.

In 1969, Eugene van Voorhis shipped the legendary 1939 Olin Stephens' 8mR, *Cheetah* (better-known as *Iskareen* in Europe), across the Atlantic to race in Scotland.[947] Eugene's new S&S 8mR, *Iroquois*, had not convincingly surpassed the pre-war *Cheetah*, so he was confident that the old boat would be competitive on the Clyde. Unfortunately, *Cheetah* missed Clyde Week due to a shipping delay. Undaunted, Eugene turned the disruption of a carefully planned summer programme into an opportunity. He left his boat on the Clyde and presented a silver trophy to the Royal Clyde for an 8-metre World Championship.

This sporting gesture turned out to be a prescient initiative, and one that materially contributed to the rise of 'classic' racing for the entire family of metre-boat classes sailing under the International Rule. Eugene and his crew flew back to re-join the Clyde 8mR fleet the following year for the new World Championship. Much to everyone's surprise the trophy stayed on this side of the Atlantic, as despite enjoying a boatload of marginal gains, *Cheetah* was edged-out for the title by Dr H. J. Weir's *Silja*, the best of the Scottish 8mRs that year. Subsequently, Erik Maxwell, one of our more accomplished metre-boat sailors, bought *Cheetah* in 1971 and returned her name to *Iskareen*. Erik had just a couple of seasons to enjoy *Iskareen* before the 8mR fleet began to break up. In 1973 there were insufficient numbers for a class start. See Chapter 30.

The 8mR World Cup is now contested regularly and last visited the Clyde in 2007. The Royal Northern welcomed the fleet for the Centennial Championships, only to inflict a week of light and fluky airs on the 22 competitors. Entrants came from as far afield as Australia, Japan, Canada, Finland, Norway, Italy, The Netherlands, Germany, Switzerland, France, and England. The 8mR association noted that "*the return of the now Australian-owned Saskia to Scottish waters, after an absence of some 70 years, gave particular pleasure locally*".

Alouette won overall, *Lafayette* finished second and *Hollandia* (all 'Moderns' with Howlett winged-keels) was third. Hard on the heels of that event, the Royal Yacht Squadron held a Centenary Metre Regatta on the Solent. Two Classics, *Athena* (Torr Holm, 1939) and *Saskia* (Fife, 1930) arrived at Cowes in time to compete against six other 8mRs and two 8CRs, the latter able, if nothing else, to tow the others home as she was fitted with a working engine. Nevertheless, *Saskia* won every race. See Appendix 3.

Eight Metre One Design Proposal (8mOD)

The final chapter in the Clyde 8-metre story was Peter Fairley's brave efforts to promote a fleet of one-design 8mRs. "*David Boyd drew two 8mR designs at the behest of the Robertson's Board in 1966 and 1969. The plan was to series-produce this type of boat in fibreglass. The first design was an elegant long-ended yacht epitomising the classic models of the class, but with separate keel and rudder and a long low coachroof. The second was a snub-ended design, like the generation of metre-boats we class as 'Moderns' today. This second iteration had an 'Intrepid-style underbody and a low Etchells-type coachroof."*[948]

The one-design 8mRs project appears to have courted Olin Stephens as a design collaborator. Ian Howlett recalls that, among other material shared during their friendship, David Boyd, at that time long retired, gave Ian the drawings of the 1967 S&S 8mR, *Iroquois*, with Boyd's own pencil modifications. Among various changes, the bow profile had been softened and rendered more traditional, perhaps to appeal to Peter Fairley and a conservative client base. Boyd was in regular correspondence with Olin Stephens and Erik Maxwell was building an S&S 6mR at that time.[949]

Peter Fairley had this to say about the proposal: *"The 8-metre One Design was my project. I was part-owner of Christina of Cascais at the time and there was difficulty in the ex-8-metre class expanding owing to a shortage of good old boats. Bringing a poor 8-metre back into racing trim was very expensive and we explored this one-design as a potential alternative, as these boats would have cost a lot less than an 8CR."* This latter class was fully fitted-out for cruising. However, times were hard in the boatbuilding industry in Scotland in the 1970s and the proposal was shelved, indefinitely as things turned out. In retrospect, this outcome brought a century of grand prix racing yacht building on the Clyde to a close.[950]

> The Clyde 8-metre fleet of the 1960s has scattered to the four winds. *Christina*, an elegant yacht with her dark blue topsides and gold cove line, sank in the North Sea. The 1936 Glen-Coats' boat, *Helen,* is active on the Solent having been restored by Duncan Walker at Fairlie Restorations (as was). *Aspacia* has been completely rebuilt. Now, sailing as K1 and under her old name of *Emily,* she currently graces Lake Constance. *If* has been brought up to *concours* condition and is now in Norway. *Margaret,* now sailing under sail number S1, has been beautifully restored. A replica has been built of the 1930 Fife, *Invader II,* which may as well be a replica of the sister-ships, *Severn* and *Finola*. And the old Fife, *Truant,* has been rebuilt by Adam Way at Crinan. Doubtless others have survived too.

The Eight Metre Cruiser Racers (8CR Class)

Post-war big boat yachting gravitated towards dual-purpose cruiser racer yachts racing under the auspices of the Royal Ocean Racing Club (RORC). The RORC rule was initially drafted in 1926 to encourage the development of faster and more seaworthy designs. In 1932, the Royal Corinthian design competition invited submissions for two 'classes', corresponding to 55ft and 35ft ratings, although there was no intention to race offshore on level-ratings – see *The Piper Calls the Tune*. Later in the

1950s, the rule would again be 'tweaked', penalising the overhangs favoured in 1932 and making the 8CRs uncompetitive.[951]

While all this was going on, and in a remarkably counterproductive move, the RORC prompted the IYRU to amend the International Rule to incorporate revised formula for a family of level-rating cruiser-racer classes. For most of the proposed size classes this idea was dead in the water.[952] However, the 8CRs took root on the Clyde, where the new class became perhaps the best-loved of all the local racing classes, and an icon of Scottish yachting.

The 8CR Class effectively supplanted the ageing fleet of International Eight Metres that had kept boat-to-boat competition alive in 'proper yachts' through the post-war years. Nevertheless, most of the new boats were built for owners who had not previously owned a Straight-eight. Unfortunately, as the 8CRs rated poorly under the RORC's own rule, they did not take off in the south, or anywhere else bar the Clyde for that matter. At least 30 'Cruiser-eights' were built worldwide, all but a dozen destined for the Scotland, as listed in Appendix 3.

The first of the 8CRs was *Sonda*, built by McGruer in 1951 for carpet manufacturer, Alastair Young, the 2nd Baronet of Partick. In 1976, after a long racing career, she left the Clyde for Wales. She was discovered in a state of disrepair in Bénodet on the French Atlantic Coast by the current owner in 2003. Following a major restoration at the Stagnol Shipyard in Brittany she was transported to Marseille, where she is now based. *Sonda* participates regularly in the classic regatta circuit, winning Les Voiles du Vieux Port in Marseille in 2010, and Les Voiles de St Tropez in 2017.[953]

Ian McKenzie tells a story about the building of *Orana* at Morris & Lorimer's yard in 1959, which provides a glimpse into the mindset of the thrifty Clyde yachtsmen of the period. While M&L built *Orana*, Ken Millar had arranged to supply the mast and rig the boat himself. At that time, British Rail innocently charged for freight on a simple weight basis. Ken had ordered the Alcan tube and the necessary components from Ian Proctor in Southampton. Having checked the logistics, he arranged transport – door-to-door.

Some months later, a 58ft package arrived at Glasgow Central Station in a 60ft freight car. No one knew what to do with it. BR was obliged to hire a lorry and drive this single light, but long, package the 80 miles over the 'Rest and be Thankful' pass to Sandbank, but they made sure it did not happen again. Years later, in the 1960s, Kilmun's amateur boatbuilders routinely ordered extruded alloy sections from the south to be made into dinghy booms. These were transported by rail and we got to know the 'freight area' of Glasgow Central Station pretty well. But then I ordered a mast-extrusion and came up hard against the '*Orana* sanction'.[954]

On masts and the railways, before we leave the subject, the following is not without interest: "*At the end of last week, the Oregon log out of which White Heather's new mast has been hewn, arrived at Fairlie. It was brought by rail from London, and being about 100 feet in length, getting it safely round the curves on the line was rather a triumph in its way.*"[955]

These wholesome boats exemplify the old-style cruiser-racer genre – where cruising yachts are raced inshore like touring cars repurposed for circuit racing. Traditionally, Scottish sailors of adequate means raced their racing yachts and kept their cruising yachts for holidays on the West Coast. However, struggling though the doldrums of a Scottish summer in an 8CR always looked like hell to me. The boats were stiff as a house, bobbing upright, and woefully under-canvassed with no shape in the sails. At least you could make a cup of tea. It was not until the 1980s that sailmakers cottoned-on to the virtues short-foot (90% of J) gossamer 'windseekers'.

That said, the 8CRs came alive when a breeze materialised, but with their old-style heavy No.1 genoas in dimensionally unstable Terylene, they became overpowered shortly thereafter. *Nan* and *Debbie* gained the advantage here with Hood sails, a class apart in the 1960s. *Inismara* was the master of the heavy air with her 48% ballast ratio. *Debbie II* was particularly stiff too. The last boats built to the rule, like *Sunburst*, were larger, with ballast ratios in the low 40s. They depended on form stability and had to be sailed upright, requiring more skill, but offering rich rewards.

Now, when these boats come up on the brokers' lists, they are perceived to be drop-dead gorgeous. It seems that the current aesthetic environment has moved the goalposts to reframe a new norm, now remote from the attenuated elegance of our youth. Boxy busses with picture windows and a barbeque on the aft terrace hardly gladden the eye.[956] Sure, there are still beautiful boats today like the TP52s, but they are few and far between, and nowhere to be seen in Scottish waters.

The original 'Cruiser Eight' fleet are now recognised as timeless classics, and many have been restored to first-class condition. But they are scattered to the four winds. James McGruer's *Namhara* (ex-*Debbie II*), a former class champion is in The Netherlands, McGruer's *Nan of Clynder* is in Canada, the McGruer-designed, M&L-built, *Orana*, has enjoyed an extended racing career and is still winning in France. *Feolinn*, another McGruer boat, now based in Denmark, is still competitive too. *Fionnuala* (ex-*Debbie I*), also McGruer, is kept in Ireland, and *Camellia of Rhu* is in Chichester. 8CRs recently appearing on current brokers' lists include: the Boyd-designed Robertson's-built *Sunburst* and the immaculate McGruer, *Inismara*. *Altricia*, another McGruer, has been restored, fire-damaged and restored again.

In the 1960s, the 8CRs were the most competitive of all Clyde classes, mainly because they alone could muster a decent fleet, thanks to the highly marketable work of James McGruer. However, in a blow to national pride, the Olin Stephens-designed *Nan of Gare* for Peter Wilson was the most elegant, best-detailed in the Clyde fleet, and quite simply, a class apart. After Peter moved on in 1970, Ninian Sanderson's second *Debbie* – the final word by James McGruer, won most of the races, until David Boyd's Robertson's-built *Sunburst* appeared in the last years of the class to share the honours.[957] As her design benefitted from Boyd's America's Cup tank-testing, *Sunburst* has since been labelled as a 'class-breaker'. However, while she was indeed a good boat, she was often just sailed better than the others in the final years of the class. See list in Appendix 3.

The Seven Metre Cruiser Racers (7CR Class)

It is sometimes forgotten that there was also an active Seven Metre Cruiser Racer fleet on the Clyde. Douglas Nesbit's McGruer's designed and built *Zaleda* was one of five 7CRs campaigned on the Clyde in the 1967 season. *Norella* was designed by Maitland Murray and built by Morris & Lorimer's at Sandbank for Mrs A. H. Poole. The other three boats were designed by Werner Seigul and built by VEB Yachtwerft in Berlin. They were *Erlin Mor*, *Shona III* and *Pelingar III*.[958] These examples do not appear to have been listed in Lloyds. The 7CRs (particularly the German imports) were conceived as a lower cost alternative to the 8CRs. As inevitably follows keen competition among well-heeled owners, the larger 8CRs were becoming increasingly expensive. However, after this initial flurry of interest, the 7CR class seldom raced as a fleet.

The Six Metre Class (6mR)

The 6-metres were the Clyde's favourite class for half a century from the inception of the International Rule in 1907 until the 1950s. Chapters 26 and 27, concerning Tommy Glen-Coats and Fred Stephen, are mainly about 6mRs. *The Piper Calls the Tune* recalls the evolution of the Fife 2nd Rule model during David Boyd's tenure and then Boyd's own development of a world-beating 3rd Rule model to lift the Seawanhaka Cup on three occasions. The notes on the 6mRs in this section are therefore limited to a few remarks.

William Fife III drew his last 6mR in 1935; that was *Eola* for a French client. Mylne's last 6mR design was *Vrana* for J. H. Maurice Clark in 1937. The last 6-metre to a David Boyd design was *Royal Thames*, built by Woodnutts for the club in 1955. James McGruer's last 6mR design was *Noa*, built in Clynder in 1947 for 'Tiny' Mitchell of the Royal Corinthian

Yacht Club at Cowes. And the last new 6-metre constructed in Scotland was *Gosling*, beautifully built for Erik Maxwell in 1971 by McGruer's in double skin mahogany over laminated frames.

In 1987, echoing a move pioneered on the Clyde with the 'ex-six metre' class, the 6mRs were split into two divisions to encourage owners to restore and modernise the large number of still-beautiful, old boats. In the current classification, a 'Classic' 6-Metre is one built before 31st December 1965, and a 'Modern' Six is one built after that date. This split is linked to the development of a hull-form with the rudder separated from the keel by an extended bustle, redistributing immersed volume, as successfully incorporated in the 12mR, *Intrepid*, in May 1967.

The 1988 Six Metre European Championships saw the boats scored separately for the first time. This worked well, so separate starts have been used since the 1995 World's. However, an unexpected result of the new interest in Classics was that very few new Sixes were built. Another issue is that boats built during a decade of design transition from 1965 to 1976 are effectively homeless. There is thus a long-running argument that the Classic/Modern cut should be moved forward to 31st Dec 1976.[959]

New 6-metre commissions are rare worldwide. After *Gosling*, we had to wait until 1981 for Erik Maxwell to build another 6mR. *Kirlo* was designed by Ian Howlett and built in England by Armstrong Mouldings. She sailed under the burgee of the Royal Yacht Squadron, so the Scottish connection is tenuous. But no matter, at least *Kirlo* was a good boat: "*She may be said to be the boat that defined modern best proportions of sail area and weight and is still widely considered to be perhaps the prettiest Modern Six.*"[960]

Ian Howlett is still very much active in the class with new designs, redesigns, new keels and all manner of optimisation. He has this to say: "*They are remarkable boats to race. When they are on-song and you really get it right, they have an extraordinary feeling of crispness. In British dinghies you only get that in boats like the National 12 or the Merlin Rocket. Sailing in events like the Olympics has tended to move towards the highly physical, whereas the cerebral part of sailing is fundamental to the Sixes, so this is much more of a thinkers' class, even though they are physically very demanding to sail.*"[961]

As the smallest of the principal metre-boat classes the 6mRs have been the most popular, with an estimated 1,234 built. They have never been cheap for their size, but for half a century they were at the leading edge of design development until the 12mRs were selected to replace the J-class for the America's Cup in 1956. This assertion should be caveated with a nod to the 5.5mR, introduced in 1949, initially to reduce the costs of Olympic participation, and now with 729 boats registered worldwide. The

5.5mR shares a similar level of continuing design evolution with the 6mR, in a lower-displacement model with lower build costs. The 5.5mR class has never been active in Scotland, but their popularity on the European lakes, where similar sailing conditions exist, suggests that perhaps Clyde sailors have missed an opportunity.

The 6-metre class was at the heart of Scottish yacht racing and design development for half a century. The class brought small-boat enthusiasts on limited professional incomes, and wealthy owners of very large boats, together in common purpose. This broad church is summed up in American commentator Bill Smart's cheeky reportage of Clyde news: *"The change in rating rules for Sixes seems now definite enough to warrant the Scots' canniness which has produced one new Six shared by thirteen owners on the Clyde."*[962] The intent might have been to perpetuate a stereotype, but the result is somewhat different. A syndicate of thirteen, all owning other boats including older sixes, agreed on the designer, builder, skipper, crew and campaign. Now, that sort of selfless collaboration is something to be proud of, is it not?

This syndicate, the size of a football team, came about for a very good reason. Six-metres were already eye-wateringly expensive before the war in 1939, let alone after it, in 1947. *"With more Eights than Sixes building, an eclipse of the latter class seems to be in process. There is no doubt a Six is relatively a very expensive boat to run in a hot class. One owner with experience of both the Sixes and Twelves going so far as to say the former actually cost him more to run."*[963]

Here, we might even the score by referencing the David Boyd-designed 6mR, *Royal Thames*, winner of the 1958 One Ton Cup. The skipper, 'Stug' Perry, had jumped ship to sidestep the dramas of the 1958 *Sceptre* campaign, a move that enabled him to emerge unscathed from the debacle, see Chapter 30.[964] The *Royal Thames* campaign foreshadowed 'crowd funding'. The boat was quick and lacked for nothing, funded by a syndicate of 250 deep-pocketed Englishmen. Glyn Foulks' brother was the 'hand' on *Royal Thames* when they won the cup. This young man had a fantastic time in Sweden, but incredibly he had to cadge his trainfare home. 'Stug' also had his cap on the pavement. *Royal Thames*' new Hood mainsail was borrowed too.

Today, the 6mR class constitutes the only reliable indicator of the progress made by generations of naval architects in the evolution of conventional, heavy displacement racing yacht design over the past century. Until recently, old boats were less competitive for a host of reasons: masts, sails, bottom finish, gear and crews. There was a transition period early in the class revival, where Classics raced on a shoestring with second-hand gear from the free-spending Modern fleet.

These days, however, ownership of Classic Sixes is an aesthetic choice. Classics campaigns are conducted at the same high level as the Moderns, with the boats sailed hard by very good sailors. What were once run-down old boats, converted into pocket-cruisers with cuddies and inboard auxiliaries, have now been restored to original specifications and brought back into full racing-trim; and indeed, a step beyond that with (removable) internal structures that allow them to be sailed hard with modern rigs, while maintaining the integrity of the old woodwork.

In full-sized racing yachts, it is difficult to assess progress in hull design through the decades, against a background of continuing improvements in materials, rigs and sail shapes. However, the 6mR bloodline has provided some insights. This is a serendipitous benefit from the 'classic yacht revival'. While the old boats generally race in a separate classic division, they also compete alongside the latest wing-keeled 6mRs, which have benefitted from generations of America's Cup funded research.

It is sobering to note that the differential between the Moderns and the Classics in the 6mR fleet is 4.5% to 5%, or less than the performance differential between crews in the top half of either fleet. *"Five percent might not sound like much but actually it's a huge number if you assess it in terms of resistance rather than in terms of speed, it's a big number in terms of the naval architecture."*[965]

This calculation of net advance was something that could never really be measured before, as each generation of new materials brought ever more efficient and more powerful rigs to obscure the contribution of the naval architect. Rig development effectively trumped hull-shape evolution, which traditionally was the major focus of design-effort. Even today, while new designs are ever-more refined, the increments are ever smaller, limited by the physics of heavy displacement, and the many other equalising parameters of the International Rule.

International Competition

The essence of Clyde yachting during its glory days might be summed up in the two most popular images in Scottish maritime art, being the Big Class off Hunter's Quay, usually with *Britannia* in the frame, and a flight of Sixes, also off Hunter's Quay, but being smaller, with the crews featuring in the depiction. Of these two icons, while the spectators may have been drawn to the drama of the Big Class, Clyde yachtsmen could never see past the nimble little Sixes. The story of the 6-metres, and particularly Scottish Sixes, is also the story of what were once the premier international yachting competitions – the British-American Cup and the Seawanhaka Cup.

The British-American Cup

The British-American Cup series was the first international team racing event. The initial idea was to race under the International Rule in Britain, and the Universal Rule in the States. Regardless of the outcome, the venue alternated between Britain and the United States. By mutual agreement, the trophy was first contested in 1921 at Cowes. Britain won this first edition of what would become a hotly contested bi-annual series. An unexpected result from the first event concerned gender equality. Sixes were often crewed by four men plus one lady (who didn't count). After Sherman Hoyt asked the host club, the Royal Yacht Squadron, to define 'lady', the rules were altered to allow five 'real' men.

When it came to defend the trophy in the USA, the British appealed to continue with the International Rule to avoid unnecessary expense. Subsequently, more 6-meters were built for the trials in 1922 than any other year in the 6mR class history. Partly as a result, in 1928 IYRU delegates agreed to use the International Rule for small boats up to 12-metres, and the Universal Rule above that. The second event saw the Americans win on Oyster Bay. At that time, Oyster Bay was the 'Hunter's Quay of America', and an important centre of international yacht racing.[966]

The Seawanhaka Cup

The Seawanhaka Cup is the oldest international trophy in American sailing and was first contested back in 1895 in little ½-raters – exciting, dinghy-like yachts. It is a best-of-five contest, with a format much like the America's Cup. This competition alone kept elite international match racing alive through the hiatus from 1937 to 1958, when first global conflict, and then post-war austerity, interrupted America's Cup racing. Over the period 1927-1987, the event was principally contested in 6-metres. Sporting challenges were accepted from yacht clubs outside the USA, with the Seawanhaka Corinthian Yacht Club always representing the United States. The competition is still around, albeit in name only.[967]

In total there were sixteen superb match-race contests in 6 Metres built to the 2nd and 3rd International Rules.[968] The Cup matches were hard fought and intensely scrutinised sea-battles, and might be considered the pinnacle for sailors, as opposed to the rarefied America's Cup, where the racing itself was overshadowed by the design battle. The Seawanhaka Cup encouraged excellence in small yacht design and showcased the match racing skills of the best amateur yachtsmen.

The Royal Northern Yacht Club won seven times – in 1922, '23, '24, '29, '31, '38 and '39, with a Scottish designer on each occasion. Fred J. Stephen's 6 Metre, *Coila III*, cruised to victory in 1922, 1923 and 1924. Then, a few years later, William Fife III's late-model 8 Metres – *Caryl* in 1929 and *Saskia* in 1931, repeated the feat.[969] All these yachts were '2nd Rule' metre boats.[970] Chronologies are included in Appendix 3.

CODA: Howden Hume's Olympics

Jimmy Howden Hume was selected to sail the 1939 McGruer 6mR, *Johan*, at the Torbay Olympics in 1948. Back-up skipper, J. Herbert Thom, and 'Tiny' Mitchell's 1947 McGruer 6mR, *Noa*, were to be held in reserve.[971] Apparently James McGruer, like many other designers of the period, had not been able to improve on his pre-war model from a decade earlier. We might speculate why *Noa* was preferred over the 1937 Boyd *Circe*, which had run Jimmy and *Johan* close in the trials. *Circe* was now owned by George Eyston but sailed in the trials by Thom, her old maestro. The official reason was that Jimmy Howden Hume would be more comfortable in a similar boat if the need for a substitution arose. *Johan* was an exceptional heavy airs boat, and *Noa* was too, so the selectors gambled on a blow with an unpadded basket of Clyde eggs.

The XIV Olympiad followed on two weeks later.[972] As events transpired, it only blew on the last day. Then, it blew like buggery and Jimmy, after an indifferent start, stormed up to join the leaders. Ironically, it was a series of extremes, tailor-made for *Circe* and Herbert Thom. *Llanoria* (Olin Stephen 1948) USA was 1st, *Djinn* (Olin Stephens 1938) of Argentina was 2nd, Sweden's *Alibaba II* (Tor Holm 1948) was 3rd. Jimmy, sailing *Johan*, was 6th. The competition saw the first appearance of a young Dane, later to become a sailing legend – Paul Elvstrom.[973]

[925] Tale of a Tub, Hunt's Yachting Magazine, Anon, 1854. Well before the Int. Rule but apt.
[926] *"If the Solent clubs are really desirous of securing really good sport, we think that they cannot do better than follow the example of the thoroughly harmonious Clyde clubs, and provide handicap races for such yachts as are outclassed. Colonel Bucknill has termed this 'pernicious handicapping', but we fail to draw any distinction between the broken-down racer and the racer that is breaking down. Both classes should, for the sake of sport, be put on an equality and this can only be achieved by handicapping each vessel according to her reputation, as has been done with triumphant success by the Clyde clubs for very many years."* The Man at the Wheel, The Yachtsman.
[927] The Piper Calls the Tune, Euan Ross and Bob Donaldson, 2017.
[928] Universal Rule 1903

$$R = \frac{0.2 \times L \times \sqrt{S}}{\sqrt[3]{D}}$$

D = Rated length (various methods)
S = Sail area (various methods)
D = Dead weight expressed in cubic feet of sea water

[929] The Kings' Britannia, John Irving, 1937. The apostrophe is after the 's' as she served two kings.
[930] Lloyds Register 1908.
[931] Data on the International Rule rating of these large cutters was provided by Nigel Sharp.
[932] Yachting, The Times, 2nd September 1910.
[933] Gerhard Barg (1858-1926), yacht designer and director of the Neptune shipyard in Rostock. In relation to the International Rule, the German designer was better known for his 12mRs.
[934] A New Racing Class, Frank B. Cooke, Baily's Magazine of Sports and Pastimes, Volume 95, Nos 611-616, January to June 1911.
[935] *Istria's* other innovations included extensive use of 'glue-lam' in structural elements and a novel 'dinghy cockpit' to reduce windage and lower the centre of gravity. When tested at rest, it was launched with a man in 9-seconds, and in a fresh breeze under full sail, the same operation took 15-seconds. On this basis, the YRA permitted its use, if kept entirely clear of gear.

936 The Season on the Clyde, The Yachtsman, 30th June 1908.

937 The Kings' Britannia, John Irving, 1937.

938 The new *Jenetta* was launched in May 2019, resplendent with a Glasgow University tartan paint job or wrap. The tartan resembles that of Mylne.

939 Division A includes *Australia II* of 1983; Division B includes *Intrepid* and all yachts built after *Intrepid*, but before *Australia II* and shall exclude *Australia II*; Division C excludes *Intrepid*; Division D is not further qualified; and Division E included gaff and Bermudian-rigged yachts and centre-boarders. There is a cautionary note with regard to restorations which may be considered replicas, as with the current *Jenetta* restoration where nothing of the hull could be salvaged: "*ITMA may assign a yacht to a division different than those given above or may determine an alternative Age/Design Correction Factor (ADCF) in special cases where: a) The construction of the yacht was completed after 1987, or b) a yacht built prior to 1987 has been so altered in hullform, appendages, or accommodation that is no longer consistent with the age date under which it was first constructed, launched, or certificated.*" 12mR Class Rules, Nov 2018.

940 *Geraldine* was an 1899 Charles Sibbick designed 32ft linear-rater, permitted by the 1st Rule to race as an 8mR until 1909.

941 British Eight Metre Association, a short history, current website.

942 IYRU Conference, Cabin tops on the Eight-metre Class, The Field, 27th February 1927.

943 Ibid

944 My Hand on the Tiller (a log of my life afloat), Gordon B. Findlay, 2006.

945 Classic Six-Metre Newsletter No. 11, 19th December 2005.

946 Ian McKenzie raced both Straight-eights and 8CRs. His experience is reflected here.

947 *Iskareen* was a pre-war Olin Stephens 8-metre and a development of the seminal 6 Metre, *Goose*. She remains a wonderful vessel; easily the best 8 metre of any era. Incredibly, in 1978, she was the overall winner of the 8 Metre World Cup forty years after her conception.

948 The Piper Calls the Tune, primary sources can be accessed in that volume.

949 Correspondence with Ian Howlett, December 2017.

950 In November 1974, Dennis Healey raised the rate of VAT on yachts from 8% to 25%. The punitive rate of value added tax remained in place for just two years before it was halved to 12.5%, but the damage had been done. For a fragile and often unprofitable industry struggling for orders amid a deepening recession, the surprise is that any yards at all survived the purge.

951 The Piper Calls the Tune, Euan Ross and Bob Donaldson, 2017.

952 There were few 7CRs built and other odds and ends like James McGruer's 13.5CR, *Stornoway*.

953 *Sonda* set the first viable Terylene/Dacron sail in 1952, see Chapter 14.

954 Being masthead rigged, 8CR masts were untapered and a straightforward DIY project.

955 Clyde, The Yachtsman, 21st July 1910.

956 Yachts like: Jeanneau Sun Odyssey 440, European Yacht of the Year – Family Cruiser 2018; Amel 50, European Yacht of the Year – Luxury Cruiser 2018. With vertical stems, they don't ride well to anchor. They are dangerously exposed on deck and are no better below, lacking hand holds and bracing points below deck.

957 Ninian Sanderson was also a fine racing driver, having won the 24hrs of Le Mans in 1956.

958 Information on the 7CR class furnished by Graham Ferguson.

959 Flawed tank testing effectively set back design development in the *Valiant* era. Boats like *Gosling*, which are no faster than *Goose* of 1938, are uncompetitive in the 'Moderns' fleet.

960 International Six-Metre Association, Modern Six-Metre's Newsletter No.1, First Revision, Tim Street,13th December 2005.

961 Extracts from Ian Howlett's thoughts on the 6mRs, which appear in the first 6-metre book by Tim Street. The Six Metre, 100 years of racing, Pekka Barck and Tim Street, 2007.

962 News from Britain, Bill Smart. Yachting, February 1947.

963 The Months Racing, Yachting Monthly, Spring 1939.

964 The thoughts of well-known Dragon sailor, Michael Crean the original helmsman, are not recorded.

965 Six-metre masterclass, Ian Howlett in conversation with James Boyd, 2nd June 2015.

966 The 'glamour' of racing 6-meters inspired the movie *Nothing Sacred*, starring Fred March and Carole Lombard, in which Briggs Cunningham and crew (all in risible wigs) sailed up the East River.

[967] The competition is still around, albeit in name only, contested in fibreglass one-designs.

[968] Toward the end of the 6mR epoch there was the odd match in 5.5 Metres and Solings, but overall, this was an epoch that embraced the glory days of the 6 Metre Class.

[969] *Caryl* beat Frank Paine's *Gypsy* and *Saskia* beat Clinton Crane's *Priscilla III*.

[970] The 1st International Rule ran from 1907 to 1919, the 2nd Rule from 1919 to 1933, and the 3rd Rule has been employed substantially unchanged since an amendment in 1937.

[971] XV Olympiad, Final Eliminating Trials Yachting World, August 1948.

[972] XIV Olympiad, International Yachting Festival at Torquay, Yachting World, September 1948.

[972] A final detail was the old Olympic scoring system which racked up thousands of points in a glorious tour de force of spurious accuracy: Points = 101 + 1000 log A − 1000 log N (A = total entries and N = finishing position). You could not make it up!

Six-metres in 1909: *Teal*, C. L'Estrange-Ewen (see Appendix 1) and *Apache*, A. Mylne (see Chapter 9)

23mR *White Heather II,* William Fife III, 1907 built for Myles Kennedy. Image: Kirk

8mR *Iskareen* (*Cheetah*), Olin Stephens built by A/B Neglinge-Varvet Sweden, 1928. Image Yuile

Six Metre yachts off Hunter's Quay 1920s, *Coila III* leading.   Image: Stephen Family Archive

6mR, *Maida*, on the hoist   19/24 *Tringa* on the slip

Six Metre yachts close reaching up the Clyde ca.1938, *Circe* K55 leading   Image: Yuile

SAIL PLAN OF 15-METRE CLASS BOAT.

DESIGN FOR THE 15-METRE CLASS

BY T. C. GLEN-COATS.

15-metre, T. C. Glen-Coats, 1906   Mylne Yacht Design

SAIL AND RIGGING PLAN OF A 12-METRE RACING YACHT, DESIGNED BY
T. C. GLEN-COATS.

Total area according to measurement rule = 3,647 sq. ft.

12-metre, T. C. Glen-Coats, 1910   Mylne Yacht Design

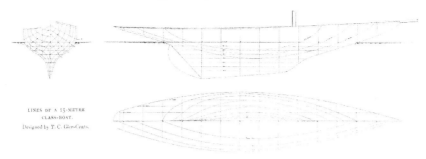

15-metre, Glen-Coats, 1906   Mylne Yacht Design

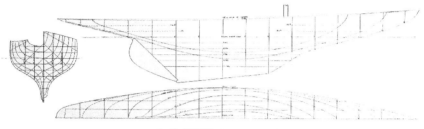

12-metre, Glen-Coats, 1910   Mylne Yacht Design

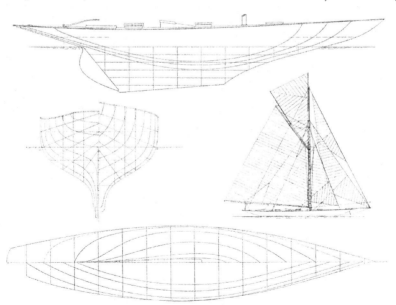

12-metre, J. P. McGregor, 1911   Reproduced in The Yachtsman
J. P. McGregor clearly had a fine eye – the lines are rather beautiful and the forward overhand is, dare-we-say, perfect. The work is not that of a dabbler. Apart from the fact Mr McGregor lived in Lenzie, little is known about him and any information is welcome.

499

Camellia of Rhu, 8CR, James McGruer, 1959   Image: Jeremy Thomson

Eight-metre yacht rigs: Marconi topsail cutter, sloop & wishbone ketch, Clyde 2007   Image: Jim McNair

Shimna, 15-metre, William Fife III, 1907   Image: David Hutchison, Robertson's Collection
The elegant *Shimna* was built by Alexander Robertson at Sandbank. She was the first boat built
to the International Rule launched in the Clyde and the lightest 15mR ever built.

Ailort, (8mR *Coila IV*) F. J. Stephen, 1927   Image: Jackson Family Archive
Image taken at Auchenlochen,1938. Young Wilfred (left) became captain of HMS *Ark Royal.*

Six-metre yachts racing off Hunter's Quay, 1930s   Artist: Montague Dawson (1890-1973)
Montague Dawson (1890-1973) had no formal art training and developed his illustration skills at a commercial art studio in 1910. After joining the Royal Navy, he continued to submit his work to publications such as *Sphere* and *The Graphic.*

6mR, *Johan,* James McGruer, 1939   Image: Yuile

6mR, *Johan,* James McGruer, 1939   Model: RNCYC collection

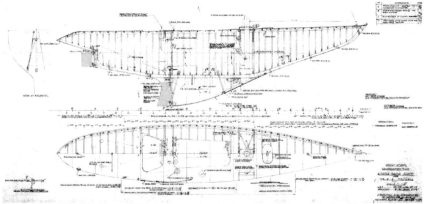

Gosling, 6mR, Olin Stephens, 1971   Note original rudder and trim-tab

Note the proposed helmsman cockpit with wheel steering and an inner concentric wheel/clutch for the trim-tab. Erik Maxwell respectfully declined the wheel option. A wheel would not appear in a 6mR until 2017 when *Bribon* was designed by Juan Kouyoumdjian with a special steering pedestal and deck-layout to cater for the physical limitations of her owner, King Juan Carlos. Also note the crew cockpit, which denies the tactician a view behind the leech of the deck-sweeping genoa.

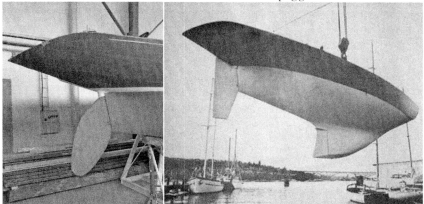

Steering: *Toogooloowoo V,* a near-sister to *Gosling* – DIY paddle blade left, barn-door blade right

Gosling, 6mR, Olin Stephens, 1971   Image: Ian Howlett collection

Chapter 25: Hot B-type Stars

In the past few years, the Pleiades have given many people, other than their owners, great pleasure. They are used for sailing courses run by the Scottish Council of Physical Recreation at Blairmore and Strone, and hundreds of young people have been taught to sail in them. Angus Whyte[974]

Through the post-war period, and until relatively recently, the Pleiades were the best-loved and most venerable one-design fleet in Scotland. The little Pleiades appeared on the Clyde in 1914. They were named after a star cluster celebrated by the Ancient Greeks. In astronomy, the Pleiades or 'Seven Sisters' refers to a star cluster tagged 'M45', comprising *"middle-aged, hot B-type stars"* in the constellation of Taurus. This might also have been written to order as a description of Pleiade owners in the 1960s.

It has been suggested that the name, Pleiade, serendipitously derives from 'plein', 'to sail' in ancient Greek, as in: 'πλεῖν ἀνάγκη, ζῆν οὐκ ἀνάγκη' which means *'to sail is necessary, to live is not'*. The heliacal rising of the Pleiades star cluster signalled the start of the sailing season in the Mediterranean. Only later was the constellation mythologized as seven divine sisters. There might have been just seven sisters but there were eventually ten Pleiades. The girls' mother, *Pleione*, was invited in to chaperone the fleet, while their father, *Atlas*, lorded over it. *Atlas* was almost immediately renamed *Oread*, after Hilda Doolittle's sestet, published to wide acclaim that spring.

> *Whirl up, sea—*
> *whirl your pointed pines,*
> *splash your great pines*
> *on our rocks,*
> *hurl your green over us,*
> *cover us with your pools of fir.*

Charles McAndrew's *Alcyone* was green, James Napier's *Electra* was white, Archie Watson's *Merope* was black, Mrs J. C. Campbell's *Sterope* was blue, Miss M. E. MacAndrew's *Calaeno* was red, Fred. J. Stephen's *Maia* was varnished, Mr R. S. Allan's *Taygeta* was yellow, Miss E. M. Allan's *Pleione* and Stewart Black's *Atlas* had yet to settle on a colour. During the German raids on Clydebank, *Calaeno* was destroyed when a stray bomb hit D. H. Munro & Son's Boatyard in Gairletter. She was effectively replaced by *Phaola* No.10, in 1951.[975] The sisters must have made quite an entrance when they first appeared on the broad catwalk of the Firth of Clyde in the spring of 1914.

The Pleiades were 20 feet 7¼" LOA, 13 feet 2½" LWL and 5 feet 8¾" beam; they were carvel-built with canvas-covered decks and sported a gunter rig of 160²ft (15²ᴹ). The scantlings reflected good Scandinavian parsimony – Siberian pine on widely spaced oak frames with a cast iron keel. They all appeared to be hogged badly by the 1960s. However, while they were indeed literally falling apart, looking at the original line drawings today, it is evident that they were designed with a very flat sheer.

The hull-form and rig were characteristic of turn-of-the-century day-sailers with a snubbed bow, cast iron rudder head and tiller, and little slatted seats on deck to keep bums dry. The Pleiades were fat and shallow, similar to the better-known, Sibbick-designed Whitewings, although the latter were rather larger at 23ft. They were also similar to Linton Hope's Broads OD Class from 1900, which is still active with new-builds today.

The Pleiades may appear as Scottish as oatcakes, but like the now better-known Loch Longs, they are Scandinavian imports masquerading in tartan. In Denmark, where the design originates, they are known as '15m² Yolle Klasse Baad (15m² Jolly Class Boats). Sir Charles MacAndrew (1888-1979) is credited with introducing the Pleiades to the Clyde.[976] In later years, Charles luxuriated in the salty and sumptuous title of 'Baron MacAndrew of the Firth of Clyde'.

MacAndrew retained a love for small boats and is cited in 'Cruising in Company' as being "*one of the most skilful helmsmen in the Clyde*" in the "*tiny Caribou*".[977] He is bracketed with T. C. Glen-Coats, G. F. Paisley and Fred J. Stephen, who although "*of substantial means*", chose to sail these and other small boats. In any event, he was a man of ability and experience who considered level-racing in small boats to provide the best sport.

Sir Charles visited Copenhagen in 1912, shopping for a class boat on behalf of a syndicate of prospective owners. There, he met Fredrick Preisler who was promoting the new Yolle Klasse. Fred had commissioned the design from Hr. A. With, a native of the same city. Charles promptly ordered six of these small yachts from Jacob Hansen, the approved Danish builder, for season-1913 delivery.

However, events in the North Atlantic prompted a change of plans. "*It is not generally known that bound up with the desire to start the new class of 20-footers on the Clyde is a pathetically romantic echo, so to speak, of the tragedy of the Titanic. The effect of the loss, it may be remembered, was a great demand for more lifeboats for ocean-going craft. Hansen, like so many other boat builders, found himself so overwhelmed with orders for lifeboats that he could not undertake construction of the little squadron.*"[978]

The *Titanic* disaster of April 1912 catalysed demand for better safety equipment on passenger ships. There was a great deal of money to be made from the lifeboat business in the aftermath of that disaster.[979] Coincidentally, Fred J. Stephen, who advised MacAndrew on design changes to the Pleiade, served on the 'Boats and Davits Committee' which drafted the new lifeboat regulations.

MacAndrew and his associates may have seen the Yolle Klasse design in the June 1912 edition of *Yachting Monthly*.[980] The magazine featured drawings of the boat and her metric specification.[981] The class-rules specified that there should be airtight compartments in the fore-peak and the stern, with a combined cubic capacity of $0.25m^3$, equal to 8 cwt of lift. Of the Scottish boats, however, only Miss Allan's *Pleione* had built-in buoyancy.

Yachting Monthly continued: "*We reproduce as a supplement the design of this useful little boat, the lines of which recently appeared in our contemporary Sejl-sport.* The cockpit was said to accommodate six persons and the write-up suggested that two bunks could be fitted under the foredeck. This optimistic prospect suggests that our forefathers were made of sterner stuff when planning a weekend away at Rothesay, not to mention fitting six adults in a cockpit less than 5ft long. "*The prices charged for the boat in Denmark, with all sails and gear, are £25 (£3,000) clench built and £29 3/6- (£3,500) for carvel-built. Working drawings and a model are lying for inspection with Mr Fredrick Preisler.*"

The magazine feature was a result of work carried out by a special-purpose committee of the Boat Racing Association (BRA). The committee of the BRA noted that the $15m^2$ Jolly Class boat was a boat that "*strikes us as eminently suitable for the purposes of the Association. It is a class that is, we understand, being taken up extensively in both Scandinavia and America, and if it were also adopted in this country possibilities of international sport would be opened up and an extensive market opened up for the sale of boats when their owners have no further use for them.*"[982]

The Scottish consortium was not deterred by the cancellation of the Danish order. They liked the boat, and they had the plans. MacAndrew approached Daniel Turner, a Dunoon boatbuilder. Up until the Pleiade contract, Turners had specialised in clinker-built vessels. However, while the new class had been designed with a clinker option, the Royal Clyde folks opted for the more up-market carvel hulls that were becoming de rigueur. The consortium was, after all, not exactly short of a bob or two.

The Pleiade contract was Dan Turner's first attempt at yacht building, and one suspects that it was probably his first attempt at carvel construction too. Nevertheless, he did a reasonable job. The Danish specifications were translated by C. L'Estrange Ewen (1877-1949), a Glasgow naval architect, yacht surveyor and something of an authority on yacht insurance.[983] Ewen was an early champion of gender equality within the all-male bastion of the Royal Clyde, as recounted in Chapter 11.

The Pleiades were lofted as per Hr. With's original plan, but with an extra 6" added to the draft, as advised by Fred. J. Stephen. This was to ensure that the boats could stand up to the conditions on the Clyde. Fred, sailing *Maia*, would go on to dominate the class whenever he could spare time from his world-beating 6-metres. European windsurfers call Denmark 'Cold Hawaii', so perhaps Fred's extra righting moment would not have gone amiss there either. Chapter 27 is devoted to the life and work of Fred. J. Stephen.

Over the course of two years, Dan Turner turned out eight smart little yachts. Writing about the class in the 1960s, Kerr Hunter marvelled that the Pleiades had cost *"less than £50"*. However, Turner's unit cost of £48 (£5,600) was more than 60% higher than the original Danish quotation for 15m² Jolly Class boats. While Scandinavian yacht builders were renowned for good value, 24 years later, J. Colquhoun & Sons, also of Dunoon, batch-produced the first Loch Longs at a cost of just £66 each (£4,500).[984] The Loch Long is a much larger boat, requiring about 50% more material.

The *London Times'* yachting correspondent noticed the new class but seems to have been unaware of its pedigree. *"Yachtsmen generally will follow the racing of the new twenty-foot Clyde class with very considerable interest. There would seem to be immense possibilities here. Nine of these boats have already been built by Turner of Dunoon, and they have many striking features. Not the least of these is their draught, well under 3ft, while they carry a sail area of slightly over 160sqft.*

I should like to see these yachts experimented with elsewhere than the Clyde, so that some true idea of the real value of the boats might then be gained, and I hope that that excellent sportsman Mr R. S. Allan, who is building two of these yachts, will assist in this direction."[985] *Pleione* would be sailed by the talented Miss E. M. Allan.

The Pleiades were mainly second boats for owners of holiday villas in Cowal. They were used for week-day races and family sailing through the summer and occasionally turned up at the weekend regattas. There are race accounts where owners sailed their principal yachts in the early starts, and their Pleiades in the late afternoon.

After the Great War, the original wealthy owners moved on to play with new toys, selling the Pleiades to cash-strapped retirees and younger men who had to work for a living. The Pleiades reformed in 1919 to sail as a class until 1931. Through the inter-war years, the class continued to give great pleasure to a less exalted, but no less competitive, racing community. However, as the thirties progressed, it became evident that the boats were approaching the end of their competitive life, condemned by their simple, low-cost carvel construction to work their seams raw and leak like baskets. The worn-out husks of the Pleiades scattered to the four winds.

In the wake of the long and dispiriting years of WW2, with peacetime came a tremendous desire to get back on the water. In 1948, with the post-WW2 yachting boom now constrained by escalating labour costs and shortages of materials for new construction, the surviving boats regrouped to sail in Clyde Fortnight after a hiatus of 17 years. A new and more egalitarian generation of sailors were game to try anything that would float. The 'Port Glasgow Pirates' epitomised this 'can-do' mentality with their converted ships lifeboats and sea-gipsy style.

In the same manner, the Pleiades were recovered and brought back into commission on the Holy Loch. *Maia* was at Loch Lomond, *Taygeta* was discovered in a coal bing at Ardrishaig, and *Orcad* was contentedly rotting at Port Bannatyne, with an opportunistic sapling growing from the deck. Another was found on the Solway, and the others were scattered around the West Coast. Angus Whyte noted that: "*Now all but one of the Pleiades are moored at Ardnadam, on the Holy Loch, where they are the mainstay of the Clyde Holy Loch Yacht Club* [sic]. *Pleione is owned by Clyde pilot, Captain Baird, who keeps her at Greenock, but he sails regularly in competitions. Many of the others are owned by local artisans who sail them with all the verve and enjoyment of their original owners.*"[986]

The class participated in the 1948 Clyde Fortnight after a hiatus of 17 years. While only four were seaworthy initially, the rest were repaired and refitted in the years that followed. In 1951, Commander E. L Reid, a "*well-known enthusiast north and south of the border*" took over from Angus Whyte and did his best to ensure that the boats were raced enthusiastically. So much so that construction was started on three new boats, the lines having been lifted from *Merope*. However, only the professionally *built Phaola* ever sailed. The two others were in the hands of amateur builders, but neither appears to have been completed.

Jock Kerr Hunter became a great advocate of the class: "*If you happened to be on holiday around the upper reaches of the Firth of Clyde during the first week of July, you must have shared, with many others, the thrill of seeing racing yachts at play. You may even have noticed eight gaily coloured small yachts, showing their keel at every puff of wind, yet carrying on quite unperturbed in the stiffest of breezes. If you did, you were watching one of the oldest one-design racing classes in Britain – the Pleiades.*"

Gybe-o! 嘲笑它:[987] On Wednesday evenings through the 1950s and 60s, the Pleiades were the only one-design keelboat to race regularly on the

Holy Loch. At that time, they were also the oldest one-design yacht racing as a class in Scotland. Today, that title is held by the Loch Longs. When the wind blew, the Pleiades lit up the loch, providing a fine spectacle for the folks in Kilmun when rounding 'Mark B'. Whole families would rush out onto the lawn to watch the boats gybe all-standing – a spectacular sight with their long, overhanging booms.

Indeed, the gung-ho exponents of the class often entertained the North Shore community with proper 'Chinese gybes' – where the boom and the lower part of the mainsail swipes across and leaves the top half of the sail on the original side – now set by the lee. The gunter rig might almost be made for this type of photogenic diversion. After the fact, it is necessary to throw in another two gybes in rapid succession, one to undo the mess and another for the second attempt. We might here define 'proper' Chinese gybes, because the widespread use of kicking straps (or boom vangs) now means that the basic scenario seldom happens today. A new generation of gung-ho round-the-world sailors imprecisely use the term for an unplanned crash gybe – an alarming event, certainly, but in no way ascribable to the seafaring practice of the Middle Kingdom. No doubt these heretical folk also disparage the fine pedantocracy of the old school who are appalled by malapropos slang.

The Pleiade fleet was keenly raced on a wing and a prayer through the 1950s and 60s, with a separate start at the Holy Loch and a regular turnout of six. The class remained together and active until the mid-1960s but was already in steep decline when the David Boyd-designed Piper arrived to sound its death knell in 1967. The last major regatta I remember the Pleiades competing in was at Hunter's Quay in 1963, but some boats lingered on beyond that date.[988]

Alan Waugh, who sailed *Alcyone*, recalls that he enjoyed the challenge of sailing the Pleiades with their old-style over-large mainsail and vestigial jib.[989] He recalls frequently having to reef the main when the wind blew. The shallow iron keel contributed little until it left the water. Reducing sail was very easy in these little boats – just a matter of pulling the boom out of the square-section gooseneck and manually rolling the sail around the boom – a system used in most day-boats and dinghies at that time.

These days, in fact since the late-1960s, we never reef small keelboats no matter how hard the wind blows; developments in sailcloth and spar technologies have changed the game entirely and a fixed sail-area can be readily depowered while maintaining neutral helm. Classes like the Pipers, Dragons and 6mRs, with large overlapping genoas, used to change down to working jibs in hard weather. While the Dragon and many 6mRs were originally designed with working jibs, with most set-ups it's a horrible compromise that ruins the overall balance.

Alan first met Alister Galbraith in 1963 after he had been forced to relocate his sailing school to Hunter's Quay following the 'requisition' of the Ardnadam Hotel and Pier by the US Navy. The British Admiralty and national strategic interests rode roughshod around the Holy Loch to accommodate the needs of the Americans. So, the old hotel now served-up greasy hamburgers and draft Budweiser in its new incarnation as a US Navy Enlisted Men's Club.

Alistair Galbraith was said to be as "*almost as much a landmark on the Clyde as Strone Buoy or the Gantocks*".[990] He was known as the 'Bishop' because he bore a startling resemblance to Archbishop Makarios III, President of Cyprus. When Dunoon Grammar won the British Schools Yachting Championship for the first time in 1966, with Rab Dallas at the helm, George Findlay, then Yachting Correspondent of *The Glasgow Herald*, commented: "*The Clark Cup winners learned their sailing in the gunter-rigged Pleiade class with Alistair Galbraith at Hunter's Quay.*" We were quite indignant about this as, while that much was true for Rab, neither Charlie Roberts nor myself, as dyed in the wool dinghy sailors in these years, had ever sailed a Pleiade. Perhaps we missed out on the Bishop and the boats?

Toward Sailing Club (TSC) was founded in 1970 by Sandy Robertson, a local farmer who had formerly crossed the bay to race his Enterprise dinghy at the Isle of Bute Sailing Club. While it seemed to be an unnecessary dilution of sailing activity at the time, it cannot be denied that Rothesay Bay is among the best venues for sailboat racing anywhere. The new TSC members bought boats from the Holy Loch and among them were *Alcyone* and *Taygeta*. The two Pleiades were used for sail training through the 1970s, however, they were long past their best. In their later years, they never did represent much in the way of a capital investment, so maintenance was often cursory. They suffered horribly at the hands of enthusiastic amateurs. Strangely nostalgic members of the TSC remember that they "*opened up like Venetian bloody blinds when it was windy!*"[991] Lying at moorings, they had to be pumped out daily.

When Norman Turner, the son of the original Pleiade builder, passed away, the Jane Street Yard was sold to a young boatbuilder from the south of England who attempted to revive the class. He faired-up one of the TSC Pleiade hulls as a plug for a fibreglass female mould. It seems to have been a poor job by all accounts, the project fell by the wayside and the yard changed hands again. To be fair, getting two halves of a plug from a Pleiade hull identical would have taxed even the best of boatbuilders.

Stan Ferguson owns the Ardmaleish Boat Building Co Ltd with his sons. Ardmaleish is the former Bute Slip Dock. Stan once worked with Norman, Dan Turner's son. Stan is a colourful character who began his career as an apprentice with the famous Stephen's Yard at Linthouse. If you are looking for a small but challenging restoration project, Stan has the last surviving Pleiade in a shipping container.[992] See list in Appendix 3.

CODA: Scottish Council for Physical Recreation

During the 1950s and 60s, most of the Pleiades were owned, or at least maintained, by the Scottish Council for Physical Recreation (SCPR a.k.a. 'The Physical Wrecks') and used as training boats. The SCPR was established as an independent body to *"promote healthy living through physical recreation"* in 1953, with separate and distinct aspirations from the British Sports administration. Together with the Sports Council for Scotland, the SCPR became the Scottish Sports Council in 1972.

Instruction programmes in dinghies, daysailers and Jock Kerr Hunter's own 1897 8-metre Sibbick yawl, *Sayonara*, were supervised by Jock himself with Angus Whyte and the inimitable Bishop in support. For many students, the cost of hotel accommodation at the Royal Marine Hotel was over their budget, so they stayed in the Blairmore guesthouse 'Creggandarroch', a fine villa in the style of Alexander 'Greek' Thomson, or for the really hard-up, Rennison's magnificent old Scottish baronial pile 'Dunselma Castle', across the Loch on Strone Point, then a youth hostel, was available.[993]

The late Jim Gibb, a 'weel-kent' Clyde yachtsman and Piper stalwart was an unlikely SPCR student in 1959. Jim and his mate, Doug Boller from the United States, jumped ship from the Pleiades to the 12-metre *Sceptre* during Clyde Week in a memorable coup de connerie described in *The Piper Calls the Tune.*

Notwithstanding the hand-to-mouth modus operandi of this motley and eccentric crew, the sailing school weathered chronic penury and rising expectations through to the mid-1960s. The Bishop, penniless throughout his life, somehow acquired the school's assets from Kerr Hunter sometime in the 1960s, before selling it on after his first heart attack in 1967.[994] The new operator had little success and the operation folded a year or so later.[995]

CODA: Pleiades in Print and the Media

The book *Sailing for Beginners* is a basic sailing primer published in 1960. It was written by J. Kerr Hunter with an excellent preface by Clyde yachting legend, J. Herbert Thom, and retailed for the princely sum of 8/6p (£8). The quite bizarre drawings were produced by A. Kennedy Smellie. The book features an image of the Holy Loch Pleiade fleet on the dust cover with a 1960s-type graphic overlay. The boats were also used in a couple of illustrations inside.[996] The book promoted the sail-training ideas of Jimmy Howden Hume and Herbert Thom and was part and parcel of the sailing courses hosted by Kerr Hunter under the auspices of the SCPR.

A 16-minute film entitled *Sailing for Sport* was made by Educational Films of Scotland in 1961 with the support of the SCPR.[997] It's a fascinating old film with the Bishop and Alec Waddell (in full RCYC boatman's regalia) as instructors. Alan Waugh and a youthful Fergie Campbell appear as enthusiastic students. The very professional narration is by Kerr Hunter in his inimitable style. By contrast, Don Sawkins attends to the camerawork with nary a care for composition or a straight horizon.[998]

There is also an 11-minute 16mm film called *Scottish Sport* sponsored by the Scottish Council for Physical Recreation from 1954 (unfortunately, not available on-line) which featured the Dragon, *Tass II*, and the Pleiades. On 18th September 1958, Kerr Hunter appeared on BBC Radio 3's *Time Out of Doors* as part of a feature on local sailing. His piece entitled: *Small-boat Sailing in Scotland* introduced some of the 'sailing masters' of the Clyde and promoted the activities of the SCPR at Hunter's Quay.

[974] Sailing for Beginners, J. Kerr Hunter, 1960.

[975] In the 1950s, *Alcyone* sported a small cuddy, and through the post-WW2 years, *Merope* always had blue sails and *Calaeno* orange sails.

[976] Sir Charles MacAndrew was knighted in 1935 and made a baron in 1959.

[977] Cruise in Company, George Blake and Christopher Small, 1959.

[978] Romance of the New Clyde Racing Class, Notes & Notions, The Yachtsman, 2nd April 1914.

[979] The first version of the International Convention for the Safety of Life at Sea (the SOLAS Treaty) was worked up in 1914 following the sinking of the RMS *Titanic*. SOLAS prescribed numbers of lifeboats and other emergency equipment, along with safety procedures. While the 1914 treaty was not universally adopted due to the outbreak of the Great War, the recommendations resulted in a sharp increase in lifeboat orders which overwhelmed the traditional lifeboat builders, such as Mercan's in Clydebank. The unit costs, and doubtless the profitability of lifeboats, also increased sharply due to higher spec.

[980] The Pleiade Story, J. Kerr Hunter, undated.

[981] "*The principal dimensions of the 15 m² Jolly Boat are as follows: Length overall, 6.28 metres; extreme draft 0.72 metres; extreme beam (to outside of skin) 1.75 metres; freeboard 0.41 metres; displacement, 660 kilos; weight of iron keel, 215 kilos. The keel is of oak, 100 millimetres broad and the stem, also of oak, 70 x 60 millimetres.*" The other scantlings were: transom timbers, 500-100 x 30; sternpost (of fir) 16; beams (fir) 35 x 25; mast beams, 50 x 25-25 by 25; distance between beams, 250; frames (of oak), 15 x 20, spaced 250; mast frame, 35 x 25; planking (of fir), 11; deck (fir, canvassed over).

[982] We can find no evidence of further involvement by the BRA in relation to the introduction of the class to Britain or the uptake in America.

[983] C. L'Estrange Ewen owned the 1884 G.L. Watson cutter *Coquette*.

[984] Loch Longs, The First 50 Years, John McMurtrie, 1987.

[985] Yachting Notes, White Ensign, Sunday Times, 24th May 1914.

[986] *Merope*, which had been changed to Bermudian rig by her naval-officer owner was restored to the less close-winded but more powerful gunter and raced by Jean McLellan, the only lady owner at that time. *Merope* had raced with the <7tons T. M. handicap class in 1947.

[987] This is Google's translation of Gybe-o, it could, of course, mean anything.

[988] *Taygeta* (A. F. Whyte) was first and *Sterope* (A. Galbraith) was second, 4½ minutes back.

[989] Two notorious Pleiade sailors of our generation were Rab Dallas and Piper stalwart, Alan Waugh, both protégés of the eccentric Bishop.

990 Sailing for Sport, 1961. 16mm colour film. Filmed by Don Sawkins.

991 Carol Gilles and Anne Douglas-Frood.

992 When Toward S. C. disposed of their Pleiades, one was used as a plug and the other was rescued by Stan, for old times' sake. While the two Pleiades were in commission at Toward, there was also a third surviving boat at Gourock. Worth tracking down perhaps.

993 Dunselma was built by the Coats family and later owned by the Bergius family – both well-known Clyde yachting dynasties.

994 Alistair Galbraith recovered from this first heart attack and bought the Piper *Tass III*, formerly *Sandbank Rebel*, and owned from new by the depot ship USS *Simon Lake* in 1972. Some years later a second attack put paid to the 'Bishop' when he was launching his dinghy to recover the Piper which had broken free of her moorings off Hafton Estate.

995 *Tass II* was the Dragon and *Tass III* was a Piper, but the original *Tass* was the Bishop's cat.

996 Sailing for Beginners, J. Kerr Hunter, 1960.

997 Sailing for Sport, 1961. 16mm colour film. Filmed by Don Sawkins.

998 Sawkins made several short films with Dunoon and sailing themes. These films are very much in the amateur category, but they provide a valuable insight into life in Cowal in the 1960s.

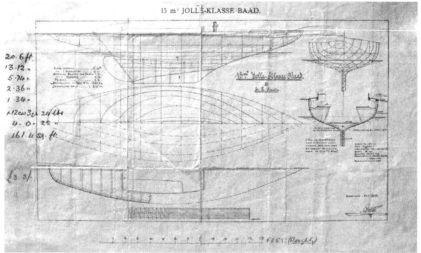

Original plans of the 15m² Jolle-Klasse Baad, 1912   Lines: Hr. A. With

The lines of the Pleiade appear on the next page. They are identical, bar the deeper keel fin as drawn by Fred J. Stephen. Stephen adapted the boat for 'Clyde conditions', where increased stiffness was deemed more important than shoal draft. The Clyde version also has wider side-decks and a narrower cockpit without the internal seats.

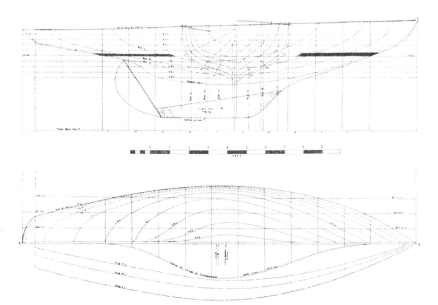

Scottish Pleiade Lines, 1913   Lines: Hr. A. With, modified by Fred J. Stephen

Under tow from Sandbank to Gourock   Images: sailing for Beginners

Pleiades racing in Clyde Week off Hunter's Quay   Image: Ian Gilchrist

The cover of *Sailing for Beginners* featuring Pleiades sailing in Holy Loch in the 1950s, with laid-up WW2 'Liberty Ships' and David Napier's villas in the background

BOOK FIVE
Northern Lights

Chapter 26: Glen-Coats – the Sorcerer's Apprentice

By next season, her designer-owner will have improved several details which will enable 'Helen' to hold her own in the best of company. Now in her first season, she takes her fair share of prizes. Besides giving much pleasure to her owner she has greatly added to the interest of the class. Uffa Fox[999]

These days we associate Scottish naval architecture with Watson, Fife and Mylne, but during the early years of the 20th century, when level-rating was at its most competitive, two talented 'amateurs' sat at the top table – Fred J. Stephens (1863-1932) and Tommy Glen-Coats (1878-1954). Fred Stephens was a scion of the famous shipbuilding dynasty, while Glen-Coats' fortune accrued from Coats of Paisley. Tommy's father took the additional name of Glen when he became a baronet. Both yachting families spared no expense in pursuit of their hobby and both had the talent to enjoy conspicuous racing success.

Sir Thomas Glen-Coats, 2nd Baronet, was a gentleman of leisure. The family firm of J. & P. Coats commanded a global business empire, enabling Tommy to devote his life to messing about in boats. Shared interests with his extended family included Arctic exploration and fine art. The Coats underwrote the Scottish National Antarctic Expedition of 1902-1904.[1000] William Speirs Bruce named a segment of Antarctica, between 20°West & 36°West, 'Coats Land' to recognise that essential contribution.

Tommy's father, Sir Thomas Glen-Coats, 1st Baronet, was a keen sailor, but not an outstanding helmsman. Nevertheless, Sir Thomas, Member of Parliament for West Renfrewshire, was active in the politics of his various yacht clubs and was a long-standing supporter of Clyde yachting. Among his yachts was the *Cruiser*, a 40-foot YRA linear-rater, designed by G. L. Watson, and originally built by Fife for James Coats Jr. in 1886. He also owned the magnificent 145ft auxiliary iron schooner, *Hebe*, built by J. & G. Thomson in Glasgow in 1869. Sir Thomas raced the *Cruiser* with some success, even though, as the name suggests, she was built for comfort rather than speed, with more beam than most 13-tonners of the period.

After tagging along for a decade, sailing with friends and family, Tommy was motivated to order his first racing yacht for delivery in 1904. With the *Thetis*, Tommy would race in the newly constituted Clyde 30-ft Restricted

Class. Alfred Mylne designed the boat, presaging a mutually beneficial business relationship in later years. She was built by McAllister of Dumbarton, the yard Mylne recommended and which enjoyed an excellent reputation for light, well-built yachts at that time.

Tommy Glen-Coats is acclaimed as an outstanding example of the Corinthian ideal, but he brought an entirely professional approach to his passion. He may not have monetised his involvement in the marine business, but then he had no need to. He was a skilled racing skipper, although his 1908 Olympic gold medal reflected his ability, rather than taxed it. This serendipitous success made him a household name even before he really got going on the design front.

In 1906, or thereabouts, Sir Thomas Glen-Coats 1st Baronet, visited the Mylne design office with a proposal. Sir Thomas's eldest son was now twenty-eight, too old to hang about the house and seemingly more interested in yachting than spinning yarn.[1001] Perhaps Alfred could see his way to take on Thomas Jr. as a 'mature' apprentice? Ian Nicolson refers to the recruitment story as *"the curious involvement of Thomas Glen-Coats"*.[1002] It was a late start. By way of comparison, in 1916 David Boyd would begin his training in naval architecture at the Ardrossan shipyard, with day release to the Royal Technical College, at the regulation age of fourteen.

However, while Tommy, or 'Tid', as he was known to intimates, might have been a little old to have his father sort out his life, he had not exactly wasted his time in the interim. He would be the first old-Etonian naval architecture apprentice, who already boasted a degree from Merton College, Oxford in his CV. Additionally, Tommy had long been a keen student of yacht design, testing his prototypes against the best at the Paisley Model Yacht Club. This club was sponsored by the Coats family and was an influential, if generally unrecognised, centre for comparative testing of free-sailing models by both amateur and professional designers.

In the Mylne's account of the discussion, Alfred acquiesced immediately, offering to waive the usual apprenticeship premium. Sir Thomas was not about to take advantage of Mylne's good nature, and after some haggling, it was finally agreed that an equivalent sum would be put in an escrow account for a 'rainy day'.[1003] Tommy's relationship with the Mylne office seems to have worked well for both men, even if the deal seems one-sided in retrospect. But we might also acknowledge that, as the years passed, Tommy sought to redress the balance through elbow-grease, enthusiasm, and finally, direct investment.

During the long Scottish winters, Tommy designed new boats for himself or his friends, and each summer he cleared the decks, disappeared from the design office, and set sail in his latest creation to lead a peripatetic existence on the regatta circuit. On his travels, the genial and well-connected apprentice acted as a useful brand ambassador for Alfred Mylne's firm. His endless passion for new projects helped the Mylne family's Bute Slip Dock through some difficult years, during which the 'rainy day money' did indeed come in useful.

Mylne was a confirmed bachelor and a gentleman. By all accounts, he was not in the least intimidating, even at the height of his success when he was mixing in rarefied circles and discussing *Britannia's* latest rig with the King. He also seems to have had a fine sense of humour. One Cowes Week, he was invited to dinner ashore with the Nicholson family. Alfred thought, wrongly as it turned out, that he must wear a dinner suit. The Scot gamely turned up in a hired outfit which was ludicrously oversized, breeks up to his armpits, bundled together with a broad leather belt, invoking the theatrical dishevelment of Charlie Chaplin.

While designers and builders in the marine industry are obliged to mix with the rich and famous, we might remember that even today, technical people in vocational work are not well-paid. Through the great years of the industry, yachtsmen liked nothing better than to chisel artists and artisans for bragging rights in the bar, even while they too tottered on the edge of bankruptcy. Self-respect is a curious thing. An entrée into fashionable company carries the risk of becoming star-struck to ape the lifestyle of wealthy clients. By their own admission, Uffa Fox comes to mind, then Ron Holland, but most are less willing to come clean. Mylne seems to have avoided this, as did Fife, but perhaps not G. L. Watson.

By normal master – apprentice standards, Alfred Mylne was generous to a fault. It appears that these two very different characters got on well together. Even so, their friendship must have been tested at times as Tommy's career blossomed. There were several seasons when the apprentice clearly outshone his illustrious mentor. But, as when William Fife II and William Fife III shared an office and maintained separate client lists, the two men shared infrastructure, they shared values and they maintained a common purpose. And, of course, their jointly owned boatyard on Bute did build the lion's share of Tommy's designs.

Since the earliest days of the marine industry, design apprenticeships have been based on learning, developing and practising core skills: making fair copies of the master's rough work, first on design details, then graduating to hull lines and construction plans. The essential numeracy, which underlies the design, specification and management of the construction of yachts, is learned from years spent as a dogsbody, then a draftsman. Creative design duties are delegated piece-by-piece and stage-by-stage, according to the candidate's ability and how busy the office is. Tommy, of course, was no ordinary apprentice. His personal spline weights were encased in fine Moroccan leather.

One can only speculate how much mentoring actually went on in the Mylne office, as in the first few months of his apprenticeship, Tommy designed *Pallas*, a Clyde 30ft Restricted Class yacht, to replace his Mylne 30-footer, *Thetis*. The boats were moderately light-displacement linear-raters, of refined design, incorporating little structural redundancy. So, as a milieu for a first design, the class presented a worthwhile challenge. Nevertheless, *Pallas* was a major departure from Tommy's previous Mylne-designed boat, being significantly larger for her rating.

No doubt Alfred would have been looking over Tommy's shoulder as the sorcerer's apprentice worked up his first design. But this is what Tommy himself had to say. "*Before proceeding further, I wish to make a personal explanation regarding the Pallas. There seems to have existed some doubt as to how far her design was original and my own. In design, Pallas is nothing if not original and was, when built, a departure in type from any of the existing boats of her class. Her lines were begun, completed and faired by me during a holiday in the autumn of 1905. Starting with certain ideas, I endeavoured to work them to their logical conclusion.*"

As might be expected of a design finalised in the Mylne office, Tommy made full use of the expertise available to specify construction and openly acknowledged Mylne's contribution. "*In construction, however, she is in almost every respect similar to the Mylne boats, Mr Mylne having all along given me free access to his construction plans. I am deeply indebted, indeed, to Mr Mylne for the advice and assistance which he generously gave whenever I sought it, and without whose practical hints and constant aid 'Pallas' could never have taken shape.*"

Glen-Coats explained how *Pallas* differed from the first generation of the class. Mylne seemed to share some of his ideas about lines of development, although in this account Tommy had yet to see *Medora's* lines. "*With her large displacement, small hollow of section, large sail area, and full ends, Pallas was quite an unknown quantity, and I was naturally somewhat anxious at the beginning of the season till I saw how my design was likely to acquit itself. I had reason to believe that the new Mylne boat Medora had some features in common with my own vessel which was reassuring.*"[1004]

Pallas was an immediate and outstanding success, with 51 prizes in the two years of Glen-Coats' ownership. *Pallas* would outperform *Medora* in the first season racing together, although Mylne's previous benchmark, *Thetis*, edged the top spot. Then, with the first publication of the draft of the International Rule in 1906 Tommy was inspired to 'cash in his chips' and move on, establishing a pattern he would follow throughout his career as a yacht designer. He sold *Pallas* to his brother, Alexander, who enjoyed two equally successful seasons in the boat. She was still winning 20 years later in the handicap class with an elegant Bermudian rig.

When Tommy joined Mylne, John Morton James was also on hand to share the workload of the practice. James joined the Mylne office fully qualified and with some experience ca.1902. He combined the positions of design partner and office manager. According to David Gray, who now owns Mylne Yacht Design, it is impossible to tell the work of James and Mylne apart, as they had a common 'eye' and a similar drawing style. Counterintuitively, James generally took charge of the firm's larger commissions. As the big boats designed in the Mylne office during the inter-war period were often sublime, it is a pity that John James remains relatively unknown.

In the autumn of 1906, even before the International Rule came into effect, Tommy published one of the very first designs to the new rule in *Yachting Monthly*.[1005] This was for a 15-metre. The object of a design exercise at this scale was to enable comparisons with the 52ft linear-raters, perhaps the most highly developed level-rating band under the old rule. *Yachting Monthly* noted: "*This is the class which it is intended shall take the place of our present 52-footers. The fullness of the ends has been modified compared to what has obtained of late (to avoid paying excessively for the tax on flare), and yet the utility of the overhangs for speed and seaworthiness has not been materially affected. A considerable margin is thus left for the increase of the other elements, and we can obtain a vessel which is slightly longer, broader, deeper, and with a displacement proportionately greater.*" The lines are reproduced at the chapter break.

The magazine noted that, compared to a 52-footer, the 15-metre would be stiffer, with the lead carried low. As for sail area, that was only slightly greater than that of *Sonya*, the benchmark 1905 Herreshoff YRA 52ft linear-rater. On the deficit side of the performance scale, *Yachting Monthly* noted that "*yachts of the 15-metre class will have to be built in accordance with the proposed scantling regulations, which would probably mean an addition of from 25% to 30% in the weight of hull, and it must also be remembered that solid masts will be compulsory for yachts of this class.*" The 15-metre design remained unbuilt; however, Tommy was already at work on a 12-metre commission.

Over the winter of 1906-1907, and not yet a year into his 'apprenticeship' with Mylne, Glen-Coats began work on the first-generation 12-metre, *Heatherbell*, for his uncle, Major Andrew Coats.[1006] In his 1927 profile of Glen-Coats, W. Dodgson Bowman stresses that there were no other metre-boats around at that time to inform the gentleman designer's first efforts.[1007] However, there must have been brainstorming sessions in the office, as Mylne was working alongside on the 15-metre, *Ma'oona*, and the 8-metre, *Baira*, although these commissions would launch later.

Andrew Coats' *Heatherbell* was one of two commissions to the new International Rule won by Alexander Robertson that year, the other being the Fife 15-metre, *Shimna*, for John Payne and Arthur Watson.[1008] The Sandbank builder was a good choice. Alexander's craftsmen were turning out yachts of exceptional lightness which hit the marks on displacement and ballast-ratio.[1009] *Shimna* was, and would remain, the lightest 15mR ever built to the International Rule.

First International Rule (1907 – 1919)

$$R \text{ (metres)} = \frac{L + B + \frac{1}{2}G + 3d + 1/3\sqrt{S}\text{-}F}{2}$$

where....

L = length (as calculated)
B = beam
G = chain girth
d = difference between skin girth and chain girth
S = sail area
F = freeboard

The other British new-builds to the new rule, as they appear in Lloyds listings for 1907, comprised: Charles E. Nicholson's 23-metre, *Brynhild*; the Fife 10-metre, *Wanda*, and his 8-metres, *Sorais* and *Ya Veremos*, the Fay 7-metre yachts, *Heroine III* and *Mignonette*; the first two Fife 6-metres, *Almoraima* and *Osborne*; and the little Payne 5-metre, *Me Too*. So, the metre-boat community formed a small and exclusive club in British waters until numbers started to build the following spring.

Heatherbell was fitted out with an elaborate cedar interior. The ladies' cabin and saloon were finished in white enamel with polished dado accents. The design was not finalised until the late spring for a launching in July. Consequently, to meet that schedule, there was a significant overtime surcharge, which added considerably to the overall cost, but no matter, Andrew could afford it. In the autumn, *Heatherbell* was back in the shed for a ruthless weight-reduction programme with the finely crafted mahogany-work on deck replaced with cedar. At the same time, more sail was added. The cruiser-racer philosophy was chucked out, along with the marble-topped escritoire.[1010] This early Glen-Coats Twelve obviously did not have much boat-to-boat competition initially, but she was a good-looking and well-mannered vessel.

Heatherbell was sold to a gentleman in Helsingfors in 1909 and represented Finland in the 1912 Olympic Games, winning the bronze medal. During the Great War, under the cash-strapped ownership of the Zetterstrom Syndicate, her lead keel was removed and replaced by internal concrete ballast. Subsequently, she was sold to Norway, then given a new keel before returning to Britain in 1924.[1011] *Heatherbell*, subsequently sailing as *Yolande*, then as *Sylva*, was based in France until the late 1960s. She is reputed to have ended up back in Norway.[1012]

Heatherbell was encouraging as a first attempt at the International Rule, so for the 1908 season, Tommy designed another 12mR for himself. This was the *Hera*. She was one of three Twelves built by McAlister in 1908, the other two being the Mylne sisterships, '*Mouchette*' and '*Nargie*'. McAlister would lose the Mylne commissions when Mylne and Glen-Coats bought the yard at Ardmaliesh.[1013] In the early season between May, when she was launched, and July, Tommy and *Hera* had already worked their way through three YRA rating certificates with sail-area and freeboard variations, reflecting changes to ballasting and trim.

Initially, she was floating a few inches light, so about a ton of lead was added to her keel. This was pinned on in sheets. The *Yachtsman* noted that *"although this must affect the 'd' measurement to some extent, it was the best way in which the addition could be made"*.[1014] Then, in July, she was in Alex Robertson's yard in Sandbank for a new mast and a new suit of sails. This was clearly a no-expense-spared optimisation programme. *Heatherbell* and *Hera* were both designed with firm bilges, the latter particularly powerful in section. *Hera* was slightly smaller than *Heatherbell*, with more 'd' (garboard hollow). She also carried a larger sail-plan, although her displacement was not much greater.

With the two Glen-Coats 12mRs now matched on the water every weekend, significant improvements in boat-speed, boat-handling and all-round competitiveness inevitably followed. In 1908, *Hera* and *Heatherbell* dominated their class on the Clyde, and *Hera* went on to triumph in the curious Olympic adventure, described in a coda to this chapter. The 1909 season was inevitably something of an anti-climax. *Hera* was sold south in 1910 and won the odd race on the Solent, although generally finishing mid-pack under her new ownership.

In the autumn of 1908, Tommy turned his attention to the 6-metre class, with a boat for his friend George Moir. *Crusader*, as she was called, performed well, winning comfortably in the early season races before Fred Stephen and *Coila II* got down to business in July. *Crusader* justified the faith that both designer and owner had invested in the project; she finished the 1909 season with 17 flags in 23 starts. The irrepressible George Moir was a larger-than-life Clyde character who became a tireless advocate of the 6-metre class. Experience with George's *Crusader* informed the lines of *Cynthia*, which Tommy would build for his own use the following year.

Towards the end of his career as a yacht designer, Tommy would consider *Cynthia* to have been his most successful design.[1015]

In 1910, Tommy was again thinking of 12-metres. He submitted a set of lines to *Yachting Monthly* and the commentary was as follows: "*Of the famous Clyde 12-metre class, Mr T. C. Glen-Coats has considerable knowledge. In its first year (1907) he was represented by Heatherbell, and in 1908 he designed for himself and steered to the top of the class Hera, a boat which is still well to the fore.*"[1016] The published design embodied practical experience with these two yachts.

Now, as an experienced designer, owner, and helmsman of 12-metres, Tommy was in a better position than most to reflect on the state of the art as it applied to 12mRs under the 1st International Rule. His 1910 design proposal was moderate in most respects. The perfect profile of the extravagant forward overhang shows a young designer now coming into his own as a master of his craft. The combination of fairly hard bilges and clean flat topsides, with barely a hint of tumblehome that would empower the 6-metre, *Cynthia*, to windward, first appeared in this bigger boat. *Yachting Monthly* confidently predicted "*success in winds with some weight in them*".

We might note at this point in the chronology that Tommy was also enthusiastic about cruising. However, he seems never to have owned a cruising yacht, although of course the mighty schooner, *Hebe*, was still in the family, and many of his close friends owned cruisers. Tommy was a founder member and served as Commodore of the Clyde Cruising Club from the club's inception in 1909 until 1923, when he handed over to Sir Thomas Dunlop. By that time, he had inherited his father's title and was also Commodore of the Royal Northern.

The winter of 1910/1911 produced two commissions for Tommy's 'branch' of the firm: *St George*, another 6-metre for George Moir, would be built by James Adams. Then there was the 8-metre, *Speedwell*, for gregarious Irish sailor Herbert Brown. *Speedwell* was built in Dumbarton by R. McAlister and Sons and replaced *Cobweb*, a 1908 Fife that Brown passed on to his brother. In the pre-war years, there was a small, but enthusiastic 8mR fleet racing on Belfast Lough. In addition, Tommy had the 6-metre, *Cynthia*, on the drawing board for himself.

It seems that, despite his considerable wealth, Glen-Coats was now canny enough to debut his ideas in a new rating band with a private client, before building the 'Mk2' for himself the following year. George Moir was always happy to oblige. He was the ideal client – enthusiastic, fully-funded and generous to a fault. In the early days of the 6-metre class, George had donated a prize of £30 (£3,500) for a contest between Fred J. Stephen's *Coila II* and *Dormy* of Burnham to establish the British 6-metre pecking order. George tagged along in his 1908 Dudley Dawson 6mR *Era* to enjoy the spectacle of his wager, see Chapter 27.

Prior to the 1911 Clyde season, *Cynthia* was transported to the Riviera for the Cannes Spring Regatta. During her sojourn in the Mediterranean, the new Six revelled in the company of the crack French and Italian 6-metres, with 9 firsts, and 5 placings in 19 starts. The English had discovered the Riviera as a winter health resort in the 18th century. Yacht racing began at Cannes in 1857, and the first Spring Regatta, organised two years later, was won by a member of the Royal Yacht Squadron.

Subsequently, the event has drifted in and out of fashion to break the ice on the Northern Hemisphere sailing season, and as an occasional forum for the 'beautiful people'. The Prince of Wales brought *Britannia* to the line in 1894, and Fife's *Ailsa* followed suit to establish a Scottish connection. However, it was not until 1929 that the event became the Régates Royales to honour Christian X of Denmark, a keen 6mR sailor.[1017]

Meanwhile, back on the Clyde, the increasing quality of the 6-metre fleet, and competition from the new Fife boats, had prompted Fred J Stephen, whose work is discussed in the following chapter, to modify *Coila II*. The old boat proved unbeatable after a comprehensive upgrade and conversion to Bermudian rig enabled her to regain her place at the head of the class that season. However, *Cynthia's* absence during her spring campaign may have flattered *Coila II's* final standing in the season-long points battle.

When Tommy brought *Cynthia* back to Scotland for the 1911 Clyde fortnight, she surprised the pundits by challenging the hegemony of *Coila II*. After a bad start, when she was in collision with *Ariel* and had to be towed into Alex Robertson's yard for repairs, she was *"the hit of the season"*. The staff correspondent covering the Royal Western Regatta enthused: *"in fine weather, at least, she is going to be a slippery little lady"*. At the end of the fortnight, Tommy's new boat topped the 6mR class. Back on the road, *Cynthia* was sent south by rail for an inter-port contest on the River Crouch. This she won, also picking up a trophy presented by the Eastern Yacht Club for the best overall performance at Burnham Week.[1018]

The *Cynthia* crew then decamped to the South Coast, where they resumed their peripatetic season with the 6-metre fleet on the Solent. The Scottish boat bested the averages during her stay. *Cynthia's* stopover coincided with the Naval Review at Spithead. She won a special trophy to mark this one-off event, organised as part of the 1911 'International Festival of the Empire'.[1019] Tommy sold *Cynthia* in the autumn, something he later regretted. As she had arguably been his best design[1020]

Cynthia has been characterised as more shapely than the designer's 12mRs, and less slab-sided (a distinction that would not afflict the 6mRs until the 3rd Rule boats came in). She was certainly a pretty boat with a classic appearance. With *Cynthia*, Tommy sought the advantages of a Marconi rig, with a tall gaff attached parallel to the mast. The details are vague, but it was described as a novel variant of the high-peaked sliding-gunter. Indeed, she carried her racing flag at the head of the gaff – ever so slightly risqué in terms of flag etiquette.

Glen-Coats' next venture was the 8-metre, *Clio*, built by McAlister in 1912. Following the successful excursion to Cannes the previous year, the new 8mR was launched in February and shipped south to make her debut on the Mediterranean. "*She is to be railed from Dumbarton to Birkenhead, then from the Mersey, she will be sent to Marseilles on the deck of a Bibby liner.*"[1021]

Clio was characterised simply as a 'bigger *Cynthia*' in the press, but she was unusual in detail. She carried a big rig of 1,200ft², with 900ft² in what was said to be the largest standing lug racing sail ever made by Ratsey, and 300 in the jib set on a short bowsprit. "*Two yachts stand out for boldness and originality, among all others Clio and Nymphea which were superior from the outset. Clio's owner and skipper, the popular Mr Glen-Coats is himself her designer and for a boat with as much freeboard her speed is amazing whether in light airs, stiff breeze or rolling sea. She won the Monaco Cup in very heavy weather.*"[1022]

While *Clio's* initial results on the Mediterranean may have been excellent, Tommy was very much aware that his new boat had yet to face top-notch competition. These reservations were not unfounded. When *Clio* raced on the Solent her results were less impressive. The Fife 8mRs, *Ventura* and *The Truant*, then fully worked-up and performing to their potential, usually prevailed.[1023] Back home on the Clyde later in the year, *Clio* lost her mast during the Clyde Fortnight in what were described as 'famously moderate' conditions, which made her the butt of some wry comment.[1024]

The *Times* correspondent recorded that mayhem was "*introduced by Mr T. C. Glen-Coats*". Three yachts were dismasted, one was run ashore in a sinking condition, and an unfortunate catalogue of broken bones and sundry other injuries 'bloodied the nose' of our most prestigious regatta.[1025] Linton Hope writes in 1913 in the first year of the Bermudian rig in 6-metres: "*Although we always carried a spare mast about wherever we raced (and I fear used regrettable language to it as a useless encumbrance), Scotia carried her original mast all through the 1913 season and the Riviera races of the following spring, when she left for Russia*".[1026] Robertson's in Sandbank did good business building spare rigs for high profile campaigns.

The 1912 season also saw the first of a number of *Red Spiders*, built to the Menai Straits Restricted Class rules for Richard Mason of Beaumaris. Alfred Mylne also designed several boats for this class. It is not clear how many of these 1-raters Glen-Coats designed, or how successful they were, but there were at least two: *Red Spider III* in 1912 and *Red Spider IV* in 1914. *Red Spyder III* was a light weather flyer, which was exactly what Mason asked for. But she was not an all-rounder, drifting to the back of the fleet when the wind came up.[1027]

The year 1913 saw Tommy return to 6-metres, building two: the radical *Euterpe*, launched in May and owned in partnership with E. G. Martin for use on the Solent, and in June, the more conventional *Ariadne* to be based on the Clyde. This was surely something of a luxury, but Tommy kept both boats in commission for two years.[1028] Tommy's partner on the Solent, Evelyn G. Martin, was an influential pioneer of offshore racing; he sailed *Jolie Brise* to win the first Fastnet Race. It is less well-known that he was also a keen and proficient small yacht sailor, racing the 6-metre, *Ejnar*, on the Crouch at Burnham. *Ejnar* was a Mylne design, built by Iversen in Norway. In 1911, the quality of Scandinavian boatbuilding was excellent, and moreover exceptionally good value for money.

Martin was certainly accomplished, but few would have placed him in the first rank of the 6-metre class. Nevertheless, he was drafted in at short notice to compete in the One Ton Cup in 1912, sailing the G. U. Laws-designed 6mR, *Bunty*, for the Royal Thames Yacht Club. There is an intriguing theory that Martin, as a practised RNVR observer, was swapped into the skipper's role at the request of the British Admiralty. The One Ton Cup was a convenient cover to make an inventory of the Imperial German fleet, then lying to moorings at Kiel. The hospitable officers of the Kaiserliche Marine fell for the ruse mudhook, line and sinker. In those circumstances, winning the regatta as Martin did, would have been an unexpected bonus. Or perhaps winning the Great War was the bonus?

Tommy's 1913 Sixes were a little longer than contemporary Fife Sixes at the measured girth stations, although this comparison is predicated on sparse details. In terms of beam, the Glen-Coats pair, at 5ft 3" and 5ft 5", were about 6" narrower than the Fifes, and on a par with the Mylnes of that year. As for draft, they appear to have been conservative. Contemporary race reports suggest that they were lacking in power, but when they settled into their sailing length, they went well upwind in a blow, and being relatively light, performed well downwind too. *Ariadne* paid for her rated length in sail area; she carried 580²ft of measured sail area in an era when most of her rivals had around 615²ft.[1029] If ever there was a boat that would have benefitted from a genoa, it was *Ariadne*. High hounds and genoa-jibs would wait in the wings for another 13 years before being invited to the party.

Euterpe was sold after the Great War and converted into a pocket cruiser, despite her limited interior space. *Ariadne*, which had been the more competitive boat, was kept in class by her subsequent owner. Post-WW2, second-string Sixes on the Solent were able to race in the 'Q class', and on the Clyde the 'Ex-Six-metre class' often had as many starters as the 'first division'. In the early years of the 6mR class, however, old and unsuccessful yachts still lacked a 'safe space' on the racecourse and were promptly repurposed as pocket-cruisers.

Tommy's early boats were all built by McAlister at Dumbarton. When Alfred Mylne acquired the old boatyard at Port Bannatyne in 1911, Tommy transferred his allegiance to the new business. Glen-Coats and Mylne were discrete in their business affairs, but it now appears likely that the Bute Slip Dock was initially a joint venture and Tommy's financial interest was significant. One reason perhaps why the boatyard did not carry the Mylne name?[1030]

Ariadne and all her successors were built on the Ardmaliesh peninsula. Charles Mylne, Alfred's brother and an ex-banker, ran the yard as a 'tight ship'. Charles had recently returned from South Africa to live in Scotland for health reasons.[1031] Southern readers, expressing astonishment at this apparent non sequitur, might not be aware that the idyllic Isle of Bute has one of the best climates for bronchial recuperation in the British Isles.[1032]

Nineteen-fourteen was lived out under the shadow of the imminent global conflict. But before all that kicked off, Tommy appeared with a substantially re-worked 6mR design. He described *Arethusa* as having less beam, more lead and much more sail, but she appears to have been markedly smaller and slightly wider than her predecessor, *Ariadne*, to gain the additional sail-area the earlier design had lacked.[1033] Contemporary Fife and Mylne 6-metres lay somewhere in between the parameters of these two consecutive Glen-Coats designs. The formula certainly worked as Tommy's new boat 'cleaned up' in that shortened and distracted season.

We have yet to establish Tommy Glen-Coats' contribution to the national war effort. He was eligible for call-up, but our research thus far has found no records of service in the military. The Mylne design office and the boatyard at Ardmaliesh were busy through both World Wars, with contracts for the Royal Navy and the Royal Naval Air Service. It is possible that he was involved in this work as a reserved occupation. More certainly, he was racing model yachts in London and still designing in his spare time. *"This month we are able, through the courtesy of Mr T C Glen-Coats, to publish the lines, sail-plan and arrangement plan of a 35-ft. load waterline fast cruiser."*[1034] A discussion on the origin and lines of this design appears in Chapter 23.

After the Great War, *Arethusa* and her crew took up the chase where they had left off. This moderate, conventional 6mR really showed her class during the 1919 Clyde regattas, besting the 12-year-old *Coila II* to win the season's averages. *Coila II* was now in the twilight of her racing career but still ran *Arethusa* a close second. In the race reports of Clyde yachting correspondents, it is clear that Fred J. Stephen's much reworked old boat was still competitive.[1035] But where were the Fifes, the Mylnes and the Nicholsons when a couple of gentleman-designers, albeit exceptionally talented, could hold such sway?

In 1920, Tommy published a particularly attractive example of a 35ft LWL cruiser-racer design to the new National Classes rule which had already been consigned to the great dustbin of history. We can only assume that something, perhaps just useful exposure, could be gained from this wasted effort, although it could have been worse; William Fife actually built one. "*Sir, I am sending you the plans of the 52 ft 6" fast cruiser as promised.*"[1036] This design appears in Chapter 23, where the debacle is recounted.

Despite his success with moderation as a design philosophy, Glen-Coats was again tempted to 'bang the corners' when the revised formula of the 2nd International Rule came out in October 1919. Beating his contemporary, Fred J. Stephen, and indeed everyone else in the industry, to the punch, Tommy designed the radical *Aurora* for the 1921 season, hedging his bets with a more conventional second design. However, it seems that the experience building and racing two boats in one season, as he had in 1913, was not to be repeated.

Second International Rule (1919 – 1933)

$$R \text{ (metres)} = \frac{L + B + 0.25G + 2d + \sqrt{S}\text{-}F}{2.5}$$

where....
L = length (as calculated)
G = chain girth
d = difference between skin girth and chain girth
S = sail area
F = freeboard

The second boat was not commissioned. This design was for a very pretty, conventional 6-metre with nipped garboards and the lead set low along a parallel keel-foot which was subtly bulbed by about 4". This was costly in rating under the 2nd Rule as the girth tax was paid in full. At 32ft 7" LOA, 20ft 3" LWL, 6ft 1" beam 4ft 7" draft, the unbuilt 6mR was slightly larger than the Mylnes of that era. *Yachting Monthly* described her as "*an average boat of the class*". In dimensions, perhaps, but the average 2nd Rule 6mR from Fife, or Mylne, had a triangular keel profile and fuller garboards. In all bar draft, still moderate in that era, the unnamed second design looks more like a small 3rd Rule boat.[1037]

Aurora, however, was the boat built, and perhaps the more interesting. She was arguably the first 'modern' 6mR. She combined a bulbed keel with a separate spade rudder. She was a small boat, designed for light weather. If you sail on the Clyde, this will give you a useful advantage six Saturdays out of seven, as the mid-season is bedevilled by oily calms. Unfortunately, after a successful international debut in light airs off Naples, *Aurora* was on the Solent for most of the summer. She had her balanced rudder altered shortly after launch and Mylne's yard carried out further alterations in June. When the wind blew, the Fife Sixes took her to the cleaners. And when she came home to the Clyde, so too did Stephen's evergreen *Coila II,* which continued to benchmark the new designs.

It seems, therefore, that *Aurora* was significantly slower than *Arethusa,* Tommy's previous Six, which had given *Coila II* a run for her money. Nevertheless, she was good enough to win her share of races and was seldom out of the top three, although she had a few dreadful results too. At this juncture, we might consider a crucial take-away from the last 50 years of metre-boat design development. There is in fact not a great deal of difference between traditional full-keel 6mRs, and the latter-day fin-and-skeg boats. *"The difference really seems to be very small. Take a boat like Nancy or Bob Kat II. Bob Kat is still in original 2ⁿᵈ Rule form, whereas Nancy has a 3ʳᵈ Rule keel. The performance differential is very small, it's less than you would imagine. Which is terrific, it just means that the rule was organised very nicely at the time."*[1038] The same was true in the 12mR class during the transition to fin-and-skeg configuration in the 1960s.

What this also means, using inductive logic, is that the early fin-and-skeg configurations were inevitably going to be significantly slower than contemporary full-keel designs, as the latter had already been filtered through countless cycles of refinement to eke out every last marginal gain. They had evolved to attain a rare level of 'perfection', as Uffa Fox would argue. In this, Uffa was not just 95% right; unusually, he was in good company. It was a commonly held view.

Another change of tack in 1922 saw Tommy, now Sir Thomas on the death of his father, return to the mainstream with *Selene,* described by the designer as long, powerful and orthodox within the frame of the 2ⁿᵈ Rule. She was a good boat in a breeze, if a little sluggish in light airs. After some alterations to her keel, *Selene* hit her numbers and gained a reputation as a fine hard-weather boat, with some good results against high quality British and American 6mRs. That said, it is not clear why Tommy should have gambled on a breezy summer. Good sailors invariably steer clear of 'heavy weather boats'; that tag is the kiss of death.

But in 1924, Glen-Coats appeared with yet another new 6mR that 'banged the corners' of the design envelope. *Echo* was configured for hard-weather and was very much in the heavy displacement, long waterline, moderate sail-area corner of the continuum. *Yachting Monthly* noted that *Echo "is of particular interest. This boat was designed by her owner and bears a strong resemblance to Cynthia, which was one of his most successful boats under the late rule. She is a long, easy-lined boat with a moderate beam and well-balanced ends, which are somewhat finer than those of Coila III and the Fife Sixes"* [1039]

Echo was lucky with the weather on the Clyde and really hit her stride in the Solent when it blew like buggery. Malden Heckstall-Smith observed that *"Echo was outstanding during the Solent Fortnight."* [1040] Dodgson Bowman cited a fine victory at Ryde in the Royal Victoria Yacht Club regatta where nine starters, including *Suzette* (Fife 1922), *Betty* (Fife 1923) and *Ayesha* (Fife 1922), took part in a thrilling contest with constant lead changes. [1041] This generation of Fife 6mRs, with David Boyd in attendance, were among the best in the world at that time; so, *Echo* cleared a high bar.

Later in the 1924 season, Glen-Coats and *Echo* were selected to sail for the British American Cup team. While *Echo*'s configuration suited Solent conditions in her designed trim, she would have been somewhat short of sail on Long Island Sound. Glen-Coats re-rated her for the trip, altering the keel and adding 36ft^2 more sail. Tommy, who routinely spent a small fortune on sails, bought two new suits of Ratsey's for this adventure. *Echo* did not let the side down, although her performance was erratic, in a class of her own in 35kts, but bringing up the rear in the light stuff. After the series concluded, *Echo* won the Noble Trophy in half-a-gale.

While British teams have won the British American Cup several times on the Solent and on the Clyde, 1924 remains the only occasion when we won the trophy in American waters. And, as recounted in the following chapter, another Scottish boat, *Coila III*, won the Seawanhaka Cup that year too. Some years later, Mr Robert Aspin told *Yachting Monthly's* correspondent that *Sulaire*, his 1928 Fife 8-metre, was the new *'Coila'* of the class. [1042] One wonders how Fife received this backhanded 'compliment' on his latest work.

Sir Thomas designed the 6mR, *Anne*, for James Allen in the spring of the 1926 season. *Anne* was built by McGruer's and is one of only two Coats designs still sailing today, the other is the 8mR, *Helen*. *Anne* was a particularly attractive Six, with a heavily raked rudder post, well-raked keel-foot and an elegant stern overhang. She was regularly raced by the Allen daughters and performed particularly well in light airs, winning on the Holy Loch.

For races further afield, James Allan chartered the 60-ton Woodnutts, M.Y. *Trident*, from Duncan Macleod, of Skeabost in Skye to act as tender to his new Six. James was a consistent back-marker, retiring often. James won once when the whole fleet in front of him sailed into a hole, and a second time after benefiting from a huge windshift. That is the 'magic' of the Holy Loch, hope springs eternal.

Anne, or *Duet*, as she was rechristened the following year when the ebullient team of Charles McAndrew and Stuart Black bought the boat, was re-rigged with a higher aspect sail-plan. Charles would later form a partnership with John G. Stephen and James Napier to campaign the radical 6mR, *Maida*. Today, sailing as *Duet*, *Anne* has lost her elegance. Her counter has been cropped, a crude rubbing strake has been added and she carries an incongruous high-aspect 'Dutch-style' gaff rig. *Anne's* original rig was Bermudian, later increased in aspect ratio.

For the 1927 season, Sir Thomas hankered after a live-aboard, clearly missed during his years with 6-metres and rail travel. So, he returned to the 12mR class. *Iris* was conceived twenty years after *Pallas*, Tommy's first design. Uffa Fox saw continuity in her design philosophy extending back to that early 30-liner-rater. Uffa also noted that *Iris "was longer than any of the then existing 12-metre yachts, which naturally forced her to carry less sail; but as the height of the sail allowed was in proportion to the length of the waterline, she had the tallest and narrowest rig of the whole lot. There is no doubt her success was largely due to her length and to her tall and narrow rig, for length is speed, and he knew that the taller and narrower the sail area the more efficient it is."*[1043]

Iris was launched as a sloop and altered to a cutter in 1928. She was the first, and possibly only, 12mR with channels cantilevered outboard to spread the shroud base. As was common with Tommy's larger boats, her interior was designed around usable accommodation with light colours and comfortable leather upholstery. Although a very wealthy man now getting on a bit, Tommy still liked to live aboard his 12mRs, and occasionally his 8mRs, during the regatta season, as the Glen-Coats entourage followed the well-established travelling-circus from port-to-port around the coastline of Britain. And, as Commodore of the Clyde Cruising Club, it was only fitting that he owned a boat that might have room down below for a few drinks and a singsong.

In 1927, *Iris* competed in both Solent and Clyde regattas and appears to have won her share of races, ranking among the top three yachts in her class. She was sold to Norwegian ship-owner, George von Erpecom, in 1932 and renamed *Irina V*. Subsequently, she enjoyed some success in Bergen Yacht Club events, participating in the Diamond Jubilee with Crown Prince Olav and Crown Princess Martha and in various Maastrand Regattas hosted by the Royal Gothenburg Yacht Club. Ragnar Fredriksen bought the boat in 1937 but had little time to enjoy her before the Nazis arrived. He removed the lead keel and concealed it during the German occupation. However, after the war Ragnar did not have the resources to recommission *Irina V*. He was reduced to selling the laboriously buried keel and the rig too, then using her as a houseboat. She was later wrecked off Hanko in Finland and lay there until 1965, when she was broken-up.[1044]

Sir Thomas designed a new 8-metre for each of the 1936, 1937 and 1938 seasons. All were built by the Bute Slip Dock. The first of this series was *Helen*, a 3rd Rule boat recently restored by Duncan Walker and his team at Hamble Yacht Services. Duncan showed us round the boat with obvious pride when we visited his office in 2016. Like other Glen-Coats designs, *Helen* is sometimes erroneously described as a Mylne, but she was drawn by Tommy for his own use. Uffa described her thus: *"Sir Thomas's new 8-metre Helen was naturally looked for with great interest by all, for we wondered what he would produce with his vast knowledge of the designing and sailing of vessels and his freedom from any restraint other than that imposed by the International Rule, which he knew so well. She is quite normal and very sweet to the eye, full advantage having been taken of the lately dropped girth measurement amidships, for the bottom of Helen's keel line is practically parallel to the waterline."*[1045] So *Helen*, designed in 1936, looks a lot like Tommy's unbuilt 6mR of 1921.

Uffa described *Helen* as a 'small boat' with generous sail-plan – in contrast to many of Tommy's earlier designs which traded light airs speed for hard-weather gains: *"The 'L' measurement is slightly less than that of the average Eight, and her larger sail area would lead one to suppose that she would be faster in light winds running.*[1046] *Her running qualities have considerably helped her in those races where she has featured in the prize list. Reaching she can hold her own even in strong breezes, but she seems to lose a little during windward work in heavy weather"*[1047] As events transpired, *Helen* gained a reputation for being quick off the wind in all conditions.

Helen enjoyed a successful racing career and would maintain her performance edge to beat her immediate successors from Tommy's board when the going was light. She was replaced by *Sapho* in 1937. *Sapho* was a longer, wider and heavier model, so it seems that Tommy was open to revisiting his design approach. *Sapho* was competitive, but like everyone sailing 8mRs on the Clyde, he found it well-nigh impossible to dislodge Jimmy Howden-Hume from the head of the leader board, no matter how much design-development he invested in. Jimmy was now coming into his own as one of the finest helmsmen ever to sail Scottish waters.

Howden-Hume bought *Froya* in the mid-1930s, after returning home from a series of engineering contracts in Shanghai and Melbourne, where he had been building power-stations for the family firm.[1048] *Froya*, a 1932

Mylne 8mR, had been undistinguished in her first life, but became the boat to beat on the Clyde under Jimmy's ownership. Jimmy's friend, Uffa Fox, rated him as an exceptional sailor, and lamented the fact that business interests and family commitments prevented Jimmy from becoming more active in international competition.[1049]

Returning to the Glen-Coats design progression; the next refinement was *Pandora*, launched in 1938. This 8mR was longer in the overhangs and slightly narrower. Like Momma Bear's porridge, she seems to have been 'just right'. However, the older boats were far from outclassed. *Froya*, sailed by the ever-consistent Howden-Hume, would take the season's honours, and Fife's veteran *Fulmar* of 1930 also had the measure of *Pandora* early in the season. Glen-Coats racked up the second places, before winning the Northern's regatta during Clyde Fortnight, along with three out of the last four races at their closing regatta. Then WW2 intervened, and the marine industry was once again directed to the war effort.

Separately from the portfolio of Alfred Mylne, Sir Thomas Glen-Coats is credited here with the lines of 29 original designs. The Mylne Design Office was responsible for the construction details and material specifications of the early boats. As would be expected with two designers operating via a common office infrastructure, all the Glen-Coats designs that were realised were built to identical standards and build quality as every other design from the Mylne office.

Designs by Sir Thomas Glen-Coats

	Yacht	Type	First Owner	Year	TM
1	*Pallas*	30ft LR	*the designer*	1906	9
2	15mR design	15-metre	-	1906	-
3	*Heatherbell (Teresita, Margit IV, Yolande, Sylva)*	12-metre	Andrew Coats	1907	27
4	Loch Fyne-type skiff design	fishing boat	-	1907	-
5	*Hera*	12-metre	*the designer*	1908	27
6	17ft c/b built by Paul Jones, Gourock	daysailer	-	1908	-
7	*Crusader (No. I, No. II, Cupidon)**	6-metre	George Moir	1909	3
8	*Cynthia*	6-metre	*the designer*	1910	4
9	12mR design	12-metre	-	1910	-
10	*St. George*	6-metre	George Moir	1911	3
11	*Speedwell (Minnie)*	8-metre	Herbert Brown	1911	9
12	*Clio (Léthé)*	8-metre	*the designer*	1912	9
13	*Red Spider III*	1-rater	Rupert Mason	1912	-
14	Six-metre built in Sweden	6-metre	Swedish client	1912	
15	*Ariadne (Rubi)*	6-metre	*the designer*	1913	4
16	*Euterpe*	6-metre	Glen-Coats/EJM	1913	4
17	*Red Spider IV*	1-rater	Rupert Mason	1914	-
18	*Arethusa*	6-metre	*the designer*	1914	3
19	18ft LWL Sloop (design exercise)	BRA-rule	-	1917	-
20	Fast Cruiser 52.5ft LOA, 35ft LWL	Cutter		1917	
21	Fast Cruiser 82.75ft LOA, 52.5ft LWL	Cutter		1920	-

22	Option B (failed to find a client)	6-metre	unbuilt	1921	4
23	*Aurora*	6-metre	*the designer*	1921	4
24	*Selene*	6-metre	*the designer*	1923	5
25	*Echo (Paula IV)*	6-metre	*the designer*	1924	5
26	*Anne (Duet)*	6-metre	J. B. Allan	1926	6
27	*Iris (Irina V)*	12-metre	*the designer*	1926	24
28	*Helen*	8-metre	*the designer*	1936	10
28	*Sapho*	8-metre	*the designer*	1937	12
29	*Pandora (Pandora of Rhu)*	8-metre	*the designer*	1938	12

* The gentlemen of the yachting press were horribly confused when Moir launched two
boats in 1909, initially known as *No. I* and *No. II*. One would become *Crusader* and the
other *Trident*, designed by Dudley Dawson, which Moir gave to his daughter.

Tommy's faithful skipper was James Mair of Saltcoats. James is credited
with a substantial contribution to his owner's success on the racecourse. The
two men were considered 'a formidable pair in a boat' and enjoyed decades
of good results. Most of Tommy's crew were Saltcoats men too.

Thomas Glen-Coats also had a life outside yachting. He became the 2nd
Baronet and 'Sir Tommy' on his father's death in 1922. Like Alfred Mylne,
he was another 'confirmed bachelor', but now at 57 years of age, he knew
he was running out of time to secure an heir to the baronetcy. Tommy
finally married on 5th April 1935 when he teamed-up with like-minded
liberal, Louise Hugon. They wed at St. Columba's Church of Scotland in
London, in the company of a dozen close friends. The modest ceremony
was followed by a honeymoon in America.

In many respects, 'Tid' and Louise were the classic 1930s Bohemian
socialite couple with the resources to live life on their own terms. Louise
became the new face of the Scottish Liberal Party. She was said to have
"*all the French woman's charm and wit as well as a thoroughly practical knowledge of
political questions*". As for the succession, Tommy and Louise failed to
produce an heir. Sir Thomas Glen-Coats, 2nd Baronet, passed away in 1954
at just 76, and his title expired with him. He was one of seven multi-
millionaire members of the Coats dynasty to die in the mid-1950s. Lady
Glen-Coats remained politically active until she too passed away in 1967.

CODA: Thomas's Doubts Allayed

"*Next day, the course was from Rothesay to Blackfarland. The wind was light
again for a while, and under Inchmarnock died completely. Pallas and Great Auk were
best placed when the new wind came. It was a fine, fresh reaching breeze, which held to
the finish. The two leaders got the breeze almost simultaneously, Pallas being about a
couple of hundred yards ahead, the others being unluckily becalmed for several minutes
longer. I shall never forget the excitement and anxiety of the next few minutes. Great
Auk was known to be fast on a reach, and there we were, heading for our mark – still
many miles distant, an ideal reaching trial in a fine, whole-sail breeze.*

Anxiously glancing at our rival from time to time we soon realised that Pallas was holding her own. This was a relief, and it came as a surprise, though a pleasant one, to her designer at any rate, seeming too good to be true. In the end we won by 4½ minutes from Great Auk, while the other five made a very close match of it several minutes astern. After the race I received the kind congratulations of my opponents and of many others; it was very good of them and much appreciated."[1050]

CODA: The 1908 Olympics

The 1908 Yachting Olympics were held at Ryde on the Isle of Wight. However, as there were no foreign entries in the International 12-metre Class and neither of the two British entries – the Clyde boat, *Hera*, owned by Tommy Glen-Coats, and the 'Mersey' boat, *Mouchette,* owned by Charles McIver, were based on the Solent, a coin was tossed to decide the Olympic venue and the Clyde won. This 'sporting compromise' was welcomed all round as *Mouchette* raced with the Scottish fleet in any case. This 1908 Olympic outlier was run off by the Royal Clyde at Hunter's Quay in mid-August of that year.[1051]

The rules of the Olympiad limited entries to two per country. Had that not been the case, the remainder of the Clyde fleet might have joined in the fun. In a speech delivered after receiving his gold medal, Glen-Coats promoted both the 12-metres as a class and the Clyde as a racing venue. He pointed out that the 12mR class on the Clyde included the Fife-designed *Alachie*, the Mylne-designed *Mouchette* and *Nargie*, and finally, *Heatherbell* and *Hera*, to his own designs.[1052] Coats continued: "*the boats have won good opinions in the Clyde this year, and the class is now firmly established. It seems surprising that it has not been built to elsewhere*".

Continuing his speech, Glen-Coats thought that "*it might be better to select a fleet of one-design boats in the waters where the Games are held and let all the crews entered draw lots for them every day, with the proviso that no crew should have the same boat twice*". Coats cited the Mylne designed 'Solent One Design Class' (63ft LOA 38ft LWL) of 1903 as an example of the type of boat he favoured. At that time, there was a good fleet of these fine 42-linear-raters, built by J. G. Fay & Co, in commission on the South Coast.[1053] Alfred Mylne, crewing for his protégé on *Hera* through the Olympic series, would have appreciated the accolade.

One of the Solent One Designs was Scottish owned. George Coats, Tommy's uncle, bought *Kelpie* to race on the Solent. A few Scottish crews commute to campaign on the Solent even today, with Steve Cowie's *Zephyr* in the Fast 40+ Class, for example, but for George, in the years before the Glasgow to Southampton shuttle flight, the racing wasn't worth the candle.

We understand that George struggled to get a full crew together. Moreover, the laid-back Scots Corinthians seem to have been a tad uncomfortable among the 'old money' crowd at the Squadron. Even in 1903, hard-core snobs disparaged our captains of industry as *nouveau riche*. Chronic stammer aside, as an old school socialite, Tommy was more confident, and able to command his own retinue, when he began to race regularly at Cowes and Cannes.

George Coats soon brought *Kelpie* up to the Clyde, where he lost the one-design competition that had been the point of the exercise but recovered his zest for the sport. *Kelpie* was altered to rate as a 12-metre following the introduction of the International Rule in October 1906. Coats clearly liked the type as he commissioned Fife to build *Alachie* to the new rule in 1908. So, while *Kelpie* is not the first 12mR, she is paradoxically the oldest as she raced in class during the first spring, before the new boats were launched.[1054]

Mylne 'Solent One Design' vs first-generation 12-metres

Yacht	Designer	LBP	LWL	Beam	Draft	TM	Year
Solent O.D.	Mylne	48.75	38.15	11	7	24	1903
Hera	Glen-Coats	52.4	39.6	11	6.1	27	1908
Mouchette	Mylne	51	42.38	10.9	6.1	24	1908
Alachie	Fife	51	-	11.55	6.1	26	1908

As can be seen from the table above, the Solent One Designs were small for a 12mR, beamier and subject to a draft penalty; so, it is unlikely that *Kelpie* would have been competitive against new yachts built specifically to the rule. The Solent OD was arguably a more wholesome boat than the new builds, optimised within the 12mR envelope, but among racing sailors that cuts little ice half-way up the first windward leg.

Kelpie is now the last survivor of Mylne's 'Solent Class'. Most of the others were stored together and destroyed in a boatyard fire.[1055] In January 2016 on the Isle of Wight, 15 yachts of the Cowes Etchells fleet and many wooden classics, including Alfred Mylne's *Fedoa of Bute*, the latter nearing completion after an extensive renovation, were lost. The 2016 fire started in an adjacent car workshop and spread to the Medina Boatyard. This yard, formerly J. Samuel White's, was bombed by the Luftwaffe in 1942.

During the Olympics, the two 12mRs from Mylne and Coats seem to have been very similar in performance. Their match-races featured endless tacking duals. It was a glimpse into the future and the tacking-duals that epitomized racing for the America's Cup during the 12mR and IACC eras. This short series has been much disparaged over the years, for obvious reasons. However, it is also true that two of the best racing yachts of that size in the world at that time, manned by two of the best crews, fought tooth and nail for Olympic honours.

The new 12mR class, adopted enthusiastically by Clyde yachtsmen for fleet-racing, would become the weapon of choice for America's Cup competitions during the fondly remembered 1958 to 1987 era, and thus eternally synonymous with match-racing. Few remember that Coats and McIver discovered the exceptional qualities of the 12mR class for this, as-yet-unexplored, branch of the sport, in 1908. Even Charlie Barr would have been blown away if he had found himself on the starting line at the helm of a US triallist in 1974.

At the medal ceremonies, the winning skipper and his mate in the 12mR received a gold medal, but in an offhand slight to the 'crew's union' the rest of his team were awarded silver. The second placed skipper and mate received silver and their crew bronze. In the smaller yachts (racing out of Ryde) the mates were relegated too, and perhaps because of the low numbers of entries, there were no medals for 3rd place. Nevertheless, the lucky skipper of the winning 7mR received a gilt commemorative medal for a sail-over. There were trophies, awards and diplomas galore for everyone associated with the event – truly a pot-hunter's paradise.

The 8mR class in the 1908 Olympics, while raced in the Solent, also has a Scottish connection. The gold medal was won by Blair Onslow Cochrane, whose grandfather, the 9th Earl of Dundonald, patented coal tar in 1781 as an alternative to copper sheathing for navy ships. Cynically, their lordships waited until the patent expired before using the system. The Earl died impoverished, but John MacAdam, his works manager, was acclaimed for his Macadamised road designs, later to be stabilised with tar in the ubiquitous tarmacadam of the motor age.

999 Sail and Power, Uffa Fox, 1936.
1000 The Coats family financed the Scottish National Antarctic Expedition of 1902-1904. The company was formed by Andrew Coats and Patrick Coats. James Coats (Andrew's son) and James Coats junior (Patrick's son) funded the undertaking, while Thomas Glen-Coats (son of James Coats) covered most of the publication costs concerning the scientific results. Expedition leader, William Spiers Bruce, has recently been rediscovered as a Scottish hero, so too with his ship, the iconic *Scotia*. The expedition was said to be 'by far the most cost-effective and carefully planned scientific expedition of the Heroic Age'. However, Bruce received no formal honours or recognition by the Westminster government and the members of this unambiguously successful scientific endeavour were not awarded the Polar Medal, routinely awarded to the coterie of self-aggrandising professional 'adventurers'.
1001 100 Years of Alfred Mylne, Ian Nicolson, Classic Boat, Dec. 1996, January & February 1997.
1002 Ibid
1003 *"However, when the Second World War broke out in 1939 yacht design and building work stopped completely. Luckily the Glen-Coats money was still sitting in the bank, some 30 years after it was lodged, and this saved both Bute Slip Dock and A. Mylne & Co"* Ian Nicolson, 2009 Mylne Regatta.
1004 The Clyde 30ft Restricted Class, Thomas Glen-Coats, the Yachting & Boating Monthly,

No.9 Volume II, January 1907.

[1005] Design for the 15-metre Class, T C Glen Coats, the Yachting & Boating Monthly. Volume I, Nos. 1 to VI, May to October 1906.

[1006] Yachting and Yachtsmen, W. Dodgson Bowman, 1927.

[1007] Ibid

[1008] Sports in Brief, The Times, 1st June 1907.

[1009] *Shimna* of 1907, Fife's first 15 Metre design demonstrated the legerdemain of Robertson's craftsmen and Alexander's knowledge of timber to achieve extremely challenging target weights and an ambitious ballast ratio.

[1010] The escritoire is artistic license, but common on gentleman's yachts of the period.

[1011] One reference has the boat in the ownership of Charles E. Nicholson for a season – one assumes with her lead back in place, but we cannot substantiate this.

[1012] International 12-metre Class Association Website, data on yachts.

[1013] Mylne went into partnership with Mr McIntyre in 1912. Tommy's involvement, uncovered by recent research by the Mylne office, appears to have been a well-kept secret.

[1014] Notes and Notions, The Yachtsman, 4th June 1908 and 2nd July 1908.

[1015] Sir Thomas Glen-Coats – Obituary, Shoes and Ships and Sealing Wax, Cabbages and Kings, the Walrus, Yachting Monthly, April 1954.

[1016] Design for a 12-metre, T. C. Glen-Coats, the Yachting Monthly and Marine Motor Magazine, Volume IX, Nos. XLIX to LIV, May to October 1910.

[1017] The Régates Royales has been resurrected as a September fixture for classic yachts, Dragons and boats built to the International Rule.

[1018] The Encyclopaedia of Sport & Games, Volume 4, C. Suffolk & Earl of Berkshire, 1911.

[1019] This was quite an event with 167 and 18 foreign warships in four lines 6 miles long presented to the newly installed King George V for his review. Then there were the passenger liners and merchant ships, and swarms of pleasure craft. It must have been quite a sight.

[1020] Yachting & Yachtsmen, W. Dodgson Bowman, 1927.

[1021] In Foreign Waters, the Mediterranean Regatta, the Yachting & Boating Monthly, Volume XIII, Nos.LXXIII to LXVIII, May to October 1912.

[1022] In Foreign Waters, the Mediterranean Regatta, the Yachting & Boating Monthly, Volume XIII, Nos.LXXIII to LXVIII, May to October 1912.

[1023] The Fife 8-metre, *Ventana*, perhaps the only candidate for this citation, was launched in 1912.

[1024] *Clio* was not the only Glen-Coats boat to drop her rig. *Arethusa* followed suit in 1923 and various others had rig problems – this was normal in the early Bermudian-era when wooden-sticks were hit or miss depending on the quality of the season's timber from North America.

[1025] The 19-metres, *Corona* and *Norada*, lost their rigs and the big Summers and Payne cutter, *Onda*, nearly sank. The Clyde Yachting Fortnight, The Times, 9th July 1912.

[1026] The Marconi or Bermuda Rig in the 6-metre Class in 1919, Linton Hope, Yachting Monthly, vol XXIX-2, 1913.

[1027] The Yachting & Boating Monthly, Volume XIII, Nos. LXXIII to LXVIII, May to October 1912.

[1028] It was difficult to fathom what was going on during the 1913 season. The Yachtsman reported that *"Mr. Coats has designed a Six for Mr Martin and one for himself"* but did not mention a partnership. Neither of the two Sixes on the stocks at Ardmaliesh that spring correlates with the registered dimensions of a third boat slated for joint ownership in the 1913 Lloyds Register. However, as *Euterpe* is captioned as being joint ownership in subsequent issues, the third boat is a ghost entry. Clyde, The Yachtsman, 17th October 1912 and through 1913.

[1029] The early Sixes carried around 510ft² to 550ft² and this increased to around 660ft² in the period before the Great War.

[1030] Discussion with David Gray re. his forthcoming book on Alfred Mylne, 31st July 2019. In 1912, however, the yard was referenced as Mylne & McIntyre.

[1031] 100 Years of Alfred Mylne, Ian Nicolson.

[1032] *"Bute's position in the Firth of Clyde (sheltered by the Isle of Arran and the Kintyre peninsula to the west, and the peninsulas of Cowal to the NE, N & NW), together with the moderating influence of the Gulf Stream that washes its shores, makes for a climate that is much milder than would otherwise be expected of a place located at 55° North latitude.*" Bute Gateway. Nevertheless, Charles passed away in 1924 and Alfred took on the additional responsibility.

[1033] Sail and Power, Uffa Fox, 1936.

[1034] 35ft Fast Cruiser, the Yachting & Boating Monthly, Volume XXII, Nos. CXXCII to CLXXIV, November 1916 to April 1917.

[1035] *Coila II's* age date is misleading as she was completely rebuilt and reconfigured in 1911.

[1036] 52.5ft Fast Cruiser, the Yachting & Boating Monthly, Volume XXIX, Nos. CLXIX to CXXXII, May to October 1920.

[1037] Design for a 6-metre Racing Yacht, the Yachting Monthly, May to October 1921.

[1038] Six-metre masterclass, Ian Howlett in conversation with James Boyd, 2nd June 2015.

[1039] The Outlook, Maldon Heckstall-Smith, the Yachting Monthly and Marine Motor, Volume XXXVII, Nos. CCXVII to CCXXII, May to October 1924.

[1040] The Outlook, Maldon Heckstall-Smith, the Yachting Monthly and Marine Motor Magazine, Volume XL, Nos. CCXXXV to CCXL, May to October 1925.

[1041] Yachting and Yachtsmen, W. Dodgson Bowman, 1927.

[1042] Clyde Notes, TWF, the Yachting Monthly and Marine Motor Magazine, 1928.

[1043] Sail and Power, Uffa Fox, 1936.

[1044] International 12-metre Class Association Website, data on yachts.

[1045] Sail and Power, Uffa Fox, 1936.

[1046] Sailing waterline, as approximated by the 3rd Rule fore and aft girth measurement points.

[1047] Sail and Power, Uffa Fox, 1936.

[1048] The Howden Heritage, David H. Hume, privately published, 2005.

[1049] After *Froya*, Jimmy acquired the Charles E. Nicholson 12mR, *Trivia*, which he converted to a cruiser, then the big Mylne yawl, *Vadura*, and finally the McGruer-designed 13.5mR, *Stornoway*, which he built in Sandbank via Morris & Lorimer – a firm he had initially acquired to carry out the extensive *Vadura* refit following that yacht's WW2 service as a barrage balloon anchor.

[1050] The Clyde 30ft (restricted) Class, T. C. Glen-Coats, the Yachting & Boating Monthly, Volume II—No.9 January 1907.

[1051] The Forth Olympiad, London, 1908 Official Report, Theodore Andrea Cook, 1909.

[1052] Builders: *Alachie* – Fife; *Mouchette* – Mylne; *Nargie* and *Hera* – Macalister; *Heatherbell* – Alex Robertson.

[1053] Mylne list nine yachts.

[1054] *Kelpie* is one of the finest classic yachts afloat today. She was converted to a cruising yawl in 1925 and sailed in that configuration until she was restored to her original specification and relaunched in 2012.

[1054] Just as the President and Vice President do not share the same aircraft, classic classes should ignore group deals and safeguard the gene-pool.

BRA 18ft-class model yachts with their designers

Left to right:
- Glen-Coats 1
- Beatty
- Vixen
- Pincher
- Glen-Coats II

The models raced on Kensington Round Pond in London during The 1914-18 War

Clyde 30ft Restricted Class, T. C. Glen-Coats, 1905 (not *Pallas*)   Mylne Yacht Design

Aurora, 6-metre, T. C. Glen-Coats, 1921   *Echo*, 6-metre, T. C. Glen-Coats, 1922

Note how the mast has moved back, the bowsprit has gone, and the aspect ratio of the rig is higher.

542

Coila II, 6-metre, Fred J. Stephen, 1908   *Crusader*, 6-metre, T. C. Glen Coats, 1909

Anne (Duet) T. G-C, 1926

Euterpe, 6mR on the Solent, T. C. Glen-Coats, 1913   Image: E. Hopkins

Heatherbell, 12-metre, T. C. Glen-Coats, 1907   Sir Thomas C. Glen-Coats, Bart.

Pallas, 30ft LWL Clyde Restricted Class, T. C. Glenn-Coats, 1903   Image: Robertson

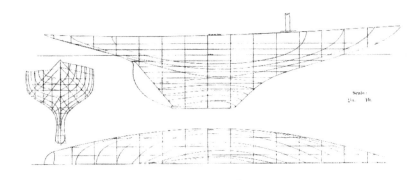

A SIX METRE RACING YACHT DESIGNED BY T. C. GLEN-COATS

L.O.A., 32ft.; L.W.L., 20.4ft.; Beam, 6.2ft.; Draught, 4.6ft. Displacement, 2.8 tons.

Six-metre, T. C. Glen-Coats, 1921   Mylne Yacht Design

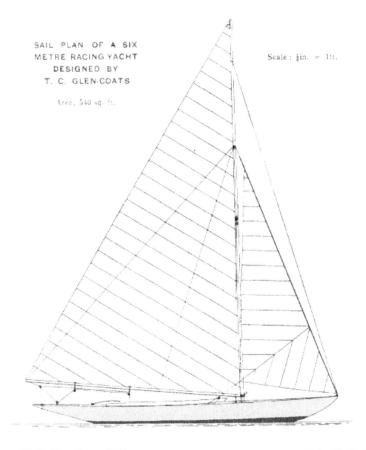

SAIL PLAN OF A SIX
METRE RACING YACHT
DESIGNED BY
T. C. GLEN-COATS

Area, 540 sq. ft.

Scale : ¼in. = 1ft.

Six-metre, T. C. Glen-Coats, 1921   Mylne Yacht Design

Chapter 27: Fred J. Stephen – Master of the 'Fife Class'

It is ironic and more than a little surprising that Fife, whose name was synonymous with the development of 6-Metres, failed to win a Seawanhaka Cup in his 'weapon of choice'. Indeed, following decades of success by boats from Fairlie, Charles E. Nicholson had dubbed the 6-Metre the 'Fife Class'. The Piper Calls the Tune[1056]

Fred J. Stephen (1863-1932) was a gifted naval architect who blended a fine grasp of contemporary scientific advances with a wealth of practical experience handed down through a renowned shipbuilding dynasty. Alexander Stephen & Sons was one of many exceptional family businesses on the Clyde. Succeeding generations built thousands of ships, without ever resting on their laurels or taking the easy option. The best of the Clyde yards were as committed to progress as profit. The Napier, Denny, Scott and Stephen families were shipbuilding royalty in Scotland, with a heritage stretching back for quarter of a millennium, see Chapter 5.

The Stephen's Shipbuilding Dynasty

The first Alexander Stephen (1722-1793) began shipbuilding on the Moray Firth ca.1750, but it was his nephew, William (1759-1838), who established the enduring dynasty. The Stephens built boats in Aberdeen, Arbroath, Dundee and Kelvinhaugh on the Upper Clyde, before moving operations to Linthouse in 1870. William's grandson, Alexander Stephen (1785-1875), was then still active in the firm.[1057] When Alexander retired in 1873, at the age of 88, he was proud of the fact that he had personally carved the hull-models for a greater tonnage of shipping than anyone else in the world.

The shipyard's connection with yachting began during the tenure of the next Alexander Stephen (1832-1899), who spent the summer months in Dunoon for 24 years, commuting to Linthouse daily from his villa 'Fearan Collie'. Alexander's first yacht was the *Coolan*, an iron cutter of 37-tons TM, apparently self-penned and built by Robinson in 1862.[1058] She safely conveyed the Stephen family up and down the West Coast for many years. Fred. J. Stephen learned his big boat sailing on *Coolan*. Alexander hoped that his vessel might match that other 'iron pot', and the most famous '50' of her time – the old *Mosquito*, then owned by the Royal Northern Yacht Club, but this ambition was never realised. Dodgson

Bowman suggests that Alexander was not dismayed. Twelve years of progress in yacht design counts for naught if the other boat is 50% bigger. Tom Waterman designed *Mosquito* in 1848 after J. Scott Russell's fanciful wave-line theory, with a long hollow bow and a full after-body. She was 59ft 2" LWL, 15ft 3" beam, and measured in at 50-tons.

Alexander's limited success on the racecourse was a minor setback; he was primarily a cruising man with a penchant for cold water voyaging. He ranged up the Outer Isles and voyaged across to Scandinavia and the Baltic. But in 1881, Alexander, although still just 49, abandoned sail after a summer of frustrating calms and missed appointments. He set to work on a series of increasingly lavish steam yachts, designed and built inhouse: *Sylvia* 136-tons and *Nerissa* 264-tons in 1885, and in 1898, *Calanthe* 429-tons, shortly before he passed away. These fine vessels were all a good advertisement for the firm's core business of commercial shipbuilding. They also spun off some spectacular superyacht commissions.

Alexander was a formidable businessman, a stalwart of the Free Church and a fine example of the Presbyterian work ethic. He was lauded as *"not so bigoted as some of his friends"* in embracing science, literature and music.[1059] In 1890, Alexander moved house to Wemyss Bay, then in 1894 passed the business on to the next generation and went sailing. His younger brother, John, dealt with the day-to-day business and eventually took over as Chairman on Alexander's death. John was another religious man, supporting missionary work by the Free Church, founding the Livingstonia Mission and investing in the Zambezi Valley. The equity of the firm was then divided up as follows:

Alex Stephen & Sons Ltd – Share Allocations 1894

Alexander Stephen	6/64ths	*retired*
A. E. Stephen (son)	21/64ths	*Engineering, Chairman 1917-1929*
Fred J. Stephen (son)	21/64ths	*Shipbuilding, Chairman 1929-1932*
John Stephen (brother)	12/64ths	*Chairman from 1900-1917*
Alexander Scott (secretary)	2/64ths	*1870-1908*
Robert McMaster (Yard Manager)	2/64ths	*served until 1901*

John Stephen (1835-1917) was considered a more 'modern man' than his elder brother. He was popular with his employees and delegated effectively. He had great faith in technology to solve the world's problems; a favourite saying was: *"Some men are as barren of ideas as angels are of trousers"*.[1060] 'Uncle John' was as impatient in habit as he was in vision. On his daily commute, he habitually jumped ship on arrival, before the ferry was secured or a gangway run out. On one occasion, he missed his footing and disappeared between the steamer and the pier. Without hesitation, one of the ferry crew dived in after him. It was not an easy rescue, but the pair were eventually picked up some way downstream. John was cold, wet and extremely lucky; not many sailors on the Clyde can swim. This then was Fred's heritage after graduation when he eased his way into the firm as the 1880s dawned. Within the decade, he would assume overall design control as Alexander Stephen & Sons' principal naval architect.

Fred Stephen's Steam Yachts

In 1902, Fred J. Stephen designed *Emerald* for Sir Christopher Furness. *Emerald*, a substantial vessel of 797-tons, was one of the first steam turbine yachts. Furness was a close friend of Charles Parsons, who pioneered the turbine, and he had great faith in this new technology. Parson's drive system was initially developed for high-speed, light-displacement applications. It comprised three turbines driving three separate shafts, with one propeller in the centre shaft and two on each of the flank shafts.

The total parasitic and interference drag from three shafts and five propellers must have been considerable, even in the most favourable circumstances. Certainly, the small-diameter, fast running propellers did not suit a deep, heavy-displacement yacht like *Emerald*. Fred Stephen recommended that the additional wing propellers be removed, and larger diameter props fitted. This improved speed, reduced noise and vibration, and became the norm for such vessels.[1061]

Emerald was the first turbine-engined ship to cross the Atlantic. On charter to Jay Gould, she followed the 12th America's Cup in 1903 when *Reliance* beat *Shamrock IV*. In 1913, when lying in the Gareloch, she was set ablaze, allegedly by the suffragettes, and became a total loss. Alexander's retirement home, Kelly House, above Wemyss Bay, suffered a similar fate. Alexander had bought the Kelly estate from the trustees of the late James 'Paraffin' Young, who features in Chapter 9. It has never been clear what the Stephen family did to upset the suffragettes, or indeed what was achieved by arson in this context.

The *Medea* of 1904 was another remarkable steam yacht and an acclaimed aesthetic masterpiece. This 137-ton vessel was designed by Fred J. Stephen and launched just 51 working-days after the team at Linthouse had laid out the keel on chocks. She went down the ways with steam up, complete to the last eggcup, to be handed over to her lucky owner two days later. This is not normal in shipbuilding, then or now. In those years, the Clyde yards were not afraid to fast-track design-and-build contracts, a skill that served the country well through two World Wars.

Medea was clearly a special boat, and looking at the lines, it is not difficult to see why; she is one of the most beautiful yachts of her size ever built. When *Medea* came on the market in 1912, she was bought back by 'Uncle' John Stephen, then Chairman of the firm. On John's death in 1917 she was sold, then loaned to the French Red Cross to serve as a hospital ship for the remainder of the Great War. Following a decade in other hands, *Medea* became available again in 1928.

Fred J. Stephen seized the opportunity to bring this lovely vessel back into the family. With deteriorating health in his mid-sixties, Fred could no longer go sailing, but he could still follow the action from the deck of *Medea*. The yacht often served as the committee vessel for the Royal Northern Yacht Club while Fred was Commodore. *Medea* is still sailing today. Paul Whittier purchased, restored and donated the much-travelled vessel to the Maritime Museum of San Diego in 1973.[1062]

However, the most impressive yacht ever built by Alexander Stephen & Co during Fred's design-tenure was the 1930 steam yacht, *Rover*, for Lord Inchcape of the P&O shipping line. *Rover* was large, at 2,115-tons, and among the most luxurious private yachts ever built. She was also a floating 'command centre' with the latest technology to allow Inchcape to run his businesses while living aboard ship. Today's Satcom billionaires have merely followed suit.

The Royal yacht, *Victoria & Albert*, was larger, but aesthetically *Rover* was in a different league entirely. James Barnett's *Nahlin*, similarly sized at 2,050-tons and built by John Brown of Clydebank, was her only rival in the thirties.[1063] It is impossible to call whether *Rover* or *Nahlin* merits the all-time contours d'elegance. The Clyde-built superyachts of the twenties and thirties are inevitably associated with sybaritic lifestyles of excess and scandal, but they were nevertheless immensely sophisticated, timeless works of art.

Among marine professionals, these opulent vessels were jealously tagged as 'sailors' homes'. For much of the year they described circles round their moorings in the lochs and bays of the Firth of Clyde "*resting far inland like weary great sea-birds*".[1064]. That said, the easy life could drive an old hand to drink. John Scott Hughes described long weeks of inactivity while serving aboard the *Vanadis*, a relatively modest steam yacht of 1,233-tons, built by A. & J. Inglis in 1908. The *Vanadis* was built for an American owner, as were many of the Clyde's finest products around the turn of the century. The Yanks admired Scottish engineering but were less impressed by our restrained good taste down below. On arrival Stateside, it was not uncommon for elegant Glasgow-school interiors to be ripped out and the bowels of the boudoir re-upholstered in brothel bling.

Sailing Yachts

The team at Linthouse also built prestigious sailing yachts. Alex Stephen & Sons was the preferred yard to realise Alfred Mylne's larger commissions. These included: *Vadura*, a composite yawl, 111-tons and 92ft LOA in 1926 for J. M. H. Clark; *Golden Hind*, a steel schooner for Commander J. H. Kitson, 144-tons and 88ft LOA in 1931; the composite ketch, *Abyn*, 82ft LOA in 1934 (now *Eileen II*); *Fulmara* (also known as *Maia III*), a steel auxiliary ketch 67ft LOA in 1934. And finally, there was *Mingary*, a 123ft LOA Cox & King steel schooner, built at Linthouse in 1926 for Kenneth Clark.[1065]

Fred J. Stephen developed an interest in sailing as a small boy mingling with the crowds watching the yacht racing at Rothesay. As a teenager crewing aboard his father's *Coolan*, it seems that Fred already had clear ideas about how the old cutter could be improved, and about yacht design more generally. Fred and his elder brother, Alexander Edward, built a small boat with the assistance of the captain of the *Coolan*, who was not only generous with his time, but also a trained carpenter. This little boat gave the brothers *"much excitement and not a little joy"*. Fred's first sail-boat design might have been just 12ft LOA, but she was a proper little yacht, drawn with an elegant counter.

Fred was destined to become a shipbuilder, but he did not formally join the firm until he had something to contribute. He took an M.A. as a first degree, before joining the maiden naval architecture course at Glasgow University in 1883.[1066] He was a prize-winning student, but the practical skills learned through his early foray into boatbuilding were always an important adjunct to his craft. Like his father before him, Fred carved his own ship models. He maintained a hands-on approach in the Linthouse drawing office, until eventually the business side of the company left little time for that, what with negotiating contracts and managing clients.

The first of Fred's racing yacht designs was the cutter, *Coila*, constructed at Linthouse in 1886 for himself and his brother, Alexander. The year 1886 would turn out to be a key pivot in the history of yacht racing, with an exciting new rating rule introduced in the autumn of that year.[1067] So, this first *Coila* was notionally obsolete on the day she was launched. She was a 3-tonner built to the old 1882 Tonnage Rule. But as events transpired, she was intrinsically fast enough to enjoy her most successful season two years later in 1888, when the old-rule 3-tonners raced as new-rule 6-raters.

The 3-tonners had made their debut on the Clyde in 1882 with two locally owned boats and two visitors. The Clyde pair were the Ailsa-designed *Mascotte* (Eyton & Quilter), and Lord Ailsa & Baden-Powell's *Snarley Yow*. The interlopers were from Plymouth: *Naida*, C. W. Courtney's homologised pre-rule boat from 1881, designed by Watson & Fox, and Lord Francis Cecil's *Chittywee*.[1068] The Clyde boats were relatively wholesome, averaging 5ft 7" beam. However, *Naida* was 5ft 4", and the Waterman-designed *Chittywee* presaged an emerging trend with a hull just 4ft 9" wide.

In 1886, the race to the bottom represented by the 'knife on edge' concept was well-established. Stephen's new *Coila* was just 4ft 7" wide from gunwale to gunwale on a LOA of about 40ft. Fred knew what was necessary to be competitive in the class, but such designs triggered the clamour for a new rating rule. This was a woeful, and thankfully short, period in British yacht design. The poisoned wellspring of the 1882 Rule produced wall-sided boats that were fast, but hideously impractical. Even so, they could be fun to sail if you were a good swimmer. The 3-tonners were known locally as 'ham knives' after the intensely satisfying way they cut to windward.

Coila was one of just five 3-tonners built under the old tonnage rule for the 1886 season: G. L. Watson designed *Rona* and *Daisie*, built by J. McQuistan of Largs for J. Stewart Clark and J. William Clark of New York respectively; then there was William Fife's *Ariel*, built for well-known Clyde yachtsman W. Peter Donaldson; and William Paton's composite *Cora*, built by M&L for the Kennedy family.[1069] Of that season's crop, *Cora* was perhaps the most life-threatening. This generation of 3-tonners featured some of the least desirable yachts ever built under any rating rule. The class averaged 40ft LOA, 29ft LWL, just 4ft 8" beam against 6ft draught, with 5 or 6 tons of lead on the keel.

While much was expected of Watson's boats, in the first two years of the 3-tonner class, Fife's *Ariel* prevailed. In the spring of 1888, Fred saw opportunities to speed up *Coila* under the changed parameters of the new Length and Sail Area Rule. He brought the boat back into the carpenter's shed at Linthouse, increased her beam and draft, and "*spread out her forebody as much as possible about the waterline*", making her longer too.[1070] The changes were subtle but complex to engineer; had he not owned the shipyard it might have made more sense to build a new boat. Following these modifications, in their third season with *Coila*, the Stephen family swept the board, picking up 23 prizes in 25 starts.

In 1890, encouraged by the success of *Coila* and motivated by the latest boats built specifically to the new rule, Fred Stephen drew an uncompromising vessel with fine ends and clean undistorted lines which was fully optimised for the 10-rater class. *Maida*, like her contemporaries, was about 35ft LWL, on a beam of 8ft. Sailing *Maida*, Fred was up against Britain's most successful designers, and indeed the best helmsmen on the Clyde, at that time, including: Fife's *Encore* (Ken Clark), *Woodcock* (Andrew Coats) and *Yvonne* (Peter Donaldson), G. L. Watson's *Phantom* (Andrew Arthur) and *Dora* (Messrs Allan). The 10-raters became one of the most competitive classes on the Clyde with no assured winners.

Through the 1890-1893 seasons, *Maida* was always in the hunt, taking her share of race wins in the weekend regattas, including the overall class win one season.[1071] Only when Andrew Coats replaced *Woodcock* with the second-generation Fife 10-rater, *Ptarmigan*, in 1892, did *Maida* struggle for her turn in the top spot. By then it was time for Fred to move on to new challenges. Meanwhile, and for many more years under new ownership, the old boat was still capable of picking up the odd handicap prize.

Maida was a good boat and the close racing in the 10-raters gave Fred invaluable feedback on his design ideas. From his conversations with his contemporaries, Stephen continuously evaluated his boat's performance, while sailing a competitive race on virtual autopilot. This allocation of mental firepower is usually a free-pass to the back of the fleet, so Fred must have been that rare thing – a 'natural' sailor. Then, from the mid-1890s on, it is possible that another, game changing factor was at work.

Alexander Stephen & Sons had built a test-tank at Linthouse, primarily to inform ship contracts that were contingent on speed and fuel-economy achieved during trials. Missing performance targets incurred serious financial penalties. Fred Stephen became engrossed in the science of tank-testing and confident in his performance predictions, as related in our discussion on the history of Scottish tank-testing in Chapter 6. So when he designed racing yachts, he brought big-ship analytics and new levels of precision to the task.

However, although Fred was familiar with G. L. Watson's innovative tank-testing at Dumbarton over the winter of 1892/83, it is unlikely that he saw such work as critical in the design of small racing yachts, or worth investing in mechanisms to introduce heel and yaw as Watson did at the Denny Tank. We know Fred used free-sailing models to inform his design choices, so he may have run simple upright resistance tests. But as an expert in the field, he understood the limitations of small model testing. Nevertheless, the ship science acquired to achieve performance specifications on his big ship contracts must have informed his racing yacht design work.

After *Maida*, sold in 1894, Fred's name appears in the race results occasionally steering other people's yachts. It may be surmised that he was just too busy at work – as the 80 ships in the Linthouse order book confirms. He would take 14 years out from competition. When he did return to round-the-cans racing, we might have expected him to build a bigger boat, as was, and indeed still is, the way in yachting. However, Fred's fascination of designing and racing small boats had not paled.[1072] The International Rule was drafted in 1906 for the 1907 season. Fred

Stephen immediately grasped its possibilities. After observing the first boats built to the rule in 1907, he set to work.

First International Rule (1907 – 1919)

$$R \text{ (metres)} = \frac{L + B + \frac{1}{2}G + 3d + \frac{1}{3}\sqrt{S}\text{-}F}{2}$$

where.... L = length (as calculated)
B = beam
G = chain girth
d = difference between skin girth and chain girth
S = sail area
F = freeboard

Scottish owners and their favoured designers were all enthusiastic about the new rule. The first metre-boat launched on the Clyde was the Fife 15-metre, *Shimna*, built at Alexander Robertson's yard for John Payne and Arthur Watson in 1907.[1073] Fife also built an 8-metre for Mrs R. G. Allen, but his other metre boats that season (*Wanda* 10-metre, *Osborne* 6-metre, *Almoraima* 6-metre, *Ya Veremos* 8-metre) were exported to clients in England and Spain. Mylne too had to travel to see his new boats in competition, these were the 15-metre, *Ma'oona*, built by R. McAlister for J. Talbot Clifton and *Baira*, an 8-metre, built by J. G. Fay & Co for export to Bilbao.

With the Clyde's long history of competitive racing in small boats, it was inevitable that a fleet of 6-metre yachts would soon muster off Hunter's Quay. Fred Stephen designed *Coila II* in 1908. She was built at Linthouse and was likely the first 6-metre launched on the estuary. The following year, Mylne designed *Correnzia* for Miss Turner-Farley, followed by *Apache* for James Napier, both McAlister-built boats. Fife's first 6-metres for a Scottish owner was *Clio* (a favoured Fife name), built as stock in 1910, then sold to A. N. Goudie, who renamed her *Ariel*; she was followed by *Cingalee* for Algernon Maudsley.[1074]

Dodgson Bowman observed that Fred Stephen's *"first two boats marked the apprenticeship stage. With Coila II he became the master."*[1075] Indeed, *Coila II* was to be outstandingly successful. Fred entered the 6mR class when the International Rule was in its second year. This cautious approach would have allowed him to evaluate the success of alternative design solutions in the first crop of new boats, then check out Fife's second-generation sister-ships, *Osborne* and *Almoraima*, in build, before they were shipped to Spain.

Looking at contemporary designs in the first years of the new rule; Mylne's 6mRs were larger, and Fife's larger yet, with longer overhangs and more beam. It is difficult to understand why Fred would have opted for a small boat. Through the history of the sport, bigger boats have almost always been quicker, and experience with any rule invariably allows the designer to grow a basic design, year by year, within the rating.

For whatever reason, Fred drew a small boat, but *Coila II* appears to have been deceptively powerful, and there are suggestions that she may have had a little more draft than most of the early 6-metres. In 1908, the first year of the class on the Clyde, *Coila II* had little opposition from *Era*, the only other 6-metre competing that year. *Era* was drawn by Dudley Dawson and built in Gourock by R. S. Banner for George Moir. In the years that followed, however, the increasingly sophisticated designs of Fife, Mylne, and later C. E. Nicholson and others, joined the fleet to form a very tough class where any success was hard won.

The 1908 Yachting Olympics were held off Ryde in the Solent. The 6-metre class attracted five entries and Britain's crew of Gilbert Laws, Thomas McMeekin and Charles Crichton won the regatta in *Dormy*. Crews from Belgium and France filled the silver and bronze positions. Both *Coila II* and *Era* had been built for selection in the 6mR class, but neither was completed in time to be considered. Consequently, at the end of the 1908 season, George Moir issued a challenge to the owner of *Dormy*, to establish who really had *"the best 6-metre yacht in the world"*. The owner of *Dormy*, H. B. Wodehouse, from Burnham on Crouch accepted the challenge.

A best-of-five format was agreed. George Moir's purse of £50 (£6,000) spiced up the racing and ensured that the event took place on the Clyde.[1076] George was generous, but not daft. *Dormy* would be up against, not just *Era*, but also *Coila II*, the Clyde champion. It is unclear who steered Wodehouse's boat in the match, but probably the designer retained that duty. The irrepressible George tagged along, although it appears that *Era* was more a spectator boat than a player in this north-south duel. After four races, *Dormy* and *Coila II* had two wins apiece. In a closely fought finale, *Coila II* took out the fifth race, and the very generous prize.

Coila II was consistently successful until 1910, when the newer boats began to get the better of her. Fred had already enlarged the old-style dual wells into a single larger cockpit. But over the winter of 1910/11, he took the boat back into the carpentry shed at Linthouse for a complete rebuild. As a rich man owning a shipyard, Fred Stephen had endless opportunities for tinkering. He resisted that urge, but when he made changes, they were substantial and invariably effective.

When *Coila II* reappeared in 1911, she was almost unrecognisable as little of the original boat remained after the rebuild. The bow was opened up and spread, as he had done with *Coila I* to increase the forward overhang and make the boat bigger. This changed the sheerline. The area of the keel-fin was increased, with a new, finer leading edge grafted on. God knows what other modifications went on under the water. Overall, he updated the design to incorporate lessons learned from the newer boats which had proved to be faster during the previous season. So, *Coila II* was effectively a new boat, and she was re-rigged too. Her bowsprit was removed, and her jackyard topsail rig replaced with a high-peaked gunter with more area in the main.[1077]

The new rig did nothing to improve her appearance, but it was clearly effective. *Coila II* reclaimed leadership of the Clyde 6-metre and remained there or thereabouts until the hiatus of the Great War. A new trophy for the season's points was presented in 1914, the sixth year of the class on the Clyde. *Coila II* secured enough points to win this, before racing was curtailed when Britain declared war on Germany on the 4th August 1914. *Coila II* remained in the Stephen family until she was broken up in 1922.

For the 1920 season, with Britain's yachtsmen now back in business after the disruption of the Great War, the YRA issued a 2nd International Rule in October 1919, re-weighting the critical measurement parameters. With what was now, in effect, a new rule, it was clear that Fred Stephen would have to sit down at his drawing board and start again from scratch. This was not something he did immediately as the demands of the family shipyard again took priority. Alex Stephen & Sons Ltd launched 30 ships in the four years of the immediate post-war period.

Second International Rule (1919 – 1933)

$$R \text{ (metres)} = \frac{L + \frac{1}{4}G + 2d + \sqrt{S} - F}{2.5}$$

where….   L = length (as calculated)
G = chain girth
d = difference between skin girth and chain girth
S = sail area
F = freeboard

The new boat would be a significantly larger and more powerful vessel than *Coila II*. With *Coila III*, Fred designed to the 'industry standard', with a boat that reflected the well-proven envelope established by William Fife. However, *Coila III's* underwater profile was more radical, tending towards a triangular planform. Such a shape reduces the girths at the measurement point and allows a deeper keel behind that point. This planform allowed her turn of bilge to be tighter than most of her contemporaries.[1078] *Coila III* was launched in 1922; she was 35ft LOA, 21ft 6" LWL, 7ft beam and drew 5ft 3". As with Fred's other boats, she was built in the carpentry shop at Linthouse, then fitted-out, rigged and commissioned at Alexander Robertson's yard in Sandbank.

Coila III was quick from the outset and was selected for the four-yacht team to represent Britain in the British American Cup races of that year.

She was shipped from the Clyde as deck cargo on the luxury Cunard liner, RMS *Scythia*, accompanied by John Stephen and his crew.[1079] The other three yachts, *Jean*, *Reg* and the syndicate boat, *Rose*, making up the British contingent were shipped separately from Southampton.[1080] The team had been selected from a fifteen-strong fleet of British 6-meters. *Rose*, for example, was sailed by her famous designer Charles E. Nicholson. The British team lost to the Americans, but ominously for the hosts, *Coila III* was the equal of any boat on Long Island Sound that year.[1081]

Seawanhaka Cup Success

Following the 1922 series on Oyster Bay, the Seawanhaka Corinthian Yacht Club invited the British team to challenge for the Seawanhaka Cup, then gathering dust in the trophy cabinet of the Manchester Yacht Club of Marblehead. This venerable trophy, presented for match-racing in yachts with a waterline of less than 25ft, had spent the best part of a decade in Canada, but it had never crossed the Atlantic.[1082] The Seawanhaka committee considered it bad form to challenge another American club, so to revive the temporarily moribund competition, the British 6-metre boys were invited to step up to the plate.

The Seawanhaka Cup is the oldest international trophy in American sailing. It was first contested in 1895 in ½-raters but is best known for the sixteen superb match-race contests held in 6-metres from 1922 to 1987.[1083] *"This competition alone kept elite international match racing alive through the hiatus from 1937 through to 1958, when first global conflict and then post-war austerity interrupted America's Cup racing."*[1084]

The Royal Northern Yacht Club had not planned to mount a challenge for the Seawanhaka Cup, so the result was a pleasant surprise. The win was initially tarnished by the rumour that the trophy was effectively 'gifted' to the Northern, as the Americans had little interest in institutionalising another 'impossible quest', like the America's Cup. The story is that the Yanks contrived to send the then-dormant trophy overseas, simply to set up the sporting prospect of winning it back.

As Sherman Hoyt noted dryly, *"Frank Paine offered 'Sakie', available in the near vicinity, as the victim"*.[1085] All this supercilious background chatter must have soured the win. But, whatever the circumstances, John G. Stephen rose to the challenge and brought the prestigious trophy home to Scotland. And as events transpired, it was not, in fact, the hollow victory engineered by the Yankees. If the Scots crew were 'gifted' the trophy, they forged a new narrative by hanging on to it.

This was a vigorous epoch in the annals of trans-Atlantic yachting. The British American Cup was held on the Solent the following year in 1923.

Fred's son, John, led the home team with *Coila III*, the top boat in the series. Then the action moved north to Rothesay on the Clyde for the Seawanhaka Cup. Fred successfully defended against the Sherman Hoyt-designed 6-metre, *Lea*, sailing for the Seawanhaka Club, although John took the helm for the final race.[1086] *Coila III* was significantly faster than *Lea* in a blow. The Scottish boat may have been less close-winded than *Lea*, but *Coila III* repeatedly demonstrated her superiority by powering through to leeward. Her velocity made good (VMG) to windward was markedly higher than the American boat.[1087]

These would become the glory days of both the Seawanhaka Cup and the 6-metre Class. The races were generally hard-fought and were intensely scrutinised in a competition that both promoted excellence in small yacht design and encouraged the development of match-racing skills among the best amateur yachtsmen. The Royal Northern Yacht Club won the cup seven times, with a Scottish designer on each occasion. Fife disciple David Boyd, would match Fred Stephen's three wins, with two for the Royal Northern with *Circe*, and a third for Canada with *Titia*.[1088]

The Royal Norwegian Yacht Club challenged for the Seawanhaka Cup in 1924. The Royal Northern nominated *Coila III* once again to defend the trophy. *Unni* was another formidable competitor. She was designed and sailed by Johan Anker, father of the Dragon One Design, and first among equals when considering Norwegian naval architects of that era. *Coila III* was again victorious, but obviously, this spectacular run of success could not last forever. The three-year-old boat was finally outclassed in 1925, when the *Lanai* team crossed the Atlantic to visit our waters en famille to challenge on behalf of the Seawanhaka Corinthians.[1089]

The 1925 Seawanhaka Cup defence presented a much more difficult task for the defender; the *Lanai* challenge was a thoroughly professional campaign. The American syndicate began by purchasing the Fife-designed *Betty* as a yardstick. There was of course only one Stephen-designed 2nd Rule 6-metre and *Coila III* was not for sale. Clinton Crane took the lines off *Betty*, inclined her and analysed every aspect of her design concept, detail and construction. Then he developed two variations – *Lanai* and *Redhead*, for a series of trials against *Betty* and the best American Sixes.[1090] After establishing that their new designs had gained a clear edge, the syndicate brought in Sherman Hoyt, one of the best helmsmen in the country, to conduct long sessions of two-boat testing.

This formidable team sailed for Scotland in June 1925, with their two new 6-metres as deck cargo. The Yanks were better prepared than any Seawanhaka Cup team before or since. Indeed, their 'no-stone-unturned' preparation was to become a model for the New York Yacht Club's successful post-war America's Cup defence campaigns in 12-metres. As the racing was to be held off Hunter's Quay, the American team took over a small temperance Hotel in Dunoon for the summer, and being sailors, slipped a sail-bag over the 'temperance' signboard.[1091]

The Seawanhaka syndicate were bemused by the phenomenon of the Scottish Sabbath and baffled by the sudden disappearance of the croquet hoops from the lawn on Sunday mornings, lest the strictures of the day be broken. Sherman Hoyt was quite at home, however. He professed to love Scotland and the Scots, and there is no reason to doubt it; he studied naval architecture at Glasgow and frequently returned to these shores to race sailboats and catch up with his many friends.

> These days, we do not associate Dunoon with temperance, quite the reverse in fact. However, the birth of the holiday industry is bound up with the Temperance Movement and Dunoon was, above all, a holiday town. When Baptist preacher Thomas Cook organised his first excursion in 1841, it was to "*employ the great powers of railways and locomotion for the furtherance of this social reform.*" Cook's early clients were temperance societies and Sunday schools. Outings to the seaside often followed this model, whether organised by benevolent employers or the church.
> The Temperance Movement in Scotland has been largely forgotten, bar the occasional derogatory references to the 'Band of Hope' when an individual's round is overdue.[1092] "*Opportunities for Scots to indulge in extremely heavy drinking had long abounded. In 1832 Glasgow provided business for 1,360 spirit dealers – a ratio of one per 14 families. The alarming factor injected into this situation from the 1840's onwards was the way an aristocratic tradition of heavy drinking was increasingly being adopted and upheld by social inferiors, and most conspicuously, by the lower classes in urban areas.*"[1093]

That summer, William Fife gave Sherman Hoyt a bunch of white heather for good luck, which *Lanai* sported on the stem-head. Fife's friendship surely veered into 'treason' on this occasion. He resented being marginalised and so was then at odds with the Royal Northern.[1094] Fife was convinced that his latest boats, *Reg* and *Saga*, were faster than the 4-year-old *Coila III*. Perhaps they were, but certainly earlier iterations of Fife's 6mR model were not. As for 1925, it was surely inevitable that *Coila III*, or indeed any other Scottish Six, should lose the Cup when we consider the strength of the American challenge.

On both sides of the Atlantic, design had moved on. William Fife's latest 6-metres were a little bigger and probably a little quicker than his *Betty* of 1922, which had both informed and benchmarked Clinton Crane's design work. That said, even if one of Fife's new boats had been nominated to defend, the result would have been the same. In 1925, the Yanks were on another level. No Corinthian sailing campaign had ever been mounted in such a smart and systematic way. Crane's measure-match-and-surpass methodology was simply more effective than anything that had gone before. This was a clear-sighted campaign based on incremental marginal gains.

In conversation with Scott Roher in 1974, David Boyd ventured, "*The American technology advantage goes back further than you might think. I remember when Clinton Crane, his brother and Sherman Hoyt brought two Sixes over to try to get the Seawanhaka Cup back in 1925. Lanai met Coila III for the cup and she dominated the match. Lanai was all anyone could talk about. One evening my father took me down to the dock at Hunter's Quay to see Lanai and her near-sister Red Head. He pointed to a round thing on the deck and asked me if I knew what it was*". "*Do you know what that was, Scott?*" "*No sir, I don't*". "*That was a sheet winch*".

> Clinton Crane's association with the Seawanhaka Cup began in 1896 when he was just 18-years old. On that occasion, sailing his first design, he beat 28 other hopefuls to defend the cup. However, despite having the bottom of the good ship, *El Heirie*, faired and polished by the Steinway Piano Company, he was beaten by the Canadians in the main event. Crane lost again in 1897 and 1898, with *Momo* and *Challenger*. The Canadians' mastery of scows and tunnel-hulls, like the controversial hybrid *Dominion*, meant that they remained unbeaten through eight challenges.[1095] The Massachusetts Yacht Club finally wrested the trophy from the Royal St Lawrence in 1905, then successfully defended it in 1910. But such had been their dominance that other clubs were disinclined to challenge. The competition appeared moribund until the Royal Northern Yacht Club was roped in, without planning or preparation in 1922, as we have described here.

The Sun Sets on a Remarkable Career

In 1927, Fred J. Stephen launched his final design. This was the composite 8-metre, *Coila IV*.[1096] That year Fred donated *Coila III* to Cardwell Bay Sailing Club for cadet training. However, three years later the club returned the boat, now called *Windward*, as they could not afford the yard bills. It seems unfortunate that nothing could be done to keep the old 6-metre in commission, as she was much-loved by the membership at Cardwell Bay.

The 8-metre, *Coila IV*, was a big powerful yacht with about 5% more volume than Fife's comparable designs of 1927. The Stephen family raced her with considerable success. Following a promising first season, she was the top boat in her class in 1928 and 1929.[1097] When Fred was forced to give up yacht racing due to ill-health, the boat was sailed by his son, 'Wee John'. There is no doubt that *Coila IV* was a good boat, and beautiful too, winning consistently on the Clyde, but she was never tested at the same high level as Fred's 6-metres.

The Stephen family's sailing skills and deep pockets were as important to their racing success as the design of their boats. When *Coila IV* was bought by Ian Fraser Marshall in 1932 and renamed *Hestia*, she seldom won. *Hestia* ended up competing in the 8-metre's 'B' fleet.[1098] George Jackson was her next owner in 1935; he renamed her *Aliort* and kept her until 1938 when she was sold south.

Fred Stephen applied his professional skills to just five full-on racing yachts. This was not enough to earn him a place atop the pantheon of acclaimed Scottish masters, but had life taken him in that direction, he would have been as well-known as Fife is today. As it was, he was content to design and build boats for himself that were notable for both their speed and their long competitive life. His series of unpretentious racing yachts represents an extraordinary outlier in the history of yacht design. Moreover, his design philosophy of continuous refinement, rather than revolution, simply defied the odds.

As an example of revolution, E. H. Bentall, is often cited. His *Jullanar* of 1875 was a 'long-odds bet' that arguably changed the course of yacht design. Successful professionals do not have this luxury, as George Lennox Watson recalled: *"The same year that Jullanar was built, I designed my first racing yacht, the 5-ton Clotilde, but whilst I had the advantage, through my friend Mr John Inglis, jun, of especially early access to Professor Froude's investigations, I cut her away in a somewhat timid fashion. Meanwhile, with splendid audacity, and with no timid reverence for precedent, Mr Bentall built the 'Jullanar'."*[1099] Fred's son, John, the subject of the next chapter, could not have been more different from his father. John matched, and arguably trumped, Bentall for 'splendid audacity'.

Working within the closely controlled design parameters of established level-rating classes, Fred Stephen's yachts competed like-for-like with the products of the best full-time yacht designers of the day. It is remarkable that his modest portfolio could exhibit a level of sophistication to win on the international scene against designers who had refined their models through countless iterations. Writing in 1935 on the trials and tribulations of a design by Fred's son, John, Uffa Fox explained that *"even if the accepted shape for 6-metres, such as seen by the lines of Bob Kat, Vorsa and Nancy is not perfect, all its details have been perfected, and so it is fast and difficult to improve upon."*[1100]

Yacht racing histories invariably include lists of racing successes. While that approach has been avoided here, in this instance, it seems appropriate: over 17 years, the two 6-metres designed, built and sailed by Fred J. Stephen, competed in 424 races and gained 166 firsts and 146 minor prizes.[1101] The extraordinary combination of antonymous factors is remarkable: 17 seasons, just two boats, a period of remarkable progress in yacht design and the presence on the racecourse of the finest sailors, the best yacht designers and the best builders the sport of yachting has ever seen. Only the racing record of *Britannia* comes close, and if we are honest, the royal yacht sailed through life on starboard tack, in a realm of suspended reality brought to ground only when sailing against the equally 'entitled' Kaiser Wilhelm II's *Meteors*.

Fred was a true Corinthian, who invariably raced with family and friends, although, as was normal then, the two hired hands dealt with deliveries and handled the logistics. With his polished shoes, Fred cut a dash on the racecourse, clad routinely in a suit and tie, topped with a 'regulation' Mudhook fedora. His son, John, continued this sartorial tradition into the 'modern' era when the opposition had all resorted to sweaters and smocks and sandshoes.

Fred's enthusiasm for competitive sport meant that he doubled-up to sail his little Pleiade One Design, *Maia*, whenever possible, see Chapter 25. This is where it helps to have the resources to 'hot bunk' your boats. Through the 1920s and 1930s, the Stephen family yachts were shepherded by the 60ft Bergius-powered launch, *Clio*, which acted as their mothership. *Clio* was originally designed and built by William Fife III for his own use in 1910. She was certainly not one of Fife's most elegant designs, but the old dog seems to have been cherished by the Stephen family.

Ashore, Fred was elected Commodore of the Royal Northern Yacht Club in the mid-1920s; the first shipbuilder to hold that position and a rare commoner.[1102] He was also Vice-Admiral of the Mudhook Yacht Club, and a member of the council of the Yacht Racing Association.[1103]

Yachts designed by Fred J. Stephen and built by the Stephen Family

	Name	Type	Designer	Builder	Year	TM
1	*Sylvia*	Steam-yacht	Stephen & Co	Alex Stephen	1882	195
2	*Nerissa*	Steam-yacht	Stephen & Co	Alex Stephen	1885	350
3	*Coila I*	Cutter	Fred J. Stephen	Alex Stephen	1886	3
4	*Calanthe*	Steam-yacht	Fred J. Stephen	Alex Stephen	1898	429
5	*Emerald*	Steam-yacht	Fred J. Stephen	Alex Stephen	1903	800
6	*Medea*	Steam-yacht	Fred J. Stephen	Alex Stephen	1904	137
7	*Maida*	10-rater	Fred J. Stephen	Alex Stephen	1890	10
8	*Coila II*	6-metre	Fred J. Stephen	Alex Stephen	1908	3
9	*Coila II* (mod)	6-metre	Fred J. Stephen	Alex Stephen	1911	3
10	*Midge*	3-metre	Alex, James, John	Alex Stephen	1913	1
11	*Coila III*	6-metre	Fred J. Stephen	Alex Stephen	1922	3
12	*Coila IV*	8-metre	Fred J. Stephen	Alex Stephen	1927	5
13	*Rover*	Steam-yacht	Fred J. Stephen	Alex Stephen	1930	2,113

Alfred Mylne-designed yachts built by Alex Stephen & Sons Ltd

1	*Vadura*	Yawl	Alfred Mylne	Alex Stephen	1926	109
2	*Mingary*	Schooner	Alfred Mylne	Alex Stephen	1926	216
3	*Golden Hind*	Schooner	Alfred Mylne	Alex Stephen	1931	144
4	*Fiumara*	Ketch	Alfred Mylne	Alex Stephen	1934	77
5	*Albyn*	Ketch	Alfred Mylne	Alex Stephen	1934	82
6	*Thendara*	Ketch	Alfred Mylne	Alex Stephen	1937	135

CODA: The Linthouse Yard

In 1919, Alex Stephen & Sons Ltd was in a strong financial position after five years of highly profitable war work. The family cashed-out and sold a controlling share to the shipping line P&O Ltd. However, cancellations and the slump in orders that accompanied the post-war depression led to bad debts and layoffs. Alexander 'Murray' Stephen

(1892-1974), Fred's eldest son and 'Wee' John's more business-minded brother, ensured that the company continued to pursue innovation, even as profitability declined throughout the industry. The Stephen shipyard was, for example, an early adopter of all-welded steel construction.

The Stephens were generally considered to be good, albeit paternal, employers, who prioritised social and physical well-being to maintain harmony in the workplace. Benefits included a welfare department, a canteen, an apprentice boys club and Coila Park at Shieldhall – 10-acres for sports and recreation. Stan Ferguson, owner of the Mylne's old yard at Ardmaliesh, started his apprenticeship at Linthouse in the 1950s. Stan recalls that the Stephens introduced scheduled tea breaks to the Clyde shipbuilding industry. While this doesn't seem like much of a concession today, old hands still recall the advent of the tea-break with misty eyes. It was a small gesture that delivered dividends in loyalty and productivity.

Murray Stephen was a tireless promoter of the shipbuilding industry on the Clyde and was knighted for his efforts. When he became chairman of the firm in 1932, he clearly had an eye to the future, setting up apprentice training schools, and upgrading and modernising plant and equipment to allow increasing prefabrication. But, in the 1960s, the company's business plan, like all Clyde yards, became unsustainable in the face of competition from Far East yards with considerably lower operational costs and government support.

The assets, work in progress and order book of Alexander Stephen & Co Ltd were transferred to Upper Clyde Shipbuilders (UCS) in 1968, although the engineering and ship repairing operations remained in family hands until 1976. The famous 'Work in' led by the charismatic Jimmy Reid lasted from June 1971 to February 1972, when a temporary reprieve was gained after a hard-fought battle to keep the yard open. However, as part of the UCS rescue package, the Linthouse yard went into liquidation. During this turbulent period, a young Billy Connolly worked for the company as an apprentice boiler maker and picked up enough stories to subsequently make a living as a stand-up comedian.

The Engine Shop at Linthouse was salvaged when the yard was demolished in 1991 and re-erected at Irvine to become the Scottish Maritime Museum. This dramatic 'Category A Listed Building' provides both shelter and context. It has hosted theatre, acrobats and highwire acts in spectacular multimedia and celebratory events that sustain repeat visits by the local population.

[1056] The Piper Calls the Tune, Euan Ross and Bob Donaldson, 2017.

[1057] This second Alexander was productive in all spheres of life. His 18 children had multiplied to 707 descendants in 1995, of whom 502 were still alive at that date. The Stephen family are linked to another well-known Scottish naval architect, Colin Mudie (1926-present). Margaret Stephen married Robert Mudie (1847-1911).

[1058] Dodson describes *Coolan* as having been designed by Alexander in 1870. Yachting and Yachtsmen, W. Dodgson Bowman, 1927. Lloyds has her as built by Robinson in 1860.

[1059] Stephen of Linthouse, a Record of Two Hundred Years of Shipbuilding – 1750-1950, published by Alex Stephen & Sons Ltd and distributed to all members of the firm by the Chairman of the Board of Directors, written by John L. Carvel, 1951.

[1060] John Stephen's favourite saying, as recorded by the Reverend John McNeil.

[1061] All the Clyde's turbine steamers benefited from the spin-off. *King Edward*, the first commercial application of the turbine, and originally a five-propeller vessel, was altered in line with Stephen's experience.

[1062] *Medea* served in two world wars, under three navies and six national flags. She was converted to oil in 1964. She is open to visitors at the San Diego Maritime Museum.

[1063] G. L. Watson passed away in 1904, so passing the baton to J. R. Barnett who managed the firm and became principal designer. *Nahlin* is now owned by a vacuum cleaner magnate. Coincidentally, one of the Stephen yard's side-lines was the manufacture of 'proper', industrial-strength, plumbed-in vacuum cleaner systems in offices and hotels like the Gleneagles.

[1064] See Sailing through Life by John Scott Hughes, 1947, where he describes his time on the *Vanadis* at her James River mooring in Virginia. Quotation pluralised.

[1065] Ken Clark's *Mingary* is not to be confused with the 1929 Mylne ketch, *Mingary*, built by the Bute Slip Dock for J. H. M Clark of the same family. There was also a *Coila* not owned by the family. This vessel was a 1901 Fife cutter 43ft LOA. Fred J. Stephen owned a 32ft 1910 twin-screw Bergius paraffin launch named *Clio*, Fife's serial 'pet' name.

[1066] Naval architecture 'came of age' as a separate and distinct profession in 1860 when the Institute of Naval Architects was formed. Glasgow University introduced a course of lectures in shipbuilding and marine engineering, with the co-operation of the Institute of Engineers and Shipbuilders, in 1881. Then, in 1883 the John Elder Chair of Naval Architecture, said to be the first in the world, was founded, with Francis Elgar (1883-1886) being appointed, doubtless through his friendship with Professor Rankine and well-known shipbuilder, John Elder.

[1067] The Encyclopaedia of Sport and Games, Vol.4, C. H. Suffolk & Earl of Berkshire, 1911.

[1068] Not to be confused with the Mylne *Chittywee*, a 5-tonner built at Burnham in 1902.

[1069] J. McQuistan of Largs built another sistership, *Pitti Sing*, which seems to have gone to a client stationed in West Africa, according to the Lloyds Register of Yachts for 1887.

[1070] Clyde, The Yachtsman, 1st June 1893.

[1071] Yacht Racing in the Clyde, The Southampton Herald, 5th July 1890; Yachting, The Southampton Herald, 12th July 1890; The Clyde Season, The Sporting Gazette, 19th July 1890; Yachting, Belfast Newsletter, 5th July 1893; Yachting, The Morning Post, 8th July 8 1893; The Royal Clyde Yacht Club Regatta, The Standard, 11th July 1893; and various other contemporary news reports.

[1072] Famous Yachtsmen No.10, F. J. Stephen, W. D. Bowman, The Yachtsman, 3rd April 1926.

[1073] Sports in Brief, The Times, 1st June 1907.

[1074] Lloyds Register of Yachts for 1910 lists 40-odd 6-metres worldwide.

[1075] Yachting and Yachtsmen, W. Dodgson Bowman, 1927.

[1076] Yachting, The Times, 7th September 1908.

[1077] The jackyard topsail incorporated what was effectively a full topmast.

[1078] Fred's son, John, would take a similar approach with *Maida* (the second yacht of that name in the family) in 1932.

[1079] British Yacht Shipped, the New York Times, 18th August 1922. The RMS *Scythia* would become the longest-serving steamship of the 20th century.

[1080] The syndicate comprised members of the Royal Yacht Squadron, the Royal Victoria Yacht Club, the Royal Thames Yacht Club and the Royal London Yacht Club. With all these institutions involved, most members must have been sleeping partners.

[1081] International Six-Meter Races, Yachting, October 1923. Baxter & Cicero 6-metre archive.

[1082] As the cup was later contested in 8-metres, which have an LWL exceeding that figure, this stipulation was dropped.

[1083] The History of the Seawanhaka Cup, Seawanhaka Corinthian Yacht Club, Oyster Bay, ed. Commodores Park Benjamin III, Bruce A. Cook William R. Denslow, Jr, Ian A. McCurdy.

[1084] The Piper Calls the Tune, Euan Ross and Bob Donaldson, 2017.

[1085] Sherman Hoyt's Memoirs, C. Sherman Hoyt, 1950. Paine was a fine designer who would later draw the J-class, *Yankee* (1930), and the ocean racer, *Highland Light* (1931).

[1086] Fifteen Years of the Six-metres, Drake H. Sparkman, Yachting, Autumn 1936. The International Six-Meter Races, Yachting, October 1923. Baxter & Cicero 6-metre archive.

[1087] The Outlook, Maldon Heckstall-Smith, the Yachting Monthly and Marine Motor Magazine, Volume XXXV, Nos. CCV to CCX, May to October 1923.

[1088] The Sandbank-built *Circe* won twice for Scotland in 1938 and 1939; then, after the hiatus of WW2, *Titia* represented the Dominion of Canada to win again in 1956. Boyd's winners were 3rd Rule 6-metres.

[1089] Clinton Crane's Yachting Memories, Clinton Crane, 1952.

[1090] The Crane brothers financed the build of *Redhead*.

[1091] This might have been the Dhailling Lodge, formerly a temperance hotel. The Cowal Hotel (Rosegarth), the best-known of Dunoon's temperance hotels, was considerably larger. The Temperance Scotland Act 1913 allowed voters to hold a poll to vote on whether their area remained 'wet' or went 'dry'. Brewers and publicans formed defence committees to fight temperance propaganda. The 1913 Act was not repealed until the Licensing (Scotland) Act of 1976. Hence the Corries' song of our youth 'There are No Pubs in Kirkintilloch'.

[1092] The introduction of temperance hotels was influenced by the Glasgow Abstainers Union, the Band of Hope, the Sabbatarian Sunday Closing Association, the United Kingdom Alliance, the Independent Order of Rechabites and the insidious International Order of Good Templars from the USA. These organisations influenced the use and operation of the Kilmun and Dunoon Seaside Homes.

[1093] Drink and Society: Scotland 1870, Norma Davies Logan, 1983. Thesis presented for the Degree of Ph.D. of the University of Glasgow.

[1094] Sherman Hoyt's Memoirs, C. Sherman Hoyt, 1950.

[1095] *Dominion's* victory was controversial to say the least. James Ross sailed a Dugan design, effectively a narrow-beam catamaran, which could be sailed on one hull to devastating effect. Dugan sportingly offered to re-sail the series with a conventional scow, but the deed (of gift) was done. A History of the Seawanhaka Corinthian Yacht Club, The Great Six Meter Era: the 1930s Decade extract, undated.

[1096] Other names include, *Hestia*, *Aliort*, *Tuctoo*, *Zadig*. The last-known owner we have is Walter Trickett of Christchurch, Hampshire, UK in 1963.

[1097] This is from the Grace's Guide account. Newspaper accounts favour *Caryl*.

[1098] Yachting, The Times, 27th June 1932.

[1099] The Badminton Library of Sports and Pastimes: Yachting, Volume 1, The Evolution of the Modern Racing Yacht, G. L. Watson, 1894.

[1100] Uffa Fox's Second Book, Uffa Fox, 1935.

[1101] Overall, including the 3-ton cutter, 10-tonner and the 8-metre, Fred J. Stephen sailed his own designs in approximately 670 races over four decades, winning some 440 prizes, of which 256 were firsts.

[1102] The more egalitarian Royal Clyde had shipbuilder John Scott as Commodore from 1895 to his death in 1903. And he followed another man 'in trade', thread manufacturer, John Clark, who held the office 1887-1894.

[1103] The Passing of Mr F. J. Stephen, Scottish News, The Yachtsman, 24th December 1932.

Calanthe, Fred J. Stephen, 1897   Image: Clydeships

Emerald, Fred J. Stephen, 1902   Image: Clydeships

British-American Cup Team, 1922   Image: press photo

Coila, 3-tonner, Fred J. Stephen, 1886   Image: W. J. Finlayson

Medea, Fred J. Stephen, 1904. Note Hydrogap rudder.   Image: Clydeships
See next page: The initial identifiers for the International Rule were letters as it was first thought that numbers (recently introduced) may have led to confusion. The 6mRs used the letter 'L'. 8mR used 'H', 12mR used 'E', 15mR used 'D' and 19mR used 'C'.

Fred J. Stephen, 1863-1932   *Coila II*, 1908 original configuration

Coila II (substantial mods), 6-metre, Fred J. Stephen, 1911   Image: Stephen Family Archive

Coila III, Fred J. Stephen, 1922   Image: Stephen of Linthouse

Coila III fetching fast with a big jib and a reefed main   Image: Stephen Family Archive
Note the mast has been moved aft and there is a new rig with a much taller foretriangle.

Coila IV, F. J. Stephen,1927   Stephen Family Archive

Clio, William Fife III, the Stephen Family's 'mothership'   Stephen Family Archive

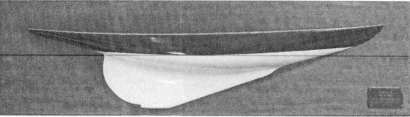

Coila III, 2nd Rule 6mR, Fred J. Stephen, 1922, (note painted WL in error)   RNCYC Collection

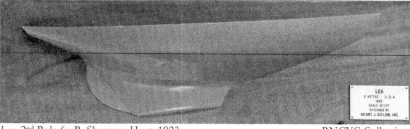

Lea, 2nd Rule 6mR, Sherman Hoyt, 1923   RNCYC Collection

It is hard to believe the model-maker has portrayed *Lea* accurately, re freeboard and body depth. Sherman Hoyt was a partner in Henry J. Gielow Inc. Olin Stephen worked as a draftsman for that firm.

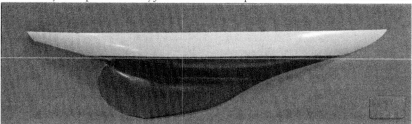

Lanai, 6mR, 2nd Rule Clinton Crane, 1925   RNCYC Collection

Lacking only an elegant sheer, *Lanai's* underbody presages the modern 6mR – unbeatable in her era.

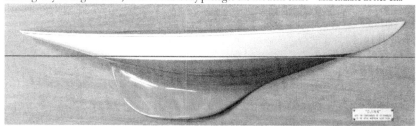

Djinn, 3rd Rule 6mR, Olin Stephen, 1938 (note painted WL in error)   RNCYC Collection

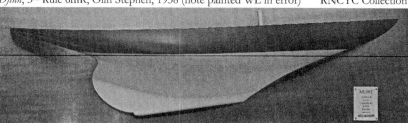

Coila IV, 8-metre, Fred J. Stephen, 1927   RNCYC Collection

Chapter 28: John G. Stephen and his Crystal Ball

In the bustled form of her afterbody Maida II predates the work of Mario Tarabocchia at S&S (12mR Intrepid etc) by some 27 years. It might be considered that the Maida II hull shape development and the advent of the wing keel in 1983 were, apart from the availability of new materials, the two most significant developments in yacht design over the last century. Ian Howlett[1104]

John G. Stephen (1894-1970) stepped into the spotlight in 1922 as skipper of *Coila III*, a new 6mR, designed by his father, Fred J. Stephen. Fred was unable to sail *Coila III* during her first season. Just before *Coila III* was launched, Fred missed his footing and fell to the ground from deck-level. A deep-keeled 6-metre sits high on its cradle, so the fall was a bad one; he broke four ribs, puncturing his lungs. Young John took over the helmsman's role, and throughout the 1922 season sailed the boat as well as his father would have done, or perhaps even a little better.

During that successful year with *Coila III*, John became famous for a tall tale told at his expense by his British American Cup teammates. As the story goes, 'Wee' John and the *Coila III* crew were engrossed in a game of golf and had to be pressured into representing the Royal Northern. The diminutive skipper was threatened *"under penalty of being held down in his bath"*.[1105] Late Victorian bath-times must have recalled untold childhood terrors as John struck his game face and lifted the famous trophy with consummate ease. Moreover, he would go on to become a serial winner of the Seawanhaka Trophy for club and country.

John G. Stephen is classed in these pages as another 'gentleman' designer, but like the rest, he was not exactly an amateur. He was a qualified naval architect, with considerable experience working in the family yard, designing ships and supervising ship construction. When John brought these same skills to bear on racing yachts, it was clear that he had inherited his father's grasp of form, and as a first-class metre-boat sailor he had no shortage of ideas on what made a fast boat. The very best sailors can often modify and 'mode' a boat to go faster than the naval architect responsible for its design. John wore both hats.

"Designers who have been producing yachts under a particular rating rule for a number of years are not likely to make any radical departure from their preconceived

ideas when creating new boats, but one who is fresh to the job approaches the problem with a virgin mind and the result may be a craft of quite novel type. To take a case in point Maida, we think, was Mr John Stephen's first 6-metre boat and in her he created a craft of most original design. She is quite unlike any other yacht hitherto produced under the International rule and possesses many novel features. Yet she proved one of the most successful yachts of her rating of the year, finishing the season at the head of her class and being selected to defend the Seawanhaka Cup."[1106]

John Stephen would surely have equalled, or perhaps surpassed, his father's success had WW2 not intervened. But there is no doubting his vision and capacity for innovation. John's work challenged the status quo and prefigured the next 30 years of yacht design under the International Rule. He rejected his father's conservative, incremental approach. His left-field design philosophy vaulted conventional development paths. The professional designers in practice on the Clyde during the immediate pre-WW2 war period must have envied his freedom. Unfortunately, however, John 'ran out of runway' to develop his ideas.

John G. Stephen began his design career at the age of nineteen. In 1913, the three Stephen boys – Alexander Murray, and the twins, James Howie Fredric and John Graeme, built *Midge*, an International 3-metre yacht, in the stables of the family home. Robert Bruce, the professional skipper of *Coila II*, sharpened the chisels and kept the lads on track. The *Midge* build replicated a similar DIY project undertaken by the boys' father and uncle in the 1880s. That project was also supervised by the family's professional skipper, but this time round the tyro boatbuilders were young men and more ambitious.

While 172 of the 'Nicholson Rule' 4-metre class (23ft LOA) have been built and the class is now enjoying a resurgence on the Swiss lakes, it seems that no other 3mRs were built.[1107] *Midge* was an elegant little yacht, smaller than a Pleiade, but better-looking, with long ends on a waterline of perhaps 12ft. She looks to be about 17ft LOA. She had a small, deep cockpit amidships and so was likely built with a full-keel, rather than a bolt-on fin. In an old image, the miniature yacht carries her sail well and moves through the water with little fuss. *Midge* would have been a valuable 'apprenticeship'.

There is a sad coda to this precocious joint venture. Of the three boat-daft boys, just two survived to take over directorships in the family firm. John's brother, James, was killed in action during the advance on Baghdad in January 1917, while the twins were with the Highland Light Infantry in Mesopotamia. James was just 22 years old, and one of 15 officers and 200 men killed that day. For a Great War battle, the proportion of officers fighting hand-to-hand and dying with their men was unusually high. Alexander, always known as 'Murray' in a family with generations of

Alexanders, became Chairman in 1932. John G. Stephen would remain as a director, 'hands-on' in the design office and on the shop floor.

Despite having helmed the boat when she first won the Seawanhaka Cup, in the United States in 1922, John Stephen dutifully crewed for his father, along with his elder brother Murray and the boat's regular crew of cronies and camp-followers, during the successful matches against the American *Lea* in 1923, and *Unni* of Norway in 1924. He crewed for his father again in 1925 when they lost the Cup to *Lanai*, as described in the previous chapter. John Stephen also blagged himself aboard both *Caryl* and *Saskia* for the 8-metre matches of 1929 and 1931. In total, he would participate in seven matches for the famous old trophy.

It is ironic, and more than a little surprising, that Fife, whose name was synonymous with the development of the 6mR class, failed to record a Seawanhaka Cup win in 6-metres to cap the consistent success of his designs. Indeed, following decades of dominance by boats from Fairlie, the great Charles E. Nicholson dubbed the 6-metre the 'Fife Class'. In these circumstances, it must have rankled that the main prize remained elusive.

Fortunately for the Fife legend, his 8-metres justified the hype. W. F. Robertson's *Caryl* recovered the Seawanhaka Cup for the Royal Northern from Frank Paine's *Gypsy* in 1929. Despite the existence of a good competitive fleet on the Clyde, *Caryl* was selected while still in-build at Fairlie. Pre-selection is not always a successful strategy, but it was one that worked on this occasion. Fife must have condescended to engage in some intense lobbying.

The Seawanhaka Corinthian Yacht Club sent over *Priscilla III* in 1931. She was defeated by *Saskia*, a 1930 Fife 8mR, in four straight races.[1108] Clinton Crane, who designed *Priscilla III*, was still designing fast boats, but it is fair to say that this challenge was an altogether more relaxed affair than Crane's exemplary campaign of 1925 with Sherman Hoyt, described in the previous chapter.

John deferred to his father until 1932. In that year, he conceived the radical 6 Metre, *Maida*, built at the family's Linthouse yard and owned in partnership with James Napier and the ebullient Charles McAndrew.[1109] *Maida* was disappointing in the early season before John Stephen was able to take charge of his new design. Her subsequent form was remarkable, particularly in fresh winds, and she finished the season at the head of the rankings with the best of the averages.

Maida is best known for losing the Seawanhaka Cup in 1932. However, like all binary sporting events, the nuances of the defeat are now forgotten. *Maida's* series against Olin Stephen's *Jill* was closely fought and arguably lost on sail design rather than hull-form. In any event, she was certainly not outclassed. During a close-fought series of racing, the lead changed frequently, and *Maida* was usually first to the weather mark.[1110] With a little more breeze, she could have had the advantage.[1111]

"Throughout the series the Scottish boat seemed to have a slight edge on Jill on the wind, but off the wind and particularly in running, Jill was markedly superior."[1112] This 'slight edge to windward' is hugely impressive when we remember that Olin Stephens and Briggs Cunningham were pulling the strings on *Jill*. *"To provide direction to his Six Metre developments JGS trialled sailing models at the model yacht Class scale of 1:7.2 (such were referred to as the 'Wee Sixes' in the 1930's) on the open water of nearby lochs. This work led to the design of Maida in 1931 as recounted in the Model Yachtsman of December 1931."* Ian Howlett[1113]

Looking at *Maida's* lines today; her fine performance scotches any conjecture that scow bows were the kiss-of-death in that era, as universally declared when David Boyd's *Sceptre* was unveiled to a sceptical yachting press.[1114] Clearly, by this stage in the game John Stephen had overcome his childhood aquaphobia, as to the untutored eye, *Maida* resembles nothing so much as a bathtub. Indeed, to extend the Seawanhaka Cup bath-tub analogy, John hijacked bath-time and reinvented it as only a wealthy man of scientific and artistic bent could have imagined.

Maida is still sailing today, and she still appears radical. The stem runs in a straight line from the knuckle above the waterline to the foot of the keel – there is no toe, like Fred Stephen's *Coila III*. This form maximises draft and allows a tight turn of the bilge under the 2nd Rule. The vestigial chin on *Coila III* is extended to form a slim, yet pronounced, bulb just below the waterline. On deck, *Maida's* hull is very full forward of the mast and the counter is long, and very fine. However, beneath the water, the entry and the run are balanced, and the diagonals are sweet. The curve of sectional areas (upright and at an angle heel of 35 degrees) are virtually identical, promoting exceptional balance. The heeled (static) waterplane at 35 degrees is almost symmetrical about a fore and aft axis, which is an aim of scow-type underbodies.

The sternpost hung rudder, cut-away at the waterline, swells to a great paddle at its foot. The oversize blade addresses the usual complement of functions in an unusual balance. The rudder-blade completes the aerofoil section of the keel-foot; it provides significant lateral resistance, and almost incidentally, it steers the boat, see Appendix 1. My old mentor, the late Peter Collyer, a marine engineer and boatbuilder, sailed on *Maida* as a young man and retained a special fondness for this most idiosyncratic of boats, a sentiment which I can well understand.[1115]

During the Great War, while the Stephen's shipyard was primarily focussed on building and repairing warships, the joiners' shop at Linthouse also played a significant role. They mass-produced almost 500 aircraft in association with J. Weir Ltd of Cathcart. These aircraft, delivered from 1915, restored the Royal Flying Corp's air superiority over the Germans.[1116] Since we have digressed to the Great War, we might also note that the model-makers workshop built 2,175 artificial feet and ankles in beechwood for disabled veterans. Truly if you can build a ship, you can build anything. The craftsmen at Linthouse were as skilled as any boatbuilders on the Clyde, but *Maida* was the last racing yacht built there.

John Stephen's first *Maida* is the only example of his work to have survived, but she was not his only design, nor by any means his most significant. John also designed two innovative 3rd Rule 6-metres which were arguably ground-breaking. Both would disappoint, but that in no way limits their importance, or their unacknowledged influence on yacht design. James McGruer-built *Eyra* for the Donaldson family in 1935, and *Maida II* for John Stephen himself in 1939. Both, as would be expected from the Clynder boatyard, were meticulously detailed.

The 3rd International Rule of 1933 dropped 'G' girth, leaving only 'd' (girth difference), which encouraged designers to increase draft and build bulbed keels.[1117] Girth difference was not measured around the keel, but to a point 'A', located 12.5% of the class rating below the waterline (about 2ft in a 6mR). The increase in righting moment allowed a reduction in beam. Less beam meant fuller ends, redistributing displaced volume from the mid-sections and increasing the prismatic coefficient. John Stephen's radical 6mR, *Eyra*, just 5ft 4" wide with a full underbody forward, led to the minimum beam stipulation advocated in 1937 by Alfred Mylne.

Third International Rule, (1933 to present[1118])

$$R \text{ (metres)} = \frac{L + 2d + \sqrt{S} - F}{2.37}$$

where… L = length (as calculated)
d = difference between skin girth and chain girth
S = sail area
F = freeboard

Minimum beam at 1ft per linear metre of rated length was introduced in September 1937

John Stephen's take on the 3rd Rule was quite radical. Worldwide, there were just four 6-metres built with a fin-and-skeg underbody prior to WW2. Two 3rd Rule boats: John Stephen's *Eyra* of 1935 and *Maida II* of 1939; and two 2nd Rule boats: *Aurora* by Glen-Coats, built at the Bute Slip Dock back in 1921, and *Josephine,* built by White of Southampton to a design by W. J. Daniels five years later in 1926, as described in Appendix 1.

As far as we are aware, none of these yachts benefitted from tank-testing, but all were informed by empirical research with free-sailing models. John Stephen built at least three models to test against a successful 'reference' design which was winning on the model 6mR circuit. Previously, both Glen-Coats and W. J. Daniels had pioneered the same development process. As might be expected with any new design direction, the fin-and-skeg boats did not represent a breakthrough on the racecourse, at least in their first season. They all failed to live up to expectations, but that was not the end of the story, more the beginning.

Josephine was the subject of a feature in *Yachting Monthly* following her difficult first season.[1119] Daniels' experiments are cited in a 1998 analysis of the fin-and-skeg development path by Ian Howlett.[1120] She was launched with a full-keel – setting the lead low-down, with the keel-foot parallel to the waterline. Behind this, a small, separate 'paddle-type' rudder, similar to the turn of the century rater, was hung off a vestigial skeg. With *Josephine's* fin-and-skeg configuration, the keel chord is not significantly reduced, although the trailing edge is partially cut-away. Subsequently, *Josephine* was rebuilt with a more conventional, triangular underwater profile, resembling the Fife sixes. She was not much faster in this form.[1121] The Stephen designs and the Glen-Coats design, described in Chapter 27, fared better.

After the mixed fortunes of the inter-war pioneers, it was not until 1950 that another 6mR appeared with an unconventional underbody. Uffa Fox designed the 6mR, *Noroda*, for F. G. 'Tiny' Mitchell. *Noroda* was an outlier in design, heavy-displacement, but styled like an old light-displacement rater, with a fin-keel and spade rudder.[1122] Uffa's enduring enthusiasm for his highly swept-back foils speaks more to his quaint jet-age vision of progress than any discernible attempt to address the function of foils.

Noroda unsettled the Americans, albeit only for a moment. *"Uffa Fox, a brilliant, puckish fellow who combines a love of the spectacular with the gift of genius, has not been content to rest on the laurels brought him by his Flying Fifteens. Embodying the same principle of cutaway fin keel and long run, he has nearly completed construction of a Flying Six Metre which promises to dynamite that super-refined, virtually one-design class into a hundred magnificent pieces."* This 'promise' was prudently ventured under an alias.[1123]

Spun Yarn's intemperate plunge into Uffa-like hyperbole was a mistake. *Noroda* was an unmitigated disaster that would damage Uffa's fragile reputation as a yacht designer and threaten the sustainability of his business. The new Six broached all over the Solent and became downright uncontrollable in a proper blow. Beside *Maida II*, which the Americans ignored entirely, *Noroda* hardly looked like a vessel designed by a man with *"the gift of genius"*.[1124]

Maida II was the third *Maida* in the Stephen family, but, while retaining the name, 'Wee' John numbered his 6-metres without regard to his father's 10-rater of 1890. To compound the muddle, John's *Maida I* and *Maida II* both carried the sail-number 6-K1, with *Maida I* somehow retrieving 6-K1 after *Maida II*'s racing days were over.[1125] This perplexing nomenclature may have contributed to the ground-breaking *Maida II* slipping below the radar in more recent years. But really, there is no excuse; when we consider the high points of Scotland's long and proud yachting heritage, the design of *Maida II* warrants a star.

Eyra was John Stephen's first fin-and-skeg design in 1935. Seen at launch, *Eyra* had a deep fine entry, with a pronounced stem and a slight clipper bow with considerable volume below the waterline. And, with the shroud base spread on 19th century channels, above the waterline the boat recalls the old 2½-raters. "*She is a particularly narrow boat, her extreme beam of 5ft 5" being over a foot less than the average width of a 6-metre.*"

"*She has a fin-and-bulb keel and a streamline rudder, but the most noticeable feature of all is the shape of her bow, which is modelled on the style of a modern liner. Instead of coming to a sharp point it is well rounded, especially at deck level where it looks more like a counter than a bow.*"[1126] The aft end of the underbody terminated with a pronounced 'bustle' and a complex faired-in rudder, featuring an odd shark-fin plate extension projecting beneath the bustle-line.

This was the first bustle seen on a Six under the International Rule and was prefigured only by the Royal Corinthian Five-metre class, *Mutt*, designed by C. E. Nicholson.[1127] "*The latest experiment has been the adoption by Mutt of a rudder of the Oertz type. Since adopting it, the boat has done extremely well and there seem great possibilities in this stream-lined rudder, which is actually part of the keel. We believe that a similar rudder was tried in the Clyde on the Six-metre boat Eyra, a craft of revolutionary design which has hitherto proved a failure.*"[1128] John Stephen was clearly inspired by the promise of the 'Oertz-type' rudder.[1129]

Eyra is so radical, and antithetical to the shallow scow entries on John's successful *Maida* of 1932, and indeed his later *Maida II* of 1939, that her owners, the Donaldson brothers, must have contributed to the concept. They were after all a knowledgeable and successful racing family. Perhaps inevitably, *Eyra*'s performance on the water was erratic. Uffa Fox reported that: "*John Stephen designed another 6-metre which was a clean break-away from the accepted shape. This daring effort to produce something entirely new in a 6-metre design failed, for she would not go to windward. This boat had a Bremen bow, and a built-on fin keel.*"[1130] John's experiments with the *Bremen* bow no doubt reflected his 'day job' building real ships. The *Bremen* was a German liner, built in 1929 with a bulbous bow incorporated within a conventional forefoot.

Novel bows are rare in the 6mR class, and for good reason, but Paul Elvstrom and Jan Kjaerulf's 1975 6mR, *Prince Alfred,* was another to break the mould, or more accurately, attempt to. This boat had a fairly normal cut-away entry, but with a long torpedo-like bulb seemingly grafted on just below the waterline. Such an appendage can only be effective in flat water and, of course all metre-boats pitch a bit. In any event, *Prince Alfred's* canoe body and the bulb did not work in concert and the gratuitous 'carbuncle' was soon removed.

The 1935 season did not begin well for *Eyra*. She was withdrawn from competition after her first few races and returned to McGruer's for major alterations. A few weeks later, she was in the shed again for more surgery. But these efforts to improve her performance ultimately came to naught. The Donaldsons borrowed *Maida* back from Lt. Col. Kenneth Barge, her new owner, to salvage their season. At the same time, they commissioned *Nike* from James McGruer for delivery later in the year. *Nike* would carry K 48, the same sail number as *Eyra*, but with considerably more success.

This left the field to what Uffa described as *"the standard and accepted type of 6-metres"*. Uffa continued: *"This shows that the rule favours the more or less standard type, and this type makes a good and serviceable boat for all purposes."*[1131] There is a note in the 1936 Lloyd's Register that *Eyra* was scheduled to be broken-up, but she was rescued by Robert Birrell in 1937 and repurposed as a pocket-cruiser. Robert would retain ownership of the boat through the war years until 1948, after which date, she disappears from the record.

Uffa noted: *"Many 6-metres are converted into little cruisers by the addition of a cabin top. With their easily driven and fast hulls they do not require an engine, as they ghost along in the lightest of airs, and their rather heavy displacement enables them to smash their way to windward even when it is blowing hard."* Of course, 6-metres are not ideal cruisers; they are narrow and cramped, perpetually damp at sea and require significant maintenance. Nevertheless, they gave their owners great pleasure. In this way, significant numbers survived until the renaissance of the class in the mid-1980s when the resources became available to restore the boats to their original racing trim.[1132]

Eyra's main impact on the sport was unrelated to her radical underbody. At the September 1937 meeting of the IYRU, Alfred Mylne called for pre-emptive action on the trend to ever narrower Sixes as *"there seemed to be a great possibility of objectionably narrow boats being built, should the minimum beam not be restricted.* He reported that his technical committee had *"thrashed the matter out, and their final decision was that the minimum beams should be 1ft per metre of linear rating"*. This was adopted for yachts built after that date and still applies to classes racing under the International Rule.[1133]

With *Maida II*, four years later in 1939, John Stephen incorporated the lessons learned from both *Maida* and *Eyra* and his extensive comparative testing with free-sailing models. *Maida II* appeared revolutionary, but her designer would have been realistic in his expectations; she was just another step along this particular development path. Unfortunately, WW2 intervened. But that year, the new boat was well-received by an enthusiastic press. *"The event which makes the 1939 6-Metre season of outstanding interest to designers is the debut of J. G. Stephen's 6mR Maida II."* [1134]

This initial optimism was based more on the pedigree of successful fin-and-skeg underbodies on model yachts by the Stephen family than the experience with *Eyra*. "*There is reason to expect the shorter keel to be a more efficient hydrofoil than that of the ordinary Six and so to reduce leeway. This is just what is claimed happens in models of this profile type. The illustration shows Maida II to be a remarkably good-looking craft.*"[1135] It was generally recognised that, while *Maida II* may have measured in as an ordinary 6mR, aesthetically, she was in a class of her own.

Maida II, like *Maida* before her, is a fine example of a metacentric shelf design, as noted in *Yachting Monthly*: "*In an earlier article it was stated that the extent to which she conforms to the metacentric shelf principle was not known at the time of that writing. Through the courtesy of her designer, it can now be stated that she conforms strictly to it.* Rear-Admiral Alfred Turner's 'metacentric shelf formula' was conceived to achieve good balance when heeled.[1136] John Stephen's design ethos favoured full scow-like entries and fine run, which did indeed produce a balanced and nicely extended heeled waterline, as in the lines of *Maida*, his first 6-metre design. And now with *Maida II*, beneath these fine aft waterlines, John had worked in a refinement of the bustle he had pioneered in the radical *Eyra* in 1935.

In Britain, amateur designer, Dr. Harrison Butler, is perhaps most closely associated with the principle, producing well-mannered boats in an age when biceps-building weather helm was not just tolerated, but often made virtue of. Now debunked, even the word 'metacentric' raises a smile today. However, as with skinning cats, there are other ways to draw hull lines which achieve the same end; that is to say, a consistent balanced feel on the helm, which is substantially unaffected by degrees of heel.

The *Yachting Monthly* review also made reference to the novel forward profile: "*We may note also that the forward profile, in its slight convexity near the waterline, is a departure, if a less noticeable one, from the stock form.*[1137] The article continued: "*however, we look at her, one must feel that her designer has performed a really notable service to the progress of yacht design.*"[1138] As events transpired, this 'noble service' was squandered. In 1939, Britain and her naval architects had more to concern themselves with than a possible revolution in racing yacht design. *Maida II* was launched at the worst possible time. However, while this limited her influence on contemporary design, it does not reduce her overall significance.

Maida II was a stunningly modern-looking boat for the period. While she was not particularly fast out of the box, her performance improved incrementally during this first season, particularly after her underwater profile was modified.[1139] Many years later (sailing as *Fane*), she would prove to be a competitive 6mR. She is remarkable for having been conceived in the 1930s, fully formed as a late 20th century yacht. This was decades before any useful precedent that might have informed the design, and decades before tank testing guided designers in that direction. All in all, it is hard to believe that 'Wee' John did not have a crystal ball!

During the hiatus of WW2, British yacht design stagnated, and in some respects, regressed. Meanwhile, in America, as in WW1, domestic innovation was uninterrupted. US rigs enjoyed the technological spin-offs from defence investment, but US naval architects missed a chance when they failed to reap the intellectual capital that John Stephen and *Maida II* had placed in the public domain. The Americans did not catch up for 28 years and it would take our yacht designers even longer. However, when they did, a general enthusiasm for all things transatlantic meant that they deferred to Olin Stephens as the pioneer of this revolution in yacht design, not John Stephen.

Nevertheless, Olin Stephens' 12-metre, *Intrepid*, of 1967, the benchmark design for fin and skeg underbodies, was prefigured in all important respects by *Maida II*. Olin Stephens' people were in Britain with *Vim* in 1939, so he may have heard about *Maida II* through the grapevine. All we know is that, almost thirty years later, he incorporated a bustle, or 'kicker' as he christened it, in the lines of *Intrepid*.

Olin Stephens recognised that his practice had not invented *Intrepid's* fin-keel and separate rudder configuration. He acknowledged the raters of the 1890s, and Dick Carter's ocean-racer *Rabbit* of 1965[1140], although curiously, he failed to credit Ricus Van de Stadt's 41ft 3" offshore flyer, *Zeevalk*, which demonstrated the viability of both the trim-tab and spade rudder in 1949.[1141] However, these three types are designed around a clean canoe-body with a discrete fin-keel and a spade rudder.[1142] Rummaging through the history of yacht design, the only useful precedents for the *Intrepid* model are *Maida II* and *Eyra*, even if Olin Stephens may have been unaware of this.

In 1939, the year of *Maida II's* launch, David Boyd's *Circe* was still the top 6-metre on the Clyde. *Circe* was a highly evolved example, optimised within a time-worn concept. Looking at the lines of the two boats, side by side, *Maida II* appears 30-years ahead of her time. But, for John Stephen, the experiment had run its course and it was time to move on. After WW2, *Maida II* was sold locally and rechristened *Fane*. She did not figure in the Clyde race results, but, since she had struggled to realise her potential even in the designer's hands this was not surprising.

All that changed during the late forties and early fifties when *Fane* was sold south. Under the skilled stewardship of Lt-Col. R. S. G. (Stug) Perry and J. Dudley Head, *Fane* began to 'hit her numbers' on the Solent. Glyn Foulkes writes: *"My father was a 6mR skipper on the Solent from 1929 to 1948. His last charge was Fane which Col. Stug Perry bought that year (1948)."* We understand that she certainly wasn't a class-breaker, but with time, effort and patience, the incremental gains began to accumulate. Eventually, Perry brought *Fane* up to the level of the best conventional models like *Circe*, then top boat in the Solent, and to which she ran a close second.[1143]

While 'Stug' Perry had a reputation as a martinet, he was certainly one of the country's best skippers. When trialling for the helmsman's spot aboard *Sceptre* in 1957, Perry had the measure of Graham Mann, but stepped aside. He dipped out again in 1964. One suspects he knew the prospect of success in America on both these occasions was limited. After excusing himself from the America's Cup, Perry took the Boyd 6mR, *Royal Thames*, over to Norway in 1958 and won the One Ton Cup in Hankø.[1144]

The changes made to *Fane* during this period were not major, but they enabled her to catch up with the 20-year start which conventional Sixes enjoyed in terms of design evolution. It is not yet known whether John Stephen or another naval architect was responsible for the makeover. While Hugh Somerville suggests that the rudder was replaced during her first season, it is more likely, however, that the modifications described, both above and below the waterline were later and concurrent.

Fane's long ends were cropped beyond the fore and aft measurement stations. Perhaps 2ft 2" was cropped from the counter and about 4" from the stem; the latter probably just to balance the revised aesthetic. These changes above the waterline look dramatic but would have delivered limited benefits in terms of performance. The reduction of weight in the ends does, of course, reduce the moment of gyration, although in this case the new rudder would have offset that to an extent. After being remodelled, *Fane* was no longer the longest 6mR afloat, but at 37ft 4" similar to her peers and the immediate post-war generation of 6mRs.

Underwater, the most obvious change was the addition of a new rudder with a surprisingly modern profile presaging the 1987 generation 12mRs, and now ubiquitous on high performance yachts. The new rudder was set further aft and faired-in behind the original blade position. With *Intrepid*, Olin Stephens tucked his under-sized rudder blade behind the bustle, like John Stephen, because he had an aversion to 'cutting the water twice'. Olin's 'cutting the water' theory is honoured in the breach these days, as designers equip their designs with more appendages than a Swiss Army knife.

Olin Stephens would also have to accept blades extending below the bustle as a real-world trade-off between rudder area and rudder angle. With

Olin's early Twelves of this configuration, the tucked-away rudder could be 'clutched in' with a large trim-tab when tacking and to facilitate pre-start manoeuvring, being then 'clutched out' to balance the boat upwind. This requires a world-class helmsman; see Chapter 30 concerning the same rudder issues on Olin's 1971 6mR, *Gosling*, for Erik Maxwell.

> The trim-tab was one of many thoughtful innovations propagated by Ricus Van de Stadt in his light-displacement, hard-chine offshore designs during the 1950s. Dick Carter adapted the Van de Stadt appendage model to a more conventional canoe-body in 1964 with his *Rabbit* and *Tina* designs.[1145] It is interesting, however, that Carter remained unconvinced that the trim-tab's benefits outweighed the increased complexity incurred. Moreover, he found that even very small angles tended to steer the boat, rather than increase lift over the fin-keel. *Fane* did not have a trim-tab, and with her initial small 'tab' rudder set-up, would have been difficult to steer, requiring speed-sapping angles to follow the breeze. The new rudder was a gamechanger.

It appears that 1" was added to *Fane's* draft. This would have brought her draft to 5ft 4" – the industry standard of that generation. She would, in any event, have been retrimmed after the weight reduction programme and the minor underwater changes. The 728 lbs of lead that were removed from the keel in 1939 were reinstated.

After her racing career was over, *Fane* sailed through the decades as a stylish cruiser. In 1965, she was re-rigged as a yawl, and no doubt missed that long counter to stay the mizzen. After many years based on the South Coast, *Fane*, now sailing as *Fern*, returned to Scotland. *Maida II* (*Fane*, *Fern*) one of the most advanced pre-war designs of any stripe, was broken-up after being sunk in Strangford Lough by 'Hurricane Charlie' in August 1986.

Sam Chamberlin of Brion Rieff Boatbuilders (Maine USA) considered the Stephen design as a potential replica project in 2008.[1146] Roger Mander obtained the lines from the late David Stephen (John Stephen's son), redrew the lines in CAD and built a model. The team at Brion Rieff Boats know what they are doing, so it would be a fine thing if this rebuild was ever commissioned, with the *Fane* underbody 'corrections' of course.[1147]

Yachts Designed by John G. Stephen

	Name	Type	Designer	Builder	Year	TM
1	Maida	6-metre	John G. Stephen	Alex Stephen	1932	3
2	Eyra	6-metre	John G. Stephen	McGruer	1935	3
3	Maida II	6-metre	John G. Stephen	McGruer	1939	3

While just three designs are listed here, it is illuminating to note that *Maida's* design drawings are marked: 6 Metre Yacht Design No.536 – just another job in the design office of a large commercial shipyard. John G. Stephen challenged orthodoxy. He had confidence in his ideas and his ability. For example, his masts were back-to-front with the aerofoil reversed – narrow at the leading edge and with a blunt trailing edge.[1148]

Maida II was launched with a gaff-headed, short foot, Bermudian mainsail on a mast 3ft longer than standard, prefiguring the square-top mains which are de-rigueur today. The gaff was about 'half-beam', or 3ft long, and extended at right angles from the mast. This set-up required a five-panel rig, with two sets of jumper struts. The lower set was by way of the hounds and must have chewed up any number of spinnaker halyards.

The innovative rig stepped in *Maida II* at launch made it difficult to identify which elements were speeding the boat up, and which were slowing it down. This temptation to try everything at once is the kiss of death when two boat testing, as every racing skipper who arranges to line up with a 'buddy' knows only too well. *"As well as being a bold experiment in hull design in giving a very promising system a real trial, Maida is trying a notable variation in rig which would certainly seem worth separate notice. Mark the shortness of the main boom. There are thus in her make-up two unknowns which may have to be isolated. It is well to remember this.*[1149]

Despite showing some promise, the gaff-headed main was soon replaced by a conventional Bermudian sail. The square-top was ahead of its time; wooden spars and cotton sailcloth compromised the concept. However, better materials were already in prospect. The 12mR, *Vim*, appeared in British waters in 1939 with a Duralumin mast, resembling that of *Enterprise* in 1930, but while such materials were already available to the aircraft industry in Britain, they were a bridge too far for the 6-metre fleet.[1150]

We discuss the history of Scottish tank tests in Chapter 6, where the pioneering work of Fred J. Stephen in the condenser-tank at Linthouse, and later in the firm's purpose-built tank, is described. However, the test-tank experiments of his son were also intriguing. John was clearly inspired by the 'junkyard wars' fought by his father and took the fight into his back garden in the 1960s. John's donut test-tank was fatally flawed, but of course the inventor himself knew that and went with the flow, as it were. His system, like David Napier's a century before, allowed an informed rule-of-thumb type of analysis.

Imagine an 'endless' tank, about 50ft in diameter, looped to resemble a giant donut. Quite bizarrely, the test rig was fixed, and the water was driven around the tank at a constant speed. With this system, the duration of a test-run was infinite as it was not constrained by the length of the tank.[1151] Moreover, the analyst could observe a dynamic test sitting tank-side in a camp-chair. Initially, the circular flow was driven by a single Seagull outboard motor.[1152] However, this proved insufficiently powerful, and a second motor was added, sited opposite. Unfortunately, no images or drawings of this phase of the work have survived.

The British Seagull company of Poole in Dorset, manufactured two-stroke outboards engines from the early 1930s until the mid-1990s. The Seagull outboards were designed by John Way-Hope and Bill Pinninger. Their iconic unshrouded motors were marketed, perhaps tongue-in-cheek, as *"The Best Outboard in the World"*, then, in times of more rigorous advertising standards, as *"The Best Outboard Motor for the World"*. The hand-wound starting-cord was lethal. These engines were famous for being rugged and long-lasting, which in practice meant that new motors were as difficult to start and as unreliable as old ones.

A second version of John Stephen's circular test-tank used racks of waterjets applied to the surface to minimise underwater turbulence. This seems to have been the definitive version, as used ca.1961-1964, referencing dates on the old home-movies of the tests. A more conventional alternative, employing a radial arm-mounted test carriage, like the rotating booms over circular sewerage treatment lagoons, appears not to have been built. With the water at rest and the model in motion, this would have ensured a cleaner flow over the test models.[1153]

The circular flow, stationary carriage set-up was easy to monitor and facilitated the use of an underwater camera to observe flow as mapped by streamers taped to the leading edge of the underwater surfaces. This Heath Robinson apparatus offered intriguing possibilities for interactive testing. If you can put up with the racket of a couple of naked Seagulls thundering in the background, you can tinker to your heart's content. You can manipulate models 'at your desk', for example, increase displacement, and alter angle-of-heel, angle-of-attack and fore-and-aft trim, all with an eye on the spring dynamometer to measure resistance and see how it changes.

The donut tank must have provided useful insights, but no more than that. John Stephen was well aware that you want to measure anything with any level of consistency, it is essential to work in the controlled circumstances of a towed model in a linear tank, indoors with constant temperature and barometric pressure. The late David Stephen inherited five of the models his father used for testing. These are 6-metre sailing models, built at the $1^2/_3$" to 1ft.[1154] The 6m model class are about 5ft long and weigh in at 20lbs. These were also tested free-sailing and the home videos of these show that sail shapes and combinations were being evaluated too.[1155]

[1104] Ian Howlett, correspondence with the author, May 2019.
[1105] A Shipbuilding History, 1750-1932 (Alexander Stephen & Sons) Grace's Guide.
[1106] From the Man at the Wheel, The Yachtsman & Motorboating, 5th November 1932.
[1107] The 4mRs are known as the 15m² class. The formula developed for the class by Charles

Nicholson in 1949 deviates from the International Rule. These are highly desirable yachts today. The Pleiade was also a 15²-metre class, but was sailed in Scotland as a one-design.

[1108] *Caryl* beat Frank Paine's *Gypsy* and *Saskia* beat Clinton Crane's *Priscilla III*. *Saskia*, a 1930 Fife design, was a slimmer and deeper development of Fife's 1928 *Caryl*.

[1109] *Maida* was rigged and launched at McGruer's, confusing the yachting press.

[1110] Seawanhaka Cup Contest, Aberdeen Journal, 19th August 1932.

[1111] From the Man at the Wheel, Yachtsman & Motorboating, 8th October 1932.

[1112] Jill brings Seawanhaka Cup home, Yachting, October 1932.

[1113] Ian Howlett; correspondence with the author, May 2019.

[1114] The Model Yachtsman, January 1933.

[1115] *Maida*, Fife's 1920 6 Metre *Caryl* and Clinton Crane's 1925 *Lanai* were tested as free-sailing models. *Caryl* and *Lanai* were pretty close, but *Maida* was found to be quicker.

[1116] Stephen of Linthouse, a Record of Two Hundred Years of Shipbuilding – 1750-1950, published by Alex Stephen & Sons Ltd, John L. Carvel, 1951.

[1117] In the 3rd Rule, 'girth' 'G' (1/4G) was dropped, leaving 'girth difference' 'd' (2d) in the rating formula – d is the difference between skin girth, measured against the skin of the boat at the designated sections, versus chain girth when the tape is stretched tight and bridges the hollow at the garboards.

[1118] The First International Rule ran from 1907 to 1919, the 2nd Rule from 1919 to 1933 and the 3rd Rule has been employed with some changes since 1933. The current definition of length is: *"The length 'L' for the formula shall be the length measured at a height of 90mm above the L.W.L. plus one and one-half times the difference between the chain girth at the bow section, measured to points 300mm above 'L' and twice the vertical height from 'L' to those points plus one-third of the difference between the chain girth, from sheerline to sheerline, at the stern ending of this length, and twice the vertical height at the side of the yacht at this station. For the purpose of calculating the rating, the minimum difference of girth at the bow station, as defined above, shall be 180mm, and minimum difference of girth at the stern station, as defined above, shall be 600mm. The requirement for a minimum value for the difference of girth at the stern station shall not apply to yachts laid down before 31st December 1961."*

[1119] Yachting Monthly, 1926, reference to *Josephine's* underbody rebuild.

[1120] The Design of Appendages, I. C. Howlett, Sailing Yacht Design: Practice, A. R. Claughton Ed. 1998.

[1121] Ibid

[1122] *Noroda* has been listed as *Norada* and cited as a pre-1940 British design. However, among F. G. Mitchell's many boats, there does not appear to have been an earlier *Noroda*. His previous 6-metre, *Nona*, was a Bjarne Aas design, which he had from new in 1935 until he bought the McGruer, *Noa*, which was replaced by *Noroda*.

[1123] Under the lee of the Longboat, Spun Yarn, Yachting, March 1949

[1124] Uffa Fox, a Personal Biography, June Dixon (Uffa's niece), 1978.

[1125] *Lintie* (ex-*Reg*) a 1926 Fife also carried K1.

[1126] Scottish News, The Yachtsman & Motor Boating Magazine, 25th May 1935.

[1127] The Royal Corinthian 5-metres foreshadowed the 5.5-metre class, both being built to an amended International Rule and intended to be cheap enough to allow experimentation.

[1128] From the Man at the Wheel, The Yachtsman & Motor Boating, 7th September 1935.

[1129] The 'streamlined rudder' was introduced by well-known German designer, Max Oertz. Within four years of the rudder becoming available, more than five million tons of British and foreign shipping had been fitted with it, improving fuel efficiency and gaining ½kt in speed.

[1130] Uffa Fox's Second Book, Uffa Fox, 1935.

[1131] Ibid

[1132] The British 6-metre revival began autumn 1985. Resurrection of the Sixes, Tim Street.

[1133] IYRU, The Yachtsman, November 1937.

[1134] Experimental 6-Metre, Yachting Monthly, June 1939.

[1135] Ibid

[1136] Cruising Yachts: Design and Performance, T. Harrison Butler, 1945.

[1137] Experimental 6-Metre, Yachting Monthly, June 1939.

[1138] Ibid

[1139] British and International Racing Yacht Classes, the International Six and Five-and-a-half Metre Classes, Hugh Somerville & Ed Whitaker, 1954.

[1140] Dick Carter Yacht Designer in the Golden Age of Offshore Racing, Dick Carter, 2018.

[1141] Great Yacht Designs, *Black Soo*, Theo Rye, Classic Boat archive. Black Soo took the *Zeevalk* model to its logical extreme in 1955, leading to Laurent Giles' *Myth of Malham*, and *Sopranino*, and the Van do Stadt's masterpiece, *Stormvogel*.

[1142] In his later work, Dick Carter was counter-influenced by the S&S portfolio and incorporated bustles in his underbodies, which retrogressively, became less dinghy-like and more yacht-like as his career progressed.

[1143] *Circe* won the Solent Cruising and Racing Association Silver Medal for the top points score of the season in 1946, 1947, 1948, 1949, 1950 and 1951 – the first two years under the command of Captain G. E. T. Eyston, the well-known racing car driver, and then in the hands of E. J. Coles for the final three seasons. Herbert Thom sailed the boat for Eyston in the 1948 season.

[1144] As a member of the design selection committee, Perry endorsed the choice of *Sceptre*. He and Frank Murdoch both sailed successful Boyd 6 Metres – *Royal Thames* and *Marletta*.

[1145] The trim tab and separate rudder are the best-known of Carter's design features, but his work on 'cleaning up' rigs to improve their aerodynamic efficiency was equally important.

[1146] Private correspondence – Roger Mander to Ian Howlett, 2008.

[1147] This yard was also understood to be interested in building a replica of Boyd's Seawanhaka Cup-winning *Circe* of 1937. *Circe* remained the best 6-metre in Britain through to 1951. The Maine boatyard carried out a fine restoration on the 1930 Fife, *Alana* (*Priscilla II*), drawn by David Boyd during his best years in the Fairlie design office. Boyd sailed her in the 1940s as a family boat to race on the Clyde with the 'Ex-Six Metre Class'

[1148] Classic Six-metre Newsletter, March 2008. Others have pursued this line of thought. 1940s World Snipe Champion Ted Wells declared that airflow is illiterate and does not always follow the rules we set for it.

[1149] Experimental 6-Metre, Yachting Monthly, June 1939.

[1150] *Enterprise* had an excellent aluminium mast in 1930, and long before that in the 1800s, steel spars were successfully used in the America's Cup, however, none of this was exactly 'mainstream' in yacht racing. It was not until the mid-1950s, that reliable mass-produced metal masts became available.

[1151] The design and commissioning of the first circular, combined current and wave test basin, David Ingram, Robin Wallace, Adam Robinson and Ian Bryden, ca.2013.

[1152] As far as we can determine, this was the first and only circular 'donut' test-tank with a rotating flow. There was a Japanese fish study using a very small circular tank. The water does not rotate but the background revolved like a diorama. There is also the new circular tank at Edinburgh University (FloWave Ocean Energy Research Facility) which has been built to study waves. This is the tank that recently recreated the 'Great Wave off Kanagawa', an early 1800s woodblock print by Japanese artist Katsushika Hokusai.

[1153] Turbulence introduced a raft of unmeasurable distortions, just like the real-world and just as maddening. The tank's value was limited to comparing the loading on the dynamometer for different models while observing underwater flow as mapped by streamers and recorded via a movie camera, then making subjective judgements as to why one shape may be faster than another. As an all-round sportsman, John also observed the performance of his fishing lures in the tank!

[1154] Keel Forms and Two Experimental Models, John A. Stewart, the Model Yachtsman, December 1932.

[1155] The 6mR scale models are very shallow draft compared to hulls built to specific model rules, like the One Metre Class, where the draft can be 0.42 metres. Nevertheless, the 6mR models are surprisingly stiff and close-winded and sail extremely well.

John, Alexander and Howie Stephen   Stephen Family Archive

Midge, 3-Metre, 1913   Stephen Family Archive

Maida sailing off Hunter's Quay in the 1950s   Images: June Collyer collection

After her racing career was over, *Maida* was repurposed as cruiser with a small doghouse and an inboard engine. She was laid up from 1972 to 1986, after which Scottish boat builder, David Spy, took her in hand. He replaced all her ribs and some planking. A further restoration was completed by Peter Wilson in Aldeburgh using the original plans. Note: *Maida* inherited *Coila III's* sail number. She now sails with her old sail No.1, as used on both *Maida* and *Maida II*.

588

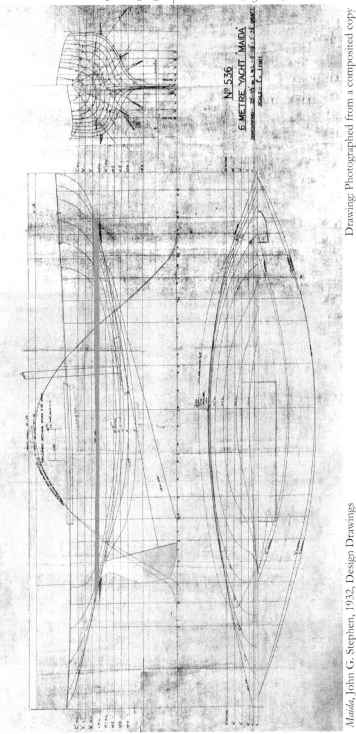

Maida, John G. Stephen, 1932, Design Drawings

Drawing: Photographed from a composited copy

Maida was an extremely innovative and quite radical design, based on extensive testing with free-sailing models. Note the curve of sectional areas (upright and at an angle heel of 35 degrees). Also note the heeled (static) waterplane at 35 degrees is almost symmetrical about a parallel fore and aft axis which is an aim of scow-type underbodies. The extension of the false keel-line to just below the waterline is similar to the John G. Stephen *Coila III*. This same feature was developed into a more pronounced chin on *Eyra* (1935). The drawing shows a spinnaker launching hatch, as later used on Dragon ODs.

Eyra, John G. Stephen, 1935   Image: feature in The Yachtsman

Note the Bremen bow, narrow beam and channels, volume in fore body, fin and bulb keel and bustle, with a complex faired-in rudder featuring a shark fin plate beneath, in an attempt to control the tip vortex on the trailing edge and increase effectiveness with a small drag penalty.

Maida II, John G. Stephen, 1939, chasing *Kini* sailed by Howden-Hume   Image: J. Hall

Maida II, John G. Stephen, 1939   Image: Stephen Family Archive

Maida II, John G. Stephen, 1939   Stephen Family Archive

Maida II, 1939 with *Intrepid*, Olin Stephens, 1967, 12mR overlaid. *Intrepid's* profile shown to scale and as it would be if interpreted under the 6-metre rule, which is proportionately deeper drafted. The press image of *Maida II* was taken on the slip at McGruer's prior to launch.   Composite: the author

Free-sailing models, 1965   Circular Test-tank 1961

Maida, John G. Stephen (rudder defined from plans)   RNCYC Collection & design drawings

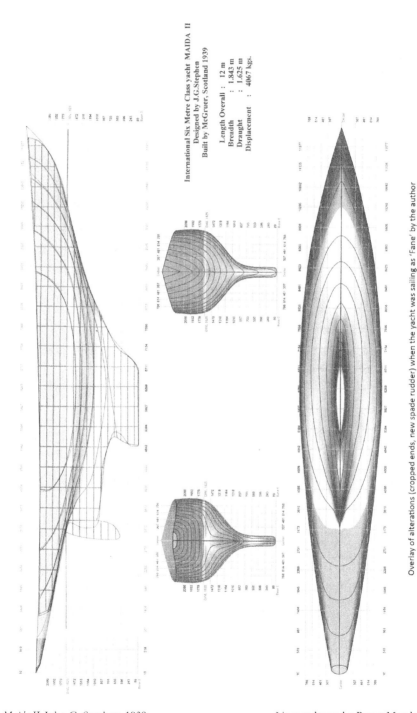

International Six Metre Class yacht MAIDA II
Designed by J.G.Stephen
Built by McGruer, Scotland 1939

Length Overall	:	12 m
Breadth	:	1.843 m
Draught	:	1.625 m
Displacement	:	4067 kgs.

Overlay of alterations (cropped ends, new spade rudder) when the yacht was sailing as 'Fane' by the author

Maida II, John G. Stephen, 1939   Lines redrawn by Roger Mander

Maida II, John G. Stephen, 1939   Image: G. L. H. Blair

Maida II is seen here re-rigged with a conventional Bermudian mainsail and a McGruer three spreader rig. The shape of the spinnaker is a perfect example of a blind design alley. Size is not everything. Note the exceptionally high gooseneck. Also note the dashing panther motif at the head of the cove line where many Fife yachts have a dragon.

594

Chapter 29: Standing on the Shoulders of Giants[1156]

Had Mr Watson not been a Britisher, whose disinclination to depart from the ways of their forefathers is inherent and rational, he would have progressed more rapidly. Being a Britisher, and a Scotch Englishman into the bargain, he has not been alert in discerning the trend of the modern racing machine, nor in following the ways which American designers have been pointing out to him and to Mr Will Fife Jun. Mr Beavor Webb, who designed the unsuccessful Genesta and Galatea, was shrewder – he emigrated to America. Caspar Whitney[1157]

Through the golden age, yacht owners and patrons of yachting on the Clyde were fortunate to enjoy access to some of the world's best naval architects on their doorstep. In the early 1880s, the Scottish marine industry was perhaps too successful. Southern builders were almost ready to throw in the towel. *"The vogue of the new racing machine from the Clyde put an end to such diversions for the owners of ordinary vessels, and the productions of Ratsey and the southern builders grew more and more scarce on the Solent as time went on."*[1158] Our English friends rose to the challenge and the crisis passed, but the Clyde's naval architects maintained a relentless pressure on the best from the Solent.

A climate of excellence was nurtured on the Clyde through respect, meaningful dialogue and even collaboration when that was to mutual benefit. Thus, for example, George Watson and William Fife III got along; so too did Watson and Alfred Mylne, at least initially while working in the same office. After establishing his own practice, Mylne valued the unassuming John James, and celebrity protégé Thomas Glen-Coats, equally. William Fife III maintained a close relationship with Peter Dickie after he left Fairlie to return to the family firm at Tarbert. Fife considered David Boyd invaluable, but let him go as a favour to Alex Robertson. Both these talented Fife disciples built fine reputations, and designed classics in the cruising and racing spheres respectively, but they always deferred to the old man across the Firth.

James Rennie Barnett, G. L. Watson's chief designer, who took over on Watson's death in 1904, mentored Boyd and others in his formidable, no-nonsense style. James McGruer, perhaps the most unassuming of all the Clyde greats, seems to have got along with just about everyone. During the unsuccessful America's Cup campaigns of 1958 and 64, we find the entire Scottish yacht design community rallying around a beleaguered David Boyd and offering support and solace. It was a tight group which included a host of second rank designers, who might have been less prominent, but were no less talented in skill or application. Men like William G. McBryde, John Bain, J. A. McCallum, Hugh Mclean, C. L'Estrange Ewen and even P. J. McGregor, a man with a rare talent for line, would have been masters of their art in any other age.

John Inglis Jr

One factor which made Clyde designers disproportionately influential on the world stage was their alliance with a prominent generation of research scientists. If there is a father of the Scottish School of yacht design, at least among the illuminati, it would be John Inglis Jr. (1842-1919), a man supported by a network of near genius in academia. This is not to diminish the importance of the harbinger of the Clyde's yacht design heritage, John Scott (1752-1837); skilled artisans, like William Fyfe (1785-1865), who whittled some fine yachts in the early 1800s; and the enduring talent of Fife II (1821-1902). But these gentlemen were patriarchs, not mentors, and their knowledge was their competitive edge.

Inglis was free to share his insights and advances as he did not compete for commissions in the yachting world. Yacht design was primarily an intellectual interest that derived from his day-job as a leading commercial shipbuilder, and occasionally, perhaps even informed it. Inglis was driven to advance the state of the art in naval architecture. To the practical ship science of the Napiers, he added the theoretical advances of Scott Russell, William Rankine and William Froude. It was a formidable 'toolbox' for commercial shipbuilding and it also informed yacht design. This syncretic approach empowered a generation of exceptional young minds.

In his youth, Inglis was an outstanding student; he studied under the formidable trio of Professors Rankine, Blackburn and Thomson from the age of fifteen to receive one of the best science-based educations of his era. When he embarked on his practical apprenticeship with the family firm, Inglis was familiar with advanced mathematics and the esoterica of fluid mechanics. And he was already enthused about the possibilities that both engineering science and tank-testing held for shipbuilding.

Inglis published *A Yachtsman's Holiday* in 1879. In that book, sandwiched between self-deprecating anecdotes and cruising yarns, Inglis set out his philosophy of yacht design.[1159] He disparaged the ponderous, workboat-derived cruisers of the day and advocated slim, fast boats. In this, Inglis recognised that high performance was an important safety factor for any cruising yacht, especially in the 1870s before auxiliary power. The first everyday engine for small yachts did not appear until 1906, when the Bergius family had James Litster of Kirn install a prototype Kelvin motor in *Dodo II*, see Chapter 34. Meanwhile, Inglis courted heresy by employing a racing spinnaker to harness the light airs of the Scottish summer.

Inglis was a 'co-conspirator' with Dixon Kemp (1838-1899) in the matter of beam. He argued that the then-current differentiation between honest 'natural stability' (beam) and dishonest artificial stability (keel weight) was wrong. Both, he said, were just 'stability', only the vanishing angle changed. In that he was certainly right, but in ridiculing centreboarders, and undervaluing the multifaceted benefits of beam, he was not just wrong, but doctrinaire – surely anathema to a thinking man. While fashions favour 'types'; and 'type-forming' may be the bane of rule-makers (or occasionally the aim), beam, draft and keel weight are all constituent elements to be evaluated and employed without prejudice.

Inglis cited the infamous case of the 143ft LOA schooner, *Mohawk*, which capsized at moorings on the Hudson River with the loss of six lives in 1876.[1160] This monologue was evoked during his account of a cruise in the *Moira*. However, while the *Mohawk* incident says much about the design of that particular vessel, it says nothing about centreboarders or the 'wide flat model'. There is no reason why yachts of this general type cannot be designed with an angle of vanishing stability that remains positive in a knock-down to horizontal (i.e. $>90^{0}$), and of course, most are.

John Inglis raced occasionally, but he was not really a 'racing man'. His own yacht designs were essentially performance cruisers. Inglis designed just six sailing yachts.[1161] There is some confusion over Inglis' own boats as he gave them fictional names in his 'yachtsman's holiday'. He warned that they could not be identified through *Hunt's Universal Yacht List,* a precursor of *Lloyds Register* which first appeared in 1878. Surely this was a coquettish and unnecessary conceit.[1162]

Sailing Yachts Designed by Dr. John D. Inglis Jnr

Year	Name	TM	Type	Owner	Notes
1872	*Hilda*	5-tons	Cutter	J. Inglis	*'Ilma'* in the book
18xx	*Viola*	5-tons	Cutter	J. Inglis	Cited by Watson
1875	*Cordelia**	9-tons	schooner	J. Inglis	*'Concordia'* in the book
1875	*Sheila**	17-tons	schooner	J. Inglis	*'Princess'* in the book
1876	*Moira*	20-tons	cutter	J. Inglis	*'Mermaid'* in the book
1876	*Irene*	20-tons	cutter	W. F Donaldson	Sistership to *Moira*

* Inglis promoted the schooner rig in small cruisers. The rig was disadvantaged for racing in those days by the rating system on the Clyde.

John Inglis Jr's first 'cruising' 5-tonner, *Hilda*, was 28ft LOA, 6ft 7" beam, with 4ft headroom under a lifting cabin top like a Norfolk Broads cruiser. To be fair to Inglis, his idea of a slim yacht was still wide enough to accommodate settee berths either side of a saloon table. *Hilda* had a beam to length ratio of 3.69, whereas *Oona*, the most extreme plank-on-edge yacht of the era (designed by his protégé Paton), came in at 7.86. In retrospect, all Inglis' designs were unequivocally wholesome, despite his advocacy of narrowness per se.

G. L. Watson suggested that John Inglis raced more than occasionally: "*There were many yachts built to beat her* (being Fife II's 5-tonner, *Pearl*, of 1873), *among them being the 5-tonners Hilda and Viola, designed, owned, and built by Mr Inglis.*[1163] As *Pearl* was launched the season after *Hilda*, this seems unlikely.[1164] The *Pearl* is well-documented. Designed by William Fife II she was built "*ahint the shed*" by Alex Fife after working hours "*by the licht o' the mune*". *Pearl* was a very successful family boat, dominating her class for three seasons with Allan Fife at the helm.[1165] Watson continued, Inglis "*also launched a very pretty schooner of 8 tons called the Cordelia, now, unhappily, lying at the bottom of the sea. She, like his other two ventures, was designed to race in the 5-ton class, and also to put the wee Pearl's nose out of joint. They were all three big boats, fully decked, and veritable ships when compared with the Pearl.*"

Inglis' pioneering work on external ballast keels, and encapsulated lead keels, as on the little steel 5-tonner, *Hilda*, in 1872, was particularly influential. The external ballast keel was enthusiastically adopted by G. L. Watson. Watson himself is ambiguous about the genesis of the idea as he recognises the prior work of Robert Steele in 1834.[1166] "*I have been unable to get any definite information as to the first application of outside ballasts, but in 1834 Messrs Steele built the Wave for Mr John Cross Buchanan, and on this vessel a metal keel was fixed.*"[1167]

Writing ten years earlier, David Pollock, who would have been aware of Steele's work, was inclined to give the benefit of the doubt to Inglis: "*The designing and sailing of yachts are favourite pursuits of Mr Inglis; and the system of yacht ballasting by means of a lead keel forming portion of the hull structure was first instituted by him in one of the many yachts built for his own use.*"[1168]

Returning to Watson, the sequence of priority becomes ever more confusing: "*Mr James Reid, of Port Glasgow, designer of the beautiful 10-tonner Florence (1876) and many other fast boats, closely followed by Mr John Inglis, of Pointhouse, and later by the writer, put all or nearly all of the ballast outside, and the practice in a few years became general.*"[1169] All we can take away from this muddled chronology is that designers, yacht builders and owners saw the benefits of external ballast, retaining lead internally as trimming ballast.

With deep-keeled steel yachts, engineering encapsulated ballast was straightforward. Where slack garboards merge into a hollow fin, it would be perverse to place the ballast anywhere else. Bolting a substantial ballast keel onto a wooden boat, however, would have presented a more complex challenge to 19th century shipwrights. Inglis's *Hilda*, a wooden boat, had a 'modern' external ballast keel, and *Moira*, built of steel and illustrated 'in section' in his book as '*Mermaid*', appears to have had the lead fitted into a hollow fin as encapsulated ballast.

A & J. Inglis built 34 yachts from 1872 to 1914, all of which John Jnr had a hand in. He was said to have made the yacht-building side of the business his own, but despite this he readily deferred to the new generation of high-profile yacht designers. Through the turn of the century, Inglis built the Watson 40-ton cutter, *Astrild*, in 1898, and the C. Francis Herreshoff-designed 60-ton cutter, *Nevada*, for Patrick McNab Inglis, John's cousin, in 1901. William Fife III drew the lines of the 66-ton cutter, *Ailsa*, in 1895, and the magnificent 154-ton schooner, *Susanne*, in 1904, see Chapter 38.

Notwithstanding John Inglis' seminal influence on a generation of naval architects, we should also recognise that his character had a dark side, recast by his friends and allies as charisma. This bonhomie obfuscated an outlook riven with social Darwinism. Inglis espoused the cult of individualism to disparage common purpose among the lower orders. While he was not alone on Clydeside in holding such views, the tide had turned. Happily, collective action would eventually transform the miserable lot of Scottish shipyard workers. The 'Workmen's Compensation Act' of 1897, so derided by Inglis, would motivate industry to review dangerous working practices and improve workplace safely.

George Watson and John Inglis

In the early part of his career as an independent yacht designer, G. L. Watson set out to challenge the old master, William Fife II (1821-1902), with whom his early work is often compared. However, the competition between Watson (1851-1904) and Fife III (1857-1944) at the peak of their powers became one of the most famous professional rivalries in yachting history. The two men were born six years apart but began their careers as recognised naval architects at the same time. After a slow start, Watson's first proper commission was *Eros*, a 10-tonner, in 1874; while Fife, working with his father, produced the 5-tonner, *Clio*, in 1875.[1170]

As apprentices, both designers spent time, hands-on, learning the ropes in commercial shipyards. After working two years with Robert Napier, young Watson transferred to A. & J. Inglis for the last three years of his premium apprenticeship, served from 1869 to 1872. It is also possible that Fife spent some time with A. & J. Inglis during his apprenticeship. There is an intriguing reference in the letters of W. P. Stephen which suggests such an attachment ca.1875. That would have been a decade after Watson's time there, and before Fife's final internship at Fullerton's

Merksworth yard, learning the intricacies of steel-framed composite construction.[1171]

John Inglis Jnr was little more than a decade older than G. L. Watson, but he was already an éminence grise in the industry when he took the young man under his wing. Watson adopted an approach to yacht design that incorporated the tools and technologies of contemporary commercial shipbuilding. William Fife, by contrast, did not. If indeed Fife worked alongside John Inglis, the contact appears to have been brief as it left no trace on his design philosophy and subsequent career. That much became clear when funding was available to conduct tank-testing during his two *Shamrock* design commissions.

John Inglis Jr saw in Watson a mind receptive to engineering science. William Fife, by contrast, would have been confident in his native design doctrine, prefigured as it was by the long-established tenets of his family's boatbuilding heritage. But then again, perhaps such a division of philosophy is merely a construct of hindsight. Inglis was an exceptionally busy man in the mid-1870s as he took on additional business responsibilities, prior to assuming overall management of the shipyard. This changeover would be precipitated by his father's death in 1882.

Inglis' role as friend and mentor in the formative years of George Watson's professional training clearly contributed to the making of a great naval architect. Young Watson was not only learning; as an active member of the Inglis brains-trust, he was supporting advances in the discipline. The Inglis shipyard pioneered scientific approaches to measuring performance and interpreting the data. Watson assisted John Inglis Jr in developing quantitative methods to establish margins of safety in ship design. A. & J. Inglis Ltd were the first shipbuilders on the Clyde to incline their vessels to assess stability, and later to estimate longitudinal hull strain, as experienced by iron vessels in a seaway. As a member of the design team in this latter phase of research, Watson was involved in one of the most important issues in the field of naval architecture at the time.

Under Inglis' direction, and following Professor William Rankine's methodology, Watson was entrusted with the critical calculations for this seminal work. The A. & J. Inglis team analysed how longitudinal strain affected two of the company's steamers, for which they had detailed design data.[1172] The results were published as curves of hogging moments calibrated to advise shipbuilders on how the distribution of weight and buoyancy should be reflected in the structure of a vessel.[1173] These advances were generously shared with the shipbuilding industry as a whole. Yacht design may have been an esoteric niche specialism, but it too profited when practitioners applied the lessons of this research. As a young professional at the heart of this work, G. L. Watson would be uniquely qualified to spearhead an explicitly scientific approach to yacht design on the Clyde. Among his peers, few could speak the same language.

While racing is the discipline that improves the breed, cruising yachts do occasionally throw up useful variations. Watson advanced Inglis' ideas on external ballast keels and used them to such effect that he influenced the course of racing yacht design for the ensuing decade.[1174] Curiously, he termed this ballasting innovation a 'lead bottom', rather than a lead keel, possibly to differentiate it from lead 'shoes', as on yachts like the old *Arrow* of 1823. Many racing yachts of that generation had a slim lead shoe bolted on externally, but primarily relied on internal ballast to stand up to their outlandish canvas.

That said, it was an American who introduced the classic yacht of the 1890s which later became known as the '*Britannia* ideal'. Nat Herreshoff was the first designer of influence to develop a genuinely modern 'wineglass' midship-section, as on the 45ft LWL *Gloriana*, which carried her external ballast low and also featured a cutaway forefoot in 1891. Launched a few days later, Watson's 35ft LWL *Dora*, may have previewed the classic spoon bow, but she still exhibited the deep convex forefoot and slack bilges of his America's Cup challenger, *Thistle*. Watson was nothing if not willing to learn. As soon as *Gloriana* hit the water, he was emboldened to draw tighter garboards, consummating his mastery of the style with *Valkyrie II* in 1893.

William Paton, Inglis and Watson

When William E. Paton (1862-1886) apprenticed himself to A. & J. Inglis in the late 1870s, John Inglis immediately recognised another kindred spirit. Consequently, he encouraged Paton, as with Watson a decade before, to take advantage of the tools the new applied sciences now had to offer the yacht designer. Paton, of course, seized the opportunity to develop his métier.

In these years there was, as yet no suitable university course in Scotland, so Paton moved south for three years to complete the formal part of his education at the Royal Naval College at Greenwich. The Institute of Naval Architects was formed in 1860, but the subject was not taught at the Royal Technical College (now Strathclyde University) until 1882.[1175]

Paton's first job, post-qualification, was with Armstrong, Mitchell & Co on Tyneside, where he worked on design details for warships. He later established an independent yacht design practice in Kensington but maintained his Scottish ties. Paton was introduced as a member of the Royal Clyde Yacht Club in 1879 when he attained his 17th birthday.[1176] His first design, the 5-tonner, *Trident*, was constructed by David Morris that same year. Morris ran his own small boatyard in Kirn, before teaming up with Robert Lorimer to form M&L at Sandbank in 1885.[1177] *Trident* was not particularly quick, but she was nevertheless an impressive self-penned effort for an 18-year-old. In subsequent ownership, the boat made her way to Bordeaux on her own bottom and proved to be tolerably seaworthy.

As his career began to take off, Paton received considerable assistance from George Watson. This was perhaps only fitting as they shared a common mentor in Inglis. Paton took full advantage of this relationship and clearly modelled elements of his style on Watson's work. Watson gave Paton the design drawings of the 5-tonners, *Clotilde* (1875) and *Finesse* (1877). *Clotilde* embodied an early and self-confessedly 'timid' interpretation of the cutaway forefoot. But her design repaid study, in that it was informed by the work of Froude, via Inglis.

Clotilde was a big boat for a 5-tonner at 6-tons TM and measured-in $1/3$-ton over rating. She could only race in Ireland, where such details were apparently less critical.[1178] Competing cheekily as a 5-tonner in her debut season on the Clyde, *Clotilde* defeated William Fife's crack *Pearl* (1873) in a £10 (£1,150) best of five wager. She lost the first two matches but won the series when the wind picked up, as might be expected of a bigger boat.

Unsurprisingly, *Clotilde* attracted a slew of protests and lost her prizes for that season. Watson was said to have been disgusted, blaming everyone but himself.[1179] It is not clear whether the designer, or David Morris the builder, was ultimately responsible, but it was unsporting to gate-crash the 5-tonners. However, as a prototype, she paved the way for the successful *Vril*, almost 10% smaller in hull volume, but nevertheless described as 'the largest size possible for a 5-tonner'.

These early Watson boats were a useful template for Paton's own 5-tonners. He would effectively retrace the development pathway trod by Watson over the preceding decade. This strategy was so successful that Watson was driven to design ever more extreme plank-on-edge designs, to compete with Paton's *Olga* (1883) which had dominated the class since her debut year. The 5-ton cutter, *Doris* (1885), was one such example. This kind of competition between designers who understood each other so well also, alas, released the self-destructive impulse of the inner lemming.

Paton's first, and coincidentally his last, client in professional practice was Irishman, Joseph Plunket, for whom he designed the successful, if short-lived, 3-tonner, *Olga*, in 1883.[1180] Other Paton designs included *Fedora*, a 4-tonner, built by Carswell & McAllister in Gourock in 1884, followed in the same year by *Currytush*, a fine 3-tonner that performed well, albeit often against limited competition. *Pansy*, another rakish 3-tonner, and *Luath*, a 5-tonner in the same mould, appeared in 1885, then came, *Brenda* an unexpectedly wholesome 5-tonner.

Paton's last two designs were *Cora*, a 3-tonner built by Morris & Lorimer's at Sandbank, and the extreme plank-on-edge *Oona*, built at the other end of the country by J. G. Fay & Co on the Itchen, for Irishman Joseph Plunket. Both yachts were launched in 1886.[1181] *Oona* became famous for all the wrong reasons. While the *Oona* tragedy has been interpreted in different ways, when this uncompromising vessel took her designer's life, she sounded a death knell for Thames Measurement. *Oona* was wrecked in the Irish Sea on a delivery trip and her designer, still just 23, died with her.

> Ironically, a knife-on-edge boat like *Oona*, if well battened-down and 'left to her own devices', is as safe as any vessel in really bad weather. With most of the boat below the waterline, the motion would have been easy. The deck might have been continually swept by heavy seas, but down below she would have been as steady as a rock. Unfortunately, lying a-hull in survival mode needs plenty of sea-room and that is what Paton did not have on the 12th May 1886.

Paton is variously credited with 30 to 40 designs, of which it seems just nine were built.[1182] It is one of the tragedies of the era that he was denied the opportunity to become a designer of distinction, rather than a footnote. Both Inglis and Watson must have grieved over this waste of a precocious talent, Watson especially, as he had been an active participant in a 'race to the bottom' that had driven the racing yacht to the edge of extinction. The great shame is that Paton did not live to test the limits of the new Length & Sail Area Rule introduced the year after he died. In that rather more inspiring forum, it is likely that he would have excelled.

Outliers

Men of ability often identify talent, ease the path of protégés, and nominate successors. Fathers favour more talented sons. This is how the baton is normally passed in all areas of human endeavour. However, outliers also rise to the top occasionally, bridging incremental progress. Through the history of yacht design, there have indeed been periods when mavericks have achieved outstanding success, but as a career-path it remains exceptional, especially today.

For those unable to underwrite their own ideas, a generous patron is required. Such sinecures, as benefitted early design pioneers like Symonds and Symington, described in Chapters 5 and 7, have never been easy to come by. The success of the outliers described in Chapters 26 and 27, concerning Thomas Glen-Coats and Fred J. Stephen, was entirely conditional on their being men of independent and considerable means, and moreover, being embedded in the marine industry with access to the tools of the trade.

Today, access to risk-capital is caveated by the high costs of skilled labour, high-tech materials and CNC milled tooling, all of which perpetuate the status quo. In these circumstances, small, cheap classes, like the Mini 6.5, which allowed David Raison to realise his offshore scow concept in 2011, provide an important service to sustain the invaluable contribution of outliers in yacht design, albeit that even the smallest boats are now becoming prohibitively expensive with the admission of foiling technologies. This is the tragedy of the materials revolution and consequent demise of self-builds in top-flight competition today. See Chapter 39.

The Flutter of Fledging

Most designers who came to prominence during the 'golden age of yachting' were generous and able to derive mutual benefit from common experience, while safeguarding the essential kernel of their success. However, small-mindedness did creep in over the years. For example, there have been suggestions of sustained animosity between George Watson and Alfred Mylne. The latter's fledging was no doubt seen as premature by his (justifiably) ego-centric boss. But, as professionals in all disciplines know, fledging is routine occurrence and even rising stars are merely a corporate resource, until they threaten to leave.

Protégés are seldom appreciated until they hand in their resignations, when the usual course of action is a rapid reappraisal of worth, followed by an offer of more money. Then, in effect, they are faced with the unhappy prospect of selling their souls to the devil. Thus, all who hanker after recognition must move on. When the owner of *Tomahawk* referred to Aage Neilson's fine design work on the 1938 S&S yawl, Olin Stephens replied: "*I have many fine draftsmen working here, but all you need to know is that the buck stops with me.*"[1183] As talented draftsmen in a similarly patriarchal design offices, Mylne knew when to move on. Certainly, the loss of a good man when the practice was busy would have been keenly felt, but surely, lasting rancour casts both men in an unfavourable light.

Ian Nicolson, who joined the Mylne office in 1959, never tired of quoting a comment attributed to 'the Watson gang': "*Watsons don't drink with Mylnes*". But Ian came along after the last whiff of genius in both firms had long-since blown out to sea. Unlike the Fifes, who improved with each generation, Alfred Mylne II, a nephew with only a name in common, remained in the shadow of his uncle. So, if there was a genuine feud, it was essentially meaningless by this time as, after J. R. Barnett retired from Watson's, neither firm could sustain the alchemy of their founder.

That said, both firms are highly reputable design houses today. After a hiatus of thirty years, the Mylne team designed their first new boat in 2011. Under David Gray, they currently enjoy specialist expertise in electric-powered vessels. Additionally, the Mylne back catalogue is a sleeping asset, which every lover of classic yachts hopes will one day burst back into life. Most recently, a rebuild of *Jenetta*, which left the Clyde for Canada in 1953, was launched with much fanfare, sporting a striking tartan wrap. Watson's, on the other hand, have long been involved in high profile rebuilds and restorations, and like Mylne, are keen to monetise their classic back-catalogue.

Mylne began his apprenticeship in 1888 with the ubiquitous Napier, Shanks & Bell and joined G. L. Watson's growing business in 1892 to further his ambitions in the specialised field of yacht design. However, the knowledge and insights he gained, came at some cost to his self-esteem. During a corporate 'marketing trip' to the States, organised in parallel with the 1895 *Valkyrie* challenge, while Watson was lionised, his young assistant was buried in work, preparing design proposals. On the surface, all this seems quite normal, but somehow Mylne became increasingly acrimonious.

The following year, Mylne left to set up on his own.[1184] It has been suggested that he 'made off' with Watson's proprietary 'scientific ratios'. However, yacht design is substantially evolutionary, and once launched, all designs are in the public domain. Moreover, each type and size-band present a unique challenge. As a new designer, Mylne may have opened shop with the entire 'intellectual property' of the Watson office between his ears, but that was simply 'experience'. He was still obliged to follow the usual career-path, building up a loyal client-base via race-winning small boats.

By the late 1890s, George Watson had substantially relinquished that type of low-margin work, although his office did design a couple of Clyde 23/30s (*Lottie* (1898) and *Vida III* (1901)) for valued big boat clients Wylie and Coats. Watson's practice now focussed on much more lucrative super-yacht projects which challenged the firm's multidisciplinary capacity. And as for the 19/24, that most competitive of small boat classes, Watson had collaborated with Fife on the class rules and had no desire to 'turn poacher'. Earlier in his career, he had resigned as Official Measurer for the YRA, on receiving commissions for yachts designed to these rules.[1185]

Tales of petty backbiting diminish a wonderful heritage. There is something unseemly about conjuring hypothetical thoughts and emotions to inhabit the minds of dead men, especially fine designers whose peak years barely overlapped. Mylne set up on his own account in 1896 and was active through two world wars. George Lennox Watson died in 1904, so Mylne had the field to himself for 47 years until 1951, when he too passed away. That said, there were many other fine designers competing for work on the Clyde throughout this period, not least William Fife III.

Additionally, if we are to consider who triumphed on the international stage, as opposed to who played a consistently good game for a legion of loyal clients, against all the odds and somewhat surprisingly, we find David Boyd, John Stephen and Tommy Glen-Coats with the best records in such competition. Despite their successes, none of these worthy gentlemen is generally considered to inhabit the pantheon of the 'all-time greats'; and the latter two, Stephen and Glen-Coats, although qualified and experienced naval architects, were not paid for their yacht design work and were, therefore, essentially hobbyists.

At Fairlie, from 1875 until 1888, the two generations of Fifes were, in effect, offering design services alongside each other with overlapping client bases. Both used the same drawing office infrastructure and offered design-and-build services. The same thing happened when Mylne brought Tommy Glen-Coats into his practice to join himself and John Morton James. All three designers' work-streams shared the resources of the Mylne drawing office and construction supervision at the Bute Slip Dock.

Acquiring a design-and-build capacity is good business in some respects, less so in others. Alfred Mylne's central Glasgow office, at 108a, Hope Street, may have worked well for initial client discussions, but once a commission was in build, the logistics faltered. A return trip down-river to Ardmaliesh to supervise construction took a full day. The Fifes, by contrast, as an efficient design and build operation, lived, worked and could cut corners 'on the job'. G. L. Watson's travel schedule, with multiple contracts running concurrently with multiple builders, was something else again and he was bound to rely increasingly on his loyal lieutenant, the similarly talented, James Rennie Barnett.[1186]

James Rennie Barnett OBE (1864-1965) joined the drawing office of G. L. Watson & Co at the age of sixteen. During his apprenticeship, he studied Naval Architecture at Glasgow University. He was a prize-winning student and went on to become a prize-winning designer. After graduation, in 1888, Barnett spent a year with William Doxford & Sons before returning to G.L. Watson & Co. as Chief Draughtsman. Barnett succeeded Watson as senior partner of the firm following Watson's death in 1904. Barnett designed over 400 yachts, lifeboats and commercial vessels including, *Liberty*, a steam yacht of 1,570-tons (1908), *Sunbeam II*, a schooner of 659-tons (1929), *Taransay*, a schooner of 166-tons (1930), *Virginia*, a schooner of 712-tons (1930), *Nahlin*, a schooner of 1574-tons (1930), *Titan*, a schooner of 103-tons (1935) and *Blue Bird*, a schooner of 161-tons (1938).[1187]

The friendship between David Boyd and James Rennie Barnett spanned a century of yacht design on the Clyde from 1881, when James began with Watson's firm, to 1979, when Boyd launched his last yacht and retired to Islay. It was an unbroken link with the original template of their common discipline; a tradition underpinned by science, but ever cognizant of the precepts of classic style in yacht design, as expressed in the inspiring words of the King James Bible, now associated with G. L. Watson. "*Judgment also will I lay to the line, and righteousness to the plummet: and the hail shall sweep away the refuge of lies, and the waters shall overflow the hiding place.*"[1188]

One of the most egregious apprentice departure stories concerns the short, but damaging, tenure of boisterous Californian Doug Peterson in Dick Carter's design office in 1973. The tale told by the man himself suggests that Peterson stayed for just four days before deciding that the East Coast was not for him. However, in that short time, it seems that he acquired all the details of *Ydra*, the Carter practice's latest world-beater. Carter himself was a 'conceptual' designer, his drawing board was a coffee table. And in his biography, he bore no real grudge.[1189]

In the design office, Mark Lindsay actually drew the boats. So, it was some time before the boss discovered that Doug Peterson had used his short stay to make off with *Ydra's* lines, sailplan, rating calculations – basically, the works. Peterson adopted the innovative characteristics of Carter's latest hull-form, reduced displacement by some 3,000lbs and cropped the ends to create the world-beating *Gambere*. Doug Peterson was obviously a talented 'shopper' in the market of emergent trends, and this secured his success. Critically, he saw that North Sails, at that time one among many good sailmakers, had stolen a decisive march on their competition and the Peterson/North association never looked back.

A Scottish Style?

In 1956, *Yachting Monthly* noted that the Scots were "*a race with a peculiar talent in naval architecture and shipbuilding. Not surprisingly they have produced some of the greatest yacht designers and builders in the country; indeed, until the genius of the late Charles E. Nicholson arose far south in Hampshire, the designers from the north of the border had things pretty well their own way.*" The magazine then went on to discuss whether there was an identifiable 'Scottish style' in yacht design, as there were distinctive Scottish schools in architecture and graphic design.

Alfred Mylne II (Mylne's nephew) contributed to the article: "*It is interesting to observe the wide separation in architectural thought between the Scottish and English designers at the present time. I think it may be attributed firstly to the wonderful stretches of deep sailing water that the Scots have on their doorstep, and secondly to their remoteness from the central influence of the RORC.*"[1190]

Certainly, the influences bearing on each and every yacht design may be complex and are often subtle, so it is difficult to separate out the individual strands. In the 20th century, a contrast was often drawn between the British and American 'schools' of design. Two very different rating systems exaggerated the differences in prevailing sailing conditions and led to yachts with very different characteristics. The two national styles (basically, deep and narrow, vs wide and shallow) also, to some extent, reflected different climates of thought and approaches to problem-solving.

While both schools encompassed errant strands that took these trends to extremes and threatened life and limb, as the discipline of naval architecture matured, the best examples on both sides of the Atlantic began to converge around a set of common characteristics. In the same way, tagging the work of all designers in the British Isles as 'British' is an over-simplification, as is the generic term 'American'. In both American and British design, many styles coexist to address specific environments.

During the inter-war years and through the post-war years until the 1970s, Scottish designers favoured relatively heavy displacement hulls, driven by more generous sailplans than were common at that time in the south. The assumption was that, with the RORC rule penalising generous sail-plans, English sailors had become accustomed to bullet-proof rigs, carrying full-sail in most conditions and resigned to weaponizing the tidal flows of the Solent in light weather.

The same *Yachting Monthly* article illustrated the difference using two relatively conventional designs for 30ft waterline cruisers, one by a Scottish designer, and one by an Englishman. The magazine noted that while the linear dimensions of the two hulls were similar, the Scottish design had approximately 10% more displacement and 20% more sail area. The additional cost on a build contract would have been a ton of lead and about 150ft^2 of canvas. Despite the higher volume hull, the Scottish boat would have used a similar schedule of material.

However, there are crucial trigger points where scantlings have to be beefed up for more powerful hull-forms, bigger sail-area and greater ballast. So too for larger rigs; metal masts might have been scaled up to the next available section. As for wooden spars, that era of Russian Roulette was thankfully drawing to a close. The best wooden stick even now remains a lash-up, belted with steel sleeves, braced with guestimates, and preserved by modern weather forecasting.

Mylne II wrote: *"To attain speeds in all winds we use a larger sail area and so have more powerful hulls than you usually have in the South. The power to carry sail depends upon ballast to a large degree, and over the years we have found that much of the displacement to carry the ballast can be worked in fairly low down in the hull, giving rather fuller garboards than normal"*. Whether full garboards are necessary for this formula to work is a matter of opinion, but certainly, the big cruising boats, designed by Mylne's uncle, used that formula to great effect.

Mylne II also suggested that this enthusiasm for powerful hulls *"prevented Scottish designers from falling so readily for the various theories of hull balance whose influence is still strong, and the effect of which was to encourage the fine-lined after bodies with tucked-in stern sections which are still a common feature of English design. They have retained the rather full, broad stern, and as far as I know, boats having it are no more ill-balanced than narrow-stern English contemporaries."*

In this respect the Scots model had more in common with Americans practice. Wide boats can, of course, be beautifully balanced in normal use.[1191] Mylne II's Uncle Alfred did indeed combine a rare elegance with generous volume in wide planform designs, but perhaps James McGruer brought the Clyde model closer to American practice than any other designer in Britain. McGruer's family of wholesome cruising yachts are perhaps the principal legacy of Scottish yacht architecture, post-WW2.

"*With their generous displacement and full hull-forms the Scottish designers have naturally been free from the pressure* (from clients to maximise) *internal space that has produced nearly straight or hogged sheerlines.* Scottish designers' "*sheerlines curve in the old, bold way, with a spring of confidence that to Southern eyes, attuned now to more inhibited curves, may seem almost flamboyant.*"[1192] These comments are a little unfair; nevertheless, English design houses such as Illingworth & Primrose and Laurent Giles were responsible for an entire generation of clever, quick, and well-balanced yachts that are forever blighted by their sheerlines.

CODA: Colin Archer

Colin Archer (1832-1921) was another, albeit remote, disciple of the 'Glasgow Boys' school of thought.[1193] He was born in Norway to Scottish parents and made his name designing sailing lifeboats and a series of seaworthy, if rather sluggish, cruising yachts. When William Spiers Bruce was looking for a vessel to explore the Antarctic, Archer recommended the 1872 *Hekla*. When the barque arrived in Scotland, Watson took one look at her and muttered that she be taken out to Ailsa Craig and scuttled. However, he was persuaded to oversee a complete pro bono redesign, rebuild and refit, funded by the Coats family, loyal Watson clients and sponsors of the expedition.[1194] Reincarnated as *Scotia*, the old *Hekla* was an outstanding polar research vessel.

In 1877, Colin Archer adapted Scott Russell's wave-line theory to incorporate Fred Chapman's displacement parabola curve, arguing that "*the immersed bulk of a vessel, in its growth from zero at the bow to a maximum at the midship section, followed by the decrease to zero at the sternpost, should follow the wave-line; thus leaving the designer at liberty in the choice of level lines of entrance and run*".[1195] It is intriguing that Archer still found value in Chapman's work. While Archer's version of the wave-line theory was as erroneous as Scott Russell's, it resulted in well-balanced hull-shapes which are reflected in the work of yacht designers into the modern era.

CODA: A Tale of Two Designers

Walter Marks, an Australian yachtsman, visited two of our great designers in 1909.[1196] Marks then owned the 1901 Arch Logan 30-linear-rater, *Culwulla*, developed from the New Zealand designer's successful raters, *Heather* and *Petrel*.[1197] His impressions of Alfred Mylne and William Fife are not without interest. The two accounts provide some fascinating insights into their respective characters and an illuminating window into past practice.

Alfred Mylne

"During my tour of Scotland, I proceeded to Glasgow to interview this great designer, and found, as in the case of Mr Laws and other yachtsmen over here, 'another white man'. This gentleman is tall, clean-shaven, fair, and young, about 35 years of age. Mr Mylne was most anxious to acquire all the knowledge possible of local conditions in Australia in the event of future orders. I had much pleasure in giving him these, and also showing my large collection of yacht pictures. The latter keenly interested him, especially those of our 'midgets' and 'eighteens'. During our lengthy interview he graciously produced the designs of many past and present champions which sprung from his board. He has had the distinction of leading the great Fife during the past few seasons where they have met in the same classes and is very aptly considered 'the designer of the day'. Needless to mention, he has as much work ahead as he can carry out, and the wish of all enthusiasts here is that his future work may include an order from Sir Thomas Lipton for the next America Cup challenger."

William Fife III

"Having received an intimation that (Fife) would be in at a certain hour; I took a train from Glasgow to Fairlie, on the Firth of Clyde, a distance of 70 miles there and back, and arrived at this historic yard after a walk of about 1½-miles in a heavy shower of rain. This was depressing enough, but nothing compared to this celebrated designer's reception of myself. It was decidedly 'chilly'. Casually glancing over my collection of Sydney yachts, which I had brought hundreds of miles for him to see and many of which he had designed, he next positively refused to design a racing yacht for Australia, on the grounds that he found 'his designs were being copied out there'.

To this I gave, of course, the direct denial, knowing it to be absolutely untrue, notwithstanding that an owner may do with his design whatever he likes. Seeing that he had made a mistake, he qualified it by remarking that he meant 'Norway and Sweden, not Australia'. On assuring him that his views would be conveyed to Australian yachtsmen, he replied, 'ah, well, as I have had many orders from Australia, I will continue to design any yacht over 10-metres, but nothing under'.

He then asked by what train I was returning to Glasgow, and not knowing their times, he informed me there was one at 1.30 pm, and considering I had arrived at 12.45 and was not invited to partake of any refreshment or lunch, and had the journey back to Glasgow to negotiate, I considered this capped everything. After viewing the yard, yachts on slips, and the shed, I walked in the rain to the station, and arrived back in Glasgow at 4 p.m. where a late lunch was more than appreciated."

The eternal value of traditional Scottish courtesy and good customer relations is shown by the fact that Marks ordered a 4-tonner from Mylne during his 1909 visit. *Culwulla II* was built the same year by W. M. Ford of Sydney. However, when he moved on to a bigger boat in 1910, he bought *Awanui* from a Mr A. C. Saxton in 1907. His 'new' *Culwulla III* was a 1907, William Fife III 16-ton cutter, with a design date of 1905. Marks clearly aspired to own a Fife yacht, despite his shabby treatment by the 'great man'. And we might note that, in this instance, the original design had most certainly been bought and paid for.

CODA: Designing Unfamiliar Classes for Overseas Markets

In 1905 Alfred Mylne received a commission to design and build a boat to the old German/Danish 7 metre rule.[1198] Alfred Mylne gave his client, Edmund Nordheim, detailed instructions on how to take key measurements off the best German yachts. Nordheim managed to size up a dozen flyers without attracting attention. The result was *Scottie*, built down to weight by Robertson's of Sandbank, with sails made by John Mackenzie in Greenock. She was an elegant, lightly built little yacht with low freeboard, fine ends and long overhangs.

In her first couple of seasons in Baltic regattas, *Scottie* won 41 races. Hans Heckmann found the yacht, then called *Seagull*, at the Berlin Yacht Club in poor condition in 1945. He bought the wreck for 500 Marks and embarked on a complete rebuild. *Scottie* now has state-of-the-art rags and still wins on the Berlin lakes, sailed by the third generation of the Heckmann family. Mylne subsequently designed a good many 7-metres to the very different specifications of the International Rule from 1908 onwards.

[1156] "*If I have seen further it is by standing on the shoulders of giants.*" Letter from Sir Isaac Newton to Robert Hooke, 1675.

[1157] The Sportsman's Viewpoint, Caspar Whitney, Outing, Volume XXXIX (1901-1902).

[1158] The Royal Yacht Squadron, Montague Guest & William B. Boulton, 1902.

[1159] A Yachtsman's Holidays or Cruising in the West Highlands, John Inglis, 1879.

[1160] The Garner-designed *Mohawk*, which capsized in 1876, was simply a poor design. Centreboard boats would dominate the America's Cup in that era. The arrival of *Madge* in 1881 showed the alternative narrow British model in a favourable light, but this was never an either-or question. Both Watson and Herreshoff designed 'compromise' hull shapes.

[1161] *Darthula* of 1889, the next yacht to be launched from the yard, was designed by John D. Inglis, John Jr's nephew.

[1162] Hunt's Universal Yacht List, 1851 to 1934 became Norrie's Yacht List. These were administrative lists and not connected with surveys.

[1163] We can find no record of a *Viola* that fits this reference.

[1164] Watson dates *Pearl* in the early 1860s, but there is no such instance in either of the Fife build lists we have to hand.

[1165] Fast and Bonnie, May Fife McCallum, 1998.

[1166] The Badminton Library of Sports and Pastimes: Yachting, Volume 1, The Evolution of the Modern Racing Yacht, G. L. Watson, 1894.

[1167] Ibid

[1168] Modern Shipbuilding and the Men Engaged in it: a Review of Recent Progress in Steamship Design, David H. Pollock, 1884.

[1169] The Evolution of the Modern Racing Yacht, G. L. Watson, 1894.

[1170] At that time Watson only had his unpromising 'apprentice piece' *Peggy Woffington* 1871 to his credit. Working with his father, Fife Jr. did not get a design credit until *Clythe* in 1877.

[1171] "*After being for a time in the big yard of A. & J. Inglis, Glasgow, he took charge of the designing in the Fairlie yard.*" The Evolution of the Yacht Designer, First Paper, English Designers, W. P. Stephen, Outing, Volume XXXIX (1901-1902). In Fast and Bonnie, May McCallum does not mention this interlude between an initial apprenticeship at Fairlie and returning to work there. But she has stressed the close relationship between Fife and Stephen (they corresponded on domestic matters, not just yacht design). May has Fife finishing his apprenticeship at Fairlie in 1878, a year after his first design credit, at the age of 21.

[1172] The form of the waves was assumed to be trochoidal. A trochoid is the curve described by a fixed point on a circle as it rolls along a straight line. Published in Engineering, 1st May 1874.

[1173] Modern Shipbuilding and the Men Engaged in it, David H. Pollock, 1884.

[1174] G. L. Watson, the Art and Science of Yacht Design, Martin Black, 2011.

[1175] As the city became famous for its shipbuilding, so naval architecture became one of the most prestigious careers a young Clydeside man might follow. David Boyd, for example, served out his 5-year apprenticeship at Ardrossan, with two evenings a week at Glasgow Tech.

[1176] This was the minimum age for membership. Cadet membership was not introduced until ca.1948 when a youthful Jeremy Thomson joined the fold. The Holy Loch Sailing Club, an offshoot that did actually cater for young people, was not formed until 1888.

[1177] David Morris passed away before M&L launched their first boat. Nevertheless, Lorimer, as a mark of respect, maintained the fiction of a partnership throughout the long life of the company.

[1178] "*Having spread in building Clotilde is 1/3rd of a ton over 5 tons but will not be protested in Ireland where 'big babies' are not at all objected to*". The Field, 31st July 1875. Sourced by Martin Black.

[1179] We might accept that *Clotilde* 'spread in building', but it is hard to see how she could have grown longer too. Her LOA and LWL were both greater than any others of her class.

[1180] *Olga* was run down and sunk in her first season. Lloyds lists an *Olga* 3-tonner designed by J. Rogers and built in 1883 in Carrickfergus for J. A. M. Heyn.

[1181] *Oona* was one of the smallest composite yachts afloat that year, but as she was a 6-tonner and the Morris & Lorimer-built *Cora* was a 3-tonner, the Sandbank boat would take that honour. The 3-tonners, *Mascotte* and *Snarley Yow*, of 1882 were composite built, three years earlier by the Marquis of Ailsa's pioneering yard at Maybole, and there are no doubt others.

[1182] Martin Black, who admires Paton and has studied him extensively, credits the designer with 40 designs, others say 31, with only 9 built. Most of Paton's short professional career was spent in the service of Armstrong Mitchell & Co. What is Luck? The Tragedy of the Oona, The Yachtsman, 6th March 1913.

[1183] Telephone conversation between the author and Richard Bond, former owner of the S&S Yawl, *Tomahawk*, October 2015.

[1184] 100 Years of Alfred Mylne, Ian Nicolson, Classic Boat, December 1996, January & February 1997.

[1185] Watson certainly appears to have behaved correctly. However, William Fife the other partner-in-crime, went directly to his drawing board to exploit every loophole he had secreted within the 19/24s rule he had jointly authored.

[1186] J. R. Barnett (1864-1965) began his apprenticeship with Watson in 1880 at the age of 16 and retired from the firm in 1957 at the age of 93. He was an incredible 76 years with the firm, and not the, surely impossible, 84 years we credited him with in The Piper Calls the Tune.

[1187] J. R. Barnett surely deserves a biography of his own as perhaps the most talented of all the many under-recognised naval architects in the world.

[1188] The King James Bible, Isaiah 28:17.

[1189] Dick Carter Yacht Designer in the Golden Age of Offshore Racing, Dick Carter, 2018.

[1190] Scottish View, Yachting Monthly, April 1956.

[1191] Today, particularly with the current scow influence, extremely wide boats, channelling the spirit of the tunnel-hulled *Dominion* of 1898, are designed to sail at angles of heel that would have embarrassed a good helmsman in the past, but now translate into efficient water-planes.

[1192] ibid

[1193] The real 'Glasgow Boys' were an 'Impressionist' art movement in the 1880s.

[1194] G. L. Watson, the Art and Science of Yacht Design, Martin Black, 2011.

[1195] As interpreted by W. P. Stevens in his incidental comments on a paper on Tank-testing. Some Experimental Studies of the Sailing Yacht, Kenneth S. Davidson, 1936.

[1196] English Yachting, Walter Marks, Sydney Morning Herald, 9th January 1909.

[1197] Walter Marks was a prominent Sydney yachtsman, lawyer and parliamentarian. He was Vice Commodore of Royal Prince Alfred Yacht Club and sometimes characterised as 'the Thomas Lipton of Australia'.

[1198] Scottish Boating Blog, 14th October 2010.

Clio, 30ft LWL Bermudian Sloop, William Fife III, 1919   Image: Fast and Bonnie

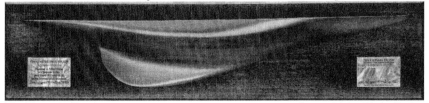

The Keepsake Trophy   Image: Mylne Yacht Design

The half-model represents the last 12-Metre designed by William Fife albeit she remained unbuilt. When offered anything in Fife's office as a memento of their friendship, Mylne chose this. It is an extraordinarily beautiful object to represent the mutual respect between two of our finest designers.

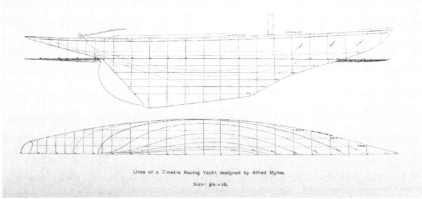

Mylne 7-metre Yacht, 1908   Mylne Yacht Design

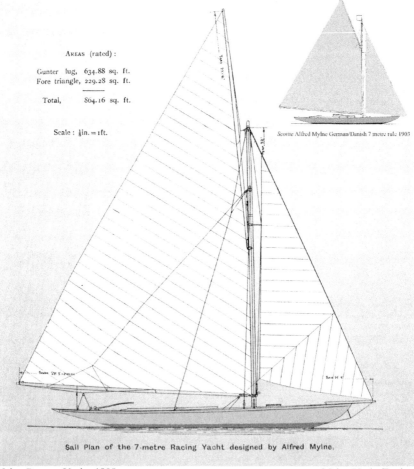

AREAS (rated):

Gunter lug, 634.88 sq. ft.
Fore triangle, 229.28 sq. ft.

Total,   864.16 sq. ft.

Scale: ⅛in. = 1ft.

Mylne 7-metre Yacht, 1908   Mylne Yacht Design
Inset profile/sailplan: Danish/German 7-metre referenced in this chapter.

614

Moira, 20-tonner, J. Inglis, 1876   Image: *A Yachtsman's Holiday*

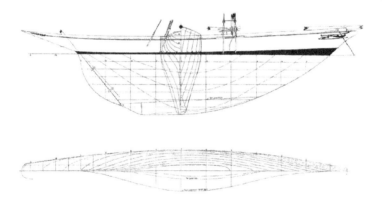

Oona, 6-tonner, William Paton, 1886   Image: *Yachting* magazine

Hilda, 5-tonner, John Inglis, 1871   Image: *A Yachtsman's Holiday*

Chapter 30: Passing the Baton, not the Buck

In the evenings, after long days of sailing and caring for the boats, we went to their parties, gave them the 'inside scoop', and danced with their daughters. We were the show, the circus come to town. And we couldn't have been happier. Dick Enersen[1199]

The Clyde's designers and boatyards have a long association with the America's Cup, starting in 1885 with *Genesta*, built by D & W Henderson & Co. for Sir Richard Sutton of the RYS. Then came *Galatea*, built by J. Reid & Co. of Port Glasgow for William Henn, an Irishman who challenged for the cup in 1886, under the flag of the Royal Northern Yacht Club. Both these boats were drawn by fashionable Irish designer John Beaver-Webb.

The Royal Clyde's challenged with *Thistle* in 1887. *Thistle* was owned by James H. Bell, designed by G. L. Watson pro bono, and built by D. & W. Henderson John Barr, then our finest sailor, skippered the boat. Dunraven's *Valkyrie* challenges of 1893 and 1895 were all-Scottish efforts too, as despite representing the Royal Yacht Squadron, they retained the same Clyde-based designer and builder. A summary of all the America's Cup matches to date appears in Appendix 3.

Glaswegian, Thomas Lipton, challenged five times: 1899, 1901, 1903, 1920 and 1930 with *Shamrocks I* to *V*, all under the banner of the Royal Ulster Yacht Club. The Irish were happy to endorse Lipton's leprechaun marketing strategies.[1200] However, Lipton's 'false flag' can also be seen, less charitably, as a slight to the land of his birth and the professional men who advised him. After the *Galatea* challenge in 1886, there would be a gap of 100 years before Harold Cudmore, a genuine Irishman, took an active part in the America's Cup, sailing for England at Fremantle in 1987.

William Fife designed the first and third of Lipton's boats and Watson the second. The first *Shamrock* was to be built by Harland & Wolff in Belfast, but the shipyard pulled out and Thorneycroft's at Chiswick eventually got the contract. *Shamrocks II & III* were built on the Clyde by Denny. *Shamrocks IV* and *V* were designed by the innovative English designer, Charles E. Nicholson, and built in his yard at Gosport. Despite Lipton's hokey Irish sentimentality, all the Lipton challenges were embraced by the Clyde's yachting community and the never-ending-story sustained a keen interest in the America's Cup among the wider population.

That same fascination and enthusiasm for the Auld Mug was revived in the autumn of 1956 when David Boyd was invited to submit 12-metre design proposals for the Royal Thames Yacht Club challenge of 1958. As I remember, even primary-school children were caught up in the excitement. The 1958 campaign features in *The Piper Calls the Tune* and elsewhere.[1201]

David Boyd and Ian Howlett

David Boyd (1902-1989) retired from full-time work as Managing Director of Robertson's yard and in-house designer in 1968, but he maintained a keen interest in America's Cup matters and ongoing 12mR design development. From their first meeting in 1978, and through his twilight years, Boyd kept in the loop via his good friend and admirer, Ian Howlett (b.1949). Ian's friendship with David Boyd, and Boyd's generosity in sharing the highs and lows of his career with Ian, has allowed us to revisit the Scottish contribution to the British challenges of 1958 and 1964; and to consider Erik Maxwell's subsequent ambitions to challenge for the America's Cup in the late 1960s and 70s.

Boyd might have appeared aloof, but he was generous with his time. After a lifetime invested in busy boatyards, he was happy to pass on his knowledge and experience. And, in so doing, he upheld our cliché of mixed metaphors to pass the baton, not the buck, to the next generation. Boyd spent hours with Chris Freer discussing 12mR design for Chris's book, the *Twelve Metre Yacht*.[1202] He freely gifted important drawings, as with the plans of *Sovereign* given to Warwick Hood, to help him with the design of the Cup contender, *Dame Pattie*. And the author can confirm that he also had time for cheeky schoolboys. From his unstinting commitment to support William Fife early in his career, Boyd was never averse to collaboration.

Ian Howlett began his America's Cup career in 1972 when he was employed to carry out design research for John Livingston's aborted challenge. Ian would go on to work through five more America's Cup cycles. Ian is now the elder statesman and undisputed authority on the arcane science of metre-boat design. If you are going to race classic 6mRs, 8mRs, or 12mRs, you need a Howlett optimisation programme, and if you have ambitions to work your way up to the front row in open competition, but can't afford a new boat, you need a Howlett winged keel.

Ian Howlett's Livingston commission involved liaison with the Scots mafia at Lloyds. The staff at the Small Craft Register in Southampton included John Leather, designer, writer, historian and the doyen of the gaff rig, Sandy Balfour, David Boyd's former assistant, later Manager of the Berthon Boat Co at Lymington, and Alastair McInnes, also a former member of the Robertson's Yard team.[1203] These were men who knew every trick in the book. They 'knew where the bodies were buried'.[1204]

Erik Maxwell encouraged David Boyd, then retired and living at the Maxwell family's bungalow by Loch Lomond, to get in touch with Ian in 1978. Ian was then chairman of the awkwardly named 'British Industry 1500 Boat Committee', a syndicate working towards the 1980 America's Cup. Erik thought that the two designers, while nearly half a century apart in years, were much closer in spirit and might enjoy each other's company. In fact, they got on famously, poring over photographs of the radical models Ian had been tank-testing for the boat that would become *Lionheart*. Ian recalls: "*He had been there before me and I recall him saying, of course just now, you will have any number of problems to sort out*." Subsequently, Boyd invited Ian to the Mudhookers' annual dinner at the Northern.[1205] The evening cemented an almost paternal relationship that would invest the young pretender with six decades of hindsight and bring great pleasure to the old man.

Cup-tied – Summarising the British Effort from 1978-2021

Lionheart, as pondered over and dissected on Boyd's dining table, would be recognised as a competitive 12mR in 1980, but she is mainly remembered for her striking flexible topmast and elliptical head mainsail which favourably altered the balance of the lift vs drag equation.[1206] This was a fruitful development path, as perhaps inadvertently the 12mR rule at that time omitted girth limitations. On *Lionheart*, the composite topmast (cored with e-glass and faired with foam[1207]) would be readily bent to a pre-set profile by the permanent backstay, and the curve locked-in by the jumper strut rigging. When the backstay was released, the mast was straight as required by the rule.[1208] In testing, there were clear aerodynamic benefits, even before measuring-in an additional 7% to the upwind sail area.

In 1980, the Australians, back for a second time with the eponymous Ben-Lexcen-designed *Australia*, out-sailed the British on their way to the final. However, the benefits of *Lionheart's* elliptical head mainsail were obvious to all. In a remarkably gutsy crash programme, Ben Lexcen copied the bendy rig during the brief interval before the Cup races proper. The Australian's clone worked perfectly, lifting their old boat's performance to such an extent that they went on to worry Dennis Connor's highly optimised choice for defender, the S&S-designed *Freedom*.

Here we might note that the challenger for the America's Cup had faster boats than the defenders in 1901 with *Shamrock II*, 1920 with *Shamrock IV*, 1931 with *Endeavour*, and 1962 with *Gretel*. But the fine performance of *Australia* in 1980 was not a false dawn; Denis Connor's 4-1 defence in 1980 did, in fact, presage the end of American dominance, not just in the America's Cup, but in grand prix yacht racing.

The British Syndicate had anticipated that the *Lionheart* rig would create a fine furore in 1980. Consequently, iron-clad protection from the ire of the New York Yacht Club was deemed absolutely essential. Ian Howlett was able to secure written permission for the bendy mast from the IYRU. Perhaps fortunately, the NYYC appears to have been blissfully unaware of the scope for 'confidential rulings' during a Cup cycle. At that time, there was a system in place, where, if a written ruling on the 12mR rules was sought and obtained within 18 months of the next America's Cup, then that ruling would remain secret for the duration of that Cup cycle.[1209]

The British were back for more punishment in 1983. Peter de Savary had contributed finance to *Lionheart* in the latter stages of the campaign and thought he could do better. De Savary's challenge certainly had a lot more money to spend but faltered at the first hurdle. *Victory '82*, designed by Ed Dubois, was an unmitigated disaster in both design and build.[1210] After this false start, it must have been a great relief when the Howlett-designed *Victory '83* was fast out of the box. *Victory '83*, re-decked and restored to concours condition, is still actively sailed in the USA and is now recognised as one of the best 12mRs of her era, and the most elegant.

However, *Victory '83* was unfortunate to come up against the game-changing *Australia II* in the challenger selection series, sponsored for the first time that year by Louis Vuitton. In 1983, in what remains the most notable yacht race in the history of the sport, the Australians would go all the way, beating the Valentijn-designed *Liberty* 4-3 and lifting the America's Cup in a very close-run series. With *Australia II*, Ben Lexcen had reworked the 12-metre model to make a small, comparatively light boat, competitive at the previously unpromising low end of the length-displacement spectrum.

The winged keel was integral to that paradigm shift. The keel combined the free spirit of Lexcen with the methodical approach and technical wizardry of Dutch aerodynamicist Joop Slooff. However, it is now forgotten that there was a third designer in the mix.[1211] Without Ian Howlett's pioneering work on the development of winged keels, and crucially, legitimising their use in America's Cup competition, the Australians would have gone home empty-handed.

Australia II commanded the headlines, but she was not the only 12mR with a winged keel in 1983. *Victory '83* also sported wings; in this instance to optimise a relatively more conventional design.[1212] Despite delivering a marginal gain, *Victory '83's* winglets, which had absorbed so much research time, were removed for the competition.[1213] This was, of course, a mistake as these appendages did indeed make the boat quicker and stripping them off rather belied the epithet '*Wing-nut*' bestowed on the boat.

Through the summer of 1983, the New York Yacht Club waged a war of attrition to avoid racing against the seemingly unstoppable *Australia II*.

The NYYC's argument hinged on the ostensibly reasonable argument that the Australian yacht's winged keel was a 'peculiarity' under Rule 27.[1214] However, both the outraged Americans and the blustering, but privately rather nervous, Australians were in for a surprise. As with *Lionheart's* bendy rig in 1980, Ian Howlett had obtained a 'confidential ruling' which adjudged winged keels to be permissible, as long as they were not adjustable or retractable and static draft was unaffected.[1215]

In retrospect, it is remarkable that the rules experts of the New York Yacht Club could stumble into this same trap once again; and that no one, not even the Australians, drew a parallel between the events of 1980 and 1983. And so, the Royal Perth Yacht Club was gifted that crucial 'get out of jail free' card to take the series and host the 1987 Louis Vuitton and America's Cup races. And by extension, Fremantle benefitted from a flurry of urban renewal, turning a neglected corner of Australia into a vibrant cosmopolitan success story. Four syndicates would chase the defender's slot and a record number of thirteen challengers made it to Perth. Clearly, the sailing world was inspired by the end of 'sports longest winning streak'.

The British *White Crusader* campaign was among the thirteen, with a two-boat challenge that included a refined design by Howlett and a radical second boat by David Hollom, notorious in these years for his left-field 'magic bullet' designs.[1216] The Hollom Twelve was more of a dog than a trial-horse and nicknamed the *Hippo* to complete an awkward troika of animal metaphors. In canine guise, she was tagged *Rover*, but they never did get her house-trained.[1217] Iain Murray, on observing a disconcerting similarity between the *Hippo's* nether regions and his new *Kookaburra III*, immediately knew he was on the wrong track and cropped her tail feathers.

The British campaign should have gone further in 1987, but the team could take some satisfaction in being generally on the pace, having achieved some good performances during the fleet racing the year before at the 1986 World Championships. The 'Fremantle Doctor', an afternoon breeze that energises the otherwise torrid climate, also turbocharged what was surely the best ever big boat regatta. In the 1987 Cup competition proper, Denis Connor *Stars & Stripes* team beat Iain Murray's *Kookaburra III* 4-0, to take the Cup home to San Diego.

British interest was briefly revived in 1988 when Peter de Savary sought to participate in Michael Fay's acrimonious 'deed of gift' challenge. Fay's 90ft LWL Farr monohull was matched against Dennis Connor's wingsail 60ft catamaran. De Savary lobbied to add his foil-stabilised outrigger, *Blue Arrow*, to the menagerie. For both defender and challenger, this was a distraction they could do without. The 1988 mismatch led to the creation of a new America's Cup Class. After two subsequent Cup cycles in San Diego, New Zealand brought the Cup back to the Antipodes in 1995. British interest was rekindled in 2003 when Peter Harrison challenged with *Wight Lightning*. Then there was another hiatus in our participation until Ben Ainslie's BAR challenge in 2013. BAR is back again, backed by a petrochemical billionaire, for another throw of the dice in 2021, for what will be the 36th challenge.

Revisiting *Sceptre* and the 17th Challenge

The 17th Challenge for the America's Cup was hatched during the height of the Cold War in 1957.[1218] So, in the spirit of the times, the syndicate met in an underground bunker built for Chamberlain's War Cabinet in 1939.[1219] Clearly, the boys were not only well-connected, but they were also thoroughly delusional too, using single-use note-pads to be collected and incinerated afterwards. As the campaign evolved, the thread of progression was scarcely discernible, so perhaps the minutes were burnt too. Paranoia is not unusual in America's Cup competitions, but the bunker highlighted British complacency. And as for espionage, that should have been *our* priority.

As an example of our unpreparedness, during one of these meetings, the subject of the spinnaker foot-length came up. Students of the Cup during the incomparable 12mR era will know that there was no limit on foot-length, as the assumption was that this was more-or-less self-limiting. So why did *Sceptre* fly a monster Herbulot spinnaker shaped like a circus marquee? As the story goes, the idea that we could get something for nothing galvanised the syndicate into life. The discussion turned into an auction until one old gentleman, armed with a Victorian ear trumpet, cried out: "*why not make it a hundred feet!*" And so, it was. That was our Monty Python-esque executive team. Foot length and half-width are now limited to J + 4.8m.[1220]

Sceptre was a much-loved boat on the Clyde, despite her poor showing in the America's Cup competition. My father took a week off from his day job to crew on the new boat during her initial trials in April 1958. It was his first experience sailing big boats. I was only six years old at the time, but I still vividly remember him coming home each day with a big grin, sunburnt and awestruck, brimming with stories. *Sceptre's* launching in April 1957 was symbolic of a new post-war optimism on Clydeside. Austerity had eased with the end of rationing in 1954, although orange juice, cod-liver oil and free school milk were still disbursed to keep the baby boomers healthy. In our collective memory, summers were endless, and the sun always shone.

The *Sceptre* model was selected through a formal design competition between Charles Nicholson, nephew of the great C. E. Nicholson, James McGruer of Clynder, Arthur Robb, a Kiwi who used to work at M&L in

Sandbank and David Boyd, director and resident designer at Robertson's Yard in Sandbank. So, it was 'Young Charlie' vs the 'Clyde mafia'. It is not clear why Angus Primrose (1938-1980), or Laurent Giles, perhaps the most successful naval architects of the day, were not involved at this stage.

Laurent Giles (1901-1969) was at that time Britain's most experienced 12mR designer and the only one with relevant tank-testing experience. Giles had tested five models for *Flicka II* in the Davidson Tank in 1937. The client was Hugh Goodison – *Sceptre's* syndicate head. *Flicka II* was used as the benchmark model in the subsequent testing. Perhaps he declined, but it seems odd that Giles, a year older than Boyd and still just 56 years old, was excluded. Although by then long in the tooth, *Flicka II* would go on to see service as a tune-up boat for *Sovereign* in 1964, and Giles' company would design *Diadem of Dewlish*, the mothership for that campaign.

The short-listed designers were required to submit two designs: one conventional ('Model A') and one just a little bit more radical ('Model B').[1221] An explicit invitation to 'think outside the box' is surely something all designers dream of. However, the response was disappointing. The four designers would all cleave to the familiar, ignoring alternative appendage configurations and choosing instead to experiment with the distribution of hull volume. However, in this respect the conventional model was already highly evolved and close to its zenith; stepping too far outside the 'envelope' almost inevitably meant regression, not progress.

Our research into John Stephen's work provokes the thought that perhaps Stug Perry, as Technical Advisor to the challenge, was keen to see how a fin-and-skeg boat, like his own 6mR, *Fane*, might perform. *Fane* was designed by John G. Stephen as *Maida II* in 1939. The visionary design of *Maida II* essentially prefigured the modern 12-metre, see Chapter 28. Fin-and-skeg boats built to the International Rule were vanishingly rare and had never been properly tank-tested against conventional full-keel models.

Perry's experience with *Fane* demonstrated the viability of fin-and-skeg designs under the International Rule. *Fane* was competitive against the best conventional models; and that after just three seasons of minor evolution and refinement. However, good as *Fane* was, she could not quite match the pace of the David Boyd-designed *Circe*, then 20 years old. Unfortunately, at this point in *Fane's* development, few appreciated that the performance gap was now no more than the difference a new mainsail might make.

Ian Howlett surmises that the pundits of the day thought *Maida II/Fane* to be a blind alley. No one, on either side of the Atlantic, was sufficiently aroused to check whether the glass was half-empty and draining, or half-full and still under the tap. As we now know, it was the latter. Sadly, the tap was turned off and yacht design was set back 20 years. So much for playing safe. That said, the Americans were certainly unadventurous too. The S&S defender, *Columbia*, a new boat, was no faster and may even have been slower than *Vim*, drawn in the same design office back in 1938. *Vim* had been converted for cruising after WW2, then hacked about extensively to restore her back to racing trim for the 1958 trials. She pushed the better equipped, better funded *Columbia* to the wire.

The *Sceptre* model was selected on the basis of tank tests which are now regarded as substantially meaningless.[1222] One of the Saunders Roe team who carried out the tests confessed many years later that *"they could not really distinguish between the nine models in 1957"*.[1223] In many respects, the testing fell short of G. L. Watson's pioneering work for *Shamrock II* in 1890/91, see Chapter 6. Nevertheless, the selection committee, made up of William Crago – Superintendent of the Saunders Roe facility, Hugh Goodison – Syndicate Head, Frank Murdoch, who had previous experience with the *Endeavour* challenges in the 1930s, and Stug Perry, made a bold call that all would agree was rash in retrospect. They played 'pin the tail on the donkey'.

Some of the differences that were detected may have arisen within the expected experimental error of the very basic testing protocol. While the constraints of small-model testing were well known at the time, it was not until the design regression of the 1970 America's Cup boats that such testing was re-evaluated objectively. It took ages to resolve the muddle, setting yacht design back by another decade.[1224] The dynamometry for the 1956 tank-tests, designed at the National Physical Laboratory (NPL) ca.1953, was fundamentally flawed. Remarkably, in light of the criticism levelled at this series of tests, in 1959, during the early days of the Red Duster syndicate, the same process was proposed for another challenge.

Summary of tank-tests from the British 1958 America's Cup Challenge

	Flicka II	Nicholson I	Nicholson II	McGruer A	McGruer B	Robb S116	Robb S117	Boyd A	Boyd B *Sceptre*
Resistance lbs			*Speed in knots to constant values of resistance with the model upright*						
200lbs	4.64	4.98	4.64	4.92	5.12	5.19	4.73	4.82	4.68
400lbs	7.48	6.93	7.05	7.05	7.22	7.22	7.26	7.38	7.48
600lbs	8.24	8.02	8.20	8.04	8.18	8.24	9.28	8.41	8.39
800lbs	8.68	8.64	8.70	8.43	8.62	8.72	8.76	8.92	8.80
Windspeed			*Speed made good to windward in knots*						
5kts true	3.07	3.10	3.10	3.01	3.01	3.06	3.06	3.15	3.19
10kts true	5.36	5.41	5.41	5.27	5.34	5.46	5.41	5.38	5.42
15kts true	6.13	6.36	6.35	6.33	6.16	6.33	6.15	6.30	6.35
20kts true	6.46	6.75	6.78	6.56	6.46	6.77	6.45	6.57	6.64

Source: An Investigation into the Hydrodynamic Characteristics of Nine 12-metre hulls. National Physical Laboratory, Report No. T/0/216, 1957.

Of interest, in this world of happenstance, is that the same deceptive dynamometry was used by the renowned Maritime Research Institute of The Netherlands (MARIN) at Wageningen for their large (one-third scale) 12mR tests in the early 1980s. This testing gave the green light to the revolutionary *Australia II*. Apparently, the 'tank crew' were unaware of the inherent systematic errors. Maddeningly, this flawed process produced an exceptionally quick boat for the 1987 America's Cup match.[1225] So while these two sets of tests 30 years apart are not directly comparable, the common link of 'garbage in, garbage out' does induce a smile. Sometimes the magic bullet is right there in the magazine.

We now consider Scotland's contribution to Britain's post-1964 America's Cup campaigns. While the Clyde marine industry's direct association with the America's Cup came to an uneasy conclusion in that year, the story continued with significant Scottish involvement. Britain has contested the Louis Vuitton challengers' selection series five more times during the post-war years, and at the time of writing a new challenge is in process for the 36th America's Cup in March 2021.[1226]

Liquid Sunshine on Islay [1227]

"Too much of anything is bad, but too much good whiskey is barely enough." So said Mark Twain, and he cannot, surely, have been referring to bourbon. The 1987 British America's Cup campaign was refinanced by Graham Walker, who had recently purchased the White Horse Whisky brand.[1228] Walker achieved great success offshore with a series of five well-sailed IOR yachts, all named *Indulgence* and all 'looking the part'. But even in those years when the Brits ruled the Admiral's Cup, the America's Cup was a tougher nut to crack. Aligning the patron's expectations with a coven of uber-competitive egos and a batch of boffins' skillsets to a common purpose is never easy, but the British seem to have found it especially challenging.

The Scotch whisky connection brought a caucus of heavy hitters from the 26th America's Cup to the West Coast of Scotland. In the summer of 1986, Ian Howlett drove north from Oxford in his little VW Polo with Lawrie Smith for company, picking up Erik Maxwell at Preston. Arriving in Islay, they took in a corporate courtesy tour of the famous Lagavulin Distillery. White Horse is a blended, mass-market whisky containing 40% malt contributed by Lagavulin, Talisker and Linkwood. The 16-year-old Lagavulin single-malt is acclaimed as one of the best whiskies distilled in the Western Isles.[1229]

These three America's Cup characters had made the long trek to Islay to confabulate with David Boyd, then living with his son and daughter-in-law in the little village of Bridgend by Loch Indaal. Boyd was hobbling along on crutches after a fall, but still game to blether about his love affair with 12-metre yachts. Boyd's advice during this trip, as Ian recalls it was: *"If I might take the liberty of offering a little advice to a young designer, it would be to keep his eyes and ears wide open and his mouth closed."* And, on the golf course, *"If I were you, I'd give it a wee kick."* and finally, *"an HB pencil, well-sharpened, is ideal for cleaning a gun."* These indeed are the secrets of an unfathomable trade.

Lawrie Smith would have lapped it all up. Lawrie has chain-smoked his way through a successful yachting career and somehow still has puff to spare. At that time, he was employed by Iain Murray's *Kookaburra* Syndicate. Smith burst into the limelight as a cocky 18-year-old at the 1974 Merlin Championships, where he came a remarkable 2nd overall. In a professional career taking in the Olympics, the Whitbread Round the World Race and the Louis Vuitton Trophy, Smith has flirted with greatness. Today, with countless championships under his belt, Lawrie is still among the best keelboat sailors with a gimlet-eyed stare that can cut unwelcome company like a cheese slice.

Erik Maxwell, the third member of the trio, was the favoured candidate to steer Sovereign, but lost out to the celebrity stardust of Peter Scott. Erik endured the purgatory of the 1964 Challenge as understudy, watching the campaign unwind. The experience had prompted him to chase the dragon of another America's Cup campaign with his old friend, David Boyd, as we describe in the following sections. So, there was a camaraderie of interest and enthusiasm as they sat down to discuss the forthcoming regatta off Fremantle.

Erik Maxwell

Erik Maxwell (1925-2000) was a successful Scottish sailor, curiously held in higher regard south of the border than in his native land. Erik was obsessed with the America's Cup and chased that dream through the best years of his life. His support for successive challenges brought him to prominence on the national stage. He was a patron of the sport in the old style of the 'tip-top sportin' chentlemen', described in Chapter 13. Erik had the resources and the confidence necessary to play in the big league; his father, John, was the man behind Associated British Pictures (ABC Cinemas) and the vast Elstree Studio complex.[1230]

John Maxwell entered the film industry in 1912, when films were silent, music was live, and the nitrate film-stock used in that era was apt to enliven the action by bursting into flames. After John bought Elstree in 1927, he maintained a policy of strategic take-overs to grow the business. In 1936, he was involved in a titanic battle to seize control of Gaumont's British operation. The combined assets of the proposed conglomerate would have totalled £24 million (£1.7 billion).[1231] The bid failed, but other acquisitions compensated, and at the peak of the business, he would control more than 500 cinemas. John's interest in filmmaking ran deep; he was very much a 'hands-on' proprietor, fully involved in screenplay and production. He broke into new markets by insisting on real-life dialogue, and curbing the clipped Oxford English proudly delivered by English actors of the time.

ABC was referred to in the House of Commons "*the rock upon which the British film industry is built*". As Producer, John Maxwell was close to completing the silent film, *Blackmail*, directed by Alfred Hitchcock, when he received news of the success of *The Jazz Singer* in the USA. Maxwell immediately made the decision to remake the film as a 'talkie' and the two versions were released simultaneously in 1929. Maxwell was one of the first to see Hitchcock's potential as a director, and gave Charles Laughton, Ray Milland, Anna Neagle, Errol Flynn, Michael Wilding and Maureen O'Hara, among other stars of the silver screen, a start in the business.

John Maxwell passed away in 1940 at the family's holiday house in Cove. The following year, John's widow, who had always taken a keen interest in her husband's business affairs, sold a little under half of the Maxwell shares in ABC to Warner Bros for £900,000 (£45 million).[1232]

Erik was then just fifteen and still a schoolboy. He would later assume responsibilities in the film distribution business, but in the meantime, he enrolled in a correspondence course to learn the saxophone. Unlikely as this route to stardom may seem, he went on to join the George Evans Orchestra. George Evans (1915-1993) jazz bandleader, arranger, tenor saxophonist, vocalist and recording artist was well-regarded in the business. And with Erik duelling on sax, we can assume that they were hot!

The magic of the America's Cup enthused Erik from childhood. As a nine-year-old in 1934, he invested his heart and soul in the *Endeavour* Challenge and his family indulged that passion. They bought him a scale model of Charles E. Nicholson's masterpiece. Erik hoisted the model's miniature racing flag with due ceremony each day of the races. As is now recognised, the Cup was there for the taking in 1934, so the boy was deeply affected when Tom Sopwith squandered the opportunity. See Chapter 15.

Erik started sailing in Loch Long keelboats at Cove & Kilcreggan, before moving on to more adventurous racing yachts. He was class champion in *Akela* in 1954, then again with *Celeano II* in 1956 and 1957. Bracketing his wins was Bert Shaw with *Blaithe*; Bert would later be a key man in the *Sceptre* crew.[1233]

Erik was still just 24 years old when he made the daunting step up to the big league. In 1949, he bought *Felma*, a 1937 Fife 8-metre, changing her name to *Cherokee*, even before he had mastered the Loch Longs. Three years later, Erik bought the 1936 Tor Holm 8-metre, *Christina*, from Rachel Pitt-

Rivers, a formidable yachtswoman (Rachel skippered her 1935 Nicholson offshore 12mR, *Foxhound of Lepe*, across the Atlantic to compete in the 1956 Bermuda Race, and then she sailed the boat back again). *Christina*, built by Abramsson & Borjesson in Sweden, was arguably the most beautiful boats on the Clyde. After Erik sold her in 1954, she became *Christina of Cascais*.[1234]

As a result of Erik's movie connections, the Loch Long, *Ripple*, featured in the 1949 J. Arthur Rank film, *Floodtide*, with Bob Haggart, Marshall Napier and of course Erik sailing the boat. The movie was written by the same George Blake, who is quoted extensively in these pages, and starred a youthful Gordon Jackson, Rona Anderson and John Laurie, later to become a much-loved grouch in 'Dad's Army'.[1235]

1959-62 Seasons

Erik Maxwell had first sailed on *Sceptre* as a guest in 1957 and knew her well. So, when he bought the boat in 1959, he was fully aware of both her potential and her defects. The purchase was the first step leading to a possible America's Cup challenge in the 1960s. David Boyd arranged for Erik to buy the boat when she was shipped back from the States. The Boyd connection was important to Erik's embryo campaign, however, the learning process, for both owner and designer, would surely have gained more from the purchase, or lease, of a good American 12mR, as subsequent Australian and French campaigns would do.[1236] *Sceptre* was cheap to buy, but ultimately, perhaps, an expensive mistake?

Unlikely as it may seem following her poor showing in the Cup, there had been genuine offers for *Sceptre* at the asking price of £15,000 (£350,000). However, the feeling in Britain was that she should be brought home, as without the benchmark of a recent trial-horse, any future 12mR challenges would have to start again from scratch. The Royal Yacht Squadron Syndicate patriotically sold *Sceptre* to Erik for £9000 (£211,000). The 1958 RYS Cup campaign had cost £70,000 (£1.6 million), so the shareholders received just 8p from each pound of their 'investment', as is invariably the way with such sporting 'wagers'.[1237]

It was reported that both Boyd and Maxwell wanted to experiment with *Sceptre*, but David Boyd's imperative was surely more personal. While he was known to have privately favoured his conventional 'Model A' design in 1957, he was still keen to vindicate *Sceptre*. It is interesting to compare Boyd's defence of the boat with his subsequent work. In 1958, he declared that just because *"Columbia had a more 'veed' bow, deeper chest, thinner keel, wider stern, lighter displacement, and straighter lines than Sceptre"* it was not necessarily the only way to go, or even a desirable design direction.[1238]

This was before the American designer Ray Hunt carried out extensive tank-testing of the *Sceptre* model, in work coordinated with Boyd in 1959. While Hunt's testing was flawed to the extent of amplifying real margins, Boyd certainly took note. Four years later, when his *Sovereign* design was revealed, the new boat had a more 'veed' bow, deeper chest, thinner keel, wider stern, lighter displacement, and straighter lines than *Sceptre*.

Meanwhile, others were also laying plans for a Cup challenge. The most substantive appeared to be the Royal Thames Yacht Club's Red Duster Syndicate, chaired by Lord Craigmyle with Arthur Robb as designer. In March 1960, they announced a £150,000 (£3.5 million) programme. This group brought the Charles E. Nicholson-designed *Norsaga* back from Norway for design research and crew training. Sailing as *Trivia*, she was formerly owned by Jimmy Howden-Hume on the Clyde. *Norsaga* was another purchase of convenience, like *Sceptre*, that did not advance the state of the art.

Over the winter of 1959-60, in consultation with Boyd, Erik sorted out *Sceptre's* handling problems; work which included moving the mast back. Through the early-season races of 1960, *Sceptre's* performance improved rapidly. That season, there were seven 12mRs, or 'ex-Twelves', based at Cowes, including those campaigned by other potential challengers; Tony Boyden's *Flica II* and Craigmyle's *Norsaga*. Initially at least, most of the boats were in cruising trim with fitted-out interiors, pre-war gear with wooden-cheeked blocks, and second-rate sails.

The unsurprising result was that *Sceptre* won nearly everything through the 1960 and 1961 seasons, attracting many column inches of favourable press coverage with her prestigious Queen's Cup wins. Prince Philip sailed the boat to victory in 1961 and '62 to guarantee more headlines.[1239] In 1962, Erik bought the *Genie Maris*, a 69-ton twin-screw ketch, to serve as a support vessel for *Sceptre* on her travels, shuttling between the Solent and the Clyde.[1240] It all seemed like the basis for a campaign.

One afternoon in the early 1960s, Erik overheard two old-timers, sitting on the quayside in Cowes looking admiringly at *Sceptre*, muttering one to the other: "*Of course she's getting going properly now that she's got a decent wooden stick in her*". In the spring of that year, following her launch at Sandbank, we turned our binoculars on *Sceptre* at her moorings with what appeared to be a wooden stick. The Kilmun kids rowed across the loch to confirm that the rivets were still there. The graphics were certainly a tour de force in the days before vinyl wraps. The old tin-leg had been 'lined' in a convincing spruce simulation, complete with the occasional knot. Kitsch or what? This treatment became quite fashionable for a while on the Clyde.

Among the syndicates still keen to challenge in 1962, Owen Aisher was said to have had an arrangement with Charles A. Nicholson to design a Twelve, but "*only when the time was right*". Tony Boyden's effort was more advanced; he had had signed-up David Boyd, with support from Laurent Giles and John Illingworth to carry out preliminary work in 1960. Boyden would then go on to fund Boyd's extensive research at the Stevens tank in the USA. By this stage, the Red Duster group had already invested in two and a half years of tank-testing at Saunders Roe, where they had, rather unsportingly perhaps, secured exclusivity.

However, Britain's patriarchal assumptions about their priority to challenge in 1962 were dashed when the New York Yacht Club announced that the Australian's were their preferred challenger, although diplomatically the NYYC said they were also open to the idea of a Commonwealth Challenge mediated by the Duke of Edinburgh. The Aussies, of course, were less than impressed by that idea. Who would want to stumble through preliminary rounds when you could proceed to the main event? Sir Frank Packer's response to the Duke was a telegram: "YOU HAVE HAD A LONG UNINTERRUPTED RUN STOP MAYBE WE WON'T DO ANY BETTER BUT EVERY NOW AND THEN YOU HAVE TO GIVE THE YOUNG FELLOW IN THE FAMILY HIS HEAD STOP".[1241]

British interests regrouped to address the 1964 spot offered by the NYYC. In January 1962, even before the Australian yacht, *Gretel*, had surprised the cognoscenti with a fine performance at Newport, Erik Maxwell told George Findlay of *The Glasgow Herald* that he was keen to see a British challenge in 1964, but he would not do it alone. Shortly afterwards, he teamed up with Michael Boyle, owner of *Vanitie*, Captain Guy Lawrence (*Evaine*) and Major Reggie Macdonald-Buchanan (*Kaylena*) to form the short-lived '12mR Owners' Syndicate' with Camper & Nicholson signed up as designers and builders. The problem, it seems, was funding.

Once again, the Red Duster group, while formed to challenge in 1962, seemed to be in the best position for a tilt at the 'Auld Mug' in 1964. Their designer, Arthur 'Robby' Robb, had an April '62 building slot booked with Groves & Gutteridge.[1242] However, instead of taking it up, the project was abandoned that same month. Craigmyle was a notable philanthropist, but he had reached the end of his tether. His barfly mates in the shipping industry mysteriously left their wallets at home when the bills came in.

Thomas Shaw, 3rd Lord Craigmyle, Commander of the Order of Pious IX, (1923-1998), was another wealthy Scot with an America's Cup obsession. 'Craigie', as he was known to his friends, was 'blessed with a total absence of snobbery'. He was said to be *"spectacularly generous on a scale unknown to most of his friends and even, sometimes, to his own family"*. Craigie struggled with alcoholism all his adult life and spent six years 'drying out'. In later life, with his roots in Rothiemurchus, the pull of the Highlands was irresistible. In 1964, after abandoning his America's Cup ambitions, he sold his family estate near Selkirk and rebuilt a ruin by Loch Nevis. His obituary in *The Glasgow Herald* recalled that *"He was happiest there, composing pibrochs and piping, lifting lobster-pots, and baking bread and bannocks"*.[1243]

This left Tony Boyden's syndicate as the only group still committed to a challenge in 1964. In terms of the bigger picture, this was a blow for Britain's chances of honing a race winner, as the *Sovereign* challenge progressed unopposed until *Kurrewa V*, a virtual sistership funded by John Livingston and Owen Aisher, entered the fray in the autumn. On the plus side, David Boyd's tank-testing at Hoboken had already been completed before the New York Yacht Club issued their game-changing memorandum in December 1962, prohibiting challengers access to American technology.

1963-65 Seasons

Tony Boyden's *Sovereign* was launched at David Boyd's Sandbank yard in April 1963. To get the 'working up' process in motion, Erik Maxwell volunteered *Sceptre* as a trial horse. Even Erik must have seen his role as 'sacrificial lamb', but in an unlikely scenario that was worrying at the time, *Sceptre* was initially quicker than *Sovereign*. However, the old boat's stirring performance had very little to do with design. *Sceptre* had been optimised, but she was still pretty average for a 1958 12mR.

What the race reports highlighted, was the fine crew work aboard *Sceptre*; an advantage she retained through the summer of 1963.[1244] Jack Knights commented: "*Maxwell's crew is the best in Britain and his helming is outstanding for his split-second starts*"[1245] *Sceptre's* red-clad crew was mainly made up of Erik's old mates from his Loch Long days: Bert Shaw, John Scaife, Tommy Steele and Dennis Royal, in addition to Bobby Bruce and Calum McLachlan from Robertson's yard.[1246]

It remains a matter of regret that both *Sovereign* and *Kurrewa V* were hobbled by arrogance, self-interest and poor executive decision-making in the run up to the 1964 Challenge. Some of the blame for this lay with the management team's failure to persevere with key lines of development, like the bendy mast programme. Boyden blamed the 'absence of a culture of excellence in British industry' for the boat's faults. Remembering the shoddy products of our manufacturing industry in the 1960s, perhaps he had a point. Then there was the skipper; Peter Scott had been a fine dinghy sailor in his youth, but his big boat experience was extremely limited.[1247]

Erik Maxwell, on the other hand, may have never sailed a dinghy at high level, but he was now a formidable metre-boat skipper with 15 years racing Eights and Twelves. However, it was Erik who had tempted fate by introducing Peter Scott to Tony Boyden. Scott was a good friend, and together with David Boyd, they all had a common interest in wildfowl. So, despite having only one 12mR race under his belt; ducks, a high profile and a winning personality won Scott the job.[1248]

Most of the crew, and indeed the yachting press, thought that if Erik had been at the helm, things might have been better.[1249] When Erik and Scott alternated, Erik nearly always had the edge. Nevertheless, he always maintained that his only interest was to raise the bar for the chosen helmsman. Erik's personal preference was for sailmaker, Bruce Banks, who had initially appeared the most likely candidate.[1250] Whatever the reason, it is certain that the end result would have been the same; the '64 rigs were dreadful, and Banks' sails were embarrassing. British challenges invariably faltered when the helmsman brought his own sails on board, as again with John Oakley's Miller & Whitworth wardrobe on *Lionheart* in 1978.

> With regard to steering heavy-displacement vs light displacement hull-forms, and notwithstanding countless successful crossovers, the two skills are quite different. The dinghy helmsman, who is used to tracking micro-shifts has to resist pinching and oversteering. Dinghy techniques are based on matching available power to available righting moment through coordinated steering and body movement. On a heavy displacement keelboat that is replaced by a more cerebral approach. He or she must forget the instant gratification of cause and effect to conceptualise a 'smoothed average' with a much longer periodicity; determined, not just by wind and sea conditions, but also by the displacement, distribution of volume and underwater profile of the vessel. It is a quite different technique and arguably harder to master. This 'smoothed' action is why the best keelboat sailors appear to be doing very little after the flurry of activity accelerating out of a tack.

In a scenario that is hard to fathom today, while *Sovereign* was launched with a double-spreader 'copy' of the American's masts, she went to America in 1964 with a single-spreader rig that recalled *Sceptre's* much-criticised set-up. It seems that the topmast was uncontrollable in 1963 and unwilling to waste any more time getting the bendy mast to work, Boyd's innate caution led him to resort to an old-fashioned straight stick.[1251] *Kurrewa V* would also go down this route, or cul de sac, to be more accurate.

Erik and his core-team accompanied our two-boat challenge to Newport in 1964, joining the pool of candidates keen to sail in the match. Erik lobbied to get more of his people on board *Sovereign* to improve the still-poor spinnaker handling, but as Tony Boyden's selection criteria favoured strength and fitness over experience and guile, it was inevitable that few 'real sailors' would make the cut.

> Erik's critics cited his lack of international experience and unadventurous tactics. However, taking a campaign to the South Coast from the Clyde is no different to sailing in France, for example. And when Erik did eventually sail *Sceptre* at Newport in 1967, he was far from intimidated. As for tactics, there is no need for the helmsman to assume that responsibility in a big boat where you have a specialist tactician (plus navigator and mainsheet trimmer) in the cockpit with you, tendering advice. While some alpha-male skippers may enjoy the challenge of 'multi-tasking', to be honest, the two key roles of helmsman and tactician are quite hard enough individually.

While he did not sail in the match, Erik made use of the time to establish contacts and plan for the future. He was playing a long game to prepare the ground for a challenge of his own. Later he would arrange for *Sceptre* to return to Newport for the 1967 America's Cup season to race against Yankee 12mRs – the only useful yardstick in these years. Boyd had argued that British 12mR crews should go and race in America in 1957. However, the Goodison syndicate elected not to charter an American 12mR for practice as poor results *"would be bad for morale"*!

1967-68 Seasons

Sceptre was shipped over to the States on the Cunard freighter, *Elysin*, and based in Newport at Port O' Call Marina for the summer of 1967.[1252] *Yachting Monthly* reported that *Kurrewa V*, then in Tony Boyden's ownership, would also sail at Newport that summer with a new mast and Hood sails.[1253] *Sceptre* had been updated to reflect David Boyd's most recent thoughts and refitted at Sandbank prior to shipping. The boat gained a new square-toed rudder, the long stern overhang was cropped to a retroussé transom and she was re-faired below the waterline. With the overhangs now in balance, *Sceptre* enjoyed a more purposeful, contemporary look to match the American Twelves.[1254]

Erik purchased a full set of sails from Hood in the USA. And, equally important, the folks at Hood gave the *Sceptre* crew essential advice on how to set them up, using much higher tensions than the British norm at that time. Eight of the crew were from Erik's loyal old Scots guard. Twelves are hyper-sensitive to sail cut and trim so, with good sails and good sailors, the old girl finally became a bit of a weapon. *Sceptre* even had the legs to act as a useful 'trial horse' for *American Eagle*, which had only been narrowly eased out of the defender's role in 1964.[1255]

It seems that in up to 15kts true of windspeed *Sceptre* and *American Eagle* were absolutely even. Once the breeze rose much above that, however, the *Eagle* would ease away.[1256] This belies *Sceptre's* characterisation as a heavy weather boat, but then the *Eagle* also had that reputation. On the New York Yacht Club Cruise in 1967, on a twelve-mile beat, *Sceptre* lost just one minute to Olin Stephen's new 'wonder boat', *Intrepid*, steered by Emil 'Bus' Mosbacher, one of the best helmsmen of the era.

So, while it had taken 10 years to get the old boat up to speed, she got there at last.[1257] This 'much of a muchness' picture of 'marginal gains' is lost in the binary arithmetic of the America's Cup, where Britain's extended losing streak against the Americans through the 20th century misrepresents a considerably more nuanced competition between the naval architects and yachtsmen of the two nations. And in these other competitions, where notable yachts from both countries crossed the Atlantic to race against local fleets in foreign waters, we often gave as good as we got. Through the history of yachting, the balance of power in racing yacht technology often lay nearer these shores.

Ultimately, posterity has assessed *Sceptre* as a 'reasonable' 1958 12mR, nothing special in terms of performance but full of nice ideas.[1258] The canoe-body was good, the scow bow prescient, and if not for her fat keel-fin, the hull shape might have been very good indeed. Through the late 1960s, Erik Maxwell invested more time and money in *Sceptre* than perhaps was wise. But the experience gained during the sojourn in Newport encouraged Erik and Boyd to make tentative plans for a future challenge.

> Ten years pushes the envelope, but even today a Maxi 76 might need two or even three seasons to become competitive. The latest scows from David Raison and Sam Manuard, and the higher volume hulls of Joubert Nivelt, for example, can also take a few years to realise their full potential. It is not just achieving optimal setup, moding and evolving sail shapes for these new modes on every point of sailing, but also developing sail-handling systems and ultimately sailing techniques, that takes the time. After all this has been accomplished, when classes approach a design plateau, as in the TP52 circuit, new boats are simply fast from the day of their launch.

Erik, together with an associate Gordon Wallace, stayed on to watch *Intrepid* trounce *Dame Pattie* in the 1967 Cup contest.[1259] He was not deterred by the one-sided contest he had just witnessed and immediately lodged a challenge through the Royal Dorset Yacht Club.[1260] Erik was described in the press at the time as a 42-year-old film distributer and *"indisputably the ablest 12mR helmsman here"*. Erik's supporting cast included the ever-faithful Reggie Macdonald-Buchanan, Chairman of the British 12mR Association.[1261] The challenge was one of four received that year, lodged by Britain, France, Australia, and in an unlikely scenario, Greece.

Erik's challenge was based on his concept of a British America's Cup Challenge Association (BACCA) to select the best from several new boats promised, or anticipated, to be built in Britain. He had a syndicate of ten signed-up and expected that number to rise to twenty. Erik had talked to Boyd and also roped in Warwick Hood, the *"brilliant young designer of Dame Pattie"*. Erik was sensibly wary of both the commitment and the scrutiny of a sceptical yachting press; so initial plans were laid in some secrecy. Resorting to clichés, the press considered that he would be *"unlikely to offend his Scots sense by risking the massive financial outlay without a good chance of success"*.

When researching the Boyd book, we came across drawings of *Sceptre* redesigned with a slimmed-down keel-fin, using a conventional (NACA 63-0123) section and with an '*Intrepid*-style' profile. The drawing was labelled 'Major Modifications, February 1968'. Other changes included nipped-in garboards, a skeg-hung rudder and a snubbed nose. The much-maligned bluff entry was retained.[1262]

The proposed changes were significant and clearly uneconomic on a 12-year-old boat as they involved a whole new centre-line structure. So, it should have been obvious that this was simply a ruse to circumvent the New York Yacht Club's recently imposed ban on foreign contenders using American facilities. Boyd was able to make full use of the Davidson Lab without alerting the NYYC. However, as events transpired, that subterfuge was the fledgling campaign's only real achievement.

1969-70 Seasons

The BACCA initiative folded in May 1969, when, if the rumour mill was correct, Erik's associates proved reluctant to get their chequebooks out.[1263] The 1970 America's Cup was an event that should not have been missed. It was the first occasion where a challenger's series was run off, and the first since *Endeavour* in 1934 to expose real weakness in the American defence. That said, the French first-timers did not really trouble the Australian's *Gretel II* in 1970. Subsequent challengers' selection series for the Louis Vuitton Trophy were hard-fought, ruthlessly establishing the strongest contenders and chipping away at American supremacy.

Going down with honour, Baron Bic took the helm of *France* himself in the last race and memorably got lost in the Newport fog. Englishman Hugh Somerville, writing for the *New York Times* wrote up the fiasco: "*even the most backward students from Britain, who have made so many ineffectual attempts at this cup business, have known that one essential for success, if you ever can get it, is to know where on earth you are.*"[1264] Ouch!

Sir Frank Packer's crew were arguably naïve, but *Gretel II* was clearly the faster boat in 1970, taking a race off *Intrepid*. Suddenly everything seemed possible and there was new interest in the Auld Mug. It appeared that the Americans were not unbeatable, so another British challenge was planned for 1974, with seed capital provided by Tony Boyden. As a first step, John Wellicome, Senior Lecturer at the University of Southampton and an excellent mathematician, carried out a parametric study of *Sovereign*; and a theoretical wave-making analysis was conducted by George Gadd, a well-known specialist at the National Physical Laboratory in Teddington. Gadd's work promised dramatic reductions in resistance with only minor adjustments to hull lines.

John Wellicome redrew the *Sovereign* lines in accordance with Gadd's recommendations and a 1:12 model tank-test model was constructed. It appears that the shoe-string programme lost momentum at this point as the finished model was set aside to gather dust. Quite why is not clear, as the tank was there to use at marginal cost. A few years later, ca.1973, Derek Coleman, then working at the Yacht Research Group, decided to test the 'improved' model. It turned out that, while the Wellicome & Gadd redesign looked good, the tank revealed that it was only "*slightly worse than the original model*.[1265] David Boyd, then happily retired at Gartocharn, must have raised his glass to that one! And so, the marginal figures in yacht design technology, and on occasion, the main players too, promise more than they can realistically deliver.

1971-73 Seasons

Erik Maxwell also had ambitions for 1974, and he would cast the net wide to get a handle on current design developments. His research programme included the earlier surrogate tank-testing with *Sceptre*-badged models at Hoboken, described in the previous section, and also an attempt to involve Olin Stephens to advise on the Robertson's fibreglass 8-metre OD – the latter repackaged as a plan to increase the marketability of the proposed class in the USA and worldwide. After the 8mR project faltered, Erik ordered the 6-metre, *Gosling*, as described in Chapter 24. As a strategy, the S&S commission cannot be faulted; a 'half-size model' should have been a fast-track to design a quick 12mR.

At that time, Olin Stephens was still considered *the* master of his craft, despite the poor showing of *Valiant* in 1970, which could not match *Intrepid* from 1967. *Valiant* was the highest-profile casualty of a tank-test glitch which favoured longer, heavier boats. All the new generation were developed using test-tank models built to a scale of 1:13.3. These were later acknowledged as too small to produce reliable results.[1266]

As the story goes, Olin Stephens, observing *Valiant's* quarter-wave on her first sail, spluttered, "*Oh damn!*". She was the greatest disappointment in his professional life. This unlovely boat got under his skin, and he was still tinkering with her during his retirement in the early 2000s. There was certainly a lot to tinker with. *Valiant* was always better on port tack than starboard. It turned out that the keel was asymmetrical, and moreover, neither side was right. After decades of modifications *Valiant's* performance is average today, but she will never be described as a 'classic'.

Notwithstanding the superb *Courageous*, which defended in 1974 and 1977, it is fair to say that when Erik turned to S&S for a new 6mR design, the firm was no longer quite the force it had been. Mario Tarabocchia had been drawing the lines since 1964, but Olin still dealt directly with his clients. Over the course of a frank exchange of letters, Erik must have been perplexed to discover that Olin was far from bullish about his 6mR designs, then frankly astonished when Olin proposed wheel-steering. Erik's boat, *Gosling*, would turn out to be heavy, short of sail area and difficult to steer.[1267] Since the whole point of the commission had been "*to gain valuable insight into the latest S&S design thinking*" for a possible America's Cup bid, this must have been hugely disappointing.[1268]

Erik's long-term planning produced nothing useful that could inform a new 12mR challenge. And, as for the subtle winnowing of ideas, there was only chaff. The gossipy *Daily Telegraph* reported that Maxwell's new Six *Gosling* was: "*an improved version of their 1970 America's Cup trialist Valiant, the new yacht could be an important asset in bringing to this country the thinking of the world's leading design team on how boats built to the metre rule should look. Gosling can thus be a valuable pattern for the Royal Thames Yacht Club 1974 Americas Cup designers*".[1269] So much for subterfuge.

A non-exclusive S&S 6-metre design in 1971 would have set you back $1,750 (£8,500 today). The 1971 model was based on the excellent 1967 12mR, *Intrepid*, however, it also incorporated the worst features of the hugely disappointing 12mR, *Valiant*. Olin even suggested using an earlier set of lines similar to *Toogoowooloo IV* (design date 1966), but *Gosling* was built to the newer *Toogoowooloo V* model (design date 1970), with minor alterations – the lateral plane was extended and the after part of the canoe-body cleaned up to ease the run.[1270] It would not have mattered much; the old design was little better than the new one, if at all.

Gosling had been a 'fishing expedition', so much so that Erik did not even race the boat. One reason for this, apart from her irrelevance, was that a more interesting prospect came on the market in 1971. The 8mR, *Iskareen*, was one of the 'magic' generation of pre-war S&S boats that included the 12mR, *Vim*, and the 6mR, *Goose*.[1271] She was a rather special boat, built by A/B Neglinge-Varvet in 1939, and extremely well-equipped after a two-decade sojourn in the United States in the ownership of Eugene van Voorhis. She would be Erik's third 8mR. The old guard – Bobby Bruce, Calum McLachlan, Bert Shaw and co ran the boat, with Erik's good friend, David Boyd, riding shotgun in the afterguard. As Erik still owned *Sceptre* in 1972, he now had a 'full set' – 6mR, 8mR & 12mR.

1974-79 Seasons

While the Royal Thames challenge was yet another promising initiative that fell through, 1974 would have been as good a time as any to challenge. There was a real window of opportunity in the 1970s, as demonstrated by the success of *Gretel II* and the ever-green *Courageous*. In spite of all the hype and talk of breakthroughs in the test-tank, design evolution had stagnated, as can happen periodically under any rule. The 1970-generation 12mRs were generally reckoned to be slower than the 1958 vintage, and they, in turn, were on a par with *Vim* from 1939.

While rigs, sails and sailing techniques were evolving rapidly on the water in the 1970s and 80s, time, money and access to test-tank time led a closeted generation of designers to favour increasingly heavy displacement. The S&S Twelves from *Constellation* (1964) onwards were all drawn by Mario Tarabocchia. Ian Howlett recalls meeting Mario and other members of the

S&S team on the Morgan Yacht, *Djinn*, during the 1974 Cup season. Tarabocchia was like a rabbit in the headlights. Clad in a raincoat and shiny city shoes, he let slip to the assembled company that this was his first view of an America's Cup race. What a contrast with tank-test pioneer David Napier, the best part of two centuries earlier, combining his rudimentary testing on the Camlachie Millpond with many hours hanging over the rail of the Belfast packet in a gale, striving to fathom the relationship between experimental testing and the real-world.

1979-84 Seasons

After sitting it out in 1977, Tony Boyden successfully brought a challenge to Newport in 1980. It seems that Boyden deeply resented Erik not contributing more in 1979/80, though he did quietly pay for the *Constellation* crew to attend the inaugural 12mR World Championships at Brighton in 1979, which *Lionheart* went on to win. Another British boat, *Victory* '82, won this 'second-tier' event in 1982 off Newport. *Victory* '83 won again at Porto Cervo in 1984, when she was owned by Consorzia Italia.[1272] The 1984 event might be considered as the first genuinely competitive 12mR Championship.

Erik Maxwell's last initiative, undertaken while he still had America's Cup ambitions, was *Kirlo*, a new Six designed by Ian Howlett and launched in 1981. Erik had for a time, the most advanced metre boat in the world. With Lawrie Smith driving, she was a class apart in the light conditions at the 1981 World Championships on Lake Constance and racked up the wins over the next few years. Tim Street noted: "*She may be said to be the boat that defined modern best proportions of sail area and weight and is still widely considered to be perhaps the prettiest Modern Six*".[1273] But Erik never sailed the boat, just as he had never raced *Gosling*. The Sixes were just 'bookmarks' in his sailing career. Erik's passion for the America's Cup remained until *Australia II* lifted the trophy in 1983. When the circus left Newport, it seems that for him at least, the magic had gone.

The Seawanhaka Cup 1987

If Erik had ended his sailing career without an opportunity to compete for the 'Auld Mug', there was still the Seawanhaka Cup; its prestige now slightly overshadowed in the age of world championships, but its heritage still intact. Erik's 6mR, *Kirlo* (Howlett 1981), fitted with a new keel had just won the 1987 British Championships. Following that event, John Prentice shipped *Battlecry V* (Howlett 1983), which had been runner-up to *Kirlo*, across the Atlantic to participate in the 1987 6mR World Cup, organised by the Seawanhaka Corinthian Yacht Club on Oyster Bay.

At this point, Erik had a light-bulb moment. As a metre-boat sailor steeped in the traditions of the genre, he had always dreamed of winning the Seawanhaka Cup. No sooner said than done: John Prentice agreed to charter *Battlecry* to Erik for a 'shilling'. Britain abolished the shilling as a unit of currency in 1971, so the transaction amounted to 5 pence. Erik and his boys from the Royal Yacht Squadron now had the use of the boat after the World Cup finished to challenge for the famous trophy, with the Cup series scheduled that year to follow-on from the 'main' event.

This would be the last Seawanhaka Cup to be contested in 6-metres. It was organised in a round-robin format to winnow-down the gaggle of contenders, before progressing to a final against the holder, the home club. As anticipated, a number of the overseas Sixes already afloat on Oyster Bay were keen to have a crack at the famous old trophy. There were challenges from two Swedish clubs and one each from Australia, Norway, Hong Kong and Britain.[1274] Now added to this list was Erik and *Battlecry*.

Lawrie Smith and Chris Mason were on-site, so Erik flew out Ian Howlett, Tony Smith, the genoa trimmer from the *Crusader* 12mR campaign in Fremantle, and Jason Holtom, a trimmer from *Kirlo* to do the foredeck. The team stayed rent-free at 'The Pink House', rented by Philip Walwyn. This ace crew ran up an enormous bar-bill at the Seawanhaka Corinthian Yacht Club, which I understand may still be as outstanding as the performance of the *Battlecry* team. The Royal Thames syndicate's efforts to mount an affordable One-ton Cup campaign in 1958 were gently ridiculed in Chapter 24, but that mob-handed endeavour was well and truly eclipsed in 1987. There can surely be no other famous international sailing event, testing design excellence and sailing skill that has been won for 5p!

[1199] Memories of a Corinthian Summer, Dick Enersen, December 2014.

[1200] Referred to as a 'Monaghan man' by Winkie Nixon, Lipton was born and bred in Glasgow. Irishman William Henn challenged in 1886 with *Galatea*, designed by John Beavor Webb, who was born in Enniskillen. Beavor-Webb also designed *Genesta*, challenger in 1885. The McCalmonts of Mount Juliet in Kilkenny were financial supporters of *Valkyrie III*.

[1201] The Piper Calls the Tune, 2017, a detailed account of this campaign also appears in Hugh Somerville's Sceptre, published in 1958. Somerville followed the campaign assiduously, but his appreciation of the designer, a good friend, is curiously limited.

[1202] The Twelve Metre Yacht, its Evolution and Design, 1906-1987, Chris Freer, 1986.

[1203] David Allan Boyd, nephew of David Boyd, also held this position.

[1204] They could cite well-known boatyards where topside planking was faired with a coarse-set plane just as soon as the Lloyd's Surveyor had knocked back his dram and tottered out the door. This is why restorations find planking of a non-standard gauge, or with odd variations, incurred as a result of fairing the skin rather than the frames With an un-planked hull frame, which is something like 5% wood and 95 % air, achieving fairness is quick, though not necessarily easy.

[1205] David Boyd enjoyed a lifetime lease on the Maxwell's Colt bungalow at Gartocharn, which later became the Boyd's retirement home.

1206 The innovative rig was a result of Ian Howlett's wind tunnel research for John Livingston. Wind Tunnel Tests in support of 12 Metre Rig Design, Report No.265, Wolfson Marine Craft Unit, University of Southampton, Dept of Aeronautics & Astronautics, November 1975.

1207 This was a simple uni-layup over a mandrel rotated during curing and postcured. The mandrel was pulled out with a tractor.

1208 The bend was introduced and locked in place with the backstay and jumper-struts before hoisting the main. The long-standing rule in nearly all classes at the time banned permanently bent masts. The appearance was not unlike the Skerry Cruisers which measured-in under the 1907 Swedish Metre Rule. Inevitably, this system (which gave 7% more sail area high-up and improved the aerodynamics overall) was effectively banned when mid (68%) and upper (41%) girth measurements were introduced.

1209 Tony Watts explained the system in 1979. Such requests were considered by a small sub-committee of the IYRU Keelboat Committee, comprising Watts, Sir Gordon Smith and Beppe Croce. The NYYC was entirely unaware of the facility, leading to unpleasant repercussions for the US measurers. The NYYC rode shotgun on a French protest running to 50 pages.

1210 Dubois (1952-2016) was a very successful IOR designer who went on to specialise in the superyacht business. The author shared helming duties on an excellent Dubois 1-tonner offshore.

1211 Peter van Oossanen, the naval architect who led the Dutch team on the development of *Australia II*, has said that he found $25,000 in his bank account, a gift from Alan Bond, after the dust had settled.

1212 The bronze winglets on the British boat were not an act of desperation like the wooden appendages Valentijin tagged on to *Magic* to placate Dennis Connor.

1213 The crew were unconvinced that dragging a set of wings around the course would deliver a net gain. Nevertheless, these magic appendages did make the boat go quicker.

1214 Rule 27: "*If from any peculiarity in the build of the yacht, or any other cause, the measurer shall be of the opinion that the rule will not rate the yacht fairly…he shall report the circumstances to the national authority*" for due enquiry before a certificate is issued. This was not done.

1215 This settled the issue, although the policy of the Keelboat Committee, as understood at that time, made no provision for confidential interpretations.

1216 David Hollom is better-known for his successful RC model yachts. *White Crusader II*, aka the *Hippo*, simply diverted time and resources away from the business in hand.

1217 When the *Hippo* failed to perform, her designer got the shore team to work long hours polishing the boat's surfboard-shaped keel-bulb on the basis that "*a speck of dust*" could destroy its efficiency.

1218 *Sceptre's* sail number of 12 K 17 was chosen to reflect this. The 1937 Nicholson 12mR, *Blue Marlin*, had previously carried this number. She now sails under FIN 1.

1219 Stories told to Ian Howlett by Erik Maxwell.

1220 'J' is the base of the fore-triangle – the distance between the aft side of the forestay where it intersects the deck and the front of the mast in its aftermost position.

1221 While he went along with the committee's selection (what choice had he?) Boyd was known to have favoured his 'Model A', developed from his very pretty *Caledonia* design of 1938.

1222 Tank-testing was used to establish an order of merit, not to refine design avenues. The tank-test models went through a total of just 41 hours of evaluation – 500 runs of five minutes each. By contrast, the Americans allocated 18 to 20 hours per model at each of 0°, 10°, 20° and 30° angles of heel. Stephens worked up seven minor variations on his *Columbia* theme before achieving a small improvement on *Vim*, the pre-war benchmark.

1223 Ian Howlett in conversation with the author.

1224 This differed from the scale of the models used by the American Davidson Lab which were even smaller at 0.9" to 1ft or 1:13.33.

1225 Ian Howlett was on-site in 1984 on behalf of the 'Consorzia Italia'.

1226 These years also saw: Peter de Savary's 1988 *Blue Arrow* foiling trimaran challenge, which was not permitted to join New Zealand's 'big boat' in the mismatch against the American wingsail catamaran, *Stars and Stripes*; Peter de Savary's 1992 challenge, which failed to build a boat; Peter Harrison's 2007 challenge failed to raise the necessary cash; and Keith Mills' Team Origin 2009 challenge was marginalised by the Deed of Gift contest in 2010. As for 2013, Mills lost interest when the AC72 catamaran class was announced for the event, nullifying Team Origin's hard-won experience and technical database.

1227 *"Whisky is liquid sunshine."* George Bernard Shaw.

1228 Other Scottish connections include Mike McIntyre, improbable winner of the Star Class at the Seoul Olympics, who was trimming the genoa. Ian Budgen would reprise that role in the 2003 Louis Vuitton Series. Ian and his brother Andy learned to sail in Pipers at Royal Gourock.

1229 Visiting Islay to research the David Boyd biography, we left the hospitality lounge pondering the etymology of 'three sheets to the wind'.

1230 Erik was a director of ABC and remained on the board after EMI's acquisition in the 1970s.

1231 Huge Cinema Deal is Completed, Aberdeen Journal, 13th October 1936. And then, No Agreement, Financial Times, 14th December 1936.

1232 £900,000 Cinema Deal, Aberdeen Journal, 12th Aug 1941.

1233 All three of these boats were built by Robertson's to David Boyd's optimised lines.

1234 Erik's 8mR interludes are confused by name changes. *Iskareen* was champion boat on the Clyde in 1949 in the hands of Douglas Taylor. The following year Erik changed the name of *Felma* to *Cherokee*. Two decades later, *Iskareen* was sailing as *Cheetah* when she returned from the United States. Erik bought *Cheetah* in 1971 and changed her name back to *Iskareen*.

1235 The plot was as follows: A man decides to become a naval architect instead of following his family's farming tradition. The Filmmakers presented the 'Floodtide Cup' to the class to mark their cinematic adventures. Loch Longs, the First Fifty Years, John McMurtrie, 1987.

1236 Sir Frank Packer leased *Vim* for 4 years for US$80,000 in 1959.

1237 An economic rate of return (ERR) of 0.871 or a loss of 87%.

1238 Britain is Risking Another Fiasco, Jack Knights, the Observer, 22nd January 1961.

1239 Daily Telegraph, Hugh Somerville, 6th August 1961.

1240 *Genie Maris* was designed by T. Munro Glass and built by Groves and Guttridge in 1948. It is difficult to ascertain her pedigree. As she was virtually rebuilt by Philip & Sons in Dartmouth in 1950, there must have been design issues. G&G was a reliable yard.

1241 Sir Frank Packer: A Biography, Bridget Griffin-Foley, 2014.

1242 The syndicate had invested heavily in tank-testing. They had been sailing *Norsaga* (extensively-instrumented) to evaluate sails and gear. It was also reported that two masts were being built at Saunders Roe and the sails were in hand at Ratsey & Lapthorn.

1243 Lord Craigmyle, obituary, Glasgow Herald, 9th May 1998, Obituary: Lord Craigmyle, The Independent, 12th May 1998.

1244 The Fun of the Fair, Sovereign and Sceptre, The Field, 1st August 1963.

1245 Scott and Maxwell go after the Cup, Jack Knights, Daily Express 5th November 1963.

1246 With the Viking spelling of Erik, what other colour could the crew wear?

1247 See The Piper Calls the Tune, where Scott's mea culpa letter is reproduced.

1248 Erik had been considered for the helmsman's role, along with yacht designer, David Thomas, sailmaker Bruce Banks, and the ubiquitous 'Stug' Perry who had jumped ship in the previous challenge to win the One-Ton Cup in the Boyd-designed 6-metre, *Royal Thames*, while Grahame Mann was wrestling with *Sceptre* in Newport.

1249 Scott and Maxwell go after the Cup, Jack Knights, Daily Express 5th November 1963.

1250 Ian Howlett writes: *"Erik was a very 'unpushy' person who enjoyed good company and wide-ranging conversation. I do not think he ever really thought of himself as the helm in 1964 or thereafter. He just wanted to be part of a group doing it right, doing it sensibly. He saw the choice of Peter Scott over Bruce Banks as absurd."* On the other hand, Ian also suggests that Banks required a white tiller, so poor was his eyesight.

1251 At launch, *Sovereign* carried upper diamonds, not jumpers. It seems likely that the section twisted and fell off to leeward. The topmast was rendered rigid with additional jumper struts.

1252 *Sceptre* was dropped off near Newport. One of Erik's mates arranged to have the ship diverted.

1253 Second British 12-Meter due here this summer, Newport Daily News, 12th April 1967.
1254 After *Sceptre's* counter was amputated in 1967, it ended up there for a time as a conversation piece, before becoming a telephone table in the Maxwells' hallway. Unfortunately, the Sceptre Preservation Society came across the old counter and reattached it in 2003.
1255 Sceptre due here Sunday, The Newport Daily News 1st July 1967. This paper reported that she would act as a trial horse for *Constellation*. Two More Twelves Arrive, Newport Daily News 3rd July 1967. The two 12mRs were *Sceptre* and *American Eagle*.
1256 Correspondence with Ian Howlett, December 2017.
1257 The old tin-leg mast, however, continued to be problematic, with earlier issues concerning cracking at the spreader roots resurfacing. The local newspapers reported that *Sceptre* was sourcing a new stick. Sceptre's Crew Suspects Mast May be Broken, Newport Daily News 25th July 1967. Four 12-Meters Get New Masts, Newport Daily News, 26th July 1967.
1258 David Boyd's *Sovereign* was an innovative boat too, with a rig that featured a flexible topmast and a system that allowed narrower sheeting angles with the lee shrouds falling in by 6". The rig was not a success, but the ideas were interesting and taken up later by others.
1259 Ibid
1260 Bold Erik Steps up America's Cup Bid, Daily Express, Jack Knights, 1967.
1261 Reggie owned the late Fife 12mR, *Kaylena* (ex-*Moyana*), of 1929 and was described as "*the doyen of 12mR owners*". He was a member of the original Goodison *Sceptre* syndicate.
1262 With regard to *Sceptre's* much-criticised full entry, overlaying her bow sections from LWL aft actually shows key similarities with *Courageous*, *Enterprise* and *Freedom*.
1263 America's Cup Profit and Loss, The Field, 8th May 1969.
1264 Why France Fell, Hugh Somerville, New York Times, 30th August 1970.
1265 Correspondence with Ian Howlett, December 2017 and January 2018.
1266 The test models were less than 5ft long and weighed about 30lbs.
1267 Bill Mavrogiannis, then troubleshooting for S&S builds, advised James McGruer to extend the rudder blade below the bustle in a crude square profile. Most S&S metre-boats of this generation were modified with arbitrarily shaped blades.
1268 Ibid
1269 Boating, six metres of thoroughbred, David Thorpe, Daily Telegraph, 31st July 1971.
1270 The Design and Building of the first 'Modern Six' in the UK, BISMA Six Metre Newsletter, Ian Howlett, October 2018.
1271 *Gosling* was named in tribute to the matrilineal design heritage of the S&S canon.
1272 The 1982 Newport event was compromised as, unlike Australia in 1986, the home teams did not take part in the championship. The winner, *Victory 82*, sailed without a valid measurement certificate.
1273 International Six-Metre Association, Modern Six-Metre's Newsletter No.1, First Revision, Tim Street, 13th December 2005. That said, Howlett's 1983 *Gitana* might be even better looking.
1274 Multiple challenges were carried over from the America's Cup in 1971 and have been accepted since.

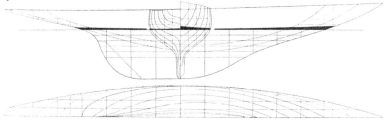

Caledonia, unbuilt David Boyd-designed 12-metre, 1938   David Boyd Archive
Caledonia, so christened by Uffa Fox, is still considered by many as the design that should have been built to challenge for the America's Cup in 1958.

Akela, one of Maxwell's Loch Longs   *Sceptre*, after mods, loading for USA in 1967

Gordon Jackson and Rona Anderson in *Floodtide* with Loch Long OD in the background

Sceptre and *Sovereign*, Image: Jeremy Thomson   *Sovereign* and *Sceptre*, Image: Ian Smith

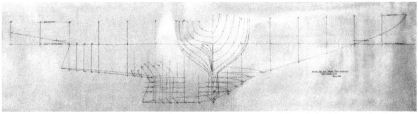

Tank Test Model, 12mR, David Boyd, 1968   David Boyd Archive, Lochgilphead

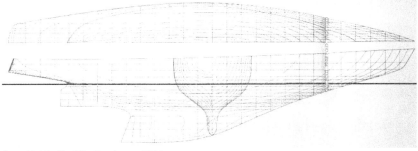

Intrepid, 12mR, Olin Stephens, 1967

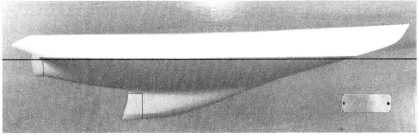

Valiant, 12mR, Sparkman & Stephens, 1970

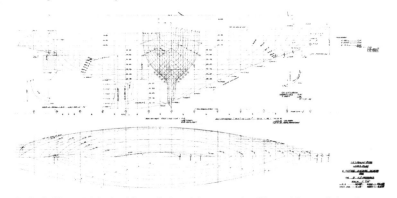

Gosling, 6mR, S&S, 1971 Original rudder and trim-tab in grey and rudder revision no.2 also shown.

Note the very considerable displacement worked into the S&S model at both 6mR and 12mR scale in comparison to the *Intrepid* generation, as represented by *Intrepid* 1967 herself and David Boyd's 'intrepidisation' of *Sceptre* from 1968. The volume below the waterline brings to mind the maxim – 'just the tip of the iceberg' to describe the appearance of the boat afloat. The design challenge in such boats is to incorporate a displaced volume that is required only by the rule.

BOOK SIX

Holy Loch - Holy Grail

Chapter 31: Covalia

To our mind, the head of the Holy Loch surpasses them one and all in its command of nature's wildest grandeur. Three mighty mountain glens here converge and send down their tributary streams to the bosom of the loch – three vast and yawning glens, each flanked with a rugged and towering mountain. Hugh MacDonald[1275]

Behind Hunter's Quay lies the Holy Loch, with its heritage, harbour and marine industry. This little loch was formed from the last 1½ miles of a fjord, once 8 miles long, that included present-day Loch Eck. The two lochs are now separated by glacial moraine. The Holy Loch is short, wide and shallow, and unlike any other loch on the West Coast. It is simultaneously one of the best and least known places in Scotland. The familiar Elysian landscape was a staple of turn of the century postcards and even now registers a million results on Google. The Holy Loch witnessed the dawn of mass-tourism in Scotland and assisted at the birth of 'the seaside'.

Hunt's yachting magazine described it thus: *"They have a perfect sheet of water for the purpose, a fine harbour from which they can start and safely come at any hour of the day or night; unlike the rapid tideways and crowded anchorages and fairways of the bonny Clyde and the dear old Cove, where the practice of amateur steering and seamanship is attended with some danger and difficulty, and all present agreed that it would be a great pity not to take advantage of such facilities for establishing a good nursery for yachtsmen."*[1276]

Accessible in the age of the steamers, sheltered and with good holding ground, the Holy Loch became one of the premier yacht harbours in the world, fêted as a Mecca for Corinthian yachtsmen. And the Holy Loch is indeed an excellent nursery. It is not impossible to get into trouble in a boat on the loch, but you do have to try extremely hard. Nevertheless, succeeding generations have mixed whisky and water, gambled with their lives and lost, as described in Chapter 33.

However, today, as conceded in these pages, Cowal is a sleepy backwater of 'white settlers', 'would-be artists' colonies and proselytising local pensioners keen to repatriate the diaspora.[1277] It is still a gateway to the Highlands, but few tourists linger at the gates these days. They bounce off the ferry with 'uncou-haste', turn right and disappear; inspired to drive ever-further north and west, blundering blindsided through the best bits, until they run out of Scotland. Carefree lemmings should be aware that there is a 300ft drop at Dunnett Head.

"Given its position within six miles of the smoke and bustle of Greenock, it seems curiously remote and withdrawn, as if it belonged not so much to the Firth as to the thinly-populated countryside of Cowal. This impression is no doubt rooted in the fact that Kilmun has a history of some ancientry and interest."[1278] The Holy Loch narrative begins centuries before the advent of recreational sailing. The archives, and the archaeology, attest to a little community that has had its moments.

The all-conquering Roman Army invaded Caledonia in AD 79. Before venturing North, the Romans already knew something of the geography of the region from the writings of Aristotle. The Roman legionaries built Antonine's Wall between 142 and AD 154 before abandoning Central Scotland in AD 162, although they briefly revisited us in AD 208. While they did not establish permanent colonies in Cowal, there are indications that they made at least a cursory exploration of the Clyde Coast and the Western Isles. *"When the Scot the whole of Hibernia stirred, and Tethys foamed with hostile oar."* Claudius Claudianus.[1279]

Robert Gordon (1580-1661) discussed the area as it featured in the writings of Ptolemy (AD100-170): *"As one goes past the peninsula the estuary Glotta opens up, little differing from the old name, for it is called the Firth of Clyde. The Cerones peoples held all that is assigned to Argyle, or Argadia as some wish, and even more. For under these peoples are assigned Covalia (Cowal) between the modern Loch Long and the previously mentioned Loch Fyne."*[1280]

Timothy Pont surveyed and mapped the whole of Scotland over the period 1560-1614, during the reign of James VI (1567-1603). It seems that Pont had precious little help when working out in the field, so the final product represents the completion of an almost Sisyphean task. While there are certainly errors, Pont's Map shows a coastline that is recognisable today. We find the Holy Loch labelled 'Loch Aint' and almost bereft of settlement in the 16th century.[1281]

The early history of the Holy Loch mainly concerns events in Kilmun. The village was named after St Fintan Munnu and has been a site of religious significance since the 7th century. The village is synonymous with Kilmun Hill, which is unusual in Cowal and indeed the Highlands generally, for its oddly regular shape. It is triangular in plan and flat-topped, presenting a long flat ridgeline when viewed from sea-level. The hills of Argyll have inspired generations of landscape painters. Our unthreatening mountains are depicted in the style of the Swiss Alps, with exaggerated profiles and Matterhorn summits, raking low clouds with knife-edge ridges. Well, apart from one. No one has ever been inspired to paint Kilmun Hill as an Alpine peak, or indeed at all.

The old name for this hill is Finnartmore, a Celtic word, alluding to the shape of a large boat or vessel. *"Anyone who glances at the huge ridge from the opposite side of the loch will at once perceive that it presents a remarkable likeness to a vast hull turned keel uppermost"*.[1282] The village on the 'prow' is Strone, from the Gaelic sròn, meaning a nose. As an amphibious child growing up in this region, in a house built by a shipbuilding legend, sited on the 'gunwale' of a big upturned-boat-shaped hill, I enjoyed a set of geomorphological and historical circumstances that could not have been more perfect to engender a lifelong interest in the sea.

The Consecration of Loch Aint

Loch Siant has long been rendered into the English language placename of Holy Loch. As to holy attributes, there are more hypotheses than insights, and all require us to suspend our disbelief to savour scepticism with a pinch of salt. The earliest story concerns Duncan Campbell, first Lord of Lochow (1390-1453), and his pilgrimage to the Holy Land. Unfortunately, the accounts of Duncan's journey are sparse and unconvincing. No matter, Colin Campbell, 1st Earl of Argyle (1428-1475), also made the trip and that pilgrimage is better recorded.

When the well-travelled Campbells sailed up the Clyde in 1641, they were, to a man, suffused with the glow of a glorious homecoming. In such circumstances, they were not the first, nor indeed the last, to neglect basic navigation. The Campbells wrecked their vessel in sight of home, on the reef off Strone Point. A barrel of Palestinian soil broke open to end up at the bottom of Loch Siant. In one account, this precious dirt was intended to consecrate Saint Kentigern's Cathedral in Glasgow. Other records suggest that it was brought home merely to sanctify Campbell graves, and God knows, they were a family that could have used sanctity.

That is one explanation. However, the toponymy and common usage of the 1600s, when the name first appeared in print, suggests another. The name Loch Aint emerges as a descriptor of what the place was known for and includes the possibility of incidents involving traces, or even boatloads, of Palestinian dirt. Siant is an old Irish word meaning a 'blessing' or a 'charm'. There are examples of the name scattered across the Highlands: 'Siant', pronounced *Shant*, also appears in Scottish Gaelic as 'sianta' or 'seanta'.[1283] In its passive form, it has morphed from 'consecrated', 'hallowed' or 'charmed', to encompass 'haunted', 'spooky' and 'otherworldly', and perhaps even 'holy' too. Indeed, the loch was known as a sacred, nay enchanted, place even in pre-Christian times.

Perhaps the most inspired Holy Loch naming myth predates all of these and concerns a youthful Saint Fintan Munnu, later patron saint of the Campbells, whose adventures are described in Chapters 1 & 2.[1284] Fintan, son of 'Niall of the Nine Hostages', was a Druid, recruited by Saint Columba as a disciple. Columba, who established the abbey on Iona, was perhaps the best known among a tide of Irish missionaries who washed up on the West Coast through the 6th century. Fintan's story lends a magical antecedent to the maritime heritage of the Holy Loch, aeons before the nature of the place was defined by the much-admired skill of our local shipwrights.[1285]

One drizzly Kilmun day a local boatbuilder, drying sawn timber in his bothy on the beach, saw a monk pass by. This humble carpenter invited the puir man in to warm his feet by the fire. It was Fintan Munnu himself who sat down and took off his chaffing brogues, more than grateful for the respite. Fintan's shoes were not just sopping wet, there was grit in them too. If you launch a skiff from Kilmun beach, you can easily replicate the miracle. Nevertheless, Munnu embarked on a long-winded explanation invoking his recent pilgrimage in company with Saint Columba, Saint Brendan and Saint Cannich. The grit, he said, was from dusty far-away lands.

One can only imagine the state of Fintan's feet after a journey of 3,500 miles over six months, especially if this was indeed the first time that he had taken off his shoes. Surely an element of penance is involved if one is to tolerate sacred grit between the toes. More likely, the canny monk espied a stairway to heaven. Fintan folded this dirt-of-undetermined-origin into his chalice cloth and carried the swaddle to his grave. I guess we have all been there, after a long day at the coast.

An alternative explanation, better supported by the chronicles, is that Saint Fintan was a certifiable masochist. He was a leper for 23 years, and in all that time his proud boast was that he never scratched an itch, or took a bath, except on Maundy Thursday, when he indulged in both luxuries simultaneously.[1286] This unabashed crank was said to welcome illness so that he might stoically endure it. After Saint Fintan Munnu died ca.635 AD, the tween-toes sand was placed in the Kilmun churchyard and the loch became a blessed place. October 21st is St Mun's Day.

The Campbells and Kilmun

Kilmun's ecclesiastical history has been entwined with the Campbells since the 1360s when the clan adopted Fintan Munnu as their patron-saint. Duncan Campbell sponsored a collegiate church in Kilmun in 1442, on the site of Munnu's ancient Culdee cell, and was himself buried there in 1453.[1287] The Campbell's new church was described as "*the aggrandisement of a pre-existing foundation upon a venerated site*".[1288] The choir of this church was re-built in 1688 to serve as Kilmun parish kirk.

Victorian villa development brought a new, more prosperous and more demanding congregation. The remainder of the old collegiate church, bar the tower, was demolished to make way for a gothic-revival replacement in 1841. The new church was designed by Thomas Burns (1781-1858) a Glasgow builder and architect.[1289] It is a fine, understated, building executed in snecked rubble. Today, the entire Grade A-listed 'religious complex' at Kilmun is nationally significant in terms of ecclesiastical continuity, and commensurately, has been the subject of enduring interest.

Returning to the Campbells and the 15th century, this mischievous dynasty was, at that time, one of the most powerful families in Scotland, so one doubts whether they actually required the services of a patron saint. However, in an age of ignorance and superstition, investing in religion was simply good business. The Campbells interred their dead in Kilmun for 600 years – initially beneath the church, and from 1794, in a four-square domed mausoleum.

There were four Kilmuns in the Campbell lands, with the one at Holy Loch in Cowal, being the best-known. In the 13th century, the Lamonts held these lands in feu for payment of a silver penny at Glasgow Fair. The droll reddendo of another local charter was a pair of Parisian gloves. These were 'blench tenures', originally rewarding service to the King in wartime. Subsequently, the Menteiths held the feu before the Campbells effected a rather underhand acquisition.

Among the Argyle Charters, there is one, under the seal of James IV, that designates Kilmun a free burgh for services rendered by the Campbells to James II and his son James III. Our little village was made a 'free burgh of barony' forever in 1490.[1290] The inhabitants were to be 'burgesses', allowed to hold weekly markets every Monday and to have two yearly fairs, one on St. Munnu's own festival, 21st October, the other on the 'Feast of the Invention of the Holy Cross' on the 3rd of May.

And so, for three hundred years, the freemen of Kilmun would be able to gaze condescendingly across the Holy Loch to Sandbank, where our friends and neighbours remained in feudal bondage through the Jacobite Rebellion of 1745, even while fighting two world wars, and on until the year 2000, when, along with the Millennium Bug, the lingering residue of indenture was eliminated via the Abolition of Feudal Tenure (Scotland) Act 2000.

David Napier 'invents' the Costa Clyde

However, all this ancient history counted for little after the Industrial Revolution and following the arrival of the steamship, when Kilmun changed overnight from a poverty-stricken highland clachan to a desirable residential address. *"Kilmun is a most pleasant place of habitation, and when seen from the water, with its handsome new church and spire, and its hoary church tower of other days, and its time-honoured and stately rows of trees, it presents, on the whole, a delicious picture of quietude and retirement."*[1291]

There was never much land for settlement on the north shore of the Holy Loch. Nevertheless, in the mid-19th century, Kilmun blossomed, first as a waypoint on the road to the Western Isles, and then as a fashionable watering-place in its own right. *"On both shores of the loch, a number of tastefully built modern residences impart liveliness to the scene, and farther down, the Lazaretto, where vessels loaded with cotton discharge their cargoes and perform quarantine, gives a fine termination to the marginal prospect."*[1292]

Kilmun's strategic location, as the best-placed deep-water landing for the onward journey through the Highlands via Loch Eck and Loch Fyne to Inveraray, provided the initial stimulus to the local economy. The village's accessibility and favourable micro-climate, courtesy of a rare south-facing aspect, made it one of the earliest coastal settlements to be gentrified in the wake of scheduled steamer services. Palm trees grow here, as they do in Torquay. Even so, the village of Kilmun evokes the little town of Macondo in *One Hundred Years of Solitude*.[1293]

In Gabriel García Márquez' *100 Years of Solitude*, Macondo has been 'off the map' for an eternity. Contact with the outside world is limited to the gipsies who pass through, peddling ice and telescopes. This timeless idyll is lost when South American intrigue, wars and violence sweep through the region. Then American agro-business arrives to plant a vast banana plantation and establish a gated community. Inevitably, there is industrial unrest. The army sides with the plantation owners and a massacre follows. There is a cover-up, and the bodies are dumped at sea. The weather gods respond to this atrocity with 5 years of ceaseless rain. After the Americans leave, the town is left to its own devices again, slips back into a state of torpor and reflects on paradise lost. Macondo might be Kilmun, or similarly in the wider context, Cowal.

In Kilmun, as in Macondo, years pass, centuries pass, and nothing changes. Of course, there have been upheavals, but they have been confined to a mere handful of decades in a long-recorded history. After the establishment of an ecclesiastical community, and after the pilgrimages and the crusades, the village lapsed back into torpor until David Napier (1790-1869), the celebrated marine engineer and a pioneer of deep-sea steam navigation, purchased an extensive feu of lands along the Holy Loch and Loch Long shores from General Campbell of Monzie in 1828.

Access was by sea; there was no road until Napier built it. But first he had to conjure up a scheduled ferry service, and the ancillary infrastructure that entails. As Napier recalled in his biography: *"About this time, I purchased the land on the north shore of the Holy Loch, which was then in a state of nature, being inaccessible by road from any part of the world. On the shore, I built piers for landing, and an hotel, and ran steamers daily to and from Glasgow. I also put a small steamer on Loch Eck, a freshwater lake about equidistant from Loch Fyne and the Holy Loch, and another across Loch Fyne, and had a road made from the Holy Loch to Loch Eck, on which I placed a steam carriage, thereby making a new route to Inveraray and the Western Highlands."*

David Napier's pioneering steam carriages have been described as carriages, but from the drawings, they were 'tugs' to pull an omnibus.[1294] Unfortunately, operating locomotives on the road wrecked the pavements of Cowal's highways and byways. Efficient motor transport did not become a reality in Argyll until the 1880s.[1295] Local motorists might observe that some things never change.

After establishing his alternative 'gateway to the Highlands', David Napier developed Kilmun as a resort. He built a stone pier and the hub of a new village – the Stag Hotel (now the Kilmun Inn) at the pier and a group of six villas for short-term let to visitors. Napier advertised the latter as *"substantial quay-side houses to let"* in 1829. After seeding the village as a resort, he subdivided his remaining land and leased it to the first wave of Glasgow businessmen and their families looking to 'take the water' of a weekend by the seaside.

Napier initially established himself in 'Glenshellish' at the north end of Loch Eck. Subsequently, he built 'Finartmore', a grander villa at Graham's Point named after the hill behind.[1296] Napier sold off the bulk of his Scottish interests ca.1837, leaving the field to other housebuilders and investors.[1297] Kilmun's transformation into a fashionable watering-place established a pattern. Other new resorts sprang up, fuelled by the steady expansion of high-speed steam navigation.

As one of the first stretches of coastline to be released by feudal landlords for private development, Kilmun prospered until a continuous string of seaside villas garlanded the shore. But soon after Napier decamped to London, development slowed, then virtually ceased. While any resort on a south-facing hillside with a God-given view might reasonably anticipate row-upon-row of housing to stack up behind the beach, in Kilmun this never happened, so our back gardens run clear o'er the hill to Ardentinny.

Hunter of Hafton

The local people consider Paradise Bay to be ironically named; the shingle beach has never been favoured for bathing and few members of the Holy Loch Sailing Club have not encountered the shoal banks there on a Wednesday-night race. But the bay certainly has a fine prospect across the loch to the imposing Hafton Estate, established by James Hunter in the 1800s. Hunter's legacy is everywhere in Cowal, although the stories handed down do not present him as a particularly likeable character.

Hunter was not a yachtsman himself, but he played a pivotal role in the establishment of our 'Highland Cowes' when he enlisted the Royal Clyde Yacht Club in his property development plans. The RCYC would lease club rooms within his new hotel at Camas Rainich. The hotel was initially unprofitable, so Hunter sold the entire operation to the Royal Clyde. The club brought its own custom and would manage the business successfully for many years, as described in Chapter 11.

The James Hunter, who features in the Clyde's yachting history, was just one among many of that name. They were described as 'Merchants of Greenock', obfuscating a wealth tarnished by involvement in sugar and slavery.[1298] The first James Hunter (1780-1834) built Hafton House in 1820, and his successors extended the estate over the years to include other Cowal properties such as Glenlean Farm and 3,000 acres of grouse moor.

The patriarch was followed by James the Younger (1814-1855), from James's second family, and at least two more Jameses, one of whom was an officer in the Indian civil service. This gentleman died 'without issue' in 1876 and left the estate to his brother, William Fredrick Hunter, who in turn left it in trust when he passed away in 1880. The last James Hunter was a nephew who styled himself as the patron of the local area. He appears to have passed away ca.1894, as the estate was again recorded as being 'in trust' in 1895.[1299]

James the Younger conducted a long-running feud with David Napier. The Glasgow upstart on the north shore of the Holy Loch was obviously a thorn in James's side. The two men had different agendas. Hunter was an old-school landowner, who sought to wring meagre returns from his land, his piers, and his property, while Napier, as a new-age entrepreneur, worked within a bigger picture. David Napier's steamers were part of a vertically integrated business, which started with his engine designs, while Hunter could only chisel pier dues from visiting steamers – easy money, certainly, but a drop in the ocean of his income.

The Lazaretto

Lazaretto Point is an exotic name for a small Scottish headland. It is a 16th-century Italian word, derived in turn from Medieval Latin. Everyone who paid attention in Sunday school is familiar with Lazarus, who came back to life after four days in Purgatory – as we did too when released from our religious instruction. Lazarus of Bethany, as he emerged from his trip to Catatonia, declaimed: "ἐδάκρυσεν ὁ Ἰησοῦς, edákrysen o Iesoús lit", or more familiarly, "*Jesus Wept.*"[1300] This is a different Lazarus, but no matter.

In the late 18th century, the age-old belief that disease was borne on a miasma of unhealthy air had been comprehensively debunked. Contagion, or human contact, was then accepted as the primary means of transmission. This led to the introduction of statutory isolation to confirm the health, or otherwise, of people, animals and goods returning from infected areas. In Biblical times, lepers were segregated for 40-days, and the same period was mandated to clear quarantine – a term derived from the Latin, *quaranti giorni*, meaning forty days.

In 1804, a notice appeared in the London Gazette confirming that 'The King's Most Excellent Majesty in Council' had designated the Holy Loch as the anchorage for vessels in-bound for Scotland's west coast ports to perform quarantine, if such was required. The 1832 'Notice to Mariners' replicated this information.[1301] Ships used to lie off the point, now known as Lazaretto, for the duration of their quarantine period, before being cleared to ascend the Clyde.

On the promontory, there were warehouses for the sequestration of incoming goods, and housing for the superintendent and his assistants. In the year 1805, the Superintendent was paid a salary of £130 (£11,130), plus 15/- (£64) per ship. The ruins of a signal tower can be found at Hunter's Quay on a small hill above the pier. It has been suggested that this may have been associated with signalling pilotage and quarantine requirements, but that would have been long before the Lazaretto was established.

Arriving seamen must have detested the place as they sulked aboard ship, barely engaged in desultory duties, counting the days. Neither was the *Imperial Gazetteer* of 1854 impressed. They found the white perimeter walls and round towers, "*more suitable for Turkey than on the Clyde – for a barbarous people than for a civilised nation*". The yachting correspondent of *Hunt's*, writing in January 1856, was similarly scathing: "*We are pleased to see that the Lazaretto, which was more fitted for a Turkish landscape than a Scottish, is entirely removed, having become wholly unnecessary, if indeed it ever was useful*".[1302] However, A decade later, Hugh MacDonald recorded that the quarantine station was still there, all be it long-abandoned.[1303] MacDonald thought it "*a lovely spot and lovely is the scenery around and a capital site for a watering village*".

Gunpowder Pilots

Before Alfred Nobel invented dynamite c.a.1860, quarrying rocks and roadbuilding required gunpowder, and lots of it. It was used to split the mantle of Mother Earth, rather than make fireworks or charge primitive firearms. "*The contractors had a hard time of it; dynamite was not then in the market, and gunpowder was the strongest ally they could employ against the old metamorphic rocks.*"(Dalradian gneiss).[1304] The development of basic infrastructure through the Highlands, involved large quantities of gunpowder. This was manufactured locally as a cottage industry to minimise the hazards of transport. The powder mills were generally located in small, isolated villages, where the inevitable accidents would not disturb the laird's siesta or devastate significant numbers of useful day-labourers.

There were four powder mills in Argyle, located at Furnace, Melfort, Millhouse and Clachaig. These mills were serial killers, with the last of many fatalities sustained while the Millhouse factory was being dismantled in 1923. The Clachaig powder mill, located by the Black Craig Burn in Glen Lean at the head of the Holy Loch, claimed the lives of perhaps 40 people before it closed in 1903. This mill was operated by Curtis's & Harvey, (later part of Nobel's) and was sufficiently large to maintain a stable of 100 brass-shod horses for the shuttle to Sandbank.

The Cooperage at Sandbank, later absorbed into Morris & Lorimer's boatyard, made barrels for the gunpowder factory and the local Brewery, which would be subsumed within Robertson's yard. In the 1950s, when our family bought the National 12 dinghy, *Hi-Jack*, the Cooperage served as the sailing base for the Cowal Sailing Club, secured on a peppercorn lease from Robert Lorimer. The club's starting box was a salvaged fishing boat wheelhouse lashed down on the rocks by Ardnadam Bay.

An incident at the Holy Loch led to a famous court case tried under the Explosives Act of 1875. The day was foggy, operations were running late, and corners were cut. It was reported that the Kames smack, *Hounslow*, had transferred a load of gunpowder to the screw-steamer, *Sardonyx*, then lying just off Ardnadam Pier, without notice, without the supervision of an officer, and after sunset. The first charge concerning the loading location was not pursued, as it raised issues of 'established custom' and differing interpretations of the statute.

However, the Harbour Trustees were of the opinion that the law required the steamer to lie off Buoy No.1 at the Tail o' the Bank during trans-shipment.[1305] The concern for safe operation was merited. In September 1892, 17 years later, the *Auchmountain*, with a hold full of gunpowder, blew up while moored to the nominated Buoy No.1 at the Tail o' the Bank.

At the conclusion of the trial, the two captains were fined a guinea each, plus costs. The facts were indisputable – fog had delayed the *Sardonyx*, it was after sunset when she arrived, and no officer was present. As for the bigger picture, that was referred to the labyrinth bureaucracy of the Board of Trade. Fortunately, on that occasion, the village of Sandbank was not blown to smithereens. Less fortunately, such an event would occur 65 years later, when the boys of HMS *Thule* inadvertently unleashed a live torpedo, which left a great crater on the beach and brought the war home to shoreline residents with a blizzard of broken glass, see Chapter 36.

The Mudflats as a Drydock

Over the years, visitors to Cowal, and locals too, have disparaged the mudflats at the head of the Holy Loch. This type of intertidal landscape is common in many parts of the world, but not on the West Coast of Scotland where the locals are proud of their deep water. We used to feel sorry for our neighbours living around the head of the loch as they lost their sea-view for a good part the day. Today, of course, we realise that wetlands are an important ecology for wildlife, as well as for local mudlarks.

Some parts of the mudflats are hard sand, and some are soft mud; the former areas have been used for centuries for transhipment. Vessels can take the ground without damage to be unloaded by horse and cart. In later years, the ubiquitous Clyde puffers with their powerful steam derricks brought this system to perfection. The loch was also used as a dry dock for minor works. In early Victorian times, there was only one dry dock on the Clyde, and it was both in demand and expensive to use. In 1874, for example, the Stephen's shipyard was conducting trials with a patent propeller and used the soft berth of the loch to alter and change blades between tides to achieve the vessel's contracted speed.

The Holy Loch also sees inadvertent groundings every other week through the summer months when visiting yachts breeze in on a falling tide without realising quite how much of the loch is about to disappear. From 'Anchorage Villa', at the head of the deep water, our family continues to enjoy such strandings as sundowner entertainment, safe in the knowledge that no damage will be done, and no daring rescues will be required.

The North British Clyde, Ardrishaig and Crinan Railway

In 1910, Councillor Anderson proposed an ambitious new multi-modal transport system for the West of Scotland.[1306] He envisaged a rail and ferry system for Argyll, linked to Ireland by a tunnel (a distance of only 14 miles), that appears hopelessly uneconomic today with current population densities, although the scenario is not so different from subsidised 'nation-building' links in Norway. It is difficult to know whether our small county missed an economic opportunity, or perhaps was spared a transient blot on the landscape that would now, post-Dr Beeching's tactless axe in 1963, be a fine network of cycle tracks.

One small section of this ambitious system was planned for Cowal. A select committee pushed a bill through the House of Commons in 1887, authorising the 'North British Clyde, Ardrishaig and Crinan Railway'. The proposed line ran from White Parlane Point at Hunter's Quay, past Ardnadam on reclaimed land, through Robertson's Yard, and still below the high tide line, along the south shore of the Holy Loch. The route then followed the River Echaig to reach Loch Eck, where it ran along the west bank to Strachur. From there, the proposed line crossed Loch Fyne on an ambitious new bridge and continued down the loch-side to Lochgilphead and the remote cul-de-sac of Crinan.

This ambitious line was another venture promoted by Hunter of Hafton and was put forward as an alternative to a more logical proposal that started in Dunoon. Despite being immensely wealthy, Hunter was always on the lookout for business opportunities, which invariably prioritised personal gain, or settling personal grudges against perceived adversaries like David Napier, over wider community interests.

When Alexander Robertson's boatyard moved to the Old Distillery site at Sandbank in 1879, he was not allowed to build a proper slipway initially as the proposed railway, ran through the middle of the yard. Morris & Lorimer's yard, established in 1885, was similarly affected.[1307] After the cancellation of the railway by an act of parliament in 1892, both yards prospered and developed extensive facilities.[1308]

CODA: Ideas Man David Napier

David Napier (1790-1869) was arguably the architect of 'doon the water'. He was born in Dumbarton, where his father, John Napier, a founder and smith, crafted the famous Carronades. John Napier moved his business to premises in Howard Street, Glasgow, when David was twelve. The boy's formal schooling, in French and mathematics, provided a valuable point of entry to study the classic French works on naval architecture. In addition, David was taught technical drawing by Peter Nicholson, something of an authority on architecture in that period. Young Napier did not serve a regular apprenticeship in the family yard but learned by *"putting his hand to everything"*. In 1810, at the age of twenty, with his father ailing, he was able to take charge of the family business. John Napier died just three years later.

Napier was a man of wide-ranging interests, some of which we described in Chapter 6. Additionally, he lobbied the Navy to make better use of steam-power from 1818 through to 1842. One of Napier's pitches to the Admiralty, ca.1820, concerned '*Monitor*-type' gunboats. On this occasion, he used the good offices of the Duke of Argyle to get a fair hearing. *"I wrote to the Admiralty, through the Duke of Argyle, suggesting a gun-boat."*

He described it thus: *"it was not to have any sides above water, only the deck, which would be eighteen inches or two feet thick; the outside of which would be iron plates, one inch thick, and the inside skin plates half-inch thick, and solid woodwork between them.* A turtledeck was proposed to afford additional buoyancy, elevate the gun turret, provide headroom, deter boarders and make it difficult for enemy shot to cause damage. The proposed vessel was *"100 feet long, and 20 feet broad, with an engine of 20 horse-power, which would impel it at a rate of seven miles an hour. Such a vessel would live in any sea, there not being a projection of any kind on her surface either on deck or anywhere else but the screw at the stern."* The Admiralty declined without citing reasons. The story of petitions to the Admiralty is a saga of missed opportunity. The hugely influential *U.S.S Monitor* was launched in the USA forty years later in 1861.[1309]

Napier's enthusiasm for innovation resulted in many patents and many more ideas left unpatented. These included: floating breakwaters; rotary engines; surface-piercing propellers, as used today in prop-rider powerboats; a 'tractor drive', resembling a dredger bucket chain buoyed to the surface; use of the double-bottom as a condenser; and a system of 'egg-box' construction with longitudinal and transverse bulkheads, to make the bottom of the ship a virtual girder, some 14 years before such a system was adopted by Scott Russell in the *Great Eastern*.

An old sparring partner, the eminent Professor Rankine, generously lauded Napier's capacity for innovation in 1859, just a year after receiving that curmudgeonly broadside from the man himself in *The Glasgow Herald* newspaper, see Chapter 6. *"The number of rotary engines that had been patented in Britain alone was upwards of two hundred, but that very few had been brought into practical operation, and these to a limited extent only. The most successful appear to have been the Earl of Dundonald's and Mr David Napier's."*[1310]

While Richard Trevithick drew the first plans for a terrestrial locomotive in 1802, and Stevenson's *Rocket* followed twelve years later, a contender for the first motor vehicle, plying for trade on a public highway, was David Napier's little-known steam charabanc, which ran from Kilmun to Loch Eck in 1827-1928, as part of his multi-modal route to the Western Highlands. Unfortunately, its weight and power destroyed the unsealed road surface – an issue at that time when communities and landowners were responsible for the maintenance and upkeep of our carriageways.

[1275] Days at the Coast. A series of Sketches descriptive of the Firth of Clyde, its Watering Places, its Scenery and its Associations, Hugh MacDonald, 1860.

[1276] Hunt's Yachting Magazine, January 1864.

[1277] 'White settlers' are folks who sell-up in the South and retire on the untaxed capital gains from the sale of a principal residence.

[1278] Days at the Coast, Hugh MacDonald, 1860.

[1279] Roman poet, Claudius Claudianus, AD 370-404.

[1280] De Antiqvitate Scotiae. Brevissima Regni Scotiae Descriptio, Joan Blaeu, Blaeu Atlas of

Scotland, commentary by Robert Gordon, 1580-1661.

[1281] Theatrum Orbis Terrarum, sive Atlas Novus Volume 5, Amsterdam, 1654. The map omits the opposing spits of Graham's Point and Lazaretto Point that protect the loch's inner waters and are its defining feature. But, in the circumstances, we can forgive Pont his errors; less so Joan Blaeu for his atlas of 1654, which simply copied Pont's surveys.

[1282] Days at the Coast, Hugh MacDonald, 1860.

[1283] The old *Statistical Accounts* have Holy Loch as Loch 'Shiant', which falls foul of pedantry with regard to both spelling and pronunciation.

[1284] 'Munnu' is, of course, a hypocoristic name (pet name), contracted from Mo-fhinnu.

[1285] The Salmanticensian Codex of Saint Munnu's life is preserved at Brussels.

[1286] Maundy Thursday marks Christ's ritual foot-washing before the Last Supper.

[1287] The Tourist's Handy Guide to Scotland, 1872.

[1288] The Origin of the Holy Loch in Cowall Argyle, N. Campbell, Scottish Historical Review Vol. 10, 1913.

[1289] The church was extensively remodelled in 1898-99 by P. MacGregor Chalmers, a commission from the laird at the time, Henry Johnston Younger of Benmore.

[1290] Kinship, Church and Culture: Collected Essays and Studies, John W. M. Bannerman, 2016. Such boroughs had no rural hinterland where they might monopolise trade; no inherent right to be represented in parliament; were not liable for cess collection; and could not participate in overseas trade, officially at least.

[1291] The Clyde from its Source to the Sea, W.J. Millar, 1888.

[1292] The Topographical, Statistical, and Historical Gazetteer of Scotland, 1843.

[1293] 100 Years of Solitude, Gabriel García Márquez, 1970.

[1294] William Symington exhibited a working model of a steam car in 1786.

[1295] Scottish engineer, John McAdam, pioneered asphalt roads in the 1820s, but it took some time to build a network. The Romans left no useful infrastructure behind north of Antonine's Wall. Attributions of building works in Cowal have not survived modern scientific scrutiny.

[1296] 'Finartmore' was a fine villa and ended its days as a geriatric hospital. After our father died, our mother worked there part-time and would retire from the matron's office. The highlight of her day was a sherry with the doctor after he had completed his rounds.

[1297] Source Historic Scotland. However, our title shows that Napier sold the property 20 years later on the 19th of October 1857. *Anchorage Villa*, together with 25 poles and 28 yds², to Alexander Scott in 1857, then to the Rev Daniel Hezekiah Cogswell in 1880, then to Captain James Ferguson and on to his son Dugald Ferguson (Steward on the *Duchess of Fife*) 1920, then to the Ross family in 1948.

[1298] The first James Hunter's business interests included: Greenock Bank; Gourock Ropeworks; Wallace & Hunter; Shaw's Water; Castle's Steamboat; the Monkland Canal; and Robertson & Hunter. He left just £30,000 (£2.5 million) in his will, a sum surely underestimated.

[1299] The information listed exhausts the data on-line and via the births, deaths, marriages and obituaries columns of our newspaper database. Other published accounts refer to 'end of the 19th century', etc and do not differentiate the multiple players in the 'James Gang'.

[1300] Gospel of John, Chapter 11, verse 35.

[1301] Nautical Magazine, Nautical Miscellany: Quarantine, 1832.

[1302] Hunt's Yachting Magazine, Volume the 5th January 1856.

[1303] Days at the Coast, Hugh MacDonald, 1860. The facility was closed in 1845; however, it was recommissioned during the 1848-1849 cholera epidemic.

[1304] The Clyde from its Source to the Sea, W.J. Millar, 1888.

[1305] Prosecution for Shipping Gunpowder in Holy Loch, Glasgow Herald, 7th March 1879. This sage judgment clarified the law in relation to the storage, loading and transhipment of explosives.

[1306] Argyll Curiosities, Marian Pallister, 2007.

[1307] M&L later constructed a slipway capable of handling vessels up to 350-tons.

[1308] Statute Law Repeals: consultation paper Abortive railway projects: proposed repeals, Scottish Law Commission, March 2011.

[1309] While 90% of the ideas the Admiralty received were certainly crackpot, these custodians Of the Navy were inclined to throw the odd baby out with the bathwater.

[1310] Admiral Cochrane 10th Earl of Dundonald, the 'Sea Wolf', was another controversial Scottish naval hero and basically 'one hell of a guy'. He was also an engineer. He experimented with steam power in the 1830s, developing a rotary engine and a propeller. He was made an Honorary Member of the Institute of Engineers and Shipbuilders in Scotland in 1857.

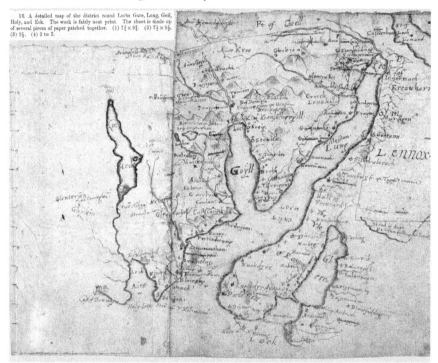

From Pont's Map of Scotland, ca.1600   Pont surveyed Scotland during the period 1560-1615

Finnartmore, the hill shaped like an upturned boat   Photocomposite, the author

Loch Eck, ca.1830 and the Napier steamer, *Aglaia*   Image: T. Nelson & Sons

Kilmun Pier, mid-19th century   Artist: Artist John Adam P. Houston

Holy Loch today, with the 'stern' of Finartmore in the background   Image: CruiseScotland

Sandbank, mid-1800s   David Boyd Jnr collection. Artist: unknown, Docherty?

Napier's steam car, or 'charabanc tug', 1827

The six 'Tea Caddies' Kilmun

Kilmun Pier, ca.1900   Image: Stengel

Loch Eck, pier and carriage terminus, 1830s   Image: Stengel

Note the volume of passenger traffic – there are around 60 passengers in this image. At this time the steam carriages had been 'retired' and horse-drawn charabancs were again in use.

The paddle steamer, *Glen Rosa*, (1893) at Kilmun Pier   Image:sourced by Dalmadan

Wetlands at the head of the Holy Loch in 1882   Artist: George Henry (1858-1943)

Chapter 32: To See Ourselves as Others See Us[1311]

Happy indeed are the merchants of Glasgow and adjacent towns to have such magnificent scenery and delightful cruising-grounds at their very door. There is no other city in the British Isles so happily situated for delightful and almost endless variety in its yachting facilities as Glasgow. Frank Cowper[1312]

Highland Cowes, the analogical subject of this book, is the village of Hunter's Quay, situated at the mouth of the Holy Loch on its southern shore. However, the first organised yacht races in the area were started from Port an Stuck (now Blairmore) and Strone, at the mouth of the loch on the north shore. The Northern Yacht Club's first encounter with a Southerly prompted a rapid change of plans. Hunter's Quay became the preferred location for major regattas on the Clyde and remained so for 150 years, even after the Royal Clyde upped sticks and moved to Rhu in the 1960s.

Counterintuitively, Hunter's Quay is an exposed promontory with a sheltered aspect. The prevailing wind from the south-west enters the Holy Loch via Glen Lean as a westerly and is then deflected down the loch west-nor-west by the "*tame, heathy, lofty hill of Finnartmore*".[1313] There is seldom an onshore breeze at Hunter's Quay and the anchorage is also well-protected from tidal flows and groundswells. In stark contrast, Strone Point, directly opposite and with a similar aspect, is a little bit like Cape Horn.

For countless summers, Hunter's Quay was the jewel in the crown of the 'Costa Clyde', a Mecca for yachts and yachting. Even as late as the 1950s and 1960s, when we looked down the Holy Loch from Kilmun, the mouth of the loch would be busy with the coming and going of the Royal Clyde fleet. And in the regatta season, it was spectacular. There was wall-to-wall sailing. The headwaters of the loch, the tidal saltings and the lower reaches of the Echaig River, also offered diversions for the sporting gentleman. The trivial pursuits of shooting and sailing were closely aligned in the early days of country life. And for unarmed children, rowing through the 1950s in clinker-built lugsail dinghies, it was an oasis in which to recreate the adventures of Swallows and Amazons – truly a heaven on earth!

Heaven, yes, but even the locals concede that a fair wind is seldom included in this otherwise idyllic package. In 1898, in a race for cruising sailboats during the HLSC's Closing Regatta, the J. L. Stephens 2½-rater,

Chiquita, from the East Coast, capsized in a vicious squall while beating up the loch. She was later recovered.[1314] It is not clear why the closing regatta, normally a September fixture, was being run-off in July.

However, in the years since, the unpredictable late-summer weather on the loch has sunk a respectable number of well-found small yachts. Occasionally, we find accounts which refer to competitors enjoying a good breeze, unfortunately, *"two of them were blowing at the same time"*. And it could sometimes 'blow dogs off chains'; *"the three-day meeting of the Clyde Club came to a conclusion in very tempestuous weather, while rain fell at frequent intervals in torrents"*. One memorable September afternoon, during which we enjoyed a mast-in-the-water knockdown a micro-second after hoisting the kite on our little ¼-tonner, the American Navy depot ship in the loch recorded 63kts.

Of course, it can also blow in July. *"Royal Corinthian Yacht Club Regatta, Narrow Escape for Britannia: It was blowing a gale of wind on Tuesday evening, and an arrangement was made that, in the event of its not moderating by the morning, the Ailsa and Britannia match would be postponed. The wind flew into the north-west just before midnight on Tuesday, sweeping down Holy Loch with hurricane-force."*

"Ailsa and Britannia dragged their anchors, and nearly drove onto the rocks at Strone Point, before a steam yacht came to their assistance. The crack 5-rater Almida was blown ashore. On Wednesday morning it broke bright and fine, the wind had steadied down, and with the prospect of less than a gale, the Ailsa and Britannia fighting flags were lashed up. A heavy squall came down the loch soon after, and burgees took the place of racing colours, and the big cutter match stood adjourned till Thursday."[1315]

Nineteenth-century yachtsmen were undaunted by the unpredictable weather, more often marvelling at the capricious magic of these waters. Seldom do we find any complaints about being robbed by 'Wee Shuey' the wind god, as we do today. *"The Clyde is, and always has been, the great yachting nursery and centre of the north. Though Clyde weather is known to yachting men as being somewhat impulsive and petulant, whipping out spars and destructive to balloon canvas unless the skipper is very weather-wise indeed. Still, for real sailing, the Clyde affords some of the best courses in the world and the grandest sport from 23-footers to 200-tonners."*[1316]

Of all the established racecourses of the Clyde, the Holy Loch is the most notorious field of play, celebrated by opportunistic backmarkers for its fluky character and 'snakes and ladders' racing. *"A tale of woe was provided for the leading boats in the four bigger classes which sailed an extra leg of a few miles in the Holy Loch. The height of the land prevented the southerly breeze from reaching the loch off Sandbank, where the leaders were becalmed for hours while slower yachts profited by their predicament and took the first flags."*[1317]

There are many idyllic little enclaves around the coasts of Britain, but most are well-kept secrets and zealously guarded. Holy Loch was different;

'weel-kent', and well-trodden from the birth of mass tourism, but somehow remaining unspoiled. Cowal was once among the better-known holiday resorts and beauty spots. But now it has slipped from the public consciousness and Dunoon is merely a waypoint rather than a holiday destination in its own right.

The local government is, perhaps belatedly, starting to fight back. Their marketing strategy is based around the concept of 'Argyll's Secret Coast'. Fortunately, this is more than a cynical rebranding exercise. The campaign seeks to popularise a remarkable coastline, hidden in plain sight, that really is quite wonderful. It is too early to suggest that it is 'secret no more', but local people do display an increased awareness of the magnificent landscape and cultural heritage they have on their doorstep, and now broadcast that pride-in-place through social media.

As recently as the 1950s and early 1960s, a great fleet of ferries, still called 'steamers' in these years, brought crowds of visitors from Glasgow to the Costa Clyde. "*It is fair to say there was never a coastal system so ample and so cheap. Considering the size of the vessels, one is astonished by the bravura of the performance*".[1318] These cheerful day-trippers would buy ice-creams and promenade the shoreline, in the interval until the arrival of the next boat.

A day out on the river offered more than fresh air and fine scenery. Sailing beyond the jurisdiction of local government licensing regulations, steamers exploited a loophole in the law which allowed 'travellers' to drink on Sundays and at other times when the terrestrial pubs were shut. This gave rise to the expression 'steaming', commonly used on the West Coast to describe that vulnerable state of joyous inebriation the Scots both pursue and dread.[1319]

Life on the North Shore

Tourism was like that up and down the Firth of Clyde. As children, we would watch the ferries come alongside at Kilmun Pier and disgorge hordes of chattering Glaswegians. Our generation saw the valedictory years of the once-great ritual. To voyage 'doon the water', whither for an afternoon or a fortnight, was the quintessential Glaswegian summer holiday for a hundred years. It was an icon of a proud urban working-class culture. As local residents, we were eternally mystified as to why this band of curiously happy people would come here, do nothing and then leave. We had no idea we lived in paradise, even though Paradise Bay lay at one end of the village.

Smug in our secluded rural backwater, we rather resented these cheerful invasions. Just up the road from our house, at the mouth of the River Echaig, Glasgow City Corporation had built a convalescent home back in 1873. This was one of many sanitoria and infectious diseases hospitals built on the Clyde coast to take advantage of the health-giving attributes of the clean sea air.[1320] Our 'homers' were on holiday in seventh heaven. Linked arm-in-arm, they took over the roads, oblivious.

Nowadays, of course, we think back with nostalgia of a time when there were more people than cars on the roads, when drivers would stop to offer you a lift, when the tinkers had horses, sapling-framed tents and jangling tinning tools, and when black and white banded Bretons rode rickety old bicycles bestrung with onions. None of this was unique to Cowal. And surely, we were not the only children to storm along a public road on a home-made land-yacht with a broomstick mast and bedsheet sails. But it conjures up an impression of the place.

Our Costa Clyde was created from scratch in the 1820s. In 1819, a survey of the Ballochyle Estate, which stretched from Dunoon to include Hunter's Quay and the whole shore of the Holy Loch to Strone Point – a distance of seven or eight miles, enumerated less than twenty buildings – churches, inns, schools, the quarantine station, a few grand houses and a handful of thatched cottages.[1321] The 19th century saw this rural idyll turned upside-down. *"Dunoon, Rothesay and the Clyde coasts of Cowal became crowded with the sandstone villas of the new industrialists. Genteel satellite settlements were built around the mouth of Loch Long like Kilcreggan, Cove and Blairmore. Often these suburban extensions of the well-to-do were related to the new cult of yachting…. Most of the houses run to size and some to the dimensions of castles."*[1322]

It is strange, even for people who devote unreasonable amounts of time to sailing, to find yachting described as a 'cult', but the sport of kings certainly bears all the hallmarks of a pagan religion. The rituals are less mysterious today but are, nevertheless, still bound up in the ancient bonhomie of rugger buggers and riding to hounds. Adherents may pursue these arcane rituals at enormous cost, compromising career prospects, threatening financial security, and marginalising family life. Good friends have literally 'bet the farm' on their hobby.

Even if the more successful businessmen and professional people from the city had no real interest in yachting, they were susceptible to Clyde-coast yachting associations and the reflected glamour that came with living in communities that boasted the richest and most celebrated families in the land. *"There are massive dwellings, not inelegant, with lawns, tennis courts, great gardens, vineries – summer houses of men retired from business or of merchant princes, who have moorings out in the bay, and nodding at them, white steam yachts that you may see in autumn in the Baltic or in Norwegian fjords, or in winter in the blue of the Mediterranean."*[1323]

The 'social elite' had always been forced to share Cowal, but from the mid-1800s on, they would be cheerfully overwhelmed during the last two weeks of July each year. Hard-working families revelled in the brief respite of the 'Glasgow Fair' holiday. From any rational perspective in today's world, the idea of everyone going on holiday in unison is quite mad. The Fair signalled logistical chaos, as to provide adequate infrastructure for such a fleeting period would have been economic madness.

However, continuous industrial processes benefit from an annual hiatus. Two week's down-time in the annual schedule allowed the furnaces in the steelworks, factories and mines to be damped down for essential maintenance. The annual shutdown cut both ways; families could holiday together. Admittedly, this caused heroic overcrowding, but nevertheless, everyone had a wonderful time, cock-a-hoop in the small boarding-houses of the resort towns, entranced by the magic of their trip doon the water and revelling in the break from a lifetime of toil.

The Glasgow Fair was first held in 1190, when Bishop Jocelin petitioned King William the Lion to sanction festivities in the grounds of Glasgow Cathedral. Even in the 1960s, many local businesses and factories still closed for a fortnight on Fair Friday. However, cumulative social change eventually democratised the Scottish summer holiday. The Fair still endures but the present incarnation barely ripples the waters of the Firth.

First came the weekend and summer houses, and after that era ran its course, the grander properties were converted into boarding houses and private hotels. Now flush with rental accommodation, the Costa Clyde became a price-competitive holiday destination, enabling cash-strapped day-trippers to stay for a week. But the new middle-class could not afford grand houses and neither did they want to bunk-up in boarding houses.

Modest three-bed and four-bedroom villas sprang up in parallel with the continued growth of the scheduled steamer services, so that a professional man might live in Kilmun year-round while working in Glasgow. When they arrived here, few such families could not afford to buy a boat, whether a small yacht, a sailing dinghy or a clinker skiff for fishing. In Kilmun, in the 1950s, we had a wonderful ferry service linking our little village to Gourock, and a Glasgow train connection. Our sailing dinghies lived on the beach before the house on a raised platform built by my father.

David Ross could commute to work in the city, a journey that took just over 1½ hours in 1952. Even so, family breakfast during the working week was always a rushed affair; my father (grey suit, Glasgow University tie and tweed fedora) munching a slice of toast, gulping down a cup of tea, while my mother (nice frock, court shoes, hair permed fifties-style) held his coat and unfeasibly large briefcase. Meanwhile, the captain of the *Maid of Ashton* sounded the klaxon to announce that he would depart in five minutes. A peck on the cheek, a flurry of last-minute activity and my father was off, jogging the 150 yards to the pier, even as the gangway was made ready to run in.

Dunoon and the 'Invention' of Tourism

Kilmun may have been the first Cowal resort, but it soon became just one of many. Dunoon enjoyed a more generous site and would expand to become the heart of the tourist industry in Cowal, providing market town services for the region. George Blake was a meticulous writer and the doyen of Clyde-coast lore, but he remained unconverted by Dunoon. *"The old hamlet expanded into a small town, with a business or shop-keeping quarter that to this day displays all the stigmata of careless, clotted, higgledy-piggledy building by a people without a tradition of civilised architecture."*[1324] This, perhaps, is a little unfair.

Like seaside towns throughout Britain, Dunoon has enjoyed mixed fortunes. In the 1960s, it was assailed by mediocre 'modernist' architects and suffered a dirth of tourists enticed elsewhere by cheap package holidays in the sun. There was also the arrival and departure of the US Navy, parachuted-in and air-lifted out without thought or consequence. It was an army of occupation. The submarine base skewed the economy for three decades, then left a costly clean-up in its wake.

But our American friends cannot be blamed for the loss of Dunoon's magnificent Victorian pavilion, which burned down in 1949, a decade before they arrived. The pavilion hosted the great music hall artists in the golden age before television killed provincial theatre. The current building, opened with some ceremony by Queen Elizabeth in 1958, was a product of its time – jerry-built, oblivious to context and lacking even a vestige of civic splendour.[1325]

Traditional music-hall was the staple theatre of the seaside. Sir Harry Lauder (1870-1950), who became world-famous as the excruciating 'Tartan Totter' was Scotland's best-known, and inexplicably most-loved, music-hall entertainer. Every rousing Scottish anthem you know is probably a Harry Lauder staple. Lauder was born in Portobello but lived in the Cowal area for many years. He bought a house in Innellan in 1908 and without a hint of self-irony named it 'Lauderville'. Later he succumbed to delusions of grandeur, moving to the 'Mansion House' at Glenbrantar.

Our great grandfather was an inspector of railways in the USA, but he moonlighted as a Harry Lauder impressionist. As the story goes, great-grandad once teamed-up with the 'the man himself' during one of Lauder's 22 tours through the States and they performed a double act on stage. Some of Lauder's best-known lyrics feature local places. So, we'd like to imagine that the duo sang *Bella, the Belle o' Dundoon* and *O'er the Hill to Ardentinny*.[1326]

Package holidays and economy air travel have changed the nature of this economic sector in the British Isles. We still have domestic tourism, but the market segments have been reversed. It is now more expensive to holiday at home and will remain so, no matter how low Sterling exchange rates fall. Today, with the exception of pensioner's bus tours, Scottish Highland holidays are the preserve of the affluent middle-class, weary of airports, sunburn and encountering embarrassing fellow-Brits overseas.

Dunoon has not adapted well to this change. Almost all of our grand hotels 'mysteriously' suffered catastrophic fires at about the time when en-suite bathrooms became de rigueur. But despite the grudging assistance of underwriters, it was all too little, too late. The grand hotel segment of the market has diminished to a few lavish hostelries dedicated to lightening the wallets of obese American golfers – Hawaiian shirts and flimsy Florida trousers, pastel polyester snapping to the onshore breeze.

Daniel Defoe, writing in 1719, was determined to take a balanced view: *"In the meantime, as I shall not make a paradise of Scotland, so I assure you I shall not make a wilderness of it."* [1327] Defoe expressed the common sentiments of the time, but he was a product of past prejudice. As the 18th century unfolded, the natural world was reappraised as a less hostile environment. Artists and writers first 'tamed' the Lake District before moving on to the Trossachs; in their wake, wild country became something to be viewed, hiked and generally enjoyed rather than feared.

The final hurdle, in this process of expanding horizons, was the commercialisation of the Swiss Alps, popularised as a holiday destination by British mountaineers in the early 1800s. Those adventurous pioneers were not passive tourists; they engaged with the landscape as a field of play, developing an entire slate of active winter sports. The Lake Poets, like Wordsworth and Coleridge, writing in the early 19th century, legitimised the wilderness. They opened the eyes of the urban literati to appreciate landscapes in a holistic sense. [1328] Subsequently, the quality of scenery has been subliminally linked to relief amplitude. [1329] Mountains manipulate space and distance, challenging perceptions of our place in the world.

Through the Victorian era, the Scottish Highlands basked in the reflected glory of the Alps. On the Clyde we are especially proud of the scenic backdrop provided by our mountains. The 'Arrochar Alps' may be on Glasgow's doorstep, but they are steep mountains with dramatic shattered summits and the romantic character of a Victorian painting. The Cobbler, seen in profile against the marbled western sky, is perhaps the most iconic of all hilltops in the Highlands, but it is only the seventh-highest of an extensive range which includes five Munros, eight Corbetts and a dozen other substantial mountains.[1330] The ethereal sentinel of the 'Arrochar Alps', floating over the northern horizon, has long been an integral part of the experience of yacht racing on the Clyde. Similarly, Goatfell and the Arran Range terminate the southern vista.

> The Arrochar Alps are clustered around the head of Loch Long and range west from Ben Lomond. This familiar name is a relatively recent designation reflecting the increasing hyperbole of Scotia today; the old name for this region, the 'Duke of Argyle's Bowling Green', recalls a time when our taciturn race held creative understatement and inverted aptronyms to be an art form and the epitome of dry humour. As for the 'bowling green' tag, the only thing horizontal in this region is the rain.

Frank Cowper, Father of 'Sailing Directions'

In the 1890s, Frank Cowper explored the coastlines of the British Isles and the English Channel.[1331] Cowper struggled to find good crews, just like that legendary pioneer of short-handed sailing and dyspeptic grouch, R. T. McMullen (1930-1891). But Frank was a past-master in the art of positive thinking, and he eschewed self-pity – a sentiment that blights McMullen's accounts of his gloomy adventures among the wastrels of the working class. Cowper was also a much better writer per se, with an easy and entertaining style. *"The fact is, I am not a sailor. I just love sailing as a delightful means to a more enjoyable end."*

Frank Cowper was ostensibly conducting research for a set of sailing directions that would be a godsend to early cruising yachtsmen. However, he found it impossible to keep to the task in hand and often digressed to write about everything under the sun. He routinely disparaged Scottish thrift, parsimony and obscurantism in acerbic language, which is still as fresh and tangy today as when he put pen to paper a century ago. Cowper's *Sailing Tours*, circumnavigating Britain in five volumes, are a must-read social commentary, whether you are interested in yachting or not.[1332]

When he visited the Holy Loch, Cowper noted that this divine body of water *"was much used by yachts during the season and at its further end during the winter for laying up purposes"*.[1333] At that time, the boatyards of the area were renowned for the small to medium-sized sailing yachts built on these shores. In these years, the slipways of Alex Robertson's and Morris & Lorimer's yards limited output in relation to both draft and tonnage.

Frank also referenced the function of the Holy Loch in Victorian and Edwardian times as a winter anchorage for large steam yachts. The elegant vessels of the period were too large to lay up ashore. Moreover, it is not easy to safeguard a 'yacht finish' amid the bustle of shipyards locked into commercial schedules. Consequently, they stayed afloat year-round with an annual trip up-river for a scrape and repaint in one of the upper-Clyde drydocks. In effect, they followed a maintenance schedule not unlike that of commercial vessels in continuous operation.

The West Coast's contingent of very large steam yachts, testifying to the collective genius of G. L. Watson, J. R. Barnett, Alex Stephen, D. & W Henderson, John Brown, and others congregated in the headwaters of the Holy Loch (and the Gareloch too) each autumn to lay-up over the winter. The 'mothball armada' comprised not only local vessels: *"One day last week Mr Cornelius Vanderbilt's SY North Star (924-tons, W. C. Storey, 1898) arrived at Sandbank from New York for her usual wintering in the Holy Loch."*[1334] Through the late 1800s, and again after the Great War, this small armada snugged down to ride out the equinoctial storms in the otherwise empty winter roadsteads. Skeleton crews had ready access to the boatyards and logistical facilities of Sandbank village with its shops and public houses.

Frank Cowper's descriptions of sailing conditions in the Firth of Clyde have been repeated faithfully over the decades. *"There is no doubt that, if variety be really charming, very charming weather can be found in the Clyde waters, even within the six-hour limit: dead calm, zephyr, good sailing breeze, rain squalls, white squalls, and the rest."*[1335] Cowper's Clyde, nevertheless, became a cruising ground of international renown. Scott Hughes loved the place, as did Anthony Heckstall-Smith and George Blake. Writing in the 1950s, this later trio were genuine experts, wore their expertise lightly and spoke directly to everyman.

George Blake wrote: *"There have been countless people like myself who can never come to the Clyde without being each time overawed by its massed beauties and grandeurs – a succession of scenes compact of all that we most care for in this world: ships, islands, beaches, deep water, mountains, soft rain, sunshine, sea smells. A morning can break with a chill, misty rain but an hour or so later the clouds will withdraw behind the hills and the sun appears in the blue sky above the blue water."*[1336] It was perhaps a high-point for wit and wisdom in a vast canon of sailing literature, blighted as it is by an absence of incident and tedious replication of stodgy old log-books.

The Clyde and the adjacent West Coast might excel as a magical cruising ground of fjord and archipelago, but few rational people would tout the local weather as an asset. The salutary experience of King Haakon IV, chronicled in the 13th century, is not atypical:[1337] *"So great was this storm that people said it was raised by the power of Magic, and the quantity of rain was prodigious, as is thus described."* Meanwhile, as I write this chapter, a 35kt squall sweeps down Glen Lean. The yachts in the Kilmun anchorage sheer violently before settling down to ride the new wind direction. Hard rain rattles on the window as the black loch turns white. A few moments later, the sun comes back out and it's 'summer' again. *After a gale, the bay at Sandbank is a lively sight with scores of yachts sheltering from the storm."*[1338]

Cowper elaborated: *"The Argyleshire shore is wilder than that of Renfrew, and a stiff breeze will often be blowing over the hills and half-way across the river when there is a dead calm along the east shore. The part of the Clyde between Holy Loch, Loch Long and the Cloch is subject to variable winds, owing apparently to the diverging arms of the lochs and river as well as the diversity of the scenery."*[1339] Frank Cowper's visit was brief, but this is indeed the experience of a lifetime. Cowper had pithy remarks to swell the chests, or draw the ire, of local denizens in all the main sailing venues: *"There is a prospect no doubt of much friendly intercourse with the natives, but the prospect hardly ever becomes a reality."*

Our Norwegian friends were even more blunt in their assessment of the character of the Scots. When the Vikings terrorised these shores, we were fortunate indeed to have a native ally like the west-coast weather: *"Now our deep-inquiring Sovereign encountered the horrid powers of enchantment and the abominations of an impious race"* – so said Snoro Starlson, Haco's bard.[1340] Of course, powers of enchantment are not always horrid. Indeed, they are the essence of this region and why the diaspora keeps coming home.

Cowper generously sang the praises of Cowal. He saw past the capricious weather and the taciturn locals to discover a little piece of Heaven on Earth. *"There are so many places where a yacht might bring up that it is not necessary to specify all; but a stay in Holy Loch should not be omitted, if only to explore Kilmun and the pretty scenery around. Kilmun with its old kirk and burying grounds nestles across the top of the Holy Loch at the foot of the wooded hill opposite. On the left is Glen Massan with its trout stream, its falls, and its potholes and borings through sandstone rock. Massive, majestic hills cluster around, and Benmore dominates the scene."*[1341]

He was less impressed with our other watering-places. Perhaps the lack of an auxiliary engine on the good ship *Lady Harvey* coloured his thoughts. Certainly, prudent navigation in the upper reaches of our Scottish fjords in a clumsy, heavy-displacement yacht of his era cannot have been easy. Cowper was at the mercy of the tide when the breeze fell below five knots. Anchoring in the steep-to sheltered spots required enormous effort with heavy, old-fashioned ground tackle. This was before a wealth of detailed sailing instructions were published. Indeed, research for the first of these was Cowper's mission.

Cowper liked Dunoon, then and now once more, something of a backwater. Through the era of the steamers, the little town grew to amalgamate with Innellan to the south, and Kirn and Hunter's Quay to the north, developing into the main conurbation on the Cowal shore. *"Dunoon is a pretty-looking, straggling collection of houses, stretching for three miles along the Cowal shore. It only dates from 1822, when Mr J. Ewing built a villa here. Previously, all it consisted of was a highland clachan, a kirk, a few cottages and a manse. The castle, certainly, has existed since 1058, in the reign of Malcolm Ceanmor, when the Lords High Stewards of Scotland held their courts here."*[1342]

Dunoon, like other Clyde-coast towns, benefitted from the years of blockade running for the Confederates in the American Civil War. Captain Leslie, adventurous, amoral and 4ft 11" in his hand-knitted socks, was one of the most successful gun-runners. He invested his fortune in Dunoon, building an entire street of villas for sale and rent with names that acknowledged the source of his ill-gotten gains – 'Bermuda Villa', 'Dixie Villa' and the like.[1343] Eventually, Leslie became Police Commissioner, continuing a long tradition of scoundrels in public office.

The *Gazetteer for Scotland* recognised Dunoon's higgledy-piggledy charm: *"The whole exhibits a charming indifference to town-like regularity, villas and cots being blended with gardens and trees; sea, wood, and mountain being all within easy access; and the views of the Clyde and its basin being as wide as they are lovely. Good bathing-ground occurs at Balgay Bay; boats may be had for hire; and the excursions alike by land and by water comprise not a little of Scotland's fairest scenery."*[1344]

Lord Dunraven was less impressed when his yacht, *Valkyrie II*, was sunk by the *Satanita* at the mouth of the Holy Loch in 1894. Like generations of shipwrecked sailors, before and since, he sought solace and a wee dram in the local pub. Alas, he declaimed, *"Dunoon is a desolate spot – no hotel, no public house"*.[1345] *Valkyrie's* designer, G. L. Watson, was obliged to take the poor man home to Glasgow for a hot bath and that much-delayed glass of malt whisky. In another telling, it was *Valkyrie's* builder, Henderson, and his wife who supplied these comforts. Quite why Dunraven disparaged the nearest hotel, the Royal Marine, owned and operated by the Royal Clyde Yacht Club, and ironically, designed by Watson's cousin, remains a mystery.

Returning to Cowper's discursive log, the southern extremity of the Rosneath Peninsula received short shrift, perhaps understandable for a man saddled with a 60lb kedge and looking for a convenient hostelry. *"Our anchor is our title deed to our real estate, and we can claim all our property all around our coasts."* Had he discovered the Minister's Rock, upon which many of us have dwelt through the intertidal interval, he might have liked the place even less: *"As neither Cove nor Kilcreggan, on the Dumbarton shore offer any attractions for yachting people, we will stand across to Gourock."*[1346] The development of this part of the Clyde coast only began with the arrival of the steamers in the 1820s, so it is likely that Kilcreggan did indeed offer few attractions for yachtsmen in these early years. Gourock was a more established town, with everything the cruising yachtsman might need.

Neil Munro took a different view, lamenting the fact that the Shaw-Stewarts had clung bitterly to their land and blocked the construction of seaside homes on the Renfrew shore. *"We see the mountain peaks sun-flecked, and covered by cloud and mist of shadow, varying in colour every hour; we see them austere and glittering under the winter snows. And in certain blessed circumstances, when the sun goes down behind Kilmun and the Cowal people sit in unhallowed dusk, we see, over them, celestial glories, vistas of crimson and gold. Why then should the Renfrew shore be dark and dwellingless?"*[1347] By contrast, across the Firth on the Cowal shore the Campbells freely traded their coastal estates when the Clyde became ripe for fashionable villa development.

Munro comes over as a begrudging lowlander here, but he was born in Inveraray and spent his early life in the Highlands. It was only when he moved across the water to work on the *Greenock Advertiser*, that this thought struck him. The best aspect of Gourock is indeed the view of Cowal, but it is only relatively recently that serried ranks of glass-fronted apartments have been built to enjoy it.

Talking of Gourock, the otherwise even-handed George Blake didn't hold back either: *"The fatal slatternliness of the Celtic west is only too obvious along a bight commanding such brilliant vistas."*[1348] He too may have overstated the case. My aunt and uncle owned Birrell's, the tobacconist and newsagent in Kempock Street. I was always entertained by Aunt Nettie's command of Royal Gourock scuttlebutt. This was a vibrant community, infused with the business of yachting, particularly after the grip of the Wee Free Church was loosened. One bright Sunday morning, bound for Inverkip, legendary yachting hack and keen cyclist Tony Heckstall-Smith was accosted by a Gourock worthy for desecrating the Sabbath by riding his bicycle. *"Mon, d'yea no ken ye're riding tae Hell?"* *"Not to, from!"* was the reply.[1349]

The refined yachtsman had no reason to tarry off Greenock either: *"Of Greenock, the less said the better, it is damp dirty and dull."*[1350] King Charles II, the so-called 'Father of Yachting', can be credited with issuing the necessary warrants to transform Greenock from a village into a powerhouse of maritime industry. In the 1890s, when Cowper visited, this was a busy working town, which had borne the brunt of industrialisation before the upper river was dredged. And for another half-century, its doughty citizens continued to grind out the dynastic fortunes which financed grand villas in more genteel parts of Clydeside, like Rhu and Cowal. Wordsworth saw the much-maligned town differently, finding magic:

> We have not passed into a doleful city,
> We who were led today down a grim dell,
> By some too boldly named 'the Jaws of Hell'[1351]

Cowper didn't know what to make of Helensburgh, then at an early stage in its development. Perhaps *"Helensburgh (was) what it looks – new, straggling and slightly common*", but the town had the last laugh when it grew through the 20th century to become one of the most desirable addresses in Scotland, housing a suspiciously high percentage of millionaires, when 'millionaires' were actually wealthy people. John Logie Baird, inventor of the short-lived mechanical television, certainly liked it well enough.

As for the fabulous islands of the Clyde, Daniel Defoe – proto-novelist, journalist, jail-bird and dodgy businessman had a low opinion: "*Here are also the islands of Arran and of Bute…. They have nothing considerable in or about them, except it be a tumultuous and dangerous sea for sailors, especially when a south-west wind blows hard, which brings the sea rowling in upon them in a frightful manner.*"[1352] Defoe's underwhelming appreciation of Clyde waters contrasts with the idyllic tropical paradise he invented for his hero Robinson Crusoe. Defoe was no friend of the Scots; he worked as a spy for the English Government. In these circumstances, we can happily disregard his fearful assessment.[1353]

Fortunately, the idyllic 'Keys' of the Clyde speak for themselves and bear comparison with Britain's more southerly islands. Bute is like Jersey, but incomparably more beautiful. Arran is a little larger than the Isle of Wight and accommodates an entire mountain range within its interior. The Cumbraes are of the same size-order as the Isles of Scilly, with Millport a wonderful time warp into the vanishing world of the Victorian seaside. Ailsa Craig and Inchmarnock complete the archipelago before we leave the Clyde for a wealth of austerely gorgeous islands on the West Coast.

The people of Cowal think they live on an island. It certainly feels like an island and we have an island mentality. When we look across the estuary to the mainland, we perceive the further shore as 'different' and subliminally less interesting. Cowal may be connected to the mainland, but the over-land route is by no means direct. If we drive to Gourock by road, the journey is more than 80-miles and takes over two hours. By ferry, its just 5 or 6 miles and takes 25 minutes, including sea-time aboard the Western Ferries.

CODA: A Poet Describes the Landscape-Weather Nexus

While local people implicitly recognise the intimate relationship between the Scottish weather and the landscape of the Highlands, it takes a poet like Robert Buchanan to get to the heart of it, as he does in his *Cruise of the Tern to the Outer Hebrides*.[1354] "*The visitor to the west coast of Scotland is, doubtless, often disappointed by the absence of bright colours and brilliant contrasts, such as he has been accustomed to in Italy and Switzerland, and he goes away too often with a malediction on the mist and the rain, and a-murmur of contempt for Scottish scenery. But what chance visitors despise becomes to the resident a constant source of joy.*

Those infinitely varied grays – those melting, melodious, dimmest of browns – those silvery gleams through the fine neutral tint of cloud! Strong sunlight dwarfs the

675

mountains so and destroys the beautiful distance. Dark, dreamy days, with the clouds clear and high, and the wind hushed; or wild days, with the dark heavens blowing past like the rush of a sea, and the shadows driving like mad things over the long grass and the landscape for minutes together to the delicate, dying thing that flutters for a moment on the skirt of the stormcloud, and dies to the sudden sob of the rain,

Two qualities are necessary to the enjoyment of these things. The first quality is quiescence or brooding-power — the patient faculty of waiting while images are impressing themselves upon you, of relinquishing your energetic identity and becoming a sort of human tarn or mirror. If you want to be 'shocked', galvanized, so to speak, you must go elsewhere, say to Chimborazo or the North Pole. What we mean to convey is, that some of the finest natural effects are vaporous, and occur only when rain is falling or impending, and that it is pitiful in a strong man to miss these from fear of a wet skin."

CODA: A Holiday by the Holy Loch

"Having an invitation to spend a few weeks with a friend, in one of those houses which of late years have rung into existence on the margin of the lochs which indent the Frith of the Clyde, I accepted it with great pleasure, and soon found myself among the romantic scenery of mountains and lakes. The substantial well-to-do citizens of Glasgow have there built retreats, to which they annually repair to enjoy the keen health-giving sea breezes and mountain air. The shores of these, but lately lonely, solitudes are now each summer thronged with town-bred beauties, in fashionable array, and with gentlemen who, in a very few days from their first arrival, experience the novel sensation of hunger, and are able to discover a sweetness and relish in plain food such as never before imagined it could be possessed of.

Viewing from the deck of the steamboat, the situation of these watering-places is most picturesque and attractive, especially to a stranger. The white houses at the foot of the mountains — on the very verge of the water — show out in striking relief, situated as they are, with such an impressive and generally wild and rugged background, and as reflected in the black-looking water close into the shore. The scene is enlivened by the number of boats which are seen in motion, propelled by oars often wielded by fair ladies who soon forget to be delicate and feeble with the opportunities and temptations here afforded for healthful exercise, in which they can pleasurably take part.

It was something new to me to sit quietly in the gently rocking boat, far away from the office. I forgot sometimes where I was altogether, as daydreams of fancy, evoked by the powers of the surroundings, overpowered me; and I was only woke up by the excitement of some of my fair friends who, naturally, when they hooked a bigger fish than usual, expected to be complimented on their skill and success.

The rowing about the loch, and to and from the places where the fish are found in greatest abundance, was a feature which lent variety to the enjoyment. I liked to feel the forward glide of the boat under me as in answer to each stroke it bounded on, dipping into the hollows, and rising above the waves. And at each fresh point of view arrived at *every few yards, the scene was noticeably different, the mountains appeared different in shape and relation to one another, and the effect was different, and the eye conveyed impressions to the silent spirit that awed, exalted, and moved."*[1355]

[1311] From the poem To a Louse, Robert Burns,1786.

[1312] Sailing Tours, Part V, The Clyde to the Thames Round North, Frank Cowper, 1896.

[1313] The Tourist's Handy Guide to Scotland, 1872.

[1314] Yacht Capsized in Holy Loch, Evening Telegraph, 25th July 1898.

[1315] Yachting, Southampton Herald, 13th July 1895.

[1316] Scottish Clubs, R. T. Pritchett and Rev. G. L. Blake. Badminton Library of Sports and Pastimes: Yachting Volume 2, 1894.

[1317] The Clyde Fortnight, from our Special Correspondent, The Times, 11th July 1949.

[1318] The Firth of Clyde, George Blake, 1952.

[1319] The Piper Calls the Tune, Euan Ross and Bob Donaldson, 2017.

[1320] In the 1930s there were over 60 convalescent homes in Scotland catering for more than 34,000 people annually. The Origins and Development of Scottish Convalescent Homes, 1860-1939, Jenny Cronin, 2003.

[1321] The Clyde, painted by Mary and Young Hunter, described by Neil Munro, 1902.

[1322] The Firth of Clyde, George Blake, 1952.

[1323] Munro has ventured into hyperbole here, there is never a groundswell in the Holy Loch that would induce a substantial steam-yacht to 'bob'. Moreover, most early steam yachts on the Clyde at that time were painted black; only later did they follow the Mediterranean fashion for white topsides.

[1324] The Firth of Clyde, George Blake, 1952.

[1325] After extensive refurbishment, the shabby old Queens Hall where we once watched bands like the Searchers has been transformed. It reopened in 2018.

[1326] Dunoon spelt 'Dundoon', usually it's an error but Lauder must have had his reasons.

[1327] A Tour thro' the Whole Island of Great Britain, Daniel Defoe, 1719.

[1328] The poets included: William Wordsworth, Samuel Taylor Coleridge, and Robert Southey, and writers: Dorothy Wordsworth, Charles Lamb, Charles Lloyd, Hartley Coleridge, John Wilson, and Thomas De Quincey.

[1329] Landscape 'amplitude' indices are used in landscape quality assessments by regional development and conservation planners.

[1330] For the non-hill walking fraternity, a 'Munro' exceeds 3,000ft and a 'Corbett' 2,500ft. Munro was a Scot, Corbett was the first Englishman to climb all the Munros. Sir Hugh Munro published his famous 'tables' of Scotland's high mountains in 1891. Munro routes that begin at sea level represent a fair hike; and the comparatively high latitudes of all these hills means that winter climbing is Alpine in character and indeed in challenge.

[1331] Sailing Tours, Part V, The Clyde to the Thames Round North, Frank Cowper, 1896.

[1332] Ibid

[1333] Cowper helpfully points out that the loch *"is two miles long, not two miles deep as one book of sailing instructions says."*

[1334] Clyde, The Yachtsman, 1910.

[1335] Scottish Clubs, R. T. Pritchett and Rev. G. L. Blake. Badminton Library of Sports and Pastimes: Yachting Volume 2, 1894.

[1336] Harbours of the Clyde, John Scott Hughes, 1954.

[1337] The Norwegian Account of Haco's Expedition Against Scotland, 1263. A translation of the saga by the Reverend James Johnstone was published in 1782.

[1338] Forgotten Scotland, Roberts J. Drumond, 1936.

[1339] Sailing Tours, Part V, Frank Cowper, 1896.

[1340] Poem of Snoro Starlson, who sailed with Haco Haakon, King of Norway in 1263. Reference the Flateyan Manuscript translated by Johnstone, Chaplain to the British Embassy in Denmark, 1779.
[1341] Sailing Tours, Frank Cowper, 1896.
[1342] Ibid
[1343] Aspects of Blockade-Running, F. MacHaffie to Clyde River Steamer Club, October 2013.
[1344] Ordnance Gazetteer of Scotland, F.H. Groome, 1884.
[1345] Dunraven might have been famously kicked into touch by the New York Yacht Club in 1896, but his 'esprit de combativité' was more successful on this occasion. When *Satanita's* Mr A. D. Clarke, was later proposed for membership of the Royal Yacht Squadron (by the Prince of Wales, no less) Dunraven engineered a blackball and reciprocally scuttled *Satanita's* owner. Past Times and Pastimes, Windham Thomas Dunraven, 1922.
[1346] Sailing Tours, Part V, Frank Cowper, 1896.
[1347] The Clyde, painted by Mary and Young Hunter, described by Neil Munro, 1902.
[1348] The Firth of Clyde, George Blake, 1952.
[1349] Island, Ben and Loch, Dr. A. Heckstall-Smith, 1932.
[1350] Sailing Tours, Part V, Frank Cowper, 1896.
[1351] Itinerary Sonnets, William Wordsworth, 1833.
[1352] A Tour thro' the Whole Island of Great Britain, Daniel Defoe, 1726.
[1353] Defoe became an adviser to the General Assembly of the Church of Scotland and committees of the Parliament of Scotland. He boasted that he was *"privy to all their folly"* but *"perfectly unsuspected as with corresponding with anybody in England"*. He published the Review promoting the English agenda for the Act of Union which came into force in 1707.
[1354] The Land of Lorne, Robert Williams Buchanan, 1871.
[1355] The Cheshire Observer, 12th June 1869.

Flying the flag at the GP14 National Championships, Largs, 2013   Image: the author

Lady Harvey, Ex fishing lugger, built in 1886 and painted by Frank Cowper. *Little Windflower*, another of Cowper's boats. Cowper also owned the cruising yachts: *Undine*, *Undine II*, *Zayda*, *Idéal* and *Ailsa*. In addition, Cowper raced his 1877 10-tonner, *Myosotis*.

Satanita, after sinking *Valkyrie II* in Holy Loch, 1894   Images: RNCYC Collection

West Bay Dunoon, ca.1955   Image: Dunoon in Old Photos

Chapter 33: Servabo Fidem

The prospect of a good ducking ought to be sufficient excitement to any reasonable being without the chance of drowning being added to enhance the interest of the sport. Drowning may be very attractive in its own way, but then a man can only be drowned once, whereas he may be ducked day after day if required. The Yachtsman[1356]

The following account of the tragic drowning of Lt. Col. Archibald McAlpine Downie, Laird of Appin, in the Holy Loch in 1958, evokes something of the atmosphere of the Cowal district in the fifties. Rod MacAlpine-Downie (1934-1986) was our most successful multihull designer through the 1960s, an exciting period of innovation and development, see Chapter 7. It is less well-known that Rod's father was also a renowned yachtsman. Lt. Col. McAlpine Downie, served with distinction through WW2. However, when peace came, like many other war heroes, he just wanted to go sailing. After being invalided out of the army, the Laird retired to his Highland seat where he became a stalwart member of the Scottish sailing community.

On the 18th April 1958, the Laird and his girl-Fridays, Anne Kellagher and Anne Chichester Constable, returned to the Holy Loch after a short cruise to Campbeltown. Their Brixham Trawler, *Servabo*, flew the swallow-tail burgee of the Royal Highland Yacht Club, which MacAlpine-Downie was entitled to fly as Rear Commodore. His first-mate, Miss Chichester Constable, was then just 22 years old, but apparently happy to exchange the glamorous whirl of a young socialite for the damp squalor of *Servabo's* forepeak. Deckhand, Kellagher, by contrast, was a schoolteacher enjoying the blessed relief of a break from the boisterous bairns of Kilmacolm.

MacAlpine-Downie brought the old ketch into the wind at the head of the loch, a cable's length from Robertson's Yard. The young crew picked up the mooring, then lent a hand to brail up the tan mainsail – a stow which gave *Servabo* the workmanlike style of a Thames Barge. Thus, was set in train a local mystery that would take months to unravel.[1357]

The 64-ton *Servabo* was built by Robert Jackson and Sons as a working boat in 1927 and converted into a yacht just a decade later. She was reputed to be the last sailing trawler built in Brixham. MacAlpine-Downie had bought the boat in Plymouth the previous year, regarding her traditional rig and 14 berths as perfect for sail training.[1358] William of Orange, the enduringly divisive 'King Billy', declared *"Servabo Fidem"* (I shall keep the faith) when he landed in England in 1688. The name implies reliability, and for many years *Servabo* was the essence of that virtue. She looked after charter parties for half-a-century and even masqueraded as a pirate ship in the 1973 film, *Mysterious Island*, starring Omar Sharif. Alas, however, *Servabo* has not endured. She was wrecked in Antigua in 1989 during 'Hurricane Hugo' and became a total loss.

The *Servabo* crew were scheduled to run a sailing course for the Scottish Council for Physical Recreation (SCPR), affectionately known as the 'Physical Wrecks'. The 'Wrecks' operated from the Royal Marine Hotel at Hunter's Quay, home of the Royal Clyde Yacht Club. It is evident that the Laird revelled in the challenge and variety of sail-training and he enjoyed the company of enthusiastic young people; he certainly didn't need the money. The same might also be said of the Laird's good friend, gentleman farmer, Major Richard Weston Brooke, who had signed up as an instructor for the forthcoming course. Richard was the second son of Sir Robert Weston Brooke, Baronet of Midfearn, but more importantly, he was a good man to have on a boat. He owned the Fife 6-metre yacht, *Sabrina*, and was Second Coxswain of the Cromarty lifeboat.

Leaving the two Annes in charge, MacAlpine-Downie rowed ashore to rendezvous with Weston Brooke, who was arriving by car. They had arranged to meet Jock Kerr Hunter, Supervisor of the 'Wrecks'. The three friends repaired to the genial fug of the Oakbank Hotel, where Jock went over the details of the impending cruise. On the morrow, an Edinburgh doctor, his wife and two children and a young chap from the East Midlands would arrive for a voyage of personal discovery. Evenings with Jock were never dull. He was an outstanding all-round sportsman, the son of a Cape Horner, and owned the elegant 1897 Sibbick yawl, *Sayonara*. Doubtless, the evening was convivial, and the talk was of West Coast Cruising.

After dinner, the *Servabo* boys bid good night to Jock and walked back through the village to Robertson's Yard, where their small clinker dinghy lay tied up by the slipway. The two shipmates were well-clad to row out to *Servabo*, with war-surplus waterproofs and waders. However, as was common at the time, and indeed is still common now, they did not wear personal buoyancy. It was early in the season, the loch was dark and foreboding, and the water was very cold, but the old boat's riding-light beckoned with the prospect of a snug cabin and a nightcap.

There was a brisk Easterly, which set up a lively chop. With this wind direction, there is a long fetch from Gourock leading to the shallow waters at the head of the Holy Loch. Indeed, it was later reported that James Hunter, the hand responsible for the anchor-watch aboard the new America's Cup Challenger, *Sceptre*, moored nearby, did not board his charge that evening. He thought it imprudent to row out and clamber onto the high-sided vessel in the dark with the wind against the tide. Coincidentally, McAlpine Downey and Weston Brooke, both keen students of the Auld Mug, had discussed plans to look over *Sceptre* the next day.

The following morning, *Servabo's* upturned tender was discovered by James McLachlan, a Sandbank dairyman and an early riser, washed up on the beach at Hafton Bay. The swamped dinghy had travelled more than a mile upwind during the hours of darkness, borne on the outgoing tide before coming to rest in the eddy behind Lazaretto Point. Of MacAlpine-Downie and Weston Brooke, there was no trace.

All this time, the girls onboard *Servabo* had been incommunicado without a dinghy. When contacted, they confirmed that the two gentlemen had not returned to the yacht, so the Sandbank police opened an investigation. Major Brooke's Rover 75 was found parked in the village. The pair hadn't been seen since they left the pub, but the sentinel, James Hunter on *Sceptre*, among others, had heard raised voices on the loch late on the Friday night. Two local lads, sent to investigate the racket, swept the anchorage with their torches but found nothing amiss.

James Ferguson owned a boatyard and a ferry business on the north shore of the Holy Loch. He was the Piermaster at Kilmun where his fleet was based. Jimmy's ferries were relatively large, seaworthy vessels and well-equipped. The Ferguson family had long been the first port of call when the authorities had official business on the loch. Jimmy had been expecting a phone call.[1359]

That day, Jimmy charged John Armour, the genial skipper of the *Sonja Tess*, with the unhappy task of dredging the loch. *Sonja Tess* was a traditional, open ferryboat, painted 'Ferguson green' with a small focs'l under a raised foredeck. Though an open launch, *Sonja Tess* had a canvas awning over battens and gas-pipe frames, extending back to midships, providing Jimmy's perennially querulous passengers with rudimentary shelter. Young Andrew Paterson was invited along as deckhand for the day. Andrew was then about 18 years old. He was a useful lad and keen as mustard; his family owned the 1906 W. H. Thomas yawl, *Moosk*.

As the crew got the boat ready, Constable McDougal from the Stronc police station arrived at the pier on his old boneshaker. All the Holy Loch policemen were obliged to assist in the search. The first order of business was to clarify the plan of attack for the afternoon's operation. The search party adjourned to the Kilmun Hotel for a yarn and perhaps a little Dutch courage. The hotel was owned by John Scott at that time; Jimmy and his wife would later take it over. The acquisition was a 'good fit' as the hotel building adjoined Ferguson's Boatyard.[1360]

Constable McDougall wheedled a wee half bottle from Mr Scott, just to keep out the cold, you understand. Then the Skipper cast off and set course for Ardnadam Pier across the loch. There, the crew picked up Sandbank's Constable Duncan MacInnes and Mr Robertson, a licensed grocer in the village. As was customary, Mr Robertson brought along another half bottle to keep spirits up on an otherwise dispiriting tour of duty. It was as well to keep the constabulary on-side; the grocer's shebeen was a popular hang-out for local yacht crews.

Once on-station at the head of the loch, Armour rigged up a grapnel trawl and instructed Andrew to steer a grid pattern, a task complicated by the extensive network of yacht moorings in the vicinity. The search area covered the stretch of water between the pub and the ghost ship, still lying to her mudhook, quiescent and now imbued with that indefinable aura of tragedy that inhabits yachts where life has been lost.

The brains trust could do nothing more for the moment, so they retired beneath the awning to address the bottle and yarn the afternoon away. To be honest, no one wanted to find anything. Andrew remembers the weight of responsibility on his young shoulders and the sense of dread as to what they might encounter. They were all going through the motions. The last thing anyone wanted was to snag the missing yachtsmen.

Unfortunately, with all this diligent cross-hatching, the trawl line became fouled on the propeller. John Armour wasn't best pleased, but there was a sense of relief in an honourable withdrawal from the scene of the crime. *Sonja Tess* limped carefully back across the loch to Kilmun Pier, where John hooked the stern of the boat up to the pier-head derrick and hoisted her up until the propeller aperture was clear of the water. Then the crew cleared the prop with boathooks from the cockpit of the *Mary Rose*. Afterwards, Andrew was sent up to the hotel to ask Mr Scott for another half bottle to keep the official enterprise on track.

With everything cleared away, there was little appetite to continue the grim search. By this time, it was about six in the evening and it was getting chilly. Andrew took charge of the *Sonja Tess* for the trip back across to Ardnadam to drop off the Sandbank contingent, while the Skipper entertained the boys below, finishing off the bottle.

Back at Kilmun Pier, Andrew slotted *Sonja Tess* into the berth alongside *Mary Rose*, a slightly smaller ferryboat with notoriously narrow side decks, as many a Cowal commuter could attest. But *Mary Rose* was a bridge too far for Constable McDougal who now hammed-up a fine impression of Buster Keaton in the 1921 silent movie 'The Boat'. The generously proportioned policeman was helped up onto the pier with some difficulty, where it became apparent that he was not just unsteady on his feet but quite insensible.

McDougal was too fou to cycle home, and it would have been indefensible to leave such a pillar of the community to his own devices. The Boss was sent for; Jimmy brought the boatyard's old tipper lorry down to the pierhead. The lads threw the bike in the bucket and 'Ferguson Transport' whisked the wobbly constable home to bed. The vehicle was uninsured, unlicensed and possibly unroadworthy, but the prospects of 'getting away with it' could not have been bettered.

Rod McAlpine Downie, then just 24 years old, arrived that evening intending to join in the search, which was set to continue the next day. But the task was clearly hopeless and after securing *Servabo*, Rod returned to Appin with Miss Chichester Constable. As he left, John Brooke, Richard Brooke's brother, arrived to encourage further efforts. So too did Glasgow businessman, Joe Deane, a regular shipmate of the two missing men.

Richard had failed to turn up for a lunch date with Joe the previous Saturday. A new pair of oars, which he had promised Joe, was found in the abandoned Rover 75. With the absence of bodies, and a drip-feed of such spurious facts, an air of mystery began to surround events. What misfortune could have overwhelmed these old hands?

Experience and reputation be dammed; none of us is immune to errors of judgement and neither were McAlpine Downey and Weston Brooke on that fateful evening. Up and down the West Coast of Scotland, in sheltered lochs and open roadsteads, through living memory, more weekend sailors have perished rowing back from the pub three sheets to the wind, than were ever lost at sea.

The local sailing community put the tragedy to the back of their minds, wrapped up as they were in the vicarious pleasures of the forthcoming *Sceptre* challenge. Then, unexpectedly, the body of Weston Brooke was discovered on the beach at Strone on 27th July. At about this time, two dumb lighters, which had been moored side-by-side at the head of the loch, had been moved to separate moorings. Perhaps the bodies had been caught between the hulls? It is possible, but MacAlpine-Downie was never found. Meanwhile, the long America's Cup summer of 1958 ground on to a disappointing conclusion off Newport.

As the new Laird, Rod had to attend to the sad business of winding up his father's affairs and dealing with the crippling death duties which now burdened the estate. Joanne, the late Laird's wife, moved back to Ireland, with her son Andrew from her first marriage, to resume the ancient MacMorrough-Kavanagh lineage. However, Borris House, the family's staggeringly opulent Irish seat, soon became untenable too and the dynasty came to earth with a bump.

CODA: Drownings in the Holy Loch

The *Servabo* tragedy was, of course, neither the first nor last drowning in the long history of sailing on the Holy Loch. Anyone can drown. The colder the water, the more dangerous are the involuntary responses that lead to drowning. Despite the ingress of wayward strands of the Gulf Stream, which ameliorate temperature fluctuations on the West Coast, the Holy Loch can be very cold indeed, especially in its headwaters where the River Echaig discharges the icy waters of Loch Eck.

When we fall overboard, there is something called 'cold shock'. Surface blood vessels constrict, and heart rate increases rapidly; blood pressure rises, and the risk of a heart attack increases significantly. Assuming that the heart keeps going, we then have to survive the hazard of our respiratory response – a great involuntary gasp followed by hyperventilation, struggling for breath. This response alone can cause drowning within minutes. You cannot physiologically prepare for cold shock, but knowledge of it can reduce panic and increase chances of survival.[1361]

If we survive initial immersion, most people will still drown fairly quickly. Blood-flow to our extremities is diverted to protect vital internal organs, so our limbs cool rapidly and their strength ebbs away. Essential muscle action is impaired as both chemical and electrical control systems break down; in short order, our capacity to help ourselves starts to diminish. The danger of hypothermia, which was ingrained into us as residents of a seaside community, is exaggerated. Even skinny people do not lose enough core-heat after half-an-hour in freezing water to die from hypothermia. When sailors go over the side, the cause of death is generally drowning – cold shock followed by rapid loss of muscle strength.

There has been useful research into the effects of alcohol on the body when there is a risk of drowning. Alcohol in the bloodstream induces what might be characterised as a 'hypersensitivity to drowning'. Studies suggest that sailors with a blood alcohol level of 100mg/100ml have about 10 times the risk of death when compared to those who have not been drinking, and alas, even small amounts of alcohol represent a hazard. For comparison, the drink driving limit in England is 80mg/100ml, and in Scotland, this has been reduced to 50mg/100ml.

Perhaps 40% of drownings are alcohol-associated and risk increases with age. Thus, looking at the demographics of Scottish yachtsmen, 20-30% of these enthusiasts are likely to drown if they go over the side.[1362] As a community, sailors have long enjoyed sundowners at sea. But whether we are bowling along in the tropics before the gentle breath of the Trade Winds or dipping nervously into the ice-strewn waters of the Furious Fifties, the stats render sobering advice. Looking through the newspaper archives, it seems that there was a drowning every few years in the vicinity of the Holy Loch, and many were poignant in the extreme.

Early one evening in February 1876, John Martin and John Blair launched their skiff at Kilmun and set off towards the lights of the Sandbank shore. The men were skilled joiners who had been working late on the Mansion House; both were sober, well-respected citizens. It is a short row of just under a mile, but the darkness had fallen, and the wind was rising. They never made it home. At some stage during the choppy crossing, they swamped the dinghy, or perhaps they overturned it.

A day or so later, one Thomas Hanley caught sight of a small boat riding low in the water off Ashton. He rowed out to find it half-full of water with a dead man on board, later identified as John Blair from a recently serviced pocket watch. It seems that he had put out the anchor to wait until daylight, but it had not caught until the boat had drifted across to Gourock. By this time, he had died of exposure. The fate of Martin was never determined.

In December 1882, three Greenock men, Murdoch McLeod, Archibald McNeil and Daniel McNeil, were working on a lighter beached at Lazaretto Point, making it ready for a tow up-river to Port Glasgow. There was a strong wind blowing and their steam-launch somehow broke free from its mooring. The three men borrowed a dinghy to chase after the launch and simply disappeared into thin air.

In September 1886, Mr Stewart, a Glasgow spirit merchant, was visiting Blairmore Farm and missed the boat back to Kirn. Charles McLeish, son of the Blairmore postmaster, offered to ferry Stewart across to Hunter's Quay. It was a dark night, but the weather was fine; nonetheless, they failed to reach the opposite shore. The following day, the master of the schooner, *T. and E. F*, of Barrow discovered a small, white-painted boat with a 'gay blue sheer strake' floating in the Firth a mile below the Cloch. Two men 'off to the fishing' had found the boat earlier, floating bottom-up between Dunoon and the Gantocks Rocks. They checked it out and left it for someone else to pick up, as in their experience, they were never rewarded for salvage. This accounted for the boat being found on an even keel by the schooner's crew.

The discovery confirmed the fate of the two men. However, severe weather then restricted search operations at the mouth of the Holy Loch. The body of young McLeish was eventually washed up at Strone Point close to their point of departure, but Stewart's battered remains somehow drifted all the way to Kerrycroy on the Isle of Bute, to be recovered 16 miles away from the incident.

One day in January 1890, as the steam trawler, *G.K. 213*, was passing Strone Buoy her tender was cast adrift when the painter gave way. This was also a mysterious tragedy which took time to reconstruct. It seems likely that the trawler circled back to retrieve the dinghy. The deckhand leant over the side to secure it but lost his footing and slipped into the icy water. His skipper immediately dived in after him. Meanwhile, the trawler was drifting rapidly away, beaching below Dunselma Castle. No bodies were ever found. Sometime afterwards an, ostensibly separate, unexplained disappearance suggested that three men may have been lost in the tragedy.

Captain William Gregory, of the schooner, *Pearl*, lost his life off Ardnadam in January 1901. Gregory, along with two seamen, had gone ashore in a small boat. However, on boarding the tender at the steps leading down from Ardnadam Pier for the return trip to the schooner, a fatal accident occurred. The good Captain, who was over 60 years of age, fell into the water. He was promptly rescued by his crew and taken back to the *Pearl* with all possible speed, but he died before reaching the vessel.

James Bruce and Robert Riddell drowned off Hunter's Quay while lifting the mooring of the yacht, *Suzette*, in September 1901. The bodies were found near the place where their boat had overturned. Riddell had a severe gash on his head. It was surmised that the lifting operation had gone awry; the heavy mooring anchors and ground chain had taken charge and upset the dinghy, which was evidently too small for the job of lifting a yacht mooring. Having courted disaster laying moorings from small dinghies ourselves, it is indeed a pointless, high-stakes, gamble.

In June 1910, the bodies of Miss Isabella Pinkerton (40 years) and Elizabeth Innes (60 years) were recovered from the shore at Kilmun where they had been washed-up. The two ladies carried on a millinery business in Edinburgh. They were dressed in the black 'widows weeds' of deep mourning. The events leading up to their deaths were a complete mystery. But, in the circumstances and with the proximity of Kilmun pier, there is little need for conjecture.

There are very clear patterns in these tragic stories, distilled from dozens retrieved from the archives: poor decision-making when weighing risks against benefits, the overconfidence of experience, or simply a lack of imagination. The accounts show how little chance there is of surviving small-boat accidents, especially at night in winter. In those days, no one wore buoyancy aids and the little clinker rowing boats used as tenders floated awash when swamped. There was no self-rescue option. Outboard-powered inflatables are certainly safer, but nothing very much has changed fundamentally today.

CODA: Surviving the Holy Loch

We might include a final cautionary tale from the author's childhood which is, by contrast, a survival story. Like most sailors, there have been more near-death experiences in my life than I care to recall, but this event from 1957 was particularly memorable. If I am celebrated for anything, it is something I did when I was a little over three years old, less than half-a-mile from home. As usual, we were running wild; my father in Iraq building a bridge over the Euphrates; my mother fully occupied with eighteen-month-old 'Baby Anne', and my eight-year-old brother, Norman, blissfully unaware of the five-year gap between us.

Norman and I are off to the 'wee shop' by the pier for the 'messages' on my soon-to-be-famous blue tricycle. I am pedalling frenetically, and Norman is standing on the treads between the back wheels, calling the shots. He is probably wearing a cowboy hat and brandishing a silver Colt 45 cap-pistol. I can visualise this precisely as there is a contemporary snapshot of just such a division of labour.

At the pier, Norman jumps off and goes into the shop. Meanwhile, Euan, lost in a daydream, pedals on down the greenheart decking and disappears over the side just by the old cargo derrick. This is fortunate, as riding off the pier-head would have resulted in almost certain death. Nevertheless, the pier is about 10ft above water-level and I take to the air, still pedalling.

Blessedly, the tide is not right-out, and the divine waters of the Holy Loch cushion my fall. This is one of my earliest memories; swallowing cold saltwater (later to become almost a way of life) and looking up at the towering masonry of the pier. As I break the surface a small cowboy is peering down at me and exhorting me to greater efforts in the language of his father: "*Attaboy, Euan; come on boy, you can do it boy*" – ad nauseam.

After a short interval, another face appears by the old derrick; it's Mr Ferguson, the Pier Master. He is wielding 'the Giant's Boathook', a three-metre-long ash spar, tipped with a great bronze spiked hook. It must weigh at least 50lbs. It has been lying on the pier for decades; like King Arthur's Excalibur, it waits patiently, ready for a situation when sufficient adrenaline can be summoned to wield it.

During the time taken to convoke these images, I have been steadily making progress towards the shore in the same uncoordinated doggy-paddle I still depend on to this day. By a logical corollary of the tide not being right out, it is not right-in either, so the distance to be covered is not very far. But even so, the struggling child remains tantalisingly out of his depth. My blond thatch dips beneath the surface as the seabed rises to meet my scuffed red sandals. As an evolving amphibian, I am now running out of time. Then I feel the reassuring punt of Excalibur's hook up my backside and my knees touch the crunchy gravel bottom.

I emerge bedraggled and dripping, and a little bit shell-shocked, oblivious to the thin applause from the small crowd now gathered above me. I am far too upset about the fate of my bike to take a bow just yet. There is no ladder on this side of the pier. I squelch off disconsolately along the shore, looking for a way up. The steps over the seawall seem to be miles away. At this point, my sense of purpose begins to wander, and at last, I start to cry. After an eternity, I struggle up the old stone treads to the road. I am greeted, matter-of-factly, by my brother. He brings the reassuring news that Mr Ferguson will recover my trike when the tide goes out.

[1356] Quotation continues: *"The wearing of a life-belt is no inconvenience whatever, and looks quite picturesque, after a fashion. As we said some time ago, this regulation used to be in force in the matches of the Clyde 3-tonners."* The Yachtsman, 13th August 1931.

[1357] The primary source of material for this story, which ran for weeks through the summer of 1958, is the Dunoon Observer and Argyllshire Standard Archive. Individual editions are not referenced here.

[1358] Brixham Heritage Sailing Trawlers Archive, http://www.brixhamsailingtrawlers.co.uk

[1359] Police Drag Loch for Missing Men, Glasgow Herald, 1958.

[1360] This story was recalled by the late Andrew Paterson and we obtained other contributions from the Ferguson Family.

[1361] Lecture by Michael Tipton, University of Portsmouth, RNZYS, 24th November 2009.

[1362] Among others: Review of the role of alcohol in drowning associated with recreational aquatic activity, T. R. Driscoll, J. A. Harrison, M. Steenkamp, 2003.

Kilmun Pier when the tide is out, 1920s   Image: sourced by Dalmadan

Servabo, R. Jackson & Sons, 1927   Image: Jarratt   Norman and Euan, ready to cycle off the pier

Holy Loch, head of the loch anchorage with the tide out   Image: Rowena Donaldson

Chapter 34: The White Heather Club

The owners call it sport. One thing was in its favour: it did not last long nor take much seamanship, apparently. However, I should be glad to have a motor in my boat. To possess one is to possess the acme of comfort, provided it does not smell, explode, get in the way, or give out just when you most need it. Frank Cowper[1363]

Today, the once-ubiquitous Kelvin launches are the stuff of memories, but sadly, they have almost disappeared from British waters. This is a pity as Kelvin was a significant and innovative company. Walter Carl Bergius had arrived in Glasgow as a German immigrant and sagely married into the Teacher's Whisky dynasty.[1364] Walter's son (also Walter) established the Bergius Car & Engine Company. He built innovative automobiles, but Edwardian motorists were hard to seduce, and sales were pitiful.[1365] In 1906, young Walter's company was on the verge of bankruptcy, kept afloat by unsecured loans from his father.

This generous spirit also kept William, the eldest son and impresario of the clan, in gainful employment as an 'ideas man' for Teacher's Whisky. To enliven the summer of 1906, or possibly just to put some work his brother's way, William commissioned a powerboat from Walter junior's car company, tongue in cheek perhaps, but not an unreasonable proposition. William and Walter were both experienced sailors. As youths, they had enjoyed gunkholing in *Dodo*, a 14ft 6" shoal-draft keelboat designed by William when he was just eighteen.[1366] Over the intervening years, William's drafting skills progressed with the 28ft *Dodo II*, styled after a Mylne 19/24 and built by James Litster of Kirn in 1903.

Consequently, for their first experiments in marine engines, the Bergius brothers naturally returned to Litster. He was subcontracted to install a 14hp Bergius car engine in a 23ft rowing gig, bought for £7 (£850) from the old schooner, *Torfrida*. The records show that, typically, there was no Bergius family discount. William's account payable included a 5/- overhead charge on the special drill-bit purchased to bore the propeller shaft. The result was the *Kelvin*, a lightweight flyer which dominated local powerboat racing to become the 'Cock o' the Clyde'. William survived to sell the over-engined gig to a reckless character with an apparent death-wish. In Mr R. I. Dobbie's ownership, *Kelvin* became known as '*Dobbie's Coffin*'.[1367]

Nevertheless, it seems that everyone wanted one. Despite Walter's initial failure to recognise a gift horse, word spread. It was clearly an idea whose time had come. William's success, and more particularly, his flamboyance on the racecourse, effectively kickstarted a whole new business. Events moved quickly. While yachtsmen would soon catch on to the possibilities of the revolution, James Litster's fishing industry contacts suggested more immediate and wider commercial possibilities. That same summer of 1906, Walter and James arranged to trial 4-cylinder 7hp Bergius units in three fishing boats, beginning with *The Brothers* from Campbeltown. And with the success of these installations, the new brand was in business.[1368]

Walter reaped the benefits, but it was William's imagination and initiative that brought Bergius engineering expertise to new markets. A lifelong filial debt ensued as Walter's company never looked back. Meanwhile, William, generously endowed with time and money through his sinecure in the Teacher's Whisky empire, progressed to a more powerful, purpose-built boat, the *Kelvin II*. She took over from her predecessor to become the 'crack' boat on the Clyde, winning nine titles through 1907-08.

The Bergius company now considered how auxiliary power might be fitted to existing small and medium-sized sailing yachts. This was something new at the turn of the century. Suitable motors only became available ca.1903. Serendipitously, the Bergius car engine was one such motor. In 1907, Litster was commissioned to install an auxiliary in *Dodo II*. A 7hp 2-cylinder motor gave the 28ft yacht a cruising speed of 5kts. The first Kelvin engine to be specifically designed as a marinised unit followed in 1908. It is remarkable that *Dodo II's* prototype installation served 28 seasons before being replaced by a new motor of the same type. The installation in *Dodo II* was significant as a successful pattern for motors in yachts that had been previously considered too small for auxiliary power.

At the turn of the century, there were certainly hybrid yachts, but steamship technology was ill-suited to sailing boats less than 100ft.[1369] The marinised internal combustion engine changed everything. Fife installed a 2-cylinder Gardner in *Minoru* (21-tons) in 1909, and then a 2-cylinder Bergius unit in *Shaheen* (83-tons) the following year. Even Herreshoff, famously reluctant to embrace auxiliary motors, capitulated in 1913 with *Vagrant* (109ft LOA) and then *Katoura* (162ft LOA) in 1914, albeit that these were hardly small yachts. By all accounts, auxiliary power was now a problem solved.[1370] The importance of this advance cannot be exaggerated.[1371]

By 1913, there were 300,000 internal combustion engines in American yachts, but only a small fraction of those motors powered sailing yachts as auxiliaries.[1372] Across the Atlantic, as here, the convenience of this type of motor led rather to an explosion in powerboating. Unlike steam engines working at pressure and subject to the vagaries of safety valves and the temptation to tie them down, the new motors did not require a certified operator. They did not so much democratise 'yachting', as clone it to form a new branch of the sport. Meanwhile, the wider yacht racing community also benefitted, as during the Royal Gourock Regatta in 1911, *"the calm was so general and so hopeless that it was only by the friendly aid of steam and motor craft that the yachts were able to get across the Clyde for the start"*.[1373]

The modern yacht is utterly dependent on auxiliary power, not just for propulsion but to charge batteries for an increasing inventory of electrically powered equipment. Virtually all yacht design concepts, and moreover, the design of yacht infrastructure from marinas to travel-lifts, depend on our boats being equipped with reliable motors. Small boats can get by with an outboard, but most yachts from about 28ft up require a dependable auxiliary for all practical purposes.

The first outboard was an electric unit designed by Gustave Trouvé in 1870 and patented in 1880. Subsequently, the American Motor Company trialled 25 internal combustion motors in 1896. However, it was not until 1909 that the first commercially successful outboard motor appeared. Norwegian-American, Ole Evinrude, created the iconic brand that is still synonymous with outboards today.

A steady stream of fishing boats arrived at James Litster's boatyard in the off-season to be beached at Kirn and have an auxiliary power unit installed. It was an efficient, rapid turnaround operation allowing Litster's business to prosper too, albeit in a more modest way. Litster's engine package required an initial 50% payment of £35 (£4,175), at the time of conversion, with the balance to be paid during the next twelve months. Litster's father was in the insurance business, so the family diversified to offer staged financing linked to anticipated increases in profits. When catches improved, which they routinely did, fishermen could afford to make the second payment. The installations were not cheap, so improvements in productivity must have been substantial to swing this notoriously conservative market.

Through the following half-century, 26,000 marine engines were sold.[1374] Kelvin engines initially became popular with fishermen, as described above, and then more widely in the marine industry as petrol/paraffin motors supplanted steam in launches, ferries and workboats. Within the decade, marine engines bearing the 'Kelvin' trademark became ubiquitous throughout the British Empire and beyond. Following the auto-trade model, the renamed 'Bergius Launch and Engine Company' also retailed motor launches from stock. Remarkably, more than 1,500 Bergius launches from 18ft to 75ft would eventually be sold. Happily, Litster, now a firm friend of the family, was not forgotten. James became an agent and an approved subcontractor, building standard hulls for fit-out at the new Bergius factory in Glasgow.

Most Kelvin launches were built by Scottish yards, but boatyards in Norway were also involved. The majority of those constructed in Scotland were exported for use as despatch launches, beach boats, naval pinnaces, passenger launches, and other such purposes in the far-flung colonies of the British Empire. After WW2, Bergius transferred the launch business to Willie Miller, of James N. Miller and Sons of St Monans, Fife, who continued to build the range under the name Miller-Kelvin until the 1960s.

The design of the launches has been attributed to Walter, who was said to be a 'competent naval architect'.[1375] However, William is the better-known of the two brothers for his design ideas incorporated in *Dodos I* to *VI*.[1376] Other sources suggest that Bergius commissioned hull-lines from established designers; the company had an association with James McCallum. Alfred Mylne, unwittingly perhaps, also appears to have benchmarked some designs. For example, Mylne's 20ft Kelvin launch of 1910 (Design No.182) scales-up to overlay a number of 'simplified' Bergius models.[1377] More certainly, the detailed design work was produced to a uniformly high standard by the anonymous draftsmen in the Bergius drawing office.

Today, the Bergius story is submerged within the corporate entity of British Polar Engines and there is little trace of their boatbuilding heritage. Nevertheless, a few oily-rag enthusiasts still revere Kelvin machinery and the whiff of paraffin combustion. And an even smaller confabulation still venerates Kelvin launches.

White Heather

The White Heather Club was an artless, but immensely popular, BBC TV Scottish variety show that ran through the 1960s. *"Haste ye back' means call again soon an 'Here's-tae-us' means good cheer but these simple words of welcome are the ones I long to hear ... Come in, come in, it's nice tae see ye how's yersel ye're lookin grand, tak yer ease we'll try to please ye man ye're welcome here's my hand."*[1378] Jeremy Paxman once cited the White Heather Club as evidence that there never was a golden age of British television. He was probably right, but shorn of embarrassing Victorian clichés, the institution has been reborn as a consortium of friends committed to keeping the *White Heather*, one of the last Kelvin launches on the Clyde, afloat.

I was invited to join the club for their annual pilgrimage 'up the water' to Glasgow on the hottest day of 2018.[1379] *White Heather* looked magnificent as we piled aboard at the Holy Loch Marina, oversized ensign fluttering proudly and varnish-work sparkling in the sunshine. Breakfast of bacon rolls and coffee was enjoyed off Greenock and a celebratory round of pre-lunch bubbly eased our passage beneath the Erskine Bridge. We berthed across the river from the BBC's city-centre headquarters, touching base, as it were, with the spirit of Andy Stewart.

After a fine lunch and a photo-session, the quick trip home on the outgoing tide was enlivened by a round of G&Ts. Fittingly, Bilgewater Gin is a Bacchanalian whimsey of Andy Thoms, the don of the White Heather Club. Andy is also a partner in the Majestic Line, a successful boutique West Coast cruise-ship operation. Then there was just time for formal afternoon tea, followed by a wee dram to round out a fine day on the river.

White Heather is a 26ft Kelvin Light-weight Utility Launch, built in 1932 to the 1919 design, by Fletcher's of Dunoon. She is planked-up in pine, with a teak gunwale and sheer strake, oak ribs and elm trim. While the lines overlay precisely with the 'authorised' product, there is some question as to the boat's pedigree. She seems to have been a custom-build, perhaps using James Litster's Kelvin launch moulds with the blessing of the Bergius family. Litster, then retired, had been an authorised builder of Kelvin launches, whereas Fletcher was not. As noted earlier, following his pioneering development work, Litster built stock boats for the Kelvin Launch and Engine Company's Glasgow showroom.

Litster and William Bergius went back a long way; apart from the boat-build connection, Alec Litster would later serve as skipper on Walter Bergius's 1927 Fife ketch, *Dodo IV*, and *Dodo V*, a 77ft Thornycroft motor launch acquired from Tom Thornycroft in 1957. *Dodo V*, formerly *King Duck*, was subsequently sold to the Marquis of Bute in 1964.[1380] The ubiquitous Bergius family still lived locally and made considerable use of Waddell's services, so it is unlikely that anything unbeknown would have taken place. Moreover, Litster and the Waddells were related.

The Fletchers delivered *White Heather* to G. & A. Waddell in 1932. The Waddell family had been boatmen since Victorian times when they secured the lease of the Ardnadam ferry-house from James Hunter of the Hafton Estate. The tenancy agreement carried an obligation to "*provide ferry services to Kilmun, day and night, throughout the year if required*". This responsibility remained even after Robert Allan, a well-known ship-owner and yachtsman, acquired the estate. Robert's extravagant fleet then included the *Torfrida*, and her yet-to-be-famous gig, the *Kelvin* prototype.

By the turn of the century, the Waddell's ferry service had developed to encompass excursions and rowing-boat hire from their base at Lazaretto Point in the Holy Loch. Gordon and Alex operated three launches – the *White Heather*, the *White Rose*, and an eponymous *Kelvin*. The ladies of the family added value to the business, selling teas and ice-cream from a kiosk. And through the long Scottish winters, as with other operations of this type, the men kept busy building clinker dinghies and repairing other small craft in their boatshed.[1381]

White Heather was originally fitted with a 15hp Kelvin E4 Ricardo side-valve Petrol/Paraffin engine, a power-unit normally associated with the larger 30ft Kelvin Utility Launch – so she has always been over-powered. In the 1970s, Alex replaced the ageing Kelvin with a 70hp Ford D4, then recently removed from Colonel Whitbread's 65ft Robert Clark ketch, *Lone Fox*, which was being re-engined at Robertson's Yard in Sandbank. The big D4 was fitted forward of the main bulkhead and required new engine beds and additional reinforcement.[1382]

Alex had the contract for safety boat duties with the Holy Loch Sailing Club in these years. He was a reassuring presence in the days of the ironically named Crewsaver buoyancy bags. *White Heather* could tow a double string of yachts down to Rothesay or Largs for the regattas at 7kts, with the revs barely above tick-over. Unencumbered, with the big D4 at full chat, she could part a shedload of water.

Over half-a-century, the Waddell family provided logistical support to all the Clyde yacht clubs – especially the Royal Clyde and the Royal Western (whose burgee Alex proudly flew). In recognition of Alex's 50 years of loyal service, the Clyde Yacht Clubs Association (CYCA) struck a special medal to honour him in the Queen's Silver Jubilee year of 1977.

Iain McAllister recalls a day spent on board the *White Heather*: "*I have a very happy memory of a day spent assisting Alex in the mid-1970s when I was a Royal Clyde Yacht Club cadet on commodore boat duty at a CYCA Saturday regatta off Kilcreggan. Although by this time the club was based at Rhu, when it came to regattas out on the open firth old traditions were upheld. Alex had motored across from Sandbank towing a beautiful, varnished clinker punt, which was used as the outer start mark flying a large red flag with the white letters START. Later I realised how lucky I was to have had this opportunity to work with such an experienced boatman and really nice man, and to experience a Clyde tradition going back to the 19th century.*"

When Alex passed away, the assets of the business were auctioned off. *White Heather* was bought by Pierre Boistelle. However, restoration was daunting, then indefinitely delayed. The old girl was rescued from an imminent Viking funeral by Kenny and Andy Love, whose grandfather, Jimmy Ferguson, formerly owned the Waddell's rival boatyard and ferry-boat operation in Kilmun. Kenny recalls that she "*was in a right old state, ribs burst, planks you could put your arm through. We had to ratchet-strap her back into shape*". The brothers doubled up the cracked ribs, rebuilt the bow with a raised forecastle and put the boat back in commission.[1383]

In 1999, to make space for another restoration challenge, Kenny sold *White Heather* to Andy and Cush Thoms. Andy replaced the monster Ford engine with a 1.5-litre BMC diesel recently removed from the UFO34, *Fascinator*. Twelve years later, the Thoms invested in a brand spanking new 30hp Yanmar. Then, keen that the boat should now enjoy more regular use, Andy invited the Boyd sisters and their underemployed husbands to share in the joy, sweat and tears of ownership in 2014, thus inaugurating the White Heather Club.

Today, the formerly anonymous old Kelvin launch brings a touch of old-world glamour to Clydeside marinas as the White Heather Club pursue their Sunday-lunch agenda through the season. While she turns heads, she is not a pampered plaything, but a utility boat maintained to working boat standards. *White Heather's* most recent restoration was in 2014, but she will be under the chisel again this winter for a new nose job to replace some ad-hoc plastic-padding surgery following a 'ladies' day' incident (which highlighted the relatively more robust construction of a 1960s polyester Piper OD).

We might close this section with an anecdote. Andy Thoms was Alex's boat-boy in the summer holidays, helping out on *White Heather*. There is also a Bergius (Teacher's Whisky) link here. Some years ago, while taking the air in Antigua, Andy hailed the owner of the big Mylne yawl, *Mariella*: *"Hello there! I used to deliver the rolls and papers to that boat when Ron Teacher had her"*. The new owner looked down his nose at Andy and straight through him. If *Mariella* ever returns to her home waters, she would be well advised to avoid the stout steel cruise ships of the Majestic Line, which no doubt, have standing orders to return the favour!

CODA: Ferry Wars

The earliest mention of a ferry-service across the Holy Loch references a boat on-station to shuttle between Hunter's Quay and Strone in 1497. The last ferry, from Ardnadam to Kilmun, crossed the loch in the 1970s. The Waddell Family and the Ferguson Family both enjoyed ferry rights; however, these were exercised from estate holdings on opposite sides of the loch. The dispute mirrored a long-running antipathy between James Hunter of Hafton and David Napier of Kilmun.[1384]

The ferry rights in the Holy Loch came up as a subject of an action at Dunoon Sheriff Court in 1928 by Dr R. S. Allan, of Hafton, whose tenant, George Waddell, was said to enjoy the rights to operate a ferry across Holy Loch from Lazaretto Point to Graham's Point, and *"sought to interdict James Ferguson, Ferry House, Kilmun, from conveying for hire by Lazaretto Point to Kilmun, and thereby interfering with pursuer and tenant's rights. The Defender held that he and his fore-fathers had held the ferry rights at Kilmun, which came under the Barony of Benmore, for over a hundred years."* [1385] The action came to naught.

CODA: Steam Launches

In the 19th century, there were a good many steam-launches operating on the Clyde – ferries, commercial vessels, navy pinnaces and tenders to the larger private steam-yachts. These stylish little vessels would have a reciprocating engine about the size of a grandfather clock, but without the complexity. These were Damoclean devices, veiled by beautifully buffed-up casings with polished copper piping and glittering brass fittings. The boilers resembled an old-fashioned steel dustbin. A bag of coal would keep a steam-launch running all day with no more effort than stoking an Aga. Steam-power was quiet, sublimely smooth, and above all, fast. The enthusiasts who have resurrected steam launches, mainly for inland waterway operation in the South, are not victims of whimsical fashion, as with some other restoration trends, but guardians of a life-affirming mode of transport, that was and remains, intrinsically worthwhile.

[1363] Sailing Tours, Frank Cowper, 1892-1909.

[1364] The Bergius Company Ltd, Jubilee Celebrations, Speech by the Chairman Mr D. W. Willocks, 11th June 1954.

[1365] Walter MacDonald Bergius, then aged just 23, founded The Bergius Car & Engine Company in May 1904, at 169, Finnieston Street, Glasgow. The first car was on the road by Christmas. The workforce of five built the engine, transmission, axles, wheel-hubs, radiator and bodywork from scratch on the premises.

[1366] *Dodo* was exhibited in the Scottish Maritime Museum at Irvine but may now be in the Scottish Transport Museum in Glasgow.

[1367] Coincidentally, the company moved to Dobbie's Loan in Glasgow in 1910. And Litster also earned a living as a coffin maker. Did Mr I. R. Dobbie even exist?

[1368] Other accounts have the first fishing boat installations in 1908.

[1369] Auxiliary yachts were large with bulky steam engines, coal bunkers and telescopic funnels like the Brassey's *Sunbeam* (St Clair Bryne, 1874) requiring commercial operational logistics. There were small steam engines and steam launches, however, installing a steam engine in a small sailing yacht involved compromises that most owners were not willing to accept.

[1370] Development of the Motor Yacht – how the internal combustion engine worked its way into the domain of steam – a review of gasoline equipment over its older rival, J. Scott Mathews, Motorboating, October 1913.

[1371] In the early days before feathering propellers, sailing days would have been accompanied by the rumble of the spinning prop shaft with the gearbox in neutral. The challenge of rating yachts with auxiliary motors for competition lay some way in the future too.

[1372] Yachting as a Sport, The Times, 13th December 1912.

[1373] Yachting, The Times, 8th July 1911.

[1374] After Walter Bergius passed away, death-duties saw the company sold in 1953. It is now Kelvin Diesels plc and is based at Uddingston.

[1375] *Vailama II*, built by Silver's, is listed as Walter's design.

[1376] William was indeed competent as his design for *Dodo III*, built by Fife, demonstrates. This innovative shoal draft weekender was the model for *Dodo IV*, a larger more complex yacht again built by Fife, but this time with the lines drawn by a recently qualified naval architect in the Fife office, one David Boyd.

[1377] In the case of the Utility Launch, the beam is increased by 15%.

[1378] 'Come in, Come in', the siren cry of the White Heather Club, lyrics by Andy Stewart.

[1379] As opposed to the proverbial 'doon the water'.

[1380] Before selling *King Duck* to Walter Bergius in 1957, Tom Thornycroft used her extensively as a mothership for regattas and carried two International 14s on deck. She served during the 1948 Torquay Olympics and the 1952 Olympics in Helsinki. Bergius had *Dodo VI* built by Berthon's in 1961. *Dodo V* was sold to Alan Fairbrother before being bought by the Marquess of Bute in 1964 and resuming her original name of *King Duck*.

[1381] Correspondence with the Waddell family, 2018.

[1382] Correspondence with the Thoms family, 2018.

[1383] Correspondence with the Love family, 2018.

[1384] The dispute concerned pier dues and steamer landing rights.

[1385] Disputed Ferry, Aberdeen Journal, 3rd July 1928.

Bergius automobile, participating in the Scottish Reliability Trials of 1906

Dodo II, Walter Bergius, built by James Litster, 1903   Fitting an auxiliary engine, James Litster, Kirn

The author on *White Heather* photographing the J-class *Lionheart*   Image: Neil and Eileen Lea.

Kelvin advertisement. Internal combustion launch prototypes: *Kelvin I left*, *Kelvin II* right

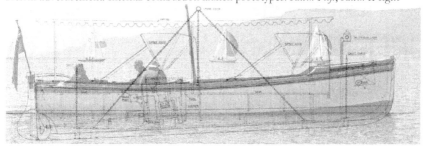

White Heather with Bergius 26ft Kelvin Light-weight Utility Launch overlay

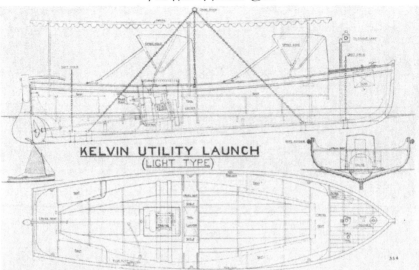

Kelvin 26ft Light Utility Launch, 1919   Image: Graces Guide to British Industrial History

White Heather, 1932, with 70hp Ford D4 from *Lone Fox*   Image: Waddell Family

Alex Waddell, 50 years of loyal service to the CYCA and the community

White Heather, 1932, arriving at Hunter's Quay in 2014   Image: Anne Ross

White Heather, 'taking up' after relaunch 2014   Image: the author

Chapter 35: Fair Play

Nothing in these Rules shall exonerate any vessel, or the owner, master or crew thereof, from the consequences of any neglect to comply with these Rules or of the neglect of any precaution which may be required by the ordinary practice of seamen, or by the special circumstances of the case. Colregs[1386]

The growth and success of yachting on the Clyde, and indeed the development of the entire Clyde coast, owed everything to the advent of what may just have been the 'best' – fast, frequent, universal, luxurious and fun – transportation system in the history of the world. The Clyde steamer network was also the most magical, in terms of the quality of the engineering proudly presented in gleaming display to bewitched passengers, and the most beautiful, in that the ferry operators sponsored generations of vessels that matched, and often surpassed, the rakish elegance of the famous racing yachts from the boards of G. L. Watson, William Fife III and Alfred Mylne.

The rise of the Clyde steamers could be viewed in the context of a love-hate relationship with the Clyde's yachtsmen, but that would be disingenuous. The steamers were simply so popular and their buccaneering masters so charismatic, that everyone loved them, even as they multiplied and ran riot to constitute an ever-present hazard to more docile forms of estuarine navigation. We might liken them to whales today. I love to see whales breach at sea, who doesn't? But when these leviathans get a little too close, admiration turns immediately to blind panic.[1387] Occasionally, however, yachtsmen and steamship masters did cross swords, and this chapter recounts a few such occasions.

Next time you leave your most treasured possession unattended on a swinging mooring and retire to the yacht club bar, raise your glass to the temerity of drunken sailors. We all enjoy a little-known dividend as a direct consequence of their apparent weakness for the demon drink. More specifically, might I suggest that my fellow yachtsmen toast the incorrigible old soaks of the Caledonian Steam Packet Company? The Holy Loch was the setting for a protracted legal battle in the early 1900s. This cause célèbre established case-law in relation to the obligations of small yachts kept on permanent moorings, unmanned and unlit at night. The story involves two small, but perfectly formed William Fife yachts, and their owners, James Arrol and Andrew Paterson.

Mr James Arrol, of the famous Glasgow engineering family, owned the *Marguerite,* a miniature Fife cutter – 21ft LOA, 17ft LWL, built at Fairlie in 1905.[1388] Lloyds suggests that James had recently bought her from George Jackson of Sandbank. Andrew's grandfather owned the *Thelma,* a larger Fife cutter – 32ft LOA, 25ft LWL from 1897, built on the other side of the North Channel by John Hilditch of Carrickfergus.[1389] The two little yachts lay at swinging moorings in front of 'Firwood', a recognised anchorage out of the fairway and well inshore of any normal approach to Kilmun pier.

James's *Marguerite* and Andrew's *Thelma* were both run down and sunk one evening in June 1912. The culprit was the *Marchioness of Breadalbane,* a fast paddle-steamer, at that time owned and operated by the Caledonian Steam Packet Company.[1390] She was 210ft LOA, capable of 17kts and built by Reid of Glasgow in 1890. A couple of years after the events related here, the *Marchioness* was requisitioned for use as a minesweeper to be based at Troon and then Portsmouth through the Great War. At the close of the conflict, the old boat brought the troops home, before resuming her original purpose on the Clyde. The *Marchioness* was eventually scrapped in 1937. Like all Clyde paddle-steamers of her era, she was as slim as a rowing eight and boasted a stem like a battle-axe.

When the *Marchioness of Breadalbane* hit the *Thelma,* the bow of the steamer fouled the yacht's rigging and dragged her some way inshore to sink in shallow water just off the Ferry House jetty. The *Marchioness* then turned her rough attentions to the *Marguerite,* cleanly cutting off the little cutter's bow. Released from her mooring and any obligation to float, the remains of the *Marguerite* went straight to the bottom of the loch, settling on top of her anchors.

James and Andrew were understandably fuming, but in the face of an unrepentant captain and intransigent Steam Packet Company, there seemed little they could do; the ferry companies had long been 'a law unto themselves'. So, James Arrol embarked on a David vs Goliath battle. He sued the ferry company for damages and his friend, Andrew Paterson, rather than lodge his own lawsuit, elected to act as James's principal witness.

In his evidence to the court, Andrew illustrated the positions of all affected vessels, having meticulously measured angles, distances and transits. He noted that the *Marchioness* usually passed 150-yards to seaward of the moored yachts. The list of supporting witnesses was long on both sides of a partisan divide and included many of the weel-kent families that still live in the village today. From the court records, it is clear that company loyalty and the side on which the witnesses' bread was buttered, trumped any concerns about the veracity of the ship's log.

Fortunately, the Scottish legal system is unimpressed by hand-on-heart perjury. The Sheriff focussed on the chain of events as they occurred that night on the bridge of the steamer. The prevailing Board of Trade Regulation, Article 10 sub-section (F) required that: "*Every fishing boat and every open-boat when at anchor between sunset and sunrise shall exhibit a white light visible around the horizon for a distance of at least one mile*". The court found the law to be clear, but not unambiguous, as there was the matter of context. The *Marguerite* lay in a safe, well-established anchorage near the head of a quiet loch, and out of the recognised path of all commercial shipping.

Sheriff Lyall, presiding, saw the matter in the light of good Scottish common sense. The steamer was off-course, and apparently, not under effective command, while the yacht was moored in such a way as to reflect the 'common practice' of generations of sailors and yachtsmen.[1391] Lyell, therefore, considered liability on the part of the owner of the *Marguerite* to be negligible. Finding against the Caledonian Steam Packet Company, he directed that the pursuer, Mr Arrol, should be reimbursed his claimed out-of-pocket expenses of £45 (£5,100).

In this judgement, we encounter common sense in a context where it is not always evident. These days, our understanding of 'common sense' is of a self-evident truth, embodied within the term. But, like many things we take for granted, it was not always thus. Thomas Reid (1710-1796) and the Scottish philosophers of the 18th and 19th centuries are credited with the 'common sense school of philosophy'.[1392] Reid considered ordinary people to be competent within the realm of common understanding: "*in a matter of common sense, every man is no less a competent judge than a mathematician is in a mathematical demonstration*".

However, such competence did not extend to "*matters beyond the reach of common understanding*" wherein "*the many are led by the few, and willingly yield to their authority*". This latter qualification is equally important. Today, the consensus on the value of expert opinion is under threat by populist politicians who declare that: "*I think that the people of this country have had enough of experts.*"[1393] The term 'common sense' acknowledges that there are areas of discussion where lay opinion can usefully complement expert opinion. It does not disparage the view of experts. Despite criticism, much of which seems pedantic today, the Scottish school prospered. Caledonian common sense exerted considerable influence on 'American pragmatism', the most distinctive contribution to philosophy tendered by our friends across the Atlantic, until they came up with 'Just do it!'.[1394]

Nothing was settled following this initial judgement, however, as an appeal had been launched and the 'court of public opinion' remained in open session. Arguments raged back and forth in the 'letters pages' of *The Glasgow Herald*, with both sides writing under pseudonyms, as was common at the time. Despite the steamer being off-course and having transits and other leading lights in place to guide her in, some regular commuters took issue with the Sheriff's verdict. They neither knew nor cared that the crew were drunk, or just possibly, they were used to visiting the bridge for a wee dram on the way home? 'Daily Traveller', 'Coaster', and others indulged in flights of hyperbole, portraying frail wooden yachts as a hazard to the stout Clyde-built steamers they were so proud of.[1395]

As might be expected, the prospect of a thousand swinging moorings becoming untenable galvanised the entire Clyde sailing community. One gentleman, writing as 'Fair Play' made the reasonable point that if the ferryboat skippers felt *"able to go messing about in the firth as they liked"* then they and 'Daily Traveller' should think again. The same correspondent returned to the fray to excoriate 'Coaster' and note that *"the decision had been well-received by the legal profession, yachtsmen and those who know anything about the subject"*, the 'known anchorages' in the Firth of Clyde being well-clear of steamer routes and pier approaches.[1396] One insightful writer observed that this was not just a local matter, it involved every yacht anchorage in the British Isles and possibly the Commonwealth too. And that is why this case has become part of the Caledonian legacy to yachting.

Everyone was aware of the elephant in the courtroom but cast and crew tiptoed around the beast. Ferryboats and the excursion business were the lifeblood of Clyde resorts. No one wanted to rock the boat. Moreover, if the steamer crew were indeed drunk, this was a serious matter, possibly leading to loss of liberty and hard labour. Article 220 of the merchant Shipping Act 1894 concerning *"misconduct endangering life or ship"*, states that: *"If a master, seaman, or apprentice belonging to a British ship, by wilful breach of duty or by neglect of duty or by reason of drunkenness, does any act tending to the immediate loss, destruction, or serious damage of the ship, or tending immediately to endanger the life or limb of a person belonging to or on board the ship, he shall in respect of each offence be guilty of a misdemeanour."*[1397]

Fortunately for the sterling reputation of Clyde seamen, and the peace of mind of their passengers, allegations of drunken sailors running amok did not appear in print; but it is a sub-text that runs through subsequent events. The presiding justices were surely not in ignorance of this crucial fact, but somehow, they were able to achieve just ends without invoking a scandal. The legal arguments rightly separated the issue of establishing case law for the country as a whole, with the secondary matter of 'coastal navigation with judgement impaired'. The latter issue was quietly deferred to be resolved later with Sir Charles Bine Renshaw of the parent railway company.

The details of the case were referred to Sydney Buxton, the President of the Board of Trade, and subsequently, a question was raised in the House of Commons in July 1912 by Mr MacCallum Scott, MP for Glasgow Bridgeton.[1398] Scott wanted to know if the yacht was at fault for failing to observe Article II of the International Regulations for Preventing Collisions at Sea 1910, or did this regulation not apply to small yachts when left unattended? Buxton, answering for the BoT, stated that since the Steam Packet had lodged an appeal, he would await the findings of the Sheriff Principal before commenting. Meanwhile, the yachting world lobbied men of influence. The July 1912 editorial of *Yachting* was devoted to the case, and thereafter, the magazine maintained a close interest in the long-running proceedings.[1399]

However, Sydney Buxton had more pressing matters to deal with. The SS *Titanic* had gone down with great loss of life a couple of months earlier. An enquiry into the sinking was in prospect, and inevitably, Buxton was under fire in the media. The BoT was undoubtedly complacent about safety, and the *Titanic* disaster occurred on Buxton's watch. The regulatory environment had failed to keep up with the rapid pace of steamship developments. Somehow, Buxton's political career survived, perhaps because the immediate past president was one Winston Spencer Churchill.

The matter of the Holy Loch moorings was raised in the Commons again in November 1912. The MP for Glasgow Bridgeton quizzed Buxton on progress and then held the floor to follow up with questions more likely to impress his constituents than advance any notional agenda. Scott invoked the Glasgow Fair, suggesting that unlit yachts interfered with the safe operation of Clyde steamers during this important holiday. Buxton wearily got to his feet and pointed out that it was a long-established practice to leave small yachts unlit and unattended in sheltered anchorages. *"No real danger was to be apprehended."* Moreover, the case was still sub-judice. MacCallum Scott's irritable retort was that if there were regulations, they should be enforced.

At the long-awaited Court of Appeal, Sheriff Gardiner Millar muddied the waters by finding both parties negligent to a degree and imposed damages of £22 10/- against Mr Arrol, cutting by half the pursuer's net damages due from the ferry company. No legal expenses were awarded to either side. Nonetheless, the Sheriff laid the blame squarely on the skipper of the *Marchioness of Breadalbane* for not maintaining a good lookout. Sheriff Millar thought it likely that the steamer would have hit the *Marguerite* regardless of riding lights.

From the record, it is apparent that Mr Arrol's case was more convincing than that of the steam-ship company, but the Sheriff felt himself bound by the letter of the law. Perhaps Miller was less confident dealing with matters of common law and common sense than his predecessor? So again, leave was given to appeal, but this time to both parties. Still, the game had been moved on. Citing the case '*ex parte* Ferguson vs Hutchison L.R.6 Q.B. 280', *Marguerite* was held to be a 'vessel' within the meaning of the 'Colregs' as she could go to sea under sail as her usual means of propulsion, although it was noted that she was also "*fitted for oars*".[1400]

In July 1913, and again in November of that year, the Glasgow MP was on his feet in the Commons. Now, he was citing anecdotal evidence from steamship captains about the dangers presented by yachts anchored in the fairway. MacCallum Scott was a panic-mongering past-master. Without apparent irony, he brought up the sinking of the SS *Titanic* and the extraordinary expense incurred by the owners of that vessel to "*mitigate the results of disasters*". Why not then "*enforce regulations aimed at preventing disaster in the first place?*" Of course, this reference to the *Titanic* would not have endeared MacCallum Scott to the beleaguered President of the Board of Trade. Buxton, to his credit, merely confirmed the case as still sub-justice. Unwilling to take no for an answer, the MP continued to petition the Board over the following months.[1401]

Correspondence also continued in the letters' columns. A disgruntled traveller, writing under the initials 'J. D.' went so far as to count the yachts lying at anchor off Hunter's Quay. On 12th July 1913, at 10.00 p.m, of 65 yachts in the anchorage, 35 displayed riding lights and 30 did not.[1402] Meanwhile, MacCallum Scott, not a man to give up easily when he had a bit between his teeth, as we have seen, again pestered the Board of Trade. The BoT coolly maintained their 'wait and see' position.

On the 18th December 1913, the second appeal came before the Scottish Court of Session, First Division. It was almost an anti-climax. This time there was no hedging of bets. The *Marchioness* was found to be unequivocally at fault, and it emerged that, had the steamer not hit the yachts, it would have run hard aground. This was a brutal assessment. The Lord President's decision to lay the entire blame on the hapless captain of the *Marchioness of Breadalbane* was unanimously signed-off on by the entire supporting panel of senior law-lords: Lord Johnston, Lord Mackenzie and Lord Skerrington.[1403]

Even with the matter settled, MacCallum Scott was unwilling to give up the dubious celebrity he had acquired through this long-running case. In July 1914, he attempted to harangue the BoT, but was admonished without ceremony by John Burns, the new President.[1404] "*An obligation on all these yachts would be a serious matter to the owners and might involve the pleasure boats being driven out of existence.*" And he followed this up with: "*Any action which might be taken would not, of course, be confined to the Clyde and I am ascertaining whether the same question arises in other parts of the United Kingdom with the object of deciding whether anything should be done in the matter generally.*"[1405]

John Burns was an unlikely champion of yachting. He held the Board of Trade position for just six months before resigning over the Liberal Government's declaration of war. As a working-class cricketer, it seems strange that he would have had any empathy with the 'sport of kings'. Moreover, it appears that he had no practical knowledge of the sea and ships. With Burns' resignation and the impending global conflict, nothing was ever done about small-craft anchorages. So, we all enjoy the mooring rights we have today. Although, to be honest, we would enjoy these rights rather more if we did not have to pay the Crown Estate for the privilege of planting mushrooms in the mud.

CODA: 'Steaming' on Steamers

The Paterson family's newspaper archive then moves on to the equally fascinating topic of 'Drinking on Steamers'; a legal anomaly pursued to the point of obsession by the Paterson clan. In this Presbyterian quest, Andrew's thirteen letters to the editor, unsurprisingly, did not get as much public support as the business of the moorings. Andrew hammered home the virtues of temperance, without referring to what was surely the main target of his ire – the crews of the steamers, rather than the odd disorderly passenger. Meanwhile, Jim Waddell, the ferryman, was writing about steamer overcrowding and painting a vivid picture of an accident waiting to happen. MacCallum Scott, the perennially quizzical M.P. for Glasgow Bridgeton, now found another, perhaps more worthwhile, axe to grind.

[1386] A Guide to the Collision Avoidance Rules, International Regulations for Preventing Collisions at Sea, 6th edition incorporating the 1981, 1987, 1989, 1993 and 2001. amendments, A. N. Cockcroft and J. N. F. Lameijer, 2004.
[1387] In the 1989-90 Whitbread Race, the maxi-yacht, *Charles Jourdan*, arrived in Auckland with a 12ft gash in the topside inflicted by a whale. Fortunately, it was above the waterline, so the crew had been able to make a temporary patch repair and complete the leg. The pod of

happy humpback whales that had entertained us all off Punta del Este didn't seem quite so entertaining after that.

[1388] My Father worked for Sir William Arrol & Co Ltd. as a civil engineer in the 1950s and early 60s. James Arrol, William's brother lived at 'Finartmore' a house originally built by Napier for his own use. The house next to ours in Kilmun was owned by the Arrol family for over 100 years. The Arrol sisters held on to 'Woodburn' (originally a David Napier property like our house 'Anchorage Villa') well into their old age to record a century of ownership. Sadly, these game 'girls' have all now passed away.

[1389] The Hilditch yard built a good many classic boats, including the recently restored 1894 Watson-designed, *Peggy Bawn*. The yard folded in 1913.

[1390] The Clyde Passenger Steamer: its rise and progress during the 19th century, James Williamson, 1904. The Caledonian Steam Packet Company was formed in 1889 to complement the services of the Caledonian Railway. The company swallowed most of its rivals before merging with MacBrayne in 1973 to become Caledonian MacBrayne.

[1391] 'Common practice' is known in case law as 'customary rights'. The legal criteria defining a custom varies with context; examples cited in contemporary references include 'customary rights to moor a vessel'.

[1392] Scottish Common-Sense Philosophy, Sources and Origins, Volume 5, edited and introduced by James Fieser, 2000.

[1393] *"I think that the people of this country have had enough of experts from organisations with acronyms saying that they know what is best and getting it consistently wrong, because these people are the same ones who got consistently wrong."* Michael Gove, 6th June 2016. As an expert who once worked for organisations with well-known acronyms, I take issue with Mr Gove and his ilk.

[1394] Common Sense in the Scottish Enlightenment, edited by Charles Bradford Bow, 2018. Thomas Reid followed Francis Hutcheson and Adam Smith as Professor of Moral Philosophy at Glasgow University.

[1395] The Holy Loch Collision, Letters to the Editor, 'Coaster', Glasgow Herald, 21st, 26th and 29th June 1912 and 'Daily Traveller' 29th June 1912.

[1396] The Holy Loch Collision, Letters to the Editor, 'Fair Play', Glasgow Herald, 27th and 29th June and 4th July 1912.

[1397] *"Offences punishable as misdemeanours: In Scotland, every offence which by this Act is described as a felony or misdemeanour may be prosecuted by indictment or criminal letters at the instance of Her Majesty's Advocate and shall be punishable with fine and with imprisonment with or without hard labour in default of payment, or with imprisonment with or without hard labour, or with both, as the court may think fit."*

[1398] Printed Answers to Questions, Holy Loch Collision, Glasgow Herald, 9th July 1912

[1399] From the Man at the Wheel, Riding Lights on Small Yachts, Yachting, 25th July 1912.

[1400] A Holy Loch Collision, Interesting Decision by Sheriff Millar, Glasgow Herald, 4th November 1912.

[1401] Debate in the House of Commons, 16th July 1913, Glasgow Herald 17th July 1913.

[1402] Clyde Small Craft & Lights, Letters to the Editor, 'JD', Glasgow Herald 22nd July 2013.

[1403] Court of Session, proceedings, Glasgow Herald, 19th December 1913.

[1404] John Burns was an interesting character: trade unionist, social progressive and pacifist, however, he was against the idea of the Welfare State and alcohol and he disparaged Jews.

[1405] Lights on Vessels in the Firth of Clyde, Glasgow Herald, 7th July 1914.

Sailing at night   Image: unknown, photomanipulated by the author

Marchioness of Bredalbane, standing room only, entering the Holy Loch at speed   Image: Adamson

Marchioness of Lorne leaving Kilmun Pier, Kilmun east anchorage at left.   Image: Stengel

Passengers on a Clyde steamer in 1884   Image: old engraving, artist unknown

Chapter 36: Damn the Torpedoes!

Smile for the camera and raise your glass. Pull up your socks till they cover your ass; say, 'goodbye'... no more mama's apple pie. Damn the torpedoes and take a bow; it'll always be now. All the children say, 'Wow!' Say, 'goodbye'... no more mama's apple pie. Spin Doctors[1406]

Classic yachtsmen of the old school pride themselves on being prepared: a 'Leatherman' multi-tool, a sailmaker's palm, a spare impeller, an assortment of cable-grips and softwood plugs tied by every skin fitting. There is, however, only so much you can prepare for. Sometimes, an event occurs under a clear blue sky that shakes the Boy Scout resolve of even the most dyed-in-the-wool diehard. Being arbitrarily torpedoed by a warship of our Senior Service is just one such event. Giving evidence to a court of enquiry in 1908, expert witness Engineer Commander A. W. Gibbs avowed that the torpedo used in the Service was *"the most perfect weapon in the world and could be depended upon to do what they wanted it to do"*. Alas, not so, and not even close.

Woodnutts of Bembridge is synonymous with the X One Design, Solent Sunbeam and Victory daysailers, designed by Managing Director, Alfred Westmacott, but they also built many successful one-off racing yachts, including the David Boyd-designed Seawanhaka Cup-winning 6-metre, *Titia*. Woodnutts can boast perhaps the best 'friendly fire' anecdote, bar none. The boatyard first crossed swords with the British Admiralty in 1908 when their vessel, *Swiftsure*, was torpedoed by HMTB *Hunter*. *Swiftsure* had the A.E.P. Payne-designed 5-metre, *Emu*, under tow at the time.

This little yacht was owned by James Ismay, younger brother of Joseph Bruce Ismay, Chairman of the White Star Line.[1407] That, of course, cut no ice.[1408] The Naval Court of Inquiry adjudged the Senior Service *"in no way responsible"* for the damage, which they held was due to the negligence of the skipper of *Swiftsure* in not avoiding the torpedo. The evidence showed conclusively, in the official opinion, that it was not the torpedo which struck the launch, but the launch which struck the torpedo. The Admiralty counter-claimed £27 (£3,200) for damage to the torpedo – and won! It took some time, but eventually, Woodnutts got their money back and more, through Admiralty contracts in WW2, building Fairmile-class patrol boats and airborne lifeboats.

Our armed forces are perennially careless with their tin fish. Robertson's Yard in Scotland, where the America's Cup 12-metres, *Sceptre* and *Sovereign*, were built, was torpedoed in a 'friendly fire' incident during the worrisome August of 1944, as we described in *The Piper Calls the Tune*. During WW2, the Royal Navy's 3rd Submarine Flotilla was based in the Holy Loch, with HMS *Forth*, a specially designed mothership built by John Brown of Clydebank, assuming station in 1942. The classic submarine war-film *We Dive at Dawn* (1943), starring John Mills, depicts HMS *Forth* and the 3rd Flotilla in the loch.

Squadron Leader, Archie Jameson (RAFVR), was assigned to 'special duties' in the Holy Loch during WW2. He was attached to the RAF Marine Aircraft Research Establishment, then squatting in splendour at 'Ardenvohr', the Royal Northern Yacht Club's elegant premises at Rhu. Whatever his specific mission, the Squadron Leader and his long-suffering wife took advantage of this opportunity to live onboard their 1908 Summers & Payne yacht, *Isola*, in the picturesque Sandbank roadstead. This 78-ton ketch, and the resident Jamesons, wintered-over on the hard at Morris & Lorimer's Yard. The following story, from 13th August 1944, may or may not have been connected with the couple's subsequent decision to decamp into more conventional married quarters.

HMS *Thule*, a split-new T Class submarine, had just returned to the Holy Loch after her first and only North Atlantic patrol, during which she had been testing Loran RDF systems. She now lay alongside the SS *Alrahda*, an old passenger ship, which had been requisitioned to provide additional berthing space. The *Thule's* high-spirited buccaneers had gone ashore for a beer and some keenly anticipated R&R, and the service crew, or 'skimmers' from HMS *Forth*, now crawled all over their vessel. Routine maintenance duties included a test firing of each tube.[1409]

The scheduled 'air shot' from *Thule's* No.11 stern tube, however, tested more than just the firing mechanism. An armed Mk.X torpedo splashed into the Holy Loch and took off like a rocket. The *Thule* crew had left the sub at action-stations with the torpedoes primed, tubes flooded and caps open. Fortunately for the absent and enervated submariners, the Officer in Charge, Lieutenant Hammer, from the HMS *Forth*, had been given written notice to that effect.

The old *Alrahda* was on a swinging mooring, so had the tide been ebbing and the prevailing sou'westerly blowing, *Thule* could have sunk the *Queen Mary* at anchor off the Tail o' the Bank. As it was, the rogue missile somehow avoided the minelayers and numerous small craft moored in the Sandbank anchorage. In the process, William Bergius discovered yet another reason for his favoured shoal draft as the missile passed directly under *Dodo III*, then a thunderstruck local fisherman in a rowing boat, before 500lbs of TNT blew a 'house-sized' crater in the foreshore just to the east of Robertson's Yard.[1410]

Young Andrew Paterson was playing on the beach at Kilmun. He still remembers the incident vividly 75 years later. He recalls that a great column of water, gravel and mussels shot skywards, and the blast broke all the windows in the neighbourhood. Andrew was not put off beachcombing and in 1985, as auctioneer, he would knock down the residual assets of Fife's Yard on the foreshore at Fairlie.

The submarine skipper, Lieutenant Commander, Alastair Campbell Gillespie Mars, was enjoying a 'Horse's Neck' (whisky and green ginger) on the 'terrace' (shelter-deck) of HMS *Forth*. Marr's view of the launch-vehicle was obscured by the *Alrahda*, but he was perfectly placed to watch the results of the unexpected action. The droll Lieutenant quipped artfully about the misadventure of "*some clot*", even as a horrible realisation began to dawn. The newly christened 'Terror of the Holy Loch' slipped out of the loch a couple of weeks later with her buttocks firmly clenched.

Base Commander, Robert Warne, must have been on good terms with the Admiral of the Fleet since a Court of Enquiry was never convened. Subsequently, however, Warne would have to deal with a £20,000 (£880,000) claim for damages from the good people of Sandbank. That would be getting on for a million today, but the claim was later settled 'in the spirit of Dunkirk' for just £5,000 (£220,000). During the Cold War, the US Navy's Subron 14 occupied the Holy Loch. They would go one better, when the SSBN *James Madison* piled into a Soviet submarine on surveillance duties off Hunter's Quay on the 3rd November 1974, as noted in Chapter 37. That unsuccessful bid to kick off World War III cost a bit more to put right.

There is a Loch Long class keelboat called *Sirocco*, still sailing today in Aldeburgh, proudly bearing an engraved plaque that commemorates an unprovoked attack on a small, unarmed yacht in peacetime. On the 3rd July 1957, warships of the Senior Service assembled for a firing exercise off Baron's Point, home to the Cove Sailing Club.[1411] The Royal Navy may have been testing the Mk.20E 21-inch torpedo for surface ships, a weapon that suffered from intractable guidance programming issues. Weighing 1,810lbs and 22ft-long, the Mk.20 was coincidentally exactly the same displacement and length as a Loch Long keelboat. However, the torpedo ran at 22kts so, unlike the little yacht, it didn't need a truculent Scotsman at the helm to inflict considerable damage.

On that fateful afternoon, a torpedo was test-launched mid-afternoon, and almost immediately, something went terribly wrong with the gyroscopic guidance system and it veered off across the loch, zigzagging erratically. Thomas Muir and his wife and son were sailing *Sirocco* across the Firth to take part in Clyde Week. The family were a quarter of a mile off the shore at Cove when Mrs Muir saw the torpedo narrowly miss another yacht farther offshore, then turn toward *Sirocco* in a wide arc at an estimated 30kts. This would have been a record for a Mk.20E 21-inch torpedo, so while the guidance system may have left something to be desired that day, the motor was running like a sewing machine.

The torpedo delivered *Sirocco* a glancing blow. The projectile was not armed, but even so, the impact seriously damaged the little yacht. Several planks were stove-in and the rudder was split. The resourceful crew trapezed from a jib halyard to keep the breach clear of the water. It was a rare moment of athleticism in the annals of Loch Long sailing. *Sirocco* was run ashore in a sinking condition near Cove Sailing Club. None of the crew was injured, but Mrs Muir was helped ashore suffering from shock.

To be fair to the Royal Navy, when challenged by a reporter from *The Times*, they immediately accepted responsibility – not always the case in these days of unexplained sinkings in the North Channel.[1412] The Royal Navy's Experimental Establishment at Greenock said that the torpedo, while under trial, had developed a fault in the guidance mechanism. *Sirocco* returned to the fray in better than new condition, accessorized with that unique, and highly desirable plaque, as a memento mori.

The same edition of *The Times* reported on another, potentially even more serious, inadvertent missile attack. The good people of Purbeck in Dorset were looking for an explanation of how a missile came in from the sea and landed near some caravans and quarry workings nearly two miles inland. Seven men were working in the quarry. A division of the Army was carrying out an exercise nearby but did not immediately accept responsibility, noting that there was also a naval gunnery range off St. Alban's Head.

We had our own rogue torpedo encounter with a Mk.24 Tigerfish, back in 1981. This torpedo had escaped during an exercise conducted by HMNB *Clyde* in Inchmarnock Water. The Tigerfish was one of several programmes disrupted by the closure of the Torpedo Experimental Establishment in Greenock in 1958 and its relocation to Portland in Dorset. Fully 60% of Tigerfish launches did not go as planned. It is, therefore, something of a blessing that they were never nuclear tipped, as once seriously proposed.[1413] Indeed, the range was such that even at the end of their run, detonation would have blown up the launch vehicle!

It was a soggy morning in May, *Bolero* was making 5.5kts in 18kts apparent, plugging painfully upwind through the raw grey morning – full main, flattening reef and 115% #2 headsail. It was the feeder race of the 1981 Scottish Series, and we were bound for Tarbert in Loch Fyne. The crew were lined up on the rail; stiff, cold and tired, in that familiar state of suspended animation inflicted by passage-racing in an IOR ¼ Tonner.

Suddenly, sliding by to weather, beneath our dangling rank of blue wellies, it's a God-damned torpedo. Almost as long as the boat and as fat as a whisky cask, with a propeller at one end and a (hopefully filleted) warhead at the other, it lies half-submerged on a reciprocal heading. As we pass, *Bolero's* bow wave runs the length of the grey steel carcass. So, for a brief moment, it appears that it is moving, and we are not. The rogue missile disappeared in our wake, a grave hazard to navigation, cruising menacingly downwind with the outgoing tide. The experience was spooky enough to raise the hairs on the back of the neck.

Following in our track and 'down the pan' already, the bold crew of the theoretically faster ½ Tonner, *Jonathan Livingston Vulture*, abandoned their race and tried to salvage this hazard to navigation. They failed miserably, but their 'catch and release' saga made for a great story in the Anchor Bar at Tarbert that evening![1414] As a post-script, the Tigerfish was so unreliable during the Falklands War that Margaret Thatcher upped our investment in marinised Cruise Missiles.

In theatres of war, of course, we can find torpedo attacks on yachts requisitioned by the world's navies. Well-known casualties included Sir Tommy Lipton's *Erin*, which served as a hospital ship in the Mediterranean until torpedoed and sunk in 1915. The Turkish royal yacht, *Ertugrul*, was torpedoed by a French submarine in the Bosporus in 1916, and in the same year another royal yacht, the *Medina*, was sunk off Plymouth. And then, during WW2, W. K. Vanderbilt II's *Alva* was torpedoed by a German U-boat off Cape Henry, Virginia. Unlikely as it may seem, yachts on active duty have occasionally redressed the balance, sinking the odd submarine, as when HMY *Lorna* sank the U74 in May 1918.

We are relatively safe in UK waters today since HMS *Conqueror*, formerly based in the Gare Loch, and the only nuclear-powered sub to have launched a torpedo in anger, was decommissioned in 1990. After sinking the *General Belgrano* in the 1982 Falklands War, the *Conqueror* maintained a low profile until she took out the *Celebration II*, a 63ft trimaran, off the coast of Florida in 1986. The Navy obligingly used their deck guns to finish off a sinking yacht. On this occasion, the *Celebration's* skipper had given his permission, and the US Coastguard were in attendance.[1415]

However, two years later, the same HMS *Conqueror*, now with a taste for polyester resin, collided with *Dalriada*, a Contessa 32 owned by the Army Sail Training Association. The unfortunate Contessa went swiftly to the bottom, leaving four crewmembers floundering in the frigid waters off the Mull of Kintyre. It was their fate to be entertained by an embarrassed Senior Service in the wardroom of the destroyer HMS *Battleaxe*, which came along later to pick up the pieces.[1416]

Yachts and torpedoes have not always been at loggerheads. Fast torpedo boats, like *HMTB Hunter*, first appeared in the 1870s. They were developed along the same slim lines as the fashionable, semi-displacement steam yachts of Vosper, Herreshoff and others. And these commuter yachts, in turn, benefitted from the design development of the motor torpedo boat (MTB) into a reliable all-weather planing vessel.

Possibly the best MTBs evolved in Germany in the 1930s. As such warships they were small enough to circumvent the rearmament restrictions imposed on Germany by the Versailles Treaty. The German torpedo boats of WW2 were based on the *Oheka II*, a 73ft luxury motor yacht built for investment banker, Otto Hermann Kahn, by the renowned Bremen yard of Luerssen in 1927.[1417] Luerssen, now trading as 'Lurssen', is still at the forefront of motor yacht design, with swanky mega-yachts such as *Octopus*, *Rising Sun* and *Azzam* to their credit in recent years.

The new boat became the much-feared Schnellboot of the Kriegsmarine. It was immediately obvious that the Germans had developed an ideal weapon for coastal defence. In Britain, the majority of our MTBs were built to standard designs developed by Noel Macklin's Fairmile Marine. Macklin persuaded the Admiralty to utilise small land-locked manufacturing facilities, such as furniture and piano workshops, to prefabricate sections of the vessels. These were then transported to coastal boatyards throughout the country for assembly. Each shipment was made up of six crates and designed to fit in a standard 15-ton lorry.

After the war, closing the circle, some MTBs were converted to serve as motor cruisers and houseboats. Most, perhaps fortunately, were sold without their massive gas-guzzling engines, as these reverted to the USA under the capricious Lend-Lease agreement. However, Uncle Sam didn't take the engines home, but bizarrely, buried them in the foundations of Cold War airbases to tease future generations of detectorists.

This last torpedo story is about the wildly romantic adventures of two famous Scottish yachts, and concerns Norway, a country that gave the

Clyde the much-loved International Dragon. In June 1940, Haakon VII, members of the Norwegian royal family and the key people for a government-in-exile were forced to flee from Oslo. The British cruiser, HMS *Glasgow*, picked up the King and his party and moved the Norwegian seat of government 600 miles north to Tromsø. Meanwhile, the gold reserves of the national treasury were taken 300 miles overland to Trondhjem for shipment overseas, although by some accounts the gold followed the King to Tromsø.

Obviously, there were fears that the ships carrying this valuable cargo might be torpedoed on the way to safety. A backstop was essential. The final plan was quite possibly brilliant, but then again it was not tested in action. The Norwegian gold was hidden in the bilges of small boats carried as deck cargo. In total 45 tonnes were carried in this way. Most of the bullion carriers were lifeboats, but two sailing yachts were drafted into the programme by shipping a liberal quota of internal ballast.[1418]

If the mothership was torpedoed, these fully rigged yachts would float free from their special cradles. They had all their sailing gear aboard and experienced crews standing by to continue the voyage to a safe haven under sail. Desmond Bagley wrote a book on these lines in 1963 called the *Golden Keel*, but his fictional protagonists went a step further to cast a new external ballast keel entirely of looted Nazi gold.

The two yachts selected were afloat in Scottish waters. James Lang's 43ft, Alfred-Mylne-designed, *Gometra* had been requisitioned for coastal defence duties at the start of WW2 and was available, lying afloat at her moorings off Greenock. The other yacht was Alan McKean's 36ft *Sinbad*, also designed by Mylne, moored on the Forth.[1419] The Annals of the Royal Vancouver Yacht Club suggest that both yachts were cruising Norwegian waters when war broke out, but Nigel Sharp's research gives us the story told here.[1420]

Sinbad was loaded onto the deck of the SS *Enterprise*, which then sailed for Tromso to rendezvous with the Royal Navy. HMS *Devonshire* would escort the freighter while evacuating the Norwegian VIPs to the relative safety of Britain. The old *Enterprise,* a steam-turbine vessel, built by John Brown in 1926, successfully avoided the U-Boat menace but came under attack from the Luftwaffe. Fortunately, she reached the sanctuary of Scapa Flow intact. From there the *Enterprise* sailed down the West Coast to Greenock to offload the *Sinbad* and the gold.

The other half of the gold was transported to Canada in the bilges of *Gometra*, 'sailing' as deck-cargo on board the *Bra Kra*, a Norwegian freighter. After the ship docked safely in Halifax, *Gometra* had effectively completed her mission. The Commodore of the Nova Scotia Royal Yacht Squadron, Ernes A. Bell seized the opportunity to buy a Mylne classic from the Admiralty at a knock-down price. After WW2, she was shipped across to Vancouver on the Pacific coast, travelling 3,000 miles on the flatbed of a Canadian Pacific Railway waggon. *Gometra* forged new legends in North America, sailing to Hawaii and Mexico on her own bottom before returning to Europe in 2006, once again as deck-cargo. She has been fully restored and is now based in the Mediterranean.

Admiral James Uchtred Farie, the first owner of *Gometra*, enjoyed some success but also endured humiliation during his navy career. He fought the Great War in destroyers and at the close of hostilities assumed command of the armoured cruiser, HMS *Cochrane*, in 1918. The *Cochrane* ran aground while being navigated by the Mersey pilot and broke her back through subsequent tides. In law, the pilot is responsible for "*the conduct of navigation during the relevant passage, while the master retains overall command*". However, this pilot denied responsibility and Captain Farie was court-martialled.[1421]

Gometra was built by the Mylne family's Bute Slip Dock at Ardmaleish and launched in 1925. The *Gometra* was named after a small island off the coast of Mull. She was initially based in Port Bannatyne. James Farie, then a widower, met his second wife during the 1928 West Highland Week. The couple moved south in 1930 and took *Gometra* with them. She was moored for a time at Lymington in Hampshire. But it seems that she was too deep for her mooring on the river, so she was sold to William Blaine Luard. Luard writes about *Gometra* in his book *Where the Tides Meet*.[1422]

Sinbad, another Mylne classic built by the Bute Slip Dock, was launched in 1928 for Alan McKean of Girvan. Alan was a keen member of the Clyde Cruising Club. His family were great supporters of the institution. Alan's brother and nephew would both serve as Commodore. *Sinbad* is listed by Lloyds as sold 'out of registration' in 1946, after her stalwart service shuttling to Norway as a treasure ship.

Quite why Alan didn't get his boat back is unclear; she may have been 'too far gone' after her war service, as many were. Nowadays, a bundle of wet firewood and a lack of imagination constitute a viable restoration project, but this was not the case during the austerity of the post-war years. In any case, McKean was not without options; he subsequently carried on sailing with his brother on the 50ft ketch, *Mingary*, another Mylne/Bute Slip Dock creation, which they had owned in partnership since her launching in 1929. *Mingary* was certainly not the most elegant of Mylne's designs, but she sails on today, immaculately restored and much-admired by 'connoisseurs' who have not seen *Mariella*.

1406 'Wow' from the album 'Here Comes the Bride', lyrics by the Spin Doctors 1999.
1407 A year before the *Titanic* tragedy, yacht-builder McAlister of Dumbarton entered into an arrangement with Captain Valdemar Engelhardt to build his patented collapsible lifeboats. McAlister delivered four Engelhardt lifeboats, 28ft x 8ft 6" x 3ft 1" to Messrs Harland & Wolff in February 1912. Lifeboat C rescued J. Bruce Ismay. Glasgow City Archives.
1408 Ismay Yacht Torpedoed! Daily Telegraph, 2nd April 1908.
1409 HMS Thule Intercepts, Alistair Marr, 1956.
1410 Memories of Dunoon and Cowal, Renee Forsyth, 1983.
1411 Loch Longs, the First 50 Years, John McMutrie, 1957.
1412 Torpedo Hits Yacht, The Times, 4th July 1957.
1413 Tigerfish data, archived by www.forecastinternational.com
1414 The Piper Calls the Tune, Euan Ross and Bob Donaldson, 2017.
1415 Torpedoed! Well, Almost! British Sub Sinks Yacht After Rescue, David Enscoe, Staff Writer on a provincial US newspaper, 7th May 1986.
1416 Hansard, HMS Conqueror (Collision) HC Deb, 21st July 1988, vol 137 cc722-3W
1417 Schnellboot (S-Boot) / (E-Boat) Motor Torpedo Boat, 7/10/2017, JR Potts, www.MilitaryFactory.com
1418 Gometra, Nigel Sharp, Classic Boat, October 2019.
1419 Troubled Waters: Leisure Boating and the Second World War, Nigel Sharp, 2015.
1420 Annals of the Royal Vancouver Yacht Club 1903-1965, Norman R. Hacking, 1965.
1421 Rear Admiral Bruen, in his evaluation, considered Farie "*of sound judgment, though perhaps not very quick in thought and action*".
1422 Luard describes the Fastnet Race in 1927, 1929, 1931 and 1935; the Channel Race in 1928 and 1934; and the Transatlantic Race in 1931 in Where the Tides Meet, William Blaine Luard, 1948.

Holy Loch, HMS *Thule* stern tube and subs rafted against HMS *Forth*. Images: Imperial War Museum

Poster for the film *We Dive at Dawn*, 1943   *Sirocco* torpedoed in 1957.   Image LL

Submarine Crew at Holy Loch   Image: Imperial War Museum

Chapter 37: Running Back-stories

The Firth of Clyde, from its landlocked character, and from the fine lochs stretching away inland from its shores, offers special facilities for yachting. The tourist, as he sails down the river on a fine summer day, will see the whole bright and sparkling waters dotted over with the white sails of pleasure-boats, from the square lug of the small rowing boat to the great white wings of the hundred-ton cutter or smart schooner. Numerous rowing boats are also to be seen, and in holiday times they literally cover the water near the shores. W. J. Millar [1423]

In the Holy Loch, the local community has fought for various essential freedoms over the years: the right to navigate our vessels unhindered; the right to secure them on permanent moorings, as discussed in Chapter 35; the right to fish these waters; and the right to have fun on, in and under them. All have been threatened and occasionally denied over the years; but while all are currently secure, we can never be complacent

Freedom of Navigation

The Holy Loch was once a Queen's Harbour; most recently via legislation which covered the loch from 16th September 1986 until 3rd June 1992, when it was revoked, although we might note that it had been under one or other ordinance since the Great War. This status was certainly not an asset, but it was less of a hindrance than it might have been.

The ordinance stated: "*Facilities to Yachtsmen. The Queen's Harbour Master will afford members of the Holy Loch Sailing Club and the Benmore Centre every facility to pursue bona fide sailing activities in the Holy Loch commensurate with the orderly regulation of the Protected Areas. In particular, the Queen's Harbour Master will normally give exemption under byelaw 5(1), to enable yachting events to take place in nominated areas or along specified racing courses provided that he is given sufficient notice to such events by the organisers. Such exemptions will generally carry a caveat giving the distance sailing craft and committee boats must keep from the ships and submarines in the Protected Areas.*"

Fortunately, the Harbour Police had no idea who was or wasn't a member of the Holy Loch Sailing Club. The Honorary Secretary was never inclined to tweak the noses of members in arrears through a discreet phone-call to invoke a summary arrest on the high seas, although, with some of the characters in that category, it must have been tempting at times. As for the 'keep-off' caveat, it was, fortunately, an American sailor's wife and her crew who sailed their Enterprise dinghy into the enticing maw of the USS *Los Alamos* (a large floating dock) as it submerged to receive a nuclear submarine for a wash and brush-up.[1424]

When the Iron Curtain came down, the American Navy and their nuclear deterrent left these shores. This was a heaven-sent peace dividend for the long-suffering people of Cowal, who lived through the Cold War sitting on a time bomb. These days, there is little evidence of officialdom, bar the odd visit of a police launch to the marina for a round of cappuccinos. However, from time to time, government agencies have imposed restrictions and prohibitions of various kinds on the use of the loch.

Ghost Ships and Skeleton Crews

In the past, the Holy Loch has been commandeered as a submarine base for both British and American navies. Another significant disruption occurred in 1905 when the Ministry of War decided to lay up a number of their obsolete and now redundant warships in the loch. The Kyles of Bute and the Holy Loch were selected as anchorages for a flotilla of superannuated cruisers, gunboats and sloops of the Senior Service. Other proposed locations were the upper Forth, the Blackwater River in the south of Ireland, and the Mother's Bank between Spithead and Southampton Water. The *Dundee Telegraph's* reporter observed cynically that Scotland had been awarded *"undue prominence"*, but such prominence was *"unenviable, as all the vessels will be obsolete"*.[1425]

In early January 1905, a group of racing yachtsmen (names withheld, apparently) met in Glasgow to discuss the proposed mothballing, which it was feared would affect freedom of navigation in the Holy Loch and the Kyles of Bute. The assembled company agreed to frame a protest against the actions of the Admiralty. The yachtsmen regarded the Kyles as difficult enough already, without the additional hazard of moored ships, while the Holy Loch should be kept clear of such uses as it was a long-standing rendezvous and anchorage for Clyde racing yachts.[1426]

The protests came to naught and the old grey ships arrived like ghosts one morning and settled into the landscape. Perhaps it's a 'boy's toys' thing, but we would have found it difficult to protest too much about the picturesque decay of the glorious behemoths of Britannia Imperium. Old photos, taken on a drizzly autumn morning, with a blanket of mist over the water, show these angst-laden old vessels adding an aura of poignancy to the local scene. The castellated silhouette and dreadnought-bow of a Victorian battleship bristling with armament remains iconic, even today.

Back then, sea-power defined the Empire, fortified the spirit and puffed up the bronchial chests of loyal Edwardians.

In 1917, *Askold*, a well-travelled cruiser of 5,300-tons, and the pride of the Imperial Russian Navy, turned up in the Holy Loch after suffering storm damage on passage from Gibraltar. She was a spectacular vessel, with a Dreadnought bow and five tall funnels, like half-smoked cigarettes. Perhaps inevitably, she was dubbed 'Woodbine Willie'. The Scots in these years were close to revolution themselves, so the boat and her crew were popular with the locals. However, things would turn ugly later: "*A revolution is not a bed of roses. A revolution is a struggle to the death between the future and the past.*"[1427]

After repairs, the *Askold's* crew sailed for Murmansk to support the new Kerensky Government. In November 1917, the Bolshevik Revolution, led by Vladimir Lenin overthrew the Provisional Government. Moored in Murmansk harbour, *Askold's* Bolshevik crew murdered the captain, imprisoned the officers and trashed the ship. *Askold* was seized by the Royal Navy after the erratic behaviour of her crew threatened the British fleet. Recommissioned as HMS *Glory IV*, she served as a depot ship in the Gareloch until the conclusion of the Russian Civil war when she was handed back with a cheeky bill for expenses incurred.[1428]

Britain's involvement in the Russian Civil War has been forgotten. The Kerensky Government of the 'February Revolution', which took office after the Tsar abdicated in March 1918, remained committed to fighting on the Eastern Front. However, following the October Revolution, Lenin appeased the Kaiser by ceding territory in the Treaty of Brest-Litovsk on 3rd March 1918. With German troops virtually in sight of Paris, the Allies were fearful that German units from the Eastern Front could now be redeployed to the West. They had no choice but to intervene as the very survival of Europe was at stake.

Scottish sea-lochs have often been used to accommodate the living dead of the maritime world. During the global depression of the 1930s, a flotilla of merchant ships was mothballed in the Gareloch. And in the 1950s, freighters – mostly line-assembled WW2 Liberty ships, were moored in the Holy Loch as surplus to requirements. From time-to-time, containerships and tankers are moored in Loch Striven off the Kyles of Bute. The old Liberty ships were part of the scenery when we were growing up. When the sinister flotilla of Subron 14 arrived in 1961, we remembered the rusting freighters and their skeleton crews sentimentally. On those long hot summer afternoons, for which the West Coast of Scotland is justly famous, my father used to swim out and invite himself aboard for a cup of tea and an Abernethy biscuit.[1429]

The Navy Lark

The Royal Navy's 3ʳᵈ Submarine Flotilla was based in the Holy Loch during WW2. Britain was fighting for its survival as a sovereign nation. As would be expected, the local people were happy to contribute in any way they could to the war effort, and service personnel were welcomed with open arms. And it helped that the submarine bases of the pre-nuclear era did not handle weapons with the potential to destroy Western Europe. Aspects of life on the British base are described in Chapter 36, specifically, misadventures by her Majesty's finest with rogue torpedoes. While in no way blunting our assessment of the later American operation, characterised as it was by a dearth of basic seamanship, reading that chapter does bring a certain relief that the crew of HMS *Thule* were not handling nuclear missiles.

Apocalypse Then

At the height of the Cold War, the United States selected the Holy Loch, *"one of the most beautiful seascapes in Europe – of longstanding aesthetic and recreational value to industrial Scotland"*, as a nuclear base and Harold Macmillan acquiesced. It was the era of the Profumo Affair and *"You've never had it so good"*. But it was also a time of heightened global tension, with the sad remains of the British Empire supine before Washington's brute power and indifference. In any case, the Westminster government prioritised the safety and landscape of Southern England.[1430] The Americans wanted a sheltered anchorage with access to deep water that was situated *"near a transatlantic airfield and a centre of population in which the American service personnel could be absorbed"*.

The Holy Loch was close to Prestwick Airport and the dancehalls, pubs and pop-up whorehouses of Glasgow; it was a sheltered harbour previously used for this purpose by the Royal Navy during WW2, and it was thought to be a spot where nuclear accidents might be contained. However, Harold Macmillan was alarmed at the prospect of stockpiling nuclear weapons just 30-miles from Glasgow and the activism of Red Clydeside. Macmillan wrote to Eisenhower suggesting that such a Soviet target *"would give rise to the greatest political difficulties and would make the project almost unsaleable in this country"*. There was a rethink, although it was a brief one. The Admiralty looked at Falmouth, where a unit of the U.S. Navy was based during WW2, Milford Haven in West Wales, and Fort William.

Macmillan's cabinet favoured the upper reaches of Loch Linnhe near Fort William.[1431] But the horny sailors of the U.S. Navy were not be denied the pre-AIDS pleasures of Glasgow's nightlife. Eisenhower would not countenance any provincial alternative, insisting that his men required the "*comfort, morale and amusement*" of a big city.[1432] This extortion falls short of the Korean 'comfort women', who were pressed into slavery during WW2, but it does show how contemptuous Eisenhower was. As for political difficulties, the campaign for nuclear disarmament (CND) and the Labour party would indeed organise high-profile protests, but they could not be sustained indefinitely. As for the other matter, prostitution and vice soared in Glasgow.

A friend of a friend worked in a currency exchange in Greenock. On Monday mornings he would open up to a queue of young ladies eager to change their US$ for Pounds Sterling. From time to time, following a crew rotation through the fleshpots of South East Asia, there would be great disappointment when the local girls discovered Vietnamese Dong and Thai Baht to be substantially worthless. Today, VND30,000 is worth about £1. On such occasions, the girls' newly acquired lower-decks expletives were strung together with a rare blend of creativity and heart-felt bile.

The U.S. Navy sailed into the Holy Loch on the 3rd March 1961 and remained a blot on the landscape for 31 years. During questions in the House of Commons in November 1960, Watkinson of the MoD gave the assurance that British control within territorial waters would be absolute: "*We have the firm assurance that these missiles would not be fired in any circumstances in United Kingdom territorial waters.*" Macmillan appeared to be "*perfectly satisfied*" that no decision to use the missiles would ever be taken without the "*fullest possible previous consultation*"[1433] Dennis Healy found this laughable, as if there was a crisis, it would all be over before anyone in our government was informed, let alone 'fully consulted'.

In fact, it was much worse than that. The maritime mission of the 'Subron 14' was characterised by arrogance, incompetence and sloppy seamanship. This was a rag-tag navy of conscription. The Vietnam War was an acknowledged conflict for 11 years (1964-1975) of the Holy Loch mission. Any kid with an interest in self-preservation could see that smoking dope, sipping Jack Daniels and chasing girls on the West Coast of Scotland was preferable to deployment and death in the monsoon mud of South East Asia.

An the publicans will aa be daein swell For it's juist the thing that's sure tae ring the bell O the dollars they will jingle They'll be no a lassie single, Even though they maybe blaw us an tae hell![1434]

Forget the CND, the Navy itself was a hotbed of anti-war activists and draft dodgers keen to hang out with the locals trading Schlitz and dope. Think the dysfunctional gunboat crew taking Martin Sheen upriver to meet Marlon Brando and engage with the 'heart of darkness' in the 1979 Francis Ford Coppola masterpiece, *Apocalypse Now*. Think the music of Jimi Hendrix and Jim Morrison, sweaty torsos, dog-tags and déshabillé. With the passing of years, the good ole' boys from Savannah eventually learned a little seamanship, even if they never aspired to the spit and polish of the Royal Navy.

Living in Kilmun, close enough to hear the ship's PA, we grew blasé about the regular and ostensibly alarming announcements: *"Fire, Fire, Fire; this is not a drill, this is not a drill!"* Three sailors were killed in November 1970, when a fire erupted on *USS Canopus*, clearly not a drill then either. Four years later, on the 3rd November 1974, the SSBN *James Madison*, a nuclear submarine armed with 16 Poseidon nuclear missiles, dived at the mouth of the Holy Loch to leave the Clyde sub-surface. Quite why is not clear as they were obliged to operate on the surface in the upper reaches of the estuary.

It seems that the Americans had not seen the *Hunt for Red October*, although, to be fair, that movie was not released until 1990. A Soviet Victor-class nuclear-powered attack submarine was lying in the shipping lane at a depth of about 10-fathoms, monitoring U.S. Naval activity. The unwary crew of *James Madison* piled straight into it. Both vessels surfaced, regarded each other warily, checked for leaks and re-submerged. The American sub was lucky not to go to the bottom. Fortunately, the *James Madison* was just a few miles from the repair-shop. The Russians, however, had a 2,000-nautical mile voyage home to Severomorsk, which they may or may not have reached.

The events were only confirmed 27-years later in 2017, although the story had appeared at the time through the investigative journalism of the *Washington Post*, among others.[1435] However, it was impossible to deny the round-the-clock presence of Russian trawlers, rigged up with aerial-arrays like Christmas trees, patrolling the three-mile limit. As to radio contact between the trawlers and a ground station at Holy Loch, denials were issued. But, as government agencies only issue denials when the facts are awkward, we pondered who among our neighbours was spying for the Soviets. Recognising local politics, there was no shortage of candidates.[1436]

After the Americans left in 1992, the Cowal community received another shock.[1437] It was revealed that 130,000 cubic metres of dangerous debris had been dumped in the sacred waters of the Holy Loch. The Edinburgh-based consultancy firm Environmental Resources Management (ERM) carried out studies for the MoD which showed high concentrations of toxins – heavy metals, PCBs and other unpleasant chemicals. All the indicators breached internationally defined safe limits. The respected quasi-academic journal *New Scientist* obtained copies of the final report; it was stamped CONFIDENTIAL and RESTRICTED.

We discovered that roughly 25% of the seabed of the loch, an area 2½-miles by ¾-mile, was covered with debris. This noxious blanket outlined the perimeter of the depot ship and floating dock. In some places it was layered 20ft deep. The MoD's underwater survey showed a remarkable variety of jetsam. There was something resembling a huge boiler, various steel girders, ladders, discarded air ducts, old oil drums, washing machines, etc. Over the years, sharp-eyed locals had seen objects as bizarre as servicemen's cars pushed over the side, so none of this was a surprise, but the sheer volume prompted a sharp intake of breath all-round. There were also nine shipwrecks, more acceptable in a seafaring community, including a Loch Long and a Dragon keelboat sunk in recent memory.

Quoting directly from the *New Scientist* article: "*Sampling carried out in December 1996 by ERM found maximum levels of nickel, chromium, zinc and copper in sediment over three times as high as in other British estuaries. One sample of sediment contained 228 milligrams per kilogram of the carcinogens known as polycyclic aromatic hydrocarbons – nearly six times the limit considered safe in The Netherlands. Concentrations of the gender-bending chemical phthalate, which mimics the hormone oestrogen, reached 245 micrograms per litre of water or 49 times the safe limit for groundwater.* [1438] *Water sampling also suggested concentrations of mercury, tin and copper in excess of European environmental quality standards.*[1439]

While ERM did not measure radioactivity, an earlier survey of sediment by the MoD detected low levels of cobalt-60 and manganese-54 from submarine reactors. A 1995 MoD survey found up to 864 micrograms of PCBs per kg of sediment at the head of the loch, among the highest levels recorded anywhere in the world.[1440] It was noted that the sampling technique likely underestimated the scale of pollution as the ERM sampling of the sediment did not measure the surface layers.

Under the NATO agreement on allied military bases in the UK, the British government was solely responsible for decontamination. The U.S. Navy was able to colonise and despoil our small paradise for 31 years without repercussions. The local community should have been outraged, but we were just happy that the clearing up programme was given the go-ahead, and the concerns of those who feared the consequences of disturbing this mess, set aside. The clean-up took three years and cost close to £6 million, but it was unequivocally worth it. More than 2,650 tons of Yankee garbage was removed from the sea bottom between February 1998 and February 2001.[1441] So much for the much-vaunted Southern courtesy.

Apocalypse Now

The Americans may have gone, but Scottish yachting is still conducted in the shadow of Britain's nuclear arsenal, now based at Faslane on the Gareloch, and innocuously known as HMNB *Clyde*. This is effectively a satellite facility of the U.S. Navy, as both the deployment and operation of

British nukes are overseen by Uncle Sam. The Gareloch was first used as a Navy base during WW2. Faslane, together with its warren of bomb-proof burrows at Coulport on Loch Long, is the second biggest single-site employer in Scotland, with around 6,500 on the payroll and thousands more in the supply chain, the whole totalling perhaps 11,000. The Royal Navy's eleven submarines will all be based there from 2020. The base is also home to ten conventional surface vessels.

Faslane was designated as a nuclear facility in 1963, just two years after the U.S. Depot ship *Proteus* sailed into Holy Loch. The location was selected from a slate that generally mirrored the earlier discussions about American submarine deployment in Britain. Scottish options included Invergordon, Loch Alsh and the other Scottish naval base at Rosyth on the East coast. There were three English sites on the shortlist: the first was Portland, near Weymouth, which became the yachting venue for the 2012 Olympics, and the Weymouth and Portland National Sailing Academy; the second was Devonport, on a site opposite the dockyard incorporating National Trust land; and finally, Falmouth. The latter would also have involved National Trust land north of the town. Two villages would be so close to the depot that they would have had to be abandoned.

The English locations were rejected for two main reasons, proximity to local populations and impacts on the watersports and tourism industries. Perish the thought that we inconvenience places like Mylor, where Ben Ainslie first dipped his toes in the water. Another option was Barrow in Furness, where the British submarines are built. However, this would have restricted the deployment to once a month when there was a full moon and a high tide. The sole Welsh location option was once again Milford Haven, and required the closure of three major petrochemical refineries and cutting off a main gas supply pipeline. It appears that the site selection study followed a technique well-established among our best and brightest regional planners.[1442] First, choose your preferred option and then identify half-a-dozen hopeless alternatives.[1443] Second, run the evaluation matrices and nod sagely at the expected result. That was my first job after graduation.

In 1963, all these alternative options were rejected and the existing naval base at Faslane was chosen. This concentrated the entire Anglo-American submarine-launched nuclear deterrent in one place where the fall-out, from either a catastrophic accident or a Russian attack, would have taken out 3½ million people. The rather cynical 1960s criteria concerning safety buffers required a gap of just one mile from any residential housing. In Kilmun, we lived half a mile from the action. The difference, of course, is no more than a few microseconds of corporeal existence.

In 1979, when the position was re-evaluated, Sir Frank Cooper of the MoD ruled out any relocation of Coulport to a new greenfield site.[1444] All this is still at the forefront of strategic discourse in the MoD today. While the Scottish Referendum on Independence failed to achieve the simple majority required to dissolve the union, Britain's imminent departure from the greater European Union has re-energised the independence movement. Scotland, as is well-known, is overwhelmingly in favour of denuclearization. *"Independence offers Scotland the chance to be what Thatcher called an ordinary country, freed from a burdensome British past of conquest, war and glory of which Trident may be the last potent symbol."*[1445] The Ministry of Defence has simply buried its head in the sand and refused to countenance any relocation on cost and logistical grounds.[1446]

The Oyster is your World

Oyster Fishing in the Holy Loch was discussed by a Select Committee of the House of Commons in 1869. Set before the honourable members was a draft bill to establish an oyster and mussel fishery in the loch. It was, and is, an industry that, if located in well-used waters, causes widespread disruption, while benefitting only a few investors and providing a small number of low-wage jobs. Consequently, the bill was opposed by many local interests. The oyster bill had been sponsored by the Board of Trade and based on an 1866 report, which evaluated suitable places for the culture of oysters. Apparently, the Holy Loch had emerged as the most feasible place for an oyster farm and an order was issued for its establishment.

Objections to the proposal were numerous: the proposed farm included mussel and cockle beds that the public have used from time immemorial; restrictions necessary for the culture of the shell-fish would be *"vexatious to the numerous excursionists who visited the loch in summer"*; coasting vessels that found harbourage in the loch would be deprived of their traditional mussel-raking privileges; and finally, the farm would *"decrease the value of house property on the shores by destroying the amenity of the loch as a watering-place"*.[1447] However, the most interesting objections concerned the suggestion that 'pleasure-seekers' visiting the loch, and encountering restrictions placed upon their freedom, might take matters into their own hands – *"discovering that they could not roam where they liked, as had been their wont, they would be inclined to riot and create disturbances"*.

James Hunter, a character by now familiar in this narrative, was the instigator. James deigned to appear at a public meeting in Sandbank in 1868 to face 300 unhappy local residents.[1448] In an extraordinary display of concern and solidarity, they appealed to Hunter's better nature. Robert Hunter (no relation) in the chair, explained that *"it was out of keeping in modern times for any landed proprietor to place such severe restrictions on a public loch in so populous a district"*. It was to no avail. Hunter restated his firm determination to carry on with his plans and was dismissive of the impacts that large-scale industrialised oyster farming in the loch would have on local businesses. The man who played 'Commodore' on the bay with his summer regattas had no interest in Cowal's lifeblood of yachting, tourism and recreation.

The meeting submitted a 'memorial of objections' to the Board of Trade so that they would not have been unaware that James stood as a minority of one. The saga dragged on until James Hunter passed away. Then, with no other business interests prepared to invest in such a speculative venture, the Board of Trade's Oyster Bill lapsed. The window of opportunity finally closed when the Royal Navy took an interest in this well-known 'harbour of refuge'.

Looking back over the years, it is encouraging to note that the crystal-clear waters which attracted the prospect of oyster farming have now returned. The waters were foul for more than a century. As Central Scotland industrialised, the first serious pollution arrived down-tide from Glasgow, then we had untreated sewerage from holiday villas, followed by the chronic oil-slicks of WW2, and finally, the garbage and obscene effluent from the Subron 14, that for decades, turned Holy Loch into the most-polluted sealoch in Western Europe.

Today, in post-industrial Clydeside, the jobs have gone but the fish are back. Surprisingly, in the cash-strapped noughties, money has been spent on reticulated sewerage systems – well, for Sandbank initially, the Kilmun community are fortunately clean of habit. We can swim again in the Holy Loch, if only on an incoming tide over a sun-baked beach. Harbour porpoises again inhabit local waters, well-fed and glad to be back. There are even reports that an enterprising dolphin has joined the Clyde porpoise pod. The grey seals have returned, as have basking sharks and the occasional dozy whale.

One Clyde Week in the 1960s we were sailing BB11 keelboats. On the first windward leg, from a start off Helensburgh, the fleet was joined by something over 200 porpoises turning the water white with unadulterated joy. While there seems little chance of Clyde Week ever returning, at least we can now recover old memories and enjoy the marine life once again.

[1423] The Clyde from its source to the sea, its development as a navigable river, the rise and progress of marine engineering and shipbuilding on its banks, and the leading historical, geological, and meteorological features of the Clyde Valley, W.J. Millar, 1888.

[1424] This matter was dealt with internally by the U. S. Navy; however, on another occasion when an HLSC club-boat was tacking off the USS *Proteus*, a delinquent sailor threw a large nut at the boat and the missile went straight through the Terylene sail. The American press may have referred to the place as 'Holy Wed-lock' due to the number of local girls marrying American sailors, but with so many thousands passing through not all were gentlemen.

[1425] Scottish Anchorages for Obsolete Warships, Dundee Evening Telegraph, 30th December 1904.

[1426] Clyde Yachtsmen's Protest, The Dundee Courier, 19th January 1905.

[1427] Fidel Castro.

[1428] Churchill's Secret War with Lenin: British and Commonwealth Military Intervention in the Russian Civil War, 1918-20, Damien Wright, 2017.

[1429] The Abernethy biscuit is an adaptation of the plain captain's biscuit or 'hardtack', with the added ingredients of sugar for energy, and caraway seeds to prevent flatulence. This was news to the author too!

[1430] Trident, the British Question, Ian Jack, the Guardian newspaper, 11th February 2006.

[1431] Scotland was pressed to accept a nuclear base on Clyde, so US servicemen could access the bright lights of Glasgow, Tony Clerkson, Daily Record newspaper, 3rd September 2016.

[1432] Britain strong-armed into having US nuclear base on Clyde, papers reveal, Marc Horne, The Times, 3rd September 2016.

[1433] In and Out of Holy Loch, the Times, 5th November 1960.

[1434] *Ding Dong Dollar*, Anti-Polaris and Scottish Republican Songs, Folkways Records, 1962.

[1435] Scottish cold war nuclear submarine collision kept secret for 43 years, Mathew Weaver, the Guardian newspaper, 25th January 2017.

[1436] Polaris Ships in Wrong Loch, The Times, 4th April 1961.

[1437] Cold War Waste Fouls the Clyde, Rob Edwards, New Scientist, 8th March 1997.

[1438] Ibid

[1439] At the time, The Netherlands was one of the few countries to have worked out marine standards for these pollutants.

[1440] Professional opinion of Graham Shimmield, then Director of the Dunstaffnage Marine Laboratory, near Oban.

[1441] The MoD, Scottish Environment Protection Agency and the Argyll and Bute Council, began clearing the loch of ferrous waste using a crane and a large electromagnet and proceeded through a comprehensive and systematic clean-up.

[1442] The author worked on this type of 'systematic' sieving of strategic alternatives for many years early on in his career, before becoming a good-governance advisor.

[1443] Other unlikely options included: combining forces with the Americans in the USA; recognising that our 'independent deterrent' was in name only; and a left-field plan to combine forces with the French and decamp to Brittany. However, the Non-proliferation Treaty states: "*Each nuclear-weapon state party to the treaty undertakes not to transfer to any recipient whatsoever nuclear weapons or other nuclear explosive devices or control over such weapons or explosives devices directly, or indirectly*". So, the MoD would have to construct separate, duplicate facilities even in an allied country.

[1444] Trident: Nowhere to Go, John Ainslie, published by the Campaign for Nuclear Disarmament, 2012.

[1445] Trident, the British Question, Ian Jack, the Guardian newspaper, 11th February 2006.

[1446] Former Chancellor Philip Hammond suggested that he could force an independent Scotland to fund the relocation of the base to an unidentified location in England.

[1447] The Oyster Fisheries of the Holy Loch, Glasgow Herald, 5th June 1869 and Oyster Fishing in the Holy Loch, Paisley Herald and Renfrewshire Advertiser, 12th June 1869.

[1448] Sandbank, Glasgow Herald, 18th February 1868.

Great War battleships moored in Holy Loch, early 1920s   Image: Unknown

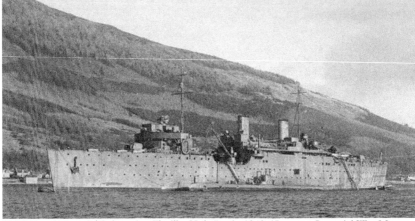

WW2 Royal Navy 3rd Submarine Flotilla, Holy Loch, 1940-45   Imperial War Museum

Holy Loch with 'Site One' the American Navy Base in residence: March 1961 – March 1992
Lower left: The author and friends sail past the USS *Holland* in the ¼-tonner *Bolero*, 1979

BOOK SEVEN
Scuttlebutt

Chapter 38: Boatbuilding in Scotland

Twenty years ago, I was talking to the members of the Paisley Model Yacht Club and asked them why the Six-metre rule was so popular with the Clyde clubs, when the rule required not only complex calculation, but very accurate building to the design. One of them said 'Well, the clubs were full of men who earned their living by working accurately to drawings'; nobody saw it as a problem. Ian Howlett[1449]

It may be wishful thinking, but there is some evidence to suggest that craftsmanship is again in the ascendance, with a new generation of shipwrights working magic in both modern and traditional materials. Some of these guys produce standards of finish that arguably exceed yesterday's past-masters, even if they do take their time about it. All the same, is it irreverent to observe that few 21st century artisans can build a 6-metre in 30 days? Not even close. That rare alchemy of eye-and-application died with fingerless gloves and open-sided corrugated iron sheds. The 21st century toolbox of labour-saving wood-working machinery appears to have done very little for productivity.

Old-time craftsmen measured twice and cut once with precision, now we rough-out and reduce, sometimes microscopically with computer-controlled milling machines. Facemasks are now de rigueur as impervious technicians work their magic through clouds of carcinogenic dust and a miasma of toxic fumes. Today, high-performance yachts are an amalgam of reinforced plastics, most of which are either unhealthy or downright dangerous to work with at home. The guy in charge of boatbuilding at Team INEOS labours under the job title of 'Construction Manager'. Perhaps this is appropriate, even if 'master shipwright' would be much more inspiring.

In *The Piper Calls the Tune*, we said: "*The very best clear-coat carbon fibre structures now invoke an alchemy that almost rivals wood. However, such boats are vanishingly rare and there is no joy whatsoever in a manufacturing process that essentially derives from elements of dressmaking and cookery. There is no romance in the new boatbuilding. Most of all, my generation regret that boatbuilding as 'theatre' no longer exists. There is nothing to see. Inside the climate-controlled plastic tents, today's prophylacticised boatbuilders wear respirators and gloves – modern boatyards are surely hellish workplaces.*"

This is a pity as, through the course of an ordinary life, few legal highs can compete with launching a boat you have built with your own hands.

As to what is fun and what is not; we are really talking about working with wood. Constructing the shell of steel, fibreglass or reinforced-concrete boat in your backyard is simply grim, with only the prospect of completion to mitigate the process. But then, no matter what the shell is made of, the fit-out highlights exactly where the joy lies – in the tactile pleasures of crafting wood and exploring its wonderful properties.

If everything goes well, you have perhaps the most uplifting blend of art and utility in the realm of man-made objects. And even if the whole process is a nightmare, you have still achieved something that 99.9% of Millennials cannot even contemplate. The keen amateur does not have to build a boat from scratch. You might fit-out a professionally-built shell, commit your life and marriage to a restoration project, repair damage, or just carry out routine maintenance to a high standard – all these activities are rewarding in a way that is rare in modern life.

It is a dimension of our sport that has been lost. In our Merlin fleet at the Holy Loch in the 1970s, perhaps half the total, seven or eight of sixteen boats, were completed from bare hulls, mostly by schoolboys. And almost all bar one of the other new boats were finished-off and fitted-out by their owners. Now, indulgent parents rig the boat and put it away, and if you keep your head down and don't 'bang the corners', you might be given a new one at regular intervals. Even if you pay your own way and sail a Laser, for example, the only way you can personalise the boat is by buying a carbon-fibre tiller extension – just like everyone else.

In a life with more life-changing adventures and sublime experiences than I can remember, I treasure a prosaic moment – the launch of our Quarter-tonner back in 1978. The fibreglass mouldings arrived on a flat-bed truck from the South and we all pitched in to have her sailing in record time. *Bolero* was hull No.4, but we splashed first and took great satisfaction in that. The licensed builders had yet to develop the necessary templates for the fit-out, so our boat was light and unique.

We towed *Bolero* down the beach with a tractor at low tide one evening after the pubs closed, set a kedge aft and a bow line to the shore then went to bed and prayed that the calm forecast would not go rogue. That night, I slept lightly with an ear for the slightest breeze and rose at first light. Skipping breakfast, I jogged along the Shore Road to the old Ferry House, where James Arrol's little Fife cutter *Marguerite,* had been sunk by the *Marchioness of Breadalbane* so many years before, to find our new boat bobbing contentedly between the cradle guides.

Obviously, we knew she was going to float; but she sat perfectly, riding light and high above her marks. It was April in Scotland, but I stripped down to my underpants, swam out sidestroke with my clothes held aloft in one hand and clambered aboard. Just sitting there on the dew-soaked deck, savouring the moment in the chilly stillness of the early morning, ranks along with some of the best moments of my life.

As children, we saw many boats christened. Launchings are important in boatbuilding communities and in the Holy Loch we were fortunate to witness the last generation of large wooden yachts, built for autocratic men of means, slip down the ways at Sandbank. The vessels were dressed overall, and the whole community was well-dressed too, enjoying the day out, thronging the rickety piers and crowding the shoreline. Naming ceremonies were done properly, and often at considerable expense.

Many of the famous names in Clyde shipbuilding also built yachts, particularly in the early days. However, when steel construction became their stock-in-trade, only steam-yachts and the very largest sailing yachts were worth a quotation. Commercial vessels are more utilitarian and so vastly more profitable to build. Corporate clients are also less inclined to require faired topsides, or to be finicky about unseen details, as long as the structure is sound, and specifications are met.

With shipbuilders moving on to bigger ships and steel construction, opportunities emerged for old-fashioned family boatyards to specialise in big wooden yachts. Yards like Alex Robertson's and Morris & Lorimer's on the Holy Loch, McGruer's and Silver's on the Gareloch, and the Mylne yard at Ardmaleish on Bute, took the lion's share of this new business.

These days, the industry has changed dramatically; construction and storage have been separated out, with boats built in factories and marinas dealing with subsequent fitouts and maintenance. Supply chains and services are increasingly specialised, so the wonderful integrated multi-sectoral operations of the past no longer exist.

While modest in scale, in comparison to the upper Clyde's commercial shipyards, the two big Sandbank boatyards, located side by side on the south shore of the Holy Loch, dwarfed anything else of that type on the Estuary. The acres of open-air hardstanding were obvious, but there was also undercover storage in cavernous corrugated-iron hangers, great draughty building sheds, tunnel-like lofts for spars, vast low-ceilinged lofts for sailmaking, and even lofts for lofting.

These artisanal boatyards mirrored the big, mechanised shipyards in their vertically integrated operation. They made boats from raw materials. There were carpentry shops, metal-working shops, rigging shops, paint shops, timber steaming apparatus and chandleries. There were on-site sawmills, forges and foundries. To move large heavy displacement yachts around, there were patented slipways, funicular railways, cranes and winches and capstans. And, of course, there were famous design offices and a legion of specialist craftsmen with the multifarious skills required to command every aspect of yacht building and maintenance.

The Small Boatbuilders of Cowal

The Robertson's story is recounted in *The Piper Calls the Tune*, and the Morris & Lorimer story will, hopefully, merit a book of its own if the means and motivation remain after this one. As for the many boatyards beyond the compass of Holy Loch, some, like Fife's of Fairlie, have been chronicled already and many more await the years of patient research necessary to do them justice.

So, in this following section, *Highland Cowes* recognises the contribution of the smaller Cowal boatyards: Dan Turner, Robert Colquhoun, the Graham brothers, the Fletcher brothers, the Sands, Neil McVicar, Ewen Sutherland, and Sinclair in Dunoon; James Litster, David Morris, and Reggie Brooks in Kirn; Gordon & Alex Waddell in Sandbank; Jimmy Ferguson in Kilmun and Duncan Munro and Mr Todd at Gairletter on Loch Long. Then, in the post-WW2 period, there was the inimitable Peter Collyer, a craftsman who built racing dinghies, very slowly and with great attention to detail. For clients of infinite patience, the 'grand piano' finish was well worth the wait.

In addition to the small businesses that traded as boatbuilders, there were also the boat hirers who commanded many of the same skills and offered similar services. These included: Neil McVicar at Wellington Street, Duncan McClarty at Agnes Street, and Walter Riddell and the McArthurs at the East Bay in Dunoon; Archie McKellar at Innellan; Alexander Dennistoun at Hunter's Quay; Colin Grey at Strone; and John McKellar at Clyde View Blairmore. Overlapping with the builders, John Turner and Norman Turner offered boat hiring boatbuilding services in the West Bay.

Daniel Turner was born in 1870, and once sailed clipper-ships on the San Francisco route. He left 'Frisco in 1906, just missing the famously destructive earthquake. On his return home, he settled down and married his fiancé. Dan established his business in Dunoon the following year.[1450] The little boatyard constructed fishing boats and rowing boats over a period of more than sixty years. During WW2, the Turners contributed to the war effort by building clinker lifeboats.

Over the decades, there would be occasional small yacht orders such as the Pleiade Class, described in Chapter 25. However, as *Merope*, built for Archie Watson Jr, was the only Turner vessel to be surveyed for the Lloyds Registry, it is difficult to determine the total output of the yard. This is the case for all small-scale workshops. Thus, the local boatbuilders' build listings, remains very much a 'work-in-progress', and is consigned to Appendix 3.

Robert Colquhoun's yard at 58, Auchamore Road, Dunoon is best known as the birthplace of the Loch Long ODs (launched as the Loch Long One Design Coronation Class). Remarkably, the initial order for five boats was underwritten by the builder himself in a time when bank loans for such businesses did not exist. The Loch Longs were sold at an agreed unit-cost of £66 (£4,460) for delivery in 1937. Colquhoun's would build another seven examples of the class over the next two years. The original Colquhoun boats are still quick, and much sought after by the cognoscenti of the Class.

Colquhoun's also built seven 'Coronation One Designs' for the Royal Lymington Yacht Club in that year. These yachts were similar to the Loch Longs, although slightly slimmer and marginally longer on the same LWL. They cost £75 (£5,260) and were delivered on the railway for a 'fiver' (£350). I can only apologise for the shameless profiteering of Dunoon folks, levying a surcharge of £9 (£610) per unit on our southern neighbours.[1451]

The Royal Lymington history notes: "*The introduction of these cheap little vessels was far from popular. Members of the established classes combined to attack the qualities of the Coronations like chickens resenting the intrusions of a newcomer, and the 'pecks' were pretty savage.*" The Lymington naysayers considered the boat both crank and too stiff, and the consensus was that they had been "*hastily constructed from old biscuit boxes and would soon fall to pieces*".[1452] In light of these scurrilous comments, perhaps we should not feel too bad about the South Coast surcharge.

Ultimately, however, the light and lively Dunoon boats could not compete with the stolid Alfred Westmacott-designed 'X' class, designed in 1909 and still mining Solent waters, to a great depth, and in great numbers. Most of the Royal Lymington's Coronation Class yachts were sold to French connoisseurs, who found them eminently suitable for the choppy waters off Cherbourg. Several are still sailing today.

The Graham Brothers arrived in Dunoon in the 1930s. They worked at Colquhoun's on occasion and took the yard over when the opportunity arose after WW2 in 1946.[1453] Johnny Colquhoun had died in the war. Bob Graham, the eldest brother, was a carpenter; Tam was a rigger and a skilled engineer who had been to sea. Tam maintained the much-abused Stuart Turner inboard-engines in the motor dinghies hired out by the Grahams and others in the West Bay. The third brother, Jim, was a joiner. Staniforth Lockheart worked the brothers' summer boat hire business in the bay and an indulgent auntie kept house for the boys.

The yard was fairly extensive with three permanent buildings. There was a large 2-storey structure with the building bay on the ground floor, a woodworking machine shop, a Nissen Hut for boat storage, and a small stone cottage, where oor Tam was aye up to his elbows in the oily bits of auxiliary engines.

There were logistical issues with a town location, half a mile from the sea. The smaller boats were trundled through the streets on bogies and launched from the slipway at the kiddies' swing park, while more substantial yachts were craned in at Dunoon Pier, or the Coal Pier. The Grahams had an arrangement with W. Wallace & Son, a local haulage contractor, when a flatbed lorry was required.

The yard was reduced to part-time operation from the mid-1950s, with occasional repairs, new-builds and winter storage of hire dinghies where the operator lacked premises of their own. Despite the access issue, loyal clients stored yachts in central Dunoon for as long as the business remained afloat. *Yvette*, a fondly remembered Fife 5-tonner from 1899, belonging to Miss M. Smith of Sandbank, was a regular winter visitor.

With orders scarce and cash-flow now a mere trickle, Bob Graham joined the workforce at Morris & Lorimer's and Tam soon followed. Jim then found work with Robertson's Yard, later moving to Fletcher's boatyard in Jane Street. Jim shaped design visualisation models for the district's most famous naval architect, David Boyd. These included half-models of Boyd's America's Cup 12-metres, *Sceptre* and *Sovereign*, and an unusual landing-craft type ferry, for use in the Western Isles. Bob died in 1970, Tam in 1985, and Jim in 2000. The yard was sold in 1978. The big tin shed became part of a builder's operation until it burnt down in 1991, with the fire spreading to the home of Rosemary Davis next door.

The Grahams' largest project was *Tonnag*, designed by W. Stewart Collie for K. B. Miller of Rhu. *Tonnag* was a Bermudian yacht of 7-tons TM with bright topsides and a raised deckhouse, launched in 1954. The yacht featured in the Summer 1955 edition of the magazine *Yachting*. Some years later, *Tonnag* was sailed across the Atlantic by the Bathgate brothers, logging in excess of 125 miles a day on their better 24hr runs. With *Tonnag*, Stewart Collie claimed a patent for the first use of the 'Hydrogap rudder' in a yacht. He promoted the concept in an article in *Yachting World* in 1939.[1454]

The Grahams built neat little pocket cruisers, specifically the two-berth Pixie Class, in the post-war period. From my own experience with *Piccolo*, the Graham boats were very nicely finished. Jimmy Kirkland of the well-known Dunoon hardware store, who supplied the gas cookers for the Pixies from 1954, also recalled being very impressed by the standard of workmanship. Published articles remarked on the Dunoon yard's excellent build quality.

In addition to yachts, during the period 1946 to 1952, the Graham Brothers built a range of standard motor launches. These measured 16ft, 18ft, 28ft and 30ft LOA. They also built 12ft and 13ft LOA motor dinghies and a standard 11ft clinker skiff. Details of the numbers built are scant, however. We know one of the larger launches went to Oban and another to Saltcoats. It appears that, in addition to the usual direct commissions for the boat-hire fleets, clinker dinghies and launches were built as yacht tenders under sub-contract to the larger yacht builders.

There are materials in the family archive suggesting a 30ft LOA sloop project, and details of a 20ft LOA yawl in 1948. Both would have been collaborations with W. A. Murray & Co, a Glasgow agent, and their consultant designer, the same W. Stewart Collie, although it is not clear if either was ever built. It appears that all the Graham Brothers' yachts (including the Pixie class and *Tonnag*) were designed by W. Stewart Collie of Kirn.

The Fletcher family's yard, based in Jane Street opposite Turner's yard, was another highly regarded small business. In particular, the quality of their pulling dinghies was second to none. In the summer they hired boats in the West Bay, and in the winter, they built dinghies. The Fletchers had a contract with the Town Council to maintain Dunoon Pier. They also ran the ferry that shuttled between Dunoon and the Cloch, later taken over by the McArthurs.

Rounding out the Dunoon operations, the Sands brothers hired boats through the summer, and built dinghies during the winter. Hugh Sands was particularly enterprising in the boat hire business. In the off-season, he transported his hire dinghies to Pitlochry, where he rented them out to anglers. Neil McVicar on the West Bay advertised *"new and second-hand boats always in stock"*. Ewen Sutherland worked out of a small workshop on Agnes Street. Finally, there was a boatbuilder called Sinclair at work in the early 1900s, constructing motor launches, but we have yet to establish his story; possibly his yard was taken over by others.

James Litster of Kirn was a small-scale but important boatbuilder in the context of Clyde yachting. The 'boxed-in' location his yard, behind the shops on Marine Parade, meant that his work on larger boats was carried out in the open, on the beach. In collaboration with the ubiquitous Bergius family, Litster pioneered the use of internal combustion engines in small yachts. The first of his many Kelvin auxiliary installations was dropped into the bilges of William Bergius's *Dodo II* in 1906. Thereafter, James and his family developed a programme to install engines in fishing smacks between tides, enabled by a performance-linked repayment plan. This influential initiative is described in more detail in Chapter 34.

David Morris built several successful racing yachts on Kirn beach at the close of the 19th century, before he teamed up with Robert Lorimer, formerly a manager at Fairfield's shipyard, to establish Morris & Lorimer's in Sandbank. Sadly, David died at just 50 years of age, shortly after the new partnership had delivered their first boat – *Verena*, a cutter for James Duncan of Benmore, who built the well-known mansion and botanic gardens and funded Kilmun Hall. The Lorimer family kept Morris's memory alive, however, as the M&L name lived on until the yard ceased trading.

While still working on his own account, Morris built the 5-tonner *Clothide* for G. L. Watson in 1875. Watson blamed Morris for the boat measuring in as a 6-tonner, suggesting that she had 'spread' in building, but that didn't entirely explain her excessive depth and length. Later, Morris built *Trident*, designed in 1879 by a precocious 18-year-old William Paton, a Watson camp-follower. Paton was only just beginning to flower as a fashionable naval architect when he drowned in 1886. Hie was aboard his plank-on-edge 6-tonner, *Oona*, when she was wrecked during a delivery trip, see Chapter 29.

The Waddell family were ferrymen who took up boatbuilding when they leased the Ardnadam ferry-house from the Hafton Estate in the 1840s. Alexander and Walter began the business, then Gordon and Alec carried it on. Jack Waddell, another brother, was a crewman on the big yachts. The Waddells specialised in clinker skiffs, rowing boats and lugsail dinghies and were still active in the 1960s.

In the 1960s, Alec built three traditional clinker sailing dinghies for the Holy Loch Sailing Club, see Chapter 20, and latterly dabbled in lightweight planing dinghies with the Seafly dinghy. The boatyard disappeared with a sale of assets in 1987 after Alec passed away. Jim Waddell, Jack's son, who had been brought up by Gordon and his wife Cissie, was expected to take over the business, but this did not transpire. Jim was already making a decent living working for M&L and Robertson's yards. The Waddell ferry, *White Heather*, features in Chapter 34.

James Ferguson in Kilmun was another boatbuilder and ferryman. He was also the Piermaster in Kilmun. James and his family operated larger ferries and excursion boats than the Waddells and their yard was mostly, although not exclusively, dedicated to the maintenance of their own fleet. The boats were hauled out on the slip at the old Ferry House and dragged along the shore road to the yard, which lay behind the Napier-built Kilmun Hotel at the pierhead. The family later bought the hotel, and it became, for a time, the heart of the community. The Ferguson ferry, *Sonja Tess*, features in Chapter 33.

D. H. Munro & Sons, formerly McKeller's Boatyard and later operated by J. J. Bell and Ian Robinson, was located at Gairletter about a mile past Blairmore on Loch Long. Munro's yard was attacked during WW2 when a stray bomb, intended for the Glasgow shipyards, scored a direct hit during the German blitz of Clydebank on the 2nd December 1939.[1455] This fire was devastating for a small operation, causing £5000 (£324,000) in damage to yachts and property. However, there was more to the Munro yard than that infamous wartime conflagration. Duncan Munro was not just an artisan, he was a talented draftsman who designed and built solid cruising boats, all with generous auxiliary installations.

The Munro yard also built high-quality racing yachts, including five of Alfred Mylne's Royal Mersey One Designs. In 1934, the Mersey Yacht Club was looking for a new open cockpit daysailer. While on holiday in Cowal, Mr S. MacLauchlan had seen a yacht built by Duncan, for export to Egypt, and had been very taken with the finish. Unfortunately, we have been unable, thus far, to identify this particular boat from the Mylne list, Clydeships, or Lloyds. This illustrates how difficult it is to recover a definitive record of the output of small builders.

MacLauchlan had a half-model of the Egypt-bound yacht made which impressed the RMYC members. Alfred Mylne was then approached to modify the design for Mersey waters. The first five Munro boats cost £185 (£13,000), ex-quay Glasgow, and mustered for their first race on the Mersey on the 11th July 1935. Of the original five, four are still racing today – *Meryl*, number 2, having been lost. A mould was made in 1980 and this has led to four fibreglass boats joining the fleet. Four wooden boats were built in 1937 by Dickies of Bangor for Trearddur Bay Sailing Club in Anglesey. These too have now joined the Mersey fleet.[1456]

Munro's operation faced the villages of Cove and Kilcreggan across the mouth of Loch Long, and being within a short boat ride, provided essential marine services that were sparse on that rocky coast. The site at Gairletter adjoins a tiny, sheltered deep-water creek, of a type common on the South Coast of England, for example, but almost unknown below the Tail o' the Bank on the Clyde. The Munro slip ran into this perfect little harbour.

Through the inter-war years, Duncan had to cope with a continuous cycle of boom and slump in new-build orders. His craftsmen must have been taken on and laid off repeatedly. Most winters, the yard was stacked with the smaller classes – 19/24s, Pleiades and Loch Longs, but Munro's could also cope with bigger boats too, in the 15 to 20-tons range. This, at least, gave a baseload of work for Duncan's core staff. And, from time to time, the boatyard secured maintenance contracts with the RNLI, the Admiralty, and the War Department – the latter two then separate clients.

After the war, Munro's yard was sold to The Marine Welding Co, who built the big shed and maintained the business until 1956, when Shirlaw Allan, auctioneers of Hamilton, sold-off *"yacht building plant and machinery, tools vessels consumable stores, scrap materials, land and buildings."* Mr Robertson, no relation to Alex Robertson & Sons, the famous Holy Loch boatbuilders, then took over the storage and maintenance business and built a few boats before selling out to the first owners of the current caravan site operation.

'Todd's boatshed' was sited on the small bay just to the south of the Munro yard, in what is now an empty field with traces of terracing. Mr Todd ran a small operation there in the early years of the 20th century. This small boatbuilder has been all but forgotten, and inquiries are still ongoing.

Peter Collyer was a qualified marine engineer and followed that trade intermittently until his retirement. He is remembered as a flamboyant 'trouble-shooter', shuttling up and down the M6 to jobs in Lymington and the Hamble in his race-tuned sporting saloons. Ironically, Peter's brother, Allister, was the time-served boatbuilder in the family, but he had moved on to work for the Forestry Commission and then the Post Office. Boatbuilding was considered as seasonal work by banks and building societies, so family men were often obliged to take steady jobs.

Stan Ferguson, a veteran of yards large and small, including the famous Stephen of Linthouse, Norman Turner's in Dunoon and his own Ardmaliesh operation, explains that he joined the police force to get a mortgage. This is a reality check which dampens the romance of honest craftsmanship and dims the sparkle of the 'golden age'. For Peter, who eternally tried the patience of his wife and family, financial security was often the last thing on his mind. Even so, he did occasionally work with the boatyards for extended periods. Peter was willing to turn his hand to any complex task and his formidable reputation allowed him to do so without provoking demarcation protests among the prickly specialist trades.

Peter was a perfectionist and knew more about boats than any man I have ever met. He was, by turns, infuriating and charming and he could be extremely unreliable. He was a man who dropped names routinely, but to our joy and amazement, the good and the great dropped his name right back; everyone in the sailing world, north and south of the border knew him. Understandably, Peter was by no means universally popular, but he was my sage and mentor in relation to both 'attitude' on the racecourse and the arcane arts of boatbuilding in wood.

Peter salvaged and retained the building lists of Alex Robertson and Morris & Lorimer. He recorded the names and details of all yachts laid up each winter at Sandbank, on the hard and afloat. He noted down the business of visiting yachts and kept details of everything, except, it seems, the boats he built himself. So, our partial list is from memory. While he occasionally hauled a larger boat into his garden for alterations or refit, those listed are mostly planing dinghies. If you ordered a boat from Peter, you had to be persistent and prepared to pay over the odds. There were some that took two years, but the finish was flawless.

Gone but Not Forgotten

The small boatyards on the north shore of the Holy Loch disappeared first, Ferguson's in Kilmun, Munro's around the corner at Gairletter, then Waddell's across the loch at Lazaretto. Next, the Dunoon and Kirn yards folded. Eventually, it was the turn of the 'big two' on the south shore of the loch, as they too failed to weather the changes that swept through the boatbuilding industry during the 1970s. Both succumbed to punitive VAT and short-term planning, as described in *The Piper Calls the Tune.*

When we look back at the wonderful story of first-class yacht-building in Scotland, it is difficult to come to terms with the fact that native craftsmanship has disappeared, almost without trace. Sadly, the late-blooming renaissance in wooden boat construction came too late for our Scottish yards. But we did cling on to the dream for a hundred years after this premature death-knell in 1883. *"Clyde Yacht-building: The building of racing yachts threatens to become one of the obsolete arts. The English yards are devoted to cruisers, and there are not many of these."*[1457]

Ewing McGruer left no books, but as a technical writer on boatbuilding topics, he left something more valuable which we might recognise here. Ewing devoted enormous time and energy to the production of detailed advice notes to support the struggling Scottish boatbuilding industry in the post-war period. This initiative was funded by the Scottish Country Industries Development Trust. Opening his 'Communication Sheet No.51', as a random example, we find: *"List of Materials Required for one 14ft pulling boat, complete in all respects"*. And it is certainly complete, down to the chrome pigskin from the Gryffe Tannery to leather the oars.

As Boatbuilding Officer, Ewing was tireless and eternally attentive to his flock. Offering advice to crusty old boatbuilders on productivity, markets and budgeting is one thing, but to possess the skill and tact required to proffer technical advice on the essence of their craft is quite another. Our window on this rare talent is his extensive correspondence with Norman Turner of Dunoon. More initiatives of this type and a more generous budget for Ewing's support to the sector might have helped our wooden-boatbuilders to weather the bleak 1970s and 80s. The few who did, transitioned from anonymous journeymen to re-emerge as artificers of the newly fashionable genre of craft industries.

Boatbuilding in Scotland Today

The 2018 Yellow Pages list 67 'Boat Builders and Repairers' in Scotland. This is a grossly misleading total in relation to the mere handful of yachts built in Scotland each year. When a new yacht is built here it is a newsworthy event. In any case, 'boatbuilder' is a trade, not a job-description. While most are keen to build a boat, few have the resources or are given the opportunity. Silvers, Crinan, and Fairlie are among the boatyards honest enough to confine their commercial ambitions to repairs and refurbishment. Similarly, the Marina-based operations do not seek to build boats. They may rig and launch most of our new yachts, but that is in the context of retail dealerships for products conceived, designed and manufactured far from these shores.

So, the long-list whittles down as we eliminate fishing boats and fish-farm contractors, winter storage, dealerships, engineering works and one-man wannabees. Stormcats of Islay, which specialises in trailable runabouts and inshore fishing boats, claims to be the largest boatbuilder in Scotland (as opposed to fitting out shells moulded south of the border). The good people of Islay deserve gainful employment through their 12-month winters in a big warm dry shed, but alas, this is not real yacht-building either.

If you want to *learn* about building wooden boats, the picture is perhaps a little brighter; well, that is if you are not contemplating a career. The Scottish Maritime Museum runs a school, and thereby gains a cheap and cheerful labour-force to support its restoration programmes, while the Portsoy Boatshed offers residential courses in the north-east. The Clyde Maritime Trust has collaborated with Galgael to run 'holistic' courses (don't ask), and there is the commune-type venture of Clydeside Boatbuilders, where apprentices and volunteers assist in the construction of traditionally styled in-house designs. Women can even learn elements of the trade from other women at the 'Archipelago Folkschool', where you will sleep in a tent and enjoy the gossip, huddled round a peat fire in a wee croft on Mull to *"challenge the gender imbalance that currently exists in the boat-building industry"*, according to their prospectus.

The Wooden Boatbuilders Trade Association lists just eight members in Scotland. Most of these guys are building clinker rowing boats or small day-boats, to generally high standards, in remote locations. The lifestyle-orientated modus operandi is an indulgence of the western world. But the glacial pace of construction doubtless stems from the fact that there are few full-time jobs available when you graduate from boatbuilding school.

Examining some of these boats at the Southampton Boat Show (well they *are* built at the back of beyond), it's apparent that there are still a few craftsmen about. While they deserve our support, we might note that more attention could be paid to traditional detailing conventions which all do indeed have a reason. Matching timber by colour and grain seems to be beyond the pale in these days when traditional hardwoods cost the Earth, but otherwise, the seeds of a craft revival are encouraging.

A. & R. Way at Lochgilphead are building small traditional clinker designs to order, and would, according to their website, "*love to build you a wooden yacht to designs by Mylne, Watson or Holman and Pye*". Unfortunately, the custodians of these back catalogues have struggled to monetise them, even as 'spirit of tradition' newbuilds establish a toehold with their blend of plagiarism and awkward angles. Clydeside Boatbuilders of Govan, based at the old Harland & Wolff site, are also keen to build you a new boat with a New England flavour, albeit perhaps not to yacht standards, as it is a training establishment with a mission to revive and propagate traditional crafts. This business also operates sail-training vessels.

The famous old Ardmaleish yard, where so many masterpieces from the boards of Alfred Mylne and Thomas Glen-Coats were built, still takes yachts for winter storage and maintenance, but their focus now is on building commercial craft in steel, which they do well. The Corpach Boatbuilding Company of Fort William, which was set up to tender for fish-farm contracts, will also consider yachts. They too are expert in steel construction, specialising in workboats, fishing boats and ferries, but can work in other materials.

That is what is left, and it is not much. No matter how we cut it, the death of the industry is a tragic loss of pan-generational skillsets and the passion that we once supposed had been instilled in our bloodstream. Today, traditional boatbuilding in wood has withered to become a niche occupation. But on the Clyde, to all intents and purposes, it has actually died. The contrast with the 1890s could not be more stark.

CODA: The Holy Loch Boatyards in 1890

Neil Munro visits the Holy Loch boatyards: "*All winter the yachts of the Firth lie 'on the hard' where they rank in rows, grotesque imaginings of the naval architect, bereft for the time of any hint of speed or grace. They look pathetic, like Greenwich pensioners who will never again go back to sea.*"[1458]

The Glasgow Herald was less elegiac: "*The Holy Loch has taken the place of Gourock Bay as the winter haven for yachts, and there is no place better fitted in Clyde* for mooring and refitting. There is complete shelter in north-west gales, when the squalls kick up a short sea but not enough to trouble any dismasted yachts. Besides the sailing and steam yachts that have been anchored in the loch all winter, the yards of Messrs Morris & Lorimer and of Mr Robertson are crowded with sailing, steam yachts, small craft, and rowing boats.

And, besides repairing, a good deal is doing is the way of building new boats. Many of the racers of last season are hauled up alongside the cruisers, and an opportunity is given of studying the progress of yacht-building. The progress of Messrs Fife may be traced by various of their yachts, from the 8-ton Zephyr to the 40-ton Annasona, and of Mr Watson from the 5-ton Vril up to the 40-ton May. The crown of beached vessels gives the best history of Clyde yacht building that could be desired.

In the yard of Mr Robertson, a whole fleet of yachts are lying, in which are various refitting for the season. The 20-ton yawl Enriqueta is among the crowd, looking as well as she did when Dan Fletcher launched her. This yawl has been sold twice since Mr Robertson of the Royal Forth owned and raced her, but she will not be raced this season. The Eclipse, Mr Henry Lamont; Olivette, Mr Aspin; Saraban, Mr McPhee; Hilda, Mr Thos. Morrison; Merope, Mr Simmons; and Cynthia, Mr Robertson, are all on the beach.

The Leveret, one of Fife's 5's, has just been sold to Mr Turner, Gourock, the 7-ton Rocket, has already changed hands. The Cocker, which has been purchased by Mr McNaughton, is being scraped and repainted, and will be launched as smart to look at as when this five was owned by the Marquis of Ailsa. Sea Star, owned by Professor Liebhausan has had new fittings and various improvements, and the 5-ton Eileen has been partially rebuilt at Sandbank. Messrs Allan have brought back their good old craft Norah, and she lies beside the Vril, G. Watson's famous five. The Gladys presents an interesting study to designers interested in prodigious keels and may be regarded as the progenitor of the 'Hummingbird' type. The old Sirius is alongside the rest, and for good carpenter work, the Irish-built clinker cutter Beatrice is a fine example.

The Zephyr, owned by Mr Thomas Reid of Paisley, is having new topsides and decks, and will look as well as she did when Captain Hays owned her. Mr Reid's new Ayrshire Lass is among the craft under cover, and several other boats have been under care. (See Chapter 35) The firm has in hand the Cowal Lass for Mr Dobie, of Dunoon. This boat measures 24-feet and has an iron keel according to rules of the Dunoon Sailing Club. Mostly decked and with high coamings, she ought to be a capital cruiser, as well as make a good show across the finishing line. The firm has also completed a 19-ft racing boat for the Holy Loch Yacht Club, for Mr Currie, Sandbank. This boat carries all her ballast inside by the rules of the club, and being designed by Mr Fife Jnr, ought to prove a 'teaser' to the other nineteens of the HLYC (See Chapter 12). Of course, a lot of new dinghies are on hand.

Messrs Morris & Lorimer have a capital show of craft in their yard, and having the advantage of a patent slip, have several large steamers beached. Among the yachts are the *twin forties of May and Annasona, lying side by side, and giving a fine opportunity of studying the lines of the rival designers. Mr P. Donaldson's Yvonne is high and dry and will shortly be refitted for the season. The 20-ton Amalthea, Mr McLellan is having new cabin fittings put in by the firm, and beside her is laying the 20-rater Windward, Mr Cross, all ready for launching to meet Dragon and Fife's new twenty. The 5-ton Lorelei, Messrs Pirie, is being scraped and painted for the season. The old Kingston craft Finola built for Mr G. B. Thomson and remembered as one of the biggest of the twenties that ever met in Clyde, is also beached in the yard, where she has had new rails and bulwarks, as well as cabin floor and new fittings. The 5-ton Carina, née Urchin, belonging at present to Mr Bulley, is also beached, as is also the famous old Terpid, the sight of which recalls many a cruising race in which the old ironclad used to have it out with the 40-ton Alceste. The S.Y. Cassandra has been sold by Mr George Clerk of Paisley to Mr Barnwell of Fairfield and she is on the firm's slip to have an overhaul since Fairfield is too busy. The S.Y. Irene, Mr Beardmore, is also in the hands of the firm for an overhaul. The 10-ton rater cutter Jess, built under the new rule for Mr G. B. Thomson, is laying in the yard for sale and unless she meets with a purchaser will not be in the hunt."*[1459]

CODA: The Ship of Theseus

Defining restorations, rebuilds and replicas is a categorisation dilemma by no means unique to yachts. As a one-time specialist in ancient Chinese timber-framed construction, I have struggled with the Nara's official definition: *"All judgements about values attributed to cultural properties as well as the credibility of related information sources may differ from culture to culture, and even within the same culture. It is thus not possible to base judgements of values and authenticity within fixed criteria. On the contrary, the respect due to all cultures requires that heritage properties must be considered and judged within the cultural contexts to which they belong."*[1460]

Nara panders to East Asiatic cultures by legitimising a view that holds built heritage to be a spiritual rather than a material concern. Fortunately, the philosophy which underpins the rejuvenation of classic yachts derives from 'anastylosis', a very different paradigm: viz, original elements are valued and maintained where possible, with reconstruction where necessary, as long as new components are incorporated honestly. Even this modest ideal is challenging, so we turn to the *Ship of Theseus*, a thought experiment that questions the nature of an object, influencing Western philosophy since Heraclitus and Plato pondered the meaning of life ca.500-400BC.

The following short explanation the *Ship of Theseus* has been prompted by an excellent video produced by Leo Sampson, a very capable young man, who is rebuilding the Albert Strange cutter, *Tally Ho!* of 1909, a powerful cruising yacht that we admired as children in the pages of *The Complete Yachtsman*.[1461] *Tally Ho!* won the Fastnet in 1927 and led an 'interesting life', in the Chinese sense, before ending up in Oregon.

Leo's yacht was surveyed in 2013 and the results were not encouraging, but neither was the prognosis terminal. Like everyone who embarks on a major restoration of a wooden boat, Leo has found that however much work you think there will be, that's not the half of it. Starting with the replacement of rotten elements in the structure, the task grows until you reach the point where the only rational course of action to justify your investment is to replace the lot, bar the indestructible ballast keel. The alternative is a bodge job fit only for weekend sailing or exhibition in a museum. But is it the same boat? Is *Tally Ho!* still the Albert Strange yacht built by Stow & Sons in 1909?

Our position is much like Leo's. If you dismantle a boat piece-by-piece, replacing each element (including the ballast keel, if need be, and in times past often sold to fund a restoration) – that is a *rebuild*. It remains the same boat, if at all times we can perceive an artefact with an independent and unique life that sustains a *continuous physical existence*. Let's call this 'Ship A'. But if you take the lines off a boat, burn the timber, then build a new one, even if you use the original lead keel – that is a *replica*, it is not the same boat. Let's call this 'Ship B'.

The *Ship of Theseus* adds an additional twist to the question. Assume that, during the protracted restoration described above, as each element was replaced, it was conserved to become dry as a crisp. Then we bring in the new technology that allows us to infuse decayed wood with epoxy to give it strength and resilience beyond its original properties. If we now put all these elements back together (let's call it 'Ship C'), is this construct still the original ship? And if it is, what is 'Ship A', the boat we have repaired over the years, afloat in the next berth, that now retains no part of the original? We are unequivocal. 'Ship C', the new epoxy construct, is a *replica* and 'Ship A', moored next door, is paradoxically the original ship.

As a student of geomorphology and the philosophy of science in my youth, I like the river analogy. Rivers retain an enduring identity, even while their material substance is being continually renewed, their course changes through the seasons, and over geological time their action reshapes their environment. Boats are like that. As for replicas, they have a place too, particularly when a historically significant vessel has been lost for posterity. But they are not the same boat, and should not use the same name, except in an unambiguous frame, such as '*Spirit of*'.

Before we leave this subject, it is interesting to note that today there are now commercially available materials like 'Ligna', which are essentially resin-infused wood. Ligna is made from a fast-growing radiata pine and marketed as a viable teak substitute for laid decks. Other brands are available.

Thus the, formerly theoretical, exercise of 'deconstruction, infusion and reconstruction using the original elements', is now possible and could even become viable. The ancient spirits of Heraclitus and Plato must be smiling.

CODA: W. Stewart Collie and the Hydrogap Rudder

W. Stewart Collie was originally a mining engineer by profession, but he had many other talents. In addition to drafting pretty yachts, he was a fine marine artist. Collie's etchings are, not only 'in the style of Wylie', but arguably close in quality too. His talent remains practically unknown, so his work does not command high prices, despite its scarcity. Nevertheless, the best Collie images are extremely desirable.

Stewart Collie's interest in the Hydrogap rudder led nowhere, but it is an interesting historical curiosity.[1462] A Hydrogap rudder is mounted hard against the sternpost or skeg, but the stock is located forward of the leading edge. Thus, a gap opens between the leading edge of the rudder and the sternpost when any degree of helm is applied. The slot is intended to give a sternpost-hung, or skeg-hung, rudder the type of clean flow over both surfaces that a spade rudder enjoys.

While we are touching base with novelty rudders, the famous 12-metre *Vim* was launched with a Flettner rudder.[1463] This was another odd device that sank, but not without a trace. The trim-tab principle was later used to operate wind-vane self-steering. While the total drag bucket is increased, the force required to activate the rudder is reduced to a fraction of that required with a single-plane rudder. The system did gain some ground in commercial shipping, but on a racing yacht – what were they thinking?

While all these 'patented' rudders have fallen by the wayside, the search for a better mousetrap continues, most recently with whale fin-like nodular leading edges, as indicated by theories of biomimicry. Juan Kouyoumdjian has been a fan of this profile on boats like the mini-maxi *Rambler*. Slim, high-performance rudder blades can thus be endowed with slightly more tolerant stall characteristics.

[1449] Personal correspondence from Russell Potts to Ian Howlett, April 2012. 6mR RC model yachts are built to the same complex rule as full-sized 6-metres.

[1450] Turner's yard was originally located on Auchamore Road in Dunoon but moved to Jane Street, which was more convenient for the West Bay, where boat-hiring, ferry services and the excursion trade formed an important part of the business. Dan's son Norman (1907-1992) took over the business after his father's death in 1957. Norman retired in the early 1970s, selling the yard.

[1451] Coronation Class: 21ft 9" LOA, 15ft LWL, 5ft 10" beam, 170²ft SA. Loch Long: 21ft LOA, 15ft LWL, 5ft 8" beam, 170²ft SA.

[1452] Royal Lymington Yacht Club 1922 – 1972, republished on the club website 2008.

[1453] Correspondence with Joe Graham, July 2019. Readers take a Bow, Boatbuilder Revealed and The Boatyard Brothers, more details revealed, Colin Cameron, Dunoon Observer & Argyllshire Standard, 12th November 2014.

1454 The Hydrogap Rudder, details of a new device giving considerable efficiency, W. Stewart Collie, Yachting World, 6th January 1939.

1455 There is a D. Munro, "Yacht and boat builder of every description; builder of the Loch Fyne skiffs", listed in Inveraray in 1903. We think this is the same Munro.

1456 Royal Mersey Mylne Class, RMYC website, current. Mylne's list 15 RMYC ODs.

1457 Clyde Yacht-building, Glasgow Herald, 3rd February 1883.

1458 The Clyde, painted by Mary and Young Hunter, described by Neil Munro, 1902.

1459 Glasgow Herald, 10th April 1890.

1460 The Nara Document on Authenticity, ICOMOS, 1994.

1461 http://sampsonboat.co.uk/ep58/ The Complete Yachtsman, Brooke. Heckstall-Smith and Captain E. Du Boulay, 1912.

1462 Tonnag, article by W. Stewart Collie, Summer 1955. Dictionary of Nautical and Yachting Terms, C. W. T. Layton.

1463 The Racing World Will Vanderbilt's Vim lead out our Twelves – proposals for 6-metres and Small Classes, H.H, Yachting Monthly, June 1939.

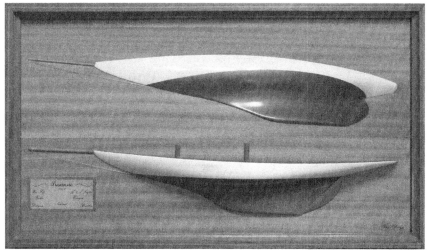

23mR, *Susanne*, composite schooner, 154-tons, William Fife III, 1911, built by A & J Inglis
This superb half-model, of what was said to be William Fife's favourite design, was carved by Peter L. Collyer as a gift for his daughter, June. The author's photo-composite illustrates both the exceptional beauty of the Fife lines and my old friend Peter's exacting craftsmanship.

Peter Collyer building N12s in the early 1960s   Images: June Collyer collection

Royal Mersey One Design, Mylne, 1934, built by Duncan Munro   Image: Emily Harris

Pixie Class, Stewart Collie, 1953. Image: Tony Webster   Lorimer girls   Image: Molly's Archive

Launching *Tonnag* at Dunoon Pier   Image: Graham Family

Tonnag, W. Stewart Collie, 1955   Image: Graham Family

Johnny Colquhoun at work on a Loch Long OD, 1937   Norman Turner, Image: Alison Turner

Peter Collyer sailing *Maida* (above) and *Hi-Jack* (right)   June Collyer Collection

Peter Collyer fitting the centreboard on the Flying Dutchman, *Flying Scotsman*   Image: June Collyer

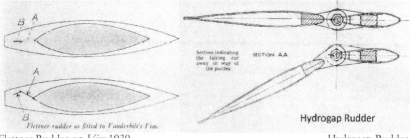

Flettner Rudder on *Vim* 1939   Hydrogap Rudder

Chapter 39: Elitist Humbug

After their own island, the sea is the natural home of the Englishman; the Norse blood is in us, and we rove over the waters, for business or pleasure, as eagerly as our ancestors. Four-fifths of the carrying trade of the world is done by the English. When we grow rich, our chief delight is a yacht. James Froude.[1464]

James Froude was a friend and disciple of Thomas Carlyle, the noted Scottish philosopher, but he still seems to have been unaware that we, who inhabit these islands, are not all English.[1465] Froude was in good company. William P. Stephen, the doyen of American yachting writers, corresponded regularly with eminent Scots in the marine business, but curiously considered them all to be English.[1466] Knocking the last of the wind from our sails, Robert Louis Stevenson, a man born and bred in Edinburgh, declared himself an 'Englishman' in *Travels with a Donkey in the Cévennes*.[1467]

While his convictions boxed the moral compass, Thomas Carlyle could turn his hand to most things, and do them well.[1468] On occasion, he even interrogated our antithetical Viking heritage, although masquerading as a mainstream historian, he struggled to contain his merciless satirical wit.[1469] *Highland Cowes* now honours the same subgenre by indulging in some deep purple prose, recognising that as a nation, we Scots innocently imagine ourselves to be blessed with a talent for wry humour. The contrast between the humbug of 3rd millennium yachtsmen and the 'rum, bum and concertina' of working seamen in the great era of sail presents an 'open goal'.[1470]

Cut loose from the domestic sanctuary of the marina, today's make-believe skippers seek out and inhabit imaginary worlds – damp microcosms in which to exercise occasional flights of tyranny. Around our coasts, harrumphs, harangues and brainless barks tumble downwind to foreshadow the passage of ten thousand bijou hell ships. When recreational sailors go to sea, they circumvent the sea's essential rites of passage and subvert the meritocracy of command. Tenure trumps ability, and the master's royal flush of pride swamps a raft of misgivings.

As a guest for the day, you smile gamely and clench your buttocks to counter that sinking feeling as you slide down the fleet and struggle to hang onto its tail end. Back at the marina, you make your excuses and disappear diplomatically before the post-race post-mortem. Then, in a rare moment of lucidity, the tongue-chewed guest might even retire gracefully from the whole shooting match to rummage the sock-drawer of yachting history in monochrome, as the author does here.

'Yachting' has long been a dirty word north and south of the border and on both sides of the Atlantic. For those who imagine themselves to be 'politically correct', the term embodies privilege, elitism and conspicuous consumption. They associate the many-facetted world of yachting with the Croesus Clan, who swagger at large through a global domain of excess beyond the ken of the common man. Like the covert tippler – who ever admits to yachting? Even our national authority, the RYA, is embarrassed and eschews our time-served terminology. You will search in vain for 'Royal Yachting Association' on its homepage.[1471]

While there is also a kindred yachting community tagged as 'boaters' across the pond, Australia and New Zealand, with an arguably more egalitarian tradition of recreational sailing, don't have such etymological issues and embrace 'yachts' and 'yachting' in their popular culture. Antipodean sportsmen incorporate the baggage of yachting's heritage with a light and ironic heart.

Perhaps it helps to separate the hard-earned qualities of what it takes to be a 'decent bloke' from the conferred attributes of wealth, rank and privilege. The crowds massing on Sydney Harbour Heads for the start of the Boxing Day race to Hobart are one example of this openness among a more knowledgeable public, and the ferry-loads of spectators who follow the spectacular Sydney Harbour Eighteen-footers are another.

Nonetheless, we are still talking about a sport that, globally, seems more egalitarian for those of us looking out through our rose-tinted bubble than for those outside, peering in. This residual, often unconscious, elitism belies the image the RYA promotes, and indeed the common platform of opinion occupied by the entire universe of yachting historians, journalists, bloggers and commentators. What can be done? Not much, to be honest; as the sardonic scorpion told the condemned frog, 'it's in our nature'.

No matter, yachting's congenital faults, in matters of class, snobbery and exclusion, make the history of the sport no less interesting from a technical perspective, and from the sociological angle, considerably more so. Dinghy sailing at club-level is less elitist, but that has never been an issue, and moreover, no one really cares very much about those few dinghy clubs which aspire to social apartheid.

But moving from impressions to substance, all these virtual barriers to entry are in truth insubstantial. Our generation, the baby boomers, moved from dinghies to daysailers to offshore racers and from there to catamarans and windsurfers and wave-boards in seamless transition. As the sport of 'yachting' expanded before our eyes through the 1960s, 70s and 80s, we had access to it all. Somehow it doesn't seem quite as easy today. Older gentlemen are no longer at liberty to take young lads in hand and show them the ropes; a tiny minority have queered the pitch.

That said, we must recognise that misperception is still a valid alternate reality. Traditional sailing clubs appear to present problems rather than solutions, so a word on their principles and politics is relevant here. I doubt if anyone, even an Australian, has ever been inspired to knock on the door of Cowes Castle – home of the Royal Yacht Squadron, to ask if they can learn to sail there. Even small sailing clubs are usually defended from public inquisition by a plethora of 'Keep Out' and 'Members Only' signage.

Ironically, these days most clubs are so desperate for new blood that even out-and-out braggarts need not fear 'black balls'.[1472] So, on behalf of the yachtsmen of Britain, we might take this opportunity to welcome anyone with so much as a passing interest in our sport to come on in. Nevertheless, for the majority, yacht clubs will probably remain aloof and intimidating for some time to come. Yawning asymmetries remain, both those we inherited from the Victorians, and new ones that have emerged as a consequence of our, rather depressing, celebrity-obsessed culture.

Today, there are two distinct, and often equally unapproachable, elites. Paid hands no longer tug their forelocks or doff their bunnets to gentlemen. Some of the current crop of professional 'rock stars' at the top-end of the sport can be as detached from the rank-and-file membership of ordinary sailing clubs as the tech billionaires and tax exiles who write their pay-cheques. Starting with the latter; wealth, particularly obscene wealth, invariably gives rise to hapless self-glorification. For the tycoons of the past, or the tech billionaires of today, success in business is somehow never enough – and has never been enough. Even outwardly modest captains of industry are motivated to compete on the public stage.

Bragging rights might involve subtle reference to the biggest and most expensive properties, private aircraft and toys. As for toys, and we are mainly talking about 'boys' toys' here, no toys are bigger or more expensive than superyachts. For the less-vulgar mogul, a more stylish braggadocio might be manifest in racing success – and in this instance, big racing yachts eclipse pedigree racehorses as perhaps the most impressive way to compete against one's peers in the public arena.

Then, there are the parties: *"For those who paid for the campaigns in after-tax dollars, the competition on the water was really an excuse for more, and better, parties. The grandest party of the summer, and indeed, of my entire life was the Sovereign party at*

The Breakers. Tony and Val Boyden, patrons of the British challenger, invited about 500 people to gather at 2200hrs for dinner and dancing (and whatever) until breakfast, which was served at 0400hrs."[1473] This is not to suggest that Boyden was just a socialite, he cared deeply about the America's Cup and was in tears in 1980 when *Lionheart* was knocked out of the competition.

In times past, the elite's aspirations to sporting success were seen as a God-given business opportunity for the canny Scots of Clydeside. Our taciturn shipwrights recognised the vulnerabilities of short, insecure men. Vaulting ambition was a sacred cow they milked for all she was worth. Sadly, as recounted in these pages, the last rites were performed over the corpse of this mythical beast half-a-century ago.

So, those days have gone now, but only here in Scotland. Super-yachting and short course racing in the new breed of 100ft super-maxis, gunwales stacked with more professionals than the active membership of many sailing clubs, is back with a vengeance. This is just the type of money-no-object proxy war that arouses hoggish robber-barons. What was unthinkable just 30 years ago has become commonplace.

How times change. Every last reminiscence about Big Class racing published in the 20th century, concluded with 'we'll nae see their likes again', or something similar in south-of-England prose. But there are many more big boats, and eye-wateringly expensive boats, afloat today than at any time in the 350-year history of the sport of yacht racing. This has transformed the earning prospects of career professionals in the yachting business, but it is a mixed blessing.

Maybe we are lucky; most summers Hunter's Quay, the now abandoned 'cradle of yachting', sees nary a glimpse of the beautiful people. That said, it would be doctrinaire not to concede that there are some modest economic benefits generated by superyachts and first-class yachting generally. Not as many benefits to society as would accrue if the 'non-dom' superyacht owners paid their taxes in full, granted, but benefits, nevertheless. And quite frankly, there are so many rogues around these days, it would indeed be remarkable if there were not boatloads at large on the water.

The conspicuous consumption of billionaires, and the mini-me drive to keep up with the Joneses among the common-or-garden millionaires, who maintain more modest family cruisers of 40ft and upwards, have empowered honourable manual trades once close to extinction. New money, conjured up through dodgy insider trading, now capitalises meaningless service employment, which in turn, funds a small residue of old-fashioned honest jobs. Perhaps this redresses the ethical balance of a terminally asymmetric society, if only to some small degree.

As the sport of yachting in Scotland developed, it cannot be denied that sailing society encompassed jaw-dropping extravagance and breath-taking snobbery. However, even among the wealthy and privileged in the early 19th century, the patrician spirit of James Hamilton shone through all that nonsense, see Chapter 15. It helped that sailing on Scottish waters has never been exclusive – there was a limitless field-of-play and a wealth of vectors for self-improvement. From its very beginnings on the Clyde, young professionals, aspiring entrepreneurs, artisans and apprentices, along with cack-handed dabblers and fanatics, found the means to get afloat.

"*Without disparaging other sports, I claim for yachting that it has all the elements of a rational recreation. If a man be not too reckless in exposing himself to the vicissitudes of weather, it has the primary recommendation of being thoroughly healthy and invigorating. To be sure, it wants the savage excitement of killing something, so dear to the British sportsman. In small craft everyone must make himself useful in some capacity, and the necessary work is just sufficient to occupy mind or body, without being harassing.*" John Inglis[1474]

The royal yacht clubs of the Clyde should receive credit for being welcoming in the main, but "*poor men who had to work for a living*" were daunted by the après sail, despite the best efforts of the Royal Gourock. And, of course, not everyone wants to hobnob with their boss. This led to comparatively humble associations of like-minded enthusiasts, sailing under the burgees of Cardwell Bay, Cove, and the unashamedly artisanal Cowal Sailing Club, serving the keen sailors who worked in the marine industry on the Holy Loch.

That said, these guilds with their duty rotas, devoted womenfolk and tea-and-biscuits, were always ancillary to the 'main event'. And we might ponder social conventions so entrenched, that by some undeclared pact, the honorary office bearers of the blue-collar societies were toffs to a man, and leading lights in one or other of the senior clubs to boot. Society as a whole was deferential. No one rocked the boat. The *Frost Report* 'Class Sketch', where John Cleese, Ronnie Barker and Ronnie Corbett all know and accept their place, comes to mind.[1475]

Playing Tennis with a Cricket Bat

Sailing in Scotland, as indeed everywhere, is sharply divided into the two main genres of racing and cruising. However, almost all yachts are marketed as cruiser-racers, even though they are generally one thing or the other. The genuine multi-purpose yacht has been an unattainable goal for generations of yacht designers and boatbuilders. Form belies function in the world of yacht racing. Thus, boxy new cruising yachts are equipped with high-tech racing sails, optimised to the nth degree, then sailed to destruction by professionals. Meanwhile, in provincial fleets, elegant old IOR racing yachts, with three-panel fractional rigs and running backstays, provide a low-cost entry-point for cash-strapped amateur crews – or at least for as long as they can keep the boat under the mast.

Unlike the heavier displacement vessels of the past, when today's specialist racing boats they enter the twilight of their competitive life, they do not retain much in the way of resale value. Caveat emptor: they are by no means a bargain. Racing sails and gear may be worthless. And repurposing such craft as cruiser-racers is challenging. Each conversion is, or certainly should be, a custom contract to ensure an efficient seaworthy outcome.

Increased displacement is inevitable and requires beefed-up scantlings, a less fragile rig and a more tolerant keel-fin. If the job is to be done properly, every engineering parameter must be recalculated to ensure that all elements under stress are 'fit for purpose'. As such work is seldom viable, the challenge is to develop a viable life-cycle model to full-on racing yachts, predicated on 'whole life costing' and recycling.

From a historical perspective, the equation is more balanced. Artless floating caravans may boss the Clyde's modest racing fleets today, but thoroughbred racing yachts have long ventured beyond the Mull of Kintyre. Wholly unsuitable vessels ranged short-handed up the West Coast from the dawn of yacht cruising. Ian Rutherford's adventures in the quirky Burgess-designed 6-metre, *Suilven*, during the 1930s were an inspiration to the shell-shocked survivors of the generation of young men who endured war service in the forties.[1476] With a positive mindset, a sack of porridge and a bottle of whisky can take you a long way.

The post-war years saw great changes in British society. Common sacrifice on the battlefields of WW2 inspired the worms to turn. The deference of centuries was overwhelmingly rejected with the election of a Labour government committed to a welfare state. Moreover, women who had done men's jobs, keeping the wheels of industry turning, wanted to keep working. Society was in turmoil, but the air was now free to breathe. For returning yachtsman, the beaches of Cowal were slick with oil-spills and the water wasn't very clean either, but at least no one was trying to kill you.

Young men with gammy limbs, 1,000-yard stares and PTSD found sanctuary, and perhaps even an element of closure, navigating the austere beauty of the West Coast. *"Bliss it was in that dawn to be alive. But to be young was very heaven."*[1477] More than a few disability pensions enabled a roving life afloat, albeit hand-to-mouth. As each spring rolled round, wooden legs and rusty prosthetics joined spars and floorboards on the trestles for a rub-down and a coat of yacht varnish.

As baby boomers, we were fortunate to avoid the mud and slaughter of global conflict and dodge conscription; set free by the sacrifice of our fathers' generation to toddle through life, piggy-backed into a bright new future. The nuclear families of the Cold War took to the water in origami boats formed from folded plywood and sponsored by daily newspapers. This new cult of unpretentious 'woolly-jumper' sailing was a modest reward for years of shortage and hardship. Canny families found their niche supping chipped mugs of stewed tea in weatherboard huts, leaving the pre-war old guard to sip G&T in the wardroom and contemplate impending ruin.

In these endless, sepia-tinted days, serene war veterans, who had seen much but said little, could take small children yachting without alerting Social Services. The baby boomers were privileged to experience the unsupervised joys of childhood in the 1950s. This was a rare window of innocence for those of us lucky enough to grow up by the seaside in the bosom of an easy-going middle-class family.[1478] My own vague oceanic ambitions grew from idyllic afternoons adrift on the miniature yacht, *Piccolo*.

Piccolo, Sheriff Bryson's pride and joy, was a Pixie Class Bermudian sloop, just 21ft LOA, 6ft 6" beam and 2ft 9" draft, designed by W. Stewart Collie and built by the Graham Brothers of Dunoon in the year of my birth. She had red cotton sails and a reliable little 4hp Stuart Turner.[1479] We never went further than Rothesay, but even that was a major voyage at a cruising speed of 4.5kts. Ours was a world of sailcloth smocks, baggy flannel shorts, gutties with the toes cut off to keep the bilges dry, jam sandwiches wrapped in greaseproof paper and mildewed kapok lifejackets that were useful only as cushions.

Life moves on. Yachting has developed as both a sport and a pastime, successfully negotiating any number of crossroads to colonise vast tracts of our lives. Today, we face more forks in the path of progress. Whether, in this era of information technology and artificial intelligence, selecting from alternative futures is more, or less fraught than it once was, remains to be seen. The sport and pastime balance, once a continuum, is now a battleground of entrenched positions and unnecessary searching for the soul of the sport. Or has it always been like that?

"Does it matter if sailing of the 70s is not the sailing of today? I think not. Women were not involved, and they had to buy drinks through a hole in the wall and sit in another room at many a club I can name right now. We have moved on with all of that, thankfully, so perhaps we can do the same with what is appealing, and what will grow the sport in all of its many manifestations."[1480] Of course, gender is no longer an issue and gay mariners have always been a part of our tradition, but

outside of Olympic squads, there are still precious few Black or Asian yachtsmen. The totalitarian might of the People's Republic of China is on the case for the latter, but whether that initiative is consistent with the essential free spirit of the sport is another matter.

Athletica-lite

The word 'athlete' derives from the Greek 'athlon', meaning a prize. Thus, an athlete is simply someone who competes for a prize. From the inception of the sport, racing sailors have taken this to heart, 'pot-hunting' rather than sailing.[1481] In so doing, we consider ourselves to be athletes, ignoring established English usage, where 'athletic' means strong, fit and active. Here, I would cite my generation's experience.

As schoolboys, yachting was an attractive alternative to the discipline and regimentation of field sports superintended by grown-up authority. But not just for gung-ho rebels, it seems. As I recall, sailing was also a godsend for the less fit, less agile and less well-coordinated legion of youngsters who couldn't make it into the school football team. These guys sought out niche sports that did not require good hand-eye coordination, gifted ball-skills or an abundance of high-twitch muscle fibres. Thus, as moderately hale and hearty youths in the early 1960s, we took our 'guns' to the 'knife-fights' of national schools' events and junior competitions, where genuine athleticism was as rare as hen's teeth.

'Relatively easy', perhaps, but my friends and I still wished away the winter, sailed until dusk in the summer and spent countless hours tinkering. Nothing was settled and everyone had an opinion in the 1960s. This was a time before sailmakers' tuning guides and definitive computer-cut sail shapes were available. We were lucky to enjoy generous logistical support to attend regional and national competitions, but we sailed through life innocent of the scars of professional coaching. And there were certainly no 'how to do it' articles of the type that now appear in *Yachts and Yachting* to strike an incongruous note. The readership of specialist sailing magazines was once assumed to be both knowledgeable and proficient.

In the 1960s and 70s, if you wanted to succeed in sailboat racing, you had to understand your (often unique) equipment, set it all up individually and coordinate the infinite variables that contribute to 'boat-speed'. Even children discussed sail-shape with their sailmakers; argued their points of view, and confidently ordered recuts, or at least this child did. Everyone who sailed did everything that a small number of full-time pros do today as a service industry. Just occasionally, when the stars aligned, you would attend a championship or an open meeting and discover you had more boat-speed than anyone else. It was bloody magic.

Much as we all disparaged golf as an old man's sport, it did not escape our notice that life afloat would be a lot more difficult if fewer 'golfers' and more 'proper athletes' cared to flex their muscles in our little pond. *"When some of the people at Cowes are not yachting or watching others yacht, some of them seek Sandown for the sterner diversion of golf. A pinnace from the Royal Yacht attracted an anticipatory crowd on Sunday, as it neared East Cowes. Instead of the King and Queen, however, its occupants were Sir Harry Stonor and Major Clive Wigram, with the bandmaster from HMY Victoria and Albert, complete with clubs and tweeds."*[1482]

Things may be slightly different today, but even as we progressed to big boats in the 1980s, nothing had really changed. Keen sailors had certainly become fitter, often jogging three or four miles several times a week and occasionally going to the gym, but stoicism was still more important than athleticism. Then as now, the journalistic hype – 'fit as track athletes', would make most big boat sailors squirm with embarrassment, and rightly so.

Competitive, big fleet boardsailing in the mid-eighties introduced your author to real athleticism, and I must confess it was a sobering baptism of fire. Some athletes sail and some (vanishingly few) sailors are athletes, but the two words are not interchangeable in any generic sense. The print and video media would do everyone a favour if they stopped referring to sailors as 'athletes'; we have our own lexicon, please use it.

Back in the mid-sixties, Beecher Moore had this to say, and I doubt if anyone has said it better since: *"Every hour less work means another hour available for play. If you are basically lazy and not very clever, the obvious hobby is sailing. It does not need the talent that is required for music, painting or sculpting. It does not need the great physical effort that is needed for swimming, tennis or hiking. Basically, it is getting 'something for nothing' that attracts. It all looks so easy.*[1483] Consequently, as sailors, we somehow feel obliged to create artificial challenges and generally make life difficult for ourselves.

Racing – Evolving Towards Extinction

Sailing is not rational. Where the rest of the world uses a chainsaw, yachtsmen use an axe with a carbon shaft and a titanium head. And what other serious sport values sportsmen who are principally good at making themselves as heavy as possible? Good mid-boat crewmen exhibit a bovine-like ability to sustain maximum leverage. But, for those of us who plied our trade among the afterguard, after an hour or so bum-to-bum with the B-max team, and some desultory attempts at conversation, we begin to lose interest in life itself. Turning again to Beecher Moore writing in 1965: *"The last twenty-five years have been very retrogressive. Certainly, the wind has never been trapped so successfully. But at what a cost of mass physical discomfort!".*[1484]

Gentlemen sail to win just as tyros, seeking 'a good time' on the water, are likely to be disappointed. When the gun goes off, there is just one item on an agenda where 'a good time' comes only after that elusive puff of smoke. Small boat competition is seldom enjoyable for its own sake: dry mouth, intense nausea in the countdown up to the gun; head spinning off the line, concentrating on boat-speed; working the waves; second-guessing the wind-shifts; knees bursting apart, calf muscles jiggling with effort, thighs cramped; upper body wracked by unequal forces; back muscles frozen; Bang! Bang! General recall. After three false starts, you are cold, wet, and stiff, and deep down you don't care anymore.

On an offshore race-boat it is even worse. They never cancel the race, no matter how hard it blows, and you never get to experience the incredible relief of a day off. On the helm, stress is relentless. If you miss a few degrees of height on a momentary lift, the soft murmur of conversation on the rail stops. A 'football-team of gorillas-in-shades' glares back at you, while some smart-arse at B-max gratuitously starts to call pressure. And if you lose the groove and the big numbers on the mast start to tumble like the countdown for a Shuttle launch, it gets pretty lonely back there.

Only winning transcends the pain and discomfort. Of course, there are some sailors out there who 'play the game' for its own sake and enjoy their time on the water regardless of results, but if you are serious about racing, you don't want these people anywhere near your boat. *"Serious sport has nothing to do with fair play. It is bound up with hatred, jealousy, boastfulness, disregard of all rules and sadistic pleasure in witnessing violence: in other words, it is war minus the shooting."* George Orwell[1485]

In the egalitarian world of post-war yachting, and through the sixties and seventies, sailors used to boast that yacht racing was the only competitive sport where a dedicated amateur could go head-to-head with a reigning World Champion and occasionally take their scalp. Even the congenital duffer was permitted to share the starting line, presenting the same gratuitous hazard to both groups. However, there are vanishingly few opportunities left where today's 100% Corinthian crews can 'mix it' with our best professionals on the racecourse. And today, no matter how dedicated you are, don't expect to remain in contact with the pros as the race progresses. It is not a disaster; that is how most sports are now.

Paediatrician Stuart Walker (1923-2018) wrote incisively on many aspects of yachting.[1486] He said this on the subject: *"What has professional sailing done for the sport? It has converted, for those involved, a game into a job, play into work. It has deprived the rest of us of the Olympics, now a professional spectacle. It has foisted judges, juries and police upon us. It has disfigured sailboats, once man's loveliest addition to the land and seascape, with advertising. And worst of all, it has attracted the attention of the media; indeed, it has developed itself expressly to serve the media, converted class into crass, substituted mass value for individual perception, and tried to make sailing a spectator sport.*"[1487]

Yacht racing demands a unique combination of specialist knowledge, hard-won experience, strategic foresight, tactical appreciation, critical thinking, problem-solving, manual skills, quick reactions and both aerobic and anaerobic fitness. If you doubt that this sport is uniquely demanding, listen to an hour of football commentary, and the beautiful game is less banal than most. Exceptionalism is something we are all prone to. And yachtsmen, almost always well-educated, relatively affluent and holding right-of-centre political views, are more prone than most. So, it is only to be expected that the sailing community would imagine that integrity was another element integral to our sport.

Cheating is as old as society itself, but in the baby-boomers' timeline, it surged in the mid-1980s. Before this watershed, traditional values generally held sway on the ocean. A good friend of mine won an important Moth regatta in New Zealand; I think it was the championships. After the final race of the series, someone at the bar remarked that it looked like he touched the wing mark. Who knew? It was impossible to say, but my old mate retired immediately. The mere possibility of an infringement soured the victory; it was not worth having. The idea anyone might think he 'got away with it' was even worse. Not so today, especially at apex events where there is on-the-water judging. No flag, no foul.

Stuart Walker has posited that yachting will soon emulate golf or tennis, where a sailor's success is judged less on who won or lost, but more on career earnings, which define the pecking order in these well-reimbursed sports. That has yet to happen. Sailors are still reticent about earnings, perhaps because they would be embarrassed to reveal just how hard it is to make a living as a second-tier pro, or a maestro in white-sail dinghies. Nevertheless, one might observe that the cat is now out of the bag. Professional sailors are no longer content to make a living as glorified 'hired hands', or to confine their activities to health and safety matters on yachts above 50ft LOA while camping in the fo'c'sle.

But seriously, surely there is no place for a professional crew aboard a J70, a docile mass-produced keelboat less than 23ft LOA. In the 2018 J70 World Championships, the first five Corinthian crews were placed 6th, 26th, 29th, 35th and 37th overall in a fleet of 91 boats. "*Sailboat racing has come full circle from the time when an advantaged few with the time and money to perfect their skills played, while a large group of professionals worked. Now we have merely combined the two groups into one."*[1488] We cannot blame the 'hired guns' for this ludicrous situation. Too many good sailors are competing for too few berths. The result is that some will have to take any pocket-money gig going, even if that means serving as human ballast and occasional nanny on the rail of a little low-tech plastic daysailer.

Of course, this is just nonsense; but even worse is the disappointment that awaits our professional elite as they seek recognition and rewards like sportsmen in other, arguably less-demanding, sports. Some still chase the holy grail of television. But today, TV serves only to consolidate the mainstream, leaving minority sports to the Internet. *"Perhaps, if the media promotion which has recently generated so many additional opportunities for professional sailors had developed sooner, the once noble Olympic regatta would not have had to be sacrificed to commercialism."*[1489]

Traditional yachting is essentially a participation sport and the many attempts to reinvent it as a spectacle have usually delivered disappointing results. A succession of new 'disciplines' present yachting as entertainment. Most have failed, and it was obvious from the outset that they would. Promoters assumed that yacht racing was interesting; that the lay spectator might care who won or lost. Sadly, this misconception has regressed to become entrenched dogma. It makes no sense; even keen sailors are less than keen to watch others set a game face and splash around pointlessly.

Success surely lies elsewhere. First, you have to secure the interest of the genuine enthusiasts who make up your core audience. This means the folk who buy yachting magazines. It is not hard to define demographic targets or establish what stimulates these constituencies. Sailors like to see technical advances explored and explained; they like spectacle and drama and balls-to-the-wall sailing, but they are content with vignettes of incredible moments. They don't want to squander an afternoon for 10 minutes of action.

Most sailing enthusiasts are, dare I say it, uninspired by speed per se, unimpressed by helmeted Ninja heroes, and frustrated by sails that change only in camber around the course – and then imperceptibly. What struck many people about the last America's Cup in Bermuda was the paradoxical 'lifelessness' of high-speed foiling. Only when the boats touched down in a ball of spray could photographers capture memorable images. As for the new AC75s, the sheer scale of these machines is certainly impressive, but alas any animation is imperceptible – like a Zeppelin passing by.

If sailing does not involve contact with the water, half the game, and perhaps the most demanding half, is lost. Steering upwind through waves is the essence of helmsmanship, while catching a wave early and holding it downwind is often equally important. Helming in flat water is merely steering, no matter how fast you go. The iconic pass in the long history of America's Cup saw *Gretel* surf past *Weatherly* in 1962. The behaviour of hull-shapes in waves was a preoccupation, and occasionally an obsession, of the post-war period. Foiling on sheltered water has lost all that.

Sure, other arcane dexterities were introduced to compensate, but these PlayStation skills were transient, and undoubtedly, better mechanised, as in a jet fighter. Ever-increasing speed, hazard and insurance liability have now cropped the ragged edge. Hence the eye-watering investment in artificial intelligence incurred by both the 36th Cup and Larry Ellison's travelling circus of recycled AC50s, now sailing as computer-aided GP50s. Who could argue? God forbid they 'crash and burn' like Nacra 17s.

Most sailors of my generation prefer to follow their passion by dipping in and out of the material available on the Internet. They have little desire to watch the action live on 'big match' television. America's Cup defences are a notable exception – or used to be before the competition format became interminable. This is why the design battle remains the essence of the Cup, the intrigues, and yes, even the court cases. And it is why one-designs have no place in our sport's apex event.

Cruising – Camembert Électrique?[1490]

Cruising is different. The novelist Henry Fielding (1707-1754) described yachting as, *"what seems to me the highest degree of amusement: that is, the sailing ourselves in little vessels of our own"*.[1491] And to this day, nothing has really changed. Cruising can be entertaining, and for those with a high boredom threshold, it can even become a lifestyle. However, passage-making is, for the most part, irredeemably tedious without a good book, or more accurately a good library on board. Not that racing is any less boring, as that too involves endless hanging around, bullshitting and drinking too much.

Quite why so many of us enjoy long-hours of limited activity is something of a mystery. But, if you have not been at sea for a while, the first moon-lit night is always magical. Coastal passage-making becomes a challenging snow-globe of lit and unlit hazards, especially for the 1 in 12 of us who are red-green colour-blind, bringing a whole new meaning to the cliché 'don't watch alone'. Responsibility for safe navigation brings heightened levels of consciousness, and occasionally raw terror, to the sensory pleasures of sailing in darkness.

More prosaically, there is always something to do on a ship at sea. The 'flying string-bag' character of a conventional sailboat demands constant adjustment and endless cycles of routine maintenance as things wear, break or just fall off. Why then is 'push-button sailing' trickling down through the size range from superyachts to family cruisers? Do the purveyors of such technology seek to bore everyone to death? Who wants to do a lap of Silverstone in a driverless car? Where is the pleasure? What is the point?

Most new yachts deny the proud owner even that most basic joy of yacht ownership – rowing off twenty yards to witness the sublime as the sun goes down. Why do so many modern yachts have portraits of classic yachts on the main bulkhead and mariners' tales from the last century on the bookshelf? Modern yachts are slightly ludicrous rendered in oil on canvas. As for modern adventures, they usually hinge on the search for a crucial spare part. Who would deny the 21st century adventurer air-conditioning and a hot shower?

Marinas that charge by the linear foot have imposed a new 'box rule'. Straight sheer, plumb ends, high freeboard, charcoal-tinted picture windows in the topsides, stumpy rig, in-mast reefing and vulgar manufacturer's graphics that overwhelm your own restrained signwriting. Uffa Fox was famous for asserting that weight is only useful in a steam road-roller, although it is likely that he nicked that axiom too. In the modern era, perhaps volume per se is only of value in a warehouse.

Yachts built on a human scale facilitate human operation. They are safer and more efficient, economical, and environmentally sustainable. Such vessels are infinitely more satisfying aesthetically than some pumped-up barn of a boat. Barn-dancing is best enjoyed in a barn, and you can leave your barbeque on the patio at home while we are on the subject. As for the widescreen TV, laptop computer and a good half of that absurd battery-bank you are so proud of, that can all be offloaded too.

As will be obvious, the author is nostalgic for the era when French sailing schools blew into West Coast anchorages in unpainted, unlined aluminium cruisers with alcohol cookers and an enormous sweep in lieu of an auxiliary motor. They captured the essence of adventure cruising, independent of shore support.

CODA: Golf, yes…. Golf

Through both world wars, shipbuilding was a reserved occupation, although many Clydeside men did join up. A significant percentage of our best yachtsmen and professional sailors brought their acknowledged leadership, stamina and technical skills to the conflict, serving on both land and sea. Murray Stephen's letters home are redolent with sangfroid: "*The present existence is stagnation, mental and physical. The Artificer has made us a cleek and an iron… these two pieces of art are really quite good. There is a field in front of the battery with some good water hazards (a couple of trenches and some shell holes). What more can you want? We spent two happy mornings laying out a 9-hole course. I wonder if you could get father to send me out some old golf-balls.*"[1492]

The Stephen family archive contains another revealing reference to golf, and the all-round sporting prowess of Clyde yachtsmen, in that era. This time it is John writing about the British American Cup, sailed in 6-metres in 1922. After several pages detailing the races, he concludes with: "*We are playing as much golf as possible. Today, Charlie and I beat two of the star members of the course here, which they did not like.*"[1493] Fortunately, even with their golf-clubs, the Scottish crew still had space in their luggage to bring home the Seawanhaka Cup, which they picked up the following week. Game set and match on this occasion, I think.

We might leave the final word to John Scott Hughes, another slave to the magic of Hunter's Quay: "*Always in Scotland, not races or even yachts, were my chief interest and joy, but friends. And, as I write that, in my mind's eye comes the scene on the lawn before the Royal Marine at Hunter's Quay. Another Clyde Fortnight has come to an end. On the lawn the pipers are playing, and the singing of 'Will ye no come back again' is led by Maurice Clark, that gracious man, who himself will not come back again.*"[1494] Alas, not just Clark, but the whole damn wonderfully flawed and exasperating company.

[1464] Oceana, James Froude, 1886.

[1465] Still, it cuts both ways. American Yachting historian Howard Chapelle, an expert if ever there was one, thought Northumberland was in Scotland, although we only had sovereignty over the county for 22 years in the 13th century.

[1466] The Evolution of the Yacht Designer First Paper – English Designers, W. P. Stephen, Outing, Volume XXXIX (1901-1902).

[1467] "*I am worthy the name of an Englishman, and it goes against my conscience to lay my hand rudely on a female*" Robert Louis Stevenson, 1879.

[1468] See the thoroughly reprehensible article – Occasional Discourse on the Negro Question, Thomas Carlyle, published anonymously in Fraser's Magazine for Town and Country of London, December 1849. Carlyle's own yachting exploits were limited to fieldtrips along the coastlines of Europe for his biographical works.

[1469] The Early Kings of Norway, Thomas Carlyle, 1800.

[1470] Quotation is the title of George Melly's autobiography, pub. 1965.

[1471] The International Yacht Racing Union (IYRU) became the more egalitarian International Sailing Federation (ISAF) in 1996 and plain old-world Sailing in 2015.

[1472] Black balls, a system where just one member could veto an application for membership anonymously. White-ball = yes, black-ball = no. The veto was called a 'black ball' even when it simply signified an objection on a show of hands.

[1473] Memories of a Corinthian Summer, Dick Enersen, December 2014.

[1474] A Yachtsman's Holidays or Cruising in the West Highlands, John Inglis, 1879.

[1475] The 'class sketch' was first broadcast in an episode of the Frost Report on 7th April 1966.

[1476] At the Tiller, Ian Rutherford, 1945. *Suilven* was launched as *Sheila* in the USA and built by the Herreshoff Manufacturing Company.

[1477] The Prelude, William Wordsworth, 1850. Inscribed on the gravestone of Sue Ross (1950-1995) in the Kilmun Churchyard by the shores of the Holy Loch.

[1478] Before nostalgia runs riot, we recognise that these were not universal privileges. Consider, for example, the 130,000 orphans shipped off to Australia into virtual domestic slavery, from the 1920s to the 1970s, by the Catholic Church, the Anglicans, the Fairbridge Society and Barnardo's. The last children were shanghaied into domestic 'slavery' in Australia in 1967, while luckier kids were ripping up and down the Holy Loch in Merlin Rockets.

[1479] *Piccolo* had a carvel hull planked-up with $^5/_8$th" mahogany over steam-bent ash frames 1" x $^7/_8$th" at 7½" in centres, with a stem and keel of English oak. She had red cotton sails by Mackenzie of Sandbank. We last saw *Piccolo* for sale in the pages of Classic Boat ca.2005. The Pixie class are beautiful yachts and small enough for your back garden; should you ever come across one – buy her!

[1480] Lower than Badminton, John Curnow, Editor, Sail-World blog, 28th April 2019.

[1481] Admittedly, most prizes are substantially worthless these days, but for much of the period covered by this book, cash rewards were pursued with enthusiasm. And mea culpa, your author scored thousands of dollars' worth of swag, particularly in his boardsailing days.

[1482] Men and Women of To-day, The Dundee Courier, 5th August 1925.

[1483] Something for Nothing, Beecher Moore, Colin Mudie, The Dinghy Yearbook, Edited by Richard Creagh-Osborne, 1965.

[1484] Ibid

[1485] Shooting an Elephant, George Orwell, 1950.

[1486] Stuart Walker could sail a bit too, competing at the Olympic Games in the Soling and winning championships in the International 14 when success in these dinghies represented the apex of our sport.

[1487] From Planing On, an article by Stuart Walker, undated.

[1488] Ibid

[1489] Ibid

[1490] Camembert Électrique (electric cheese) was an album by French jazz/prog rock band Gong, released in 1971. Is 'yacht à voile èlectrique' not equally ridiculous?

[1491] Henry Fielding – a Memoir, including newly discovered letters and records, with illustrations from contemporary prints, G. M. Godden, 1909.

[1492] Letter from Murray Stephen to his mother, Mabel, on 10th December 1915.

[1493] Letter from John Stephen to his father, Fred, on 10th September 1922.

[1494] Harbours of the Clyde, John Scott Hughes, 1954.

Mariette, Nat Herreshoff, 1915, sailing at the 2008 Fife Regatta on the Clyde   Image: the author.

The Lady Ann, William Fife III, 1912, 2008 Fife Regatta on the Clyde   Image: the author

Viola, William Fife III, 1908 on the Clyde   Image: the author

Halloween, William Fife III, 1925, sailing at the 2008 Fife Regatta on the Clyde   Image: the author

Racin' every day of the week, every day except Sunday;
We finishes up of a Saturday night, and goes racin' again on Monday.

The Masthead Man's Lament, trad. anon

Appendices

Appendix 1: Adding Insult to Injury

You'll be doin' it for pleasure, I suppose?" "Yes" said the singlehander, "I'm doing it for pleasure. E. S. Turner, 1910[1495]

The following technical notes are intended to support the chapters that bear on yacht design and equipment. They are ancillary but not entirely irrelevant to the central narrative of the book.

Comparing Dimensions

In the 19th century, with all the gear and carbuncles hanging off the bow and stern of the yachts (bowsprits, bumkins, figureheads, cutwaters, etc), 'overall length' (LOA) was not particularly meaningful in 'sizing' a yacht. In these circumstances, when comparing dimensions published in Lloyds and builders' lists, this may be 'length between perpendiculars' (the distance from the outside face of the stem to the aft face of the rudder post) as used to calculate Thames Tonnage. Another Thames measurement that crops up is 'depth of hold', a proxy for draft, which was difficult to measure, especially when the vessel was afloat. Hold depth is measured from the upper side of the rabbet to the bottom of the deck-beams at centre.

Difficulties also arise when comparing designs built under the International Rule; builders' lists often use the rated length, which approximates to actual sailing length, and lies between the LWL and the LOA. Alfred Benzon, an industrialist and sportsman from Denmark with a keen interest in the science of sailing, is credited with the method used in the Rule. He proposed bow and stern girth taxes to quantify 'effective sailing length', rather than static waterline length. Benzon also proposed the 'd' measurement, which penalises hollows in the midship section to prevent 'skimming dishes'.[1496] Scottish designer, C. L'Estrange Ewen, found a way round this: see annexe note on 'The *Teal* Case'.

"Length – the length 'L' for the formula is to be the length measured at a height of 1.5% of the class rating above the LWL plus one-and-a-half times the difference between the girth at the bow section measured to points of 5% cent of the rating above 'L' and twice the vertical height of the rating from 'L' to these points, plus one-third of the difference between the girth, covering-board to covering-board, at the stern ending of this length and twice the vertical height at the side of the yacht at this station. The minimum difference of girth at bow station, as above defined, to be 30%, or twice the said vertical height."[1497]

We might use the Sixes to illustrate how yachts under the International Rule got bigger over the years. This phenomenon occurs with most rules, whether there is a maximum LOA or not, and reached a peak with the International Offshore Rule (IOR), where level-rating classes at the end of that era were a full rating band larger than they were at the beginning. Even today, in the offshore box rule classes like the Class 40s and IMOCA 60s, new boats cannot be longer, but they do tend to increase in volume, with the prevailing scow influence and ever higher prismatic coefficients.

The 1st Rule boats are delicate in appearance, and above the water, not unlike the Raters they replaced, but of course, much heavier. They were shallow with low freeboard and extreme overhangs. The 2nd Rule boats were perhaps the 'best balanced' aesthetically of any era with good internal volume and moderate in all respects, although the triangular underwater profile made slipping difficult. The 3rd Rule did not necessarily represent progress across all fronts, as in order to foster wholesome boats it required arbitrary manipulation and even then, a minimum beam of 7ft vs 6ft would have been preferable to support a second life after top-flight competition. The following table illustrates how dimensions evolved through the lifetime of the rule.

Six-metre Yachts – Evolution of Principal Dimensions 1908-1948

Year	Name	Designer	LBP	LWL	Beam	Depth
First International Rule 1907-1919						
1908	*Elsa*	Hope	23.0	21.2	6.2	4.0
1908	*Coila II*	Fred Stephen	26.8	20.55	5.7	-
1910	*Elise-Clair*	Morgan Giles	-	20.3	5.93	-
1910	*Cingalee*	Fife	27.1	20.2	5.92	4.0
1910	*Cynthia*	Glen-Coats	27.0	-	5.67	-
1913	*Ariadne*	Glen-Coats	29.8	20.0	5.4	3.9
1914	*Gonda*	Morgan Giles	28.14	20.46	5.67	4.0
Second International Rule 1919-33			*LOA*			*Draft*
1921	Coats 'B'	Glen-Coats	37.6	20.4	6.2	4.6
1921	*Margaret*	Morgan Giles	36.0	20.7	6.9	5.1
1922	*Patience*	Nicholson	33.0	21.2	6.9	5.0
1922	*Coila III*	Fred Stephen	-	-	7.0	-
1922	*Ayesha*	Fife	35.0	21.3	6.9	5.1
1922	*Gairney*	Fife	35.5	-	6.65	5.1
1931	*Cresta*	Nicholson	35.9	25.3	6.58	-
1931	*Vorsa*	Mylne	-	23.0	7.0	-
Third International Rule 1933-present						
1936	*Senoia*	Nicholson	37.4	23.3	6.5	5.4
1937	*Circe*	Boyd	38.6	23.5	6.1	5.4
1938	*Erica*	Nicholson	36.2	23.6	6.0	5.4
1938	*Djinn*	Rod Stephens	37.0	23.7	6.0	5.4
1939	*Maida II*	John Stephen	39.5	23.2	6.1	5.3
1939	*Johan*	McGruer	37.8	23.6	6.3	5.4
1947	*Marletta*	Boyd	37.2	23.5	6.0	5.4
1948	*Juno*	Nicholson	37.5	23.7	6.0	5.4

Note: prior to ca.1919, LOA and Draft are not given only TM measurements of LBP and Depth. Tumblehome may be ignored as the International Rule limits it to 2%.

After 1937, when the minimum beam was introduced, most designs of the 'classic era' shared the same design envelope. Deviations from the norm carried heavy rating penalties to be paid for in sail area reductions.

Metal Masts

In pursuing new metal masts, at seemingly any cost, disregarding health and safety, and perhaps also ethics and financial propriety, the Clyde Straight-eight fleet actually had it right. Whatever latter-day connoisseurs may favour, when restoring Bermudian-rigged yachts from the 1920s through to the post-WW2 period, metal masts are preferable in every way. Only the most perverse and pernickety restorations employ natural fibre materials for sails and cordage and eschew modern fastenings, paints and varnishes, so why return to antediluvian rigs? Yachting is dangerous enough without one's weather eye constantly distracted by every creak and groan; that is the sole business of the mainsail trimmer and the nervous owner.

Moreover, metal spars have been around for a long time and have been essential race winning kit since the 1930s. The G. L. Watson designed America's Cup challenger, *Valkyrie III*, built by D & W Henderson, successfully stepped one of the first steel masts in 1895. Such spars became de rigueur for Cup competition until more exotic alloys arrived in the 1930s. Tom Sopwith's J Class, *Endeavour*, carried perhaps the ultimate steel mast in 1934. Had they been more readily available, every racing yacht designer since the Great War would have specified a metal mast.

Scottish designers were very much alive to the potential of new materials with such innovations as composite construction. Iron masts had been introduced successfully in the Clyde 19ft luggers back in 1881. They were, allegedly, as light as wooden spars but much stiffer even with small tube sizes. Stock boiler tube was used as there was an almost infinite variety available from a shipbuilding industry famous for its steam engines. The lower mast was generally about 4" in diameter, with a 3/16" or 1/4" wall. These spars were 'tapered' by socketing progressively smaller tubes from the root up.[1498]

Why then would anyone go back to wood – inconsistent, unreliable and expensive? In her first season, *Britannia* went through three lower masts, one topmast, a gaff and two bowsprits. Every one of these failures was a life-threatening episode. Wood endured as a spar material only because expertise in metal mast construction was limited and conservatism ingrained. One of the best early alloy rigs was stepped on the American J Class, *Enterprise*, in 1930. *Enterprise's* Duralumin mast was engineered by Charles Burgess, brother of Starling, her designer.[1499]

However, before manufacturing good-practice could 'trickle down' to smaller yachts and mass-markets, decades of epic failures were required to pave the way for reliable rigs. Early metal masts were no more reliable than wooden sticks.[1500] Moreover, the transition to alloy was complicated by the introduction of flexible rigs, which began in the 1940s with the Star class.

Unfortunately, too few bendy rigs were built initially to allow evolution to run its course, and there was an unfortunate period of regression which gave straight masts an extended lease on life and gave birth to bendy booms and zippers – bonkers aberrations about which the less said the better.

Technology stalled until the 12mR, *Vim*, visited Britain in 1939. *Vim* sported an efficient, controllable alloy rig that delivered clear performance gains.[1501] In terms of hull design, contemporary wooden-sparred British 12mRs were probably little slower, if at all, than the Americans. Much was expected of William Burton's new *Jenetta* that season.[1502] Alfred Mylne was a designer renowned for his "*highly structured and mathematical approach*". However, he belied that reputation by frustrating his clients' express interest in using Duralumin for the mast, as stepped on *Vim*.[1503] Mylne had an irrational dislike of metal masts, so *Jenetta* stepped an already-obsolete wooden stick. With this prejudice, he condemned one of his finest creations to the second division. Now *Jenetta* has been reincarnated with another wooden mast which denies the technical advances of her era.

Following cumulative innovations in aircraft engineering during WW2, reliable metal mast sections at last became widely available in the UK. Initially, they were built-up by Camper & Nicholson, and from 1955 they were mass-produced by Proctor using Alcan sections.[1504] It had been a long wait, but sailors could finally engage the breeze with confidence.[1505]

Rudders

The Scottish 'hobby' designers, like their professional peers, ran the gamut of rudder designs without resolution. From the helmsman's perspective, it has taken a century or more to get rudders into the right ballpark. Going back to basics, the traditional rudder-blade on a lugsail dinghy was shaped like a fat paddle and cocked back at 45-degrees from the vertical. Such blades deflected the water, with attached flow only on one side, rather than the blade 'tacking' through the medium with attached flow on both sides, taking the stern of the boat with it.

Other factors steered development away from rational solutions. When deep-keel yachts were still based on working boats, they were required to take the ground. Nearly all traditional yachts used keel-hung rudders. The rudder post, and occasionally the stem, were heavily raked to reduce the running keel length that took the ground – one of just two factors used to calculate port dues, and then rating, when organised yacht racing began.[1506] After the system was amended to measure length from the stem to the rudderpost on deck, keel length continued to shorten through the 1880s, but in those years for performance reasons. Rudder-post rake was coupled with increasingly radical forward cut-away to reduce wetted area.

In these circumstances, the planform of yacht rudders was dictated by the 'safe' triangular area between the sectional centreline and the ground. So, when the tide leaves the boat on its side, the fragile blade is fairly safe from damage – even if the tiller is not lashed centrally. Scandinavian yacht designers, more concerned with hitting rocks than mud, lifted the rudder foot and adopted especially narrow profiles. Such traditional shapes are sub-optimal if you just want to steer the boat. Moreover, with sternpost rake, when upright, the rudder blade acts as a brake and pulls the stern down. When heeled, weather helm lifts the stern and reduces righting moment; and at extreme heel angles, the rudder breeches the surface, air is sucked down the blade, it stalls out and a broach ensues.

However, apart from a short, but fertile, period of innovation driven by the turn of the century linear-rater rule, rudder design stagnated for a hundred years. Archaic profiles prevailed throughout the classic period of yacht design with few outliers. John Stephen's *Maida* was an example of a desire to redistribute the area lower down for greater efficiency, while trusting to luck that the blade would stay clear of the seabed.

The rudder on *Maida* is so large that, when allied to a triangular keel-profile, it effectively endows the boat with a 'gybing' keel-foil. Her massive lower rudder bearings suggest that Fred did indeed intend for the blade to provide a significant percentage of the total lateral resistance. However, as the helmsman is obliged to constantly change the angle of attack when working to windward, especially in a seaway, this reduces, and even reverses, the intended effect and increases leeway.

In the last decades of the keel-hung rudder on racing yachts, designers used *Maida*-style rudders, albeit they were less extreme – roughly triangular and wide at the base, ostensibly to maximise the area in undisturbed water. Through the 1960s, metre-boats on both sides of the Atlantic by Olin Stephens and David Boyd used this planform. But the long-keel configuration was already obsolete and only the exceptional refinement allowed it to be retained for so long. Designers who were tied to delivering 'an equal or better boat' to a conservative client remained shackled to the classic profile.

However, talented owner-designers spending their own money, like the Stephens (father and son) and Glen-Coats, could go out on a limb and experiment, and therein lies their importance. When the idea of separating the keel and the rudder was revived in the inter-war period, there was a temptation to return to the rudder shapes used in the old raters. This regression ignored the fact that the smaller classes of these old raters were often sailed on shallow weedy waters, and so used self-shedding shapes.

That said, the rater-era spawned considerable innovation. Separating the functions of lateral resistance from buoyancy in hull-form, engineering fin-and-bulb keels, and employing separate spade-rudders represented real progress. However, the virtues of that slate obscured some really bad and quite unnecessary ideas. Both the flat-section steel-plate keels and swept-back plate rudders are needlessly inefficient – it would not have been difficult to add correctly profiled wooden cheeks.[1507]

With the old rater type of set-up, the boat must be trimmed so that the keel-fin is assigned 90% of the job of resisting side-force. Disconcertingly, if a swept-back rudder-blade is to remain 'unloaded', that implies a small amount of lee-helm. In this balance, the rudder is adding to wetted area without contributing upwind efficiency.[1508] Rudders can, of course, provide lateral resistance effectively. Sailboards can go to windward efficiently solely on the skeg, while Hobiecat crews, on a boat which has no keel foil, rake the whole rig over the transom to sail on the rudders, rather than using the flat lee wall of the asymmetric hulls, as the designer intended.

When *Maida II* was optimised in 1950, the small skeg-hung rudder was replaced. The boat had no trimtab and the rudder was just too small to steer the boat efficiently. The re-design featured a much deeper blade, extending for two-thirds of its depth below the bustle, which then acted as a vestigial skeg. In profile, this 70-year-old design would not look out of place on a modern racing yacht.

Today, thanks to parallel advances in materials, we can have the rudders talented helmsmen always wanted; impossibly deep, impossibly narrow and profiled to the micron. Look at a TP52 or a Fast40; they illustrate where the state-of-the-art should have been half a century ago. And this works just fine with heavy-displacement yachts like 6mRs too. That said, for most amateur helmsmen, a larger rudder with around 20% greater chord than the professionals use is invariably lower in drag and faster all round.

Altering the Equation with Genoa Jibs

The sail-area/sailing-length trade-off in the International metre-boat classes varied over the years, until the advent of genoa jibs. Foresails were measured at just 85% of the foretriangle. Even in an era before efficient winch packages, it is remarkable that free sail area was spurned for so many years. The power of a genoa and the ability it gives to 'change gears' – accelerating a heavy displacement hull after a tack or footing off to maintain boat-speed through a chop, is undeniable. However, it took a number of drubbings by the Americans to drive this point home to British crews. Our professional hands certainly didn't help; they were resistant to overlapping jibs, mainly because of the extra work involved. Eventually, the clear benefits of these sails motivated owners to lay down the law.

However, as the port of 'Genoa' is neither in the USA or Scotland, the credit should go to the Italians. In February 1926, following months of brain-storming and empirical testing, Raimondo Panario and Francesco Tagliafico built a new flat-cut windward foresail, based on the panels of a second-hand British mainsail. The new sail was tested, and first used in competition, on Giuseppe Roggero's then new Baglietto-designed 6mR, *Cora IV*. Helming the boat, Panario enjoyed an unforgettable year, beating the French, British, Dutch, Norwegian and Danish boats at the 1926 Genoa Spring Regatta.[1509]

A Swede, Sven Salén, is generally given credit for popularising the genoa in America with his 6mR, *May-Be*, during the Scandinavian Gold Cup races of 1927 in Oyster Bay. Sven had seen the sail at Genoa and ordered one. The early 6mR 'genoas' had a 120% overlap, but this grew until it became established at an optimum at about 150%. The Skerry Cruisers in Scandinavia, by contrast, scorned diminishing returns. Some use 220% genoas, extending well past the end of the mainboom, despite the fact that beyond 150% or 160% real benefits become imagined.

Nevertheless, even after the genoa had convincingly proved its worth in competition, the Scots were loath to abandon their working jibs. So there were a few backward steps before genuine progress was established. What makes this reluctance puzzling in retrospect, is that in the days when 6-metres, for example, stepped gaff rigs, they carried powerful, long-hoist jibs, often to windward. See the images of the early designs from the boards of Glen-Coats and Fred J. Stephen in Chapters 26 and 27.

There is a well-known story concerning Johnston de Forest's challenge for the Seawanhaka Cup against A. S. L. Young of the Royal Northern. The competition was sailed in 8-metre yachts on the Clyde.[1510] Johnston claimed to have lost the 1931 match as his boat was unable to tack quickly. With a constant, penetrating drizzle, *Priscilla III's* light cotton genoa stuck to her mast like a wet tee-shirt, while the canny Scots in *Saskia*, with their unfashionable working jib, sailed off into the distance.

However, when the sun came out, the conservative paid-hands, skippers and designers of the British metre-classes eventually followed the Americans and reappraised their interpretation of the International Rule to design bigger, heavier boats with less measured sail-area, employing the free power of large overlapping jibs to make up the difference. Today, we have completed a full circle. When all sail area is measured, the jib area in the overlap is less efficient than it would be within the parameters of the foretriangle.

As a result, at the cost of elegance and to the detriment of teamwork, overlapping genoas have gone out of fashion under new measurement rules. However, they are still very useful sails. Consequently, just as soon as the paradigm shift to non-overlapping headsails was consummated, sailmakers were enjoined to engineer spinnakers that set like genoas. The so-called 'code-zero' sails are effectively mast-head genoas, built at enormous development cost and with great ingenuity to fit within the spinnaker measurement box.[1511]

Free-sailing Model Yacht Testing

Thomas Glen-Coats, Fred J. Stephen and John G. Stephen all designed and sailed model yachts; some were avenues of research, while others were miniature 'prototypes' of proposed full-sized yachts.[1512] All three designers were very much concerned with 'balanced' hull lines, and all variously referenced Rear-Admiral Alfred Turner's 'metacentric theory' – a questionable, but undoubtedly useful, rule of thumb when seeking good balance in a free-sailing model.

Model yachting boasts a proud history. Virtually all the great turn of the century yacht designers considered free-sailing models a useful adjunct to their profession, and some were prime movers in organised model yacht clubs. Albert Strange, artist and self-taught yacht designer, was a leading light. Dixon Kemp and his friend, G. L. Watson, sailed models of *Shamrock II* on Loch Lomond and found the exercise useful. William Fife, Charles E. Nicholson and others were keen observers of model design trends and experiments. Yachting luminaries such as the Marquis of Ailsa, Lord Brassey, Brooke Heckstall-Smith and Sir William Burton were also keen students of this vicarious branch of our many-faceted sport.

"One of the best-known and most delightful traits in the character of Mr William Fife Snr, now an elderly man, is that he still has a boy's fondness for the making and sailing of model boats. Trade is dull at Fairlie just now, and to help to keep the youths about the yard in amusement, Mr Fife offered prizes for a race for models. To further countenance the regatta, he sailed a model of his own making. The first prize fell to Mr Adam French, and to the amusement of all, the model of the great builder himself was last. She was of the old school, and the more fortunate boats had all a strong dash of the Wenonah (Herreshoff 'skimming dish') *breed in them."*[1513]

The first models to the International Rule were built and sailed in competition by the London Model Yacht Club.[1514] Tommy Glen-Coats and YRA stalwart, E. R. Tatchell, both tested their initial ideas there. The first race to the new International Rule was held on the Round Pond in Kensington Gardens in March 1907. This was a few months before any full-size yachts, built to the rule, had been launched. The models were designated '1-metre' boats. The first fleet had three examples designed by Glen-Coats, three by Tatchell, and three by John Odgers.

The Paisley Model Yacht Club benefitted from an enviable level of support from the wealthy Clyde yachting community. The captains of Clydeside industry donated trophies and quietly sponsored club facilities and activities. There was naturally considerable interest among local designers, builders and yacht owners, many of whom followed the latest race results on the specially constructed pond at Barshaw Park.

Seventeen 12-metre model yachts competed in the racing at Barshaw in 1928. One of these little yachts was *Iris*, said to be a model of Tommy Glen-Coats full-size 12mR yacht, *Iris*, built in 1926. Also competing was a model of *Coila III*, Fred J. Stephen's successful 6mR design, scaled-up as a 12mR and sailed then by Willy Robertson, who crewed with the Stephen family. Willy was a high-powered 'pit-man'; he was chairman of the Clyde Navigation Trust and owner of the Gem Line. Parenthetically, Willy's son Kenneth, an inveterate gambler and something of a dilettante, is reputed to be 'the man that broke the bank of Monte Carlo'.

John G. Stephen experimented with two 6-metre models in 1931, match racing them at Whiteinch Boating Pond in Glasgow, the Lake of Monteith and on the 'open sea' of the Gareloch against *Ailsa*, a successful fin-keeler.[1515] Stephen's Model No.1 had a constant chord bulb-fin, with vertical leading and trailing edges, and a small rater-type rudder. This model had a short static waterline length, increasing rapidly when heeled. Stephen's Model No.2 had a triangular underwater profile and a long waterline with a canoe stern. The sections of this boat were markedly different from contemporary Fife, or Mylne 6-metres.

The fin-and-skeg configuration of Model No.1 proved to be significantly faster up-wind in light to moderate conditions, and less-so reaching and running. The more conventional hull-form of Model No.2 was outstanding to windward in a blow. Stephen was convinced of the value of model yacht testing, and we can see some of the concepts trialled in this way appearing on his successful full-sized boats. It is unclear to what extent a 'live' helmsman (as opposed to Braine gear) would have affected these results.

W. J. Daniels (1882-1959) was an important contributor in the world of model-yachts and design theory.[1516] He is credited by some with the first rigorous analytics to determine hull balance with his model yacht *XPDNC* of 1906.[1517] Daniels' analyses involve the calculation of sectional 'wedges'; the 'in wedge' is the immersed area as the boat heels and the 'out wedge' is the resultant area raised out of the water. If these are in balance, the hull will track straight as it heels. In a displacement boat, it is also desirable that long-ended hull-forms extend effective waterline length through rotation via immersed sections that are less buoyant than the sections revealed. Using these principles, Daniels designed the full-scale fin-and-skeg 6mR, *Josephine*, in 1926,

In the 1950s, the Paisley club sailed model 6-metres and the 'Marblehead' class.[1518]George Braine's quadrant steering gear appeared in the 1930s, a considerable advance on the 'weighted rudder' method. Subsequently, vane steering was employed (later essential equipment for full-size singlehanders before the advent of Autohelm). Interestingly, when vane gear was pioneered in model yacht competition in 1875, it was considered unsporting. However, in 1935, a cad using vane steering won a big race and then it became a free for all, accelerating development. Radio control was introduced in the 1980s. This allowed infinitely more complex forms of fleet racing with tacking duals and calls for water at the marks.

The *Teal* Case – Following the Rule to the Letter

It is almost always possible to take advantage of inadvertent loopholes in a rating rule. Glasgow naval architect, C. L'Estrange Ewen (1877-1949), found one in the 1st International Rule and drove a cart and horses through it in 1909. The opportunity was presented by the wording used to define the 'd' measurement – the difference between the skin girth and the chain girth.[1519]

As the rule is now written, girths and girth difference are measured at 0.55 of LWL back from the fore end of the waterline. As the rule was written in 1907, the measurement was taken at the point of maximum chain girth. Everyone expected this to be roughly at the midships point, where the current rule mandates measurement. L'Estrange Ewen realised that if he designed a boat with a stern-hung rudder, and radically ramped the sheerline up at the stern, this would be the point of maximum depth which would, de facto, become the measurement point. There can be no girth difference on a parallel-sided sternpost

This produced several clear benefits. A tight turn-of-bilge and an efficient keel section could be incorporated in a lighter displacement hullform without any girth difference penalty whatsoever. And, without the usual trade-offs that other designers were forced to accept, a bigger boat with more sail area was possible. Moreover, the design actually gained chain girth and freeboard credits. Apart from the odd-looking kicked-up sheerline, the boat looked like a scaled-up Clyde 19/24, but with a Scandinavian-style canoe-stern.

As the story goes, Herbert Brown wanted a more useful boat to sail on Belfast Lough than the narrow-bodied conventional Sixes. Ewen resurrected some ideas he had sketched out in 1906 and worked them up. Whether this unlikely, but still feasible, tale was concocted as an 'alibi' and Brown and Ewen were simply cheating the rule, is best left to the reader. *Teal* was built by Dickie's of Tarbert and launched in May 1909.

The published IYRU instructions gave the measurer clear instructions regarding the definition of the covering board and measuring sternposts at the termination of the waterline (items 14 & 20), suggesting that the rule had been drafted with unconventional designs in mind. These provisions no doubt allayed any concerns with regard to item XXI concerning 'peculiarities', which meant that *"the rule will not rate the yacht fairly"*. This old chestnut was revived by the New York Yacht Club in connection with the winged keel on *Australia II*, see Chapter 30.

Then the fun started. The Secretary of the YRA made out the certificate, but did not issue it, as *"the measurement of the freeboard did not appear to be taken amidships as well as forward and aft."* The rule at that time required no such thing. Referred to the Measurement Committee in October, the certificate was denied on the grounds that the girth measurement had not been taken *"according to the intention of the rule"*. The Committee invoked Clause XXI, citing a 'peculiarity' of build that did not allow the yacht to be rated fairly.

Ewen summarised the situation as follows: *i) one of the rules which was distinctly stated (Clause I.) to be in force for ten years from Jan. 1, 1908, has now been modified; ii) such modification has been made without notice; iii) the modification affects measurements made before ratification; iv) the Permanent Committee considers equitable a modification of the rule by which the option vested in the designer is transferred to the Permanent Committee in the case of one boat only; v) that boat having been measured and found to be of 6-metres rating by the YRA official, and having raced for a season in the 6-metre class, two months after the close of the season they say the boat never was 6-metres.*

The Permanent Committee decided that, uniquely in the case of *Teal*, the girth station would be placed where the chain girth (covering-board to covering-board) measured 3% less than the maximum (as previously measured). This was an extraordinary decision that defined a unique measurement procedure for one boat only. Moreover, the resolution applied only to the *"trim in which she was measured on May 17th 1909"*.

That much was bad news, but to a certain extent, understandable. What it implied and what came next was, as Ewen asserted, wholly *"untenable in law and equity, and also transgresses the ethics of sport"*. The Permanent Committee added that: *"The yacht must, however, be in the same trim as she was on that date of the original measurement and the hull unaltered, because the ruling of the Committee only applied to the specific case of the Teal laid before them. If the hull of the yacht is altered the ruling of the Committee ceases to apply, and the yacht, as altered, will again be liable to be measured in whatever way the YRA deem equitable."*

So, what this means is that the YRA claimed the right to fix the position of chain girth measurement in any position in order to bring *Teal* over her class measurement. The 'max chain girth plus 3%' ruling could not be used to re-rate the boat to measure as a 6mR. The Committee appeared determined to keep *Teal* out of the 6mR class, even if she reduced sail area to shed the excess rating. If any alterations were made to reduce *Teal's* rating, the committee declared a willingness to set a new position for the chain girth measurement that would specifically rule her out of her class again. In these circumstances, not knowing where the Committee might choose to place the girth difference measurement, and with the chain girth location now effectively a 'moving target, Ewen could see no means of achieving a successful remeasurement to bring the boat back into class.

It seems that the Permanent Committee of the IYRU, were being overprotective of the new rule, or perhaps they just had no sense of humour. The committee declined to countenance such an 'evasion of the spirit of the rating formula' and decreed that *Teal* be penalised in such a way to keep her out of class. Normally, when you find a clear loophole that is not subject to interpretation, the Measurement Committee will meet over the winter and amend the rule. You get a season to make hay before the weight of common interest forces you to fall into line. That much can be expected, but the manner of handling this case was arbitrary and duplicitous. Even after *Teal* had been sold-on as a cruiser, Ewen's arguments with the IYRU continued, as he fought on for a fair resolution.[1520]

Girth measurements, until modified to an arbitrary point below the waterline, simply acted as a spur to rule cheating. This was evident from the immediate lapse into radical triangular profiles in the 19/24s and was later taken to similar extremes in the 6-metres with the Stephen family boats, *Coila III* and *Maida*. These boats, with their maximum depth behind the measurement point, are so difficult to slip and manage out of the water that holes with knock-out plugs were drilled in the keel to strap the boats forward and prevent them popping out the back of the cradle like a lozenge.

Looking over the history of rule-cheating, this was an extraordinary case. Despite having a waterline beam more than 20% wider than her peers, *Teal* was fast. In the early season, Ewen reports that she was a match for the best Sixes on the estuary. *"This boat is quite a daring departure from Coila, Era, Dormy and Mr Moir's new boat. She is a high-sided beamy boat with an unusual amount of sheer. Before the race was five minutes old, she showed a rare capacity to ghost."*[1521] However, with the measurement debacle, things fell apart. Perhaps this was just as well, *Teal* was not a 'looker'; she resembled a fishing boat and would have lowered the tone of an otherwise elegant class.

[1495] E. S. Turner, in the Evening News, 1910.

[1496] Notes on the First International Rule, Ian Howlett, July 2018, 6-metre Class website.

[1497] Lloyds Register of Shipping, Rules for the Construction and Building and Classification of Yachts intended for racing in the International Rating Classes, Section 2, 1921.

[1498] Manual of Yacht and Boat Sailing and Architecture Dixon Kemp, 6th edition, 1888. Contribution by G. L. Watson.

[1499] *Enterprise's* Sailing Master was a Scotsman, George Monsell.

[1500] Aspirants to defend the America's Cup in the 1930s had to have at least one complete spare rig on the dockside if they were even to be considered as eligible.

[1501] The American yacht, *Gesture*, an S&S sloop from 1941, is likely to have been the first ocean racer with an extruded aluminium mast, drawn by the Fuller Brush Company from Alcoa Aluminium in the 1940s.

[1502] Mylne and Burton's Last Boat, Clair McComb, Classic Boat, November 2019.

[1503] The Twelve Metre Yacht, its Evolution and Design, 1906-1987, Chris Freer, 1986.

[1504] Proctor was taken over by the Swedish company, Seldon, in 1996.

[1505] History of Sailing Yacht Masts, Rigging and Sails: 1900-Present day, James Gilliam, web-post.

[1506] 'Builders' Old Measurement' was used for commercial craft from ca.1650 to 1854 when it was replaced by the 'Moorsom System' (L x B x ½B). For racing yachts, the old system was replaced by the RTYC's 'Thames Measurement' in 1855, adopted by the YRA in 1876. Running keel length was replaced by a stem to rudderpost (position on deck) measurement called 'length between perpendiculars' (LBP). The change to Thames Measurement and the heyday of the cutter saw few designers prepared to deviate from a straight forefoot to 'maintain grip on the water', until *Jullanar* in 1875. Meanwhile, rudderposts were raked at extreme angles of up to 55-degrees.

[1507] Modern 'River Cruiser' class yachts on the Norfolk Broads take a rating hit similar to stepping a carbon-fibre mast if they use a rudder blade with a profiled section.

[1508] When the GP14 class allowed the swept-back rudder-blade to be dropped to vertical, the boat was transformed. It is mystifying why 200,000 Laser dinghies still persevere with a swept-back blade. The Frank Bethwaite-designed Laser 2, with a very similar hull-shape to Bruce Kirby's Laser 1, has a deep narrow rudder blade and is a joy to sail.

[1509] Sailmaker: Raimondo Panario, J. Dumon, Classic Six newsletter, No.13, March 2008. Sourced from Genoa Jib: cento anni di vela in Italia, C. Tagliafico and T. Delfino ca.1988.

[1510] The Seawanhaka Corinthian Yacht Club, John Parkinson, 1965.

[1511] After a phase of big, but inefficient sails, the major sailmakers all now have their cable-less technologies to achieve this end. Countless examples, historical and current, of rule-cheating in yachting not only evade penalties but are accepted and institutionalised.

[1512] History and Heritage of Paisley Model Yacht Club, Robert Rooney and the staff of Paisley Central Library Heritage Centre, Paisley.org.uk.

[1513] Clyde, The Yachtsman, 30th November 1893.

[1514] While the whole idea of a social hierarchy in model yacht racing seems ridiculous, the Paisley Club's documentation suggests that the Londoners 'took themselves too seriously'.

[1515] Keel Forms and Two Experimental Models J. A. Stewart, December 1932.

[1516] Daniels built his first full-size keel boat, the elegant *Onward*, for himself in 1913. This was a half-rater fin-and skeg scow, based on the design of *Onward*, his second model design. Life and Times of Bill Daniels, Russell Potts, Vintage Model Yacht Group, August 2015.

[1517] That Peculiar Property: Model Yachting and the Analysis of Balance in Sailing Hulls, Earl Boebert, The 18th Chesapeake Sailing Yacht Symposium, March 2007.

[1518] The Marblehead owners sailed for the McGruer Trophy, donated by the yacht-building family in memory of Heather McGruer.

[1519] The Teal Case, C. L'Estrange Ewen, Yachting Monthly, Volume 5, 1909.

[1520] *Teal* was re-measured without her topsail and rated 5.97mR without the topsail. But the measurer did not follow the specifically prescribed guidelines.

[1521] Clyde, The Yachtsman, 27th May 1909.

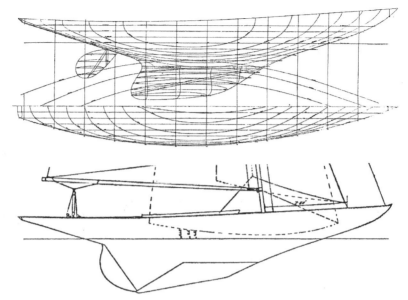

Josephine, W. J. Daniels 1926, built by White of Southampton for Philip Runciman. *Josephine* was rebuilt with a conventional, triangular underwater profile, to resemble the contemporary Fife sixes, an outstandingly successful model drafted by David Boyd. *Josephine*, alas, lacked that stardust. *Yachting Monthly* had this to say: *"Taking first Josephine's certificate of rating from the YRA handbook, it is to be noticed that whilst her girth difference is greater and her sail area is rather less than that of the majority of the class, she comes very close in her measured elements to such boats as Lanai and Coila III, so that it may be taken that no error was made in this. Some novelties were introduced, all seams being glued, and the hull bound together fore and aft by stays with bottle screws (the forward pair taking the thrust of the mast from the forefoot. Leakage under the mast being not an uncommon complaint in racing craft."*

The magazine also observed: *"It is true that the old 'length and sail area' and 'first linear rating rule' boats had detached rudders and fins, but their hulls were of a much shallower bodied type, and even then, instances occurred where filling in the deadwood and hanging the rudder on it, greatly improved speed and handling as was the case with Josephine. The principal alterations as shown by the second set of lines were the change to normal profile and the adjustments to weight of keel necessary to bring her to her designed waterline.*

The body of the boat was left unaltered and any alteration would be difficult and costly. Though the wetted surface is now somewhat greater, the all-round result of the alterations has been that with careful tuning up the boat is anything up to 20-minutes faster round a 14-mile course." Clearly there was a lot more going on here than the *Yachting Monthly* correspondent could have been aware of. The main issue appears to have been that the boat was overweight. Objectively, the apparent speed difference is nonsense.

Left: The first true upwind-capable Genoa jib. Designed by sailmaker, Raimondo Panario and cut from a second-hand British mainsail. Seen here on the 6mR, *Cora IV*, designed by V Baglietto for Giuseppe Roggero. Subsequent sails were usually built of lighter cloth which drew into a hollow clew.

TEAL

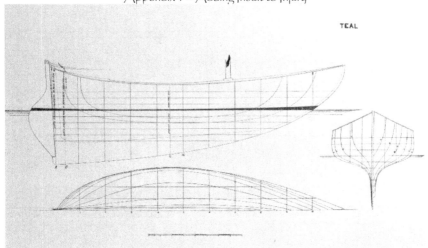

Lines of *Teal* 1909   C. L'Estrange Ewen

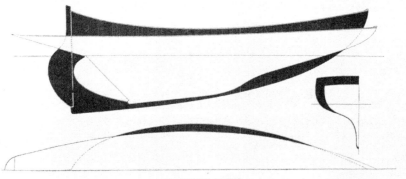

A COMPARISON OF TYPE.

Teal compared to a conventional 6mR   C. L'Estrange Ewen

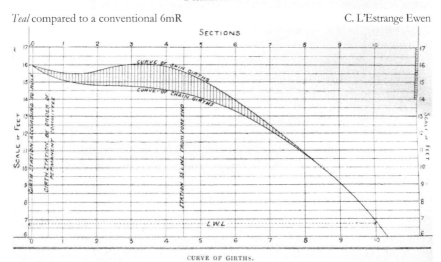

CURVE OF GIRTHS.

Teal graph of girth difference   C. L'Estrange Ewen

Appendix 2: Yachting Literature

The author does not, however, think any apology necessary; as, if the public lose time unprofitably over his pages, he considers the blame attachable to them not him.
Patrick Matthew (1790-1874).[1522]

Scotsman Patrick Matthew's eccentric views on the selection of timber for shipbuilding made no significant contribution to naval architecture; indeed, he was generally dismissed as a crackpot. But if we dig deeper, we find that there was nothing wrong with his mind. Patrick's thoughts on natural selection were both inspired and insightful, and predated both Wallace and Darwin. So, 'don't judge a book by its cover', as they say. Mind you, as far as this volume goes, you are welcome to assess it by Olga Darroch's cover image, and of course, its heft.

Perhaps the first account of a yachting cruise in the modern idiom was written by Roger North (1653-1734), who has left us a chatty log of a yachting cruise ca.1687.[1523] Uffa Fox featured this adventure in one of his 'big books'.[1524] Here is late 17th century yachting, described in the inimitable style of Mr North. It has the essential ring of authenticity that conjures up messing about in boats, in those far-off days, or indeed in any era.

"Another of my mathematical entertainments was sailing. I was extremely fond of being master of anything that would sail, and consulting Mr John Windham about it, he encouraged me with a present of a yacht, built by himself, which I kept four years in the Thames, and received great delight in her. This yacht was small, but had a cabin and a bedroom athwartships, aft the mast, and a large locker at the helm; the cook-room, with a cabin for a servant, was forward, with a small chimney at the very prow. Her ordinary sail was a boom-mainsail, stay-foresail, and jib.

She was no good sea-boat, because she was open aft, and might ship a sea to sink her, especially before the wind in a storm, when the surge breaks over faster than her way flies; but in the river she would sail tolerably and work extraordinarily well. She was ballasted with cast lead. It was a constant entertainment to sail against smacks and hoys, of which the river was always full. At stretch they were too hard for me; but by, I had the better; for I commonly did in two what they could scarce get in three boards. And one reason of the advantage they had at stretch was their topsail, which I could not carry.

The seasons of entertainment were the two long vacations, Lent and autumn, especially towards Michaelmas, for the summer is too hot and calm; unless by accident, those times are cool and windy, without which the sea is a dull trade. But these were for long voyages, which lasted for the most part five or six days. I sent for the yacht, which had lain all Trinity term in the heat uncaulked, so that her upper work was open, though her bottom was as tight as a dish. We went aboard, and when the vessel began to heel the water came in at her seams and flowed into the cabin, where the company was, who were too warm to perceive such an inconvenience, till at last they were almost up to the knees, and they powdered out. We called for boats and went ashore, and the yacht was run ashore to prevent sinking downright."

The next record of recreational yachting unearthed in this brief review describes a sailing holiday 80 years later in the 18th century.[1525] The Clarks and the Smiths, two upper middle-class English families, enjoyed a 10-day cruise in the *Lovely Mary*, a Hampshire vessel, in 1768. Meanwhile, on the Norfolk Broads, pleasure-craft were available for all to hire. As ever in those days, the sport of yachting not only appealed to enthusiasts, but also offered discreet and even luxurious accommodation to host clandestine out-of-wedlock liaisons and alcohol-fuelled fun and games.

Almost a century later, *Hunt's Magazine* appeared on 1st August 1852 as the first specialist sailing periodical, testing a new market for the printed word. *Hunt's* served every club in the British Isles with equal dedication: *"The jolly young watermen who strive, against each other, for the Coat and Badge… we shall imitate their example… strong in the knowledge that we have… as yet no rival either ahead, or astern, or abreast of us… And we nail our colours to the mast!"*[1526] The first edition of *The Field*, a magazine that addressed yachting as just one aspect of the complete 'sporting life', came out five months later, on 1st January 1853. 'Aquatics' would soon take on a life of its own in the pages of *The Yachtsman*, first published in April 1891 (*"Our progress towards perfection will be continuous, although the road is a long one to travel, and the end of it is not on earth."*) and then *Yachting Monthly*, 15-years later in May 1906.

As for books, cross-over publications like *Hunt-Room Stories and Yachting Yarns*, *A Yacht Voyage Round England* and *Sketches of a Yachting Cruise*, and their tradition of self-deprecation, would yield to hubristic narratives in the modern idiom. This style had been pioneered decades earlier by Robert Buchanan's *The Cruise of the Tern to the Outer Hebrides*, and John Inglis, design guru, cruising enthusiast, and 'one of the boys', with his lively account of *A Yachtsman's Holiday*.[1527]

While there were some exceptions, like R. T. McMullen, a man of no-nonsense Scottish Presbyterian heritage, it was not until the turn of the century that gentlemen would accede to having their given names appear in print. The convention was to snipe from the fenestration of pseudonyms, or initials, like 'the Governor' or 'AJ'. Frank Cowper published as 'Jack-all-alone', 'Diogenes Jr', 'Nomad', 'Undine', 'Little Windflower', 'Guardian Angel', 'Psyche', 'Ubique', 'Old Hand' and many more. William Kingston wrote as 'Barnaby Brine', before coming clean, and even the well-known Irish hack, William Cooper, wrote under the name of 'Vanderdecken' after Willem van der Decken, master of the legendary ghost ship, *Flying Dutchman*.[1528]

For the student of Caledonia's maritime heritage, substantive yacht racing literature began with the two-volume *Yachting*, published in 1894, as part of the *Badminton Library of Sports and Pastimes*. Badminton's wide-ranging *Yachting* puts the state of the art today to shame; it is still one of the most insightful and useful works to have been published in any era.

The Badminton Library was named after the country house of its founder, the Duke of Beaufort, and ran to 33 volumes to address every sporting whim of the leisured late-19th century gentleman. The series was exceptional in securing the best experts of the day and endowing the generally surface-skimming encyclopaedic format with the credibility of specialist literature.[1529] *"It is astonishing how much one can learn in one winter if he devotes only an hour a night to the acquirement of nautical lore."*[1530] Scottish yachting was represented in a fulsome contribution by our very own George Lennox Watson, then the recognised master of his craft. Watson's opinions in the year 1893, and his illustrations, still crop up occasionally, unattributed – sometimes three or four times removed from the original text.

To this day, Badminton's *Yachting* remains the geographically best-balanced of yachting histories and compendia. It was edited with a light touch and an even hand, characterised by the following: *"There are cruising grounds on the West Coast of Scotland which may well make yachtsmen in England envious, and some lovely harbours and rivers along the South Coast of England, which would delight the heart of many a Clyde yachtsman."*

The seminal *Yachts and Yachting*, written by Caledophile, William Cooper, under his 'Vanderdecken' by-line, and Dixon Kemp's first edition (1878) of the ever-expanding *Manual of Yacht and Boat Sailing* are also significant works in this context, by any measure.[1531] However, while these volumes touch on yachting history, they focus primarily on yacht sailing, the state of the art in Victorian times, and yacht designing in a 'how-to' format.

Moving through the decades, it is understandable that in their dense and detailed 1902 history of the RYS, with *"an enquiry into the history of yachting and its development in the Solent"*, Montague Guest and William B. Boulton made only passing mention of Scottish yachting in the main body of their work. However, that chronicle, like all accounts of the RYS, considers the club to be so intrinsically linked with the genesis of the sport that they incorporate potted yachting histories along the way.

For example, referring to the 1880s, Guest and Boulton noted that, *"The vogue of the new racing machines from the Clyde put an end to such diversions for the owners of ordinary vessels, and the productions of Ratsey and the southern builders grew more and more scarce on the Solent as time went on. The Squadron still made some efforts to improve matters by attempting a modification of the Association Rules, in the races which were confined to their own yachts, by a system of handicapping which might give the older type of vessel a chance, but with little success."*[1532]

The excellent *British Yachts and Yachtsmen*, published in 1907 by *The Yachtsman* magazine, attempted to balance the north/south canvas, with a generous section on Scottish yachting and the inclusion of many well-known Scottish luminaries in their 'Who's Who'.[1533] I used this as a basis for an expanded list of Scottish yachtsmen judged to have been prominent through the 'golden years' of sailing on the Clyde. As will be obvious, I blanched at the prospect of adding another hundred pages to this book; so that remains a work in progress.

Peter Heaton's *Yachting, a History*, first published in 1955, was for many years the go-to volume for everyman. It is informative, well-written and charming in its obliquity, but it is also curiously light on Scottish matters. Of 109 illustrations, only 2 are from Scotland.[1534] Phillip Birt's *History of Yachting* tells the story with a transatlantic twist and an emphasis on the America's Cup, which leaves little room for the kind of detail we are interested in here.[1535] It is an attractive coffee-table book, nonetheless, and fleetingly recognises the contribution of the marine industry north of the border: *"To be Clyde, rather than Solent, built was for a period the proudest claim for yachts steam or sail."*

A century on, we are still waiting for a narrative that places Scotland at the heart of the story, where it surely belongs. Mike Bender, in his introduction to *A New History of Yachting*, published in 2017, seeks to eschew the usual South Coast bias.[1536] *"In the years before the Great War, the Firth of Clyde and the yacht clubs in it, could lay claim to be the leading location in British Yachting."* So, Bender makes a good start, but since much of his Scottish perspective appears to reflect the bountiful marginalia of Martin Black's elegant Watson biography, it understandably tails-off when Watson leaves the scene early in the 20th century.[1537]

George Blake (1893-1961) and Neil Munro (1863-1930) were essentially novelists. They were not specifically yachting writers or sailing historians, nevertheless, they elevated 'writing about sailing' to literature that can hold its own with the work of their contemporaries. Both were friends of Joseph Conrad (1857-1924). *"On Saturday 20th April 1923, on the eve of his departure for the States, Munro and some other Glasgow admirers dined with Conrad in the North British Hotel on George Square. It was presumably on this convivial evening that Munro, so an account given by his friend George Blake tells, took Conrad out into George Square and persuaded him that he could become an honorary Glaswegian by throwing a stone into the outstretched top hat of the George Square statue of James Oswald MP."*[1538] Rather poignantly, Conrad passed away the following year.

In Scotland, while there is no yachting history as such, we do have a considerable number of excellent sectoral books and chronicles, as a browse in the dusty warren of McLaren's specialist nautical bookshop in Helensburgh will confirm. As always in sailing literature, the oldest are the best. For students of Scotland's yachting heritage, I would recommend the following from my own library:[1539]

- *Days at the Coast. A series of Sketches descriptive of the Firth of Clyde, its Watering Places, its Scenery and its Associations*, Hugh MacDonald, 1860
- *The Cruise of the Kate*, E. E. Middleton, 1870
- *The Voyage Alone in the Yawl Rob Roy*, John MacGregor, 1867
- *The Land of Lorne, including the Cruise of the Tern to the Outer Hebrides*, Robert Williams Buchanan, 1871
- *Yachts and Yachting*, Vanderdecken (William Cooper), 1873
- *A Yachtsman's Holidays or Cruising in the West Highlands*, John Inglis, 1879
- *Evolution of the Modern Racing Yacht*, G. L. Watson, *Yachting – the Badminton Library, Volume I*, 1894
- *Sailing Tours, Part V, The Clyde to the Thames Round North*, Frank Cowper, 1896
- *The Clyde*, painted by Mary & Young Hunter and described by Neil Munro, 1902
- *Sailing Boats from around the World*, Henry Colman Folkard, 1906
- *British Yachts and Yachtsmen, a complete history of British yachting from the middle of the sixteenth century to the present day*, The Yachtsman, 1907
- *Yachting and Yachtsmen*, W. Dodgson Bowman, 1927
- *Island, Ben and Loch*, S. Heckstall-Smith, 1932
- *Sailing Orders*, Captain J. R. Harvey, 1935
- *Down to the Sea*, George Blake, 1937
- *The Yachtsman's Annual and Who's Who*, K. Adlard Coles & Terrance L. Stocken, 1938
- *At the Tiller*, Ian Rutherford, 1945
- *Sherman Hoyt's Memoirs*, C. Sherman Hoyt, 1950
- *The Firth of Clyde*, George Blake, 1952
- *Harbours of the Clyde*, John Scott Hughes, 1954
- *Sceptre*, Hugh Somerville, 1958
- *Cruise in Company, the History of the Royal Clyde Yacht Club*, George Blake and Christopher Small, 1959
- *Memories of Dunoon and Cowal*, Renee Forsyth, 1983
- *Fast and Bonnie*, May Fife McCallum, 1998
- *G. L. Watson, The Art and Science of Yacht Design*, Martin Black, 2011

The Designer Writes

Dixon Kemp (1839-1899) may have passed away more than a century ago, but arguably, he remains yachting's most influential writer. When Kemp was just twenty, working as a reporter on the *Isle of Wight Observer*, he was assigned to cover the yachting news. Work became his life and he immersed himself in a comparative study of the design of yachts, taking off lines and comparing dimensions in the manner of Fincham and Marett. In 1862, at just 23 years of age, he left Cowes for London, where he would take up the position of Yachting Editor for *The Field*. Kemp remained 'in post' until his death in 1899.

From such inauspicious beginnings, as an over-confident self-taught amateur, Dixon Kemp would become an acknowledged authority on the sport of yachting, leading to his appointment as the first and longest-serving Secretary of the Yacht Racing Association (1876-1898). He first published *Yacht Designing* in 1876, republished as *Yacht Architecture* in 1885. This weighty volume was followed two years later by *Yacht and Boat Sailing* in 1878, which grew to encyclopaedic proportions by its thirteenth edition.

Thus, Kemp had a finger on the pulse of British yachting and another in the pie-charts of its institutions. He was what we now tag an 'opinion leader'. His writings ran the gamut of the sport and his authority was seldom challenged. Kemp's writing commanded particular respect as his readership knew that authorities such as G. L. Watson had contributed their thoughts, often without attribution.

In the USA, Cary Smith and Edward Burgess, also self-taught yacht designers, boned-up on the writings of Philip Marett and Dixon Kemp to become experts in the field, despite subscribing to the wave-line inheritors, Colin Archer and John Hyslop – Archer's American shadow. However, Kemp himself was no more than competent as a naval architect. His only design that today's reader might know is *Firecrest* – a ponderous gaff cutter, designed in 1892, in which Frenchman Alain Gerbault, a three-time Grand Slam tennis champion, circumnavigated the world in 1923-29.

Uffa Fox (1898-1972) was another prominent yachtsman and yacht designer who made his mark on the sport through his writing. Uffa was a shameless self-promoter; but for his loyal admirers, claiming credit for ideas already in circulation was part of his roguish charm. Schoolboys didn't know and didn't care. Not many people can pull this off. Uffa did design some excellent dinghies in his early career, but his lasting contribution lies in his prolific published output, written in conjunction with his 'journalistic mentor', Charles Willis. The large-format 'annuals' are coffee table books par excellence. Most keen yachtsmen of a certain age have these books in their libraries, so as they shuffle off this mortal coil, a good supply of Uffa's 'big books' are now on the market at reasonable prices.

Caledonia was Uffa's second home. He loved the Clyde, both as a racing venue and a ready source of material for his series of 'big books'.

He was on intimate terms with many of our designers and boatbuilders and knew everyone's business. He had a rare talent to wheedle the lines of current vessels from our taciturn designers. We appreciated his presence at all the important launches and his promotion of all things Scottish. Uffa's great-great-grandfather on his mother's side was a Scot; perhaps this ancestral link made him feel at home on the Clyde and encouraged him to be on his best behaviour.[1540]

Ian Proctor wrote extensively and impartially, as did Colin Mudie. In Scotland, Ian Nicolson, now in his 90s, is from the same mould. Ian's primary contribution to the sport has been in print. Everyone remembers his *Designer's Diaries*, but bar the idiosyncratic *St Mary*, few will recall his other work. And this, despite being associated with Mylne Yacht Design for decades.

Historic Images of Clyde Yachting

In terms of photographic records and access to them, the Clyde comes a poor second to the Solent, with Beken, for example, producing excellent large-format books and an annual calendar featuring classic yachting images. At the present time, there are no comparable publications depicting the great years of Scottish Yachting. This situation should improve with the recent rescue of *The Glasgow Herald's* Outram archive by Clyde photographer, Marc Turner. Hopefully, this crucial side of the story will be marketed in the near future. Mark's father, Harry, was an institution through the 1960s and 70s at regattas large and small with *Smile Please*, his little motorboat.

Clyde Yachting Correspondents

"The Clyde has every reason to be proud of its yachting correspondents as one can say without fear of contradiction that even the recognised headquarters of yachting (Cowes) has no such gifted writers." Craig McGovern[1541]

Among Scottish yachting journalists from the 'great days of yachting', two names stand out – James Meikle and Harry Horne. Meikle was a carpenter with Steele, Scott and Fife before G. L. Watson encouraged him to become a yachting correspondent. Early advice from an old colleague at the bench was *"see you hand the scales level; deid level, min' you, 'atween the Fifes and Watsons"*. Meikle's best work was for the *North British Daily Mail* and the short-lived *Yachting Gazette,* but he wrote for many newspapers and journals and enjoyed a fine international reputation.[1542] A New York journalist said in 1903 *"if you can't win the cup you have at any rate a man who can write the best description of a yacht race"*. He was long connected with *The Yachtsman* magazine, an important source of material for *Highland Cowes*.

Among the rest, the next best known on the Clyde was Robert Smith, who wrote for *The Herald* and *Scottish Country Life*, succeeding J. D. Bell at the *Herald*. He was said to be 'almost as well informed as Mr Meikle'. A third well-respected Clyde correspondent was Mr John Fearon, who contributed regularly for *The Glasgow Evening News* before taking up a post 'down south'. During his time in Glasgow, Fearon was Clyde correspondent for *Yachting World*, and unlike the majority of his colleagues, he was a good helmsman. When Fearon left Glasgow, Mr Ferguson, yachting correspondent for the *Scotsman*, took up Fearon's duties with *Yachting World*. Mr J. D. Bell, the first regular yachting correspondent of *The Herald*, had moved from his native East Coast as *"an invalid medical student in search of health"*. This man loved yacht racing and the West Coast so much that he stayed, abandoning his medical studies. Bell devoted himself to journalism and painting, as a member of the Royal Society of Water Colour Painters.

There were also the freelancers, of which the best-known included Robert Smith of *The Glasgow Herald*, and Robert McIntyre, who wrote under the alias 'Pennant'. McIntyre's particular skill was ingratiating himself with owners and skippers to scoop the latest news. Hughie Houston, a nephew of John Houston who skippered the 'terrible' *Fiona* (Fife 1865), was another highly rated freelancer. Houston trained for the Law but gave up that career to write for *The Glasgow Citizen* and the *Boston Herald*.

In the post-war years we had the likes of George Blake and Ian Gilchrist (also a fine yacht photographer) contributing to *The Field*, and *The Glasgow Herald's* inimitable George Findlay, as described in *The Piper Calls the Tune*.

[1522] On Naval Timber and Arboriculture, Patrick Matthew, 1831.

[1523] Posthumously published in a consolidated volume of his writings, The Lives of the Norths, Roger North, 1890.

[1524] Thoughts of Yachts and Yachting, a 17th Century Cruising Yachtsman, Uffa Fox, 1938.

[1525] A New History of Yachting, Mike Bender, 2017.

[1526] Hunts Yachting Magazine, 1855.

[1527] The Land of Lorne, including the Cruise of the Tern to the Outer Hebrides, Robert Williams Buchanan, 1871; A Yachtsman's Holiday, The Governor (John Inglis) 1879; A Yacht Voyage round England, William Henry Giles Kingston, 1879; Hunt-Room Stories and Yachting Yarns, Anon; 1884 Sketches of a Yachting Cruise, Major Gambier Parry, 1889.

[1528] See the Cruise of the Frolic, Barnaby Brine, Esq, RN. (William Kingston) 1860; and Yachts and Yachting, Vanderdecken (William Cooper) 1873 and others by these two gentlemen.

[1529] The Duke was of the 'Trump school of gentlemen' as the following quotation demonstrates. *"Some women – I speak it with all respect – bear being 'squeezed' and 'pinched', they almost seem to like it, at any rate they don't cry out; while others will cry out immediately and vigorously; so will yachts."* At least he was right about yachts.

[1530] Ibid

[1531] Manual of Yacht and Boat Sailing, Dixon Kemp, 1878.

[1532] The Royal Yacht Squadron, Montague Guest & William B. Boulton, 1902.

[1533] British Yachts and Yachtsmen, a complete history of British yachting from the middle of the sixteenth century to the present day, The Yachtsman, 1907.

[1534] Yachting, a History, Peter Heaton, 1955.

[1535] A History of Yachting, Douglas Phillips Birt, 1974.

[1536] A New History of Yachting, Mike Bender, 2017.

[1537] Bender is in equal parts historian and sociologist; so, understandably, his work is elaborated in the style of an academic paper. That said, the 'history' is a useful contribution to the genre.
[1538] Conrad and the Clyde, Brian D Osborne, weblog.
[1539] Note: Major Brooke Heckstall-Smith was secretary of the YRU (World Sailing), his brother Maldon Heckstall-Smith was a naval architect, his nephew Anthony Heckstall-Smith was a writer, and Anthony's uncle, S. Heckstall-Smith was an Essex doctor.
[1540] As schoolboys in the autumn of ca.1970, we were in Cowes for the Owen Aisher Award. One of the promised highlights of the week was an audience with Uffa Fox. Alas, it was too late. The legendary old codger was draining away – a sad bundle of blankets slumped in a wheelchair, animated only by that distinguished beak of his. Each morning, the shell of Uffa was trundled out to take the air. Nevertheless, I think every one of us made a special effort to do the job right when we gybed round the bottom mark in front of the 'Commodore's House'.
[1541] Famous Clyde Yachting Correspondents, Craig McGovern, The Yachtsman & Motor Boating magazine, 22nd November 1924.
[1542] James Meikle worked for The North British Daily Mail, The Yachting Gazette, The Daily Record, The Glasgow Citizen, The Scottish Field and The Yachtsman, with articles for a number of American journals.

Clyde Yachting Journalists, 2nd September 1897   Image: William Robertson & Co, Gourock
Standing: Angus McLeod, Robert McIntyre, James Meikle, Robert Smith, Tom Ferguson.
Sitting: John Fearon, Harry Horn, H. R. Houston.

Appendix 3 – Class Lists, Builders Lists, Competitions

Clyde 19ft One Design fleet – G. L. Watson, 1886

	Yacht	Date	Builder	Owner	Notes
1.	Red	1886	McAlister	Clyde Canoe Club	Royal Western Yacht Club
2.	White	1886	McAlister	Clyde Canoe Club	Royal Western Yacht Club
3.	Blue	1886	McAlister	Clyde Canoe Club	Royal Western Yacht Club
4.	tba	1887	McAlister	Royal Clyde	*Shamrock?*
5.	tba	1887	McAlister	Royal Clyde	*Thistle?*
6.	tba	1887	McAlister	Royal Clyde	*Daffodil?*
7.	tba	1891	Paul Jones	Royal West	In Black's text but not listed
8.	tba	1891	Paul Jones	Royal West	In Black's text but not listed
9.	tba	1891	Paul Jones	Royal West	In Black's text but not listed
10.	Enid	188?	tba	tba	Image only
11.	Nell	1888	J Adam	N B Stewart Jr	Different design, deep-keel
12.	tba	tba	tba	tba	Others are likely

Clyde 17/19 fleet – Restricted Class, various designers, 1887

	Name	Designer	Builder	Year
1.	Nelie	Wm Fife III	W. Fife & Son	1887
2.	Caprice	Wm Fife III	W. Fife & Son	1888
3.	Nellie II	Wm Fife III	W Fife & Son	1888
4.	Banshee	G L Watson	McLaren, Kilcreggan	1888
5.	Dorothy	Wm Fife III	W Fife & Son	1888
6.	Lapwing	Wm Fife III	W Fife & Son	1888
7.	Harlequin	G L Watson	Peter McLean	1890
8.	Welcome (Celia)	G L Watson	Robert Logan	1892
9.	Cutty Sark (Rosalind)	G L Watson	Peter McLean	1892
10.	Katydid	Wm Fife III	W Fife & Son	1892
11.	Snarlyow I	Wm Fife III	W Fife & Son	1893
12.	Saucy Kipper	Wm Fife III	W Fife & Son	1893
13.	Puckerirera	G L Watson	Peter McLean	1893
14.	Daisy Bell	G L Watson	James Adam	1894
15.	Pirouette	G L Watson	Peter McLean	1894
16.	Olea	G L Watson	Ramage & Ferguson	1894
17.	Hatasoo	Wm Fife III	W Fife & Son	1894
18.	Fricka	Wm Fife III	W Fife & Son	1896
19.	Snarlyow II	Wm Fife III	W Fife & Son	1896
20.	Yvette	A Mylne	McGruer	1897

Likely to be one of the above: *Golden Plover*

Clyde 19/24 fleet – Restricted Class, various designers, 1896

No.	Name	Sail No.	Designer	Builder	Year	Owner
1.	Susette		A Mylne	tba	1896	x2 in Mylne design list
2.	Brenda		A Mylne	tba	1897	in Mylne design list
3.	Verenia		W Fife	Paul Jones	1897	A W Stephen
4.	Trebor		McLean	McLean	1897	DA Wilson
5.	Memsahib	3	A Mylne	McGruer	1897	J K Tullis
6.	Vishnu		Linton Hope	MacAlister	1897	Robert Clark
7.	Moti		Linton Hope	MacAlister	1897	James Forsyth

8.	*Hinemoa*		Linton Hope	MacAlister	1897	Rev Bruce Taylor
9.	*Vashti*		A Mylne	Ninian	1898	R Clark
10.	*Zitella*	8	A Mylne	McGruer	1898	R S Allan
11.	*Ceres*		A Mylne	MacAlister	1898	Andrew Eadie
12.	*Mimosa*		McLean	McLean	1898	W Russell
13.	*Tringa*	9	Wm Fife III	W Fife & Son	1898	Wm C & J H Teacher
14.	*Jean*	18	A Mylne	McGruer	1898	A Murdoch & A Sutton
15.	*Valmai*		A Mylne	Robertson	1900	Robert Clark
16.	*Memsahib II*	3 (III)	A Mylne	McGruer	1900	J. K. Tullis
17.	*Shireen*	7	A Mylne	McGruer	1900	R S Allan
18.	*Sapphire*		A Mylne	McLean	1900	John Stewart
19.	*Lunga*		McLean	McLean	1900	A Kedey
20.	*Gertrude*	5	A Mylne	McGruer	1901	Andrew Eadie
21.	*Ulidia*		Wm Fife III	W. Fife & Son	1901	Sir William Corry
22.	*Estrella*	12	A Mylne	Malcolm	1902	R S Allan
23.	*Tringa II*	9	Wm Fife III	W Fife & Son	1902	Wm. C. & J H Teacher
24.	*Susette II*	1	A Mylne	Robertson	1903	John Thom
25.	*Valtos*		A Mylne	Robertson	1903	Robert Clark
26.	*Lorelei*	7	A Mylne	McAlister	1904	J D Allison
27.	*Sunbeam*	6	A Mylne	Robertson	1904	A S Ormond

Likely to be one of the above: *Lyvinda*, surveyed in 1973 and ascribed to McGruer 1905, however, as McGruer did not build any 19/24s after 1901, this is incorrect.

Clyde 23/30 fleet – Restricted Class, various designers, 1890/1893

	Yacht	Date	Designer	Builder	Owner	Notes
1.	*Mayflower*	1890	G L Watson	McAlister	RCYC	4-tons
2.	*Thistle*	1890	G L Watson	McAlister	RCYC	4-tons
3.	*Shamrock*	1890	G L Watson	McAlister	RCYC	4-tons
4.	*Volunteer*	1890	G L Watson	McAlister	Robert Wylie	4-tons
5.	*Verve III*	1891	G L Watson	Alex Robertson	Robert Wylie	Counter '89
6.	*Fab Tan*	1882	G L Watson	McAlister	Chas. Henderson	2 ½ rater
7.	*Majel*	1892	G L Watson	Peter McLean	J K Tullis	23/30 Rule
8.	*Vida I*	1893	G L Watson	Alex Robertson	W A Wylie	23/30 Rule
9.	*Pike*	1893	G L Watson	Alex Robertson	George Coats	23/30 Rule
10.	*Shuna*	1893	G L Watson	Peter McLean	J S Clark	23/30 Rule
11.	*Thaber*	1893	Wm Fife III	Fife	Peter Coats	23/30 Rule
12.	*Lala*	1893	Wm Fife III	Fife	Norman Clark	23/30 Rule
13.	*Norka*	1893	Wm Fife III	Fife	R M Donaldson	23/30 Rule
14.	*Badgewr*	1894	G L Watson	Alex Robertson	George Coats	23/30 Rule
15.	*Vida II*	1895	G L Watson	Wylie & Lockhead	W A Wylie	23/30 Rule
16.	*Klysma*	1895	Wm Fife III	Fife	R M Donaldson	23/30 Rule
17.	*Thella*	1896	Wm Fife III	Fife	K M & N Clark	23/30 Rule
18.	*Rona*	1897	Wm Fife III	Fife	J Stewart Clark	23/30 Rule
19.	*Dincella*	1897	Wm Fife III	Fife	A Davidson	23/30 Rule
20.	*Espada*	1898	Wm Fife III	Fife	Andrew Bain	23/30 Rule
21.	*Mavis*	1898	Wm Fife III	Fife	Henry Allen	23/30 Rule
22.	*Fuji*	1898	Wm Fife III	Fife	Andrew Coats	23/30 Rule
23.	*Cora*	1898	Wm Fife III	Fife	D. Ralston	23/30 Rule
24.	*Lottie*	1898	G L Watson	Alex Robertson	George Coats	23/30 Rule
25.	*Hawk*	1898	G L Watson	Alex Robertson	R G Allan	23/30 Rule
26.	*Psyche*	1898	A Mylne	McGruer	J S Dunn	23/30 Rule
27.	*Lola*	1899	A Mylne	P. Jones & Son	M H Patterson	23/30 Rule
28.	*Vida III*	1901	G L Watson	Wylie & Lockhead	W A Wylie	23/30 Rule

Innellan One Design – J. & H. M. Paterson, 1895

	Name	Owner	Builder	Year
1.	Butterfly	Col Wadding	P Jones, Greenock	1896
2.	Coryphee	J Shankland	P Jones, Greenock	1896
3.	Eva, Tangerine	J Maitland	P Jones, Greenock	1896
4.	Go Bang	H Shankland	P Jones, Greenock	1896
5.	Jeanette	D Blanche	P Jones, Greenock	1896
6.	Midge	E S Coats	P Jones, Greenock	1896
7.	Quharrie, McDyff	W Shankland	P Jones, Greenock	1896
8.	Skipper	A Douglas	P Jones, Greenock	1896
9.	Speedwell	V Houston	P Jones, Greenock	1896
10.	Swallow	D C Shankland	P Jones, Greenock	1896
11.	Valerie	E Houston	P Jones, Greenock	1896
12.	Ya Soong	J Dick	P Jones, Greenock	1896
13.	Xantho	J Spiers	P Jones, Greenock	1896
14.	Ranee Laut	A R Grieve	P Jones, Greenock	1898
15.	Elsa, Neomi, Red Rose	W A Thomson	J Ninian, Largs	1896
16.	Smudge	D & N Croal	J Ninian, Largs	1896
17.	Fantaise	tba	J Ninian, Largs	1896
18.	Ariel, Santo	tba	J Ninian, Largs	1896
19.	Idaho	tba	J Ninian, Largs	1896
20.	Lola	tba	J Ninian, Largs	1896
21.	Tatum, Lettice,Whaup	tba	J Ninian, Largs	1897
22.	Brilliant Idea	B R Wood	J Ninian, Largs	1897
23.	Amelia, See See	tba	J Ninian, Largs	1897

Holy Loch One Design – Alfred Mylne, 1898

No.	Name	Designer	Builder	Owner
1.	Tatiana	A Mylne	McGruer	R M Mann
2.	Olive	A Mylne	McGruer	K & H Tullis
3.	Winsome, Memsahib	A Mylne	McGruer	J K Tullis
4.	Gollywog	A Mylne	McGruer	D H Kemp

Holy Loch Redwing One Design – Alfred Mylne, 1903

No.	Name	Designer	Builder	Owner
1.	Sunbeam	A Mylne	Alex Robertson	G P Collins
2	Coraline	A Mylne	Alex Robertson	tba
3.	Diana	A Mylne	Alex Robertson	tba
4.	Redwing II	A Mylne	Alex Robertson	tba

Clyde 30ft-rating Restricted Class – various designers, 1904

	Name	Designer	Builder	First Owner	Year*
1.	Andrum*	Wm Fife III	Fife	Capt J Orr-Ewing	1903
2.	Lilian	Wm Fife III	Fife	James S Craig	1904
3.	Mikado	Wm Fife III	Fife	Sir W Corry	1904
4.	Armyne	A Mylne	McAlister	R G Allen	1904
5.	Thetis	A Mylne	McAlister	T C Glen-Coats	1904
6.	Psyche	A Mylne	Malcolm**	J S Dunn	1904
7.	Corrie	A Mylne	Robertson	W A Collins	1904
8.	Vladimir (Medea)	A Mylne	Robertson	Robert Clark	1904
9.	Great Auk	Wm Fife III	Fife	Andrew Coats'	1905
10.	Tarpon	Wm Fife III	Fife	T K Laidlaw	1905
11.	Medora	A Mylne	McAlister	R G Allan	1906
12.	Pallas	Glen-Coats	McAlister	T C Glen-Coats	1906

13.	*Lilian II*	Wm Fife III	Fife	James Craig	1907
14.	*Corrie*	Wm Fife III	Robertson	W A Collins	1908
15.	*Sunbeam*	A Mylne	Robertson	Godfrey Collins	1908

*A number of YRA 30ft-linear-raters were built before the Clyde Restricted Rule and after, for use elsewhere. **The Ardmaleish Yard, later acquired by Mylne & Glen-Coats

Pleiade One Design – Hr. A. With, 1912

	Name	Owners				
		1914	1948	1953	1956	1963
1.	*Alcyone*	C MacAndrew	tba	Dr. R C MacLeod	G Rodger	Neely Blair (Alan Waugh)
2.	*Electra*	James Napier	tba	J G Walker & Dr. T C McInnes	Dr. T C McInnes	Davie Parker
3.	*Merope*	Archibald Watson Jr	Jean McLellan	Messrs Pierpoint & Davidson	N Davidson	Alec Crampsie
4.	*Sterope*	J. C. Campbell	tba	C A S Parker	J Sloan	A. Galbraith (Rab Dallas)
5.	*Calaeno*	Ms MacAndrew	Bombed by the Luftwaffe 1940			
6.	*Maia*	Fred J. Stephen	tba	E L Reid	A Galbraith	A. Galbraith (Jennifer Lambert)
7.	*Taygeta*	Miss C. J. Allan	tba	A F Whyte	A F Whyte	Angus Whyte (later Melville Lang)
8.	*Pleione*	Miss A. E. Allan	Capt. Baird	Capt Baird	Capt Baird	tba
9.	*Orcad**	J. Stewart Black	tba	*tba*	tba	tba
10.	*Phaola*	tba	tba	D S Leishman	tba	tba

*Originally *Atlas*

Scottish Islands One Design – Alfred Mylne, 1928

No.	Name	Year	Builder	First Owner
1.	*Westra*	1929	McGruer & Co	Thomas Dunlop Jr & George Jackson
2	*Cara*	1929	McGruer & Co	J M Christie
3.	*Bernara*	1929	McGruer & Co	R K Sharp
4.	*Stroma*	1929	McGruer & Co	George Nisbet
5.	*Sanda*	1929	McGruer & Co	William & Thomas E Russell
6.	*Jura*	1930	Bute Slip Dock	Thomas Dunlop Jr
7.	*Fidra*	1930	Bute Slip Dock	William Wordie
8.	*Iona*	1931	Bute Slip Dock	James Buchanan
9.	*Gigha*	1931	Bute Slip Dock	J Herbert Thom
10.	*Canna*	1938	Bute Slip Dock	J Herbert Thom
11.	*Isla*	1958	Bute Slip Dock	Mr & Mrs P Simpson
12.	*Shona*	2000	Richard Pierce	Martin Webster

International One Design (IOD) Bjarne Aas 1936 *Scottish fleet 1968-2008*

No.	Sail	Date	Name	Owners
1.	K1	1966	*Stallion*	Tom Merret; Willie Kerr; Bob Shaw; J Macqueen; R Finlayson; W Rennie & D Jackson; Gillian Manuel
2.	K2	1961	*Mighty Mo*	Monsiuer Bassompierre; Brian Tunstil; Marshal Napier & Douglas Miller; Hugh & Robert Napier; David Witten, Tim Lightholler; Peach Prothers & Jo Fairlie
3.	K3	1956	*Arrow*	John Gibb
4.	K4	1958	*Wahoo*	Lt Commander Pat Brians; Blair Forbes
5.	K6	1954	*Susie*	Bert D'Agistino; Jack Robertson; Will Rudd
6.	K7	1967	*Wiffenpoof*	Robert D Brown; J Paver; Tony Thain; N Henderson; Marshal Napier; Gilmour Manuel
7.	K8	1954	*Tadpole*	George Steadman; Eddie Gamley; Howard Fowler; Collin & Constance Carmichael; John Macdonald; Gilmour & Gilli Manuel; Bob Napier & Michael Pollet
8.	K9		*Starlight*	Shona Young

9.	K10	1954	Kyla	James Leask; Harold Haswell Smith; Christina Manuel; Mike McEwan, Chris Roddis & Ian Broadley
10.	K11	1955	Pirate 11	Bill Maitland
11.	K13	1955	Happy Go Lucky	Tom Merret; Tom Cuthell; Evan Young;
12.	K17	1958	Mitzi	Karry Holmes, C Connors, Campbell Macaulay
13.	K18		Seil, Diana 2	Ian Woolward, Fraser Mills

Eight Metre Cruiser Racers 1951 (restricted class, various designers)

No.	Sail	Name	Date	Designer / Builder
1.	K1	Sonda	1951	McGruer / McGruer
2.	K2	Delphin	1953	Arthur Robb / Timbercraft (Shandon)
3.	K3	Josephine IV	1953	McGruer / Moodie
4.	N8	Isolde	1953	Torr Holm / Gamleby Varv (Norway)
5.	-	-	1954	Knud H. Reimers (Sweden, yawl)
6.	-	-	1954	Knud H. Reimers (Ireland, yawl)
7.	K4	Adastra X	1954	McGruer / Woodnutts
8.	K5	Namahra	1955	McGruer / Bute Slip Dock
9.	-	Scharhorn IV	1955	Ouhlmann / Matthiesen & Paulssen (yawl)
10.	K6	Nan of Clynder	1956	McGruer / McGruer
11.	F1	Jabadao	1958	Eugène Cornu / Jézéquel (France)
12.	-	Suzette	1958	Molich / Christensen (Norway)
13.	K7	Tinto (II)	1957	MacMillan/ Fairlie Yacht Slip
14.	K8	Orana	1959	McGruer / Morris & Lorimer
15.	K9	Camellia of Rhu*	1959	McGruer / McGruer
16.	K10	Gigi of Clynder *	1960	McGruer / McGruer (yawl)
17.	RM1	Tomis*	1961	McGruer / McGruer Export to Romania
18.	K17	Feolinn	1961	McGruer / McGruer
19.	K11	Debbie (Feonnuala)	1961	McGruer / Morris & Lorimer
20.	K12	Charm of Rhu	1963	McMillan / Fairlie Yacht Slip
21.	K15	Inismara	1963	McGruer / McGruer
22.	202	Orani	1964	McGruer / Cuthbertson (Hobart)
23.	K16	Nan of Gare	1965	Sparkman & Stephens / McGruer
24.	K18	Altricia	1965	McGruer / McGruer
25.	K22**	Debbie (Arbella)	1966	McGruer / McGruer
26.	K23	Sunburst	1967	Boyd / Alex Robertson
27.	KA24	Celeste III	1968	McGruer /Duncanson (Adelaide)
28.	KA1	-	-	Jack Savage / (Australia)
29.	-	Hermes	-	McGruer / built in Belgium of steel
30.	-	Marie Louise III	-	France

*sisterships ** K19, K20 & K21 unknown – may not have been taken up.

British 8-Metre Fleet 1968 (restricted class, various designers)

	Sail	Name	Designer	Builder	Owner	Notes
1.		Aspasia (Esmeralder, Emily)	1924	William Fife	Fife of Fairlie	Ms M Prichard	Cut down rig cruiser
2.	K3	Sirus	1925	M Giles	Giles	T Crawford	Clyde
3.	K4	Margaret	1926	J Anker	Anker & Jensen	M Dumfries Ballantyne	Clyde
4.	K5	Pleiades of Rhu (Thamar)	1926	J Anker	Anker & Jensen	K Todd & W Jordan	Yawl, cruiser
5.	K7	Vaguant II (Thora, Southern Cross, Caryl)	1927	William Fife	Fife of Fairlie	Dr J Kennedy Young	
6.	K15	Sposa II	1929	Bjarne Aas	Bjarne Aas	G Hughes	Yawl, cruiser
7.	K12	June	1929	J Anker	Anker & Jensen	I Rose	Clyde cropped
8.	K33	Finola (Violetta, Verity, Finola)	1930	William Fife	Fife of Fairlie	P Lang	Cutdown rig cruiser
9.	K23	Severn	1930	William Fife	Fife of Fairlie	A Wheeler	Left UK '68
10.	N26	Silja	1930	J Anker	Anker & Jensen	Dr H Weir	Clyde fleet
11.	N27	If (Whill, Wif)	1930	Bjarne Aas	Bjarne Aas	T Rose	Clyde, cropped

12.	K30	*Severn II of Ardmaleish*	1934	A Mylne	Bute Slip Dock	A Hardie		Clyde fleet
13.	K2	*Carron (Jean, Esme, Carron)*	1934	William Fife	Fife of Fairlie	W. L. Downie		Clyde fleet
14.	N34	*Turid III (Froya)*	1934	Bjarne Aas	Bjarne Aas	J Wolf		Clyde fleet
15.	K32	*Wye*	1935	C E Nicholson	Camper & Nicholson	G Findlay, K Findlay, C Craig		Clyde fleet
16.	K16	*Christina of Cascais (Ilderim)*	1936	Torr Holm	Abrahamsson & Borjessons	K Gall		Clyde fleet
17.	K34	*Idothea (Meme, Rosa)*	1938	C E Nicholson	Camper & Nicholson	M Green & A Green		Cut down rig cruiser
18.	-	*Aina*	192?	-	-	Ken Baird		Clyde fleet
19.		*Iskareen*	1938	S&S	Neglinge-Varvet	Erik Maxwell		From 1971

Dunoon Boatbuilders (work in progress)

Daniel Turner

Year	Name	TM	LOA	Type	Owner
1909	Various	-	20.6	Pleiade	9 built
1939-45	tba		-	Lifeboats	tba

James Colquhoun & Sons

Year	Name	TM	LOA	Type	Owner
1931	*Ladye Louise*	11	35.5	Motoryacht	Client in Gloucester
1933	*Greywing*	7	29.5	Motoryacht	Client in Southampton
1933	*Janey*	5	26.0	Motoryacht	Client in Greenock
1934	*Sruth Ban*	10	31.3	Ketch 50/50	Client in Greenock
1937	Various	-	21.5	RLYC Coronation OD	7 one-designs built
1937-39	Various	-	21.0	Loch Long OD	12 built

Graham Brothers

Year	Name	TM	LOA	Type	Owner
1946-52	-	-	11.0	Clinker skiff	various
1946-52	-	-	12.0	Motor dinghy	various
1946-52	-	-	13.0	Motor dinghy	various
1946-52	-	-	16.0	Motor launch	various
1946-52	-	-	18.0	Motor launch	various
1946-52	-	-	28.0	Motor launch	various
1946-52	-	-	30.0	Motor launch	various
1946-52	-	-	30.0	Sailing yacht	-
1946-55	-	-	20.0	Sailing yacht	-
1953-55	Various	-	21.0	Pixie Class sloop	various
1954	*Tonnag*	7	29.5	Auxiliary Ketch	K.B. Miller

Interim data on yachts designed by W. Stewart Collie

Year	Name	TM	LOA	Type	Owner
1928	-		62.0	Motor Yacht	Pub. in *Yachting Monthly*
1951	-		21.0	Sloop	Pub. in *Yachting Monthly*
1953-55	Various		21.0	Pixie Class sloop	This was a series build
1954	*Tonnag*	7	29.5	Auxiliary Ketch	-

Fletcher Brothers

Year	Name	TM	LOA	Type	Owner
1932	*White Heather*	-	26.0	launch	G & A Waddell
tba	tba	tba	tba	tba	tba

Sinclair

Year	Name	TM	LOA	Type	Owner
1907	*White Knight*		26.0	Motor launch	tba

Fletcher Brothers

Year	Name	TM	LOA	Type	Owner
1932	*White Heather*	-	26.0	launch	G & A Waddell

James Litster

Year	Name	TM	LOA	Type	Owner
	Olga	-	-	2½-rater	James Martin
1903	Dodo II	7	27.8	Gaff Sloop	William Bergius (designer)

David Morris

Year	Name	TM	LOA	Type	Client
1875	Clothide	6	-	cutter	G. L. Watson (sold to Ireland)
1879	Trident	-	-	-	William Paton

D. H. Munro & Sons, formerly McKeller's and later J. J. Bell and Ian Robinson

Year	Name	TM	LOA	Type	Client
1913	Marjorie	19	42.0	Auxiliary Ketch	Reg in Shoreham
1914	Unknown	-	36.6	Aux Lugger	Reg in Ayrshire
1917	Ben	18	45.6	Motor Vessel	Reg in London
1920	Arabian II	24	48.2	Aux Schooner	Reg in Greenock
1921	Nighean Donn	7	27.6	Aux Lugger	Clyde Client
1922	Thalia	8	30.6	Motor Vessel	Reg in Glasgow
1922	Commodore Trunnion	25	45.0	Auxiliary Ketch	Reg in Greenock
1922	Kelvinia	7	30.8	Motor Vessel	Reg in London
1924	Manora	14	35.6	Auxiliary Ketch	Reg in Greenock
1924	Coya	16	36.8	Auxiliary Ketch	Reg in Greenock
1925	West Star	10	33.8	Auxiliary Sloop	Reg in Greenock
1925	Anita	8	24.4	Auxiliary Sloop	Reg in Greenock
1925	Unknown	4	24.8	Mylne OD	Egypt Client
1930	Rosemary V	12	33.4	Auxiliary Sloop	Reg. in Guernsey
1934	Ocean Wave	18	40.7	Motor Vessel	Carrickfergus Client
1934	Mermaid	4	24.8	R M Mylne OD	Mersey Client
1935	Mersey	4	24.8	R M Mylne OD	Mersey Client
1935	Meryl	4	24.8	R M Mylne OD	Mersey Client
1935	Merk	4	24.8	R M Mylne OD	Mersey Client
1935	Merlin	4	24.8	R M Mylne OD	Mersey Client
1936	Mallard	19	39.3	Auxiliary Ketch	Reg in Greenock
1950-53	Elizabeth & Ira	-	21.0	Loch Long OD	2 built

Peter Collyer

Year	Name	Type	Owner	Notes
1951	Hi-Jack	National 12	the builder	Deck and fit-out of Holt shell
1964	Suzy	National 12	Lady Anne	Roscoe Squid 2, Sail No. 2228
1964	Joy	National 12	-	Roscoe Squid 2, Sail No. 2229
-	-	National 18	-	Sail No. 248?
-	Sabun	National 18	D. Davidson	Sail No. 252
-	Flying Scotsman	Flying Dutchman	the builder	Sail No. K24
-	-	Flying Dutchman	-	Sail No. K31
-	-	Cowal Class	the builder	Fit-out, lengthened, ketch rig

Seawanhaka Cup 1922-1987

Year	Location	Club	Yacht	Owner	Result
1922	Massachusetts	Manchester YC	Sakie	Frank C Paine	
	(6-metres)	R Northern & Clyde YC	Coila III	Fred J Stephen	win
1923	Clyde	R Northern & Clyde YC	Coila III	Fred J Stephen	win
	(6-metres)	Seawanhaka CYC	Lea	J F Bermingham	
1924	Clyde	R Northern & Clyde YC	Coila III	Fred J Stephen	win
	(6-metres)	R Norwegian YC	Unni	L S Skourgaard	
1925	Clyde	R Northern & Clyde YC	Coila III	Fred J Stephen	
	(6-metres)	Seawanhaka CYC	Lanai	Clinton H Crane	win
1927	Oyster Bay	Seawanhaka CYC	Clytie II	H B Plant	
	(6-metres)	R Norwegian YC	Noreg	HRH C P Olav	win

1928	Hanko	R Norwegian YC	*Figaro*	V T Olsen	
	(6-metres)	Seawanhaka CYC	*Akaba*	Clinton H Crane	win
1929	Oyster Bay	Seawanhaka CYC	*Gypsy*	Frank C Paine	
	(8-metres)	R Northern & Clyde YC	*Caryl*	W F Robertson	win
1931	Clyde	R Northern & Clyde YC	*Saskia*	A S L Young	win
	(8-metres)	Seawanhaka CYC	*Priscilla III*	J DeForest	
1932	Clyde	R Northern & Clyde YC	*Maida*	MacAndrew/ Stephen	
	(6-metres)	Seawanhaka CYC	*Jill*	J S Johnson	win
1934	Oyster Bay	Seawanhaka CYC	*BobKat II*	R B Meyer	win
	(6-metres)	R Northern & Clyde YC	*Kyla*	W Russell	
1935	Oyster Bay	Seawanhaka CYC	*Challenge*	P V Shields R	win
	(6-metres)	R Norwegian YC	*Norma IV*	HRH C P Olav	
1937	Oyster Bay	Seawanhaka CYC	*Rebel*	P V Shields	win
	(6-metre)	R Norwegian YC	*Buri*	O D Simonsen	
1938	Oyster Bay	Seawanhaka CYC	*Goose*	G Nichols	
	(6-metres)	R Northern & Clyde YC	*Circe*	J Herbert Thom	win
1939	Clyde	R Northern & Clyde YC	*Circe*	J Herbert Thom	win
	(6-metres)	R Norwegian YC	*Noreg III*	R Svinndal	
1947	Clyde	R Northern & Clyde YC	*Johan*	J Howden Hume	
	(6-metres)	Seawanhaka CYC	*Djinn*	R B Meyer	win
1948	Oyster Bay	Seawanhaka CYC	*Llanoria*	H F Whiton	win
	(6-metres)	R Swedish YC	*Maybe VI*	S Salen	
1953	Oyster Bay	Seawanhaka CYC	*Llanoria*	M Konow	win
	(6-metres)	Royal Yacht Squadron	*Marylette*	J E Harrison	
1956	Oyster Bay	Seawanhaka CYC	*Goose*	H F Whiton	
	(6-metres)	R Canadian YC	*Titia*	E Barker	win
1976	Oyster Bay	Seawanhaka CYC	*Teal*	Harry Melges Jr	win
	(Solings)	R Northern & Clyde YC	*Bullet III*	J Watson	
1987*	Oyster Bay	Seawanhaka CYC	*St Francis*	G Foster	
	(6-metres)	Royal Yacht Squadron	*Battlecry*	Erik Maxwell	win

*last 6-metre participation, Lawrie Smith on helm, sailing for RYS.

British-American Cup 1921-1955 in 6-metres.

Year	Location	British Team	USA Team	Winner

First trophy donated in 1921

1921	Solent	*Victoria, Polly, Flya, Jean*	*Jeannie, Nontaulk, Grebe, Sheila*	Britain
1922	Oyster Bay	*Caryl, Coila III, Jean, Reg*	*Clytie, Grebe, Lea, L'esprit*	USA
1923	Solent	*Coila III, Reg, Suzette, Capelle*	*Lea, Clytie, Hawk, Ingomar*	Britain
1924	Oyster Bay	*Echo, Zenith, Betty, Thistle*	*Lea, Paumonok. Heron, Dauphin*	Britain

Britain retires the first trophy. Second trophy donated 1927

1928	Clyde	*Naushabah, Fintra, Felma, Finvola*	*Akaba, Heron, Lanai, Readhead*	Britain
1930	Oyster Bay	*Coral, Fintra, Prudence, Felma*	*Lucie, Cherokee, Mars, Aphroditie*	USA
1932	Solent	*Vorsa, Ancora II, Fineta* Nada**	*Bob-Kat II, Lucie, Jill, Nancy*	USA

USA retires the second trophy. The third trophy, a silver 6mR model, presented 1934.

1934	Oyster Bay	*Kyla, Vorsa, Melita, Saskia II*	*Bob-Kat II, Challenge, Lucie, Anis***	USA
1936	Clyde	*Lalange, Melita, Nike, Vorsa*	*Indian Scout, Jill, Lucie, Mood*	USA
1938	Oyster Bay	*Erica, Vrana, Circe, Solenta*	*Fun, Goose, Rebel, Djinn*	USA

Second World War, hiatus

| 1949 | Solent | *Thistle, Johan, Circe, Lalange* | *Goose, Star Wagon, Firecracker, Llanoria* | USA |

USA retires the third trophy. The fourth trophy was donated in 1951 as a perpetual challenge

1951 Solent   *Circe, Marletta, Johan* ****   *Llanoria, Firecracker, Goose*   USA
1953 Oyster Bay   *Titia, Marylette, Marletta, Bibos****   *Llanoria, Goose, Fun, Maybe VII*   USA
1955 Solent   *Royal Thames, Noresca, Marylette, Thistle Llanoria, Goose, Ondine, MayBe VII*   USA
Decline of 6-metre class, hiatus
1974 Clyde   *Soling OD Team led by John Watson and Gilmour Manuel*   Britain

The series has subsequently continued in various one-design yachts
*ex *Felma*, **ex *Dana*, ***ex *Totem*, *** *Bibos Canadian boat*, **** *three boat teams*

The America's Cup 1870-2017

Rule	Year	Venue	Club	Defender	Score	Challenger	club
Fleet racing	1851	IoW	RYCS	-	0–1	*America*	NYYC
Fleet racing	1870	New York	NYYC	*Magic*	1–0	*Cambria*	RTYC
Schooners	1871	New York	NYYC	*Columbia* & *Sappho*	4–1	*Livonia*	RHYC
Schooners	1876	New York	NYYC	*Madeleine*	2–0	*Countess of Dufferin*	RCYC
65 ft cutter	1881	New York	NYYC	*Mischief*	2–0	*Atalanta*	BQYC
NYYC 85ft	1885	New York	NYYC	*Puritan*	2–0	*Genesta**	RYS
NYYC 85ft	1886	New York	NYYC	*Mayflower*	2–0	*Galatea**	RNYC
NYYC 85ft	1887	New York	NYYC	*Volunteer*	2–0	*Thistle**	RCYC
SCYC 85ft	1893	New York	NYYC	*Vigilant*	3–0	*Valkyrie II**	RYS
SCYC 90ft	1895	New York	NYYC	*Defender*	3–0	*Valkyrie III**	RYS
SCYC 90ft	1899	New York	NYYC	*Columbia**	3–0	*Shamrock**	RUYC
SCYC 90ft	1901	New York	NYYC	*Columbia**	3–0	*Shamrock II**	RUYC
SCYC 90ft	1903	New York	NYYC	*Reliance**	3–0	*Shamrock III**	RUYC
Universal 75	1920	New York	NYYC	*Resolute*	3–2	*Shamrock IV*	RUYC
J-Class	1930	Newport	NYYC	*Enterprise*	4–0	*Shamrock V*	RUYC
J-Class	1934	Newport	NYYC	*Rainbow*	4–2	*Endeavour*	RYS
J-Class	1937	Newport	NYYC	*Ranger*	4–0	*Endeavour II*	RYS
12mR	1958	Newport	NYYC	*Columbia*	4–0	*Sceptre**	RYS
12mR	1962	Newport	NYYC	*Weatherly*	4–1	*Gretel**	RSYS
12mR	1964	Newport	NYYC	*Constellation*	4–0	*Sovereign*	RTYC
12mR	1967	Newport	NYYC	*Intrepid*	4–0	*Dame Pattie*	RSYS
12mR	1970	Newport	NYYC	*Intrepid*	4–1	*Gretel II*	RSYS
12mR	1974	Newport	NYYC	*Courageous*	4–0	*Southern Cross*	RPYC
12mR	1977	Newport	NYYC	*Courageous*	4–0	*Australia*	SCYC
12mR	1980	Newport	NYYC	*Freedom*	4–1	*Australia*	RPYC
12mR	1983	Newport	NYYC	*Liberty*	3–4	*Australia II*	RPYC
12mR	1987	Fremantle	NYYC	*Kookaburra III*	0–4	*S&S '87*	SDYC
DoG match	1988	San Diego	SDYC	*S&S '88*	2–0	*KZ-1*	MBBC
IACC	1992	San Diego	NYYC	*America³*	4–1	*Il Moro*	CDVV
IACC	1995	San Diego	NYYC	*Young America*	0–5	*Black Magic*	RNZYS
IACC	2000	Auckland	RNZYS	*NZL-60*	5–0	*Luna Rossa*	YCPA
IACC	2003	Auckland	RNZYS	*NZL 82*	0–5	*Alinghi*	SNG
IACC	2007	Valencia	SNG	*SUI-100*	5–2	*NZL-92*	RNZYS
DoG match	2010	Valencia	SNG	*Alinghi 5*	0–2	*USA-17*	GGYC
AC72	2013	San Frisco	GGYC	*Oracle, USA 17*	9–8	*Aotearoa*	RNZYS
AC50	2017	Bermuda	GGYC	*Oracle, 17*	1–7	*Aotearoa II*	RNZYS
AC75	2021	Auckland	RNZYS	*TNZ (Defender)*	-	*Luna Rossa (CoR)*	CVS

*_Scottish designer, builder, skipper or challenging club

The Author

Euan Ross was born in Dunoon and spent his childhood on the north shore of the Holy Loch, where his family still retains a house. Euan was one of the last 'colonial' officers sent overseas by Her Majesty's Crown Agents to manage the rump of our empire. Subsequently, he became an international development consultant trespassing through many and diverse fields of expertise. He has been a life governor of the RNLI and a life member of the RYA since 1982. He is a member of the Association of Yachting Historians, an associate of the British National Yachting Archive, a member of the Holy Loch Sailing Club and an honorary life member of the Piper Class Association. Euan has raced sailboards, dinghies, catamarans, and most types of yacht, from sports-boats to maxis, with immense pleasure and occasional success. He gave up competitive sailing in 1992 and now enjoys exercising his stable of thoroughbred bicycles on the South Downs.

Ailsa and the author at the Piper's Golden Jubilee in 2016   Image: Jim McNair
David Boyd design 1966, built Alex Robertson's 1973, owned by the author from 2009 to 2018

Ah! you should have seen me go in the good old times;
the white loam smoking up under my bowsprit,
a shower of spray like the spouting of a whale
sparkling like a rainbow on my weather beam,
and a ton or two of water on the lee side of the deck.

A Tale of a Tub, Hunt's, April 1854

'Classic Boat' magazine – Best Books of 2017
'The Sailors Annual Yachting Year 2018' – Best Books for 2018

The Piper Calls the Tune is an account of the life and works of David Boyd (1902-1989), who experienced both great success and great frustration through his 60-year career. We review Boyd's contribution to the maritime heritage of the Clyde Estuary and celebrate his enduring legacy. The book is a nostalgic appreciation of a wonderful world of inspired designers, beautiful yachts, eccentric owners and skilled craftsmen. It records the memories of a generation of proud old men who have been pleased to revisit the golden age they experienced, before it is swept away in the revisionist accounts of today that sometimes seem to focus only on Fife, Watson and Charles E. Nicholson.

Wheelsagley is a celebration of adventure cycling. Cycling can transport you in many ways beyond the obvious; the humble bicycle is so much more than an uncannily efficient conveyance. If we are mountain-biking, the landscape we roam far exceeds the compass

of the heartiest rambler. On a road-bike, for the same effort, we can travel 6 times as fast for twice as long as the fittest jogger. Our world is simply bigger on a bike, and it's better too. If we ride regularly the activity imbues fitness, almost magically. Cycling is a sport that allows you to 'empty the tank' and yet still roll home. The phlegmatic bicycle may even promote long life and happiness, although I am less sure about the first of these.

Both books are available post-free from Amazon UK, USA and Europe.